"This is indeed a complete guide to portfolio performance. The authors have described a range of possible measures and evaluated their usefulness in theory and in practice. It will serve as both an introduction to this important subject and a reference work for those concerned with measuring and analyzing the performance of investment portfolios."

William F. Sharpe, Professor Emeritus, Stanford University

"Performance measurement has expanded in many directions over the last decades. François and Hübner provide a much needed, ambitious synthesis. Their Complete Guide to Portfolio Performance *is the reference that should always be within immediate reach, with the confidence that insightful answers about any question related to portfolio performance will be found. The authors do not only effectively synthesize the state-of-the-art knowledge in the field, but they also bring their own original and specific contributions on many occasions. A massive* tour de force.*"*

Frank J. Fabozzi, Professor of Practice, The Johns Hopkins University, Carey Business School. Editor of The Journal of Portfolio Management

"The book analyzes many facets of performance appraisal but also explains how it is integrated within the portfolio management process. Each topic is reviewed with rigor and augmented with practical and easy-to-implement examples."

Naïm Abou-Jaoudé, Chief Executive Officer,
New York Life Investments Management

The Complete Guide to Portfolio Performance

The Complete Guide to Portfolio Performance

Appraise, Analyze, Act

Pascal François

HEC Montréal

Georges Hübner

HEC Liège, Liège University

WILEY

This edition first published 2024

Registered Office(s)
John Wiley & Sons Ltd, The Atrium, Southern Gate, Chichester, West Sussex, PO19 8SQ, UK
John Wiley & Sons, Inc., 111 River Street, Hoboken, NJ 07030, USA
John Wiley & Sons Singapore Pte. Ltd, 134 Jurong Gateway Road, #04-307H, Singapore 600134

For details of our global editorial offices, customer services, and more information about Wiley products visit us at `www.wiley.com`.

Wiley also publishes its books in a variety of electronic formats and by print-on-demand. Some content that appears in standard print versions of this book may not be available in other formats.

Library of Congress Cataloging-in-Publication Data is Available

ISBN 9781119930174 (Paperback)
ISBN 9781119930181 (ePDF)
ISBN 9781119930198 (ePub)

Cover Design: Wiley
Cover Image: © Olivier Le Moal/Shutterstock

Set in 10.5/12.5pt and STIX Two Text by Straive, Chennai, India.

SKY10070016_032124

This book is dedicated to

Laurence, Marianne and Perrine
Pascal François

Fabienne, Philippe and Hélène
Georges Hübner

Contents

Preface

WHY THIS BOOK?

Someone who wishes to invest in financial assets necessarily makes a bet on the future. The outcome of the portfolio management process results from a mixture of efforts, skills, and luck. If the investor is involved in the decision-making process, they take at least part of the responsibility for the result. To maximize their chances of success, they should be knowledgeable in *portfolio management*. The editorial offering in this domain is vast and highly qualitative: whatever the reader's initial expertise, there is a reasonable chance of progressing through an adapted learning material. However, the vast majority of people do not manage their portfolio themselves. Rather, they appoint professional asset managers to do it on their behalf. Thus, the challenge is much less to participate in the investment decisions, but rather to control their quality through *portfolio performance* tools. In designing and writing this book, we have been driven by our empathy toward these numerous persons who entrust finance specialists and, in turn, legitimately expect them to defend their interests in the best possible way.

Animated with this state of mind, we have continuously attempted to address the following question throughout the book: "*Given my position in the value chain, from the final customer to the experienced professional, can I get the information that really matters regarding my portfolio's performance?*" If we had the firm conviction that a definite answer could be found in a single already-existing source, we would probably not have written this book. However, we feel that this is not the case. To date there are a few excellent reference books, but none of them does fully encompass all fields that we consider relevant to answer our question. Some of them put a strong focus on specific topics such as benchmarking, performance measurement, asset pricing, or performance attribution. Some others are generalist, but way too short to cover the full spectrum of portfolio performance. Furthermore, the literature on the subject has literally exploded recently. It has become necessary to provide a contemporaneous synthesis. This means that we feel endowed with a key responsibility that underlies the book's title: to propose a "complete guide" involves a promise to the reader, and we must give our best efforts to deliver accordingly.

Our subtitle: *Appraise – Analyze – Act* represents the second principle that has guided us throughout the conception and production process. Studying portfolio performance is not a meditative activity. As this topic belongs to the field of financial management, there must be a concrete application associated with every single facet covered within this book. Inspired by this duty toward the reader, and with the *carte blanche* of our publisher, we have attempted to mercilessly discard superfluous digressions or material that is too theoretical. Conversely, driven by the obsession to always leave a useful takeaway for the reader, we have tried to provide recaps, roadmaps, or dashboards whenever we found it appropriate. This has resulted in material that, we hope, consistently addresses the three dimensions that underlie our title. In the first half of the book, we roll out the measures that can be used to appraise performance. In the third quarter, we show how to use these tools to analyze the performance achieved by the manager. In the final part, we examine various ways of using performance for action.

WHO IS THIS FOR?

The primary readership targeted by our book is the community of finance professionals who are involved, through whichever vector, in performance measurement issues. This includes, but is not necessarily limited to, individual and collective (fund) portfolio managers, risk managers, analysts, wealth managers, private bankers, supervisors in the asset management sector, and all the persons involved in associated activities. There is no geographical limitation, as the themes addressed here and the way we have presented them are truly universal. There is no restriction either regarding the size of the organization for which this book is relevant. Some aspects are more interesting to large institutions, whereas others explicitly target the individual investor and their professional advisor.

We also consider that many people who wish to prepare themselves for a position in the portfolio management industry would potentially benefit from the contents of this book. Having served ourselves as instructors for the preparation of some major finance certifications, we have consciously designed the book's material in accordance with the types of requirements that should be expected in this context.

Even though this is not an educational type of book, with its associated learning material (exercises, simplified examples, mini-cases, summary questions, or quizzes), we have carefully taken care of the pedagogical character of the structure and presentation. Some of our choices are particularly suitable for adoption as a main or support reference for a finance course. The parts, chapters, and sections are rigorously structured according to our own experience of teaching at the graduate and MBA levels. In most chapters, we develop a numerical example that is rolled out throughout the sections. Because we believe that it can be useful, we have also made excel files with all data, formulas, and graphs available in the companion website. Furthermore, each chapter is accompanied by a complete powerpoint presentation that is available to the book's owner. These can be freely used provided that the authors' credits are duly mentioned. Thus, we believe that many instructors would benefit from prescribing our book as main reference (for performance-dedicated courses) or, at least, as supplementary reference (for portfolio management or wealth management courses, for instance).

Finally, would the non-professional reader be interested in our book? For someone who is reasonably literate and interested in portfolio management, we believe that the answer is positive. This is a "complete guide," and it is always interesting to have this book on one's shelf in order to better understand the challenges of performance evaluation and, in particular, to meaningfully challenge the claims made by finance professionals around this topic.

HOW TO READ IT?

Because of its ambition to encompass a large variety of relevant topics in portfolio performance, this is a pure reference book. It means that we neither develop a single set of consecutive ideas as in a monograph, nor wish to propose a study guide for pure teaching purposes. Nevertheless, there is a red wire, reflected in our subtitle. Our three themes are organized with a logical progression that corresponds to the three time-related perspectives that underlie the keywords: Appraise = backward; Analyze = current; Act = forward. All chapters are designed in such a way as to address a specific topic on a stand-alone basis, with the supporting cross-references to other chapters for technical details whenever needed.

We view our main competitors as being search engines, financial information platforms, and artificial intelligence companions. In contemporaneous times, professional managers would want to rely on a few trustworthy documents that go beyond those almost unlimited resources. Through our choices of themes and their presentation through texts, tables, figures, and equations, we have always tried to walk in the shoes of our readers with the same question in mind: "*What's in it for me?*" This book aims to provide relevant answers at two levels. First, through the coverage of an extensive set of topics, it is more likely than not that a specific solution can be found on a specific problem. By staying within immediate reach of the reader, a simple gesture – opening it at the table of contents or the index section – is sufficient to jump to the right section and get, if not the complete answer, at least the directions for further investigations. Second, by the construction of the chapters, the user who wants to explore a particular theme can dig deep into it. We provide two specific tools that ease this perspective: complete numerical examples, built with realistic (i.e., actual but transformed) data, and reproducible thanks to the transparent excel files available in the companion website; and a systematic end-of-chapter "key takeaways and equations" section that provides a useful technical summary.

Pedagogical applications are not forgotten either. Backed by comprehensive slide decks, many chapters could lend themselves quite easily to the preparation of teaching, training, or study material. When writing the book, we have constantly been concerned with the clarity of exposition and the anchoring of the contents in the scientific and professional literature.

Despite our efforts regarding the completeness and correctness of the material contained in this book, we are aware that some mistakes or omissions might remain. We would strongly appreciate that anyone who wishes to provide a constructive comment with the aim of improving the book contacts us by e-mail. We will carefully consider every message and thank all contributors in advance.

Acknowledgements

We would like to thank the following persons who helped us to bring improvements to the book through various types of contributions: Philippe Bertrand, Aymeric Block, Philippe Cogneau, Vincent Colot, Alberto Desirelli, Louis Esch, Cédric Gillain, Roman Goossens, François-Valéry Lecomte, Bertrand Maillet, Elena Manola-Bonthond, Pruthvin Naveen Batham, Alexandre Scivoletto, Célina Thonus, Philippe Van Damme, and Johan Vankelecom. Pascal gratefully acknowledges the financial support of HEC Montréal. Georges is also grateful to Wilfried Niessen, Dean of HEC Liège, for his warm support and encouragements, Christelle Lecourt for her hospitality at Aix-Marseille University, and the National Fund for Scientific Research of Belgium (FNRS) for financing a temporary research allowance.

We are especially grateful to Gemma Valler, our Commissioning Editor and Richard Samson, our Managing Editor for their trust and continuous support. We also wish to thank Wiley's wonderful editorial team, Rathi Aravind, Alice Hadaway, Gajalakshmi Sivakumar, and all the persons who diligently intervened in the production process for their high-performing work.

Finally, Georges would like to express his deepest gratitude to Pierre-Armand Michel for sowing the seed of finance in his life. This book would not exist without him.

About the Website

Thank you for purchasing this book.

You may access the following additional resources provided for your use by visiting:

www.wiley.com\go\francoishubner\cgpp

This website includes:

- **Excel spreadsheets** for all through-the-chapter examples, including the supporting data, tables, graphs, and the implementation of all associated formulas
- **Powerpoint presentations** for all chapters (except Chapter 11), in normal (4/3) as well as widescreen (16/9) formats

CHAPTER 1

The Scope of Portfolio Performance

INTRODUCTION

The notion of "portfolio performance," which is at the core of the present book, is related to the quality of the management process of a financial investment. Even though it is part of the control function, we view its importance as essential for the success of the whole venture. We claim in this chapter that the feedback loop generated by the performance evaluation process has implications for the preparation and execution steps in the process. This motivates the subtitle of our book: "Appraise–Analyze–Act."

In the first section, we decorticate portfolio management by analogy with a production process. The important takeaway of this matching exercise is the identification of performance as a measure of how efficiently the inputs are transformed into an output being the terminal portfolio value. Accordingly, its inputs are *cash outlay, costs, time*, and, most critically, *risk*. According to this point of view, a risk-adjusted performance measure can be defined as an *efficiency indicator* or an *output gap*. These two structures are shared by many performance measures developed throughout the consecutive chapters.

Pursuing on the same logic, we are in a position to explain the structure of the rest of the book. It is split into four parts. The first two are dedicated to the identification and interpretation of the many portfolio performance measures that exist nowadays. This is the "appraisal" dimension. The second one, namely "analysis," mostly tries to capture and understand the drivers of performance. This is the subject matter of the third part of the book. Finally, we dare a forward-looking dimension through the "act" motto. In the fourth part of the book, we use performance measures as a real adjuvant to the investor's or the manager's decision-making process. In doing so, we close the loop of the portfolio management cycle.

For the purpose of the book's technical developments, we need to clarify a certain number of notions. The third section is therefore dedicated to laying out some basic definitions regarding returns, risk, and benchmarks. Specifically, we briefly describe the different rules for compounding and averaging returns and for incorporating cash flows into the calculation of returns. We also review the economic and probabilistic foundations of risk, elaborate on some specific risks associated with combining assets into a portfolio, and present some axioms for relevant risk measures. Finally, we stress the relevance of portfolio benchmarking and discuss some practical issues related to a comparative assessment of portfolio performance.

1.1 FROM PORTFOLIO MANAGEMENT TO PORTFOLIO PERFORMANCE

Different reference books or summary articles devoted to portfolio performance address the scope of their subject matter in various ways. Since our book will be released perhaps decades later than some of them, we do not have the ambition to reinvent the wheel. Nevertheless, our critical reading of our peers' introductory chapters reveals very diverse standpoints and structuring of thoughts. There are some disagreements on the terms, the objectives, or even the definitions surrounding the notion of portfolio performance. Since our main goal is to propose a guided tour of the matter, it is necessary that we restart from a blank page and, notwithstanding the existence of many insightful contributions in the same field, come up with our own vocabulary and structure.

We first attempt to understand where the question of portfolio performance evaluation arises in the investment decision-making process. Then, we focus on what the notion of performance itself covers in that particular context. This allows us, in a third stage, to provide more explanations about the subtitle that we have chosen for this book: "Appraise–Analyze–Act."

1.1.1 The role of portfolio performance in the investment management process

Like any well-constructed management process, the investment in a financial portfolio generally obeys a three-stage procedure, *prepare, execute, and control*, that repeats itself in a feedback loop. This process leads, in particular, to what Bailey, Richards, and Tierney (2007) call "performance evaluation." From the most general perspective, we can represent it with the chart shown in Figure 1-1, inspired from the process depicted by Maginn, Tuttle, McLeavey, and Pinto (2007).

The sequence presented in Figure 1-1 clearly shows that the preparation phase (left part of the chart) features two complementary exercises. The first one, on the upper side, consists of understanding the investor and translating this knowledge into usable parameters. The outcome of the process is to determine a portfolio policy (very long term) and associated

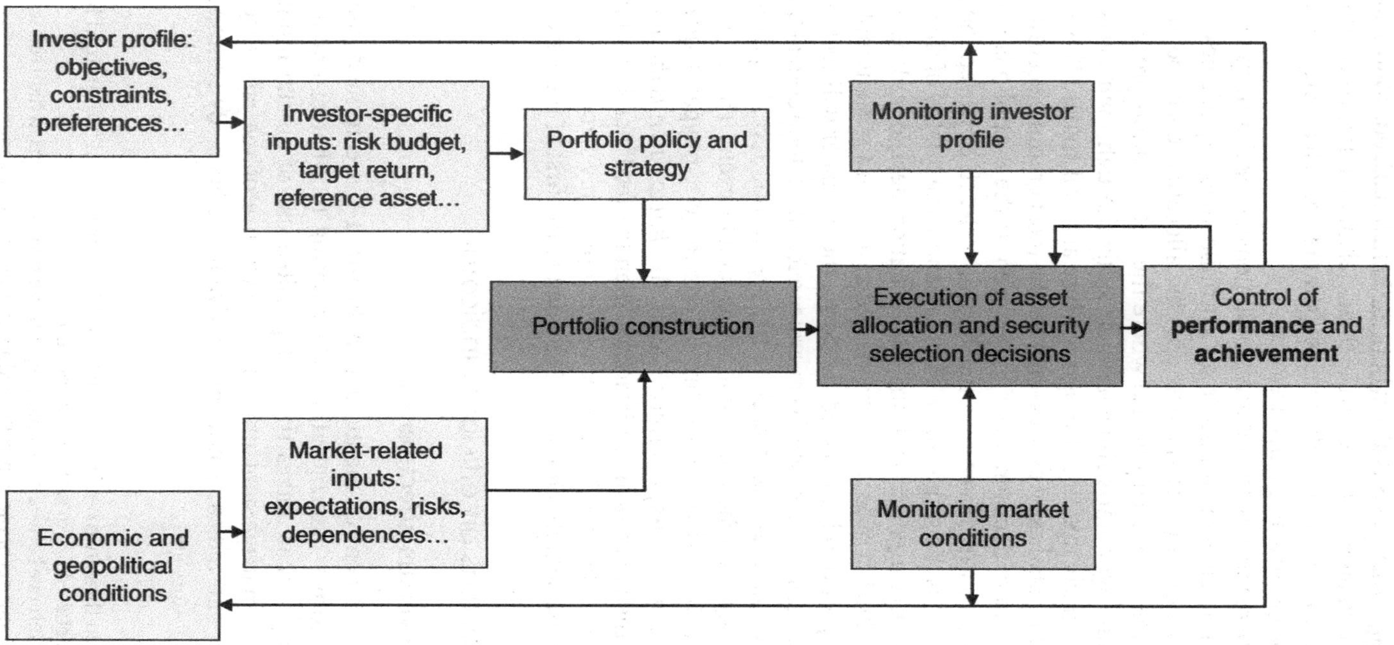

FIGURE 1-1 Steps in the portfolio management process. *Source*: Adapted from Maginn et al. (2007), Exhibit 1-1.

strategy (medium long term).[1] This is also where the benchmark portfolio, if applicable, will be determined.[2] The second module relates to the financial market. It involves the economic intelligence that leads to the calibration of the market parameters that are necessary to parametrize the risk and return properties of financial assets.

The meeting point of the market and investor dimensions is the inception of the actual execution process. It first involves creating a "real" portfolio, made up of stocks, bonds, and other instruments, with the aim of being the best possible allocation corresponding to the inputs. This is the construction phase. This is also where the optimization process is implemented. Then, the portfolio manager starts showing their skills through their decisions. The portfolio composition is regularly updated through the buy and sell trades. This can be performed from the upper level of global asset classes down to the most granular securities selection decisions, with a continuum of decision levels in between. If the portfolio is managed passively, the rebalancing decisions are driven by a mechanical rule. If, however, the manager has an active strategy, then this is the stage where they can show the quality of their decisions.

The last stage occurs *a posteriori* from the execution decisions. It is about monitoring and control. The monitoring process can be viewed as a continuous attempt to challenge and improve the way the portfolio is managed. To do so, the manager will seek information from the market and the investor's sides, which generates a feedback loop both at the execution level (by generating trades) and even going back to the preparation level by possibly changing the assumptions underlying the whole portfolio management cycle. The control level occurs at the end of the process. It consists of providing an answer to two types of questions: "*How has the portfolio management process performed?*" and "*To what extent has the outcome achieved its stated objectives?*". If the answers are satisfactory, then the feedback is positive. If not, it may certainly impact the way the mandate is executed but probably some of the assumptions used in the preparatory phase as well. Our scope is related to the first of these two questions.[3]

1.1.2 Performance as an efficiency indicator

1.1.2.1 Efficiency versus effectiveness

The two dimensions of control mentioned in Figure 1-1 are termed "performance" and "achievement." The former concept aims at evaluating to what extent the whole process has delivered an output that makes the best possible use of all the inputs that were put at the disposal of the management unit. It is a measure of the *efficiency* of the portfolio management process and indicates how productive it has been. By contrast, the concept of

[1] The articulation between these two terms for actual portfolio construction is examined in Chapter 13.
[2] See Section 1.3.3 for a detailed discussion on this notion.
[3] We come back to the difference between the meaning of these two questions, which reflect the "performance" and "achievement" components of the control function, in the next subsection.

achievement reflects how successful the portfolio has been: It is a measure of *effectiveness*. There is necessarily an objective that is associated with it.

Consider that we are interested in a specific portfolio P that has been managed according to the principles of Figure 1-1. Adapting the concepts of efficiency (performance) and effectiveness (achievement) to the particular case of the management of a financial portfolio, we can simultaneously translate them under the form of a summary equation:

$$\{X_{P,1}, \ldots, X_{P,K}\} \underset{\text{efficiency}}{\Rightarrow} Y_P \underset{\text{effectiveness}}{\Leftrightarrow} Y_P^* \tag{1-1}$$

where $\{X_{P,1}, \ldots, X_{P,K}\}$ is the set of K inputs in the portfolio management process, Y_P is the observed output (that, for simplicity, we consider to be unique at a single point in time), and Y_P^* is the objective set by the target user, who in our case is the investor. The right arrow "$\Rightarrow$" symbolizes the whole transformation process that uses the inputs in order to produce the output, whose quality reflects its efficiency level. The double arrow "$\Leftrightarrow$" symbolizes the gap between the observed and the desired output. The magnitude of this gap reflects the effectiveness of the process.

It is not the purpose of this section to discuss at length the notion of an efficient production frontier, but we can simply posit that the process aims at consuming the least possible inputs. Thus, the smaller the quantity of each input $X_{P,i}$ producing the same level of output Y_P, the higher efficiency is. A well-performing portfolio management process will thus seek to be as parsimonious as possible for the same result or, equivalently, to produce the largest possible result with a given set of available inputs.

The issue of effectiveness involves setting and disclosing a measurable output objective. The portfolio management process will have achieved its goal if the observed output exceeds this target. It does not matter here whether the inputs have been wisely used or simply wasted as long as the objective is attained. Thus, a process can be effective without being efficient and *vice versa*. Consider a simple example of someone who absolutely needs to obtain \$120 at the end of their investment horizon. They have the choice between two mutually exclusive accounts. The first one requires an initial outlay of \$100 and delivers a final amount of \$115. The second one requires an initial outlay of \$115 and delivers a final amount of \$120. Because it makes better use of the available money, the first process is more efficient than the second one. However, since the second process allows the investor to attain their objective and not the first one, it is effective and the other one is not.

1.1.2.2 Performance evaluation as a function of inputs and output

Since we are primarily interested in the notion of "portfolio performance," our focus is on the left part of Equation (1-1). Identifying the inputs of the process involves answering a simple question: *What do we want to minimize or even avoid in the hope of obtaining the output Y_P?* The qualitative answer leads to the identification of four types of inputs: cash outlay, costs, time, and risk.

1. *Cash outlay*: This is the initial amount that the investor has committed in order to start the process. Sometimes, this amount is released gradually over the portfolio lifetime, as in the case of private equity investments (see Chapter 12). This outlay can be viewed, as for any investment decision, as a temporary sacrifice of immediate consumption in order to obtain the possibility to consume more in the future. Everything else being equal, any rational investor would like to minimize this outlay to generate a given output.
2. *Costs*: This is the natural extension of the previous item. Fees, charges, taxes, and any other outflow represent an erosion of the final output. Even though, for many managed portfolios, these various costs are deducted from the investor's account, in reality this should be viewed as an add-on to the initial cash outlay.
3. *Time*: The portfolio management process is not instantaneous; it requires a certain amount of time in order to produce its output. In the meantime, the investor's money is frozen and cannot be used for any other purpose, which corresponds to a missed opportunity. The longer they have to wait to obtain their output, the lower their satisfaction.[4]
4. *Risk*: This is the most "controversial" input. We assume that the standard investor who cares about their net worth and commits a substantial amount of their own wealth in a portfolio exhibits risk aversion. This means that, *ceteris paribus*, they prefer to take less risk for the same expected outcome. There are numerous real-life examples where this assumption is violated, but these happen under specific circumstances and can be considered exceptions in the field of portfolio management.[5]

Consequently, we can generically write the set of inputs in the following way:

$$\{X_{P,1}, \ldots, X_{P,K}\} \equiv \{V_{P,0}, C_{P,H}, H, \mathcal{R}_{P,H}\} \tag{1-2}$$

[4]This statement assumes that the opportunity cost of having money committed to an investment is positive. This translates concretely into a positive interest rate. Even though there have been numerous recent examples of periods of negative nominal interest rates for many currencies, we assume that these situations are artificial and do not reflect the representative investor's time-related preferences.

[5]We discuss some of these exceptions in the context of behavioral finance, which is the subject matter of Chapter 10.

where $V_{P,0}$ stands for the initial value of portfolio P at time 0 expressed in currency units (e.g., US Dollar), $C_{P,H}$ is the total cost incurred by the investor during the whole horizon H of the portfolio management process (expressed at time H for simplicity), and $\mathcal{R}_{P,H}$ represents the total risk borne by the investor during this time frame. The symbol "≡" means "identity," i.e., the terms on both sides are identical. The arguments of the right-hand side of Equation (1-2) represent the four inputs, in their order of presentation.

The unequivocal quantitative outcome of the portfolio management process is an amount of money that crystallizes the portfolio value at the end of the period under consideration, including all reinvested interim cash flows received by the investor. This final amount can be distributed to the investor or simply available for liquidation. Thus, if the portfolio has been managed over a given investment horizon H, we can simply identify the output as

$$Y_P \equiv V_{P,H} \tag{1-3}$$

where $V_{P,H}$ stands for the value of the portfolio P at time H.

To address the link between the inputs (Equation (1-2)) and the output (Equation (1-3)), we proceed in two steps. The first one consists of eliminating the scale-related factor in the portfolio management process because most performance measures do not consider this issue explicitly.[6]

$$R_{P,H} \equiv f_{\text{scale}}(V_{P,H}; V_{P,0}, C_{P,H}) = \frac{V_{P,H} - C_{P,H}}{V_{P,0}} - 1 \tag{1-4}$$

where $f_{\text{scale}}(V_{P,H}; V_{P,0}, C_{P,H})$ is the transformation function that relates the output with two of its inputs, and $R_{P,H}$ is the cumulative net (from costs and fees) rate of return of the portfolio.

Similarly, if the time dimension is simultaneously taken into account, another simple and well-known function can be used to assess the efficiency of the portfolio management process:

$$\overline{R}_P \equiv f_{\text{scale+time}}(V_{P,H}; V_{P,0}, C_{P,H}, H) = \sqrt[H]{\frac{V_{P,H} - C_{P,H}}{V_{P,0}}} - 1 \tag{1-5}$$

where $\overline{R}_P$ is the (geometric) average net rate of return of the portfolio. Note that we can simplify this function by simply stating that the return itself reflects the impact of scale on the process. Equation (1-5) can be simply rewritten as $\overline{R}_P \equiv f_{\text{scale+time}}(R_{P,H}; H) = \sqrt[H]{1 + R_{P,H}} - 1$.

Since functions $f_{\text{scale}}(\cdot)$ and $f_{\text{scale+time}}(\cdot)$ explicitly relate the output with (some of) its inputs, the cumulative and average net portfolio returns are undoubtedly performance

[6]The main exception to the principle of scale-free performance measurement is the "first dollar alpha," that explicitly foresees decreasing returns to scale. This issue is discussed in Chapter 18.

measures.[7] This is why, in practice, there are plenty of documents that use the words "returns" and "performance" interchangeably. Nevertheless, this way of making the concepts equivalent does not meet our preference. Our reasoning is that these versions of portfolio returns do not *fully* reflect the efficiency level of the portfolio management process. A very important input is missing: risk.

We therefore generically define a *risk-adjusted performance measure* as a function that connects, explicitly or implicitly, the portfolio return not only with time but also with risk. It is interesting to distinguish two main cases, depending on whether the efficiency level of the portfolio is assessed in absolute terms or relative to an external, but comparable portfolio management process. Accordingly, our definitions are generically written as follows:

$$\mathrm{PM}_P^{\mathrm{abs}} \equiv f_{\mathrm{all}}(R_{P,H}; H, \mathcal{R}_{P,H}) \tag{1-6}$$

$$\mathrm{PM}_P^{\mathrm{rel}} \equiv f_{\mathrm{all}}(R_{P,H}; H, \mathcal{R}_{P,H}, R_{B,H}, \mathcal{R}_{B,H}) \tag{1-7}$$

where $R_{B,H}$ and $\mathcal{R}_{B,H}$ are the return and risk of a "benchmark" portfolio B, respectively, that is supposed to be comparable to portfolio P regarding the portfolio management process.

In general, the most popular types of measures encountered in practice are of two kinds. For the absolute ones (Equation (1-6)), the majority of them involve a ratio: $\mathrm{PM}_P^{\mathrm{abs}} = \frac{\mathcal{P}(R_{P,H})}{\mathcal{R}_{P,H}}$, where $\mathcal{P}(R_{P,H})$ stands for an increasing function of portfolio return. The interpretation as an *efficiency ratio* is quite obvious: The ratio increases with the numerator (output) and decreases with the denominator (input). This is the case for the Sharpe ratio, as discussed in Chapter 3, for instance. For the relative measures (Equation (1-7)), most measures use a differential operator: $\mathrm{PM}_P^{\mathrm{rel}} = \mathcal{P}(R_{P,H}) - \mathcal{P}(R_{B,H})$, where the benchmark risk is implicitly subsumed under its rate of return. This simple expression, equivalent to an *output gap*, covers Jensen's alpha, which is also discussed in Chapter 3.

However, the ways to measure performance are not limited to these simple examples. In total, we list 116 performance measures, summarized in Chapter 11, that correspond to the definition of Equation (1-6) or (1-7). In addition, for some specific cases, some adaptations are also examined in Chapters 12 and 16. However, they all share a common characteristic: The transformation function $f_{\mathrm{all}}(\cdot)$ can be of many different types, but it must account for portfolio risk in one way or another.

A final note is worth mentioning here. Some performance measures mix some elements of efficiency and effectiveness. This is the case of measures that use a notion of reservation rate

[7]Some authors, like Bailey et al. (2007), indeed associate the name "performance measure" with only the rate of return defined in Equations (1-4) or (1-5) and contrast them with the notion of "performance appraisal," which takes into account all inputs in order to assess the skills of the portfolio manager. While we acknowledge the correctness of their point of view, we diverge from their terminology by associating the term (risk-adjusted) "performance measure" to a function that takes all inputs (including risk) into account and refer to "performance appraisal" as the use and interpretation of the measures.

(i.e., minimum acceptable rate of return) or target return (for specific investment goals). They are mostly studied in Chapter 10, which is devoted to the study of performance measures that are adapted to a behavioral finance context.

1.1.3 Why appraise, analyze, and use performance in decision-making

From the above discussion, it appears that our focus is on the last phase of the process. Even though it occurs in the end, after the output of the portfolio management decisions has been observed, Figure 1-1 clearly shows that the control stage is part of a circuit. It can thus be viewed as the beginning of a new cycle in the decision-making process. This statement motivates the whole philosophy that we pursue in this book.

Zooming in on the last part of Figure 1-1 provides a first visual insight into our red wire. Leaving aside the "achievement" function, the cyclical character of the investment management process can be very clearly connected to the three dimensions that are covered throughout the book, as shown in Figure 1-2.

Figure 1-2 clearly shows the interaction between different dimensions involving the use of performance-related tools. It starts with an *ex post* appraisal method, out of which an analysis is carried out in order to gain insights and prepare for potential action for the future.

The retrospective application of performance evaluation consists of appraising how efficiently the portfolio management process has been carried out. This is where we need to put in place a measurement approach that detects how the manager has performed their job with the inputs that they have consumed. Since there are a variety of ways to approach the "risk" input, and also to treat the characteristics of a properly designed benchmark, it is not surprising to realize that this dimension is particularly bushy and requires a lot of attention.

The next step is to properly analyze how the performance has been generated. From a very wide perspective, it can be viewed to encompass the performance measurement stage. Nevertheless, Amenc and Le Sourd (2003) point out that "*Performance analysis is the final stage in*

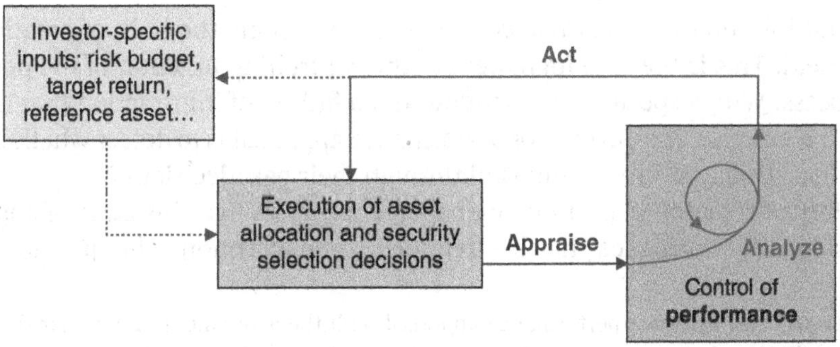

FIGURE 1-2 The feedback loop of performance evaluation.

the portfolio management process. It provides an overall evaluation of the success of the investment management process in reaching its objective and also identifies the individual contribution of each phase to the overall result." We stand at the heart of the control function. Leaving aside the effectiveness check (see above), the key objective is to understand and explain. This means that it might be necessary to (i) account for the specificities of the portfolio that does not lend itself easily to a plain appraisal approach and (ii) use some specific tools, such as attribution models (Chapters 13 and 14), in order to gain insight into the sources of overperformance or underperformance.

Lastly, performance appraisal and analysis can serve as a basis for decision-making. This "act" dimension starts with good communication and understanding from the receiver. Feedback on performance can then be used to revise the investment management process, at least, not only operationally (this is the solid arrow, going back directly to the execution engine) but also potentially strategically. It serves not only as an internal guidance for the manager but also as a selection criterion for the investor. Incidentally, performance can be used to reward, penalize, hire or fire managers. One must ensure that the signal sent by the retrospective evaluation is properly processed because in the end, it is all about people.

1.2 ROLLING OUT THE THREE LAYERS OF PERFORMANCE EVALUATION

The three layers of performance evaluation presented in Figure 1-2 involve dealing with the past (appraise), the present (analyze), and the future (act). Because of the cyclical character of the process, these dimensions are heavily intricated: The future of the current time is also the past of the next control period. Nevertheless, we can identify several themes that more closely correspond to each of these dimensions. The whole book's structure, including all 17 chapters following this introductory one, is designed in accordance with the cyclical view. Each of them is discussed below.

1.2.1 Understanding the past: Performance appraisal

Designing and interpreting performance measures represents the bulk of creative contributions in the field. This is the core ingredient of the controlling function of the portfolio management process. With a specific time window and a full set of information that is considered relevant for the exercise, the purpose of performance appraisal is to detect whether the portfolio manager has displayed investment skill through their past decisions.[8]

The history of research in portfolio management reveals that this issue of appraisal is the first dimension of performance that has retained some attention. The question of whether

[8]Bailey et al. (2007) also associate performance appraisal with the assessment of whether the manager can preserve their skill. We adopt a more granular perspective and associate this predictive assessment with the "act" dimension.

active portfolio managers are able to "beat the market" through a representative stock index is central to the article of Jensen (1968). Since the 1960s, hundreds of researchers and practitioners have designed measures aimed at diagnosing as precisely as possible if, and how, managers have actually been able to manage their portfolio in the most efficient way. This plethora of measurement approaches, many of which are very meaningful, explains why this topic represents a substantial fraction of our material. Figure 1-3 represents the logic underlying our structure.

Figure 1-3 shows how first two parts of the book, which are devoted to the "appraisal" dimension, organize the corresponding nine chapters. The figures featuring in each box correspond to the numbers of remarkable performance measures that we list and analyze further in Chapter 11 (whose scope is explained in the next subsection).

Part I, entitled "Classical Performance Measurement," is entirely dedicated to the in-depth study of the performance measures that were developed in the early days of the Standard Portfolio Theory (SPT) – generally known in the literature as the Modern Portfolio Theory but that we prefer to rename according to a more contemporaneous perspective – introduced by Markowitz (1952), and the consecutive Capital Asset Pricing Model (CAPM) developed by Treynor (1962), Sharpe (1964), Lintner (1965), and Mossin (1966). Whereas Part I comprises four chapters, Figure 1-3 only displays one of them. Due to the historical importance and the popularity of the classical measures, the other chapters discuss their theoretical underpinnings (Chapter 2), the rationale for their choice (Chapter 4), and the difficulties associated with their application (Chapter 5).

Part II investigates the other ways to measure performance – including extensions of the original measures – that coexist in the literature or in market practice, or that we propose ourselves within this book. They can be split into three categories. The first one covers the extensive set of measures that can be viewed as variations from the classical ones (Chapter 6). The second one examines measures that have been developed with a view to reveal how the

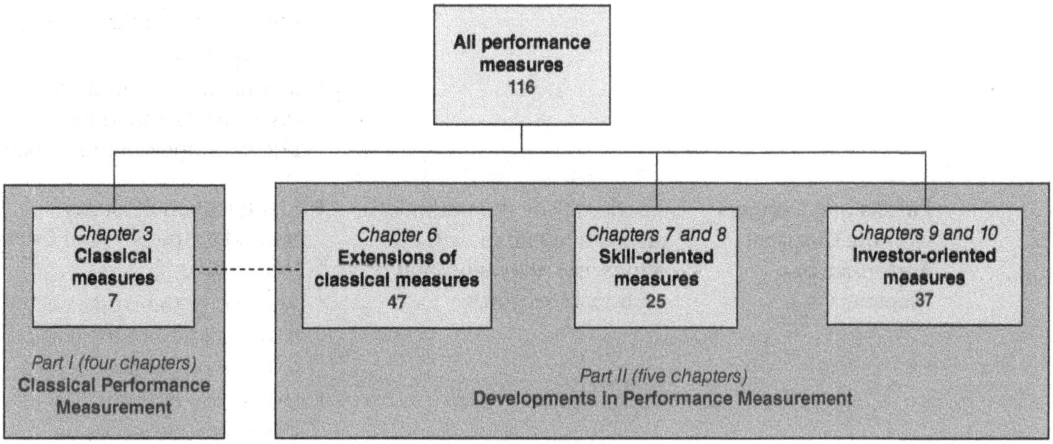

FIGURE 1-3 Structure of the "appraisal" dimension in the book.

portfolio manager has implemented their skills through (i) the identification of their risk factor sensitivities (Chapter 7) or (ii) the uncovering of their market timing skills (Chapter 8). The third one focuses on the investor's preferences and makes a distinction between the assumption of a standard (i.e., fully rational) or a behavioral investor (Chapters 9 and 10, respectively).

The summaries in Tables 1-1 and 1-2 provide a high-level description of each chapter for Parts I and II.

TABLE 1-1 Overviews of the chapters contained in Part I.

Chapter	Title	Objective	Key features
2	**Standard Portfolio Theory and the CAPM**	To develop and explain the theoretical underpinnings of the classical performance measures	• Presentation of the SPT and the CAPM • Practical insights on how to implement the CAPM • Presentation of multifactor extensions
3	**Classical Portfolio Performance Measures**	To present the main classical performance measures based on total risk, systematic risk, and specific risk	• Definition of each measure • Practical and statistical significance criteria • Discussion of strengths and weaknesses
4	**Selecting a Classical Performance Measure**	To discuss the criteria to be considered for the choice of the most suitable classical performance measure	• Categorization of measures on the risk and measurement dimensions • Choice criteria from the normative and the positive standpoints • Identification of how to discriminate managers based on their performance
5	**Pitfalls and Dangers with the Classical Performance Measures**	To identify all the potential issues associated with the practical implementation of classical measures	• Identification of issues related to the SPT and CAPM frameworks • Analysis of the statistical issues related to the sample and the regressions • Discussion of the interpretation issues

TABLE 1-2 Overviews of the chapters contained in Part II.

Chapter	Title	Objective	Key features
6	**The Classical Performance Measures Revisited**	To review relevant alternative performance measures that build on the classical ones	• Presentation of refined or altered versions of the Sharpe ratio • Alternative versions of the other performance measures • Design of risk-adjusted forms of classical measures
7	**Performance Measurement in Multifactor Models**	To examine how performance can be measured when the manager is exposed to several risk factors	• Identification of the different families of multifactor models • Presentation of classical performance measures adapted to a multifactor context • Special cases of multifactor models
8	**Performance Measurement with Market Timing**	To examine how performance can be measured when the manager attempts to time the market	• Measurement of performance with non-linear regressions • Capture of market timing with return-based and holding-based exposures • Roadmap for the choice of market timing appraisal method
9	**Preference-based Performance for the Standard Investor**	To determine how performance must be appraised when the investor's risk aversion is taken into account	• Definition of the structure of the standard investor's preferences • Identification of preference-based measures in the mean–variance framework • Use of standard utility functions for performance measurement
10	**Preference-based Performance for the Behavioral Investor**	To determine how performance must be appraised when the investor's behavioral traits are taken into account	• Definition of the structure of the behavioral investor's preferences • Use of behavioral utility functions for performance measurement • Extensions to ratios of gains over losses • Assessing performance with mental accounts

1.2.2 Explaining the present: Performance analysis

With (at least) 116 ways to assess the past performance of a portfolio manager, anyone would presumably be lost without further guidance. Fortunately, there exist tools in order to make sense of all this information. In Part III, devoted to the analysis of performance-related information and made up of four chapters, we propose some guidance on three dimensions.

First and foremost, we find it necessary to provide the reader with some keys in order to find a way out of the maze of performance measures. Chapter 11, which attempts to perform this task, should be viewed as the bridge between the appraisal and the analysis of performance. This chapter applies different methods to sort the measures in a logical way and concludes by providing a dashboard for the selection of one or several approaches that are suited to the analysis.

The second dimension, addressed in Chapter 12, focuses on the necessary adaptations to faithfully reflect how performance should be analyzed in specific portfolio management contexts. The purpose is not to reinvent performance measures but to adapt the framework to the specificities of particular asset classes that go beyond the traditional equity or global allocation portfolios for which many measures have been designed.

The last two chapters (Chapters 13 and 14) of Part III are dedicated to a set of processes that are generally considered at the core of performance analysis, namely contribution and attribution. Consistent with our philosophy, the purpose of these two chapters is neither to replace the very detailed treatment of some qualitative and highly specialized textbooks on the matter nor to present the sometimes very sophisticated practical systems that are made available to the analyst by premium vendors. Rather, they aim at providing some insight regarding the approach and some useful applications in order to get started with a thorough analysis of the performance drivers in many circumstances.

The key insights of the chapters covered in Part III are reported in Table 1-3.

1.2.3 Preparing the future: Using performance for action

Because of its richness, performance analysis can serve as basis in the decision-making process. There are various ways to consider this matter, but the first element to consider is a proper transmission mechanism from the issuer to the consumer of performance information. This is the reason why Part IV, which is dedicated to the use of performance for action, starts with the issue of the communication of performance-related information in Chapter 15. This involves not only a faithful disclosure but also the possibility for the receiver to verify the correctness and exhaustiveness of information that serves as the basis for their own decision-making process.

The next two chapters propose a thorough investigation of two important themes belonging to this dimension. The first one, which is the focus of Chapter 16, examines how performance measures themselves can be used as a decision-making tool for several strategies or investor types. This is where we analyze more closely the link between financial and non-financial (i.e., sustainability-driven) performance. The second chapter (Chapter 17) studies the link between past and future performance, generally associated with the term

TABLE 1-3 Overviews of the chapters contained in Part III.

Chapter	Title	Objective	Key features
11	**Navigating the Maze of Portfolio Performance**	To sort and structure the main 116 measures presented in the first two parts	• Structured list and glossary of the 116 measures • Analysis of analytical and statistical sorting procedures • Dashboard for the selection of measures
12	**Performance Design for Specific Asset Classes**	To determine how performance analysis must be adapted to reflect specificities of some portfolio management strategies	• Adaptation of the performance framework for fixed-income portfolios • Specificities of illiquid investments • Design of performance analysis for hedge funds and private equity
13	**The Granular Analysis of Performance**	To introduce the processes of performance contribution and attribution of performance measures	• Dissection of the fundamentals of performance decomposition • Defining performance attribution • Applying attribution to performance ratios
14	**Performance Attribution Methods**	To develop the main practical methods to attribute portfolio performance	• Introduction to the BHB attribution analysis framework for single and multiple periods • Extension of the framework to different portfolio types • Adaptation to statistical attribution analysis

"persistence," extending the scope to other relevant indicators for the investment decision-maker.

The final chapter explores the delicate topics of agency conflicts and illusions regarding performance. It aims at identifying many situations in which performance must be considered with great caution. These situations concern remuneration issues, temptation to artificially embellish the outcome of the portfolio management process, or simply disentangling skill from luck. Chapter 18 can be viewed as a synthetic *vade mecum* for the decision-maker who wishes to avoid being mistaken throughout the process.

The contents of Part IV are summarized in Table 1-4.

TABLE 1-4 Overviews of the chapters contained in Part IV.

Chapter	Title	Objective	Key features
15	**Disclosing and Verifying Portfolio Performance**	To identify the challenges of properly communicating and understanding performance-related information	• Main features of the Global Investment Performance Standards (GIPS) • Discussion of the challenges of effective performance communication • Introduction to fund rating and portfolio analysis systems
16	**Applications of Performance in Investment Decisions**	To use performance-related approaches as an aid in the investment decision-making process	• Determination of investment universe and strategy design using performance analysis • Use of performance criteria for specific typologies of investors • Reconciliation of ESG criteria and financial performance
17	**Performance and Predictability**	To analyze the link between past and future performance-related characteristics	• Discussion of the drivers of predictability in portfolio management • Identification of absolute persistence in performance • Methods for studying relative persistence
18	**Agency Issues and Illusion of Performance**	To distinguish the cases in which performance should not be considered at face value for decision-making	• Examination of the implications of performance measure in agency conflicts • Design principles for adequate performance measurement • Distinction between skill and luck in performance

1.3 RETURNS, RISK, AND BENCHMARKS

This section is dedicated to the definition and some technical clarifications regarding the three major ingredients of portfolio performance appraisal, namely the return, its associated risk, and the benchmark.

1.3.1 Returns

A portfolio return seems to be the most intuitive economic notion related to performance. However, the precise notion of a return requires a few specifications that we examine below.

1.3.1.1 Compounding

Using the notations introduced in Section 1.1, the gross and net returns on portfolio P between dates t_1 and t_2 are given by

$$R_{P,t_2}^{\text{gross}} = \frac{V_{P,t_2}}{V_{P,t_1}} \tag{1-8}$$

$$R_{P,t_2}^{\text{net}} = \frac{V_{P,t_2} - V_{P,t_1}}{V_{P,t_1}} = R_{P,t_2}^{\text{gross}} - 1 \tag{1-9}$$

For clarity of exposition, we will work with net returns whenever possible, and the notation $R_{P,t}$ will by default refer to a net return at the period ending at time t. For instance, the presentation of the STP in Chapter 2 relies on net returns.

Returns can be compounded discretely or continuously, depending on how the passing of time is envisioned. This distinction yields two different methods for calculating cumulative returns over several periods. The discrete compounding of \$1 over N (equally spaced) periods yields

$$(1 + R_{P,t_1})(1 + R_{P,t_2}) \ldots (1 + R_{P,t_N}) = \prod_{i=1}^{N} (1 + R_{P,t_i}) \tag{1-10}$$

where all the R_{P,t_i} are periodic returns (i.e., expressed in reference to the duration of the period). The continuous compounding of \$1 over N (equally spaced) periods yields

$$\mathrm{e}^{R_{P,t_1}^c} \mathrm{e}^{R_{P,t_2}^c} \ldots \mathrm{e}^{R_{P,t_N}^c} = \prod_{i=1}^{N} \mathrm{e}^{R_{P,t_i}^c} = \exp\left(\sum_{i=1}^{N} R_{P,t_i}^c \right) \tag{1-11}$$

where superscript "c" indicates that the R_{P,t_i}^c are continuously compounded.

Equations (1-10) and (1-11) do not just reflect two compounding conventions. They also involve two different types of returns: Discretely compounded (or, simply, "discrete") returns take on values above −1, whereas continuous returns are real values.

1.3.1.2 Average returns

Another issue that arises when performance is evaluated over several periods is how to compute average returns. There are two methods for averaging returns whose use depends on the context of application.

When an investor aims at assessing the average financial profitability of their investment, they should use the *geometric average* return given by

$$\overline{R}^{\text{geo}}_{P,t_N} = \sqrt[N]{\prod_{i=1}^{N}(1 + R_{P,t_i})} - 1 \tag{1-12}$$

The geometric average return reflects the average economic conditions under which the portfolio owner or manager actually invests their money. Suppose the end-of-month values of portfolio P (with initial cash outlay 100) turn out to be 102 in January, 99 in February, and 103 in March. The periodic net returns are $\left(\frac{102}{100} - 1\right) = 2\%$, $\left(\frac{99}{102} - 1\right) = -2.94\%$, and $\left(\frac{103}{99} - 1\right) = 4.04\%$ for the first, second, and third months, respectively. Over the three-month period, the portfolio has experienced an average monthly return of $\overline{R}^{\text{geo}}_{P,t_N} = \sqrt[3]{(1 + 2\%)(1 - 2.94\%)(1 + 4.04\%)} - 1 \approx 0.99\%$. Indeed, compounding the initial investment at this rate over three months yields the same terminal value: $100(1 + 0.99\%)^3 \approx 103$.

For statistical purposes, it might be relevant to use the *arithmetic average* return defined as

$$\overline{R}^{\text{ari}}_{P,t_N} = \frac{1}{N}\sum_{i=1}^{N}(1 + R_{P,t_i}) - 1 \tag{1-13}$$

To extrapolate the portfolio profitability, one may wish to generate scenarios for future periodic returns. If one assumes that the observed past returns represent independent draws from an identical (not necessarily known) distribution, then one can consider that, on average, the investor should expect their portfolio to yield $\overline{R}^{\text{ari}}_{P,t_N}$ for the upcoming periods. Using the same numerical example, we obtain $\overline{R}^{\text{ari}}_{P,t_N} = \frac{1}{3}(1 + 2\% + 1 - 2.94\% + 1 + 4.04\%) - 1 \approx 1.03\%$.

Note that, by construction, $\overline{R}_{P,t_N}^{\text{geo}} < \overline{R}_{P,t_N}^{\text{ari}}$, and the financial explanation for this difference is the compounding of interests over several periods that the geometric average captures while the arithmetic average does not.

1.3.1.3 Multiperiod returns with interim cash flows

During their management, portfolios often receive additional deposits or experience partial withdrawals. These interim cash inflows and outflows clearly affect the value of the portfolio. However, they should not interfere with the calculation of the value created by the portfolio manager. To this end, one should use *time-value weighted returns* defined as geometric average returns with periodic returns given by

$$R_{P,t_i} = \frac{V_{P,t_i} - (V_{P,t_{i-1}} + \mathrm{CF}_{t_i})}{V_{P,t_{i-1}} + \mathrm{CF}_{t_i}} \tag{1-14}$$

where CF_{t_i} denotes the net cash flow affecting portfolio P between dates t_{i-1} and t_i. Other similar methods are available (such as the modified Dietz method). A more detailed discussion on this issue can be found in Chapter 15.

In those cases where the value of the portfolio cannot be marked to market on a frequent basis such as, for instance, investments in illiquid segments (e.g., private equity or real estate), one must resort to *money-value weighted returns*. These can be calculated as an internal rate of return (IRR) over the whole period of evaluation. That is, the IRR is the solution to

$$V_{P,t_0} = \sum_{i=1}^{N} \frac{\mathrm{CF}_{t_i}}{(1+\mathrm{IRR})^i} + \frac{V_{P,t_N}}{(1+\mathrm{IRR})^N} \tag{1-15}$$

The IRR reflects the average periodic growth rate of the investment, but its determination is biased by the timing of cash flows.

1.3.2 Risk and risk measure in portfolio performance

As discussed in Section 1.1.2, risk is one of the most important inputs in the assessment of portfolio performance, and it turns out to be one of the most difficult to define and measure. The very notion of risk is related to danger,[9] and one fundamental assumption in economics and finance is that investors are non-satiable (they always prefer more to less) and risk averse.

[9] The word "risk" allegedly stems from "*resecum*" (literally "something that cuts" in Latin), which designated a reef and, by extension, the hazard threatening supplies shipped by boat.

Since the semantic distinction made by Frank Knight in 1921, it is commonly admitted that risk, in contrast to uncertainty, is measurable. Thus, the characterization of risk in performance appraisal is subject to a twin problem: One needs to rely on a definition of risk and a corresponding *risk measure*. We briefly review the major approaches followed in the finance literature to provide a representation of risk. Then, we touch upon the specific additional issues while dealing with *portfolio risk*. Finally, we present some axioms related to measuring risk and provide examples of some commonly used risk metrics.

In what follows, the representations and measures of risk refer, without any loss in generality, to *total risk*. Depending on the investment context, they can also be applied to systematic risk or idiosyncratic risk. These alternative specifications will yield different dimensions for portfolio performance appraisal and, accordingly, different performance metrics (see Chapters 3 and 6).

1.3.2.1 Representations of risk

1. The utility-based representation

In neo-classical economics, the formal treatment of decision under uncertainty relies on the expected utility theory. Consider an investment universe comprised of N risky assets with (stochastic) gross returns $R_{i,H}$ over horizon ($i = 1, \ldots, N$). Endowed with a utility function $U(\cdot)$ assumed to be monotonically increasing (for non-satiability) and concave (for risk aversion), the rational investor allocates the amount x_i in asset i, and solves the following optimization problem:

$$\max_{x_i} \mathrm{E}[U(V_{P,H})] \qquad \text{(1-16)}$$
$$\text{s.t.} \sum_{i=1}^{N} x_i = V_{P,0}$$

where $V_{P,H} = V_{P,0} + \sum_{i=1}^{N} x_i R_{i,H}$ stands for the value of the portfolio P at time H.

To avoid resorting to utility functions, the utility maximization problem above can be reformulated as risk minimization. More specifically, the measure of risk $\mathcal{R}_{P,H}$ is said to be *consistent* with the order relation induced by the utility function $U(\cdot)$ if Equation (1-16) is equivalent to (see Ortobelli, Svetlozar, Rachev, Stoyanov, Fabozzi, and Biglova, 2005, for more details):

$$\min_{x_i} \mathcal{R}_{P,H}(V_{P,H}) \qquad \text{(1-17)}$$
$$\text{s.t.} \sum_{i=1}^{N} x_i = V_{P,0} \text{ and } \mathrm{E}(V_{P,H}) \geq m$$

where m denotes a minimal requirement on expected terminal wealth.

The formulation (1-17) of portfolio investment puts the risk measure at the center of the problem. Alternatively, the utility maximization program of Equation (1-16) offers another representation of risk through the notion of *stochastic dominance*.[10] Indeed, it has been shown (see, e.g., Levy, 1992) that having $\mathrm{E}[U(V_{P_1,H})] \geq \mathrm{E}[U(V_{P_2,H})]$ for two portfolios P_1 and P_2 and for any increasing, concave utility function (where the inequality is strict for at least one particular $U(\cdot)$) is equivalent to portfolio P_1 being second-order stochastically dominating portfolio P_2.

2. Probabilistic representation

The representation of risk through stochastic dominance is particularly insightful because it reflects the idea that the risk associated with the investment problem (1-16) can be directly measured from the distribution of terminal wealth $V_{P,H}$.

The probabilistic approach also represents a shift in the focus on risk: While the utility function is inherently related to the investor's attitude toward risk (a subjective measure), the distribution of terminal wealth (or, equivalently, return) can be objectively constructed from the data using, for instance, statistical inference or parametric modeling. Nevertheless, the subjective assessment of risk is not entirely ruled out in the probabilistic approach. Once the distribution of returns is determined, the investor must decide which aspects of that distribution they like or dislike.

In this regard, the investor's attitude toward risk can be conveniently subsumed within their tastes for the different moments of the return distribution. It is usually acknowledged that rational investors enjoy higher odd moments and lower even moments. As a matter of fact, a non-satiable investor likes a higher expected terminal wealth, all else being equal. A risk-averse investor dislikes the variance surrounding that terminal wealth. However, even if the attitude toward the third moment is usually a preference for positive skewness, such behavior may not hold for all agents in all markets. The fourth moment (also known as kurtosis) represents the variance of the variance and indicates the likelihood of extreme events, which investors typically dislike. It is conceptually difficult to associate investors' behavioral traits with moments of order higher than four.[11]

It therefore appears that, for a given return distribution, a measure of risk can be designed by penalizing to various extents the exposure to variance, negative skewness, and kurtosis. A technical limitation associated with this approach is the aggregation over time. When portfolio performance must be evaluated over several periods, the return expectation and variance grow proportionally with time under mild assumptions, but no similar rule exists regarding skewness and kurtosis.

---

[10]Stochastic dominance is a preference rule between two outcomes that involves the shapes of their cumulative distribution functions (CDFs). See Chapter 16 for a formal analysis.

[11]A more detailed analysis of the structure of investors' preferences is carried out in Chapter 9.

3. Downside and upside risks

An important question affecting the representation of risk is whether the investor should only worry about the potential losses or if they should find a way to trade off the exposures to gains and losses. There are, in fact, three ways to address this dilemma. The first one (and oldest one in the development of portfolio theory) is to penalize upside and downside wealth variations equally. This only makes sense if the return distribution is symmetric (like the normal distribution, for example). Such behavior leads to adopting a risk measure such as the standard deviation.

A second attitude is to focus exclusively on downside risk. Assuming investment portfolios are made of long positions in assets, risk exposure is then assessed from the shape of the left tail of the return distribution. Note that this behavior can be motivated by subjective reasons (such as aversion to regret) or by objective reasons (avoidance of costly frictions such as illiquidity or bankruptcy). Examples of corresponding risk measures[12] include the negative semi-variance, the Value-at-Risk (VaR), the Conditional Value-at-Risk (CVaR), and Young's (1998) minimax criterion.

Finally, an investor with a more comprehensive view might want to adjust their appreciation of downside risk with the potential for gains. This leads to performance metrics combining gains and losses (typically in the form of a ratio), that are examined in a greater detail in Chapter 10.

1.3.2.2 Risks of portfolios

The discussion up to this point has considered the risk affecting the terminal wealth $V_{P,H}$ as a whole (i.e., as if it were composed of a single asset). However, since P is a portfolio made of many different assets, its overall risk is the sum of all individual risks of its components. As such, the portfolio risk is impacted by the *diversification* effect and by *correlation risk*.

Diversification refers to the gradual elimination of idiosyncratic risk as the number of assets in the portfolio increases. Indeed, correlation among many assets tends to cancel out shocks in returns that go in opposite directions. When this mechanism is applied on a large scale, mostly co-movements in asset returns affect the portfolio value, and such exposure to covariance risk can be interpreted as systematic risk. However, diversification not only reduces total risk but also alters the moments of the portfolio return distribution and thereby the nature of risk that the investor is exposed to.

To illustrate this, Figure 1-4 shows the evolution of the portfolio return standard deviation (σ), skewness (s), and kurtosis (k) as a function of the number of assets (N). The individual

[12]Ortobelli et al. (2005) refer to them as "safety-first" risk measures.

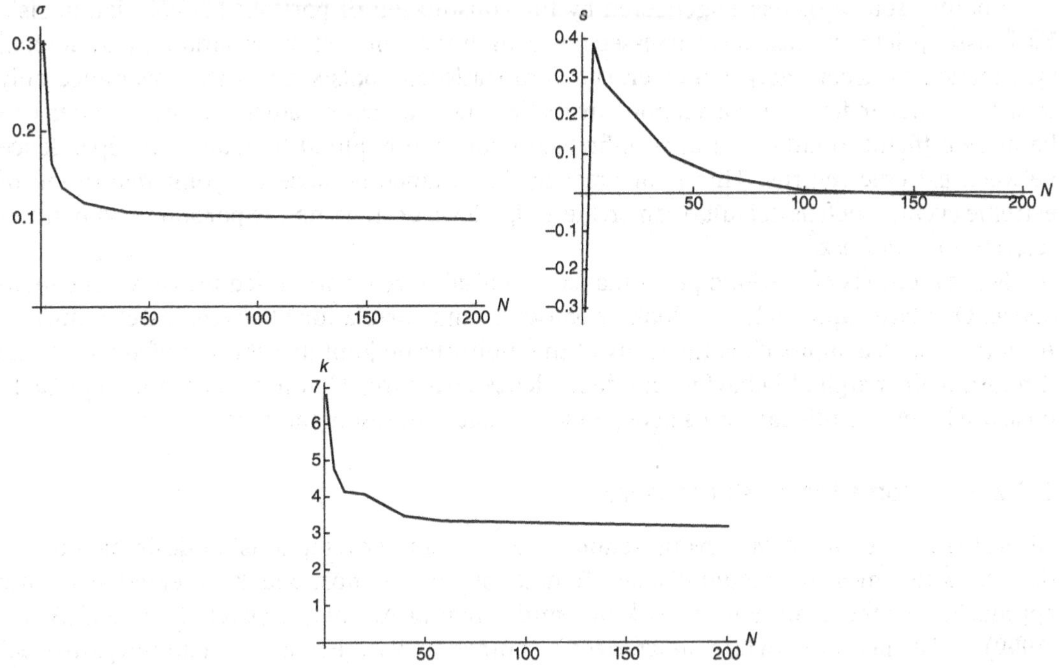

FIGURE 1-4 Example of diversification on portfolio return standard deviation σ, skewness s, and kurtosis k.

asset returns are generated by a Cornish–Fisher expansion that accommodates slight deviations from normality.[13] To simplify the exposition, all individual asset returns display similar characteristics (same σ, s, and k) and are linked by the same pairwise correlation coefficient (equi-correlation). More specifically, these returns are slightly negatively skewed, leptokurtic (i.e., the tails of their distribution are fatter than the normal tails), and they are positively correlated with one another.

The example displayed in Figure 1-4 is only one among many different situations depending on the characteristics of the individual assets. It, however, highlights some common effects of diversification. First, the standard deviation rapidly decreases with N and stabilizes at some incompressible level, its amount of systematic risk. Second, a similar phenomenon applies to the kurtosis: The exposure to some extreme outcomes cannot be fully diversified away. These two diversification effects should be welcomed by the risk-averse investor. However, the behavior of skewness is more complex. The individual negative skewness is quickly flipped into a positive value for a small number of assets. Then, the portfolio skewness erodes with portfolio size and can ultimately revert to negative values. Depending on the investor's preferences, the combined impact of diversification on portfolio skewness and kurtosis may or may not be favorably perceived.

[13]See Chapter 6 for a detailed presentation of the Cornish–Fisher expansion.

Another source of risk engendered by the constitution of portfolios is correlation risk. Early asset pricing models have assessed correlation risk with return covariance and defined systematic risk accordingly. However, standard statistical tools such as the covariance only measure a linear form of correlation. In reality, the way asset returns move together can be more difficult to fathom, and specific techniques are required to gauge the dependence between extreme returns. This is of practical importance because the joint realization of extreme events (such as defaults) can create a high level of stress on the portfolio – sometimes referred to as *tail risk*.

Some methods of portfolio performance appraisal have incorporated measures of dependence. One basic approach is to look at pairwise rank correlations between asset returns.[14] A more advanced approach is the study of the multivariate joint distribution of asset returns through their marginal behavior and dependence structure. That approach uses *copulas* to measure highly non-linear forms of dependence that manifest in tail risk.

1.3.2.3 Axioms for a risk measure

Given the discussion above, several scholars have tried to develop a list of desirable properties that a risk measure should display. To date, one of the most widely accepted axiomatic approaches for the definition of a risk measure is that of Artzner, Delbaen, Eber, and Heath (1999). A risk measure can be characterized as a function $\mathcal{R}_{P,H}$ that assigns a non-negative real number (a score) to the random variable "the value of portfolio P at horizon H." Artzner et al. (1999) posit that $\mathcal{R}_{P,H}$ is a *coherent* risk measure if it satisfies the following properties:

- *Subadditivity*: For two portfolios P_1 and P_2, $\mathcal{R}_{P,H}(P_1 + P_2) \leq \mathcal{R}_{P,H}(P_1) + \mathcal{R}_{P,H}(P_2)$. This property implies that the risk score should reflect the benefits of diversification.
- *Positive homogeneity*: For any positive scalar c, $\mathcal{R}_{P,H}(cP) = c\mathcal{R}_{P,H}(P)$. This property implies that any leveraged portfolio should increase the risk score in proportion to the leverage factor.
- *Translation invariance*: For any scalar c and denoting by R_f the periodic risk-free rate, $\mathcal{R}_{P,H}(P + c(1 + R_f)^H) = \mathcal{R}_{P,H}(P) - c$. This property implies that any investment in the risk-free asset should diminish the risk score by the invested amount.
- *Monotonicity*: If in all states of the world, $P_1 \leq P_2$, then $\mathcal{R}_{P,H}(P_2) \leq \mathcal{R}_{P,H}(P_1)$. This property implies that the risk measure should focus on the downside risk.

Alternatively, the first two properties can be replaced with a convexity condition, i.e., for two portfolios P_1 and P_2 and any scalar c between 0 and 1, $\mathcal{R}_{P,H}(cP_1 + (1 - c)P_2) \leq c\mathcal{R}_{P,H}(P_1) + (1 - c)\mathcal{R}_{P,H}(P_2)$. The convexity property being less stringent than combined subadditivity and

[14] The main corresponding statistical tool is Kendall's tau discussed in Chapter 17.

positive homogeneity, a risk measure that complies with convexity, translation invariance and monotonicity is said to be weakly coherent (Carr, Geman, and Madan, 2001).

This list of axioms serves as a guideline for a proper assessment of risk. As we will see, several (but not all) portfolio performance metrics rely on risk measures that meet some (but not all) of these criteria. Table 1-5 (inspired by Ortobelli et al., 2005) lists some of the classic risk measures used in portfolio performance appraisal and checks their conformity with coherence.

Note also that all the risk measures listed in this table are consistent with second-order stochastic dominance (Section 1.3.2.1), except for the Value-at-Risk.

In a recent simulation study on nearly 200 000 portfolios of US stocks, Righi and Borenstein (2018) examine the rankings of portfolio strategies that solve either a risk minimization problem such as Equation (1-17) or a risk-adjusted value maximization problem such as Equation (1-16). The optimization problems are solved using 11 popular risk measures. The authors' major finding is that, despite some variations in the portfolio rankings, there is no risk measure that is clearly preferable to the others, in the sense that it allows us to achieve a significantly better optimum. This result does not mean that risk measures are pointless. Rather, it calls for a robust analysis of risk in the appraisal of portfolio performance.

1.3.3 Benchmarks

The concept of a benchmark is pervasive in the asset management literature. The reason is that for most investors, performance must be evaluated in relative terms.[15] Indeed, the comparative approach in appraising an (active) investment strategy reflects the scarcity of investable

TABLE 1-5 Properties of some common risk measures (adapted from Ortobelli et al., 2005).

Risk measure	Subadditivity	Positive homogeneity	Translation invariance	Monotonicity	Convexity
Standard deviation	✓	✓	X	X	✓
Mean absolute difference	✓	✓	X	X	✓
Value-at-Risk (VaR)	X	✓	✓	✓	X
Conditional VaR	✓	✓	✓	✓	✓
Minimax criterion	✓	✓	✓	✓	✓

[15]Notable exceptions are hedge funds that design and market investment strategies with the goal of generating performance in absolute terms.

resources and the associated opportunity cost. Simply put, the investor wants to know not only "*How much money have I made?*" but also "*How much money could I have made considering the (less expensive, less time-consuming, passive) alternatives?*"

The assessment of performance therefore requires the proper identification of a benchmark. We first address the gap between the ideal market reference in theory and the available benchmarks in practice. Then, we briefly elaborate on the qualities that a relevant benchmark should have.

1.3.3.1 The market portfolio and the benchmark

From the onset of its development, the SPT has established that efficient financial markets would reward only those active asset managers that can do better than what everybody else obtains with buy and hold strategies. In equilibrium, the positions of all these passive investors result in the so-called *market portfolio*, i.e., the sum of all investable assets weighted by their market capitalization. Therefore, in theory at least, the market portfolio turns out to be the proper benchmark for active investors.

Unfortunately, the market portfolio is hardly observable in practice. Given the complex investment universe, it is virtually impossible (or excessively too costly) to replicate all positions in all investable assets.[16] Thus, we are left to resort to more or less imperfect proxies for benchmarking (such as market indices or ETFs).

These approximations of the market portfolio lead to several practical challenges for portfolio performance evaluation. Chapter 5 provides a thorough discussion of these issues in the context of a one factor asset pricing model. In a multifactor framework, the discrepancy between the analytical benchmark underlying the multifactor model and the self-reported benchmark adds another layer of difficulty in finding the correct proxy for performance assessment (see Chapter 7).

The imperfect identification of a benchmark also has implications for performance attribution, whose goal is to adequately recognize the talents of portfolio managers (ability to select securities and/or market timing skills). This is analyzed in Chapter 13.

1.3.3.2 Some desirable properties for a benchmark

Even though the choice of a relevant benchmark is a case-by-case decision impacted, among other things, by the type of strategy, investment style, and asset classes, there are some

[16] It might be more feasible if the universe is restricted to an asset class. However, then the question is whether the strategy should be benchmarked with such a restriction in the first place.

fundamental properties that a benchmark should display. We shall emphasize four of them and claim that a benchmark should be:

- *Transparent*: The construction method for the benchmark should be accessible and clear to everyone (the investor, the portfolio manager, the portfolio manager's supervisor, any external auditor, . . .).
- *Investable*: The benchmark should represent a feasible alternative for passive investment. This condition also applies to the position sizes that the manager can achieve.
- *Representative*: A significant proportion of assets managed in the portfolio should be present in the benchmark.
- *Manipulation proof*: The portfolio manager should behave as a price taker for all the constituents of the benchmark.

Related to transparency, Hamilos and Ribando (2016) advocate that investors should understand the implications of the benchmark construction method. They argue that benchmarks never truly reflect a passive investment, but rather implicit allocation decisions made by the benchmark provider. They cite the example that market-cap-weighted indices overweight high momentum securities (see also, Treynor, 2005, for a related point).

In terms of representativeness, Bailey (1992) further points out that the benchmark turnover should be low (for a sound comparison over the long run), and that the correlation between the manager's performance against the market and the benchmark's performance against the market should be high.

With numerical experiments to support their claim, Amenc, Goltz, and Lodh (2012) note that beyond the selection of constituents, the weighting scheme of the benchmark also has an impact on the assessment of strategies.

Key Takeaways and Equations

- The management of a financial portfolio, analogously with any transformation process, follows a three-stage procedure: *prepare, execute, and control.* A feedback loop is triggered by the controlling step, which combines the verification of the performance and the achievement of the process.
- Portfolio performance corresponds to the concept of efficiency of the process, whereas the achievement of initial objectives indicates the process's effectiveness. These concepts are summarized by the following equation:

$$\{X_{P,1}, \ldots, X_{P,K}\} \underset{\text{efficiency}}{\Rightarrow} Y_P \underset{\text{effectiveness}}{\Leftrightarrow} Y_P^* \tag{1-1}$$

(continued)

(continued)

- The inputs of the process are mainly fourfold: cash outlay, costs, time, and risk:

$$\{X_{P,1}, \ldots, X_{P,K}\} \equiv \{V_{P,0}, C_{P,H}, H, \mathcal{R}_{P,H}\} \tag{1-2}$$

  whereas the output is generally considered to be the final portfolio value:

$$Y_P \equiv V_{P,H} \tag{1-3}$$

- The rate of return is a measure of performance, but it does not account for risk. The two main versions of a *risk-adjusted performance measure* are generically written as

$$\text{PM}_P^{\text{abs}} \equiv f_{\text{all}}(R_{P,H}; H, \mathcal{R}_{P,H}) \tag{1-6}$$

$$\text{PM}_P^{\text{rel}} \equiv f_{\text{all}}(R_{P,H}; H, \mathcal{R}_{P,H}, R_{B,H}, \mathcal{R}_{B,H}) \tag{1-7}$$

  - The first version is usually written in the form $\text{PM}_P^{\text{abs}} = \frac{\mathcal{P}(R_{P,H})}{\mathcal{R}_{P,H}}$ and is interpreted as an *efficiency ratio*.
  - The second version is usually written as $\text{PM}_P^{\text{rel}} = \mathcal{P}(R_{P,H}) - \mathcal{P}(R_{B,H})$ and is interpreted as an *output gap*.
- We consider the feedback loop surrounding the performance evaluation process as a circuit that connects the preparation, execution, and control stages. Consequently, it constitutes the red wire of the book:
  - *Performance appraisal* refers to understanding the past. Parts I and II of the book are dedicated to this dimension. It results in the identification of 116 measures analyzed through nine chapters.
  - *Performance analysis* corresponds to explaining the present. It features in particular the very important performance attribution analysis, which can take many forms, studied in Part III.
  - *Acting upon performance* involves preparing the future. Part IV proposes different applications of this point of view, including the use performance in predictive analyses.
- For the purpose of the book's technical developments, we need to define some key concepts. These involve the *returns*, *risk* and its measurement, as well as the identification of *benchmarks*.

- Returns can be expressed in discrete or continuous time, leading to slightly different compounding rules. Their mean can be computed with a *geometric average* (that reflects the actual compounding over several periods)

$$\overline{R}_{P,t_N}^{\text{geo}} = \sqrt[N]{\prod_{i=1}^{N}(1 + R_{P,t_i}) - 1} \tag{1-8}$$

  or with an *arithmetic average* (that reflects, from a statistical standpoint, the compounding conditions to be expected):

$$\overline{R}_{P,t_N}^{\text{ari}} = \frac{1}{N}\sum_{i=1}^{N}(1 + R_{P,t_i}) - 1 \tag{1-9}$$

- In the presence of significant interim cash flows, the actual portfolio growth rate should be measured with *time-weighted returns*. If the value of the portfolio cannot be updated regularly, an internal rate of return can be calculated.
- Risk can be apprehended from the expected utility theory or from a probabilistic approach. In the latter case, the attitude toward risk can be fully captured from the asset return distribution. A simplified approach consists of gauging the preference toward the *moments of the distribution*.
- Aggregating assets into portfolios exposes the investor to the effects of *diversification* (affecting the moments of the return distribution) and to *correlation risk*.
- Many risk measures have been used in the field of portfolio performance appraisal. *Consistency* (with respect to second-order stochastic dominance) and *coherence* (with respect to the axioms of Artzner et al., 1999) help appreciate the quality of a risk measure.
- The wedge between the unobservable market portfolio and the benchmark used in practice is a source of errors in performance appraisal. Several chapters elaborate on how to mitigate the impact of these errors.
- Educated investors should understand the limitations in any benchmark, not only in relation to the strategy under assessment but also inherently associated with its construction method.

REFERENCES

Amenc, N., and V. Le Sourd (2003), *Portfolio Theory and Performance Analysis.* Wiley Finance.

Amenc, N., Goltz, F., and A. Lodh (2012), Choose your betas: Benchmarking alternative equity index strategies. *The Journal of Portfolio Management*, Vol. 39 (1), pp. 88–111.

Artzner, P., Delbaen, F., Eber, J. M., and D. Heath (1999), Coherent measures of risk. *Mathematical Finance*, Vol. 9, pp. 203–228.

Bailey, J. V. (1992), Evaluating benchmark quality. *Financial Analysts Journal*, Vol. 48 (3), pp. 33–39.

Bailey, J. V., Richards, T. M., and D. E. Tierney (2007), Evaluating portfolio performance. In: Maginn, J. L., Tuttle, D. L., Pinto, J. E., and D. W. McLeavey, Eds., *Managing Investment Portfolios: A Dynamic Process, 3rd Edition.* CFA Institute Investment Series, pp. 717–780.

Carr, P., Geman, H., and D. B. Madan (2001), Pricing and hedging in incomplete markets. *Journal of Financial Economics*, Vol. 62, pp. 131–167.

Hamilos, P. A., and J. M. Ribando (2016), Benchmark buyer beware: How well do you know your index? *Journal of Asset Management*, Vol. 17 (2), pp. 89–99.

Jensen, M. (1968), The performance of mutual funds in the period 1943–1964. *The Journal of Finance*, Vol. 23, pp. 383–416.

Levy, H. (1992), Stochastic dominance and expected utility: Survey and analysis. *Management Science*, Vol. 38, pp. 555–593.

Lintner, J. (1965), The valuation of risk assets and the selection of risky investments in stock portfolios and capital budgets. *Review of Economics and Statistics*, Vol. 47, pp. 13–37.

Maginn, J. L., Tuttle, D. L., McLeavey, D. W., and J. E. Pinto (2007), The portfolio management process and the investment policy statement. In: Maginn, J. L., Tuttle, D. L., Pinto, J. E., and D. W. McLeavey, Eds., *Managing Investment Portfolios: A Dynamic Process, 3rd Edition.* CFA Institute Investment Series, pp. 1–62.

Markowitz, H. (1952), Portfolio selection. *The Journal of Finance*, Vol. 7, pp. 77–91.

Mossin, J. (1966), Equilibrium in a capital asset market. *Econometrica*, Vol. 34, pp. 768–783.

Ortobelli, S., Rachev, S. T., Stoyanov, S., Fabozzi, F. J., and A. Biglova (2005), The proper use of risk measures in portfolio theory. *International Journal of Theoretical and Applied Finance*, Vol. 8, pp. 1107–1133.

Righi, M. B., and D. Borenstein (2018), A simulation comparison of risk measures for portfolio optimization. *Finance Research Letters*, Vol. 24, pp. 105–112.

Sharpe, W. F. (1964), Capital asset prices: A theory of market equilibrium under conditions of risk. *The Journal of Finance*, Vol. 19, pp. 425–442.

Treynor, J. (1962), Toward a theory of market value of risky assets, Unpublished manuscript. Reprinted in *Asset Pricing and Portfolio Performance*, 1999, R. A. Korajczyk, ed., London: Risk Books, pp. 15–22.

Treynor, J. (2005) Why market-valuation-indifferent indexing works. *Financial Analysts Journal*, Vol. 61 (5), pp. 65–69.

Young, M. R. (1998), A minimax portfolio selection rule with linear programming solution. *Management Science*, Vol. 44, pp. 673–683.

PART I - *Appraise (1/2)*

CLASSICAL PERFORMANCE MEASUREMENT

The foundations of portfolio management as we know it today find their roots in the second half of the twentieth century. They rest on two complementary theoretical contributions: The Standard Portfolio Theory (SPT), published in 1952, that proposes a robust risk-return framework, and the Capital Asset Pricing Model (CAPM), appearing in the 1960s, that explains how to price financial securities at equilibrium. Building on these solid pillars, the first wave of portfolio performance measures soon followed. This early group, although with a very limited number of members, is still widely used nowadays. It represents the set of what we call the classical performance measures. Their in-depth study is the subject matter of the first part of this book, which is organized in four chapters.

In **Chapter 2**, we begin by setting the scene through some preparatory material. The chapter summarizes the SPT and the CAPM and their associated implementation issues. It also introduces some of their main extensions and alternatives, to the extent that this proves to have implications about how to appraise and analyze performance. Chapter 2 does not provide any specific discussion of performance appraisal, but it can be a useful reference to familiarize the reader with the remainder of the book.

The core of this part of the book can be found in **Chapter 3**. It introduces and discusses a set of classical performance measures that we restrict to seven members: The peer group comparison return, the Sharpe ratio, the Treynor ratio, Jensen's alpha, the modified Jensen's alpha, the Information ratio, and the Appraisal ratio. Each of these measures is thoroughly examined in a structured fashion around two dimensions: their significance and their strengths and weaknesses.

Following the objective examination of the classical performance measures, **Chapter 4** proposes a set of guidelines regarding their selection in order to appraise portfolio performance in the most appropriate fashion. It is shown that the differences in risk definition and performance presentation have a potentially strong influence on the relevance of each of the classical measures. The chapter adopts both the perspective of the investor and the one of the portfolio manager.

Finally, we list and analyze in **Chapter 5** a large set of difficulties related to the implementation of classical performance measurement. These issues range from applying the SPT and CAPM frameworks in practice, to the statistical problems related to the sample or the estimation, and to the interpretation of the outcome of performance measurement. For each topic, the potential solutions are explored, either directly or through references to subsequent chapters that explicitly deal with the sources of the problems.

CHAPTER 2

Standard Portfolio Theory and the CAPM

INTRODUCTION

This chapter presents what historically stands out as the first rigorous framework for addressing the portfolio allocation problem. The Standard Portfolio Theory (SPT), initially developed by Markowitz (1952), analyzes portfolios of assets according to the mean and variance of their returns over a given horizon.[1] The mean–variance framework has the double advantage of representing reasonable investors' attitudes toward risk and offering a tractable resolution of the portfolio allocation problem.

The analysis of Markowitz is further extended by several researchers including Treynor (1962), Sharpe (1964), Lintner (1965), and Mossin (1966) to formalize the first asset pricing model in the history of Finance, namely the Capital Asset Pricing Model (CAPM). The CAPM provides an elegant view of the way efficient markets function: In equilibrium, the only source of risk that is rewarded is the systematic exposure to market risk – all forms of idiosyncratic risk being diversified away through portfolio allocation. Systematic risk is captured by the beta, i.e., the covariance of an asset return with the market return divided by the market return variance. The CAPM establishes two fundamental linear relations. The first one, referred to as the *Capital Market Line* (CML), addresses the famous risk–return trade-off that lies at the very heart of the field of finance. It states that expected excess return of *mean–variance efficient* asset allocations must be proportional to the return standard deviation, and that the coefficient

[1]The theory has been coined the "Modern Portfolio Theory" for several decades (see, for instance, the reviews of Elton and Gruber, 1997, or Fabozzi, Gupta, and Markowitz, 2002). Yet, many developments have appeared since the original work of Markowitz, and we argue that the theory has gained enough maturity to earn its "standard" status.

of proportionality is the unit price of market risk, also known as the Sharpe ratio. The second one, referred to as the *Security Market Line* (SML), states that the excess return of *any* asset must be proportional to its beta, and that the coefficient of proportionality is the market risk premium.

The first linear relation leads to the two-fund separation theorem: Any efficient allocation consists in holding the market portfolio and the risk-free asset, the relative investment weights being only a matter of personal attitude toward risk. From a practical point of view, this result can be regarded as a theoretical justification for passive portfolio management. The second linear relation opens up the way for individual security performance analysis. Any asset return deviating from the SML can be viewed as abnormal and should call for deeper investigation. This is where active portfolio managers come into play, which promptly raises the question of evaluating the quality of their intervention. Most importantly, these two linear relations enable an easy implementation and test of the model, which has greatly contributed to the popularity of the CAPM among academics and practitioners.

Of course, any model, despite its intrinsic elegance, has its limitations. We review some of the major challenges faced by the implementation of the CAPM. A more thorough examination of the pitfalls associated with CAPM-related performance measures (including their potential fixes) is presented in Chapter 5. Finally, we also take a look at multifactor models, which, over the last decades, have appeared as natural extensions to the CAPM. These models have earned their inclusion into the SPT, judging by their growing popularity in the portfolio management and asset pricing literature. We present a broad classification of multifactor models and briefly discuss their implications for portfolio management. Most importantly, resorting to these models requires adjusting the CAPM-based performance metrics – a topic that is addressed in Chapter 7.

The Marko Invest Inc. Example

Marko Invest Inc. has access to the risk-free asset and to four different funds for a one-year horizon investment. The risk-free rate is at 3%. The risk–return profiles of the four funds are summarized in Table 2-1:

TABLE 2-1 Risk–return profiles.

Fund	A	B	C	D
Expected return	7%	11%	15%	4%
Standard deviation of return	15%	26%	33%	18%

The return correlation matrix between those four funds is shown in Table 2-2.

TABLE 2-2 Return correlation matrix.

	A	B	C	D
A	1.00	0.32	0.77	−0.14
B		1.00	0.21	0.05
C			1.00	−0.22

Marko Invest Inc. aims at determining the optimal portfolio allocation. In particular, how to quantify the risk–return trade-off at the portfolio level? Which risky assets should be invested in? How should the risk-free asset be included in the strategy? Does the optimal allocation depend on the attitude toward risk? Marko Invest Inc. applies the SPT to address these questions.

2.1 THE PORTFOLIO ALLOCATION PROBLEM

2.1.1 Mean–variance framework

Consider a financial market on which N risky assets and one risk-free asset are traded. Investors share a common horizon and intend to form portfolios over that period (i.e., they all follow buy and hold strategies). Let R_i, $i = 1, \ldots, N$, denote the returns on these assets over the horizon, R_f referring to the risk-free asset return. The subsequent analysis posits that risky asset returns are fully characterized by their first two moments: Expectation $E(R_i)$ and standard deviation $\sigma(R_i)$ (that is, the square root of the variance, also called "volatility"). To simplify the exposition, the following notations will be used throughout: $\mu_i \equiv E(R_i)$ and $\sigma_i \equiv \sigma(R_i)$.

The so-called mean–variance framework (where the word "mean" stands for "expectation") can be justified in two ways, either through the distribution of returns or through the investors' attitude toward risk:

- If returns are assumed to be normal, then the expectation and standard deviation uniquely determine their distribution.[2]

[2]Under normality, the probability that R_i lies within $[a, b]$ is given by $\frac{1}{\sigma_i\sqrt{2\pi}} \int_a^b \exp\left(-\frac{(x-\mu_i)^2}{2\sigma_i^2}\right) dx$, which only depends on μ_i and σ_i.

- In line with standard economic theory, investors evaluate their current wealth not according to their expected payoff but according to the expected utility derived from that payoff. That is, investors assess the profitability of asset i by calculating $E(U(R_i))$, where $U(\cdot)$ is an increasing, concave function. Assuming investors are risk averse and measure risk using the variance (dispersion around the mean), their expected utility can be written as $E(U(R_i)) = E(R_i) - \frac{\gamma}{2}\sigma^2(R_i)$, where γ denotes the risk-aversion parameter.[3]

Each of these two assumptions has been challenged empirically. On the one hand, for most financial assets, time series of returns more or less exhibit strong departures from normality. On the other hand, behavioral experiments have highlighted complex attitudes toward risk that are not consistent with the expected utility theory (see, e.g., Kahneman and Tversky, 2013). Despite these limitations, the mean–variance framework should be seen as the cornerstone of standard portfolio theory. As shown below, its analytical approach allows for an elegant and insightful solution to the portfolio allocation problem. Extensions of the SPT are discussed in detail in Chapter 6.

Figure 2-1 shows the mean–variance representation of a universe of 12 asset returns. It is in fact more convenient to plot the returns in the standard deviation–expectation space. A risk-averse investor aims at maximizing the expected return of their portfolio given a certain (accepted) level of risk. Conversely, that same risk-averse investor could aim at minimizing risk given a targeted expected return. In both cases, the most attractive assets are the ones with their returns located in the northwest portion of the figure.

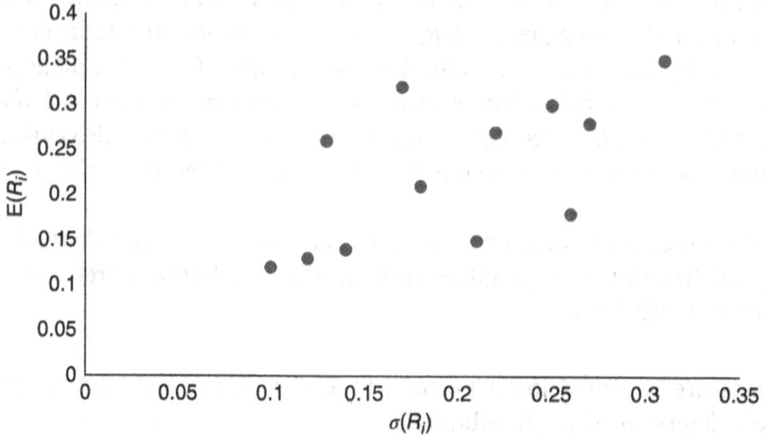

FIGURE 2-1 Asset returns in the standard deviation–expectation space.

[3]The expected utility theory is examined in detail in Chapter 9, entirely devoted to this topic.

A portfolio P is defined as a weighted sum of the $N+1$ assets, where the weight w_i, $i = 0, \ldots, N$ (with the convention that subscript 0 refers to the risk-free asset), represents the fraction of initial wealth invested in asset i. By construction, the weights add up to 1, and they can be positive or negative (i.e., leverage and short selling are allowed). The expectation and variance of the return on portfolio P are given by

$$E(R_P) \equiv \mu_P = \sum_{i=0}^{N} w_i \mu_i \tag{2-1}$$

$$\mathrm{Var}(R_P) \equiv \sigma_P^2 = \sum_i \sum_j w_i w_j \sigma_{ij} \tag{2-2}$$

with $\sigma_{ij} \equiv \mathrm{Cov}(R_i, R_j) = \sigma_i \sigma_j \rho_{ij}$ for all i,j, where ρ_{ij} is the Pearson correlation coefficient between the returns of asset i and asset j $(-1 \leq \rho_{ij} \leq +1)$.

2.1.1.1 The efficient frontier

To understand the impact of forming a portfolio on the expectation and the standard deviation of returns, we can start by analyzing the situation of a two-asset fund. In that case, we have

$$\mu_P = w_1 \mu_1 + (1 - w_1)\mu_2 \tag{2-3}$$

$$\sigma_P^2 = w_1^2 \sigma_1^2 + (1 - w_1)^2 \sigma_2^2 + 2w_1(1 - w_1)\sigma_1 \sigma_2 \rho_{12} \tag{2-4}$$

Figure 2-2 shows, for all combinations of assets 1 and 2 (i.e., all values of w_1), various standard deviation–expectation profiles that can be achieved. The asset risk–return characteristics are $\mu_1 = 0.12$, $\sigma_1 = 0.15$, $\mu_2 = 0.35$, $\sigma_2 = 0.31$, and $\rho_{12} = 0.2$. Each point represents an

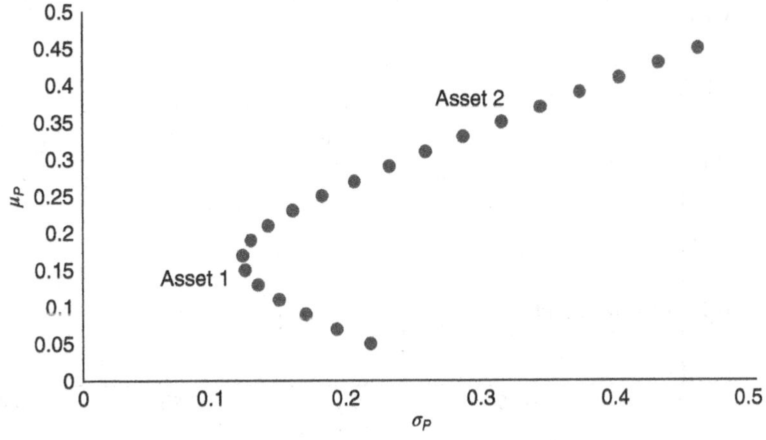

FIGURE 2-2 Two-asset portfolio returns in the standard deviation–expectation space.

allocation from $w_1 = -1.5$ to $w_1 = +1.5$ by increments of 0.1. All combinations of assets 1 and 2 form a hyperbola in the standard deviation–expectation space.

Of special interest is the case where the two-asset fund comprises the risk-free asset. Since $\mu_0 = R_f$ (the risk-free rate) and $\sigma_0 = 0$, we obtain

$$\mu_P = w_0 R_f + (1 - w_0)\mu_1 \tag{2-5}$$

$$\sigma_P = (1 - w_0)\sigma_1 \tag{2-6}$$

Therefore, all combinations of the risk-free asset and asset 1 are represented by two half-lines in the standard deviation–expectation space, as shown in Figure 2-3, where we set $R_f = 0.05$. The two half-lines originate at the risk-free asset coordinates $(0, R_f)$. The increasing (decreasing) half-line corresponds to long (short) positions in the risky asset.

The two preceding results obtained with two assets can be extended to the general case of a market with N risky assets. On the one hand, all portfolios forming any combination of any of these N risky assets are represented by a surface delineated by a hyperbola in the standard deviation–expectation space. This first property is illustrated by the shaded area in Figure 2-4. On the other hand, all portfolios including the risk-free asset and any combination of risky assets are represented by a half-line originating at $(0, R_f)$. That second property is illustrated with the two examples of portfolios combining the risk-free asset and fund J or fund K (yielding the return R_J and R_K, respectively).

In the investment universe depicted by Figure 2-4, the mean–variance investor aims at the most northwest portfolio that is attainable. Among the set of risky assets (i.e., the shaded area), only the allocations representing the upper portion of the hyperbola are worth considering. For instance, portfolio K is strictly preferred to portfolio J since it exhibits higher expected return and lower risk.

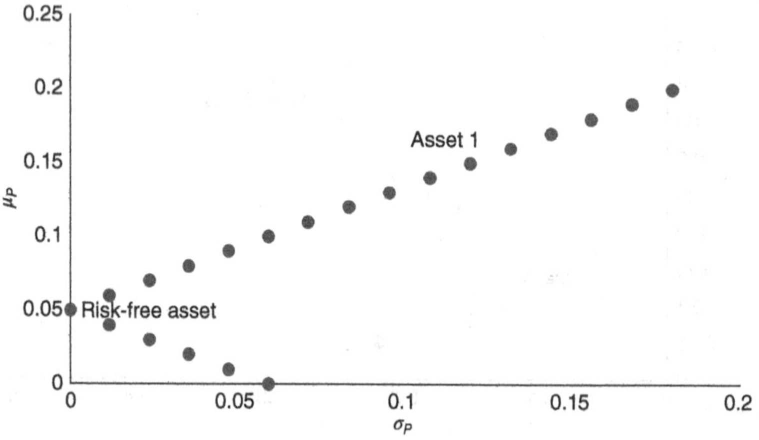

FIGURE 2-3 Two-asset portfolio returns in the standard deviation–expectation space when one asset is risk-free.

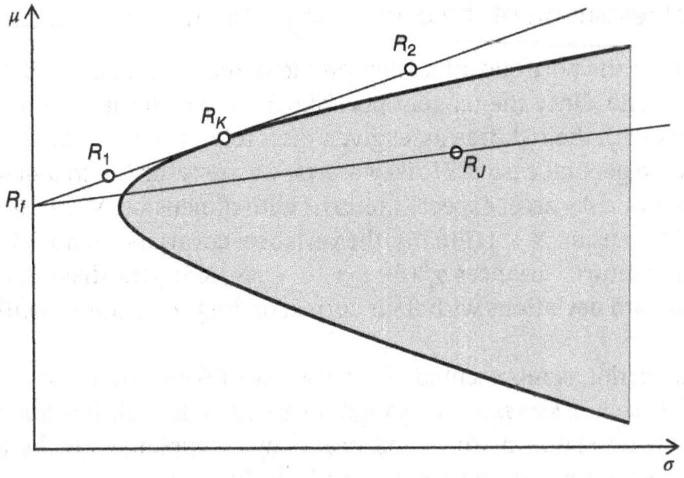

FIGURE 2-4 Investable portfolios in the standard deviation–expectation space when one asset is risk free.

The introduction of the risk-free asset allows the investor's welfare to improve even further. Indeed, the set of attainable portfolios is enriched with all the half-lines that can be drawn from the risk-free asset coordinates $(0, R_f)$ and joining the risk–return characteristics (σ_J, μ_J) of the risky asset under study. For asset J for example, these new allocations do not make the investor better off since that half-line is below the upper portion of the hyperbola. But for asset K, whose risk–return characteristics (σ_K, μ_K) form the tangency point with the hyperbola, the half-line of new attainable portfolios represents the best allocations that can be achieved. That half-line therefore appears as the *efficient frontier* in the investment opportunity set.

The notion of an efficient frontier is extremely insightful. It entails that, within the investment universe of N risky assets and one risk-free asset, the only mean–variance efficient allocations are the ones combining the *tangent portfolio*[4] with the risk-free asset. This is the so-called *two-fund separation theorem* originally formulated by Markowitz and Tobin.

The practical implication is that, despite their differences in risk tolerance, all mean–variance investors should optimally build a combination of the tangent portfolio and the risk-free asset. The only way that their portfolio strategies will differ is through the weight allocated to each of these two funds.[5] While all portfolios will stand on the same half-line, more risk-averse investors will allocate more of their wealth into the risk-free asset yielding a low risk–return profile, like the point R_1 in Figure 2-4. By contrast, less risk-averse investors will position their allocation further away from the origin of the half-line, like the point R_2 in Figure 2-4.

[4]In Figure 2-4, the tangent portfolio is asset K. In practice, it may not be a single asset but rather a certain combination of assets (a fund) such that its risk–return characteristics aligned with those of the risk-free asset form the tangent half-line.

[5]Let us recall here that the two-fund separation theorem has been derived under the assumption of a common investment horizon and under the restriction to buy-and-hold strategies.

2.1.1.2 Formal resolution of the allocation problem

We formally solve for the portfolio allocation problem, that is, we determine the composition of the tangent portfolio. Once the tangent portfolio is found, all the investor has to do is find their preferred mix with the risk-free asset given their tolerance for risk.

To cope with the general case of N risky assets, we are resorting to a matrix notation. Let $\boldsymbol{\mu}$ denote the vector of risky asset expected returns with dimension $N \times 1$. Similarly, $\mathbf{1}$ denotes the unit vector of dimension $N \times 1$. Finally, the variance–covariance matrix is $\mathbf{V}$. It is an $N \times N$ matrix with all asset return variances σ_i^2 (for $i = 1, \ldots, N$) along the diagonal and the products of all pairwise standard deviations with their corresponding correlation coefficients $\sigma_i \sigma_j \rho_{ij}$ for all $i \neq j$.

A portfolio allocation is represented by a vector $\mathbf{w}$ of dimension $N \times 1$ containing all the weights assigned to each risky asset. The weight invested in the risk-free asset is deduced from $w_0 = 1 - \mathbf{w}^T\mathbf{1}$, where $\mathbf{w}^T$ stands as the transpose of $\mathbf{w}$. As explained at the beginning of this section, the investor's optimization program can be written as

$$\max_P \mathrm{E}(R_P) - \frac{\gamma}{2}\sigma^2(R_P) \tag{2-7}$$

where γ is a risk-aversion parameter. Using our matrix notation, this program can be reformulated as follows:

$$\max_w (1 - \mathbf{w}^T\mathbf{1})R_f + \mathbf{w}^T\boldsymbol{\mu} - \frac{\gamma}{2}\mathbf{w}^T\mathbf{V}\mathbf{w} \tag{2-8}$$

The first-order condition yields

$$-R_f\mathbf{1} + \boldsymbol{\mu} - \gamma\mathbf{V}\mathbf{w} = 0 \tag{2-9}$$

$$\mathbf{w} = \frac{1}{\gamma}\mathbf{V}^{-1}(\boldsymbol{\mu} - R_f\mathbf{1}) \tag{2-10}$$

Given that $\gamma > 0$, Equation (2-10) characterizes the half-line where all efficient portfolio allocations are located (for various values of γ). It also holds for the tangent portfolio, which means that there exists a specific γ_τ such that the tangent portfolio allocation is

$$\mathbf{w}_\tau = \frac{1}{\gamma_\tau}\mathbf{V}^{-1}(\boldsymbol{\mu} - R_f\mathbf{1}) \tag{2-11}$$

Since the tangent portfolio allocation in the risk-free asset is nil, it verifies $\mathbf{w}_\tau^T\mathbf{1} = 1$, which yields

$$\frac{1}{\gamma_\tau} = \frac{1}{\mathbf{1}^T\mathbf{V}^{-1}(\boldsymbol{\mu} - R_f\mathbf{1})} \tag{2-12}$$

and therefore

$$\mathbf{w}_\tau = \frac{\mathbf{V}^{-1}(\boldsymbol{\mu} - R_f\mathbf{1})}{\mathbf{1}^T\mathbf{V}^{-1}(\boldsymbol{\mu} - R_f\mathbf{1})} \tag{2-13}$$

Marko Invest Inc. (continued)

All the portfolios that can be built from the four risky funds A, B, C, and D are plotted in the graph below. Figure 2-5 shows the risk–return profiles of these portfolios in the standard deviation–expectation space. It is typically referred to as a mean–variance plot. For clarity of exposition, only non-negative weights by increments of 0.1 are shown on the graph.

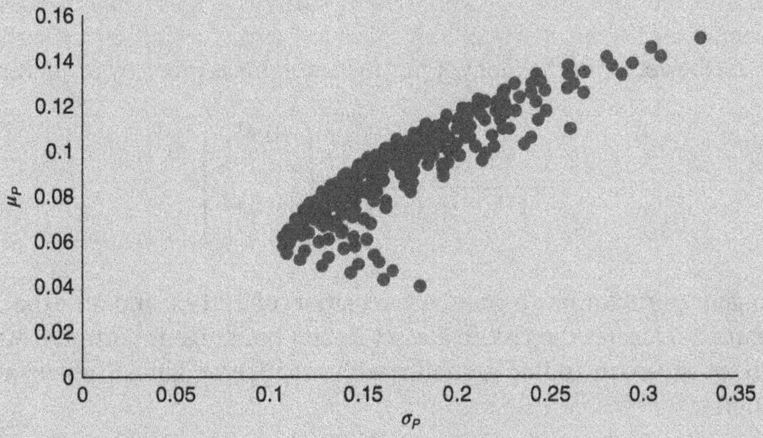

FIGURE 2-5 Attainable portfolios (with non-negative weights).

The combinations of two, three, and four funds form hyperbolas, and the envelope of all these portfolios also forms a hyperbola in the standard deviation–expectation space.

To determine the tangent portfolio, we first compute the variance–covariance matrix:

$$\mathbf{V} = \begin{pmatrix} +0.0225 & +0.0125 & +0.0381 & -0.0038 \\ +0.0125 & +0.0676 & +0.0180 & +0.0023 \\ +0.0381 & +0.0180 & +0.1089 & -0.0131 \\ -0.0038 & +0.0023 & -0.0131 & +0.0324 \end{pmatrix}$$

The inverse of that matrix is

$$\mathbf{V}^{-1} = \begin{pmatrix} +116.746 & -11.057 & -39.199 & -1.391 \\ -11.057 & +16.682 & +0.852 & -2.151 \\ -39.199 & +0.852 & +23.335 & +4.777 \\ -1.391 & -2.151 & +4.777 & +32.784 \end{pmatrix}$$

(*continued*)

(continued)

The vector of excess returns is

$$\mu - R_f\mathbf{1} = \begin{pmatrix} 0.04 \\ 0.08 \\ 0.12 \\ 0.01 \end{pmatrix}$$

Moreover, the vector of the tangent portfolio weights is given by (Equation (2-13))

$$\frac{\mathbf{V}^{-1}(\boldsymbol{\mu} - R_f\mathbf{1})}{\mathbf{1}^{\mathrm{T}}\mathbf{V}^{-1}(\boldsymbol{\mu} - R_f\mathbf{1})} = \begin{pmatrix} -0.452 \\ +0.472 \\ +0.654 \\ +0.326 \end{pmatrix}$$

The tangent portfolio has a standard deviation of 22.17% and an expected return of 13.14%. Figure 2-6 locates the risk-free asset R_f and the tangent portfolio. More combinations have been added (including portfolios with negative weights) to obtain a more precise representation.

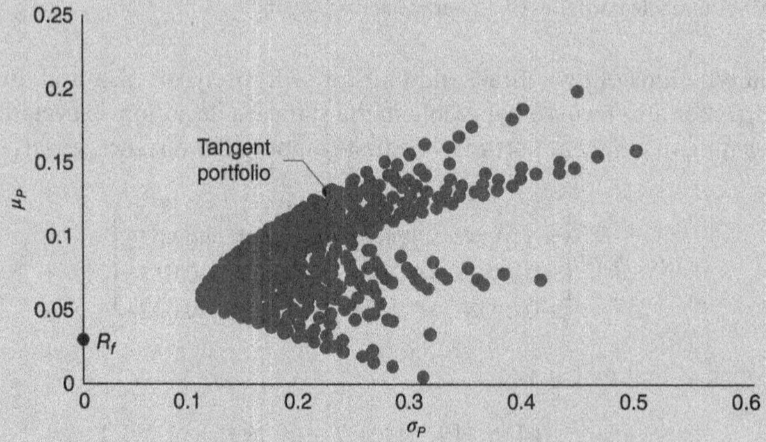

FIGURE 2-6 The tangent portfolio and the investment opportunity set.

2.1.2 The Capital Market Line

From the previous analysis, we concluded that all optimal portfolio allocations lie on the efficient frontier, i.e., the half-line joining the risk-free asset with coordinates $(0, R_f)$ and the tangent portfolio whose coordinates will be denoted by (σ_M, μ_M) from then on. In the standard deviation–expectation space, the equation of that half-line is

$$\mu_P = R_f + \left(\frac{\mu_M - R_f}{\sigma_M}\right)\sigma_P \tag{2-14}$$

Equation (2-14) applies to any efficient portfolio P and establishes a linear relationship between expected return μ_P and risk σ_P. Specifically, the expected excess return of an efficient portfolio is proportional to the standard deviation of its return by a factor of $(\mu_M - R_f)/\sigma_M$. That ratio can be interpreted as the unit price of risk for the market portfolio or the market's reward-to-variability ratio (RVR). That is, it is the extra remuneration over the risk-free rate offered by the tangent portfolio divided by its quantity of risk. As shown in Chapter 3, that ratio is also known as the Sharpe ratio for the tangent portfolio when it is considered *ex post*, with observed data.

The next crucial development in the SPT consists of characterizing the tangent portfolio with risk–return coordinates (σ_M, μ_M). If we still rely on the assumption that all investors share the same horizon and that they all form the same anticipations regarding the risk–return profiles of the N assets on the market, then they all share the same representation of the investment opportunity set, i.e., they all build the same Figure 2-4. As a result, all investors identify the same tangent portfolio. Following the two-fund separation theorem, all investors invest in the same combination of risky assets and only differ through their allocation in the risk-free asset. We can therefore interpret the tangent portfolio as the *market portfolio*, that is, the portfolio containing all risky assets in proportions of their relative market capitalization.[6]

The tangent portfolio being recognized as the market portfolio, the SPT labels the efficient frontier as the CML as illustrated in Figure 2-7.

2.2 THE MARKET PORTFOLIO AND THE SECURITY MARKET LINE

2.2.1 The standard formulation

We showed the linear relationship between expected return and risk for efficient portfolios. The question now is: What kind of relationship between expected return and risk is there for any (inefficient) asset?

[6]That interpretation relies on an equilibrium argument. If the tangent portfolio requires investing a fraction w in risky asset i, then the aggregated demand for that asset i will represent a fraction w of all the wealth invested on the market. Note that this argument only focuses on the demand for risky assets, and it is therefore a partial equilibrium argument – the supply of securities from corporations being ignored.

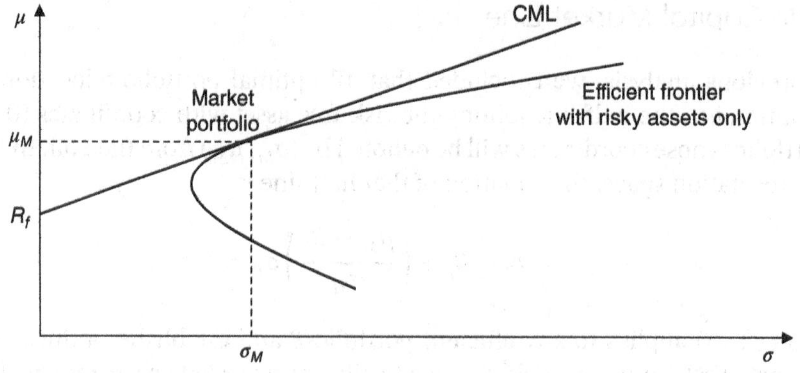

FIGURE 2-7 The Capital Market Line (CML).

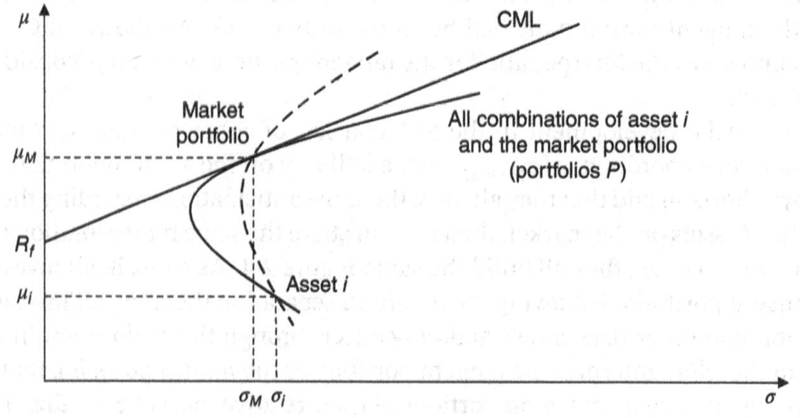

FIGURE 2-8 Combinations of an individual asset and the market portfolio.

Consider an individual asset i among the N risky assets. Let us build a portfolio P including asset i (with weight w) and the market portfolio (with weight $1-w$). By construction, we obtain

$$\mu_P(w) = w\mu_i + (1-w)\mu_M \tag{2-15}$$

$$\sigma_P^2(w) = w^2\sigma_i^2 + (1-w)^2\sigma_M^2 + 2w(1-w)\sigma_{iM} \tag{2-16}$$

For varying values of w, portfolios P are combinations of two funds, and, as such, they form a hyperbola in the standard deviation–expectation space (see Section 2.1.1.1). Since the market portfolio is on the CML, no portfolio P can exhibit a superior risk–return profile. In other words, the hyperbola formed by portfolios P cannot stand above the CML. This argument is illustrated in Figure 2-8.

All combinations of asset i and the market portfolio are represented by the hyperbola with a solid line, which remains below the CML. Hypothetically, if these combinations were represented by the hyperbola with a dashed line, then some portfolios P above the CML could be used in conjunction with the risk-free asset to build a half-line of portfolio allocations that would be more efficient than the portfolios located on the CML. This is in contradiction with the way that the tangent portfolio was initially identified.

Since the hyperbola of all portfolios P must remain below the CML, it must be tangent to the CML at the point representing the market portfolio. That is, its slope must be equal to the slope of the CML when portfolio P is simply the market portfolio (i.e., when $w = 0$). Formally,

$$\left.\frac{d\mu_P(w)}{d\sigma_P(w)}\right|_{w=0} = \frac{\mu_M - R_f}{\sigma_M} \tag{2-17}$$

Using the composition rule from calculus, the term of the left-hand side of Equation (2-17) can be written as

$$\left.\frac{d\mu_P(w)}{d\sigma_P(w)}\right|_{w=0} = \left.\frac{d\mu_P(w)/dw}{d\sigma_P(w)/dw}\right|_{w=0} = \frac{\mu_i - \mu_M}{\sigma_{iM} - \sigma_M^2}\sigma_M \tag{2-18}$$

Combining Equations (2-17) and (2-18) and rearranging, we obtain

$$\mu_i = R_f + \frac{\sigma_{iM}}{\sigma_M^2}(\mu_M - R_f) \tag{2-19}$$

Equation (2-19) addresses the question asked at the beginning of this section. Just like for efficient portfolios, there also exists a linear relationship between expected return and risk for individual assets. When it comes to individual assets, however, risk is measured by the covariance between their and the market portfolio return. Indeed, Equation (2-19) indicates that the expected excess return of an individual asset is proportional to σ_{iM} by a factor of $(\mu_M - R_f)/\sigma_M^2$.

Equation (2-19) highlights another proportionality between the individual expected excess return and the market portfolio expected excess return. The coefficient between the two is commonly referred to as the beta, and Equation (2-19) can be reformulated as follows:

$$\beta_i = \frac{\sigma_{iM}}{\sigma_M^2} = \rho_{iM}\frac{\sigma_i}{\sigma_M} \tag{2-20}$$

$$\mu_i = R_f + \beta_i(\mu_M - R_f) \tag{2-21}$$

Equation (2-21) is the cornerstone of the CAPM originally developed by Treynor, Sharpe, Lintner, and Mossin. It establishes a linear relation between an individual asset expected excess return and its beta. Graphically, this linear relation is referred to as the SML.

Figure 2-9 provides a representation of the SML. In equilibrium all assets should be located on the SML, and their exact position depends on their beta, i.e., on the extent to which their return is correlated with the market portfolio return. The risk-free asset, for instance, yields the return R_f which, by design, is uncorrelated with R_M (its beta is nil). The risk-free asset therefore stands at the intercept of the SML. The market portfolio is located at the coordinates $(1, \mu_M)$ since $\beta_M = 1$.

Figure 2-9 shows the position of two other assets. Asset 1 has a beta greater than 1, which implies a return that is higher in expectation but also a return that amplifies the market movements. Indeed, since the return of asset 1 strongly covaries with that of the market portfolio, asset 1 will perform very well during market growth periods. Conversely, it will perform poorly when the market is in a bearish phase. Asset 1 is sometimes referred to as an aggressive asset. By contrast, asset 2 has a beta lower than 1. Its return will damp the market movements. Because of its low correlation with the market portfolio, asset 2 will moderately benefit from bullish periods, but its performance will not drastically deteriorate during recessions. Asset 2 can be viewed as a defensive asset.

The economic insight underlying the SML is that individual assets generate some excess return only thanks to their exposure to the market portfolio risk, also referred to as *systematic risk*. Thus, if total risk can be decomposed as the sum of idiosyncratic risk and systematic risk, only the latter source of risk is rewarded on the financial market equilibrium. This property can be related to the notion of portfolio *diversification*. In a portfolio containing a sufficiently high number of assets, the idiosyncratic shocks affecting individual returns tend to cancel out with one another, and their contribution to the portfolio risk will eventually fade out.

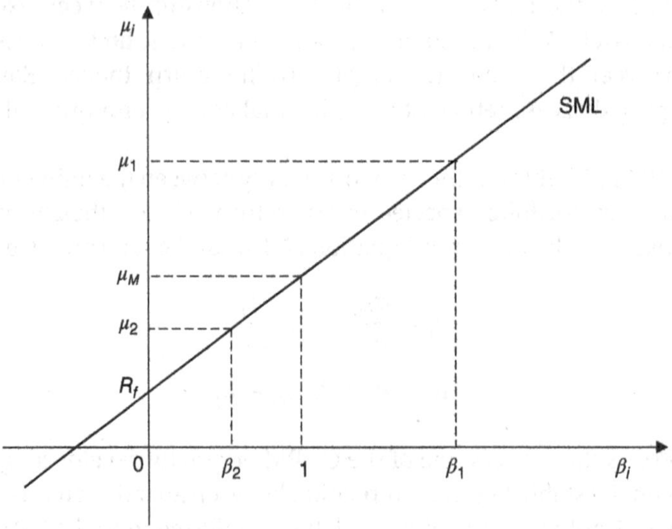

FIGURE 2-9 The Security Market Line (SML).

Marko Invest Inc. (continued)

The market (tangent) portfolio has been identified as

$$M = -0.452A + 0.472B + 0.654C + 0.326D$$

Assuming that the CAPM holds, we can infer the betas of the four funds:

$$\beta_A = \frac{\mu_A - R_f}{\mu_M - R_f} = \frac{0.07 - 0.03}{0.1314 - 0.03} = 0.3945$$

$$\beta_B = \frac{\mu_B - R_f}{\mu_M - R_f} = \frac{0.11 - 0.03}{0.1314 - 0.03} = 0.7890$$

$$\beta_C = \frac{\mu_C - R_f}{\mu_M - R_f} = \frac{0.15 - 0.03}{0.1314 - 0.03} = 1.1834$$

$$\beta_D = \frac{\mu_D - R_f}{\mu_M - R_f} = \frac{0.07 - 0.03}{0.1314 - 0.03} = 0.0986$$

Given that the volatility of the market portfolio is $\sigma_M = 22.17\%$, we can also infer the covariance between the fund returns and the market portfolio return:

$$\sigma_{AM} = \beta_A \sigma_M^2 = 0.3945 \times 0.2217^2 = 0.0194$$

$$\sigma_{BM} = \beta_B \sigma_M^2 = 0.7890 \times 0.2217^2 = 0.0388$$

$$\sigma_{CM} = \beta_C \sigma_M^2 = 1.1834 \times 0.2217^2 = 0.0582$$

$$\sigma_{DM} = \beta_D \sigma_M^2 = 0.0986 \times 0.2217^2 = 0.0048$$

Using $\rho_{iM} = \frac{\sigma_{iM}}{\sigma_i \sigma_M}$, the correlation matrix can be augmented with the market portfolio (Table 2-3):

TABLE 2-3 Return correlation matrix including the market portfolio.

	A	B	C	D	M
A	1.00	0.32	0.77	−0.14	0.58
B		1.00	0.21	0.05	0.67
C			1.00	−0.22	0.80
D				1.00	0.12

(continued)

(continued)

Funds A and D are the most defensive assets as they exhibit the lowest correlation with the market portfolio. Only fund C has a beta greater than 1, which is reflected with a very high correlation with M.

2.2.2 Major extensions

There have been many extensions of the standard CAPM proposed in the literature. Although we do not deny their importance and validity, we focus on two of them that are important for performance evaluation, namely Black's (1972) zero-beta version and the international CAPM originally developed by Solnik (1974).

2.2.2.1 The zero-beta Capital Asset Pricing Model

Black (1972) proposes an extension of the CAPM that does not require any identification of the risk-free asset. This extension yields an alternate version of the SML that can be helpful when the investor cannot or does not wish to take position into the risk-free asset.[7]

Consider all portfolios whose return R_Z is uncorrelated with the market portfolio return R_M. In other words, the beta of these portfolios is nil, $\beta_Z = 0$. These portfolios are graphically represented in Figure 2-10. The CML intercepts the y-axis at $\mu = \mu_Z$ (not necessarily identified as the risk-free rate). The horizontal line at $\mu = \mu_Z$ crosses the investment opportunity set at Z. All portfolios located on that line and on the right-hand side of Z (portfolio A for example) have a zero beta. Among these zero-beta portfolios, Z is the one with the minimum variance.

The portfolio Z with weight vector $\mathbf{w}$ formally results from the resolution of the following optimization program:

$$\min_{\mathbf{w}} \mathbf{w}^{\mathrm{T}}\mathbf{V}\mathbf{w} \tag{2-22}$$

subject to

$$\mathbf{w}^{\mathrm{T}}\mathbf{V}\mathbf{w}_M = 0 \tag{2-23}$$

$$\mathbf{w}^{\mathrm{T}}\mathbf{1} = 1 \tag{2-24}$$

---

[7]One can think of instances when the risk-free asset is difficult to identify because of multiple yield curves (e.g., treasury yields versus interbank rates) or when the investment horizon does not match with any available maturity of liquid risk-free securities. Another instance is a period of stochastic inflation which makes it impossible to achieve a risk-free investment in real terms.

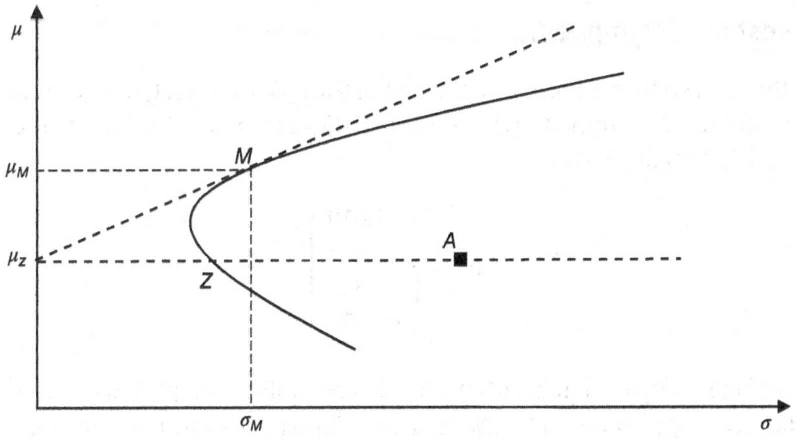

FIGURE 2-10 Portfolios uncorrelated with the market portfolio.

As Figure 2-10 shows, the coordinates of the zero-beta portfolio can be identified as the intercept of the straight line that is tangent to the efficient frontier at the level of the market portfolio.

Once this minimum variance zero-beta portfolio has been numerically identified, it is possible to compute its expected return:

$$\mu_Z = \mathbf{w}^T \boldsymbol{\mu} \tag{2-25}$$

The SML equation for any asset i is then given by

$$\mu_i = \mu_Z + \beta_i(\mu_M - \mu_Z) \tag{2-26}$$

The zero-beta CAPM therefore appears as a generalization of Equation (2-21), which nests the standard CAPM as a special case. If the risk-free asset exists, then it is, by definition, the asset that is uncorrelated with the market portfolio with minimum variance (in this case, zero variance). Therefore, $\mu_Z = R_f$. However, if the risk-free asset is not investable, then the premium for exposure to systematic risk is $\mu_M - \mu_Z$, and assets are rewarded with their excess return being proportional to that premium (with coefficient beta).

Marko Invest Inc. (continued)

Assuming that Marko Invest Inc. cannot invest in the risk-free asset, the minimum variance zero-beta portfolio is determined as the solution to Equation (2-22) subject to the constraints (2-23) and (2-24), which yields

$$\mathbf{w} = \begin{pmatrix} +1.019 \\ -0.072 \\ -0.323 \\ +0.376 \end{pmatrix}$$

That portfolio is uncorrelated with the market portfolio, its expected return is $\mathbf{w}^{\mathrm{T}}\boldsymbol{\mu} = 3\%$, and its volatility is $\sqrt{\mathbf{w}^{\mathrm{T}}\mathbf{V}\mathbf{w}} = 11.71\%$. It is the closest proxy to the risk-free asset, but it induces an irreducible level of volatility that Marko Invest Inc. must bear in its portfolio allocation.

2.2.2.2 The international Capital Asset Pricing Model

As discussed previously, the premium for systematic risk is a consequence of the benefits of diversification. This economic insight can be extended to an international context. The access to foreign markets increases the number of assets and portfolios that can be invested in. Consequently, one should expect the benefits of international diversification to surpass those of domestic diversification.[8]

Considering the world as a global financial market, it is possible to derive an international version of the CAPM (see, in particular, Solnik, 1974). Following the same mean–variance framework, an investor in country C can represent all possible portfolios in the standard deviation–expectation space, where returns are expressed in their own currency. Given R_{f_W}, the world risk-free rate, the investor can determine the tangent portfolio and the corresponding CML for their investment universe denominated in their own currency.[9] Let μ_{M_W} and σ_{M_W} denote the expected return and volatility of that portfolio. Then, a reasoning similar to the domestic case leads to the following equation for the international SML:

$$\mu_{i_C} = R_{f_C} + \beta_{i_W}(\mu_{M_W} - R_{f_C}) \qquad (2\text{-}27)$$

[8]A caveat to this claim is the exposure to currency risk. However, evidence shows that exchange rates exhibit very low correlation with domestic market portfolios. Furthermore, exchange rates are not perfectly correlated with one another, and therefore global currency risk can be, at least partially, diversified away within an international investment strategy.

[9]The identification of R_{f_W} is one obstacle to implementing the international CAPM. Empirical proxies include the yield on US Treasury Inflation-Protected Securities (TIPS) or GDP-weighted real rates from a selection of developed countries.

where R_{f_C} denotes the risk-free rate in country C and

$$\beta_{i_W} = \frac{\sigma_{iM_W}}{\sigma^2_{M_W}} \tag{2-28}$$

stands for asset i beta with respect to the world market portfolio.

2.3 IMPLEMENTING THE CAPM

Implementing the CAPM involves the rigorous application of specific estimation techniques discussed hereafter. Furthermore, this raises a number of important questions that need to be addressed in an adequate manner in order to trustfully appraise the performance of a portfolio manager in this context. These topics are discussed below.

2.3.1 Statistical estimation

2.3.1.1 Beta estimation

Equation (2-21) suggests that the beta of any asset i can be estimated by means of an ordinary least-square (OLS) regression. By regressing a time series of asset i returns $\{R_{i,t}\}, t = 1, \ldots, T$, on a time series of market portfolio returns $\{R_{M,t}\}, t = 1, \ldots, T$, we obtain the following OLS model:

$$R_{i,t} = \alpha_i + \beta_i R_{M,t} + \varepsilon_{i,t} \tag{2-29}$$

where $\varepsilon_{i,t}$ is an error term with zero mean and no correlation with $R_{M,t}$. Equation (2-29) is commonly referred to as the *market model*. It can be viewed as an *ex post* version of the CAPM, that is, a regression of observed returns allowing to characterize expected returns. The slope coefficient of Equation (2-29) is

$$\widehat{\beta}_i = \frac{\widehat{\sigma}_{iM}}{\widehat{\sigma}^2_M} \tag{2-30}$$

and therefore it serves as an estimate of asset i beta. By identification with Equation (2-21), the intercept coefficient $\widehat{\alpha}_i$ is an estimate for $(1 - \beta_i)R_f$, or, more generally under the zero-beta CAPM, for $(1 - \beta_i)\mu_Z$.[10]

Expressed in terms of variances, the market model of Equation (2-29) implies that

$$\sigma_i^2 = \beta_i^2 \sigma_M^2 + \sigma_{\varepsilon_i}^2 \tag{2-31}$$

[10] We revert back to the interpretation of this intercept estimate and the associated interpretation issues in Chapter 5.

which recalls the decomposition of asset i total risk into the sum of its systematic risk $\beta_i^2\sigma_M^2$ and its idiosyncratic risk $\sigma_{\varepsilon_i}^2$. It should be noted that the R^2 of Equation (2-29) regression precisely indicates the estimated fraction of systematic risk over total risk. Indeed, for a univariate OLS regression,

$$R^2 = \rho_{iM}^2 = \frac{\widehat{\sigma}_{iM}^2}{\widehat{\sigma}_i^2\widehat{\sigma}_M^2} = \frac{\widehat{\beta}_i^2\widehat{\sigma}_M^2}{\widehat{\sigma}_i^2} \tag{2-32}$$

The estimation of the market model (2-29) requires a time series of market portfolio returns. Such time series is difficult to construct in practice. Data limitations make it almost impossible to measure the returns of all risky assets in the economy.[11] A common practice consists of proxying the market portfolio with a market index. The relevance of that practice is discussed below and examined further in detail in Chapter 5.

To implement the market model, one must determine the window and frequency of estimation. A couple of constraints apply. First, the statistical noise surrounding returns usually increases with the observation frequency. Second, the OLS estimation requires a minimum number of points to obtain statistically significant estimates. However, that requirement implies using old data when the observation frequency is low, and these old data may no longer reflect the actual economic conditions. A trade-off between these two conflicting constraints, derived from early tests of the market model (e.g., Fama and MacBeth, 1973), is to run the OLS regressions of Equation (2-29) with five years of monthly returns. This criterion, however, sounds more like a conventional wisdom rather than a firmly established econometrics principle.

Whatever the chosen estimation window and frequency, estimated betas have been shown to vary substantially over time. This beta instability is partly explained by the fact that the fraction of systematic risk ($\beta_i^2\sigma_M^2$) is typically small compared to the total risk of an individual stock. In other words, the R^2 coefficient in Equation (2-32) is usually low when Equation (2-29) is estimated at the individual security level, and this hinders the accurate estimation of beta. To mitigate this issue, it has been shown (e.g., Alexander and Chervany, 1980) that applying the market model on diversified (but not necessarily large) portfolios reduces the instability of betas. Repeating the estimation on several portfolios, it is possible to retrieve individual betas using the linearity of the covariance operator. That is, for a portfolio P invested in K risky assets with weights w_i,

$$\beta_P = \sum_{i=1}^{K} w_i\beta_i \tag{2-33}$$

Therefore, assuming that there is a total of N risky securities on the market, estimating the market model on N different portfolios of size $K \leq N$ yields a system of N equations (the N estimated $\widehat{\beta}_P$) and N unknowns (the N individual betas).

[11] Some asset classes are simply not marketed (e.g., human capital), and other asset classes are thinly traded on illiquid markets (e.g., private debt, real estate, luxury goods, etc.).

Beyond the statistical argument, there is also a fundamental, economic reason for betas to be instable over time. As firms regularly update their investment and financing policies, they constantly change their exposure to systematic risk. Acknowledging time-varying betas leads to the notion of a *conditional* CAPM (e.g., Jagannathan and Wang, 1996). Considering a set of discrete dates $0, 1, \ldots, t-1, t, \ldots, T$, the expected return on asset i in period $[t-1, t]$ conditional on the information available at the preceding date $t-1$ is given by

$$E_{t-1}(R_{i,t}) \equiv \mu_{i,t} = R_{f,t-1} + \beta_{i,t-1}(\mu_{M,t-1} - R_{f,t-1}) \tag{2-34}$$

where $R_{f,t-1}$, is the one-period risk-free rate observed at date $t-1$, $(\mu_{M,t-1} - R_{f,t-1})$ is the market risk premium calculated at date $t-1$, and

$$\beta_{i,t-1} = \frac{\mathrm{Cov}_{t-1}(R_{i,t}, R_{M,t})}{\mathrm{Var}_{t-1}(R_{M,t})} \tag{2-35}$$

By restricting its application to one period after the other, the conditional version of the CAPM is more flexible than the original version. Its implementation, however, requires specifying the way betas change over time. The literature has presented several versions of the conditional CAPM, and its superiority over the unconditional version remains open to debate.[12]

Marko Invest Inc. (continued)

It has been established that the beta of fund A is $\beta_A = 0.3945$. This is a theoretical beta assuming that the CAPM holds. Marko Invest Inc. wishes to assess its ability to correctly estimate the beta of fund A from observed returns. Given that $\mu_A = 0.07$, $\sigma_A = 0.15$, $\mu_M = 0.1314$, $\sigma_M = 0.2217$, and that the correlation between fund A and the market portfolio is $\rho_{AM} = 0.58$, a set of simulations is run assuming that the returns R_A and R_M are normally distributed. Specifically, Marko Invest Inc. builds 100 scenarios of monthly returns over a 10-year period (120 months). Thus, each scenario is a vector of pairs $\{R_{A,t}, R_{M,t}\}_{t=1,\ldots,120}$. In each scenario, the returns $\{R_{A,t}\}$ are regressed over the returns $\{R_{M,t}\}$, and the slope coefficient is an estimation of the beta. An average beta can be calculated from the 100 scenarios as well as additional metrics measuring the precision of that average beta.

(continued)

[12] Empirical support for various versions of the conditional CAPM is, for instance, found in the works of Ang and Chen (2007), Guo, Wu, and Yu (2017), or Cenesizoglu and Reeves (2018). Rebuttals of the conditional CAPM include Ghysels (1998) and Lewellen and Nagel (2006). Furthermore, we examine the consequences of the adoption of the conditional CAPM for performance measurement in Chapter 5, and, for the multifactor version, in Chapter 7.

(continued)

Table 2-4 reports the results from the numerical experiment. Three windows have been considered for the regressions: (i) the whole 10 years, (ii) the last 5 years (months 61–120), and (iii) the last 3 years (months 85–120).

TABLE 2-4 Statistics on estimated betas.

Estimation period	Average beta	Standard deviation	5th percentile	95th percentile
Last 10 years	0.3970	0.0518	0.2988	0.4721
Last 5 years	0.4047	0.0768	0.2859	0.5170
Last 3 years	0.3879	0.1021	0.2249	0.5628

These results indicate that the accuracy of estimation increases as the regression uses a longer set of data. The point estimate gets closer to the theoretical β_A, and dispersion (both measured with the standard deviation and with extreme percentiles) around that point estimate decreases.

However, that exercise has assumed a constant beta over the whole period. The incentive to use a longer set of data to increase statistical accuracy must be contrasted with the possibility that fund A can change its beta over time (due, for example, to a different fund composition). That latter concern calls for restricting the estimation window to the most recent data.

2.3.1.2 The *Ex Post* SML

Once the betas have been estimated, it is possible to verify *ex post* the linear relation between returns and betas predicted by the CAPM. The procedure consists of regressing the observed asset excess returns (over a given period) on the estimated betas $\widehat{\beta}_i$ using a model of the following form:

$$R_i - R_f = \gamma_0 + \gamma_1 \widehat{\beta}_i + \eta_i \tag{2-36}$$

Note that we have omitted the time index t as the regression is done on a cross-section of data, involving no time variations. The outcome of that regression is the construction of an empirical, *ex post* SML in contrast with the theoretical, *ex ante* SML defined in Equation (2-21).

If the predictions of the CAPM hold true, then we should obtain that the intercept γ_0, and the beta coefficient γ_1, are not statistically different from zero and $R_M - R_f$ respectively.

The *ex ante* SML must have a positive slope, given that investors are risk averse (and therefore demand a positive premium for exposure to systematic risk). This is not necessarily the case for the *ex post* SML. After a period of bearish market, the return on the market portfolio can be negative and that will cause a downward slope of the *ex post* SML. Figure 2-11 illustrates that situation. Every black diamond represents an asset with coordinates (β_i, R_i), and the estimated OLS regression line is the *ex post* SML.

This negative slope is not a rebuttal of the CAPM. It is merely a manifestation of exposure to risk: Favorable as well as unfavorable states of nature can happen. The CAPM predicts that the linear relation between returns and betas should hold in all states of nature, no matter the slope coefficient.

2.3.1.3 Cross-sectional application

The *ex post* SML can be used as a benchmark for security performance because the residual in Equation (2-36) can be interpreted as an abnormal return. In line with this reasoning, we can extend the regression of excess returns over beta to multiple assets. This leads to the cross-sectional approach initially presented by Fama and MacBeth (1973).

Let $\mathbf{Z}_t$ denote the vector of excess returns calculated over a period t for the set of N risky assets.[13] Assuming that the betas for these N assets have been calculated, the following cross-sectional regression can be estimated:

$$\mathbf{Z}_t = \gamma_{0t}\mathbf{1} + \gamma_{1t}\widehat{\boldsymbol{\beta}} + \eta_t \tag{2-37}$$

where $\mathbf{1}$ denotes the unit vector of dimension N, $\widehat{\boldsymbol{\beta}}$ is the vector of estimated asset betas, and η_t is a vector of normally distributed innovations.

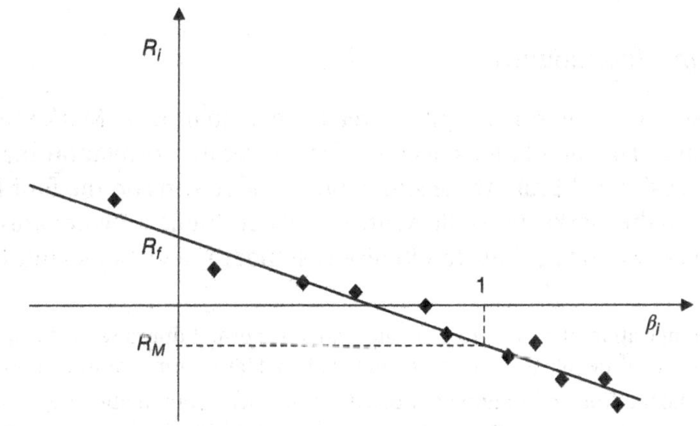

FIGURE 2-11 An example of an *ex post* SML.

[13]The maturity of risk-free rate should match with the horizon of the period.

The next step is to repeat the estimation of regression (2-37) over T periods. This yields the time series of T estimates for the intercept γ_{0t} and the beta coefficient γ_{1t}. The average of these estimates across time $\hat{\gamma}_j$ and their variance $\hat{\sigma}_j^2$ are given by

$$\hat{\gamma}_j = \frac{1}{T}\sum_{t=1}^{T}\hat{\gamma}_{jt}, j = 0,1 \quad (2\text{-}38)$$

$$\hat{\sigma}_j^2 = \frac{1}{T(T-1)}\sum_{t=1}^{T}(\hat{\gamma}_{jt} - \hat{\gamma}_j)^2, j = 0,1 \quad (2\text{-}39)$$

Since the residuals of regression (2-37) are independent and normally distributed, the same holds for the estimated $\hat{\gamma}_0$ and $\hat{\gamma}_1$. It is therefore possible to apply a Student $\boldsymbol{t}$-test on these values. Define the following $\boldsymbol{t}$-statistic:

$$\hat{\boldsymbol{t}}_{\gamma_j=0} = \frac{\hat{\gamma}_j}{\hat{\sigma}_j}, j = 0,1 \quad (2\text{-}40)$$

It follows a Student $\boldsymbol{t}$-distribution with $T - 1$ degrees of freedom.

These so-called Fama–MacBeth regressions thus allow to fully take advantage of the cross-sectional distribution of asset returns to estimate and test the CAPM. Indeed, according to the CAPM, the true value of the intercept should be $\gamma_0 = 0$, and the true value of the beta coefficient should be the market risk premium, i.e., $\gamma_1 = R_M - R_f$. Consequently, the statistical test on $\hat{\gamma}_0$ determines the level of confidence at which one can reject the hypothesis that γ_0 is nil, in compliance with the SML. Furthermore, the calculation of $\hat{\gamma}_1$ provides a point estimate of the market risk premium, and the statistical test on $\hat{\gamma}_1$ determines a confidence interval for it. This premium, in turn, can be used, in conjunction with the beta, to assess whether a specific asset generates an abnormal return over a subsequent period.

Marko Invest Inc. (continued)

We use a set of simulated monthly returns over 10 years to provide Marko Invest Inc. with a historical sample. The simulations account for the return correlation matrix using the Cholesky decomposition.[14] From these simulations, the returns on the four funds A, B, C, and D and those on the market portfolio M are calculated. Table 2-5 compares the empirical average (annualized) returns, their (annualized) standard deviations, and the betas with

[14]The Cholesky decomposition allows us to generate standard normal draws with the appropriate correlation structure. Let $\mathbf{u} = (\varepsilon_k)^T$ denote a vector of n simulated standard normal draws whose elements are, by construction, independent from one another. Consider the linear combinations $e_i = \sum_{k=1}^{i} \alpha_{ik}\varepsilon_k$, for $i = 1, \ldots, n$. These variables are normally distributed with zero mean. We further require that $\sigma^2(e_i) = 1$ and $\mathrm{Cov}(e_i, e_j) = \rho_{ij}$, where $(\rho_{ij})^T$ is the correlation matrix one wishes to simulate. These last two equalities turn into $\sum_{k=1}^{i} \alpha_{ik}^2 = 1$ and, for all $j < i$, $\sum_{k=1}^{j} \alpha_{ik}\alpha_{jk} = \rho_{ij}$, which represents a system of n equations and n unknowns (the coefficients α_{ik}). Note that the Cholesky factorization is equivalent to decomposing the covariance matrix into the product of a lower triangular matrix $\mathbf{L} = (\alpha_{ik})^T$ and a vector $\mathbf{u} = (\varepsilon_k)^T$ of uncorrelated standard normal draws.

their theoretical counterparts (the betas are estimated from regressing the corresponding returns on R_M over the 10-year period).

TABLE 2-5 Empirical and theoretical average returns, standard deviations, and betas.

	A	B	C	D	M
Empirical $\hat{\mu}_i$	0.1442	0.0254	0.1632	−0.0955	0.0504
Theoretical μ_i	0.07	0.11	0.15	0.04	0.1314
Empirical $\hat{\sigma}_i$	0.1599	0.2438	0.3497	0.1952	0.2501
Theoretical σ_i	0.15	0.26	0.33	0.18	0.2217
Empirical $\hat{\beta}_i$	0.3807	0.6289	1.1426	−0.0064	1
Theoretical β_i	0.3945	0.7890	1.1834	0.0986	1

The table highlights a standard issue in time-series econometrics, namely the fact that accurate estimates of growth rates are difficult to pin down using a small sample. In the historical scenario we have generated, we see that the market is more bearish than theoretically anticipated ($\hat{\mu}_M < \mu_M$), and this is driven by the poor performance of funds B and D. By contrast, standard deviations of returns and their correlations (not reported) are fairly well estimated from the historical sample. As a consequence, the differences between empirical and theoretical betas are limited though the betas of funds B and D are strongly underestimated.

Marko Invest Inc. aims at deriving the *ex post* SML. For an accurate estimation, one should consider an arbitrarily large number of portfolios providing a wide dispersion in systematic risk. This, in turn, would reduce the impact of measurement error in estimating the betas of individual funds.

For clarity of exposition (and given that the investment universe is restricted to four funds), Marko Invest Inc. considers only 50 portfolios with randomly selected weights. The betas of these 50 portfolios are estimated in the same way as for the individual funds, i.e., by regressing the portfolio returns on the tangent portfolio returns over the 10-year period.

The graph in Figure 2-12 shows the excess returns on the 50 portfolios (the risk-free rate is still 3%) over their corresponding betas. The regression line is an estimation of the *ex post* SML.

(continued)

(continued)

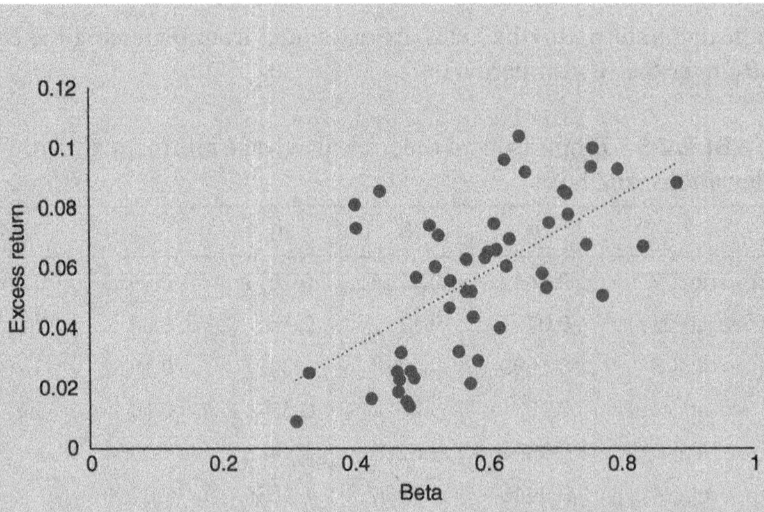

FIGURE 2-12 Estimation of the *ex post* SML.

Detailed results of the regression are gathered in Table 2-6.

TABLE 2-6 Regression results for the *ex post* SML.

Coefficient	γ_0	γ_1
Estimate	−0.0168	0.1261
p-value	0.2452	2.91×10^{-6}

The adjusted R^2 of the regression is 36%. This is a crude estimation of the *ex post* SML because of the limited number of portfolios. However, the intercept is not statistically different from zero as it should be. In addition, the empirical market risk premium is statistically significant and estimated at 0.1261, whereas its theoretical counterpart is $\mu_M - R_f = 0.1314 - 0.03 = 0.1014$. The slope of the *ex post* SML is a bit higher than that of the *ex ante* SML.

2.3.2 Major issues to consider

2.3.2.1 Unobservability of the market portfolio

A major caveat when implementing the CAPM is formulated by Roll (1977) and is commonly referred to as Roll's critique. The argument directly challenges the SPT claim that the market portfolio is mean–variance efficient. In fact, the validity of the CAPM and the efficiency of the market portfolio are two sides of the same coin, that is, they represent two joint assumptions that cannot be tested separately. This, according to Roll, raises a first empirical concern. Since the market portfolio is not observable, it is *ipso facto* impossible to test if it is mean–variance efficient.

In practice, the market portfolio is proxied by various market indices. This is cause for additional empirical issues. Let Π denote the proxy for the market portfolio. If Π is mean–variance efficient, then computing individual betas from Π automatically yields a linear relation between the expected return and the beta. All asset returns will be located on the SML. This might create the illusion that the CAPM is valid while the market portfolio might well be inefficient (which remains undetermined).

The zero-beta CAPM helps explain Roll's critique. Recall that it is possible to characterize the portfolio Z, uncorrelated with M and with minimal variance, to derive Equation (2-41):

$$\mu_i = \mu_Z + \beta_i(\mu_M - \mu_Z) \tag{2-41}$$

However, the reasoning underlying the zero-beta CAPM can be applied to *any* mean–variance efficient portfolio, not necessarily the market portfolio. Figure 2-13 shows how any efficient proxy Π can be associated with its zero-beta counterpart.

For instance, working with portfolio Π_1 as the market portfolio proxy, the derivation of CAPM leads to

$$\mu_i = \mu_{Z_1} + \beta_{i,\Pi_1}(\mu_{\Pi_1} - \mu_{Z_1}) \tag{2-42}$$

Thus, the linear relation between expected return and beta still holds, but the beta is measured relative to the market portfolio proxy Π_1.

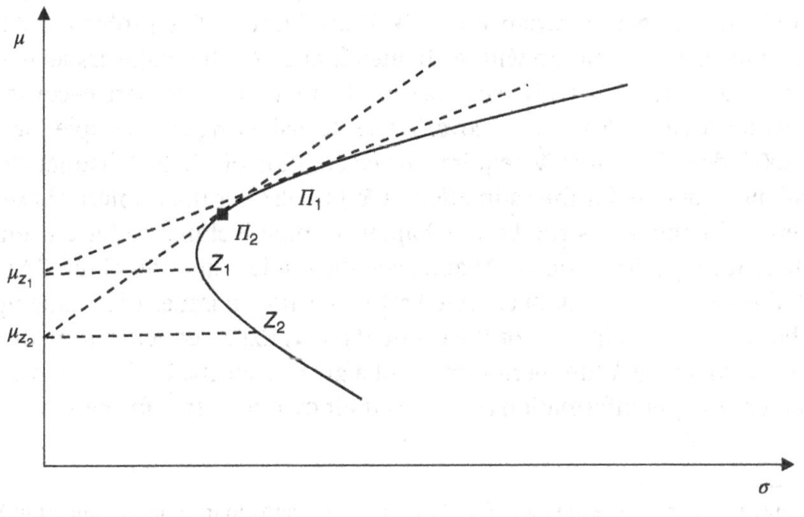

FIGURE 2-13 Market portfolio proxies and their zero-beta portfolios.

Conversely, if Π is mean–variance inefficient, one may find a nonlinear relation between expected return and beta. However, the detected abnormal performance depends on the chosen proxy and therefore is not fully reliable. When the CAPM is applied to multiple assets, the ranking of performance can be very sensitive to the chosen proxy.

To summarize Roll's critique, the mismatch between the proxy and the market portfolio is the source of two potential mistakes. One is to wrongfully validate the CAPM because the portfolio proxy is mean–variance efficient when the market portfolio is not. The other is to wrongfully reject the CAPM because the portfolio proxy is not mean–variance efficient when the market portfolio is.

The general message sent by Roll's critique is that econometric tests of the CAPM or of any asset pricing model involving the market portfolio should be interpreted with caution. Beyond that simple warning, some authors have tried to assess whether the possible inefficiency of the market portfolio proxy is an empirical issue. Kandel and Stambaugh (1987) and Shanken (1987) show that working with a proxy (Π) or with the true market portfolio (M) leads to the same CAPM rejection rule provided the returns on Π and M are sufficiently correlated (their studies indicate a minimum correlation of 0.7). Prono (2015) extends these works to multifactor models and finds even lower thresholds. Pollet and Wilson (2010) examine the time-series implications of Roll's critique. They argue that the weak relation between stock market risk and future stock returns is a symptom of the market portfolio containing important non-stock assets. The empirical relevance of Roll's critique is still open to debate.[15]

2.3.2.2 Incorporating private information

As shown in Section 2.1, the derivation of CAPM is straightforward once the vector of expected returns $\boldsymbol{\mu}$ and the variance–covariance matrix $\mathbf{V}$ are known. The problem for the portfolio manager, of course, is to come up with estimates $\hat{\boldsymbol{\mu}}$ and $\hat{\mathbf{V}}$. The major issue associated with $\hat{\mathbf{V}}$ is the size of the matrix. Given N securities on the market, the variance–covariance matrix contains N variances and $N(N-1)/2$ covariances. Considering for example the constituents of the S&P 500 index, the matrix $\hat{\mathbf{V}}$ requires the calculation of 125 250 distinct elements. This poses a challenge not only for the estimation of $\hat{\mathbf{V}}$ but also for the numerical execution of all computations involving $\hat{\mathbf{V}}$. As shown in Chapter 5, some techniques have been specifically developed to reduce the dimension of $\hat{\mathbf{V}}$ and keep the implementation of the CAPM tractable. By contrast, the size of the vector of expected returns is not an issue. The challenge is that it is difficult to build reliable estimates for the elements of $\hat{\boldsymbol{\mu}}$. Expected returns are directly related to how investors view the future performance of a given security. In this regard, the portfolio manager can use market information as well as their own private information.

[15] We further investigate the consequences of Roll's critique for performance measurement in Section 5.2.2.2 of Chapter 5.

Black and Litterman (1992) develop a methodology to effectively combine these two sources of information. Suppose the manager has some private views about K assets ($K \leq N$). The views are formally represented by three quantities:

- A $K \times N$ matrix $\mathbf{P}$ containing the weights associated with each view. If the view is relative (e.g., "*Asset A will outperform asset B by x%*"), the corresponding weights add up to 0, reflecting the gain of $x\%$ obtained from a long–short strategy in A and B. If the view is absolute (e.g., "*The return on asset C will be y%*"), the corresponding weights add up to 1.
- A $K \times 1$ vector $\mathbf{Q}$ containing the returns for each view.
- A $K \times K$ variance–covariance matrix $\mathbf{\Omega}$ accounting for the uncertainty surrounding the views. For simplicity, we assume that the views are uncorrelated. Therefore, $\mathbf{\Omega}$ is merely a diagonal matrix containing all the view variances.

For example, consider an investor with two views out of four assets. The views are: (i) "*I believe, with a 10% standard deviation (according to a centered normal distribution), that asset #2 will outperform asset #4 by 4%*"; (ii) "*I believe, with a 20% standard deviation, that asset #1 will return 3%.*" Then, we obtain

$$\mathbf{P} = \begin{pmatrix} 0 & 1 & 0 & -1 \\ 1 & 0 & 0 & 0 \end{pmatrix}; \mathbf{Q} = \begin{pmatrix} 0.04 \\ 0.03 \end{pmatrix}; \mathbf{\Omega} = \begin{pmatrix} 0.1^2 & 0 \\ 0 & 0.2^2 \end{pmatrix} \tag{2-43}$$

The Black–Litterman approach allows the portfolio manager to revisit the portfolio allocation problem by adjusting the vector of expected returns $\hat{\boldsymbol{\mu}}$ and the variance–covariance matrix $\hat{\mathbf{V}}$. The adjustment consists in tilting the CAPM-based expected returns (the market view) to incorporate private views.[16]

The portfolio manager starts with the following inputs:

- $\hat{\mathbf{V}}_{\text{mkt}}$, the variance–covariance matrix of security returns estimated from market data.
- An estimate of the market risk premium, $\mu_M - R_f$.

Assuming that the market is in equilibrium, a vector of expected returns can be backed out from the CAPM. The approach proposed by Best and Grauer (1991) considers the reverse engineering of the solution of the allocation problem formulated in Equation (2-10). Indeed, market equilibrium entails that the market perfectly clears the supply and demand for financial assets. The resulting weights of each asset in the market portfolio corresponds to its market capitalization relative to the global market, i.e., $w_i^* = \frac{\text{mktcap}_i}{\sum_{i=1}^{N} \text{mktcap}_i}$. Since this condition holds for

[16]More specifically, the adjustment results from a Bayesian update of market information using private information. See, e.g., Cheung (2010) for more details.

every asset i, its application leads to the vector of equilibrium weights $\mathbf{w}^*$, which is supposed to result from the global resolution of the allocation problem. Plugging the equilibrium weights into Equation (2-10) leads to the identification of the vector of market-implied expected risk premiums:

$$(\hat{\boldsymbol{\mu}}_{\text{mkt}} - R_f\mathbf{1}) = \gamma^* \hat{\mathbf{V}}_{\text{mkt}} \mathbf{w}^* \tag{2-44}$$

where γ^* is the market-wide level of risk aversion that matches the risk premium of the market portfolio, i.e., $\gamma^* = \frac{\mu_M - R_f}{\sigma_M^2}$.

Then, the Black–Litterman adjusted vector of expected returns is given by

$$\hat{\boldsymbol{\mu}}_{\text{BL}} = R_f + [(\tau\hat{\mathbf{V}}_{\text{mkt}})^{-1} + \mathbf{P}^{\text{T}}\Omega^{-1}\mathbf{P}]^{-1}[(\tau\hat{\mathbf{V}}_{\text{mkt}})^{-1}\hat{\boldsymbol{\mu}}_{\text{mkt}} + \mathbf{P}^{\text{T}}\Omega^{-1}\mathbf{Q}] \tag{2-45}$$

and the adjusted variance–covariance matrix is

$$\hat{\mathbf{V}}_{\text{BL}} = [(\tau\hat{\mathbf{V}}_{\text{mkt}})^{-1} + \mathbf{P}^{\text{T}}\Omega^{-1}\mathbf{P}]^{-1} \tag{2-46}$$

where τ is a risk multiplier, with $0 < \tau \leq 1$, that accounts for the estimation error made on $\hat{\mathbf{V}}_{\text{mkt}}$. A rule of thumb is to set τ equal to the inverse of the number of observation dates. For instance, if the variance–covariance matrix has been estimated from five years of monthly data, then $\tau = \frac{1}{5\times 12} \approx 0.017$.

Once private information has been incorporated into asset return expectations, variances and covariances, the portfolio manager can address the portfolio allocation problem (that is, solve for the tangent portfolio and re-apply the CAPM) using $\hat{\boldsymbol{\mu}}_{\text{BL}}$ and $\hat{\mathbf{V}}_{\text{BL}}$ as revised inputs.

2.4 MULTIFACTOR MODELS

As a natural extension of the discussion of the SPT and the CAPM, in this section we provide an introduction to multifactor models. An in-depth coverage of this topic is provided in Chapter 7, which is fully devoted to the development of performance measurement approaches that aim to capture the skills of a manager whose return-generating process is characterized with a multifactor model of the kind discussed here.

2.4.1 General formulation

Among the possible limitations of the SPT, one obvious objection is that the market portfolio may not be the only factor to explain the cross-section of asset returns. To address that issue, a natural extension of the CAPM is a multifactor model of the form

$$R_{i,t} = \alpha_i + \sum_{k=1}^{K} \beta_{i,k} F_{k,t} + \varepsilon_{i,t} \tag{2-47}$$

where the return on asset i over the period t is driven by a linear combination of K factors. The loadings $\beta_{i,k}$ account for the sensitivity of $R_{i,t}$ with respect to the factor $F_{k,t}$.

For a proper estimation of Equation (2-47) by means of an OLS regression, it is typically assumed that the factors have zero mean and that the error terms $\varepsilon_{i,t}$ are white noises with

$$\mathrm{Cov}(\varepsilon_{i,t}, \varepsilon_{j,t}) = \mathrm{Cov}(\varepsilon_{i,t}, F_{k,t}) = \mathrm{Cov}(\varepsilon_{i,t_1}, \varepsilon_{j,t_2}) = 0 \tag{2-48}$$

for all i, j, k, t_1, and t_2.

Assuming Equation (2-48), we obtain that $\mathrm{E}(R_{i,t}) = \alpha_i$, that is, we can correctly interpret α_i as the expected return on asset i. The variance–covariance matrix of asset returns is then given by

$$\sigma_i^2 = \sum_{k=1}^{K} \beta_{i,k}^2 \sigma_{F_k}^2 + \sigma_{\varepsilon_i}^2 \tag{2-49}$$

$$\sigma_{ij}^2 = \sum_{k=1}^{K} \beta_{i,k}\beta_{j,k}\sigma_{F_k}^2, \forall i, \forall j \neq i \tag{2-50}$$

Note that for $K = 1$, Equation (2-47) simply boils down to the market model (Equation (2-29)), where the unique factor is the market return.

As far as the factors are concerned, it is usually more convenient to work with uncorrelated $F_{k,t}$. Depending on how these factors are chosen, it might therefore be necessary to orthogonalize them before building the multifactor model as specified in Equation (2-47). There has been a vast literature on asset pricing, testing a wide variety of factors, or as famously put by Cochrane (2011), a "zoo of factors." The following subsections, which by no means aim at being exhaustive, examine three different ways to construct the factors, leading to three different types of multifactor models.

The first approach shows that the linear model of Equation (2-47) can be motivated by the assumption of arbitrage-free financial markets. It entails that well-behaved (i.e., with zero mean and orthogonal to one another) but non-interpretable factors can be uncovered from a factor analysis, provided the sample of asset returns is sufficiently large. The second approach appeals to the economic and financial theory to limit the selection of factors to observable quantities, such as macroeconomic, industry-related, or firm-specific variables. Such factors are clearly interpretable but exogenously specified. The third approach is inductive and aims at unraveling factors with high explanatory power from econometric analysis. The factors are interpretable but hardly related to the financial theory.

2.4.2 Types of models

2.4.2.1 Arbitrage factors

Ross (1976) shows that the factors can be obtained from applying the no-arbitrage principle, which states that a portfolio built from no wealth must earn zero return on average. This approach led to the so-called arbitrage pricing theory (APT).

Consider an investor building an arbitrage portfolio, that is, buying and selling some assets in such a way that the strategy costs nothing at inception. Formally, the amounts w_i invested in assets i ($i = 1, \ldots, N$) and expressed as a fraction of the investor's total wealth must satisfy

$$\sum_{i=1}^{N} w_i = 0 \tag{2-51}$$

Assuming the multifactor structure (2-47), the return on the arbitrage portfolio over one period is (time subscripts are dropped for clarity)

$$R_P = \sum_{i=1}^{N} w_i \alpha_i + \sum_{i=1}^{N} w_i \beta_{i,1} F_1 + \ldots + \sum_{i=1}^{N} w_i \beta_{i,K} F_K + \sum_{i=1}^{N} w_i \varepsilon_i \tag{2-52}$$

The goal of the arbitrage strategy is to eliminate all risk, both idiosyncratic and systematic. Regarding idiosyncratic risk, if the investor selects a high number of assets and very small investment weights (i.e., $w_i \approx 1/N$), then the strategy will diversify away the error terms ε_i. This is because the law of large numbers states that $\sum_{i=1}^{N} w_i \varepsilon_i \to 0$ as $N \to \infty$. Regarding systematic risk, the investor can always choose a combination of weights to obtain zero exposure to any factor. Formally, if

$$\sum_{i=1}^{N} w_i \beta_{i,k} = 0, \text{for all } k, \tag{2-53}$$

then the arbitrage portfolio is orthogonal to all sources of systematic risk. In the absence of arbitrage, such an investment (whose initial outlay is nil) must earn a zero return, which yields

$$R_P = \sum_{i=1}^{N} w_i \alpha_i = 0 \tag{2-54}$$

Since Equations (2-51) and (2-53) entail Equation (2-54), then it results from linear algebra that there exists a set of coefficients $\lambda_0, \lambda_1, \ldots, \lambda_K$ such that, for every asset i,

$$\alpha_i = \lambda_0 + \sum_{k=1}^{K} \lambda_k \beta_{i,k} \tag{2-55}$$

If there is a risk-free asset, then all its sensitivities $\beta_{0,k}$ are nil and therefore $\lambda_0 = R_f$. The APT thus states the following arbitrage, linear pricing relation for excess returns:

$$\alpha_i - R_f = \sum_{k=1}^{K} \lambda_k \beta_{i,k} \tag{2-56}$$

Since the $\beta_{i,k}$ represent the sensitivities (factor loadings) to each factor, the coefficients λ_k can be interpreted as the prices of risk for each factor.

Inspection of Equation (2-56) shows that the CAPM can be subsumed as a special case of the APT. Indeed, considering only one factor ($K = 1$), and defining $\beta_i = \sigma_{iM}/\sigma_M^2$ as the sensitivity to the market portfolio return (that is, R_M is the only factor priced by the market), the risk premium (the price of risk) is $\lambda = \mu_M - R_f$. By contrast to the CAPM, the APT relies on a much weaker set of hypotheses. No assumption is made about the distribution of asset returns or about the preferences of investors. The market portfolio plays no special role in the APT (whereas it is required to be mean–variance efficient by the CAPM). In addition, Equation (2-56) theoretically holds for any subset of assets, which means that the empirical validation of the APT does not require working with the entire universe of assets.

That being said, implementing the APT is not exempted of challenges. The first step is to collect the time series of log returns for a set of assets and to compute the variance–covariance matrix of these returns. Next, a factor analysis (with a maximum likelihood criterion) must be run to determine the number of factors and the factor loadings $\beta_{i,k}$. The maximum likelihood method provides a chi-square test that helps decide, for a given accuracy, whether a kth factor should be included. However, this method comes at the cost of assuming the normality of returns.

The major drawback of APT implementation is that the identified factors are not interpretable. They are merely combinations (portfolios) of existing securities. For that reason, some investors might prefer to apply their own view of the market and select their own factors from interpretable, economic quantities (see the next two subsections).

2.4.2.2 Exogenous factors

A direct way to implement the multifactor model in Equation (2-47) is to pick up factors $F_{k,t}$ from a list of macroeconomic variables. The literature[17] has investigated a long list of candidates among which are the GDP growth rate, inflation, returns on treasury bills, the slope of the yield curve, the default risk premium, and the index dividend yield.

The specification (2-47) entails that the selected factors must be zero mean. Practically speaking, this means that one should only consider the unanticipated variations of the macroeconomic factors listed above. Such variations are difficult to estimate. They can be, for instance, extrapolated from past observations.

[17] See, for example, Chen, Roll, and Ross (1986), Burmeister and McElroy (1988), Antoniou, Garrett, and Priestley (1998), Flannery and Protopapadakis (2002), and Maio and Philip (2015).

Alternatively, factors can also be selected among industry-specific or microeconomic variables. Industry-related variables are relevant because they may capture the value specifically created from the business model and its environment (including the technology, regulatory constraints, and the labor market). One example is oil and mining companies whose stock returns are affected by the price of the commodity they are operating (or by the price differential between different commodities). Microeconomic (or fundamental) variables refer to firm-specific financial items, such as leverage, dividend yield, market capitalization, measures of liquidity, and price-earnings ratio.

Several multifactor models in the financial industry combine the two types of exogenous factors (i.e., macro and micro). Among popular examples are the Barra and Wilshire models. The Barra Global Equity Model (licensed by MSCI), for instance, relies on common factors grouped into world, country, industry, style, and currency components.

2.4.2.3 Empirical factors

Factors can be selected using an inductive approach that "lets the data speak." In this regard, the three-factor model of Fama and French (1992, 1993) has become a standard benchmark both in the academic literature and in the industry practice.

The Fama–French three-factor model can be viewed as an extension of the CAPM. It posits that the expected excess return on asset i is a linear function of the market risk premium and two additional factors, labeled high minus low (HML) and small minus big (SMB). That is,

$$\mu_i = R_f + \beta_{i,M}(\mu_M - R_f) + \beta_{i,\text{SMB}}\text{SMB} + \beta_{i,\text{HML}}\text{HML} \tag{2-57}$$

The factor SMB represents the difference in expected excess returns between companies with small market capitalization (small stocks) and companies with big market capitalization (big stocks). The factor HML represents the difference in expected excess returns between companies with a high book-to-market ratio (value stocks) and companies with a low book-to-market ratio (growth stocks).[18] The inclusion of the HML and SMB factors into the asset pricing model is motivated by an empirical observation: Despite their relatively comparable betas, value stocks and growth stocks on the one hand, and small stocks and big stocks on the other hand, exhibit a large spread in their historical returns.

The HML and SMB factors are computed and regularly updated on Kenneth French's website (`https://mba.tuck.dartmouth.edu/pages/faculty/ken.french/index.html`). Calculations are reported from the daily to the annual frequency. Since the factors are easily identified, the beta coefficients of Equation (2-57) can be obtained by running an OLS regression of stock excess returns on the index excess returns (proxy for the market factor) and the HML and SMB factors.

---

[18] Section 7.2.1.3 of Chapter 7 details the computation of these factors.

In the search of additional relevant empirical factors, we can cite two extensions of the Fama–French three-factor model which have received some empirical attention. The four-factor model of Carhart (1997) adds momentum to obtain the following specification:[19]

$$\mu_i = R_f + \beta_{i,M}(\mu_M - R_f) + \beta_{i,\text{SMB}}\text{SMB} + \beta_{i,\text{HML}}\text{HML} + \beta_{i,\text{UMD}}\text{UMD} \tag{2-58}$$

In its original application, the Carhart (1997) specification uses monthly returns. The up minus down (UMD) factor is the difference in one-month lagged returns between the top 30% of stocks that best performed over the last 11 months and the bottom 30% of stocks (return averages are equally weighted). The momentum effect captures the fact that past stock winners (losers) tend to overperform (underperform) during the following period – a market anomaly initially observed by Jegadeesh and Titman (1993). The importance of the momentum phenomenon has been questioned in recent research.[20]

Fama and French (2015) propose a five-factor model that includes profitability and investment as additional factors. The robust minus weak factor is the return spread of the most profitable firms minus the least profitable. The conservative minus aggressive factor is the return spread of firms that invest conservatively versus aggressively.

Although interpretable, the empirical factors have been criticized for not being related to an explicit financial theory. It has been argued that the explanatory power of the Fama–French model stems from the fact that their empirical factors capture fundamental, but still unraveled economic effects. For instance, the exact relation between Fama–French factors and systematic default risk (which could drive a risk premium on equity markets) is a current empirical question (Campbell, Hilscher, and Szilagyi, 2008; Anginer and Yilidizan, 2018). Other studies have pointed toward information on macroeconomic risk factors embedded in the Fama–French factors (Vassalou and Xing, 2004; Aretz, Bartram and Pope, 2010).

2.4.3 Portfolio implications

Multifactor models posit a linear relation between the excess returns and the factors. Hence, just like the CAPM, they can easily be estimated by means of an OLS regression. The estimated betas keep a simple interpretation as sensitivity coefficients with respect to the associated factor. In this respect, estimation is a relatively easy task for multifactor models since they are not subject to Roll's critique. In fact, estimation is even easier than it is for the CAPM, as statistical significance of betas is usually achieved with much fewer observations. The major empirical

[19]This equation matches Equation (7-5) of Chapter 7 that describes the corresponding return-generating process.

[20]Bollen and Busse (2005) document that performance persistence of mutual funds is short-lived. Choi and Zhao (2021) find that the momentum effect has faded away over the past two decades.

challenge with multifactor models is identification. The number and choice of factors is always a delicate issue, as orthogonality and interpretability often create empirical tensions.

Single-factor and multifactor models also have different implications for portfolio performance appraisal. The CAPM provides a clear assessment of the portfolio's risk–return trade-off. The reward for exposure to systematic risk (through beta) draws a simple line between what should be expected from passive versus active portfolio management. Classic performance metrics for portfolio management have been constructed along this insight, as examined in Chapter 3. By contrast, a multifactor model helps the investor better understand how their portfolio reacts to various sources of risk, like macroeconomic factors for instance. But the evaluation of the portfolio management performance becomes a multidimensional issue. Adjusting the performance metrics is possible but not always straightforward (see Chapter 7).

Marko Invest Inc. (continued)

We use the same set of simulated monthly returns on the four funds A, B, C, and D over 10 years to estimate a two-factor model. In addition to portfolio M, two macroeconomic factors are considered. One, say industrial production (IP), has exhibited a drift of 3% and a volatility of 25% over the 10-year period. The other, say the consumers price index (CPI), has exhibited a drift of 2% and a volatility of 15% over the same time. A 10-year monthly path is simulated for these two series.

Before including the macroeconomic factors into a multifactor model, the log returns on IP and on CPI are orthogonalized with respect to the returns on the market portfolio. That is, we first run the following regressions:

$$R_{\mathrm{IP},t} = a_1 + b_1 R_{M,t} + e_{1,t}$$

$$R_{\mathrm{CPI},t} = a_2 + b_2 R_{M,t} + e_{2,t}$$

The returns on the orthogonal factors are then calculated as the difference between the observed and the estimated returns:

$$R_{\mathrm{IP},t}^{\perp M} \equiv R_1 = R_{\mathrm{IP},t} - \widehat{a}_1 - \widehat{b}_1 R_{M,t}$$

$$R_{\mathrm{CPI},t}^{\perp M} \equiv R_2 = R_{\mathrm{CPI},t} - \widehat{a}_2 - \widehat{b}_2 R_{M,t}$$

Finally, the excess returns on funds A, B, C, and D are regressed on $R_M - R_f$ (single-factor model) or, alternatively, on R_M and R_1 (two-factor model with industrial production), or on R_M and R_2 (two-factor model with inflation). The results are gathered in Table 2-7 ("**" and "*" mean statistical significance at the 1% and 5% levels, respectively).

TABLE 2-7 Regression results from single- and two-factor models.

	Intercept	Market	IP	CPI	Adj. R^2
	0.0037	0.3807**			0.3491
Fund A	0.0037	0.3807**	−0.0748		0.3581
	0.0037	0.3775**		−0.0554	0.3464
	−0.0012	0.6289**			0.4114
Fund B	−0.0012	0.6289**	0.1325*		0.4260
	−0.0012	0.6326**		0.0660	0.4081
	0.0048	1.1426**			0.6651
Fund C	0.0048	1.1426**	−0.2017**		0.6843
	0.0048	1.1400**		−0.0465	0.6627
	−0.0065	−0.0064			−0.0084
Fund D	−0.0065	−0.0064	0.0788		−0.0062
	−0.0065	−0.0100		−0.0647	−0.0144

As previously analyzed by Marko Invest Inc., the estimation of the single-factor model correctly pins down the beta for funds A and C, slightly underevaluates the beta of fund B and fails to accurately measure the beta of fund D. Coupling the market factor with industrial production yields a two-factor model with a higher explanatory power. Since the additional factor is orthogonal to market returns, the estimation of the market beta is unaffected.

Moreover, the R_1 factor turns out to be significant and improves the goodness-of-fit (measured by the adjusted R^2) for funds B and C. By contrast, the R_2 factor does not bring any benefit. It is never significant and only deteriorates the quality of estimation. Clearly, inflation is not to be considered as a second factor.

Key Takeaways and Equations

- The SPT addresses the portfolio allocation problem in a one-period, mean–variance framework. The optimal allocation (two-fund separation theorem) is a combination of the risk-free asset and the tangent portfolio, i.e., the portfolio located at the tangency point of the hyperbolic efficient frontier and the CML whose intercept is the risk-free rate.
  - The vector of weights (adding up to 1) for the tangent portfolio is $\mathbf{w}_T = \frac{1}{\gamma_T}\mathbf{V}^{-1}(\boldsymbol{\mu} - R_f\mathbf{1})$.
  - The relative allocation between the risk-free asset and the tangent portfolio depends on the investor's risk tolerance.
- The CAPM posits that the market portfolio is mean–variance efficient and therefore must be the tangent portfolio. In equilibrium,

$$\mu_i = R_f + \beta_i(\mu_M - R_f) \tag{2-21}$$

  - Only systematic risk, i.e., the covariance of the asset return with the market portfolio return, is rewarded.
  - The linear relation between expected return and beta is referred to as the SML whose slope is the market risk premium.
- Zero-beta CAPM: Equation (2-21) can be extended to the case without any risk-free asset, by replacing R_f with μ_Z, the expected return on the asset, with minimum variance, that is uncorrelated with the market portfolio.
- Beta coefficients can be estimated with the market model, an OLS regression of the form

$$R_{i,t} = \alpha_i + \beta_i R_{M,t} + \varepsilon_{i,t} \tag{2-29}$$

- A statistical validation of the CAPM consists in regressing observed excess returns on estimated betas, yielding the *ex post* SML:

$$R_i - R_f = \gamma_0 + \gamma_1\widehat{\beta}_i + \eta_i \tag{2-36}$$

  - The intercept should not be statistically different from zero.
  - The slope is an estimation of the realized market risk premium.
- A standard test of the CAPM is by means of cross-sectional (Fama–MacBeth) regressions (where bold notations indicate vectors across all available assets):

$$\mathbf{Z}_t = \gamma_{0t}\mathbf{1} + \gamma_{1t}\widehat{\boldsymbol{\beta}} + \boldsymbol{\eta}_t \tag{2-37}$$

- Cross-sectional regressions are repeated over several periods.
- Intercept and slope coefficients are averaged over time. Their Student *t*-distribution allows for statistical testing.

- The CAPM is subject to Roll's critique stating that the market portfolio is unobservable, let alone its mean–variance efficiency. The empirical challenge consists in working with the security index that best proxies for the market portfolio.
- The expected returns on individual assets can be estimated by a combination of market and private information (Black–Litterman method).
  - The market view is backed out from the CAPM.
  - Private information reflects the portfolio manager's personal views on the future performance (in absolute or relative terms) of some individual assets.
- The single-factor CAPM can be extended to multifactor models with generic specification:

$$R_{i,t} = \alpha_i + \sum_{k=1}^{K} \beta_{i,k} F_{k,t} + \varepsilon_{i,t} \tag{2-47}$$

  - The factors $F_{k,t}$ have zero mean.
  - Error terms are uncorrelated with the factors, as well as uncorrelated in the time series and in the cross-section.
- Different types of factors lead to different types of multifactor models:
  - The APT proceeds with a factor analysis. The resulting factors are not interpretable, but they are constructed in such a way to prevent arbitrage opportunities.
  - Factors can be exogenously selected among a list of plausible candidates that includes macroeconomic, industry-specific, or firm-specific variables.
  - Fama–French factors (most notably HML and SMB) have been shown to display high explanatory power over the cross-section of equity returns.

REFERENCES

Alexander, G., and N. Chervany (1980), On the estimation and stability of beta. *Journal of Financial and Quantitative Analysis*, Vol. 15, pp. 123–137.

Ang, A., and J. Chen (2007), CAPM over the long run: 1926–2001. *Journal of Empirical Finance*, Vol. 14, pp. 1–40.

Anginer, D., and Ç. Yildizhan (2018), Is there a distress risk anomaly? Pricing of systematic default risk in the cross-section of equity returns. *Review of Finance*, Vol. 22, pp. 633–660.

Antoniou, A., Garrett, I., and R. Priestley (1998), Macroeconomic variables as common pervasive risk factors and the empirical content of the arbitrage pricing theory. *Journal of Empirical Finance*, Vol. 5, pp. 221–240.

Aretz, K., Bartram, S., and P. Pope (2010), Macroeconomic risks and characteristic-based factor models. *Journal of Banking & Finance*, Vol. 34, pp. 1383–1399.

Best, M. J., and R. R. Grauer (1991), On the sensitivity of mean–variance-efficient portfolios to changes in asset means: Some analytical and computational results. *The Review of Financial Studies*, Vol. 4, pp. 315–342.

Black, F. (1972), Equilibrium without restricted borrowing. *Journal of Business*, Vol. 45, pp. 444–454.

Black, F., and R. Litterman (1992), Global portfolio optimization. *Financial Analysts Journal*, Vol. 48, pp. 28–43.

Bollen, N., and J. Busse (2005), Short-term persistence in mutual fund performance. *The Review of Financial Studies*, Vol. 18, pp. 569–597.

Burmeister, E., and M. McElroy (1988), Joint estimation of factor sensitivities and risk premia for the arbitrage pricing theory. *The Journal of Finance*, Vol. 43, pp. 721–733.

Campbell, J., Hilscher, J., and J. Szilagyi (2008), In search of distress risk. *The Journal of Finance*, Vol. 63, pp. 2899–2939.

Carhart, M. (1997), On persistence in mutual fund performance. *The Journal of Finance*, Vol. 52, pp. 57–82.

Cenesizoglu, T., and J. Reeves (2018), CAPM, Components of beta and the cross section of expected returns. *Journal of Empirical Finance*, Vol. 49, pp. 223–246.

Chen, N. F., Roll, R., and S. Ross (1986), Economic forces and the stock market. *Journal of Business*, Vol. 59, pp. 383–403.

Cheung, W. (2010), The Black–Litterman model explained. *Journal of Asset Management*, Vol. 11, pp. 229–243.

Choi, J., and K. Zhao (2021), Carhart (1997) mutual fund performance persistence disappears out of sample. *Critical Finance Review*, Vol. 10, pp. 263–270.

Cochrane, J. (2011), Presidential address: Discount rates. *The Journal of Finance*, Vol. 66, pp. 1047–1108.

Elton, E., and M. Gruber (1997), Modern portfolio theory, 1950 to date. *Journal of Banking & Finance*, Vol. 21, pp. 1743–1759.

Fabozzi, F., Gupta, F., and H. Markowitz (2002), The legacy of modern portfolio theory. *Journal of Investing*, Vol. 11, pp. 7–22.

Fama, E., and K. French (1992), The cross-section of expected stock returns. *The Journal of Finance*, Vol. 47, pp. 427–465.

Fama, E., and K. French (1993), Common risk factors in the returns on stocks and bonds. *Journal of Financial Economics*, Vol. 33, pp. 3–56.

Fama, E., and K. French (2015), A five-factor asset pricing model. *Journal of Financial Economics*, Vol. 116, pp. 1–22.

Fama, E., and J. MacBeth (1973), Risk, return, and equilibrium: Empirical tests. *Journal of Political Economy*, Vol. 81, pp. 607–636.

Flannery, M., and A. Protopapadakis (2002), Macroeconomic factors do influence aggregate stock returns. *The Review of Financial Studies*, Vol. 15, pp. 751–782.

Ghysels, E. (1998), On stable factor structures in the pricing of risk: Do time-varying betas help or hurt? *The Journal of Finance*, Vol. 53, pp. 549–573.

Guo, H., Wu, C., and Y. Yu (2017), Time-varying beta and the value premium. *Journal of Financial and Quantitative Analysis*, Vol. 52, pp. 1551–1576.

Jagannathan, R., and Z. Wang (1996), The conditional CAPM and the cross-section of expected returns. *The Journal of Finance*, Vol. 51, pp. 3–53.

Jegadeesh, N., and S. Titman (1993), Returns to buying winners and selling losers: Implications for stock market efficiency. *The Journal of Finance*, Vol. 48, pp. 65–91.

Kahneman, D., and A. Tversky (2013), Prospect theory: An analysis of decision under risk. In: L. MacLean, L. and W. Ziemba, Ed., *Handbook of the Fundamentals of Financial Decision Making: Part I*. World Scientific, pp. 99–127.

Kandel, S., and R. Stambaugh (1987), On correlations and inferences about mean–variance efficiency. *Journal of Financial Economics*, Vol. 18, pp. 61–90.

Lewellen, J., and S. Nagel (2006), The conditional CAPM does not explain asset-pricing anomalies. *Journal of Financial Economics*, Vol. 82, pp. 289–314.

Lintner, J. (1965), The valuation of risk assets and the selection of risky investments in stock portfolios and capital budgets. *Review of Economics and Statistics*, Vol. 47, pp. 13–37.

Maio, P., and D. Philip (2015), Macro variables and the components of stock returns. *Journal of Empirical Finance*, Vol. 33, pp. 287–308.

Markowitz, H. (1952), Portfolio selection. *The Journal of Finance*, Vol. 7, pp. 77–91.

Mossin, J. (1966), Equilibrium in a capital asset market. *Econometrica*, Vol. 34, pp. 768–783.

Pollet, J., and M. Wilson (2010), Average correlation and stock market returns. *Journal of Financial Economics*, Vol. 96, pp. 364–380.

Prono, T. (2015), Market proxies as factors in linear asset pricing models: Still living with the Roll critique. *Journal of Empirical Finance*, Vol. 31, pp. 36–53.

Roll, R. (1977), A critique of the asset pricing theory's tests. *Journal of Financial Economics*, Vol. 4, pp. 129–176.

Ross, S. (1976), The arbitrage theory of capital asset pricing. *Journal of Economic Theory*, Vol. 13, pp. 343–360.

Shanken, J. (1987), Multivariate proxies and asset pricing relations: Living with the Roll critique. *Journal of Financial Economics*, Vol. 18, pp. 91–110.

Sharpe, W. F. (1964), Capital asset prices: A theory of market equilibrium under conditions of risk. *The Journal of Finance*, Vol. 19, pp. 425–442.

Solnik, B. (1974), An equilibrium model of the international capital market. *Journal of Economic Theory*, Vol. 8, pp. 500–524.

Treynor, J. (1962), Toward a theory of market value of risky assets, Unpublished manuscript. Reprinted in Korajczyk, R. A., Ed., *Asset Pricing and Portfolio Performance* (1999). Risk Books, pp. 15–22.

Vassalou, M., and Y. Xing (2004), Default risk in equity returns. *The Journal of Finance*, Vol. 59, pp. 831–868.

CHAPTER 3

Classical Portfolio Performance Measures

INTRODUCTION

The simplest means of measuring portfolio performance is to directly inspect realized portfolio returns. If this inspection is performed without caution, doing so leads to a "too simple to be true" diagnosis, i.e., it considers only the output (return) of the management process without considering the associated input (risk) hence discards essential information and thus provides an incomplete picture. Essentially, the mean or cumulative realized return is not a measure of performance because it provides no insight on the amount of risk taken to achieve such returns, and thus does not allow us to assess the efficiency of the portfolio management process. However, under certain circumstances, *comparing* average portfolio returns with those of a *relevant* peer group can be at the same time relevant and useful. The analysis of the so-called *peer group comparison return* is our starting point.

To explicitly take risk into account in performance measurement, one needs to do so in a rigorous manner. The Standard Portfolio Theory (SPT) provides guidance for that. It has led to an equilibrium asset pricing relationship through the Capital Asset Pricing Model (CAPM) that we reviewed in Chapter 2. Unlike any previous attempt to develop a theoretical framework to connect securities' risk and returns and upon the condition that its underlying assumptions are respected, the CAPM entails a normative behavior for rational, risk-averse investors regarding their portfolio choice. Consequently, it is possible to control the *ex post* efficiency of their decision-making process through a set of appropriate performance measures.

In this chapter, we review the four classical performance measures that are consistent with the CAPM framework: the *Sharpe ratio*, *Jensen's alpha*, the *Treynor ratio* (and the almost equivalent *modified Jensen's alpha*, also called the Black–Treynor ratio), and the *Information ratio* (whose specific version within the CAPM framework is called the *Appraisal ratio*). We do not follow the chronological order of their appearance in the literature, but rather a logical flow in which each measure is shown to belong to a specific family of performance measures. Their distinctive feature is the definition of risk that underlies the assessment of portfolio management efficiency.

While analyzing the significance and the pros and cons of each performance measure, we take for granted the validity of the assumption of an independent and identically distributed (i.i.d.) Gaussian distribution of asset returns. The underlying statistical issues are analyzed in Chapter 5. Throughout the text, we illustrate the concepts with a simple but realistic example built with a sample of fund and index returns.[1]

The XYZ example – Part I

We have collected one year of monthly total returns for three mutual funds X, Y, and Z belonging to the long/short equity strategy, for a stock market index (M) and for an equally weighted portfolio of other funds belonging to the same peer group (B). The time series of monthly rates of returns are reported in Table 3-1.

TABLE 3-1 XYZ example – Monthly rates of return.

Month	X	Y	Z	M	B
Jan	−1.58%	−1.64%	−2.92%	−1.38%	−0.59%
Feb	2.66%	1.58%	2.28%	3.00%	1.68%
Mar	−0.41%	−1.23%	1.23%	−2.40%	−2.00%
Apr	−0.33%	−0.67%	−0.99%	2.44%	0.61%
May	1.40%	1.92%	5.13%	2.69%	0.83%
Jun	−1.44%	1.37%	0.22%	−2.00%	−0.40%
Jul	3.27%	2.95%	0.26%	5.75%	2.88%
Aug	−2.08%	0.57%	3.37%	−1.58%	−0.22%
Sep	1.10%	−1.63%	−2.37%	0.96%	0.00%
Oct	1.02%	1.32%	1.87%	1.29%	0.89%
Nov	−1.67%	−2.20%	−1.52%	−1.94%	−1.31%
Dec	1.87%	2.50%	3.12%	1.10%	0.84%

[1]The example is designed with one year of monthly data (12 observations) for the sake of visual parsimony. Obviously, it is extremely dangerous to draw statistical inference with a time series of 12 data points, and we strongly recommend adopting longer time windows and/or a higher data frequency (e.g., weekly returns) for practical applications.

The subsequent exploitation of this example requires the use of their means, volatilities (the financial name for standard deviation), and Pearson correlations. Their estimates are provided in Table 3-2.

TABLE 3-2 XYZ example – Means, volatilities, and correlations.

		X	Y	Z	M	B
Mean return		0.32%	0.40%	0.81%	0.66%	0.27%
Standard deviation		1.81%	1.79%	2.47%	2.55%	1.32%
	X	1.00				
	Y	0.65	1.00			
Correlations	Z	0.32	0.70	1.00		
	M	0.87	0.61	0.22	1.00	
	B	0.81	0.77	0.29	0.93	1.00

Figure 3-1 represents the cumulative total returns for each investment vehicle.

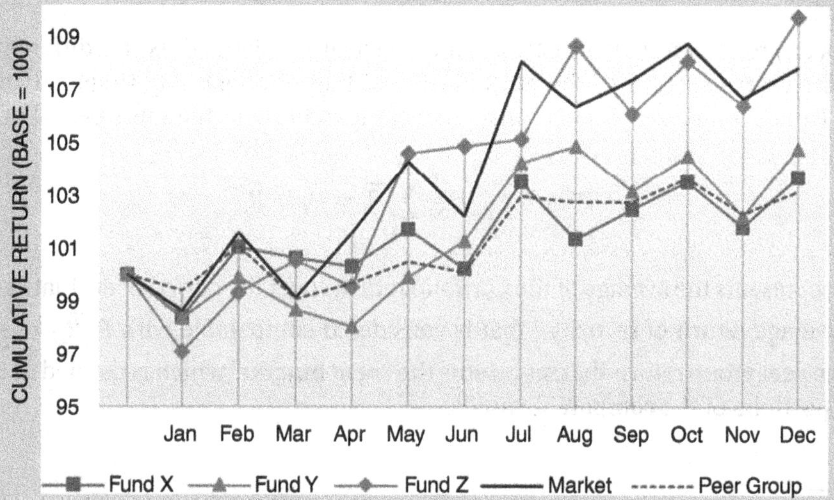

FIGURE 3-1 XYZ example – Cumulative rates of return.

(continued)

(continued)

Thus, the graphical information in Figure 3-1 indicates that Fund Z has "performed" closely to the stock index and better than its peers X and Y. The peer group index (dotted line) has evolved in a less volatile fashion, but its final value is close to X and Y. Beyond the visual impression, little can be said about the actual absolute and relative performance of these funds without further analysis. This example is developed and extended throughout this chapter.

3.1 PEER GROUP COMPARISONS

3.1.1 Definition

In the absence of (or ignoring) the equilibrium relation between risk and expected returns, it is not possible to engineer an efficiency measure that connects a necessary level of input (risk) to produce a desired output (realized return). The peer group comparison, which has historical roots long before the development of the SPT, disconnects risk from return by *implicitly* accounting for risk in performance measurement. It only focuses on the realized return of funds or other portfolios that are *implicitly* supposed to share similar risk levels or objectives.

The peer group comparison performance measure is defined as the differential return between the average return of the portfolio P and that of an equally weighted[2] portfolio of securities (funds or indexes) that is considered comparable over the same period of reference:

$$\mathrm{PG}_P = \overline{R}_P - \frac{1}{N}\sum_{i=1}^{N}\overline{R}_i = \overline{R}_P - \overline{R}_G \tag{3-1}$$

where $\overline{R}_P$ represents the average of the portfolio returns over the period of evaluation, and each $\overline{R}_i$ is the average return of security i that is considered comparable with P. $\overline{R}_G = \frac{1}{N}\sum_{i=1}^{N}\overline{R}_i$ is the average peer group return that represents the "benchmark," which is defined as the equally weighted portfolio of the comparable funds.

[2]Other weighting schemes can also be considered. When the funds' Assets Under Management are available, it can be useful for asset managers to construct value-weighted portfolios in order to match the industry structure.

3.1.2 What is a good peer group differential return?

3.1.2.1 Practical significance

From an economic perspective, the decision rule regarding the peer group comparison return is simple; the portfolio has outperformed its peer group when PG_P is positive.

Nevertheless, as discussed below, information conveyed by the peers' returns is richer than the benchmark return. The peer group comparison return criterion is often used to check the percentile reached by the portfolio in comparison to its comparable investment vehicles. From this perspective, a "good" portfolio is one whose average return belongs to the xth top percentile. The threshold is the median, but one may commit to an objective of belonging to the first quartile (top 25%) or quintile (top 20%), for instance.

3.1.2.2 Statistical significance

As the PG is a difference between two arithmetic averages,[3] the assessment of its significance, from a statistical point of view, is rather straightforward. Defining the benchmark return $R_G \equiv \frac{1}{N}\sum_{i=1}^{N} R_i$, the t-statistic for hypothesis testing is of the form

$$\hat{t}_{PG_P=0} = \frac{PG_P}{\sqrt{\frac{1}{T-1}(\sigma_P^2 + \sigma_G^2 - 2\rho_{PG}\sigma_P\sigma_G)}} \equiv \frac{\sqrt{T-1}}{\sigma(R_P - R_G)} PG_P \tag{3-2}$$

It follows (under the null hypothesis of zero performance) a Student's t-distribution with $T-1$ degrees of freedom, where T is the number of observations, σ_P^2 and σ_G^2 are the variances of the portfolio and benchmark returns, respectively, and ρ_{PG} is the Pearson correlation coefficient between the returns of the portfolio and the benchmark. The last identity shows that the denominator of the t-statistic features the standard deviation of the differential return between the portfolio and the benchmark return. This expression is explained again later when we discuss the Information ratio.

XYZ example (continued)

Fund Z has the highest returns of all three funds. To verify whether it significantly outperforms its peer group, we calculate the following sample estimates: $PG_Z = 0.81\% - 0.27\% = 0.54\%$; $\sigma(R_Z - R_G) \equiv \sigma_{Z-G} = 2.44\%$. Therefore, the t-statistic for this fund is equal to

(continued)

[3] The differences between the uses of arithmetic and geometric returns are discussed in Chapter 1.

(continued)

$\hat{t}_{PG_Z} = \frac{\sqrt{11}}{2.44\%}0.54\% = 0.73$. Since this value is lower than the critical value of the Student distribution with 11 degrees of freedom at the 95% confidence level, namely 1.796, we cannot reject the null hypothesis of the equality between the expected returns of fund Z and those of the peer group index.[4]

3.1.3 Strengths and weaknesses

3.1.3.1 Strengths

As seen in the first part, the challenge of performance measurement is to find a single synthetic measure of efficiency in the portfolio management process. Here, unlike many other performance measures, we obtain the PG value by aggregating information retrieved from a set of N comparable funds. Using raw data about the returns of these funds provides potentially helpful information about the percentile ranking of the portfolio among its peers. Furthermore, the availability of several time periods allows for carrying out both a cross-sectional (spatial) and a time-series (historical) ranking analysis. This is the only simple performance measure that makes this type of synoptic analysis possible.

The standard presentation for the fund ranking analysis is the "box-and-whisker plot" (or simply boxplot). It is a chart that visually displays the quartiles of the sample average returns of the funds that belong to the peer group. The graph generally sets the range of average returns on the vertical axis, and it represents a box whose upper and lower sides correspond to the first and third quartiles, respectively, and which is cut by a horizontal line showing the median. The upper and lower whiskers show the distance to the maximum and minimum or, occasionally, to a very high and very low percentile. If the whiskers do not span the whole range of the distribution, outliers can then be represented with a dot or a small circle.

XYZ example (continued)

The peer group G, identified as the benchmark B in Table 3-1, features 62 funds. The descriptive statistics in Table 3-1 show that its one-year geometric mean return is 3.16%. Additionally, we obtain the following percentile information for the one-year, three-year, and five-year time windows (Table 3-3).

[4] Even though the difference in the mean returns between Z and B appears to be economically large (9.68% − 3.21% = 6.47% on a yearly basis), the low number of observations (12) does not enable us to make any powerful statistical inference. Had the number of observations been higher, e.g., 5 years (60 months), the t-statistic would amount to $\hat{t}_{PG_Z} = \frac{\sqrt{59}}{2.44\%}0.54\% = 1.69$, higher than the critical value of 1.671; thus, the difference in mean returns would have become statistically significant.

TABLE 3-3 XYZ example – Percentile information for different time periods.

Percentile	Symbol	One-year return	Three-year return	Five-year return
1	Lower whisker	−6.56%	+0.00%	−0.51%
25 (1st quartile)	Lower box side	+0.71%	+3.75%	+3.58%
50 (median)	Middle box line	+2.97%	+5.16%	+5.13%
75 (3rd quartile)	Upper box side	+5.68%	+6.82%	+6.40%
99	Upper whisker	+13.00%	+10.93%	+10.26%
Peer group (mean)	Cross	+3.16%	+5.22%	+5.04%
X	Square	+3.69%	+5.06%	+5.25%
Y	Triangle	+4.77%	+6.79%	+7.74%
Z	Diamond	+9.75%	+3.93%	+2.19%

Figure 3-2 translates this information into boxplots, showing simultaneously the three periods of estimation.

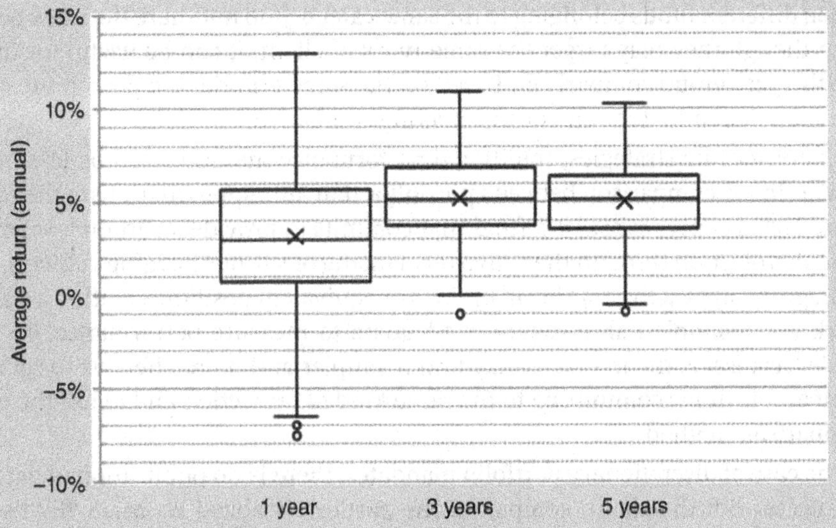

FIGURE 3-2 XYZ example – Box-and-whisker plot over different time periods.

(continued)

(continued)

A visual inspection of Figure 3-2 enables us to place in perspective the very positive one-year return of fund Z. It is considerably higher risk than the other funds (see Table 3-2), and the benchmark translates into more volatile multi-year returns, which shows that its recent outperformance is not the reflection of a longer trend relative to its peers. Such a multidimensional analysis, featuring space and time, is made possible due to the granular information about all funds across all years.

The peer group comparison method, although relatively simplistic, is very popular among institutional asset managers and investors. There are several potential reasons for that:

- Many active portfolio managers do not consider that they should compete with either a market index, which is not in the same league as they are, or a predefined risk-based benchmark, considered an artificial construction. Pragmatically, they consider that their real competitive landscape is the population of their fellow asset managers who are supposed to do the same job as them. This inclination to refer to the peer group as the relevant benchmark is reinforced by the importance of fund classification systems, which usually pool funds into homogeneous categories and rank each fund relative to their own group members.
- When different funds belonging to the same category do not share the same benchmark, even though they may target the same types of client, it can be useful for investors to use the peer group comparison. Based on the same criteria, the peer group stands as a common denominator and permits making comparisons.
- For very specific strategies, traditional performance measures can be less informative than a simple comparison between portfolios that are supposed to share the same objectives. For instance, consider a fund that commits to provide a certain level of dynamic capital protection through the active rebalancing of various hedging vehicles. Since this strategy involves active trading in options or equivalent positions, neither a static benchmark nor a simple risk measure is adequate to measure performance. To avoid any model risk issue, the manager may find it simpler and more effective to set a group of comparable funds committing to the same kind of protection and to use the peer group comparison method.
- In the case of discretionary portfolio mandates, there is no publication of data. To communicate with the client, comparing the portfolio realized returns with a set of published funds or indexes considered to strive for the same types of objectives is a simple and pedagogical reporting approach.

- Beyond the comparison of realized returns, analyzing the risk of competing funds may prove instructive. A fund or portfolio manager may want to position themselves jointly as a good performer in terms of return maximization and risk minimization. This approach leads to a two-dimensional analytic framework in which a weakness in one dimension could be compensated for by a strength in the other dimension.

XYZ example (continued)

The manager of Fund Y (triangle) strives to simultaneously outperform the median average return (2.97%) and the median risk level (4.93%) in the peer group. This behavior corresponds to the upper-left part (shaded zone) in Figure 3-3.

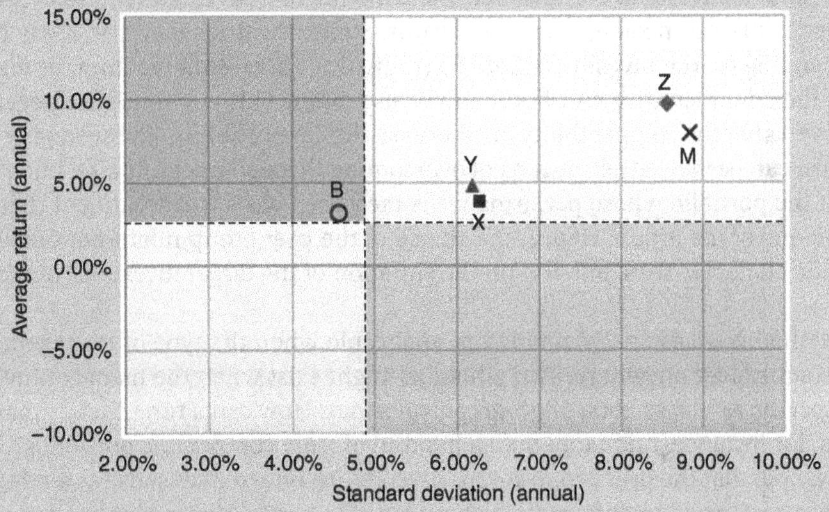

FIGURE 3-3 XYZ example – Peer group positioning in the mean-volatility framework.

We observe that none of the three funds manages to simultaneously achieve a risk level below the median and a return level above the median. Only the peer group index does so in the sample.

3.1.3.2 Weaknesses

It is tempting to constitute a relatively large peer group to achieve meaningful benchmark risk and return. However, for active portfolio managers, identifying the true competitors usually results in a relatively narrow group of "peers" that one can only outperform because of genuine skills. Thus, a too large group implies some loss in comparability. On the other hand, if the group becomes too narrow, the value of PG_P could be mostly due to good or bad luck, and nothing could be concluded about its significance. Furthermore, a tiny group of comparable portfolios hinders one of the major advantages of the approach, namely, the analysis of percentile rankings. The trade-off between homogeneity and representativeness is thus a matter of a fairly arbitrary (and thus occasionally suspicious) peer selection process.

There is also an issue of consistency over time. Some comparable funds appear; others disappear or change their strategy. The choice of a peer group may be valid at some point in time but may make less sense at another point in time, with a great importance of judgment; thus, it is difficult to consider that the peer group comparison return results from a fully objective process.

The choice of a peer group is not only a question of similarities in the portfolio management strategy. Another difficulty to consider is the set of regulatory and institutional differences that may arise from one jurisdiction to another. A key consideration is the tax treatment of the fund and its investors. For instance, there are notable tax treatment differences regarding dividends, interest income, and capital gains. Some countries may also apply transaction taxes. Depending on the investment vehicle (mutual fund, alternative fund, or discretionary portfolio), the administrative cost burden may also differ. This result might altogether create confusion and alter the comparability of otherwise similar portfolios. The averaging of the peer group return can be viewed as a means of overcoming these sources of noise, but a key condition is that the portfolio whose performance is measured has a cost treatment that is close to the average one of the group. Hence, the choice of the peer group might not only depend on fund-specific characteristics, but also on the situation of the target investors (jurisdiction, tax status, etc.).

The method is occasionally simply not applicable when the type of management has no reasonable equivalent anywhere. This situation might exist when the manager invests in certain very specific assets, sectors, or geographical zones. How can a fund that primarily invests in fine arts, for instance, find more than a handful of truly comparable portfolios?

Finally, note that the peer group comparison return only makes sense as a relative performance measure. It provides information about how the portfolio manager has done in relation to a group of other portfolios but says nothing about the absolute performance of the portfolio. If the investor has specific return objectives, it does not make sense for them to know that the manager that they have trusted has, e.g., "achieved a negative return, but not as catastrophic as the peer group." For them, the portfolio performance should have been positive, and the fact that the whole set of comparable portfolios has headed south is no consolation.

3.1.3.3 Conclusion

The technique of peer group comparison return is conceptually very simple and relatively straightforward, and it is not necessarily inconsistent with the CAPM. Nevertheless, its compatibility with the normative framework hinges on an important condition: the risk of each portfolio must be identical or at least fairly similar. Obviously, it would not make sense to compare the realized return of an aggressive all-equity fund whose yearly volatility exceeds 15% with that of a very defensive money market fund with a volatility of less than 3%. However, even when the difference in risks is lower, the comparative approach entails a practical problem: at what level can we consider the difference "not significant"? Instead of trying to justify a rather arbitrary heuristic rule for the application of the comparative approach, it is often preferable to explicitly account for the differences in risk. This point is true for the risk-adjusted performance measures presented in the following sections. Through their ability to control for risk, they allow in principle the comparison of heterogeneous portfolios.

3.2 THE SHARPE RATIO

3.2.1 Definition

Since the investor's objective is to maximize their expected utility in the mean–variance framework, a necessary condition in the CAPM is that they must then maximize the slope of the reward-to-variability ratio (RVR). Because all investors are *ex ante* rational, they all mix an investment in the risk-free asset and in the market portfolio. Doing so, they know that their resulting portfolio will plot on the Capital Market Line. From an expectations point of view, it is not possible to find any portfolio whose risk premium per unit of total risk will exceed that of the market portfolio. These statements summarize some of the major takeaways retrieved from Chapter 2.

Unlike the process imposed on them by this normative decision-making process, many investors will (voluntarily or not) depart from the market portfolio. In particular, some of them will deliberately manage their portfolio in an active fashion because they anticipate that their realized returns will favorably compare to those of a perfectly diversified, but passive, portfolio. In other words, even though the market portfolio is *ex ante* mean–variance efficient, some investors believe that it will not be *ex post* and choose an alternative portfolio composition that they hope will "beat the market."

Sharpe (1966) demonstrates that, in this context, the evaluation of the performance of a portfolio P held by an investor should be measured by the ratio of its excess return (over the risk-free interest rate) divided by its total risk:

$$\text{SR}_P = \frac{\overline{R}_P - R_f}{\sigma_P} \tag{3-3}$$

where $\overline{R}_P$ and σ_P represent the mean and standard deviation of the portfolio returns, respectively, and R_f is the rate of return of the risk-free asset, which is considered constant over the period.[5]

[5]We consider measurement issues in Chapter 5.

The Sharpe ratio displays a decisive advantage over the peer group comparison return; it explicitly adjusts for risk and is thus able to consistently rank portfolios with different volatilities. The rationale of this ratio intimately hinges on the validity of the CAPM assumptions regarding the behavior of financial investors. In particular, the assumption of homogeneous information across all investors enables them to precisely assess each portfolio's risk. Furthermore, the existence of a risk-free asset that investors are free to buy or sell at the rate of return R_f gives them access to "homemade leverage," that is, to all possible portfolios that combine a weight w in a risky asset or portfolio and a weight $1 - w$ in the risk-free asset. The resulting coordinates of the risk–return characteristics of all these possible portfolios will plot on a straight line, known *ex ante* as the Capital Allocation Line (CAL).

Two portfolios, L and H, which display different mean returns and volatilities during the period of reference will each obtain a unique value of the Sharpe ratio according to Equation (3-3). Consider the graph of Figure 3-4. L is less risky but also less profitable than H: $\sigma_L < \sigma_H$ and $\overline{R}_L < \overline{R}_H$. Drawing a straight line originating from the risk-free rate R_f, the slope of this line is clearly greater for L than for H: $\frac{\overline{R}_L - R_f}{\sigma_L} > \frac{\overline{R}_H - R_f}{\sigma_H}$. Since this slope is precisely equal to the Sharpe ratio of each portfolio, $SR_L > SR_H$, and we can conclude that portfolio L has outperformed portfolio H.

Due to the homemade leverage possibility, any investor can adjust the risk level of their portfolio along its CAL. Someone who invests in portfolio L and who wishes to reach the same risk level as H will simply borrow at the risk-free rate and invest the proceeds of the loan in L up to the point where the desired level of volatility is reached at leveraged portfolio L'. This technique is represented by the dotted line on the graph. Likewise, someone who initially invested in H could have sold a fraction of their portfolio and invested the proceeds in the

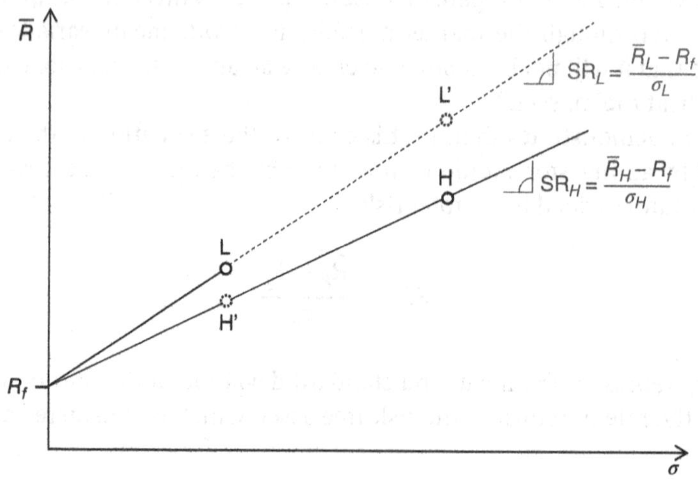

FIGURE 3-4 Graphical representation of the Sharpe ratio.

riskless asset up to a portfolio H' that is equally risky as L. Whatever the risk level sought by the investor, the coordinate on the upper line provides a higher utility to the rational, risk-averse investor: $\overline{R}_L < \overline{R}_{H'}$ while $\sigma_L = \sigma_{H'}$, and $\overline{R}_{L'} < \overline{R}_H$ while $\sigma_{L'} = \sigma_H$. The performance of L is thus unequivocally better than that of H, as shown by the difference in their Sharpe ratios.

The Sharpe ratio is also called the "reward-to-variability ratio," with reference to its *ex ante* interpretation. It translates the value of each input unit of volatility in terms of output rate of return, as shown by the following transformation of formula (3-3):

$$\overline{R}_P = R_f + \text{SR}_P \times \sigma_P \tag{3-4}$$

For instance, if the Sharpe ratio is 0.5, each additional percentage point of volatility taken translates into a 0.5 percentage point of additional realized return. If the risk-free rate is 1% and the volatility is 12%, the resulting return will thus be $\overline{R}_P = 1\% + 0.5 \times 12\% = 7\%$.

Note that it is customary to represent and interpret the Sharpe ratio in yearly terms. According to the assumption that all returns are i.i.d., we have a simple rule that links the Sharpe ratio computed with one frequency to another. Consider that the data are computed with a frequency of n times per year. The link between the Sharpe ratios is as follows:

$$\text{SR}_P^{1y} = \frac{\overline{R}_P^{1y} - R_f^{1y}}{\sigma_P^{1y}} = \frac{n \times \left(\overline{R}_P^{1y/n} - R_f^{1y/n}\right)}{\sqrt{n} \times \sigma_P^{1y/n}} = \sqrt{n} \times \text{SR}_P^{1y/n} \tag{3-5}$$

In other words, one has to multiply the Sharpe ratio by the square root of the number of compounding periods to obtain the yearly Sharpe ratio.

XYZ example (continued)

The monthly risk-free interest rate for the period is 1.44% per annum (0.12% on a monthly basis).[6] Table 3.4 summarizes the calculations for the three funds and two indexes.

TABLE 3-4 XYZ example – Sharpe ratios.

Measure	X	Y	Z	M	B
Mean (monthly)	0.32%	0.40%	0.81%	0.66%	0.27%
Volatility (monthly)	1.81%	1.79%	2.47%	2.55%	1.32%
SR (monthly)	0.11	0.16	0.28	0.21	0.11
SR (yearly)	**0.38**	**0.55**	**0.96**	**0.73**	**0.39**

(continued)

[6]The interest rate is expressed on a yearly basis, and its reported level is proportional to the periodic interest rate applicable during the compounding period.

(continued)

The graphical representation of the Sharpe ratios of the funds and the market index is provided in Figure 3-5.

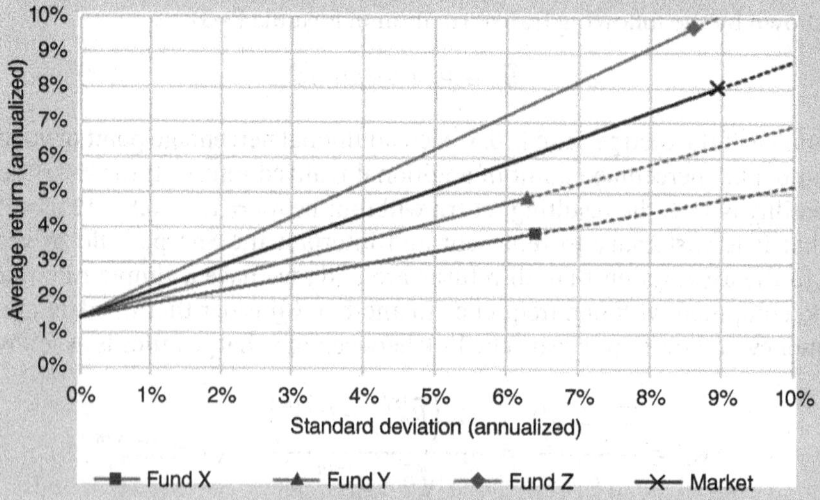

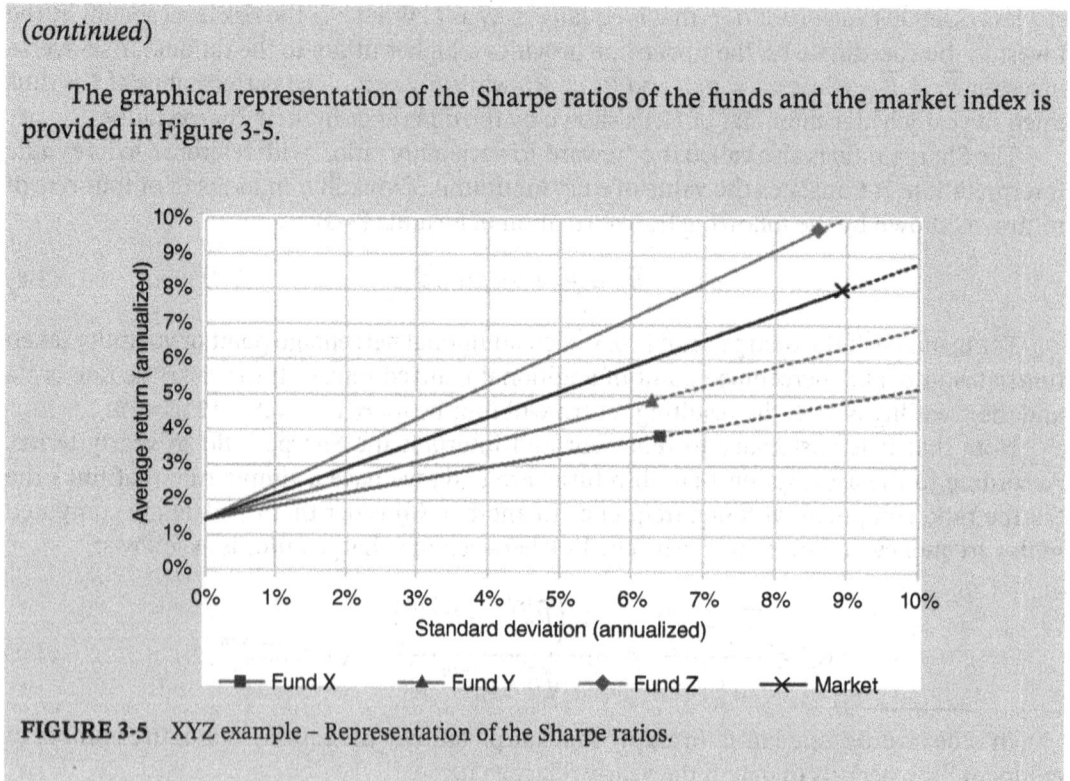

FIGURE 3-5 XYZ example – Representation of the Sharpe ratios.

3.2.2 What is a good Sharpe ratio?

3.2.2.1 Practical significance

The Sharpe ratio delivers a scalar (decimal) number, so its value does not say anything readily interpretable.

As, in general, the expected returns of risky investments are supposed to be positive and greater than the risk-free rate and because volatility is a strictly non-negative number, the Sharpe ratio should usually be positive. This point also holds true for *passive* investments. A risky investment that would yield a Sharpe ratio equal to zero in the long term would essentially provide the risk-free return and would not reward the investor for the risk taken. This result is possible of course (for instance, for funds that are completely uncorrelated with the market portfolio), but the investment would in general be considered a poor performer. Thus, $SR_P = 0$ is a mediocre figure; it should be easy to beat.

On the other hand, contrarily to a misconception that is pervasive on popular but imprecise websites, there is no particular reason that the Sharpe ratio of a fund or portfolio should exceed 1, which is in no way a "magic number." Consider for instance the monthly standard deviation of the S&P 500 index from 1950 to 2018 (828 data points), which is 4.11%, corresponding to an annualized return of 14.24%. It would not make sense to require an excess return (over the risk-free rate) of 14.24% from any active portfolio over the same period to be considered *average*. Incidentally, the excess return of this index during the same period has "only" been in the neighborhood of 9%, depending on the interest rate considered.

Thus, the cutoff point between a "bad" and a "good" Sharpe ratio is somewhere between 0 and 1. In their comprehensive study of global financial markets in the long term, Jordà, Knoll, Kuvshinov, Schularick, and Taylor (2019) obtain results for equally weighted average indexes over 16 countries (Australia, Belgium, Denmark, Finland, France, Germany, Italy, Japan, the Netherlands, Norway, Portugal, Spain, Sweden, Switzerland, the United Kingdom, and the United States) that are summarized in Table 3-5.

Table 3-5 suggests that equities achieve a Sharpe ratio close to 0.30 in the long term, which many professional asset managers would consider insufficient. Real estate has constantly performed better, but it refers to an illiquid investment vehicle. Due to portfolio diversification, however, it is possible to achieve better figures by combining different asset classes. In other words, over a long period, the Sharpe ratio of a diversified portfolio will always be better than the one of an undiversified one.

The Sharpe ratio that can reasonably be targeted by an active portfolio manager is not only a matter of their strategic asset allocation, their tactical bets, and their asset selection abilities, but also contingent on the market conditions that prevail during the holding period of measurement. Consider for instance a portfolio manager who would passively invest for five years in a portfolio of domestic US stocks (S&P 500), of world stocks (MSCI World), or of an equally weighted average of world stocks and corporate bonds (S&P International Corporate

TABLE 3-5 Sharpe ratios for global financial markets in the long term.

Time period[7]	Measure	Bonds	Equity	Housing
1870–2015	Mean excess return	1.50%	6.15%	6.46%
	Standard deviation	8.91%	22.78%	10.70%
	Sharpe ratio	**0.17**	**0.27**	**0.60**
1950–2015	Mean excess return	1.91%	7.59%	6.91%
	Standard deviation	9.80%	25.09%	10.15%
	Sharpe ratio	**0.19**	**0.30**	**0.68**

Source: Jordà et al. (2019), authors' computations.

[7] Periods covered diverge across countries, but the coverage is consistent within countries.

Bond Index). The starting point is anywhere between April 2002 and December 2013, but the manager obviously does not know what the market will do over the next five years. If they enter the market at a random point in time, the Sharpe ratio at exit, five years later, will plot as shown in Figure 3-6 for all three portfolios.

As expected from the potential impact of diversification benefits, an international portfolio of stocks tends to outperform a domestic one, although it will not always actually do so. Furthermore, opening the portfolio to other asset classes may also increase the risk–return trade-off. However, even though the average Sharpe ratio of the manager's portfolio is roughly consistent with what could be expected in the long term (see the dotted horizontal lines), its range is quite wide. If they have unluckily been exposed to the global financial crisis of 2008, they will carry a disappointing Sharpe ratio for a long subsequent period. This result can be verified in the descriptive statistics of the three time series as shown in Table 3-6.

Overall, the target value of the Sharpe ratio of an active portfolio manager is not a constant number but rather heavily depends on how the market rewards risk during the period. However, in the long term, a well-diversified, passive portfolio is likely to achieve a Sharpe ratio that would be closer to 0.5 than to 0 or to 1.

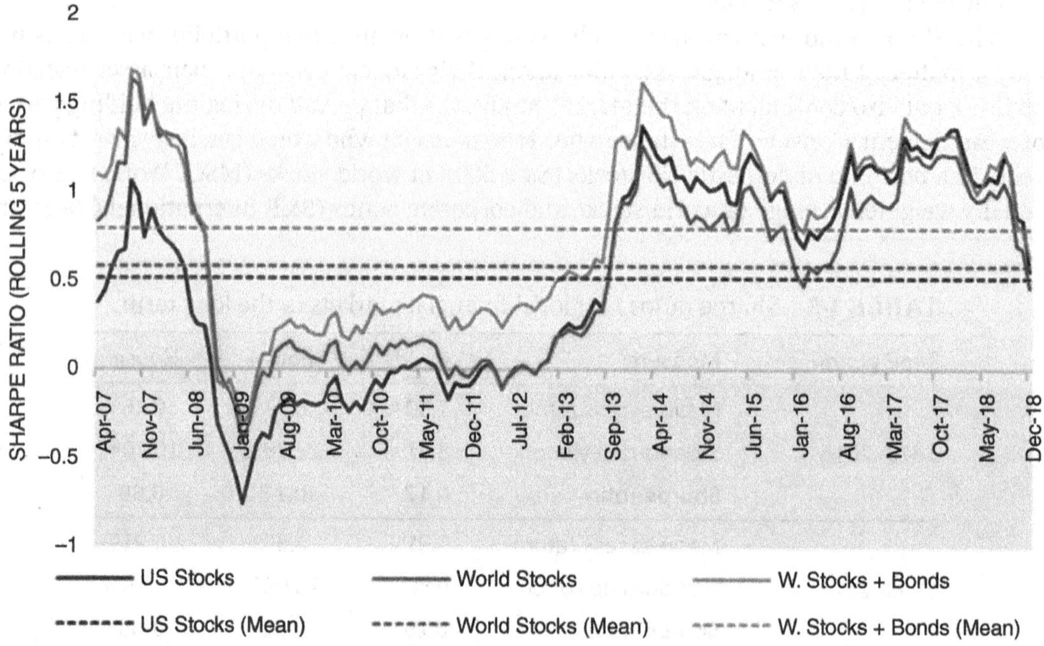

FIGURE 3-6 Time series of the rolling five-year Sharpe ratios for three portfolios: US stocks, world stocks, and equally weighted average of world stocks and corporate bonds.

TABLE 3-6 Descriptive statistic of rolling five-year Sharpe ratios.

	US stocks	World stocks	World stocks and bonds
Mean	0.51	0.58	0.79
Standard deviation	0.58	0.50	0.49
Min	−0.76	−0.40	−0.32
Max	1.37	1.63	1.68

3.2.2.2 Statistical significance

Unlike many other performance measures, the fact that there is no critical value of the Sharpe ratio makes it relatively useless to perform hypothesis tests against theoretical constant values such as 0 or 1. However, statistical inference remains insightful for other purposes.

When the Sharpe ratio is studied in isolation, it is interesting to construct confidence intervals around its observed value. On the basis of the work of Jobson and Korkie (1981), Lo (2002) obtains a very simple formulation for the asymptotic distribution of the Sharpe ratio estimator when the returns are i.i.d. and normally distributed. The confidence interval for the true Sharpe ratio of portfolio P with a $1-x$ confidence level around its estimated value is written as follows:

$$SR_P \pm z_{1-\frac{x}{2}} \times \sqrt{\frac{1}{T}\left(1+\frac{SR_P^2}{2}\right)} \tag{3-6}$$

where SR_P is the statistical estimate of the Sharpe ratio,[8] T is the number of observations, and $z_{1-\frac{x}{2}}$ is the $\left(1-\frac{x}{2}\right)$th percentile of the standard normal distribution. The square root term is the asymptotic standard error of the estimator of the Sharpe ratio.

Because the expression for the confidence interval is only asymptotically valid, it is hazardous to try to make an inference for small samples. Nevertheless, Lo (2002) provides some insight about the relation between the asymptotic standard error and the level of the Sharpe ratio for various values of the sample size. It is interesting to address the following reverse question: "*How many observations would be necessary, for each estimated value, to exclude the value of zero from the confidence intervals?*" From a hypothesis testing point of view, this query would be similar to asking the question of the sample size that would be required to reject the

[8]In all rigor, we should denote the statistical estimate of the Sharpe ratio by $\widehat{SR}_P$, but this representation would probably cause unnecessary confusion, as we always deal with estimated performance measures.

TABLE 3-7 Minimum number of observations necessary to exclude 0 from the confidence interval around the estimated Sharpe ratio.

	Significance level (x)									
$\widehat{SR}_P$	1%	2%	3%	4%	5%	6%	7%	8%	9%	10%
0.2	170	139	121	108	98	91	84	79	74	69
0.4	45	37	32	29	26	24	23	21	20	19
0.6	22	18	16	14	13	12	11	11	10	9
0.8	14	12	10	9	8	8	7	7	6	6
1.0	10	9	8	7	6	6	5	5	5	5
1.2	8	7	6	6	5	5	4	4	4	4

null hypothesis of the absence of any reward for the risk taken by each portfolio. This critical number of observations T_P^* can be readily retrieved from Equation (3-6):

$$T_P^* = \left\lceil z_{1-\frac{x}{2}}^2 \left(\frac{1}{2} + \frac{1}{SR_P^2} \right) \right\rceil \quad (3\text{-}7)$$

where $\lceil \cdot \rceil$ stands for the ceiling (smallest integer greater than or equal to) of the argument. Naturally, the critical number increases with the confidence level considered and decreases when the Sharpe ratio increases. What is important is that the behavior of T_P^* is inversely proportional to the square of the Sharpe ratio. Thus, when the general level of Sharpe ratios is rather low because the market does not generously reward risk, it takes a potentially very long period to safely consider that a portfolio has created extra return for the risk taken. The behavior of T_P^* as a function of confidence level and estimated Sharpe ratio is summarized in Table 3-7.

XYZ example (continued)

As an illustration of the order of magnitude of confidence intervals, we apply Equation (3-6) to the three funds and two indexes of the example (even though with $T = 12$, we should not draw any conclusion from this exercise).

The lower and upper bounds of the confidence intervals and the critical number of observations T_P^* necessary to exclude 0 from the confidence intervals are reported in Table 3-8.

TABLE 3-8 XYZ example – Confidence intervals around estimated Sharpe ratios.

Measure	$\frac{x}{2}=5\%$			$\frac{x}{2}=2.5\%$			$\frac{x}{2}=1\%$		
$z_{1-\frac{x}{2}}$	1.645			1.960			2.326		
	Upper	Lower	T_P^*	Upper	Lower	T_P^*	Upper	Lower	T_P^*
X	0.87	−0.11	21	0.96	−0.21	29	1.07	−0.32	41
Y	1.06	0.04	11	1.15	−0.06	15	1.27	−0.17	21
Z	1.54	0.39	5	1.65	0.28	7	1.77	0.15	9
M	1.27	0.20	7	1.37	0.10	10	1.49	−0.02	13
B	0.88	−0.10	20	0.97	−0.20	28	1.08	−0.31	39

If we consider the true Sharpe ratio of each portfolio equal to the estimation of the SR volatility, there are very few instances where we can be confident that the true value is contained in the intervals. Only Fund Z has lower bounds that are consistently positive. The intervals for Fund X and the peer group index B, on the other hand, all contain value zero; even with a relatively weak confidence level of 90%, the observed value is not inconsistent with a true Sharpe ratio of 0.

Going one step further than Lo (2002), there is also an analytical approach to obtain the asymptotic distributions when returns are i.i.d. but not normally distributed.[9] This method makes use of the "delta method" for the quotient of random variables described by Stuart and Ord (1994). Applying it to the Sharpe ratio, Mertens (2002) and Opdyke (2007) derive an extended version of Equation (3-6) by taking the third (skewness) and fourth (kurtosis) moment of the returns into account:

$$\mathrm{SR}_P \pm z_{1-\frac{x}{2}} \times \sqrt{\frac{1}{T}\left(1 + (\mu_{P,4} - 1)\frac{\mathrm{SR}_P^2}{4} - \mu_{P,3}\mathrm{SR}_P\right)} \tag{3-8}$$

where $\mu_{P,3} \equiv \frac{\mathrm{E}(R_P - \overline{R}_P)^3}{\sigma_P^3}$ and $\mu_{P,4} \equiv \frac{\mathrm{E}(R_P - \overline{R}_P)^4}{\sigma_P^4}$ are, respectively, the normalized third and fourth moments of the portfolio returns, known as their "skewness" and "kurtosis."[10]

Rather than studying the Sharpe ratio of a portfolio in isolation, it usually makes more sense to compare the ratio with that of another portfolio or index measured over the same

[9]The most general case, when returns are neither Gaussian nor i.i.d., is covered in Christie (2005).

[10]We discuss in greater detail the role of skewness and kurtosis for performance measurement in Chapters 5 and 6.

period. Here again it is possible to perform simple statistical inference over the asymptotic behavior of the Sharpe ratios, provided that we still accept the i.i.d. and normality assumptions.

Under this simplified setup, Jobson and Korkie (1981), corrected by Memmel (2003), provide the asymptotic test statistic for the difference in Sharpe ratios between two portfolios P and Q (expressed in the same frequency as in the sample, i.e., in monthly terms if we have monthly observations):[11]

$$\hat{z}_{\mathrm{SR}_P-\mathrm{SR}_Q=0} = \frac{\bar{r}_P\sigma_Q - \bar{r}_Q\sigma_P}{\sqrt{\frac{1}{T}\left[2(1-\rho_{PQ}) + \frac{1}{2}\left(\mathrm{SR}_P^2 + \mathrm{SR}_Q^2 - 2\rho_{PQ}^2\mathrm{SR}_P\mathrm{SR}_Q\right)\right]}} \tag{3-9}$$

where $\bar{r}_i \equiv \bar{R}_i - R_f$ and σ_i are respectively the excess return and volatility of portfolio i, ρ_{PQ} is the Pearson (linear) correlation coefficient between the returns of P and Q, and Z follows a standard normal distribution with expectation of 0 and variance of 1.

The correlation between the returns of the matched portfolios is crucial to assess the significance of the difference. Imagine that you compare two portfolios whose managers have completely remote investment styles, areas, or assets; a large deal of their realized returns is generated by risk sources that are unconnected. It is very likely that a small difference between their Sharpe ratios would be primarily due to good or bad luck. Oppositely, consider two managers who implement (almost) exactly the same strategy, but one charges higher fees and commissions than the other; thus, their net-of-fee Sharpe ratio is only slightly lower. The difference in their Sharpe ratios is purely deterministic (different fee levels) and thus must be very highly significant. In expression (3-9), the denominator is minimized, and significance is thus highest when $\rho_{PQ} = +1$.

We have one word of caution concerning the test presented in Equation (3-9) – it is not very powerful. That is, if the *true* Sharpe ratios of two portfolios are different, the Z-statistic does not recognize this fact often enough and instead leads to a no-rejection of the hypothesis of equal Sharpe ratios. Specifically, if the observed value of Z is high enough to reject this null hypothesis, the confidence that we could have in this decision can be reasonably high. Conversely, failing to discriminate two Sharpe ratios on the basis of this test does not necessarily mean that the managers are indeed equally good. Thus, to achieve at the same time a greater power and more flexibility in testing the Sharpe ratio differences, it is preferable to turn to "robust" approaches based on bootstrapping the returns distributions, such as in Ledoit and Wolf (2008).[12]

---

[11]Note that this test has been designed using figures expressed in percentage points. Thus, if portfolio i has a volatility of 3%, the formula features $\sigma_i = 3$ and $\sigma_i^2 = 9$. Otherwise, the figures do not make sense.

[12]In the next section, a simple illustrative numerical application is presented on the modified Jensen's alpha.

XYZ example (continued)

To meaningfully compare the three funds and the indexes, it is necessary to use the correlations between the time series reported in Table 3-2. They range from 0.22 (between the market M and Fund Z) to 0.93 (between the market M and the peer group B). Thus, we can expect the outcome of the pairwise comparison test to be contrasted from one matched pair to another.

For the sake of the illustration, consider that the number of observations is $T = 36$ (three years). The results are summarized in Table 3-9, which is presented in the form of a double entry table.

TABLE 3-9 XYZ example – Pairwise Z-statistics of the Sharpe ratio (using $T = 36$ observations).

		X	Y	Z	M
	SR_P	*0.38*	*0.55*	*0.96*	*0.73*
Y	*0.55*	1.08			
Z	*0.96*	**3.41**	**3.44**		
M	*0.73*	**4.74**	1.51	−1.70	
B	*0.39*	0.07	−0.90	*−2.38*	*−4.40*

There are only five significant differences: three positive ones (in bold) and two negative ones (in italics). If we zoom in on the largest absolute values, they correspond to the following: $SR_M(= 0.73) \gg SR_X(= 0.38)$ and $SR_M(= 0.73) \gg SR_B(= 0.39)$. These comparisons are the two for which the correlations are highest. Even though its Sharpe ratio is by far the highest one, Fund Z does not significantly outperform the market from a statistical viewpoint; its management style is too remote from the market portfolio to draw any conclusion on the basis of the test.

This example illustrates the fact that the Sharpe ratio of different portfolios results from two effects: the inherent risk–return relationship of the market in which the manager is active and the impact of the intrinsic quality of the manager. In the case of the manager of Fund Z, the generation of the Sharpe ratio cannot be decisively attributed to better skills. On the other hand, Fund X tracks the stock market reasonably well, and the lower reward-to-risk ratio that it achieves compared to the index (difference of −0.35) can be considered large enough to draw conclusions about its underperformance.

3.2.3 Strengths and weaknesses

3.2.3.1 Strengths

The major advantage of the Sharpe ratio over any other performance measure based on total risk is its theoretical robustness. Being perfectly consistent with the optimal behavior of a rational decision maker in the context of the SPT, this performance measure is the ultimate reference for the "best" risk–return trade-off when risk is measured by the volatility of returns. Of course, there are practical hindrances to its measurement, but these difficulties are not inherent to the Sharpe ratio; rather, they are an issue with the implementation of the model itself.

In the CAPM framework, a well-known issue with *ex post* analysis with realized return, first identified by Roll (1977), is the practical impossibility of identifying the market portfolio.[13] Any attempt to measure portfolio performance relative to a market benchmark is literally cursed by this critique. The Sharpe ratio escapes the curse by not relying on the market portfolio at all; it is an absolute performance measure. In many respects, this aspect raises a potential issue of comparability, but from a conceptual point of view, it is a substantial advantage. Additionally, the fact that the measure is not associated with the results of the asset pricing model (which corresponds to the Security Market Line, SML) also insulates the Sharpe ratio from the many issues surrounding the identification of the risk factors that influence asset returns. Thus, the Sharpe ratio can be viewed as carrying the advantages, not the drawbacks of the equilibrium asset pricing model.

Another quality of the Sharpe ratio is its malleability. The ratio is a generic measure of "excess return per unit of risk." Many of the modern performance measures that have emerged since the publication of Sharpe's paper borrow the same type of interpretation as a reward-to-total-risk ratio. However, unlike the vast majority of performance measures of this family, there is no reliance on any arbitrary assumption with the Sharpe ratio. When one gives up the special features of other commonly used measures, such as the Sortino ratio, the Roy "safety-first ratio," and even the Information ratio discussed below, the fallback is the Sharpe ratio itself.

Finally, the popularity of the Sharpe ratio is probably the highest of all the (numerous) performance measures that are disclosed to investors. It has stood for more than 50 years and generally appears in the top-three performance measures disclosed by major institutional asset managers (e.g., JPMorgan Chase, Fidelity, …) in their factsheets. Why is popularity a strength? Not necessarily because it crowns the best possible performance measures but simply because a performance measure is only legitimate if it is widely disseminated. A proprietary performance measure that was invented and intellectually protected by an outstanding scholar, for instance, could dominate any other performance measure from an intellectual point of

[13] We refer the reader to Section 2.3.2 of Chapter 2 for a discussion.

view. From a practical viewpoint, however, such a measure would be worthless because performance measurement is primarily about monitoring and controlling the outcome of a process, and no one can control anything without precisely knowing how the efficiency process has been assessed, i.e., which performance measure has been used.

3.2.3.2 Weaknesses

For many people who are regularly confronted with individual investors without any financial literacy, the Sharpe ratio is a nightmare to explain. Since it stands as a ratio of two figures expressed as a percentage, it yields a scalar without any economic unit of measurement. What does it mean for a normal person to have a Sharpe ratio of 0.5? 0.5 *what*? One should expect a performance measure that is very popular, such as the Sharpe ratio, to be readily interpretable and explainable. We could call it "*the user-friendliness test*"; if an unsophisticated investor does not understand your explanations, then you are only speaking in your financial jargon. You may even create some feeling of distrust if the customer feels that you want to confuse them. The popularity of the Sharpe ratio in the retail investment market can be considered puzzling in this respect.

Beyond the difficulty with explaining the Sharpe ratio as such, interpreting its level is also an issue. The discussion of the ratio above shows that there is no "magic number," such as 0 or 1, that discriminates the good from the bad portfolio manager. This lack is a drawback shared by many absolute performance measures and most likely explains why many professionals prefer to compare the Sharpe ratios of a set of competing portfolios or funds rather than trying to make sense of its absolute level.

A third notable weakness of the Sharpe ratio resides in its dependence on "homemade leverage" to compare portfolios with different risk levels. Even though such an assumption is a cornerstone of the CAPM, its justification in practice is questionable, especially from an *ex post* perspective for individual investors. Not only is it difficult for many investors to assess *a priori* what might be the risk that would actually be taken by various portfolios they are considering, but also, even if they could reasonably gauge the volatility level of their funds (which is made possible through standardized information documents), they would definitely not spontaneously *first* choose their portfolio *only* on the basis of their Sharpe ratio, *then* deliberately modify its volatility level through lending or borrowing at the riskless rate of interest over their investment horizon. Even if they were sophisticated enough to do so (which could be true for the more financially literate or better advised persons), they would be confronted with the practical difficulty of finding a Lombard loan at the risk-free rate, all the more in the case of high leverage. Fortunately, in such cases, there exists a solution for performance measurement. Some measures explicitly take into account the investor's risk aversion and the absence of leverage, and are entirely consistent with the CAPM (except for the ability to use homemade leverage). They are termed "preference-based" performance measures (see Chapter 9).

Finally, the Sharpe ratio is dangerous when misused or misinterpreted, which happens when the true portfolio risk is not adequately reflected by the volatility of returns. We are not dealing here with a "simple" measurement error but rather with the more fundamental issue of alterations in the risk profile of the portfolio that make the use of volatility completely misleading. This occurs, for instance, when the manager heavily employs or replicates option strategies. Options create a convex (if bought) or concave (if sold) sensitivity pattern of the portfolio returns with respect to the contracts' underlying asset. Thus, the resulting portfolio returns may depart too significantly from the Gaussian distribution to warrant the use of a standard deviation measure. Some managers may even use options on purpose to artificially inflate their Sharpe ratio. This phenomenon is called "performance manipulation" and is studied in Chapter 18.

3.2.3.3 Conclusion

Almost every factsheet of every fund in every part of the world reports the Sharpe ratio. As it is the *a posteriori* version of the CAPM's RVR, the case to defend the relevance of the Sharpe ratio as a performance measure is not even open to discussion. However, like any tool that summarized a complex reality with a single digit, it has its limitations and suffers from several weaknesses. Two main such limitations are its nature as a ratio, which induces a challenging interpretation for retail investors, and the absence of a magical number for its level, making it mostly a comparative tool rather than an absolute reference. Furthermore, its reliance on the investor's capacity to freely adjust their risk level limits the scope of its application. Again, this calls for no use of the Sharpe ratio in isolation but to complement it with other indicators of performance.

Nevertheless, it is worth concluding that it remains a keystone of performance measurement and comparison for well-diversified portfolios. There have been many avatars of the Sharpe ratio proposed in the literature, both by researchers and practitioners. This attention is a recognition of the importance of this approach to measure portfolio efficiency through a simple input (risk)/output (return) ratio. This approach is still, by far, the leading means of controlling the quality of the portfolio management process, and the Sharpe ratio is its undisputed ambassador.

3.3 THE TREYNOR RATIO, JENSEN'S ALPHA, AND THE MODIFIED JENSEN'S ALPHA

3.3.1 Definitions

3.3.1.1 The Treynor ratio

From an *ex ante* perspective, rational investors choose a single optimal risky portfolio at equilibrium, namely, the market portfolio. The Sharpe ratio follows this normative *a priori* rule and asks whether one could design a portfolio that achieves *a posteriori* a better risk–return trade-off than the market. Starting from the same framework, we now go one step further and deal with the logical consequences of the equilibrium risk–return relationship regarding individual securities and portfolios. As shown in Chapter 2, the SML shows a linear relationship between the expected return of any asset and its systematic risk, measured by the beta. Once the investor is supposed to be perfectly diversified through their holding of the market portfolio, the SML provides the expected remuneration of the risk of each component of this market portfolio that cannot be diversified away, reflected in the beta.

What if the investor is convinced that some assets will outperform others within the market portfolio? Considering the *ex post* perspective, and assuming away the issue of potential underdiversification, the quality of their choice will be assessed with a logic similar to that of the Sharpe ratio. Their performance will be measured by the amount by which the portfolio's excess return rewards its systematic risk.

Treynor (1965) defines the corresponding performance measure as the slope of the reward-to-systematic-risk (RTSR) linear function. The Treynor ratio of a portfolio P, called TR_P, is the ratio of its excess return (over the risk-free interest) divided by its systematic risk:

$$\text{TR}_P = \frac{\overline{R}_P - R_f}{\beta_P} \tag{3-10}$$

where $\overline{R}_P$ represents the mean portfolio return, R_f is the rate of return of the riskless asset, which is considered constant over the period, and $\beta_P = \frac{\text{Cov}(R_P, R_M)}{\sigma_M^2} \equiv \rho_{PM}\frac{\sigma_P}{\sigma_M}$ is the beta of the portfolio with respect to the market portfolio (see Chapter 2).

Because of its similarity to the Sharpe ratio, the Treynor ratio shares many of its characteristics regarding its ability to control for risk (here the systematic one, whereas it is total risk for the Sharpe ratio) and the possibility to compare portfolios with different betas through the recourse to the notion of "homemade leverage" explained in Section 3.2.1.

3.3.1.2 Jensen's alpha

Instead of trying to compare the slopes of the RTSR function, it is tempting to adopt a more straightforward approach by directly comparing the portfolio's realized and required average rates of return. The former is just $\overline{R}_P$, while the latter is the image of the SML corresponding to the portfolio beta. Jensen's (1968) alpha, called α_P, refers to this difference:

$$\alpha_P = \overline{R}_P - [R_f + \beta_P(\overline{R}_M - R_f)] \tag{3-11}$$

where $\overline{R}_M$ represents the mean return of the market portfolio. The other inputs are the same as in Equation (3-10).

Equation (3-11) is usually estimated through the linear regression used to test the CAPM:

$$R_{P,t} - R_f = \alpha_P + \beta_P[R_{M,t} - R_f] + \varepsilon_{P,t} \tag{3-12}$$

where $\varepsilon_{P,t}$ represents the error term of the regression with zero mean.[14]

Together with the Sharpe ratio, Jensen's alpha is probably the most popular performance measure. The term "alpha" has even become generic in the asset management world. The simple figure it provides reflects the additional return that the portfolio has actually generated over what it should have generated on the basis of its systematic risk. This aspect is the reason why the alpha is generally called the portfolio's *abnormal return*.

3.3.1.3 The modified Jensen's alpha

Because they both directly derive from the SML equation, there is an obvious familiarity between the Treynor ratio and Jensen's alpha. Smith and Tito (1969) propose a "rescaled" version of Jensen's alpha by dividing it by the portfolio beta, thereby enabling a direct comparison between the active and the market portfolios for equivalent risks. This ratio is called the modified Jensen's alpha ($m\alpha_P$), occasionally also referred to as the Black–Treynor ratio:

$$m\alpha_P = \frac{\alpha_P}{\beta_P} \tag{3-13}$$

As shown later, even though the modified Jensen's alpha features a number of advantages over Jensen's alpha, its conditions of use are relatively delicate, which explains its lack of popularity compared to the original alpha.

3.3.1.4 Relations between the measures

The Treynor ratio, Jensen's alpha, and the modified Jensen's alpha can be viewed as three perspectives of the same reality. Their connection is straightforward:

$$\text{TR}_P = \frac{\alpha_P}{\beta_P} + (\overline{R}_M - R_f) = m\alpha_P + (\overline{R}_M - R_f) \tag{3-14}$$

$$\alpha_P = \beta_P \text{TR}_P - \beta_P(\overline{R}_M - R_f) = \beta_P m\alpha_P \tag{3-15}$$

Since the excess market return $\overline{R}_M - R_f$ is exogenous to the portfolio management process, the Treynor ratio is nothing other than the modified Jensen's alpha plus a constant. Jensen's

[14]Under the assumption that returns are independent and identically distributed (i.i.d.) and Gaussian, this equation can be estimated using the ordinary least-squares (OLS) method. Potential issues and pitfalls related to this estimation are treated in Chapter 5.

alpha, however, differs from the other two measures in a multiplicative fashion. This characteristic can lead to substantial differences in the ranking of portfolios with different betas.

Since all three measures share a common definition of risk (the beta), they can be jointly interpreted in a single graph, in the same vein as Figure 3-4 for the Sharpe ratio. Nevertheless, they all feature a key difference from the Sharpe ratio as each of them explicitly refers to the market portfolio through the computation of the portfolio beta. Referring to the discussion of portfolios L and H proposed in Section 3.2.1, it is meaningful to introduce the market portfolio M in their interpretation.

Two active portfolios L and H that display different mean returns and betas during the period of reference will each obtain a unique value of the Treynor ratio, Jensen's alpha, and the modified Jensen's alpha according to Equations (3-10), (3-11), and (3-13). The market portfolio, by its very definition, has a Jensen's alpha (and thus modified Jensen's alpha) of zero, while its Treynor ratio will be equal to the slope of the SML.

Consider the graph of Figure 3-7. The performance measures of portfolios L and H are both reported. L has a beta lower than 1, while H has a beta higher than 1. Both portfolios have a positive alpha, but L has a smaller abnormal return than H: $\beta_L < 1 < \beta_H$ and $0 < \alpha_L < \alpha_H$. Their ranking based on Jensen's alpha is clear, and it is graphically represented as the vertical distance between the coordinates of each portfolio and the image of their beta on the SML.

Next, we draw a straight line originating from the risk-free rate R_f. It is interpreted as the RTSR. On the graph, the slope of this line is clearly greater for L than for H: $\frac{\bar{R}_L - R_f}{\beta_L} > \frac{\bar{R}_H - R_f}{\beta_H}$, and so is its Treynor ratio: $TR_L > TR_H$. Finally, since the RTSR of L is always above that of H, it is also true at the level of $\beta = 1$, corresponding to the coordinates of L^* and H^* on the

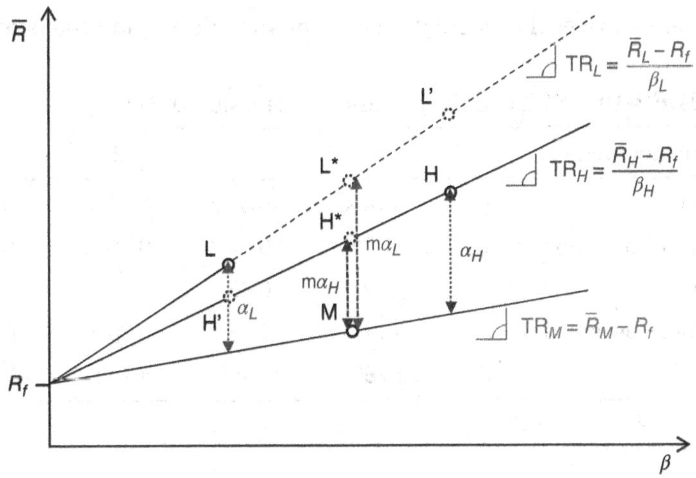

FIGURE 3-7 Graphical representation of the Treynor ratio, Jensen's alpha, and the modified Jensen's alpha.

graph. The modified Jensen's alpha is represented as the vertical distance between each line and the coordinates of the market portfolio. Based on this, $m\alpha_L > m\alpha_H$, and we can conclude that portfolio L has outperformed portfolio H.

The notion of homemade leverage discussed in the context of the Sharpe ratio also pertains here. This aspect is the key source of the difference in rankings between Jensen's alpha and the other two measures. A visual inspection of Figure 3-7 clearly shows that the alpha of H exceeds that of L, but it appears to be comparing apples with oranges, as the risk levels of both portfolios largely differ. The modified Jensen's alpha aims at neutralizing this difference to create a level playing field. However, if portfolio L could not be leveraged, neither L' nor L^* could be reached and the whole argument around a higher return for the same risk would collapse. In other words, in the absence of leveraging possibilities, Jensen's alpha is the relevant measure. However, if the investor has the possibility to freely modify their portfolio beta through gearing, then the alpha provides a biased view of performance. In particular, as shown later, the use of the alpha opens up the way to performance manipulation by artificially altering portfolio risk to inflate reported performance.

XYZ example (continued)

We calculate each fund's alpha and beta using the ordinary least-squares (OLS) regression method, which is expressed as follows:

$$R_{i,t} - R_f = \alpha_i + \beta_i[R_{M,t} - R_f] + \varepsilon_{i,t}$$

with $R_f = 0.12\%$ on a monthly basis.

Table 3-10 summarizes the calculations for the three funds and the peer group index.

TABLE 3-10 XYZ example – Linear regression outputs.

Regression outputs	X	Y	Z	B
Alpha	−0.14%	0.05%	0.57%	−0.11%
Standard deviation alpha	0.28%	0.44%	0.75%	0.15%
Beta	0.62	0.43	0.21	0.48
Standard deviation beta	0.11	0.18	0.30	0.06
R^2	75.26%	37.40%	4.75%	87.30%

Applying the formulas, the set of three performance measures (expressed on a yearly basis) follows as shown in Table 3-11:

TABLE 3-11 XYZ example – Treynor ratio, Jensen's alpha, and the modified Jensen's alpha.

Performance measure	X	Y	Z	M	B
Treynor ratio	3.84%	7.93%	39.01%	6.49%	3.67%
Jensen's alpha	−1.63%	0.62%	6.87%	0.00%	−1.36%
Modified Jensen's alpha	−2.65%	1.44%	32.52%	0.00%	−2.82%

A graphical representation of the performance measures for the three funds and the market portfolio is provided in Figure 3-8.

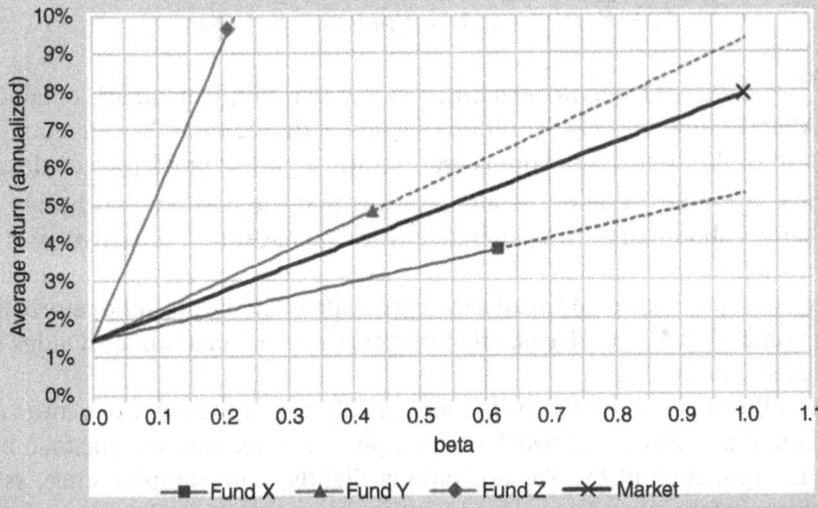

FIGURE 3-8 XYZ example – Representation of the Treynor ratio, Jensen's alpha, and the modified Jensen's alpha.

The fact that is immediately striking on this chart is the difference in behaviors between Funds X and Y, on the one hand, and Fund Z, on the other hand. While Z has a very large volatility, it appears to have a very small beta. Combined with a very high Jensen's alpha, this result causes the slope of its RTSR line (Treynor ratio) to become huge. Its modified Jensen's alpha is so high (greater than 30%) that it is not represented in the graph. There are two attitudes that one could adopt in the face of this phenomenon: either acknowledge

(continued)

(continued)

that Fund Z is incredibly good and provides a tremendous remuneration for the systematic risk taken or express doubts about the validity of the model and especially the choice of the market index that proxies for the market portfolio. This issue is discussed in Section 5.5 of Chapter 5.

3.3.2 What is a good Treynor ratio, Jensen's alpha or modified Jensen's alpha?

3.3.2.1 Practical significance

First consider Jensen's alpha, obtained from Equation (3-11). Rearranging this equation yields a very useful expression:

$$\alpha_P = \overline{R}_P - [\beta_P \overline{R}_M + (1 - \beta_P) R_f] \equiv \overline{R}_P - \overline{R}_B^{CAPM} \qquad (3\text{-}16)$$

where $\overline{R}_B^{CAPM} = \beta_P \overline{R}_M + (1 - \beta_P) R_f$ is defined as the portfolio benchmark obtained directly from the CAPM. Comparing this definition of alpha with Equation (3-1), it simply stands as a specific form of the peer group comparison return. In other words, we could write $\alpha_P = PG_P^{CAPM}$. Thus, a positive value of the alpha means that the portfolio has beaten its benchmark and that the abnormal return generated by the manager over a passive asset allocation combining the market portfolio and the riskless asset is positive. Very pragmatically, even an alpha of zero could be considered as satisfactory provided that the portfolio return, net of costs and fees, surpasses that of a passive one that mirrors the benchmark, like an index fund or an exchange traded fund (ETF).

Because of the linear relation between Jensen's alpha and the other two measures, a positive alpha entails a positive modified Jensen's alpha, provided that the portfolio beta is positive.[15] The interpretation of the Treynor ratio is slightly more complex since, as shown in Figure 3-7, the portfolio must be compared with the market. A good Treynor ratio must be higher than the market excess rate of return $\overline{R}_M - R_f$. This difficulty in interpreting the absolute value of the Treynor ratio might partly explain why it is much less commonly reported than Jensen's alpha.

There is another important application of Jensen's alpha in the context of portfolio choice. This performance measure drives the marginal increase in the Sharpe ratio of the investor's portfolio when the ratio is included in their asset allocation. If the investor has allocated a

[15]The issue of negative betas is discussed in Section 5.5 of Chapter 5.

weight w in the market portfolio and $1 - w$ in the risk-free asset, then the marginal increase in their Sharpe ratio by including a weight w_i in portfolio i with performance α_i is given by the following expression:

$$\left.\frac{\partial \text{SR}_P}{\partial w_i}\right|_{w_i=0} = \frac{\alpha_i}{w\sigma_M^2} \tag{3-17}$$

Equation (3-17) reveals that, beyond its ability to detect whether a manager outperforms the market, Jensen's alpha also acts as a contributor to the global efficiency of a well-diversified portfolio. Since w and σ_M^2 are not under the responsibility of the portfolio manager, their alpha is the key ingredient that enables the investor to increase their global portfolio's risk–return trade-off.

XYZ example (continued)

Since Fund Y has a positive alpha, a well-diversified, moderately risk-averse investor could be tempted to include it into their portfolio worth \$1 000 000 that is currently equally weighted between the market index and the risk-free asset ($w = 0.5$). In this case, Equation (3-17) shows that the first dollar invested in this fund would result in a rate of increase in the Sharpe ratio equal to $\frac{\alpha_Y}{w\sigma_M^2} = \frac{0.62\%}{0.5 \times 8.85\%^2} = 1.575$.

Thus, if the investor considers a very small investment (say, \$5000) in this fund ($w_Y = 0.5\%$), their resulting Sharpe ratio would increase by approximately $1.575 \times w_Y = 0.0079$. Of course, this approximation will be valid for very small increments because the gain in alpha will increasingly be offset by the loss in portfolio diversification. This trade-off is further investigated in Section 3.4.

3.3.2.2 Statistical significance

Regarding the statistical significance of the trio of performance measures, there is (only) good news about Jensen's alpha. Since evidence of good performance is warranted if the alpha is positive, it suffices to show that it is significantly different from zero. Under the usual probabilistic assumptions of the OLS regression (3-12), the test statistic takes the form

$$\hat{t}_{\alpha_P=0} = \frac{\alpha_P}{\sigma_{\alpha_P}} \tag{3-18}$$

It follows (under the null hypothesis of zero performance) a Student t-distribution with $T - 1$ degrees of freedom, where T is the number of observations, and σ_{α_P} is the volatility of the estimate of α_P.

In general, we can expect that if Jensen's alpha is insignificant, so also will be the modified Jensen's alpha because it is just equal to the original alpha divided by a noisy estimate; therefore, it is even less precise. Nevertheless, when Jensen's alpha is statistically significant, testing whether the modified Jensen's alpha significantly differs from zero could be very useful.

Still using the OLS framework, the modified Jensen's alpha features the ratio of the intercept (alpha) over the slope (beta) of the regression line. As a rule of thumb, we can associate the issue of its significance with that of the whole regression model. In the one-factor regression model such as in Equation (3-12), the significance of the regression model derives from the significance of the beta. If the model is poorly specified (i.e., if the R^2 of the regression is low), the significance of alpha could be altered by a beta that would be so noisy that the ratio of alpha over beta itself would become estimated with a very large error, leading it to become insignificant. Thus, a significant Jensen's alpha does not entail that the modified Jensen's alpha will be significant. Oppositely, if Jensen's alpha is insignificant, so will be the modified Jensen's alpha. The latter metric can thus be viewed as a more stringent performance measure than the alpha.

Although the ratio is simple, its statistical properties are not, even if the estimators of alpha and beta are supposed to be normally distributed (i.e., when the number of observations is large).[16] Since we cannot go much further using an analytical approach, the assessment of the significance of the modified Jensen's alpha should in practice be performed using numerical bootstrapping procedures. This approach consists of reusing historical returns of portfolio and index returns to create a large (potentially unlimited) number of sequences of returns. On each sequence, regression (3-12) is re-estimated and the resulting pair (alpha, beta) is recorded. With the large number of pairs, we can simply construct confidence intervals for their ratio and perform hypothesis testing in a similar vein as Equation (3-6) for the Sharpe ratio.

Alternatively, if we posit a Gaussian distribution of the estimates of alpha and beta with a nonzero correlation, it is relatively easy to perform a numerical (a.k.a. "Monte Carlo") simulation of many possible pairs (alpha, beta) and construct similar confidence intervals. The algorithm for the Monte Carlo procedure is relatively simple and can even be carried out in an Excel sheet:

1. Perform the OLS linear regression of the portfolio excess returns over the market index as in Equation (3-12), $R_{P,t} - R_f = \alpha_P + \beta_P[R_{M,t} - R_f] + \varepsilon_{P,t}$, and obtain the estimates $\widehat{\alpha}_P$ and $\widehat{\beta}_P$.

[16]In this case, it is possible to approximate the probability distribution of the ratio. If the alpha and beta were uncorrelated, it would follow a Cauchy distribution. However, since the OLS estimates of alpha and beta are correlated, the expression is more complex. The interested reader can refer to Hinkley (1969). Alternatively, one can use the "delta method" of a ratio of random variables, as in Stuart and Ord (1994) (see Section 3.2.2.2).

2. Retrieve the standard deviations of the estimates of alpha and beta, which are given by the formulas of the OLS regression: $\sigma_\alpha = \sigma_\varepsilon\sqrt{\frac{1}{T} + \frac{(\bar{R}_M - R_f)^2}{(T-1)\sigma_M^2}}$ and $\sigma_\beta = \frac{\sigma_\varepsilon}{\sqrt{T-1}\sigma_M}$. The correlation coefficient is $\rho_{\alpha\beta} = \frac{-(\bar{R}_M - R_f)}{\sqrt{\frac{T-1}{T}\sigma_M^2 + (\bar{R}_M - R_f)^2}}$.
3. Generate two uncorrelated random variables following a standard normal distribution (expectation zero and variance 1), denoted by $\tilde{z}_1^{(1)}$ and $\tilde{z}_2^{(1)}$ (superscript$^{(1)}$ means that this term represents the first pair of simulated draws).
4. Obtain a simulated realization of the pair $(\hat{\alpha}_P^{(1)}, \hat{\beta}_P^{(1)})$ by computing $\hat{\alpha}_P^{(1)} = \hat{\alpha}_P + \sigma_\alpha \tilde{z}_1^{(1)}$ and $\hat{\beta}_P^{(1)} = \hat{\beta}_P + \sigma_\beta(\rho_{\alpha\beta}\tilde{z}_1^{(1)} + \sqrt{1-\rho_{\alpha\beta}^2}\tilde{z}_2^{(1)})$.
5. Repeat steps 3 and 4 a large number N times to obtain N pairs $(\hat{\alpha}_P^{(i)}, \hat{\beta}_P^{(i)})$ and compute their associated modified Jensen's alpha $\widehat{m\alpha}_P^{(i)} = \frac{\hat{\alpha}_P^{(i)}}{\hat{\beta}_P^{(i)}}$.
6. Rank the $\widehat{m\alpha}_P^{(i)}$ from the lowest (#1) to the highest (#N) and obtain the lower and upper bounds of the confidence interval with confidence level of $1 - x$, called $Q_{\frac{x}{2}}$ and $Q_{1-\frac{x}{2}}$, by selecting the observations ranked $\#\frac{x}{2}N$ (lower bound) and $\#\left(1 - \frac{x}{2}\right)N$ (upper bound).

This process is performed in the example with a correlation between alpha and beta set to $\rho_{\alpha\beta} = -0.2$ as shown in Table 3-12.

In the table, $Q_{2.5\%}$ stands for the lower bound of the interval at the 95% confidence level obtained with Monte Carlo simulations ($N = 10\ 000$ runs), i.e., the observation ranked #250. The values in italics represent the estimates and lower bound for the beta ($\hat{\beta}$, second row) and the alpha ($\hat{\alpha}$, third column), while the framed values in the lower-right part of the table represent the estimates for their ratio (modified Jensen's alpha). Values in bold are significantly positive. As expected, the case tagged "alpha significant–beta insignificant" (upper-right cell in the frame) reflects the impact of the joint condition on the intercept ("the alpha must be high") and the model quality ("the beta must not be low"), driving a conclusion that the ratio

TABLE 3-12 Significance level of the modified Jensen's alpha compared to those of alpha and beta.

			beta ($\sigma_\beta = 0.3$)	
		$\hat{\beta}$	*1.0*	*0.3*
		$Q_{2.5\%}$	*0.41*	*−0.29*
	$\hat{\alpha}$	*1.0%*	**1.00%**	3.33%
alpha	$Q_{2.5\%}$	*0.41%*	0.34%	−30.61%
($\sigma_\alpha = 0.3\%$)	$\hat{\alpha}$	*0.30%*	0.30%	1.00%
	$Q_{2.5\%}$	*−0.29%*	−0.27%	−12.67%

is insignificant. Because the beta is low, the lower bound of the confidence interval becomes negative. The influence of the correlation between the estimates of alpha and beta is reflected in the very high absolute value of the percentile.

If the sample size for the estimation is very large, it is possible to associate the significance of the modified Jensen's alpha with that of the difference between the Treynor ratio of the portfolio and the market. This possibility is discussed below.

Indeed, with respect to comparing portfolios, a partial solution of this significance issue is provided by examining the Treynor ratio. It is shown previously that portfolio rankings are the same when the modified Jensen's alpha or the Treynor ratio are used, as clearly shown in Figure 3-7. Thus, if a fund has a significantly greater Treynor ratio than another one, the same conclusion will apply to their modified Jensen's alphas. Jobson and Korkie (1981) provide an asymptotic test statistic that allows for portfolio comparisons.

Consider two portfolios P and Q. The Gaussian Z-statistic for the difference in their Treynor ratios (expressed in the same frequency, i.e., in monthly terms with monthly observations) is written as[17]

$$\hat{Z}_{\mathrm{TR}_P-\mathrm{TR}_Q=0} = \frac{\bar{r}_P\beta_Q - \bar{r}_Q\beta_P}{\sigma_M\sqrt{\frac{1}{T}[\sigma_P^2\sigma_Q^2(\rho_{PM}^2+\rho_{QM}^2-2\rho_{PQ}\rho_{PM}\rho_{QM})+\bar{r}_P^2\sigma_Q^2(1-\rho_{QM}^2)+\bar{r}_Q^2\sigma_P^2(1-\rho_{PM}^2)-2\bar{r}_P\bar{r}_Q\sigma_P\sigma_Q(\rho_{PQ}-\rho_{PM}\rho_{QM})]}} \tag{3-19}$$

where $\bar{r}_i \equiv \bar{R}_i - R_f$ is the excess return of portfolio i, ρ_{ij} is the Pearson (linear) correlation coefficient between the returns of i and j, and Z follows a standard normal distribution.

Although Jobson and Korkie (1981) do not specifically study it, their test statistic for the difference between the Treynor ratio of a portfolio P and the proxy for the market portfolio M is a much simplified version of Equation (3-19):

$$\hat{Z}_{\mathrm{TR}_P-\mathrm{TR}_M=0} = \frac{\alpha_P}{\sigma_P\sigma_M\sqrt{\frac{1}{T}[(1-\rho_{PM}^2)(\bar{r}_M^2+\sigma_M^2)]}} \tag{3-20}$$

If the observed value of the Z-statistic is significant, then the modified Jensen's alpha of the portfolio is also significantly different from zero. Equation (3-20) even suggests that the Jobson and Korkie statistic might serve as a direct test for the significance of the modified Jensen's alpha. This "good news" should however be placed in perspective; the Z-statistic is based on an approximation that is only valid for a very large number of observations. In small samples, its power is quite limited, and the Treynor ratio test is even weaker than the Sharpe ratio test.

[17]Note that this test has been designed using figures expressed in percentage points. Thus, if portfolio i has a volatility of 3%, the formula features $\sigma_i = 3$ and $\sigma_i^2 = 9$. Otherwise, the figures do not make sense.

XYZ example (continued)

From Table 3-10, we can directly compute the ***t***-statistic for the alpha by dividing their estimated values by their respective standard deviations. For instance, for Fund X, this yields $\hat{t}_{\alpha_X} = \frac{-0.14\%}{0.28\%} = -0.5$.

The application of Equations (3-19) and (3-20) to different funds and the market portfolio is presented in Table 3-13, with a form similar to Table 3-9, for the Sharpe ratio discussed above. For the sake of the illustration, consider that the number of observations is $T = 36$ (three years).

TABLE 3-13 XYZ example – Pairwise Z-statistics of the Treynor ratios (with 36 observations).

		X	Y	Z	M
	TR_P	*3.84%*	*7.93%*	*39.01%*	*6.49%*
Y	*7.93%*	**0.58**			
Z	*39.01%*	**1.43**	**1.47**		
M	*6.49%*	**0.81**	**−0.20**	**−1.28**	
B	*3.67%*	**−0.04**	**−0.72**	**−1.43**	**−1.30**

Unlike Table 3-9, which featured significant values for the difference in Sharpe ratios, Table 3-13 does not display any significant differences in Treynor ratios. Thus, despite its very high Treynor ratio, even Fund Z cannot be said to significantly dominate the others, including the market portfolio.

This example illustrates two issues with this test: (i) the necessity to have a high number of observations to obtain insightful results and (ii) the weak connection between the absolute value of the Treynor ratio and its statistical reliability for a portfolio with an unusual performance, such as Fund Z in this case.

3.3.3 Strengths and weaknesses

3.3.3.1 Strengths

The trio of systematic risk-based performance measures shares a common philosophy; they aim at measuring the added value of a portfolio compared to a passive investment in the market portfolio. They have a strong theoretical justification by relying on the key takeaway from the CAPM, namely, the equilibrium linear risk–return relationship for individual securities and portfolios. As they can be used for a wide variety of portfolios, they represent rather universal measures of performance.

From a theoretical standpoint, the benchmark for performance appraisal is supposed to be the market portfolio. However, beyond the world of the CAPM, all three measures are also quite flexible. Not only the portfolio benchmark can be practically any relevant comparable portfolio, but also the structure of the asset pricing model used to compute the portfolio beta can be extended to multifactor models, like the ones studied in Chapter 7. The potential scope of their applications is thus relatively wide.

In addition, each of these measures has several interesting properties that distinguish them from one another:

- The Treynor ratio has a similar form to the Sharpe ratio and provides an assessment of the remuneration per unit of risk. As shown above, it is insensitive to portfolio leverage, and its use enables a statistical comparison of the performance of portfolios that do not have the same level of systematic risk. On a side note, the Treynor ratio also provides a means of revealing potential issues with the application of the CAPM; if the ratio is unusually high or low, as in the case of Fund Z in our XYZ example, it should cast doubt on the application of the model. The alpha does not display a similar advantage; when the market model has a poor fit, the level of the alpha can still seem to make sense economically, even though it has been derived with a wrong model.
- Jensen's alpha, together with the Sharpe ratio, has the merit of its fame. Every single actively managed portfolio with a benchmark will naturally disclose its alpha. Because a performance measure, despite its potential weaknesses, only exists in practice when it is widely shared and commonly understood, Jensen's alpha is certainly a dominant one. As a corollary, it is also very easy to understand and to explain. This characteristic is in obvious contrast with the Sharpe ratio, which, while probably equally popular, does not pass the "user-friendliness test."
- The modified Jensen's alpha corrects for the leverage issue of the original alpha; as with the Treynor ratio, it provides a tool to compare the performance of portfolios with different betas and has a similar ability to uncover any suspicion about the validity of the regression model. At the same time, it carries the same interpretation of an abnormal return as Jensen's alpha. In a sense, it can be said to represent the best of two worlds.

3.3.3.2 Weaknesses

Unlike the peer group comparison return, all three performance measures explicitly refer to the CAPM. They make use of the (theoretically justified) "market portfolio" and assume that the portfolio beta remains constant during the period of measurement. From an *ex post* perspective, the CAPM raises several serious implementation issues. First, as Roll (1977) demonstrates in a famous article,[18] it is virtually impossible to justify the use of any market proxy for the market portfolio, which is essentially unobservable and "unbenchmarkable." Next, even if one could live up to this fundamental but unsolvable issue for pragmatic reasons, the use of a stock market index as the portfolio benchmark creates tracking difficulties such as inapplicable high-frequency rebalancing, asset replacement costs, tracking errors (TEs) and fees when using ETFs, and tax inefficiencies. One could argue that the resulting risk is of a specific nature and does not impact the beta, but there is also a potential deadweight cost that may affect the alpha and thus overall absolute performance. Finally, the portfolio contractual benchmark can also experience a different behavior from the market portfolio proxy; a beta that would be relevant one day could become biased the next day if the portfolio benchmark has diverged. Thus, in general, the anchoring of systematic risk-based performance measures on the CAPM can be seen as too strict a constraint to properly reflect portfolio performance.

The assumed linear relation between the portfolio return and the market index is also a source of concern with respect to appraising its performance. The drivers of a manager's performance are their skills in selecting mispriced securities (asset selection) or in anticipating market movements (market timing). Typically, market timing skills involve a nonlinear relation between the portfolio returns and its associated benchmark. In the presence of such skills, all three measures will deliver a distorted picture of the true performance of the manager.

Finally, the necessity to run through an empirical model to estimate the beta and the alpha generates potentially important measurement errors that do not contaminate total risk-based measures (such as the Sharpe ratio) or heuristic approaches (such as the peer group comparison return). The additional estimation issue weakens the statistical inference that can be carried out with measures based on the beta, such as the Treynor ratio, Jensen's alpha, or modified Jensen's alpha.

On top of these general criticisms, each specific measure may also suffer from specific sources of weakness:

- Even though its output is a rate of return in percentage points (unlike the Sharpe ratio, for instance), the Treynor ratio does not truly provide a readily interpretable assessment of performance. This shortcoming makes the communication and interpretation of this ratio quite challenging. It might also be difficult to explain extremely high or negative values of the ratio while at the same time the alpha delivers a reasonable figure.
- Jensen's alpha can be manipulated because it is sensitive to portfolio leverage. For a given portfolio with a certain alpha, the manager or the intermediary between the manager and the investor could artificially inflate the alpha by leveraging their investment. Therefore, Modigliani and Pogue (1974) firmly conclude that Jensen's alpha is unequivocally dominated by the Treynor ratio or the modified Jensen's alpha on a theoretical basis. In a corollary to this problem, only portfolios with similar betas should be compared on the basis of Jensen's alpha. This limitation considerably restricts the scope of its application.

[18]This very important perspective on the actual possibility of testing the CAPM is discussed in Chapter 5.

- From a conceptual point of view, and in addition to the general criticism about this family of performance measures, the modified Jensen's alpha does not truly display weaknesses. It can yield strange figures for low or negative beta portfolios, such as the Treynor ratio, but this result would only be a symptom of model misspecification and not a drawback of the measure *per se*. From a statistical point of view, inference based on the ratio of alpha over beta appears to be a real challenge, while the alpha alone can easily be tested from the linear regression outputs. However, perhaps the major weakness of this measure is its lack of recognition and use among professional asset managers and, consequently, its relative obscurity with final investors.

3.3.3.3 Conclusion

The three measures presented in this section are very close to each other in their genesis. Nevertheless, only one has truly become famous – Jensen's alpha. It is by far the simplest approach to expressing and explaining portfolio performance. It would not be fair to write that this characteristic is its only merit, but this point is, in our view, largely true. Whatever portfolio is considered, its alpha will almost always (seem to) make sense. Be it +1.5% or −2.8%, for instance, its reported value does not truly create any skepticism regarding how this figure has been generated. This measure is a convenient, "no-brainer" means of communicating portfolio performance. Our discussion of the alternatives, the Treynor ratio, and the modified Jensen's alpha clearly shows that these measures are conceptually superior to the mere alpha, but they are also more complex to calculate, to test, and to explain. These difficulties are probably not sufficiently serious to disregard the alternatives, especially when there is suspicion regarding the model underlying the computation of an alpha. In contrast, it is worth recalling the famous quote of Henry Louis Mencken: "*Explanations exist; they have existed for all time; there is always a well-known solution to every human problem – neat, plausible, and wrong.*"

3.4 THE INFORMATION RATIO

3.4.1 Definition

The Information ratio, occasionally also called the Appraisal ratio in the context of the CAPM, was originally introduced by Treynor and Black (1973).[19] While the Sharpe ratio and the Treynor ratio respectively focus on measures of total and systematic risk, the Information ratio accounts for specific (a.k.a. idiosyncratic or residual) risk as the "cost" input for the generation of abnormal return.

[19]More precisely, Treynor and Black (1973) initially define their Appraisal ratio as the square of the Information ratio as defined hereunder.

This performance measure hinges on the identification of a benchmark portfolio B. The perspective of a portfolio manager who wishes to maximize the Information ratio is intimately related to the presence of this benchmark, which is more important for this measure than for any other. Since the manager is responsible for tracking, and hopefully beating, their benchmark, the notions of risk and return have to be understood through the divergence of the portfolio with respect to this benchmark. If the benchmark delivers, for instance, −10% over a period, the portfolio will have outperformed it if it managed to control the damage and yielded −8%, thereby obtaining a differential return of +2%. Thus, the abnormal return is simply equal to the difference between the average returns of the portfolio and the benchmark. In this context, it is called the tracking difference (TD): $TD_P = \overline{R}_P - \overline{R}_B \equiv \overline{R}_{(P-B)}$. The benchmark can be a peer group (in which case, the TD is the peer group comparison return; see Section 3.1), a leveraged investment in the market portfolio (in which case the TD is Jensen's alpha; see Section 3.3), or an index, be it composite or proprietary. Because the TD reflects the outcome of the decisions made by the manager to move away from the benchmark, it is generally associated with the notion of *active return* of the portfolio.

Likewise, risk must be viewed as the variability of the portfolio returns around the benchmark. It results from the manager's conscious willingness to deviate from the benchmark, creating a source of noise for the investor, with the hope of achieving higher returns. Consequently, it is called the portfolio's *active risk*. This notion, which is truly a measure of specific risk, is estimated by the standard deviation of the return difference between the portfolio and the index. It is termed the tracking error (TE). In symbolic form, it also writes $\sigma_{(P-B)}$ and is defined as follows:

$$\sigma_{(P-B)} \equiv \sigma(R_P - R_B) = \sqrt{\sigma_P^2 + \sigma_B^2 - 2\rho_{PB}\sigma_P\sigma_B} \tag{3-21}$$

where σ_P^2 and σ_B^2 are the variances of the portfolio and benchmark returns, respectively, and ρ_{PB} is the Pearson correlation coefficient between the returns of the portfolio and the benchmark.[20]

The Information ratio is the ratio of active return (the reward) over active risk (the cost), and its equation is as follows:

$$IR_P = \frac{TD_P}{TE_P} = \frac{\overline{R}_{(P-B)}}{\sigma_{(P-B)}} \tag{3-22}$$

The active risk/active return framework resembles the ordinary risk/return graph, except that a portfolio with no risk and no return would locate at the origin of the axes. Two portfolios L and H that display different TDs and TEs during the period of reference will each obtain a unique value of the Information ratio according to Equation (3-22). Consider the graph of Figure 3-9. Portfolio L not only exhibits less active risk but also a lower active return than H: $TE_L < TE_H$ and $TD_L < TD_H$. The slope of a straight line originating from the origin of the

[20]This expression is similar to the one derived in Equation (3-2) in the context of the peer group comparison return.

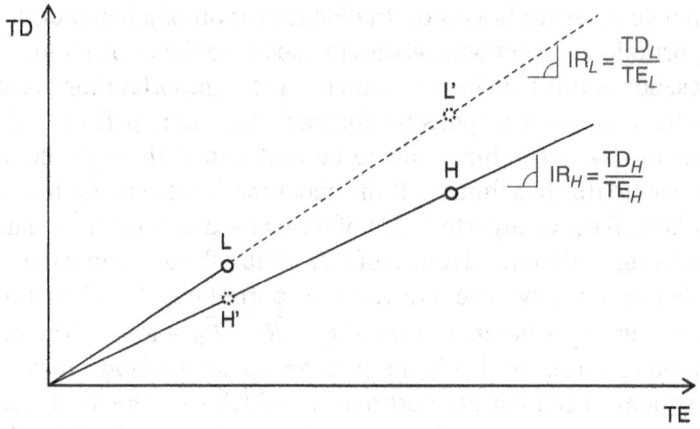

FIGURE 3-9 Graphical representation of the Information ratio.

axes is clearly greater for L than for H: $\frac{TD_L}{TE_L} > \frac{TD_H}{TE_H}$. Because $IR_L > IR_H$, using the now familiar notion of homemade leverage, we can conclude that portfolio L has outperformed portfolio H.

Sharpe (1994) insists on the fact that the expression of the Information ratio looks very similar to the Sharpe ratio. He contends that the original version of the Sharpe ratio that he had introduced in 1966 should be considered as a special case of the Information ratio, in which the risk-free asset replaces the benchmark. If $\overline{R}_B = R_f$ and $\sigma(R_P - R_B) = \sigma(R_P - R_f) = \sigma(R_P)$, then Equation (3-22) indeed collapses to the expression of the Sharpe ratio.

This simplification could be interpreted in two different ways. Some managers may consider that their benchmark should be a riskless asset because they bear absolutely no systematic risk, and all the risk supported by their investors is of a specific nature. The required return should be the risk-free rate, and the active risk of the portfolio is its total volatility. This philosophy is that of *Absolute Return* funds. Another point of view is to consider that this simplification reflects an abuse of the notions of active risk and return. Replacing the benchmark by the riskless asset is an admission of weakness, as the TE collects all sources of risk, be they systematic or specific, without further analysis.

In the context of the CAPM, we remember that the benchmark of the active portfolio is a mixture of the market portfolio and the risk-free asset, whose return is expressed as follows: $R_{B,t}^{CAPM} = \beta_P R_{M,t} + (1 - \beta_P) R_f$. If we consider the linear regression used to estimate the model in Equation (3-12), the difference between the return of the portfolio and its benchmark takes a simple form

$$R_{P,t} - R_{B,t}^{CAPM} = \alpha_P + \varepsilon_{P,t} \tag{3-23}$$

Since $\overline{R}_P - \overline{R}_B^{\text{CAPM}} = \alpha_P$ and $\sigma(R_P - R_B^{\text{CAPM}}) = \sigma(\varepsilon_{P,t}) \equiv \sigma_{\varepsilon_P}$, the expression for the Information ratio proposed in Equation (3-22), which bears the name of Appraisal ratio, in reference to the analysis proposed by Treynor and Black (1973), immediately translates to the following:

$$\text{AR}_P = \frac{\text{TD}_P}{\text{TE}_P} = \frac{\alpha_P}{\sigma_{\varepsilon_P}} \tag{3-24}$$

which is nothing other than Jensen's alpha divided by the specific risk of the portfolio, i.e., the standard deviation of the residual returns.

With respect to the Sharpe ratio, the Information ratio is typically expressed and interpreted in yearly terms. According to the assumption that all returns are i.i.d., the yearly Information ratio is equal to its periodic estimate multiplied by the square root of the number of periods in the year:

$$\text{IR}_P^{1y} = \frac{\overline{R}_P^{1y} - R_B^{1y}}{\text{TE}_P^{1y}} = \frac{n \times (\overline{R}_P^{1y/n} - \overline{R}_B^{1y/n})}{\sqrt{n} \times \text{TE}_P^{1y/n}} = \sqrt{n} \times \text{IR}_P^{1y/n} \tag{3-25}$$

XYZ example (continued)

We again start from the OLS regression applied to the three funds and the peer group index with respect to the proxy for the market portfolio. This time, we focus on each fund's alpha and on the standard deviation of the error term of the regression. Table 3-14 summarizes the calculations.

TABLE 3-14 XYZ example – Appraisal ratio.

Regression outputs	X	Y	Z	B
Alpha	−0.14%	0.05%	0.57%	−0.11%
Standard deviation epsilon	0.90%	1.42%	2.42%	0.47%
AR (monthly)	−0.15	0.04	0.24	−0.24
AR (yearly)	**−0.52**	**0.13**	**0.82**	**−0.84**

The Appraisal ratio of the peer group index B is much worse than those of the individual funds, including X. Because it represents the average returns of the individual funds, index B is better diversified. Its specific risk is thus reduced, but its alpha remains the same. Consequently, its performance indicator depreciates compared to its Sharpe ratio or its Treynor ratio. This example shows that, in general, individual portfolios will display Appraisal ratios

(continued)

(continued)

that are closer to zero than a peer group index, whose active risk is typically lower than those of its constituents.

The graphical representation of the Information ratio for the three funds is shown in Figure 3-10.

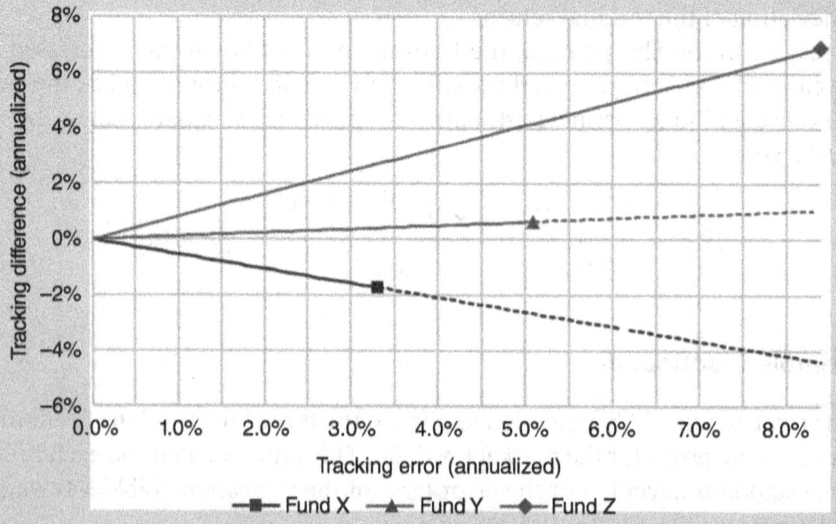

FIGURE 3-10 XYZ example – Representation of the Appraisal ratio.

The diagnostics previously carried out for the three funds regarding their Treynor ratios are confirmed here: X underperforms the market, and Z is much better than Y. There is, however, an important difference with respect to Table 3-11. Because Y has a much lower specific risk than Z does, the distance between their respective performances is much lower with the Appraisal ratio; Z has achieved a better active return but at the expense of a higher active risk. This aspect contrasts with their systematic risk (betas), which was also lower for Z than for Y and that drove the systematic risk-based performance measure to extremely high values.

3.4.2 What is a good Information ratio?

3.4.2.1 Practical significance

The natural cutoff point to determine whether the Information ratio is considered to reflect superior performance should be zero, just as for Jensen's alpha. Nevertheless, the fact that this ratio explicitly accounts for a measure of specific risk reflects a particular care for the lack of diversification induced by a portfolio that deliberately deviates from its benchmark. This specific risk is a sort of sacrifice made by the investor, and it calls for due compensation in terms of abnormal returns.[21] Therefore, in contrast to the straightforward interpretation of the sign of the alpha, the practical significance of the Information ratio for an active portfolio manager goes beyond a mere check of its positive sign.

To see why the Information ratio should be largely positive to be convincing, one has to understand that it truly enjoys a huge popularity in the community of professional asset managers. It mostly stems from the adequacy between what it measures *ex post* (tracking difference over tracking error) and what most managers feel to be their duty *ex ante* toward their clients–investors, namely, to generate active return as a reward for active risk.[22] Thus, it is not surprising to witness relatively ambitious targets regarding the levels of the IR that are considered "good." The reference in the field is the discussion begun by Grinold and Kahn (1995) and completed by Goodwin (1998).

From an *ex post* perspective, even though Grinold and Kahn (1995) report that approximately 10% of all their observed before-fees IR lie above 1 (and thus there would exist the same proportion of exceptional managers, which makes the notion of "exceptional" quite common), they do not substantiate these values with empirical evidence or a theoretical argument. Empirical evidence reported by Goodwin (1998) on 212 asset managers spanning a period of 10 years shows that, with the exception of those who invest in small capitalization stocks and sector bonds, the proportion of managers who are able to achieve net (after fee) Information ratios above 1.0 is zero and that achieving an IR greater than 0.5 is a challenge that is met by less than 15% of managers on average.

Moreover, as we show below, the question of the practical significance of the Information ratio cannot be disentangled from the discussion about the frequency of the data and the length of the estimation window. We explain this point in the next subsection.

3.4.2.2 Statistical significance

The genuinely relevant approach for assessing the significance of the Information ratio is the statistical one because, unlike the other ratios discussed above, hypothesis testing with the *IR* is straightforward, at least under the usual distributional assumptions of i.i.d. and normally distributed returns.

Recall Equation (3-23), which defines $R_{P,t} - R_{B,t}^{\text{CAPM}} = \alpha_P + \varepsilon_{P,t}$ and results in $\text{TD}_P = \overline{R}_P - \overline{R}_B^{\text{CAPM}} \equiv \alpha_P$ and $\sigma(R_P - R_B^{\text{CAPM}}) = \sigma(\varepsilon_{P,t}) \equiv \sigma_{\varepsilon_P}$. If we want to test whether the tracking difference TD_P is significant, we can compute a Student t-statistic in a very similar vein as in

[21] This argument is formalized in Fama's performance decomposition framework, discussed in the Section 13.1 of Chapter 13.

[22] We discuss the use of the Information ratio from an *ex ante* perspective in the context of institutional investments in Chapter 16.

Equation (3-2) for the peer group differential return PG_P – the only difference being that the benchmark return is defined as the required return under the CAPM:

$$\hat{t}_{\mathrm{TD}_P=0} = \frac{\sqrt{T-1}}{\sigma(R_P - R_B)}\mathrm{TD}_P = \mathrm{IR}_P\sqrt{T-1} \tag{3-26}$$

In other words, all that is required to assess the significance of the IR is its level (of course) and the number of observations. Adopting the same logic as for the significance of the Sharpe ratio, one obtains a simple expression for the necessary number of observations to draw conclusions about the significance of the Information ratio for a given confidence level:

$$T_P^* = \left\lceil \left(\frac{t_{(T_P^*-1);1-\frac{x}{2}}}{\mathrm{IR}_P}\right)^2 + 1 \right\rceil \tag{3-27}$$

where $t_{(T_P^*-1);1-\frac{x}{2}}$ is the $\left(1-\frac{x}{2}\right)$th percentile of the Student t-distribution with $T-1$ degrees of freedom, and $\lceil\cdot\rceil$ stands for the ceiling (least integer greater than or equal to) of the argument. The equation is theoretically difficult to solve, as its solution T_P^* appears on both sides of the equality. Nevertheless, for practical purposes, we note that $t_{(T_P^*-1);1-\frac{x}{2}} \approx z_{1-\frac{x}{2}}$ when T_P^* is sufficiently large. For instance, for $T = 120$ and $x = 10\%$, we have $t_{(119);95\%} = 1.658$, while $z_{95\%} = 1.645$. However, for a lower number of observations or a higher confidence level, the values can largely diverge, and the estimation of T_P^* must be carried out numerically. Table 3-15, whose construction is similar to that of Table 3-7, provides solutions to the above equation for selected pairs of values of the periodic IR (measured on the basis of the frequency of estimation) and desired levels of significance.

TABLE 3-15 Minimum number of observations necessary to obtain Information ratio significance.

	Significance level (x)									
$\widehat{\mathrm{IR}}_P$	1%	2%	3%	4%	5%	6%	7%	8%	9%	10%
0.2	171	140	122	110	100	92	86	80	75	71
0.4	47	38	34	30	28	26	24	23	21	20
0.6	23	19	17	16	14	13	12	12	11	11
0.8	15	13	11	10	9	9	8	8	8	7
1.0	11	9	8	8	7	7	6	6	6	6
1.2	9	8	7	6	6	6	5	5	5	5

Unlike Table 3-7, whose practical usefulness is limited (the value of 0 has no particular meaning for the Sharpe ratio), Table 3-15 is extremely important for the Information ratio. It provides the right tool for its practical significance level depending on the frequency of observations, size of the time window, and desired level of significance. As a "dashboard," the Table 3-16 delivers the critical level of the yearly Information ratio that must be observed to draw conclusions about the skill of the manager by using the statistical inference tool of Equation (3-26).

If we associate target significance levels with plain adjectives, such as "weak significance = good," "medium significance = very good," and "strong significance = exceptional," Table 3-16 provides a practical answer to the question of the discriminant levels of the Information ratio. An IR of 0.5 is "good" if measured over 10 years, but not outstanding for a shorter horizon. A portfolio manager must achieve an IR of at least 0.75 over five years to be "good." If they manage to keep the same level over 10 years, they are "excellent" because this indicates a substantial ability to sustain superior performance over time.[23] When a more traditional three-year period is considered, only levels close to or above 1.0 are sufficient to conclude that the manager has significantly outperformed their benchmark ("good"). For any lower value, nothing can be faithfully concluded about their superior quality. This analysis places in perspective the evidence reported by Goodwin (1998) over 10 years. He finds that 1% of the portfolio managers (2 out of 212) reach the mark IR > 1.0 and 15% (32 out of 212) manage to obtain IR > 0.5. Given the figures shown in Table 3-16, several of them would simply beat the market by chance. We can only trust the fact that some (probably approximately 10% of the managers) might exceed an Information ratio of 0.5% because of their skill, but the two managers who exceeded 1.0 might simply have been lucky to obtain such a high value.[24]

TABLE 3-16 Critical values of the yearly Information ratios in various contexts.

Horizon	Weak $\left(\frac{x}{2} = 5\%\right)$			Medium $\left(\frac{x}{2} = 2.5\%\right)$			Strong $\left(\frac{x}{2} = 1\%\right)$		
	Daily	Weekly	Monthly	Daily	Weekly	Monthly	Daily	Weekly	Monthly
1 year	1.65	1.69	1.88	1.97	2.03	2.30	2.35	2.43	2.84
2 years	1.17	1.18	1.24	1.39	1.41	1.49	1.65	1.68	1.81
3 years	0.95	0.96	0.99	1.13	1.14	1.19	1.35	1.36	1.43
5 years	0.74	0.74	0.75	0.88	0.88	0.90	1.04	1.05	1.08
10 years	0.52	0.52	0.53	0.62	0.62	0.63	0.74	0.74	0.75

[23] This ability is called "performance persistence" and is examined in detail in Chapter 17.

[24] This issue of "false discoveries" is analyzed more thoroughly in Chapter 18.

XYZ example (continued)

The outputs of the regression presented in Table 3-14, together with the knowledge of the number of observations ($T = 12$), provide enough information to perform statistical inference on the three funds and their peer group. Table 3-17 summarizes the outputs of the analysis, including the critical number of observations T_P^* necessary to reject the null hypothesis of no abnormal performance:

TABLE 3-17 XYZ example – Significance of the Appraisal ratio.

Statistics	X	Y	Z	B
AR (monthly)	−0.15	0.04	0.24	−0.24
t-statistic	−0.50	0.12	0.79	−0.80
$T_P^* \left(\frac{x}{2} = 5\%\right)$	123	2061	51	50

There are definitely too few observations to draw any conclusion about the significance of any of the Appraisal ratios. Considering the monthly values achieved by each fund, it would take more than four years to finally draw a conclusion about the outstanding quality of manager Z. Despite its negative AR, manager X would not be diagnosed as "bad" before 10 years (120 observations) elapsed.

In reality, the simple test proposed in Equation (3-26) suffers from a drawback; it relies on the statistical estimate of the TE in the denominator of the Student t-statistic. Taking the estimation error into account leads to an asymptotic distribution of the IR derived by Bertrand and Protopopescu (2010), which is very similar to that of the Sharpe ratio proposed by Lo (2002) (see Equation (3-6)):

$$\mathrm{IR}_P \pm z_{1-\frac{x}{2}} \times \sqrt{\frac{1}{T}\left(1 + \frac{\mathrm{IR}_P^2}{2}\right)} \tag{3-28}$$

Furthermore, when returns are not Gaussian, Durham (2015) also provides confidence intervals adjusted for the returns' skewness and excess kurtosis, similar to Equation (3-8) for the Sharpe ratio:

$$\mathrm{IR}_P \pm z_{1-\frac{x}{2}} \times \sqrt{\frac{1}{T}\left(1 + \frac{\mathrm{IR}_P^2}{4}(\mu_{P,4} - 1) - \mu_{P,3}\mathrm{IR}_P\right)} \tag{3-29}$$

Comparing these two equations with (3-26) reveals an increase in the variance of the Information ratio and thus a reduction of its significance, especially if the distribution of returns is leptokurtic ($\mu_{P,4} > 3$) and left-asymmetric ($\mu_{P,3} < 0$). As an illustration, in his study of a momentum strategy on duration-neutral US government bonds from 1985 to 2013, Durham (2015) obtains average levels of the Information ratio of approximately 0.40 with 337 monthly observations. This time window corresponds to a standard deviation of the IR equal to $\sigma_{IR} = \sqrt{1/(337-1)} = 5.46\%$. With an IR of 0.40, applying Equation (3-28) results in an increase of σ_{IR} by a factor of $\sqrt{\left(1+\frac{IR_P^2}{2}\right)} = 1.039$. Applying Equation (3-29) to his data, Durham obtains that σ_{IR} rises by a factor ranging from 1.06 for low IRs (approximately 0.2) to 1.15 for high IRs (approximately 0.6). Thus, the adjustment can be substantial and typically reduces the significance of the estimated performance, but it has a larger impact when the Information ratio is itself already high, thus not truly impacting the nature of the decision about whether the performance is significant.

3.4.3 Strengths and weaknesses

3.4.3.1 Strengths

From a theoretical point of view, the Information ratio has great merits, especially from an *ex ante* perspective. It represents the key building block of the core-satellite approach, discussed in Chapter 16, by determining the marginal increase in the Sharpe ratio that can be achieved through optimal allocation in actively managed portfolios or assets. It also determines the maximum surplus of return, adjusted for residual risk, that can be expected by an investor.

From the practical point of view of many asset managers who run "benchmarked portfolios," the Information ratio would certainly be considered a very, if not the most, relevant performance measure regarding the assessment of their quality. Compared to Jensen's alpha (Section 3.3) or the peer group differential return (Section 3.1), the Information ratio explicitly takes into account a dimension that corresponds to the essence of the portfolio manager, namely, the extent to which they have chosen to depart from their portfolio of reference. Because the IR simultaneously accounts for their active risk and their active return in a synthetic measure, many managers would find it a useful means of measuring their skills. Additionally, since mutual funds usually disclose their benchmark, their managers can meaningfully compare one another at any point in time by removing the effect of this "fixed point" around which they actively manage their positions. This popularity among professional asset managers represents, in turn, a very useful piece of information for investors, institutional and professional alike. Knowing that the IR serves as a ranking metric among the managers, their clients or employers can faithfully use this information (which is easy to compute and cannot be easily manipulated) to make their portfolio choice, trust or reward the best performing managers, or sanction the worst ones.[25]

The determinants of the Information ratio are also an interesting reflection of the portfolio manager's skills. This performance measure represents the cornerstone of the so-called "Fundamental Law of Active Management" introduced by Grinold and Kahn (1995). It is represented by a simple multiplicative formula that (approximately) links the IR to its constituents:

$$\mathrm{IR}_P = \mathrm{IC}_P\sqrt{\mathrm{BR}_P} \tag{3-30}$$

where BR_P represents the *breadth* of the strategy, defined as the number of times the manager makes an active forecast per year (i.e., decides to diverge from the benchmark), and IC_P is the *information coefficient* of the manager, measured by the correlation coefficient between the manager's forecast of expected return and actual portfolio return, i.e., $\mathrm{IC}_P = \rho(\mathrm{E}_{t-1}(R_{p,t}), R_{p,t})$. Equation (3-30) can only be estimated with detailed holding and forecast data. It is of limited use for investors or clients, but it can be useful as a monitoring tool for professional asset management firms, provided that an adequate reporting system is implemented.

Another noticeable strength of the Information ratio is the relative ease of (basic) hypothesis testing. Even though, as for any other performance measure, accurate statistical inference is obviously far more sophisticated than the simple *t*-test, the Information ratio is the only "ratio" measure examined in this chapter whose testing, under the usual Gaussian assumption, is obvious and straightforward. The significance levels obtained with the *t*-test might be approximate, but they nevertheless give valuable insight on the outperformance of an active portfolio manager.

Finally, the Information ratio appears to be designed for the assessment of the performance of ETFs or other types of index trackers. The key statistical metric used to estimate the risk of an ETF is the tracking error relative to its benchmark. Moreover, the most important cost component of the ETF is the regular management fee that makes its compound net return diverge in a deterministic way from that of the index that it is supposed to track. In other words, the key cost metric is the ETF's tracking difference. The first intuitive comparison approach between cost (TD) and risk (TE) is naturally the ratio of the former over the latter, i.e., the IR. However, as shown in Chapter 16, this intuition is sometimes wrong, and a more appropriate use of the ingredients (TD and TE) provides a better picture of the true quality of the tracker.

[25] A practical limitation to this property comes from the fact that it can take many years to identify good performers, as shown in Table 3-16. Thus, it might happen that it is too late to take advantage of this information at the moment it is known.

3.4.3.2 Weaknesses

More than any other performance measure examined here above, and especially Jensen's alpha or the peer group comparison return, the quality of the measure is related to that of the portfolio benchmark. A poorly specified benchmark will certainly drive the alpha up or down, but its realized value will always look reasonable and bear some interpretation. If we consider the structure of Equation (3-21), which simply expresses the tracking error as $TE_P = \sqrt{\sigma_P^2 + \sigma_B^2 - 2\rho_{PB}\sigma_P\sigma_B}$, we can see where the danger lies; a poorly specified benchmark will display a weak correlation with the portfolio. Since the interaction term is the only element in the square-root argument that reduces the level of the TE, a too small correlation will destroy the hedging property of the benchmark. Consider the extreme case where $\rho_{PB} = 0$, which implies that $TE_P^2 = \sigma_P^2 + \sigma_B^2$. The residual risk, expressed in variance terms, would then become the *sum* of the portfolio and benchmark risks. Such an odd situation is simply the reflection of a wrong benchmark choice, which will inflate the denominator of the IR and make its level meaningless.

As with the Sharpe ratio, the Information ratio does not pass the "user-friendliness" test depicted in Section 3.2.3. The value that one obtains by applying the formula does not correspond to any economic quantity, such as percentage terms or dollars. This drawback is nevertheless slightly less pronounced. Unlike the SR, the sign of the IR already means something. A positive Information ratio is good, and a negative one is bad. This relationship is at least something that is easy to explain to a unsophisticated investor.

3.4.3.3 Conclusion

Unlike the other metrics discussed previously in this chapter, the Information ratio represents more than a mere performance measure. Being the cornerstone of the justification of active portfolio management, the *ex ante* version of the IR can be considered the primary source of the mandate of any active portfolio manager who has to refer to a benchmark. Not surprisingly, this notion of abnormal portfolio return per unit of specific risk has become the playing field of many professional asset managers. Being generic enough to encompass various specifications for the benchmark (practical, by identifying an index, or analytical, by specifying a return generating process), the Information ratio can be considered a flexible tool to measure performance, which explains why it is so popular among finance professionals. The next milestone, namely, to become a widely accepted and communicated measure toward retail investors, remains hard to reach. The fact that this ratio is probably less intuitive than its simple numerator (the alpha) probably largely explains why it is still relatively ignored by consumers of financial portfolios.

Key Takeaways and Equations

- The *peer group comparison return* PG_P is defined as the difference between the realized return of the portfolio and that of a benchmark comprising a group of peers:

$$PG_P = \overline{R}_P - \frac{1}{N}\sum_{i=1}^{N}\overline{R}_i = \overline{R}_P - \overline{R}_G \tag{3-1}$$

- A well-performing portfolio should deliver a value of $PG_P > 0$. Its statistical significance is assessed through a Student *t*-statistic:

$$\hat{t}_{PG_P=0} = \frac{\sqrt{T-1}}{\sigma(R_P - R_G)} PG_P \tag{3-2}$$

- The main strengths of the peer group comparison return are its simplicity and its use of a large set of information that can be used to refine the analysis of performance. Its major weakness is related to the arbitrary character of the benchmark.
- The *Sharpe ratio* SR_P is defined as the ratio of the excess return of the portfolio over the risk-free interest rate divided by its total risk, measured by the volatility of returns:

$$SR_P = \frac{\overline{R}_P - R_f}{\sigma_P} \tag{3-3}$$

- It is difficult to assess the SR_P minimum value that a well-performing portfolio should deliver, but it should probably exceed a mark between 0.30 and 0.50. Its statistical significance is assessed with a confidence interval around the estimated value:

$$SR_P \pm z_{1-\frac{x}{2}} \times \sqrt{\frac{1}{T}\left(1 + \frac{SR_P^2}{2}\right)} \tag{3-6}$$

It is also usual to assess the significance of the difference between the Sharpe ratios of two portfolios with a Gaussian Z-statistic, valid asymptotically:

$$\hat{z}_{SR_P - SR_Q = 0} = \frac{\overline{r}_P \sigma_Q - \overline{r}_Q \sigma_P}{\sqrt{\frac{1}{T}\left[2(1-\rho_{PQ}) + \frac{1}{2}(SR_P^2 + SR_Q^2 - 2\rho_{PQ}^2 SR_P SR_Q)\right]}} \tag{3-9}$$

- The main strengths of the Sharpe ratio are its theoretical robustness and its generic form of "excess return per unit of risk" that has made this measure very popular. Its major weakness is its difficulty of interpretation and communication.
- The three performance measures based on systematic risk are the Treynor ratio, Jensen's alpha, and the modified Jensen's alpha.
  - The *Treynor ratio* SR_P is defined as the ratio of the excess return of the portfolio over the risk-free interest rate divided by its systematic risk, measured by the beta:

$$\mathrm{TR}_P = \frac{\overline{R}_P - R_f}{\beta_P} \tag{3-10}$$

  - *Jensen's alpha* α_P is defined as the difference between the realized return of the portfolio and its required return on the SML:

$$\alpha_P = \overline{R}_P - [R_f + \beta_P(\overline{R}_M - R_f)] \tag{3-11}$$

  - The *modified Jensen's alpha* ($\mathrm{m}\alpha_P$), occasionally also referred to as the Black-Treynor ratio, is defined as the ratio of the abnormal return of the portfolio, measured by Jensen's alpha, divided by its systematic risk, measured by the beta:

$$\mathrm{m}\alpha_P = \frac{\alpha_P}{\beta_P} \tag{3-13}$$

- Depending on the measure used, a well-performing portfolio should deliver a Treynor ratio greater than the market excess rate of return $\overline{R}_M - R_f$, a positive alpha $\alpha_P > 0$, or a positive modified Jensen's alpha $\mathrm{m}\alpha_P > 0$.
- The significance of Jensen's alpha is usually assessed through a Student ***t***-statistic:

$$\hat{t}_{\alpha_P=0} = \frac{\alpha_P}{\sigma_{\alpha_P}} \tag{3-18}$$

It is much more difficult to assess whether the other two ratios are significantly different from zero. Nevertheless, the significance of the difference between the Treynor ratio of an active portfolio and the market is assessed with a Gaussian Z-statistic, valid asymptotically:

$$\hat{Z}_{\mathrm{TR}_P-\mathrm{TR}_M=0} = \frac{\alpha_P}{\sigma_P\sigma_M\sqrt{\frac{1}{T}\left[\left(1-\rho_{PM}^2\right)\left(\overline{r}_M^2+\sigma_M^2\right)\right]}} \tag{3-20}$$

(continued)

(continued)

- The main strengths of the three systematic risk-based performance measures are their firm grounding in the CAPM and their relative ease of interpretation. In addition, Jensen's alpha is a simple and rather universal performance measure, while the modified Jensen's alpha cannot easily be manipulated and is therefore very reliable. The major weakness of these measures is related to issues with the implementation of the CAPM. Moreover, Jensen's alpha may provide a misleading picture of portfolio performance, while the Treynor ratio and the modified Jensen's alpha occasionally deliver weird values when the CAPM cannot be applied.
- The *Information ratio* IR_P is defined as the ratio of the portfolio tracking difference (realized differential return of the portfolio over its benchmark) divided by tracking error (volatility of this differential return):

$$IR_P = \frac{TD_P}{TE_P} = \frac{\overline{R}_{(P-B)}}{\sigma_{(P-B)}} \tag{3-22}$$

- In the context of the CAPM, this performance measure bears the name of *Appraisal ratio*. It is then defined as the ratio of Jensen's alpha over specific risk:

$$AR_P = \frac{TD_P}{TE_P} = \frac{\alpha_P}{\sigma_{\varepsilon_P}} \tag{3-24}$$

- A well-performing portfolio should deliver a positive value of the IR_P. Nevertheless, since it is also interpreted as the ratio of active return over active risk, it is commonly expected that a good active portfolio manager should deliver an IR_P of at least 0.5 before fees. Its statistical significance is assessed through a Student ***t***-statistic:

$$\hat{t}_{TD_P=0} = \frac{\sqrt{T-1}}{\sigma(R_P - R_B)} TD_P = IR_P\sqrt{T-1} \tag{3-26}$$

- The main strength of the Information ratio is its economic and practical suitability for active portfolio management. Its major weaknesses are related to the arbitrary character of the benchmark and its difficulty of interpretation and communication.

REFERENCES

Bertrand, P. and C. Protopopescu (2010), The statistics of the Information ratio. *International Journal of Business*, Vol. 15 (1), pp. 71–86.

Christie, S. (2005), Is the Sharpe ratio useful in asset allocation? MAFC Research Paper No. 31, Applied Finance Centre, Macquarie University.

Durham, J. B. (2015), Can long-only investors use momentum to beat the US Treasury market? *Financial Analysts Journal*, Vol. 71 (5), pp. 57–74.

Goodwin, T. H. (1998), The Information ratio. *Financial Analysts Journal*, Vol. 54 (4), pp. 34–43.

Grinold, R. C. and R. N. Kahn (1995), *Active Portfolio Management*, Irwin.

Hinkley, D. V. (1969), On the ratio of two correlated normal random variables. *Biometrika*, Vol. 56, pp. 633–639.

Jensen, M. (1968), The performance of mutual funds in the period 1943–1964. *The Journal of Finance*, Vol. 23, pp. 383–416.

Jobson, J. D., and B. M. Korkie (1981), Performance hypothesis testing with the Sharpe and Treynor measures. *The Journal of Finance*, Vol. 36, pp. 883–908.

Jordà, Ò., Knoll, K., Kuvshinov, D., Schularick, M., and A. M. Taylor (2019), The rate of return on everything, 1870–2015. *The Quarterly Journal of Economics*, Vol. 134, pp. 1223–1298.

Ledoit, O., and M. Wolf (2008), Robust performance hypothesis testing with the Sharpe ratio. *Journal of Empirical Finance*, Vol. 15, pp. 850–859.

Lo, A. W. (2002), The statistics of Sharpe ratios. *Financial Analysts Journal*, Vol. 58 (4), pp. 36–52.

Memmel, C. (2003), Performance hypothesis testing with the Sharpe ratio. *Finance Letters*, Vol. 1, pp. 21–23.

Mertens, E. (2002), Comments on variance of the IID estimator in Lo (2002). Research Note.

Modigliani, F., and G. A. Pogue (1974), An introduction to risk and return: Concepts and evidence. *Financial Analysts Journal*, Vol. 30 (3), pp. 63–86.

Opdyke, J. P. (2007), Comparing Sharpe ratios: So where are the p-values? *Journal of Asset Management*, Vol. 8 (5), pp. 303–326.

Roll, R. (1977), A critique of the asset pricing theory's tests. Part I: On past and potential testability of the theory. *Journal of Financial Economics*, Vol. 4, pp. 123–176.

Sharpe, W. F. (1966), Mutual fund performance. *Journal of Business*, Vol. 39, pp. 113–138.

Sharpe, W. F. (1994), The Sharpe ratio. *The Journal of Portfolio Management*, (Fall), pp. 43–58.

Smith, K. V., and D. A. Tito (1969), Risk–return measures of ex post portfolio performance. *Journal of Financial and Quantitative Analysis*, Vol. 4, pp. 443–471.

Stuart, A., and K. Ord (Eds.) (1994), *Distribution Theory, Vol. 1 of Kendall's Advanced Theory of Statistics, 6th ed.* Oxford University Press.

Treynor, J. L. (1965), How to rate management of investment funds. *Harvard Business Review*, Vol. 43 (1), pp. 63–75.

Treynor, J. L., and F. Black (1973), How to use security analysis to improve portfolio selection. *Journal of Business*, Vol. 46, pp. 66–86.

CHAPTER 4

Selecting a Classical Performance Measure

INTRODUCTION

The Standard Portfolio Theory (SPT) and its related market equilibrium relationship, the Capital Asset Pricing Model (CAPM), have generated many portfolio performance measures such as the Sharpe ratio, the modified Jensen's alpha, and the Information ratio.[1] All of them are consistent with a measure of efficiency in the active portfolio management process, and they bear their own theoretical justifications. All of them also being *a priori* legitimate, their coexistence makes the issue of the selection of one of them a nontrivial exercise. This point has surprisingly drawn little attention in the asset management literature.

In this chapter, we perform a 360° analysis on the criteria that should influence the choice of the most relevant performance measure in different contexts. To achieve that objective, we first identify their key discriminating features, namely, how they measure the risk dimension as an input, and how they relate the input to the return output. This process leads us to produce a *synoptic view of performance measures* that serves as a guide throughout the rest of the chapter.

There are two main perspectives through which the selection of the right way to measure portfolio performance makes sense, namely, that of the customer (the investor) and that of the producer (the asset manager). Both points of view are defendable, but they may produce different outcomes. The point of view of the investor can take two forms. The *normative approach* considers the investor's rational behavior when they are confronted with an actively managed fund that potentially enhances the risk–return properties of their asset allocation. This view is

[1]See Chapter 3 for a detailed review of these measures.

mostly an *ex ante* one, in which the observed performance of the portfolio serves as an indicator of its potential added value in the future. The *positive approach*, by contrast, associates the most relevant performance measure with the natural destination of the portfolio or the most likely situation of the investor who currently holds it. For both approaches, the good news is that there is room for the application of total, systematic, or specific risk as an input. Therefore, it is occasionally best to use the Sharpe ratio, but at other times, the modified Jensen's alpha or the Information ratio is more appropriate.

The portfolio manager's viewpoint can also be relevant regarding the choice of a performance measure. This perspective is important for ranking, rewarding, or sanctioning the persons who are in charge of actively managing their customers' assets. The key message here is that one should faithfully rely on the classification produced by the selected performance measure. The notion of *stability of portfolio rankings* under various sampling conditions is a useful tool that enables the outside observer to make a choice among the set of candidate performance measures.

Throughout the text, we work through a simple but realistic example of a fund offering for which the challenge – either for the investor or for the asset manager – is to select the right performance measure in the right context.

The Global–Thematic–Neutral (G–T–N) Asset Management Company Example

We introduce the G–T–N Asset Management Company, which runs three active funds:

1. The Global fund is an aggressive asset allocation fund with a large exposure to world equities.
2. The Thematic fund tries to take advantage of the particular skills of the firm's senior portfolio managers. It focuses on the company's domestic market (USA) and invests mostly in corporate bonds.
3. The Neutral fund is a relative value alternative fund that aims to implement quasi-arbitrage trades while keeping a very low exposure to equity markets.

The returns of the funds and the world market index (**M**) have been recorded over a period of 10 years. The relevant risk and return statistics of the funds are represented in Table 4-1, with the addition of data corresponding to the risk-free asset (**F**).

TABLE 4-1 G–T–N example – Means, volatilities, and correlations.

	Global	Thematic	Neutral	M	F
Mean return	6.39%	4.72%	2.55%	7.39%	1.44%
Standard deviation	7.12%	6.41%	3.90%	8.83%	0.00%
Correlation with market	0.97	0.48	0.04	1.00	0.00

The risk–return properties of the three funds, the market portfolio, and the riskless asset are represented in Figure 4-1. The dotted straight line represents the *ex post* Capital Market Line (CML).

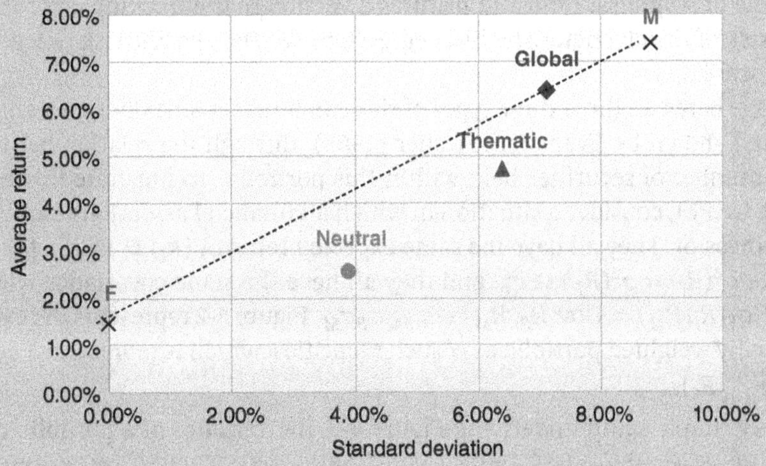

FIGURE 4-1 G–T–N example – Risk–return properties of the three funds.

From a pure risk–return trade-off perspective, only the Global fund outperforms the market as this fund is the only one that lies slightly above the CML. Nevertheless, drawing definite conclusions from this visual inspection would be too simplistic as the other two funds display much lower correlations with the market portfolio, whose influence on performance does not appear on the graph.

4.1 RISK AND MEASUREMENT DIMENSIONS

4.1.1 The risk dimension of the input

An asset manager generally aims to maximize their realized return over a certain period. This result is the natural output of the portfolio management process. However, to measure the manager's performance, one also needs to specify the corresponding input. With the exception of the peer group comparison return – which is a useful but purely heuristic tool – the classical performance measures discussed in Chapter 3 all explicitly consider that portfolio risk is the input of the asset management process. The Sharpe ratio builds on the portfolio total risk, measured with the volatility (i.e., standard deviation) of returns. The Treynor ratio, Jensen's alpha, and the modified Jensen's alpha are all derived from the *ex post* security market line (SML). Under this approach, portfolio risk is measured with the beta, which accounts for systematic risk. Finally, when represented in the CAPM framework, the Information ratio bears the name of Appraisal ratio and features a version of the tracking error that is equal to the residual risk of the characteristic line regression, i.e., the specific risk (a.k.a. idiosyncratic risk) of the portfolio.

The linkage between these three types of risk can be schematically represented in the SPT context, as first shown by Evans and Archer (1968), through the relation between portfolio risk and the number of securities held within this portfolio. To illustrate this relation in the context of the CAPM, consider a situation in which all financial assets i are similar to portfolio P held by an investor. They all have the same expected return $\mathrm{E}(R_i) = \mathrm{E}(R_P)$, they all have the same variance $\sigma^2(R_i) = \sigma^2(R_P) \equiv \sigma_P^2$, and they all have the same covariance with the market portfolio M: $\mathrm{Cov}(R_i, R_M) = \mathrm{Cov}(R_P, R_M) \equiv \rho_{PM}\sigma_P\sigma_M$. Figure 4-2 represents the evolution of the risk of an equally weighted portfolio of N such securities, which is represented as the function $\sigma_N^2 = \sigma^2\left(\frac{1}{N}\sum_{i=1}^{N} R_i\right)$.

In the very simple setup underlying Figure 4-2, the variance of a portfolio comprising N securities is always equal to $\sigma_N^2 = \frac{1}{N}\sigma_P^2 + \left(N - \frac{1}{N}\right)\rho_{PM}\sigma_P\sigma_M$. That is, total portfolio risk (measured by its variance) is a weighted average of each of its components' total risk (represented by σ_P^2) and systematic risk (represented by $\rho_{PM}\sigma_P\sigma_M$). This average decays toward a horizontal asymptote whose level is equal to systematic risk. Thus, the difference between total risk and systematic risk, which equals $\sigma_P^2 - \rho_{PM}\sigma_P\sigma_M$, is the specific risk that is eliminated with portfolio diversification.

The link between the measures of risk used as inputs of the classical performance measures and those derived from the Evans and Archer (1968) approach is summarized in Table 4-2.

The representations of the three types of risks are different. However, Table 4-2 clearly shows that the Sharpe ratio reflects the whole risk of a portfolio, the Treynor ratio (and both Jensen's alpha and the modified Jensen's alpha) accounts for the undiversifiable risk that

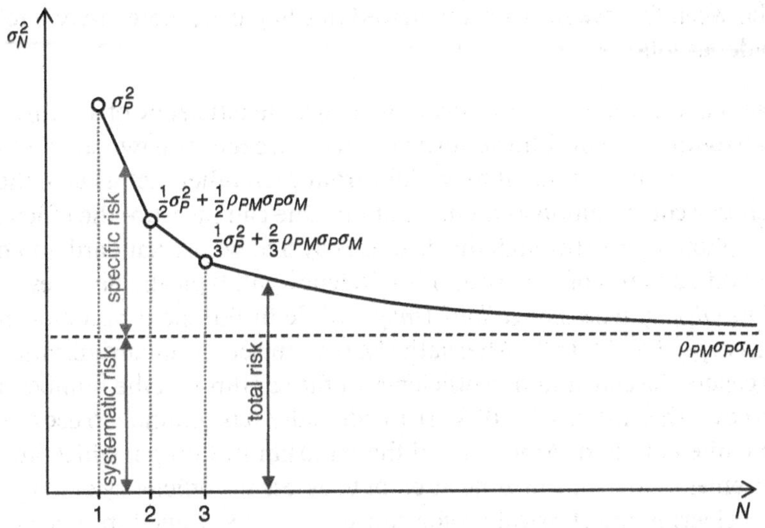

FIGURE 4-2 Decomposition of the three types of portfolio risk.

TABLE 4-2 Link between risk decomposition and performance measures.

	Risk in performance	Risk in decomposition	Analogy
Total risk	σ_P	σ_P^2	Only based on variance
Systematic risk	$\beta_P = \frac{\rho_{PM}\sigma_P}{\sigma_M}$	$\rho_{PM}\sigma_P\sigma_M$	Based on volatility × correlation
Specific risk	$\sigma_{\varepsilon_P} = \sigma_P\sqrt{1-\rho_{PM}^2}$	$\sigma_P(\sigma_P - \rho_{PM}\sigma_M)$	Based on difference between total and systematic risk-based measures

remains after the portfolio has fully seized all possible diversification opportunities, and the Information ratio only considers the diversifiable risk, i.e., the one that the portfolio manager could remove through their diversification efforts and thus deliberately chooses to be exposed to.

4.1.2 The measurement dimension of the relation between input and output

The classical performance measures not only differ from each other by the choice of risk measure as input but also distinguish themselves on the basis of the type of result that they provide, i.e., how the efficiency of the portfolio management process is measured. To ensure a proper comparison between the five measures reviewed in Chapter 3, there are two relevant dimensions to consider as follows:

1. *The measurement unit*: As it is meant to gauge the efficiency of a transformation from inputs to outputs, a portfolio performance measure relies on two sources of information whose units of measurement may differ from each other. Let us take the analysis of a car's energy consumption as an illustration. One can measure the efficiency of the gas consumption process through the distance covered with a standard unit of gas volume. In the United States of America, this efficiency will typically be assessed through the ratio "*number of miles per gallon*" (*mpg*), while in Europe it becomes the "*number of kilometers per liter*" (*km/l*). Alternatively, we can set a standard distance (say 100 km) and measure the consumption efficiency of the car through the number of liters necessary to cover this distance (*l*/100 km). Incidentally, it is common to use the *mpg* measure in the United States of America and the *l*/100 km in Europe, which are two different measurement units for the same attempt to assess the efficiency of a process.

   Considering the classical performance measures studied in this chapter, we have seen that the output (gain) is always measured through a rate of return, in percentage points (%). The difference between each measure lies in how risk is assessed (either in percentage points or as a scalar), which leads to two types of measurement units for the assessment of performance, namely, either a *decimal number* or a value in *percentage points*.
2. *The measurement scale*: Two performance measures may share the same units of measurement for the input and the output of the process, but they can still differ in how they model the relation between these two variables.

   Going back to the example of the gas consumption of a car, if everyone agrees that the standard distance that should be used to compare the efficiency of two cars is 100 km, the performance measure would be the number of liters of gas. The ranking of two cars then becomes "Car X is more efficient than Car Y because it consumes 5.4 l instead of 6.0 l," since everyone knows that the distance has been standardized to 100 km. However, using an absolute rather than a relative measure of performance may lead to misleading results when the unit of input is not standardized. Take the same example, but now consider that Car X has a gas tank of 54 l, while that of Car Y is 72 l. If the performance measure is the distance covered with one full tank, it is 1000 km for Car X but 1200 km for Car Y. By not standardizing the measure of input, the performance measure provides the false impression that Car Y is more efficient than Car X simply because there is a distortion in the scale of the input.

   In the context of the appraisal of portfolio performance through an absolute measure, one has to consider the same potential issue about how its risk is measured. If it is measured as a standard quantity, then the measure is *scale-independent* (i.e., the performance is independent of the quantity of risk that has been taken). If the measure of performance delivers a value that is affected by the quantity of risk taken, it is *scale-dependent*.

TABLE 4-3 Measurement units and scales of the classical performance measures.

Performance measure	Equation	Measurement unit	Measurement scale
Sharpe ratio	$SR_P = \frac{\overline{R}_P - R_f}{\sigma_P}$	Decimal number	Scale-independent
Treynor ratio	$TR_P = \frac{\overline{R}_P - R_f}{\beta_P}$	Percentage point	Scale-independent
Jensen's alpha	$\alpha_P = \overline{R}_P - \left[R_f + \beta_P\left(\overline{R}_M - R_f\right)\right]$	Percentage point	Scale-dependent
Modified Jensen's alpha	$m\alpha_P = \frac{\alpha_P}{\beta_P}$	Percentage point	Scale-independent
Information ratio	$IR_P = \frac{TD_P}{TE_P} = \frac{\overline{R}_P - \overline{R}_B}{\sigma(R_P - R_B)}$	Decimal number	Scale-independent

In Table 4-3, we characterize each of the classical performance measures on both dimensions.

The natural way to measure efficiency is to report the number of outputs per unit of input. However, in the context of portfolio performance, the measurement unit of the input (risk) and the output (gain) is often the same: one percentage point (%). Taking the ratio of two variables whose measurement units are similar leaves a scalar as a result, which has the unwelcome characteristic of being difficult to communicate and to explain.[2] This difficulty exists for the Sharpe ratio and the Information ratio, whose outcomes do not correspond to returns in percentage form.

To avoid this difficulty and directly report a rate of return, it is possible to either (i) change the measurement unit of one of the ingredients or (ii) disclose a measure of performance that is absolute instead of relative, i.e., replace a ratio by a measure of output, taking for granted the quantity of input that has been used. Because they use the portfolio beta as input, the Treynor ratio and the modified Jensen's alpha keep the properties of a relative measure of efficiency, but their outcome can be interpreted as a rate of return, expressed as a percentage. Jensen's alpha takes the route of an absolute performance measure, but it does not fix the value of the beta taken as an input. In that sense, it is a scale-dependent measure; everything else remaining equal, a portfolio will double its performance by doubling its beta.

4.1.3 A synoptic view of performance measures

Matching the risk and measurement dimensions associated with each of the classical performance measures in a single synoptic table is a simple but useful exercise for two reasons. First,

[2]We refer to it as the "user-friendliness test" in Chapter 3.

it provides a dashboard that enables an immediate comparison between them, while its empty cells also reveal potential "loopholes" in the portfolio performance evaluation process. Second, it paves the way for the construction of a similar table in other situations, i.e., when one tries to classify performance measures that are either not classical or adapted to more complex asset pricing frameworks than the CAPM, such as for instance multifactor asset pricing specifications. Aggregating information from the previous subsections leads to the following synoptic table (Table 4-4).[3]

The cells corresponding to decimal-based measures suffer from the drawback of making the interpretation and communication of performance difficult. The cells corresponding to scale-dependent measures are prone to being manipulated, be it voluntarily or not, by altering portfolio risk. Unsurprisingly, the only measures that avoid any of these two drawbacks are the Treynor ratio TR_P and the modified Jensen's alpha $m\alpha_P$, which essentially measure the same thing – return (excess for TR_P and abnormal for $m\alpha_P$) per unit of beta.

The key takeaway of this section is that there is only one risk dimension (namely, systematic risk) for which there exist classical measures that simultaneously provide a readily interpretable figure (in %) and cannot be mechanically altered by changing portfolio risk. In a corollary to this statement, the assessment and disclosure of performance when total or specific risk is used as an input remains a challenge. This challenge partly explains why the practitioners' and academic literatures have developed alternative measures that are meant to overcome this difficulty.

When classifying funds or actively managed portfolios, it is tempting to use the information of Table 4-4 in an opportunistic way, i.e., to strategically push forward the metric anticipated to make the best impression. Quite often, the rankings produced under different risk dimensions or by not taking the risk level into account will be different. A portfolio manager may wish to adopt a particular performance measure on the sole basis of where their ranking will be most favorable. This approach is of course not at all the purpose of such a table. The

TABLE 4-4 Synoptic table of the classical performance measures.

Measurement dimension		Risk dimension		
Unit	**Scale**	***Total risk***	***Systematic risk***	***Specific risk***
Decimal (%/%)	Dependent			
	Independent	SR_P		IR_P, AR_P
Percentage (%)	Dependent		α_P	
	Independent		TR_P, $m\alpha_P$	

[3]The complete table is presented in Section 6.4.3 of Chapter 6 after new performance measures are presented and examined.

choice of a performance measure should be well justified and understood and, above all, be adapted to the purpose of the analysis. There are two main such purposes, namely, reporting to investors and assessing the quality of portfolio managers. They are not necessarily equivalent, as shown in the remainder of the chapter.

G–T–N example (continued)

Recall Table 4-1, which introduces the key risk and return statistics.

	Global	Thematic	Neutral	M	F
Mean return	6.39%	4.72%	2.55%	7.39%	1.44%
Standard deviation	7.12%	6.41%	3.90%	8.83%	0.00%
Correlation with market	0.97	0.48	0.04	1.00	0.00

Table 4-5 reports the values of the classical performance measures retrieved from the data.

TABLE 4-5 G–T–N example – Outcomes of the classical performance measures.

Measure	Global	Thematic	Neutral	M
Sharpe ratio	0.70	0.51	0.28	0.67
Treynor ratio	6.33%	9.42%	62.85%	5.95%
Jensen's alpha	0.30%	1.21%	1.00%	0.00%
Modified Jensen's alpha	0.38%	3.47%	56.90%	0.00%
Information ratio	0.17	0.21	0.26	0.00

Applying these values to the synoptic table leads to the rankings reported in Table 4-6, and reveals the complexity engendered by adopting different risk measures in the context of performance measurement. While only fund **G** dominates the market portfolio from a total risk perspective, all funds produce a positive Jensen's alpha and thus post positive abnormal returns. Each fund dominates all the others in at least one dimension; the Thematic fund has the best alpha, and the Neutral fund displays the largest Information ratio. Thus, each manager could be tempted to boast about their superiority over their colleagues by choosing her favorite risk dimension. Moreover, while the Neutral fund has a lower alpha than the

(continued)

(continued)

Thematic one, the ordering is reversed when their risk levels (measured by their beta) are taken into account. This phenomenon has to be interpreted with great caution, however, given that the correlation of fund **N** with the market is extremely low (0.04).

TABLE 4-6 G–T–N example – Synoptic table of the classical performance measures.

Measurement dimension		*Risk dimension*		
Unit	**Scale**	*Total risk*	*Systematic risk*	*Specific risk*
Decimal (%/%)	Dependent			
	Independent	G > M > T > N		N > T > G > M
Percentage (%)	Dependent		T > N > G > M	
	Independent		N > T > G > M	

4.2 CHOOSING A MEASURE FOR THE INVESTOR: THE NORMATIVE APPROACH

Reporting the *ex post* performance of a portfolio is a means of controlling the quality of the manager's work. Thus, the selection of the measure should not be driven by the manager's own choice because doing so would lead to a conflict of interest with the other stakeholders. Ultimately, the performance of a portfolio impacts the customer's welfare; it is natural that the measure adopted corresponds to the investor's needs. The client can be institutional or professional, in which case a simple solution is to communicate a variety of performance measures and even the raw returns data. The investor is then equipped to make up their own opinion on the basis of a complete set of information.

The matter becomes more delicate for the nonprofessional investor. Considering Table 4-4, and even if we restrict ourselves to the five classical performance measures, it does not make sense to literally throw all of them to the investor without placing them in perspective. If several measures are simultaneously shown, there should be a clear roadmap enabling the client, who is often not a specialist in portfolio management, to identify which of all these measures would be more suitable for their situation and purpose. Additionally, if only one measure is to be selected, the choice should be made carefully, not to embellish the situation but to inform the investor in a suitable manner, especially if different measures do not strongly correlate with each other.[4]

In general, looking at Table 4-4, the risk dimension (columns) matters much more than the measurement dimension (rows). The latter dimension simply refers to how performance is presented but does not truly alter the nature of the type of efficiency that is measured. Of course, when a risk dimension is chosen, it is generally preferable to adopt a measure that is scale-independent and reported in percentage points, which is why it might be worthwhile to replace the Sharpe ratio and the Information ratio with alternative presentation methods; this idea is examined in Chapter 6. If one chooses the systematic risk dimension, it is also better to use the modified Jensen's alpha or the Treynor ratio rather than the simple Jensen's alpha.[5] There is a notable exception to this principle, however; when the level of the portfolio beta is well known and understood by the investor, the Jensen's alpha may suffice to adequately reflect portfolio performance, and it might be superfluous to add further complexity by dividing it with the beta. Simple is beautiful when simple is sufficient.

A first way to look at the choice of the relevant performance measure of a portfolio is to consider the criteria that the investor *should* adopt to make their investment decision. This normative point of view takes the stance of portfolio selection on the basis of expectations.[6] The investor is confronted with a certain situation with objectives and constraints and considers placing money in an actively managed portfolio. They have to adopt a criterion based on risk and expected return to select the portfolio and determine the amount to be invested in it. However, the application of this criterion is subject to constraints on this invested amount. The investor could try to find the best possible allocation between the market and active portfolios, in which case the optimization is not constrained at all. However, they may also commit to allocate all their wealth, or a predetermined fraction of it, to the active portfolio. In fact, the nature of these constraints will often be linked to an associate classical performance measure, as shown below.

4.2.1 The fully constrained case

Consider an investor whose investment decision can be summarized by allocating all their wealth in a single well-diversified portfolio to the exclusion of any other one. This "fully constrained" case of optimal portfolio selection is the simplest situation because the Sharpe ratio itself results from an optimization process (Figure 4-3). Indeed, in the CAPM framework, the

[4]This remains a very contemporaneous issue in the practice of portfolio management. After a careful examination of the rank correlations between the major performance measures over a long period (1950–2023), Horstmeyer and Li (2023) conclude: "*So, if a fund manager reports their Sortino or Information ratio but goes silent on their Sharpe and Treynor ratios, it may reflect a strategic play and warrant further investigation.*"

[5]We refer to Chapter 3 for a complete discussion of the pros and cons of these measures.

[6]To ensure consistency with the statistical notation of the performance measures, we here assume that the expected return is adequately estimated by the sample mean, i.e., $E(R_P) = \overline{R}_P$. This simplified notation is for the sake of exposition throughout the whole chapter.

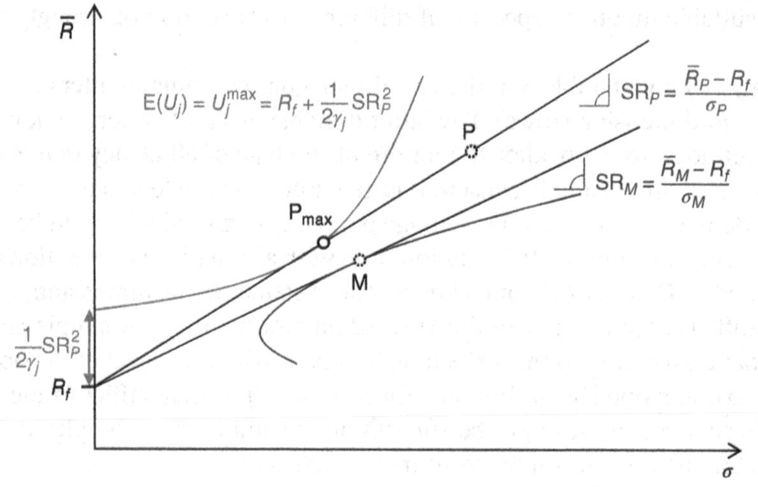

FIGURE 4-3 Fully constrained optimal portfolio selection process.

rational, risk-averse investor has to select a portfolio that maximizes their expected utility. In the risk–return graph, this process consists of running a two-stage procedure: (i) finding a portfolio *P* on the efficient frontier that is tangent to the Capital Allocation Line starting from the coordinates of the risk-free asset (i.e., the riskless rate R_f on the vertical axis); (ii) once this portfolio is identified, levering it by investing a fraction of wealth in the risk-free asset to reach the risk–return trade-off that maximizes expected utility. This property is known as Tobin's (1958) two-fund separation theorem. From an *ex ante*, probabilistic perspective, the application of this theorem results in an equilibrium in which every investor chooses the same risky asset, namely, the famous market portfolio *M*. The Capital Allocation Line that links R_f with the coordinates of *M* is the CML, and the optimal portfolio for a given investor *j* corresponds to the allocation whose coordinates are tangent to one of their indifference curves.[7]

In the context of practical optimal portfolio selection, we have to acknowledge that the market portfolio is unobservable. The investor can choose from among many passively and actively managed funds and portfolios and will try to implement the same kind of rational process as above but with no particular prejudice about the identity of the best possible portfolio on the basis of historical information. From this "agnostic" point of view, the estimators of the risk and return are the sample standard deviation and mean return, and any portfolio will be tested as a potential candidate. The selected one in this context is the portfolio *P* whose Sharpe ratio is the maximum across all risky assets in the investment universe. Then, once it

[7]The full development of this equilibrium relationship framework is detailed in Chapter 2.

is identified, the investor will try to maximize their expected utility by choosing the fraction of their wealth to be invested in this portfolio by the solving the following program:

$$\max_{w} \mathrm{E}\left(U_j\left(wR_P + (1-w)R_f\right)\right) = w\overline{R}_P + (1-w)R_f - \frac{1}{2}\gamma_j w^2 \sigma_P^2 \tag{4-1}$$

where $U_j(\cdot)$ is the quadratic utility function of investor j, and γ_j stands for their risk-aversion coefficient; $\overline{R}_P$ and σ_P^2 represent the mean and variance of the portfolio returns, respectively; and R_f is the rate of return of the riskless asset, which is considered constant over the period.

Because of the two-fund separation theorem, we know that the optimal weight is $w_{\max} = \frac{\sigma_{P_{\max}}}{\sigma_P}$, where $P_{\max}$ is the optimal portfolio and $\overline{R}_{P_{\max}} = w_{\max}\overline{R}_P + (1 - w_{\max})R_f$. The solution is obtained by a straightforward application of the first-order condition applied to Equation (4-1) and yields the following:

$$w_{\max} = \frac{\overline{R}_P - R_f}{\gamma_j \sigma_P^2} = \frac{1}{\gamma_j \sigma_P}\mathrm{SR}_P \tag{4-2}$$

Thus, both the identification of the best possible portfolio P and the optimal allocation in this portfolio $w_{\max}$ depend on its Sharpe ratio. It is therefore not surprising to realize that the expected utility extracted by the investor is equal to the following:

$$\max \mathrm{E}(U_j(R_P)) \equiv U_j^{\max} = R_f + \frac{1}{2\gamma_j}\mathrm{SR}_P^2 \tag{4-3}$$

Equation (4-3) bears an interesting interpretation.[8] It shows the maximum potential surplus, expressed in terms of additional satisfaction, brought by the portfolio. Since the investor can achieve a riskless return of R_f, the added value of choosing portfolio P and mixing it up with the risk-free asset f is equal to the difference between the expected utility of the optimal portfolio and the riskless rate, namely, $\frac{1}{2\gamma_j}\mathrm{SR}_P^2$. In the graph, this surplus in expected utility is represented by the vertical distance between the intercept of the investor's indifference curve and the risk-free rate.

Thus, from a normative point of view, the only criterion that an investor should consider to choose their optimal portfolio is the Sharpe ratio. It is a matter of not only maximizing the mean return per unit of risk but also choosing the amount of leverage in the optimal portfolio

[8] In Chapter 9, we further elaborate on this result by designing performance measures that explicitly account for the investor's risk profile.

allocation through w_{max} and of estimating the gain in expected satisfaction retrieved from this best allocation through U_j^{max}.

G–T–N example (continued)

Consider a private bank that wishes to offer three different portfolios to its customers: an Aggressive (a), a Median (m), and a Defensive (d) one. The corresponding risk-aversion coefficients of the representative customer in each category are the following: $\gamma_a = 4$, $\gamma_m = 8$, and $\gamma_d = 12$.

The sequence of decisions that the bank must follow is the following:

(i) Choice of the best-performing fund. From Table 4-5, every investor should pick the portfolio that achieves the best Sharpe ratio among the potential candidates, namely, the Global fund (**G**).

(ii) Choice of the optimal level of leverage. The weight invested in portfolio **G** is obtained by applying Equation (4-2), $w_{max} = \frac{1}{\gamma_j \sigma_P} SR_P$, with $j = a, m$, and d. The results are reported in Table 4-7.

TABLE 4-7 G–T–N example – Fully constrained optimal portfolios for different investor types.

Investor	Risk aversion γ_j	Weight w_{max}	Volatility $\sigma_{P_{max}}$	Mean return $\bar{R}_{P_{max}}$	Utility surplus
Aggressive	4	244%	17.38%	13.52%	6.04%
Median	8	122%	8.69%	7.48%	3.02%
Defensive	12	81%	5.79%	5.47%	2.01%

The first two portfolios (Aggressive and Median) involve leveraging the initial portfolio P, i.e., their weights invested in the risky portfolio exceed 100%. Thus, the risk and mean return of both allocations are also greater than those of the Global fund. From Equation (4-2), we can observe that these portfolio characteristics are inversely related to the risk-aversion coefficient of the representative investor.

The last column of Table 4-7 reports the utility surplus that each investor obtains from their optimal allocation. It decreases as the investor's risk aversion increases but is always positive as long as the investor is not infinitely risk averse. This analysis is visually represented in Figure 4-4.

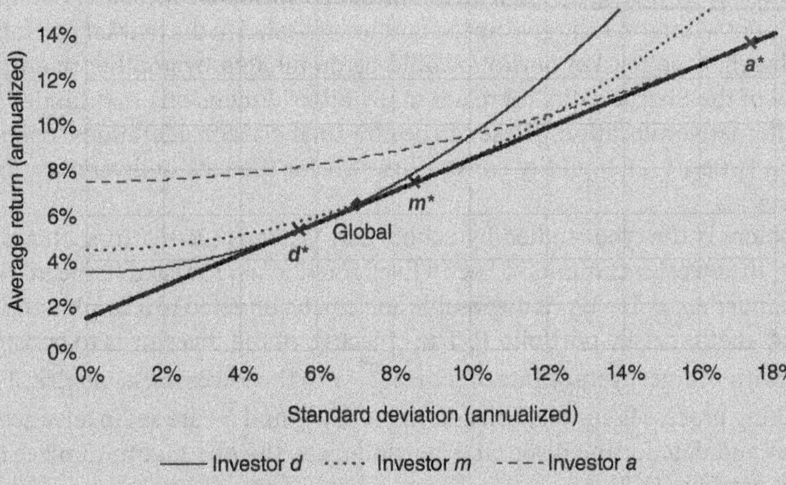

FIGURE 4-4 G–T–N example – Determination of the optimal fund offering mix.

In Figure 4-4, the optimal portfolio for each investor type is represented by a cross along the Capital Allocation Line constructed with the Global fund. The concave lines, which are tangent to the optimal portfolios, represent the best achievable indifference curve for investor *a* (right curve), *m* (middle), and *d* (left). The more risk averse the investor is, the steeper will be their indifference curves, which explains that the value added of portfolio d^* is the lowest one. This graph clearly shows that even though investors are heterogeneous in their attitudes toward risk, they share the same selection criterion for their global optimal portfolio, namely, the Sharpe ratio.

4.2.2 The partially constrained case

In the context of the CAPM, the systematic risk of a given asset is captured by its beta. The risk reflects the quantity of nondiversifiable risk that is compensated for through a risk premium. The specific risk of the asset is meant to be diversified away. This phenomenon theoretically arises because the investor's holding of it is supposed to be infinitesimal. Thus, when an investor has to choose an optimal allocation, they know that each individual security or asset should have an expected return related to its beta, but this knowledge is presumably of very little use in their decision-making process about the global portfolio choice.

The issue becomes different when the investor has access to portfolios whose risk–return trade-offs seemingly exceed that of the market portfolio. In the previous subsection, we have seen that the criterion of maximizing the Sharpe ratio suffices to guide the investor toward the best (in terms of expected utility maximization) mutually exclusive allocation. However, this case also suggests that the investor commits to fully switch from the (passive) market portfolio to an actively managed one with a superior performance measure. In most situations, the investor is not willing to fully give up the amount invested in the market portfolio. Although they recognize that the market portfolio could be dominated by another one from the strict point of view of the Sharpe ratio, there are many other dimensions that hinder a full switch toward the alternative allocation. These can be non-financial considerations (operational risks, concentration issues, ...), liquidity constraints, fear for the lack of diversification, or simply emotional reasons.

This problem is the type studied by Scholz and Wilkens (2005). In such a partially constrained case, the investor commits to keep a fixed fraction w_M invested in the market portfolio, and the remainder $w_D = 1 - w_M$ is disposable and can be invested in a combination of the riskless asset and another risky portfolio P. The objective of the investor is to construct a global portfolio Ω^* with a target average rate of return $\overline{R}^*$ with the lowest possible risk. The investor's decision-making process is simple; considering that w_M and $\overline{R}^*$ are set in advance, what is the best possible candidate for the disposable portfolio, i.e., the one that minimizes the total risk of the overall portfolio Ω^*?

Considering a candidate portfolio P, the risk of the total portfolio is obtained in three steps:

(i) retrieve the target mean return of the disposable portfolio on the basis of the target global rate of return equal to $\overline{R}_D = \frac{\overline{R}^* - \overline{R}_M}{w_D} + \overline{R}_M$, where $\overline{R}_M$ is the mean return of the market portfolio;

(ii) determine the weight that needs to be invested in P to achieve this target mean return of the disposable portfolio, equal to $w_P = w_D \frac{\overline{R}_D - R_f}{\overline{R}_P - R_f}$; and

(iii) compute the volatility of the global portfolio; the selected candidate will be the one that minimizes this volatility, which is simply computed with the usual expression for the portfolio standard deviation $\sigma_{\Omega^*} = \sqrt{w_P^2\sigma_P^2 + (1 - w_D)^2\sigma_M^2 + 2w_P(1 - w_D)\rho_{PM}\sigma_P\sigma_M}$.

Following this sequence, Scholz and Wilkens (2005) show that the expression to be maximized for the selection of the disposable portfolio that maximizes the investor's expected utility is the investor-specific performance measure (ISM_P), which is defined as follows:

$$\text{ISM}_P = -w_D\left(\frac{\overline{R}_D - R_f}{\sigma_M \text{SR}_P}\right)^2 - 2(1 - w_D)\frac{\overline{R}_D - R_f}{\text{TR}_P} \tag{4-4}$$

where σ_M represents the standard deviation of the market portfolio returns, SR_P and TR_P are the Sharpe ratio and Treynor ratio of portfolio P, respectively, and $\overline{R}_D$ is the average rate of return of the disposable portfolio.

Figure 4-5 provides a graphical representation of the investor's decision-making process in the risk–return framework.

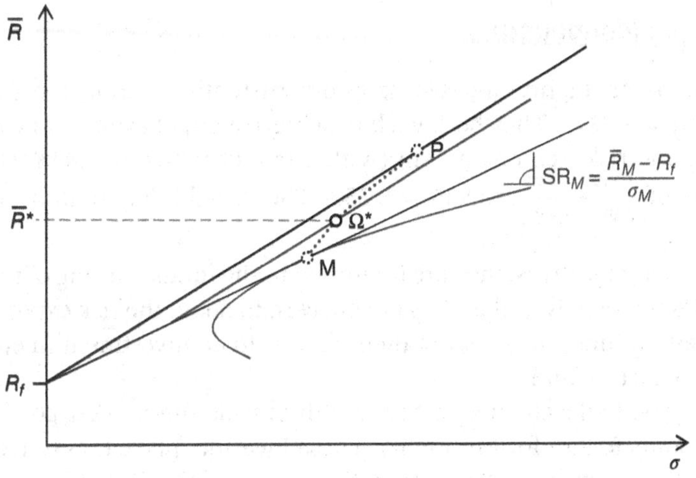

FIGURE 4-5 Optimal partially constrained portfolio selection process.

In this illustration, the weight in the disposable portfolio is $w_D = 50\%$. This figure corresponds to a point on the CML that is equidistant between the coordinates of the market portfolio and the risk-free asset. We start from that point on the CML, and to obtain the optimal portfolio Ω^*, we draw the straight line, which is parallel to the Capital Allocation Line of portfolio P. The optimal portfolio respects the target average return constraint $\bar{R}_{\Omega^*} = \bar{R}^*$. The concave dotted line that connects portfolios M and P represents the enhanced constrained efficient frontier.

Thus, according to Equation (4-4), the criterion that must be applied for the choice of a complement to the market portfolio features a mixture of the Sharpe ratio and the Treynor ratio of the candidate fund. Interestingly, the formulation of the ISM_P resembles that of a weighted sum of the inverse of these two performance measures. If the weight of the disposable portfolio w_D is high, the first term dominates and the selection criterion is driven by the Sharpe ratio. This situation leans toward the case of the fully constrained selection process discussed above. Conversely, when most of the investment is kept in the market portfolio, the main driver of portfolio selection is the Treynor ratio. In particular, Scholz and Wilkens (2005) note that if the required return is infinitesimally higher than that of the market portfolio, the appropriate performance measure for choosing the complement portfolio is solely the Treynor ratio. This approach matches the logic of using a systematic risk measure only for very small fractions of the market portfolio. The ISM simply reflects the balance between the two extreme cases of constrained portfolio selection, from the fully disposable portfolio (Sharpe ratio only) to the almost null disposable portfolio (Treynor ratio only).

G–T–N example (continued)

Mrs. Twenty and Mr. Eighty are two investors currently holding the market portfolio ($\overline{R}_M = 7.39\%, \sigma_M = 8.83\%$). They both wish to achieve a target average rate of return of 7%. They could use the risk-free investment (with a rate of return of 1.44%), but they would then bear a risk of $\frac{7.00\% - 1.44\%}{7.39\% - 1.44\%} \times 8.83\% = 8.25\%$. They would like to limit their risk budget to 8% at most.

To achieve their objectives, they are interested in the funds offering of the G–T–N Asset Management Company. Given that they are not certain about the risk exposures that would apply to the Neutral fund, they restrict their choices to an investment in either the Global (**G**) or the Thematic (**T**) fund.

Mrs. Twenty will allocate 20% of her wealth outside the market portfolio, while this proportion amounts to 80% for Mr. Eighty. These investors place themselves in the conditions of a partially constrained allocation with a weight of the disposable portfolio equal to $w_D = 20\%$ for Mrs. Twenty and $w_D = 80\%$ for Mr. Eighty. Their common return objective is a target $\overline{R}^* = 7.00\%$.

The application of the ISM entails, for each investor, successively (i) retrieving the required mean return of the disposable portfolio $\overline{R}_D = \frac{\overline{R}^* - \overline{R}_M}{w_D} + \overline{R}_M$; (ii) determining the weight to be invested in the best candidate portfolio $w_P = w_D \frac{\overline{R}_D - R_f}{\overline{R}_P - R_f}$; and (iii) computing the volatility of the global portfolio. This volatility will be minimized for the portfolio with the highest ISM.

We apply this sequence to the portfolio choices between the Global and Thematic fund investments to be made by Mrs. Twenty and Mr. Eighty and obtain the results as shown in Table 4-8.

TABLE 4-8 G–T–N example – Partially constrained optimal portfolios for different investor types.

			Global		Thematic	
Investor	Disposable weight w_D	Disposable portfolio return $\overline{R}_D$	Weight w_G	Volatility σ_{P*}	Weight w_T	Volatility σ_{P*}
Mrs. Twenty	20%	5.44%	16.16%	8.19%	**24.39%**	**7.94%**
Mr. Eighty	80%	6.90%	**88.28%**	**8.01%**	133.23%	9.52%

Both investors succeed in reducing their global portfolio volatility with the add-on of a fund, but that volatility differs from one person to another.

Mrs. Twenty, who largely sticks to the market portfolio, will be interested in a fund that brings significant active return compared to its required rate of return. She should thus naturally favor a fund with a high Treynor ratio. For her, the ISM criterion leads to $ISM_T = -0.84 > ISM_G = -1.10$. She prefers the Thematic fund, whose Treynor ratio dominates that of the Global fund. The allocation of Mrs. Twenty is $w_M = 80\%$ and $w_T = 24.39\%$. She must borrow 4.39% of her wealth at the risk-free rate to fund her risky positions.

Mr. Eighty is willing to largely depart from the market portfolio, with only a residual investment of 20% in the passive index. His selection criterion is close to that of the fully constrained case (previous subsection). The application of the ISM rule yields $ISM_T = -1.40 < ISM_G = -0.98$. He prefers the Global fund that achieves the highest Sharpe ratio. His allocation is $w_M = 20\%$ and $w_T = 88.28\%$. He must borrow 8.28% of his wealth at the risk-free rate to fund his risky positions.

4.2.3 The unconstrained case

In the discussions of the previous subsections, the investor tries to act rationally but at the same time imposes on themselves holding requirements that hinder the potential risk–return trade-off of the optimal allocation. The fully constrained case entails that the investor can only hold mutually exclusive portfolios without the possibility of combining them. The partially constrained case is less drastic, but it still assumes that the investor deviates from the market portfolio with a predefined allocation rule. Nothing guarantees, of course, that the discretionary disposable weight w_D will be the one that maximizes their expected utility.

Ultimately, the rational investor who does not want to specify any constraint on their asset allocation should try to maximize the Sharpe ratio of the global risky portfolio and then use the risk-free asset to obtain the level of portfolio risk that maximizes their expected utility, as shown in Figure 4-3. However, unlike what happens on that graph, they should remain indifferent to the mix between the market portfolio and any candidate risky portfolio P and test every possible allocation between them. In this context, the investor implements a *core–satellite allocation* process, in which the "core" is the allocation in the passive market portfolio, and the "satellite" is the remaining allocation in the actively managed portfolio. Unlike the core, the satellite is not necessarily meant to have either a constant weight or a unique component.[9]

The Appraisal ratio has a particular role in this context. The AR reflects the potential increase in the Sharpe ratio of the optimal global portfolio held by a rational investor who has access to the risk-free asset, the market portfolio M, and an active portfolio P. Treynor and

[9]We investigate the implications of core–satellite investing in terms of trade-off between risk exposures and performance in more details in Section 16.2.1 of Chapter 16.

Black (1973) show that, provided that the Appraisal ratio of the active portfolio is positive, the optimal weight invested in that portfolio Ω^* will be equal to the following:

$$w_P^* = \frac{x_P}{1 + (1 - \beta_P)x_P} \tag{4-5}$$

where $x_P = \frac{\alpha_P/\sigma_{\varepsilon P}^2}{\overline{R}_M/\sigma_M^2}$, while the remainder is $w_M^* = 1 - w_P^*$ invested in the market portfolio.

The global portfolio Ω^* thus consists of two components: the "core," passive portfolio with weight w_M^*, and the "satellite," active portfolio with weight w_P^*. Under this condition, the maximum Sharpe ratio that can be achieved by the investor will then be the following:

$$SR_{\Omega^*} = \sqrt{SR_M^2 + AR_P^2} \tag{4-6}$$

where $SR_M = \frac{\overline{R}_M - R_f}{\sigma_M}$ is the Sharpe ratio of the market portfolio. SR_{Ω^*} will improve the risk-return trade-off achieved with a passive investment (the market portfolio), provided that AR_P is positive.

Since SR_M is exogenous, the only way for the investor to leverage their Sharpe ratio is to identify a portfolio with a positive value of the Appraisal ratio, presumably as high as possible. Once the optimal risky portfolio is identified, the investor can still use the riskless asset to achieve the allocation that maximizes their expected utility, as shown in Figure 4-3. Figure 4-6 illustrates this optimization process.

The logic underlying the identification of the globally optimal allocation does not need to restrict the choice to a single portfolio. Drilling down into the composition of portfolio P,

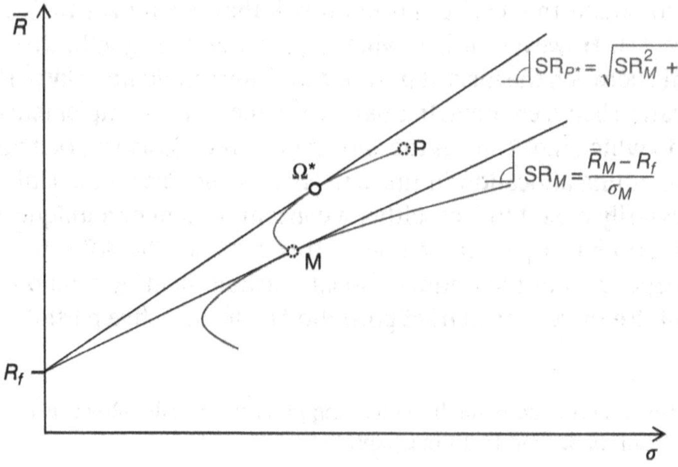

FIGURE 4-6 Unconstrained optimal selection process with the market portfolio (core) and a satellite.

Treynor and Black (1973) further show that the optimum weight of each asset i held within this portfolio P should also be determined by its own Appraisal ratio with the relation

$$w_i^* = \frac{\mathrm{AR}_i/\sigma_{\varepsilon i}^2}{\sum_{i=1}^{N} \mathrm{AR}_i/\sigma_{\varepsilon i}^2} \tag{4-7}$$

Therefore, to build an optimal active portfolio to maximize their Sharpe ratio, the rational investor should adopt the following procedure:

(i) compute the w_i^* according to Equation (4-7) based on each component's Appraisal ratio;
(ii) create the satellite portfolio P whose returns are $R_{P,t} = \sum_{i=1}^{N} w_i^* R_{i,t}$ and calculate its own Jensen's alpha $\alpha_P = \sum_{i=1}^{N} w_i^* \alpha_i$, beta $\beta_P = \sum_{i=1}^{N} w_i^* \beta_i$, and residual risk $\sigma_{\varepsilon P} = \sqrt{\sum_{i=1}^{N} w_i^{*2} \sigma_{\varepsilon i}^2}$;
(iii) determine its optimal weight w_P^* by applying Equation (4-5), while $w_M^* = 1 - w_P^*$.

The resulting portfolio, in which each asset is held with a proportion equal to $w_i^* \times w_P^*$, maximizes the risk–return trade-off with no constraint on the weights invested in each individual asset.[10]

G–T–N example (continued)

With the offering of the G–T–N Asset Management Company, a rational investor could try to create an optimal allocation with the market portfolio. There are two ways through which this allocation can be implemented:

(a) ***By combining the market portfolio with an optimal weight in a single fund***
In such a case, the fund's optimal weight is $w_P^* = \frac{x_P}{1+(1-\beta_P)x_P}$, where $x_P = \frac{\alpha_P/\sigma_{\varepsilon P}^2}{\bar{R}_M/\sigma_M^2}$. Applying this approach to the Global, Thematic, and Neutral funds, we obtain the results as shown in Table 4-9.

(continued)

[10] If no short selling is allowed, i.e., every asset can only be held with a non-negative weight, the same procedure can be applied with the restriction that $w_i^* = \begin{cases} \frac{\mathrm{AR}_i/\sigma_{\varepsilon i}^2}{\sum_{i:\mathrm{AR}_i \geq 0} \mathrm{AR}_i/\sigma_{\varepsilon i}^2} & \text{if } \mathrm{AR}_i > 0 \\ 0 & \text{if } \mathrm{AR}_i \leq 0 \end{cases}$.

(continued)

TABLE 4-9 G–T–N example – Unconstrained optimal portfolios with a single fund.

Fund	Optimal weight w_P^*	Mean return $\overline{R}_{\Omega^*}$	Volatility σ_{Ω^*}	Sharpe ratio SR_{Ω^*}
Global	85.45%	6.54%	7.34%	0.69
Thematic	31.93%	6.54%	7.22%	0.71
Neutral	**41.43%**	**5.38%**	**5.48%**	**0.72**

The best candidate for completing the initial allocation is the Neutral fund (**N**). By combining 58.57% of the investor's wealth in the market portfolio and 41.43% in that fund, the investor obtains the largest improvement of the market Sharpe ratio: $SR_M = 0.67$. Consistent with Equation (4-5), it is the fund with the largest Appraisal ratio, namely, **N** (see Table 4-5), that leads to the best risk–return trade-off $SR_{\Omega^*} = \sqrt{SR_M^2 + AR_N^2} = \sqrt{0.67^2 + 0.26^2} = 0.72$, even though its Sharpe ratio (0.28) is much lower than that of the market (0.67). This outcome, which is strange at first sight, results from the very low correlation between the fund and the market portfolio, thus yielding a very high diversification potential.

(b) ***By combining the market portfolio with an optimally weighted portfolio of each fund***

In such a case, we apply the following sequence: (i) compute the optimal weight invested in each fund inside the satellite portfolio; (ii) retrieve the characteristics (alpha, beta, and AR) of the satellite portfolio; and (iii) compute the optimal weight of the satellite.

The first two steps are summarized in Table 4-10.

The last row of Table 4-10 enables us to apply step (iii) and obtain $x_P = \frac{\alpha_P/\sigma_{\varepsilon P}^2}{\overline{R}_M/\sigma_M^2} = \frac{0.70\%/(1.85\%)^2}{7.39\%/(8.83\%)^2} = 2.15$ and $w_P^* = \frac{x_P}{1+(1-\beta_P)x_P} = \frac{2.15}{1+(1-0.45)\times 2.15} = 98.80\%$.

The optimal portfolio features:

- a core investment in the market portfolio of $w_M^* = 1 - w_P^* = 1.20\%$;
- a satellite investment in funds **G**, **T**, and **N** of respectively $w_G^* \times w_P^* = 48.2\%$, $w_T^* \times w_P^* = 18.5\%$, and $w_N^* \times w_P^* = 32.1\%$.

The mean return and risk of the globally optimum portfolio are $\overline{R}_{\Omega^*} = 4.86\%$ and $\sigma_{\Omega^*} = 4.45\%$, which leads to a "best possible" Sharpe ratio that is indeed equal to the expression of Equation (4-6): $SR_{\Omega^*} = \sqrt{SR_M^2 + AR_P^2} = \sqrt{0.67^2 + (0.70\%/1.85\%)^2} = 0.77$.

TABLE 4-10 G–T–N example – Construction of the optimally weighted portfolio of each fund.

	Step (i)	Step (ii)		
Fund	optimal weight w_i^*	alpha α_i	beta β_i	Residual variance $\sigma_{\varepsilon i}^2$
Global	48.80%	0.30%	0.78	$(1.73\%)^2$
Thematic	18.73%	1.21%	0.35	$(5.62\%)^2$
Neutral	32.47%	1.00%	0.02	$(3.90\%)^2$
Weighted sum	100%	0.70%	0.45	$(1.85\%)^2$

The risk–return properties of the optimal portfolio obtained in Case b are indeed higher than in Case a, as shown in Figure 4-7.

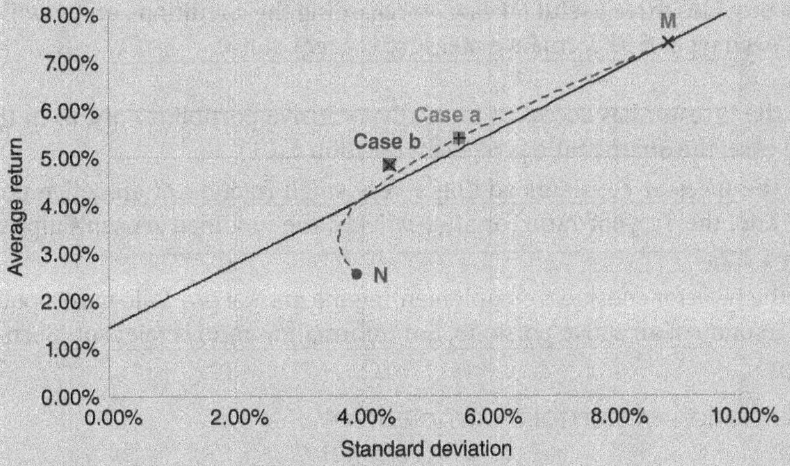

FIGURE 4-7 G–T–N example – Risk–return properties of the optimal portfolios in Case a (single fund) and Case b (weighted combination of the three funds).

Figure 4-7 displays, with the dashed curve, the set of portfolios obtained by combining the market portfolio **M** with the Neutral fund **N**. Even though it has the lowest Sharpe ratio of the three active funds, its very low correlation with the market enables the investor to create a combination with a very high Sharpe ratio, shown on the square located on the curve ("Case a"). However, when all three funds can be combined, the optimal asset allocation achieves a risk–return trade-off that is even better. It is displayed through the square above the curve ("Case b") that lies to the left of the "Case a" portfolio. Both portfolios are above the CML, which confirms that they represent a fruitful improvement over the market portfolio.

4.3 CHOOSING A MEASURE FOR THE INVESTOR: THE POSITIVE APPROACH

In the Section 4.2, we adopted the point of view of an investor who holds (or has access to) the market portfolio and tries to optimally allocate their wealth between different types of funds. The person is supposed to be rational and risk averse and to have relevant information about the risk and return properties of all portfolios before making their choice. The only difference between the three studied cases was the type of constraint that applied to the weights invested in different components of their global portfolio.

From a real-life perspective, the above analysis is probably of limited use for two reasons: (i) it assumes that the investor uses the realized risk and returns as a means of predicting future performance, which is highly questionable as long as there is no strong evidence of persistence in performance;[11] and (ii) since the investor is meant to be rational, they should try to achieve the best Sharpe ratio. Therefore, they should not apply any weighting constraint at all since doing so would devalue the risk–return trade-off of their overall portfolio. Nevertheless, this analysis provides three useful takeaways regarding the conditions under which we might suspect that each type of performance measure is adequate:

- When the investor has access to mutually exclusive portfolios only, as in the fully constrained case, the Sharpe ratio is relevant (Section 4.2.1).
- When the investor considers adding a very small fraction of an active portfolio to an existing one, the Treynor ratio (or alternatively, the modified Jensen's alpha) is relevant (Section 4.2.2).
- When the investor considers complementing the market portfolio with a potentially substantial fraction of an active portfolio, the Information ratio is relevant (Section 4.2.3).

4.3.1 The notion of portfolio complement

In the normative case discussed above, the market portfolio represents the baseline of the asset allocation decision. This initial position is then possibly incremented with an investment in one or several actively managed portfolios or funds to shape the investor's global allocation.

However, in reality, when the performance of a particular portfolio is reported to the customer, we are usually in an *ex post* perspective. The baseline information that is known by the relationship manager is the amount actually or to be allocated in that very portfolio. The remainder of the investor's wealth and how it is itself invested represent information that must be retrieved – or guessed – to assess how the global asset allocation has been constructed. Thus, the logic is reversed compared to the previous situation; the actively managed portfolio is the core of the allocation, and the rest gravitates around it.

[11]The issue of performance persistence is discussed in Chapter 17.

The above leads to the notion of a "complement" portfolio (Cavé, Hübner, and Lejeune, 2013). Knowing its composition is necessary to ascertain which performance measure should be used to meet the investor's legitimate expectations about how their active portfolio has been managed. Even though there is a potentially infinite number of situations that can arise, Bodie, Kane, and Marcus (2018) identify three of them that are relevant for the selection of an appropriate performance measure.[12] These three cases are examined in detail below.

- *No complement*: The active portfolio is considered the sole exposure to financial assets of the investor.
- *Active complement*: The active portfolio is complemented by a significant amount invested in other actively managed portfolios that, altogether, constitute a well-diversified allocation in financial assets.
- *Passive complement*: The active portfolio is complemented by a significant amount invested in a passive, well-diversified allocation in financial assets.

The investor naturally knows whether they have a complement portfolio and presumably also the type of complement. On the other side of the table, however, the portfolio manager does not necessarily hold the same level and quality of information. It could then be necessary to retrieve information from the customer. This task is not an easy one, though. A professional fund manager typically does not have detailed information about their individual investors. Even the relationship manager, who has direct contacts with their wealthy client in the scope of a discretionary or advisory mandate, might have difficulty obtaining information about the rest of the customer's assets. Therefore, it is often useful to anticipate the reasons for which each of the three cases (no, passive, or active complement) is likely to prevail. These reasons can be of two kinds: (i) the *nature of the managed portfolio* corresponds to one of the three cases; or (ii) the *situation of the investor* is such that it can be deduced that one of the three cases applies to them. For each case, we will try to identify the most obvious circumstances – without necessarily being exhaustive – that call for the use of a performance measure that would be more relevant than the others.

4.3.2 The case with no complement

The simplest case is the one where the investor is not supposed to hold any significant stake in a portfolio of financial assets other than the one whose performance is appraised because such a case is merely the equivalent of the "fully constrained case" described in Section 4.2.1. Since the investor is supposed to have invested all their wealth in a single portfolio, its total risk is the only matter of interest regarding the input of performance measurement. The *Sharpe ratio* is thus the right measure on which the performance of the portfolio manager is to be assessed.

[12]While the authors previously used the terminology of "complementary portfolios," they no longer explicitly refer to this notion in the 11th edition of their famous *Investments* textbook. However, they still apply the same logic in their analysis.

4.3.2.1 Nature of the portfolio

There are different types of portfolios whose performance is naturally prone to be appraised on the basis of their total risk:

- *Globally diversified funds in risky asset classes*: The clear ambition of these portfolios is to resemble as much as possible the theoretical market portfolio. Even though their risk level might not correspond to each investor's risk appetite, they can be combined with investment in fixed-income securities or portfolios to modify their risk level without altering their Sharpe ratio. Such funds position themselves as substitutes for the market portfolio; therefore, their total risk adequately reflects the input to be considered for performance measurement.
- *Allocation funds*: Compared with the previous type of portfolio, an allocation fund completes the allocation in risky assets with investment in fixed-income securities to achieve a desired level of allocation in asset classes that is supposed to remain steady over time. Such funds, ranging from the most aggressive (high equity risk) to the most defensive (low equity risk) ones, combine the choice of the global allocation fund with that of portfolio leverage into one single patrimonial vehicle. They target people who look for a one-size-fits-all portfolio corresponding to their whole investment in financial assets.
- *Lifecycle funds*: These types of fund, which include most pension fund investments, simultaneously consider the investor's risk aversion and investment horizon to determine the portfolio's strategic allocation. As time passes, the investment horizon becomes closer, and the fund reduces its risk level by changing the mix between more or less risky assets. Since the fund managers consider that, at the end of the investment horizon, the investor will need the liquidation value of the fund to sustain their standard of living, this portfolio is naturally associated with the full financial investment of the beneficiary.

4.3.2.2 Situation of the investor

- *Diversified discretionary portfolio management mandate*: This situation is the wealth management counterpart of allocation funds but possibly tailored for individual investors or families. The manager may suspect or even know that the investor has one or several other investments besides that mandate, and even that the same mandate coexists among different private banks. Nevertheless, the portfolio ought to be managed as though there was no complement portfolio because that is the nature of the contract that has been sealed with the customer. Thus, total risk should be the input for performance measurement.
- *Portfolio aggregation*: Some investors or groups of investors simultaneously hold stakes in different portfolios, be it to diversify the asset management counterparties or because each portfolio has a particular set of characteristics (in terms of asset classes, levels of

liquidity, or identity of the owners). Often, these people appoint an "orchestra conductor" whose holistic view will enable them to allocate funds in different compartments to maintain a global coherence. This task is typically performed by a family office in the case of ultrahigh-net-worth individuals or families, but it can also be performed at a more modest scale by a competent finance professional. At the level of the aggregate portfolio that by definition has no complement, the appropriate measure to be considered is thus total risk.

- *Single significant investment*: The investor might not, for various reasons, behave with the rationality that underlies the SPT framework. Some people hold a large portfolio of assets or occasionally even a single financial asset. There can be several reasons for this seemingly strange behavior. Some persons may have accidentally inherited a portfolio and do not truly care about reallocating it. Others may voluntarily choose to concentrate their investments in a very limited number of assets because they firmly believe that the expected rate of return is so high that it largely compensates for their idiosyncratic risk.[13] There are even investors who simply do not want to diversify more than their underdiversified existing portfolio, for instance who may suffer from a "home bias" or a "sector bias," or who deliberately restrict their investment universe with ESG criteria.[14] In all cases, the principle is the same; even if the portfolio is known to largely diverge from the market portfolio, for good or bad reasons, the investor is fully exposed to total risk, and the Sharpe ratio will have to be applied to evaluate portfolio performance.

4.3.3 The case with an active complement

The case in which the investor considers that an actively managed portfolio also has an active complement looks similar to a mirroring situation because the portfolio under study is itself the active complement of the rest. To grasp the investor's point of view, it is necessary to consider the rationale for having only active portfolios or funds in their global allocation. Their intent is probably to build up a well-diversified aggregate portfolio by combining various specific investments in different asset classes, geographical zones, sectors, and styles. Even though each component alone is not necessarily very diversified, the combination clears away specific risk with the same mechanism as depicted in Figure 4-2. Specifically, expressing the portfolio's excess rate of return according to the market model,

$$R_{P,t} - R_f = \alpha_P + \beta_P(R_{M,t} - R_f) + \varepsilon_{P,t} \tag{4-8}$$

[13]This scenario describes the situation of an entrepreneur, for instance, who is led to concentrate their investments in a single venture with the hope of capturing a significant upside from the project. Another relevant situation is the one of a real estate investor who engages in a buy-to-let transaction. Those two situations are analyzed in detail in Section 16.3.3 of Chapter 16.

[14]The performance of funds that include sustainability criteria is studied in Section 16.4 of Chapter 16.

where β_P and $\varepsilon_{P,t}$ represent, respectively, the beta and the residual return of the portfolio. The goal of the investor is to combine many assets such that the impact of each of their residual returns on the global portfolio becomes negligible through the benefit of portfolio diversification.

For this bottom-up approach to work well, the weight of each individual portfolio holding should be low enough. Specifically, if each actively managed portfolio i is present with a weight w_i in the investor's global portfolio Ω, we have the following:

$$\sigma_\Omega = \sqrt{\sum_{i=1}^{N} w_i^2 \beta_i^2 \sigma_M^2 + \sum_{i=1}^{N}\sum_{j=1}^{N} w_i w_j \rho_{\varepsilon_i\varepsilon_j} \sigma_{\varepsilon_i} \sigma_{\varepsilon_j}} \approx \sqrt{\left(\sum_{i=1}^{N} w_i^2 \beta_i^2\right)} \sigma_M \tag{4-9}$$

where σ_{ε_i} is the specific risk of portfolio i, and $\rho_{\varepsilon_i\varepsilon_j}$ is the Pearson correlation coefficient between the specific component of portfolios i and j.

Note that the term that almost disappears from the square root in Equation (4-9) is $\sum_{i=1}^{N}\sum_{j=1}^{N} w_i w_j \rho_{\varepsilon_i\varepsilon_j} \sigma_{\varepsilon_i} \sigma_{\varepsilon_j} = \sum_{i=1}^{N} w_i^2 \sigma_{\varepsilon_i}^2 + 2\sum_{i=1}^{N}\sum_{\substack{j=1 \\ j \neq i}}^{N} w_i w_j \rho_{\varepsilon_i\varepsilon_j} \sigma_{\varepsilon_i} \sigma_{\varepsilon_j}$. For this result to occur, both terms of the latter expression must be close to zero. Thus, what the expression for σ_Ω simply means is that it is possible to build a well-diversified global portfolio if its individual components have (i) low weights and (ii) low correlations between their specific components. A successful bottom-up portfolio construction approach therefore entails that each individual portfolio should be held in a small proportion and that there is no "shadow" source of risk that would commonly influence many individual portfolios.

If Equation (4-9) holds, i.e., if the aggregate portfolio Ω successfully evacuates most of the specific risk, then we can also express the global portfolio return as a function of an active portfolio P and the $N-1$ other assets: $R_{\Omega,t} = w_P R_{P,t} + \sum_{i=1}^{N-1} w_i R_{i,t}$. Since the idiosyncratic risk of the second part of this equation fades away in this portfolio, we can conveniently re-express it as

$$R_{\Omega',t} \approx w'_P R_{P,t} + (1 - w'_P) R_{M,t} \tag{4-10}$$

where $R_{\Omega',t} = \frac{R_{\Omega,t} - \sum_{i=1}^{N-1} w_i \alpha_i}{w_P + \sum_{i=1}^{N-1} w_i \beta_i}$ is the deleveraged normal return of the aggregate portfolio, and $w'_P = \frac{\sum_{i=1}^{N-1} w_i \beta_i}{w_P + \sum_{i=1}^{N-1} w_i \beta_i}$ is the weight of the return of P in that portfolio.

Equation (4-10) suggests that we are in precisely the same case as in Section 4.2.2, which analyzed the partially constrained case, but with the special circumstance that w'_P (which has the same meaning as the weight of the disposable portfolio w_D under that analysis) is very small. This case corresponds to what Scholz and Wilkens (2005) obtain as a corollary to Equation (4-4):

$$\text{ISM}_P|_{\overline{R}^* \to R_M} > \text{ISM}_Q|_{\overline{R}^* \to R_M} \Leftrightarrow \text{TR}_P > \text{TR}_Q \tag{4-11}$$

Thus, in the context of a multitude of small investments in actively managed portfolios that aim to globally constitute a well-diversified portfolio, the quality of each manager should be assessed on the basis of their systematic risk-adjusted performance. Because the rankings of portfolios based on the *Treynor ratio* and the *modified Jensen's alpha* are identical, both measures can be used interchangeably, for that matter.

In the case of a benchmarked portfolio, we obtain a result similar to that of Equation (4-10). Consider, for instance, a mutual fund whose investment universe is restricted to Canadian stocks and whose benchmark is the S&P/TSX index. The portfolio rate of return can be expressed as $R_{P,t} - R_f = \alpha_P + \beta_{P,B}(R_{B,t} - R_f) + \varepsilon_{P,B,t}$, where $\beta_{P,B}$ and $\varepsilon_{P,B,t}$ represent, respectively, the beta and the residual return of the portfolio with respect to its benchmark index $B \equiv$ S&P/TSX. Meanwhile, the benchmark itself is connected to the (worldwide) market portfolio through the same CAPM relation but without any alpha since the index is a passive portfolio with no abnormal return; thus, $R_{B,t} - R_f = \beta_{B,M}(R_{M,t} - R_f) + \varepsilon_{B,M,t}$. Combining both equations yields $R_{P,t} - R_f = \alpha_P + \beta_P(R_{M,t} - R_f) + \varepsilon_{P,t}$, where $\beta_P \equiv \beta_{P,B}\beta_{B,M}$ and $\varepsilon_{P,t} \equiv \varepsilon_{P,B,t} + \beta_{P,B}\varepsilon_{B,M,t}$, and we return to the logic of Equation (4-9). However, given that the beta of the benchmark with respect to the market portfolio is beyond the reach of the portfolio manager, it is practically appropriate to use the benchmark beta, and not the aggregate market beta, as the measure of systematic risk underlying the computation of the risk-adjusted performance.

4.3.3.1 Nature of the portfolio

Portfolios that are prone to being analyzed with performance measures using systematic risk are those that address a very specific, relatively small component of the market portfolio, whatever it is. It is impossible to provide an exhaustive list of all types of portfolios that share these characteristics, but there are a few archetypes:

- Thematic *equity or bond funds*: Many fund managers have a commitment that restricts them to a specific group of equities or fixed-income instruments. Such commitments can be contractual – the investment policy is restricted by a charter or a mandate – or convictional – the manager wants to limit the scope of their investments to the regions, zones, or styles in which they feel better armed to outperform a passive benchmark. A portfolio whose eligible investment universe is deliberately narrow can pretend to play neither the role of the market portfolio (as in Section 4.3.2.1) nor the role of a diversifying satellite (as in Section 4.3.4.1). Rather, it falls under the scope of the natural contributor of a global portfolio made up of actively managed components.
- *Funds that represent a subset of an asset class*: There are many funds that do not fully exploit the diversification possibilities within a particular asset class. A European commercial real estate fund or a southeast Asian buyout private equity fund, for instance, is not representative of the real estate or private equity classes. Even though such funds have their merits, for the same reason as above, they should not be considered by their nature a suitable single add-on of a passive portfolio.

- *Direct line investments*: Many portfolios feature direct lines, i.e., investments made in a single stock, bond, or other financial asset issued by a single counterparty. The reasons for holding these individual assets can be very diverse, but the decision to keep them must be somehow related to the hope of achieving a superior rate of return. Given that, in the context of the CAPM, their required rate of return is computed according to the SML and depends on their beta, their *ex post* performance should also be appraised through a measure that takes systematic risk into account.

4.3.3.2 Situation of the investor

- *Part of a* global *portfolio patchwork*: Such a situation is the mirror case of the first two items of the list above but considered from a holistic perspective. If the investor has chosen to devote several fractions of their global portfolio to thematic investments in stocks, bonds, or other asset classes, with a clear ambition to outperform a benchmark index or portfolio for each of these compartments, this case is clearly one justifying the use of systematic risk. Even though the global portfolio performance is to be evaluated with the Sharpe ratio, its thematic components require the use of the Treynor ratio or the modified Jensen's alpha.
- *Subportfolio mandate with identified expertise*: Some investors may choose to dedicate a small portion of their managed assets to a thematic investment in which they consider having access to particular expertise. This choice can be driven not only by objective considerations, such as access to a portfolio manager with a proven track record, but also by very subjective motivations. This case includes the self-management of a small pocket of the portfolio with a trading approach or a "home bias" – the conviction that local asset managers have superior skills for the selection of local or national assets. Irrespective of how the rest of the investor's wealth is managed, and provided that the weight of these portfolios is very peripheral, it is likely that the suitable measure of risk is the beta with respect to the corresponding benchmark.

4.3.4 The case with a passive complement

Why would an investor who holds the market portfolio want to allocate part of their resources in an actively managed fund or portfolio? How this question is phrased suggests that the case of a passive complement actually corresponds to an incremental asset allocation approach; the passive complement is the starting point, the "core" of the allocation, and the investor departs from this anchor with the hope of generating an extra return that more than compensates for the extra risk that has been taken.

There are different ways to answer the question above. The first one is to consider that the investor acts rationally in the context of the Treynor and Black (1973) framework described in Section 4.2.3. The sequence proceeds as follows: they (i) start from a full investment in the market portfolio, then (ii) optimally combine it with the best possible actively managed portfolio, and finally (iii) choose a level of leverage to maximize their expected utility. In this normative framework, the Sharpe ratio of the global optimum Ω^* is given by Equation (4-6): $SR_{\Omega^*} = \sqrt{SR_M^2 + AR_P^2}$.

The second answer is still related to a rational behavior but adopts a different – and presumably more realistic – sequence: they (i) start from a full investment in the market portfolio, then (ii) choose a level of leverage to maximize their expected utility, and finally (iii) combine this utility-maximizing portfolio with the best possible actively managed portfolio to further enhance their satisfaction. This case is discussed by Grinold and Kahn (1995).[15] To solve this sequential optimization problem, they introduce the notion of the investor's level of residual risk aversion, which they denote by λ_R. The objective is to maximize the additional expected utility of the portfolio, called the value added (VA_P). They obtain that the value added of the global optimum Ω^* is given by the following:

$$VA_{\Omega^*} = \frac{IR_P^2}{4\lambda_R} \tag{4-12}$$

The last answer is not normative but simply results from a discretionary decision to allocate part of the investor's wealth in an actively managed portfolio without explicitly attempting to meet any quantitative utility maximization criteria. This approach is the "real-life" case in which the investor extracts $w\%$ of their initial allocation in a well-diversified portfolio M to invest in an actively managed one P. The return of the global (but not necessarily optimal this time) portfolio Ω of the investor (before investing in the risk-free asset) is thus equal to $R_{\Omega,t} = wR_{P,t} + (1-w)R_{M,t}$, and its global performance is measured by its Sharpe ratio SR_Ω.

How does SR_Ω depend on the performance of portfolio P? The answer is given by Hallerbach (2005) with simple algebra. It suffices to note that, in general, this Sharpe ratio can be written as follows:

$$SR_\Omega = \rho_{\Omega M} SR_M + \sqrt{1-\rho_{\Omega M}^2} AR_\Omega \tag{4-13}$$

where $\rho_{\Omega M}$ is the Pearson correlation coefficient between the returns of portfolios Ω and M.

Hallerbach (2005) notes that, in this configuration, $\rho_{\Omega M} = \rho_{PM}$ and $AR_\Omega = AR_P$. Applying this property to Equation (4-13), he immediately obtains the following identity:

$$\Delta SR_\Omega \equiv SR_\Omega - SR_M = \sqrt{1-\rho_{PM}^2} AR_P - (1-\rho_{PM}) SR_M \tag{4-14}$$

Thus, the improvement brought to its passive complement by the actively managed portfolio P depends on two factors: (i) its correlation with the market portfolio (i.e., its diversifying power) and (ii) its performance, measured by the Appraisal ratio.

[15]See Section 16.3.1 of Chapter 16 for a detailed analysis.

Overall, whatever route is pursued to answer the introductory question of this subsection, the answer will always depend on a single type of performance measure – the one that uses specific risk as an input, namely, the *Information ratio* or its CAPM-related version, the *Appraisal ratio*.

4.3.4.1 Nature of the portfolio

In general, funds or portfolios whose performance should preferably be appraised on the basis of their specific risk are meant to achieve a positive outcome of Equation (4-14). There are two ways of attaining it: through the diversification potential of the portfolio (ρ_{PM}) and/or due to a superior active risk/active return trade-off (IR_P). Various types of portfolios supposedly feature these characteristics. We refer to three families of funds based on their strategy types (multi-strategy hedge funds, managed futures funds, and alternative asset classes) and a broad category of funds based on their risk or return objectives (absolute return funds and total return funds), keeping in mind that there are possible overlaps between them (for instance, many hedge funds aim at achieving an absolute return objective).

- *Multi-strategy hedge funds*: Hedge funds are not a homogeneous asset class, and there is no single definition of a "hedge fund." Rather, there are a set of characteristics that are common to most hedge funds and probably help in determining whether an actively managed fund can be considered a hedge fund: their investor base (usually targeting private or institutional clients), their legal and regulatory structure (usually less strict than mutual funds), their low level of liquidity, their use of sophisticated financial instruments or strategies, and their uncommon risk and return objectives (usually driven toward absolute returns with little or no systematic risk).[16] It is possible to find hedge funds that do not correspond to any one or several of the above criteria, but what is important here is their aim to diverge from traditional investment strategies (i.e., buying and selling stocks, bonds and money market instruments) to generate returns that are not easily explained by traditional asset pricing models. They are in principle never meant to replace a well-diversified portfolio but rather stand as their complement. Therefore, they naturally correspond to the "passive complement" case, and not, unlike what many fact sheets of hedge funds suggest, the "no complement" case in which the Sharpe ratio or similar performance measures would be appropriate.
- *Managed futures funds*: These funds, also historically called "Commodity Trading Advisors", represent the other category of so-called "modern alternative investments" (Lhabitant, 2006). Managers of these funds seek to exploit anomalies in the functioning of financial markets. To do so, they can implement various trading mechanisms (from algorithmic-based to purely discretionary) with rebalancing at various frequencies

[16] Many hedge funds involve complex risk and return property characteristics. They will be studied in more detail in Section 12.4 of Chapter 12.

(from multiple times per day or even second to several weeks or months), but they have a preference for the use of derivatives – especially futures contracts – because of their usually high liquidity, low transaction costs, and huge leverage possibilities. There is much empirical evidence about their substantial diversification properties (low correlation with stock or bond indexes) across time periods, including under very severe market stress. Thus, even though they might not generate very large alphas, their merits are mostly to be found in the low value of ρ_{PM} in Equation (4-14).[17]

- *Alternative asset classes*: In addition to investment in stocks and bonds, financial investors also have access to a very large set of investment possibilities in other asset classes, which are essentially securitized versions of real or illiquid assets. These assets include (but are not limited to) real estate, private equity, art and collectibles, leveraged loans, etc. Although these are theoretically part of the market portfolio, they are seldom considered in traditional asset allocation, possibly due, for some of them, to their relatively low liquidity, the investor's reluctance to allocate funds in some types of assets, their relative economic insignificance in the market portfolio, or simply because they are neglected in the allocation process. They can be viewed as return enhancers (reaping an illiquidity premium), risk diversifiers (being exposed to uncommon sources of risk), or both. Thus, when they are considered in isolation, funds that are specialized in alternative asset classes should preferably be analyzed according to their exposure to specific risk.
- *Target risk or return funds or portfolios*: This category of funds, without necessarily belonging to the hedge fund world, pursues the objective of achieving a target rate of return or not exceeding a target level of risk regardless of the market circumstances. These funds are termed "total return funds" and "absolute return funds," respectively. Unlike allocation funds described above, their compass is not based on asset allocation but on risk or return control. For them, the end justifies the means; they must accept a certain variability of their asset allocation over time, and they often use hedge fund-like techniques such as gearing, short selling, or derivative trading as ways to fulfill their goal. Even though these funds typically refuse to have a well-defined benchmark, their performance should usually be assessed from the point of view of the investor with a passive complement simply because they do not replace the market portfolio but rather complete it.

4.3.4.2 Situation of the investor

- *Core–satellite investment mandate*: This type of management typically corresponds to the reasoning made initially by Treynor and Black (1973). Even when there is no explicit attempt to optimize the weight invested in the satellite portfolio, the philosophy of the

[17]We can also associate Global Macro hedge funds, which do not necessarily use the same tools but share a similar philosophy, with the category.

mandate is to associate a passive, well-diversified portfolio (the "core") with an actively managed one (the "satellite"). From the point of view of the satellite, the "core" is a passive complement; thus, the performance of the active portfolio should be evaluated with the Information ratio or a similar measure.

- *Stuck investment*: There are many situations in which the investor's global portfolio does not fully result from a voluntary and dynamic asset allocation process. Some investments are frozen, occasionally for a long period. These can be intrinsically illiquid investments, such as a participation in a private equity fund, or portfolios in which the investor has committed to keep their stake up to a certain level, such as a loan to a related business. Whatever the rationale for the initial investment decision, it is represented in the global portfolio. The leading principle should be that the stuck investment, as it does not correspond to a decision to invest in a portfolio that mimics the market portfolio, should be appraised according to its specific risk.

4.3.5 Wrap-up: When to use or not to use a performance measure

The list of situations in which the three kinds of classical performance measures are likely to be adequate is not meant to be exhaustive but rather representative of several situations. They can be summarized in Table 4-11.

In addition to some minor cases that are also relevant but ignored in Table 4-11, there are several situations in which *none* of the three sets of performance measures can be considered suitable. They include the following three particular cases:

- *Single-strategy hedge funds or equivalent*: A single-strategy hedge fund is usually a rather concentrated portfolio following a strategy that is very remote from the behavior of traditional asset classes (stocks and bonds) dominant in the market portfolio. Such funds represent a hybrid vehicle between target risk or target return funds (requiring specific risk-based performance measurement) and funds that represent a subset of an asset class – in this case, the hedge funds universe (requiring systematic risk-based performance measurement). The huge specific risk of such funds prevents them from bringing reasonable added value to a passive complement as suggested in Equation (4-12). On the other hand, the very low significance of the relation between their returns and those of the market portfolio hinders the application of a measure such as the Treynor ratio, for which the beta appears in the denominator. Many managers or analysts are tempted to use the Jensen's alpha alone or the Sharpe ratio to appraise the performance of single-strategy hedge funds, but the solution is fallacious in both cases; Jensen's alpha is meaningless if the market model is misspecified, while the Sharpe ratio is not appropriate at all in this context. These types of funds require the development and use of alternative performance measures (see Eling and Schuhmacher, 2007, for a discussion), which is the subject of Chapter 6.
- *Market timing portfolio strategies*: An active portfolio manager who seeks to "beat the market" must retain some skills. These skills belong to two families: asset selection and

TABLE 4-11 Summary of the situations pertaining to the use of different types of risks.

Type of risk	Type of complement	Nature of the portfolio	Situation of the investor
Total risk	None	• Globally diversified funds in risky asset classes • Allocation funds • Lifecycle funds	• Diversified discretionary portfolio management mandate • Portfolio aggregation • Single significant investment
Systematic risk	Active	• Thematic equity or bond funds • Funds that represent a subset of an asset class • Direct line investments	• Part of a global portfolio patchwork • Subportfolio mandate with identified expertise
Specific risk	Passive	• Multi-strategy hedge funds • Managed futures funds • Alternative asset classes • Target risk or return funds	• Core–satellite investment mandate • Stuck investment

market timing. If the manager heavily relies on the second, doing so involves trying to modify their exposure to the market portfolio (i.e., the beta) according to their anticipation of the sign and magnitude of market movements. None of the classical measures developed in the context of the CAPM are adapted to that kind of situation. The Sharpe ratio does not use the beta as input, but its value does not fully reflect the nonlinear dependence between the active portfolio return and that of a passive index. The other performance measures are simply not able to reflect the impact of time variability of betas in the true abnormal return and will generally deliver a biased estimate of portfolio risk-adjusted performance. The case of market timing funds is studied in Chapter 8.

- *Structured funds*: For reasons that are technically similar to those described with market timing funds, many structured funds cannot be analyzed with classical performance measures.[18] The explanation lies in the fact that these funds typically use options or similar trading strategies to reach their desired objective. Therefore, neither their volatility nor their beta or tracking error can reflect their true risk. As a famous example, consider the simple case of a world index fund. When gross-of-fee-returns are considered, its Sharpe ratio should be roughly equal to that of the passive index. If a manager decides to implement a traditional covered call strategy with the same index, i.e., simultaneously hold it and write out-of-the-money call options on that same

[18] We study the case of these kinds of products in Section 16.2.2 of Chapter 16.

index, they will presumably observe a lower average excess rate of return, but most importantly a more-than-proportional decrease in the volatility of returns. The joint impact of these two effects on the Sharpe ratio will thus be positive. Thus, by implementing a mechanical strategy (i.e., "passive" from the point of view of the objective of delivering active returns), the manager can enhance their risk-adjusted performance. Is that a "free lunch"? Of course not; the price to pay for raising the Sharpe ratio is a decrease in upside potential that is triggered by the sale of the options. This kind of situation, in which traditional performance is obviously not appropriate, is analyzed in Chapter 18.

G–T–N example (continued)

Mr. November, who died recently, was the father of three daughters: May, June, and July. One year ago, he had anticipated his demise and decided to make a donation of $450 000 to each of his beloved children. May left her money in a savings account. June decided to split her investments into various mutual funds taken from a list, prepared by her private banker, of selected active managers in different types of markets, but she has no exposure to her domestic (US) bond market. Finally, July bought global equity and global bond ETFs with an allocation that corresponded to her investor's profile.

Today, the three sisters each obtain an additional $50 000 from their father's heritage. This time, they decide to coordinate their investment decisions. They call a relationship manager of the G–T–N Asset Management Company to obtain advice about the best possible allocation of their available financial resources within the firm's funds offering.

Based upon the information provided by each sister, the relationship manager should formulate the recommendation as summarized in Table 4-12.

TABLE 4-12 G–T–N example – Fund advice corresponding to each investor's situation.

Investor name	Amount	Complement	Type of mandate	Type of suitable fund	Fund name	Performance measure
May	$500 000	None	Diversified discretionary portfolio management	Globally diversified funds in risky asset classes	**Global (G)**	SR_P
June	$50 000	Active	Global portfolio patchwork	Thematic equity or bond funds	**Thematic (T)**	$m\alpha_P$
July	$50 000	Passive	Core–satellite investment	Target risk or return funds	**Neutral (N)**	IR_P

It appears from the table that the range of G–T–N's funds offering perfectly matches the needs of the firm's customers. Furthermore, how these funds were managed to date should provide comfort to the three sisters:

- For May, who cares about total risk and who should refer to the Sharpe ratio, Table 4-6 reveals that **G** > **M** > **T** > **N**, where **M** stands for the market portfolio.
- For June, who cares about systematic risk and who should refer to the modified Jensen's alpha, Table 4-6 reveals that **T** > **G** > **M**, while, from a qualitative point of view, fund **N** is not suitable because she should complete her allocation with an investment in her domestic bond market, which this fund does not provide.
- For July, who cares about specific risk and who should refer to the Information ratio, Table 4-6 reveals that **N** > **T** > **G** > **M**.

4.4 CHOOSING A MEASURE FOR THE MANAGER

In the asset management world, the relations between the manager and the ultimate investor can be very diverse, from very close to very remote. At one end of the spectrum, some customers want to be directly involved in their portfolio management decisions. In such cases, the manager cannot ignore the situation of the investor and the exact scope of the mandate given. The previous section fully applies to their choice of performance measures and excludes almost any other consideration. At the other end of the spectrum, a vast majority of mutual funds have a multitude of anonymous clients, with various needs and situations. Their managers can – and probably should – anticipate what could be the most suitable performance measures for their clientele based on the nature of their fund, as indicated in the third column of Table 4-11. In that "investor-driven" case, they must try to maximize the efficiency of their active management according to this sole criterion. However, in their professional world, managers should also care about how they will be assessed by their hierarchy and by their peers, which might lead them to prioritize the performance measure on which they know that they will be judged, regardless of their client's interest. This scenario is the "manager-driven" case.

Why would the manager's situation matter for the selection of a performance measure? There are many potential reasons, but we highlight two of them. First, taking the manager's point of view may lead to a correct assessment of their true active management skills over a certain fixed period, which could ease the comparison with other asset managers who are active in similar markets or instruments. This matter is of importance not only for investors, who should legitimately care about the quality of the person who will manage their assets, but also for the asset management companies that need some objective metrics to select, reward, or sanction their employees.

A second reason for considering the manager's perspective is related to the detection of persistence in performance. This notion refers to the evidence of the reproducibility of active returns over time. Indeed, if there exist superior skills among a set of managers, this observation should not be limited to one period; such an approach would simply be nothing but luck. Rather, a manager's quality does not fade away rapidly; thus, one should normally be able to detect it over several periods of time. There is however a double condition to be fulfilled, i.e., not only the presence of superior portfolio management skill but also the adequate measurement of this skill. Thus, understanding how the manager works, and how their performance should be evaluated, is a necessary condition to identify their ability to display persistent performance over time.

The issue of choosing the right performance measure from the manager's point of view is not restricted to the classical performance measures studied in this chapter. Since there are many other ways to assess the performance of an actively managed portfolio beyond the traditional Sharpe, Treynor, or Information ratios, the discussion presented below can be generalized to any analogous context with alternative performance measures.

4.4.1 The ranking stability criterion

Both justifications for adopting the manager's perspective are mostly related to a comparison of performances. Thus, we are less interested in their absolute levels than in their relative standings. Therefore, the preliminary condition for choosing the appropriate measure is to construct a peer group. Then, assuming that we have the right group of competing managers, the selection of the most relevant performance measure will be driven by the quality of how it ranks the portfolios. This quality is assessed by the statistical notion of *ranking stability*.

From a rigorous perspective, this concept was introduced in the context of bioinformatics by Siebourg, Merdes, Misselwitz, Hardt, and Beerenwinkel (2012) on the basis of the stability selection approach by Meinshausen and Bühlmann (2010). When adapted to the classification of portfolios, it provides a measure of a fund's stability associated with some cutoff percentile k by computing the probability that the fund will be ranked among the top $k\%$ ones under alternative validation experiments, i.e., rankings according to the same performance measures but in different conditions. If we fix a threshold for the minimum level of frequency π that is necessary for a fund to be considered stable, the quality of the performance measure can be assessed by the number of funds fulfilling this condition, called the "stable set." Formally, if there is a set N of funds or portfolios to be ranked and we create m alternative classifications using a given performance measure, then the stable set is expressed as

$$\hat{\Lambda}_{k,\pi}^{\text{perf.}} = \left\{ n \in N \mid \hat{\Pi}_k^n \geq \pi \right\} \tag{4-15}$$

where $\widehat{\Pi}_k^n = \frac{1}{m}\sum_{i=1}^{m} 1_{\{n\in\Lambda_k(i)\}}$ is the frequency at which portfolio n belongs to the stable set $\Lambda_k(i)$ generated with each alternative classification $i = 1, \ldots, m$, and $1_{\{n\in\Lambda_k(i)\}}$ is a binary function that takes value 1 if $n \in \Lambda_k(i)$ and 0 otherwise.

For instance, imagine that we have $N = 100$ funds that are ranked, from the best (#1) to the worst (#100), according to their Sharpe ratio over a period of three years with weekly observations. We are interested in the top quintile funds, i.e., $k = 20$. We decide to divide the period in quarters and recompute the Sharpe ratio of each fund for each of the 12 quarters. Some funds will often be included in the top 20, some much less frequently. Suppose that we consider "stable" a fund that is in the first quintile during at least 9 quarters out of 12, i.e., $\pi = 75\%$. This condition is satisfied by a stable set $\widehat{\Lambda}_{20;75\%}^{SR}$ of 15 funds. Alternatively, consider the Information ratio. We repeat the same procedure and obtain a stable set $\widehat{\Lambda}_{20;75\%}^{IR}$ of 12 funds. According to the ranking stability criterion, the Sharpe ratio produces a larger stable set than does the Information ratio.

A valuable side result of this criterion is to provide an assessment of each fund's real rank under a considered performance measure. Siebourg et al. (2012) observe that stable sets are nested; if a portfolio is in the top-k list, then it will also be in the top-k' list for $k' > k$. Thus, the best fund (the one that first enters the top-k list when k increases) will also be in the list of the best-two funds, which means that the other fund must be the second-best one and so on. The "true" rank of a fund according to a performance measure is thus equal to the order in which it enters the stable set:

$$\mathrm{rk}_{\pi}^{\mathrm{perf.}}(n) = |\widehat{\Lambda}_{k^*;\pi}^{\mathrm{perf.}}|, \text{where } k^* = \min\{k|\widehat{\Pi}_k^n \geq \pi\} \tag{4-16}$$

where $|\widehat{\Lambda}_{k^*;\pi}^{\mathrm{perf.}}|$ is the cardinality of the stable set at value k^*, i.e., the number of funds that will be in the top-k^* list with probability π. The relation between the ranking cutoff k and the number of stable funds is represented in Figure 4-8 with the figures used in the above example.

The graph simultaneously shows the size of the stable set for each cutoff value (which permits identifying the ranking of each fund by observing the order in which it enters the stable set) and the ranking quality of each performance measure. In our example, the Sharpe ratio lets funds enter the stable set more quickly, i.e., provides more stable rankings, than does the Information ratio.

In practice, however, this approach is difficult to apply in the context of portfolio performance for different reasons. First, the ranking stability criterion heavily relies on the fact that there exists a true, hidden ranking, and there is one performance measure that is able to reproduce this ranking better than any other one. In reality, however, there is a strong uncertainty about whether there is any deterministic order in the quality of the funds. Perhaps only a minority of the managers exhibit skills that translate into superior risk-adjusted returns; therefore, there is no truly accurate ranking scheme. Second, the stability criterion depends on two

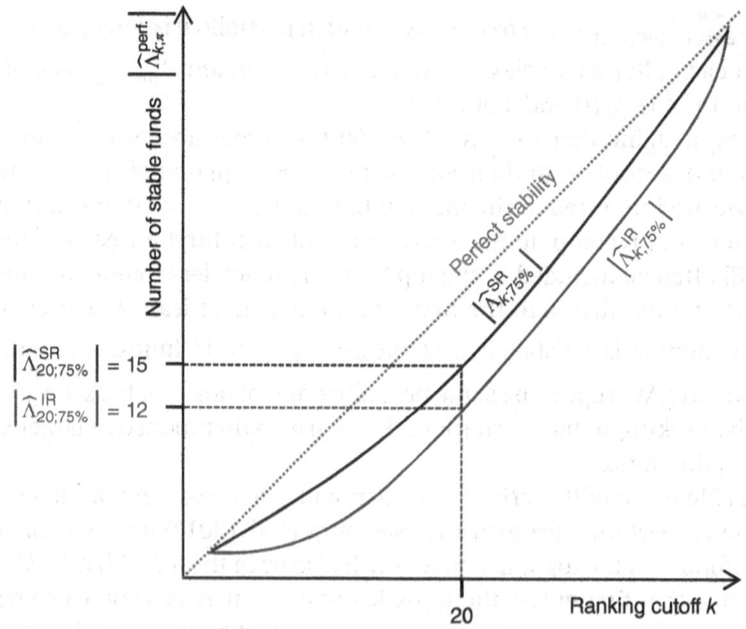

FIGURE 4-8 Illustration of stability selection for a specific ranking cutoff k under two performance measures.

parameters: the cutoff level k and the threshold probability π. Choosing different combinations of this pair may lead to contradicting results about the quality of performance measures, especially given the uncertainty about the existence of a dominant one. Grau-Carles, Doncel, and Sainz (2019) attempt to combine different performance measures to estimate the stability of individual funds, but there has thus far been no attempt to generalize the stability criterion to discriminate performance measures themselves. Finally, applying the criterion involves generating many rankings for each performance measure. In practice, there are only a few possibilities to create "random perturbations" in the measurement of performance without changing the conditions under which a manager's performance is judged. Considering the above illustration, the conclusions about the stable set are only valid if each quarterly sample of returns is perfectly comparable to another. If fund managers change, if market conditions largely differ, or if the managers' strategies evolve, the true rankings of the first and the last quarters will also surely differ. The ranking stability criterion is only reliable if each drawing of the controlled experiment is carried out under similar conditions. In human sciences, this technique is much harder to justify than in genomics, for which the stability criterion was developed.[19]

[19]In spite of the difficulties associated with the use of the stability criterion in this field, we examine how this technique can be adapted and used within the context of persistence in performance in Chapter 17.

4.4.2 The two-by-two ranking stability approach

To study the stability of rankings, a simpler approach is to perform two-by-two comparisons of classifications obtained under the same performance measure but according to alternative situations. Schematically, a table that looks similar to the one proposed in Table 4-13 with illustrative figures needs to be analyzed.

In such a setup, applying the rank stability criterion of Equation (4-15) is impossible since there are only $m = 2$ alternative classifications. However, the information conveyed by matching two rankings is potentially very valuable because we have two full ranges of rankings, and we can study the distance between the performance values or the ranks of the same fund from one list to another.

The quality of a performance measure applied to a sample of N funds will simply be reflected in the intensity of the "association" between the portfolio classifications. Trying to measure some kind of association between two series of random variables naturally leads to a measure of linear (Pearson) correlation (there is no question of causality between two rankings). However, the notion of association is wider than this parametric correlation, and there are many different ways to address it. In his study of the stability of performance measures, Hübner (2007) uses four of them:

- Two parametric measures that are based on the values of the performance measures themselves:
  - Pearson's correlation coefficient, defined as $\rho^P_{XY} = \frac{\text{Cov}(V_i^X, V_i^Y)}{\sigma(V_i^X)\sigma(V_i^Y)}$;
  - Lin's (2000) concordance correlation coefficient, which is more appropriate when the variables are continuous, defined as $\rho^C_{XY} = \frac{2\text{Cov}(V_i^X, V_i^Y)}{\sigma^2(V_i^X) + \sigma^2(V_i^Y) + (\overline{V}_i^X - \overline{V}_i^Y)^2}$
- Two nonparametric measures that are based on the ranks:
  - Spearman's rank correlation coefficient, in which the values of the funds' performances are replaced with their ranks, defined as $\rho^\Sigma_{XY} = \frac{\text{Cov}(S_i^X, S_i^Y)}{\sigma(S_i^X)\sigma(S_i^Y)}$.

TABLE 4-13 Structure of the two-by-two performance ranking comparisons.

Fund	Value under condition X (V_i^X)	Rank under condition X (S_i^X)	Value under condition Y (V_i^Y)	Rank under condition Y (S_i^Y)
A	0.51%	14	0.35%	17
B	0.33%	19	0.48%	13
⋮	⋮	⋮	⋮	⋮

- Cohen's (1960) kappa, which is a measure of the agreement of judgments made by different raters (in our case, these raters are the performance measures themselves). It is based on the 2×2 contingency table, in which the funds are considered "winners" if their rank is above the median, and "losers" otherwise. Cohen's kappa measure is defined as $\rho_{XY}^{\kappa} = \frac{2}{N}\left[\sum_{i=1}^{N} 1_{\left\{S_i^X < \frac{N}{2} \,\&\, S_i^Y < \frac{N}{2}\right\}} + \sum_{i=1}^{N} 1_{\left\{S_i^X > \frac{N}{2} \,\&\, S_i^Y > \frac{N}{2}\right\}}\right] - 1$.

To assess the stability of the rankings produced by competing performance measures on a list of funds, the author proposes to use the lower bound L^j of the confidence intervals for each association measure $j = P, C, \Sigma, \kappa$ and to use an interpretation scale that maps this lower bound to intervals $L^j \in [0.0,0.2],]0.2,0.4],]0.4,0.6],]0.6,0.8]$, and $]0.8,1.0]$ with levels of associations considered "slight," "fair," "moderate," "substantial," and "almost perfect," respectively.

This notion of two-by-two ranking stability can be used in the contexts of a cross-sectional (contemporaneous) comparison of managers, discussed below, and of the assessment of their (temporal) persistence in performance. The issue of temporal stability is intimately related to the identification of persistence in portfolio performance, which is studied in detail in Chapter 17. The postulate underlying the analysis is that the portfolio managers of the peer group exhibit skill differences that have durable effects on their performance. Therefore, their ranking over a given period should not substantially differ from their ranking over another, not too remote period. A multiperiod extension of the two-by-two ranking stability approach has been proposed by Menardi and Lisi (2012) to identify the performance measure that would reveal in the best possible way persistence in performance, but this approach has not become a dominant one in the field, most likely because Menardi and Lisi (2012) have the ambition of *simultaneously* selecting a performance measure and assessing performance persistence, while the stability criterion only focuses on the first dimension, and most of the persistence studies are dedicated to the second one.

4.4.3 Cross-sectional stability

For both the rank stability criterion and the two-by-two ranking stability approach, the intent is to analyze portfolio rankings generated with the same performance measure but subject to a noisy perturbation that is independent from the underlying source of performance, i.e., the skill of each manager. We infer the most relevant performance measure, from the point of view of the managers themselves, by selecting the one that results in the best stability output.

To apply this procedure, it is logical to study portfolio performance rankings produced for the same time window but according to different measurement conditions. The variations may include the identification of the benchmark (market portfolio), the hypotheses for the measurement of risk (volatility, beta, or tracking error) and mean return (arithmetic or geometric), and the identification of the risk-free rate or the currency of denomination (local currency, common currency, with or without hedging). All these variants contribute to the study of the cross-sectional stability of the rankings produced according to each competing performance measure.

In summary, the selection of the most relevant performance measure involves the following steps:

1. Identify the universe of actively managed portfolios constituting a relevant "peer group".
2. Select the performance measures that could be relevant to ranking the active managers.
3. For each performance measure, rank the portfolios according to the most realistic measurement conditions (choice of the benchmark, risk-free rate and currency, and measurement method for the statistical risk and average return estimates).
4. Choose a set of credible alternative measurement conditions and repeat the ranking of step 3.
5. Apply association measures to all pairs of rankings generated with each performance measure.
6. Select the performance measure that achieves the best association between the rankings.

Note that the "best" performance measure from the point of view of the managers might not be the most suitable one from the point of view of the investor. Additionally, some performance measures that are "dominated" by others according to Table 4-4, such as Jensen's alpha (dominated by the modified Jensen's alpha and the Treynor ratio), should not necessarily be discarded outright from the analysis. Indeed, many managers are likely to compete with one another according to their Jensen's alpha, even though they are – or should be – aware that the choice of that measure is not in the best interest of their customers.

G–T–N example (continued)

The lead manager of the Thematic fund (**T**) has the objective of featuring in the top quintile (i.e., top 20%) of the competing funds in the universe of US corporate bond large fund managers. The peer group of fund **T** comprises the other nine large funds active in the same segment, called B1, B2, ..., B9 (*step* 1).

Even though each manager of this category aims at maximizing their abnormal return, the management of G–T–N wants to determine whether the funds should preferably be ranked according to their (raw) Jensen's alpha, their modified Jensen's alpha (because their betas might largely differ from each other), or their Information ratio (because the right way to appraise the risk that they take would be their tracking error rather than their beta).

(*continued*)

(*continued*)

G–T–N considers that performance should be measured according to one of these three performance measures, without any particular prejudice (*step* 2).

The fund manager knows that the G–T–N Asset Management Company has adopted the world market index **M** (with mean return $\overline{R}_M = 7.39\%$ and volatility $\sigma_M = 8.83\%$) as a single benchmark for all its funds, in accordance with the SPT. Therefore, under these theoretically justifiable measurement conditions, the performance of fund **T** should be computed according to the estimates reported in Table 4-1 (*step* 3). However, to assess the stability of the rankings, the most realistic alternative measurement configuration for these funds would replace the world market portfolio by its bond-only counterpart **M′**, with mean return $\overline{R}_{M'} = 4.88\%$ and volatility $\sigma_{M'} = 5.12\%$ (*step* 4). According to the same two measurement methods as those applied for the fund, the relevant risk and return statistics of the whole peer group are represented in Table 4-14.

As before, the risk-free rate $R_f = 1.44\%$. With the information reported in Table 4-14, the computation of the Jensen's alpha, the modified Jensen's alpha, and the Information ratio under both measurement conditions leads to the rankings shown in Table 4-15a–c.

TABLE 4-14 G–T–N example – Means, volatilities, and correlations for the peer group of fund T.

Fund	Mean	Standard deviation	Correlation (M)	Correlation (M′)
Thematic	4.72%	6.41%	0.48	0.56
B1	4.51%	5.75%	0.63	0.75
B2	5.12%	7.65%	0.45	0.35
B3	4.11%	3.96%	0.61	0.72
B4	6.28%	6.23%	0.90	0.88
B5	7.01%	8.21%	0.79	0.78
B6	3.99%	4.52%	0.85	0.62
B7	3.52%	3.79%	0.53	0.65
B8	4.39%	5.43%	0.51	0.56
B9	4.22%	5.90%	0.75	0.90

TABLE 4-15a G–T–N example – Match of peer group rankings with Jensen's alpha.

α_P (M)	Fund	Fund	α_P (M′)
1.36%	B2	B2	1.88%
1.21%	**Thematic**	B5	1.27%
1.20%	B5	B4	1.16%
1.08%	B8	B8	0.91%
1.06%	B4	**Thematic**	**0.87%**
1.04%	B3	B3	0.75%
0.73%	B7	B6	0.67%
0.63%	B1	B7	0.42%
−0.04%	B6	B1	0.17%
−0.20%	B9	B9	−0.79%

TABLE 4-15b G–T–N example – Match of peer group rankings with the modified Jensen's alpha.

$m\alpha_P$ (M)	Fund	Fund	$m\alpha_P$ (M′)
3.81%	B3	B2	3.60%
3.49%	B2	B8	1.53%
3.47%	**Thematic**	B3	1.35%
3.46%	B8	**Thematic**	**1.24%**
3.20%	B7	B6	1.22%
1.68%	B4	B4	1.08%
1.64%	B5	B5	1.01%
1.54%	B1	B7	0.88%
−0.09%	B6	B1	0.20%
−0.40%	B9	B9	−0.76%

(continued)

(continued)

TABLE 4-15c G–T–N example – Match of peer group rankings with the Information ratio.

IR_P (M)	Fund	Fund	IR_P (M′)
0.39	B4	B4	0.39
0.33	B3	B3	0.27
0.24	B5	B2	0.26
0.23	B8	B5	0.25
0.23	B7	B8	0.20
0.21	**Thematic**	B6	0.19
0.20	B2	**Thematic**	**0.16**
0.14	B1	B7	0.15
−0.02	B6	B1	0.05
−0.05	B9	B9	−0.31

Regarding the Thematic fund, the greatest rank change occurs with Jensen's alpha (Table 4-15a), for which the fund loses three places (from #2 to #5). Nevertheless, a visual inspection of the transitions (represented with the lines at the center of each table) reveals that the highest stability seems to be achieved with the use of Jensen's alpha, and the situation of fund **T** is an outlier. This outcome is confirmed in Table 4-16, summarizing the outcomes of the measures of association (*step* 5).

TABLE 4-16 G–T–N example – Association measures for the candidate performance measures.

Performance measure	Pearson $\rho^P_{MM'}$	Lin $\rho^L_{MM'}$	Spearman $\rho^\Sigma_{MM'}$	Cohen $\rho^\kappa_{MM'}$
Jensen's alpha $\propto_P$	80.79%	77.09%	87.88%	80.00%
Modified Jensen's alpha $m\propto_P$	61.40%	44.47%	78.18%	60.00%
Information ratio IR_P	78.19%	73.35%	76.97%	40.00%

For all four association measures, Jensen's alpha stands out as the one that achieves the best scores. It is thus most likely that, among the three performance measures that have been tested, the majority of fund managers of the peer group compete with one another according to their Jensen's alpha (*step* 6).

To verify that the manager of the Thematic fund has indeed achieved their objective of featuring among the top quintile of the peer group (i.e., top 2 here), further analysis is needed. With Jensen's alpha, the alternative rankings place fund **T** as #2 under measurement conditions **M** and as #5 under **M′**. To determine the most likely true position of fund **T**, it is necessary to apply the ranking stability criterion methodology described in Section 4.4.1.1 and to generate many different rankings under alternative measurement conditions.

Note that we had previously concluded that for fund **T**, the use of systematic risk was preferable to assess its performance from the point of view of the investor; however, from their perspective, the modified Jensen's alpha would dominate the "simple" alpha because of the potential manipulation issues. These results are contradictory, but they may coexist; on the one hand, the investor should use the modified Jensen's alpha to select the best managers (normative standpoint), but on the other hand, the managers actually compete with each other on the basis of Jensen's alpha (descriptive standpoint).

The results of the above example must however be considered with caution. From the analysis, we infer as a "best estimate" that the alpha is the most likely method to classify the fund managers who belong to the peer group. However, this result is only the outcome of a statistical exercise based on a limited set of performance measures. It is possible that some, but not all, managers try to differentiate each other on the basis of a given way to measure their performance, but there might be no consensus among them. Even worse, it is possible that they try to maximize another performance measure that is not considered in the list of candidates. It would thus be dangerous to draw definite conclusions with this approach, and it is always better to try to understand how portfolio managers truly work rather than trying to infer their collective behavior on the basis of pure statistical data.

Key Takeaways and Equations

- Classical portfolio performance measures distinguish themselves on two dimensions: the definition of risk as an input and how the relation between the input and the output is measured (in terms of unit, either as a decimal number or a value in percentage points, and in terms of risk scale, either scale-independent or scale-dependent). The classical performance measures are classified as follows:
  - The *Sharpe ratio* $SR_P = \frac{\overline{R}_P - R_f}{\sigma_P}$ uses total risk as input, produces a decimal number, and is scale-independent.
  - The *Treynor ratio* $TR_P = \frac{\overline{R}_P - R_f}{\beta_P}$ and *modified Jensen's alpha* $m\alpha_P = \frac{\alpha_P}{\beta_P}$ use systematic risk as input, produce a number in percentage points, and are scale-independent.

(continued)

(continued)

- *Jensen's alpha* $\alpha_P = \overline{R}_P - [R_f + \beta_P(\overline{R}_M - R_f)]$ uses systematic risk as input, produces a number in percentage points, and is scale-dependent.
- The *Information ratio* $\mathrm{IR}_P = \frac{\mathrm{TD}_P}{\mathrm{TE}_P} = \frac{\overline{R}_P - \overline{R}_B}{\sigma(R_P - R_B)}$ uses specific risk as input, produces a decimal number, and is scale-independent.

- From the perspective of the investor, the selection of the appropriate performance measure for a given portfolio can be considered either from a *normative point of view*, i.e., the *ex ante* choice of a portfolio to invest in, or from a *positive point of view*, i.e., the *ex post* situation of assessing the added value that a given portfolio has achieved.
- In the normative approach, three main cases have to be distinguished regarding the investor's allocation constraints in determining their optimal investment in an active portfolio *P*:
  - *The fully constrained case*: If investor *j* wants to invest all their wealth in a single portfolio *P*, then they have to maximize the expected utility of a combination of that portfolio *P* and the riskless asset, which is expressed as

$$\max \mathrm{E}(U_j(R_P)) \equiv U^{\max} = R_f + \frac{1}{2\gamma_j}\mathrm{SR}_P^2 \tag{4-3}$$

The relevant performance measure in this context is the Sharpe ratio.

  - *The partially constrained case*: If the investor wants to achieve a target average global return $\overline{R}^*$ by investing a constant fraction of their wealth w_D in a disposable portfolio combining managed portfolio *P* and the riskless asset, the expected utility-maximizing portfolio is the one that maximizes the ISM_P:

$$\mathrm{ISM}_P = -w_D\left(\frac{\overline{R}_D - R_f}{\sigma_M \mathrm{SR}_P}\right)^2 - 2(1 - w_D)\frac{\overline{R}_D - R_f}{\mathrm{TR}_P} \tag{4-4}$$

If w_D is very high, the Sharpe ratio is the most important contributor of the ISM. If w_D tends to zero, i.e., if the investor considers a marginal investment in portfolio *P*, then the Treynor ratio (or, equivalently, the modified Jensen's alpha) is the key selection criterion.

  - *The unconstrained case*: If the investor does not wish to constrain the weight to be invested in active portfolio *P*, then the maximum Sharpe ratio of their optimized global portfolio Ω^* is given by the following expression:

$$\mathrm{SR}_{\Omega^*} = \sqrt{\mathrm{SR}_M^2 + \mathrm{AR}_P^2} \tag{4-6}$$

Thus, the determining criterion for choosing the best portfolio is its Appraisal ratio.

- In the positive approach, three main cases have to be distinguished regarding the investor's type of remaining allocation next to their investment in the actively managed portfolio P:
  - The *no-complement case*: If the investor has invested all their wealth in a single portfolio P, then they have to care about total risk, and the Sharpe ratio is the right measure on which the performance of the portfolio manager is to be assessed. This case typically applies for (i) globally diversified funds in risky asset classes, (ii) allocation funds, (iii) lifecycle funds, (iv) diversified discretionary portfolio management mandates, (v) portfolio aggregation, and (vi) a single significant investment.
  - The *active complement case*: If the investor has invested the remainder of their wealth in a combination of other actively managed portfolios whose aggregation is well diversified, then they have to care about systematic risk, and the Treynor ratio or the modified Jensen's alpha is the right measure on which the performance of the portfolio manager is to be assessed. This case typically applies for (i) thematic equity or bond funds, (ii) funds that represent a subset of an asset class, (iii) direct line investments, (iv) part of a global portfolio patchwork, and (v) subportfolio mandates with identified expertise.
  - The *passive complement case*: If the investor has invested the remainder of their wealth in a well-diversified passive fund mimicking the market portfolio, then they have to care about specific risk, and the Information ratio is the right measure on which the performance of the portfolio manager is to be assessed. This case typically applies for (i) multi-strategy hedge funds, (ii) managed futures funds, (iii) alternative asset classes, (iv) target risk or return funds, (v) core–satellite investment mandates, and (vi) stuck investments.
- From the perspective of the manager of an actively managed portfolio, the selection of the appropriate measure to appraise their performance is related to the reliability level of the ranking of their peer group according to the selected performance measure. It can be assessed through the stability of the portfolio rankings under alternative measurement conditions.
  - When many different sets of conditions can be generated, the most rigorous approach is to use the *ranking stability criterion* associated with some cutoff percentile k and a threshold for the minimum level of frequency π that is necessary for a fund to be considered stable. If there is a set N of funds or portfolios to be ranked and we create m alternative classifications using a given performance

(*continued*)

(*continued*)

measure, the most stable performance measure is the one that maximizes the stable set defined as

$$\hat{\Lambda}_{k;\pi}^{\text{perf.}} = \{n \in N | \hat{\Pi}_k^n \geq \pi\} \tag{4-15}$$

where $\hat{\Pi}_k^n = \frac{1}{m}\sum_{i=1}^{m} 1_{\{n \in \Lambda_k(i)\}}$ is the frequency at which portfolio n belongs to the stable set $\Lambda_k(i)$ generated with each alternative classification $i = 1, \ldots, m$.

- A simpler approach is to compare the *two-by-two ranking stability* through a measure of association between the alternative rankings generated with a given performance measure but different measurement conditions. The measure of association can be a correlation coefficient (Pearson, Spearman, or Lin's concordance coefficient) or a nonparametric measure of agreement (Cohen's kappa). It is typically used to assess the cross-sectional stability of rankings produced with a single performance measure but different measurement conditions (alternative benchmarks, various risk measurement choices, or changes in the market-related inputs).

REFERENCES

Bodie, Z., Kane, A., and A. J. Marcus (2018), *Investments, Eleventh Edition*. McGraw-Hill Education.

Cavé, A., Hübner, G., and T. Lejeune (2013), Evaluating portfolio performance: Reconciling asset selection and market timing. In: Baker, H. K., and G. Filbeck, Eds., *Portfolio Theory and Management*. Oxford University Press, pp. 467–489.

Cohen, J. (1960), A coefficient of agreement for nominal scales. *Educational and Psychological Measurement*, Vol. 20, pp. 37–46.

Eling, M., and F. Schuhmacher (2007), Does the choice of performance measure influence the evaluation of hedge funds? *Journal of Banking & Finance*, Vol. 31, pp. 2632–2647.

Evans, L. J., and H. S. Archer (1968), Diversification and reduction of dispersion: An empirical analysis. *The Journal of Finance*, Vol. 23, pp. 761–767.

Grau-Carles, P, Doncel, L. M., and J. Sainz (2019), Stability in mutual fund performance rankings: A new proposal. *International Review of Economics and Finance*, Vol. 61, pp. 337–346.

Grinold, R. C., and R. N. Kahn (1995), *Active Portfolio Management*. Irwin.

Hallerbach, W. G. (2005), The information ratio as a performance metric. Working Paper.

Horstmeyer, D., and K. Li (2023), How do performance metrics correlate? Might fund managers cherry-pick? *Enterprising Investor* blog, CFA Institute (September).

Hübner, G. (2007), How do performance measures perform? *The Journal of Portfolio Management*, Vol. 33 (Summer), pp. 64–74.

Lhabitant, F.-S. (2006), *Handbook of Hedge Funds*. John Wiley & Sons, Wiley Finance Series.

Lin, L.-K. (2000), A note on the concordance correlation coefficient. *Biometrics*, Vol. 56, pp. 324–325.

Menardi, G., and F. Lisi (2012), Are performance measures equally stable? *Annals of Finance*, Vol. 8, pp. 553–570.

Meinshausen, N., and P. Bühlmann (2010), Stability selection. *Journal of the Royal Statistical Society: Series B*, Vol. 72, pp. 417–473.

Scholz, H., and M. Wilkens (2005), Investor-specific performance measurement: A justification of Sharpe ratio and Treynor ratio. *The International Journal of Finance*, Vol. 17, pp. 3671–3691.

Siebourg, J., Merdes, G., Misselwitz, B., Hardt, W.-D., and N. Beerenwinkel (2012), Stability of gene rankings from RNAi screens. *Bioinformatics*, Vol. 28, pp. 1612–1618.

Tobin, J. (1958), Liquidity preference as behavior towards risk. *Review of Economic Studies*, Vol. 25, pp. 65–86.

Treynor, J. L., and F. Black (1973), How to use security analysis to improve portfolio selection. *Journal of Business*, Vol. 46, pp. 66–86.

CHAPTER 5

Pitfalls and Dangers with the Classical Performance Measures

INTRODUCTION

Built upon the foundations of Standard Portfolio Theory (SPT), the Capital Asset Pricing Model (CAPM) is an elegant framework. As shown in Chapter 2, the asset pricing equations (the Capital Market Line and the Security Market Line) derive from an equilibrium situation but remain analytically simple, each of them reflecting a linear relation between expected return and risk. All the classical performance measures discussed in Chapters 3 and 4 are the direct emanations of this framework.[1]

In spite of its intuitiveness and its renown, what if the framework was simply wrong? Would all these eminent performance measures, the great Sharpe ratio, the prestigious Jensen's alpha, and the famous Information ratio, simply suffer from a "garbage-in, garbage-out" syndrome? To what extent are the various possible model weaknesses impact on the validity or accuracy of these measures? Are there solutions to these issues, and how to implement them? These are the questions that we attempt to address in this chapter.

With such a huge potential list of pitfalls and dangers, it would be particularly pretentious to claim we are enumerating and comprehensively handling all of them in a single chapter. Nevertheless, we can be ambitious here.

With a structured approach, we propose to isolate *five clear categories*, organized in consecutive sections, of issues related to these classical performance measures. The first two categories have a theoretical underpinning. We examine how the SPT and CAPM can be challenged in such a way that the application of their associated performance measures (mostly the Sharpe

[1]The peer group comparison return discussed in Chapter 3, being a heuristic performance measure, stands as an exception. Nevertheless, it is very similar in meaning and even sometimes in interpretation with the Jensen's alpha.

ratio for the SPT and the other ones for the CAPM) would be mistaken, at least in their native form. The next two categories belong to the order of statistics. There are a number of problems associated with the *sampling* of data, one the one hand, and with the execution of *regression models*, on the other hand. Finally, once the outcomes of performance measurement are produced, a last category of potential dangers relates to their *interpretation*.

Many of the issues that we list, and perhaps also many more, have been already discussed here and there in the portfolio performance literature. We try to gather them, discuss them, but most importantly, we do not want to leave the reader with too many question marks. Some issues might be more severe or difficult to solve than others, but we make it a point of honor to systematically propose ways to get *solutions for these identified issues.* Some are straightforward and discussed directly in the chapter; some others are more sophisticated and are treated in separate chapters. Interestingly, some solutions, like radically changing the way the beta is estimated or wholly inverting the interpretation of Jensen's alpha, are even very surprising.

The G–T–N Asset Management Company Example – Part II

We reuse the Global–Thematic–Neutral (G–T–N) Asset Management Company example that was introduced in Chapter 4. The summary of statistical information about these three funds (the Global, Thematic, and Neutral funds), the market portfolio, and the risk-free rate is provided in Table 5-1. These data were obtained using a sample of monthly returns over three years.

TABLE 5-1 G–T–N example – Summary statistics and performance measures.

	Global	Thematic	Neutral	M	F
Mean return	6.39%	4.72%	2.55%	7.39%	1.44%
Standard deviation	7.12%	6.41%	3.90%	8.83%	0.00%
Correlation with market	0.97	0.48	0.04	1.00	0.00
Sharpe ratio	0.70	0.51	0.28	0.67	
Treynor ratio	6.33%	9.42%	62.85%	5.95%	
Jensen's alpha	0.30%	1.21%	1.00%		
Modified Jensen's alpha	0.38%	3.47%	56.90%		
Information ratio	0.17	0.21	0.26		

The empty cells correspond to irrelevant information (zeros). Note that we had already concluded that the unusually high values for the Treynor ratio and modified Jensen's alpha of the Neutral fund were doubtful as the CAPM did not seem to explain well how this fund's return had been generated.

Initially, the company's three marketed portfolios each have their own merits. The Global one (**G**) achieves the highest Sharpe ratio, the Thematic one (**T**) has the best alpha, and the Neutral fund (**N**) obtains the best Information ratio. Their position with respect to each other is summarized in the radar chart shown in Figure 5-1, which reflects for each fund its standardized relative performance (i.e., the measure minus the average across the three funds and divided by the range).

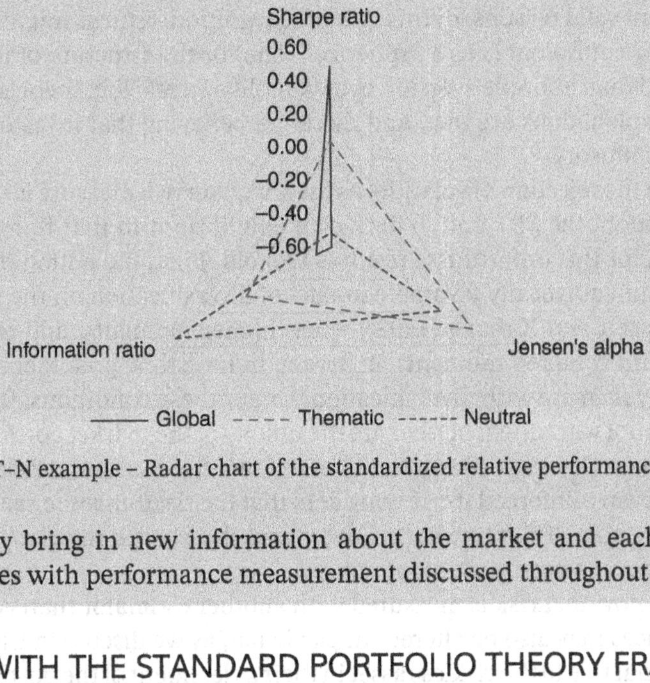

FIGURE 5-1 G–T–N example – Radar chart of the standardized relative performance measures.

We gradually bring in new information about the market and each fund as we go through the issues with performance measurement discussed throughout the chapter.

5.1 ISSUES WITH THE STANDARD PORTFOLIO THEORY FRAMEWORK

The Standard Portfolio Theory (SPT) represents the core of classical performance measurement and is the framework that directly justifies the Sharpe ratio as the relevant *ex post* measure of portfolio performance when total risk is considered. Before considering estimation issues, we have to wonder whether the major assumptions underlying the use of the Sharpe ratio are warranted. This is not necessarily an attack against the logic of the whole framework. Rather, we are concerned here with two aspects of the problem: (i) the relevance of the input (risk) and output (excess return) chosen for the efficiency measure, and (ii) the generalization of the application of the Sharpe ratio for all portfolios thanks to homemade leverage.

5.1.1 Rebutting the risk and return components of the Sharpe ratio

The Sharpe ratio of a portfolio measures, from an *ex post* perspective, the slope of its risk–return relation obtained during a period of reference.[2] This is a very powerful meaning because it reflects the outcome of the optimization program of any rational, risk-averse investor who tries to select a global portfolio that maximizes their expected utility. There are two crucial assumptions underlying this quest for an optimal portfolio: (i) the acceptance that the risk of any asset is adequately estimated with its volatility, and (ii) the identification of the excess return over the risk-free rate as the measure of gain.

Challenging how risk is measured is at the same time the simplest and most serious way to put the Sharpe ratio into question. Investors may not consider that the risk of an asset should not be assessed thanks to its variance (and therefore its square root, i.e., the volatility). There can be very different valid reasons for this lack of recognition: returns might not follow a Gaussian distribution or equivalent (i.e., a "spherical" one) or the structure of their preferences is more sophisticated than a simple aversion over volatility. In real life, there is indeed ample evidence that both explanations are met, and therefore believing that investors only care about volatility is largely illusory.

The issue with the rejection of volatility as the adequate risk measure is that it is then much more difficult to adopt the SPT and to derive an equilibrium in that framework. The major underlying reason for this unfortunate result is twofold. First, the notion of an efficient frontier hinges on the unequivocally favorable impact of diversification on the portfolio variance. As shown by Brockett and Kahane (1992), when higher moments, and especially the portfolio skewness (third centered moment), intervene in investors' preferences, then risk might sometimes actually *increase* with diversification. Under these conditions, the concavity of the efficient frontier is not warranted; neither are the unicity of the market portfolio or the linearity of the relation between leverage (the quantity of the risk-free asset) and risk. All these sources of complexity are even reinforced if one considers that the fixed-income security is itself risky. In a nutshell, the whole SPT framework shivers and the Sharpe ratio no longer reflects the right measure of excess return per unit of risk.

Consider thus now that risk is measured with another estimator than volatility. Then, the investor's preferences may also be altered. In particular, as we discuss in Chapter 6, they may not assign any special role to the riskless asset in their assessment of the portfolio's reward. This leads to Roy's (1952) "safety first" criterion, which introduces the notion of a reservation rate that is investor-specific and plays the role of a pivot between the perception of gains (returns above this rate) and losses (returns below this rate). This means that not only the numerator but also the denominator of the Sharpe ratio is no longer accurate.[3]

[2]As a reminder, this is the classical interpretation that the literature and financial practice have given to this measure, in spite of Sharpe's initial intent to consider it rather as a special case of the Information ratio using the risk-free asset as the benchmark.

[3]The Roy ratio is discussed in detail in Chapter 6.

5.1.2 Discarding the homemade leverage assumption

Homemade leverage is crucial for the use of the Sharpe ratio when portfolios with different risks are simultaneously considered and matched with each other. Without this ability to freely borrow or lend at the risk-free rate, it is impossible to conclude that one portfolio dominates the other after controlling for the risk of their allocations. There are two main issues with the homemade leverage assumption: differences in lending and borrowing rates, and the practical inability to activate the leveraging process.

5.1.2.1 Different borrowing and lending rates

The first issue is related to the investor's ability to benefit from the same interest rate conditions whenever they lend or borrow money in order to leverage the portfolio. Such an issue had been initially discussed by Blume and Friend (1973). They show that if an investor must borrow at a higher rate than the one they get for lending, they have only access to a curvilinear mean–variance space.[4] Then, several efficient portfolios can be held at equilibrium, and the Capital Market Line is not unique.

From the perspective of performance appraisal, two Sharpe ratios must be defined for a single portfolio P: one with the lending rate R_f^l that prevails for any allocation involving a positive weight in the riskless asset (and thus a lower volatility than the portfolio) and the other with the borrowing rate R_f^b that prevails for any allocation involving a negative weight in the riskless asset (and thus a higher volatility than the portfolio). Formally, this is represented by the following equations:

$$\mathrm{SR}_P^l = \frac{\overline{R}_P - R_f^l}{\sigma_P} \text{ for } \sigma_{P'} \leq \sigma_P \quad \text{(5-1a)}$$

$$\mathrm{SR}_P^b = \frac{\overline{R}_P - R_f^b}{\sigma_P} \text{ for } \sigma_{P'} > \sigma_P \quad \text{(5-1b)}$$

where $\overline{R}_P$ and σ_P represent the mean and standard deviation of the portfolio returns, respectively; R_f^l and R_f^b are the interest rates at which the investor can lend and borrow in order to alter the risk level of their portfolio, and $\sigma_{P'} \equiv (1 - w_f)\sigma_P$ is the volatility of the investor's global portfolio in which w_f is the weight invested in the riskless asset. Obviously, because $R_f^l < R_f^b$, we obtain that $\mathrm{SR}_P^l > \mathrm{SR}_P^b$: the slope of the reward-to-volatility ratio of the portfolio suddenly shifts downward at its risk–return coordinates.

[4]A more drastic standpoint considers that, in addition to being charged a higher interest rate, investors are also constrained regarding the borrowed amount. Typically, a Lombard loan (backed by a portfolio of financial assets) must be overcollateralized at a rate that is directly related to the riskiness of the portfolio. A full equity portfolio, for instance, can only be leveraged by a fraction close to 50% of its market value. This constraint makes the difference between lending and borrowing even more acute and reinforces Blume and Friend's (1973) reasoning.

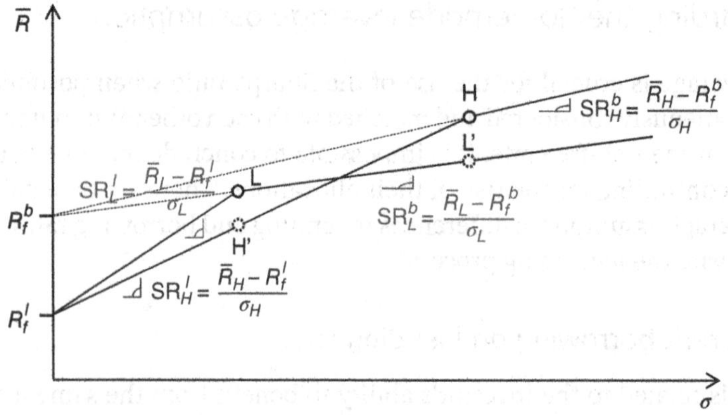

FIGURE 5-2 Graphical representation of the Sharpe ratio with different lending and borrowing rates.

This result has profound implications regarding portfolio rankings. It makes it much more difficult to compare Sharpe ratios across risk levels and puts the notion of dominance into perspective. The reason for this difficulty is illustrated in Figure 5-2.

This graph mirrors Figure 3-4 of Chapter 3, with the difference being that the lines drawn to the right of portfolios *L* and *H* originate from the borrowing rate R_f^b and are thus flatter than the ones starting from R_f^l up to the coordinates of the portfolios. When lending only is considered, the conclusions are the same as with the Sharpe ratio: portfolio *L* dominates *H*, whose unlevered version with the same risk, denoted *H'*, delivers a lower average rate of return. This corresponds to $SR_L^l > SR_H^l$ on the graph. However, the story drastically changes when it comes to borrowing. Homemade leverage becomes costly, and leveraging portfolio *L* so as to reach the same risk as *H* can only be done by borrowing at such a high rate that it substantially deteriorates the performance of the leveraged portfolio. If the investor wants to achieve the same risk as *H*, they have to accept the return of portfolio *L'*. Because $SR_L^b < SR_H^b$, the riskier version of *L* is outperformed by portfolio *H* that achieves the same risk and a higher return. This means that neither portfolio strictly dominates the other from the point of view of the investor: the choice depends on the level of risk that they want to adopt. Depending on the shape of their indifference curves, it is also possible that they would be indifferent between two distinct portfolios that maximize their expected utility, one involving lending with *H* and the other one involving borrowing with *L*.

This situation resembles the one of the Roy ratio, based on the "safety first" criterion, described in Chapter 6, with different interest rates replacing the investor-specific reservation rates. As in that case, the higher the borrowing interest rate, the more favorable it is for the riskier portfolio. There is a key difference between both frameworks though. With the Roy ratio, the investor chooses their reservation rate on the basis of their own preferences. There are thus as many values of the ratio as there are different investors. With different borrowing and lending rates, these values are imposed on the investor. It is only the difference in borrowing conditions of different categories of investors that matters here. We can expect the groups of investors to be much more homogenous (individuals and institutional investors of various sizes) and identified with objective criteria. This is a very important distinction as far as performance measurement is involved.

5.1.2.2 Investor's ability to use leverage

The second important issue related to homemade leverage is the realism of this assumption. For many investors, especially those non-sophisticated individual ones who engage a contractual relationship with a professional asset manager, the choice of their portfolio takes the form of a "take it or leave it offer." This happens, for instance, when the investor's risk profile is estimated by their financial advisor and they have to select one of a range of "off-the-shelf" model portfolios or flagship allocation funds in order to match this risk profile. In that case, it is advisable to compute the certainty equivalent return according to the expected utility equation:

$$u_j(R_P) = \overline{R}_P - \frac{1}{2}\gamma_j\sigma_P^2 \tag{5-2}$$

where $u_j(\cdot) \equiv \mathrm{E}(U_j(\cdot))$ is the expected quadratic utility of investor j, and γ_j stands for their risk-aversion coefficient; $\overline{R}_P$ and σ_P^2 are the mean and variance of the portfolio returns, respectively. The outcome of the analysis might reveal that a portfolio might dominate another one according to its Sharpe ratio, but simultaneously deliver a lower expected utility when the investor's particular attitudes toward risk are taken into account. This kind of situation is summarized in Figure 5-3.

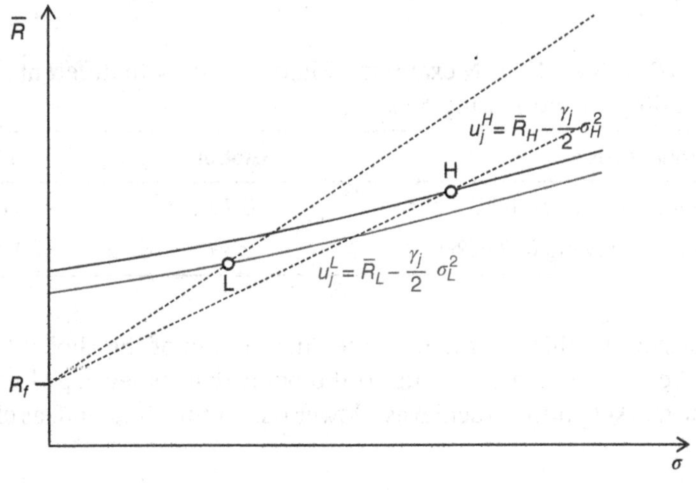

FIGURE 5-3 Graphical representation of the investor's choice between two portfolios of different risk levels.

Portfolios L and H are the same as before. In terms of their Sharpe ratios, L dominates H. However, if we consider an investor j with a very moderate risk aversion, denoted by γ_j, the indifference curve intersecting portfolio H corresponds to a higher expected utility $u_j^H = \overline{R}_H - \frac{\gamma_j}{2}\sigma_H^2$ than the one going through L. From their perspective, portfolio H delivers the most appealing risk–return trade-off in spite of a lower Sharpe ratio. This performance measure is useless from their point of view because they cannot leverage portfolio L so as to reach a higher return, very desirable from their point of view, at the expense of a higher risk that is less important.

In general, less risk-averse investors will prefer riskier portfolios, even if their Sharpe ratios are lower than more conservative ones. Thus, combined with the issue of lending and borrowing rates, there is clearly a captive clientele for high risk portfolios whose performance might look somewhat disappointing compared to less risky ones, but that cannot be matched through simple leveraging.

G–T–N example (continued)

The Global fund's asset manager considers that "the fund outperforms the market thanks to its higher Sharpe ratio, after fees. Furthermore, it is a perfect substitute to the market index (portfolio M) for all our customers." The issues related to homemade leverage make this claim too assertive.

If we consider that this fund targets individual investors who have access to Lombard credit at a borrowing rate of 3.60% per annum, we can challenge the first part of the asset manager's claim. With the market inputs, we can use Equations (5-1a) and (5-1b) to construct the table showing the investor's Sharpe ratio considering their lending and borrowing rates (Table 5-2):

TABLE 5-2 G–T–N example – Sharpe ratios with different lending and borrowing rates.

Sharpe ratio	Global	M
with lending (@1.44%)	0.70	0.67
with borrowing (@3.60%)	0.39	0.43

Indeed, considering this information, the Sharpe ratio of the Global fund in the borrowing region becomes much lower, up to the point that its leveraged version with the same risk as the market portfolio achieves a lower risk–return trade-off, as clearly shown in Figure 5-4.

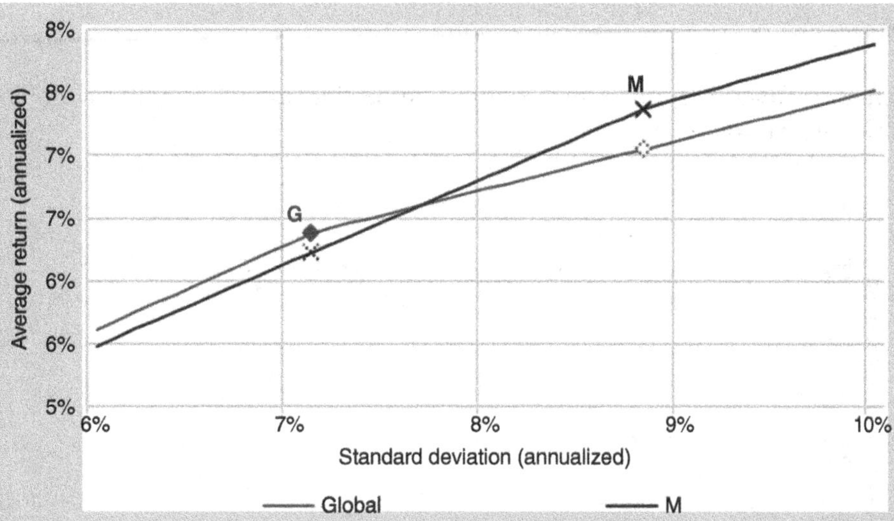

FIGURE 5-4 G–T–N example – Sharpe ratios of G and M with different lending and borrowing rates.

Thus, it is not correct to say that **G** outperforms **M** as it is practically impossible for an investor holding the Global fund to leverage it up to the risk of **M** and obtain a higher return.

Consider now that the investors to whom the Global portfolio is marketed are not offered to combine it with any investment in the risk-free asset. We can roughly categorize the customer base of G–T–N in two groups: a "low risk aversion" group with a risk-aversion coefficient of 4, and a "high risk aversion" group with a risk-aversion coefficient of 12. Using formula (5-2) for the certainty equivalent of the portfolios, we can rebut the second part of the asset manager's claim because we obtain the results shown in Table 5-3:

TABLE 5-3 G–T–N example – Certainty equivalents with different risk-aversion coefficients.

Certainty equivalent	Global	M
Low risk aversion ($\gamma_j = 4$)	5.38%	5.83%
High risk aversion ($\gamma_j = 12$)	3.35%	2.71%

The low risk-aversion group gets a greater level of satisfaction, reflected in the expected utility score, from the market portfolio than for the Global fund.

This situation, resulting from identifying two categories of investors according to their risk aversion, is illustrated in Figure 5-5 that shows both portfolios and the

(continued)

(continued)

indifference curves corresponding to their respective expected utilities for the two categories of investors.

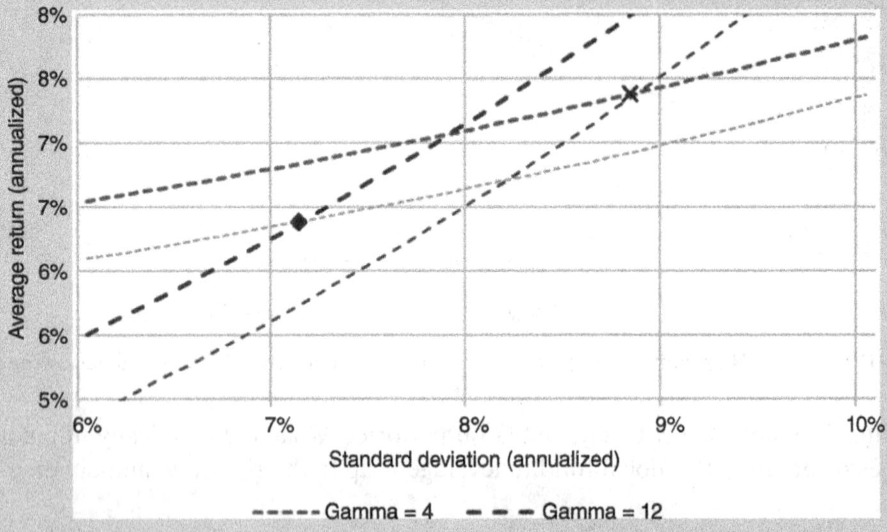

FIGURE 5-5 G–T–N example – Indifference curves going through G and M for the two investor types.

Thus, it is not correct to say that **G** is a better substitute for **M** as low risk-aversion investors consider that the market index provides them with a higher expected utility than the fund.

5.1.3 Challenging the riskless character of the interest rate

The existence and use of a riskless interest rate (possibly different for lending and borrowing purposes) constitutes the bridge between the SPT and the CAPM. Thanks to a safe-haven investment with neither positive variance nor (*a fortiori*) correlation with an existing risky asset or portfolio, the investor can allocate their wealth between any combination of risky assets and this risk-free investment, ensuring that the risk–return trade-off of their investment is a constant. This is the basis for Tobin's (1958) two-fund separation studied in Chapter 2 that underlies the equilibrium on the financial market.

The SPT and the CAPM were imagined and published in the middle of the Bretton Woods fixed-rate system, in which the convertibility of the US Dollar in a fixed quantity of gold was assuring a very low volatility of most financial variables, including interest rates. The assumption of a very sticky interest rate, even though it was not exactly respected, was largely acceptable in practice. However, since the abandonment of this system in 1971, the world has

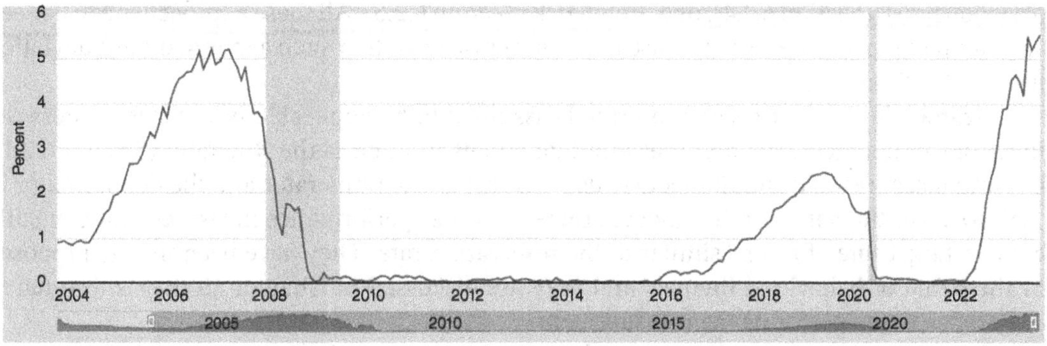

FIGURE 5-6 Evolution of the one-month US Treasury Bill rate over time. *Source*: Board of Governors of the Federal Reserve System (US) (`https://fred.stlouisfed.org/series/DGS1MO#`)

changed and volatility has surged on all financial variables. Interest rates are no exception, with some periods of very low variability, but also some periods of very strong and rapid swings. The graph in Figure 5-6 shows the evolution of the one-month constant maturity US Treasury Bill rate over a period of 20 years (September 2003 to September 2023).

Over that period, the average level of this proxy for the riskless interest rate was 1.29%, evolving in a range between 0.00% after the recessions of 2009 and 2020 (shaded areas in the graph) and up to 5.54% in August 2023. The volatility of the series was 1.63%, corresponding to an approximate 0.13% standard deviation of the monthly rate of return of the T-Bill. Thus, there is no such thing as a constant interest rate in the real world, and this assumption can be questioned – especially in periods of high interest rate volatility, such as during the 2002–2007 period or since the start of 2022.

From an *ex ante* perspective, the variability of interest rates does not challenge the validity of the CAPM framework. In theory, the investor identifies their investment horizon and matches the duration of their fixed-income investment with this investment horizon. By doing so, they immunize their portfolio against interest rate movements. Thus, as a one-period model, the CAPM remains valid and resists the variability of actual interest rates. The issue arises in the context of *ex post* performance assessment of a portfolio. The investor's horizon is often unknown and usually unused for the estimation of the risk and performance metrics. A periodical interest rate, in line with the estimation method, is used instead. The interest rate volatility becomes incompatible with the theoretical underpinning of the model.

5.1.4 Solutions

5.1.4.1 Finding the risk and return inputs

Questioning the way risk and excess return are measured according to the SPT framework is indeed a major theme discussed in Section 6.2 of Chapter 6. We examine how to replace volatility with alternative distance risk measures (Section 6.2.2), downside risk (Section 6.2.3), drawdown risk (Section 6.2.4), or extreme risk (Section 6.2.5). All these approaches can be seen as potential improvements to the use of a symmetric deviation such as the standard deviation used by the Sharpe ratio.

Meanwhile, when a reservation rate is assumed to be applicable in order to express the investor's preferences, the first measure that comes to mind is the Roy ratio (Section 6.2.1), but also measures that simultaneously use this rate as the numerator and the denominator of the ratio, like the Sortino ratio. Indeed, there are other performance measures that explicitly adopt a target rate of return similar to the reservation rate. They have been mostly proposed in the scope of behavioral finance, and they are discussed in Chapter 10 that is devoted to preference-based performance measurement.

There is an important caveat to be brought in the case where a reservation rate is used though. As shown by Hoechner, Reichling, and Schulze (2017), when the investor specifies an arbitrary target return, this cannot be used as a substitute to the riskless interest rate in order to leverage the portfolio. Thus, unless the reservation rate is equal to the interest rate, homemade leverage – that is crucial in order to adopt avatars of the Sharpe ratio for performance measurement – is simply not possible. Only portfolios with the same risk could then be faithfully ranked, which obviously reduces the attractiveness of such measures.

5.1.4.2 Dealing correctly with homemade leverage

The corrective actions targeting the two homemade leverage issues identified here are very different.

The existence of different lending and borrowing rates applicable to the investor is a complex issue to deal with. There are potentially as many cases as there are different investors. From the portfolio manager's point of view, it is totally beyond their control. Thus, this reality makes the comparison of portfolios with very different levels of risks and returns potentially tricky, and there is no simple solution for it. Nevertheless, it does not mean that managers are not completely unaware of this lack of comparability and even may take advantage of it. Hübner and Lambert (2019) show that instead of a straight line, the empirical reward-to-volatility ratio resembles a curve, and the net-of-fee mutual fund performance seems to deteriorate when their risk increases. This phenomenon, which suggests that some managers might capture part of the abnormal returns through their own remuneration, is studied in more detail in Chapter 18.

Regarding the lack of homemade diversification possibility, the solution in terms of performance measurement is indeed relatively straightforward: it is given by Equation (5-2). Because the investor's point of view is taken into account and that their attitudes toward risk are reflected in the risk-aversion coefficient, the certainty equivalent of the portfolio represents its *preference-adjusted* performance. This is the starting point of the numerous attempts to appraise performance adjusted for risk *and* preferences, which is the topic of Chapter 9.[5]

[5] In Section 16.3.2 of Chapter 16, we also examine the particular situation in which a tracker (ETF or index fund) is used as a substitute for an index in the context of an actively managed portfolio. This, to some extent, is also an issue related to the impossibility for the investor to apply a perfect homemade leverage strategy.

5.1.4.3 Accounting for interest rate variability

It is indeed possible to adapt the measurement of performance based on total risk in the context of volatile interest rates. There are essentially two approaches. The first one is proposed by Sharpe (1994). He proposes to consider a fixed-income security that matches the investor's horizon as the portfolio benchmark and to interpret the Sharpe ratio as a special case of the Information ratio. This is explained in detail in Section 6.1.2 of Chapter 6. The second one, introduced by Graham and Harvey (1997), leads to "curbing" the reward-to-volatility relation and proposes a set of performance measures expressed as risk-adjusted rates of return but consistently with the approach of the Sharpe ratio. This is discussed in Section 6.4.1 of Chapter 6.

If the notion of "risk-free rate" is accepted in spite of its variability, the issue of its identification becomes important. Yet, this issue has not gained much attention in the performance measurement literature. It is common practice to adopt a short-term reference interest rate of the currency of denomination (e.g., three-month US T-Bill for USD), considering that taking slightly different maturities (such as the one-month rate) does not make much difference. The chosen rate will typically be the same as the one used in the regression for the estimation of the required return. From a statistical point of view, this makes sense: the use of a short-term rate usually allows to deliver high regression R^2 and this choice ensures a sort of consistency between estimation of beta and performance appraisal. However, from an economic standpoint, this is probably a mistaken approach. We have to revert back to Sharpe's (1994) clarification to understand that. He clearly shows that the ratio that bears his name results from a zero-investment strategy. Accordingly, the interest rate should apply to a maturity that matches the investment horizon of the portfolio. By extension, this logic also applies to performance measures based on systematic risk as they are built upon the same central model. Thus, when one wishes to appraise portfolio performance in a multi-year period (like three or five years), the best choice of the risk-free rate would be the initial yield (at inception of the period) of a fixed-income instrument whose duration matches the sample. In other words, when the Sharpe ratio is measured using T observations with a frequency of n times per year, it makes full sense to associate the risk-free rate with the interest rate for $\frac{T}{n}$ years that was prevailing at the beginning of the period, i.e., $\frac{T}{n}$ years ago:

$$\mathrm{SR}_P^{(T/n)} = \frac{\overline{R}_P - R_{f,T/n}^{(T/n)}}{\sigma_P} \tag{5-3}$$

where $R_{f,T/n}^{(T/n)}$ is the yield-to-maturity of a treasury security maturing in $\frac{T}{n}$ years that was observed exactly $\frac{T}{n}$ years before the estimation of the ratio.[6]

[6]We should specify a duration of $\frac{T}{n}$ years instead of a maturity of $\frac{T}{n}$ years for the sake of correctness. Nevertheless, for low values of the rate or of the maturity, the difference is not material and the approximation does not make much difference.

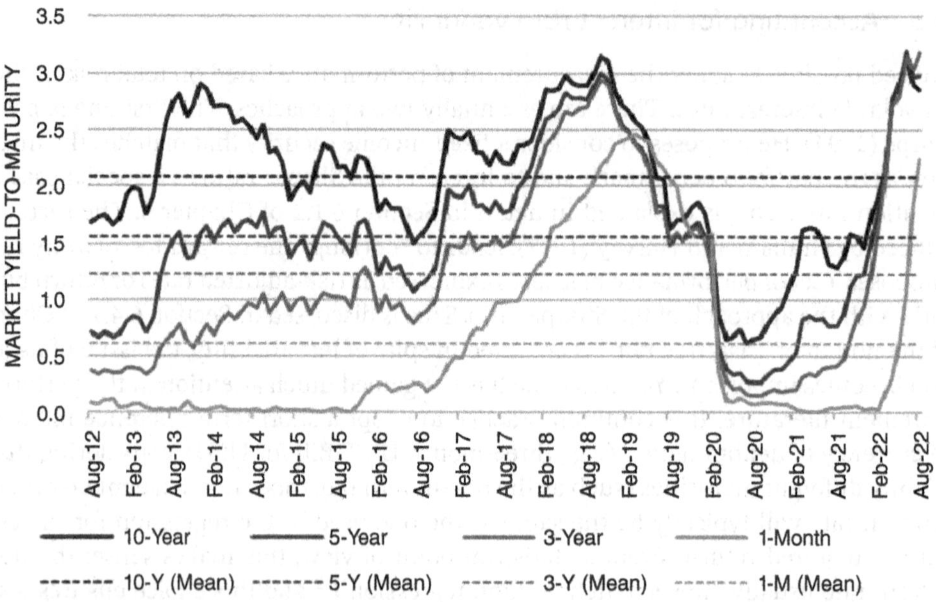

FIGURE 5-7 Joint evolution of the US Treasury market yields-to-maturity over time. *Source*: Board of Governors of the Federal Reserve System (US), own calculations

The implementation of the principle set forth in Equation (5-3) can deliver surprising results. Compared to the one-month T-Bill rate that is often – and relatively automatically – adopted, longer term yields are typically higher, with a positive relation between the maturity and the rate level – with some exceptions, usually shortly before recession periods. This is illustrated in Figure 5-7:

Figure 5-7 not only suggests that the average interest rate over time largely differs as a function of the chosen maturity, but also that various yields can experience swings that can be sudden and not necessarily perfectly similar from one maturity to another. As a numerical illustration, we below report the values of the Sharpe ratios of a hypothetical portfolio whose average rate of return would be a flat 5% over time with a constant volatility of 10% measured at different moments and with different horizons as shown in Table 5-4.

Even though the average value of the ratio does not seem to differ very much from one horizon to another, the gap between the uses of the one-month and 10-year yields is important (one-third of the absolute value of the ratio in this case). More importantly, the appraisal of performance is very different according to the initial year considered. For instance, in August 2020, it did not really matter what maturity was chosen as rates were flat for all tenors. Oppositely, when the slope of the yield curve was steep as was the case in 2014, the Sharpe ratio built with the short-term rate was almost the double of its long-term counterpart. These market conditions have definitely to be accounted for when performance has to be appraised.

TABLE 5-4 Sharpe ratios for a hypothetical portfolio across time and investment horizons.

Horizon (years)	Initial measurement time						
	2012	2014	2016	2018	2020	2022	Average
Standard (1 month)	0.49	0.50	0.47	0.31	0.49	0.28	**0.44**
3 years	0.46	0.41	0.41	0.23	0.48	0.18	**0.38**
5 years	0.43	0.34	0.39	0.22	0.47	0.20	**0.34**
10 years	0.33	0.26	0.34	0.21	0.44	0.21	**0.29**

5.2 ISSUES WITH THE CAPITAL ASSET PRICING MODEL

When measures of systematic risk are used in order to assess the performance of a portfolio, we move one step further than SPT, and rely on Sharpe's CAPM. This model is at the origin of Jensen's alpha, the Treynor ratio, and the modified Jensen's alpha, but also the version of the Information ratio that emanates from the CAPM, namely Treynor and Black's Appraisal ratio. We list here three types of issues related to the application of the framework: the underspecification problem, the inputs of the model, and the assumption regarding the stability of the coefficients.

5.2.1 Failing to identify relevant risk factors

Historically, the CAPM has been the first model of its kind. When it was published, in the middle of the 1960s, its simplicity and apparent effectiveness in explaining stock (and thus portfolio) returns made it an immediate success. It was sufficient to identify the market portfolio and observe the variations of its returns over time, and this was enough to simultaneously obtain the alpha, beta, and specific risk of every single asset.[7]

Besides its character of an equilibrium model, the CAPM is nothing else than a "one-factor model" to explain the cross section of asset returns. This means that it posits that a single random variable – the periodic return of the market portfolio – is necessary and sufficient in order to characterize the common source of risk of financial asset returns so that their remaining variability is idiosyncratic and cannot be explained by any other random variable. This characteristic is important regarding the interpretation of the Jensen's alpha. Indeed, we can reshuffle Equation (3-12) of Chapter 3 in order to represent it in the following way:

$$\alpha_P + \varepsilon_{P,t} = R_{P,t} - [R_f + \beta_P(R_{M,t} - R_f)] \equiv R_{P,t} - R_{P,t}^{\text{req}} \tag{5-4}$$

[7]As Roll (1977) thoroughly explained in his critique, this process is actually much more complicated than it seems at first sight. This is examined in more detail in the next sections.

where $R_{P,t}^{\text{req}} = R_f + \beta_P(R_{M,t} - R_f)$ is the portfolio required return at time t according to the model, and $\varepsilon_{P,t}$ is a random variable with a zero mean. Let us call $u_{P,t} = \alpha_P + \varepsilon_{P,t}$ the unexplained return, i.e., the part of the portfolio return that is not explained by the regression model, whatever the quality of the estimation.[8]

According to the one-factor model, the story ends here and there is nothing to exploit from the variations of this error term $\varepsilon_{P,t}$ that behaves like white noise. The linear model becomes underspecified if there exists another random variable that can be interpreted as a risk factor and that can further explain the variations of the unexplained return over time for a multitude of assets or portfolios. In other words, we can successfully estimate a regression of the type:

$$u_{P,t} = c_{P,0} + \sum_{k=1}^{K-1} c_{P,k} F_{k,t} + \eta_{P,t} \tag{5-5}$$

where $c_{P,0}$ is the intercept of the regression and each $c_{P,k}$ represents the linear return sensitivity (also known as the exposure) to the kth factor, and $F_{k,t}$ stands for the realization of the corresponding factor return at time t.

The idea is to exhaust all potential explanatory factors in such a way that the remaining part of the return that is still left unexplained by the market portfolio (factor 1) and the other $K-1$ factors, namely $c_{P,0} + \eta_{P,t}$, cannot be explained by any other factor. Thus, if the factors are adequately chosen, the "true" alpha of the portfolio, i.e., the abnormal return that remains after all sources of systematic risk have been taken into account, is equal to the intercept of the second regression $c_{P,0}$.

The issue regarding the alpha is simple: if the mean of the sum of the risk factor exposures is not equal to zero (i.e., $\sum_{k=1}^{K-1} c_{P,k}\overline{F}_k \neq 0$), then the intercept of Equation (5-5) has a different value from the alpha: $c_{P,0} \neq \alpha_P$. In short, we can say that "Jensen's alpha is not the true alpha" because the one-factor model is misspecified and suffers from an omitted variables problem.

This issue, in turn, affects the beta. If the factors $F_{k,t}$ that influence the unexplained return $u_{P,t}$ are not independent from the market return $R_{M,t}$, then it is necessary to estimate the whole model as a multiple regression in which the explanatory variables are introduced simultaneously rather than sequentially as we did in Equations (5-4) and (5-5). This gives birth to a special case of a K-factor model, in which the first factor is the market portfolio return.[9] The estimation techniques become more sophisticated, and it is highly likely that the resulting coefficient of $R_{M,t}$ will take a different value from the market beta β_P obtained in Equation (5-4).

In a nutshell, the suspicion of omitted variables in the estimation procedure irrevocably questions both the values taken by the alpha and the beta, and all associated performance measures (Jensen's alpha, Treynor ratio, modified Jensen's alpha, and Appraisal ratio). This

[8]The main statistical issues are discussed in Section 5.4.

[9]There are many versions of K-factor models in which the market portfolio does not play any particular role. We refer to Chapter 7 for more details.

is a potentially very serious issue in practice. Indeed, in many cases, we can anticipate that the average value of the additional risk premiums carried by an actively managed portfolio, namely $\sum_{k=1}^{K-1} c_{P,k}\overline{F}_k$, would be positive in most situations: this corresponds to a realistic case in which the portfolio manager tries to capture some alternative sources of risk with an associated reward. If that is the case, then $c_{P,0} < \alpha_P$: Jensen's alpha overestimates the true alpha. The use of the single factor model provides a false impression of an abnormal return that is higher than the actual one, taking into account all relevant risk factors.

There is in reality ample evidence (as discussed in Chapter 7) that the empirical translation of the CAPM through the market model of Equation (5-4) is underspecified. However, this is a complex topic, mostly because of the joint issue of uncovering the right identity and number of factors. Yet, once a set of candidates is known, the application of the model to a particular portfolio can quickly lead to the conclusion that it is better to move away from the CAPM. In general, a simple and effective indicator of the accuracy of a multiple regression is its adjusted R-squared or R^2_{adj}, which represents the coefficient of determination of the linear regression model with a correction for the number of variables: $R^2_{\text{adj}} = 1 - (1 - R^2)\frac{T-1}{T-K-1}$, where T is the number of observations. Note that in the case of a single factor, the R-squared is simply the square of the correlation coefficient between the returns of the portfolio and the market so that $R^2_{\text{adj}} = 1 - (1 - \rho^2_{PM})\frac{T-1}{T-2}$.

If the value of the adjusted R-squared of the K-factor model is higher than the one of the market model (Equation (5-4)), which corresponds to the special case $K = 1$, then it is very likely that it is necessary to bring more explanatory factors and that the Jensen's alpha and all associated performance measures are inaccurate.[10]

G–T–N example (continued)

A simple look at correlation coefficients suggests that the quality of the fit with a single-factor regression is very different for the three funds. In order to assess whether it is necessary to extend the model to a two-factor model, the risk manager decides to include a well-known candidate as a second explanatory factor and obtains the following values of the R^2: 94.16% for **G**, 57.04% for **T**, and 17.21% for **N**. As for the initial sample, we use monthly data for a period of three years ($T = 36$).

(continued)

[10]There are much more sophisticated ways to assess the quality of the information brought by alternative specifications. They are mostly based on the use of a function that penalizes the log-likelihood function with a penalty for the number of parameters used, such as the Akaike information criterion (AIC) or the Bayesian information criterion (BIC). We refer the reader to the specialized literature for more insight on this topic.

(continued)

On the basis of these results, we can challenge the informativeness of the one-factor regression by comparing the adjusted *R*-squared as in Table 5-5:

TABLE 5-5 G–T–N example – Comparison of the adjusted *R*-squared.

No. of factors	Global	Thematic	Neutral
1	93.92%	20.78%	−2.78%
2	93.81%	54.44%	12.19%

With the market return as a single risk factor, the Global fund achieves a very high goodness of fit and a second factor does not appear to be necessary. For the other two funds, the addition of a second factor clearly adds value. Note that, for the Neutral fund, the correlation coefficient is so low (4%) that the adjusted *R*-squared yields a negative value $R^2_{\text{adj}}(\text{N}) = 1 - (1 - 0.04^2)\frac{36-1}{36-2} = -2.78\%$.

5.2.2 Missing the right benchmark inputs

It all starts with Roll's (1977) critique of the CAPM, as discussed in Chapter 2. Without attacking the theoretical framework as such, the author explains how difficult it is to test it empirically. The common root of all difficulties is that the proxy chosen for the market portfolio is never equal to the optimized portfolio featuring all existing assets. The latter "market portfolio" is essentially unobservable, but it is easy to be mistaken as it is possible to find out an infinity of portfolios that are *ex post* mean–variance efficient without having decisive evidence that one of them is the *ex ante* market portfolio, which can even not be *ex post* efficient.

Even though Roll's arguments mostly address how arduous it is to try to test the theory, they have important implications for performance measurement as well. This is explained in the next section.

5.2.2.1 Choice of the proxies

Without rejecting the CAPM as a model, Roll (1980) questions the quality of its *ex post* measures. Focusing on Jensen's alpha, he defines the performance evaluation error for the portfolio, denoted by δ_P, as follows:

$$\delta_P = \widehat{\alpha}_P - \alpha_P \tag{5-6}$$

where $\widehat{\alpha}_P = \overline{R}_P - \left[\widehat{R}_f + \widehat{\beta}_P\left(\widehat{\overline{R}}_M - \widehat{R}_f\right)\right]$ is the "estimated alpha," equal to the difference between the realized return of the portfolio and its estimated required return using the chosen proxies for the market portfolio and the risk-free rate; and $\alpha_P = \overline{R}_P - [R_f + \beta_P(\overline{R}_M - R_f)]$ is the "true alpha," equal to the difference between the realized return of the portfolio and its estimated required return using the genuine (but unknown) market portfolio and risk-free rate. Because of the particular definition of the alphas, we can also obtain the performance evaluation error through the difference in the portfolio's true and estimated rates of return:

$$\delta_P = \left[R_f + \beta_P\left(\overline{R}_M - R_f\right)\right] - \left[\widehat{R}_f + \widehat{\beta}_P\left(\overline{\widehat{R}}_M - \widehat{R}_f\right)\right] \tag{5-7}$$

Roll (1980) considers that the assessment of performance evaluation error can be contaminated by three (cumulative) types of non-statistical errors:

(a) *The inaccurate assessment of portfolio risk*: It is perfectly possible that the chosen proxy for the market portfolio delivers an excess return that is equal to the true one, which means that the slope of the *ex post* SML is correct, but the resulting – and accurately estimated – portfolio beta $\widehat{\beta}_P$ with this proxy differs from the true one β_P. This is not an estimation issue as such, because the beta is correctly estimated, but it relates to a wrong identification of the market portfolio.

(b) *The incorrect intercept and slope of the SML*: Since the development of the zero-beta CAPM by Black (1972), many empirical studies have concluded that the nearest linear relation between asset betas and average returns are closer to the specification that he proposes rather than the original CAPM developed by Sharpe. Black (1972) replaces the risk-free rate R_f by an intercept, called $\overline{R}_Z$, that corresponds to the average return of a portfolio with no systematic risk (the "zero-beta portfolio"). This intercept, associated with $\widehat{R}_f$ under our notation, is typically higher than most proxies for the riskless rate of interest. This also means that the slope of the empirical SML $(\overline{R}_M - \widehat{R}_f)$ is flatter than the theoretical one under the CAPM. As a consequence, portfolios with a beta lower than 1 have an estimated required return that is higher than the true one, and vice versa for portfolios with a beta higher than 1.

(c) *The wrong market portfolio*: This is the core of Roll's case. The use of a market proxy, whatever it is, instead of a properly optimized portfolio featuring an extremely large number of assets, results in a candidate for the market portfolio that is *ex ante* mean–variance inefficient. Thus, its average rate of return $\overline{\widehat{R}}_M$ is also likely to differ (either positively or negatively, depending on the *ex post* efficiency of this proxy) from the true market return $\overline{R}_M$.

The joint impact of these three errors is illustrated in Figure 5-8.

The graph shows the situation of a portfolio whose estimated alpha is positive whereas the true one is negative. The difference in alphas results from the combination of (i) the underestimation of the beta $\widehat{\beta}_P < \beta_P$ that lowers the required return and (ii) the underestimation of the slope of the true SML $\overline{\widehat{R}}_M - \widehat{R}_f < \overline{R}_M - R_f$, which is only partly compensated by the

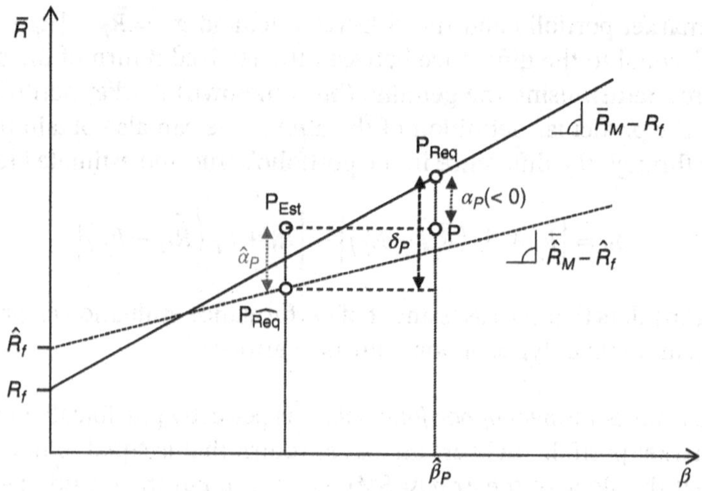

FIGURE 5-8 Decomposition of the true alpha into performance evaluation error and estimated alpha.

favorable effect of the overestimation of the risk-free rate. Because of the error in the measurement of beta, we have the illusion that the portfolio coordinates correspond to the point P_{Est} whereas the portfolio truly locates at point P.

5.2.2.2 Benchmark manipulation

The asset management industry excels at creating benchmarks. We have already addressed numerous issues related to the specification of a reference index or portfolio that is supposed to reflect the manager's required rate of return.

When a benchmark is identified for a particular portfolio, it lies somewhere in a continuum between a pure passive index that obeys unambiguous construction rules, like a broad market index, and a very specific portfolio combining a number of comparable funds or portfolios, generally termed as a "peer group." However, whenever, in the context of performance measurement, the benchmark is neither considered within the scope of a multifactor model nor meant to be used in order to compare very specific strategies in a total risk perspective, then it is used to compute an alpha (be it Jensen's alpha in the CAPM framework or a peer group comparison return).

Focusing again on the CAPM, Roll (1980) explains how difficult it is to approach the true market portfolio. One may indeed be tempted to voluntarily depart from it. Kryzanowski and Rahman (2008) argue that some asset managers have the incentive to voluntarily choose an inefficient benchmark, i.e., one that exhibits a significant idiosyncratic risk relative to the correctly specified benchmark. Doing so, they can achieve positive and significant alphas without exhibiting any particular skill (neither selectivity nor timing). The more inefficient the benchmark, the more interesting it is in order to artificially generate a significant abnormal return and the performance measures that use it as an input.

On the other hand, ignoring the fund's own self-defined benchmark is also a potential source of error. Even if the analyst's motivation is virtuous, the act of replacing a reference portfolio that the manager is committed to track with another based on expert judgment may introduce a substantial level of noise. Worse still, this can create a potential disagreement by the manager with the performance appraisal made by the external stakeholder, with endless disputes.

G–T–N example (continued)

We reuse the data on alternative benchmarks exploited in Section 4.4 of Chapter 4. Instead of using the world market index **M** (with mean return $\overline{R}_M = 7.39\%$ and volatility $\sigma_M = 8.83\%$) as a single benchmark for all its funds, we replace it by an optimized portfolio featuring stocks and bonds **M′**, with mean return $\overline{R}_{M'} = 4.88\%$ and volatility $\sigma_{M'} = 5.12\%$. The correlation of the fund with **M** is $\rho_{TM} = 0.48$ whereas the correlation with the alternative benchmark is $\rho_{TM'} = 0.56$. Furthermore, it stands clear that the relevant risk-free rate regarding the horizon with which the portfolio is managed should correspond to a longer maturity, with $R_{f'} = 2.24\%$.

Will all information about the competing benchmarks, we obtain the results as shown in Table 5-6.

TABLE 5-6 G–T–N example – Performance measures for the Thematic fund under alternative benchmarks.

Thematic fund	M	M′
Beta	0.35	0.70
Required return	3.51%	4.09%
Alpha	1.21%	0.63%
Modified alpha	3.47%	0.90%
Information ratio	0.21	0.12

The fund's performance evaluation error is equal to the difference between the true and the estimated required returns ($\delta_T = 4.09\% - 3.51\% = 0.58\%$) or, equivalently, to the difference between the estimated and the true alpha ($\delta_T = 1.21\% - 0.63\% = 0.58\%$). Since delta is positive, it indicates that the fund's estimated alpha overstates its true performance.

5.2.3 Ignoring the portfolio manager's decisions

The CAPM was originally designed to characterize the risk–return relationship of financial assets, with a focus on listed equities. If the company pursues a consistent strategy over time, then both its total risk and its correlation with the market portfolio should remain relatively steady. This leads to a constant beta. In order to estimate it statistically, the analyst must identify the adequate sample period for which the model's assumption of a constant beta can be satisfied. Thus, the measurement issue is purely statistical and does not as such lead to invalidation of the model.

However, beyond its ambition to determine the expected return of listed equities, the CAPM stands as an equilibrium model that aims at pricing all financial assets, including bonds, commodities, and even unlisted assets through a buy-and-hold strategy applicable during one full period of time. By extension, it is also supposed to be relevant to address the issue of the risk and return relation of many types of financial portfolios, including – and this is the issue here – actively managed ones. Applying the model thus "forces" the portfolio to comply with its assumptions; otherwise, the model outputs are likely to be invalid.

The problem here is that a portfolio manager who tries to "beat the market" does not necessarily behave like the CEO of a listed company. Of course, it is possible to justify a kind of analogy when the portfolio manager holds a certain allocation over time and tries to outperform a passive benchmark by carefully choosing the securities that are likely to produce a positive abnormal return. In practice, multiperiod versions of the CAPM can be implemented to accommodate this behavior. However, if the manager regularly changes their allocation with tactical bets in an anticipation of upward or downward market movement, this certainly does not correspond to what is expected from the top manager of a company. This becomes a serious issue when the manager voluntarily and substantially changes the market exposure of their portfolio over time because the fundamental model is not able to accommodate such a behavior through a constant beta.

Grinblatt and Titman (1989) posit this issue in a clear manner. They define the first category of successful active portfolio manager as someone who has "selectivity information." Using our own words, this person obtains an abnormal return unexplained by the model that is positive for at least one period. That is, there exists a moment τ for which $E(R_{i,\tau} - R_{i,\tau}^{req}) > 0$ for some asset i held in the portfolio. As shown, this is consistent with a positive alpha. Portfolio managers who possess this type of selectivity skill are sometimes called "stock pickers" when they are specialized in equities.

By contrast, the successful second category of manager (the one who anticipates market movements) has "timing information." This so-called "market timer" manages over time the portfolio's exposure to the market in such a way that there exists a moment τ for which $E(R_{P,\tau}^{req} - R_P^{req}) > 0$, where R_P^{req} is the required return of the portfolio for the whole time period. This condition can only be satisfied if the portfolio beta changes over time. It cannot be captured by Jensen's alpha.

The authors illustrate the issue of using the CAPM in the presence of a market timer. In their example, the portfolio manager can adopt two levels of beta at each point in time. On average, the manager makes correct decisions: they adopt a low beta when the market delivers a low return and a high beta when the market provides a better reward. Besides, the manager has no selectivity information (neither positive nor negative). Thus, overall, the manager's performance must be evaluated as positive.

The issue arises when the variability in betas is not properly accounted for in the estimation procedure. If one tries to estimate the alpha and beta according to the regression of Equation (5-4), the results can be surprising, as shown in Figure 5-9 extracted from their article (with coordinates D and B′ being added on the original graph).

The solid straight lines correspond to the characteristic lines of the portfolio in the high beta and in the low beta environment. The coordinates of points A and B on these lines represent the mean of the market excess return under each environment on the horizontal axis, and the corresponding excess return obtained by the portfolio on the vertical axis. Thus, for each market environment taken in isolation, the portfolio has not beaten the market (the average return is equal to its required one), but it is clear that the manager is a good timer as they manage to increase their exposure when the market premium is larger. However, the regression line that moves through A and B, represented graphically with the dotted straight line, has a negative intercept, i.e., a negative alpha (point C on the graph). Thus, applying the standard

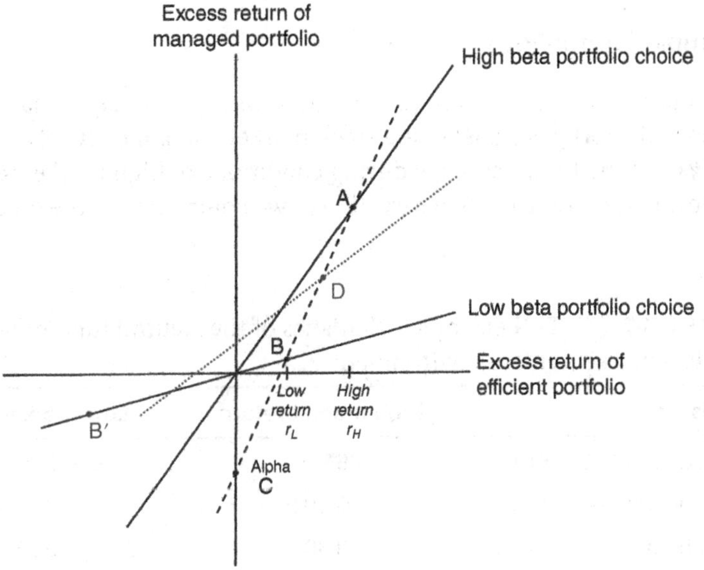

FIGURE 5-9 Illustration of wrong alpha and beta estimations in the case of a market timer. *Source:* Grinblatt and Titman (1989). Points B′ and D and the thin dotted line have been added to the original graph.

CAPM estimation technique here results in a misleading impression of an underperforming manager (all classical measures based on alpha are negative), whereas in reality the manager is at the same time a good market timer and a neutral stock picker. The empirical consequences of failing to account for the market timing behavior of the portfolio manager are documented by Bunnenberg, Rohleder, Scholz, and Wilkens (2019).

Note that the outcome will not necessarily always produce a negative alpha. If the low beta coordinates had been to the left of the vertical axis at point B′, for instance, the straight line that connects A and B′ would have delivered a positive alpha. Furthermore, the reality is a bit more complicated than what the graph shows. Presumably, the estimated global beta with all observations taken into account will yield a weighted average between the "high beta" and the "low beta" situations, i.e., a line whose slope is somewhere between the solid lines (thin dotted line on the graph). As this line moves through point D corresponding to the coordinates of the average excess market and portfolio returns (the midpoint between A and B), it intersects the vertical axis above the origin, producing a positive alpha. Again, this alpha is likely to be biased as it results from the combination of "normal" portfolio returns in high and low market return environments.

All we can conclude is that failing to account for market timing behavior is very likely to deliver unreliable alphas and makes the application of the classical performance measures developed in Chapter 3 misleading.

G–T–N example (continued)

The Neutral fund's beta is almost zero ($\beta_N = 0.02$), but this is indeed a market neutral fund that takes long and short positions on the stock market using mostly ETFs. Based upon an in-depth analysis of the fund's strategy during conditions of high market return (18 observations) and low market return (18 observations), we come up with the outcome presented in Table 5-7:

TABLE 5-7 G–T–N example – Statistics of the Neutral fund in high and low market returns environments.

Statistics	High market return	Low market return
Average market return	8.94%	5.84%
Average fund return	3.69%	0.28%
Fund beta	0.30	−0.26
No. of observations	18	18

Applying the CAPM relation under each environment (with a constant interest rate at 1.44%), we can see that the manager has not beaten the market in either case:

$$\overline{R}_{\mathbf{N},\,\text{high}} = 3.69\% = 1.44\% + 0.30(8.94\% - 1.44\%) = R_f + \beta_{\mathbf{N}}(\overline{R}_{M,\,\text{high}} - R_f)$$

$$\overline{R}_{\mathbf{N},\,\text{low}} = 0.28\% = 1.44\% + (-0.26)(5.84\% - 1.44\%) = R_f + \beta_{\mathbf{N}}(\overline{R}_{M,\,\text{low}} - R_f)$$

However, the fund has globally delivered a positive alpha when the average figures are considered:

$$\overline{R}_{\mathbf{N},\,\text{average}} = 2.55\% = 1.00\% + 1.44\% + 0.02(7.39\% - 1.44\%)$$

This phenomenon is illustrated in Figure 5-10.

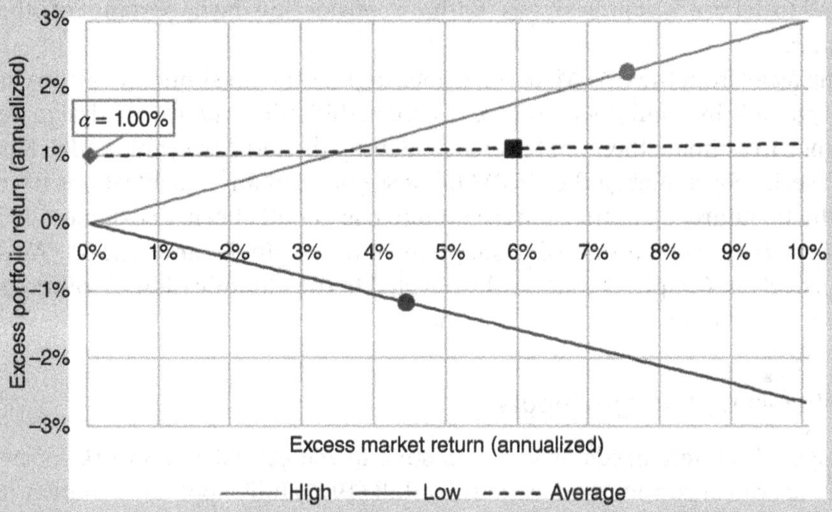

FIGURE 5-10 G–T–N example – Characteristic lines of the Neutral fund in different market environments.

5.2.4 Solutions

5.2.4.1 Identifying relevant risk factors

It is tempting for a portfolio manager to deny, voluntarily or not, the issue of underspecification of the single-factor model. The popular Jensen's alpha generally benefits from this ignorance as many omitted risk factors would contribute to the portfolio required return and thus erode abnormal return accordingly. From an absolute value standpoint, sticking to a (wrong) pricing model with only the market return as explanatory variable can substantially embellish portfolio performance. From a statistical point of view though, the absence of relevant risk factors in the model weakens hypothesis testing and reduces significance, but this issue is too often overlooked in practice.

An interesting "acid test" in this respect is the use of the modified Jensen's alpha and the attempt to perform statistical inference on that basis. Unlike tests of the significance of the original Jensen's alpha, the advantage of testing the modified Jensen's alpha is that it jointly assesses the significance of the estimate and the validity of the model. If the portfolio beta is too low or if the coefficient of determination (R^2) is insufficient, the test will fail to reject the null hypothesis of zero performance, even if the alpha is very high (like in the case of the Neutral fund in the example). Using the modified Jensen's alpha as a preferred classical performance measure is not sufficient to detect whether additional factors should be used, but it can already be very useful to discard one-factor specifications that are totally irrelevant. This can be interesting, for instance, in order to challenge some alternative investment strategies that pretend to deliver "absolute alphas" without considering the importance of other potential risk premiums.

Moving away from the CAPM, performance appraisal with similar measures to the classical ones is possible in a multifactor setup. The main difficulty is neither to design performance measures nor to estimate them, but rather to identify the most relevant model. Since the first attempt to seriously challenge the CAPM by Ross (1976), many specifications have been proposed in the literature, up to the point that there has literally been an exponential increase in the number of risk factors proposed to supplement the original market model. We discuss this issue extensively in Chapter 7 that is fully devoted to the identification of solutions regarding performance measurement in multifactor models.

5.2.4.2 Selecting the right inputs

If the analyst absolutely needs or wants to stick to the CAPM framework for performance appraisal, the critical considerations made by Roll (1977) fully apply, and there is no easy way to escape from them. Nevertheless, in a companion paper to the one explaining the issues surrounding performance errors, Roll (1981) proposes an avenue for a partial solution regarding the benchmark choice. He suggests a kind of two-step procedure in which (i) the long-run mean return of each stock (with stationary returns) is estimated according to a weighted regression on the average return of all stocks and (ii) the performance evaluation error of a stock is computed by subtracting the estimate of its required return using a market index from its expected return obtained in step (i). Thus, the evaluation error of any diversified portfolio is the weighted average of those of its constituents.

In order to construct a version of the market portfolio with market data, the solution that has proven most popular is the one introduced by Best and Grauer (1985). They propose the use of market capitalizations, the variance–covariance matrix, and a market-wide risk aversion to construct a proxy for the market portfolio and its required return. This approach has later been adopted by Black and Litterman (1991) as the basis for their Bayesian approach to characterize the expected rate of return of stocks and indexes. Their procedure is explained in Section 2.3.2 of Chapter 2.

Another, more pragmatic step toward the reduction of the benchmark error is the adoption of a market index whose construction lends itself as little as possible to Roll's critique. For instance, the MSCI All Countries World Index (ACWI) features 2934 constituents from 47 markets with a coverage of 85% of their total market capitalization. Even though the optimization procedure underlying this index does not necessarily correspond to the true market portfolio, this index is logically closer to the theoretical optimal portfolio than the MSCI World, which only features stocks from the most developed markets.

The question raised by the choice of an inefficient benchmark is naturally solved if one genuinely attempts to approach the optimized market portfolio as described above. If one does not want to adopt a passive index for performance computation, Kryzanowski and Rahman (2008) suggest the use of a peer group. However, instead of choosing the peers by trying to compose a homogeneous group who are close to the portfolio (for instance, direct competitors, funds with the same region of incorporation), the criterion should be that they have adopted the same benchmark. Starting with the assumption that most active managers would not outperform the market on average, their alpha should average out and therefore picking their average return as benchmark should reduce as much as possible the performance evaluation error. Eventually, as Angelidis, Giamouridis, and Tessaromatis (2013) point out, it is dangerous to diverge from the self-defined benchmark of the portfolio manager as it may induce a substantial measurement error. The best solution would be, from the investor's point of view, to induce (or force) the portfolio manager to select a benchmark that becomes an undisputed reference – hard to beat, and obviously an anchor for the portfolio.

There is also a possibility to account for the benchmark inefficiency by directly applying a correction for the portfolio's inefficiency level. This approach is discussed in Section 6.1.4 of Chapter 6.

5.2.4.3 Accounting for market timing behavior

Unlike solutions proposed for performance appraisal in multifactor models, the treatment of market timing involves the creation of new performance measures specifically designed for that purpose. The issue is not necessarily more complex than the extension to multiple factors, but the evidence of dynamic market exposures involves a relatively sophisticated treatment of information.

There are two chapters that deal with this issue. In Chapter 8, we investigate approaches that have been specifically developed in order to isolate and measure the impact of market timing skills on portfolio performance. They can be of different kinds: based on the results of nonlinear regressions, based on dynamic regressions, or even calibrated with information on portfolio holdings. In this latter case, when rich and detailed information is known about how the portfolio has been actually managed over time, we can use performance attribution models which, as an output, will precisely quantify the impact of timing information on the generation of abnormal return (see Chapter 14).

5.3 ISSUES WITH THE SAMPLE

Let us assume now that the model is suitable, different issues with the inputs are adequately fixed, and that there are no particular specificities (such as market timing skills) that would contaminate performance measurement with the classical performance measures. A key difficulty remains to be overcome: make the best possible use of the available data in order to faithfully estimate the necessary inputs. We distinguish two types of issues: the ones associated with the sample of observed returns, and others related to statistical estimation of the parameters.

5.3.1 Selecting an inadequate sample

5.3.1.1 Time window

It has been known for many years that the estimated portfolio performance is sensitive to the size and the location in time of the sample of observations. Friend and Blume (1970) had already concluded that the choice of a too small time window – regardless of the frequency of the computation of returns – produced very different portfolio rankings regarding their risk-adjusted performance. Thus, one is tempted to select the longest possible time length in order to reach two objectives: (i) capture as faithfully as possible the key risk metrics (standard deviation, beta, and tracking error) that reflects the portfolio manager's risk-taking behavior, and (ii) obtain an estimate of the market risk premium that resembles the true expected return on the financial market.

This maximalist approach bounces on several obstacles that cast doubt on the validity of the performance measures:

- The longer the estimation period that is chosen, the more likely it is that the portfolio manager will have substantially shifted their strategy, and that the average beta or risk level measured over the full time period will not reflect the dynamic changes of the fund's exposures to different risk factors.
- Performance measurement mostly attempts to identify the skills associated with an active portfolio manager. If performance is estimated over a long period, it is possible that the initial manager has been replaced at some point in time. This can obviously be controlled for at the individual portfolio level, but this can become a major issue if the same time period is used in order to rank a large number of funds, for which a significant proportion of managers might have changed.
- Even if a manager decides to pursue a very steady strategy, the underlying securities held in their portfolio could themselves experience a sensible change in their risk

characteristics. A well-known example is the banking sector, whose stocks were generally considered as defensive (beta lower than one) before the global financial crisis and suddenly became aggressive (beta higher than one) once the dust settled and the world discovered that banking was a riskier business than it was previously thought. Extending the period under consideration increases the probability that the estimated risk of the portfolio actually corresponds to the average of different risk levels over time.

- Finally, past performance might not be very persistent over time. Measuring a Sharpe ratio or an alpha over a 10-year period implicitly assumes that the manager has been able to consistently achieve the average performance during the whole period. However, in reality, there is very little evidence that active portfolio managers are able to steadily outperform their peers or benchmark, and their rankings may change substantially from one period to another. Trying to appraise performance over a too long period could result in an "averaging out" effect, destroying much of the information that could be retrieved with shorter periods.

Some of these issues are illustrated in Figure 5-11. It corresponds to a five-year period during which the "true" portfolio beta equals one during the first 20 months, then collapses to zero (e.g., because of a shift in strategy) during the next period of 20 months, and then goes back to one again.

The bold line represents the evolution of the true portfolio beta over time. The average beta is equal to $\frac{1}{3} \times 1 + \frac{1}{3} \times 0 + \frac{1}{3} \times 1 = \frac{2}{3}$ and would be close to the one estimated using the full time window. Shrinking the sample to 12, 18, or 24 months would produce beta estimates at each point in time that correspond to the values taken by the dashed and dotted lines. We

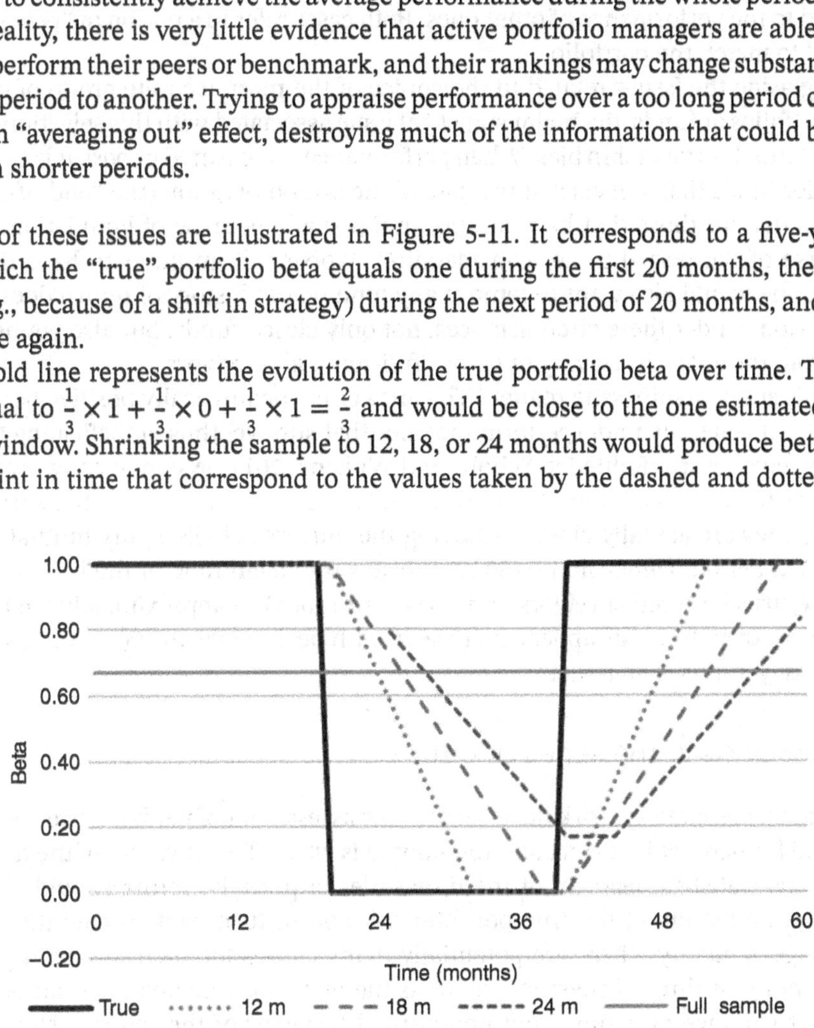

FIGURE 5-11 Illustration of the influence of the time window on the estimation of the beta.

can clearly see that the sample size that would produce at the same time the closest behavior to the true U-shaped function and the best reactivity (i.e., the shortest lag between the changes in true and estimated betas) corresponds to the shortest time window (12 months).

5.3.1.2 Cross-section

Talking about the cross-section makes sense when a panel of observations are used for performance appraisal, i.e., a combination of time series of returns and a cross-section of different funds or portfolios. Thus, this discussion applies when (i) the benchmark for performance evaluation uses data from several other portfolios or when (ii) the performance of a single portfolio is compared to the performance of other ones. Both cases refer to a notion of "peer group" that is supposed to match the portfolio.

Leaving aside the issues related to the choice of the most accurate group of comparable indexes, portfolios or funds, the major statistical issue associated with this selection is the presence of a potential survivorship bias. When performance is measured *ex post*, it is convenient to only consider funds that still exist at the date of the last observation (the "end-of-sample survivors") and discard those that have disappeared (usually because of liquidation or merger) in the course of the period under consideration. Worse still, in order to have the cleanest peer group, one would also want to remove any fund whose history of return does not totally span the period. Under these circumstances, not only closed funds, but also young funds are excluded from the analysis, leaving only the "full-sample" survivors.

Does this survivorship issue matter? The answer is unequivocally positive because funds that are left out generally underperform the ones that survive, thus embellishing their cross-sectional average return. Rohleder, Scholz, and Wilkens (2011) systematically investigate the magnitude of the bias and show that closed funds largely underperform the surviving ones years before they are actually closed. Studying the universe of US equity mutual funds over the 1991–2020 period, Dimensional (2020) assesses the magnitude of the bias (difference in abnormal returns between survivors and graveyard funds) to approximately 0.60% per year. On average, 5% of all funds disappear every year, with peaks of 9% in 2001 and more than 11% in 2011. Thus, yes, this is an issue.

5.3.2 Mishandling the series of returns

Imagine that all preparatory work necessary for the assessment of performance has been done properly: the framework is correct and the sample is clean. The question of the data set itself remains. Some statistical features of the time series of portfolio returns could substantially influence the estimation of the true portfolio risk and in turn contaminate the assessment of the manager's quality. There are potentially many causes for such misleading diagnosis, but it turns out that three of them stand out as the most documented ones: autocorrelation, non-constant variance over time, and non-normal behavior of the returns. Note that these issues are not necessarily mutually exclusive and will mostly affect the Sharpe ratio.

5.3.2.1 Autocorrelation

Autocorrelation or serial correlation of a time series of returns means that the observed return at time t partly depends on the realization of the lagged returns at time $t - l$ (when $l = 1$, we have evidence of first-order autocorrelation, i.e., the return depends on its immediate predecessor). Formally, an autoregressive (AR) process of order L, also denoted by AR(L), can be written as

$$R_{P,t} = \rho_0 + \sum_{l=1}^{L} \rho_l R_{P,t-l} + \varepsilon_{P,t} \tag{5-8}$$

where ρ_0 is a constant and ρ_l represents the coefficient of the lth lag of the process.

The existence of such a phenomenon would imply that returns would be at least partly predictable by "simply" using their past observations, which represents a breach of the weak form of the informationally efficient market hypothesis. Beyond very short-term market microstructure effects that can be exploited by high-frequency trading algorithms, there is limited evidence of autocorrelation of stock returns for low-frequency data, like weeks or months. For various reasons however (discussed in Chapter 12), some evidence of serial correlation can be found in the returns of actively managed portfolios. Thus, a fraction of their variability is not stochastic anymore but depends on a deterministic trend. Computing the standard deviation without any adjustment will result in a misleading assessment of the portfolio's risk and, consequently, in a bias in performance measurement. In general, if the process is an AR(1) – the most common scenario – we have the following inequality:

$$\sigma_P > (\text{resp.} <)\ \hat{\sigma}_P \text{ if } \rho_1 > (\text{resp.} <)\ 0 \tag{5-9}$$

where σ_P is the true (unobserved) volatility of the portfolio returns, $\hat{\sigma}_P$ is its estimated one, and ρ_1 represents the autocorrelation coefficient in the process $R_{P,t} = \rho_0 + \rho_1 R_{P,t-1} + \varepsilon_{P,t}$.

Thus, evidence of positive autocorrelation, which means that returns keep a sort of memory of their past values, would presumably lead to a lower estimation of risk than the actual one. The Sharpe ratio, which features risk at the denominator, will then probably be overstated.

5.3.2.2 Heteroscedasticity

Heteroscedasticity is a scholarly word that translates the fact that the residuals of a process display a variance that is not constant across observations. When applied to the world of financial time series, this mostly addresses the fact that returns are likely to experience a phenomenon called "volatility clustering." Even though the sign of relative price changes evolves almost randomly, their magnitude (in absolute value) seems to cluster over time in a relatively predictable way. Some periods are quiet, and some others are excited. This is illustrated in the

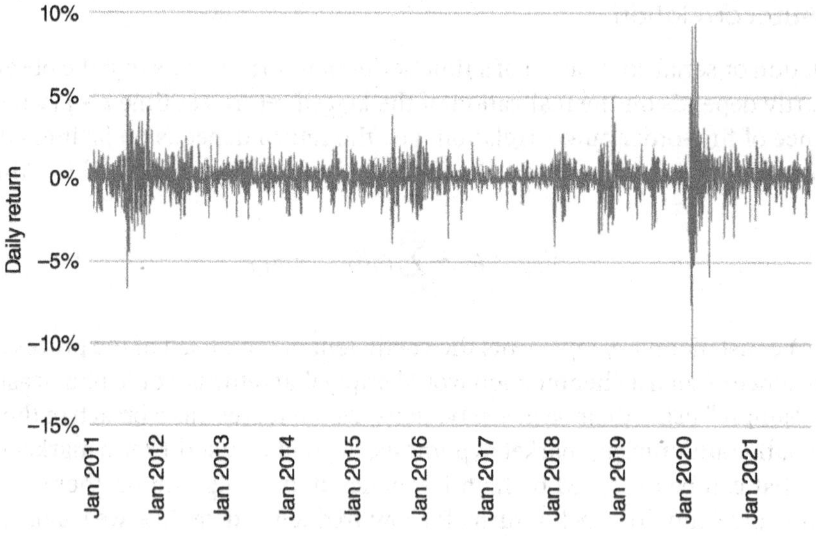

FIGURE 5-12 Daily returns of the S&P500 Index, 2011–2021.

chart presented in Figure 5-12, which displays the daily returns of the S&P500 Index over the 2011–2021 period.

The visual impression left by Figure 5-12 confirms the presence of volatility clustering in the data. There are a few excited periods (mid-2011, end 2018, and March 2020) that contrast with quiet or even very quiet moments, such as in 2017. Keeping the assumption of normally distributed returns but trying to account for this phenomenon leads to the following formulation:

$$R_{P,t} = \mathrm{E}(R_{P,t}) + \varepsilon_{P,t}, \text{ with } \varepsilon_{P,t} \rightsquigarrow \mathcal{N}(0, \sigma^2_{P,t}) \tag{5-10}$$

where $\mathrm{E}(R_{P,t})$ stands for the expectation of the return conditional on all information known up to time t, and $\sigma^2_{P,t}$ is its conditional variance. The square root of this conditional variance is the conditional volatility $\sigma_{P,t} = \sqrt{\sigma^2_{P,t}}$.

Why would this be an issue for the assessment of portfolio performance? Because the aggregation of daily, weekly, or monthly estimated conditional volatilities might substantially differ from the point estimate traditionally obtained from the sample, this will not only affect the Sharpe ratio but also potentially all performance measures. In particular, if we measure performance *ex post* on the basis of a specific sample, we obtain the following inequality:

$$\sigma_P > (\text{resp.} <) \, \hat{\sigma}_P \text{ if } \overline{\sigma}_P > (\text{resp.} <) \, \hat{\sigma}_P \tag{5-11}$$

where $\hat{\sigma}_P$ is the unconditional estimate of the volatility of portfolio returns, and $\overline{\sigma}_P = \frac{1}{T}\sum_{t=1}^{T} \sigma_{P,t}$ is the average of the conditional volatilities during the same period.

The same reasoning holds if there is evidence of volatility clustering at the level of the residual of the market model regression or the tracking error of the portfolio versus its benchmark. In that case, the Information ratio (or the Appraisal ratio) must be adjusted as well.

5.3.2.3 Non-normality

The simplest justification for the use of the standard deviation of returns as a risk measure is that they follow a Gaussian distribution. In Section 5.1.1, it is observed that this assumption is very hard to sustain in practice, and it is appealing to simply discard volatility and replace it with another more sophisticated notion for the purpose of assessing a manager's performance. Nevertheless, if the departure from normality is not too pronounced, another pragmatic approach is to keep adopting volatility as the risk measure and to neglect the consequences of this departure on the investor's apprehension of the portfolio riskiness. In doing so, precious information may be wrongfully discarded.

By looking at each moment in isolation, we can try to analyze the influence of higher moments than the variance on the way investors perceive the riskiness of a portfolio. Although it is possible to inspect moments of every order larger than two (i.e., the variance), in practice only the third one ("skewness," denoted by $\mu_{P,3}$) and fourth one ("excess kurtosis," denoted by $e\mu_{P,4}$) appear to matter. As a reminder, their formulas are

$$\mu_{P,3} \equiv \frac{\mathrm{E}[(R_P - \overline{R}_P)^3]}{\sigma_P^3} \tag{5-12a}$$

$$e\mu_{P,4} \equiv \frac{\mathrm{E}[(R_P - \overline{R}_P)^4]}{\sigma_P^4} - 3 \tag{5-12b}$$

These definitions of the skewness and excess kurtosis use the centered moments of orders 3 and 4, respectively, "normalize" them by the corresponding power of the standard deviation to get a scale-free index, and, in the case of the kurtosis, deduce 3 in order to center it around 0 such that in the case of the Gaussian distribution, $\mu_{P,3} = 0$ and $e\mu_{P,4} = 0$. Note that the unbiased estimators of these coefficients with a sample of T observations that are independent and identically distributed (i.i.d.) are the following:

$$\hat{\mu}_{P,3} = \frac{T}{(T-1)(T-2)} \sum_{t=1}^{T} \left(\frac{R_{P,t} - \overline{R}_P}{\hat{\sigma}_P} \right)^3 \tag{5-13a}$$

$$e\hat{\mu}_{P,4} = \frac{T(T+1)}{(T-1)(T-2)(T-3)} \sum_{t=1}^{T} \left(\frac{R_{P,t} - \overline{R}_P}{\hat{\sigma}_P} \right)^4 - 3\frac{(T-1)^2}{(T-2)(T-3)} \tag{5-13b}$$

where $\overline{R}_P$ and $\hat{\sigma}_P$ are the sample mean and standard deviation of portfolio returns, respectively.

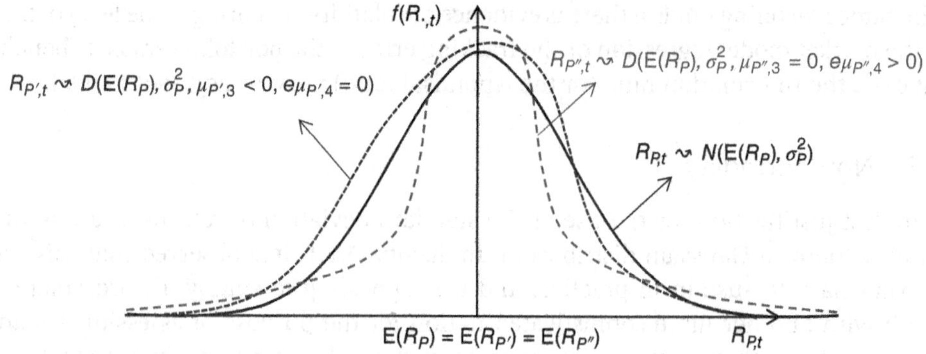

FIGURE 5-13 Illustration of the three concepts related to extreme risk.

In general, investors dislike portfolio returns displaying a negative skewness ("left-asymmetric" distributions) and a positive excess kurtosis ("leptokurtic" distributions).[11] Figure 5-13 shows why this is usually the case.

The graph illustrates the probability distribution function (also known as "density function") $f(R_{.,t})$ for three portfolios P, P', and P''. As a benchmark, the returns of portfolio P are normally distributed with expectation $E(R_P)$ and variance σ_P^2. The density function corresponds to the continuous line adopting the emblematic "bell shape" of the Gaussian distribution.

Returns of portfolio P' follow another distribution compared to the Gaussian one but have the same expectation and variance, but also excess kurtosis, as those of P. Nevertheless, its skewness $\mu_{P',3}$ is negative. Visually, this corresponds to a density function (thin dotted curve) that "leans" to the left of the expectation. This means that the likelihood of observing a very negative return is greater for P' than for P, which corresponds to a fatter left tail of the distribution of P'. This higher dispersion to the left is compensated by a thinner right tail and a greater concentration around the mode (peak of the density function) which is higher than the expectation. To write it in a simple way, we could say that *with P', when you have a surprise, it is more likely to be a bad one than with P*. Thus, if they are given the choice between P and P', a vast majority of risk-averse investors would choose the former, because they would be deterred by the perspective of having a bigger probability of losing large amounts of money with P'.

The returns of portfolio P'' also follow another distribution compared to the Gaussian one, still with the same expectation and variance as those of P. This time, its skewness is zero (the distribution is symmetric around the expectation), but its excess kurtosis $\mu_{P'',4}$ is positive. The density function (thick dashed curve) is fatter than the one of P at both ends. This implies that the likelihood of observing extreme returns (of either sign) is greater for P'' than for P.

---

[11]This is not an absolute truth: there are many counterexamples of situations to be found when skewness and kurtosis effects are mixed in such a way that these preferences paradoxically switch.

Because their variances are the same, the fatter tail of the distribution of P'' is compensated by a narrower density in the middle. Again, expressing the phenomenon in simple words, it means that *with P'', you are more likely to have a surprise than with P.* Usually, investors dislike surprises, because their feeling of joy when they obtain larger gains is less strong than their feeling of distress when they bear large losses. Hence, if they are given the choice between P and P'', a vast majority of risk-averse investors would also choose the former, whose profile of gains and losses is more reassuring.

The combination of skewness and kurtosis can produce situations with undetermined effects on investors' preferences, but in general, the skewness effect dominates up to a certain point. A positive skewness combined with a large kurtosis, for instance, is probably appreciated (*you are more likely to have a surprise, and it is more likely to be a good one*) until the point where the kurtosis effect becomes too large (*you are very likely to have a surprise, even though it is more likely to be a good one*). We can summarize the typical impact of the interaction of skewness and kurtosis in Table 5-8.

The parentheses indicate a weaker combined effect. The lower left and upper right corners of the table leave unequivocal results because skewness and kurtosis influence the subjective assessment of portfolio risk in the same direction. The situations in which skewness is very pronounced compared to kurtosis also leave little doubt on the investor's reaction. For the rest, this is mostly a matter of individual risk profile, and in particular the sensitivity to behavioral aspects.[12]

To wrap up, if one tries to perform adjustments to the portfolio volatility based upon the effect of higher moments of the distribution of portfolio returns, we can reach the following principles, expressed as inequalities:

$$\sigma_P^{\text{adj}} > (\text{resp.} <)\ \hat{\sigma}_P \text{ if } \begin{cases} \mu_{P,3} < (\text{resp.} >)\ 0 \text{ and } e\mu_{P,4} \geq (\text{resp.} \leq)\ 0 \\ e\mu_{P,4} > (\text{resp.} <)\ 0 \text{ and } \mu_{P,3} \leq (\text{resp.} \geq)\ 0 \end{cases} \tag{5-14}$$

TABLE 5-8 Anticipated impact of the combination of skewness and kurtosis on investor's assessment of risk.

Skewness	Excess kurtosis			
	Very negative	Negative	Positive	Very positive
Very negative	?	(−)	−	−−
Negative	?	?	−	−
Positive	+	+	?	?
Very positive	++	+	(+)	?

[12]These issues are discussed in detail in Chapters 9 and 10.

where $\sigma_P^{adj} = \hat{\sigma}_P + \ell(\hat{\sigma}_P, \mu_{P,3}, e\mu_{P,4})$, for some function $\ell(\cdot)$, is an estimate of the volatility reflecting an adjustment for the portfolio's skewness and kurtosis.

As indicated in Table 5-8, the other combinations of signs are less easy to characterize. Nevertheless, it is interesting to note that most time series of returns exhibit simultaneously a negative skewness and a (very) positive kurtosis. For instance, the daily returns of the S&P500 Index used in Figure 5-12 exhibit skewness and kurtosis that are respectively equal to $\mu_{S\&P,3} = -0.62$ and $e\mu_{S\&P,4} = 16.51$. The very high estimate of the kurtosis can be explained by the presence of sudden and very extreme negative returns, such as −6.66% on 8 August 2011 and −11.98% on 16 March 2020. This latter observation, which corresponds to the burst of the COVID-19 crisis and its unanticipated lockdown decisions, corresponds to deviation from the mean (0.05% per day) equal to a multiple of more than 11 times the daily volatility (1.08% per day). If one believes that the S&P500 returns are normally distributed, this corresponds to a probability of occurrence lower than $1\% \times 10^{-100}$. That is, an impossible event; it simply means that the Gaussian distribution does not work in this case.

The case where $\mu_{P,3} < 0$ and $e\mu_{P,4} > 0$ that matches many series of portfolio returns unfortunately corresponds to a "clear" situation accounted for in Equation (5-14). This calls for an upward adjustment of the estimate of the volatility of portfolio returns if one still wishes to use performance measures that are based on that type of risk measure, like the Sharpe ratio.

G–T–N example (continued)

We assume that three years of data are used in order to perform three statistical estimation exercises in an independent way so that we obtain a better picture of the potential issues with the data. The exercises are: (i) to calibrate an AR(1) process for the returns, (ii) to obtain an estimation of the average conditional volatilities of the monthly portfolio returns over the whole sample window, and (iii) to assess the higher moments of the returns of the funds.

The estimation outcomes are reported in Table 5-9.

TABLE 5-9 G–T–N example – Relevant estimates for volatility adjustments.

	Symbol	Global	Thematic	Neutral	M
Mean return	$\overline{R}_P$	6.39%	4.72%	2.55%	7.39%
Volatility	$\hat{\sigma}_P$	7.12%	6.41%	3.90%	8.83%
Autocorrelation	ρ_1	0.14	−0.11	0.37	0.01
Average volatility	$\overline{\sigma}_P$	7.64%	6.29%	4.63%	8.91%
Skewness	$\mu_{P,3}$	−0.27	0.35	−1.65	−0.34
Excess kurtosis	$e\mu_{P,4}$	1.23	1.49	4.96	0.98

Checking with these data the inequalities of Equations (5-9) (for autocorrelation), (5-11) (for heteroscedasticity), and (5-14) (for higher moments), the outcome is summarized in Table 5-10:

TABLE 5-10 G–T–N example – Summary of the directions of necessary volatility adjustments.

	Global	Thematic	Neutral	M
Original volatility	7.12%	6.41%	3.90%	8.83%
Autocorrelation	↗	↘	↗↗	=
Heteroscedasticity	↗	↘	↗↗	=
Higher moments	↗	?	↗↗	↗

We bear in mind that (i) an upward volatility adjustment induces a reduction of the Sharpe ratio, and vice versa, and (ii) each adjustment is considered in isolation: they might overlap but are not necessarily substitutes to each other. Thus, we can conclude that the Sharpe ratios of the Global and Neutral funds are likely to be overstated, while it is the opposite for the Thematic fund.

5.3.3 Overlooking measurement error

Even though the best efforts are enforced to obtain a sample of highest quality data with a very clear vision on the specific features of the time series, this remains a sample and not the whole population. This difference induces some noise that is generically termed "measurement error." This noise is inevitable and its influence on the quality of the estimation of the inputs of the various performance measures should be recognized and, if possible, accounted for.

Error is important when it comes to the point estimates of the relevant risk and return metrics: the expectation, the variance, and the two-by-two correlations of asset returns. This has a direct impact on the Sharpe ratio because its estimation of risk (volatility at the denominator) contains the combination of the genuine portfolio risk and the contribution of the measurement error to the risk estimation. This can be understood with the approach of Kan and Zhou (2007) for portfolio optimization. They consider that the returns of all assets $i = 1, \ldots, N$ are i.i.d. and follow a multivariate normal distribution throughout the population. Then, the distributions of the vector of their sample means $\overline{\mathbf{R}} = (\overline{R}_1, \ldots, \overline{R}_N)^{\mathrm{T}}$ and of the sample variance–covariance matrix $\hat{\boldsymbol{\Sigma}}$ are known:

$$\overline{\mathbf{R}} \rightsquigarrow \mathcal{N}\left(\boldsymbol{\mu}, \frac{\boldsymbol{\Sigma}}{T}\right) \tag{5-15a}$$

$$\hat{\boldsymbol{\Sigma}} \rightsquigarrow \frac{W_N(T-1, \boldsymbol{\Sigma})}{T} \tag{5-15b}$$

where $\mathcal{W}_N(T-1, \boldsymbol{\Sigma})$ denotes a Wishart distribution with $T-1$ degrees of freedom and covariance matrix $\boldsymbol{\Sigma}$.

Even though, for very large samples, the estimated values will be very close to the true parameters, a smaller number of observations induces a potentially substantial estimation noise, which has to be accounted for as an additional layer of risk for the investor in risky assets. For an investor j with a certain risk-aversion coefficient γ_j, the optimal portfolio choice should obey the optimization program discussed in Section 4.2.1 of Chapter 4 (Equation (4-1)). Nevertheless, the authors show that, if the sample estimates are used as such in the program (the "plug-in" approach), the resulting portfolio is too risky (because of the additional estimation risk) and thus inefficient. The extent of the inefficiency of the optimized portfolio – and thus the reduction of the Sharpe ratio – is positively associated with the severity of measurement error. Obviously, this directly relates not only to the number of observations but also the number of different assets used in the estimation.

5.3.4 Solutions

5.3.4.1 Designing the right sample

In general, it is better to manage surplus than deficit. It is also the case for the design of the sample of data. With a large sample size, both in terms of the length of the time series and the breadth of the universe of comparable assets of portfolios, it is always possible to shrink it; the reverse is unfortunately not true.

To obtain a complete and accurate picture of the performance of mutual and pensions funds, Bauman and Miller (1995) study a long period of data and come to the conclusion that "*the ranking of investment performance of mutual funds and pension funds is more consistent over time when evaluations are made over complete stock market cycles.*" Under these conditions, and provided that the sample contains all funds that have existed and posted returns during this period (in order to avoid the survivorship bias), this represents an exhaustive and premium quality basis material for the analysis of performance (benchmarking, ranking of managers, persistence analysis, ...).

This solution is not very practical. Considering all the issues listed in Section 5.3.1.1 related with the choice of a too long time window, a shorter period of time seems to be the logical solution. However, there are two important statistical obstacles regarding a low number of observations. This first one is of statistical order and refers to noise in the estimation. Trying to appraise portfolio performance with monthly data over a yearly time period, for instance, is not to be envisaged. It would use only 12 data points, and would lead to a much too high variance of any estimator, even simple ones like the volatility or the beta. One may retort that the issue can be solved using a higher frequency. For instance, taking weekly returns would inflate the sample size to 52, which can be viewed as reasonable for many practical purposes. However, this would ignore the second major hindrance for the use of short windows, namely, the interpretability of the estimate of the measure itself. Performance measurement is used in order to appraise the skills of a manager (usually after deducing their remuneration). It might take time for their qualities to be reflected in actual results. Consider the Fundamental Law of Active Management discussed in Chapter 3 and take the example of a portfolio manager whose skills are more tilted toward the information content of their trades rather than the breadth of their mandate. If this manager makes *really* good decisions only a few times per year, it will take some time before the data reveals it. Constraining the time window to be too small, regardless of the frequency of observations, might not be sufficient to uncover this type of skill.

What is the "acceptable" trade-off between the pros and cons of a too short or a too long sample size? An answer is given by the asset management practice. It has become relatively standard to adopt time periods ranging between three years (the practical norm) to five years, with the possible extension to ten years. The three-year, monthly returns benchmark for the sample window is, for instance, adopted as the lower bound and base case for the assessment of the Morningstar Rating™ and the Refinitiv Lipper scores. According to the Global Investment Performance Standards (GIPS®), the same three-year milestone is considered as the threshold over which asset management firms should disclose the fund's and benchmark's standard deviation, thus implicitly paving the way to risk-adjusted performance appraisal.[13] Nevertheless, one has to bear in mind that this is not a miracle solution for all issues discussed above. There are other more sophisticated and to-the-point potential approaches introduced in Section 5.4.

Regarding the cross-section issue, there is only one reasonable answer to address this point: avoiding the survivorship bias, by making sure that all funds or portfolios that need to be considered for the comparison are accounted for, irrespective of whether they have disappeared or not in the meantime. This also entails that a proper approach is implemented in order to faithfully estimate the last (delisting) return for the funds that suddenly disappear from the database. This usually requires some manual investigation to detect the cause and consequence of the disappearance.

5.3.4.2 Dealing correctly with the properties of the data

To each of the three potential issues identified in Section 5.3.2 (autocorrelation, heteroscedasticity, and non-normality), a rather simple, explicit and dedicated solution exists in the scope of performance measurement. They are all discussed in Section 6.1.3 of Chapter 6. Regarding autocorrelation, the Sharpe ratio can be adapted in a straightforward manner, not only in the case of the presence of an AR(1) process but also for any potentially more complex structure of the serial correlation of returns. The issue of heteroscedasticity is usually treated through the family of generalized autoregressive conditional heteroscedasticity (GARCH) models. It has the advantage of not only delivering estimates of the past but also the future expected volatility that are potentially more informative for the Sharpe ratio than the simple point estimator of the standard deviations. Finally, the same section of Chapter 6 examines the adjustments

[13] We will study the performance ranking systems and disclosure standards in more details in Chapter 15.

that can be brought to the volatility by approximating the impact of skewness and kurtosis on the portfolio risk.

Sometimes, however, there are other, more sophisticated treatments that can also be implemented, providing more drastic ways to cure the identified problems than "simply" adapting the performance measure. This is particularly true for the case of the time dependence of the returns. These can display various structures of autoregressive, but also moving average processes stemming from artificial sources and that require a specific and in-depth treatment. This is particularly the case for portfolios that heavily invest in illiquid assets (real estate and private equity) or trading strategies (hedge funds). These issues are discussed in Chapter 12.

The other complex issue is the influence of higher moments on the risk assessment of the portfolio. Because investors do indeed care about skewness, kurtosis, and potentially other indicators of asymmetry or tail risks, many risk measures other than the standard deviation can be used with the ambition of reflecting the investors' attitudes toward risk. This is essentially the topic of the whole Section 6.2 of Chapter 6. However, it is possible to go further in the personalization of performance appraisal by explicitly recognizing the structure of an investor's risk profile. Unsurprisingly, many developments in preference-based performance measurement feature the intervention of higher moments; this is a major topic studied in Chapter 9. Finally, higher moments also play a role in the factors that potentially explain how the portfolio returns are generated. This is also discussed, in the specific context of hedge funds, in Chapter 12.

5.3.4.3 Mitigating the impact of measurement error

There is no definite way to eradicate the measurement error issue simply because of the inherent unobservable character of the market portfolio. However, even though the problem does not bear any perfect solution, all possible efforts must be mobilized to mitigate it. A first approach is to recognize it and take corrective actions in the right direction. For instance, as shown by Kan and Zhou (2007), a solution to improve the Sharpe ratio of an optimized portfolio with measurement error is to combine it with the minimum variance portfolio (again resulting from the sample). A stream of research has originated from their original paper, with the objective of making decisions that lead to the improvement of the Sharpe ratio of the global portfolio.

Another, pragmatic improvement approach in the context of performance measurement is to work on the estimation of the risk parameters. It is clear that understanding the correct dynamics of market risk, like for instance fitting a well-specified GARCH-type model, is a precious asset here. However, the major part of the issue resides in the correlations between the returns of the various assets because they are very numerous and potentially noisy: for a universe of N assets, it amounts to $\frac{N\times(N-1)}{2}$ parameters to estimate with usually a limited number of T observations. Many of their estimates might just represent noise and contaminate the ones for which there is a genuine interdependence. The most standard approach is the use of *shrinkage estimation*, introduced in the field of asset management by Ledoit and Wolf

(2003; 2004). The principle is simple: finding the best possible compromise between, on the one hand, the estimated covariance matrix and, on the other hand, the one that is theoretically anticipated. The general formulation for the shrinkage formula is

$$\widehat{\boldsymbol{\Sigma}}_{\text{shrink}} = \delta^* \, \boldsymbol{\Theta} + (1 - \delta^*) \, \widehat{\boldsymbol{\Sigma}} \tag{5-16}$$

where $\widehat{\boldsymbol{\Sigma}}$ is the $N \times N$ sample variance–covariance matrix, $\boldsymbol{\Theta}$ is the shrinkage target, i.e., the covariance matrix that would be theoretically anticipated considering the data (for instance, a diagonal matrix as in Ledoit and Wolf (2003) or a matrix with constant two-by-two correlation coefficients as in Ledoit and Wolf (2004), but many other sophisticated structures are possible), and δ^* is the shrinkage constant. The shrinkage estimator of the covariance matrix $\widehat{\boldsymbol{\Sigma}}_{\text{shrink}}$ is thus a trade-off between the two extremes.[14] The principle is thus simple, although its implementation, through (i) the choice of the target and (ii) the determination of the shrinkage constant, is not straightforward. Nevertheless, there is ample evidence that using this principle leads to substantial improvements in optimized portfolios and their associated performance.

5.4 ISSUES WITH THE REGRESSIONS

We dig further into the statistical problems that can arise with the estimation of the market model regression coefficients underlying the CAPM, namely, the alpha and the beta. We split these issues in two main types: the pure estimation problems related to statistical issues with the data and the bias in the coefficients arising from missing relevant information about the structure of the relation.

5.4.1 Estimating coefficients with error

5.4.1.1 Errors-in-variables

Measurement error does not only complicate the estimation of the parameters that characterize the distribution of returns. A second level of concern is its impact on the quality of regressions that lead to estimations of alpha, beta, and residual risk, as well as the associated statistical inference. The key issue here is the errors-in-variables (EIV) present in the regressors, whose presence tends to lead to inconsistent ordinary least-squares (OLS) estimators in linear regression models. The story is a bit different from the one described in the previous section because we are less concerned here with the sampling effect – still valid in this context – than with the approximation effect.

[14] To justify their approach, Ledoit and Wolf (2004) make a simple analogy: *Most people would prefer the compromise of one bottle of Bordeaux and one steak to either extreme of two bottles of Bordeaux (and no steak) or two steaks (and no Bordeaux).*

The presence of EIV can be summarized in the following way:

$$R_{M,t} = \tilde{R}_{M,t} + \nu_t, \text{with } \nu_t \rightharpoonup \mathcal{N}(0, \sigma_\nu^2) \tag{5-17}$$

where $\tilde{R}_{M,t}$ is the return of the true, but unobserved market portfolio and ν_t reflects the error-in-variable whose variance σ_ν^2 translates the severity. If the CAPM is applicable on the true market portfolio, but if the proxy of Equation (5-17) is used instead, the outcome of the market model regression (Equation (3-12) in Chapter 3) becomes

$$R_{P,t} - R_f = \alpha_P + \beta_P[\tilde{R}_{M,t} - R_f] + \varepsilon_{P,t} - \beta_P \nu_t, \tag{5-18}$$

Hence, in a single-factor regression like the market model used to estimate the CAPM, the presence of the last term (noise) alters the estimation results. Cragg (1994) underlines the existence of an "attenuation effect" because the measurement error biases the slope coefficient toward zero.[15] The consequence of this phenomenon can be immediately understood: in general, the more substantial the EIV issue, the lower the estimated slope (beta) and the higher the intercept (alpha) in case the excess portfolio return is positive.

5.4.1.2 Microstructure effects

Because of the constraints related to the sample size of asset returns, the time period considered for the estimation of the CAPM parameters is often relatively short. To increase the number of observations and obtain more efficient estimates of the alpha and beta, the natural reaction is to adopt the highest possible frequency of observations, i.e., on a weekly or even daily basis. A three-year time window, for instance, only leaves 36 monthly observations – a very low number for solid statistical inference – but 156 weeks and even more than 750 trading days. We observed in Chapter 3 that this can clearly make a difference for the assessment of significance of performance measures such as the Treynor ratio or the Information ratio, for instance. There is a price to pay for this type of improvement, however. This is related to the influence of actual trading mechanisms on the formation process of asset prices, also known as "market microstructure effects."

When daily data are used, the main issue with the time series is that of *thin trading*, i.e., the low frequency of transactions for a certain number of stocks (generally small caps with low float). Thin trading artificially impacts their daily price change: sometimes, prices do not move, and then suddenly experience a large swing because of an imbalance between buy or sell orders. In the regression that aims to estimate a stock or portfolio beta, this issue can arise on the left-hand side (the portfolio return) or on the right-hand side (the index return). If it affects the portfolio return, this issue is to be solved directly within the sample. But sometimes,

[15] In multiple regressions, there is a second effect called "contamination effect" that produces a bias of the opposite sign on the intercept coefficient when the average of the explanatory variables is positive.

thin trading impacts the index as well. Of course, for some indexes that only track large cap stocks, this is essentially a non-issue. However, if the proxy for the market portfolio is meant to be a broad combination of securities of all sizes, such as – for instance – the MSCI ACWI or the Wilshire 5000 indexes, the presence of such stocks with infrequent trades can represent a material issue. As a consequence, the index might display a significant level of serial correlation whose structure (like a traditional autoregressive process) is not necessarily straightforward. In this case, the resulting daily beta is likely to be affected as well as all performance measures that build on it.

Turning to weekly returns is often considered as a good trade-off between the microstructure issues that contaminate high-frequency data and the drop in the amount of observations inherent to the choice of monthly observations. This appealing solution also bears its own problems, which are this time mostly associated with calendar anomalies, and more specifically the *day-of-the-week* effect. It appears that the days surrounding the weekend, during which no trades take place, are likely to witness a different stock return behavior than the other days (usually a higher than average Friday return and lower than average Monday return). This phenomenon, which is understandable considering informational efficiency explanations, fluctuates in intensity over time and markets (see Chang, Pinegar, and Ravichandran, 1995, and Dubois and Louvet, 1996, for a review). When it is present, it may impact the estimation of the regression coefficients, which can differ depending on what particular day of the week is chosen in order to compute the weekly price changes.

5.4.2 Neglecting nonlinearities

Investors' preference for higher moments discussed in Section 5.3.2.3 impacts the assessment of the alpha and the beta as well. Leland (1999) considers the case of a portfolio manager who deliberately chooses to invest or divest in "fairly priced" index options as an overlay to their linear exposure to the market. This choice does not involve any specific skill, and thus it should be reflected in neither superior nor inferior performance. Nevertheless, the presence of these contracts in the portfolio changes the relation between the market and portfolio returns: instead of being linear, as in the "plain-vanilla" CAPM, it becomes concave (if options are sold) or convex (if they are bought). Noticeably, selling options – be them calls or puts – involves adopting a negative skewness because of the positive quadratic sensitivity of the option contract to its underlying, which takes a negative sign with a short position. Since investors tend to dislike negative skewness, this strategy is risk-taking and obtains a corresponding reward, which is not recognized by the CAPM. In other words, for a given beta and exposure to the market portfolio, and everything else remaining equal, the call option seller who adopts a so-called "rebalancing" or "covered call" strategy (long the index + short calls) reaps an "alpha" that is not really portfolio performance but merely the capture of a risk premium. Oppositely, the manager who chooses to ensure the portfolio through the simultaneous purchase of the index and put options adopts a "protective put" or "momentum" strategy that delivers a negative

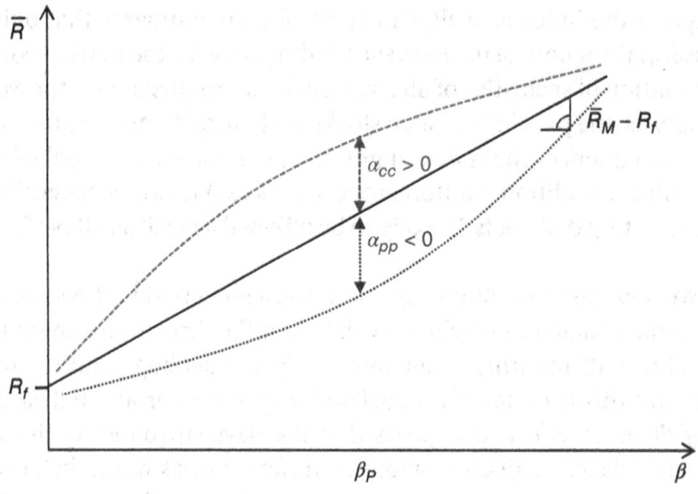

FIGURE 5-14 Risk–return relation of portfolio insurance and covered call strategies.

alpha, even though the manager has not underperformed at all. This logic is best understood in Figure 5-14.

The graph shows the patterns of required returns for three types of portfolios. The linear one (continuous line) with no options, the "covered call" (*cc*) one (thick dashed lines) whose manager combines a long linear position and a short call option position on the index, and the "protective put" (*pp*) one (thin dotted lines) whose manager combines a long linear position and a long put option position on the index. Leland (1999) shows that these curves will be obtained by gradually increasing (resp. decreasing) the strike price of the option as the beta increases for the covered calls (resp. protective puts) strategy. For a given β_P, assuming that all three portfolio managers exhibit no particular skill, the resulting mean return of the covered call strategy will lie on the upper curve, delivering $\alpha_{cc} > 0$, whereas the protective put strategy will provide the impression of a negative abnormal return ($\alpha_{pp} < 0$). In both cases, the diagnosis is flawed as the outperformance is nil.

5.4.3 Ignoring conditioning information

Performance measurement mostly deals with actively managed portfolios. Some managers genuinely adapt their market exposure over time, in line with their convictions, in order to generate an abnormal return based on their market timing skills. Their beta becomes dynamic, and performance measures must be adapted (see Section 5.2.3). Often, however, portfolio management strategies involving a time-varying beta obey a structure that can be reverse engineered with public information. The beta at time t would then depend on this information observed one period earlier, i.e., at time $t - 1$. This idea of a beta whose value is conditioned by previously observed information was initially brought forward by Ferson and Schadt (1996). It entails that the beta is not constant over time anymore but does not behave in a totally random way either.

The authors assume that the prices (and thus the returns) of many financial assets reflect public information about market conditions that can be observed beforehand. Because they observe such information, asset managers may be induced to use it in order to let their factor betas change accordingly. For instance, if someone could realize that the change in unexpected inflation at time $t-1$ (yesterday), represented by some random variable z_{t-1}, is negatively correlated with the return of a stock index at time t (today), they could decide to proportionally reduce their market beta after each increase in inflation and to increase the beta consecutively to a decrease in inflation. In this case, the change in unexpected inflation is interpreted as a conditioning instrument whose lagged observation negatively influences the market beta adopted be the portfolio manager. Note that, since the conditioning information is public, its use in order to let betas vary over time is not synonymous of abnormal returns *per se* since anyone could apply the same mechanical strategy in order to construct a portfolio.

The fact that, at the same time, (i) the beta varies over time and (ii) its variations are deterministic once the instrument has been observed can be understood thanks to the simple three-dimensional example shown below.

We assume in Figure 5-15 that the portfolio manager decides to set their market beta at each point in time as the sum of (i) a constant sensitivity coefficient $\beta_{P,0}=1$ plus (ii) the realized value of the conditioning instrument (e.g., the change in the VIX index), which is thus multiplied by a unit coefficient $\beta_{P,z}=1$. Consider for the sake of the illustration that the excess market return can take three values: $R_{M,t}-R_f=-10\%, 0\%, +10\%$. Furthermore, the lagged instrument can also take three values: $z_{t-1}=-1, 0, +1$. We report the dots corresponding to the

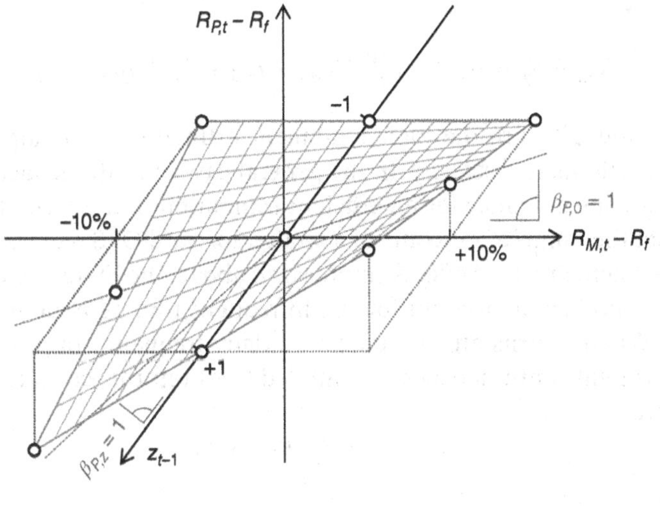

FIGURE 5-15 3D representation of the impact of the conditional instrument on portfolio returns.

nine outcome combinations on the graph. When $z_{t-1} = -1$, the two components offset each other and the resulting aggregate beta is equal to zero. When $z_{t-1} = 0$, the beta is just equal to the constant sensitivity coefficient $\beta_{0,P} = 1$. Finally, when $z_{t-1} = +1$, the resulting market sensitivity is equal to the constant coefficient (+1) plus the value of the conditioning instrument (+1), and thus the portfolio has a resulting beta of 2. Taking all possible combinations of these two effects on the total beta results in a smooth surface represented graphically by the hashed grid, it clearly shows two phenomena: the CAPM does not apply anymore as the portfolio beta is clearly not a constant, but once the instrument is identified and its realization is known (which is the case at any time t because the instrument is observed at time $t-1$), the beta is known for sure. Thus, this calls for an adaptation of performance measurement, but it is not likely to be as drastic as if the beta is supposed to be completely time varying without any particular structure, like in the case for a market timer.

5.4.4 Solutions

5.4.4.1 Mitigating the impact of estimation error

The EIV issue is a rather complex one to solve because one essentially deals with the gap between what is observable and what is not, i.e., a matter of uncertainty. The generic approach is to use artificial regressions, as suggested by Davidson and MacKinnon (1993). An elegant solution, adapted from Dagenais and Dagenais (1997), consists of regressing the market portfolio returns on rolling estimated of its higher moments (skewness and kurtosis) and gathers the residuals of this regression, denoted by $\widehat{\omega}_{M,t} = R_{M,t} - \widehat{R}_{M,t}$, where $\widehat{R}_{M,t}$ is the market return predicted with the artificial regression. This residual stands as the proxy for the error-in-variable at time t. Then, a second pass multiple regression is performed on the observed market return and this residual:

$$R_{P,t} - R_f = \alpha_P^{\mathrm{HM}} + \beta_P^{\mathrm{HM}}[R_{M,t} - R_f] + \psi_P^{\mathrm{HM}}\widehat{\omega}_{M,t} + \varepsilon_{P,t} \tag{5-19}$$

where α_P^{HM}, β_P^{HM}, and ψ_P^{HM} are the higher moment estimates of the alpha, beta, and EIV coefficient of the portfolio, respectively. In the general case of multiple factors, Dagenais and Dagenais (1997) provide guidance for an efficient estimation of these coefficients, which are (unfortunately) not the "simple" outcome of a straightforward OLS regression estimation.[16]

Regarding the microstructure effects emphasized above, the literature is prolific on adaptations of the portfolio beta to account for the infrequent trading issue in the proxy for the market portfolio. When returns are observed on a daily frequency over T trading days, it is common to regress total continuously compounded (log) returns, considering that the daily risk-free rate is zero:

$$R_{P,t} = \alpha_P + \beta_P^{(0)} R_{M,t} + \varepsilon_{P,t} \tag{5-20}$$

[16]This approach is especially useful for the estimation of hedge fund performance.

where $\beta_P^{(0)}$ is the OLS estimate of the beta with daily data and simultaneous market observations.

The major beta adjustment methods reported in the literature, ranked chronologically, are as follows:[17]

- The *Scholes and Williams* (1977) (SW) method.
  - Run regressions similar to (5-20) with lead and lagged market returns (usually one day on each side, but this can be extended to n days): $R_{P,t} = \alpha_P + \beta_P^{(+1)} R_{M,t+1} + \varepsilon_{P,t}$ and $R_{P,t} = \alpha_P + \beta_P^{(-1)} R_{M,t-1} + \varepsilon_{P,t}$.
  - Record the first-order autocorrelation of market return: $R_{M,t} = \rho_0 + \rho_1 R_{M,t-1} + \eta_{M,t}$.
  - Obtain the Scholes–Williams beta by the formula

$$\beta_P^{SW} = \frac{\beta_P^{(-1)} + \beta_P^{(0)} + \beta_P^{(+1)}}{1 + 2\rho_1} \tag{5-21}$$

- The *Dimson* (1979) (D) method.
  - Run a single multiple regression with lead and lag market returns (usually one day on each side as well): $R_{P,t} = \alpha_P + \beta_P^{m(+1)} R_{M,t+1} + \beta_P^{m(0)} R_{M,t} + \beta_P^{m(-1)} R_{M,t-1} + \varepsilon_{P,t}$.
  - Obtain the Dimson beta by simply summing up the coefficients:

$$\beta_P^{D} = \beta_P^{m(-1)} + \beta_P^{m(0)} + \beta_P^{m(+1)} \tag{5-22}$$

- The *Hansen and Hodrick* (1980) (HH) method.
  - Record the set of autocorrelation coefficients of the market return up to order $H-1$: $R_{M,t} = \rho_0 + \sum_{l=1}^{H-1} \rho_l R_{M,t-1} + \eta_{M,t}$.
  - Run a single overlapping-observation regression with returns measured every day on a horizon of H days in arrears: $\left(\sum_{l=0}^{H-1} R_{P,t-l}\right) = \alpha_P^{HH} + \beta_P^{HH} \left(\sum_{l=0}^{H-1} R_{M,t-l}\right) + \varepsilon_{P,t}$.
  - Because the overlapping-observation regression is contaminated by the autocorrelation issues, the estimators of the coefficients of this regression are obtained by

$$\begin{pmatrix} \alpha_P^{HH} \\ \beta_P^{HH} \end{pmatrix} = (\mathbf{X}\mathbf{X}^T)^{-1}\mathbf{X}^T\mathbf{\Omega}^{-1}(\mathbf{X}^T\mathbf{X})^{-1} \tag{5-23}$$

[17]The old age of this literature can be explained by the fact that thin trading was a material issue for most stock indexes, including the leading US ones, in the twentieth century. Nowadays, most indexes are largely insulated from the problem, but it is still highly relevant for some geographical zones or for indexes whose composition features a large fraction of illiquid securities, such as all-shares indexes, some bond indexes, or indexes for specific asset classes.

where $\mathbf{X}$ is the $T \times 2$ matrix of observations $\begin{pmatrix} 1 & R_{M,1} \\ \vdots & \vdots \\ 1 & R_{M,t} \end{pmatrix}$ and $\boldsymbol{\Omega}$ is a "band" matrix with the variances and autocovariances of the regression errors:

$$\boldsymbol{\Omega} = \sigma^2_{\varepsilon_P} \begin{pmatrix} 1 & \rho_1 & \cdots & \rho_{H-1} & 0 & 0 \\ \rho_1 & 1 & \rho_1 & \cdots & \rho_{H-1} & 0 \\ \cdots & \rho_1 & 1 & \rho_1 & \cdots & \rho_{H-1} \\ \vdots & \vdots & \vdots & \vdots & \vdots & \vdots \\ 0 & \rho_{H-1} & \cdots & \rho_1 & 1 & \rho_1 \\ 0 & 0 & \rho_{H-1} & \cdots & \rho_1 & 1 \end{pmatrix} \tag{5-24}$$

- The *Fowler and Rorke* (1983) (FR) method.
  - Compute the market return during an interval of ranging from L days ahead to L days before time t, i.e., $R_{M,t}^{[-L,+L]} = \sum_{l=-L}^{+L} R_{M,t+l}$.
  - Obtain the FR beta by applying the formula

$$\beta_P^{\mathrm{FR}} = \frac{\mathrm{Cov}(R_P, R_M^{[-L+L]})}{\mathrm{Cov}(R_M, R_M^{[-L+L]})} \tag{5-25}$$

- The *Cohen, Hawawini, Maier, Schwartz, and Whitcomb* (1983) (CHMSW) method.
  - Run a regression similar to (5-20) with an interval of length l_1, greater than one day $R_{P,t} = \alpha_P + \beta_{P,l_1} R_{M,t} + \varepsilon_{P,t}$, where $R_{P,t}$ and $R_{M,t}$ are computed over a period of l_1 days.
  - Repeat the procedure for longer intervals (one week, two weeks, etc.) L times to obtain a series of betas $\beta_{P,l_1}, \beta_{P,l_2}, \ldots, \beta_{P,l_L}$.
  - Obtain the CHMSW beta by regressing the estimated betas on a power of its corresponding interval and retrieving the intercept:

$$\beta_{P,l_i} = \beta_P^{\mathrm{CHMSW}} + \theta_P (l_i)^{-n} + \eta_P \tag{5-26}$$

  where, according to the authors, the most accurate power value is $n = 0.8$.

In a comprehensive study made by Sercu, Vandebroek, and Vinaimont (2008), it turns out that there is apparently no miracle when these methods are applied with simulated and real data: less bias (thus an estimated beta whose expected value is closer to the real one) comes at the cost of a lower efficiency (thus a more volatile estimator of the beta). This is intuitively understandable: one needs larger intervals in order to reduce the thin trading issue, but this goes along with a higher standard error of the estimate.

Finally, the day-of-the-week effect being the main issue when weekly data are used, there is indeed a simple workable solution. If daily observations are used but returns are observed on a weekly frequency, it consists of avoiding problematic days when setting the price observation dates. Thus, as the days surrounding the weekend are troublesome, picking any other day is fine. A common choice is Wednesday, but this is not a general obligation.

5.4.4.2 Reflecting the nonlinear trading behavior

The option trades (or similar synthetic trading strategies) executed by a portfolio manager are often largely unobservable by their customer. Of course, some of them can be the result of a proactive hedging strategy in some circumstances or the willingness to increase the market exposures in some others. If these choices are not mechanical, but discretionary or algorithmic, then some kind of attempt to time the market is to be suspected. There are tools available in order to assess the performance of such a manager, and we are essentially back to the set of solutions adapted to this environment, as discussed in Section 5.2.4.3. As a reminder, an extensive discussion of suitable methods for performance appraisal of market timers is the subject of Chapter 8.

The story is essentially different when a systematic investment plan in option-related products is designed by the portfolio manager. In that case, the graph shown in Figure 5-14 leads to a biased assessment of portfolio performance using standard estimation techniques, even if great care has been taken to tackle all statistical issues. The answer is provided by Leland (1999) under the assumption of lognormally distributed prices and if investors have a power utility function.[18] He suggests a change in the estimation of the nonlinearity-adjusted beta through the following formula:

$$\beta_P^{(\gamma)} = \frac{\text{Cov}(R_P, -(1+R_M)^{-\gamma})}{\text{Cov}(R_M, -(1+R_M)^{-\gamma})} \tag{5-27}$$

where $\gamma = \dfrac{\log(\text{E}(1+R_M)) - \log(1+R_F)}{\sigma^2(\log(1+R_M))}$ is the market-implied risk-aversion coefficient. The nonlinearity-adjusted alpha (also called "Leland's alpha") simply follows from replacing the traditional beta with the one of Equation (5-27):

$$\alpha_P^{(\gamma)} = \overline{R}_P - [R_f + \beta_P^{(\gamma)}(\overline{R}_M - R_f)] \tag{5-28}$$

Leland (1999) analytically shows that a passive portfolio using options will automatically obtain a nonlinearity-adjusted alpha of zero. Of course, a difficulty resides in the determination of the market risk aversion γ.

5.4.4.3 Recognizing conditioning information

The influence of an instrumental variable whose realization drives the evolution of the beta, as discussed above, can be directly modeled in a single regression framework used in order to measure portfolio performance, as shown by Ferson and Schadt (1996). This results in the conditional CAPM, which can be expressed by the following equation:

$$R_{P,t} - R_f = \alpha_P + \beta_{P,0}(R_{M,t} - R_f) + \beta_{P,z}[z_{t-1} \times (R_{M,t} - R_f)] + \varepsilon_{P,t} \tag{5-29}$$

---

[18]We study the most important utility functions in Chapter 9.

where $\beta_{P,0}$ is the constant sensitivity coefficient toward the market, and $\beta_{P,z}$ is the conditional sensitivity coefficient that multiplies the interaction factor between the lagged realization of the instrument z_{t-1} and the contemporaneous excess return $R_{M,t} - R_f$ (in the example of Figure 5-15, we used $\beta_{P,0} = 1$ and $\beta_{P,z} = 1$). We can therefore define the time-varying conditional beta as follows:

$$\beta_P(z_{t-1}) = \beta_{P,0} + \beta_{P,z} z_{t-1} \equiv \beta_{P,t} \tag{5-30}$$

This beta varies over time, but it is not random conditionally on the realization of the instrumental variable. It is thus "conditionally deterministic." The intercept of Equation (5-29) represents the alpha corrected for conditional information.[19]

G–T–N example (continued)

We have applied Dagenais and Dagenais's (1997) higher moment-based regression approach for the correction of EIV (Equation (5-19)), Leland's (1999) nonlinearity-adjusted beta approach (Equation (5-27)) using an estimate of the market risk aversion based on the mean return and the risk-free rate $\gamma = \dfrac{\log(1 + 7.39\%) - \log(1 + 1.44\%)}{8.83\%^2} = 7.30$, and Ferson and Schadt's (1996) conditional CAPM (Equation (5-29)). This leads to Table 5-11, for which the first four rows were already known.

TABLE 5-11 G–T–N example – Adjusted betas.

	Symbol	Global	Thematic	Neutral	M
Mean return	$\overline{R}_P$	6.39%	4.72%	2.55%	7.39%
Volatility	σ_P	7.12%	6.41%	3.90%	8.83%
Correlation with market	$\rho_{P,M}$	0.97	0.48	0.04	1.00
CAPM beta	β_P	0.78	0.35	0.02	1.00
EIV-corrected beta	β_P^{HM}	0.85	0.34	0.05	1.00
Nonlinearly adjusted beta	$\beta_P^{(\gamma)}$	0.82	0.33	0.17	1.00
Constant sensitivity	$\beta_{P,0}$	0.87	0.35	0.07	1.00
Conditional sensitivity	$\beta_{P,z}$	1.23	0.03	−0.96	0.00

[19] In Chapter 7, we introduce conditional multifactor models and the associated conditional multifactor alpha that can be made time varying as well.

In order to compute the conditional alpha, we need to obtain the average interaction term (brackets in the equation). It is equal to $z_{t-1} \times (R_{M,t} - R_f) = -0.45\%$.

The resulting alphas are reported in the graph shown in Figure 5-16 which shows them using histograms in order to visualize the relative impact of the adjustments for each of the funds.

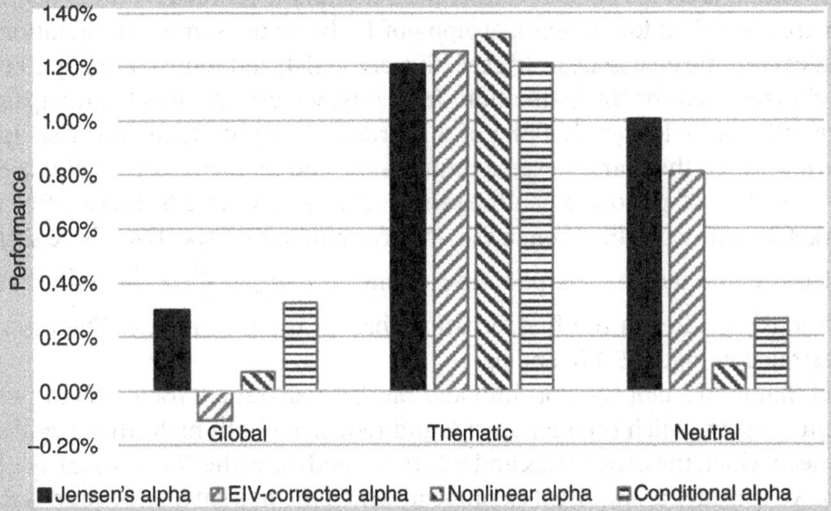

FIGURE 5-16 G–T–N example – Adjustments of the alpha.

The graph confirms that the alpha of the Thematic fund appears to be reliable. It hardly suffers from different types of adjustments. Regarding the Global fund, there seems to be a substantial impact of the EIV issue. Nevertheless, when conditioning information is taken into account, the manager is still diagnosed to perform a relatively good job. The results are most puzzling for the Neutral fund, whose alpha does not resist well to the treatment of nonlinearities or conditioning. This suggests again that the fund manager does not really adopt a flat but rather a concave exposure to the market.

5.5 ISSUES WITH THE INTERPRETATIONS

Whatever care taken to produce performance estimates that conform to the data according to all the principles (and solutions) discussed in this chapter, the output is a figure that needs to be interpreted with caution and honesty. We list three types of issues that can arise in this context. The first one is the meaning associated with the result, regardless of any statistical consideration, but taking into account the market environment. The second one refers to the difficulty of making sense of negative figures. The third one relates to the problem of low or negative betas.[20]

5.5.1 Overlooking market conditions

When performance is assessed against a benchmark, as in the case of all measures based on abnormal return, it is tempting to get rid of the benchmark characteristics as soon as its risk and return are controlled for. A Jensen's alpha of 1% bears the same interpretation – putting aside statistical significance issues – irrespective of the risk and return of the market portfolio or the benchmark used for the estimation. In reality, we can intuitively anticipate that it is much more difficult to deliver an alpha of this order of magnitude in "low risk–low return" periods during which the market excess return is 2% and its realized volatility is 6% than in "high risk–high return" periods when the same index return exceeds the risk-free rate by 8% with a market volatility of 24%. From a risk–return trade-off perspective, these situations are indistinguishable: the market Sharpe ratio is identical $\left(SR_M = \frac{2\%}{6\%} = \frac{8\%}{24\%} = \frac{1}{3}\right)$, but the challenge is obviously greater in the first situation than in the second one. The essence of this issue is illustrated in Figure 5-17a and b.

On each figure, we plot the portfolio and market risk–return trade-offs in two different environments: one in which the market risk and return are both high (the "High" case), and the other one in which the market risk and return are both low (the "Low" case). For the sake of illustration, we consider a simplified example in which the market Sharpe ratio is the same in both cases, and the portfolio P mimics the market and has thus exactly the same risk (total and systematic) as its benchmark but delivers a positive abnormal return equal to some constant λ irrespective of the market environment.

Figure 5-17a shows that the market environment makes a difference. A constant abnormal return inflates the Sharpe ratio of portfolio P to a much higher extent when the market risk (and thus the one of the portfolio) is low. This result is rather intuitive. Consider the numerical example presented above. If the excess return of the portfolio is 3% whereas the market delivers 2%, this is one-third better, and that for a risk of 6%. The merit of the manager is likely to be greater than if the market posts an 8% excess return and the portfolio obtains 9%, especially when the volatility is as high as 24%.

The graph illustrated in Figure 5-17b is very contrasted. The abnormal return of the portfolio is equivalent to its Jensen's alpha. Whatever the market conditions, it remains a constant, so is the manager's performance. Using the modified Jensen's alpha does not help either: since the portfolio beta is the same in both environments, it does not change the diagnosis about the portfolio performance in this case. Note that the issue is the same when the Information ratio is used instead of a performance measure based on systematic risk. The problem lies in the

[20] More complex issues with the interpretation of performance, such as the suspicion of performance manipulation or the distinctions between luck, skill, and performance delivered to the investor, are discussed in Chapter 18.

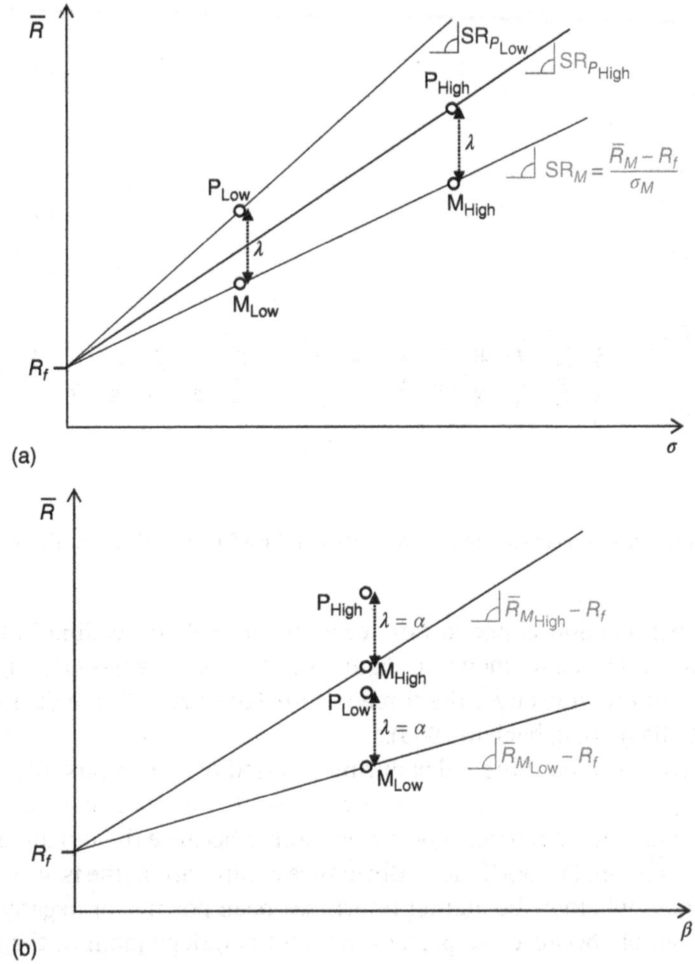

FIGURE 5-17 Graphical representation of (a) the Sharpe ratio and (b) Jensen's alpha in high and low market environments.

alpha: being equal to the difference between the portfolio's mean and required returns, the level of the latter is controlled for in the performance appraisal. What seems to be an advantage might turn out to become a drawback as the information about the market environment is neglected.

5.5.2 Handling negative Sharpe and Information ratios

Sometimes – too often perhaps – financial markets are negatively oriented. Even for a long period of time, stock indexes can deliver stubbornly disappointing excess returns. Similarly, actively managed portfolios can also behave. Their average excess return can even become

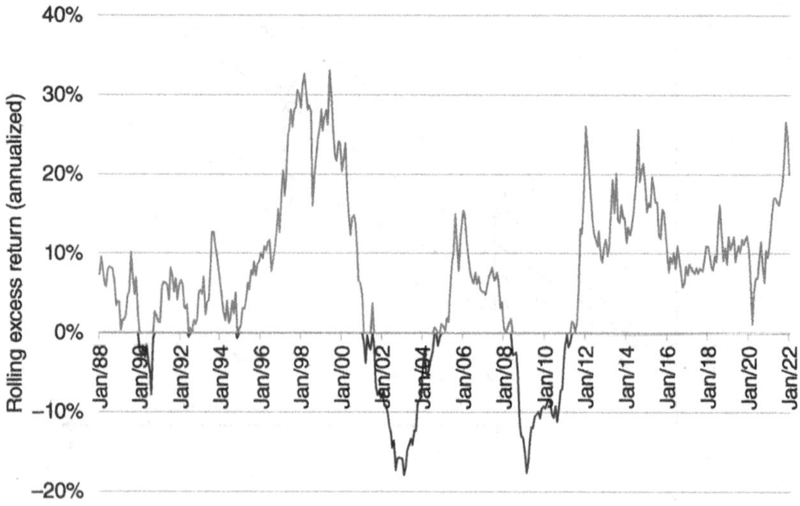

FIGURE 5-18 Three-year *ex post* rolling excess returns of the S&P500 Index over the T-Bill rate.

negative. This phenomenon is not so rare, even at the scale of leading indexes such as the S&P500 for instance. The chart shown in Figure 5-18 tracks the *ex post* rolling three-year average excess return of the index over the three-month Treasury Bill rate during the 1988–2022 period (thus with data going back to 1985).

If someone wishes to hold the index during a period of three years, they would naturally want to secure a positive excess return. However, nobody can really choose the entry and exit moments so as to maximize returns *a posteriori* simply because the outcome is not known at the moment of inception. For portfolio performance computation, the issue is similar: the analyst does not choose whether the market return has been positive or negative at the moment of the appraisal simply because the present moment is independent of the past market outcome. In the example of the chart, the proportion of three-year negative average excess return periods is 22% of the total number of observations. This means that, historically, someone who had to measure the performance of a fund or portfolio benchmarked over the S&P500 Index had approximately one chance out of five to get trapped in a negative market excess return environment. Naturally, the periods of negative returns tend to cluster at specific periods of time (this is logical as we are rolling over overlapping periods of time), but nonetheless this is a material issue.

If a portfolio's excess return is negative, this is also necessarily the case of its Sharpe ratio simply because the denominator (standard deviation of returns) is always positive. This phenomenon is represented in the graph shown in Figure 5-19.

The situation represented in Figure 5-19 is rather straightforward. The average market portfolio return $\overline{R}_M$ is negative. Portfolio A has the same excess return as M, i.e., $\overline{R}_A - R_f = \overline{R}_M - R_f$, but has a lower volatility ($\sigma_A < \sigma_M$). In terms of their Sharpe ratios, since both are

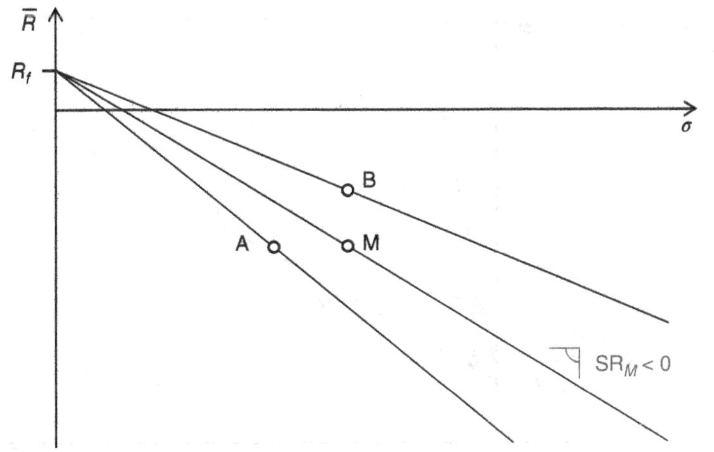

FIGURE 5-19 Representation of the case of negative Sharpe ratios.

negative, this translates into $SR_A = \frac{\bar{R}_A - R_f}{\sigma_A} < \frac{\bar{R}_M - R_f}{\sigma_M} = SR_M$. Likewise, portfolio B has the same risk as the market ($\sigma_B = \sigma_M$) but a better return: $\bar{R}_B - R_f > \bar{R}_M - R_f$. Again, this is reflected in the difference in their Sharpe ratios: $SR_B = \frac{\bar{R}_B - R_f}{\sigma_B} > \frac{\bar{R}_M - R_f}{\sigma_M} = SR_M$.

What can we really extract from this graph? Naturally, the situation is bad for all portfolios. But *how* bad? Is it the sole fault of the portfolio managers? There should be some nuance in the judgment we pose there. Furthermore, the comparison of the three portfolios is also puzzling. M is undoubtedly dominated by B: it has the same risk level but a better return (less negative return than the market). For A, this is much less obvious. On the one hand, we may argue that *A delivered the same return as the market, but took less risk. Since investors dislike risk, this was a laudable choice.* Under that point of view, A has outperformed M. This contradicts the sense of the inequality of their Sharpe ratios. On the other hand, another reasoning is possible: *The return of A was as disappointing as that of M, but this negative result is more under the responsibility of the manager since A was more conservatively managed than M*. According to this reasoning, we can conclude that A has underperformed M as indicated by the ordering of their Sharpe ratios. The issue of interpretation gets even more complicated when portfolios with concurrently different risks and returns are compared, such as A versus B: which one dominates then?

Note that the very same reasoning as above can be applied to the case of the Information ratio. It suffices to replace total risk with the tracking error. The issues are wholly similar.

5.5.3 Getting confused with low or negative betas

When we consider performance measures based on systematic risk such as the Treynor ratio, Jensen's alpha, and the modified Jensen's alpha, the issues with the figures are of two kinds.

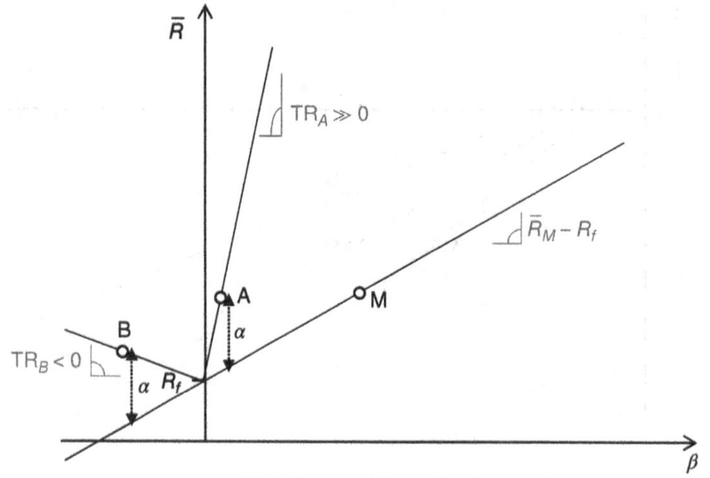

FIGURE 5-20 Representation of the case of low or negative values of betas.

First, when market returns are negative, we retrieve the same issues as those of the Sharpe ratio. We do not repeat the arguments here. Second, when market returns are positive, we still may observe strange results because, unlike volatility, betas can potentially take any value, including zero (or very low values) and negative ones. The cases that can arise and be puzzling to interpret are represented in the graph shown in Figure 5-20.

In Figure 5-20, both actively managed portfolios *A* and *B* display the same level of Jensen's alpha. However, their situations are very different.

Portfolio *A*'s beta is extremely low, almost indistinguishable from zero. The graph reports its Treynor ratio, defined as the slope of the straight line originating from the risk-free rate and going through its coordinates. Since the scale of the beta is largely not commensurate to its alpha, the associated performance measures – both the Treynor ratio and the modified Jensen's alpha – are absurdly high, leaving no possibility to associate any economically meaningful interpretation. Imagine for instance an alpha of 1% – it reads reasonable – and a beta of 0.02 – very close to zero, but why not after all. This would result in a modified Jensen's alpha of $\frac{1\%}{0.02} = 50\%$. This would mean that if the portfolio was leveraged so as to reach the same systematic risk as the market, it would outperform it by 50% *per year*. There is a problem somewhere.

The case of portfolio *B* is very different, even though it is reported on the same graph. Its beta might be economically substantial but negative. There can be only one explanation: its correlation with the market ρ_{BM} is negative. When the market is up, it tends to go down and *vice versa*. This can happen if the manager is "net short" of the market, i.e., if they adopt short selling or bearish derivative strategies, like some hedge funds for instance, or when the portfolio holds a majority of contrarian stocks like some gold mines. Here, the issue resides in the completely opposite picture delivered by various performance measures. The Jensen's alpha α_B

is positive. However, since the beta is negative, so is its modified Jensen's alpha: $m\alpha_B = \frac{\alpha_B}{\beta_B} < 0$. The Treynor ratio is also negative as can be visually checked on the figure. Is the portfolio performance positive or negative? Which performance measure to believe? Here again, negative values pose the question of their correct interpretation.

5.5.4 Solutions

5.5.4.1 Accounting for market conditions in performance appraisal

The influence of market conditions on the assessment of a manager's performance only makes sense in situations when heterogeneous market conditions are simultaneously considered. This is the case in two kinds of circumstances: (i) when different periods in time are considered for one or several portfolios, with notable differences in their common benchmark average returns across time, and (ii) when different portfolios whose benchmarks markedly differ from each other – and so do their mean excess returns too – are compared during a single period of time. For all "ordinary" cases of unity in space and time (i.e., comparison of performances is considered over the same period on the same market), the differential market conditions are a non-issue.

From the discussion of Section 5.5.1, we can also narrow the issue at the level of performance measures that adopt Jensen's alpha as an ingredient. The question to solve is thus *when the benchmark return is likely to matter for different periods or locations, how to explicitly account for it in performance measures that use the alpha?*

An interesting answer is given by adopting a notion of performance adjusted with the risk and excess return of the benchmark that, for the time being, we can call π_P and define as follows:[21]

$$\pi_P = \frac{\sigma_M}{\sigma_P}(\overline{R}_P - R_f) - (\overline{R}_M - R_f) \tag{5-31}$$

We can interpret π_P as the portfolio's excess return differential with the market return, rescaled so as their risks are matched. So far, the alpha does not intervene here. But once we formulate the portfolio's excess return in the CAPM framework, it eventually shows up as we can write it as $\overline{R}_P - R_f = \alpha_P + \beta_P(\overline{R}_M - R_f)$. Combining this expression with Equation (5-31) and noticing that $\beta_P \equiv \rho_{PM}\frac{\sigma_P}{\sigma_M}$, this brings a very useful decomposition:

$$\pi_P = \frac{\sigma_M}{\sigma_P}\alpha_P + (\rho_{PM} - 1)(\overline{R}_M - R_f) \tag{5-32}$$

This equation disentangles total portfolio differential performance in two parts. The first one $\frac{\sigma_M}{\sigma_P}\alpha_P$ reflects the contribution of its active return (reflected in its Jensen's alpha) and can

[21]This performance measure is indeed shown to be called the *relative risk-adjusted performance*, denoted by $RRAP_P$, and is thoroughly analyzed in Chapter 6.

be either positive or negative. Provided that the market portfolio return exceeds the risk-free rate, the second term $(\rho_{PM} - 1)(\overline{R}_M - R_f)$ is negative because $\rho_{PM} \leq 1$ by definition. It reflects the penalty that must be associated with the active portfolio risk: the lower the value taken by ρ_{PM}, the greater the freedom taken by the portfolio manager to diverge from the market. Interestingly, this penalty increases with the level of the market excess return. For instance, consider a portfolio with the same risk as the market ($\sigma_P = \sigma_M$) and a correlation of $\rho_{PM} =$ 0.5. In order to justify their underdiversification, the portfolio manager must deliver an alpha greater than 50% of the market excess return: $\pi_P > 0 \Leftrightarrow \alpha_P > \frac{1}{2}(\overline{R}_M - R_f)$. If the market excess return is 6%, the alpha must exceed 3%. If the market is more generous, so must be the manager. Thus, this approach brings an answer to our question.[22]

5.5.4.2 Resolving the negative performance puzzles

When it comes to interpreting Sharpe ratios, there are two questions regarding negative values: (i) how to interpret the observed negative Sharpe ratio of a given portfolio and (ii) how to run the comparison of negative Sharpe ratios of different portfolios?

A negative Sharpe ratio is something every portfolio manager wants to avoid. However, if the market itself does not pay off for the risk taken, it is very hard to expect that a well-diversified portfolio whose performance is measured according to total risk would be so good as to avoid landing in negative territory. The interpretation of a negative performance should thus always relate to the market conditions. Question (i) is not really interesting as such: at times, it indeed happens that risk does not pay off as expected, and there is a statistical likelihood that, for a certain period of time, a negative excess return is observed. Nevertheless, providing a more precise and quantitative answer to this question helps in addressing the second one.

Consider the probability of observing a negative average excess return over different periods of time as a function of the portfolio's expected return and risk under the assumption of a Gaussian distribution. This is represented (assuming continuously compounded returns) by the following equation:

$$\Pr\left[\overline{R}_P^{Hy} - R_f^{Hy} < 0\right] = \Phi(-\mathrm{E}(\mathrm{SR}_P)\sqrt{H}) \qquad (5\text{-}33)$$

where $\overline{R}_P^{Hy} - R_f^{Hy}$ is the average portfolio excess return over the H years considered, $\mathrm{E}(\mathrm{SR}_P)$ is the portfolio's expected Sharpe ratio, and $\Phi(x) \equiv \Pr[Z \leq x]$ with $Z \rightsquigarrow \mathcal{N}(0,1)$, i.e., it represents the probability that a standard normal random variable is lower than or equal to x.

Equation (5-33) also holds for the market portfolio. The probability of observing a negative excess return over a certain period of time thus depends on the market's "generosity," i.e., the

[22] The properties of Equation (5-32) are studied in more detail in Section 13.3 of Chapter 13 as it serves as the basis for the Sharpe ratio attribution approach.

TABLE 5-12 Gaussian probability of observing negative excess returns under various market conditions.

Period	Low ($E(R_M) - R_f = 3\%$)			Medium ($E(R_M) - R_f = 5\%$)			High ($E(R_M) - R_f = 8\%$)		
	$\sigma = 10\%$	$\sigma = 15\%$	$\sigma = 20\%$	$\sigma = 10\%$	$\sigma = 15\%$	$\sigma = 20\%$	$\sigma = 10\%$	$\sigma = 15\%$	$\sigma = 20\%$
$H = 1$	38%	42%	44%	31%	37%	40%	21%	30%	34%
$H = 3$	30%	36%	40%	19%	28%	33%	8%	18%	24%
$H = 5$	25%	33%	37%	13%	23%	29%	4%	12%	19%
$H = 10$	17%	26%	32%	6%	15%	21%	1%	5%	10%

expected reward-to-volatility ratio that a well-diversified investor can expect. Table 5-12 shows the assessment of the probability of observing a negative market excess return under various possible risk and expected return conditions, considering that we evolve in a Gaussian world.

As long as the market expected return is positive, the probability of observing negative excess returns decays as the period of reference increases. Nonetheless, this probability is never really negligible. We can reconcile here the empirical results shown in Figure 5-18: they correspond to an expected Sharpe ratio that is slightly below 40%, which is close to the historical average.

Considering the situation of any portfolio P for which we observe a negative Sharpe ratio as in Figure 5-19, the logical interpretation of Equation (5-33) is applicable as well. The greater the portfolio volatility, the bigger the portfolio's expected return in order to match the same expected Sharpe ratio. We can thus make the following statements:

- Two portfolios with different volatilities but the same negative Sharpe ratio have the same probability of reaching their situation by chance. They should thus be assigned the same performance.
- If two portfolios X and Y have the same volatility, but the average return of X is less negative than that of Y, there is a higher probability that X reached that level by chance compared to Y. Thus, the performance appraisal for X should be better than for Y (this is the situation of B and M in Figure 5-19, with B better than M).
- If two portfolios X and Y have the same negative average return, but the volatility of X is greater than that of Y, there is a higher probability that X reached that level by chance compared to Y. Thus, the performance appraisal for X should be better than for Y (this is the situation of A and M in Figure 5-19, with M better than A).

What these three statements imply altogether is that whatever the situation, when returns are negative, the rankings provided by the Sharpe ratios are valid in order to assess the ordering of portfolio performance. This interpretation is consistent with the line of thought initially developed by McLeod and van Vuuren (2004) who first associate the Sharpe ratio with the probability of exceeding the risk-free rate. In this regard, we share the standpoints of Akeda (2003) and Bacon (2021), and the latter author expresses it in a colorful way: *Perversely for negative returns it is better to be more variable not least because the chance of returning into positive territory is higher than when variability is low.*

An analogous storyline can be adopted for the case of the Information ratio. In a Gaussian world, under the null hypothesis of zero abnormal return ($E(\alpha_P) = 0$), the probability of observing an average differential return between the portfolio and its benchmark that is worse than its alpha is directly related to its Information ratio by the relation

$$\Pr\left[\overline{R}_P^{Hy} - \overline{R}_B^{Hy} \leq \alpha_P\right] = \Phi(\mathrm{IR}_P\sqrt{H}) \tag{5-34}$$

where $\overline{R}_P^{Hy} - \overline{R}_B^{Hy}$ is the average portfolio abnormal return above its benchmark B over the N years considered, $\alpha_P \equiv \overline{R}_P - \overline{R}_B$ is the observed (negative) alpha, and $\mathrm{IR}_P = \frac{\overline{R}_P - \overline{R}_B}{\sigma(R_P - R_B)}$ is the (negative) Information ratio (or Appraisal ratio $\frac{\alpha_P}{\sigma_{\varepsilon P}}$ in the context of the CAPM – see Chapter 3). Equation (5-34) essentially states that the Information ratio plays the role of an iso-probability function in the active risk-active return space. Thus, if portfolio X has a more negative Information ratio than portfolio Y, then according to Equation (5-34), the probability of observing this or a lower value of the abnormal return than the observed one by chance is lower for X than for Y. In other words, the negative outcome of X is more extreme than the one of Y, and it is less likely to be the mere outcome of bad luck. Consequently, as indicated by the rank of their Information ratios, Y has outperformed X.

Our reasoning is in sharp contrast with an approach that seems to have been conventional wisdom for years. It all started with Israelsen's (2005) idea that the ranking of portfolios according to their Sharpe and Information ratios in negative territories was wrong and had to be reversed. His point of view rests of the rather intuitive reasoning exposed in Section 5.5.2.1: *if two portfolios have the same excess or abnormal return (whether positive or negative), the less risky one is necessarily the best.* If this is correct, Israelsen's (2005) claim is right.[23] Accordingly, he proposes two alternative versions of the Sharpe and Information ratios that lead to a reversal of portfolio rankings when the numerator of the equation is negative:

$$\mathrm{iSR}_P = \frac{\overline{R}_P - R_f}{(\sigma_P)^{\phi_P}} \tag{5-35a}$$

$$\mathrm{iIR}_P = \frac{\mathrm{TD}_P}{\mathrm{TE}_P} = \frac{\overline{R}_P - \overline{R}_B}{(\sigma(R_P - R_B))^{\phi_P}} \tag{5-35b}$$

[23] Israelsen's (2005) reasoning appears to be valid in the particular case of trackers (ETFs or index funds) regarding the use of the Information ratio when they display the same tracking difference because the logic of the use of trackers is one of substitution (the tracker replaced the index) rather than the one of complement. Nevertheless, as we show in Section 16.3.2 of Chapter 16, the very applicability of the Information ratio in this context is highly questionable, and other selection methods should be preferred.

where $\phi_P = \frac{|\overline{R}_P - R_f|}{\overline{R}_P - R_f}$ takes value 1 if $\overline{R}_P - R_f \geq 0$ and -1 if $\overline{R}_P - R_f < 0$. The ratios are thus unadjusted when the numerator is positive and is multiplied (instead of divided) by portfolio risk otherwise. The author insists that, in that latter case, the performance measure does not have any economic meaning anymore and should only be used in order to rank portfolios or funds according to the logic "a lower risk means, *ceteris paribus*, a higher performance" – a logic upon which we disagree here, as explained above.

5.5.4.3 Making sense of unusual betas

The two situations depicted in Figure 5-20 demand very different types of treatments. They are both very intuitive.

The case of a very low beta (portfolio *A* in the graph) has already been identified in Chapter 3. When the significance level of the market model is very low, while at the same time the average portfolio return is substantially higher than the risk-free rate, the beta tends to zero and the alpha captures most of the excess return. It would be natural to consider such a positive alpha associated with a poor explanatory power of the model as suspicious. There are several ways to handle this, ranked by order of sophistication:

- First, report the modified Jensen's alpha preferably to the mere Jensen's alpha: if the former is particularly high, then the model should be severely challenged, if not abandoned.
- Second, in order to validate (or not) the estimated performance, test the significance of the modified Jensen's alpha. Such a test is a useful tool in order to simultaneously check the quality of the model and the existence of a true outperformance.
- Third, if necessary, extend the regression with the addition of one or several relevant risk factors, in order to inflate the quality of the model and lend more credibility to the resulting alpha. This is the subject of Chapter 7, which is fully devoted to the discussion of performance measurement applied to multifactor models.

The situation that arises when the beta is negative (and sufficiently high not to be confused with zero), like portfolio *B*, bears a mechanical, but surprising solution. Since we are in the context of the CAPM, the challenge posed with this portfolio is to match the return that this fund obtains if its risk is matched with that of the market portfolio, whose beta is (by definition) equal to one. The portfolio should thus be *shorted* in order to transform its negative beta into a positive one. This means that an investor who wishes to compare oranges with oranges must adopt a contrarian strategy with this portfolio. If portfolio *B* has a positive alpha as in the figure, this is bad news: the negative holding will impose additional losses to the investor. Paradoxically, a negative alpha going along with a negative beta is therefore synonymous of a negative performance for the investor. This is illustrated in the graph shown in Figure 5-21, which shows a continuation of Figure 5-20.

The diagnosis posed with the Treynor ratio is confirmed with the modified Jensen's alpha: a fund or portfolio that goes against the market, and thus has a negative systematic risk, is

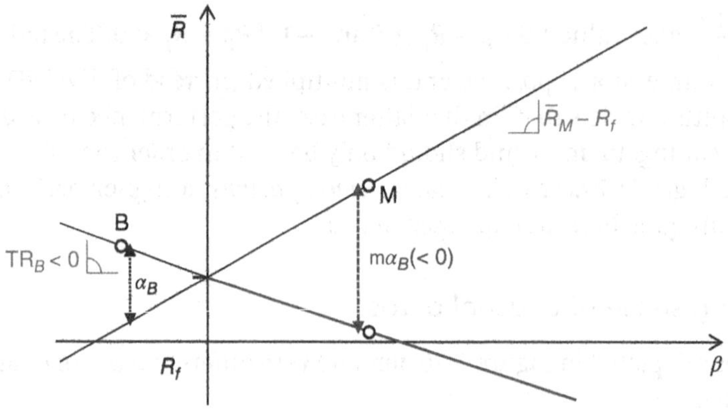

FIGURE 5-21 Performance of a portfolio with a negative beta.

expected to do even *worse* than its expected return in order to be associated with a positive performance. The conclusion is also without appeal: Jensen's alpha has to be interpreted in a wholly opposite manner as in the "normal" world of positive betas. The lower the alpha, the better it is. This counterintuitive outcome may indeed signal that the benchmark is poorly chosen. If the beta is negative, this induces a negative correlation between the portfolio and its benchmark, which is not a natural situation. Hence, if negative betas are observed during several periods, this might call for a full reevaluation of the whole benchmarking process.

Fortunately, this strange phenomenon neither extends to the Treynor ratio nor to the modified Jensen's alpha, whose normalization process (through their denominator) ensures a correct assessment of portfolio performance.

G–T–N example (continued)

The three-year risk and return data of each fund and the market portfolio have been split in sub-periods of one year. The summary of the results is provided in Table 5-13.

The periods are contrasted regarding the market risk and return: An excellent first year, with a market Sharpe ratio of $SR_M^{(y1)} = 1.36$; a disastrous second year ($SR_M^{(y2)} = -0.66$); and a good third year ($SR_M^{(y3)} = 0.99$). Logically, the three funds tend to follow more or less closely the same trends. Furthermore, the managers seem to reap an alpha that is positive in the first period and negative in the second one. These statements are visually confirmed by the impressions retrieved from the pair of bar charts shown in Figure 5-22.

In the second (bearish) period, the three funds' Information ratios are negative. Applying the formula of Equation (5-34) (with $N = 1$), we can reconcile the observed levels of the IR with the probability of observing performance values that are lower than or equal to them for each fund: $\Phi(IR_G) = 40\%$, $\Phi(IR_T) = 31\%$, and $\Phi(IR_N) = 32\%$. Since the larger the probability, the better it is, we can conclude that the funds' Information ratios rank them correctly regarding the quality of their management under these circumstances.

TABLE 5-13 G–T–N example – Summary statistics and performance measures per year.

	Year 1 (bullish)				Year 2 (bearish)				Year 3 (good)			
	G	T	N	M	G	T	N	M	G	T	N	M
Mean	15.63%	10.96%	4.35%	16.46%	−2.36%	−2.30%	0.69%	−3.35%	5.90%	5.50%	2.61%	9.06%
SD	9.41%	8.88%	4.03%	11.05%	5.53%	5.02%	3.54%	7.28%	5.74%	4.38%	4.11%	7.68%
Correlation	0.98	0.51	0.19	1.00	0.99	0.48	−0.35	1.00	0.99	0.54	0.28	1.00
SR	1.51	1.07	0.72	1.36	−0.69	−0.75	−0.21	−0.66	0.78	0.93	0.28	0.99
TR	17.00%	23.23%	41.99%	15.02%	−5.05%	−11.30%	4.41%	−4.79%	6.03%	13.18%	7.82%	7.62%
Alpha	1.66%	3.36%	1.87%		−0.20%	−2.15%	−1.57%		−1.18%	1.71%	0.03%	
Modified alpha	1.98%	8.21%	26.97%		−0.26%	−6.51%	9.20%		−1.59%	5.56%	0.20%	
IR	0.88	0.44	0.47		−0.25	−0.49	−0.47		−1.46	0.46	0.01	

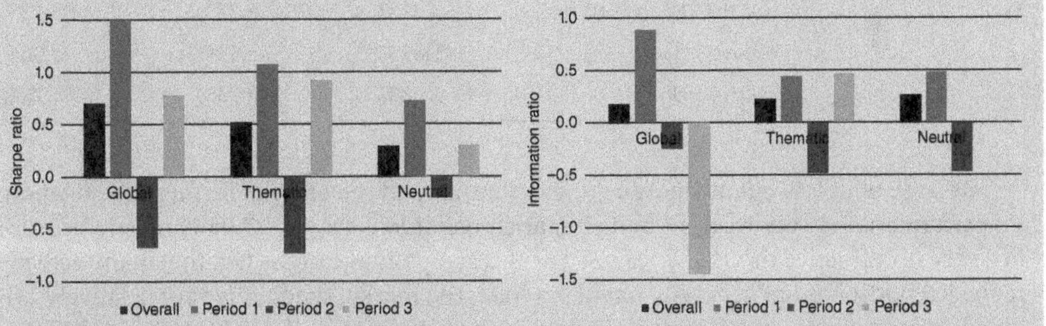

FIGURE 5-22 G–T–N example – Split of the Sharpe ratios (left) and Information ratios (right) over time.

Under these very different market conditions, it is tempting to conclude that all funds have nicely outperformed the market during the first period and underperformed during the second one. Nevertheless, this impression is largely flawed. Table 5-14 summarizes the outcome of the split of the funds' excess return differential over the market according to Equation (5-32).

(continued)

(continued)

TABLE 5-14 G–T–N example – Contributors to differential returns per period.

		Global	Thematic	Neutral
Three years	Excess diff. return π_P	0.19%	−1.43%	−3.44%
	Active return	0.37%	1.66%	2.28%
	Active risk	−0.18%	−3.09%	−5.71%
Year 1 (bullish)	Excess diff. return π_P	1.64%	−3.17%	−7.04%
	Active return	1.94%	4.19%	5.13%
	Active risk	−0.30%	−7.36%	−12.17%
Year 2 (bearish)	Excess diff. return π_P	−0.21%	−0.63%	3.25%
	Active return	−0.26%	−3.12%	−3.22%
	Active risk	0.05%	2.49%	6.47%
Year 3 (good)	Excess diff. return π_P	0.91%	2.23%	−3.43%
	Active return	−1.81%	3.45%	0.06%
	Active risk	−0.06%	−2.74%	−4.28%

Because of its low but unstable beta, the Neutral fund is worthy of further investigation. Its performance is very weak in bullish market conditions ($\pi_N = -7.04\%$) mostly because of a very strong active risk that does not pay. It is symptomatic of the fact that many actively managed portfolios are generally unable to track the market when it is very positively oriented, as in the first year. However, in year 2, the picture radically differs. The fund posts a very positive performance, even though its Information ratio is negative (see Table 5-13). The reason is that taking systematic risk did not get rewarded during that period: the market's excess return is negative. Thus, **N**'s manager was well inspired to diverge from the market, which is translated in a positive contribution of active risk to the total performance.

Finally, still regarding the Neutral fund, we can relate the negative second year alpha $\alpha_N^{(y2)} = -1.57\%$ with its positive modified Jensen's alpha $m\alpha_N^{(y2)} = +9.20\%$. This can simply be explained by the manager's adoption of a negative beta during this period. If an investor had wanted to use this fund and short it in order to reach the same beta as the market, the negative alpha would then have turned positive, leaving a positive abnormal return. Even though its alpha was negative, the fund has outperformed the market during bearish times.

Key Takeaways and Equations

- We list five types of pitfalls associated with the use of classical performance measures:
  1. Issues with the Standard Portfolio Theory, which challenge the relevance of the Sharpe ratio.
  2. Issues with the Capital Asset Pricing Model, which challenge the relevance of Jensen's alpha, the Treynor ratio, the modified Jensen's alpha, and the Appraisal ratio.
  3. Issues with the sample of data that is used in order to generate the performance measurement estimates.
  4. Issues with the linear regression model that is used in order to estimate the parameters of the CAPM.
  5. Issues with the interpretation of the results generated from the data, irrespective of the resolution of all the ones discussed above.
- Major issues with the Standard Portfolio Theory belong to three main categories:
  - The refutation of the validity of the *risk and return components* because of the lack of justification of volatility as an adequate measure of risk.
  - The inapplicability of the *homemade leverage assumption* because of the practical existence of different lending and borrowing rates and limitations to leverage.
  - The inexistence of a *riskless interest rate* that applies for all portfolios.
- Potential solutions to these three types of issues feature:
  - Regarding risk and excess return components, a number of adjusted versions of the Sharpe ratio are proposed in Chapter 6.
  - Regarding the homemade leverage assumption, the major answer is provided by the use of preference-adjusted performance measures as developed in Chapter 9.
  - Regarding the riskless interest rate, several ways to solve the difficulty to identify the risk-free rate are proposed in Chapter 6. Another approach is to use the initial yield of a fixed-income instrument whose duration matches the sample:

$$\mathrm{SR}_P^{(T/n)} = \frac{\overline{R}_P - R_{f,T/n}^{(T/n)}}{\sigma_P} \tag{5-3}$$

- Major issues with the Capital Asset Pricing Model belong to three main categories:
  - The failure to identify *relevant risk factors*, beyond or even instead of the market portfolio return.

(continued)

(continued)

  - The unobservability of the *true benchmark inputs*, along with Roll's (1977) critique of the CAPM.
  - The ignorance of the actual *portfolio manager's decisions*, especially regarding their decisions to time the market ("market timing").
- Potential solutions to these three types of issues feature:
  - Regarding relevant risk factors, the issue is studied in detail in Chapter 7.
  - Regarding the true benchmark inputs, there are various ways to approximate as closely as possible the properties of the market portfolio.
  - Regarding the portfolio manager's decisions, this is the subject of Chapter 8.
- Major issues with the sample used for estimation belong to three main categories:
  - The selection of an *inadequate sample* either because of an inappropriate time window or because of a wrong cross-section of comparable funds or portfolios.
  - Mistakes in the usage of the *series of returns*, mostly regarding phenomena such as autocorrelation, heteroscedasticity, on non-normality of returns.
  - The ignorance of *measurement error* in the data, which could lead to biased estimates of performance.
- Potential solutions to these three types of issues feature:
  - Regarding the choice of an adequate sample, a workable approach is to use periods ranging from three to (maximum) ten years, and avoid the survivorship bias.
  - Regarding the series of returns, their treatment and associated modified performance measures are studied in detail in Chapter 6.
  - Regarding measurement error, several statistical treatments exist. A particularly interesting one is the use of shrinkage estimation for the variance–covariance matrix:

$$\hat{\Sigma}_{\text{shrink}} = \delta^* \, \Theta + (1 - \delta^*) \, \hat{\Sigma} \tag{5-16}$$

- Major issues with the regression models belong to three main categories:
  - The estimation of *coefficients with error* either because of the error-in-variable problem with the data or because of microstructure issues for high-frequency data.
  - The neglecting of *nonlinearities* that can be present in the relation, especially when the manager uses options or equivalent strategies.
  - The ignorance of *conditioning information*, based on the observation of past public information, in the manager's market exposures.

- Potential solutions to these three types of issues feature:
  - Regarding the coefficients with error, there are various estimation techniques that aim to correct the estimated beta to address the impact of the documented issues.
  - Regarding the nonlinearities, it is useful to use Leland's (1999) adjusted beta:

$$\beta_P^{(\gamma)} = \frac{\text{Cov}(R_P, -(1+R_M)^{-\gamma})}{\text{Cov}(R_M, -(1+R_M)^{-\gamma})} \tag{5-27}$$

  - Regarding conditioning information, it is recommended to use the conditional CAPM proposed by Ferson and Schadt (1996):

$$R_{P,t} - R_f = \alpha_P + \beta_{P,0}(R_{M,t} - R_f) + \beta_{P,z}[z_{t-1} \times (R_{M,t} - R_f)] + \varepsilon_{P,t} \tag{5-29}$$

- Major issues with the interpretation of the results belong to three main categories:
  - The overlooking of *market conditions*, which may put in perspective the importance of the performance generated by the manager.
  - The explanation of *negative performance measures*, especially in the case of the Sharpe and Information ratios.
  - The handling of *low or negative betas*, which might create misunderstandings regarding the true risk-adjusted performance of the manager.
- Potential solutions to these three types of issues feature:
  - Regarding the market conditions, it is advisable when relevant to disentangle the contribution of active return and active risk in performance:

$$\pi_P = \frac{\sigma_M}{\sigma_P}\alpha_P + (\rho_{PM} - 1)(\overline{R}_M - R_f) \tag{5-32}$$

  - Regarding the negative performance measures, this is essentially a non-issue: negative Sharpe and Information ratios are adequate reflections of performance.
  - Regarding unusual betas, values close to zero should be regarded as unreliable, whereas negative values lead to the reversal of the interpretation of Jensen's alphas.

REFERENCES

Akeda, Y. (2003), Another interpretation of negative Sharpe Ratio. *Journal of Performance Measurement*, Vol. 7 (3), pp. 19–23.

Angelidis, T., Giamouridis, D., and N. Tessaromatis (2013), Revisiting mutual fund performance evaluation. *Journal of Banking & Finance*, Vol. 37, pp. 1759–1776.

Bacon, C. R. (2021), *Practical Risk-Adjusted Performance Measurement, 2nd Edition*. Wiley, Wiley Finance Series.

Bauman, W. S., and R. E. Miller (1995), Portfolio performance rankings in stock market cycles. *Financial Analysts Journal*, Vol. 51 (2), pp. 79–87.

Best, M. J., and R. R. Grauer (1985), Capital asset pricing compatible with observed market value weights. *The Journal of Finance*, Vol. 40, pp. 85–103.

Black, F. (1972), Capital market equilibrium with restricted borrowing. *Journal of Business*, Vol. 45, pp. 444–454.

Black, F., and R. Litterman (1991), Asset allocation: Combining investor view with market equilibrium. *Journal of Fixed Income*, Vol. 1 (1), pp. 5–18.

Blume, M. E., and I. Friend (1973), A new look at the Capital Asset Pricing Model. *The Journal of Finance*, Vol. 28, pp. 19–34.

Brockett, P. L., and Y. Kahane (1992), Risk, return, skewness and preference. *Management Science*, Vol. 38, pp. 851–866.

Bunnenberg, S., Rohleder, M., Scholz, H., and M. Wilkens (2019), Jensen's alpha and the market timing puzzle. *Review of Financial Economics*, Vol. 37, pp. 234–255.

Chang, E. C., Pinegar, J. M., and R. Ravichandran (1995), European day-of-the-week effects, beta asymmetries and international herding. *European Financial Management*, Vol. 1, pp. 173–200.

Cohen, K. J., Hawawini, G. A., Maier, S. F., Schwartz, R. A., and D. Whitcomb (1983), Estimating and adjusting for the intervalling-effect bias in beta. *Management Science*, Vol. 29, pp. 135–148.

Cragg, J. G. (1994), Making good inferences from bad data. *Canadian Journal of Economics*, Vol. 27, pp. 776–800.

Dagenais, M. G., and D. L. Dagenais (1997), Higher moment estimators for linear regression models with errors in the variables. *Journal of Econometrics*, Vol. 76, pp. 193–221.

Davidson, R., and J. MacKinnon (1993), *Estimation and Inference in Econometrics*. Oxford University Press.

Dimensional (2020), Why worry about survivorship bias? Retrieved from `https://www.dimensional.com/us-en/insights/why-worry-about-survivorship-bias`.

Dimson, E. (1979), Risk measurement when shares are subject to infrequent trading. *Journal of Financial Economics*, Vol. 7, pp. 195–226.

Dubois, M., and P. Louvet (1996), The day-of-the-week effect: The international evidence. *Journal of Banking & Finance*, Vol. 20, pp. 1463–1484.

Ferson, W. E., and R. Schadt (1996), Measuring fund strategy and performance in changing economic conditions. *The Journal of Finance*, Vol. 51, pp. 425–462.

Fowler, D. J., and H. C. Rorke (1983), Risk measurement when shares are subject to infrequent trading: Comment. *Journal of Financial Economics*, Vol. 12, pp. 295–283.

Friend, I., and M. Blume (1970), Measurement of portfolio performance under uncertainty. *American Economic Review*, Vol. 60, pp. 561–575.

Graham, J. R., and C. R. Harvey (1997), Grading the performance of market-timing newsletters. *Financial Analysts Journal*, Vol. 53 (6), pp. 54–66.

Grinblatt, M., and S. Titman (1989), Portfolio performance evaluation: Old issues and new insights. *The Review of Financial Studies*, Vol. 2, pp. 393–421.

Hansen, L. P., and R. J. Hodrick (1980), Forward exchange rates as optimal predictors of future spot rates: An econometric analysis. *Journal of Political Economy*, Vol. 88, pp. 829–853.

Hoechner, B., Reichling, P., and G. Schulze (2017), Pitfalls of downside performance measures with arbitrary targets. *International Review of Finance*, Vol. 17, pp. 595–610.

Hübner, G., and M. Lambert (2019), Performance sharing in risky portfolios: The case of hedge fund returns and fees. *The Journal of Portfolio Management*, Vol. 45 (4), pp. 105–118.

Israelsen, C. L. (2005), A refinement to the Sharpe ratio and Information ratio. *Journal of Asset Management*, Vol. 5, pp. 423–427.

Kan, R., and G. Zhou (2007), Optimal portfolio choice with parameter uncertainty. *Journal of Financial and Quantitative Analysis*, Vol. 42, pp. 621–656.

Kryzanowski, L., and A. Rahman (2008), Portfolio performance ambiguity and benchmark inefficiency revisited. *Journal of Asset Management*, Vol. 9, pp. 321–332.

Ledoit, O., and M. Wolf (2003), Improved estimation of the covariance matrix of stock returns with an application to portfolio selection. *Journal of Empirical Finance*, Vol. 10, pp. 603–621.

Ledoit, O., and M. Wolf (2004), Honey, I shrunk the covariance matrix. *The Journal of Portfolio Management*, Vol. 30 (4), pp. 110–119.

Leland, H. (1999), Beyond mean–variance: Performance measurement in a nonsymmetrical world. *Financial Analysts Journal*, Vol. 55 (1), pp. 25–36.

McLeod, W., and G. van Vuuren (2004), Interpreting the Sharpe ratio when excess returns are negative. *Investment Analysts Journal*, Vol. 33 (59), pp. 15–20.

Rohleder, M., Scholz, H., and M. Wilkens (2011), Survivorship bias and mutual fund performance: Relevance, significance, and methodical differences. *Review of Finance*, Vol. 15, pp. 441–474.

Roll, R. (1977), A critique of the asset pricing theory's tests. Part I: On past and potential testability of the theory. *Journal of Financial Economics*, Vol. 4, pp. 125–176.

Roll, R. (1980), Performance evaluation and benchmark errors (I). *The Journal of Portfolio Management*, Vol. 6 (4), pp. 5–12.

Roll, R. (1981), Performance evaluation and benchmark errors (II). *The Journal of Portfolio Management*, Vol. 7 (2), pp. 15–22.

Ross, S. A. (1976), The arbitrage theory of capital asset pricing. *Journal of Economic Theory*, Vol. 13, pp. 341–360.

Roy, A. D. (1952), Safety first and the holding of assets. *Econometrica*, Vol. 20, pp. 431–449.

Scholes, M., and J. Williams (1977), Estimating betas from non-synchronous data. *Journal of Financial Economics*, Vol. 5, pp. 308–328.

Sercu, P., Vandebroek, M., and T. Vinaimont (2008), Thin-trading effects in beta: Bias v. estimation error. *Journal of Business Finance & Accounting*, Vol. 35, pp. 1196–1219.

Sharpe, W. F. (1994), The Sharpe ratio. *The Journal of Portfolio Management*, Vol. 21 (Fall), pp. 45–58.

Tobin, J. (1958), Liquidity preference as behavior towards risk. *Review of Economic Studies*, Vol. 25, pp. 65–86.

PART II - *Appraise (2/2)*

DEVELOPMENTS IN PERFORMANCE MEASUREMENT

The field of performance measurement has considerably evolved since the first classical measures were introduced. Even though the Sharpe ratio, Jensen's alpha or the Information ratio remain popular and have their merits, there are many ways to improve on how the quality of the portfolio management process can be appraised. This can be done in several ways, depending on the perspective adopted. Some are very well-justified from a theoretical perspective, whereas others mainly aim at responding to very practical issues. In total, there are more than one hundred performance measures that coexist today. In this second part of the book, which presents itself as the continuation of the previous one under the "appraisal" dimension, we propose a structured journey into the bushy field of developments in performance measurement.

The opening chapter provides a direct connection with the previous part. In **Chapter 6**, we study in detail how the classical measures can be adapted, extended or reinterpreted in order to meet the challenge of enhanced performance appraisal. This induces a thorough revisit of the notions of "risk", "excess return" or "required return" that are historically central to performance assessment. At the end of the chapter, we attempt to reconcile the various types of measurement approaches within a unified framework.

One of the key extensions of the classical framework induces the use of multiple risk factors to explain portfolio returns. **Chapter 7** focuses on the numerous approaches that have been developed to fulfill this objective. Performance measurement methods have also been adapted to this evolving landscape. This explains why we dedicate a chapter to review and analyze how performance appraisal must be conducted within the scope of multifactor models.

Another substantial field of development of new performance measurement approaches is the assessment of market timing skills of portfolio managers. This is the subject of **Chapter 8**, in which we discuss how researchers and practitioners have attempted to capture this essential component of portfolio performance. Because of the diversity of such methods, we also aim at providing a roadmap to assist the reader in the selection of the adequate performance measures.

The last two chapters of this part are entirely dedicated to the assessment of performance with an explicit treatment of the investor's own preferences. This entails that the appraisal of performance becomes largely customer-oriented. In **Chapter 9**, we adopt the perspective of a "standard" investor who applies a fully rational investment decision-making process. **Chapter 10** enlarges the perspective by addressing the consequences of behavioral considerations on the performance measurement process. This does not only encompass theoretical adjustments to expected utility, but also more heuristic approaches as well as the extension of performance appraisal in the context of goal-based investment decisions.

CHAPTER 6

The Classical Performance Measures Revisited

INTRODUCTION

The five original performance measures that were developed within the scope of the Capital Asset Pricing Model (CAPM) framework and discussed in Chapters 4 and 5 are far from covering the whole spectrum of performance appraisal. Several studies, such as Cogneau and Hübner (2009a; 2009b), Caporin, Jannin, Lisi, and Maillet (2013), or Bacon (2021), literally list hundreds of formulas that are all meant to capture some kind of risk-adjusted performance of a portfolio manager. Obviously, unless they are utterly redundant, all these formulas do not aim to capture the same notion of output (gain) and input (loss). It is necessary to tidy up this abundance of measures.

In this chapter, we choose to develop a number of performance measures (all in all, we list 60 of them in the text) that are close, in one way or another, to the CAPM. It is important to provide a structured approach in order to discuss all these avatars. Some of them attempt to correct a drawback of one of the original measures; we call them "refinements." Some go one step further and replace an ingredient of the measure with another one, claiming that it is more appropriate to appraise performance; we call them "alterations." Finally, some other measures change the unit of measurement and transform ratio-based measures into risk-adjusted returns, sometimes with further refinements or alterations.

Throughout the chapter, we uncover some famous performance measures that belong to one of these families, especially in the context of the Sharpe ratio. To name a few of them, the *adjusted Sharpe ratio* accounts for higher moments of the returns distribution, the *Roy ratio* replaces the risk-free rate with an investor-specific reservation rate, the *Sortino ratio* uses downside volatility as a risk measure, the *Calmar ratio* adopts the maximum drawdown instead of volatility, the *modified Sharpe ratio* uses an estimate of Value-at-Risk that accounts for higher moments, and the M^2 transforms the Sharpe ratio into a risk-adjusted return. As a collateral, but useful takeaway of the chapter, we will be able to complete the synoptic table of performance measures presented in Section 4.1.3 of Chapter 4 by filling the empty cells corresponding to the scale-independent percentage returns when total or specific risk measures are used as inputs.

Note that this chapter mostly focuses on the positive side of CAPM-based risk measures, with all the possibilities that they create. It has to be mirrored with Chapter 5, which was devoted to the pitfalls and difficulties encountered with measuring performance in the context of the CAPM. Notably, several sections provide direct solutions to some pitfalls with the use of classical performance measures listed and discussed in Chapter 3.

The XYZ example – Part II

We reuse the data of the three funds X, Y, and Z from Chapter 3. Since we are interested in more sophisticated risk and return characteristics of these portfolios than the mere sample means and volatilities, we have completed Table 3-2 with some additional sample statistics that are useful in this chapter.

The last column of Table 6-1 corresponds to the fixed-income security f, namely, a one-month Treasury Bill whose return is not considered to be riskless anymore: It displays a material level of volatility, and its correlation with the funds and the market portfolio varies from very negative to positive figures.

TABLE 6-1 XYZ example – Means, volatilities, higher moments, and correlations.

		X	Y	Z	M	f
Mean return		0.32%	0.40%	0.81%	0.66%	0.12%
Standard deviation		1.81%	1.79%	2.47%	2.55%	0.66%
Skewness		0.18	−0.15	0.09	0.49	0.05
Excess kurtosis		−1.34	−1.60	−0.83	−0.50	1.19
Correlations	X	1.00				
	Y	0.65	1.00			
	Z	0.32	0.70	1.00		
	M	0.87	0.61	0.22	1.00	
	f	0.46	−0.83	−0.24	−0.14	1.00

Figures 6-1 to 6-3 represent the coordinates of the funds and market portfolio in the risk–return framework according to the three versions of risk: total (represented by the volatility), systematic (represented by the beta), and specific (represented by the tracking error).

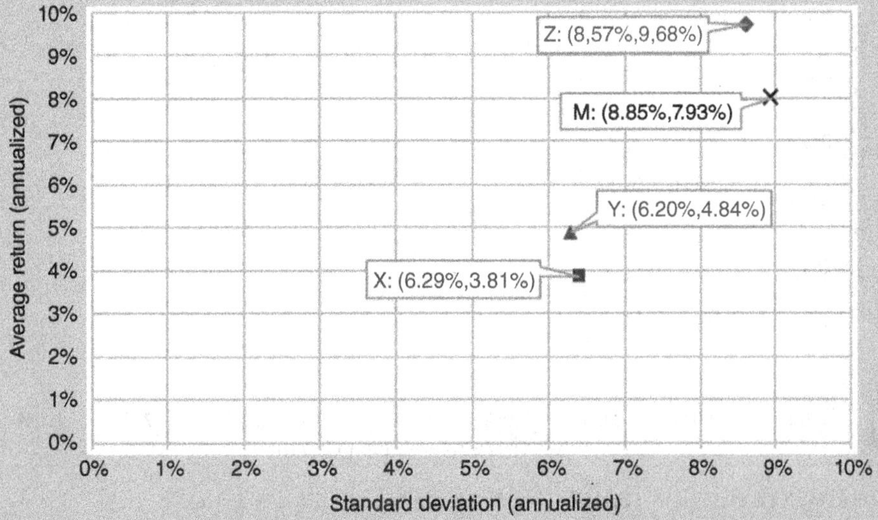

FIGURE 6-1 XYZ example – Portfolio coordinates in the total risk space.

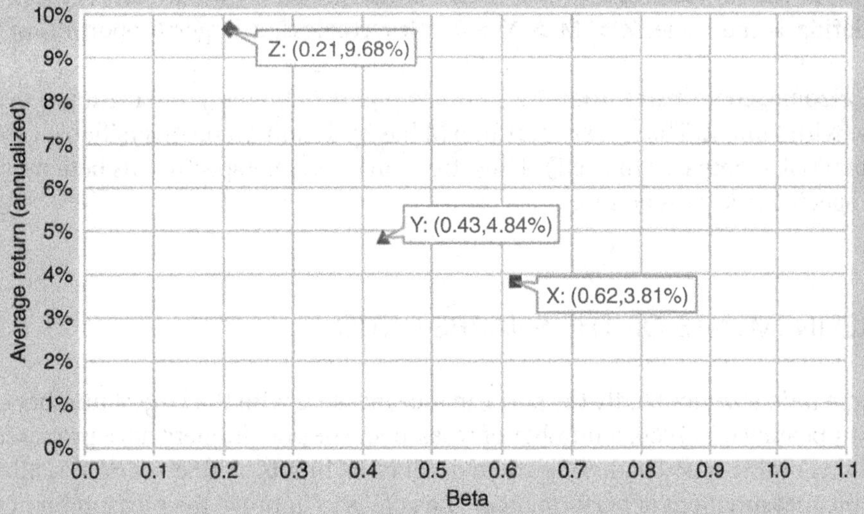

FIGURE 6-2 XYZ example – Portfolio coordinates in the systematic risk space.

(continued)

(continued)

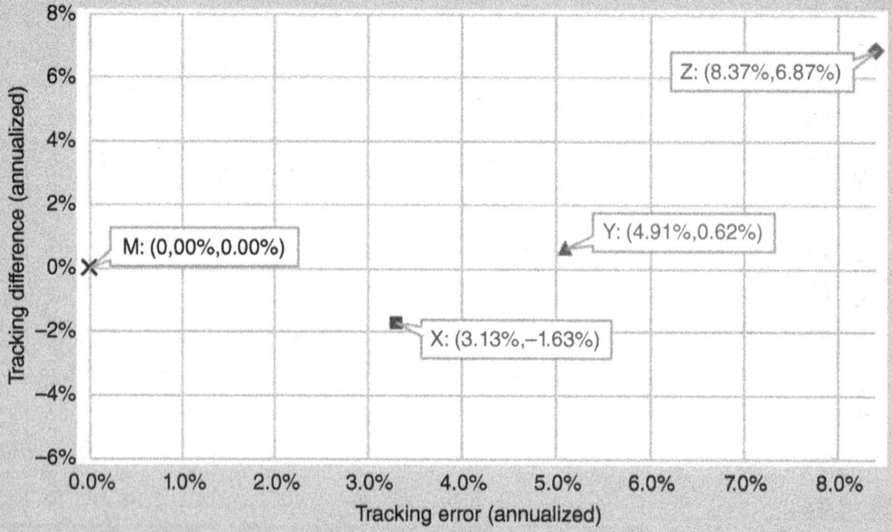

FIGURE 6-3 XYZ example – Portfolio coordinates in the specific risk space.

In the first two graphs, there is an obvious difference between the ordering of the four portfolios on the vertical and the horizontal spaces. From the point of view of mean returns, the ordering is the same: Z > M > Y > X. Nevertheless, a larger proportion of the risk of Fund Y is diversifiable compared to Fund X. This explains the reversal of the order of their horizontal coordinates from Figure 6-2 to Figure 6-3. This phenomenon is even more extreme with Fund Z. The market portfolio M has by definition no diversifiable component in its total risk (compared to itself). Thus, from an *ex post* perspective, its beta must be one and its specific risk must be zero.

6.1 REFINEMENTS OF THE SHARPE RATIO

The Sharpe ratio is undoubtedly the performance measure with the largest number of avatars. Since its appearance in 1966, a number of researchers or practitioners have proposed alternative versions of this ratio by altering some or all of its inputs. A first set of measures aims at *refining* the measurement of performance. The goal is to improve the measurement quality of the ratio's ingredients, thereby providing a more faithful representation of performance without changing the original meaning of the measure (ratio of excess return per unit of volatility).

In order to organize this section in a logical order, we simply represent the original Sharpe ratio in its most generic form:

$$\mathrm{SR}_P = \frac{\text{average portfolio return} - \text{risk-free rate}}{\text{portfolio volatility}} \times \text{(no) adjustment factor} \qquad (6\text{-}1)$$

From expression (6-1), there are four (not mutually exclusive) ways of refining the measurement of performance: through the two terms of the numerator, through the denominator, or through an adjustment factor that may differ from the neutral value of 1. We examine the main such types of adaptations hereunder.

6.1.1 Adapting the portfolio return

Using the average portfolio return as a measure of output is not really challenged in the context of the Sharpe ratio.[1] A more delicate issue is the appraisal of performance for much longer horizons than the frequency of the observation of portfolio returns because of the impact of compounding that may then become important, especially in the case of highly volatile returns. Instead of using the arithmetic mean of portfolio returns, it then becomes necessary to adapt the ratio to geometric returns. Under the standard assumption of an independent and identically distributed (i.i.d.) Gaussian distribution of portfolio returns with an expectation of $\mathrm{E}(R_P) = \mu_P$ and variance σ_P^2, the compound portfolio return for a horizon of H periods, denoted by $R_P(H) \equiv \prod_{t=0}^{H}(1 + R_{P,t})$, has an expectation $\mathrm{E}(R_P(H)) = \mathrm{e}^{H(\mu_P+\sigma_P^2/2)} - 1$ and variance $\sigma^2(R_P(H)) = \mathrm{e}^{H(2\mu_P+\sigma_P^2)}(\mathrm{e}^{\sigma_P^2} - 1)$.

If one replaces the expected return μ_P by the sample mean $\overline{R}_P$, the annualized *geometric Sharpe ratio* is given by the formula proposed by Lin and Chou (2003):[2]

$$\mathrm{SR}_P^g = \frac{\mathrm{e}^{H(\overline{R}_P+\sigma_P^2/2)} - \mathrm{e}^{HR_f^c}}{\mathrm{e}^{H(\overline{R}_P+\sigma_P^2/2)}\sqrt{\mathrm{e}^{H\sigma_P^2} - 1}} \times \sqrt{\frac{n}{H}} \qquad (6\text{-}2)$$

where $R_f^c = \log(1 + R_f)$ is the continuous periodic risk-free rate and n is the frequency of the computation of portfolio returns per year. It is important to note that, even though its first two moments can be computed, $R_P(H)$ is lognormally distributed and therefore departs from the Gaussian distribution. Thus, statistical inference of the Sharpe ratio discussed in Chapter 3 cannot be applied here, and one has to resort to numerical analysis in this case.

This version of the Sharpe ratio is a decreasing function of the investment horizon. Because of the power of compounding, it favors large volatility portfolios for short horizons but low

[1]When other metrics than the mean return are used in order to appraise the portfolio reward, the associated performance measures belong to other families to be discussed in later chapters.
[2]Note that their formula contains a typo, which is corrected here.

volatility portfolios for long horizons. This is illustrated in the following example, in which two portfolios with different risk profiles are compared. The "High" portfolio has a monthly mean return of 0.75% and a volatility of 4.40%. For the "Low" portfolio, the mean return and volatility are 0.40% and 1.60%, respectively. With a risk-free rate of 0.20% per month, both portfolios share the same arithmetic Sharpe ratio of $SR_{High} = SR_{Low} = \frac{0.75\%-0.2\%}{4.4\%} \times \sqrt{12} = \frac{0.4\%-0.2\%}{1.6\%} \times \sqrt{12} = 0.43$. Applying formula (6-2) for horizons ranging from one month to five years leads to the graph shown in Figure 6-4.

For very long horizons, the negative impact of the volatility adjustment might become overly penalizing for very risky portfolios compared to their arithmetic Sharpe ratio. Furthermore, for some portfolios featuring regular inflows and outflows like mutual funds, the retrospective computation of performance over T periods on the basis of arithmetic average returns makes sense since every period can be viewed as an independent portfolio management process.

A solution to reconcile the opposite perspectives (arithmetic for retrospective and geometric for prospective) when the investment horizon exceeds the sample time window ($H > T$) is to average the two versions of the Sharpe ratio, in the spirit of Blume's (1974) approximation, originally developed for expected rates of return:

$$\overline{SR}_P = \frac{H-T}{H-1} SR_P^g + \frac{T-1}{H-1} SR_P \tag{6-3}$$

This measure is very heuristic and has to be considered as such, but it can somehow correct the discrepancies of geometric Sharpe ratios for portfolios with very different levels of volatilities.

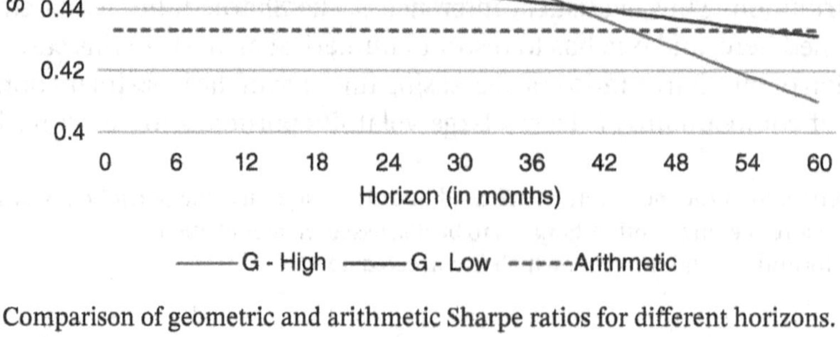

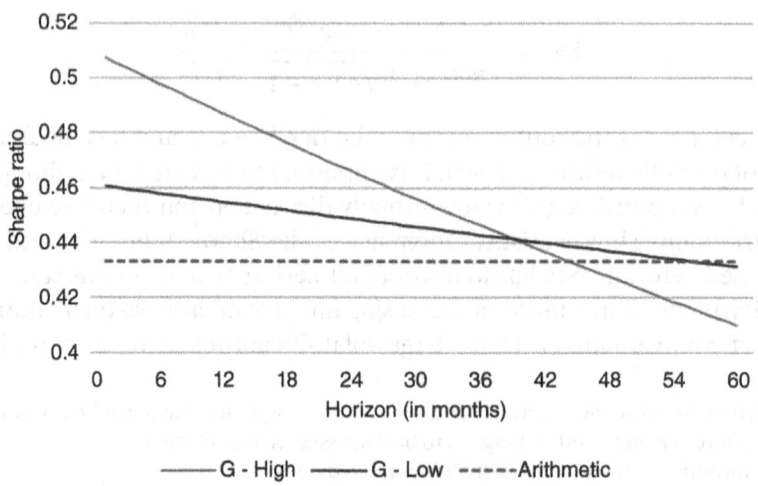

FIGURE 6-4 Comparison of geometric and arithmetic Sharpe ratios for different horizons.

XYZ example (continued)

Three investors are contemplating an investment in the XYZ funds and hesitate with a pure passive investment in the market portfolio. These investors have an investment horizon of 5, 10, and 25 years, respectively. Applying formula (6-2) on the basis of the monthly mean and volatilities, they obtain Table 6-2.

TABLE 6-2 XYZ example – geometric and average Sharpe ratios.

Measure	Horizon (in months)	X	Y	Z	M
Mean		0.32%	0.40%	0.81%	0.66%
Volatility		1.81%	1.79%	2.47%	2.55%
Arithmetic Sharpe ratio	12	0.38	0.55	0.96	0.73
Geometric Sharpe ratio	60	0.38	0.53	0.81	0.65
	120	0.36	0.48	0.66	0.55
	300	0.29	0.37	0.39	0.35
Average Sharpe ratio	60	0.38	0.53	0.84	0.67
	120	0.36	0.49	0.69	0.57
	300	0.30	0.38	0.41	0.37

The values of the five-year geometric Sharpe ratios are close to the original ones for funds X and Y, while they are already substantially impacted by the high volatilities for Fund Z and the market portfolio M. For the latter one, it even becomes dominated by Fund Y for very long investment horizons (25 years). Because of the very short estimation time window (1 year = 12 months), the average Sharpe ratios obtained with Blume's (1974) formula are largely dominated by their geometric versions.

6.1.2 Adapting the risk-free rate

Anyone who works in the area of asset management would inevitably express some skepticism regarding the assumption of a risk-free rate, defined as a constant interest rate for the reference period. This issue is not straightforward: for instance, when determining the corporate cost of capital, it is often accepted to posit a long-term interest rate corresponding to the yield-to-maturity of a default-free bond whose duration matches the investment horizon. However, in the context of performance measurement using historical data retrieved from a sample of portfolio returns and market data, the interest rate exhibits some volatility and correlation with risky asset returns. Even though the scale of those variations might be limited, still this riskiness can be relevant because (i) acknowledging this phenomenon enhances the precision of the Sharpe ratio anyway, and (ii) sometimes the volatility can become material, for instance when the central bank actively revises its monetary policy.[3]

In line with this more realistic point of view, Sharpe (1994) considers the case where the fixed-income security providing a short-term interest income is taken as the portfolio benchmark. The *revised Sharpe ratio* of portfolio P, denoted by rSR_P, then becomes a special case of the Information ratio with formula

$$\text{rSR}_P = \frac{\overline{R}_P - \overline{R}_f}{\sigma_{(P-f)}} \tag{6-4}$$

where $\overline{R}_P$ and $\overline{R}_f$ represent the means of the portfolio and fixed-income security returns, respectively, and $\sigma_{(P-f)} \equiv \sigma(R_P - R_f) = \sqrt{\sigma_P^2 + \sigma_f^2 - 2\rho_{Pf}\sigma_P\sigma_f}$, where σ_f is the volatility of the return of the fixed-income asset and ρ_{Pf} is its correlation with the portfolio return. Like in the definition of the Information ratio proposed in Chapter 3, the numerator of Equation (6-4) is the portfolio tracking difference, while its denominator is defined as the tracking error of the portfolio return over its fixed-income benchmark.

Compared with the original Sharpe ratio, the revised Sharpe ratio can be greater or lower as a function on the behavior of the tracking error. It depends on the sign of $\sigma_f^2 - 2\rho_{Pf}\sigma_P\sigma_f$: If this expression is positive, i.e., if $\rho_{Pf} < \frac{\sigma_f}{2\sigma_P}$, then taking into account the variability of the fixed-income asset deteriorates performance. In particular, the revised Sharpe ratio is greater than the original one in the case of perfect correlation ($\rho_{Pf} = 1$) between the portfolio and the fixed-income returns. Conversely, when the correlation is nil or negative, the revised Sharpe ratio reports a lower portfolio performance than the original one.

It is standard to represent this performance measure as a special case of the Information ratio in the context of the tracking difference/tracking error risk–return framework. Nevertheless, it is probably more intuitive to show how this version of the Sharpe ratio differs from the traditional one in the mean–volatility framework, as in the graph shown in Figure 6-5.

The initial situation, represented by the two dotted lines emanating from the vertical axis, is similar to Figure 3-4 from Chapter 3: The Sharpe ratio of portfolio L exceeds that of portfolio H. We represent the random behavior of the fixed-income security through the point whose coordinates are $(\sigma_f, \overline{R}_f)$. In order to represent the revised Sharpe ratio on the graph, we compute the tracking error for each portfolio. For portfolio L, $\sqrt{\sigma_L^2 + \sigma_f^2 - 2\rho_{Lf}\sigma_L\sigma_f} > \sigma_L$, and thus the slope of the corresponding reward-to-volatility line is lower than its original Sharpe ratio. On the contrary, the revised Sharpe ratio of portfolio H is greater than its original one. These two evolutions are represented by the solid lines on the graph. We can see that the difference could lead to a reversal of the portfolio ranking. Because H is strongly correlated with

[3]See Section 5.1.3 of Chapter 5 for a discussion.

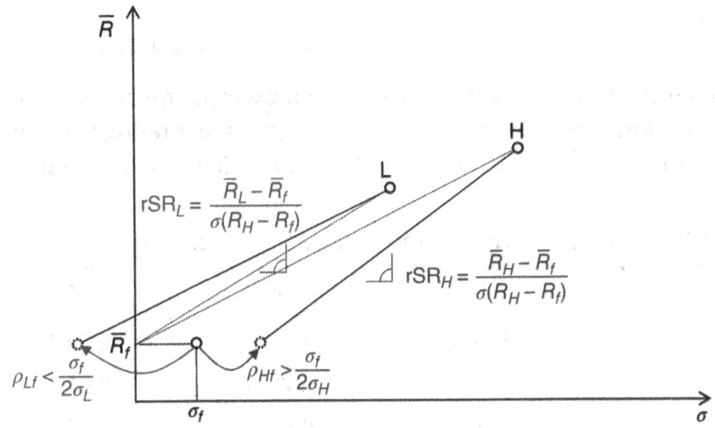

FIGURE 6-5 Graphical representation of the revised Sharpe ratio.

the fixed-income asset, its tracking error is lower than its total risk. Oppositely, L is weakly or negatively correlated with the fixed-income security, which depredates its tracking error. Thus, while $SR_L > SR_H$, we finally conclude that $rSR_L < rSR_H$.

The influence of the variability and correlation of the fixed-income asset f on portfolio performance can become significant when portfolios investing in different asset classes are compared with each other. By nature, f is close to a short-term Treasury Bill or equivalent. Its return increases when the interest rate increases. Generally, there is a negative correlation between the periodic returns of stocks and bonds and the evolution of interest rates. We can therefore expect that most classical funds would display a negative correlation with the fixed-income asset. Nevertheless, some less conventional strategies, like for instance some that are used by hedge fund managers, can provide a positive correlation with the short-term interest rate. For these funds, it is likely that the revised Sharpe ratio favorably compares to the original one.

XYZ example (continued)

With the data of Table 6-1, we can update the calculations of the Sharpe ratios of the three funds and the market index as shown in Table 6-3 (all figures are expressed in yearly returns).

Because of its very negative correlation with the fixed-income security, the risk of Fund Y largely increases when the variability of the interest rate is accounted for. Conversely, Fund X positively correlates with the interest rate. Thus, its manager achieves to some extent a form of hedging of its return compared to the T-Bill. This has a positive

(continued)

(continued)

influence on their revised Sharpe ratio, which even exceeds the one of manager Y, thereby changing their ranking relative to each other. The graphical representation of the revised Sharpe ratios of the funds and the market index is provided in Figure 6-6.

TABLE 6-3 XYZ example – Original and revised Sharpe ratios.

Measure	X	Y	Z	M
Mean	3.81%	4.84%	9.68%	7.93%
Volatility	6.29%	6.20%	8.57%	8.85%
Sharpe ratio	**0.38**	**0.55**	**0.96**	**0.73**
Tracking error	5.61%	8.20%	9.39%	9.44%
Revised Sharpe ratio	**0.42**	**0.41**	**0.88**	**0.69**

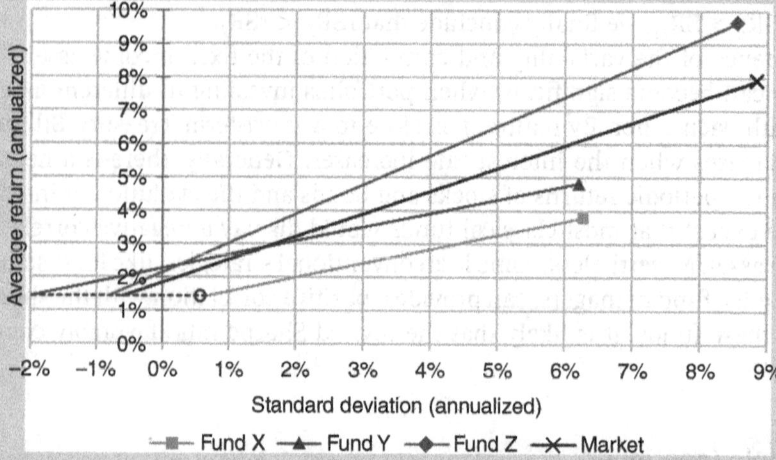

FIGURE 6-6 XYZ example – Representation of the revised Sharpe ratios.

The circle corresponds to the coordinates of the Treasury Bill. Only Fund X, whose correlation with the interest rate is positive, improves its tracking error compared to its total risk. The graph shows that the revised Sharpe ratios of Funds X and Y become very similar, which contrasts with the differences in their Sharpe ratios shown in Figure 3-5 from Chapter 3.

6.1.3 Adapting the total risk measure

The third ingredient of the Sharpe ratio that can be refined is its denominator, namely, the portfolio volatility. The objective is not to replace this risk measure but to provide a fairer value of the Sharpe ratio by improving the assessment of portfolio risk over the sample period used for the estimation. There are many such ways with different levels of complexity. Thus, it is impossible to provide an exhaustive list of those improvement approaches. Nonetheless, three directions stand out as good compromises between sophistication and practical applicability. In all cases, the Sharpe ratio consecutive to the adjustment can be written as $SR'_P = \frac{\overline{R}_P - R_f}{\sigma_P^{\text{corrected}}}$. Note that these corrections correspond to the pitfalls identified in Section 5.3.2 of Chapter 5.

6.1.3.1 Correcting for autocorrelation of returns

Autocorrelation refers to the situation in which portfolio returns linearly depend on the realization of their lagged values. As a reminder of Equation (5-8) of Chapter 5, an autoregressive process of order L, also denoted by AR(L), can be written as

$$R_{P,t} = \rho_0 + \sum_{l=1}^{L} \rho_l R_{P,t-l} + \varepsilon_{P,t} \tag{6-5}$$

where ρ_0 is a constant and ρ_l represents the coefficient of the lth lag of the process.

In general, finding evidence of autocorrelation (a.k.a. serial correlation) of returns is good news for an active portfolio manager. It represents a simple breach of the weak form of the informationally efficient market hypothesis. In other words, it entails that it is possible to outperform the market by trading on the basis of this historical information.

In portfolio management, the story is not so straightforward. Uncovering the presence of serial correlation of portfolio returns is often associated with a significant level of illiquidity in the portfolio's asset or liability structure. As explained in Chapter 12, this primarily happens for some hedge fund strategies, most real estate funds (including notably infrastructure, farmland, and timber), and private equity. In these circumstances, obtaining a marked-to-market valuation of all assets with the same frequency as the publication of the portfolio's net asset value is not possible at reasonable costs. This introduces an artificial smoothing of the series of prices, which is not in line with the genuine – but hidden – economic values. This phenomenon of "stale pricing," reflected in the positive autocorrelation of returns, leaves the impression of returns that are relatively stable over time. Unfortunately, many funds that are concerned with this issue do not permit investors to freely step in or out at the same frequency as the one of the publication of returns.[4] In other words, returns seem to be predictable, but this information is useless for investment purposes.

[4] We study this phenomenon of stale prices, and potential remediation approaches, in Chapter 12.

Lo (2002) shows how to adapt the computation of total risk when returns are observed n times per year and the autocorrelation process obeys Equation (6-5) with $L < n$:

$$\sigma_P^{(L)} = \sigma_P \times \sqrt{1 + \frac{2}{n}\sum_{l=1}^{L}(n-l)\rho_l} \tag{6-6}$$

In the case where $L = 1$ and $\rho_1 \equiv \rho$, Lo (2002) shows that this expression bears a closed-form solution:

$$\sigma_P^{(1)} = \sigma_P \times \sqrt{1 + \frac{2\rho}{1-\rho}\left(1 - \frac{1-\rho^n}{n(1-\rho)}\right)} \tag{6-7}$$

Of course, it makes little sense to report a periodic Sharpe ratio in this context since a minimum of L lagged returns are necessary to retrieve the full spectrum of the autocorrelation pattern. Thus, the annualized corrected Sharpe ratio can be written as $\mathrm{SR}_P^{(L)} = \sqrt{n}\frac{\overline{R}_P - R_f}{\sigma_P^{(L)}}$.

6.1.3.2 Accounting for conditional heteroscedasticity

For most risky assets, including stocks and indexes, there is very limited evidence of substantial predictability of the level of returns (notwithstanding evidence of stale prices that mostly affect less liquid portfolios). However, such a statement does not hold for the magnitude (in absolute value) of these returns. There is indeed ample evidence of time-varying volatility that evolves in a well-structured fashion (see Chapter 5 for an illustration). In most of such models, the variance of returns is typically represented as an autoregressive process. They are generically termed as "autoregressive conditional heteroscedasticity" (ARCH) models.

The first version of these models was introduced by Engle (1982) and was subsequently followed by many avatars. The most popular of these versions is the one proposed by Bollerslev (1986), who defines the generalized autoregressive conditional heteroscedasticity (GARCH) model as an autoregressive moving average model (ARMA) with parameters q (the order of the moving average process) and p (the order of the autoregressive process) for the variance of asset returns.

When adapted to a portfolio context, the GARCH(p, q) can be generically represented as follows:

$$R_{P,t} = \mathrm{E}(R_{P,t}) + \varepsilon_{P,t}, \text{with } \varepsilon_t \rightsquigarrow \mathcal{N}(0, \sigma_{P,t}^2) \tag{6-8a}$$

$$\sigma_{P,t}^2 = a_{P0} + \sum_{i=1}^{q} a_{Pi}\varepsilon_{P,t-i}^2 + \sum_{j=1}^{p} b_{Pj}\sigma_{P,t-j}^2 + \eta_{P,t} \tag{6-8b}$$

where $\mathrm{E}(R_{P,t})$ stands for the conditional expectation of the return (for instance determined with the CAPM) and $\sigma_{P,t}^2$ is its conditional variance and a_{P0} is a constant. For the volatility process to be stationary, it is sufficient that all coefficients in Equation (6-8b) are positive, and $\sum_{i=1}^{q} a_{Pi} + \sum_{j=1}^{p} b_{Pj} < 1$.

The system depicted in Equations (6-8a) and (6-8b) has to be estimated jointly. If the model is validated, its coefficients provide a very useful refinement for the assessment of the volatility of portfolio returns and therefore of its Sharpe ratio.

There are essentially two practical uses of the outputs of the GARCH model for performance measurement. The first one merely uses the time series of estimated conditional volatilities $\hat{\sigma}_{P,t}$ in order to obtain a refined estimate of the average risk taken by the portfolio manager during the sample period used for the computation of the Sharpe ratio:

$$\overline{\sigma}_P = \frac{1}{T}\sum_{t=1}^{T} \hat{\sigma}_{P,t} \tag{6-9}$$

The second approach is more forward-looking. It consists of using information contained in the estimation of the GARCH(p, q) process in order to assess the long-term unconditional volatility $\sigma_{P,\infty}$, which is defined as

$$\sigma_{P,\infty} = \sqrt{\frac{a_{P0}}{1 - \sum_{i=1}^{q} a_{Pi} - \sum_{j=1}^{p} b_{Pj}}} \tag{6-10}$$

In both cases, the original estimate of the portfolio volatility is replaced with the one obtained from the GARCH model. Note that it is also possible to use the point-in-time information at the time of the last observation (i.e., at the end of the sample window, when the Sharpe ratio is observed) in order to assess the future expected variance of the portfolio returns for any subsequent period τ, which is given by

$$\mathrm{E}(\sigma^2_{P,T+\tau} | \sigma^2_{P,T}) = \sigma^2_{P,\infty} + \left(\sum_{i=1}^{q} a_{Pi} + \sum_{j=1}^{p} b_{Pj}\right)^{\tau} (\sigma^2_{P,T} - \sigma^2_{P,\infty}) \tag{6-11}$$

This expression can prove to be very useful in order to (try to) forecast future portfolio performance.

Many other specifications can be implemented. Their choice should be driven by simultaneously considering the quality of the fit and the appropriateness of the assumptions, usually estimated through the maximum likelihood techniques. Naturally, the GARCH family models have been developed in the context of market data; they are not specifically meant to address the situation of actively managed portfolios, whose returns are the joint result of the dynamics of asset returns and managerial trading decisions. Nevertheless, for some portfolios or funds that involve relatively infrequent rebalancing decisions (such as buy-and-hold strategies), the quality of the model fit can still be substantial.

6.1.3.3 Adjusting for higher moments

There are numerous variations of the Sharpe ratio that replace the volatility of portfolio returns with alternative measures of risk. If the portfolio returns follow a Gaussian distribution, these variations are economically useless. Any measure of risk is a monotonically increasing function of the variance, and portfolio rankings according to their risk are therefore unaffected by the shift in risk measure. If returns are not normally distributed, the situation is different. Distinct ways of measuring risk could lead to very different diagnoses. However, before departing from the theoretically robust framework underlying the Sharpe ratio, it is worth attempting to adjust the volatility in order to adequately reflect the impact of the non-Gaussian behavior of portfolio returns.

The implementation of the Cornish and Fisher (1938) expansion proves to be useful in this context. This formula provides an approximation for the percentiles of the returns distribution that accounts for its skewness and kurtosis. It is mostly used to model the negative part of the distribution of returns and is especially useful when the skewness is negative and the kurtosis is high. In this case, the left tail of the distribution is fatter than the Gaussian one, and it is worthwhile to adapt the measurement of risk to this phenomenon.

Formally, if $R_{P,t} \rightsquigarrow \mathcal{N}(\mathrm{E}(R_P), \sigma_P^2)$, we know that the xth percentile of the distribution of returns is equal to $Q_x(R_P) = \mathrm{E}(R_P) + z_x \times \sigma_P$, where z_x is the xth percentile of the standard normal distribution (i.e., corresponding to $Z \rightsquigarrow \mathcal{N}(0, 1)$).

Consider now that the portfolio return follows an unknown distribution $\mathcal{D}$, but sufficiently close to the Gaussian one, in which moments of order three and four are supposed to be known, such that $R_{P,t} \rightsquigarrow \mathcal{D}(\mathrm{E}(R_P), \sigma_P^2, \mu_{P,3}, \mu_{P,4})$, where $\mu_{P,3} \equiv \frac{\mathrm{E}(R_P-\overline{R}_P)^3}{\sigma_P^3}$ and $\mu_{P,4} \equiv \frac{\mathrm{E}(R_P-\overline{R}_P)^4}{\sigma_P^4}$ are, respectively, the normalized third and fourth moments of the portfolio returns, known as their "skewness" and "kurtosis." Applying the Cornish–Fisher (C–F) expansion delivers the following relation:

$$Q_x(R_P) \cong \mathrm{E}(R_P) + z_{x,P}^* \times \sigma_P \tag{6-12a}$$

$$z_{x,P}^* = z_x + (z_x^2 - 1)\frac{\mu_{P,3}}{6} + (z_x^3 - 3z_x)\frac{e\mu_{P,4}}{24} - (2z_x^3 - 5z_x)\frac{\mu_{P,3}^2}{36} \tag{6-12b}$$

where $e\mu_{P,4} \equiv \mu_{P,4} - 3$ is the "excess kurtosis." For the Gaussian distribution $\mu_{P,3} = 0$ and $e\mu_{P,4} = 0$. We are interested in the far tail of the distribution, which corresponds to very low values of x (typically below 5%).

Once the value of $z_{x,P}^*$ is estimated, it is possible to rescale the return volatility by using the ratio of the adjusted percentile $z_{x,P}^*$ over the initial Gaussian one corresponding to the same percentile z_x, which leads to the modified volatility $m\sigma_P^{(x)}$:

$$m\sigma_P^{(x)} = \sigma_P \times \frac{z_{x,P}^*}{z_x} \tag{6-13}$$

This formula may be appealing, but has to be used with great caution. First, it is not compatible with any percentile or skewness level. Given the interpretation of the higher moments, one reasonably expects that $z^*_{x,P}$ is an increasing function of the skewness and decreasing in kurtosis. Because expression (6-12b) is nonlinear in both z_x and $\mu_{P,3}$, Cavenaile and Lejeune (2012) show that it behaves well only for $x < 4.16\%$ and when the skewness is positive or, if negative, is reasonably close to zero.[5] Second, the volatility multiplier $\frac{z^*_{x,P}}{z_x}$ can provide contrasted output depending on the joint situation resulting from the choice of x and the values taken by the returns' skewness and excess kurtosis. The graph shown in Figure 6-7 illustrates this sensitivity.

Besides the base case of the normally distributed returns ("Sk 0/K 0"), we report four situations depending on the pair skewness – excess kurtosis ($\mu_{P,3}, e\mu_{P,4}$). For each case, "Sk +" corresponds to a positive skewness $\mu_{P,3} = +0.5$ (right-asymmetry) and "Sk –" corresponds to $\mu_{P,3} = -0.5$ (left asymmetry). Regarding excess kurtosis, "K +" corresponds to $e\mu_{P,4} = +1$ (leptokurtic, higher than normal) and "K –" corresponds to $e\mu_{P,4} = -1$ (platykurtic, lower than normal). For sufficiently high percentiles, the multiplier converges to a value whose main driver is the skewness. Nevertheless, in the far tail of the distribution, the impact of the kurtosis may become very important and even supersedes the one of the skewness. For instance,

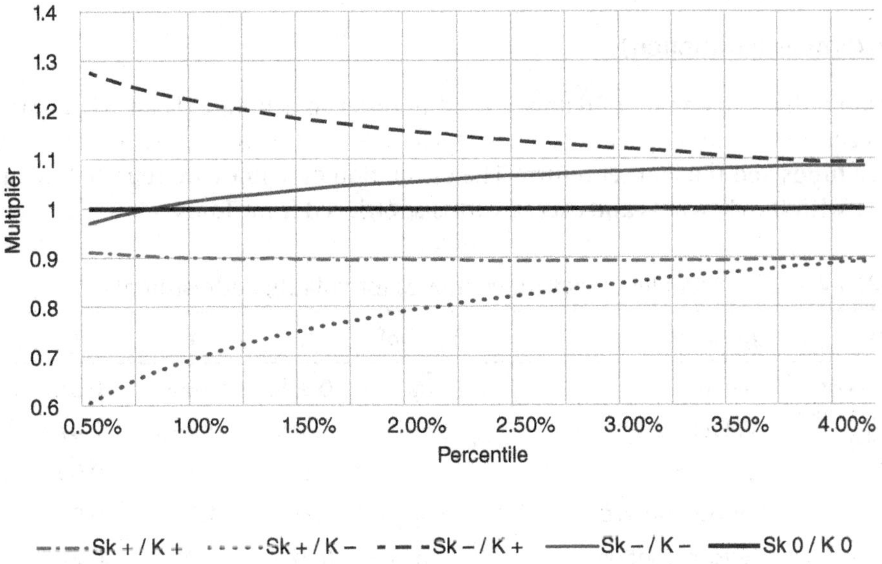

FIGURE 6-7 Evolution of the volatility multiplier $\frac{z^*_{x,P}}{z_x}$ in different situations.

[5] The critical value of the skewness depends on the percentile x. For instance, if $x = 4\%$, the skewness $\mu_{P,3}$ must be greater (less negative) than -3.13. If $x = 0.5\%$, the critical value for the skewness becomes -0.79.

observing simultaneously negative values for the skewness and the kurtosis may lead to values of the multiplier above or below one, depending on the chosen percentile (light increasing curve). Even though there is no general rule, it seems that percentile values around $x = 2.50\%$ lead to a balanced influence of the skewness and the kurtosis, which might be the intention of the procedure in many cases.

This approach of adjusting the volatility of portfolio returns can be used in conjunction with the other ones, provided that the skewness and kurtosis are re-estimated consistently with their respective econometric specification.

Another way of dealing with higher moments is to directly reward/penalize the volatility estimate with a function of the skewness and kurtosis. This is the route followed by Watanabe (2014), who proposes the following volatility adjustments:

$$\sigma_P^{(S-K)} = \begin{cases} \sqrt{\sigma_P^2 + \left(\dfrac{1}{1+\mu_{P,3}}\right)^2 + e\mu_{P,4}^2} & \text{if } \mu_{P,3} \geq 0 \\ \sqrt{\sigma_P^2 + (\mu_{P,3} - 1)^2 + e\mu_{P,4}^2} & \text{if } \mu_{P,3} < 0 \end{cases} \tag{6-14}$$

Note however that this adjustment is largely arbitrary and some other approaches deal more rigorously with this issue.

XYZ example (continued)

We assume that three years of data are used in order to calibrate (i) an AR(1) process for the returns and, in an independent exercise, (ii) a GARCH (1,1) process for the variance of all three funds and the market return. The estimation outcomes are reported in Table 6-4, together with the skewness and excess kurtosis retrieved from Table 6-1.

TABLE 6-4 XYZ example – Relevant estimates for volatility adjustments.

Dimension	Measure	Symbol	X	Y	Z	M
Moments of the distribution (monthly)	Mean	$\overline{R}_P$	0.32%	0.40%	0.81%	0.66%
	Volatility	σ_P	1.81%	1.79%	2.47%	2.55%
	Skewness	$\mu_{P,3}$	0.18	−0.15	0.09	0.49
	Excess kurtosis	$e\mu_{P,4}$	−1.34	−1.60	−0.83	−0.50
AR(1)	Autocorrelation	ρ	−0.07	0.21	0.22	0.05
GARCH(1,1)	Intercept (sq. root)	$\sqrt{a_{P0}}$	0.25%	0.29%	0.37%	0.33%
	Coeff. lagged sq. residual	a_{P1}	0.09	0.11	0.22	0.10
	Coeff. lagged variance	b_{P1}	0.89	0.86	0.75	0.88

Based on that, we can apply different formulas in order to obtain the adjusted volatility. For instance, we show the computations for Fund X, whose volatility is $\sigma_X = 1.81\%$:

- With the first-order autocorrelation coefficient $\rho_X = -0.07$, applying formula (6-7), the resulting volatility equals $\sigma_X^{(1)} = 1.81\% \times \sqrt{1 + \frac{2\times(-0.07)}{1-(-0.07)}\left(1 - \frac{1-(-0.07)^{12}}{12\times(1-(-0.07))}\right)} =$ 1.70%. Note that the adjustment is favorable because the serial correlation is negative, which induces that the original series of returns features an oscillating character whose removal leaves a lower standard deviation. Nevertheless, the coefficient is quite close to zero and might be insignificant.
- With the parameters of the GARCH(1,1) process, we can use Equation (6-10) to obtain the long-term estimate equal to $\sigma_{X,\infty} = \sqrt{\frac{(0.25\%)^2}{1-0.09-0.89}} = 1.77\%$. This figure, lower than the sample estimate, indicates that the average level of volatility measured during the sample period seems to exaggerate its long-term unconditional level.
- With the fund's skewness and excess kurtosis, we set a percentile of $x = 2.5\%$, corresponding to $z_{2.5\%} = -1.96$ in order to apply the Cornish–Fisher expansion. Equation (6-12a) leads to $z^*_{2.5\%} = -1.96 + ((-1.96)^2 - 1)\frac{0.18}{6} + ((-1.96)^3 - 3\times(-1.96))\frac{(-1.34)}{24} - (2\times(-1.96)^3 - 5\times(-1.96))\frac{(0.18)^2}{36} = 1.78$. Hence, applying Equation (6-13), the modified volatility equals $m\sigma_X^{(x)} = 1.81\% \times \frac{(-1.78)}{(-1.96)} = 1.65\%$. Here again, the positive value of the skewness, which indicates an asymmetry of the distribution on the right side, favors Fund X.

The application of the same method to the three funds and the market index results in Table 6-5 for the yearly Sharpe ratios.

TABLE 6-5 XYZ example – Refined Sharpe ratios with the different volatility adjustments.

Adjustment type	X	Y	Z	M
Autocorrelation	0.40	0.45	0.78	0.70
Heteroscedasticity	0.39	0.59	1.11	0.80
Higher moments	0.42	0.56	1.01	0.87
Original	*0.38*	*0.55*	*0.96*	*0.73*

6.1.4 Directly adjusting the Sharpe ratio

Instead of attempting to tackle one of the three inputs of the Sharpe ratio in isolation, it is possible to directly correct the global figure in order to simultaneously address the numerator and the denominator. We list three main approaches: an economic adjustment aiming to reflect the efficiency level of the portfolio, a "through-the-cycle" adjustment that overcomes this issue of negative market returns discussed in Chapter 5, and a statistical adjustment addressing the impact of higher moments.

6.1.4.1 Adjusting for the efficiency level

The dominance of one portfolio over another one on the basis of the Sharpe ratio hinges on the investor's ability to freely use leverage in a frictionless manner in order to modify portfolio risk by simply lending or borrowing money at the riskless rate. This "homemade leverage" is a key justification for the use of the Sharpe ratio to compare portfolios with different risk levels.

In reality, for most investors, portfolio choice is a "take-it-or-leave-it" offer. Two portfolios with different risk levels cannot be simply compared on the basis of homemade leverage if the investors, for one reason or another (ignorance of the true risk, prohibitive leverage costs, firm portfolio offerings, cash constraints, ...), cannot switch their risk levels to make them fully comparable. In such cases, a relevant approach is to assess the investor's risk-aversion level and compute certainty equivalents for portfolio returns in order to reflect the preferences, as shown in Chapter 9. Nevertheless, absent this information about individual preferences, it is still interesting to gauge the intrinsic properties of different portfolios regarding the efficiency in the risk–return space.

Cantaluppi and Hug (2000) suggest applying the relative efficiency measure developed by Kandel and Stambaugh (1995) in the context of the Sharpe ratio. Their measure considers the distance between the coordinates of the portfolio in the risk–return space and the one of an *ex post* efficient portfolio with the same risk, but a mean return that is higher than or equal to the one of the portfolio. Their *efficiency measure* eSR_P is expressed through the comparison of their Sharpe ratios:

$$\text{eSR}_P = \text{SR}_P \times \left(\frac{\overline{R}_P^* - \overline{R}_f}{\sigma_P} \right)^{-1} = \frac{\overline{R}_P - \overline{R}_f}{\overline{R}_P^* - \overline{R}_f} \tag{6-15}$$

where $\overline{R}_P^* = \max_i \overline{R}_i$ subject to $\sigma_i = \sigma_P$ is the mean return of the *ex post* mean–variance efficient portfolio with the same risk as P. The efficient frontier can be the unconstrained one (all weights can be positive or negative) or, more realistically, the constrained one with all asset weights forced to be non-negative. By construction, the efficiency ratio can never exceed one.

The logic underlying the eSR_P is illustrated in Figure 6-8, which is directly adapted from Figure 3-4 of Chapter 3:

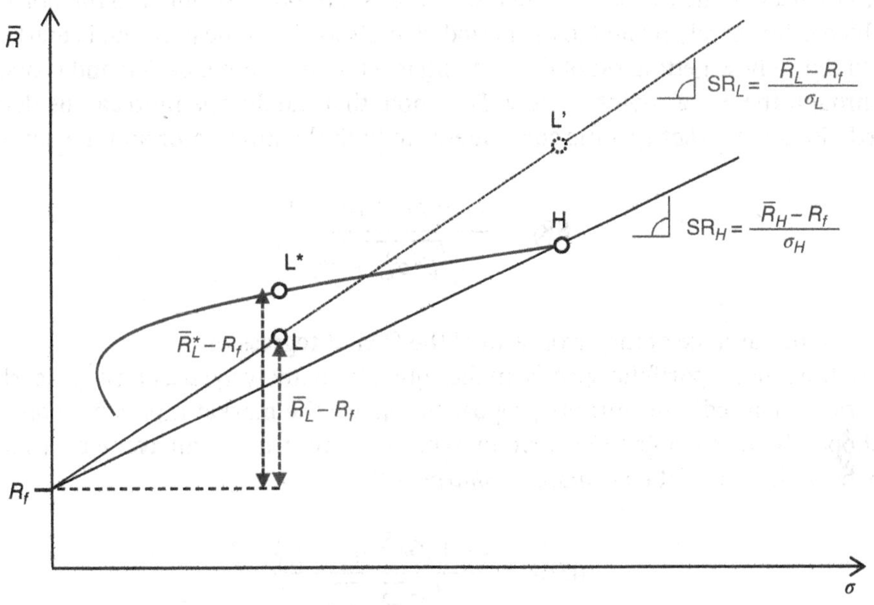

FIGURE 6-8 Graphical representation of the efficiency ratio.

As with the discussion of the original Sharpe ratio, portfolio H is dominated by L because of its lower Sharpe ratio. The argument of homemade leverage allows the investor to gear the risk of L up to the same one as H, with the dominating portfolio L'. However, what if portfolio H is lying on the risk–return efficient frontier while L is not? This means that, without using any form of leverage – the argument is important here – it is possible to find a combination of risky assets with the same risk as that of L but with a higher return. The lower the distance between the coordinate of L with the ones of this combination, called L^*, the better its performance. Note that the market index might not necessarily lie on the *ex post* efficient frontier.

The scope of utilization of the efficiency ratio should be well understood. It only makes sense in two types of circumstances: when the use of leverage is not an option for the investor or when performance is appraised in order to assess the intrinsic quality of portfolio managers, irrespective of the identity of the final investor.

6.1.4.2 Adjusting for the "through-the-cycle" return

Even though this can statistically happen (as shown in Chapter 5), the occurrence of negative excess returns on the market portfolio makes the analysis of portfolio performance more complex, as those "point-in-time" situations do not reflect what can be considered as "normal" market conditions. Setting a fixed period of 3, 5 or even 10 years for retrospective analysis presumably makes this issue unavoidable. Yet, Krimm, Scholz, and Wilkens (2012) propose an approach to disentangle the part of the return that should be attributed to the portfolio manager (which is intimately related to the period of analysis) from the part that is market-related, for which they advise getting rid of the straightjacket of the sample period and propose adopting a "through-the-cycle" point of view. They note that the Sharpe ratio can be decomposed into portfolio- and market-specific components in both the numerator and the denominator:

$$\mathrm{SR}_P = \frac{\alpha_P + \beta_P(\overline{R}_M - R_f)}{\sqrt{\beta_P^2\sigma_M^2 + \sigma_{\varepsilon_P}^2}} \tag{6-16}$$

where $\sigma_{\varepsilon_P}^2$ is the variance of the error term of the CAPM regression.

Everything that is portfolio specific in the equation, namely α_P, β_P, and $\sigma_{\varepsilon_P}^2$, clearly belongs to the period analyzed. The authors propose to replace the market inputs by their long-term values, hopefully reasonable (a positive market excess return and an average variance). This leads to the definition of the *normalized Sharpe ratio*:

$$\mathrm{nSR}_P = \frac{\alpha_P + \beta_P(\overline{R}_{lM} - R_{lf})}{\sqrt{\beta_P^2\sigma_{lM}^2 + \sigma_{\varepsilon_P}^2}} \tag{6-17}$$

where $\overline{R}_{lM} - R_{lf}$ and σ_{lM}^2 represent the long-term ("through-the-cycle") estimates of the mean excess return and variance of the market portfolio, respectively.

This approach has the advantage of overcoming the need to justify and interpret negative Sharpe ratios. Nevertheless, it may raise difficulties in communicating performance as the formula introduces a disconnection between the observed (point-in-time) portfolio risk and return and their normalized (through-the-cycle) counterparts, which are both hybrid constructions of inputs that are not contemporaneously observed.

6.1.4.3 Adjusting for higher moments

Instead of correcting portfolio volatility in order to account for the non-normality of the returns distribution, a more comprehensive approach consists of reflecting the adjustment directly on the Sharpe ratio. In general, it is necessary to posit some structure of investors' preferences over risk and return in the expected utility framework, with an explicit identification of the investor-specific risk profile parameters.[6]

[6] These measures are studied in more detail in Chapter 9, dedicated to preference-based performance.

In the context of the exponential utility function, Pézier and White (2008) derive an *adjusted Sharpe ratio*, aSR_P, that does not explicitly depend on risk aversion:

$$aSR_P = SR_P \times \left(1 + \frac{\mu_{P,3}}{6} SR_P - \frac{e\mu_{P,4}}{24} SR_P^2\right) \tag{6-18}$$

By separating the effect of skewness and kurtosis, this approach has the drawback of failing to reflect their joint effect on the investor's satisfaction.[7] For instance, a very positive skewness is magnified by a high kurtosis. This joint effect is potentially better reflected by the use of the Cornish–Fisher formula or by explicitly taking investors' preferences into account.

XYZ example (continued)

Using information of Table 6-1 (excluding the fixed-income security because of the unavailability of leverage), and using the same technique as in Chapter 2 to construct the efficient frontier on the basis of assets X, Y, Z, and M, we obtain the results shown in Table 6-6 with Equation (6-15).

TABLE 6-6 XYZ example – Computation of the efficiency ratios.

	X	Y	Z	M
Mean return	0.32%	0.40%	0.81%	0.66%
Mean efficient return	0.68%	0.67%	0.92%	0.95%
Standard deviation	1.81%	1.79%	2.47%	2.55%
Efficiency ratio	**0.36**	**0.52**	**0.86**	**0.65**

Considering a long-term market excess return of $\overline{R}_{IM} - R_{lf} = 8.20\%$ and volatility $\sigma_{IM} = 17.40\%$, we obtain the normalized Sharpe ratio of each fund according to Equation (6-17) as shown in Table 6-7.

(continued)

[7] A heuristic additive adjustment is proposed by Watanabe (2006): $SR_p + \frac{\mu_{P,3}}{e\mu_{P,4}}$. This version, although relatively simple, has the major drawback of being very noisy when the excess kurtosis is close to zero. It can be interesting for making quick comparisons of portfolios with very similar Sharpe ratios in order to assess how they can be rewarded/penalized by their higher moments.

(continued)

TABLE 6-7 XYZ example – Computation of the normalized Sharpe ratios.

	X	Y	Z
Jensen's alpha	−1.63%	0.62%	6.87%
St. dev. epsilon	3.13%	4.91%	8.37%
Beta	0.62	0.43	0.21
Normalized Sharpe ratio	**0.31**	**0.46**	**0.94**

Using data on the skewness and kurtosis, the adjusted Sharpe ratios are reported in Table 6-8.

TABLE 6-8 XYZ example – Computation of the adjusted Sharpe ratios.

	X	Y	Z	M
Mean return	0.32%	0.40%	0.81%	0.66%
Standard deviation	1.81%	1.79%	2.47%	2.55%
Skewness	0.18	−0.15	0.09	0.49
Excess kurtosis	−1.34	−1.60	−0.83	−0.50
Adjusted Sharpe ratio	**0.38**	**0.55**	**1.01**	**0.79**

6.2 ALTERATIONS OF THE SHARPE RATIO

In Section 6.1, we examined a first set of modifications of the Sharpe ratio that aim to *refine* the measurement of performance. The second set is more drastic, as the alternative formulas *replace* a measure of reward (numerator) or risk (denominator), or both. As before, we successively deal with the numerator and denominator of the original Sharpe ratio as depicted in Equation (6-1).

For the numerator (excess return), the main modification is the replacement of the risk-free rate. The case of the denominator of the Sharpe ratio provides a richer set of avatars. If returns follow a Gaussian distribution, every measure of risk can be analytically expressed as a function of the first (expectation) and second (variance) moment. Replacing volatility with another definition of risk is of limited or even of no use if the objective is to rank funds and portfolios. Nevertheless, if returns depart from normality – which is the case in practice for most financial assets – then it can be relevant to associate the mean excess return of a portfolio with a notion of risk that is more appropriate, either from a statistical or an economic point of view, or both. This is the area in which researchers and practitioners in the field have been the most creative. Even though performance is still measured using excess return divided by total risk, we leave the world of the pure Sharpe ratio and create mutations that are more or less close to the original measure.

We will cover the main alternative risk measurement approaches that have been adopted as well as the most representative performance measures belonging to each family.[8] Note that, in several cases using the notion of reservation rate as discussed hereafter, the numerator is modified as well.

6.2.1 Modifying the portfolio excess return

The "safety first" approach of Roy (1952) represents a very influential contribution to the field of performance measurement. It introduces a notion of reservation rate or "disaster level" $\underline{R}$, which is investor-specific, as a substitute for the risk-free rate. Instead of trying to maximize their expected utility in the mean–variance framework, the investor tries to minimize the shortfall probability, i.e., $\min_P \Pr(R_P < \underline{R})$. This program is known as the safety-first criterion.

If returns are Gaussian and if the investor has access to leverage, the safety-first criterion maximizes the expected excess return over the reservation rate per unit of volatility. In an *ex post* world, the relevant performance measure for the investor is the *Roy ratio* (RoyR_P):

$$\text{RoyR}_P = \frac{\overline{R}_P - \underline{R}}{\sigma_P} \tag{6-19}$$

The replacement of R_f by $\underline{R}$ is both theoretically and practically important. By not recognizing the specific role of the riskless asset, which is necessary for the "homemade leverage" argument, we depart from the CAPM framework. A portfolio with a higher Roy ratio than another one does not necessarily dominate it in the SPT framework, in contrary to the key theoretical argument that supports the use of the Sharpe ratio. The Roy ratio is more heuristic than its famous counterpart.

From a practical standpoint, with the reservation rate, the author introduces an important degree of freedom in the equation. The choice of $\underline{R}$ is investor-specific; there are thus potentially as many values as there are different investors. The "usual suspects" are the following:

- $\underline{\mathbf{R}} = \mathbf{0\%}$: This corresponds to an investor who absolutely wants to avoid recording a loss in nominal terms. This is a purely psychological threshold that is shared by many investors.

[8] For a complete discussion of this list, we refer the reader to Cogneau and Hübner (2009a; 2009b) and Bacon (2021), but also to the set of analyses performed throughout Chapter 11.

- **$\underline{R} = R_f$**: Considering the opportunity cost of any investment as the rate that one could earn with a riskless security, the investor wants to make sure that the risk taken with the portfolio is rewarded with a positive premium. Note that the investor can consider different maturities for the fixed-income security, depending on their investment horizon.
- **$\underline{R}$ = inflation rate**: The investor considers that the investment should at least protect their purchasing power, represented by the (expected) inflation rate.
- **$\underline{R}$ = GDP growth rate + inflation rate**: Irrespective of the nominal interest rate, this value corresponds to the nominal growth rate in the economy, which is the sum of real growth and the increase in price levels.

Even though the reservation rate is specific to each investor, this is not equivalent to a level of risk aversion. Rather, the safety-first criterion can be seen as a precursor of the loss-aversion indicators in the context of behavioral finance. Indeed, $\underline{R}$ reflects a switching point between the notions of "satisfaction" and "dissatisfaction," with very different investor's attitudes toward risk and return in each of these moods.[9] Importantly, the choice of the reservation rate has a direct influence on portfolio rankings and may alter the ones obtained with the Sharpe ratio. This is illustrated in Figure 6-9.

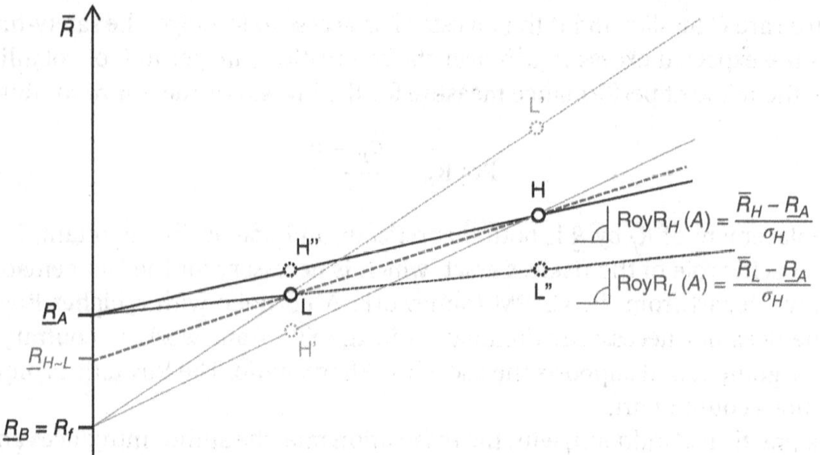

FIGURE 6-9 Graphical representation of the Roy ratio.

[9]We examine these notions in detail in Chapter 10, which introduces investor-specific behavioral attitudes toward risk and return in the assessment of portfolio performance. We will revert to the notion of reservation rate in this context. Nevertheless, because the reservation rate is used in many avatars of the Sharpe ratio without explicitly referring to the investor's profile, we already find it adequate to discuss this notion in the current chapter.

Besides the intercept of the reward-to-risk linear functions, the interpretation of this graph is very similar to the one of the Sharpe ratio. However, because different investors choose different reservation rates, the slopes of these lines can deliver very contrasted pictures. In the illustration, investor B adopts a very rational point of view that is consistent with the CAPM. Considering that they are risk averse, they require a positive excess return that is proportional to the level of total risk taken. This investor uses the Sharpe ratio, which is nothing else than the Roy ratio with a reservation rate of R_f (represented in light gray on the graph). For that investor, the performance of L is better than that of H. On the other hand, investor A ambitiously sets a much higher reservation rate $\underline{R}_A > R_f$. This investor obviously runs a greater risk of being disappointed with any portfolio because the probability of failing to achieve their reservation rate increases with the rate itself. For this investor, return matters more than risk, which explains that $\text{RoyR}_H(A) > \text{RoyR}_L(A)$.

In corollary, it is interesting to identify the break-even reservation rate $\underline{R}_{P\sim Q}$ that makes an investor indifferent between two portfolios P and Q, i.e., $\text{RoyR}_P(P\sim Q) = \text{RoyR}_Q(P\sim Q)$.

$$\underline{R}_{P\sim Q} = \frac{\overline{R}_Q\sigma_P - \overline{R}_P\sigma_Q}{\sigma_P - \sigma_Q} \tag{6-20}$$

If this ratio is negative or if it is higher than the larger mean return, it means that no reasonable value of the reservation rate makes the investor indifferent. Then, it is fair to say that the portfolio with the greater Roy ratio (and thus also the larger Sharpe ratio) economically dominates the other one for every type of investor. Geometrically, this break-even rate corresponds to the intercept of a straight line that connects the coordinates of both portfolios. On the graph, this corresponds to the origin of the dotted line. Naturally, we obtain $\underline{R}_A > \underline{R}_{H\sim L} > R_f$ here.

This illustration shows that, *ceteris paribus*, the relative performance of riskier portfolios increases with the level of the reservation rate. It also suggests that it does not make sense to compare values of the Roy ratio across different levels of the reservation rate: the higher the $\underline{R}$, the lower the Roy ratio for any portfolio. Thus, issues related to the interpretation of the level of the Sharpe ratio, as discussed in Chapter 3, are all more complicated in this new context.

XYZ example (continued)

Instead of using the risk-free rate, we consider the case of an investor who does not want to record any capital loss and sets a reservation rate $\underline{R} = 0\%$. The results are illustrated in Figure 6-10.

The solid lines corresponding to the Roy ratio emanate from the origin of the axes. As it can be seen from the comparison with the Sharpe ratios, the ordering of the portfolios is unaffected by the change of reservation rate from $R_f = 1.44\%$ to $\underline{R} = 0\%$. The values of the Roy ratios and the two-by-two break-even rates are reported in Table 6-9.

(continued)

(continued)

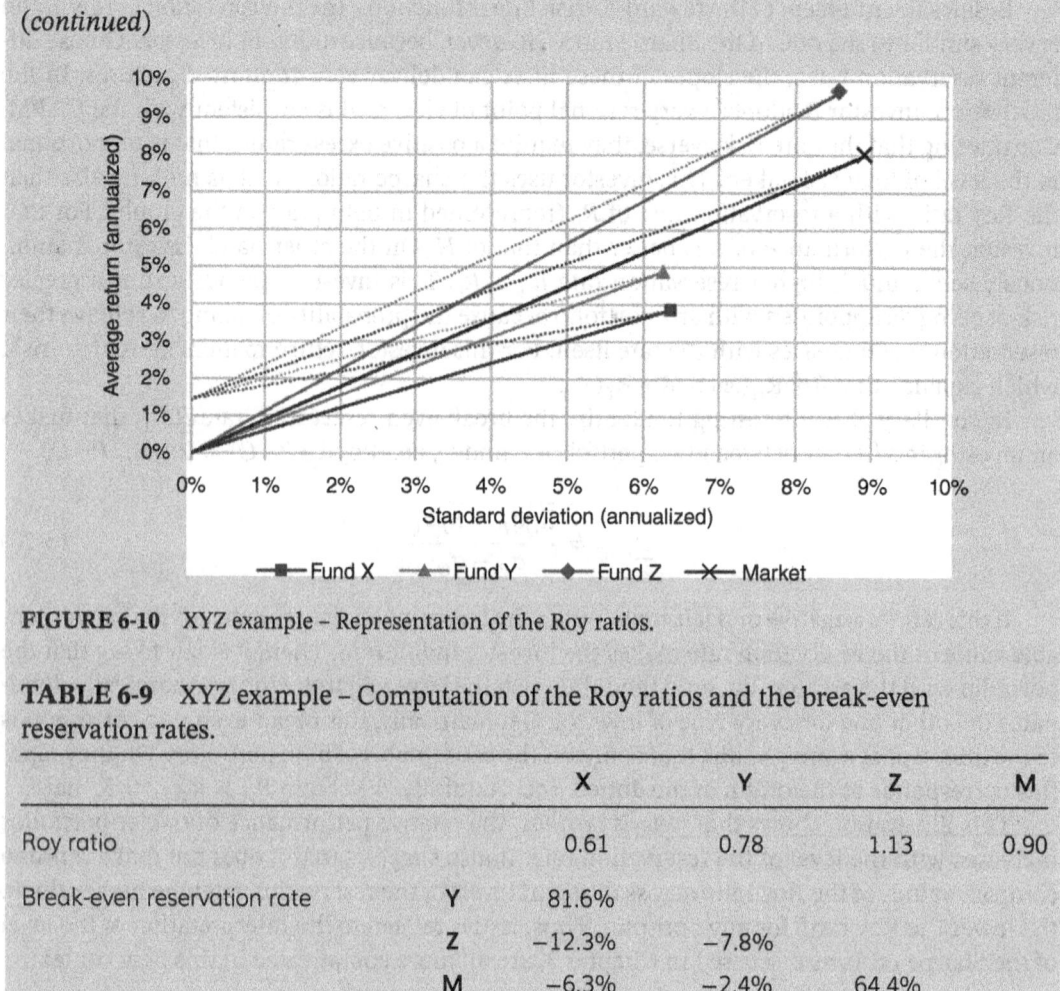

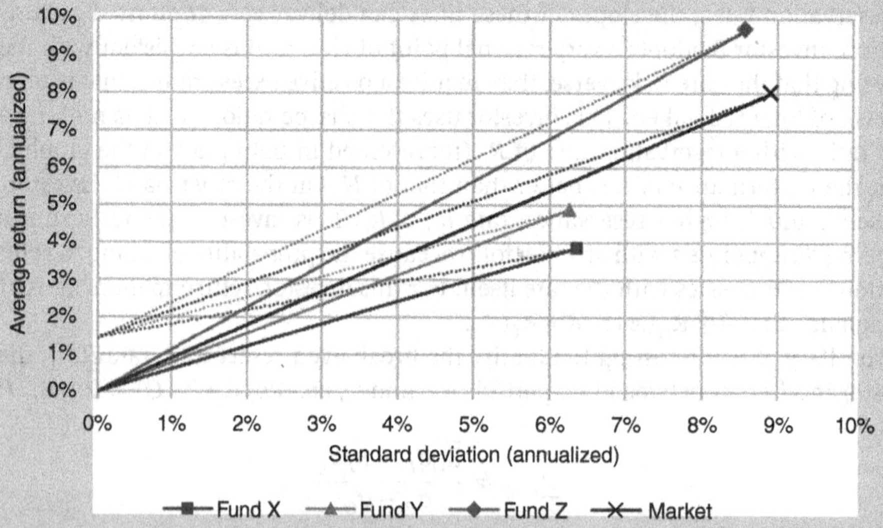

FIGURE 6-10 XYZ example – Representation of the Roy ratios.

TABLE 6-9 XYZ example – Computation of the Roy ratios and the break-even reservation rates.

		X	Y	Z	M
Roy ratio		0.61	0.78	1.13	0.90
Break-even reservation rate	Y	81.6%			
	Z	−12.3%	−7.8%		
	M	−6.3%	−2.4%	64.4%	

6.2.2 Replacing volatility with alternative distance risk

6.2.2.1 Defining alternative distance risk

The simpler way of changing the measure of risk is to adopt a formulation that is different from the standard deviation of returns, without necessarily trying to modify the underlying interpretation as an indicator of return variability. The purpose is similar to the original volatility measure: one attempts to assess a relevant measure of distance from a "good" to a "bad" realization of the portfolio return. Performance measures that belong to this category can be viewed as mere substitutes to the original Sharpe ratio, without substantial change in its interpretation.

6.2.2.2 Measuring performance with alternative distance risk

The main measures proposed in this context are as follows:

- The *MAD ratio* (Konno and Yamakazi, 1991):

$$\text{MADR}_P = \frac{\overline{R}_P - R_f}{\text{MAD}_P} \tag{6-21}$$

  where $\text{MAD}_P = \frac{1}{T-1}\sum_{t=1}^{T}|R_{P,t} - \overline{R}_P|$ is the mean absolute deviation of the portfolio returns. In general, it assigns a lower weight to extreme returns than the volatility.
- The *Minimax ratio* (Young, 1998):

$$\text{mMR}_P = \frac{\overline{R}_P - R_f}{\text{mM}_P} \tag{6-22}$$

  where $\text{mM}_P = \max_{t=1,\ldots,T}(R_{f,t} - R_{P,t})$ is the maximum of the negative excess portfolio returns. This ratio corresponds to a portfolio optimization program in which the objective function is to minimize the maximum loss incurred during the estimation period. The value of mM_P is the sample estimate of the actual risk taken. Note that the Minimax ratio can also be considered as a measure using an estimate of extreme risk (see Section 6.2.5).
- The *Gini ratio* (Yitzhaki, 1982):

$$\text{GiR}_P = \frac{\overline{R}_P - R_f}{\text{Gi}(R_P - R_f)} \tag{6-23}$$

  where $\text{Gi}(R_P - R_f) = \frac{2}{T(T-1)}\sum_{t=1}^{T-1}\sum_{s=t+1}^{T}|(R_{P,s} - R_{f,s}) - (R_{P,t} - R_{f,t})|$ represents Gini's rescaled mean difference of the portfolio excess returns.
- The *Range ratio* (Caporin and Lisi, 2011):

$$\text{RgR}_P = \frac{\overline{R}_P - R_f}{\text{hRg}_P} \tag{6-24}$$

  where $\text{hRg}_P = \frac{1}{2}\left(\max_{t=1,\ldots,T}(R_{P,t}) - \min_{t=1,\ldots,T}(R_{P,t})\right)$ is the half-range of the portfolio returns.

XYZ example (continued)

We build different performance measures for the three funds and the market on the basis of their time series of monthly rates of returns (similar to those of Table 3-1 in Chapter 3) reproduced as shown in Table 6-10.

TABLE 6-10 XYZ example – Monthly rates of return.

Month	X	Y	Z	M
Jan	−1.58%	−1.64%	−2.92%	−1.38%
Feb	2.66%	1.58%	2.28%	3.00%
Mar	−0.41%	−1.23%	1.23%	−2.40%
Apr	−0.33%	−0.67%	−0.99%	2.44%
May	1.40%	1.92%	5.13%	2.69%
Jun	−1.44%	1.37%	0.22%	−2.00%
Jul	3.27%	2.95%	0.26%	5.75%
Aug	−2.08%	0.57%	3.37%	−1.58%
Sep	1.10%	−1.63%	−2.37%	0.96%
Oct	1.02%	1.32%	1.87%	1.29%
Nov	−1.67%	−2.20%	−1.52%	−1.94%
Dec	1.87%	2.50%	3.12%	1.10%

Considering a risk-free rate of 0.12% per month, we build the risk measures as shown in Table 6-11.

TABLE 6-11 XYZ example – Computation of the alternative variability measures.

	X	Y	Z	M
MAD	1.71%	1.71%	2.21%	2.29%
Minimax	2.20%	2.32%	3.04%	2.52%
Gini	1.72%	1.64%	2.19%	2.58%
Range	2.68%	2.58%	4.03%	4.08%

In order to compare the rankings of the four portfolios according to the corresponding performance measures, we center each of them around their mean and represent them along a radar chart as illustrated in Figure 6-11.

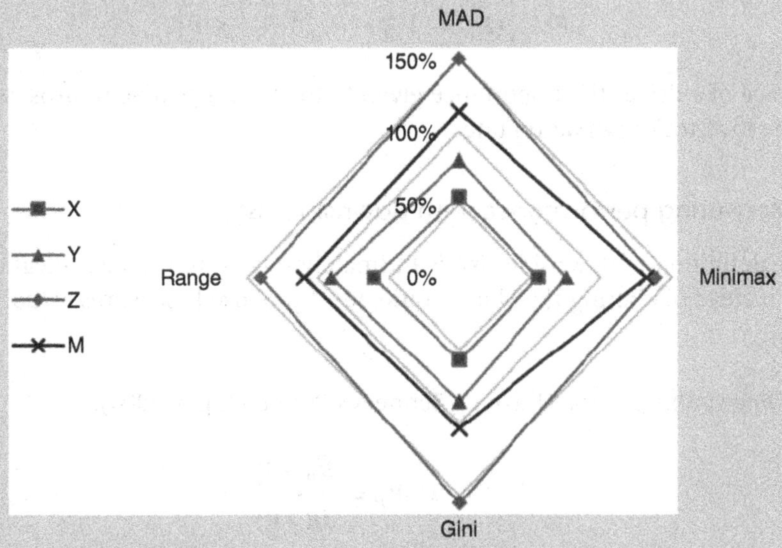

FIGURE 6-11 XYZ example – Radar chart of the ratios using alternative variability measures.

Even though the rankings of the three funds and the market portfolio remain unchanged, it clearly stands out that the market portfolio is favorably impacted by the use of the whole range of returns, which can be explained by the larger positive skewness of this index compared to the funds. Conversely, M and Y are very close to each other from the points of view of the Gini and Range ratios.

6.2.3 Replacing volatility with downside risk

6.2.3.1 Defining downside risk

Downside risk measures directly result from the challenges associated with the symmetric character of the Gaussian returns distribution. Since returns are, in general, asymmetrically distributed around their mean, and because investors mostly care about what happens on the downside, a number of risk measures focus on the left (negative) part of the distribution of returns. Furthermore, given that we clearly distinguish downside risk from upside potential, the notion of reservation rate, i.e., the threshold that separates the satisfactory versus unsatisfactory returns, is directly applicable here.

From a generic perspective, downside risk measures all make use of a lower partial moment (LPM) of the returns distribution. The LPM of order k with respect to a threshold $\underline{R}$ is similar to its kth centered moment, except that (i) it replaces the expectation by the threshold level and (ii) it only considers negative deviations from this threshold. The corresponding formula is

$$\text{LPM}_{k,P}(\underline{R}) = \text{E}[(\underline{R} - R_{P,t})^k | R_{P,t} \leq \underline{R}] \tag{6-25}$$

The choice of k drives the importance given to the most negative returns, while $\underline{R}$ corresponds to the investor's reservation rate.

6.2.3.2 Measuring performance with downside risk

Because the definition of downside risk is intimately related to the identification of a reservation rate, instead of altering the Sharpe ratio, most proposed measures actually modify the Roy ratio.[10]

- The *Omega-Sharpe ratio* (Kazemi, Schneeweis, and Gupta, 2004):

$$\Omega\text{SR}_P = \frac{\overline{R}_P - \underline{R}}{d\overline{R}_P(\underline{R})} \tag{6-26}$$

  where $d\overline{R}_P(\underline{R}) = \frac{1}{T}\sum_{t=1}^{T} \max(\underline{R} - R_{P,t}, 0)$ is the downside mean of the portfolio return relative to the reservation rate $\underline{R}$.

  This ratio is directly connected to the Omega performance measure Ω_P, which is extensively discussed in Chapter 10, by the relation $\Omega\text{SR}_P = \Omega_P - 1$. The merit of Equation (6-26) is thus to show how an altered version of the Sharpe ratio can be connected to that very popular, although very controversial, performance measure.[11]
- The *reward to half-volatility and reward to semi-volatility* (Ang and Chua, 1979):

$$\text{RHV}_P = \frac{\overline{R}_P - R_f}{h\sigma_P} \tag{6-27}$$

$$\text{RSV}_P = \frac{\overline{R}_P - R_f}{s\sigma_P} \tag{6-28}$$

[10]Most of the alterations of the Sharpe ratio based on downside risk represent specific cases of the family of "gains/loss ratios" that are studied in Chapter 10. We revert to their properties in that particular chapter.

[11]The Omega is problematic because, instead of taking the root of a quasi-moment of order two (for the variance) or higher, the denominator of the formula uses an average deviation (something that is inconsistent in the context of the full distribution of returns because, by definition, the average deviation of the mean is always zero). We discuss it further in Chapter 10.

where $h\sigma_P = \sqrt{\frac{1}{T-1}\sum_{t=1}^{T}(\max(\overline{R}_P - R_{P,t}, 0))^2}$ and $s\sigma_P = \sqrt{\frac{1}{T}\sum_{t=1}^{T}(\max(R_f - R_{P,t}, 0))^2}$ are the half-volatility and the semi-volatility of the portfolio returns, respectively.[12] They are interpreted as the part of the volatility that locates below a threshold, being equal to the mean return $\overline{R}_P$ in the first case and the risk-free rate R_f in the second one.

These two measures, initially presented in the context of a specific form of the investor's utility function, can be seen as the grandparents of the downside risk measures. While $h\sigma_P$ is a pure statistical concept that only depends on the sample of portfolio returns, $s\sigma_P$ takes an economic viewpoint by assigning to the risk-free rate the role of a reservation rate.

- The *Sortino ratio* (Sortino and van der Meer, 2011):

$$\text{SorR}_P = \frac{\overline{R}_P - \underline{R}}{d\sigma_P(\underline{R})} \tag{6-29}$$

where $d\sigma_P(\underline{R}) = \sqrt{\frac{1}{T}\sum_{t=1}^{T}(\max(\underline{R} - R_{P,t}, 0))^2}$ is the downside volatility of the portfolio return relative to the reservation rate $\underline{R}$.

Compared to the measures proposed by Ang and Chua (1979), the Sortino ratio has become more popular thanks to its flexibility (through the choice of the reservation rate $\underline{R}$) but also its consistency: From the moment that departure from the mean–variance framework is acted through the use of a downside risk measure, there is no reason anymore to clinch to the risk-free rate as the pivotal point between gains and losses. Thus, allowing the investor to display their own minimum acceptable rate of return induces an associated measure of gain (excess return) as an output and a measure of potential loss (downside volatility) as an input.

The special case in which $\underline{R} = 0\%$ is called the *downside risk Sharpe ratio* (Ziemba, 2005). There also exist versions of the Sortino ratio proposed by Watanabe (2014) including ad hoc adjustments for downside skewness and downside kurtosis.

- The *Kappa ratio* (Kaplan and Knowles, 2004):

$$\kappa\text{R}_P = \frac{\overline{R}_P - \underline{R}}{dm_{3,P}(\underline{R})} \tag{6-30}$$

where $dm_{3,P}(\underline{R}) = \sqrt[3]{\frac{1}{T}\sum_{t=1}^{T}(\max(\underline{R} - R_{P,t}, 0))^3}$ is the downside third centered moment of the portfolio return relative to the reservation rate $\underline{R}$. It gives an even greater weight to extreme negative returns than the Sortino ratio.

A closer examination of the structure of the Omega-Sharpe ratio, the Sortino ratio, and the Kappa ratio reveals that they all represent specific cases of the generic performance measure

---

[12]For the half-volatility, we have to divide the sum by $T-1$ in order to obtain an unbiased estimate because the use of the sample mean consumes a degree of freedom, whereas it is not the case for the semi-volatility (neither for the partial moments discussed hereunder).

defined as $\frac{\overline{R}_P-\underline{R}}{dm_{k,P}(\underline{R})}$, where $dm_{k,P}(\underline{R}) = \sqrt[k]{\frac{1}{T}\sum_{t=1}^{T}(\max(\underline{R}-R_{P,t},0))^k}$, is the kth root of the corresponding downside sample centered moment of the distribution.[13] This intriguing finding calls for further discussion, whose right place to be held is in Chapter 10.

XYZ example (continued)

We repeat the same process as above and obtain the results shown in Table 6-12 and Figure 6-12.

TABLE 6-12 XYZ example – Computation of the downside risk measures.

	X	Y	Z	M
Mean downside	0.63%	0.61%	0.65%	0.78%
Half-vol	1.26%	1.31%	1.74%	1.72%
Sortino	1.04%	1.05%	1.26%	1.28%
Kappa	4.77%	4.80%	5.41%	5.46%

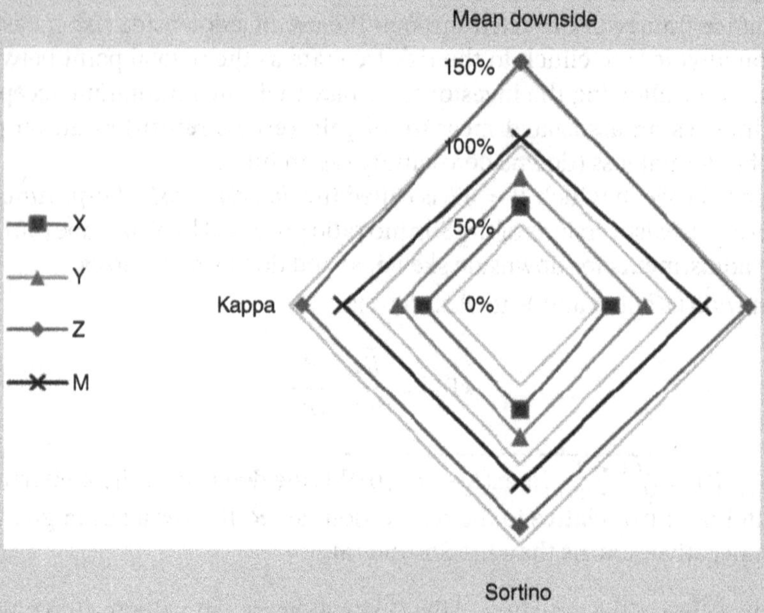

FIGURE 6-12 XYZ example – Radar chart of the ratios using downside risk measures.

[13]This class of measures is called by Kaplan and Knowles (2004) the "Sortino–Satchell" set of performance measures.

6.2.4 Replacing volatility with drawdown risk

6.2.4.1 Defining drawdown risk

From a behavioral perspective, regret avoidance is an important concept. Regardless of the actual gain or loss experienced by the investor at the end of a reference period, the journey toward this final outcome is also important. Some investors may perceive a strong discomfort related to their inability to divest from their portfolio at a peaking point, even though they may eventually obtain a gain from their investment. This generates a feeling of regret, whose intensity is directly related to a notion of risk.

The most intuitive way of measuring the extent of this discomfort, which is path dependent, is the concept of portfolio drawdown $dd_{P,t}$. It corresponds to the largest loss in return observed with respect to a previous maximum or, in short, the "peak-to-valley" in total return. This is represented by the following formula:

$$dd_{P,t} = \frac{\max\limits_{\tau=1,\ldots,t} V_{P,\tau} - V_{P,t}}{\max\limits_{\tau=1,\ldots,t} V_{P,\tau}} \tag{6-31}$$

where $V_{P,\tau}$ is the net asset value of the portfolio at time τ.

The notion of drawdown corresponds to the intensity of the regret borne by the investor at any time t. It increases as consecutive negative returns accumulate: The maximum level reached by the drawdown, or "maximum drawdown," reflects the risk taken by the investor over the whole period. It can be associated with a complementary measure: the recovery time from the drawdown $td_{P,t}$, which translates the amount of time during which the investor felt some regret. Both types of measures are illustrated in Figure 6-13.

Visually, the identification of drawdowns is similar to finding the "lakes" that appear after pouring some water on the graph. Starting from time t_0, the portfolio has experienced in total two significant drawdowns (in general, very small price drops are disregarded), represented with the gray hatches. With the second one, the investor has reached a bottom point that is lower than the initial portfolio value. The largest drawdown is thus equal to $dd_2 = V^+ - V^-$, whose normalized value is $\frac{V^+ - V^-}{V^+}$. This is neither equal to the relative range, as the maximum price is larger than V^+, nor to the most negative return since inception because $V^+ > V_{t_0}$.

The graph illustrates the difficulty associated with the correct identification and treatment of drawdowns. For the same portfolio, the drawdowns would be very different for investors whose initial investment in the portfolio occurs at different dates. If, instead of committing the investment at t_0, someone enters at time t_0' (left case), they incur three drawdowns, all smaller than dd_2, but included in it. Importantly, the drawdowns for this investor are all distinct from the initial case. Furthermore, someone investing in t_0'' (right case) has a first drawdown that is distinct from the left case, but the second one is the same. Thus, in the case of a fund whose investors enter and exit at different points in time, for instance, the notion of drawdown may deliver drastically different pictures even though the fund's history is the same.

It is also useful to represent the evolution of the portfolio drawdown, as defined in Equation (6-31), at each point in time by simply plotting the size of the hatched region as a

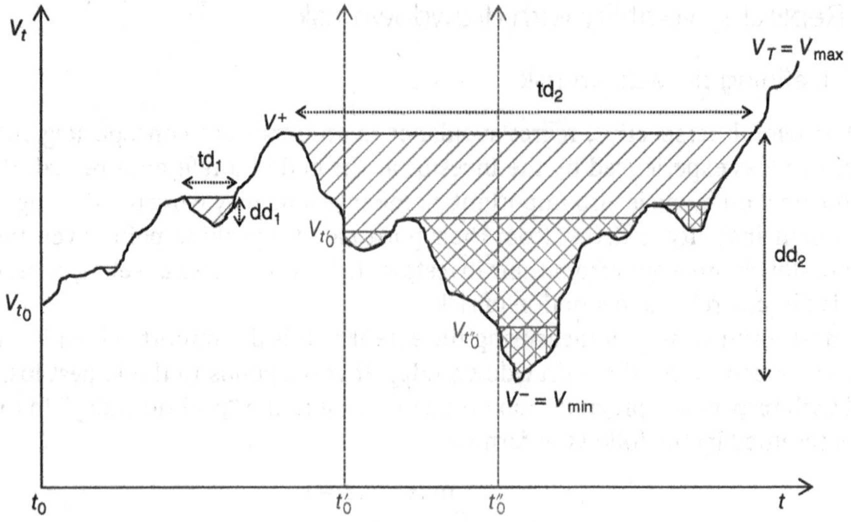

FIGURE 6-13 Graphical representation of the drawdown concept.

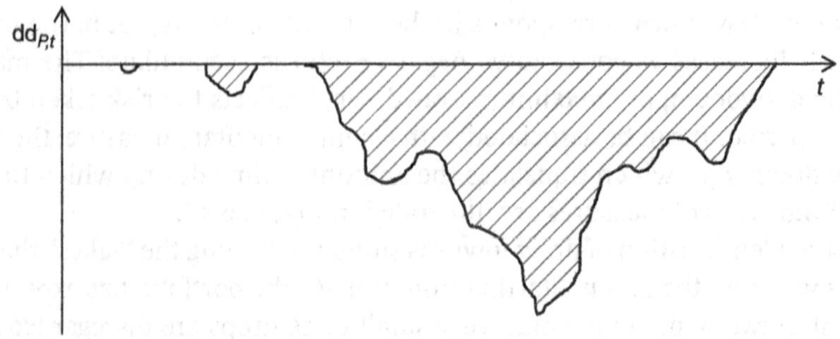

FIGURE 6-14 Drawdown evolution over time.

function of time. Figure 6-14 shows the result when applied to the portfolio represented in Figure 6-13.

6.2.4.2 Measuring performance with drawdown risk

Because it calls upon the practitioner's and the customer's intuition and it is very visual, the use of drawdown in performance measurement has become very popular. Here are some of the most famous measures:

- The *Calmar ratio* (Young, 1991):

$$\mathrm{CalR}_P = \frac{\overline{R}_P - R_f}{\mathrm{dd}_{P,\max}} \tag{6-32}$$

where $dd_{P,max} = \max_t(dd_{P,t})$ is the maximum drawdown experienced during the period. "Calmar" is the acronym of Young's company, California Managed Annual Reports, according to which the measurement period is set to three years. This ratio has the advantage of being simple and unequivocal as there is no question of the threshold for counting a negative return as a drawdown or not.

- The *Sterling ratio* (Kestner, 1996):

$$\text{SteR}_P = \frac{\overline{R}_P - R_f}{\overline{dd}_{P,\text{signif}}} \tag{6-33}$$

where $\overline{dd}_{P,\text{signif}} = \frac{1}{d}\sum_{i=1}^{d} dd_{P,\text{signif}}$ is the average of the d most significant non-overlapping drawdowns experienced during the period.[14] For instance, in Figure 6-13, this corresponds to dd_1 and dd_2, which are the largest values of the drawdowns observed during distinct periods.

Bacon (2021) proposes the *Sterling–Calmar ratio* StCaR_P, a hybrid performance measure that overcomes the difficulty of identifying the most significant drawdowns through selecting the maximum drawdown for each sub-period y (typically one year) during the whole time window:

$$\text{StCaR}_P = \frac{\overline{R}_P - R_f}{\overline{dd}_{P,\max}} \tag{6-34}$$

where $\overline{dd}_{P,\max} = \frac{1}{Y}\sum_{y=1}^{Y} dd_{P,\max}(y)$ is the average of the maximum drawdowns observed during sub-period y, defined as $dd_{P,\max}(y) = \max_t(dd_{P,t}(y))$.

- The *Sharper ratio* (Burke, 1994):

$$\text{ShR}_P = \frac{\overline{R}_P - R_f}{\sigma_{dd_{P,\text{signif}}}} \tag{6-35}$$

where $\sigma_{dd_{P,\text{signif}}} = \sqrt{\frac{1}{d}\sum_{i=1}^{d} (dd_{P,\text{signif}})^2}$ is the square root of the average squared most significant drawdowns.[15]

[14]The original ratio, proposed by Deane Sterling Jones, adds a penalty of 10% to the denominator in order to ease the comparison with the Calmar ratio. As this penalty is largely arbitrary, Bacon (2021) suggests to drop it.

[15]The original ratio proposed to take only the sum and not the average, but this version ensures a better comparability with the other drawdown-based performance measures.

- The *Pain ratio* and the *Ulcer ratio* (Martin and McCann, 1989):

$$\mathrm{PR}_P = \frac{\overline{R}_P - R_f}{\overline{\mathrm{dd}}_P} \quad (6\text{-}36)$$

$$\mathrm{UR}_P = \frac{\overline{R}_P - R_f}{\sigma_{\mathrm{dd}_P}} \quad (6\text{-}37)$$

where $\overline{\mathrm{dd}}_P = \frac{1}{T}\sum_{t=1}^{T} \mathrm{dd}_{P,t}$ and $\sigma_{\mathrm{dd}_P} = \sqrt{\frac{1}{T}\sum_{i=1}^{T} (\mathrm{dd}_{P,t})^2}$ are the mean of all drawdowns and the square root of the average squared drawdowns, respectively.

These ratios directly use the drawdown function of Equation (6-31) and have the merit of combining information about the intensity and the length of the drawdowns.

XYZ example (continued)

We repeat the same process as above and obtain the results shown in Table 6-13 and Figure 6-15 (we take the first and second semesters for the Sterling–Calmar ratio).

TABLE 6-13 XYZ example – Computation of the drawdown-based measures.

	X	Y	Z	M
Calmar	0.57	0.67	1.41	1.35
Sterling–Calmar	0.58	0.68	1.40	1.34
Pain	0.51	0.68	1.66	1.16
Ulcer	0.54	0.68	1.54	1.24

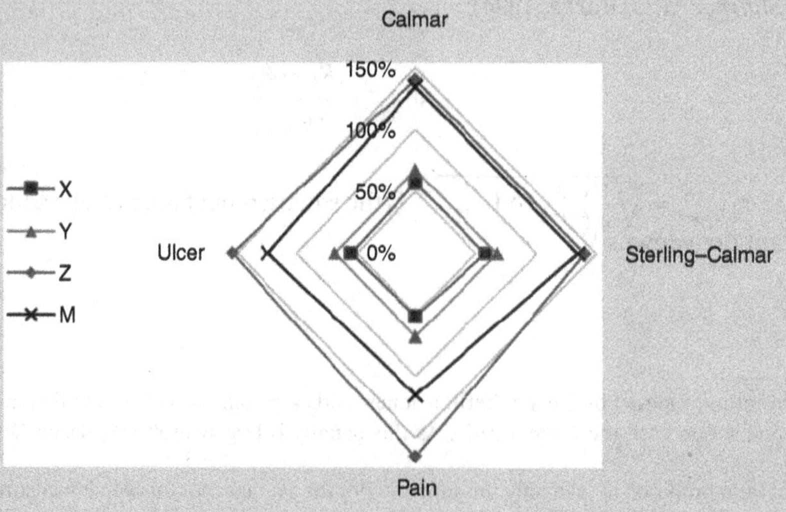

FIGURE 6-15 XYZ example – Radar chart of the ratios using drawdown-based measures.

The results are more contrasted: Fund Z is much better rated with the Pain and Ulcer (thus using information about the whole history of drawdowns) than with the maximum drawdown-based measures. Furthermore, Funds X and Y more severely underperform the other two portfolios with all measures. This can be understood by comparing, for instance, the evolution of drawdowns for X and Z as shown in Figure 6-16:

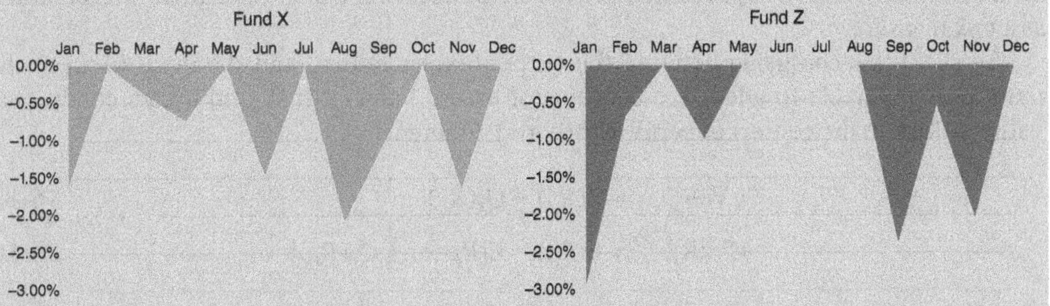

FIGURE 6-16 XYZ example – Evolution of drawdowns for X and Z.

Because of its seesaw pattern of returns, Fund X exhibits many periods of drawdowns, creating several potential regret situations. There are only two drawdown periods for Fund Z, with fewer periods of stress for its investor.

6.2.5 Replacing volatility with extreme risk

6.2.5.1 Defining extreme risk

If the investor cares about downside risk, it is logical to consider that what matters most to them is what happens in the tail of the distribution of returns, i.e., what happens in the worst $x\%$ of the times. There are two main types of risk measures that address the estimation of extreme risk: the Value-at-Risk $\text{VaR}_P^{(1-x)}$ and the conditional Value-at-Risk $\text{CVaR}_P^{(1-x)}$ (also equivalently called "expected shortfall").[16] Their definitions are generally expressed in absolute value:

$$\text{aVaR}_P^{(1-x)} \equiv -Q_x(R_P) = -\arg(\Pr[R_{P,t} \leq \text{aVaR}_P^{(1-x)}] = x\%) \tag{6-38}$$

$$\text{aCVaR}_P^{(1-x)} = -\text{E}[R_P | R_P \leq Q_x(R_P)] \tag{6-39}$$

where $Q_x(R_P)$ is the xth percentile of the distribution of returns and $1 - x$ is the associated confidence level, i.e., the probability that the return is above that percentile. In Equation (6-39), the expectation is considered conditionally on $R_{P,t} \leq Q_x(R_P)$.

[16]Even though the Value-at-Risk measure is the reference in the banking industry, notably for the determination of capital requirements, it suffers from the fact that it is not a "coherent" measure of risk according to the axioms of Artzner, Delbaen, Eber, and Heath (1999) (see Chapter 1 for a discussion). This is the reason why the conditional Value-at-Risk, which is a coherent measure of risk, tends nowadays to be favored in the asset management industry.

These definitions are problematic in the context of portfolio returns, especially in comparison with the Sharpe ratio, whose denominator expresses a distance with respect to the average return. The absolute VaR and CVaR are positively influenced by this average. Because it is also present in the numerator, this creates a double counting problem: portfolios with a higher mean obtain, *ceteris paribus*, a greater numerator and a lower denominator. Furthermore, if the portfolio returns are tilted toward positive values, it is possible that the realized values of Equations (6-38) and (6-39) become close to zero or negative, which ruins their interpretation as a risk measure.

To avoid this confusion between the output (excess return) and the input (risk) of the ratio, it is preferable to adopt the concepts of excess Value-at-Risk and excess conditional Value-at-Risk in the context of performance measurement:

$$\text{VaR}_P^{(1-x)} = \text{E}(R_P) - Q_x(R_P) \tag{6-40}$$

$$\text{CVaR}_P^{(1-x)} = \text{E}(R_P) - \text{E}[R_P | R_P \leq Q_x(R_P)] \tag{6-41}$$

All these concepts are illustrated in Figure 6-17.

The graph shows a distribution of returns that is obviously negatively skewed (left asymmetry), which is often the case in reality. The absolute Value-at-Risk corresponds to minus the xth percentile of the distribution. The absolute conditional Value-at-Risk corresponds to minus the expectation of the area located below that percentile. The excess VaR and CVaR are the distances between the expected return and the corresponding absolute risk measures.

Using extreme risk measures for performance measurement makes little sense if returns are assumed to be normally distributed. In that case, both the VaR and the CVaR are directly related to the expected return and its standard deviation through the following formulas:

$$\text{gVaR}_P^{(1-x)} = z_{1-x} \times \sigma_P \tag{6-42}$$

$$\text{gCVaR}_P^{(1-x)} = q_{1-x} \times \sigma_P \tag{6-43}$$

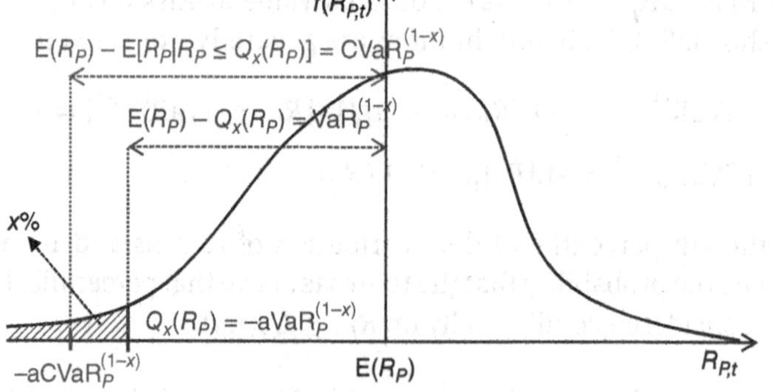

FIGURE 6-17 Illustration of the three concepts related to extreme risk.

TABLE 6-14 Multipliers of the volatility for the Gaussian VaR and CVaR.

Confidence level $1 - x$	VaR multiplier z_{1-x}	CVaR multiplier q_{1-x}
90%	1.282	1.755
95%	1.645	2.063
97.5%	1.960	2.338
99%	2.326	2.665
99.9%	3.090	3.367

where $q_{1-x} = \frac{1}{x}\phi(z_{1-x})$ in which $\phi(z_{1-x}) \equiv \frac{e^{-z_{1-x}^2/2}}{\sqrt{2\pi}}$ is the value of the density function of the standard normal distribution taken at percentile z_{1-x}. Note that $z_{1-x} = -z_x$ and $q_{1-x} = q_x$ as the distribution is symmetric around the expectation.

Table 6-14 reports their expressions for traditional values of the confidence levels, from the least to the most conservative one.

Besides multiplying volatility at the denominator, the expressions for the Gaussian VaR and CVaR do not bring much insight to performance measurement: As Table 6-14 suggests, the volatility multiplier increases monotonically with the confidence level.

If returns depart from normality, using extreme risk measures can become relevant. Then, four main techniques can be applied: (i) the parametric approach, according to which a distribution is calibrated on the data and the associated percentiles are estimated with the corresponding parameters; (ii) the historical approach that uses the observed returns in order to infer the extreme risk measures (with possible extrapolations using bootstrapping techniques or with a filtering technique using a parametric model on the data and historical percentile on the residuals) directly from the sample; (iii) the numerical (a.k.a. Monte Carlo) approach that constructs virtual return distributions using simulation techniques; and (iv) the extreme value theory (EVT) approach that attempts to directly model the tail of the returns distributions using some specific statistical properties of the data.[17]

6.2.5.2 Measuring performance with extreme risk

Several performance measures derived from the Sharpe ratio have been proposed, generally with historical-based measures of extreme risk (using merely sample data) at the denominator.[18]

[17]It has to be noted that, despite the high relevance of the EVT approach for the estimation of tail risk measures in this context, it has to our knowledge not been applied to the creation of associated performance measures.
[18]Some measures were originally developed with the absolute VaR or CVaR measure, but we plead here for consistency across performance measures and use the excess VaR and CVaR throughout.

- The *Reward to VaR ratio* (Dowd, 1999):

$$\mathrm{VR}_P^{1-x} = \frac{\overline{R}_P - R_f}{\mathrm{hVaR}_P^{(1-x)}} \tag{6-44}$$

where $\mathrm{hVaR}_P^{(1-x)} = \overline{R}_P - R_{P,n_x}$ is the historical VaR, with R_{P,n_x} is the return that is ranked at the n_xth place in the list of the portfolio returns ordered from the highest to the lowest one, i.e., $n_x = \lceil \mathrm{T}(1-x) \rceil$ in which $\lceil \cdot \rceil$ stands for the ceiling (least integer greater than or equal to) of the argument. For instance, if we use monthly data for a period of 10 years ($\mathrm{T} = 12 \times 10 = 120$) and the confidence level is $(1-x) = 95\%$, $n_x = \lceil 120 \times 0.95 \rceil = 114$, i.e., R_{P,n_x} is the return ranked 114th or the seventh one from the minimum.

- The *Stable Tail Adjusted Return ratio* (Martin, Rachev, and Siboulet, 2003), also more simply called the *Reward to CVaR ratio*:

$$\mathrm{CVR}_P^{1-x} = \frac{\overline{R}_P - R_f}{\mathrm{hCVaR}_P^{(1-x)}} \tag{6-45}$$

where $\mathrm{hCVaR}_P^{(1-x)} = \overline{R}_P - \frac{1}{T-n_x} \sum_{i=1}^{\mathrm{T}-n_x} R_{P,i}$ is the mean return minus the average of the returns $R_{P,i}$ that are lower than the VaR. For instance, in the former example, $\mathrm{T} - n_x - 1 = 120 - 114 = 6$, and we take (minus) the average of the six lowest returns.

- The *Tail ratio* (Bacon, 2021):

$$\mathrm{TVR}_P^{1-x} = \frac{\overline{R}_P - R_f}{\mathrm{hTVaR}_P^{(1-x)}} \tag{6-46}$$

where $\mathrm{hTVaR}_P^{(1-x)} = \overline{R}_P - \sqrt{\frac{1}{T-n_x} \sum_{i=1}^{T-n_x} (R_{P,i})^2}$ is the mean return minus the square root of the average squared returns that are lower than the VaR. This ratio provides an even more conservative assessment of extreme risks by increasing the weight of the most negative returns.

In this context however, estimation quality becomes a sensitive issue because, by nature, the associated risk measures feature returns that are observed with scarcity. If the time window (e.g., 3–5 years) and/or the frequency of returns observations (e.g., monthly) imply a relatively limited sample size, there might be too few observations in order to produce a reliable estimate of the VaR or the CVaR. This is the reason why a parametric approach, using the Cornish–Fisher expansion as introduced in Section 6.1.3, has become popular:

- The *Modified Sharpe ratio* (Favre and Galeano, 2002):

$$\mathrm{mVR}_P^{1-x} = \frac{\overline{R}_P - R_f}{\mathrm{mVaR}_P^{(1-x)}} \tag{6-47}$$

where $mVaR_P^{(1-x)} = -z^*_{x,P} \times \sigma_P$ in which $z^*_{x,P}$ is computed along Equation (6-12b).[19]

- The *Modified Reward to CVaR ratio*:

$$mCVR_P^{1-x} = \frac{\overline{R}_P - R_f}{mCVaR_P^{(1-x)}} \tag{6-48}$$

where $mCVaR_P^{(1-x)} = q^*_{x,P} \times \sigma_P$ in which q^*_x is obtained by the Cornish–Fisher formula:

$$q^*_{x,P} = q_x \times \left(1 + z_x \frac{\mu_{P,3}}{6} + (z_x^2 - 1)\frac{e\mu_{P,4}}{24} - (2z_x^2 - 1)\frac{\mu^2_{P,3}}{36}\right) \tag{6-49}$$

where $q_x = \frac{1}{x}\frac{e^{-z_x^2/2}}{\sqrt{2\pi}}$. Building on Table 6-14, we can assess the impact of skewness and kurtosis on the Cornish–Fisher adjustment through the illustration presented in Table 6-15.

The illustration shows how sensitive the volatility multiplier becomes – and thus the associated value of the CVaR – to the higher moments of the distribution, especially when the confidence level becomes very conservative. For funds or portfolios with a very adverse skewness and kurtosis, this can seriously penalize their performance.

It is worth mentioning that there is no evidence of the use of the Modified Reward to CVaR ratio in the literature, in spite of its technical superiority over its Modified Sharpe ratio counterpart, which is only based on the VaR. Furthermore, for both ratios, we believe that it is more effective – both from the computational as well as the interpretative standpoints – to use the

TABLE 6-15 Multipliers of the volatility for the CVaR (Gaussian case and Cornish–Fisher adjustment).

Confidence level	Gaussian	C–F with $\mu_{P,3} = 0, e\mu_{P,4} = 6.9$	C–F with $\mu_{P,3} = -0.5, e\mu_{P,4} = 6.9$
90%	1.755	2.079	2.251
95%	2.063	3.074	3.309
97.5%	2.338	4.248	4.536
99%	2.665	6.046	6.394
99.9%	3.367	11.643	12.085

[19]Note that $-z^*_x \neq z^*_{1-x}$ unlike in the Gaussian case because the distribution of returns is no longer assumed to be symmetric.

outputs of the Cornish–Fisher expansions to directly adapt the volatility in the Sharpe ratio rather than switching to a performance measure based on extreme risk measures. In other words, if one wants to use a VaR-like performance measure with the Cornish–Fisher expansion, it is more convenient to use formula (6-13) to adjust the volatility. Likewise, if the CVaR is adopted instead, then the alternative modified volatility can be written as

$$\widetilde{\text{m}\sigma}_P^{(x)} = \sigma_P \times \frac{q_x^*}{q_x} \tag{6-50}$$

where q_x^* is computed according to Equation (6-49).

XYZ example (continued)

Given the small number of observations (12 per fund), this part of the example can only be viewed as a crude estimation exercise.

For the historical VaR and CVaR, we focus on the 90% confidence level. This leads to $n_x = \lceil 12 \times 0.90 \rceil = 11$. This means that the absolute VaR is equal to the next-but-last observation, and the corresponding absolute CVaR is the last (= lowest) one.

For the modified VaR and CVaR, we use a confidence level of 97.5%. We then obtain the results shown in Table 6-16 and Figure 6-18.

TABLE 6-16 XYZ example – Computation of the VaR-based measures.

	X	Y	Z	M
hVaR	1.99%	2.04%	3.18%	2.66%
hCVaR	2.40%	2.95%	5.13%	5.75%
mVaR	3.23%	3.43%	4.61%	4.24%
mCVaR	3.29%	3.58%	5.05%	4.41%

The results are much more contrasted than before, especially when the historical approach is adopted. This is simply the result of the important sensitivity of these measures to outliers, especially when the sample size is very small (as it is obviously the case here). The results using the modified (Cornish–Fisher) versions of the VaR and CVaR are less sensitive to the tail events and provide performance values that are more comparable across portfolios.

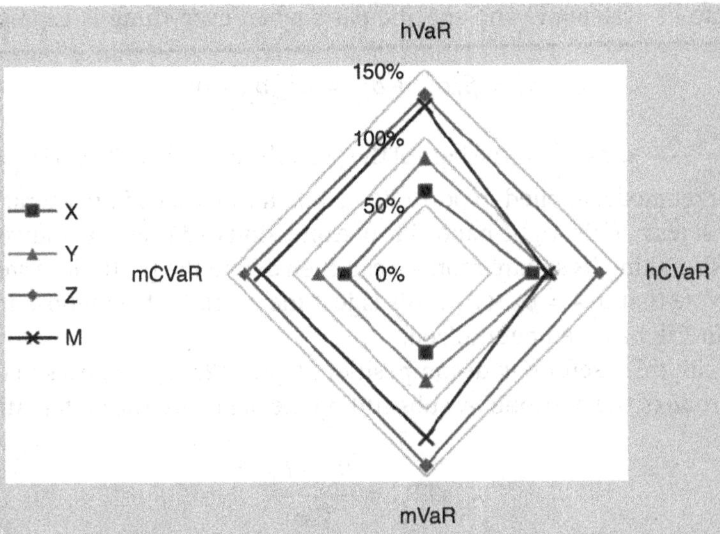

FIGURE 6-18 XYZ example – Radar chart of the ratios using VaR-based measures.

6.3 ALTERNATIVE VERSIONS OF THE OTHER CLASSICAL PERFORMANCE MEASURES

Even though the attempts to modify the inputs of the other classical performance measures are less numerous, there are interesting avatars of the measures based on systematic risk (the Treynor ratio and the modified Jensen's alpha) as well as specific risk (the Information ratio).[20]

6.3.1 Alternative versions of the Treynor ratio and the modified Jensen's alpha

Both the Treynor ratio and the modified Jensen's alpha examined in Chapter 3 deliver a rate of return as a measure of portfolio performance. While, from a practical point of view, this is an intuitive and economically meaningful property, it does not allow any comparison with the Sharpe ratio, whose measurement dimension is in decimal units (see Chapter 4).

In some cases, it can be very useful to reconcile the measurement units of the Sharpe ratio and the Treynor ratio. This can be carried out by adapting the latter performance measure. It suffices to note that, in the context of the CAPM, the total risk of the portfolio can be

[20]We leave aside Jensen's alpha from this discussion, as this particular performance measure is the main subject of Chapters 7 and 8.

decomposed into its systematic and specific parts when everything is expressed in terms of variances:

$$\sigma_P^2 = \beta_P^2\sigma_M^2 + \sigma_{\varepsilon P}^2 = \rho_{PM}^2\sigma_P^2 + \sigma_{\varepsilon P}^2 \tag{6-51}$$

where $\beta_P = \frac{\text{Cov}(R_P,R_M)}{\sigma_M^2} \equiv \rho_{PM}\frac{\sigma_P}{\sigma_M}$ is the beta of the portfolio and $\sigma_{\varepsilon P}^2$ is the variance of the residual term of the market model applied to portfolio P, which reflects its idiosyncratic risk. One can interpret the first term of the right-hand side of expression (6-51) as the undiversifiable part of the portfolio risk. Taking its square root, we can then define the portfolio systematic volatility $\sigma_{\rho P} \equiv \rho_{PM}\sigma_P$. Note that $\sigma_{\rho P} = \beta_P \times \sigma_M$: this is just the portfolio beta whose influence on the market portfolio risk has been neutralized.

Endowed with this useful risk decomposition, Bacon (2021) proposes to define the *alternative Treynor ratio* of the portfolio by substituting the beta with the systematic volatility:

$$\text{aTR}_P = \frac{\overline{R}_P - R_f}{\sigma_{\rho P}} \tag{6-52}$$

In a similar fashion, the *alternative modified Jensen's alpha* is defined as

$$\text{am}\alpha_P = \frac{\alpha_P}{\sigma_{\rho P}} \tag{6-53}$$

Note that the relation between these performance measures and their original counterpart is just a rescaling through the market portfolio volatility: $\text{mTR}_P \times \sigma_M = \text{TR}_P$ and $\text{am}\alpha_P \times \sigma_M = \text{m}\alpha_P$.

This reformulation of systematic risk-based performance measures allows a graphical representation in the same dimension as the Sharpe ratio, as shown in the graph shown in Figure 6-19:

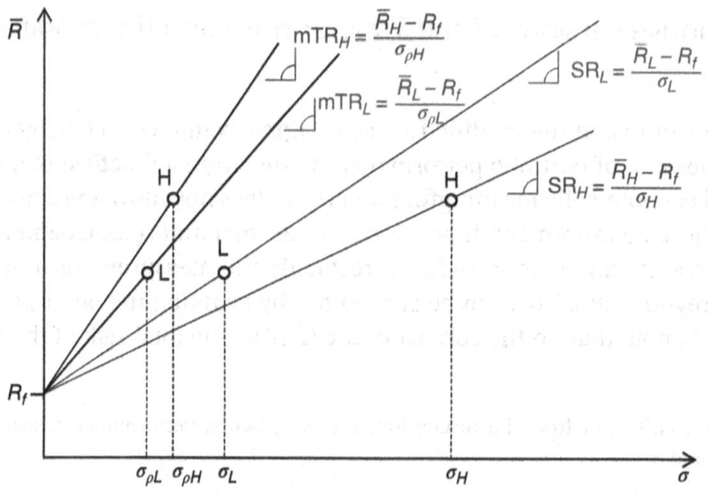

FIGURE 6-19 Graphical representation of the modified Treynor ratio.

In the picture, the vertical coordinates of portfolios L and H are the same: the graph simply shows two versions of the same portfolio – and therefore the same mean returns – according to two different measures of risk that can be displayed on the horizontal axis. Figure 6-19 shows how the Sharpe and modified Treynor ratios can deliver contrasted views of performance. Whereas portfolio L dominates H according to their Sharpe ratios, its lack of diversifying power leads to a reversal of the rankings when risk is measured with its systematic version.

Note that another version of this analysis is proposed by Fama (1972) who provides a comprehensive decomposition of portfolio performance. His approach is examined in detail in Section 13.1 of Chapter 13.

XYZ example (continued)

The information needed in order to construct the modified Treynor ratio and the alternative modified Jensen's alpha is linked to the implementation of the CAPM. For the three funds, this is summarized in Table 6-17, considering that the monthly volatility of the market portfolio is 2.55%.

TABLE 6-17 XYZ example – Computation of the alternative systematic risk-based measures.

	X	Y	Z
Beta	0.62	0.43	0.21
Alpha	−0.14%	0.05%	0.57%
Systematic volatility	5.45%	3.79%	1.87%
Modified Treynor ratio	0.43	0.90	4.41
Alternative modified Jensen's alpha	−0.30	0.16	3.68

The Modified Treynor ratio for the three funds is larger than their Sharpe ratios as the systematic volatility cannot be higher than total risk. Nevertheless, the reduction in risk is very contrasted as Fund X is highly correlated with the market, whereas Fund Z is almost uncorrelated, as shown in Figure 6-20.

The empty geometric forms correspond to the coordinates of the funds according to their Sharpe ratio, whereas the filled ones are the reflections of their modified Treynor ratios. The horizontal distance between the corresponding forms reveals the extent of the diversifying power of each fund. Unsurprisingly, Fund Z, whose correlation with the market index is the lowest, achieves by far the highest systematic risk-adjusted performance. This outcome has to be interpreted with caution since, as already discussed in Chapter 3, this

(continued)

(continued)

fund's returns are unlikely to be adequately explained with the chosen proxy for the market portfolio.

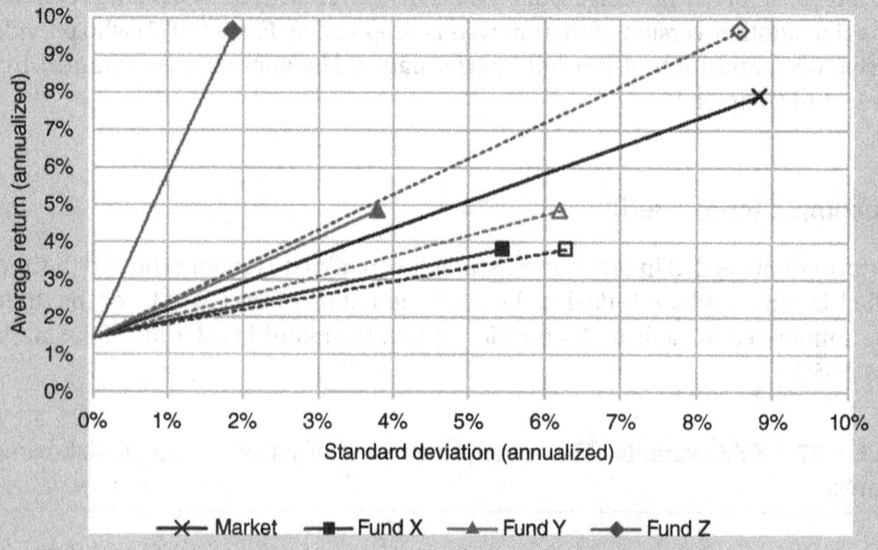

FIGURE 6-20 XYZ example – Representation of the modified Treynor ratio.

6.3.2 Alternative versions of the Information ratio

Since specific risk is usually estimated using a measure of standard deviation, it is not surprising to realize that most alternative versions of the Information ratio adopt the same routes as the ones of the Sharpe ratio. Therefore, we classify these alternatives using the same logic as in the first two sections of this chapter.

We start with the definition of the Information ratio as described in Chapter 3, namely,

$$IR_P = \frac{\text{average excess return over the benchmark}}{\text{volatility of the excess return over the benchmark}} \tag{6-54}$$

and subsequently examine the proposals to either refine the way the Information ratio is measured or to alter the inputs of the formula.

6.3.2.1 Refinements of the Information ratio

- The *geometric Information ratio*

  In order to compound differences in returns (over the risk-free rate or the benchmark portfolio return), it is necessary to define the geometric differential returns as $R^g_{(P-j),t} \equiv \frac{1+R_{P,t}}{1+R_{j,t}} - 1$, where if $j = f$, it represents the geometric excess return, and if $j = B$, this is the differential return over the benchmark (which can be the market portfolio). With the new series of returns, the *geometric Information ratio* can be written as

$$\mathrm{gIR}_P = \frac{\overline{R}^g_{(P-B)}}{\sigma^g_{(P-B)}} \tag{6-55}$$

  where $\sigma^g_{(P-B)} \equiv \sigma(R^g_{(P-B),t})$ is the sample standard deviation of the geometric differential return. In other words, after the transformation of arithmetic into geometric returns, the definition is unchanged.

- The *adjusted Information ratio*

  There exists an adjustment for higher moments analogous to the one of the Sharpe ratio proposed in Equation (6-18) applied to the Information ratio. Instead of estimating the skewness and kurtosis of the portfolio returns, it is performed for the portfolio differential return with respect to its benchmark. The adjusted Information ratio can be written as

$$\mathrm{aIR}_P = \mathrm{IR}_P \times \left(1 + \frac{\mu_{(P-B),3}}{6}\mathrm{IR}_P - \frac{e\mu_{(P-B),4}}{24}\mathrm{IR}_P^2\right) \tag{6-56}$$

  where $\mu_{(P-B),3} \equiv \frac{E((R_P-R_B)-(\overline{R}_P-\overline{R}_B))^3}{\sigma^3(R_P-R_B)}$ and $e\mu_{(P-B),4} \equiv \frac{E((R_P-R_B)-(\overline{R}_P-\overline{R}_B))^4}{\sigma^4(R_P-R_B)} - 3$ are the skewness and excess kurtosis of the differential portfolio returns over its benchmark, respectively.

6.3.2.2 Alterations of the Information ratio

- The *downside Information ratio*

  For a benchmarked portfolio, it is rather natural to consider that the reservation rate applicable in the context of downside risk measurement is the mean return of the benchmark itself. Thus, the *downside Information ratio* dIR_P is revealed to be the special case of the Sortino ratio in which the reservation rate is set to the mean benchmark return:

$$\mathrm{dIR}_P = \frac{\overline{R}_{(P-B)}}{d\sigma_P(\overline{R}_B)} \tag{6-57}$$

where $\overline{R}_{(P-B)} = \overline{R}_P - \overline{R}_B$ is the tracking difference of the portfolio return relative to the benchmark B, and $d\sigma_P(\overline{R}_B) = \sqrt{\frac{1}{T-1}\sum_{t=1}^{T}(\max(\overline{R}_B - R_{P,t}, 0))^2}$ is the downside tracking error.

- The *drawdown risk-based Information ratios*

  Drawdown risk is particularly relevant in the context of active risk and return, but also for the assessment of the quality of a fund or portfolio whose objective is to track a reference index at the lowest cost and distance, like Exchange Traded Funds or index funds. In both cases, part of the active risk taken by the portfolio manager may materialize through an unexpected stalling, whose translation is provided by the extent of active portfolio drawdown, defined as

$$\text{add}_{P,t} = \frac{\max\limits_{\tau=1,\ldots,t}(V_{P,\tau} - V_{B,\tau}) - (V_{P,t} - V_{B,\tau})}{\max\limits_{\tau=1,\ldots,t}(V_{P,\tau} - V_{B,\tau})} \tag{6-58}$$

where $V_{P,\tau}$ and $V_{B,\tau}$ are the net asset values of the portfolio and the benchmark, respectively, at time τ.

In relation with this concept, performance measures that are proposed in this context are the *active Calmar ratio* (Bradford and Siliski, 2016), *active Pain ratio*, and *active Ulcer ratio*:

$$\text{aCR}_P = \frac{\overline{R}_{(P-B)}}{\text{add}_{P,\max}} \tag{6-59}$$

$$\text{aPR}_P = \frac{\overline{R}_{(P-B)}}{\overline{\text{add}}_P} \tag{6-60}$$

$$\text{aUR}_P = \frac{\overline{R}_{(P-B)}}{\sigma_{\text{add}_P}} \tag{6-61}$$

where $\text{add}_{P,\max} = \max\limits_t(\text{add}_{P,t})$, $\overline{\text{add}}_P = \frac{1}{T}\sum_{t=1}^{T}\text{add}_{P,t}$, and $\sigma_{\text{add}_P} = \sqrt{\frac{1}{T}\sum_{t=1}^{T}(\text{add}_{P,t})^2}$ are the maximum active drawdown, the mean of all active drawdowns, and the square root of the average squared active drawdowns, respectively.

- The *Reward to relative VaR*

  Even if many extreme risk-based versions of performance measures have been proposed in the context of total risk, there is no such abundance of measures for active risk. The *Reward to relative VaR* can be written as

$$\text{aVR}_P^{1-x} = \frac{\overline{R}_{(P-B)}}{\text{VaR}_{(P-B)}^{(1-x)}} \tag{6-62}$$

where $\text{VaR}^{(1-x)}_{(P-B)} = (\overline{R}_P - \overline{R}_B) - Q_x(R_P - R_B)$ is the active excess Value-at-Risk at the associated $1 - x$ confidence level. It makes little sense to use the Gaussian VaR, since it simply leads to a multiple of the original Information ratio, but it is possible to use the historical, modified, or any other estimation method of the VaR as discussed in Section 6.2.5.2.

XYZ example (continued)

We consider the CAPM-based version of the Information ratio (i.e., the "Appraisal ratio") as a starting point. The original regression outputs and the association performance measures are displayed in Table 6-18 (they are similar to Table 3-15 in Chapter 3).

TABLE 6-18 XYZ example – original Information ratio.

Regression outputs	X	Y	Z
Alpha	−0.14%	0.05%	0.57%
St. dev. epsilon	0.90%	1.42%	2.42%
IR (monthly)	−0.15	0.04	0.24
IR (yearly)	**−0.52**	**0.13**	**0.82**

Those results are based on the time series of active returns, defined as the difference between the monthly fund returns and their CAPM-based benchmark. Their time series and relevant statistical estimates are reproduced in Table 6-19.

Since the use of geometric excess returns for such a short time period does not lead to substantial differences, we focus on the other alternative versions of the Information ratio. With the data of Table 6-19, they are summarized in Table 6-20.

Unlike the various alterations of the Sharpe ratio, for which one usually expects to produce a positive figure, the alternative versions of the Information ratio may deliver very divergent results depending on which measure of active risk is adopted. For Fund X, the fact that the alpha is negative leads to very different results, especially with the drawdown-based measure (Active Calmar) since a higher risk makes the IR less negative (closer to zero), thereby providing a better picture. On the other hand, as shown in Table 6-20, Fund Z benefits from a much lower downside tracking error than its original one (roughly 50% lower), which inflates its downside IR compared to its peers. This is a dangerous consequence of the fact that the regression is almost insignificant for Z, which means that the measures of this fund's tracking error are all but reliable. The radar chart shown in Figure 6-21, in

(continued)

(continued)

which each performance is standardized (i.e., centered and divided by the range), illustrates these results.

TABLE 6-19 XYZ example – Statistics of the active returns.

	X	Y	Z
Jan	−0.78%	−1.12%	−2.72%
Feb	0.76%	0.22%	1.55%
Mar	1.02%	−0.27%	1.64%
Apr	−1.88%	−1.79%	−1.60%
May	−0.30%	0.70%	4.47%
Jun	−0.25%	2.16%	0.55%
Jul	−0.32%	0.42%	−1.05%
Aug	−1.15%	1.18%	3.61%
Sep	0.46%	−2.11%	−2.67%
Oct	0.18%	0.70%	1.50%
Nov	−0.52%	−1.44%	−1.20%
Dec	1.15%	1.96%	2.79%
Mean	**−0.14%**	**0.05%**	**0.57%**
Standard deviation	**0.90%**	**1.42%**	**2.42%**
Skewness	**−0.30**	**−0.11**	**0.09**
Kurtosis	**−0.28**	**−1.10**	**−1.21**
Downside volatility	**0.74%**	**1.00%**	**1.34%**
Max drawdown	**3.86%**	**2.93%**	**2.72%**

TABLE 6-20 XYZ example – Alternative Information ratios.

Performance	X	Y	Z
Original IR	−0.52	0.13	0.82
Adjusted IR	−0.53	0.13	0.83
Downside IR	−0.64	0.18	1.48
Active Calmar	−0.12	0.06	0.73
Reward to relative VaR	−0.25	0.06	0.45

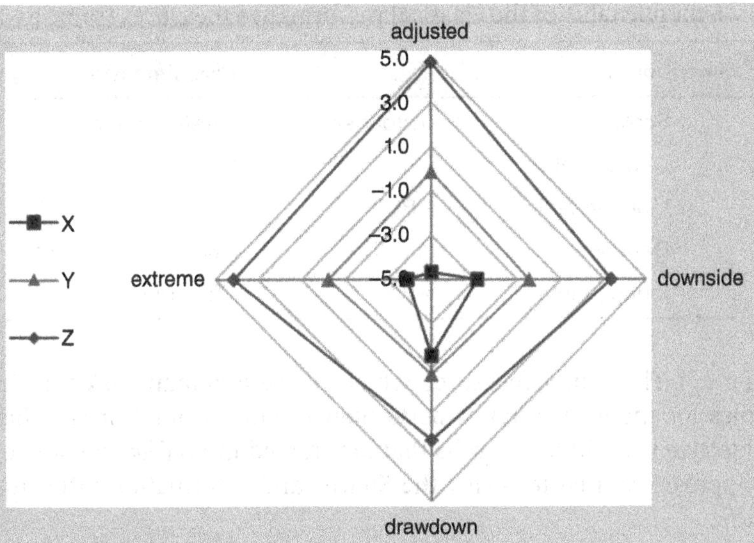

FIGURE 6-21 XYZ example – Radar chart of the alternative Information ratios.

6.4 CLASSICAL PERFORMANCE MEASURES AS RISK-ADJUSTED RETURNS

In Chapter 4, we discussed two issues related to the measurement dimensions of the relation between risk and return: the unit and the scale of the performance measure. These considerations led us to propose a synoptic table featuring the major classical performance measures presented in Chapter 3. We reproduce it here, as it serves as the starting point of the current section.

Even though both the Sharpe ratio SR_P and the Information ratio IR_P are invariant to portfolio leverage, they share the unfortunate property of expressing portfolio performance through a decimal number. Such a presentation does not ease its understanding by the user, especially when they are a non-specialist investor. Furthermore, the question of the practical significance of these measures is also not trivial. Regarding the Sharpe ratio, there is no magic number: neither 0 nor 1 have any particular meaning regarding the portfolio management's quality. The threshold between a "good" and a "bad" Sharpe ratio over the long run seems to be somewhere in the neighborhood of 0.30. For the Information ratio, the issue appears to be even more complicated, as its attractiveness also depends on the investor's aversion to active risk.

The difficulties associated with the Sharpe and Information ratios contrast with the simplicity of interpreting the three other measures represented in Table 6-21. Both the Jensen's alpha α_P and the modified Jensen's alpha $m\alpha_P$ are expressed as rates of return whose sign immediately signals portfolio quality (the Treynor ratio TR_P being simply a homothetic

TABLE 6-21 Synoptic table of the classical performance measures (same as Table 4-4).

Measurement dimension		Risk dimension		
Unit	**Scale**	*Total risk*	*Systematic risk*	*Specific risk*
Decimal	Dependent			
(%/%)	Independent	SR_P		IR_P, AR_P
Percentage	Dependent		α_P	
(%)	Independent	–	TR_P, $m\alpha_P$	–

translation of $m\alpha_P$). Thus, these measures, which all use systematic risk as an input, represent useful examples for the expression of performance built on total or specific risk. In other words, the objective is to fill in the cells that are framed in bold in the last row of the table. The various approaches used to revisit the Sharpe and Information ratios in that spirit are discussed below.

6.4.1 Risk-adjusted return performance measures with total risk

6.4.1.1 Transforming the Sharpe ratio into a risk-adjusted return

The pure translation of the major systematic risk-based performance measures in the context of total risk is attributed to Modigliani and Modigliani (1997). They generically define the portfolio *risk-adjusted performance*, denoted by RAP_P, as the average return of the leveraged portfolio so as to achieve the same volatility as the market portfolio:

$$RAP_P \equiv M_P^2 = R_f + \frac{\sigma_M}{\sigma_P}(\overline{R}_P - R_f) \tag{6-63}$$

Note that the RAP is more commonly called the "M-squared" (M_P^2) as a tribute to the intergenerational association of the prestigious Nobel Prize winner Franco Modigliani and his granddaughter Leah Modigliani who acted as co-authors of the paper proposing this influential performance measure.

The link between the risk-adjusted performance and the Sharpe ratio is straightforward since we can rewrite it as $RAP_P = \overline{R}_P + SR_P \times (\sigma_M - \sigma_P)$. Nevertheless, a further adjustment is necessary in order to fully match the interpretation of this performance measure as an "abnormal" return of the portfolio over its benchmark. This is why the notion of *relative risk-adjusted performance*, denoted by $RRAP_P$, also proposed by the authors, proves to be useful.[21] It is defined as

$$RRAP_P = RAP_P - RAP_M = \frac{\sigma_M}{\sigma_P}(\overline{R}_P - R_f) - (\overline{R}_M - R_f) \tag{6-64}$$

[21] It is also called the *excess standard deviation adjusted return* (eSDAR) according to Statman (1987) who appears to be the inventor of this measure.

Note that $\text{RAP}_M \equiv \overline{R}_M$ and therefore we can simply define the RRAP_P as $M_P^2 - \overline{R}_M$ or, in terms of the portfolio Sharpe ratio, $\text{RRAP}_P = (\overline{R}_P - \overline{R}_M) + \text{SR}_P \times (\sigma_M - \sigma_P)$. Obviously, ordering portfolios on the basis of the RAP_P or the RRAP_P will lead to the exact same rankings.

If we follow the quest for analogies between performance measures based on volatility and on beta as risk measures, it is interesting to consider the total risk version of the plain Jensen's alpha. According to the interpretation of the latter measure as the difference between the observed and the required portfolio return, we can define the *total risk alpha* of the portfolio, called $\text{T}\alpha_P$, which refers to the manager's "net-selectivity" by Fama (1972), with a formula that resembles the one of the original alpha but in which the required return is obtained by the Capital Market Line instead of the Security Market Line:

$$\text{T}\alpha_P = (\overline{R}_P - R_f) - \frac{\sigma_P}{\sigma_M}(\overline{R}_M - R_f) \tag{6-65}$$

Just like the link between Jensen's alpha and the modified Jensen's alpha is determined by the intensity of portfolio leverage (measured through its beta), the total risk alpha is a leveraged version of the relative risk-adjusted performance through the relation

$$\text{T}\alpha_P = \text{RRAP}_P \times \frac{\sigma_P}{\sigma_M} \tag{6-66}$$

Thus, the $\text{T}\alpha_P$ can be artificially inflated with portfolio leverage, while the RRAP_P is leverage-invariant. Note as well that the total risk alpha can be expressed using the market portfolio's Sharpe ratio as $\text{T}\alpha_P = \overline{R}_P - R_f - \text{SR}_M \times \sigma_P$.

It is possible to represent these various performance measures on a single graph that looks very similar to Figure 3-7 proposed in Chapter 3.[22]

The figure clearly shows the analogy between the M^2 and the RRAP and their equivalence in terms of portfolio rankings. It also allows us to visually understand the main drawback of using the total risk alpha when comparing portfolios of different risks. In the graph shown in Figure 6-22, portfolio L has a greater Sharpe ratio than portfolio H. This dominance appears clearly when they are compared according to similar risk levels: portfolio L' obtains a higher return than H with the same risk level, and likewise L achieves a higher return than H' for the same risk. Nevertheless, we also obtain that $\text{T}\alpha_H > \text{T}\alpha_L$: thanks to its higher risk, the manager of portfolio H gathers a risk premium that is sufficient to obtain a higher markup with respect to their required return than the manager of portfolio L.

[22]A further and complete graphical comparative analysis between these risk-adjusted performance measures and the analogous ones based on systematic risk is proposed by Scholz and Wilkens (2005).

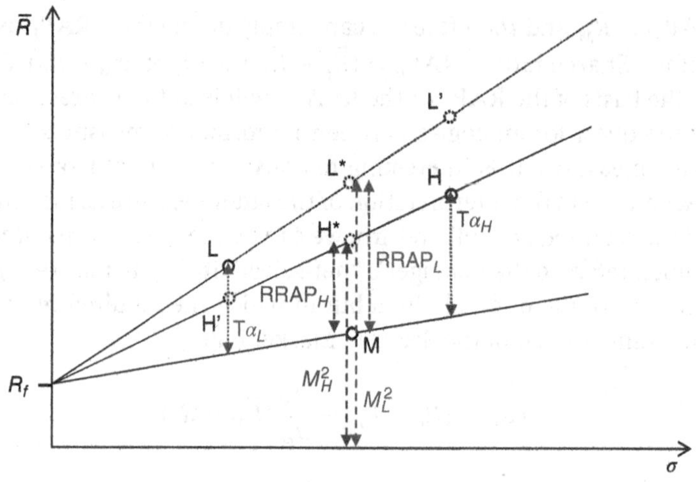

FIGURE 6-22 Graphical representation of the risk-adjusted return transformations of the Sharpe ratio.

XYZ example (continued)

According to their Sharpe ratios, the rankings of the three funds and the market index are the following: Z > M > Y > X. Only Fund Z outperforms the market. Consequently, this is the only fund whose risk-adjusted performance measures will exceed those of the market. Table 6-22 summarizes the results.

TABLE 6-22 XYZ example – Risk-adjusted return transformations of the Sharpe ratio.

Performance	X	Y	Z	M
Sharpe ratio	0.38	0.55	0.96	0.73
Risk-adjusted performance (or M^2)	4.77%	6.29%	9.94%	7.93%
Relative risk-adjusted performance	−3.16%	−1.64%	2.01%	0.00%
Total risk alpha	−2.24%	−1.15%	1.95%	0.00%

Interestingly, for the measures yielding a null performance of the market portfolio (the RRAP and the $T\alpha$), the underperforming funds (Fund X and Fund Y) produce a negative value. This considerably eases their interpretation. Note as well that $T\alpha_Z$ and $RRAP_Z$ are very close to each other because the risk of Fund Z is close to the one of M. This is not the case for the other two funds, whose lower risk leads to a larger difference between their scale-dependent and scale-independent measures.

6.4.1.2 Adjusting risk-adjusted returns for risky interest rates

Because it measures the slope of a straight line, the ability of the Sharpe ratio to appraise portfolio performance is limited if the risk–return relation is not linear. This is the case if the interest rate is applicable to the least risky, but not riskless investment in fixed-income securities. Instead of being a straight line, the Capital Market Line then becomes a concave curve. Furthermore, any combination of a risky portfolio with the fixed-income security also lies on a curve whose curvature mostly depends on the correlation coefficient of their returns. It can even be that the curves might cross each other for two different portfolios.

In such a complex world, the relative risk-adjusted performance and the total return alpha appear to be much more appealing ways to represent the ability of a portfolio manager to beat the market than any avatar of the Sharpe ratio. In particular, the revised Sharpe ratio discussed in Section 6.1.2 (Equation (6-4)) is theoretically interesting but bumps into the impossibility of reflecting the impact of leveraging the portfolio through a constant risk premium. Graham and Harvey (1997) thus propose adaptations of the $RRAP_P$ and the $T\alpha_P$ when the interest rate is not riskless. The authors have simply called their measures according to their initials, namely, $GH1_P$ as the counterpart of the total risk alpha and $GH2_P$ for the relative risk-adjusted performance. These two measures are respectively defined as follows:

$$GH1_P = \overline{R}_P - [w_M^* \overline{R}_M + (1 - w_M^*)\overline{R}_f] \tag{6-67}$$

where $w_M^{*2}\sigma_M^2 + (1 - w_M^{*2})\sigma_f^2 + 2w_M^*(1 - w_M^*)\rho_{Mf}\sigma_M\sigma_f = \sigma_P^2$, which means that the target weight w_M^* invested in the market index is chosen in such a way that the resulting combination with the fixed-income security yields exactly the same risk as portfolio P:

$$GH2_P = [w_P^* \overline{R}_P + (1 - w_P^*)\overline{R}_f] - \overline{R}_M \tag{6-68}$$

where $w_P^{*2}\sigma_P^2 + (1 - w_P^{*2})\sigma_f^2 + 2w_P^*(1 - w_P^*)\rho_{Pf}\sigma_P\sigma_f = \sigma_M^2$, which means that the target weight w_P^* invested in the portfolio P is chosen in such a way that the resulting combination with the fixed-income security yields exactly the same risk as the market index.

Note that for both equations, the target weight bears an analytical solution as the positive root of a second degree polynomial.[23] After some simplifications, w_M^* and w_P^* can be written as follows:

$$w_M^* = \frac{\sigma_f^2 - \rho_{Mf}\sigma_M\sigma_f + \sqrt{\sigma_P^2\sigma_{(M-f)}^2 - \sigma_M^2\sigma_f^2(1 - \rho_{Mf}^2)}}{\sigma_{(M-f)}^2} \tag{6-69a}$$

$$w_P^* = \frac{\sigma_f^2 - \rho_{Pf}\sigma_P\sigma_f + \sqrt{\sigma_M^2\sigma_{(P-f)}^2 - \sigma_P^2\sigma_f^2(1 - \rho_{Pf}^2)}}{\sigma_{(P-f)}^2} \tag{6-69b}$$

[23]The second root of the polynomial is negative for most reasonable parameter values and is therefore economically meaningless.

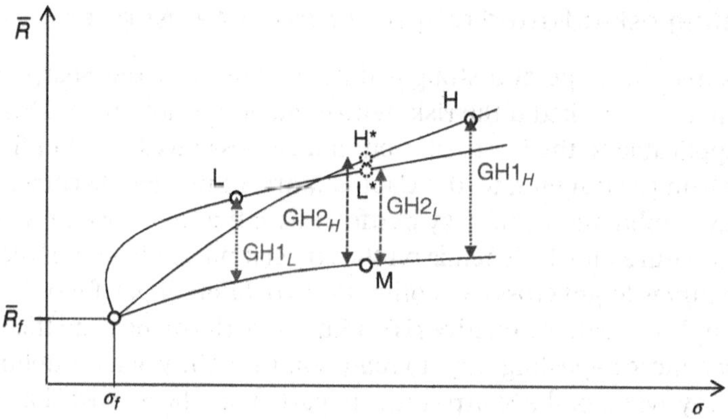

FIGURE 6-23 Graphical representation of the Graham–Harvey measures.

where, like in Section 6.1.2, $\sigma_{(M-f)} \equiv \sigma(R_M - R_f)$ and $\sigma_{(P-f)} \equiv \sigma(R_P - R_f)$ are defined as the tracking error of respectively the market return and portfolio return over the fixed-income security.

The graphical interpretation of the Graham–Harvey ratios features a mixture of Figures 6-5 and 6-22, summarized in Figure 6-23.

Figure 6-23 shows the analogy between the GH performance measures and the ones represented in the previous graph. The GH1_P measure reflects the distance between the portfolio realized and required returns, while the GH2_P neutralizes the effect of portfolio risk and compares its rescaled return with the one of the market index, both having the same volatility.

In this very stylized graph (given that one should expect the volatility of R_f to be rather small), the very different concavity levels of the curves that link the coordinates of the fixed-income security with the ones of portfolios *L* and *H* lead to a drastically different picture than in Figure 6-22. Because of its low (and perhaps even negative) correlation with the fixed-income asset, portfolio *L* enjoys a great benefit of diversification. However, this becomes a double-edged sword when it is leveraged so as to reach a higher risk level. In that case, the weight invested in the fixed-income security is negative, and the diversification benefit largely vanishes. Because portfolio *H* does not experience the same phenomenon, the two curves are not parallel, and they cross each other at a lower risk level than that of the market index. Hence, we have the surprising result that $\text{GH2}_H > \text{GH2}_L$, even though it is clear that $\text{SR}_H < \text{SR}_L$, and as in Figure 6-22, $\text{RRAP}_H < \text{RRAP}_L$. Thus, accounting for the potential variability of the return of the risk-free asset might lead to surprising outcomes.

Under this perspective, the GH1 measure has specific merits compared to GH2: the curve that links the coordinates of the market index and the fixed-income asset is unique and is thus the same for all portfolios. Therefore, the GH1 values are much easier to compare from one portfolio to another, provided that their riskiness is not too remote from each other. Furthermore, one may argue that it is much easier to leverage the market portfolio than an actively managed portfolio, especially when it involves borrowing. Finally, considering the market portfolio as a full equity benchmark, using the GH1 measure usually involves lending (because most portfolios look like *L* in the graph), which many investors are in a position to do without constraint, unlike the case of borrowing.

XYZ example (continued)

The relevant data for the fixed-income security are retrieved from Table 6-1. According to these parameter values, the application of the GH1 and GH2 formulas for the three funds and the market index produces the outputs shown in Table 6-23.

TABLE 6-23 XYZ example – Graham–Harvey performance measures.

Performance		X	Y	Z
GH1	Target weight	71.72%	70.78%	97.01%
	Performance	−2.28%	−1.19%	1.94%
	Difference	−0.04%	−0.04%	−0.01%
GH2	Target weight	147.87%	132.50%	103.00%
	Performance	−2.99%	−1.98%	2.00%
	Difference	0.17%	−0.34%	−0.02%

For each performance measure, the "Difference" row reports the delta between the Graham–Harvey version and the one without interest rate variability. The results are particularly noticeable for Fund X. For the GH1 measure, we obtain $GH1_X - T\alpha_X = (-2.28\%) - (-2.24\%) = -0.04\%$: this result is in the ballpark of the other two funds, with a rather small performance difference when the variability of the interest rate is taken into account. By contrast, $GH2_X - RRAP_X = (-2.99\%) - (-3.16\%) = +0.17\%$. Because of its high correlation with the fixed-income security, a leveraged portfolio involving almost 150% invested in X and a short position of −50% (i.e., borrowing) in the riskless asset generates some diversification that improves the fund's performance. This phenomenon is exactly opposite for Fund Y, whose very negative correlation with the fixed-income security ($\rho_{Yf} = -0.83$) is detrimental in the case of the leveraged portfolio. This explains the deterioration of its GH2 measure in comparison with the RRAP.

6.4.1.3 Changing the inputs in risk-adjusted returns

If it is possible to change the risk measure at the denominator of the Sharpe ratio, then the same adaptation is achievable for its risk-adjusted transformations. The generic formulas for the three adjusted performance measures are always of the same form:

$$\widetilde{\text{RAP}}_P \equiv R_f + \frac{\text{risk}_M}{\text{risk}_P}(\overline{R}_P - R_f) \tag{6-70a}$$

$$\widetilde{\text{RRAP}}_P = \frac{\text{risk}_M}{\text{risk}_P}(\overline{R}_P - R_f) - (\overline{R}_M - R_f) \tag{6-70b}$$

$$\widetilde{\text{T}\alpha}_P = (\overline{R}_P - R_f) - \frac{\text{risk}_P}{\text{risk}_M}(\overline{R}_M - R_f) \tag{6-70c}$$

where risk_i stands for the estimate of the risk of portfolio i ($i = P$ or $i = M$) according to the chosen metric. A noteworthy performance measure belonging to this category is the M^2 measured for downside risk in the spirit of the Sortino ratio (Bacon, 2021), called $\text{SM}^2_P(\underline{R})$, in which $\text{risk}_i \equiv d\sigma_i(\underline{R}) = \sqrt{\frac{1}{T}\sum_{t=1}^{T}(\max(\underline{R} - R_{i,t}, 0))^2}$ for both the portfolio and the market.

Any other risk transformation is possible in that context. Nevertheless, if one wants to keep the original axes of the risk–return graph but wishes to include the information contained in higher moments (skewness and kurtosis), a very useful avatar of the performance measures is the replacement of volatility with its modified version as in Equation (6-13) for both the portfolio and the market, namely, $\text{risk}_i \equiv \text{m}\sigma_i^{(x)} = \sigma_i \times \frac{z^*_{x,i}}{z_x}$.

Another approach to change in inputs in the risk-adjusted performance measures features the direct adaptation of the reward per unit of risk, i.e., the Sharpe ratio itself, in the formulas in the same way as in Equation (6-16). This yields the adapted versions of the measures, which can be written as follows:

$$\text{aRAP}_P = \overline{R}_P + \text{aSR}_P \times (\sigma_M - \sigma_P) \tag{6-71}$$

$$\text{aRRAP}_P = (\overline{R}_P - \overline{R}_M) + \text{aSR}_P \times (\sigma_M - \sigma_P) \tag{6-72}$$

$$\text{aT}\alpha_P = \overline{R}_P - R_f - \text{aSR}_M \times \sigma_P \tag{6-73}$$

where $\text{aSR}_i \equiv \text{SR}_i \times \left(1 + \frac{\mu_{i,3}}{6}\text{SR}_i - \frac{e\mu_{i,4}}{24}\text{SR}_i^2\right)$ for portfolio i ($i = P$ or $i = M$) stands for the adjusted Sharpe ratio. These adjusted performance measures have the advantage of using the portfolio's own adjustments for skewness and kurtosis for the computation of the risk-adjusted performance measures (aRAP_P and aRRAP_P), thereby rewarding or penalizing the portfolio according to its exposure to higher moments, whereas the $\text{aT}\alpha_P$ takes into account the market remuneration of risk through its own higher moments.

6.4.2 Risk-adjusted return performance measures with other types of risk

6.4.2.1 Transforming the Information ratio into a risk-adjusted return

In the context of the CAPM, when a combination of the market portfolio and the risk-free asset is defined as the portfolio benchmark (leading to the specific case of the Appraisal ratio), there exists no such transformation of the Information ratio that bears the interpretation of a risk-adjusted return. This unfortunate outcome is due to the fact that the market portfolio has a zero tracking error with respect to itself, and thus no performance measure analogous to those developed in the previous subsection can be computed. For the same reason, the same shortage of performance measures also holds for whichever benchmark portfolio is directly used for the analysis.

There remains a third case: The comparison of two portfolios P and Q that share the same benchmark. It is possible to consider the differential risk-adjusted performance of one portfolio compared to another one, which we call *incremental relative risk-adjusted performance* of P over Q or iRRAP_{P-Q} according to the same formula as before, but replacing total risk estimates with tracking errors:

$$\text{iRRAP}_{P-Q} = \frac{\sigma_{(Q-B)}}{\sigma_{(P-B)}}(\overline{R}_P - \overline{R}_B) - (\overline{R}_Q - \overline{R}_B) \tag{6-74}$$

where $\sigma_{(j-B)} \equiv \sigma(R_j - R_B)$ stands for the tracking error of portfolio j ($j = P$ or $j = Q$) with respect to its benchmark B whose average return is $\overline{R}_B$. In the context of the CAPM, the measure simplifies to $\text{iRRAP}_{P-Q} = \frac{\sigma_{\varepsilon Q}}{\sigma_{\varepsilon P}}\alpha_P - \alpha_Q$.

Besides this incremental approach, some heuristic approaches can also be adopted in order to capture the essence of the Information ratio in terms of a risk-adjusted return. We propose two adaptations that build on the intuition of Equation (6-51), which splits the total variance into an undiversifiable and a specific component. Instead of defining active risk by the tracking error, we identify the *relative active risk* $\sigma^2_{\varepsilon_P/P}$ by the ratio of the idiosyncratic variance over the total variance of the portfolio returns. The *normalized Excess return* (nER_P) and the *specific Excess return* (sER_P) are both constructed using this notion of relative active risk:

$$\text{nER}_P = \frac{\overline{R}_P - R_f}{\sigma^2_{\varepsilon_P/P}} \tag{6-75}$$

$$\text{sER}_P = (\overline{R}_P - R_f)(1 - \sigma^2_{\varepsilon_P/P}) \tag{6-76}$$

where $\sigma^2_{\varepsilon_P/P} \equiv \frac{\sigma^2_{\varepsilon P}}{\sigma^2_P}$ is the fraction of the total variance of portfolio returns due to idiosyncratic risk.[24]

[24] It is also possible to replace the excess return $\overline{R}_p - R_f$ by the alpha in formulas (6-75) and (6-76), leading to respectively the normalized Information ratio nIR_p and the specific alpha $s\alpha_p$. Note as well that in the special case in which the benchmark is based on the output of a linear regression, we can write the performance measures as $\text{nER}_p = \frac{\overline{R}_P - R_f}{1 - R^2}$ and $\text{sER}_p = (\overline{R}_p - R_f) \times R^2$, where R^2 is the regression R-squared.

Both ratios have the merits of (i) expressing performance as a rate of return, (ii) taking explicitly into account a penalty for the portfolio's exposure to active risk in the equation, and (iii) allowing the comparison of different portfolios that might not share the same benchmark by focusing on the fraction of their active risk rather than its absolute value. They are not specifically backed by a theoretical justification, but because of the third property above, they can be very useful for the analysis of persistence in performance as proposed in Chapter 17.

Another approach to measure the added value of a portfolio manager who chooses to bear some active risk is proposed by Moses, Cheyney, and Veit (1987). Instead of defining a portfolio's specific risk as its tracking error with respect to the benchmark, they view it as the difference between the beta of a perfectly diversified portfolio and the one of the portfolio under study, i.e., $\beta_P^{\text{specific}} = \beta_P^{\text{diversified}} - \beta_P = \frac{\sigma_P}{\sigma_M}(1-\rho_{PM})$. They then consider the portfolio abnormal return (alpha) per unit of specific beta in the spirit of the modified Jensen's alpha. Finally, they normalize their ratio by dividing further $\beta_P^{\text{specific}}$ by the market excess return so as to reflect the normal remuneration of this part of the beta to which the manager has decided to be exposed. Accordingly, their measure of risk-adjusted performance, which we simply call the *normalized alpha*, can be written as

$$\text{n}\alpha_P = \frac{\alpha_P}{\frac{\sigma_P}{\sigma_M}(1-\rho_{PM})} \times (\overline{R}_M - R_f) \tag{6-77}$$

This expression reflects a measure of abnormal return corrected for the portfolio underdiversification and that is scale-independent. Thus, in essence, it can be seen as the return adjusted for specific risk that we were looking after in the introduction of this subsection.

XYZ example (continued)

With the alphas and tracking errors of the three funds relative to their CAPM-based benchmark, we retrieve a two-by-two table of their incremental relative risk-adjusted performance (Table 6-24).

TABLE 6-24 XYZ example – Incremental risk-adjusted performance of the funds relative to each other.

Fund	X	Y	Z
X	0.00%	−0.92%	−3.24%
Y	0.58%	0.00%	−1.68%
Z	1.21%	0.99%	0.00%

The sign of each iRRAP depends on two effects: the difference in alphas and the effect of leveraging through the ratio of standard deviations. In the case of the Funds X, Y, and Z, the difference in their alphas is so large that the picture is always the same: Fund Z dominates Fund Y that dominates Fund X. Nevertheless, the outperformance of Fund Y over X, equal to $\text{iRRAP}_{Y-X} = 0.58\%$, appears to be smaller in absolute value than the underperformance of Fund X over Y, equal to $\text{iRRAP}_{X-Y} = -0.92\%$. This is due to the fact that the tracking error of Y is greater than that of X, and therefore it is necessary to leverage X in order to reach the risk of Y, with a multiplicative effect on X's negative alpha.

The computation of the specific alpha for the funds yields $\text{s}\alpha_X = -1.63\% \times \left(1 - \frac{0.90\%^2}{1{,}81\%^2}\right) = -1.23\%$, $\text{s}\alpha_Y = 0.62\% \times \left(1 - \frac{1.42\%^2}{1.79\%^2}\right) = 0.23\%$, and $\text{s}\alpha_Z = 6.87\% \times \left(1 - \frac{2.42\%^2}{2.47\%^2}\right) = 0.33\%$. The performance of Fund Z is clearly penalized by its low R^2, casting doubt on the validity of the model, and reducing its specific alpha to almost zero.

Finally, the Moses–Cheyney–Veit normalized alphas are close to the specific alphas. They are respectively equal to $\text{n}\alpha_X = \frac{-1.63\%}{\frac{1.81\%}{2.55\%}(1-0.87)} \times (7.93\% - 1.44\%) = -1.12\%$, $\text{n}\alpha_Y = 0.15\%$, and $\text{n}\alpha_Z = 0.59\%$.

6.4.2.2 Accounting for specific and total risk in risk-adjusted return

It is tempting to let different types of risks coexist in a single performance measure that produces a risk-adjusted rate of return. This is the approach proposed by Muralidhar (2000) who adopts a normative approach. He considers an extension of the M^2 measure in which the portfolio is held together with the benchmark and the risk-free asset so as to maximize the total return of the global portfolio G, keep the same volatility as the benchmark σ_B, and respect an upper bound on the tracking error TE_G^*. The solution of the program is the M-cube (M_P^3) whose expression is given by

$$M_P^3 = a_3\overline{R}_P + b_3\overline{R}_B + (1 - a_3 - b_3)R_f \tag{6-78}$$

where $a_3 = \frac{\sigma_B}{\sigma_P}\sqrt{\frac{1-\rho_{GB}^2}{1-\rho_{PB}^2}}$ and $b_3 = \rho_{GB} - a_3\frac{\sigma_P}{\sigma_B}\rho_{PB}$ in which $\rho_{GB} = 1 - \frac{(\text{TE}_G^*)^2}{2\sigma_B^2}$ stands for the optimized correlation between the global portfolio and the benchmark. In the context of the CAPM, we simply change the variables by $\rho_{PB} = \rho_{PM}$, $\sigma_B = \beta_P\sigma_M$, and $\overline{R}_B = \beta_P\overline{R}_M + (1 - \beta_P)R_f$.

It is obviously paradoxical to design an *ex post* performance measure on the basis of a sophisticated *ex ante* optimization program. Bacon (2021) criticizes the ambition to simultaneously deliver a target absolute rate of return and to control the tracking error. Furthermore, the measurement of performance requires a discretionary choice of the target tracking error TE_G^*. If this target is too large compared to the benchmark return, there can even be no solution for the optimized correlation ρ_{GB}. However, in spite of these drawbacks, the M^3 approach has two appealing features: (i) it allows us to appraise the performance of actively managed portfolios in the context of various investors' levels of residual risk aversion (as defined in Chapter 4); and (ii) it explicitly takes into account the structure of the correlation between the portfolio and its benchmark in the computation of the M^2, to which Muralidhar (2000) directly refers.

XYZ example (continued)

We adopt the portfolio optimization program underlying the M^3 measure, considering the benchmark of each fund as the one retrieved from the CAPM. The graph shown in Figure 6-24 plots the evolution of each fund's M^3 as a function of the global portfolio's target tracking error TE_G^*.

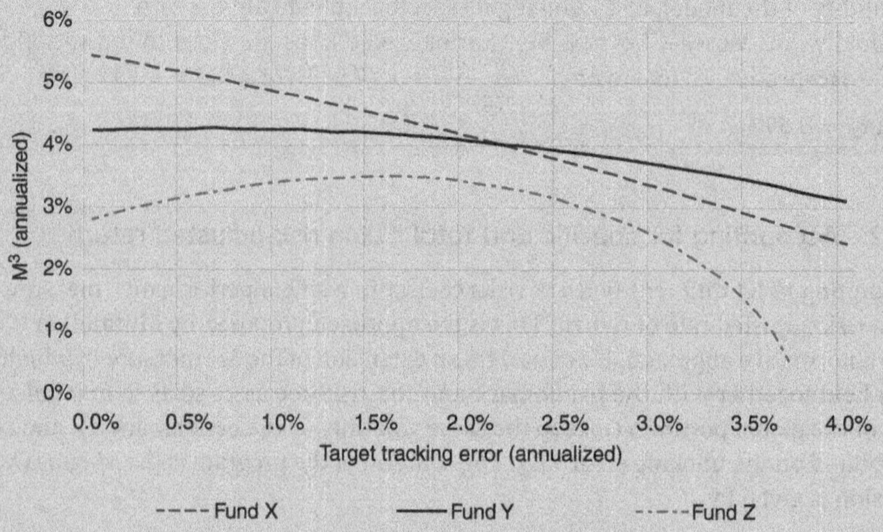

FIGURE 6-24 XYZ example – M^3 as a function of the target tracking error.

For Funds X and Y, the M^3 is a decreasing function of TE_G^*. This is rather logical as the market portfolio has a better Sharpe ratio than these two funds. "Forcing" a certain level of tracking error therefore leads to a deterioration of the risk-adjusted performance in both cases. Interestingly, Fund X dominates Fund Y for low tracking errors until a break-even level, where $TE_G^* = 2.14\%$, in which case $M_X^3 = M_Y^3 = 4.04\%$. For low target tracking errors, the higher correlation of Fund X with the market is a valuable characteristic as it entails investing a larger proportion of the benchmark, with a more attractive return, in the optimized portfolio than for Fund Y.

Fund Z features the expected behavior for a fund whose Sharpe ratio dominates that of its benchmark: There appears to be a maximum achievable level of global portfolio return at $TE_G^* = 1.53\%$, in which case $M_Z^3 = 3.50\%$. Paradoxically, in spite of its higher Sharpe ratio than the market, the M^3 of portfolios made up with this fund is disappointing. This is due to its very high tracking error, and thus it is necessary to put a large weight in the risk-free asset, whose return is lower than both M and Z, in order to satisfy the target tracking error. This example clearly shows that the optimization program imposed for the computation of the M^3, which imposes a level of tracking error, may lead to very counterintuitive results and is probably dominated by the normative approach of Treynor and Black discussed in Chapter 4.

6.4.3 A complete synoptic view of performance measures

Thanks to the material developed in this section, we can eventually redesign as completely as possible the synoptic table of classical performance measures introduced in Chapter 4. The new version, bringing together the original measures and some of their risk-adjusted return counterparts, looks as shown in Table 6-25.[25]

Even though the M^2 is sometimes considered as the counterpart of the modified Jensen's alpha in the context of total risk, it is indeed the relative version (the relative risk-adjusted performance) that bears the same interpretation. The total risk alpha rightfully bears its name, but it is (like its famous systematic risk-based counterpart) dependent on the risk scale.

Regarding specific risk, we have included the Moses–Cheyney–Veit normalized alpha measure in the table as it is the one that meets the necessary three conditions: (i) being based on a measure of specific risk, (ii) being expressed as a percentage, and (iii) being

TABLE 6-25 Complete synoptic table of the classical performance measures.

Measurement dimension		Risk dimension		
Unit	*Scale*	*Total risk*	*Systematic risk*	*Specific risk*
Decimal	Dependent			
(%/%)	Independent	SR_P	mTR_P, $am\alpha_P$	IR_P, AR_P
Percentage	Dependent	$T\alpha_P$	α_P	sER_P
(%)	Independent	$RRAP_P$	TR_P, $m\alpha_P$	$n\alpha_P$

[25] A very similar, although slightly different, classification of performance measures is discussed in the "jigsaw puzzle" approach of Scholz and Wilkens (2005).

insensitive to portfolio leverage. Nevertheless, the way specific risk is estimated in that context (i.e., through the difference between two betas) does not make it fully comparable with the Information ratio.[26]

This table is still far from exhaustively covering the spectrum of performance measures. It "only" deals with the classical ones, i.e., the ones that are fully compatible with the original CAPM. In Chapters 7 to 10, we develop many more ways to appraise portfolio performance, and the whole synthesis – together with the comparison with other authors' approaches to classify performance measures – is presented in Chapter 11.

Key Takeaways and Equations

- The Sharpe ratio is the classical performance measure that has experienced the most numerous refinements. They are of four kinds, according to the corresponding ingredients of its generic equation $\text{SR}_P = \frac{\text{average portfolio return}-\text{risk-free rate}}{\text{portfolio volatility}} \times$ (no) adjustment factor:
  - The Sharpe ratio with adapted portfolio returns adopts its geometric form. It can be combined with the original (arithmetic) one according to the investor's investment horizon H as

$$\overline{\text{SR}}_P = \frac{H-T}{H-1}\text{SR}_P^g + \frac{T-1}{H-1}\text{SR}_P \qquad \text{(6-3)}$$

  - When the interest rate is assumed to be risky, the revised Sharpe ratio corresponds to a special case of the Information ratio:

$$\text{rSR}_P = \frac{\overline{R}_P - \overline{R}_f}{\sigma_{(P-f)}} \qquad \text{(6-4)}$$

  - There are several adaptations of the total risk measure that do not alter its interpretation as portfolio volatility but aim to deliver a corrected version of the measure as $\text{SR}'_P = \frac{\overline{R}_P-\overline{R}_f}{\sigma_P^{\text{corrected}}}$. The volatility can be adjusted for autocorrelation, for conditional heteroscedasticity, or for higher moments (skewness and kurtosis). In that case, the use of the Cornish–Fisher expansion leads to the estimation of the modified volatility, useful for performance measurement, that can be written as

$$\text{m}\sigma_P^{(x)} = \sigma_P \times \frac{z_{x,P}^*}{z_x} \qquad \text{(6-13)}$$

[26] We will see that, in the context of the performance decomposition proposed by Fama (1972) in Chapter 13, there is another, intuitive way to reconcile the three risk dimensions in a single framework.

- The two important direct adjustments of the Sharpe ratio are driven by (i) the portfolio's efficiency level, with the efficiency measure:

$$\mathrm{eSR}_P = \mathrm{SR}_P \times \left(\frac{\overline{R}_P^* - \overline{R}_f}{\sigma_P} \right)^{-1} = \frac{\overline{R}_P - \overline{R}_f}{\overline{R}_P^* - \overline{R}_f} \qquad (6\text{-}15)$$

and (ii) the portfolio return's higher moments, with the adjusted Sharpe ratio:

$$\mathrm{aSR}_P = \mathrm{SR}_P \times \left(1 + \frac{\mu_{P,3}}{6}\mathrm{SR}_P - \frac{e\mu_{P,4}}{24}\mathrm{SR}_P^2 \right) \qquad (6\text{-}16)$$

- Alterations of the Sharpe ratio aim to replace a measure of reward (numerator) or risk (denominator), or both.
  - The "safety first" approach of Roy (1952) introduces a notion of reservation rate or "disaster level" $\underline{R}$, which is investor-specific, as a substitute for the risk-free rate. The Roy ratio can be written as

$$\mathrm{RoyR}_P = \frac{\overline{R}_P - \underline{R}}{\sigma_P} \qquad (6\text{-}19)$$

  - Some measures replace the portfolio volatility with an alternative distance metric, such as the MAD ratio, the Minimax ratio, the Gini ratio, and the Range ratio.
  - Some measures replace the portfolio volatility with an estimate of downside risk. The most renowned of such performance measures is the Sortino ratio

$$\mathrm{SorR}_P = \frac{\overline{R}_P - \underline{R}}{d\sigma_P(\underline{R})} \qquad (6\text{-}29)$$

  - Some measures replace the portfolio volatility with an estimate of drawdown risk. The most renowned of such performance measures is the Calmar ratio

$$\mathrm{CalR}_P = \frac{\overline{R}_P - R_f}{\mathrm{dd}_{P,\max}} \qquad (6\text{-}32)$$

  - Some measures replace the portfolio volatility with an estimate of extreme risk. The most renowned of such performance measures is the modified Sharpe ratio

$$\mathrm{mVR}_P^{1-x} = \frac{\overline{R}_P - R_f}{\mathrm{mVaR}_P^{(1-x)}} \qquad (6\text{-}47)$$

(continued)

(continued)

- There are no substantial alterations of the systematic risk-based measures. Nevertheless, replacing the beta with the systematic part of the volatility, we define the alternative Treynor ratio and the alternative modified Jensen's alpha:

$$\text{aTR}_P = \frac{\overline{R}_P - R_f}{\sigma_{\rho P}} \tag{6-52}$$

$$\text{am}\alpha_P = \frac{\alpha_P}{\sigma_{\rho P}} \tag{6-53}$$

- Most refinements and alterations of the Information ratio are very similar to the ones of the Sharpe ratio.
- In order to ease the interpretation of the Sharpe ratio, Modigliani and Modigliani (1997) propose a version expressed in terms of risk-adjusted performance. Their measure, called "risk-adjusted performance" and subsequently renamed "M^2" as a tribute to the authors, can be written as

$$\text{RAP}_P \equiv M_P^2 = R_f + \frac{\sigma_M}{\sigma_P}(\overline{R}_P - R_f) \tag{6-63}$$

- A proper comparison of risk-adjusted returns based on total risk with the Jensen's alpha and the modified Jensen's alpha is provided by two modifications of the M^2, the relative risk-adjusted performance and the total risk alpha:

$$\text{RRAP}_P = \text{RAP}_P - \text{RAP}_M = \frac{\sigma_M}{\sigma_P}(\overline{R}_P - R_f) - (\overline{R}_M - R_f) \tag{6-64}$$

$$\text{T}\alpha_P = (\overline{R}_P - R_f) - \frac{\sigma_P}{\sigma_M}(\overline{R}_M - R_f) \tag{6-65}$$

- An adjustment for random interest rates is proposed by Graham and Harvey (1997) through their GH1 and GH2 measures:

$$\text{GH1}_P = \overline{R}_P - [w_M^* \overline{R}_M + (1 - w_M^*)\overline{R}_f] \tag{6-67}$$

$$\text{GH2}_P = [w_P^* \overline{R}_P + (1 - w_P^*)\overline{R}_f] - \overline{R}_M \tag{6-68}$$

- Risk-adjusted versions of the Information ratio do not exist per se, but it is possible to compare two actively managed portfolios on the basis of their tracking error with respect to a common benchmark through the incremental relative risk-adjusted performance:

$$\text{iRRAP}_{P-Q} = \frac{\text{TE}_Q}{\text{TE}_P}(\overline{R}_P - \overline{R}_B) - (\overline{R}_Q - \overline{R}_B) \tag{6-74}$$

- The performance measure whose interpretation is the closest to the one of the scale-independent risk-adjusted abnormal return in the spirit of the modified Jensen's alpha is the normalized alpha proposed by Moses, Cheyney, and Veit (1987):

$$n\alpha_P = \frac{\alpha_P}{\frac{\sigma_P}{\sigma_M}(1-\rho_{PM})} \times (\overline{R}_M - R_f) \tag{6-77}$$

- The RRAP (for total risk) and the normalized alpha (for specific risk) are the two performance measures that complete the modified Jensen's alpha (for systematic risk) in that they simultaneously meet three conditions: (i) being based on a measure of specific risk, (ii) being expressed as a percentage, and (iii) being insensitive to portfolio leverage.

REFERENCES

Ang, J. S., and J. H. Chua (1979), Composite measures for the evaluation of investment performance. *Journal of Financial and Quantitative Analysis*, Vol. 14, pp. 361–384.

Artzner, P, Delbaen, F., Eber, J.-M., and D. Heath (1999), Coherent measures of risk. *Mathematical Finance*, Vol. 9, pp. 203–228.

Bacon, C. R. (2021), *Practical Risk-Adjusted Performance Measurement, 2nd Edition.* Wiley, Wiley Finance Series.

Blume, M. (1974), Unbiased estimates of long-run expected rates of return. *Journal of the American Statistical Association*, Vol. 69, pp. 634–638.

Bollerslev, T. (1986), Generalized autoregressive conditional heteroskedasticity. *Journal of Econometrics*, Vol. 31, pp. 307–327.

Bradford, D., and D. Siliski (2016), Performance drawdowns in asset management: Extending drawdown analysis to active returns. *Journal of Performance Measurement*, Vol. 21 (1), pp. 34–48.

Burke, G. (1994), A sharper Sharpe ratio. *Futures*, Vol. 23 (3), p. 56.

Cantaluppi, L., and R. Hug (2000), Efficiency ratio: A new methodology for performance measurement. *Journal of Investing*, Vol. 9 (2), pp. 1–7.

Caporin, M., and F. Lisi (2011), Comparing and selecting performance measures using rank correlations. *Economics, The Open-Access, Open-Assessment E-Journal*, Vol. 5 (2011–10), pp. 1–34.

Caporin, M., Jannin, G. M., Lisi F., and B. B. Maillet (2013), A survey of the four families of performance measures. *Journal of Economic Surveys*, Vol. 28, pp. 916–942.

Cavenaile, L., and T. Lejeune (2012), A note on the use of modified Value-at-Risk. *Journal of Alternative Investments*, Vol. 14 (4), pp. 79–83.

Cogneau, P., and G. Hübner (2009a), The (more than) 100 ways to measure portfolio performance: Part 1: Standardized risk-adjusted measures. *Journal of Performance Measurement*, Vol. 13 (4), pp. 56–71.

Cogneau, P., and G. Hübner (2009b), The (more than) 100 ways to measure portfolio performance: Part 2: Special measures and comparison. *Journal of Performance Measurement*, Vol. 14 (1), pp. 56–69.

Cornish, E. A., and R. Fisher (1938), Moments and cumulants in the specification of distribution. *Review of the International Statistical Institute*, Vol. 5, pp. 307–320.

Dowd, K. (1999), A Value at Risk approach to risk–return analysis. *The Journal of Portfolio Management*, Vol. 25 (4), pp. 60–67.

Engle, R. F. (1982), Autoregressive conditional heteroscedasticity with estimates of variance of United Kingdom inflation. *Econometrica*, Vol. 50, pp. 987–1008.

Fama, E. F. (1972), Components of investment performance. *The Journal of Finance*, Vol. 27, pp. 551–567.

Favre, L., and J.-A. Galeano (2002), Mean-modified Value-at-Risk optimization with hedge funds. *Journal of Alternative Investments*, Vol. 5 (2), pp. 21–25.

Graham, J. R., and C. R. Harvey (1997), Grading the performance of market-timing newsletters. *Financial Analysts Journal*, Vol. 53 (6), pp. 54–66.

Kandel, S., and R. F. Stambaugh (1995), Portfolio inefficiency and the cross-section of expected returns. *The Journal of Finance*, Vol. 50, pp. 157–184.

Kaplan, P. D., and J. A. Knowles (2004), Kappa: A generalized downside risk-adjusted performance measure. *Journal of Performance Measurement*, Vol. 8 (3), pp. 42–54.

Kazemi, H., Schneeweis, T., and R. Gupta (2004), Omega as a measure of performance. *Journal of Performance Measurement*, Vol. 8 (3), pp. 16–25.

Kestner, L. N. (1996), Getting a handle on true performance. *Futures*, Vol. 25 (1), pp. 44–46.

Konno, H., and H. Yamakazi (1991), Mean-absolute deviation portfolio optimization model and its application to Tokyo stock market. *Management Science*, Vol. 37, pp. 519–531.

Krimm, S, Scholz, H., and M. Wilkens (2012), The Sharpe ratio's market climate bias: Theoretical and empirical evidence from US equity mutual funds. *Journal of Asset Management*, Vol. 13, pp. 227–242.

Lin, A., and P. H. Chou (2003), The pitfall of using Sharpe ratio. *Finance Letters*, Vol. 1, pp. 84–89.

Lo, A. W. (2002), The statistics of Sharpe ratios. *Financial Analysts Journal*, Vol. 58 (4), pp. 36–52.

Martin, P., and B. Mc Cann (1989), *The Investor's Guide to Fidelity Funds: Winning Strategies for Mutual Fund Investors*. John Wiley & Sons.

Martin, R. D., Rachev, S., and F. Siboulet (2003), Phi-alpha optimal portfolios and extreme risk management. *Wilmott*, Vol. 2003 (6), pp. 70–83.

Modigliani, F., and L. Modigliani (1997), Risk-adjusted performance. *The Journal of Portfolio Management*, Vol. 23 (2), pp. 45–54.

Moses, E. A., Cheyney, J. M., and E. T. Veit (1987), A new and more complete performance measure. *The Journal of Portfolio Management*, Vol. 13 (2), pp. 24–33.

Muralidhar, A. S. (2000), Risk-adjusted performance: The correlation correction. *Financial Analysts Journal*, Vol. 56 (5), pp. 63–71.

Pézier, J., and A. White (2008), The relative merits of alternative investments in passive portfolios. *Journal of Alternative Investments*, Vol. 10 (4), pp. 37–49.

Roy, A. D. (1952), Safety first and the holding of assets. *Econometrica*, Vol. 20, pp. 431–449.

Scholz, H., and M. Wilkens (2005), A jigsaw puzzle of basic risk-adjusted performance measures. *Journal of Performance Measurement*, Vol. 9 (Spring), pp. 57–64.

Sharpe, W. F. (1994), The Sharpe ratio. *The Journal of Portfolio Management*, Vol. 21 (Fall), pp. 45–58.

Sortino, F. A., and R. van der Meer (1991), Downside risk. *The Journal of Portfolio Management*, Vol. 17 (4), pp. 27–31.

Statman, M. (1987), How many stocks make a diversified portfolio? *Journal of Financial and Quantitative Analysis*, Vol. 22, pp. 353–363.

Watanabe, Y. (2006), Is Sharpe ratio still effective? *Journal of Performance Measurement*, Vol. 11 (Fall), pp. 55–66.

Watanabe, Y. (2014), New Prospect ratio: Application to hedge funds with higher order moments. *Journal of Performance Measurement*, Vol. 19 (Fall), pp. 41–53.

Yitzhaki, S. (1982), Stochastic dominance, mean variance and Gini's mean difference. *American Economic Review*, Vol. 72, pp. 178–185.

Young, M. R. (1998), A minimax portfolio selection rule with linear programming solution. *Management Science*, Vol. 44, pp. 673–683.

Young, T. W. (1991), Calmar ratio: A smoother tool. *Futures*, Vol. 20 (1), p. 40.

Ziemba, W. T. (2005), The symmetric downside-risk Sharpe ratio. *The Journal of Portfolio Management*, Vol. 32 (1), pp. 108–122.

CHAPTER 7

Performance Measurement in Multifactor Models

INTRODUCTION

The Capital Asset Pricing Model (CAPM) underlies the most famous performance measures used by researchers and practitioners. Nevertheless, using a simple linear relation between the portfolio return and the one of a market index, be it highly relevant, often proves to be insufficient to properly capture the causes of the portfolio's required return. Starting with Ross's (1976) Arbitrage Pricing Theory (APT), a vast literature has managed this issue over the years by proposing linear relations that are similar to the CAPM one but with multiple factors (generally between three and five) instead of one. These so-called *multifactor (linear) models* essentially belong to three main families. The first one directly derives from the APT and attempts to identify macroeconomic or statistical factors using the argument of the absence of arbitrage in financial markets. The second focuses on the fundamental characteristics of listed firms and tries to relate them to well-documented market anomalies. The third, probably most pragmatic one, has no other ambition than to try to explain as well as possible portfolio returns through the use of a passive one replicated with market indexes. Because it is important to find one's way in this bushy literature, we devote a significant part of this chapter to a discussion of the ins and outs of a model's choice.

Among the classical portfolio performance measures examined in Chapter 3, the one that bears the most natural extension in this context is Jensen's alpha. The *multifactor alpha* essentially retains the same interpretation, but also the strengths and weaknesses, as its CAPM counterpart. Perhaps less famous, the *multifactor modified alpha* also provides an insightful extension of the modified Jensen's alpha (or, equivalently, the Treynor ratio) in the richer context of models with multiple explanatory variables. Remarkably enough, this measure is also relatively simple to compute and interpret, which makes it a valuable add-on to the manager's or analyst's toolkit.

Even though the definitions of the classical Sharpe and Information ratios do not depend on the type of model used in order to explain portfolio returns, we also propose in this chapter how to measure performance based on total and specific risks when the self-reported portfolio benchmark differs from the analytical benchmark that underlies the multifactor regression. In that context, it is also important to stress that the use of a single-factor model could lead to performance measures that may differ from the CAPM Jensen's alpha or modified Jensen's alpha.

Finally, as a kind of transition toward Chapter 8 that studies performance measurement in the context of market timing, we introduce the family of conditional multifactor models and their associated ways to measure portfolio performance.

The Kay Faktory Fund (KFF) example

The KFF is an actively managed portfolio belonging to the "medium allocation" category. The fund is allowed to invest in world equities and in investment-grade bonds, with the possibility of using cash to leverage or deleverage the portfolio. Its self-reported benchmark is a passively indexed portfolio with the following weights: 30% Equities-Europe, 10% Equities-North America, 5% Equities-Japan, 5% Equities-Rest of World, 40% Bonds-Developed, and 10% Bonds-Emerging Markets. In the fund's home currency, the interest rate is 1.8% per year (15 basis points per month).

The fund has existed for the past three years. The summary statistics of the fund and the relevant stock and bond index monthly returns are summarized in Table 7-1. The indexes have been ordered by decreasing order of correlation with the fund (Equities-North America, Equities-Japan, Equities-Rest of World, Bonds-Developed, Equities-Europe, and Bonds-Emerging Markets).

TABLE 7-1 KFF example – Means, volatilities, and correlations with the KFF fund.

	KFF	Eq-N.Am.	Eq-Jap	Eq-RoW	Bd-Dev	Eq-Eur	Bd-EM
Mean return	0.91%	0.67%	0.88%	0.93%	0.26%	0.59%	0.22%
Standard deviation	2.69%	4.77%	5.20%	5.42%	1.68%	4.49%	1.15%
Correlation with fund		81.90%	77.75%	75.66%	66.73%	64.58%	10.51%

The outcome of the linear regressions, estimated through the ordinary least-squares (OLS) method, of the fund's excess returns over different asset classes is summarized in Table 7-2.

TABLE 7-2 KFF example – Coefficients of the multiple linear regressions.

	Intercept	Eq-N.Am.	Eq-Jap	Eq-RoW	Bd-Dev	Eq-Eur	Bd-EM	R^2
Coefficient (standard deviation)	0.52% (0.26%)	0.46 (0.06)						67.1%
	0.50% (0.27%)	0.39 (0.15)	0.07 (0.14)					67.4%
	0.48% (0.27%)	0.30 (0.18)	0.07 (0.14)	0.09 (0.10)				68.2%
	0.49% (0.27%)	0.25 (0.18)	0.07 (0.13)	0.08 (0.10)	0.29 (0.22)			69.9%
	0.50% (0.25%)	0.05 (0.20)	0.02 (0.13)	0.05 (0.10)	0.71 (0.30)	0.24 (0.12)		73.3%
	0.48% (0.26%)	0.06 (0.20)	0.03 (0.14)	0.06 (0.10)	0.62 (0.46)	0.23 (0.14)	0.10 (0.37)	73.4%

Each cell reports the estimated regression coefficient and the standard deviation of this estimate. The first row corresponds to a regression with a single factor (Equities-Europe), the second row uses a second factor (Equities-North America), and so on. The incremental order corresponds to the same ordering as in Table 7-1 and does not necessarily correspond to the best possible ordering of the factors to maximize the explanatory power of the model (which will be examined through the development of the example).

From this table, we can observe that the fund has delivered a positive average return (intercept) beyond the fraction of its returns that are explained by the regression model. The material of this chapter helps determine what information can be inferred from this kind of data and analysis.

7.1 TYPES OF LINEAR MULTIFACTOR MODELS

7.1.1 Defining linear multifactor models

7.1.1.1 From the CAPM to factor models

The CAPM introduced in Chapter 2 displays many advantages (derivation from equilibrium, simplicity, elegance, ...), but also some major drawbacks, mostly from a practical standpoint. Roll's (1977) famous critique outlines the quasi-impossibility of identifying the true market portfolio and to perform adequate tests of the theory. Following this line of thought, the CAPM empirically boils down to a postulated affine relation between two financial assets whose returns co-vary with each other. In other words, it is merely a one-factor model of the form

$$R_{i,t} = a_i + b_i F_t + \varepsilon_{i,t} \tag{7-1}$$

where $R_{i,t}$ represents the return of asset i at time t, F_t is the return of the factor, $\varepsilon_{i,t}$ is the residual term of the model with $E(\varepsilon_i) = 0$ and $Cov(\varepsilon_i, F) = 0$, and a_i and b_i represent the intercept and the slope of the regression line.[1]

Linking this expression with the market model, we can interpret F_t as the excess return of the candidate market portfolio, denoted by $R_{M,t} - R_f$ in the context of the CAPM, the slope coefficient b_i is equivalent to the asset beta β_i, and the intercept a_i relates to Jensen's alpha defined in Chapter 3 by the identity $a_i = \alpha_i + R_f(1 - \beta_i)$. The residual return $\varepsilon_{i,t}$ reflects the specific risk of the asset.

Reducing the CAPM to a simple linear model with a single factor underlines its empirical shortcomings. Since Equation (7-1) is supposed to reflect a causality relation between the factor and the asset returns, it is natural to suspect that other factors, beyond a market index, may also explain part of the variability of the returns over time. An interesting indicator in that respect is the regression's R-squared (R^2), which represents the proportion of the variance of returns that is explained by the regression model. If the R^2 is low, it is reasonable to anticipate that the addition of one or more explanatory variables might potentially explain a larger proportion of the asset return variance. In other words, increasing the number of factors could lead to a significant improvement in the explanatory power of the model. This, in turn, would bring several other advantages in the context of portfolio management:

- It allows us to understand the underlying drivers of the returns during the time window of the analysis. This sheds light on the risks taken by the portfolio manager to achieve their returns.
- It permits the mapping of the outcomes of a particular portfolio strategy to different sources of systematic risk, with their associated sensitivities.
- Last but not least, it makes it possible to identify the value created by a portfolio manager over a passive investment with a better precision than with a single explanatory variable. Thus, identifying an accurate multifactor model enhances the appraisal of the genuine performance of a portfolio manager.

If a set of K distinct factors are included in the regression model, then Equation (7-1) bears a multifactor linear extension that takes the following form, which matches the generic definition of a multifactor model provided in Equation (2-47) of Chapter 2:

$$R_{i,t} = a_i + \sum_{k=1}^{K} b_{i,k} F_{k,t} + \varepsilon_{i,t} \tag{7-2}$$

[1] In the general formulation of a factor model, $E(F) = 0$ and thus $a_i = E(R_i)$. Nevertheless, to ease the exposition, we drop this technical requirement in our developments.

where each $b_{i,k}$ represents the asset's linear return sensitivity (also known as the exposure) to the kth factor and $F_{k,t}$ stands for the realization of the corresponding factor return at time t. The interpretations of a_i and $\varepsilon_{i,t}$ are unchanged.

It is usually more convenient to express Equation (7-2) in excess returns:

$$R_{i,t} - R_f = \alpha_i^{\mathrm{MF}} + \sum_{k=1}^{K} \beta_{i,k}(F_{k,t} - R_f) + \varepsilon_{i,t} \tag{7-3}$$

where each $\beta_{i,k}$ represents the "factor beta" and α_i^{MF} is the portfolio's incremental (or abnormal) return that is analyzed in more detail in the next section.

In general, the specification of a K-factor model such as the one of Equation (7-3) poses two main challenges: the choice of the number of factors and the identification of each factor. We discuss these two issues below.

7.1.1.2 Determining the optimal number of factors

There is nowadays a large consensus that considers a single factor is in general insufficient to adequately explain the variability of asset returns. On the other hand, in order to explain differences in the return generating process of N assets, it would be useless to consider N distinct factors because they would not explain any commonality at all.

In general, there is a trade-off to be found between parsimony – the smaller the number of factors, the more meaningful each systematic risk exposure, and exhaustiveness – if a relevant source of systematic risk that is priced on the financial market is omitted in the model, its absence contaminates all coefficients as well as the residual term, inducing potential biases and incorrect statistical inference. Because of this latter issue, one may be tempted to inflate the number of explanatory factors in order to ensure that no relevant source of risk will be missed. Nevertheless, adding superfluous factors to the model is not a good idea as they could destroy most of the economic insight, introduce some risk premiums without economic significance, and blur the individual interpretation of the coefficients through collinearity issues.[2]

The optimal number of factors that should be used indeed depends on both spatial (asset classes and number of securities considered)[3] and temporal dimensions (the time window used for the analysis). Hence, there is no "one-size-fits-all" definite number. However, as the financial research evolves, there seems to be a convergence toward a relatively thin range of acceptable values for K when a homogeneous set of financial assets (for instance, US equities) is considered:

- From the theoretical standpoint of the maximization of the investor's expected utility, the number of factors should correspond to the number of moments of the distribution of returns for which a "representative investor" would express clear preferences. The CAPM is consistent with investors showing some aversion for the variance

[2] When the focus is on performance measurement, a dissonant point of view is defended by Lewellen (2022), as discussed hereunder.

[3] See for instance the extensive review by Cazalet and Roncalli (2014).

of returns (second moment). Kraus and Litzenberger (1976) and Fang and Lai (1997), among others, provide evidence that equity investors like the skewness (third moment) and dislike the kurtosis (fourth moment) of returns. Logically, it should be possible to find factors associated with these moments. Mitton and Vorkink (2007) successfully extend the analysis to the case of the "lottery investor," who expresses a preference for idiosyncratic skewness. Finally, behavioral finance opens up the way to a different structure of preferences depending on whether asset returns are above or below a certain threshold (see Chapter 10), leading to a potential additional corresponding factor. Thus, there seems to be a reasonable scope for three to five factors that would encompass the spectrum of investors' preferences over risk.

- Some researchers have strived to identify the common drivers of the variance–covariance matrix of asset returns. The most famous of such attempts are probably the papers by Roll and Ross (1980), who identify at most four distinct "priced" dimensions in this matrix, and then by Chen, Roll, and Ross (1986), who propose five macroeconomic factors to encompass these dimensions. Bai and Ng (2002) present a simple method to identify the optimal number of factors based on information criteria and propose only two relevant factors in most cases. Later, other researchers, such as Ericsson and Karlsson (2004) or Hwang and Lu (2007), have systematically screened multiple possible specifications using a large set of factors and also reached the conclusion that a very limited set of factors (typically three or four, depending on the sample and time window considered) prevails in most cases.
- Finally, letting the market speak, we can simply observe which are the leading multifactor models in the financial literature. Several famous models have become very popular, all with a limited number of factors: four for the models of Cremers, Petajisto, and Zitzewitz (2012), Hou, Xue, and Zhang (2015) and Stambaugh and Yuan (2016), and five for the model of Fama and French (2015). In their comparative study of 10 widely used multifactor models, Ahmed, Bu, and Tsvetanov (2019) do not provide a number of desirable factors outside that range.

Thus, in many cases, it appears that no more – and perhaps even fewer – than five factors are sufficient in order to explain most of the cross-sectional variation of the expected returns of a relatively homogeneous group of financial assets. There are, however, three noticeable exceptions to this consensual finding. First, for some specific asset classes like hedge funds, it can be necessary to inflate the number of factors in order to address the variety of "alternative betas" that hedge fund managers tend to adopt with their non-standard strategies.[4] Second, some multifactor models are developed with a different ambition of explaining the sources of variability of stock returns. This is the case for the so-called style analysis (discussed hereunder), whose major objective is to create a tradable passive portfolio that mimics, as well as possible, the behavior of an active one. Third, as Lewellen (2022) shows, inflating the number

[4] We discuss that in detail in Chapter 12 devoted to performance measurement for specific asset classes.

of factors, even with potentially redundant ones, can be helpful in order to estimate portfolio performance more accurately. His argument is that if the specific focus is on the intercept of the regression equation (7-3), adding superfluous factors does not really harm inference but potentially improves the efficiency of the estimator.

Finally, it is also worth pointing out that, in order to explain the returns of assets belonging to very different asset classes and regions of the world, it might be necessary to use different groups of factors that correspond to the levels of segmentation of the financial markets considered. We study the influence of this type of situation on performance measurement later in this chapter.

7.1.1.3 Identifying the factors

Given the relatively small number of factors that supposedly explain most of the cross-sectional variation of asset returns, identifying them properly is a crucial challenge. As discussed in the remainder of this section, there are several families of models that propose very different ways to construct or identify the factors. Nevertheless, we can identify four common desirable properties that should be met by any multifactor model aiming to explain how asset returns are generated in the financial market.

1. *Feasibility*: Whichever factors are included in the model, it must be possible to unequivocally and quickly construct them and compute their returns using transparent and publicly available data. As they are supposed to reflect common sources of returns for a large array of assets, this property is a necessary condition for the applicability of the model. It explains why, for instance, models that build factors through the application of statistical methods must map these constructs to financial or economic variables.
2. *Intuitiveness*: A multifactor model is supposed to reflect a causality relationship between an explained variable (the asset return) and a set of K explanatory variables (the factors). Causality is stronger than mere covariation: It is possible to find, by chance, many variables whose behavior is statistically close to one or a combination of the true factors. In order to avoid the *a priori* suspicion of a spurious causality, each of the selected factors should thus fulfill its economic role and provide a valid reason for its presence.
3. *Parsimony*: The number of factors should be as low as possible in order to avoid overfitting. As indicated above, superfluous factors could confuse the interpretation of the model and contaminate the statistical interpretation of the sensitivity parameters (betas). Furthermore, the overfitting problem reduces the quality of the out-of-sample performance of the factor model.
4. *Accuracy*: The ultimate aim of a multifactor model is to explain how the returns of financial assets are generated using a few sources of common variations. The explanatory power of the model, as measured by an information criterion, should thus be high enough so that the residual "noise," represented by the residual term $\varepsilon_{i,t}$ of each of the N assets used in the investment universe, is as small as possible. The simplest of such

accuracy indicators is the adjusted R-squared or R^2_{adj}. It represents the coefficient of determination of the linear regression model of Equation (7-3) with a correction for the number of variables: $R^2_{\text{adj}} = 1 - (1 - R^2)\frac{T-1}{T-K-1}$, where T is the number of observations.

It is important to note that the factors used in the analysis primarily owe their presence to their ability to capture a substantial variability of returns (either historically or cross-sectionally, or both) and not to their nature or interpretation. This means that some factors can be interpreted as risk premiums that are supposed to remunerate the investor for some sort of risk, while some others are the reflection of a market anomaly (for instance due to taxes or behavioral biases) that provides a positive remuneration and that tends to persist over time. In the context of performance measurement, since the point of view is retrospective, both types of interpretations are warranted. In the next sections, we present the three major families of multifactor models: the ones with a macroeconomic or statistical view that rely on a no-arbitrage reasoning on financial markets; the ones that adopt a microeconomic view and associate risk premiums to fundamental characteristics of stocks; and the ones that adopt a pure empirical view of trying to find multiple indexes in order to best replicate portfolio returns.

KFF example (continued)

The last column of Table 7-2 reports the raw value of the R^2 for each regression model. Mechanically, it increases with the number of factors. Nevertheless, some factors may happen to overlap with others or simply fail to explain the variation of the fund's returns beyond the mere consumption of one degree of freedom in the regression (Figure 7-1).

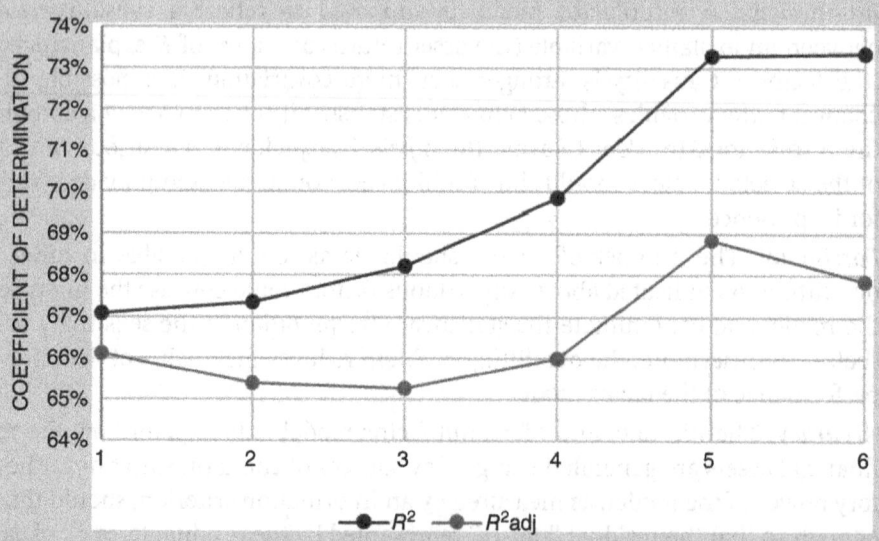

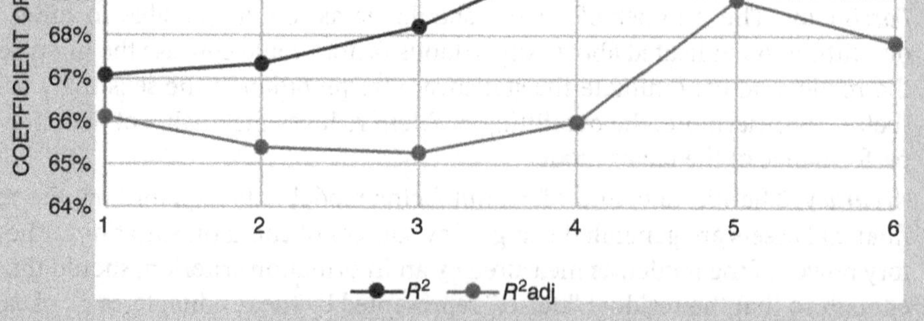

FIGURE 7-1 KFF example – Evolution of the R^2 and R^2_{adj} as a function of the number of factors.

Applying the R^2_{adj} formula pleads for a model with more than one factor, as the coefficient of determination is highest with the five-factor specification. Nevertheless, it seems that the second and third factors (Equities-Japan and Equities-Rest of World) do not add significant explanatory power over the first one (Equities-North America). Thus, the ordering of the entry list of the factors can be improved.

7.1.2 Arbitrage-based multifactor models

Historically, arbitrage-based multifactor models represent the first family of multifactor models. Inspired by Roll's (1977) critique, the APT introduced by Ross (1976) stands as a reaction to the equilibrium relation that underlies the CAPM. Instead of imposing assumptions that lead to an equilibrium on financial markets, Ross (1976) posits a relation similar to Equation (7-2) that explains the returns of financial assets, with $\mathrm{E}(\varepsilon_i) = 0$, $\mathrm{Cov}(\varepsilon_i, F_k) = 0$, and $\mathrm{Cov}(\varepsilon_i, \varepsilon_j) = 0$. Provided that investors have a frictionless access to the financial market, they are free to engage in unlimited portfolio diversification, which enables them to get rid of their idiosyncratic risk.

In this context, the author shows that in the absence of any arbitrage opportunity, the expected rate of return of a financial asset is given by $\mathrm{E}(R_i) = R_f + \sum_{k=1}^{K} \beta_{i,k}(\mathrm{E}(F_k) - R_f)$, whose estimation equation is precisely the one of expression (7-3). If $K = 1$ and F_k is the return of the market portfolio, the APT nests the CAPM as a special case but without the need for a particular theory underpinning it. This approach has directly led to two kinds of multifactor models, namely, the factor models based on macroeconomic variables, or "macroeconomic factor models," and the factor models based on statistical properties of returns or "endogenous factor models."[5]

7.1.2.1 Macroeconomic factor models

The association of the factors with macroeconomic variables corresponds to the most natural application of the APT in a practical context. The seminal paper in this area is the study by Chen, Roll, and Ross (1986). They propose a specification of Equation (7-2) in which the factors are associated with (i) the term spread (difference between long and short interest rates), (ii) the change in expected inflation, (iii) the change in unexpected inflation, (iv) the change in industrial production, and (v) the credit spread (difference between yields of low- and high-grade bonds). Remarkably, they discard the market excess return from their list of factors, thereby justifying the APT as an alternative, and not a mere extension, of the CAPM.

[5] There are naturally other taxonomies proposed in the literature. It does not really matter for the purpose of measuring performance in the multifactor context.

Since the publication of the Chen, Roll, and Ross (1986) paper, many other articles have tried different sets of factors.[6] However, this family of macroeconomic models, although theoretically appealing and economically meaningful, has not become the dominant form of multifactor model. However, it has left some very useful traces in different areas, such as the implementation of pricing models adapted to very segmented national or regional markets, the extension to other types of factors for some specific asset classes, such as hedge funds or real estate, or the identification of instrumental variables in the context of conditional multifactor models, as discussed in Section 7.3.

7.1.2.2 Endogenous factor models

After the publication of the theoretical development of the APT in 1976, the first concern was to assess the number of factors that would bear a risk premium on the stock market. The Roll and Ross (1980) paper provides an answer to this question by performing a statistical factor analysis on the variance–covariance matrix of the returns $\mathbf{\Omega}$. The outcome of the analysis expresses this matrix as $\mathbf{\Omega} \approx \mathbf{B\Lambda B}^{\mathrm{T}} + \mathbf{\Theta}$, where $\mathbf{B}$ is an $N \times K$ matrix of the first K eigenvectors (ranked by decreasing levels of their corresponding eigenvalues) of the original matrix $\mathbf{\Omega}$, $\mathbf{\Lambda}$ is the variance–covariance matrix of the factors, and $\mathbf{\Theta}$ is a diagonal matrix of the own asset variances $\sigma_{\varepsilon i}^2$. Each element of $\mathbf{B}$ corresponds to coefficient $\beta_{i,k}$ of Equation (7-3). The major practical application of this technique is called the principal components analysis with rotated factors. Its general objective is to reduce the dimensionality of that matrix to a limited number of common factors that are easily interpretable through their association with observed financial or economic variables.

While the literature has mostly taken a route that diverges from this pure statistical approach, the literal logic of the original APT has been pursued in industrial applications.[7] Statistical factors are extracted from the database of returns and are thus specific to that particular sample. One of the key advantages of this approach is to "let the data speak" and thus ensure the integrity of the results. In particular, it allows us to group portfolios in homogeneous clusters based on the statistical properties of their returns, irrespective of their self-reported investment styles or impressions of external analysts. The drawback is the potential lack of economic meaning of the factors: What emerges from the data could simply make no economic sense because there is no such guarantee at any stage of the factor construction procedure.

7.1.3 Fundamental multifactor models

By contrast with arbitrage-based multifactor models, another approach trades off theoretical rigor ("for the beauty of it") against practical effectiveness ("the end justifies the means") by

[6]See Section 2.4.2 of Chapter 2 for a further discussion.

[7]For instance, the company Advanced Portfolio Technology (APT) had initially adopted the same acronym as the model. Its solutions are now part of the FIS group.

directly relating the factors to firms' characteristics or attributes. The underlying idea is simple: If some characteristic that differs across firms (such as their size, for instance) involves an associated economically significant difference in their stock returns, there must be a corresponding risk premium entering the multifactor model.

In order to assess the relevance of a factor, it has become standard to apply a procedure inspired by the seminal paper of Fama and MacBeth (1973) as discussed in Chapter 2. The approach essentially involves the successive application of two regressions. The first one is similar to Equation (7-3). Its outcome is a set of estimated factor sensitivities for individual securities or portfolios, denoted by $\hat{\beta}_{i,k}$. The second is a cross-sectional regression across all securities, whose purpose is to assess whether there is a significant risk premium that is associated with each candidate risk factor. The equation of this "second pass" regression is

$$\overline{R}_i = \lambda_0 + \sum_{k=1}^{K} \hat{\beta}_{i,k}\lambda_k + \eta_i \tag{7-4}$$

where $\overline{R}_i$ is the mean asset return, λ_k is the risk premium associated with factor k, and λ_0 is the average stock or portfolio return that is not explained by the model. A proposed fundamental multifactor model is "successful" if the estimated values of λ_k are significantly different from zero while simultaneously λ_0 is insignificant.

The pragmatism of this approach explains why, in the race among families of models that use several factors to explain financial returns, fundamental models have become so popular, both in the academic and professional communities. In the world of scientific research, the so-called "empirical factor models" have become largely dominant, while financial practice has also adopted in parallel the "microeconomic factor models" initially developed by BARRA Inc. in the 1970s.

7.1.3.1 Empirical factor models

After the publication of the CAPM, some puzzling anomalies are quickly documented. Basu (1977) and Reinganum (1981) detect that, after controlling for their beta, the so-called "value stocks," i.e., with a low price-earnings ratio or market-to-book ratio, tend to generate higher returns. Banz (1981) finds a similar phenomenon for stocks with a low market capitalization (the so-called "small caps"). Later, Jegadeesh and Titman (1993) also discover a puzzling "momentum effect": Those stocks that have outperformed their peers in the recent past (3–12 months) have the tendency to keep beating their peers and vice versa. In other words, winners remain winners, and losers remain losers, as if the prices of all these stocks were benefiting (or suffering) from a kind of momentum. Logically, these anomalies are good candidates for playing a role in multifactor models.

In two famous papers, Fama and French (1992) (for size and value) and Carhart (1997) (for momentum) put all this together and inaugurate the long series of papers belonging to the category of empirical factor models. The most famous specification of Equation (7-3) is the version of Carhart (1997) that extends the Fama–French model to include the effect of momentum:

$$R_{i,t} = \alpha_i^{\mathrm{MF}} + \beta_{i,M}(R_{M,t} - R_{f,t}) + \beta_{i,\mathrm{SMB}}\mathrm{SMB}_t + \beta_{i,\mathrm{HML}}\mathrm{HML}_t + \beta_{i,\mathrm{UMD}}\mathrm{UMD}_t + \varepsilon_{i,t} \tag{7-5}$$

where SMB_t ("small minus big"), HML_t ("high minus low"), and UMD_t ("up minus down," also known as WML_t for "winners minus losers") represent the risk premiums corresponding to the size, value, and momentum effects, respectively.[8] The three additional factors are "self-financing" portfolios, i.e., based on long–short positions that theoretically do not need to be funded, and therefore they do not need to be expressed as excess returns.

To construct the first two empirical factors, Fama and French (1992) propose to allocate all stocks into six long–short portfolios on the basis of the partitioning in small/big market capitalization and high/medium/low book-to-market ratio (thus, BH= Big–High, BM= Big–Medium, etc.). Then, the premiums are given by the average returns of the intersection portfolios: $\mathrm{SMB}_t = \frac{\mathrm{SH}_t+\mathrm{SM}_t+\mathrm{SL}_t}{3} - \frac{\mathrm{BH}_t+\mathrm{BM}_t+\mathrm{BL}_t}{3}$ and $\mathrm{HML}_t = \frac{\mathrm{SH}_t+\mathrm{BH}_t}{2} - \frac{\mathrm{SL}_t+\mathrm{BL}_t}{2}$. The factors are constructed with NYSE, AMEX, and NASDAQ data, but the breakpoint for size is based on NYSE only. All portfolios are value-weighted (i.e., returns are weighted according to market capitalization) and not equally weighted (in order to avoid dominance of micro-caps, whose lack of liquidity creates an issue for their actual tradability).[9] Carhart (1997) uses an analogous approach to compute the momentum premium.

After the initial success of such a model to explain the cross-sectional expectation of stock returns, there has been a blossoming of papers proposing their own candidate(s) for the inclusion in multifactor models, with associated evidence of a significant risk premium.[10] However, as shown by Harvey, Liu, and Zhu (2016), ordinary statistical inference provides too generous results when confronted with the inflation of the number of tested factors. Indeed, if you test multiple factors, you may get to select some of them simply because, statistically, one of twenty (=5%) will emerge by chance if you have a confidence level of 95%. Thus, one needs a much more discriminating multiple testing approach, such as the familywise error rate (FWER) (including the Bonferroni test) that deems it unacceptable to make a single false discovery. The easiest of such FWER multiple tests is the Holm (1979) method, whose criterion is

$$\mathrm{RH}_0 \text{ if } p_k < \frac{x}{K+1-k} \tag{7-6}$$

[8]Note that the rate of return of the risk-free asset is time varying in the regression, in accordance with the fact that interest rates move over time, and recognizing that generally improves the outcome of the regression.
[9]Several papers have challenged the methodological choices made by Fama and French (1992), and especially the simultaneous partitioning of the sample into size and value categories (see Lambert, Fays, and Hübner, 2020, for a review of these methodological choices and their impact on the pricing performance of the model).
[10]Section 2.4.2 of Chapter 2 discusses some of these proposed models.

where RH_0 stands for "reject the null hypothesis of the absence of statistical significance of the factor," p_k is the p-value (i.e., the probability of observing a value of the test statistic that is greater, in absolute value, than the one tested in the null hypothesis is true) associated with the kth factor, ranked from the most ($k = 1$) to the least ($k = K$) significant, and $1 - x$ is the confidence level. For instance, if 10 factors are tested ($K = 10$) and the significance level of each associated risk premium is $1 - x = 95\%$, the hurdle for the "best" factor is $0.05/(10 + 1 - 1) = 0.5\%$. For the second, it is 0.55% and so on.

In a paper that they updated regularly until 2019, Harvey and Liu (2020) counted the number of factors proposed in top finance journals and applied their multiple testing approach in order to distinguish those factors that are very likely to faithfully explain stock returns from those that are just significant by pure "luck." The quintessence of their results is summarized in Figure 7-2.

With the application of the Holm criterion (dotted line), we see from the graph that four factors clearly emerge as undisputedly significant: the Value factor (HML), the Momentum factor (MOM, equivalent to UMD in Equation (7-5)), the Durable Consumption Goods (DCG)

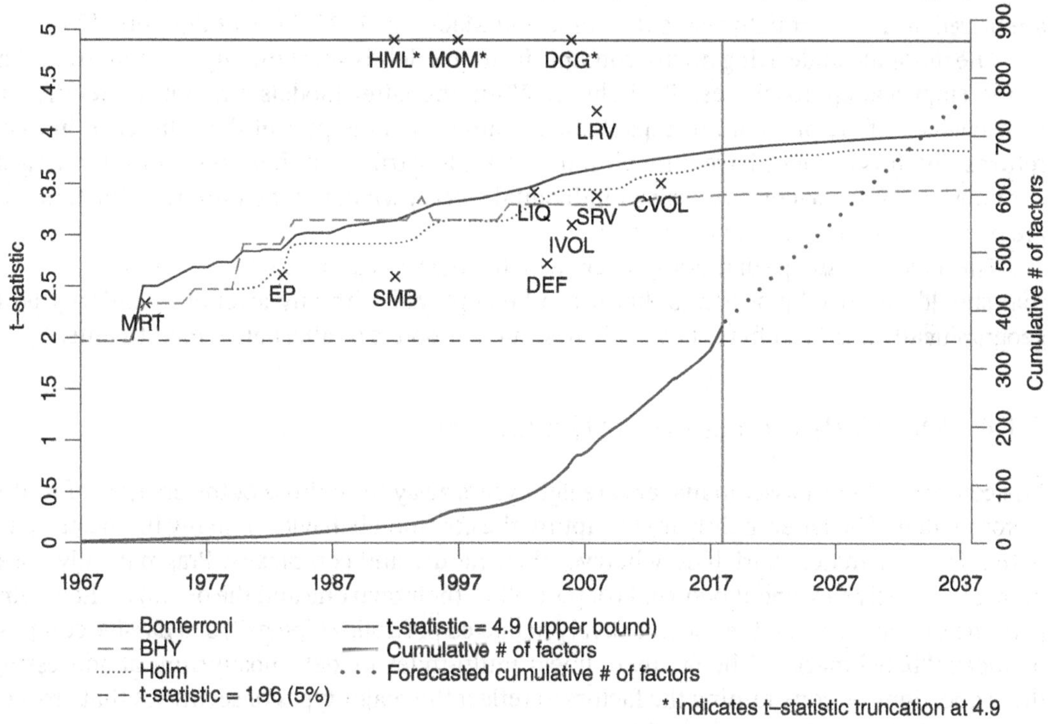

FIGURE 7-2 Summary of the multiple testing approach on a selected set of empirical factors. Source: Harvey and Liu (2020), retrieved from `https://papers.ssrn.com/sol3/papers.cfm?abstract_id=3341728`.

of Yogo (2006), and the Long Run Volatility (LRV) of Adrian and Rosenberg (2008). Two additional factors are just above the bar: the Market (MKT) factor initially used by Fama and MacBeth (1973) and the Liquidity (LIQ) factor proposed by Pastor and Stambaugh (2003). Thus, even though the evidence presented in the Harvey and Liu (2020) paper does not constitute an ultimate proof, it confirms that, in spite of the considerable efforts made for many years by researchers across the world to discover new factors, only a very limited set of those factors would presumably be sufficient to explain the major part of stock returns.

7.1.3.2 Microeconomic factor models

The approach was initially introduced by Sharpe (1982), but the BARRA model,[11] commercially implemented since 1975 and now part of the MSCI group, is the most scalable example of such an approach. The key insight is that the company's stock returns are determined by a set of specific fundamental characteristics. Some overlap with the factors used in leading empirical multifactor models (size, value, growth, ...), but some may not (industrial sector, trading activity, yield, ...). For a given set of firms, what is observable is the set of the exposures to these characteristics, and the challenge is to determine whether the associated factors are priced or not, essentially using the Fama and MacBeth (1973) logic of Equation (7-4).

The rationale underlying microeconomic factor models is substantially different from that of the empirical approach described above. While the latter models attempt to identify the restricted set of factors that are capable of explaining a large part of the difference in asset returns, the former ones have a much more down to earth ambition: to capture the largest possible part of the average returns of individual stocks, whatever the number of factors that are necessary in order to reach this goal.

The major advantage of this approach, which is *a priori* agnostic with respect to the factors that should be priced globally, is that it can be deployed with any level of granularity both geographically and for different asset classes, such as bonds or alternative investments.

7.1.4 Multi-index models and style analysis

The concerns of most asset managers are light years away from those of the creators of multifactor models. The latter mainly try to capture the common behavior of many financial assets with a few explanatory variables, whatever their nature and complexity. Pragmatically, asset managers mostly care about two kinds of portfolios: their own one and the one(s) of their competitor(s), which can be either other actively managed portfolios ("peers") or a passive composite index ("benchmark"). The family of linear multi-index models mostly aims at addressing these questions by constraining the factors to reflect the major types of securities that are – or could be – held by a fund or a portfolio.

[11] See Grinold and Kahn (2000) for a complete description of the original BARRA approach.

7.1.4.1 Characterizing a multi-index model

The general form of a multifactor model entails a change in the nature of the factors employed in Equation (7-3). Instead of the original equation, we write

$$R_{i,t} - R_{f,t} = \alpha_i^{\mathrm{MF}} + \sum_{k=1}^{K} \beta_{i,k}(I_{k,t} - R_{f,t}) + \varepsilon_{i,t} \tag{7-7}$$

where $I_{k,t}$ represents the return of the kth index to which the return is supposed to be sensitive and $\beta_{i,k}$ is its associated asset beta.

The first attempt to develop such a model can be attributed to Elton, Gruber, Das, and Hlavka (1993). Inspired by a study of Ippolito (1989), they propose to explain stock returns with three indexes (the market, an index for small stocks, and an index for bonds) through the regression approach of Equation (7-7). The clear intention underlying this approach is to build a benchmark portfolio, invested in the corresponding indexes, representing the passive investment that would replicate the behavior of the asset without delivering abnormal performance.

To some extent, the study of Elton et al. (1993) opens a Pandora's box. Instead of only three indexes, it could be advisable to include additional indexes in order to enhance the quality of the benchmark associated with the portfolio. Building on this idea, Siegel (2003) provides some guidance for the selection of a benchmark index.[12] He lists eight desirable properties that should be met by each index in the process of the multi-index modeling approach, whose aim is to statistically build a composite benchmark. We re-express here these individual index features with our own wording. In sum, each index should be

1. *Proportional*: It features the market that it is supposed to cover in an adequate way. This imposes the use of market cap-weighted indexes.
2. *Representative*: It covers the whole spectrum of the market that it represents with similar proportions of each sub-class of assets.
3. *Investable*: It provides the investor with the opportunity to invest in replicating financial products (ETFs, index funds, futures, or swaps) at reasonable costs.
4. *Transparent*: It should be governed with clear published and open rules.
5. *Accurate*: It should be covered with complete and unambiguous data.
6. *Acceptable*: It should undoubtedly reflect its underlying asset class in the eyes of the investors.
7. *Hedgeable*: It should display a set of derivatives and other negotiable products that enable the investors to implement various trading strategies.
8. *Liquid*: It should be associated with a low turnover and related transaction costs.

---

[12] Siegel's (2003) discussion deals with a single index that is supposed to encompass a homogeneous market, namely, US stocks. We thus extend his logic to the selection of several indexes in order to feed the multi-index model.

Because we simultaneously deal with several indexes for the construction of the benchmark, it is necessary to bring four additional conditions. In addition to the eight features listed above, each index should be

9. *Exclusive*: It covers a set of financial assets that is not covered, in part or in full, by any other index.
10. *Comprehensive*: It should be such that, combined with all the other indexes in the benchmark, the whole market in which the portfolio or fund invests is wholly covered.
11. *Distinctive*: It ensures that its returns are not too correlated with those of the other indexes in order to avoid any collinearity issue in statistical analyses.
12. *Relevant*: It reflects a significant share of the investments made by the portfolio or fund that is not covered elsewhere.

Naturally, any list of indexes that fulfills these 12 conditions also respects the "feasibility," "intuitiveness," and "accuracy" criteria that should apply to a multifactor model (see Section 7.1.1.3) but not necessarily the "parsimony" requirement.

In addition to this list, Sharpe (1992) notices that, for performance measurement purposes, the benchmark portfolio should be "not easily beaten." Thus, it is important to use indexes whose construction or behavior lends credibility to the approach. Several vendors commercialize a wide set of indexes that aim to fulfill these 12 properties. Nowadays, it is possible to feed multi-index models for any type of portfolio without any difficulty.

KFF example (continued)

The six indexes were selected according to the eight conditions set forth by Siegel (2003). Checking the four additional conditions that apply to their combination yields the results shown in Table 7-3.

TABLE 7-3 KFF example – Additional checks of the index selection criteria.

	Exclusive?	Comprehensive?	Distinctive?	Relevant?
Eq-N.Am.	✓	✓	✓	✓
Eq-Jap	✓	✓	✓	✓
Eq-RoW	✓	✓	×	✓
Bd-Dev	✓	✓	✓	✓
Eq-Eur	✓	✓	✓	✓
Bd-EM	✓	✓	✓	×

When examining their correlation matrix, we find that the correlation between Equities-Rest of World and Equities-North America stands above 90% (92.4%). Even though indexes can be correlated in multi-index analyses, this level of redundancy appears not to be acceptable here. The least relevant index for the fund (Equities-Rest of World) is thus rejected.

Since the fund is supposed to invest only in sovereign or corporate bonds of the most developed countries, it is not necessary to include an emerging bond index in order to construct the benchmark. The corresponding index is thus irrelevant and consequently discarded.

Re-estimating the linear multi-index model with only the retained indexes results in the following four-index model (standard errors of coefficients between parentheses):

$$\begin{aligned} R_{\text{KFF},t} - R_{f,t} = &\ \underset{(0.25\%)}{0.51\%} + \underset{(0.18)}{0.09}\,(I_{\text{Eq-NAm},t} - R_{f,t}) + \underset{(0.13)}{0.02}\,(I_{\text{Eq-Jap},t} - R_{f,t}) \\ &+ \underset{(0.29)}{0.73}\,(I_{\text{Bd-Dev},t} - R_{f,t}) + \underset{(0.12)}{0.25}\,(I_{\text{Eq-Eur},t} - R_{f,t}) + \underset{(1.40\%)}{\varepsilon_{\text{KFF},t}} \end{aligned}$$

where $R_{f,t}$ is a constant set at 0.15% per month. The R^2 of this new model is 73.1%, very close to that of the original six-factor model reported before.

7.1.4.2 Return-based style analysis

In parallel with the study of Elton et al. (1993), Sharpe (1992) revisits the Standard Portfolio Theory with the ambition of designing a framework for the direct identification of adequate benchmark portfolios through a multi-index model. He introduces the notion of "return-based style analysis" (RBSA), in which the statistical properties of portfolio returns are directly used in order to infer a multi-index benchmark portfolio.[13] To do so, the multifactor model is re-expressed through the following equations:

$$R_{i,t} = \alpha_i^{\text{MF}} + \sum_{k=1}^{K} w_{i,k} I_{k,t} + \varepsilon_{i,t} \tag{7-8}$$

$$\sum_{k=1}^{K} w_{i,k} = 1 \tag{7-9}$$

where $w_{i,k}$ represents the weight of the kth index in the benchmark of asset i, which explains the constraint of Equation (7-9) that these weights must add up to 1.

[13]The Holding-Based Style Analysis (HBSA), in which the benchmark is determined by the evolution of the actual portfolio holdings, is examined in Chapter 8.

From this general setup, it is possible to distinguish three forms of RBSA, depending on the sign constraints set on the weights. Under the weak form, no further requirement applies, and any weight can be positive or negative. With the semi-strong form, some weights cannot be negative, in order to avoid short selling some assets, such as real estate. Finally, the strong form imposes that all weights must be non-negative. This latter form leads to the identification of benchmarks as long-only mimicking portfolios. This is the standard form that applies to most mutual funds that are not supposed to have net short positions in any asset class.

Whatever the form of the RBSA is retained, traditional statistical procedures used in linear regressions do not readily apply for the estimation of the style weights because of the presence of at least one constraint, namely the weights summing up to one in Equation (7-9). Rather, one should use quadratic programming techniques in order to minimize the variance of the error term in Equation (7-8).

7.1.4.3 Isolating leverage in style analysis

Reconciling style analysis with generic multi-index models, and therefore easing the estimation of the model, is perfectly doable, at least in the weak form.[14] As shown by McGuire and Tsatsaronis (2009), the adaptation is done at the expense of allowing the existence of an additional explanatory variable, interpreted as a leverage, that plays the role of an adjustment factor. It re-expresses Equation (7-7) as follows:

$$R_{i,t} = \alpha_i^{\text{MF}} + (1 - \rho_i)R_{f,t} + \rho_i \sum_{k=1}^{K} w_{i,k} I_{k,t} + \varepsilon_{i,t} \tag{7-10}$$

where $\rho_i = \sum_{k=1}^{K} \beta_{i,k}$ is the leverage coefficient of the portfolio and $w_{i,k} = \frac{\beta_{i,k}}{\rho_i}$ is the weight of the leverage-free portfolio invested in index k. If $\rho_i > 1$, the portfolio has positive leverage, and the weight invested in the risk-free asset is negative (net borrower).

Note that Equation (7-10) can be readily expressed as a style index model with $K + 1$ factors, i.e., $R_{i,t} = \alpha_i^{\text{MF}} + w_{i,0}^* R_{f,t} + \sum_{k=1}^{K} w_{i,k}^* I_{k,t} + \varepsilon_{i,t}$ in which $w_{i,k}^* = \beta_{i,k}$ and $w_{i,0}^* = 1 - \sum_{k=1}^{K} \beta_{i,k}$.

KFF example (continued)

In the four-factor model that explains the fund's returns, the coefficients of the indexes sum up to $0.09 + 0.02 + 0.73 + 0.25 = 1.09$. Thus, we can deduct that the fund has used a leverage coefficient of 109%, which can have several explanations (cash borrowing, betas

[14]Provided that the indexes are adequately chosen, all forms of style analysis provide the same results for most long-only portfolios, such as the majority of mutual funds or discretionary personal portfolios.

of the stocks higher than one, durations of the bonds higher than the average ones of the indexes, ...). We can therefore re-express the multi-index model in the form of a five-factor RBSA equation:

$$R_{KFF,t} = 0.51\% - 0.09R_{f,t} + 1.09(0.08\, I_{Eq-NAm,t} + 0.02\, I_{Eq-Jap,t} + 0.67\, I_{Bd-Dev,t} + 0.23\, I_{Eq-Eur,t}) + \varepsilon_{KFF,t}$$

7.1.4.4 Choosing the right set of indexes

Traditional variable selection procedures used in standard econometrics do not readily apply in style analysis. Since the set of indexes is chosen *ex ante* and the estimation of coefficients results from a quadratic programming procedure, it is possible that some indexes that are redundant with other ones (collinear) or superfluous (insufficient explanatory power) are kept in the analysis while they should be discarded. In order to reduce the number of indexes used to those that are only relevant for the analysis, Lobosco and DiBartolomeo (1997) propose a simple iterative method that allows us to rationalize the final choice of the indexes included in the analysis. Their approach rolls out as follows:

1. Conduct the style analysis on the initial K style indexes $R_{i,t} = \alpha_i^{MF} + \sum_{k=1}^{K} w_{i,k} I_{k,t} + \varepsilon_{i,t}$ and retrieve the estimated style weights $\hat{w}_{i,k}$ and the idiosyncratic risk of the portfolio $\sigma_{\varepsilon i}$.
2. For each style index k, perform a regression of its returns on the $K-1$ remaining style indexes: $I_{k,t} = \alpha_k^{MF} + \sum_{l=1, l\neq k}^{K-1} \beta_{k,l} I_{l,t} + \nu_{k,t}$. The standard deviation of the residual provides the idiosyncratic risk $\sigma_{\nu k}$ of the style index. The higher the value of $\sigma_{\nu k}$ is, the larger the added value of the corresponding index.
3. Compute the standard error of the style weight by applying the formula $\sigma_{w_{i,k}} = \frac{1}{\sqrt{T-K-1}} \frac{\sigma_{\varepsilon i}}{\sigma_{\nu k}}$.
4. Construct the confidence interval for the style weight of index k with a $1-x$ confidence level as follows: $\hat{w}_{i,k} \pm z_{1-\frac{x}{2}} \times \sigma_{w_{i,k}}$, where $z_{1-\frac{x}{2}}$ is the $\left(1-\frac{x}{2}\right)$th percentile of the standard normal distribution.
5. Discard each index whose confidence interval includes 0.
6. Repeat steps 1–5 until no index is discarded anymore.

KFF example (continued)

We start with the four-index model retained (with a leverage of 1.09). The standard deviation of the residual term is $\sigma_{\varepsilon i} = 1.40\%$. Applying steps 2–4 of the procedure with a confidence level of 95% (which corresponds to a value of $z_{1-\frac{x}{2}} = 1.645$), we obtain the results shown in Table 7-4a:

TABLE 7-4a KFF example – Confidence intervals for the four initial style indexes.

	$\hat{w}_{i,k}$	$\sigma_{\nu k}$	Lower bound	Upper bound
Eq-N.Am.	0.08	1.37%	−0.23	0.39
Eq-Jap	0.02	1.95%	−0.20	0.24
Bd-Dev	0.67	0.86%	0.18	1.17
Eq-Eur	0.23	2.10%	0.03	0.43

Only the lower bounds of the last two indexes (Bonds-Developed and Equities-Europe) are positive, which means that the corresponding confidence intervals do not contain 0, unlike for the other two indexes. The "Bonds-Developed" index is retained mostly because of its very high weight, in spite of its low idiosyncratic variation. For the "Equities-Europe" index, the effects are the opposite: Its style weight is relatively modest, but it has a very high idiosyncratic risk, which indicates a high marginal added value of this index.

With the two remaining indexes, we run again the Lobosco–DiBartolomeo procedure on the new model, with a leverage coefficient of 1.23 and a residual volatility of $\sigma_{\varepsilon i} = 1.41\%$. It is very close to that of the original model, which indicates that discarding the other two indexes has not largely impacted the explanatory power of the model. The new table is Table 7-4b.

TABLE 7-4b KFF example – Confidence intervals for the two retained style indexes.

	$\hat{w}_{i,k}$	$\sigma_{\nu k}$	Lower bound	Upper bound
Bd-Dev	0.74	1.37%	0.44	1.03
Eq-Eur	0.26	1.95%	0.06	0.47

This time, no confidence interval contains zero anymore, and we can consider the procedure as complete. The final version of the two-index style index equation now stands as

$$R_{\mathrm{KFF},t} = 0.52\% - 0.23R_{f,t} + 1.23(0.74\, I_{\mathrm{Bd-Dev},t} + 0.26\, I_{\mathrm{Eq-Eur},t}) + \varepsilon_{\mathrm{KFF},t}$$

The model has an R^2 of 72.6%, corresponding to an adjusted one of $R^2_{\text{adj}} = 71\%$, which is higher than any level of the different index models presented before. The standard deviation of the residual term is $\sigma_{\varepsilon\text{KFF}} = 1.84\%$.

The return-based style benchmark corresponding to the KFF eventually consists of −23% invested in the riskless asset (negative cash account), +91% invested in the Bonds-Developed index, and +32% invested in the Equities-Europe index.

7.2 THE MULTIFACTOR ALPHA AND THE MULTIFACTOR MODIFIED ALPHA

The primary difference between a one-factor model such as the CAPM and any linear multi-factor discussed in Section 7.1, whatever its kind, lies in the multiplicity of coefficients. Instead of having a single beta that reflects the systematic risk exposure of a portfolio in the original version of the model, every declination of Equation (7-3) features an intercept and several sensitivity coefficients.

In relation to the material of Chapter 3, the set of classical performance measures that explicitly refer to the portfolio beta are the Treynor ratio, Jensen's alpha, and the modified Jensen's alpha. It is of primary interest to examine how these three measures bear the migration from a single beta to multiple regression coefficients, each of which can be interpreted as a "multifactor beta" in that context. We distinguish the extension of Jensen's alpha, on the one hand, from that of the modified Jensen's alpha, on the other hand.[15]

7.2.1 Definitions

7.2.1.1 The multifactor alpha

The adaptation of the Jensen's alpha of a portfolio P in the context of a multifactor model represented by Equation (7-3) is straightforward:

$$\alpha_P^{\text{MF}} = \overline{R}_P - \left[\overline{R}_f + \sum_{k=1}^{K} \beta_{P,k}(\overline{F}_k - \overline{R}_f)\right] \equiv \overline{R}_P - \overline{R}_B^{\text{MF}} \tag{7-11}$$

where $\overline{R}_P$ represents the mean portfolio return, $\overline{R}_f$ is the average rate of return of the riskless asset prevailing at each period of time, $\beta_{P,k}$ is the beta of the portfolio with respect to the kth factor, and $\overline{R}_B^{\text{MF}} = \overline{R}_f + \sum_{k=1}^{K} \beta_{P,k}(\overline{F}_k - \overline{R}_f)$ represents the average return of the regression-based

[15]Given that the Treynor ratio and the modified Jensen's alpha share very similar properties, we concentrate on the latter measure as it is directly comparable to the alpha.

benchmark. In their methodological paper devoted to performance measurement in the context of APT, Connor and Korajczyk (1986) show that this expression is the unambiguous extension of Jensen's alpha in a multifactor model.

The multifactor alpha can thus differ from the portfolio abnormal return obtained by using its "official" (self-reported) benchmark, be it a composite passive index or a peer group portfolio: $\alpha'_P = PG_P = \overline{R}_P - \overline{R}_B$, where $\overline{R}_B$ stands for the average return of the self-reported benchmark, and α'_P is nothing other than the peer group comparison return PG_P as defined in Chapter 3. This distinction between α_P^{MF} and α'_P will prove to be very important later on.

Representing graphically the multifactor alpha is only possible in a two-factor setup ($K = 2$). In order to represent any kind of model (arbitrage-based, fundamental, or multi-index) as discussed in Section 7.1, we have to acknowledge that (i) the factors might or might not be orthogonal to each other, without impairing the empirical validity of the model and (ii) the remuneration of the factors might differ from each other. These two facts do not alter the interpretation of the multifactor alpha. Figure 7-3 reflects these features by (i) not imposing that the axes are orthogonal (obviously, the horizontal axes do not have a 90° angle) and (ii) showing that the mean return of the two factors can be different (which is reflected in the different angles of the projection of each risk premium above its corresponding axis, represented in light gray on the graph).

Consider two active portfolios L and H, represented on the graph, that display different mean returns and multifactor betas during the period of reference. Since $\beta_{L,1} < \beta_{H,1}$ and $\beta_{L,2} < \beta_{H,2}$, the required return on L is necessarily lower than that on H. This is represented by the two solid lines originating from the coordinate of the risk-free rate $\overline{R}_f$: their extremities correspond to a mean return of $\overline{R}_f + \beta_{L,1}(\overline{F}_1 - \overline{R}_f) + \beta_{L,2}(\overline{F}_2 - \overline{R}_f)$ for L (represented by the lower line)

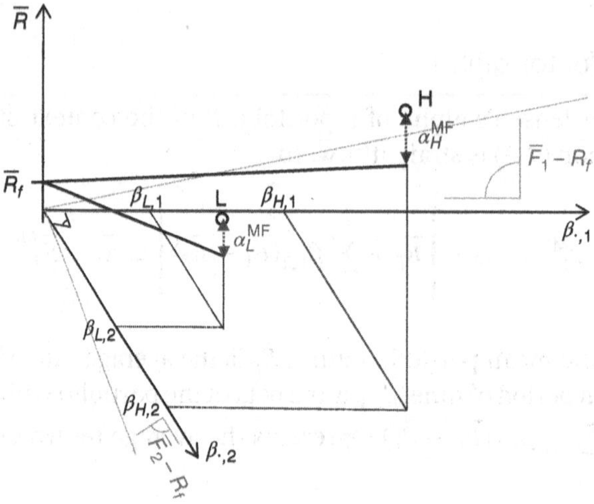

FIGURE 7-3 Graphical representation of the multifactor alpha.

and of $\overline{R}_f + \beta_{H,1}(\overline{F}_1 - \overline{R}_f) + \beta_{H,2}(\overline{F}_2 - \overline{R}_f)$ for H (upper line). According to Equation (7-11), the multifactor alphas of these two portfolios are represented by the distance between their coordinates and their corresponding required return. This is shown by the vertical pairs of arrows on the graph. As the one for H is longer than the one for L, we can deduce from that evidence that $0 < \alpha_L^{\text{MF}} < \alpha_H^{\text{MF}}$, i.e., portfolio H has outperformed portfolio L.

7.2.1.2 The multifactor modified alpha

Both the structure of the generic multifactor model of Equation (7-3) and the inspection of Figure 7-3 leave the impression of a great difficulty to extend the modified Jensen's alpha, defined as the alpha divided by the beta, in a multifactor setup. Nevertheless, it is possible and, at the end of the day, it delivers a relatively simple measure.

As discussed by Hübner (2005), a performance measure derived from a linear multifactor model is a proper generalization of the modified Jensen's alpha if it satisfies seven conditions.[16] The first four conditions apply to the modified Jensen's alpha, while the last three are specific to the multifactor model.

1. *Ratio of Euclidean distances*: The measure should reflect a vertical distance (alpha) on the numerator and a horizontal distance (beta) on the denominator.
2. *Homogeneity*: The measure should be strictly proportional to the level of abnormal return, strictly inversely proportional to the level of risk, and invariant to the portfolio leverage.
3. *Proportionality*: The measure should apply proportionally to a portfolio's abnormal return and inversely proportionally to a portfolio's risk.
4. *Reference portfolio*: The measure for the portfolio's benchmark should be equal to its multifactor alpha.
5. *Model irrelevance*: The measure for the portfolio applied on two competing multifactor models should not change if they deliver the same required return.
6. *Reducibility*: The measure simplifies to the modified Jensen's alpha in a single-factor model.
7. *Parsimony*: Among all measures that respect the above conditions, the measure should be the simplest one.

Considering condition 4, it only makes full sense to compute the *multifactor modified alpha*, called $m\alpha_P^{\text{MF}}$ as in Chapter 3, if there is a benchmark associated with the portfolio – indeed, this applies as well in the context of the CAPM, as the market portfolio plays the role of the benchmark in that case. In this case, Hübner (2005) shows that the portfolio performance

[16]In the paper, the measure is called the "generalized Treynor ratio" by reference to the original article.

is written as the multifactor alpha divided by the ratio of the portfolio's over the benchmark's required excess return:

$$m\alpha_P^{MF} = \frac{\alpha_P^{MF}}{\left(\frac{\sum_{k=1}^{K}\beta_{P,k}(\overline{F}_k-\overline{R}_f)}{\sum_{k=1}^{K}\beta_{B,k}(\overline{F}_k-\overline{R}_f)}\right)} = \alpha_P^{MF}\frac{\overline{R}_B-\overline{R}_f-\alpha_B^{MF}}{\overline{R}_P-\overline{R}_f-\alpha_P^{MF}} \tag{7-12}$$

where, as before, $\overline{R}_B$ stands for the average return of the self-reported benchmark associated with portfolio P, and the application of the same multifactor model as for the portfolio yields the relation $\overline{R}_B = \alpha_B^{MF} + \overline{R}_f + \sum_{k=1}^{K}\beta_{B,k}(\overline{F}_k - \overline{R}_f)$ so that α_B^{MF} is the multifactor alpha of the benchmark portfolio.

The intuition underlying the formula of Equation (7-12) is as follows. Starting from the same multifactor model as above, the whole "trick" consists of considering a virtual multifactor model with factors $F_1^*, \ldots, F_K^*$ in which (i) all factors are independent of each other, (ii) each factor delivers the same average return $\overline{F}_k^* = \overline{F}^* = \frac{1}{K}\sum_{k=1}^{K}\overline{F}_k$, and (iii) for each portfolio, the new factor betas are identical and equal to $\beta_{P,k}^* = \beta_P^* = \frac{\sum_{k=1}^{K}\beta_{P,k}(\overline{F}_k-\overline{R}_f)}{\sum_{k=1}^{K}(\overline{F}_k-\overline{R}_f)} = \sum_{k=1}^{K} w_k\beta_{P,k}$, where $w_k = \frac{(\overline{F}_k-\overline{R}_f)}{\sum_{k=1}^{K}(\overline{F}_k-\overline{R}_f)}$ is simply the weight of the kth factor in the total excess returns of the factors. We call β_P^* the "*representative beta*" of the portfolio.

Under these conditions, the required return of each portfolio is unchanged and is equal to $\overline{R}_f + \sum_{k=1}^{K}\beta_{P,k}(\overline{F}_k - \overline{R}_f) = \overline{R}_f + \sum_{k=1}^{K}\beta_{P,k}^*(\overline{F}_k^* - \overline{R}_f) = \overline{R}_f + K\beta_P^*(\overline{F}^* - \overline{R}_f)$. Since $\overline{F}^*$ is identical for all portfolios, the only driver of their risk is their β_P^*, which is strictly proportional to their required excess return $\sum_{k=1}^{K}\beta_{P,k}(\overline{F}_k - \overline{R}_f)$. Thus, the greater the required excess return is, the greater the representative beta, regardless of how the factors are priced and are correlated with each other. In fact, we can rewrite the multifactor modified alpha in terms of representative betas as follows:

$$m\alpha_P^{MF} = \alpha_P^{MF}\frac{\beta_B^*}{\beta_P^*} \tag{7-13}$$

Figure 7-4 shows a graphical representation of the insight underlying the derivation of the multifactor modified alpha.

The performance measures of portfolios L and H, which are supposed to have a common benchmark B, are reported with the vertical pairs of arrows. L has a lower required return than B, while it is the opposite for H. Three changes have been made compared to Figure 7-3: the horizontal axes have been made orthogonal to each other; the excess returns of the factors have become identical; and each portfolio beta is the same for both factors. Therefore, the projection of each portfolio coordinates on the horizontal plane draws a perfect square, whose diagonal

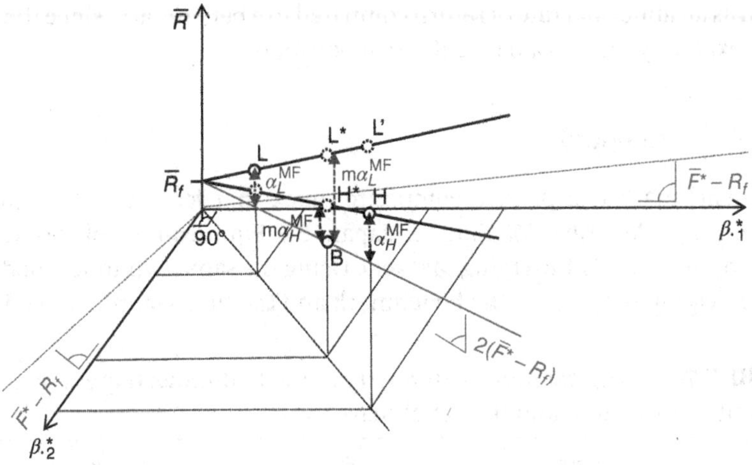

FIGURE 7-4 Graphical representation of the multifactor modified alpha.

is the oblique line starting from the origin. The benchmark *B*, whose multifactor alpha is null in the example, has a return that is equal to its required one.[17]

The alphas are actually the same as in the previous figure, and thus we still have $\alpha_L^{\mathrm{MF}} < \alpha_H^{\mathrm{MF}}$. L^* and H^* are the leveraged versions of portfolios *L* and *H* whose risk (and therefore whose required returns as well) has been made equal to that of their benchmark. Consistent with the interpretation of the original measure, the multifactor modified alpha is represented as the vertical distance between each line and the coordinates of the benchmark. On that basis, $\mathrm{m}\alpha_L^{\mathrm{MF}} > \mathrm{m}\alpha_H^{\mathrm{MF}}$, and we can conclude that portfolio *L* has outperformed portfolio *H*.

This graph is the exact counterpart of Figure 3-7 in Chapter 3, but adapted to a multifactor (three-dimensional) context. It relies on the same principle of homemade leverage, i.e., it shows that the multifactor modified alpha corrects for different levels of risk that could be adopted by different portfolio managers in spite of the fact that they belong to the same group, i.e., that they share the same (or at least very similar) benchmarks.

The specific case of the ***absolute modified multifactor alpha*** in which this performance measure is used without the formal identification of a benchmark – which is indeed the case when the multifactor alpha is used – boils down to dividing the alpha by the portfolio's representative beta:

$$\mathrm{m}\alpha_P^{\mathrm{MF,abs}} = \frac{\alpha_P^{\mathrm{MF}}}{\beta_P^*} \tag{7-14}$$

It still allows a meaningful comparison of portfolios with different risks, especially for ranking purposes. However, it loses one interesting property of the modified alpha, namely, its

[17]The more general case where the benchmark portfolio delivers a non-zero multifactor alpha is examined in Section 7.2.2.

interpretation as an abnormal rate of return compared to a benchmark, since the representative beta does not explicitly refer to a particular real portfolio.

KFF example (continued)

The fund's benchmark is a passive composite index that features 30% Equities-Europe, 10% Equities-North America, 5% Equities-Japan, 5% Equities-Rest of World, 40% Bonds-Developed, and 10% Bonds-Emerging Markets. Using the same two-index model as KFF, we obtain the regression outputs for the benchmark and the funds summarized in Table 7-5.

TABLE 7-5 KFF example – Summary of the two-index regression outputs for the fund and the benchmark.

	Average exc. return	α	$\beta_{\text{Bd-Dev}}$	$\beta_{\text{Eq-Eur}}$	σ_ε	R^2
KFF	0.76%	0.52%	0.91	0.32	0.69%	72.6%
Benchmark	0.31%	0.04%	0.77	0.43	0.03%	98.7%

The application of formula (7-12) provides the following value of the multifactor modified alpha:

$$m\alpha_{\text{KFF}}^{\text{MF}} = \alpha_{\text{KFF}}^{\text{MF}} \frac{\overline{R}_B - \overline{R}_f - \alpha_B^{\text{MF}}}{\overline{R}_{\text{KFF}} - \overline{R}_f - \alpha_{\text{KFF}}^{\text{MF}}} = 0.52\% \frac{0.31\% - 0.04\%}{0.76\% - 0.52\%} = 0.58\%$$

The factors' weights in excess return are $w_{\text{Bd-Dev}} = \frac{(\overline{I}_{\text{Bd-Dev}} - \overline{R}_f)}{(\overline{I}_{\text{Bd-Dev}} - \overline{R}_f) + (\overline{I}_{\text{Eq-Eur}} - \overline{R}_f)} = \frac{0.11\%}{0.11\% + 0.44\%} =$ 20% and $w_{\text{Eq-Eur}} = 80\%$. The representative beta of KFF is equal to $\beta_{\text{KFF}}^* = w_{\text{Bd-Dev}}\beta_{\text{KFF,Bd-Dev}} + w_{\text{Eq-Eur}}\beta_{\text{KFF,Eq-Eur}} = 20\% \times 0.91 + 80\% \times 0.32 = 0.44$, whereas that of the benchmark is $\beta_B^* = 20\% \times 0.77 + 80\% \times 0.43 = 0.50$. We can easily check that the multifactor modified alpha of KFF equals its alpha multiplied by the ratio of representative betas:

$$m\alpha_{\text{KFF}}^{\text{MF}} = \alpha_{\text{KFF}}^{\text{MF}} \frac{\beta_B^*}{\beta_{\text{KFF}}^*} = 0.52\% \frac{0.50}{0.44} = 0.58\%$$

7.2.2 What is a good multifactor alpha or multifactor modified alpha?

7.2.2.1 Practical significance

The answer to the issue of the multifactor alpha's and modified alpha's practical significance is *a priori* straightforward. Since they are direct extensions of the Jensen's and modified alphas, respectively, which are estimated using the intercept of a regression, the arguments put forward in Chapter 3 are also applicable here: In order to beat its benchmark, the portfolio should deliver a positive multifactor alpha. Indeed, the argument is valid if the only benchmark considered is the one retrieved from the regression, whose return is $\overline{R}_B^{MF} = \overline{R}_f + \sum_{k=1}^{K} \beta_{P,k}(\overline{F}_k - \overline{R}_f)$.

However, unlike in the CAPM case in which there is a single reference portfolio for all usages, relying on a multifactor model typically confronts two benchmarks in practice: the statistical one and the self-reported one B with return $\overline{R}_B$, and usually their compositions will only coincide by chance. The significance issue becomes threefold:

1. The multifactor alpha must be positive to justify the added value of the active management beyond the factor exposures.
2. Considering that the self-reported benchmark itself delivers a multifactor regression output α_B, the portfolio should also justify a better abnormal return, adjusted for its systematic risk when considering the respective exposures to the set of the factors: $\alpha_P^{MF}\frac{\beta_B^*}{\beta_P^*} > \alpha_B^{MF}$. This relates to the argument of Angelidis, Giamouridis, and Tessaromatis (2013), who claim that the portfolio's abnormal return should be explicitly measured with respect to the self-defined benchmark's own risk-adjusted performance (RAP).
3. Moreover, because the self-reported benchmark is the reference portfolio for the investors, the choice to diverge from it has to pay off. Thus, regardless of the value of α_P^{MF}, the portfolio manager must at least deliver a positive peer group comparison return or, in other words, $\alpha'_P = PG_P = \overline{R}_P - \overline{R}_B > 0$.

Combining these three conditions, the portfolio manager will have delivered a positive performance if the following condition is satisfied:

$$\alpha_P^{MF} > \max\left[0, \alpha_B^{MF}\frac{\sum_{k=1}^{K} \beta_{P,k}(\overline{F}_k - \overline{R}_f)}{\sum_{k=1}^{K} \beta_{B,k}(\overline{F}_k - \overline{R}_f)}, \alpha_B^{MF} + \sum_{k=1}^{K}(\beta_{B,k} - \beta_{P,k})(\overline{F}_k - \overline{R}_f)\right] \tag{7-15}$$

where the arguments of the square bracket depend on three inputs: the benchmark's own alpha, the portfolio's, and the benchmark's required excess returns.

KFF example (continued)

Checking the three conditions in inequality (7-15), we first note that the fund's multifactor alpha is positive.

From the example above, we obtain that the benchmark's own alpha is $\alpha_B^{MF} = 0.04\%$. Furthermore, the table immediately gives the required excess returns. For the benchmark, this required return is equal to $0.77 \times 0.11\% + 0.43 \times 0.44\% = 0.27\%$. For KFF, it is $0.91 \times 0.11\% + 0.32 \times 0.44\% = 0.24\%$

The application of inequality (7-15) gives the following result:

$$\alpha_{KFF}^{MF} = 0.52\% > \max\left[0,0.04\% + (0.27\% - 0.24\%), 0.04\% \times \frac{0.24\%}{0.27\%}\right] = \max(0,0.07\%,0.03\%)$$

Thus, all three conditions are satisfied.

7.2.2.2 Statistical significance

Regarding the multifactor alpha, the general approach used for hypothesis testing is the check of only condition (1), i.e., the positivity of the performance measure. The test of statistical significance corresponds to the one of the intercepts of a linear regression model. Similar to Jensen's alpha, under the usual probabilistic assumptions applied to the least squares multiple regression (7-7), the test statistic of the form

$$\hat{t}_{\alpha_P^{MF}=0} = \frac{\alpha_P^{MF}}{\sigma_{\alpha_P^{MF}}} \tag{7-16}$$

follows (under the null hypothesis of zero performance) a Student t-distribution with $T-1$ degrees of freedom, where T is the number of observations, and $\sigma_{\alpha_P^{MF}}$ is the volatility of the estimate of α_P^{MF}. Essentially, this is the same test as for the univariate (one-factor) regression, i.e., Jensen's alpha.

Testing the significance of the multifactor modified alpha is unfortunately much more complicated. First, it does not make sense to only test the positivity of $m\alpha_P^{MF}$ in isolation, since this would explicitly acknowledge the existence of a benchmark portfolio (whose existence is necessary to justify the use of this measure) without taking its own alpha into account. Thus, at least condition (2) above must be included, and the null hypothesis to be tested must be a twin condition:

$$H_0: \alpha_P^{MF} \frac{\sum_{k=1}^{K} \beta_{B,k}(\bar{F}_k - \bar{R}_f)}{\sum_{k=1}^{K} \beta_{P,k}(\bar{F}_k - \bar{R}_f)} - \max[0, \alpha_B^{MF}] = 0 \tag{7-17}$$

Second, the test is necessarily performed numerically. The difficulty resides in the fact that, unlike for the original modified Jensen's alpha, it would be necessary to simultaneously generate three ingredients in order to challenge inequality (7-15). Therefore, we recommend here to preferably use numerical bootstrapping procedures as described in Chapter 3. This approach consists of reusing historical portfolios, benchmarks, and multiple index returns to create an arbitrarily large number of sequences of returns. On each sequence, regression (7-3) is re-estimated on the portfolio and the benchmark, so that the resulting quadruplet whose components are $\left[\alpha_P^{MF}, \alpha_B^{MF}, \sum_{k=1}^{K} \beta_{P,k}(\overline{F}_k - \overline{R}_f), \sum_{k=1}^{K} \beta_{B,k}(\overline{F}_k - \overline{R}_f)\right]$ is recorded. With a large number of quadruplets, we can simply construct a confidence interval for expression (7-17) and check whether it includes zero or not.

7.2.3 Strengths and weaknesses

7.2.3.1 Strengths

In a nutshell, the multifactor versions of the alpha and modified alpha share, at least, the same advantages as their single-factor counterparts. They reflect the abnormal return that remains after all relevant sources of risks have been taken into account. Indeed, both performance measures are the simplest ones that precisely bear the same interpretation as the original Jensen's alpha and modified alpha in the multifactor setup. This can be readily seen by comparing Figure 7-4 in this chapter with Figure 3-7 in Chapter 3: The former is literally a 3-D version of the latter.

Thanks to the formulation of the alpha in Equation (7-11), both measures also allow the identification of the benchmark portfolio that is most relevant for the determination of the portfolio's required return during the time window considered for the analysis. This piece of information can be highly relevant in order to understand the choices made by the portfolio manager and, in particular, the extent to which they have diverged from the self-reported benchmark that the portfolio was supposed to track and to outperform.

In addition to their common strengths, each measure has its own specific advantages. The multifactor alpha displays at least four desirable properties:

- Not surprisingly for the experienced reader, the main strength of the multifactor alpha in this context is that everyone knows it in the asset management profession. Even more than with the CAPM, which many researchers and practitioners appreciate but hardly find realistic, the multifactor alpha is "the" famous performance measure that is meant to reflect the abnormal rcturn of a portfolio.
- Regarding the nature of the measure, its simplicity is another advantage. Whatever the specific form adopted by the linear model described in the first section, the multifactor alpha can always be computed as its estimated intercept. Not only the measure that it brings is generally reasonable (provided that the factors used in the analysis are also reasonable), but statistical inference is not complicated either. For researchers, the

alpha is also often used as a tool in order to test the validity of a model specification or the relevance of a risk factor.

- The alpha is also essentially benchmark-free. Of course, its nature as an abnormal return entails the construction of a regression-based benchmark, but it does not depend upon any reference portfolio determined externally. Here again, this ensures the applicability of this measure in any context, including the one of so-called "absolute return" funds for which, even though a multifactor model would be informative, the strategy hinges on the absence of a benchmark (besides a hurdle rate).
- From Figure 7-3, another clear advantage of the multifactor alpha measure immediately stands out: For any given model, it delivers a unique value of performance associated with every single portfolio, whatever their difference in factor sensitivities and, in particular, the relevance of the model. It is thus truly universal.

On the other hand, the multifactor modified alpha also reveals a set of advantages over the simple version of multifactor alpha:

- From a purely conceptual standpoint, the multifactor modified alpha dominates the straight multifactor alpha for the same reasons as the dominance of the modified alpha over Jensen's alpha in the CAPM case. It is scale independent and delivers a normalized picture of portfolio performance, whatever its risk level could be. This reason alone is presumably sufficient to justify the adoption of this measure in many performance appraisal contexts.
- The modified alpha displays other advantages beyond that conceptual reason. Whereas a self-reported benchmark portfolio exists otherwise, it is recommended to adopt the modified alpha whenever a linear multifactor model is used in order to understand how the portfolio return has been generated. This situation corresponds to a practical concern for many investors: How to simultaneously address the outperformance of a portfolio compared to its benchmark *and* its model? Clearly, the answer is unambiguously given in inequality (7-15), and one needs the multifactor modified alpha for that purpose.
- The fact that the alpha is normalized by the portfolio required return in expression (7-12) also induces that the multifactor modified alpha literally acts as an acid test of the underlying model validity. Computing the alpha of a poorly specified model that shows a very small required return makes no sense, but the resulting alpha itself will not take an absurd value. However, if the required return is low, the modified alpha will likely be ridiculously high (in absolute value). Do not shoot the messenger: The problem is not with the performance measure but with the model. The modified alpha allows the analyst to put the finger on a potential modeling issue.

7.2.3.2 Weaknesses

Probably, the major weakness associated with this pair of performance measures is their reliance on a model that might not reflect the reality of (i) the risk–return relationship on the financial market and (ii) the true nature of the manager's skill.

The first issue directly refers to the long discussion about the model specification and its associated questions: How many factors? Which ones should be included? Are there redundancies or, on the contrary, missing factors? Are these factors the reflection of some sort of systematic risk that should be remunerated, or the mere outcome of a market anomaly? Nothing can be inferred from the performance measures in order to answer each of these important questions. If the model is garbage, the alpha will be garbage, but the observed level of the alpha does not tell it.

The second issue is not related to the quality of the asset pricing model, but rather to the way it applies to the portfolio manager. In particular, it does not allow the observer to identify the impact of market timing skills on performance. The multifactor alpha and modified alpha may be completely biased (upward or downward) as a consequence of this shortcoming. This issue is discussed in Chapter 8.

Finally, both versions of the alpha (the original and the modified ones) are also supposed to reflect the net performance of the portfolio as it is returned to the investors. This notion should not be confused with the diagnosis that should be posed about the manager's skill in generating abnormal returns by their very decisions, irrespective of the portfolio's size or fee structure. In order to understand this skill, it is necessary to dissect the alpha further, as discussed in Chapter 18.

Not surprisingly, each measure has its own list of weaknesses. For the multifactor alpha, we can list the following:

- The last listed strength of the alpha, namely, its ability to always deliver a simple and unique value for the performance, is a double-edged sword. The multifactor alpha cannot possibly alert its user against deficiencies in the model used for the analysis. Be it a lack of significance, a shortage of relevant factors, or any other misspecification, none of these issues really alters the reassuring indication brought by the alpha. This problem also induces a potential danger of performance manipulation: If a relevant factor with a positive excess return is omitted – which is a real issue for some sophisticated portfolios like hedge funds – the alpha usually captures a large part of the premium and can thus be artificially inflated. This might be an incentive for unethical (or simply lazy) portfolio managers themselves not to make the effort of attempting to explain their returns in the best possible way, knowing that this could eventually embellish the presentation of their performance.
- Another issue, which actually precisely justifies the use of the modified Jensen's alpha instead, is its "scale dependence" as defined in Chapter 4. The illustration of Figure 7-4 clearly shows that portfolio H (higher risk) dominates portfolio L (low risk) on the basis

of their alphas, but the ordering switches when the difference in their risks (materialized by their required return) is explicitly taken into account in the measurement of performance. Thus, the multifactor alpha is not suitable at all in order to compare funds or portfolios whose risk levels are very different.

- Finally, in the presence of a self-reported benchmark, it must be underlined that the multifactor alpha is necessary but not sufficient to address the issue of the manager's outperformance. Equation (7-10) certainly expresses this outperformance in terms of the portfolio's alpha, but the conditions use all the ingredients that compose the modified alpha, whose use is warranted for that purpose.

In spite of its advantages, why is the multifactor modified alpha not dominant in that field, either for asset management professionals or researchers? There are also some legitimate explanations:

- On the one hand, the multifactor modified alpha is less straightforward, less "classical," and less intuitive than the alpha. All these reasons dampen its popularity for practitioners. The measure may appear here and there in some detailed reports, but it clearly bumps into the difficulty of replacing simpler measures to compute and to explain, such as the alpha.
- On the other hand, the testability issue with the multifactor modified alpha is a clear hindrance for researchers. Not only is a simple statistical inference tool similar to the Student *t*-statistic not available, but one also needs to identify a specific benchmark in order to assess the significance of the estimates. Furthermore, the very high sensitivity of this performance measure to model quality renders the analysis of multiple portfolios very difficult. It suffices to observe one or a few outliers for which the model does not work, and the whole interpretation of the results can be impaired. Therefore, there is still much to do in order to adapt the multifactor modified alpha to the requirements of most empirical papers in the field.
- In the absence of a well-identified benchmark portfolio *B*, the performance measure can still be computed, and it allows the comparison of multiple portfolios. Nevertheless, it loses much of its intuitiveness as the notion of a "representative beta" of a portfolio only stands as an arbitrary scaling factor when it is not matched with that of a benchmark. In other words, the absolute version of the modified alpha $m\alpha_P^{\text{MF,abs}} = \frac{\alpha_P^{\text{MF}}}{\beta_P^*}$ delivers a rate of return that can be used for comparative purposes, but that does not correspond to any self-explanatory definition.
- Finally, it is worth mentioning that simplicity has its merits when sophistication is useless. For simple situations, with portfolios that have more or less the same risk, the added value of computing the modified version of the alpha could be very limited compared to its drawbacks listed above.

7.3 OTHER CLASSICAL PERFORMANCE MEASURES ADAPTED TO MULTIFACTOR MODELS

The extension of a single-factor model, such as the CAPM, to a linear multifactor specification mostly affects systematic risk exposures of a portfolio. Nevertheless, there are still a number of issues that may affect performance when a notion of total risk or specific risk comes is considered. The main – but not only – reason for the rise of such issues resides in the simultaneous presence of several types of benchmarks: the multifactor one, which is an analytical construction based on Equation (7-3); the self-reported one, which is a discretionary choice that can be either a passive index or an actively managed portfolio; and even the theoretical market portfolio itself. They all have their own risk and their own correlation with the returns of the analyzed portfolio, leading to a potential need to measure performance in a different way from the multifactor alpha or its modified version examined in Section 7.2.

What are we talking about in this section? If we apply Equation (7-3) to an actively managed portfolio, its total risk (expressed in terms of its variance), can be split into its factor-related part and the idiosyncratic part:

$$\sigma_P^2 = \sigma_{BMF}^2 + \sigma_{\varepsilon_P}^2 \qquad (7\text{-}18)$$

where $\sigma_P^2 = \sigma^2(R_P)$ is the variance of portfolio returns, $\sigma_{BMF}^2 \equiv \sigma^2\left(\sum_{k=1}^{K} \beta_{P,k}(F_{k,t} - R_f)\right)$ is the variance of the factor exposures, and $\sigma_{\varepsilon_P}^2 \equiv \sigma^2(\varepsilon_{P,t})$ is the variance of the residual term, also known as the idiosyncratic variance.

The Sharpe ratio and the Appraisal ratio are defined on the basis of σ_P and $\sigma_{\varepsilon P}$, respectively. We investigate below how these measures – and other ones – evolve when the specificities of a multifactor model are considered.

7.3.1 Performance measures based on total risk

The Sharpe ratio (according to its commonly accepted definition) is a performance measure based on total risk.[18] By nature, this notion does not depend upon the asset pricing model, whatever its kind used in order to explain the required returns of the portfolio. Thus, using a multifactor model rather than a single-factor one (such as the CAPM) has no effect on the Sharpe ratio of a portfolio; this is a non-issue.

Nevertheless, it becomes interesting to use a measure of total risk in performance measurement when alternative portfolios (a competing one or the multifactor benchmark) are considered in the analysis. By introducing this additional dimension, the objective is to explicitly take into account the responsibility of the style adopted by the manager, which is often

[18] Note that this definition does not correspond to Sharpe's (1994) own interpretation of the performance measure called by his own name, which is now generally called the Information ratio. We discuss this issue in Chapter 3.

not a free choice on their side (like in many mutual funds, for which the fund charter largely constrains the manager to adopt a particular style and an associated benchmark).

7.3.1.1 The relative risk-adjusted performance measure

A useful avatar of the Sharpe ratio for the purpose of the chapter is the Modigliani and Modigliani (1997) "risk-adjusted performance", also called the M^2, presented in Chapter 6. This measure essentially restates the Sharpe Ratio in the form of a normalized rate of return generated by the actively managed portfolio when its risk is made comparable to that of the market portfolio. As a reminder, the original measure is written as $\text{RAP}_P = R_f + \frac{\sigma_M}{\sigma_P}(\overline{R}_P - R_f)$, where σ_M stands for the volatility of the market portfolio returns.

A portfolio manager can achieve a high or low value of the RAP – and thus a high Sharpe ratio – because their benchmark itself has obtained an attractive risk–return trade-off during the same period. This is the reason why Lobosco (1999) proposes, in the context of style analysis, the explicit inclusion of the model-based benchmark's RAP in the analysis. His idea is to distinguish the effect of the self-reported benchmark B that replaces the market portfolio in the RAP from the effect of the style (model-based) benchmark that drives the portfolio's required rate of return. The so-called *multifactor relative risk-adjusted performance* (RRAP) is written, according to our notation, as

$$\text{RRAP}_P^{\text{MF}} = \text{RAP}_P - \text{RAP}_{B\text{MF}} = \frac{\sigma_B}{\sigma_P}(\overline{R}_P - R_f) - \frac{\sigma_B}{\sigma_{B\text{MF}}}\left(\overline{R}_B^{\text{MF}} - R_f\right) \tag{7-19}$$

In this expression, the benchmark only appears as a risk-normalization device. It is interesting to note that, as $\sigma_{B\text{MF}} = \sqrt{\sigma_P^2 - \sigma_{\varepsilon_P}^2}$ from Equation (7-18), the factor exposure risk $\sigma_{B\text{MF}}$ must be lower than the total risk σ_P, and therefore the risk multiplier of the first term of the RRAP is greater than that of the second one. In order to deliver a positive performance, the portfolio manager must therefore obtain a ratio of excess return over its multifactor benchmark that is greater than the ratio of their risks: $\text{RRAP}_P > 0 \Longleftrightarrow \frac{\overline{R}_P - R_f}{\overline{R}_B^{\text{MF}} - R_f} > \frac{\sigma_P}{\sigma_{B\text{MF}}} > 1$.

7.3.1.2 The split risk–return performance measure

Another approach to explicitly include total portfolio risk in performance measurement is to separate the issue of the remuneration of risk on the financial market from the actual generation of excess return. Aftalion and Poncet (1991) propose this idea by introducing a performance index in which they split the actual extra portfolio return over its multifactor benchmark (i.e., its multifactor alpha), on the one hand, and the market-based reward that the portfolio should obtain for its extra risk, on the other hand. We refer to this measure as the *split risk–return performance* (SRRP) of the portfolio:

$$\text{SRRP}_P = \left(\overline{R}_P - \overline{R}_B^{\text{MF}}\right) - \text{MRP} \times (\sigma_P - \sigma_{B\text{MF}}) = \alpha_P^{\text{MF}} - \text{MRP} \times (\sigma_P - \sigma_{B\text{MF}}) \tag{7-20}$$

where MRP stands for the market risk premium, i.e., the prevailing remuneration for volatility risk that stands on the financial market at that moment. In the CAPM context, this would be equal to the Sharpe ratio of the market portfolio (MRP $= \frac{\overline{R}_M - R_f}{\sigma_M}$), but it remains to be determined what market proxy should be used. Aftalion and Poncet (1991) conjecture that the MRP would likely stand between 0.20 and 0.40 annually, which is in line with long-term values of the Sharpe ratios observed for broad asset classes documented in Chapter 3.

The graphical representation of both performance measures is given in Figure 7-5. On the graph, the risk of the benchmark σ_B stands at the level where the RRAP is reported: This performance measure simply corresponds to the vertical distance between the coordinates of the risk-scaled version of the portfolio ($\frac{\sigma_B}{\sigma_P}P$) and the one of its multifactor benchmark ($\frac{\sigma_B}{\sigma_{B^{MF}}}B^{MF}$). The SRRP is computed as the vertical distance between these two portfolios (α_P), diminished with the required excess return linked to the difference in their risks (the vertical pair of arrows, which comes in deduction of the performance).

It is important to note that both performance measures have a legitimate justification. The RRAP explicitly recognizes the existence of an analytical (multifactor) benchmark portfolio and a self-reported one. Its role is to express the incremental total-risk-adjusted performance in the presence of these two benchmarks for an investor who cares about total risk (see Chapter 4 for a discussion of the circumstance in which it is warranted). The SRRP is "benchmark-free" instead. Rather than looking at factual abnormal returns, it addresses a pure normative perspective through the question: *How much should an investor earn on their portfolio knowing the risks of their portfolio and the one that they cannot avoid (through the factor exposure risk)?*

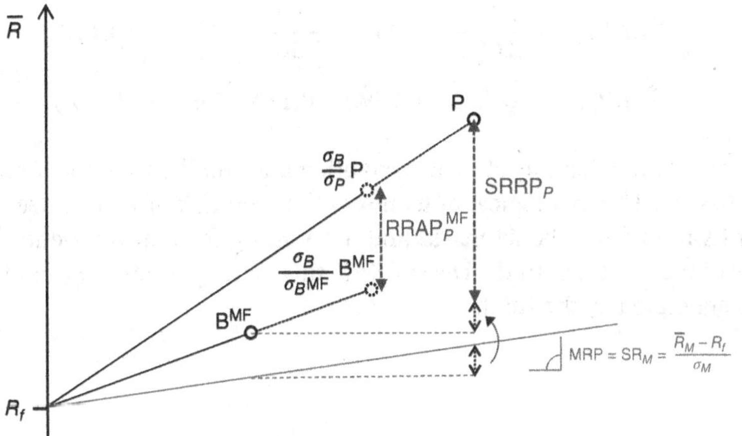

FIGURE 7-5 Graphical representation of the multifactor relative risk-adjusted performance (RRAP) and the split risk–return performance (SRRP).

KFF example (continued)

It is considered for the sake of the SRRP computation that the market portfolio M is made up with a weighted average of equity returns (40% North America, 25% Europe, 5% Japan, and 25% Rest of World). In order to assess portfolio performance according to the two measures, we simply need the excess return and total risk (volatility) of the different portfolios considered in the calculations.

The results are summarized in Table 7-6.

TABLE 7-6 KFF example – Excess returns and volatilities of the portfolios.

Portfolio	Average exc. return	Volatility
KFF	0.76%	2.65%
Benchmark	0.31%	2.49%
Benchmark MF	0.24%	2.26%
Market	0.59%	4.48%

The proxy for the market portfolio delivers a risk premium equal to $MRP = \frac{0.59\%}{4.48\%} = 0.13$, corresponding to a yearly Sharpe ratio of $SR_M = 0.13\sqrt{12} = 0.45$, which is a realistic figure.

The computation of the total risk-based performance measures gives

$$RRAP_{KFF} = \frac{2.49\%}{2.65\%} \times 0.76\% - \frac{2.49\%}{2.26\%} \times 0.24\% = 0.45\%$$

$$SRRP_{KFF} = (0.76\% - 0.24\%) - 0.13 \times (2.65\% - 2.26\%) = 0.47\%$$

Both figures are incidentally close to each other and smaller than the fund's multifactor alpha ($\alpha_P = 0.52\%$). This is a logical outcome as the total risk of KFF is necessarily higher than that of its multifactor benchmark, and accounting for that difference penalizes the performance of the portfolio. In the case of KFF, this penalty is not large enough to destroy all the alpha generated by the fund.

7.3.2 Performance measures based on residual risk

7.3.2.1 The multifactor ("pure") Information ratio

In his article attempting to put the ratio called by his own name in perspective, Sharpe (1994) addresses the question of performance measurement in the framework of RBSA. In his view, the spirit of the reward-to-risk ratio underlying the original Sharpe ratio entails the identification of a reference portfolio that serves as a benchmark. In the CAPM framework, the risk-free asset plays this role. Accordingly, he advocates the use of the multifactor benchmark in the context of style analysis. In fact, this corresponds to the same definition as the one that we have given to the Information ratio in Chapter 3. We call this the *pure Information ratio*:

$$\mathrm{IR}_P^{\mathrm{pure}} = \frac{\overline{R}_P - \overline{R}_B^{\mathrm{MF}}}{\sigma(R_P - R_B^{\mathrm{MF}})} = \frac{\alpha_P^{\mathrm{MF}}}{\sigma_{\varepsilon P}} \tag{7-21}$$

The definition is exactly the same as in Chapter 3. Thus, in a multifactor context, when specific risk is taken into account in order to measure the abnormal return per unit of risk, one has to "simply" record the intercept and the standard deviation of the residual term of regression (7-3), respectively, as the numerator and the denominator of the performance measure.

7.3.2.2 The "misfit" and "global" Information ratios

Like the multifactor alpha, the Information ratio expressed in Equation (7-21) ignores the existence of a self-reported, portfolio-specific benchmark B that can differ from the regression-based one, obtained analytically. These notions can be related to the determination of the Information ratio applied to both benchmarks.

According to this logic, we can split the active return of the portfolio, defined from the investor's perspective as $\alpha_P' = \mathrm{PG}_P = \overline{R}_P - \overline{R}_B$, into two components. The regression-based benchmark drives the "true active return" of the portfolio, thus defined by its multifactor alpha $\overline{R}_P - \overline{R}_B^{\mathrm{MF}} = \alpha_P^{\mathrm{MF}}$, whereas the difference between the regression-based and the self-reported benchmark is the "misfit active return" $\overline{R}_B^{\mathrm{MF}} - \overline{R}_B = \left(\sum_{k=1}^{K}(\beta_{P,k} - \beta_{B,k})\left(\overline{F}_k - \overline{R}_f\right)\right) - \alpha_B^{\mathrm{MF}}$.

To compute the Information ratios, it is necessary to associate their active risk with each of these two active returns. The "pure active risk" is simply $\sigma_{\varepsilon P}$ described in Equation (7-21) above. Thus, the pure Information ratio reflects the genuine performance attributable to the portfolio manager. The "misfit active risk" represents $\sigma(R_B^{\mathrm{MF}} - R_B)$, which depends on (i) the difference in factor sensitivities between the portfolio and its benchmark, and (ii) the specific risk of the benchmark. Consequently, we can characterize the *misfit Information ratio* of portfolio P as

$$\mathrm{IR}_P^{\text{misfit}} = \frac{\overline{R}_B^{\mathrm{MF}} - \overline{R}_B}{\sigma(R_B^{\mathrm{MF}} - R_B)} = \frac{\left(\sum_{k=1}^{K}(\beta_{P,k} - \beta_{B,k})(\overline{F}_k - \overline{R}_f)\right) - \alpha_B^{\mathrm{MF}}}{\sqrt{\sigma^2\left(\sum_{k=1}^{K}(\beta_{P,k} - \beta_{B,k})(F_{k,t} - R_f)\right) + \sigma_{\varepsilon B}^2}} \tag{7-22}$$

where $\sigma_{\varepsilon B}^2 = \sigma^2\left(R_B - \alpha_B^{\mathrm{MF}} - \overline{R}_f - \sum_{k=1}^{K}\beta_{B,k}(F_{k,t} - R_f)\right)$ stands for the variance of the residual term of the multifactor regression model applied on the benchmark portfolio.

The misfit Information ratio reflects the level of satisfaction felt by the investor regarding the actual benchmark chosen by the portfolio manager compared to the self-reported one. There are two drivers of sign of this ratio: the difference in remuneration of the factor risk exposures (the higher the one of the portfolio, the better it is) and the multifactor alpha of the benchmark (the higher this alpha, the worse it is).

Finally, the *global Information ratio* combines the pure and misfit active risks and returns. It corresponds to the combined impact of the portfolio manager's skill and the satisfaction of the benchmark choice. Considering that the correlation between the residual terms of the portfolio and the benchmark is negligible, we can write this ratio as

$$\mathrm{IR}_P = \frac{\overline{R}_P - \overline{R}_B}{\sigma(R_P - R_B)} \approx \frac{\alpha_P^{\mathrm{MF}} - \alpha_B^{\mathrm{MF}} + \left(\sum_{k=1}^{K}(\beta_{P,k} - \beta_{B,k})(\overline{F}_k - \overline{R}_f)\right)}{\sqrt{\sigma^2\left(\sum_{k=1}^{K}(\beta_{P,k} - \beta_{B,k})(F_{k,t} - R_f)\right) + \sigma_{\varepsilon P}^2 + \sigma_{\varepsilon B}^2}} \tag{7-23}$$

The decomposition of specific risk-based performance between the true and misfit components is very useful when one attempts to "correct" the impact of misfit risk through the use of so-called completeness funds (see Tierney and Winston, 1990, for a discussion). The underlying rationale is to find a complement portfolio whose risk properties allow a realignment of the behavior of the global portfolio with the benchmark chosen by the investor.

KFF example (continued)

The pure Information ratio can readily be computed using the multifactor alpha $\alpha_{\mathrm{KFF}}^{\mathrm{MF}} = 0.52\%$ reported in Table 7-5 and the standard deviation of the residual of the two-factor model specification for the KFF fund, which is equal to $\sigma_{\varepsilon\mathrm{KFF}} = 0.69\%$.

Regarding the other two ratios (misfit and global IR), it is necessary to obtain four more ingredients: (i) the multifactor alpha of the benchmark, (ii) the mean and (iii) the standard deviation of the difference between the required returns of the KFF fund and its self-reported benchmark, and (iv) the standard deviation of the residual term of the multifactor regression model applied on the benchmark portfolio.

(i) The multifactor alpha of the benchmark is given in Table 7-5 as $\alpha_B^{MF} = 0.04\%$.
(ii) From Table 7-5, the mean difference between the required returns of KFF and its self-reported benchmark is $(\overline{R}_{KFF} - \alpha_{KFF}^{MF}) - (\overline{R}_B - \alpha_B^{MF}) = (0.76\% - 0.52\%) - (0.31\% - 0.04\%) = -0.03\%$.
(iii) By reconstructing the series of differential returns, i.e. $(\beta_{KFF,Bd-Dev} - \beta_{B,Bd-Dev})(I_{Bd-Dev,t} - R_f) + (\beta_{KFF,q-Eur} - \beta_{B,q-Eur})(I_{q-Eur,t} - R_f)$, we obtain the standard deviation of this expression equal to 0.48%.
(iv) Finally, Table 7-5 immediately delivers the specific risk of the benchmark: $\sigma_{\varepsilon B} = 0.03\%$.

The application of formulas (7-21) to (7-23) provides the following outputs:

$$IR_{KFF}^{pure} = \frac{0.52\%}{0.69\%} = 0.75$$

$$IR_{KFF}^{misfit} = \frac{-0.03\% - 0.04\%}{\sqrt{(0.48\%)^2 + (0.03\%)^2}} = \frac{-0.07\%}{0.48\%} = -0.14$$

$$IR_{KFF} \approx \frac{0.52\% - 0.04\% - 0.03\%}{\sqrt{(0.48\%)^2 + (0.69\%)^2 + (0.03\%)^2}} = \frac{0.45\%}{0.85\%} = 0.53$$

Naturally, these ratios are generally expressed in annualized terms, i.e., multiplied by the square root of 12 in the case of monthly returns.[19] This then gives $IR_{KFF}^{pure} = 2.59$, $IR_{KFF}^{misfit} = -0.50$, and $IR_{KFF} = 1.84$. Interestingly, considering the qualitative assessment related to these values (see Section 3.4.2 of Chapter 3), it would correspond to the diagnosis that the way KFF is managed is "excellent" from a qualitative perspective ($IR_{KFF}^{pure} > 1$), but from the investor's point of view (who only cares about the self-reported benchmark), it is reduced by almost one third of its pure value.

The graphical representation of the three versions of the Information ratio is provided in Figure 7-6.

(continued)

[19] See Chapter 3 for an explanation of the adjustment.

(continued)

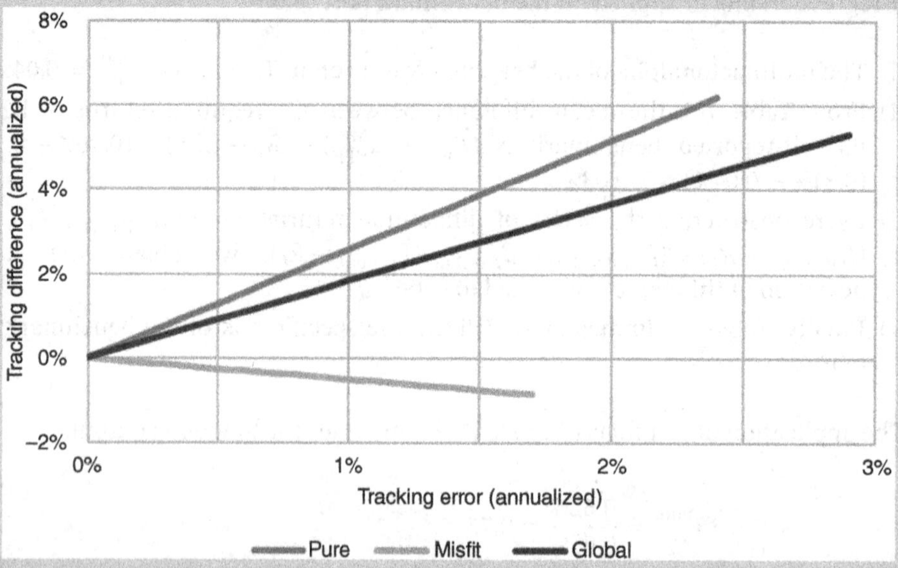

FIGURE 7-6 KFF example – Representation of the pure, modified, and global Information ratios.

The Information ratio corresponds to the slope of each line.

The middle line, which represents the global active return/active risk trade-off of KFF, reflects the aggregation of active returns (vertical axis) and active risks (horizontal axis) present in the pure (upper line) and misfit (lower line) IRs. The graph clearly shows the difference in the treatment of return and risk. While active returns are additive (the vertical coordinate of the middle line equals the sum of the coordinates of the other two), active risks are sub-additive (the horizontal coordinate of the middle line is lower than the sum of the coordinates of the other two). This reflects the effect of diversification between the residual risks of the factor exposures and the specific risk of the benchmark.

7.4 MEASURING PERFORMANCE IN SPECIAL CASES OF MULTIFACTOR MODELS

Linear multifactor models are very diverse, but their formulation is rather generic. Before considering nonlinear alterations of this model in order to accommodate particular skills such as market timing, two special cases of factor models are worth discussing within the scope of this chapter. The first one involves a simplification: When there is a single factor considered, performance measurement according to the principles of the previous sections may still differ from the classical way to appraise performance in the context of the CAPM. On the contrary, the second special case involves an additional complexification: When we add the possibility to condition the portfolio management strategy on previously observable information, we are still within the scope of linear multifactor models but with a more sophisticated structure. This so-called conditional model also involves the adaptation of portfolio measurement approaches.

7.4.1 Single-factor models

We saw in the beginning of this chapter that the CAPM can be viewed as a special case of a multifactor model, in which the market portfolio return is identified as the single factor influencing portfolio returns in a systematic way.

What would then differ between the theoretical approach depicted in Chapter 2 (and its associated performance measures developed in Chapter 3), on the one hand, and the use of a single-factor model that would be considered sufficient to explain returns on the other hand? The answer lies in the identification of the benchmark. In the CAPM, there is an identity between the factor and the risky component of the benchmark: They are both identified as the market portfolio. In a single-factor model, nothing prevents the factor and the benchmark to be distinct from each other. This creates two potential differences that are meaningful for performance measurement. First, the benchmark mean returns, i.e., $\overline{R}_B^{SF} = \overline{R}_f + \beta_P(\overline{F} - \overline{R}_f)$ for the single-factor model and $\overline{R}_B = \overline{R}_f + \beta_B(\overline{F} - \overline{R}_f)$ for the self-reported benchmark, may differ. Second, the portfolio and the benchmark display different specific risks. This all entails some adaptations of the classical performance measures.[20]

7.4.1.1 The single-factor modified alpha

Even though the same logic as with the multifactor modified alpha would lead to Equation (7-12) in the single-factor version of the model, it is convenient to use instead a simplified version of Equation (7-13), which uses the representative beta. The single-factor modified alpha can be written as

$$m\alpha_P^{SF} = \alpha_P \frac{\beta_B}{\beta_P} \tag{7-24}$$

This expression simply means that the modified alpha of a portfolio is equal to its alpha normalized by the ratio of the betas. If $\beta_B = 1$, i.e., if the benchmark has a unit systematic risk, the ratio boils down to the ordinary modified Jensen's alpha described in Chapter 3.

[20]Note that the single-factor alpha is unchanged compared to equation (7-11). It is therefore not discussed further.

The question of the significance of the single-factor modified alpha is also simplified. Using the same arguments as the ones leading to inequality (7-15), we can conclude about the outperformance of a portfolio manager if (i) they have delivered a positive performance ($\alpha_P > 0$); (ii) they have a better model-based abnormal return than the benchmark ($\alpha_P \frac{\beta_B}{\beta_P} > \alpha_B$), and (iii) they have directly beaten the benchmark ($\alpha'_P = \overline{R}_P - \overline{R}_B > 0$). Altogether, portfolio outperformance entails that

$$\alpha_P > \max\left[0, \alpha_B \frac{\beta_P}{\beta_B}, \alpha_B + (\beta_B - \beta_P)(\overline{F} - \overline{R}_f)\right] \tag{7-25}$$

Finally, statistical inference can be performed according to a relatively simple version of the null hypothesis of the form

$$H_0 : \alpha_P \frac{\beta_B}{\beta_P} - \max[0, \alpha_B] = 0 \tag{7-26}$$

7.4.1.2 The single-factor Information ratio

In the context of the decomposition of the Information ratio discussed in Section 7.3.2, the analysis considerably simplifies. The pure Information ratio remains identical and is called the Appraisal ratio: $\text{IR}_P^{\text{pure}} = \text{AR}_P = \frac{\overline{R}_P - \overline{R}_B^{\text{SF}}}{\sigma(R_P - R_B^{\text{SF}})} = \frac{\alpha_P}{\sigma_{\varepsilon P}}$. Regarding the misfit and global versions of the ratio (Equations (7-22) and (7-23)), the complexity of estimating the variance of the factor vanishes: As there is a single factor left, there is no covariance term in the expressions of active risk. Using the same notation as before, we can rewrite the single-factor versions of the ratios as

$$\text{IR}_P^{\text{misfit}} = \frac{\overline{R}_B^{\text{SF}} - \overline{R}_B}{\sigma(R_B^{\text{SF}} - R_B)} = \frac{(\beta_P - \beta_B)(\overline{F} - \overline{R}_f) - \alpha_B}{\sqrt{(\beta_P - \beta_B)^2 \sigma^2(F) + \sigma_{\varepsilon B}^2}} \tag{7-27}$$

$$\text{IR}_P = \frac{\overline{R}_P - \overline{R}_B}{\sigma(R_P - R_B)} \approx \frac{\alpha_P - \alpha_B + (\beta_P - \beta_B)(\overline{F} - \overline{R}_f)}{\sqrt{(\beta_P - \beta_B)^2 \sigma^2(F) + \sigma_{\varepsilon P}^2 + \sigma_{\varepsilon B}^2}} \tag{7-28}$$

where $\sigma^2(F)$ stands for the variance of the returns of the factor.

KFF example (continued)

The portfolio manager has chosen to select the index with the highest correlation with the KFF fund, namely, Equities-North America, in order to implement the single-factor model. The regression outputs for the fund and the factor are provided in Table 7-7.

TABLE 7-7 KFF example – Summary of the single-index regression outputs for the fund and the benchmark.

	Average exc. return	α	$\beta_{Eq-N.Am}$	σ_ε	R^2
KFF	0.76%	0.52%	0.46	0.83%	67.1%
Benchmark	0.31%	0.04%	0.51	0.18%	92.0%

Not surprisingly, the R^2 is lower and the specific risk is higher for this regression than for the two-factor model presented in Table 7-5. From Table 7-1, we know that the mean and standard deviation of the excess index returns are $\overline{I}_{Eq-N.Am} - \overline{R}_f = 0.52\%$ and $\sigma_{Eq-N.Am} = 4.77\%$.

The modified alpha of KFF is equal to $m\alpha^{1F}_{KFF} = 0.52\%\frac{0.51}{0.46} = 0.57\%$.

The three components of the Information ratio are the following:

$$IR^{pure}_{KFF} = \frac{0.52\%}{0.83\%} = 0.62$$

$$IR^{misfit}_{KFF} = \frac{(0.46 - 0.51) \times 0.52\% - 0.04\%}{\sqrt{(0.46 - 0.51)^2 \times (4.77\%)^2 + (0.18\%)^2}} = \frac{-0.07\%}{0.28\%} = -0.24$$

$$IR_{KFF} \approx \frac{0.52\% - (0.46 - 0.51) \times 0.52\% - 0.03\%}{\sqrt{(0.46 - 0.51)^2 \times (4.77\%)^2 + (0.83\%)^2 + (0.18\%)^2}} = \frac{0.45\%}{0.88\%} = 0.51$$

Note that these figures are close to but lower than the ones formerly obtained with the two-factor model. The active returns are actually very similar, but, as a price to pay for the improvement in model parsimony, the active risks of both the fund and the benchmark are higher, thereby increasing the denominator for the pure and the global Information ratios. On the contrary, the misfit active risk is lower in the case of a single factor because of the very similar factor betas of the fund and the benchmark.

7.4.2 Conditional multifactor models

7.4.2.1 Defining a conditional multifactor model

Whatever the number of factors (one or several) used in the model, every specification considered so far has kept factor sensitivities constant. Indeed, some asset managers deliberately let their factor exposures change over time. This is the case for so-called "market timers," who manage their betas dynamically in order to increase their factor exposures when they anticipate high associated returns and reduce their exposures when they have an opposite view. In Chapter 8, how their performance can be appraised in such contexts is discussed.

Halfway between stubbornly static betas and wildly dynamic ones, it is possible to alter the model represented by Equation (7-3) by imposing a specific structure of time-varying factor exposures. This corresponds to the family of conditional multifactor models, as proposed by Ferson and Schadt (1996) in the context of a single-factor specification (i.e., the conditional CAPM, as introduced in Chapter 5). Here, we develop the multifactor extension of this framework, with the possibility of not only increasing the number of factors from one (single-factor model) to K but also inflating the set of conditioning instruments from one to L, with the constraint that $L < K$ (i.e., the number of different instruments cannot exceed the number of factors).

To construct a conditional multifactor model, it is necessary to identify the set of conditioning instruments – which can, and typically will, differ from the factors – and to assess the relation between the realizations of these instruments and the factor betas of a given asset or portfolio i. Ferson and Schadt (1996) address these questions by considering a functional form in which the market factor beta is linearly linked with the instruments. Adapted to the context of a multifactor model, this gives

$$\beta_{i,k}(\mathbf{z}_{t-1}) = \beta_{i,k,0} + \mathbf{B}^{\mathrm{T}}_{i,k}\mathbf{z}_{t-1} \equiv \beta_{i,k,t} \tag{7-29}$$

where $\mathbf{z}_{t-1}$ is a normalized column vector of dimension $L \times 1$ representing the deviations of the conditioning instruments from their unconditional (long-term) means at time $t-1$, i.e., $\mathbf{z}_{t-1} = \mathbf{Z}_{t-1} - \mathrm{E}(\mathbf{Z})$; $\mathbf{B}^{\mathrm{T}}_{i,k}$ is a line vector $(\beta_{i,k,1} \ \ldots \ \beta_{i,k,L})$ of dimension $1 \times L$ of the sensitivities of the kth factor beta to the instruments; and $\beta_{i,k,0}$ can be interpreted as the "average factor beta" of the asset. The last identity of the equation reflects the fact that the beta becomes time-varying as a consequence of the dependence on the instruments, which themselves evolve randomly over time.

Considering that Equation (7-29) is potentially applicable for all K factors, the conditional version of the multifactor model can be written as

$$R_{i,t} - R_f = \alpha_i^{\mathrm{MF}} + \sum_{k=1}^{K} \beta_{i,k,0}(F_{k,t} - R_f) + \sum_{k=1}^{K}\sum_{l=1}^{L} \beta_{i,k,l}[z_{l,t-1} \times (F_{k,t} - R_f)] + \varepsilon_{i,t} \tag{7-30}$$

Even though it might look complicated, this conditional model is no more than a linear multiple regression model with $K \times (L+1)$ variables: the K original factors, plus $K \times L$ interaction variables, representing the products of the K factors with the L instruments.

It is important to stress that, even though the factor betas are dynamics, they do not evolve randomly but rather through a deterministic structure resulting from the decision of the manager to condition their levels on the realization of the instruments.

The choice of instruments is a delicate matter because it has to respect principles that are similar to those applicable for the choice of factors, in particular parsimony and accuracy. Among the natural macroeconomic and macro-financial candidates adopted in the literature, we typically find the term spread (difference between the 10-year and 3-month Treasury bond yields), the credit spread (difference between the 10-year Treasury bond yields and the 10-year

Moody's Baa or S&P BBB-rated bond yield), the dividend yield of the stock index, the implied volatility index, the unemployment rate, or the consumer price index. Naturally, since the instruments drive the factor sensitivities adopted by a portfolio manager, there is no single set that should necessarily apply to all actively managed portfolios or funds.

7.4.2.2 The conditional multifactor alpha

As such, the conditional factor specification proposed in Equation (7-30) does not change the way performance should be measured in the multifactor model. Nevertheless, Christopherson, Ferson, and Turner (1999) propose to extend the conditional multifactor model to include a similar dependence structure for the alpha and for the betas:

$$R_{i,t} - R_f = \alpha_{i,0}^{\mathrm{MF}} + \sum_{l=1}^{L} \alpha_{i,l}^{\mathrm{MF}} z_{l,t-1} + \sum_{k=1}^{K} \beta_{i,k,0}(F_{k,t} - R_f)$$
$$+ \sum_{k=1}^{K} \sum_{l=1}^{L} \beta_{i,k,l}[z_{l,t-1} \times (F_{k,t} - R_f)] + \varepsilon_{i,t} \qquad \text{(7-31)}$$

Compared with the preceding specification, we add L more variables (the time-varying alphas), but the model remains linear.

If we apply this approach to an actively managed portfolio P, this gives its so-called conditional multifactor alpha, which aggregates the time-varying conditional alphas:[21]

$$\alpha_P^{\mathrm{cMF}} = \alpha_{P,0}^{\mathrm{MF}} + \mathbf{A}_P^{\mathrm{T}} \overline{\mathbf{z}} \qquad \text{(7-32)}$$

where $\alpha_{P,0}^{\mathrm{MF}}$ is the unconditional (=constant share of the conditional) multifactor alpha, $\mathbf{A}_P^{\mathrm{T}}$ is again a line vector $(\alpha_{P,1}^{\mathrm{MF}} \; \ldots \; \alpha_{P,L}^{\mathrm{MF}})$ of dimension $1 \times L$ of sensitivity coefficients that reflects the fluctuation of the abnormal performance due to each of the conditioning instruments, and $\overline{\mathbf{z}}$ is the column vector of average instrument values $(\overline{z}_1 \; \ldots \; \overline{z}_L)$.

In terms of statistical inference, it is important to make a distinction between two types of tests. First, we can use the standard deviation of the estimate of the "unconditional average alpha" $\sigma_{\alpha_{P,0}^{\mathrm{MF}}} \equiv \sigma(\alpha_{P,0}^{\mathrm{MF}})$ for the appraisal of the manager's selectivity through the usual Student t-test statistic $\hat{\boldsymbol{t}}_{\alpha_{P,0}^{\mathrm{MF}}=0} = \frac{\alpha_{P,0}^{\mathrm{MF}}}{\sigma_{\alpha_{P,0}^{\mathrm{MF}}}}$ since, in general, by construction $\mathbf{A}_P^{\mathrm{T}} \overline{\mathbf{z}} = 0$. This is the approach adopted by Christopherson et al. (1999).[22] Second, since the conditional multifactor alpha is

[21] Of course, if the instruments are normalized so that their average is zero, the conditional multifactor alpha equals the original one. Expression (7-32) will differ if the mean instrument values are themselves not different from zero.

[22] Ferson, Sarkissian, and Simin (2008) warn however that spurious regression effects might generate large biases in the estimates of the regression coefficients. Thus, even the $\boldsymbol{t}$-statistic obtained for the unconditional alpha has to be considered with great caution.

itself time-varying, it is useful to test whether the mean of expression (7-32) statistically differs from 0. Again, because the expression features combinations of several random variables, this can only be reasonably performed numerically. However, as a first, heuristic estimate of the significance of the average conditional alpha, it is still possible to use a simplified approach by checking the value of the ratio $\frac{\alpha_{P,0}^{MF}}{\sigma(\mathbf{A}_P^T \mathbf{z}_{t-1})/\sqrt{T}}$ where T is the number of observations (provided that it is large), i.e., using the sample standard deviation of the variable part of the conditional alpha. Of course, this approach ignores the statistical measurement error in the estimation of the regression coefficients, and does not replace a rigorous statistical inference. Nevertheless, if the value of this ratio is large enough for a sufficiently long sample period, one can be confident that the average conditional multifactor alpha is not null.

In addition, there is, to the best of our knowledge, no conditional version of the multifactor modified alpha.

KFF example (continued)

The manager of the KFF fund has implemented an approach in which they decide not only to change the portfolio composition, namely, the allocation between stocks and bonds, but also the selection of individual securities, on the basis of observed lagged values of the spread between BBB/Baa-rated and AAA/Aaa-rated bond yields, i.e., the credit spread: An increase in the spread triggers a reduction in allocation in fixed-income securities, while a decrease in the spread induces a larger allocation to equities. Consequently, analyzing the returns of this fund entails the use of a conditional two-factor model (the same as before, i.e., with the Bonds-Developed and Equities-Europe indexes) with a single instrument (lagged normalized difference in Credit Spread, or $z_{\text{Cr.Spr},t-1}$), which means $K = 2$ and $L = 1$.

The output of the conditional multi-index linear regression is summarized in the following equation (standard errors of coefficients between parentheses):

$$\begin{aligned} R_{\text{KFF},t} - R_{f,t} = {} & \underset{(0.25\%)}{0.66\%} + \underset{(0.20)}{0.45}\, z_{\text{Cr.Spr},t-1} + \underset{(0.22)}{0.52}\, (I_{\text{Bd-Dev},t} - R_{f,t}) + \underset{(0.05)}{0.29}\, (I_{\text{Eq-Eur},t} - R_{f,t}) \\ & - \underset{(6.94)}{9.09}\, z_{\text{Cr.Spr},t-1}(I_{\text{Bd-Dev},t} - R_{f,t}) + \underset{(3.84)}{1.11}\, z_{\text{Cr.Spr},t-1}(I_{\text{Eq-Eur},t} - R_{f,t}) + \underset{(1.40\%)}{\varepsilon_{\text{KFF},t}} \end{aligned}$$

The direct (constant) sensitivities to the bond and equity indexes are lower than in the original specification. The interaction terms are on the second line. Although the coefficients are large in absolute value, the associated variables (the product of the lagged instrument with the corresponding index) are relatively small. Consequently, the variations in betas are limited.

The components of the conditional (time-varying) two-factor alpha correspond to the first two terms. The intercept is larger ($\alpha_{\text{KFF},0} = 0.66\%$) and more significant ($\hat{t}_{\alpha_{\text{KFF},0}=0} =$

$\frac{0.66\%}{0.25\%} = 2.63$) than in the unconditional model (in that case, $\alpha_{\text{KFF}} = 0.52\%$ and $\hat{t}_{\alpha_{\text{KFF}}=0} = \frac{0.52\%}{0.24\%} = 2.13$). Moreover, there is a significant sensitivity of the alpha to the realization of the factor. The positive coefficient means that the manager is better at "beating the market" when the credit spread increases ($z_{\text{Cr.Spr},t-1} > 0$).

The graphical representation of the evolution of the cumulative alpha over time can be informative about the genesis of the evolution of this alpha (Figure 7-7).

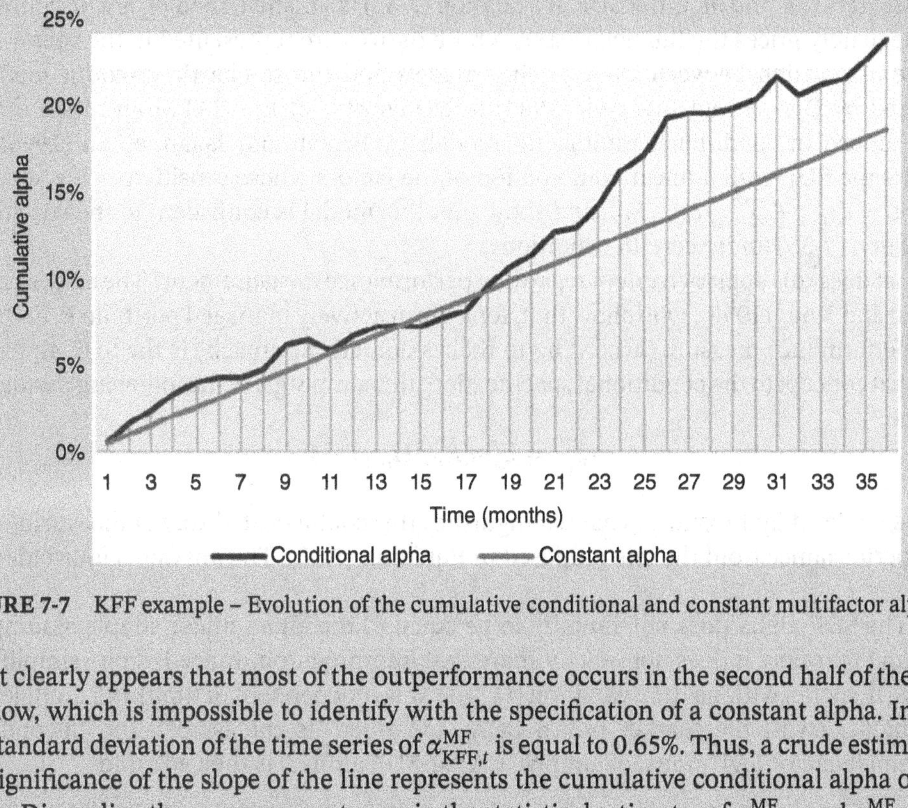

FIGURE 7-7 KFF example – Evolution of the cumulative conditional and constant multifactor alphas.

It clearly appears that most of the outperformance occurs in the second half of the time window, which is impossible to identify with the specification of a constant alpha. In fact, the standard deviation of the time series of $\alpha^{\text{MF}}_{\text{KFF},t}$ is equal to 0.65%. Thus, a crude estimate of the significance of the slope of the line represents the cumulative conditional alpha on the graph. Discarding the measurement error in the statistical estimates of $\alpha^{\text{MF}}_{\text{KFF},0}$ and $\alpha^{\text{MF}}_{\text{KFF,Cr.Spr.}}$, we obtain a heuristic significance ratio of $\frac{\alpha^{\text{MF}}_{\text{KFF},0}}{\sigma(\alpha^{\text{MF}}_{\text{KFF,Cr.Spr.}} z_{\text{Cr.Spr},t-1})/\sqrt{T}} = \frac{0.66\%}{0.65\%/\sqrt{36}} = 6.14$. This value exaggerates of course the true significance of the ratio because it ignores the measurement error of the coefficients, but it already indicates that we can expect a high significance of the slope of the conditional alpha over time.

7.4.3 The stochastic discount factor conditional alpha

In general, every linear multifactor model such as the one depicted in Equation (7-3) can be viewed as a special case of a stochastic discount factor (SDF) model of the form

$$\mathrm{E}(m_t\mathbf{R}_t - \underline{\mathbf{1}}|\Omega_{t-1}) = 0 \tag{7-33}$$

where $\mathrm{E}(\cdot|\Omega_{t-1})$ denotes the expected value of the argument conditional on the information set known at time $t-1$ symbolically represented as Ω_{t-1}, $\underline{\mathbf{1}}$ is a vector of ones, $\mathbf{R}_t$ is the vector of total asset returns, and m_t is the SDF. If Equation (7-33) is satisfied, then m_t is a discount factor that adequately prices the financial assets whose returns are represented in the vector $\mathbf{R}_t$.

The association between asset pricing models and the stochastic discount model was pioneered by Dybvig and Ingersoll (1982) in the context of the CAPM and then extended to the context of conditional multifactor models by Ferson and Jagannathan (1996). They associate the SDF with a linear combination of the factors whose sensitivities are set at time $t-1$: $m_t = c_{0,t-1} + \sum_{k=1}^{K} c_{k,t-1}F_{k,t}$, and show that this model is equivalent to the specification of Equation (7-33) under certain conditions.

What does this approach entail regarding performance measurement? The answer is given by Chen and Knez (1996), who show that, for a given actively managed portfolio P, an "admissible" performance measure (according to their axiomatic approach) is the SDF alpha. If we adapt that concept to the conditional specification, this simply gives the following performance measure:

$$\alpha_{P,t}^{\mathrm{SDF}} = \mathrm{E}(m_t R_{P,t}|\Omega_{t-1}) - 1 \tag{7-34}$$

The reader might wonder what distinguishes this sophisticated way of measuring conditional performance from the one proposed in Equation (7-32). The answer is fourfold:

- The SDF alpha does not simplify to be equal to the alpha under simple assumptions, and therefore it does not exactly share that interpretation. Indeed, if one simplifies the SDF model with no time variation ($\Omega_{t-1} \equiv \Omega$ is independent of time) and a single-factor model (with the market return being identified as the factor), the unconditional single-factor SDF alpha, or simply "CAPM-SDF alpha," is then equal to

$$\alpha_{P,t}^{\mathrm{uSF-SDF}} \equiv \alpha_P^{\mathrm{SDF,CAPM}} = \alpha_P(\overline{R}_m - R_f) \tag{7-35}$$

  Thus, as shown by Aragon and Ferson (2006), there is a difference between the SDF and the standard (Jensen's or multifactor) alphas, but it is just a matter of scale.
- The structure of the product of $m_t R_{P,t}$ in the expectation operator is rather generic and not particularly meant to be estimated with standard linear regression procedures.

Thus, it is recommended to estimate expression (7-34) with sophisticated statistical estimation techniques based on the generalized method of moments (GMM), which essentially sets estimation conditions on all relevant moments of the distributions of m_t, $R_{P,t}$, and their cross-product.

- Equation (7-34) fully makes sense in the presence of a benchmark B that is fairly priced on the market. In this case, we can rewrite the alpha as $\alpha_{P,t}^{SDF} = \mathrm{E}(m_t(R_{P,t} - R_{B,t})|\Omega_{t-1}) - 1$. As indicated by Aragon and Ferson (2006), the SDF alpha is not unique unless markets are complete. Since this condition is essentially not testable, we are back again to Roll's (1977) critique: One cannot empirically ensure that $\alpha_{P,t}^{SDF}$ is unique.
- Finally, there is a strong justification of the SDF approach that is rooted in expected utility theory. We can interpret a positive sign of the SDF alpha as leading to an increase in the investor's overall utility by putting their money in the portfolio.

Key Takeaways and Equations

- A *linear multifactor model* is a statistical linear regression model that aims to explain the excess return of a financial asset with K distinct explanatory factors:

$$R_{i,t} - R_f = \alpha_i^{MF} + \sum_{k=1}^{K} \beta_{i,k}(F_{k,t} - R_f) + \varepsilon_{i,t} \quad (7\text{-}3)$$

  Even though there is no golden rule to identify the optimal number of factors, there are many elements pointing to an amount of three to five being necessary and sufficient. A good model should have four properties: feasibility, intuitiveness, parsimony, and accuracy.
- There are three major families of multifactor models:
  - The family of *arbitrage-based multifactor models* builds on the no-arbitrage reasoning underlying Ross's (1976) Arbitrage Pricing Theory. The factors are built using statistical techniques or chosen from a set of macroeconomic factors.
  - The family of *fundamental multifactor models* associates the factors with stock characteristics by trying to identify those that deliver a significant risk premium. The models can be purely empirical, trying to associate factors with market anomalies, or microeconomic, by investigating the stock characteristics that best explain differences in returns.

(continued)

(continued)

- The family of *multi-index models* mostly attempts to explain returns using traded indexes. In particular, RBSA is a technique that builds passive replicating portfolios by setting constraints on factor sensitivities:

$$R_{i,t} = \alpha_i^{\text{MF}} + \sum_{k=1}^{K} w_{i,k} I_{k,t} + \varepsilon_{i,t} \tag{7-8}$$

$$\sum_{k=1}^{K} w_{i,k} = 1 \tag{7-9}$$

- Two performance measures are straight extensions of the classical ones developed in the context of the CAPM:
  - The *multifactor alpha* is defined as the difference between the average portfolio return and that of its model-based benchmark:

$$\alpha_P^{\text{MF}} = \overline{R}_P - \left[\overline{R}_f + \sum_{k=1}^{K} \beta_{P,k}(\overline{F}_k - \overline{R}_f)\right] \equiv \overline{R}_P - \overline{R}_B^{\text{MF}} \tag{7-11}$$

  - The *multifactor modified alpha* is defined as the alpha divided by the ratio of the portfolio's over the self-reported benchmark's required excess return:

$$m\alpha_P = \frac{\alpha_P^{\text{MF}}}{\left(\frac{\sum_{k=1}^{K} \beta_{P,k}(\overline{F}_k - \overline{R}_f)}{\sum_{k=1}^{K} \beta_{B,k}(\overline{F}_k - \overline{R}_f)}\right)} = \alpha_P^{\text{MF}} \frac{\overline{R}_B - \overline{R}_f - \alpha_B^{\text{MF}}}{\overline{R}_P - \overline{R}_f - \alpha_P^{\text{MF}}} \tag{7-12}$$

  or, in short, as the alpha multiplied by the ratio of the benchmark's and the fund's representative betas:

$$m\alpha_P = \alpha_P \frac{\beta_B^*}{\beta_P^*} \tag{7-13}$$

  where $\beta_{\cdot}^* = \sum_{k=1}^{K} w_k \beta_{\cdot,k}$ and $w_k = \frac{(\overline{F}_k - \overline{R}_f)}{\sum_{k=1}^{K} (\overline{F}_k - \overline{R}_f)}$.

  - The *absolute multifactor modified alpha* simplifies the $m\alpha_P^{\text{MF}}$ in the absence of any benchmark:

$$m\alpha_P^{\text{MF,abs}} = \frac{\alpha_P^{\text{MF}}}{\beta_P^*} \tag{7-14}$$

- Because of the existence of two different types of benchmarks (a self-reported benchmark and a model-based benchmark), the portfolio can be considered to have outperformed on both dimensions if the following condition is respected:

$$\alpha_P^{MF} > \max\left[0, \alpha_B^{MF}\frac{\sum_{k=1}^{K}\beta_{P,k}(\overline{F}_k - \overline{R}_f)}{\sum_{k=1}^{K}\beta_{B,k}(\overline{F}_k - \overline{R}_f)}, \alpha_B^{MF} + \left(\sum_{k=1}^{K}(\beta_{B,k} - \beta_{P,k})(\overline{F}_k - \overline{R}_f)\right)\right] \quad (7\text{-}15)$$

- Two performance measures based on total risk are applicable in the context of multifactor models.
  - The *relative risk-adjusted* performance can be written as

$$\text{RRAP}_P^{MF} = \text{RAP}_P - \text{RAP}_{B^{MF}} = \frac{\sigma_B}{\sigma_P}(\overline{R}_P - R_f) - \frac{\sigma_B}{\sigma_{B^{MF}}}(\overline{R}_B^{MF} - R_f) \quad (7\text{-}19)$$

  - The *split risk–return performance* can be written as

$$\text{SRRP}_P = (\overline{R}_P - \overline{R}_B^{MF}) - \text{MRP} \times (\sigma_P - \sigma_{B^{MF}}) = \alpha_P - \text{MRP} \times (\sigma_P - \sigma_{B^{MF}}) \quad (7\text{-}20)$$

- Considering residual risk as an input of performance measurement, the classical Information ratio can be split into three components:
  - The *pure Information ratio*, which corresponds to the ratio of active return over active risk with respect to the model-based benchmark:

$$\text{IR}_P^{\text{pure}} = \frac{\overline{R}_P - \overline{R}_B^{MF}}{\sigma(R_P - R_B^{MF})} = \frac{\alpha_P^{MF}}{\sigma_{\varepsilon P}} \quad (7\text{-}21)$$

  - The *misfit Information ratio*, which accounts for the difference between the risk and return of the model-based and multifactor benchmarks:

$$\text{IR}_P^{\text{misfit}} = \frac{\overline{R}_B^{MF} - \overline{R}_B}{\sigma(R_B^{MF} - R_B)} = \frac{\left(\sum_{k=1}^{K}(\beta_{P,k} - \beta_{B,k})(\overline{F}_k - \overline{R}_f)\right) - \alpha_B^{MF}}{\sqrt{\sigma^2\left(\sum_{k=1}^{K}(\beta_{P,k} - \beta_{B,k})(F_{k,t} - R_f)\right) + \sigma_{\varepsilon B}^2}} \quad (7\text{-}22)$$

  - The *global Information ratio* combines the other two:

$$\text{IR}_P = \frac{\overline{R}_P - \overline{R}_B}{\sigma(R_P - R_B)} \approx \frac{\alpha_P^{MF} - \alpha_B^{MF} + \left(\sum_{k=1}^{K}(\beta_{P,k} - \beta_{B,k})(\overline{F}_k - \overline{R}_f)\right)}{\sqrt{\sigma^2\left(\sum_{k=1}^{K}(\beta_{P,k} - \beta_{B,k})(F_{k,t} - R_f)\right) + \sigma_{\varepsilon P}^2 + \sigma_{\varepsilon B}^2}} \quad (7\text{-}23)$$

(continued)

(continued)

- In the special case of a single-factor model, the alpha remains unchanged. When a self-reported benchmark portfolio is provided, the criterion for identifying portfolio outperformance becomes

$$\alpha_P^{SF} > \max\left[0, \alpha_B^{SF}\frac{\beta_P}{\beta_B}, \alpha_B^{SF} + (\beta_B - \beta_P)(\overline{F} - \overline{R}_f)\right] \quad (7\text{-}25)$$

- As a more sophisticated approach, conditional multifactor models allow the factor loadings and the multifactor alpha to vary over time as a linear function of lagged values of instrumental variables:

$$R_{i,t} - R_f = \alpha_{i,0}^{MF} + \sum_{l=1}^{L} \alpha_{i,l}^{MF} z_{l,t-1} + \sum_{k=1}^{K} \beta_{i,k,0}(F_{k,t} - R_f)]$$
$$+ \sum_{k=1}^{K}\sum_{l=1}^{L} \beta_{i,k,l}[z_{l,t-1} \times (F_{k,t} - R_f)] + \varepsilon_{i,t} \quad (7\text{-}31)$$

The *conditional multifactor alpha* aggregates the time-varying intercepts:

$$\alpha_P^{cMF} = \alpha_{P,0}^{MF} + \mathbf{A}_P^T\overline{\mathbf{z}} \quad (7\text{-}32)$$

- The generic specification of multifactor models is the stochastic discount factor approach. When applied to the conditional modeling approach, the *SDF conditional alpha* can be written as

$$\alpha_{P,t}^{SDF} = \mathrm{E}(m_t R_{P,t} | \Omega_{t-1}) - 1 \quad (7\text{-}33)$$

which, in the context of the CAPM, is equal to the unconditional single-factor SDF alpha:

$$\alpha_{P,t}^{uSF-SDF} \equiv \alpha_P^{SDF,CAPM} = \alpha_P(\overline{R}_m - R_f) \quad (7\text{-}34)$$

REFERENCES

Adrian, T., and J. Rosenberg (2008), Stock returns and volatility: Pricing the short-run and long run components of market risk. *The Journal of Finance*, Vol. 63, pp. 2997–3030.

Aftalion, F., and P. Poncet (1991), Les mesures de performance des OPCVM: problèmes et solutions. *Revue Banque*, Vol. 517 (June), pp. 582–588.

Ahmed, S., Bu, Z., and D. Tsvetanov (2019), Best of the best: A comparison of factor models. *Journal of Financial and Quantitative Analysis*, Vol. 54, pp. 1713–1758.

Angelidis, T., Giamouridis, D., and N. Tessaromatis (2013), Revisiting mutual fund performance evaluation. *Journal of Banking & Finance*, Vol. 37, pp. 1759–1776.

Aragon, G. O., and W. E. Ferson (2006), Portfolio performance evaluation. *Foundations and Trends in Finance*, Vol. 2, pp. 83–190.

Bai, J., and S. Ng (2002), Determining the number of factors in approximate factor models. *Econometrica*, Vol. 70, pp. 191–221.

Banz, R. W. (1981), The relationship between market value and return of common stocks. *Journal of Financial Economics*, Vol. 9, pp. 3–18.

Basu, S. (1977), Investment performance of common stocks in relation to their price-earnings ratios: A test of the efficient market hypothesis. *The Journal of Finance*, Vol. 32, pp. 663–682.

Carhart, M. M. (1997), On persistence in mutual fund performance. *The Journal of Finance*, Vol. 52, pp. 57–82.

Cazalet, Z., and T. Roncalli (2014), Facts and fantasies about factor investing. Working Paper, available at SSRN: `https://ssrn.com/abstract=2524547`.

Chen, Z., and P. J. Knez (1996), Portfolio performance measurement: Theory and applications. *The Review of Financial Studies*, Vol. 9, pp. 511–555.

Chen, N.-F., Roll, R., and S. A. Ross (1986), Economic forces and the stock market. *Journal of Business*, Vol. 59, pp. 383–403.

Christopherson, J. A., Ferson, W. E., and A. L. Turner (1999), Performance evaluation using conditional alphas and betas. *The Journal of Portfolio Management*, Vol. 26 (1), pp. 57–72.

Connor, G., and R. A. Korajczyk (1986), Performance measurement with the Arbitrage Pricing Theory. *Journal of Financial Economics*, Vol. 15, pp. 373–394.

Cremers, M., Petajisto, A., and E. Zitzewitz (2012), Should benchmark indices have alpha? Revisiting performance evaluation. *Critical Finance Review*, Vol. 2, pp. 1–48.

Dybvig, P., and J. Ingersoll (1982), Mean-variance theory in complete markets. *Journal of Business*, Vol. 55, pp. 233–251.

Elton, E. J., Gruber, M. J., Das, S., and M. Hlavka (1993), Efficiency with costly information: A reinterpretation of evidence from managed portfolios. *The Review of Financial Studies*, Vol. 6, pp. 1–22.

Ericsson, J., and S. Karlsson (2004), Choosing factors in a multifactor asset pricing model: A Bayesian approach. Working Paper, Stockholm School of Economics.

Fama, E. F., and K. R. French (1992), The cross-section of expected stock returns. *The Journal of Finance*, Vol. 47, pp. 427–465.

Fama, E. F., and K. R. French (2015), A five-factor asset pricing model. *Journal of Financial Economics*, Vol. 116, pp. 1–22.

Fama, E. F., and J. D. MacBeth (1973), Risk, return, and equilibrium: Empirical tests. *Journal of Political Economy*, Vol. 81, pp. 607–636.

Fang, H., and T. Y. Lai (1997), Co-kurtosis and capital asset pricing. *Financial Review*, Vol. 32, pp. 293–307.

Ferson, W. E., and R. Jagannathan (1996), Econometric evaluation of asset pricing models. In: Maddala, G. S. and C. R. Rao, Eds., *The Handbook of Statistics. Vol. 14: Statistical Methods in Finance.* North Holland, pp. 1–30.

Ferson, W. E., and R. Schadt (1996), Measuring fund strategy and performance in changing economic conditions. *The Journal of Finance*, Vol. 51, pp. 425–462.

Ferson, W. E., Sarkissian, S., and T. Simin (2008), Asset pricing models with conditional betas and alphas: The effects of data snooping and spurious regression. *Journal of Financial and Quantitative Analysis*, Vol. 43, pp. 331–354.

Grinold, R. C., and R. N. Kahn (2000), *Active Portfolio Management: A Quantitative Approach for Producing Superior Returns and Controlling Risk*. New York: McGraw-Hill.

Harvey, C. R., and Y. Liu (2020), A census of the factor zoo. Working Paper, available at SSRN: `https://ssrn.com/abstract=3341728`.

Harvey, C. R., Liu, Y., and H. Zhu (2016), ... and the cross-section of expected returns. *The Review of Financial Studies*, Vol. 29, pp. 5–68.

Holm, S. (1979), A simple sequentially rejective multiple test procedure. *Scandinavian Journal of Statistics*, Vol. 6, pp. 65–70.

Hou, K., Xue, C., and L. Zhang (2015), Digesting anomalies: An investment approach. *The Review of Financial Studies*, Vol. 28, pp. 650–705.

Hübner, G. (2005), The generalized Treynor ratio. *Review of Finance*, Vol. 9, pp. 415–435.

Hwang, S., and C. Lu (2007), Too many factors. Do we need them all? Working Paper, available at SSRN: `https://ssrn.com/abstract=972022`.

Ippolito, R. A. (1989), Efficiency with costly information: A study of mutual fund performance. 1965–84. *Quarterly Journal of Economics*, Vol. 104, pp. 1–23.

Jegadeesh, N., and S. Titman (1993), Returns to buying winners and selling losers: Implications for stock market efficiency. *The Journal of Finance*, Vol. 48, pp. 65–91.

Kraus, A., and R. H. Litzenberger (1976), Skewness preference and the valuation of risk assets. *The Journal of Finance*, Vol. 31, pp. 1085–1100.

Lambert, M., Fays, B., and G. Hübner (2020), Factoring characteristics into returns: A clinical study on the SMB and HML portfolio construction methods. *Journal of Banking & Finance*, Vol. 114, 105811.

Lewellen, J. (2022), How many factors? Working Paper, Dartmouth College.

Lobosco, A. (1999), Style/risk-adjusted performance. *The Journal of Portfolio Management*, Vol. 25 (Spring), pp. 65–68.

Lobosco, A., and D. DiBartolomeo (1997), Approximating the confidence intervals for Sharpe style weights. *Financial Analysts Journal*, Vol. 53 (July–August), pp. 80–85.

McGuire, P., and K. Tsatsaronis (2009), Estimating hedge fund leverage. BIS Working Paper, No. 260.

Mitton, T., and K. Vorkink (2007), Equilibrium underdiversification and the preference for skewness. *The Review of Financial Studies*, Vol. 20, pp. 1255–1288.

Modigliani, F., and L. Modigliani (1997), Risk adjusted performance. *The Journal of Portfolio Management*, Vol. 23 (Winter), pp. 45–54.

Pastor, L., and R. F. Stambaugh (2003), Liquidity risk and expected stock returns. *Journal of Political Economy*, Vol. 111, pp. 643–85.

Reinganum, M. (1981). A misspecification of capital asset pricing: Empirical anomalies based on earnings yields and market values. *Journal of Financial Economics*, Vol. 9, pp. 17–46.

Roll, R. (1977), A critique of the asset pricing theory's tests. Part I: On past and potential testability of the theory. *Journal of Financial Economics*, Vol. 4, pp. 125–176.

Roll, R., and S. Ross, (1980), An empirical investigation of the Arbitrage Pricing Theory. *The Journal of Finance*, Vol. 35, pp. 1073–1103.

Ross, S. A. (1976), The arbitrage theory of capital asset pricing. *Journal of Economic Theory*, Vol. 13, pp. 341–360.

Sharpe, W. F. (1982), Factors in NYSE security returns, 1931–1979. *The Journal of Portfolio Management*, Vol. 8, (Summer), pp. 5–19.

Sharpe, W. F. (1992), Asset allocation: Management style and performance measurement. *The Journal of Portfolio Management*, Vol. 18 (Winter), pp. 7–19.

Sharpe, W. F. (1994), The Sharpe ratio. *The Journal of Portfolio Management*, Vol. 21 (Fall), pp. 47–58.

Siegel, L. B. (2003), *Benchmarks and Investment Management, 13th Edition*. The Research Foundation of AIMR (CFA Institute).

Stambaugh, R. F., and Y. Yuan (2016), Mispricing factors. *The Review of Financial Studies*, Vol. 30, pp. 1270–1315.

Tierney, D., and K. Winston (1990), Defining and using dynamic completeness funds to enhance total fund efficiency. *Financial Analysts Journal*, Vol. 46 (July–August), pp. 47–54.

Yogo, M. (2006), A consumption-based explanation of expected stock returns. *The Journal of Finance*, Vol. 61, pp. 537–580.

CHAPTER 8

Performance Measurement with Market Timing

INTRODUCTION

The skills of an active portfolio manager who produces abnormal returns for their customers are of two main kinds: asset selection and market timing. Many performance measures have been developed in order to appraise the former one, which focuses on a superior ability to detect and purchase assets that will outperform their peers. Market timing, by contrast, appears when the manager successfully anticipates market movements and modifies their risk factor exposures accordingly. This entails that linear models explaining portfolio returns, such as the plain-vanilla Capital Asset Pricing Model (CAPM) presented in Chapter 2 or those discussed in Chapter 7, are as such not suited to capture the market timing skills of a manager. Some specific approaches, and their associated performance measures, have to be developed.

This chapter discusses three main approaches for assessing market timing. In the first two sections, we examine two models in which the portfolio beta varies in a nonlinear but structured way with the realization of market returns. The *Henriksson and Merton (*1981*) model* posits that the beta reacts in a piecewise-linear fashion, depending on whether the associated market portfolio return is high (calling for a high beta) or low (low beta). The *Treynor and Mazuy (*1966*) model* proposes a quadratic relation between the beta and market returns. For both models, the intercept (alpha) of the nonlinear regression of portfolio excess returns on market returns appears not to fully capture the value of the portfolio manager's market timing. We propose different ways to adjust this alpha upward, which all produce fairly similar results. We also review several ways to improve these two models to enhance their ability to capture market timing in a more accurate manner.

The second type of market timing estimation approach is the family of *return-based dynamic exposures models*. Instead of considering that the portfolio beta remains constant over time, this family of models explicitly acknowledges that the manager may regularly adjust their exposures to the risk factor(s) according to their views. There are some sophisticated ways to estimate time-varying betas that allow the development of associated performance measures. We review some of them, indicating what type of benchmark portfolio is considered in order to assess the quality of the manager's market timing-related decisions.

Finally, the most convenient way to address the challenge of measuring market timing is to make direct use of the detailed portfolio holdings (and trades) over time. A precise appraisal of performance can then be performed through the *holding-based dynamic exposures models*. For the preceding case, the suitable performance measure mostly depends on the kind of benchmark considered. The assessment of a manager's performance under these circumstances can be systematically processed in attribution models, which are discussed in Chapters 13 and 14.

We are well aware that the number of performance measures presented in this chapter is large (we count eight different families). In order to ease the selection process for the reader, our last section is devoted not only to a discussion of potential biases (wrong detection of the presence or absence of timing) but also to the presentation of a *decision tree* for the choice of a final formula. We hope that this equipment will represent a useful guide for your journey in the fascinating world of market timing.

The ConveX-Timing Company Example

The executive team of ConveX-Timing is convinced that most of the outperformance that the company can generate relates to the market timing skills of its three fund managers. They all track a common composite index and have the mandate to manage their portfolios defensively (with an average beta lower than one) while generating abnormal returns from their successful ability to anticipate market movements. The managers now have a two-year track record, and the corresponding series of monthly excess returns over the risk-free rate, which is a constant 0.2% per month, are represented in Table 8-1 together with their sample mean and standard deviation.

TABLE 8-1 CX-T example – Monthly rates of return.

Date	CX-A	CX-B	CX-C	Market
Jan	−0.40%	−0.34%	−0.88%	−1.91%
Feb	0.69%	3.24%	1.05%	1.96%
Mar	−0.52%	0.63%	0.38%	0.50%
Apr	0.74%	−0.65%	−1.10%	−0.67%
May	0.78%	1.68%	0.00%	1.25%
Jun	−0.73%	0.92%	1.25%	−0.12%
Jul	−0.51%	0.80%	0.05%	−0.07%
Aug	−1.27%	0.73%	−1.13%	−4.11%
Sep	0.08%	−0.19%	0.18%	0.85%
Oct	−1.71%	−1.04%	−0.04%	−3.93%
Nov	5.29%	3.60%	1.58%	3.50%
Dec	2.55%	2.49%	0.87%	2.43%
Jan	3.10%	2.27%	0.76%	1.25%
Feb	2.37%	1.35%	1.26%	1.73%
Mar	−0.91%	0.14%	−0.92%	−2.56%
Apr	1.61%	1.62%	2.26%	2.23%
May	2.23%	2.40%	0.96%	1.74%
Jun	0.74%	−0.48%	−0.82%	−0.98%
Jul	2.02%	1.53%	1.40%	1.26%
Aug	0.35%	1.66%	0.21%	0.31%
Sep	2.10%	1.18%	1.39%	1.44%
Oct	0.48%	1.08%	0.52%	0.60%
Nov	0.84%	0.37%	−0.02%	0.50%
Dec	−1.62%	0.24%	−0.67%	−4.70%
Mean excess return	**0.76%**	**1.05%**	**0.36%**	**0.10%**
Standard deviation	**1.64%**	**1.18%**	**0.93%**	**2.11%**

(continued)

(continued)

From these time series of returns, we first calculate each fund's alpha and beta using the ordinary least-squares (OLS) regression method, whose equation is as follows:

$$R_{i,t} - R_f = \alpha_i + \beta_i[R_{M,t} - R_f] + \varepsilon_{i,t}$$

with i = CX-A, CX-B and CX-C, and $R_f = 0.20\%$ on a monthly basis. The regression outputs for each of the three funds are reported in Table 8-2.

TABLE 8-2 CX-T example – Linear regression outputs.

Regression outputs	CX-A	CX-B	CX-C
Alpha	0.70%	1.01%	0.32%
St. dev. alpha	0.20%	0.17%	0.13%
Beta	0.64	0.41	0.34
St. dev. beta	0.09	0.08	0.06
R^2	67.76%	52.90%	60.04%

Apparently, the market timing strategies of all three managers have been successful. Figure 8-1 represents the cumulative total returns for each investment vehicle.

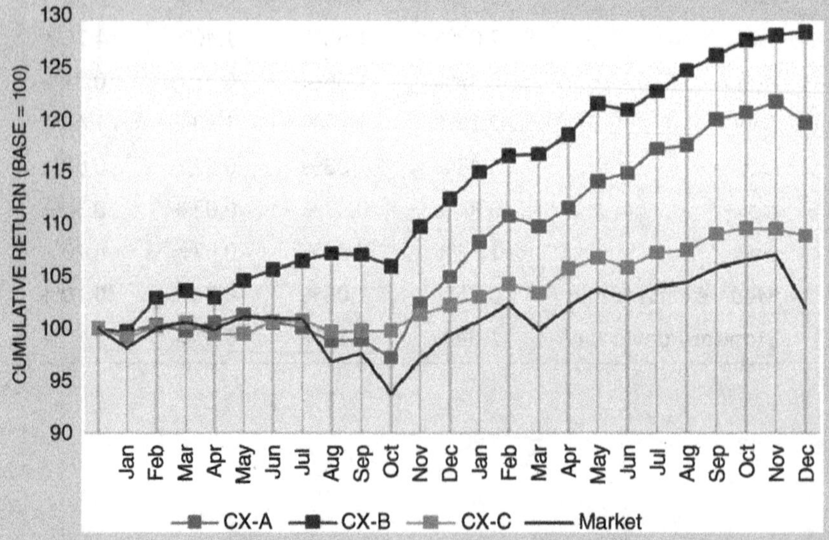

FIGURE 8-1 CX-T example – Cumulative rates of return.

The market has experienced two substantial drawdowns that the funds largely avoided. In this chapter, we investigate how performance measures can be adapted in order to identify, as precisely as possible, the value of each manager's capacity to anticipate market movements.

8.1 PIECEWISE-LINEAR REGRESSION APPROACH

8.1.1 The Henriksson and Merton (HM) model

What is a good market timer in the context of the CAPM setup? Obviously, because the intercept of the market model (the alpha) is a constant that does not depend on market conditions, this is not the right standpoint to manage the problem. Rather, studying the portfolio beta's behavior over time is more relevant. Since the beta reflects the sensitivity of the portfolio return to that of the market, a manager that successfully anticipates market movements will tend to increase the beta when markets are positively oriented and decrease it otherwise. However, how should these variations in betas be measured if, for statistical purposes, we still want to remain within the context of a regression analysis?

The answer provided by Henriksson and Merton (1981) in their parametric approach is rather dichotomous.[1] According to them, a fund manager with good market timing chooses between two distinct levels of the portfolio beta: a high one when they guess that the market return will exceed the risk-free rate and a low one when they anticipate that the market return will be lower than this hurdle rate. In terms of the regression equation, this translates into the inclusion of a second variable in the market model with excess portfolio returns:

$$R_{P,t} - R_f = \alpha_P^{(\mathrm{hm})} + \beta_P^{(\mathrm{hm})}[R_{M,t} - R_f] + \gamma_P^{(\mathrm{hm})}\max[R_f - R_{M,t}, 0] + \varepsilon_{P,t} \tag{8-1}$$

where $R_{P,t}$ represents the return of portfolio P at time t, R_f is the rate of return of the riskless asset, which is considered constant over the period, $\alpha_P^{(\mathrm{hm})}$ and $\beta_P^{(\mathrm{hm})}$ are the intercept (alpha) and the linear sensitivity (beta) of the portfolio with respect to the market portfolio, respectively, $\gamma_P^{(\mathrm{hm})}$ is the market timing coefficient, and $\varepsilon_{P,t}$ represents the error term of the regression.[2]

[1]Merton (1981) also introduces a purely nonparametric version in which the manager chooses to invest all the assets into either equities or cash, depending on their anticipation of the market movement. The model is then estimated in a probabilistic regression. Given its relative lack of realism (the manager is essentially constrained to have 100% of the allocation in one asset class), it has not really become popular. Therefore, we do not discuss it here.

[2]Note that Equation (8-1) is sometimes equivalently represented with the use of a dummy (binary) variable, i.e., $R_{P,t} - R_f = \alpha_P^{(\mathrm{hm})} + \beta_P^{(\mathrm{hm})}[R_{M,t} - R_f] + \gamma_P^{(\mathrm{hm})}[1_{\{R_f > R_{M,t}\}}(R_f - R_{M,t})] + \varepsilon_{P,t}$, where $1_{\{R_f > R_{M,t}\}}$ is a binary variable that takes value 1 if $R_f > R_{M,t}$ and 0 otherwise.

The portfolio manager's ability to successfully time the market is represented by coefficient $\gamma_P^{(hm)}$ in the regression. If this coefficient is positive, the manager succeeds in switching their market beta from a high level equal to $\beta_P^{(hm)}$, called the "upside beta" when the market return exceeds the risk-free rate to a lower level of $(\beta_P^{(hm)} - \gamma_P^{(hm)})$ (the "downside beta") otherwise.

The formulation of the model, which corresponds to the original idea put forward by Merton (1981) and Henriksson and Merton (1981), suggests that the investment strategy of the manager can be replicated with two components: a first long (positive) position in the market portfolio with intensity $\beta_P^{(hm)}$ and a second long position in an at-the-money put option on the market portfolio, i.e., an option whose strike (exercise) price is equal to the risk-free rate.[3] Expression (8-1) simply reflects the return obtained from this trading strategy. The geometrical interpretation of the model is reflected in Figure 8-2.

In the illustration, the small dots on the graph represent the individual pairs of observations $(R_{M,t} - R_f, R_{P,t} - R_f)$ of excess returns. The visual inspection confirms that the alignment of the points follows linear trends that are distinct depending on whether they are on the left or the right of the vertical axis. This is translated into the different slopes of the associated regression lines.

The solid line draws a piecewise-linear function of the market excess returns. If $\gamma_P^{(hm)}$ is positive, as it stands on the graph, this function is convex. It translates the protective benefits of an option-like payoff, whose gains are relatively more pronounced than losses. The level of gamma drives this convexity and thus characterizes the intensity of the downside protection offered by the portfolio manager to their investors through their superior market anticipation skills.

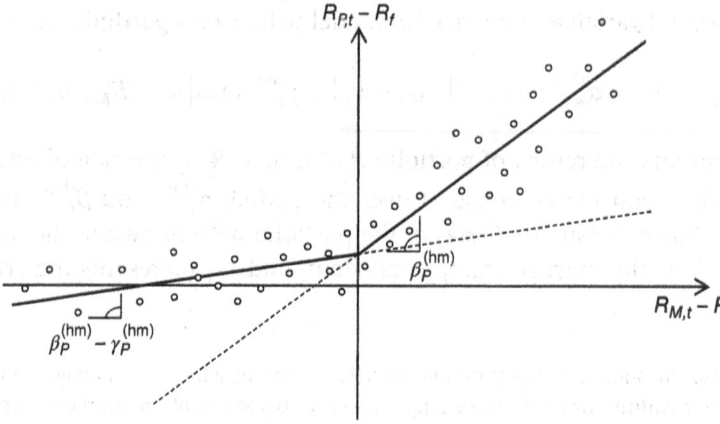

FIGURE 8-2 Graphical representation of the Henriksson and Merton (1981) model.

[3] Another classical representation of the model entails the use of a call option instead of a put. This alternative is written as $R_{P,t} - R_f = \alpha_P^{(hm)} + \beta_P^{\prime(hm)}[R_{M,t} - R_f] + \gamma_P^{(hm)} \max[R_{M,t} - R_f, 0] + \varepsilon_{P,t}$. Since $\max[R_{M,t} - R_f, 0] = [R_{M,t} - R_f] + \max[R_f - R_{M,t}, 0]$, then only the beta is affected. Coefficient $\gamma_P^{(hm)}$ and the intercept $\alpha_P^{(hm)}$ are unchanged.

The CX-T example (continued)

Instead of the linear one-factor regression, we have applied the HM piecewise-linear model on each of the three funds:

$$R_{i,t} - R_f = \alpha_i^{(\mathrm{hm})} + \beta_i^{(\mathrm{hm})}[R_{M,t} - R_f] + \gamma_i^{(\mathrm{hm})}\max\,[R_f - R_{M,t}, 0] + \varepsilon_{i,t}$$

The regression outputs are displayed in Table 8-3.

TABLE 8-3 CX-T example – Henriksson–Merton (HM) regression outputs.

Regression outputs	CX-A	CX-B	CX-C
Alpha_{HM}	−0.11%	0.28%	−0.01%
St. dev. alpha_{HM}	0.30%	0.26%	0.22%
Beta_{HM}	1.23	0.95	0.58
St. dev. beta_{HM}	0.20	0.17	0.14
Gamma_{HM}	0.94	0.85	0.38
St. dev. gamma_{HM}	0.29	0.25	0.21
R^2	78.37%	69.68%	65.61%

The improvement in the model fit, represented by the R^2, is substantial compared to the linear model (Table 8-2). The gains in significance range from 5 percentage points for CX-C up to almost 17 percentage points for fund CX-B. All betas and gammas are statistically significant (their *t*-statistics are all above 1.80), but this is no longer the case for their alphas.

The contrast between both sets of regressions (the linear and the piecewise-linear ones) is best reflected in the graphs shown in Figure 8-3.

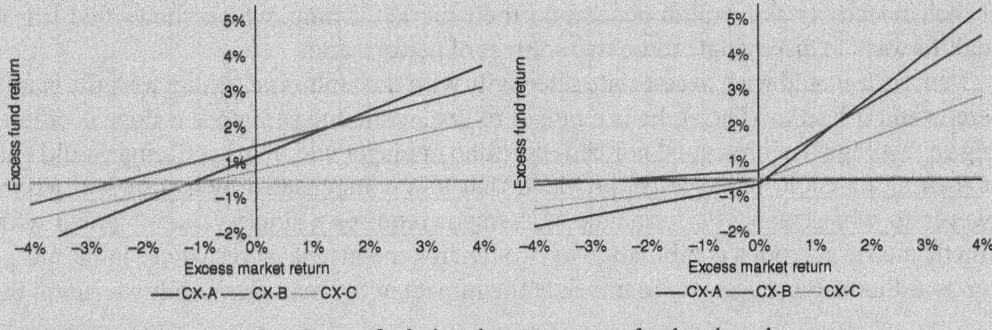

FIGURE 8-3 CX-T example – Types of relations between excess fund and market returns.

(continued)

(continued)

The left figure graphically represents the relation between each fund and the market as estimated linearly in Table 8-2. In contrast, the right figure shows the broken lines that reflect how successful each fund is at modifying its beta according to the market conditions. The first two funds (CX-A and CX-B) more drastically change their exposure to the market portfolio according to the prevailing market conditions than fund CX-C does. However, only CX-B manages to simultaneously keep a positive intercept, which entails that this fund's performance is undoubtedly positive (both a positive alpha and a positive timing coefficient).

8.1.2 The Henriksson–Merton-adjusted alpha

It is tempting to measure the outperformance of a portfolio manager by separately considering selectivity and timing in regression (8-1). According to this point of view, the intercept, namely $\alpha_P^{(hm)}$, reflects the manager's asset selection skills, while the coefficient of the put option $\gamma_P^{(hm)}$ would be the measure of their talent at timing the market. Unfortunately, this simple vision would be both fallacious and of little practical use.

The fallacy of this reasoning can be readily understood by looking at Figure 8-2. The dashed straight lines that extend the solid ones would reflect the situations of two managers exhibiting the same alpha as the portfolio but no timing skill at all. Each of these two managers has a different beta however. The one with the steepest line has a beta of $\beta_P^{(hm)}$, whereas the other one has a beta of $\beta_P^{(hm)} - \gamma_P^{(hm)}$. Thus, according to the CAPM and considering that it is necessary to correct performance for leverage, the second manager has a better performance, measured by the modified Jensen's alpha (see Chapter 3), than the first one. Portfolio *P*, with upside and downside betas that are equal to these managers' linear betas, would thus have a selectivity lying somewhere in between, i.e., it would depend on the value of $\gamma_P^{(hm)}$. Meanwhile, $\gamma_P^{(hm)}$ is supposed to measure the manager's market timing. Thus, it would mean that their selectivity skill would depend on their market timing, which shows that it is not straightforward to disentangle these two sources of performance.

Even if one would wish to associate selectivity with the alpha and timing with the gamma, where would it lead to? The alpha is a rate of return, while the gamma is a slope coefficient. Being an "average" (neither good nor bad) portfolio manager with market timing would entail that their alpha could be negative, provided that it is compensated by a sufficient gamma. However, to what extent? Performance assessment requires a single value obtained with a synthetic metric and not a combination of two heterogeneous measures whose joint interpretation is arduous. It is necessary to translate the impact of the manager's ability to adapt their beta to prevailing market circumstances into an equivalent rate of return that adds up to the regression alpha. This is the essence of the HM-adjusted alpha, denoted by $\pi_P^{(hm)} = \alpha_P^{(hm)} + f(\gamma_P^{(hm)})$, where the second term represents the adjustment to the alpha that depends on the level of the portfolio's convexity. This adjustment is positive when gamma is itself positive and increases with the level of gamma, i.e., $f'(\gamma_P^{(hm)}) > 0$. This also entails that an average (i.e., with no superior performance) manager whose global performance should not differ from zero ($\pi_P^{(hm)} = 0$) but who has a positive gamma will, as a consequence, have a negative alpha.

8.1.2.1 Option-based adjustment of the HM alpha

The most accurate and elegant answer to the issue of reflecting the optional value created by the manager is provided by Merton (1981) in a companion paper to that of the HM article. He proposes to directly reflect the value of the option replicated by the portfolio manager in the performance adjustment through the following equation, where superscript "o" on the performance measure reflects that it corresponds to the "option" approach:

$$\pi_P^{(hm,o)} = \alpha_P^{(hm)} + \gamma_P^{(hm)} \times (1 + R_f) \times \overline{\text{Put}}\left(1, \frac{1}{n}, 1 + R_f\right) \tag{8-2}$$

where $\overline{\text{Put}}\left(1, \frac{1}{n}, 1 + R_f\right)$ is the average price over time of a put with remaining time to maturity equal to the time interval expressed as a fraction of a year ($\frac{1}{n}$ represents one unit of time, being a day, a week, or a month depending on the sample period frequency) and strike price of $1 + R_f$ written on the market portfolio M, whose price is normalized to 1. This strike price corresponds to a forward at-the-money put option.

The reasoning underlying Equation (8-2) is the following. In order to replicate the pattern of portfolio returns of Equation (8-1), it is necessary to simultaneously adopt a long position of $\beta_P^{(hm)}$ in the market portfolio and another one of $\gamma_P^{(hm)}$ in a put on the same index. This put only delivers a positive payoff if the index return is lower than the riskless rate. The remaining amount equal to $(1 - \beta_P^{(hm)} - \gamma_P^{(hm)})$ is invested (if positive) or borrowed (if negative) at the risk-free rate. The cost of adopting such a strategy is the initial put premium $\overline{\text{Put}}\left(1, \frac{1}{n}, 1 + R_f\right)$ per unit of gamma. It should be capitalized to represent the realized opportunity cost of the strategy versus a linear one.

In spite of its correctness and economic appeal, the implementation of $\pi_P^{(hm,o)}$ requires the use of the price of put options on the market index at each observation date. Since these put options are not traded, they must be estimated analytically. A relatively classical approach entails the application of the Black and Scholes formula, which delivers an analytical valuation for the European option (i.e., that can only be exercised at maturity, as is the case here) that depends on five parameters: the current price S_t, the time-to-maturity τ, the strike price K, the annualized continuously compounded interest rate R_f^c, and the annualized volatility $\sigma(S_t) \equiv \sigma$.[4] For call and put options, the respective formulas are written as

$$\text{Call}(S_t, \tau, K) = S_t \Phi(d_1) - K e^{-R_f^c \tau} \Phi(d_2) \tag{8-3a}$$

$$\text{Put}(S_t, \tau, K) = K e^{-R_f^c \tau} \Phi(-d_2) - S_t \Phi(-d_1) \tag{8-3b}$$

$$d_1 = \frac{\log\left(S_t/K\right) + \left(R_f^c + \frac{1}{2}\sigma^2\right)\tau}{\sigma\sqrt{\tau}} \tag{8-3c}$$

$$d_2 = d_1 - \sigma\sqrt{\tau} \tag{8-3d}$$

where $\Phi(x) \equiv \Pr[Z \leq x]$ with $Z \rightsquigarrow \mathcal{N}(0,1)$ is the cumulative density function of a standard normal random variable taken at value x, i.e., it represents the probability that it is lower than or equal to x, and $R_f^c/n = \log(1 + R_f)$ is the continuously compounded interest rate.

In the context of the HM model, we obtain $S_t = 1$, $\tau = \frac{1}{n}$, and $K = 1 + R_f = e^{R_f^c/n}$. Considering that the standard deviation of the periodic returns of the market portfolio is a constant σ_M (i.e., its yearly volatility is equal to $\frac{\sigma_M}{\sqrt{\tau}}$), Equation (8-2) considerably simplifies as

$$\pi_P^{(hm,o)} = \alpha_P^{(hm)} + \gamma_P^{(hm)} \times (1 + R_f) \times \left(2\Phi\left(\frac{\sigma_M}{2}\right) - 1\right) \tag{8-4}$$

Because $\frac{\sigma_M}{2} > 0$, $\Phi\left(\frac{\sigma_M}{2}\right) > 0.5$ and the argument of the last parenthesis is positive.[5] Thus, the sign of the adjustment to the HM alpha is the same as that of $\gamma_P^{(hm)}$.

8.1.2.2 Other adjustments of the HM alpha

There are two other, simpler approaches to compute the adjustment brought to the alpha in order to reflect the value of market timing. They are primarily motivated by the potential absence of liquid traded options on the market proxy that would have the desired characteristics.

The first of these approaches was proposed by Coles, Daniel, and Nardari (2006). Expressing the portfolio beta as time-varying $\beta_{P,t}^{(hm)} = \beta_P^{(hm)} + \gamma_P^{(hm)} 1_{\{R_f > R_{M,t}\}}$, where $1_{\{R_f > R_{M,t}\}}$ is a binary

---

[4] For the sake of clarity, we leave aside the dependence of the dividend (level or rate) here as we focus on total returns.

[5] The general case where the market volatility is time varying but deterministic leads to a similar equation, i.e., $\pi_P^{(hm,o)} = \alpha_P^{(hm)} + \gamma_P^{(hm)} \times (1 + R_f) \times \frac{1}{T}\sum_{t=1}^{T}\left(2\Phi\left(\frac{-\sigma_{M,t}}{2\sqrt{n}}\right) - 1\right)$. The difference is that the last factor is equal to the average of the put option value over time.

variable that takes a value of 1 if $R_f > R_{M,t}$ and 0 otherwise, they obtain the following approximate adjusted performance measure, where superscript "a" on the performance measure reflects that it corresponds to the "approximate" approach:

$$\pi_P^{(hm,a)} = \alpha_P^{(hm)} + \gamma_P^{(hm)} \times \left(\overline{\max}\,[R_{M,t} - R_f, 0] - q_M^+(\overline{R}_M - R_f)\right) \tag{8-5}$$

where $\overline{\max}\,[R_{M,t} - R_f, 0] = \frac{1}{T}\sum_{t=1}^{T} \max\,[R_{M,t} - R_f, 0]$ is the average value of the excess market return floored to zero when it is negative, and $q_M^+ = \frac{1}{T}\sum_{t=1}^{T} 1_{\{R_f < R_{M,t}\}}$ is the observed frequency of positive excess market returns.

The second alternative way to adjust the HM alpha to the presence of market timing is much simpler and has become the most popular one in the related literature. Bollen and Busse (2004) start from (8-1) and, taking the average of both sides of the equation, they note that the mean portfolio abnormal return is $\overline{R}_P - R_f - (\beta_P^{(hm)} - \gamma_P^{(hm)})[\overline{R}_M - R_f] = \alpha_P^{(hm)} + \gamma_P^{(hm)}\overline{\max}\,[R_{M,t} - R_f, 0]$. The left-hand side is considered the required return for a portfolio with a constant downside beta, and the right-hand side can be considered its abnormal return. Thus, under this basic approach, where superscript "s" on the performance measure reflects that it corresponds to the "simplified" approach, we obtain

$$\pi_P^{(hm,s)} = \alpha_P^{(hm)} + \gamma_P^{(hm)} \times \overline{\max}\,[R_{M,t} - R_f, 0] \tag{8-6}$$

It is straightforward to note that $\pi_P^{(hm,s)} > \pi_P^{(hm,a)}$ if the market excess return $\overline{R}_M - R_f$ is positive and vice versa. In terms of theoretical correctness and accuracy, it is preferable to use $\pi_P^{(hm,o)}$, then $\pi_P^{(hm,a)}$, and finally $\pi_P^{(hm,s)}$. However, the optional approach requires more assumptions, and the difference between the other two adjusted performance measures is often rather small.

Note that all three types of adjustments are multiplicative. Thus, in every case, we obtain an add-on to the alpha of the kind $f(\gamma_P^{(hm)}) = \gamma_P^{(hm)} \times g_M$, where the "$g_M$" factor provides the market remuneration per unit of gamma.

8.1.2.3 Disentangling selectivity and timing

The price to pay for adjusting the HM alpha for the manager's ability to switch betas, which is inevitable in this context, is that the resulting composite performance measure cannot reasonably be split into a selectivity and a timing component. For the reasons explained at the beginning of the previous section, the modified alpha depends on the upside and downside betas. Therefore, it would be wrong to simply posit on the one hand "$\alpha_P^{(hm)}$ = selectivity" and, on the other hand, "$\gamma_P^{(hm)} \times g_M$ = timing."

Nevertheless, we consider that it is possible to approximate the value of selectivity and timing in the context of the modified Jensen's alpha (the portfolio alpha divided by its beta).

The average portfolio beta is equal to $\overline{\beta}_P = q_M^+ \beta_P^{(hm)} + (1 - q_M^+)(\beta_P^{(hm)} - \gamma_P^{(hm)}) = \beta_P^{(hm)} - (1 - q_M^+)\gamma_P^{(hm)}$, where, as before, $q_M^+ = \frac{1}{T}\sum_{t=1}^{T} 1_{\{R_f < R_{M,t}\}}$ is the observed frequency of positive excess market returns. Thus, the modified HM-adjusted alpha $\mathrm{m}\pi_{P,\mathrm{HM}}$ is written as

$$\mathrm{m}\pi_P^{(hm)} = \frac{\alpha_P^{(hm)} + \gamma_P^{(hm)} \times g_M}{\beta_P^{(hm)} - (1 - q_M^+)\gamma_P^{(hm)}} \tag{8-7}$$

where $\gamma_P^{(hm)} \times g_M$ is the level of the adjustment to the HM alpha.

In that case, the decomposition of the numerator into a selectivity and a timing component can be performed because the denominator also accounts for the impact of the manager's timing behavior into their average beta:

$$\mathrm{m}\pi_P^{(hm)}(\text{selection}) = \frac{\alpha_P^{(hm)}}{\beta_P^{(hm)} - (1 - q_M^+)\gamma_P^{(hm)}} \tag{8-8a}$$

$$\mathrm{m}\pi_P^{(hm)}(\text{timing}) = \frac{\gamma_P^{(hm)} \times g_M}{\beta_P^{(hm)} - (1 - q_M^+)\gamma_P^{(hm)}} \tag{8-8b}$$

This decomposition approach becomes meaningful when the performance of the manager is compared with other funds or portfolios, with or without market timing skills, and that may differ with respect to their beta.

Nevertheless, Equations (8-8a) and (8-8b) have to be used with great caution. Consider the case of a manager who delivers absolutely no performance because they have chosen to simply adopt a beta of $\beta_P^{(hm)}$ and to systematically buy an equivalent of $\gamma_P^{(hm)}$ forward at-the-money put options on the index. The manager would obtain a performance $\pi_P^{(hm)} = 0$ and, consequently, an unadjusted alpha of $\alpha_P^{(hm)} - \gamma_P^{(hm)} \times g_M < 0$. In spite of this negative alpha, it would be incorrect to consider that this portfolio has a negative selectivity: they have just no skill, neither positive nor negative. Thus, the decomposition approach is only meaningful to analyze funds or portfolios that do not trade derivative securities, be they traded options or synthetic replicating strategies.

The CX-T example (continued)

In order to compute the necessary adjustments to the HM alpha of the three funds, we need three more inputs, namely the components of g_M according to each method.

1. For the option approach, we need the cumulative density function of the standard normal distribution $\Phi\left(\frac{\sigma_M}{2}\right) \equiv \Pr\left[Z \leq \frac{\sigma_M}{2}\right]$. From Table 8-1, $\sigma_M = 2.11\%$ and $\Phi(1.05\%) = 50.42\%$.

2. There are 15 positive values of market returns out of a total of 24. Therefore, $q_M^+ = \frac{15}{24} = 62.5\%$.
3. Finally, the average of the positive market returns can be computed using the data of Table 8-1 and is equal to $\overline{\max}\,[R_{M,t} - R_f, 0] = 0.90\%$.

The aggregation of the results for all three funds is presented in Table 8-4.

TABLE 8-4 CX-T example – Adjusted HM alphas according to the three methods.

Fund	$\alpha_P^{(hm)}$	$\gamma_P^{(hm)}$	$\alpha_P^{(hm)} + \gamma_P^{(hm)} \times g_M$		
			Option	Approximate	Simplified
CX-A	−0.11%	0.94	0.68%	0.67%	0.73%
CX-B	0.28%	0.85	1.00%	0.99%	1.04%
CX-C	−0.01%	0.38	0.31%	0.31%	0.33%

Compared to the option approach of Equation (8-4), which is in principle the most accurate one, the approximate approach (Equation (8-5)) delivers very similar results for all three funds. Note that these values are very close to the original (linear) Jensen's alphas reported in Table 8-2, as the differences never exceed four basis points per month – probably within the tolerance of statistical noise. As could be expected from a more generous adjustment, the simplified approach (Equation (8-6)), in spite of its popularity, probably overstates the true funds' performances.

Finally, the modified HM-adjusted alpha also builds on the weighted average beta computed with the help of q^+. The results of the analysis are reported in Table 8-5.

TABLE 8-5 CX-T example – Identification of selectivity and timing in modified HM-adjusted alphas.

Fund	$\overline{\beta}_P$	$m\pi_P^{(hm)}$	Selectivity	Timing
CX-A	0.88	0.78%	−0.12%	0.90%
CX-B	0.63	1.59%	0.44%	1.15%
CX-C	0.44	0.72%	−0.02%	0.74%

Compared to raw adjusted HM alphas, fund CX-C largely catches up on its rivals. With a defensive strategy, it turns out that the difference between the upside and downside betas,

(continued)

(continued)

reflected in a value of $\gamma_{\text{CX-T}}^{(\text{hm})} = 0.38$, is relatively large when compared with its systematic risk exposure. This explains why the modified adjusted alpha stands at a much closer level to the CX-A fund than its raw adjusted alpha.

8.1.3 Model extensions

Without necessarily aiming to be fully exhaustive on this vast literature, we can identify two types of extensions to the original HM model. The first one attempts to inflate the number of factors on which the market timing ability of the manager is measured. The second one adds some flexibility in the HM model, either by introducing another potential asset class or by focusing on the cutoff point between the upside and the downside beta decisions made by the portfolio manager. All these extensions are briefly discussed below.

8.1.3.1 Multifactor versions

What would constrain a manager to apply their timing skill on a single market index? In principle, nothing: What is valid in the context of the market portfolio can be extended to any relevant risk factor for which a manager could realistically attempt to anticipate its realization. Generally, we can thus expect a multifactor model of the form

$$R_{P,t} - R_f = \alpha_P^{(\text{hm})} + \sum_{k=1}^{K} \beta_{P,k}^{(\text{hm})}(F_{k,t} - R_f) + \sum_{k=1}^{K} \gamma_{P,k}^{(\text{hm})} \max\left[R_f - F_{k,t}, 0\right] + \varepsilon_{P,t} \tag{8-9}$$

where each $\beta_{P,k}^{(\text{hm})}$ represents the portfolio's linear exposure to the kth factor and $F_{k,t}$ stands for the realization of the corresponding factor return at time t.[6] This is the approach proposed, for instance, by Chan, Chen, and Lakonishok (2002), who adapt the Fama and French three-factor model described in Chapter 7 (Section 8.1.3) in the context of the US mutual fund industry.

Another approach to assess the manager's ability to time the market is to complement this potential skill with the use of conditioning information (based on lagged realization of signal variables) in order to let the beta vary over time. In Chapter 7, we studied the family of conditional multifactor models, insisting on the difference between "reading" public information to automatically adjust the beta – which itself is not a particular market timing skill – and "anticipating" the market to modify the portfolio's exposure on the basis of such anticipations – which is what we are trying to measure. Ferson and Schadt (1996) thus naturally consider the complementarity between their conditional asset pricing approach and the definition of timing

[6] Note that, if the factor is a self-financing portfolio such as the Fama–French size or value factors, it is not necessary to deduce the risk-free rate from the factor return.

under the HM specification. They define an upside and a downside conditional beta adopted by the manager according to their anticipation of favorable or unfavorable market conditions. This leads to the conditional HM model:

$$R_{P,t} - R_f = \alpha_P^{(hm)} + (\beta_{P,0}^{(hm)} + \beta_{P,z}^{(hm)} \times z_{t-1})[R_{M,t} - R_f] + (\gamma_{P,0}^{(hm)} + \gamma_{P,z}^{(hm)} \times z_{t-1})\max[R_f - R_{M,t}, 0] + \varepsilon_{P,t} \quad (8\text{-}10)$$

where $\beta_{P,0}^{(hm)} - \gamma_{P,0}^{(hm)}$ is equal to the unconditional downside beta, $\beta_{P,z}^{(hm)} - \gamma_{P,z}^{(hm)}$ is the conditional downside beta, and z_{t-1} represents the deviations of the conditioning instrument from its unconditional (long-term) mean at time $t-1$, i.e., $z_{t-1} = Z_{t-1} - E(Z)$.[7] Indeed, one great merit of the conditional specification of Equation (8-10) is that it allows the modeling of both the capacity of the manager to dynamically manage their beta on the basis of conditioning information and their ability to anticipate the sign of market returns independently of that conditioning information.

Finally, a worthy extension of the original model is provided by Henriksson (1984) himself. Applying the HM model to a sample of mutual funds, he notices a significant negative correlation between the estimates of the HM alphas and gammas using Equation (8-1). This is not surprising if one considers that, on average, fund managers exhibit no or limited performance ($\overline{\pi}_P^{(hm)} = \overline{\alpha}_P^{(hm)} + \overline{\gamma}_P^{(hm)} \times g_M \approx 0$): Unskilled managers with a larger gamma would then tend to trade options more intensively than the others, whose cost would be reflected in a negative alpha. However, Henriksson (1984) proposed another potential explanation: This negative correlation could also be due to an omitted variable simply because the market index used for the estimation of the regression is not the true market portfolio. In order to circumvent this issue, he proposes amending the model in two steps:

1. First, select a sample of comparable, well-diversified mutual funds and run a linear regression of the returns of an equally weighted portfolio of these funds, called $R_{EW,t}$, on the market index: $R_{EW,t} - R_f = \alpha_{EW} + \beta_{EW}[R_{M,t} - R_f] + \varepsilon_{EW,t}$. The unexplained fraction of the return, namely $\widetilde{R}_{EW,t} = \alpha_{EW} + \varepsilon_{EW,t}$, is supposed to represent the market-wide rate of return that is not reflected in the market index used for the regression.

[7] It is naturally possible to extend the model to K factors and L instruments, as in Chapter 7, but we only present here the one-factor version in order to save space. It is also possible to include the conditional alpha in the model, without prejudice of the identification of the pure market timing skill (i.e., the one that is independent from any conditional information), which is still represented by coefficient $\gamma_{P,0}^{(hm)}$ in the equation.

2. Second, expand the HM model with this new factor while keeping the same type of specification:

$$R_{P,t} - R_f = \alpha_P^{(hm)} + \beta_P^{(hm)}[R_{M,t} - R_f] + \gamma_P^{(hm)} \max[R_f - R_{M,t}, 0] + \beta_P'^{(hm)}[\widetilde{R}_{EW,t} - R_f] + \gamma_P'^{(hm)} \max[R_f - \widetilde{R}_{EW,t}, 0] + \varepsilon_{P,t} \quad (8\text{-}11)$$

The interpretation of the model remains unchanged as, by construction, the two variables identified in the regression are uncorrelated with each other.

8.1.3.2 Flexible versions

Instead of extending the Henriksson and Merton (1981) model toward the inclusion of a larger number of explanatory variables, another direction points to the introduction of more flexibility for the portfolio manager to change their exposure. The focus is thus not so much in increasing the "number of gammas" (which is the common feature of Equations (8-9) to (8-11)), but rather in changing the "argument of the maximum" operator in the regression equation.

This is the route adopted by Weigel (1991). He considers that, in a generic active asset allocation framework, the portfolio manager typically has the choice between three – instead of two – traditional asset classes: stocks, bonds, and cash. The latter asset class is primarily meant to act as a shelter when the first two classes are not interesting. Furthermore, the manager would not only like to time the stock market but also the bond market in a similar fashion. Thus, they adopt two different strategic allocation betas and decide to modify one of these betas according to whether stocks will outperform bonds or vice versa. The corresponding measurement equation becomes

$$R_{P,t} - R_f = \alpha_P^{(hm)} + \beta_{P,M}^{(hm)}[R_{M,t} - R_f] + \beta_{P,D}^{(hm)}[R_{D,t} - R_f] + \gamma_P^{(hm)} \max[R_f - R_{D,t}, R_f - R_{M,t}, 0] + \varepsilon_{P,t} \quad (8\text{-}12)$$

where $R_{D,t}$ is the return of a bond (debt) index, and $\beta_{P,M}^{(hm)}$ and $\beta_{P,D}^{(hm)}$ respectively represent the target allocation to stocks and bonds.

The implications of the model regarding the manager's tactical asset allocation decisions can be understood through Table 8-6, which displays the resulting portfolio weights under different prevailing market conditions.

Clearly, the timing coefficient $\gamma_P^{(hm)}$ plays the role of an adjustment coefficient. When cash is unattractive ($\min[R_{M,t}, R_{D,t}, R_f] = R_f$), the portfolio adopts its target allocations. When the manager perceives that stocks or bonds will underperform, they withdraw a proportion $\gamma_P^{(hm)}$ of that asset class and store it in cash.

The main interest in the Weigel (1991) model is that it provides an intermediate and rather straightforward trade-off between the simplistic version of the basic HM model and a thorough

TABLE 8-6 Portfolio weights as a function of market conditions.

$\min[R_{M,t}, R_{D,t}, R_f]$	Weight in equities $w_{M,t}$	Weight in bonds $w_{D,t}$	Weight in cash $w_{F,t}$
$R_{M,t}$	$\beta_{P,M}^{(hm)} - \gamma_P^{(hm)}$	$\beta_{P,D}^{(hm)}$	$1 - \beta_{P,M}^{(hm)} - \beta_{P,D}^{(hm)} + \gamma_P^{(hm)}$
$R_{D,t}$	$\beta_{P,M}^{(hm)}$	$\beta_{P,D}^{(hm)} - \gamma_P^{(hm)}$	$1 - \beta_{P,M}^{(hm)} - \beta_{P,D}^{(hm)} + \gamma_P^{(hm)}$
R_f	$\beta_{P,M}^{(hm)}$	$\beta_{P,D}^{(hm)}$	$1 - \beta_{P,M}^{(hm)} - \beta_{P,D}^{(hm)}$

holding-based performance attribution approach, such as the ones examined in Chapter 14, with the advantage that it does not require the full knowledge of portfolio holdings and can be estimated in the context of a statistical regression framework.

Another way to introduce some flexibility in the HM model, although not documented in the literature, is to try to maximize the explanatory power of the model by letting the strike price of the put option vary, i.e., by not constraining the portfolio beta to switch exactly at the level of the risk-free rate. Indeed, from a theoretical standpoint, the portfolio manager is right when they decide to adopt an upside beta when the market posts positive returns, and to diminish the market exposure otherwise. However, in reality, this condition imposes a severe constraint on the empirical regression specification. Perhaps the market timing skill of the manager is not that strict, and they are able to switch their beta when they feel that the market return will be lower than another threshold return. This corresponds to the following equation to be estimated:

$$R_{P,t} - R_f = \alpha_P^{(hm)} + \beta_P^{(hm)}[R_{M,t} - R_f] + \gamma_P^{(hm)} \max\,[R_L^* - R_{M,t}, 0] + \varepsilon_{P,t} \tag{8-13}$$

where R_L^* is the strike price of the put option that maximizes the R^2 of the regression.

At first sight, the simultaneous estimation of all parameters of Equation (8-13) might look arduous because we are no longer in the framework of a simple linear regression. Nevertheless, a simple algorithm makes it perfectly doable with limited efforts:

1. Estimate the original HM model (Equation (8-1)) and record the associated R^2, denoted by $R^2(\#0)$.
2. Rank the market returns below the risk-free rate from the highest to the lowest, with rank $\#{-1}$ to $\#{-n}$, and rank the market returns above the risk-free rate from the lowest to the highest, with rank $\#{+1}$ to $\#{+m}$.
3. Set $R_L = R_{M,\#+1}$ and run the HM model, whose corresponding coefficient of determination is $R^2(\#+1)$. Likewise, set $R_L = R_{M,\#-1}$ and run the HM model again, with associated $R^2(\#-1)$.

4. If $\max(R^2(\#0), R^2(\#{+}1), R^2(\#{-}1))$ is $R^2(\#0)$, keep the original HM model and stop there. Otherwise, if $R^2(\#{+}1) > R^2(\#{-}1)$, set $R_L = R_{M,\#+2}$ and continue the incremental procedure until the situation when $R^2(\#{+}(k{+}1)) < R^2(\#{+}k)$. Otherwise, if $R^2(\#{-}1) > R^2(\#{+}1)$, set $R_L = R_{M,\#-2}$ and continue the incremental procedure until the moment when $R^2(\#{-}(k{+}1)) < R^2(\#{-}k)$.
5. The final flexible HM model is the one whose $R_L^* = R_{M,\#k}$ maximizes the R^2 of the regression.

When the optimal value R_L^* is set, it is then necessary to compute a new value of the adjusted HM alpha. For instance, the corresponding value of the approximate method (Equation (8-5)) is written as

$$\pi_P^{(hm,a),L} = \alpha_P^{(hm)} + \gamma_P^{(hm)} \times \left(\overline{\max}\,[R_{M,t} - R_L^*, 0] - q_M^{L+}(\overline{R}_M - R_L^*)\right) \tag{8-14}$$

where $\overline{\max}\,[R_{M,t} - R_L^*, 0] = \frac{1}{T}\sum_{t=1}^{T} \max\,[R_{M,t} - R_L^*, 0]$ and $q^{L+} = \frac{1}{T}\sum_{t=1}^{T} 1_{\{R_L^* < R_{M,t}\}}$.

The CX-T example (continued)

We apply the algorithm for the determination of R_L^* to each of the three funds. The results are summarized in the Table 8-7.

TABLE 8-7 CX-T example – Outcomes of the algorithm for the search of R_L^*.

	#−6	#−5	#−4	#−3	#−2	#−1	#0	#+1	#+2	#+3	#+4
R_L	*−2.36%*	*−1.71%*	*−0.78%*	*−0.47%*	*0.08%*	*0.13%*	*0.20%*	*0.51%*	*0.70%*	*0.70%*	*0.80%*
R^2(CX-A)						78.2%	78.4%	79.0%	79.2%	**79.2%**	79.1%
R^2(CX-B)		71.3%	**73.9%**	73.5%	70.0%	69.8%	69.7%	68.7%			
R^2(CX-C)	70.1%	**71.1%**	70.5%	69.5%	65.8%	65.7%	65.6%	65.1%			
$\overline{\max}\,[\cdot]$	2.88%	2.34%	1.60%	1.37%	0.98%	0.94%	0.90%	0.70%	0.59%	0.59%	0.54%
$\overline{R}_M - R_L^*$	2.67%	2.02%	1.09%	0.78%	0.22%	0.17%	0.10%	−0.21%	−0.40%	−0.40%	−0.50%
q^{L+}	87.5%	83.3%	79.2%	75.0%	70.8%	66.7%	62.5%	62.5%	58.3%	54.2%	50.0%

Applying the algorithm to the three funds reveals very different timing behaviors. For CX-A, it is necessary to search above the risk-free rate (equal to 0.20% per month) with a limited gain in significance. The other two funds have a negative optimal strike price, with a substantial gain in the significance of the HM regression. This means that, for CX-B and CX-C, the manager tends to switch the beta while protecting the portfolio against tail risks (i.e., very large losses) rather than trying to fully capture the upside and shelter against the downside, as underlies the interpretation of the original HM framework. For each optimal regression (figures in bold in Table 8-7), the summary results are reported in Table 8-8.

TABLE 8-8 CX-T example – Adjusted HM alphas associated with the optimal strike price.

Fund	R_L^*	$\alpha_P^{(hm)}$	$\beta_P^{(hm)}$	$\gamma_P^{(hm)}$	$\pi_P^{(hm,a)}$
CX-A	0.70%	−0.38%	1.37	1.01	0.44%
CX-B	−0.78%	0.45%	0.87	1.01	1.19%
CX-C	−1.71%	0.08%	0.55	0.69	0.53%

Compared with the results of Table 8-4, the performance remains positive for all three funds, but it becomes much smaller (by more than 20 bps) for fund CX-A, and increases by about 20 bps for the other two funds. More importantly, the search for the best inflexion point reveals a very different behavior compared to the HM model, which imposes excessive constraints on the piecewise-linear regression. This is represented in Figure 8-4.

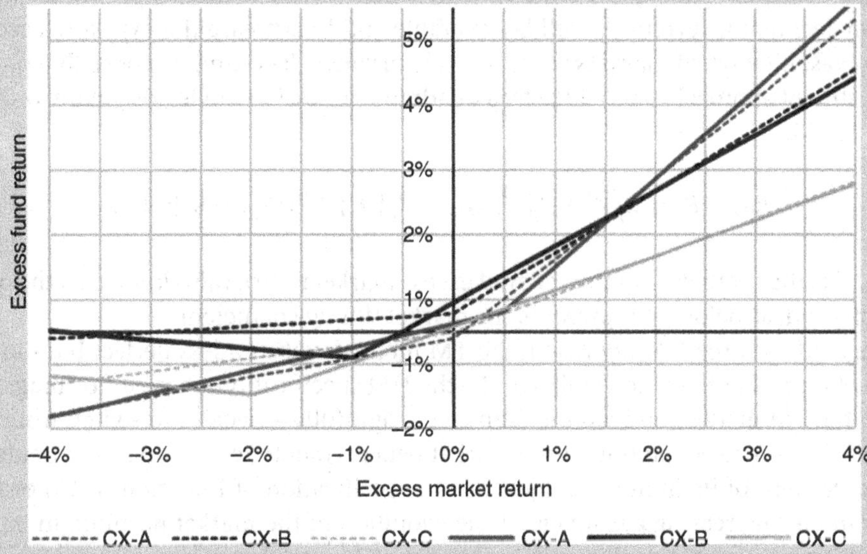

FIGURE 8-4 CX-T example – Regression lines under the original and flexible HM models.

The dashed lines reproduce the lines of the right graph of Figure 8-3, while the continuous lines represent the graphical translation of Table 8-8. The lines look very similar for fund

(continued)

(continued)

CX-A, whereas there is a large difference in their behavior for the other two funds in the region of negative excess market returns. Apparently, the managers of both CX-B and CX-C succeed in taking advantage of very negative returns in order to switch to a net negative beta. The original HM model is not tailored to uncover this behavior.

All in all, the evidence shown in this section suggests that the HM model does a reasonably good job in explaining how the manager of CX-A attempts to time the market, but it is certainly improvable regarding the return generating processes of funds CX-B and CX-C.

8.2 POLYNOMIAL REGRESSION APPROACH

8.2.1 The Treynor and Mazuy (TM) model

Even though the idea of adopting polynomial regression models in order to assess the market timing skill of a manager is older than the HM approach discussed in the preceding section, it is paradoxically more flexible. Instead of being constrained to only choose between two levels of fixed betas, the manager is allowed to gradually increase their exposure to the market when they feel that its evolution will be favorable and to decrease the exposure according to a similar reasoning when markets are negatively oriented. The simplest of such a progressive beta adjustment approach is provided by a quadratic regression model, originally proposed by Treynor and Mazuy (1966):

$$R_{P,t} - R_f = \alpha_P^{(\text{tm})} + \beta_P^{(\text{tm})}[R_{M,t} - R_f] + \gamma_P^{(\text{tm})}[R_{M,t} - R_f]^2 + \varepsilon_{P,t} \tag{8-15}$$

where $\gamma_P^{(\text{tm})}$ is the coefficient of the squared excess market return (also known as the quadratic coefficient) and, as before, it represents the market timing coefficient.

Compared with the HM approach, the TM model involves a less perfect but more intensive type of market anticipation skill. Unlike the HM specification, there is no "magic turning point" in the TM model in which the manager – rightfully – decides to switch from a low to a high beta level. The adaptation of the market beta is smooth, continuous and gradual. Nevertheless, because of its limitless convexity, the specification of Equation (8-15) enables the manager to take increasing advantage of the evolution of the market portfolio in both directions. As shown below, the flexibility brought by the TM model translates into the analogy with options as well.

Graphically, the interpretation of the model can be readily contrasted with that of the HM regression that was proposed in Figure 8-2.

The illustration takes the same set of observations as in Figure 8-2 but with a different fitted regression line (Figure 8-5). The curve represents a quadratic function of the excess market

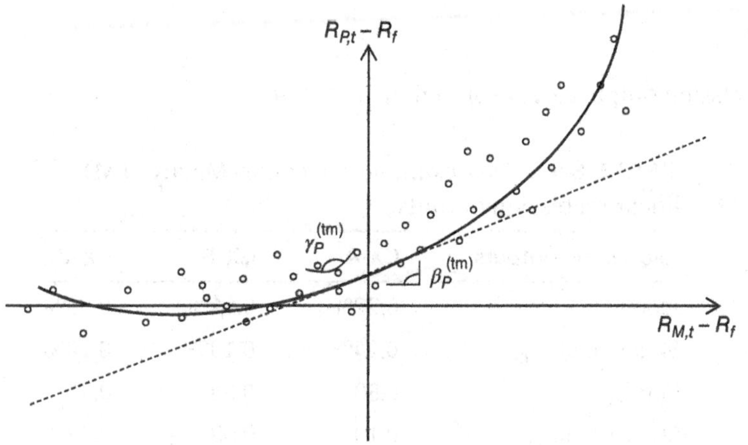

FIGURE 8-5 Graphical representation of the Treynor and Mazuy (1966) model.

returns that is supposed to minimize the vertical squared distance between the coordinates of the points and the corresponding ones on the curve, as in a traditional least-squares estimation.

The graph shows how the linear (beta) and quadratic (gamma) coefficients combine with each other in order to produce the fitted regression curve. First, $\beta_P^{(tm)}$ indicates the trend adopted by the portfolio manager, and corresponds to a kind of middle exposure to the market across market conditions.[8] Second, $\gamma_P^{(tm)}$ completes the linear picture by showing how the ability of the manager to anticipate market movements allows them to gradually increase their exposure in the positive quadrant and decrease it in the negative quadrant.

The CX-T example (continued)

Instead of the linear one-factor regression, we have applied the TM quadratic model on each of the three funds:

$$R_{i,t} - R_f = \alpha_i^{(tm)} + \beta_i^{(tm)}[R_{M,t} - R_f] + \gamma_i^{(tm)}[R_{M,t} - R_f]^2 + \varepsilon_{i,t}$$

(continued)

[8]The TM beta should not be interpreted as the average linear exposure of the portfolio. It would only be the case if, by chance, the dispersions of negative and positive market excess returns were very similar, which is hardly the case in practice, especially for a long period of time in which we can reasonably expect the average excess returns to be positive.

(continued)

The regression outputs are displayed in Table 8-9.

TABLE 8-9 CX-T example – Treynor–Mazuy (TM) linear regression outputs.

Regression outputs	CX-A	CX-B	CX-C
$Alpha_{TM}$	0.22%	0.51%	0.08%
St. dev. $alpha_{TM}$	0.24%	0.19%	0.16%
$Beta_{TM}$	0.80	0.58	0.42
St. dev. $beta_{TM}$	0.10	0.08	0.07
$Gamma_{TM}$	10.18	10.76	5.16
St. dev. $gamma_{TM}$	3.56	2.81	2.39
R^2	76.80%	72.29%	67.27%

Similar to the HM model (Table 8-3), the quadratic specification greatly improves the quality of the fit compared to the linear regression. Nevertheless, this improvement is lower than with the HM model for fund CX-A (76.80% for TM vs. 78.37% for HM). Note as well that the gamma coefficient has a much larger scale than the one of the HM model. This outcome is logical as the unit of measurement of the squared market return is different as well.

The contrast between the piecewise-linear (HM) and quadratic (TM) regressions for the three funds is shown in Figure 8-6.

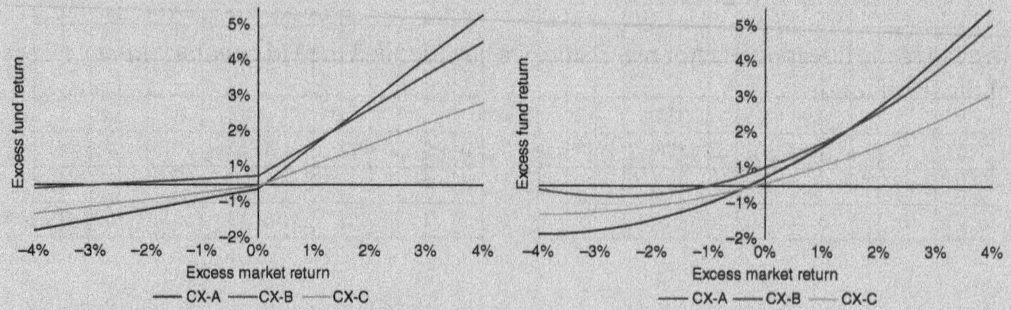

FIGURE 8-6 CX-T example – Types of relations between excess fund and market returns.

The relations look similar for the HM and TM models, which could be expected given that both approaches aim at uncovering the same kind of behavior. The convexity of the relation is more pronounced for fund CX-B than for the other two funds in both cases, but the Treynor–Mazuy curve even leads to a net bearish market exposure for extreme negative returns. Note as well that all three alphas become positive on the right graph. Given that the positive convexity ($\gamma_i^{(tm)} > 0$) indicates superior timing, we can conclude that none of the three funds has underperformed the market since they all have at the same time a positive alpha and a positive gamma.

8.2.2 The Treynor–Mazuy-adjusted alpha

As in the HM model, the overall performance of a portfolio whose returns are explained by Equation (8-15) should take the intercept into account - the higher the alpha, the higher the performance, but also the quadratic coefficient - the more pronounced the convexity, the greater the market timing skill of the manager. Thus, we should also expect that the TM-adjusted alpha adopts the same additive structure as the HM-adjusted alpha: $\pi_P^{(tm)} = \alpha_P^{(tm)} + f(\gamma_P^{(tm)})$, with $f'(\gamma_P^{(tm)}) > 0$. However the functional form of $f(\gamma_P^{(tm)})$ will be different in this case.

8.2.2.1 Option-based adjustment of the TM alpha

What mostly differentiates the TM Equation (8-15) from the HM Equation (8-1)? It is the nature of the convexity adjustment on top of the portfolio's exposure to the market portfolio. In the piecewise-linear model, it reflects the return of a put option on the market that matures exactly over one period. This explains the form of the gamma term, which resembles the terminal payoff of an option at its maturity date.

In the case of the Treynor–Mazuy model, the analogy with options is slightly less straightforward, but it can be supported if one accepts more flexibility in the choice of the option that replicates the slope and convexity of the fitted regression curve. Hübner (2016) suggests comparing the form of the quadratic regression to that of a synthetic replicating portfolio $\widetilde{P}$ composed of (i) a weight $w^{\tau,\kappa}$ in a long position in a call option on the index M with a moneyness (defined as the ratio of the strike price over the current price) of $\frac{K}{M_t} = \kappa$ and whose maturity τ is longer than a single period of time, and (ii) the remainder $1 - w^{\tau,\kappa}$ invested in the riskless asset.[9] The rate of return of such a portfolio, which we denote by $R_{\widetilde{P},t}$, can be approximated thanks to the so-called "Greeks" using a Taylor series development. It is equal to

$$R_{\widetilde{P},t} = w^{\tau,\kappa}\left(\Delta^{\tau,\kappa} R_{M,t} + \frac{1}{2}\Gamma^{\tau,\kappa} R_{M,t}^2 + \Theta^{\tau,\kappa}\right) + (1 - w^{\tau,\kappa})R_f + o_t \qquad (8\text{-}16)$$

[9]We develop the argument for the case of a positive beta and a positive gamma. The other cases (negative or null beta; negative gamma) are discussed later.

where $\Delta^{\tau,\kappa} = \frac{\partial \text{Call}^{\tau,\kappa}}{\partial M}$, $\Gamma^{\tau,\kappa} = \frac{\partial^2 \text{Call}^{\tau,\kappa}}{(\partial M)^2}$, and $\Theta^{\tau,\kappa} = \frac{\partial \text{Call}^{\tau,\kappa}}{\partial t}$ are the option's delta, gamma, and theta, respectively, and o_t is a term related to the numerical approximation of the return of the optional position.

Obviously, Equations (8-15) and (8-16) display great similarities, even though the first one corresponds to the return of an actively managed portfolio, while the second one reports the return of a mechanical, passive portfolio strategy. If one considers, for sufficiently small values of R_f, that $[R_{M,t} - R_f]^2 \approx R_{M,t}^2$ and that the residual terms of the equations reflect a pure specific risk in both cases, the linear and quadratic coefficients are respectively equal if $w^{\tau,\kappa} \times \Delta^{\tau,\kappa} = \beta_P^{(\text{tm})}$ and $w^{\tau,\kappa} \times \frac{1}{2}\Gamma^{\tau,\kappa} = \gamma_P^{(\text{tm})}$. This is the case if $\frac{2\Delta^{\tau,\kappa}}{\Gamma^{\tau,\kappa}} = \frac{\beta_P^{(\text{tm})}}{\gamma_P^{(\text{tm})}}$. This entails that the option chosen should have a ratio of its delta over its gamma that is strictly proportional to the ratio of the regression's beta over gamma coefficients. Furthermore, we obtain that $w^{\tau,\kappa} = \frac{\beta_P^{(\text{tm})}}{\Delta^{\tau,\kappa}} > \beta_P^{(\text{tm})}$ since the option delta is always lower than one.

Under these conditions, the intercepts of the regressions will also become equal to each other if $\alpha_P^{(\text{tm})} = -c_{\widetilde{P}} \equiv (\beta_P^{(\text{tm})} - w^{\tau,\kappa})R_f + w^{\tau,\kappa}\Theta^{\tau,\kappa}$. Note that $\beta_P^{(\text{tm})} - w^{\tau,\kappa} < 0$ and $\Theta^{\tau,\kappa} < 0$ in the case of a call option on a no-dividend underlying, which means that both terms on the right-hand side are negative. Thus, if the manager of portfolio P neither outperforms nor underperforms the synthetic portfolio $\widetilde{P}$, their resulting alpha will be negative and equal to $-c_{\widetilde{P}}$. This value represents the opportunity cost, expressed as a rate of return, of trying to replicate the portfolio's beta and gamma using options. Among the many options allowing this replication, the manager will choose the one whose moneyness κ^* and maturity τ^* minimize the cost: $c_{\widetilde{P}}^* = \min_{\tau,\kappa}(w^{\tau,\kappa} - \beta_P^{(\text{tm})})R_f - w^{\tau,\kappa}\Theta^{\tau,\kappa}$.

The minimum replication cost $c_{\widetilde{P}}^*$ corresponds to the adjustment that must be brought to the regression intercept in order to faithfully represent the performance of the portfolio manager:

$$\pi_P^{(\text{tm},o)} = \alpha_P^{(\text{tm})} + \beta_P^{(\text{tm})}\left(\frac{1}{\Delta^{\tau^*\kappa^*}} - 1\right)R_f - \frac{\beta_P^{(\text{tm})}}{\Delta^{\tau^*\kappa^*}}\Theta^{\tau^*\kappa^*} \tag{8-17}$$

where $\Theta^{\tau^*\kappa^*}$ is the theta of the cheapest option that verifies $\frac{2\Delta^{\tau,\kappa}}{\Gamma^{\tau,\kappa}} = \frac{\beta_P^{(\text{tm})}}{\gamma_P^{(\text{tm})}}$, and $w^{\tau^*\kappa^*} = \frac{\beta_P^{(\text{tm})}}{\Delta^{\tau^*\kappa^*}}$.

How to interpret the adjustment term? It features two components. The first one reflects the savings made by the portfolio manager by "only" investing $\beta_P^{(\text{tm})}$ in the market index, whereas to replicate the same linear exposure, one has to invest a weight of $w^{\tau^*\kappa^*}$ in the call option. The difference, which is positive, can be stored in a riskless security that provides a rate of return of R_f. The second component represents the savings made by the portfolio manager by creating the same linear and convex exposure to the market without having to use options. They avoid the erosion of the value of the option over time, which is represented by its (negative) theta.

The adjustment term only depends on the quadratic coefficient $\gamma_P^{(\text{tm})}$ in an indirect fashion through the identification of the replicating option that has the desired properties. However, what is new, compared to the different adjustments presented in the context of the HM model, is that the adjustment explicitly depends on the portfolio beta $\beta_P^{(tm)}$ too. This is rather logical: The cost of creating the convexity shown in Figure 8-5 using options is likely to also depend on what option is to be used in order to create the linear slope shown in the graph.

In the context of the Black and Scholes option pricing approach corresponding to Equations (8-3a) to (8-3d), the "Greeks" (delta, gamma, and theta) associated with a European call option also adopt an analytical expression:

$$\Delta(S_t, \tau, K) = \Phi(d_1) \tag{8-18a}$$

$$\Gamma(S_t, \tau, K) = \frac{\Phi'(d_1)}{S_t \sigma \sqrt{\tau}} \tag{8-18b}$$

$$\Theta(S_t, \tau, K) = -\frac{S_t \Phi'(d_1)\sigma}{2\sqrt{\tau}} - R_f^c\, K e^{-R_f^c \tau}\Phi(d_2) \tag{8-18c}$$

where $\Phi'(d_1)$ is the value of the density function of the standard normal distribution taken at value d_1, defined in Equation (8-3c).

We can illustrate the logic underlying the adjustment with a simple example. We set $K = \kappa$ and $S_t = 1$ because we work with rates of return. Consider a portfolio whose returns are explained by the Treynor and Mazuy quadratic regression with $\beta_P^{(tm)} = 1$ and $\gamma_P^{(tm)} = 6.11$. The TM alpha of this fund is $\alpha_P^{(tm)} = 0.3\%$. The continuously compounded risk-free rate is 2% per year (which corresponds to a monthly interest rate of $e^{2\% \times 1/12} - 1 = 0.17\%$), and the volatility of the underlying index is $\sigma_M = 10\%$. The cheapest option whose replicating portfolio matches the slope and curvature of the index is a call with maturity $\tau^* = 0.5$ year and moneyness $\kappa^* = 1.02$, i.e., the strike price is set at 102% of the current price of the underlying. Normalizing the price of the market index to 1, we obtain the following: $\Delta^{\tau^*\kappa^*} = 0.459$, $\Gamma^{\tau^*\kappa^*} = 5.611$, and $\Theta^{\tau^*\kappa^*} = -0.0001$ per trading day or -0.20% per month. This option satisfies the constraint on the fund's relative curvature: $\frac{2\Delta^{\tau,\kappa}}{\Gamma^{\tau,\kappa}} = \frac{2\times 0.459}{5.611} = \frac{1}{6.11} = \frac{\beta_P^{(tm)}}{\gamma_P^{(tm)}}$. Furthermore, the weight invested in the option in the replicating portfolio is equal to $w^{\tau^*\kappa^*} = \frac{\beta_P^{(tm)}}{\Delta^{\tau^*\kappa^*}} = 2.18$. Thus, if the frequency of observations is 1 month (20 days), we obtain a value of the adjustment that is equal to 0.64%: $(w^{\tau^*\kappa^*} - \beta_P^{(tm)})R_f - w^{\tau^*\kappa^*}\Theta^{\tau^*\kappa^*} = (2.18 - 1) \times 0.17\% - 2.18 \times (-0.2\%) = 0.2\% + 0.44\%$.

The performance adjustment is illustrated in Figure 8-7, in which the portfolio regression outputs are in bold and the replicating portfolio is represented by thin lines.

With the numerical data used in the illustration, Figure 8-7 shows the geometric argument that is at stake. The fund's slope and curvature, on top of the graph, are perfectly reproduced by the option-based replicating portfolio, lying below. The total performance of the portfolio simply sums up its alpha (the intercept of the quadratic regression) and the opportunity cost of the replicating portfolio.

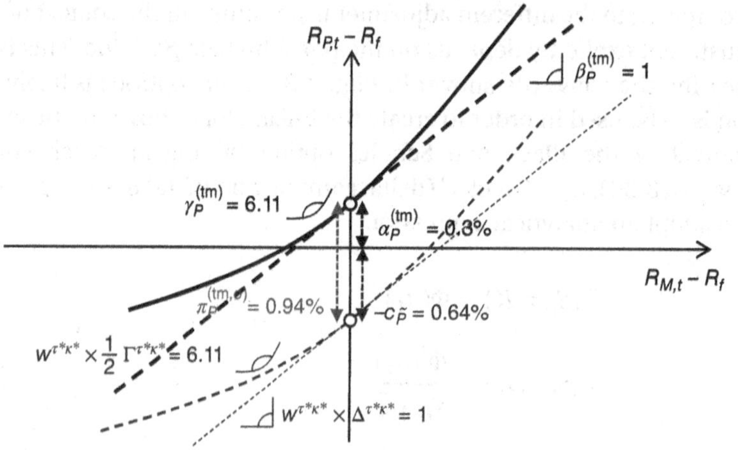

FIGURE 8-7 Illustration of the optional adjustment to the TM model.

There are two difficulties to overcome for the implementation of this adjustment method. The first one involves the choice of the optimal option characteristics, namely, its moneyness κ^* and time-to-maturity τ^*. Even though the choice of the cheapest option has to be done on a case-by-case basis, Hübner (2016) suggests that, in general, the shorter the maturity of the option, the lower its cost; as a rule of thumb, it is interesting to match the option maturity with the periodicity of the returns. Once the maturity is set, the moneyness remains to be identified on the basis of the level of the ratio of delta over gamma that is looked after.

The second difficulty is to adapt the methodology to the various cases that can arise in practice. Here again, the analogy between the linear and quadratic sensitivities of the portfolio returns with the delta and gamma of an option-based portfolio appears to be helpful. If one distinguishes the situations with a positive, zero, and negative beta, on the one hand, and those with a positive or a negative gamma, on the other hand, the option trades that need to be used in order to construct the replicating portfolio are summarized in Table 8-10.

TABLE 8-10 Synthesis of option-based replicating strategies.

Directional exposure	Quadratic exposure	
	$\gamma_P^{(tm)} > 0$	$\gamma_P^{(tm)} < 0$
$\beta_P^{(tm)} > 0$	Long call	Short put
$\beta_P^{(tm)} = 0$	Long straddle	Short straddle
$\beta_P^{(tm)} < 0$	Long put	Short call

When the portfolio has a directional exposure (long or short), one option suffices. If the regression shows that the portfolio is market-neutral, such as some hedge fund strategies for instance, it is necessary to use a straddle, which is a combination of a put and a call option with the same strike prices. If gamma is positive, the strategy involves the purchase of both options (long straddle), whereas a negative gamma requires the sale of the options (short straddle).

It remains to be noted that this approach, based on an arbitrage argument, can also be applied when the proxy for the market portfolio is an index that is the underlying of traded options. Rather than relying on a numerical or analytical adjustment (as in the illustration above with the Black and Scholes formula), the actual cost of purchasing the option and keeping it during one period can be used instead. This has the merit of considering the true opportunity cost of replicating the manager's convexity in real life, including the trading costs of buying and selling derivatives or the variations in option premiums in times of market stress, for instance.

8.2.2.2 Other adjustments of the TM alpha

In the same spirit as the Merton (1981) approach for the replication of the HM payoff with a put option, there is another way of calling upon option pricing theory in order to provide the adjustment in the TM model. In their discussion of the properties of "manipulation-proof performance measures," Goetzmann, Ingersoll, Spiegel, and Welch (2007) identify that the counterpart of Equation (8-4) can be developed using a security that would pay a fraction of the squared market return.[10] They propose the following adjustment:

$$\pi_P^{(\text{tm},q)} = \alpha_P^{(\text{tm})} + \gamma_P^{(\text{tm})} \times (1 + R_f)^2 \times (e^{\sigma_M^2} - 1) \tag{8-19}$$

where, as before, σ_M^2 is the variance of the market portfolio return over the time interval. The superscript "q" on the performance measure reflects that it corresponds to the "quadratic" approach.

Another way to correct the Treynor–Mazuy alpha for the presence of a market timing skill of the investor is proposed by Admati, Bhattacharya, Pfleiderer, and Ross (1986) and Grinblatt and Titman (1994). These authors characterize the properties of an optimally managed active market timing portfolio if the returns are normally distributed and if the investor exhibits a constant absolute risk aversion utility function. They assume that the manager linearly adjusts their beta to the information they receive about market returns. In this case, the adjusted performance measure $\pi_P^{(\text{tm},v)}$ (superscript "v" corresponds to the "variance-based" approach) adopts a simple expression:

$$\pi_P^{(\text{tm},v)} = \alpha_P^{(\text{tm})} + \gamma_P^{(\text{tm})} \times \sigma_M^2 \tag{8-20}$$

[10] At the same time as they propose this adjustment, the authors concede that this particular performance measure is itself prone to being manipulated. We discuss this notion of "manipulation" in Chapter 18.

Finally, in the exact same spirit as for their simplified approach in the HM model that led to Equation (8-6), Bollen and Busse (2004) propose the same type of adjustment in the quadratic case. They propose to define the market timer's performance as

$$\pi_P^{(tm,s)} = \alpha_P^{(tm)} + \gamma_P^{(tm)} \times \overline{[R_M - R_f]^2} \tag{8-21}$$

where $\overline{[R_M - R_f]^2} = \frac{1}{T}\sum_{t=1}^{T}[R_{M,t} - R_f]^2$ is the average squared market excess return, which is always positive. As in the previous section, superscript "*s*" on the performance measure reflects that it corresponds to the "simplified" approach. When the frequency of observations is large (for daily or weekly returns, for instance), the difference between Equations (8-20) and (8-21) can be considered negligible.

Compared with the option-based approach, the alternative adjustment methods appear to be much simpler to apply. Nevertheless, the adjustment made with the help of options has two major advantages. First, it explicitly acknowledges the influence of the choice of the portfolio beta on the value of convexity, through its influence on the identification of the option. For complex problems that involve very convex or concave behaviors, or negative betas, for instance, this may lead to large differences compared to simpler adjustments. Second, it allows us to better understand what the portfolio manager exactly does through the option characteristics that underlie the adjustment.

The CX-T example (continued)

We start with the choice of the cheapest option applied to each fund in the option-based approach. Setting a target maturity $\tau = 1/12$ and using the Black–Scholes formula for the Greeks with inputs $M_t = 1$, $\sigma_M = 2.11\% \times \sqrt{12} = 7.32\%$, $R_f^c = \log(1 + 2.4\%) = 2.37\%$, we obtain the results shown in Table 8-11.

TABLE 8-11 CX-T example – Option characteristics for the replicating portfolio in the TM model.

Option features	CX-A	CX-B	CX-C
Maturity τ^* (fixed)	0.083	0.083	0.083
Moneyness κ^*	0.993	1.001	0.992
Ratio $\frac{2\Delta^{\tau,\kappa}}{\Gamma^{\tau,\kappa}} = \frac{\beta_P^{(tm)}}{\gamma_P^{(tm)}}$	0.0788	0.0540	0.0822
Delta $\Delta^{\tau^*\kappa^*}$	0.67	0.51	0.69
Gamma $\Gamma^{\tau^*\kappa^*}$	17.07	18.87	16.72
Theta (per day) $\Theta^{\tau^*\kappa^*}$	−0.00017	−0.00017	−0.00016
Weight $w^{\tau^*\kappa^*}$	1.19	1.14	0.61
Cost c_P^*	**0.48%**	**0.49%**	**0.23%**

The application of the four adjustment approaches delivers extremely similar results as shown in Table 8-12.

TABLE 8-12 CX-T example – Adjusted TM alphas according to the four methods.

Fund	$\alpha_P^{(tm)}$	$\gamma_P^{(tm)}$	$\alpha_P^{(tm)} + f\left(\gamma_P^{(tm)}\right)$			
			Optional	Quadratic	Variance	Approx.
CX-A	0.22%	10.18	0.70%	0.68%	0.68%	0.68%
CX-B	0.51%	10.76	1.00%	0.99%	0.99%	0.99%
CX-C	0.08%	5.16	0.31%	0.31%	0.31%	0.31%

In general, the optional approach provides slightly higher adjustments than the other three methods, which are very close to each other by design. Because the TM and HM approaches have very similar regression results, the adjusted performance measures presented in Table 8-12 also look much like those of Table 8-3 for the HM model applied to the three funds. This is in sharp contrast with the levels of HM and TM alphas, which are very different.

It is useful to graphically represent the behavior of the replicating portfolio applied to each of the three funds (Figure 8-8). To this end, we report on the same graph the fitted regression outputs and those resulting from applying Equation (8-16) with the inputs of Table 8-11.

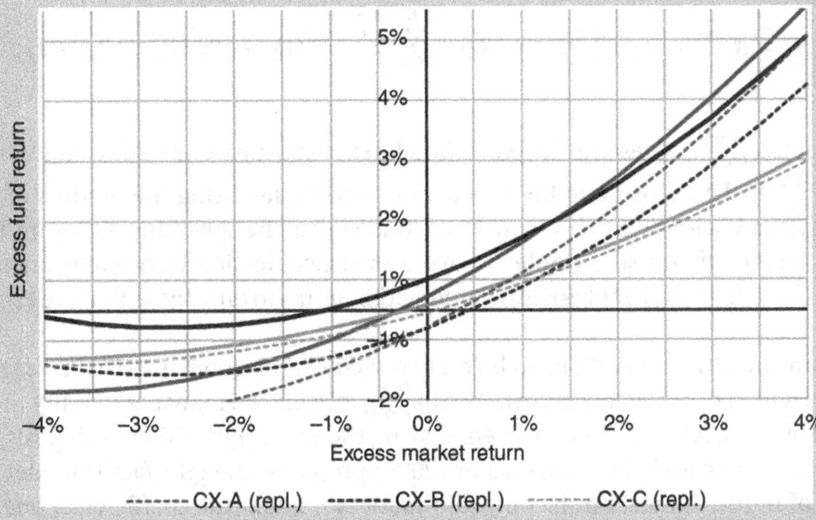

FIGURE 8-8 CX-T example – Comparison between the quadratic regression and the replicating portfolios.

(continued)

(continued)

The larger the distance between the solid and dotted lines of the corresponding tones, the larger the associated fund's performance. The graph clearly shows why CX-B is the best performer: The manager not only delivers the largest alpha but also mimics the option that has the largest value (together with fund CX-A).

8.2.3 Model extensions

The types of extensions brought to the original Treynor–Mazuy model are essentially of the same two types as the ones presented for the HM model above. Some authors propose to increase the number of explanatory variables, including those that aim to assess the market timing skills of the manager. Others introduce some more flexibility in the model in order to better capture the potential nonlinearities of the portfolio, without necessarily augmenting the model. Of course, these different approaches can be combined with each other, but we present them one by one.

8.2.3.1 Multifactor versions

The possibility to use at the same time several risk factors and a quadratic term opens up possibilities that are absent in a multifactor model: the creation of interaction variables that feature the product of the returns of two potential explanatory factors. The most general form of the model is written as follows:

$$R_{P,t} - R_f = \alpha_P^{(tm)} + \sum_{k=1}^{K} \beta_{P,k}^{(tm)}(F_{k,t} - R_f) + \sum_{k=1}^{K}\sum_{l=1}^{K} \gamma_{P,kl}^{(tm)}(F_{k,t} - R_f)(F_{l,t} - R_f) + \varepsilon_{P,t} \quad (8\text{-}22)$$

where, as before, $\beta_{P,k}^{(tm)}$ represents the portfolio's linear exposure to the kth factor whose return is $F_{k,t}$ and $\gamma_{P,kl}^{(tm)}$ is the exposure to the interaction variable featuring the product of the excess returns of factor k with factor l. When $k = l$, this is just the quadratic exposure to the corresponding factor. Of course, in order to avoid overspecification (too many variables), it is necessary to limit the number of potential interaction terms to only those that are economically relevant.

Lehmann and Modest (1987) introduce a two-factor extension with a stock (M) and a bond (D) index, in which the interaction coefficient $\gamma_{P,MD}^{(tm)}$ reflects the manager's ability to anticipate movements of the stock and bond markets sharing the same sign, either both positive or both negative. In a more classic fashion, Comer (2006) proposes an eight-factor model to explain the returns of mutual funds, but he only allows for two quadratic coefficients, one for stocks and one for bonds.

A variant involves the estimation of volatility timing, as proposed by Busse (1999) and Chen and Liang (2007). They consider that when market volatility is allowed to be time varying (like with a generalized auto-regressive conditional heteroscedasticity (GARCH) setup), fund managers may attempt to anticipate when the market is nervous (highly volatile) or calm through a specification similar to (8-22), in which the volatility factor is defined as the demeaned standard deviation of market returns $F_{\sigma,t} \equiv \sigma_{M,t} - \overline{\sigma}_M$. In this case, it makes little sense to simultaneously use the squared market return with the squared volatility factors because of their extremely high correlation. Rather, the interaction coefficient $\gamma_{P,M\sigma}^{(tm)}$ that multiplies the product of the market return and the volatility factor is of great interest. A negative value indicates that the portfolio manager is successful at increasing their market exposure when they feel that the volatility is going to decrease.

Another important extension of the Treynor–Mazuy model involves its adaptation to conditional asset pricing models. In the same spirit as the conditional HM model, Ferson and Schadt (1996) present a conditional TM model, that we propose again in the single-factor version for ease of exposition:

$$\begin{aligned} R_{P,t} - R_f &= \alpha_P^{(tm)} + (\beta_{P,0}^{(tm)} + \beta_{P,z}^{(tm)} \times z_{t-1})[R_{M,t} - R_f] \\ &\quad + (\gamma_{P,0}^{(tm)} + \gamma_{P,z}^{(tm)} \times z_{t-1})[R_{M,t} - R_f]^2 + \varepsilon_{P,t} \end{aligned} \tag{8-23}$$

where the interpretation of the gamma coefficients in the equation is similar to that in the original model. If market volatility is itself used as an instrument, the difference between the conditional specification and the volatility timing approach discussed above lies in the fact that the former model uses the lagged value of this volatility variable, while the latter one uses the observation that is contemporaneous with the market return.

Note that, in many empirical papers that have aimed at measuring market timing in the scope of the TM approach, the conditional specification (usually with multiple factors) has proven to be much more effective than the unconditional versions of the model.

It is also possible to deploy the TM version of the Henriksson (1984) omitted variable model, but this route has not been adopted in the related literature.

8.2.3.2 Flexible versions

The Treynor–Mazuy model is the simplest case of a polynomial regression approach. A natural way to bring more flexibility to the model can be through higher degrees of the polynomial, i.e., raising the market excess return to a higher power. Jagannathan and Korajczyk (1986) suggest adopting this approach in order to test the specification of the quadratic model rather than really trying to bring an additional insight regarding the curvature of the polynomial regression. This approach – even though not formally tested in the original Jagannathan and Korajczyk (1986) paper – has led to a cubic regression that has been empirically examined on many markets (see, for instance, the Bauer, Otten, and Tourani-Rad (2006) application in New Zealand):

$$R_{P,t} - R_f = \alpha_P^{(\mathrm{tm})} + \beta_P^{(\mathrm{tm})}[R_{M,t} - R_f] + \gamma_P^{(\mathrm{tm})}[R_{M,t} - R_f]^2 + \delta_P^{(\mathrm{tm})}[R_{M,t} - R_f]^3 + \varepsilon_{P,t} \quad (8\text{-}24)$$

where $\delta_P^{(\mathrm{tm})}$ is the coefficient of the cubic market return. In the spirit of Jagannathan and Korajczyk (1986), a significant value of this coefficient may indicate that the quadratic model is itself misspecified. However, there is a more positive way of interpreting the cubic regression. A significant cubic coefficient could imply some kind of asymmetric timing ability of the manager that is not captured by the original TM model. Specifically, if $\delta_P^{(\mathrm{tm})} > 0$, the manager could be able to better decrease their market beta in the case of severe market downturns than the Treynor–Mazuy model itself predicts. Some may argue that this argument is stretching slightly far from the spirit of the polynomial model, and this has not yet substantively been backed by the empirical literature.

Another interesting development of the model goes in the direction of reconciling the insights underlying the economic rationale of the HM model, namely the manager's ability to distinguish bullish and bearish market conditions, with the larger flexibility offered by the TM quadratic specification. An elegant solution is provided by Chen and Liang (2007) who introduce a sort of piecewise-quadratic regression that mixes the HM with the TM approach in a single estimation:

$$\begin{aligned} R_{P,t} - R_f = \alpha_P^{(\mathrm{tm+hm})} &+ (\beta_{P+}^{(\mathrm{tm+hm})} 1_{\{R_f < R_{M,t}\}} + \beta_P^{(\mathrm{tm+hm})})[R_{M,t} - R_f] \\ &+ (\gamma_{P+}^{(\mathrm{tm+hm})} 1_{\{R_f < R_{M,t}\}} + \gamma_P^{(\mathrm{tm+hm})})[R_{M,t} - R_f]^2 + \varepsilon_{P,t} \end{aligned} \quad (8\text{-}25)$$

where $\beta_{P+}^{(\mathrm{tm+hm})}$ and $\gamma_{P+}^{(\mathrm{tm+hm})}$ respectively stand for the add-on to the portfolio beta and gamma when the market excess return is positive. It is also possible to use the same approach for different market volatility or reward-to-volatility levels, as suggested by Chen and Liang (2007).

In order to perform the adjustment to the alpha of the portfolio in such a setup, it is no longer possible to use the option replication approach. Rather, a mixture of the simpler adjustments proposed in the HM model (to account for the two different regimes) and in the TM model (to account for the quadratic term) is warranted. The joint application of the approximate HM method and the simplified TM approach in this context yields the following expression:

$$\begin{aligned} \pi_P^{(\mathrm{tm+hm})} &= \alpha_P^{(\mathrm{tm+hm})} + \beta_{P+}^{(\mathrm{tm+hm})} \left(\overline{\max}\,[R_{M,t} - R_f, 0] - q_M^+(\overline{R}_M - R_f) \right) \\ &+ \gamma_P^{(\mathrm{tm+hm})} \times \overline{[R_M - R_f]^2} + q_M^+ \gamma_{P+}^{(\mathrm{tm+hm})}\, \overline{\max}\,[R_{M,t} - R_f, 0]^2 \end{aligned} \quad (8\text{-}26)$$

where $\overline{\max}\,[R_{M,t} - R_f, 0]^2 = \left(\frac{1}{T}\sum_{t=1}^{T} \max\,[R_{M,t} - R_f, 0]\right)^2$ is the squared mean value of the excess market return floored to zero when it is negative.

The CX-T example (continued)

The mixed HM–TM approach proposed by Chen and Liang (2007) is applied to all three funds. The results are summarized in Table 8-13 (noting, as before, that $q^+ = 62.5\%$)

TABLE 8-13 CX-T example – Mixed TM–HM linear regression outputs.

Regression outputs	CX-A	CX-B	CX-C
$\alpha_P^{(tm+hm)}$	−0.07%	0.56%	0.10%
$\beta_P^{(tm+hm)}$	−0.14	0.84	0.83
$\beta_{P+}^{(tm+hm)}$	1.01	−0.20	−0.18
$\gamma_P^{(tm+hm)}$	−11.40	17.01	15.30
$\gamma_{P+}^{(tm+hm)}$	26.17	−10.39	−20.95
R^2	80.52%	73.09%	71.80%
$\pi_P^{(tm+hm)}$	**0.54%**	**1.04%**	**0.42%**

The sensitivities of these funds to the market index are very different as illustrated in Figure 8-9.

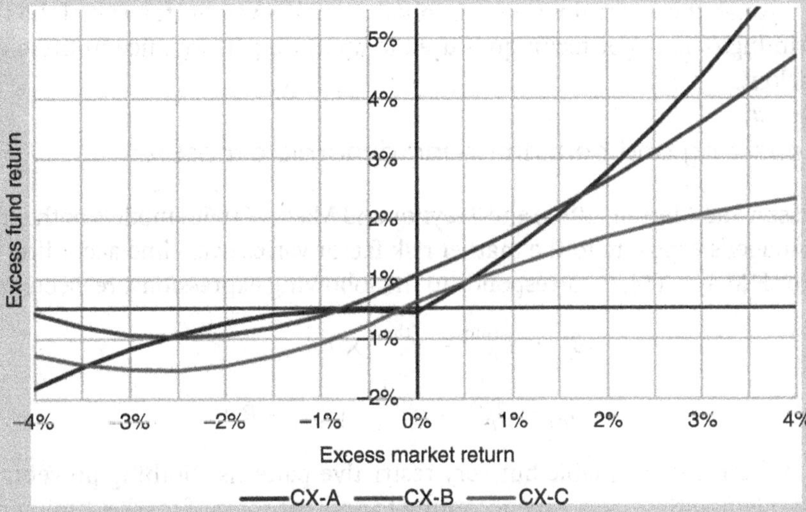

FIGURE 8-9 CX-T example – Mixed TM–HM regression curves.

(continued)

(continued)

The results displayed in this table and shown in the graph suggest a very different behavior for funds CX-A compared to CX-B and CX-C. The first fund has a concave behavior when market excess returns are negative (negative estimate of $\gamma_{CX-A}^{(tm+hm)}$) but it becomes positive when excess market returns are positive ($\gamma_{CX\text{-}A+}^{(tm+hm)} > \gamma_{CX\text{-}A}^{(tm+hm)}$). The other two funds are more convex in the negative area than in the positive area. For CX-C, the convexity even becomes negative when excess market returns are positive ($\gamma_{CX\text{-}C}^{(tm+hm)} + \gamma_{CX\text{-}C+}^{(tm+hm)} < 0$).

8.3 RETURN-BASED DYNAMIC EXPOSURES APPROACH

The nonlinear regression approaches examined in Sections 8.1 and 8.2 are rather parsimonious in terms of inputs. They use periodic portfolio and factor returns data, and only lead to the estimation of a few parameters. This is paradoxical, considering the aim of identifying the dynamic behavior of the portfolio manager who adapts their factor exposures to anticipated market movements.

It is therefore natural to raise the level of ambition and to try to capture the market timing skill of a manager in a more sophisticated manner than "merely" fitting a regression curve, as accurate as it could be. With the portfolio returns as raw material, there are essentially two ways of achieving this objective: through a more comprehensive use of statistical data and techniques and through the determination of implied portfolio weights for a portfolio that exhibits no market timing. The major techniques used to appraise performance in these contexts are examined below.

8.3.1 Measuring and benchmarking dynamic exposures

The Henriksson and Merton (1981) and Treynor and Mazuy (1966) models both entail that the portfolio manager's exposure to the market risk factor varies over time according to a certain structure. For HM and TM, it corresponds to the following expressions, respectively:

$$\beta_{P,t} = \beta_P^{(hm)} - \gamma_P^{(hm)} \times 1_{\{R_f > R_{M,t}\}} \tag{8-27a}$$

$$\beta_{P,t} = \beta_P^{(tm)} + \gamma_P^{(tm)} \times [R_{M,t} - R_f] \tag{8-27b}$$

These are perfectly justifiable but very restrictive patterns. Nothing prevents a portfolio manager from letting their beta vary according to another form of market timing rule.

With the same raw material as in the first part of the chapter, the question is: *How to implement a statistical model that enables the factor exposures (i.e., the betas) to be truly and freely time varying according to the decisions made by the portfolio manager?* A first answer could be to adopt a conditional model, in which the betas change according to the realization of instrumental variables, but we have seen before that this might not, as such, fully capture the manager's timing behavior. Another, the "low-tech" approach, entails the use of rolling betas to capture the manager's drift in factor exposures in a relatively smooth manner. The idea underlying rolling-beta regressions is simple: Instead of using the full sample of size T for a single statistical estimation of the parameters, it is split into sub-samples of equal size $n < T$, the first one featuring the first n observations $\{R_{P,1}, \ldots, R_{P,n}\}$, the second one using the same sample but dropping the first observation and adding the first next consecutive one $\{R_{P,2}, \ldots, R_{P,n+1}\}$, and so on until the last sub-sample featuring the last n observations $\{R_{P,T-n+1}, \ldots, R_{P,T}\}$. For each of the sub-samples denoted by $\tau = 1, \ldots, T-n+1$, the same multifactor model is estimated:

$$R_{P,t} - R_f = \alpha_P^{\mathrm{MF}(\tau)} + \sum_{k=1}^{K} \beta_{P,k}^{(\tau)}(F_{k,t} - R_f) + \varepsilon_{P,t} \tag{8-28}$$

From this repeated estimation procedure, the resulting $\alpha_P^{\mathrm{MF}(\tau)}$ and $\beta_{P,k}^{(\tau)}$ are stored, and their behavior is examined. This might be useful in order to detect whether the portfolio has experienced a "style drift," i.e., a progressive shift in the allocation between the different types of factors.

A more powerful and rigorous treatment of information should lead to the use of the full sample in one single estimation procedure. The objective is to detect as accurately and quickly as possible any change in the factor loadings in order to track the manager's decisions. The most common of such methods is the Kalman filter approach that was successfully applied in the mutual funds literature by Mamaysky, Spiegel, and Zhang (2008), and is nowadays extensively used in the hedge funds literature. It hinges on the assumption of multivariate normality of the returns and builds on two statistical regressions that need to be estimated simultaneously: (i) a measurement equation that relates variables whose realized values are observable and (ii) a set of transition equations used in order to deduce the exposure values at each time t of the historical series. Using the same type of notation as above, the system is written as

$$R_{P,t} - R_f = \alpha_{P,t}^{\mathrm{MF}} + \sum_{k=1}^{K} \beta_{P,k,t}(F_{k,t} - R_f) + \varepsilon_{P,t} \tag{8-29a}$$

$$\alpha_{P,t}^{\mathrm{MF}} = \alpha_{P,t-1}^{\mathrm{MF}} + \xi_{P,0,t} \tag{8-29b}$$

$$\beta_{P,k,t} = \beta_{P,k,t-1} + \xi_{P,k,t} \tag{8-29c}$$

where $\alpha_{P,t}^{\mathrm{MF}}$ is the time-varying alpha at time t, $\beta_{P,k,t}$ is the time-varying factor loading at time t, and the residual terms $\varepsilon_{P,t}$, $\xi_{P,0,t}$ and $\xi_{P,k,t}$ are all normally distributed with an expectation of 0.

Figure 8-10, similar to the one presented in Section 5.3 of Chapter 5, illustrates the outcomes of both estimation procedures in a simple one-factor case: The manager of the portfolio has kept their beta equal to one for 20 months, then set it to zero for the next 20 months, and

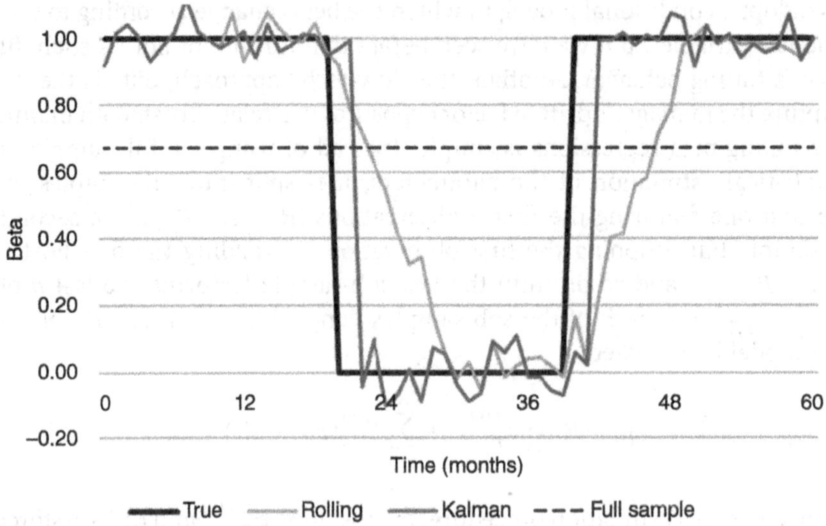

FIGURE 8-10 Illustration of different estimation procedures for dynamic betas.

finally pulled it back to one during the last 20 months. In addition, the manager has also taken some idiosyncratic risk.

The black line represents the evolution of the true portfolio beta over time. With a simple linear regression over the whole time window, the estimated beta is close to $\frac{1}{3} \times 1 + \frac{1}{3} \times 0 + \frac{1}{3} \times 1 = \frac{2}{3}$. This corresponds to the fully horizontal line. With a rolling-window regression, taking sub-sample windows of 12 months, the estimation of the time-varying betas starts after one year. When the actual portfolio beta drops to zero, the estimated beta only decreases very gradually and approaches zero only after one full year. The same phenomenon occurs when the beta jumps back to one again. This behavior is reflected in the V-shaped line, which seems to lag and smooth the true beta. By contrast, the beta estimated with the Kalman filter (U-shaped) reacts much faster and tracks the beta with a small delay and the noise associated with the estimation procedure.

Once the model has been estimated with dynamic exposures, the model-based benchmark (in the spirit of the ones discussed in Chapter 7) can be determined by considering the average factor betas and completing the benchmark portfolio weights with lending or borrowing at the risk-free rate:

$$R_{B,t} = \sum_{k=1}^{K} \overline{\beta}_{P,k} F_{k,t} + \left(1 - \sum_{k=1}^{K} \overline{\beta}_{P,k}\right) R_f \tag{8-30}$$

where $\overline{\beta}_{P,k} = \frac{1}{T}\sum_{t=1}^{T}\beta_{P,k,t}$ is the average beta with respect to the kth factor. This analytical benchmark directly derives from the data and can coexist with a self-defined benchmark whose weights can totally differ from those obtained with the regression.

8.3.2 Measuring performance with statistical dynamic exposures

At first sight, the richness of the information contained in the time-varying betas should prove to be useful in order to distinguish selectivity and market timing skills in the evaluation of portfolio performance. This is indeed the case. An intuitive answer is given by the estimation of the difference between the mean returns of the portfolio and the one of its benchmark $\overline{R}_P - \overline{R}_B$. Combining Equations (8-29a) and (8-30), it is given by the following expression:

$$\overline{R}_P - \overline{R}_B = \overline{\alpha}_P^{\mathrm{MF}} + \frac{1}{T}\sum_{t=1}^{T}\sum_{k=1}^{K}(\beta_{P,k,t} - \overline{\beta}_{P,k})F_{k,t} \tag{8-31}$$

where $\overline{\alpha}_P^{\mathrm{MF}} = \frac{1}{T}\sum_{t=1}^{T}\alpha_{P,t}^{\mathrm{MF}}$ is the average time-varying alpha over the period.

This expression is indeed fully in line with the logic underlying classical performance attribution models (see Chapter 14). The second term represents the pure impact of the market timing decisions on the portfolio's excess return over the model-based benchmark. The first term reflects the residual portfolio abnormal return, i.e., any component of the abnormal return that is not explained by pure market timing. In particular, it encompasses the asset selection skills of the manager.

Even though it was originally developed in a single-factor context, the Cornell (1979) and Grinblatt and Titman (1989a) approach essentially reaches an analogous performance decomposition, but in the scope of asymptotic theory and in the presence of a self-reported benchmark portfolio that might differ from the analytical one. Adapted to the context of the dynamic model of Equation (8-29a), it is necessary to go through an intermediary step by considering the relation between each factor and the benchmark:

$$F_{k,t} - R_f = \beta_{k,B}(R_{B,t} - R_f) + \varepsilon_{k,t} \tag{8-32}$$

where $\beta_{k,B}$ is the linear sensitivity of the kth factor to the benchmark. The regression bears no intercept as the factor excess return should display no alpha when considered over a long time window.

Inserting this relation into the dynamic regression equation and rearranging leads to a generalized version of the Cornell (1979) performance measure, denoted by GC_P, that should be valid asymptotically:

$$\mathrm{GC}_P = \overline{\alpha}_P^{\mathrm{MF}} + \mathrm{plim}\left(\frac{1}{T}\sum_{t=1}^{T}(\beta_{P,t} - \overline{\beta}_P)R_{B,t}\right) \tag{8-33}$$

where *plim* stands for the probability limit of the argument, which can be intuitively interpreted as the very long run average, $\beta_{P,t} = \sum_{k=1}^{K} \beta_{P,k,t} \times \beta_{k,B}$ is the global time-varying beta of the portfolio with respect to the benchmark, and $\overline{\beta}_P = \frac{1}{T} \sum_{t=1}^{T} \beta_{P,t}$. As in the previous version of the performance measure, the first term serves to appraise the portfolio manager's selectivity, and the second one corresponds to their ability to time the market.[11]

The CX-T example (continued)

The manager of Fund CX-C has deliberately changed their market beta over time. The outcome of the Kalman filter for the last 24 months is reported in Table 8-14.

TABLE 8-14 CX-T example – Monthly rates of return and beta for fund CX-C.

Date	Market excess return	CX-C	
		Excess return	Beta
Jan	−1.91%	−0.88%	0.17
Feb	1.96%	1.05%	0.41
Mar	0.50%	0.38%	0.44
Apr	−0.67%	−1.10%	0.44
May	1.25%	0.00%	0.50
Jun	−0.12%	1.25%	0.48
Jul	−0.07%	0.05%	0.46
Aug	−4.11%	−1.13%	0.30
Sep	0.85%	0.18%	0.45
Oct	−3.93%	−0.04%	0.31
Nov	3.50%	1.58%	0.38
Dec	2.43%	0.87%	0.41
Jan	1.25%	0.76%	0.44
Feb	1.73%	1.26%	0.43
Mar	−2.56%	−0.92%	0.44

[11] Grinblatt and Titman (1989a) add a term that is related to the small-sample bias in the measurement of the portfolio beta, which aims at overcoming the difficulty in identifying a benchmark that is representative of the market portfolio.

TABLE 8-14 *(continued)*

Date	Market excess return	CX-C	
		Excess return	Beta
Apr	2.23%	2.26%	0.54
May	1.74%	0.96%	0.75
Jun	−0.98%	−0.82%	0.81
Jul	1.26%	1.40%	0.74
Aug	0.31%	0.21%	0.66
Sep	1.44%	1.39%	0.61
Oct	0.60%	0.52%	0.68
Nov	0.50%	−0.02%	0.46
Dec	−4.70%	−0.67%	0.22

A visual way to check how successful the manager has been in trying to time the market is by ordering the market excess returns by increasing order, and tracking the joint evolution of the portfolio beta, which is shown in Figure 8-11.

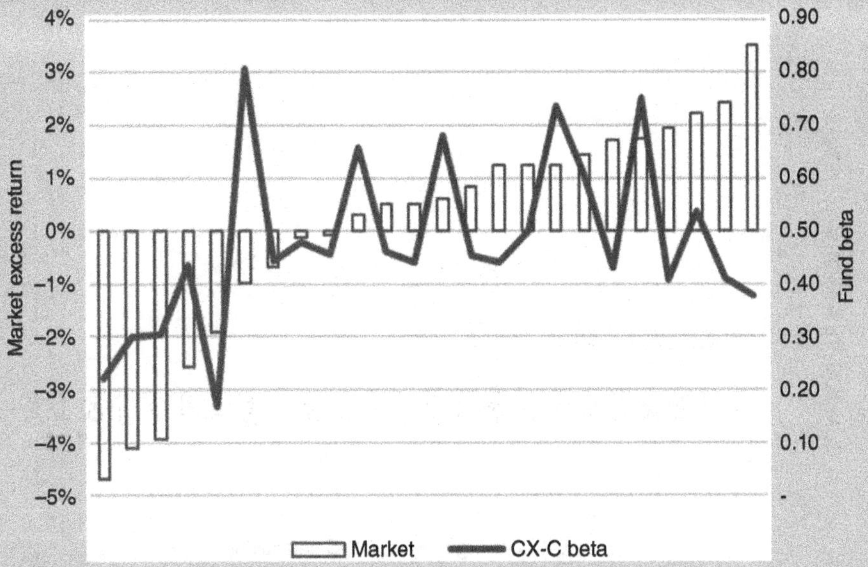

FIGURE 8-11 CX-T example – Joint evolution of market excess return and CX-C beta.

(continued)

(*continued*)

As it is apparent from Figure 8-11, the fund manager has mostly been successful in reducing their exposure to the market at times of very negative returns. In addition, no specific visual pattern arises at times of average or positive outcomes for the market factor.

The average portfolio beta is $\overline{\beta}_{CX-C} = 0.48$. Therefore, applying Equation (8-30), the fund's benchmark portfolio is defined as $R_{B,t} = 0.48 \times R_{M,t} + 0.52 \times R_f$, whose average return is $\overline{R}_B = 0.25\%$.

Implementing Equation (8-31) with a single factor ($K = 1$) results in the following outcome:

$$\text{Timing} = \frac{1}{24}\sum_{t=1}^{24}(\beta_{\text{CX-C},t} - 0.48) \times R_{M,t} = 0.15\%$$

$$\text{Selectivity} = \overline{\alpha}^{\text{MF}}_{\text{CX-C}} = \overline{R}_{\text{CX-C}} - \overline{R}_B - \text{Timing} = 0.56\% - 0.25\% - 0.15\% = 0.16\%$$

The manager of CX-C has thus succeeded in simultaneously achieving a positive outcome both for asset selection and market timing.

Indeed, there is more information to retrieve from the model than simply the performance measure and its decomposition because it is possible to identify the period-by-period time-varying timing and selectivity (alpha) measures. By doing so, one can analyze how the fund's performance has gradually been built over time. The graph in Figure 8-12 shows how the cumulative performance of the fund has been generated.

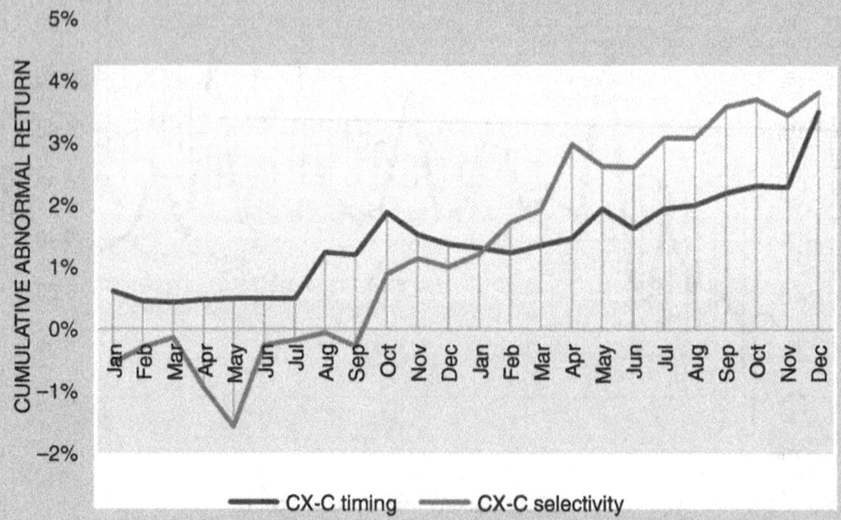

FIGURE 8-12 CX-T example – Evolution of the cumulative values of timing and selectivity for CX-C.

8.3.3 Measuring performance with implied dynamic periodical weights

By construction, the multifactor model with dynamic exposures leads to the identification of time-varying betas with respect to risk factors. These betas, in turn, allow us to make a connection between the portfolio returns and those of its benchmark. Thanks to them, the defined performance measures provide an elegant way to identify market timing and selectivity skills – something that is much more arduous with nonlinear regressions examined in Sections 8.1 and 8.2. Nevertheless, there are also drawbacks associated with this approach. There is a potentially important estimation error that could lead to biased coefficient estimates. Furthermore, the use of incorrectly specified benchmarks would result in flawed performance appraisal.

In order to detect market timing in a setup that is much less constrained by statistical estimation or benchmark identification, Grinblatt and Titman (1989a; 1989b) propose an alternative approach. They consider that a manager who exhibits genuine market timing skills should be able to durably enhance the expected utility of the investor over a passive investment. They assign time-varying weights to each of the portfolio's periodic excess returns, interpreted as the investor's marginal utility, in such a way that these weights would result in null performance for a portfolio that would not exhibit any market timing skills. Formally, they define the *positive period weighting measure* of a portfolio, denoted by PPWM_P through the following equation:

$$\text{PPWM}_P = \sum_{t=1}^{T} \dot{w}_t (R_{P,t} - R_f) \tag{8-34}$$

where $\dot{w}_t$ denotes the neutral weight assigned to the return at time t, with $\dot{w}_t \geq 0$ and $\sum_{t=1}^{T} \dot{w}_t = 1$. The weights are such that, for some reference passive portfolio (which can be the portfolio benchmark or not) B, its positive period weighting measure level is null: $\text{PPWM}_B = \sum_{t=1}^{T} \dot{w}_t (R_{B,t} - R_f) = 0$.

The PPWM_P measure is quite general. Grinblatt and Titman (1989b) show that Jensen's alpha, as defined in Chapter 3, stands as a special case with $\dot{w}_t = \frac{\sigma_M^2 - (R_{M,t} - \bar{R}_M)\bar{R}_M}{T\sigma_M^2}$.

Unfortunately, there is a potentially infinite set of weights, and their associated construction methods that respect the above constraints. Thus, the advantage of not having to estimate dynamic factor exposures is, to some extent, offset by the necessity to impose a certain structure on the construction of the period weights $\{\dot{w}_1, \ldots, \dot{w}_T\}$. As a workable solution, Grinblatt and Titman (1989b) suggest using the power utility function defined as $U(W_t) = \frac{1}{1-\theta} W_t^{1-\theta}$, where W_t is the wealth at the end of period t (W_0 being normalized to 1).

Once the utility function is known, the determination of the weights can be achieved numerically, but quite simply, as follows. For someone who invests in a combination x of a reference portfolio B and $1 - x$ in the risk-free asset, this investor obtains at each period a terminal wealth equal to $W_t(x) = 1 + xR_{B,t} + (1 - x)R_f$. They try to determine the optimal value of x, denoted by x^*, by maximizing their expected utility, which leads to the condition

$E(W_t(x^*)^{-\theta}(R_{B,t} - R_f)) = 0$ over the total investment horizon. This means that x^* solves the equation:

$$\sum_{t=1}^{T}(1 + x^* R_{B,t} + (1 - x^*)R_f)^{-\theta}(R_{B,t} - R_f) = 0 \tag{8-35}$$

Once the optimal value of x^* is set, the weights are simply defined as

$$\dot{w}_t = \frac{(1 + x^* R_{B,t} + (1 - x^*)R_f)^{-\theta}}{\sum_{t=1}^{T}(1 + x^* R_{B,t} + (1 - x^*)R_f)^{-\theta}} \tag{8-36}$$

For instance, in their application to international mutual funds, Cumby and Glen (1990) set the investor's risk-aversion coefficient to $\theta = 6$ and apply the numerical procedure above in order to obtain their individual estimates of the positive period weighting measure.

Note that the PPWM performance measure also belongs to the family of so-called preference-based performance measures that is studied in more detail in Chapter 9. Nevertheless, as it primarily aims at isolating the market timing skills of an active portfolio manager by creating implied periodic weights that differ from the actual frequencies of returns, we have chosen to discuss it here.

The CX-T example (continued)

It is assumed that, according to the prevailing market conditions, the representative investor has a power utility function with a risk-aversion coefficient equal to $\theta = 8$. By choosing the market index as the benchmark, the application of the procedure presented in Equation (8-35) yields $x^* = 0.8$. Consequently, Table 8-15 reveals the positive period weighting measure computed for the market index and each of the three funds.

TABLE 8-15 CX-T example – Determination of the positive period weighting measure.

Date	Utility $W_t(0.8)^{-8}$	Weight w_t	Market	CX-A	CX-B	CX-C
Jan	1.11	4.69%	−0.08%	−0.01%	−0.01%	−0.03%
Feb	0.87	3.67%	0.08%	0.04%	0.16%	0.06%
Mar	0.95	4.02%	0.03%	−0.01%	0.04%	0.03%

TABLE 8-15 *(continued)*

Date	Utility $W_t(0.8)^{-8}$	Weight w_t	Market	CX-A	CX-B	CX-C
Apr	1.03	4.33%	−0.02%	0.04%	−0.02%	−0.04%
May	0.91	3.83%	0.06%	0.05%	0.09%	0.01%
Jun	0.99	4.18%	0.00%	−0.02%	0.05%	0.07%
Jul	0.99	4.17%	0.01%	−0.01%	0.05%	0.01%
Aug	1.28	5.42%	−0.21%	−0.05%	0.04%	−0.04%
Sep	0.93	3.93%	0.04%	0.01%	0.00%	0.02%
Oct	1.27	5.35%	−0.20%	−0.07%	−0.04%	0.01%
Nov	0.79	3.33%	0.12%	0.26%	0.18%	0.08%
Dec	0.84	3.56%	0.09%	0.13%	0.13%	0.05%
Jan	0.91	3.83%	0.06%	0.15%	0.12%	0.05%
Feb	0.88	3.72%	0.07%	0.12%	0.07%	0.07%
Mar	1.16	4.89%	−0.12%	−0.03%	0.02%	−0.03%
Apr	0.86	3.61%	0.09%	0.09%	0.09%	0.12%
May	0.88	3.72%	0.07%	0.11%	0.12%	0.05%
Jun	1.05	4.42%	−0.03%	0.04%	−0.01%	−0.03%
Jul	0.91	3.83%	0.06%	0.10%	0.08%	0.07%
Aug	0.96	4.07%	0.02%	0.03%	0.09%	0.02%
Sep	0.90	3.79%	0.06%	0.11%	0.06%	0.07%
Oct	0.95	3.99%	0.03%	0.03%	0.06%	0.03%
Nov	0.95	4.02%	0.03%	0.05%	0.03%	0.01%
Dec	1.34	5.63%	−0.25%	−0.07%	0.02%	−0.02%
Sum	**23.72**	**1**	**0.00%**	**1.08%**	**1.41%**	**0.63%**

The last row provides the value of each fund's performance. All of them display a positive timing skill. Compared with the outcomes of the HM and TM models above, the ranking is relatively similar: CX-B is the best fund, followed by CX-A and then CX-C. Nonetheless, the PPWM is considerably higher (by an order of magnitude of ca. 0.4% in general) than the adjusted performance measures obtained above. The level of the PPWM is highly contingent on the choice of the utility function and the calibration of the risk-aversion parameter.

8.4 HOLDING-BASED DYNAMIC EXPOSURES APPROACH

Knowing the evolution of the detailed portfolio holdings happens to be very valuable information in order to assess the manager's performance. Instead of only observing the portfolio returns from the outside, it is equivalent to having the full transparency about the portfolio from the inside. Formally, this means that information about the portfolio invested in N different assets is summarized by the following equation:

$$R_{P,t} = \sum_{i=1}^{N} w_{P,i,t} R_{i,t} \tag{8-37}$$

where $w_{P,i,t}$ is the weight (in terms of economic exposure) of asset i held in the portfolio at the beginning of period t, with $\sum_{i=1}^{N} w_{P,i,t} = 1$, and $R_{i,t}$ is the periodic return of the asset.[12]

Unlike the approaches discussed in Section 8.3, information underlying Equation (8-37) is rich enough to allow the precise determination of portfolio performance at each point in time. The performance over a complete period of time T then simply results from the aggregation of each individual periodic value. It only summarizes the available information, while there might be other useful ways to treat it in order to track the performance of the manager over time.

This portfolio transparency is indeed the main input used for the whole range of performance attribution analyses discussed in Chapter 14. Nevertheless, before turning to such an analytical framework, it is necessary to determine how performance measures can be designed in order to make full use of the available information. We can distinguish four approaches in this context, depending on which type of benchmark is chosen for the comparison of the manager's abnormal return: benchmark-free, with a characteristic-based benchmark, with a peer group-based benchmark, and with a return-based benchmark.

8.4.1 Measuring performance without an external benchmark

With only the raw material consisting of the asset weights and returns, it is possible to do without a benchmark portfolio and still measure performance. Not having to rely on a benchmark, whatever it may be (analytical or self-reported), has two main advantages: it avoids Roll's (1977) famous critique about the validity of index to proxy for the market portfolio and it allows us to analyze performance before fees and transaction costs.

8.4.1.1 The self-benchmarked performance measure

Wermers (2006) suggests applying a so-called "self-benchmarking" approach in order to assess the manager's capacity to anticipate the evolution of the portfolio's asset returns. The starting

[12] Equivalently, some authors write $w_{P,i,t-1}$ as weight of asset i in the portfolio at the end-of-period $t-1$.

point of his analysis is to define a portfolio holding measure ($PHM_{i,t}$) at each point in time, computed as the covariance between the lagged portfolio weight and the current return of each asset, i.e., $PHM_{i,t} = Cov(w_{P,i,t}, R_{i,t})$, as the building block of benchmark-free performance measurement.

With some assumptions on the structure of the asset returns, one can simplify the covariance as $Cov(w_{P,i,t}, R_{i,t}) = E[(w_{P,i,t} - E(w_{P,i,t}))R_{i,t}]$. Grinblatt and Titman (1993) consider that the past weight (with a sufficient time distance) invested in the security as a relevant proxy for the expected weight. Thus, they set $E(w_{P,i,t}) = w_{P,i,t-l}$ for some number of periods l in the past. This entails that we have a sufficiently large number of observations so that the noise of this estimator is averaged out. Furthermore, using that method induces that the first l observations are dropped out for the computation of the performance measure.

Aggregating the value of $PHM_{i,t}$ across assets leads to the *self-benchmarked performance measure* $SBP_{P,t}$ of Grinblatt and Titman (1993), defined as $SBP_{P,t} \equiv \sum_{i=1}^{N}(w_{P,i,t} - w_{P,i,t-l})R_{i,t}$. Finally, taking the average of this measure across time yields the measure of portfolio performance SBP_P:

$$SBP_P \equiv \frac{1}{T-l}\sum_{t=l+1}^{T} SBP_{P,t} = \frac{1}{T-l}\sum_{t=l+1}^{T}\sum_{i=1}^{N}(w_{P,i,t} - w_{P,i,t-l})R_{i,t} \tag{8-38}$$

How to disentangle market timing from selectivity skills in this context? The challenge is to determine how the manager can anticipate market movements without relying on any external benchmark. The authors suggest working on each asset return and to partition $R_{i,t}$ into two parts: the corresponding sector (or asset class) return and the asset-specific return. This allows them to propose the following decomposition:

$$SBP_{P,t} = \sum_{i=1}^{N}(w_{P,i,t} - w_{P,i,t-l})R_{i,t}^{IND} + \sum_{i=1}^{N}(w_{P,i,t} - w_{P,i,t-l})(R_{i,t} - R_{i,t}^{IND}) \tag{8-39}$$

where $R_{i,t}^{IND}$ is the return of the industry group to which asset i belongs at time t (or, for other asset classes, a similar notion). The first term reflects the manager's performance that can be attributed to their ability to pick the most promising industry at the right moment (market timing). The second term stands for the manager's asset selection skill (asset picking). The aggregation of the $SBP_{P,t}$ over time provides the same interpretation for the whole period.[13]

[13]Equation (8-39) adopts a structure that is very similar to the classical attribution model developed in Chapter 14. The main difference lies in the definition of the benchmark, which is endogenous and based on historical information about the portfolio in the Grinblatt and Titman (1993) approach. Note as well that there exist conditional versions of the self-benchmarked performance measures.

Since the portfolio holdings are observed and thus do not need to be statistically estimated, traditional inference can be used in order to test the null hypothesis of zero abnormal performance. Thus, under the assumption of normally distributed returns, an assessment of the significance of the SBP_P measure is given by

$$\hat{t}_{SBP_P=0} = \frac{\sqrt{T-1}}{\sigma(SBP_P)} SBP_P \tag{8-40}$$

where $\sigma(SBP_P)$ is the sample standard deviation of the time series of the $SBP_{P,t}$. When the measure is decomposed as in Equation (8-39), the same equation holds for both terms.

8.4.1.2 The adjusted self-benchmarked performance measure

The SBP_P measure makes use of only portfolio-specific information and makes full sense for large sample sizes. Because of the endogeneity of the benchmark creation, it potentially avoids the issues related to the use of exogenous benchmarks. Nevertheless, if the manager has adopted a certain style drift in their dynamic management of the asset allocation, there still might be some systematic risk exposures associated with this measure. As a second-order estimation of performance, Wermers (2006) proposes regressing the time series of the $SBP_{P,t}$ on the risk factors on which the portfolio is suspected to be dynamically exposed. This leads to the *adjusted self-benchmarked performance measure:*

$$aSBP_P = SBP_P - \sum_{k=1}^{K} b_{P,k}\overline{F}_k \tag{8-41}$$

where each $b_{P,k}$ is the coefficient associated with the kth factor in the linear regression of the time series of the $SBP_{P,t}$ on the risk factors considered, i.e., $SBP_{P,t} = a_P + \sum_{k=1}^{K} b_{P,k}F_{k,t} + v_{P,t}$.

The CX-T example (continued)

Focusing on Fund CX-C, we re-use information contained in Table 8-14 in which the last column corresponds to the actual holding of the proxy for the market index at the beginning of each month; the remainder is invested in cash at a monthly rate of 0.2%. We consider a 12-month seasonality of the market index. Accordingly, we use 12 lagged observations in order to implement Equation (8-38); thus, $l = 12$. The computation of $SBP_{CX\text{-}C}$ is detailed in Table 8-16.

TABLE 8-16 CX-T example – Computation of the self-benchmarked performance for CX-C.

Date	Holding $w_{CX-C,M,t}$	Lagged holding $w_{CX-C,M,t-12}$	Difference	$SBP_{CX-C,t}$
Jan	0.44	0.17	0.27	0.54%
Feb	0.43	0.41	0.02	0.24%
Mar	0.44	0.44	−0.01	0.21%
Apr	0.54	0.44	0.09	0.41%
May	0.75	0.50	0.25	0.64%
Jun	0.81	0.48	0.33	−0.12%
Jul	0.74	0.46	0.28	0.55%
Aug	0.66	0.30	0.36	0.31%
Sep	0.61	0.45	0.15	0.42%
Oct	0.68	0.31	0.38	0.43%
Nov	0.46	0.38	0.08	0.24%
Dec	0.22	0.41	−0.19	1.10%
Average	**0.56**	**0.40**	**0.17**	**0.41%**

By averaging the monthly values of the self-benchmarked performance measure for the fund, we obtain 0.41%. The series reported in the last column is very consistently positive, with only one exception. Its sample standard deviation is 0.29%. As expected, the Student *t*-statistic used to test the null hypothesis of the absence of outperformance is very high: $\hat{t}_{SBP_{CX\text{-}C}=0} = \frac{\sqrt{11}}{0.29\%} \times 0.41\% = 4.67$. This confirms the evidence of a strong market timing skill of the manager during the second year of their tenure.

As a next step, we regress the time series of the $SBP_{CX\text{-}C,t}$ on the excess market returns. This gives the following outputs: $b_{CX\text{-}C,M} = 0.04$ and $a_{CX\text{-}C,M} = 0.42\%$ with a standard deviation of $\sigma_{a_{CX\text{-}C,M}} = 0.09\%$, which corresponds to a *t*-stat of $\hat{t}_{a_{CX\text{-}C}=0} = \frac{0.42\%}{0.09\%} = 4.93$. Nevertheless, the very low R^2 of the regression (7.9%) casts doubts about its relevance, which explains why the test statistics are so close to each other.

8.4.2 Measuring performance with a characteristic-based benchmark

Combining information about portfolio holdings and external benchmark returns has pros and cons compared to the previous method. It brings in all the potential issues related to the specification of the benchmark (discussed in Chapter 1), but it also allows the performance measure to explicitly account for information that is objectively relevant for the assessment of the portfolio manager's quality.

Detailed data about portfolio holdings over time can ease the determination of a fully relevant benchmark for the portfolio. This can be done by matching each asset with a "control portfolio" of similar securities (i.e., sharing the same relevant characteristics) and tracking its evolution over time. This is the idea put forward by Daniel, Grinblatt, Titman, and Wermers (1997). They propose to decompose the total portfolio return at time t into three components: one that can be interpreted as the required return (the "average style" measure $AS_{P,t}$), one that evaluates the manager's selectivity (the "characteristic selectivity" measure $CS_{P,t}$), and one that appraises the manager's timing (the "characteristic timing" measure $CT_{P,t}$). They are defined by the following set of equations:

$$R_{P,t} = AS_{P,t} + CS_{P,t} + CT_{P,t} \tag{8-42a}$$

$$AS_{P,t} = \sum_{i=1}^{N} w_{P,i,t-l} R_{i,t}^{b_{t-l-1}} \tag{8-42b}$$

$$CS_{P,t} = \sum_{i=1}^{N} w_{P,i,t}(R_{i,t} - R_{i,t}^{b_{t-1}}) \tag{8-42c}$$

$$CT_{P,t} = \sum_{i=1}^{N} (w_{P,i,t} R_{i,t}^{b_{t-1}} - w_{P,i,t-l} R_{i,t}^{b_{t-l-1}}) \tag{8-42d}$$

where $R_{i,t}^{b_{t-j}}$ is the return of a (value-weighted) control portfolio of assets sharing the same characteristics as asset i at time $t-j$.

The first component $AS_{P,t}$ is a reflection of the manager's required rate of return. Thus, the total performance at time t is the sum $AS_{P,t} + CS_{P,t}$, and the average over time provides the total performance of the portfolio and its decomposition. The authors suggest selecting the stocks composing the control portfolio by using the same types of risk factors as those uncovered in the asset pricing literature and discussed in Chapter 7.

8.4.3 Measuring performance with a peer group-based benchmark

It is not unrealistic to consider that if one knows detailed information about the holdings of one portfolio, the same person would also have access to similar data about other comparable portfolios or funds. Such information can be valuable in order to assess a manager's performance – the challenge is of course how to process it.

Cohen, Coval, and Pástor (2005) propose a systematic approach for determining the portfolio's abnormal return in this context. Instead of focusing on the returns of comparable assets, they control for the asset weights in the measurement of performance. Specifically, they consider the other asset managers' investments (weights) and trades (changes in weights) in the same assets and use information about their own performance in order to assess the performance of every single portfolio manager. They define two performance measures on the basis of this analysis: one that is based on holdings $\delta_P^{(H)}$ and the other that is based on trades, $\delta_P^{(\Delta H)}$. The first one mostly addresses the comparative asset selection skills of the reviewed manager, whereas the second one deals with their market timing abilities.

8.4.3.1 The peer group holding-based performance measure

We are interested in appraising the performance of the manager of portfolio P who belongs to a group of Q relevant peers who also actively manage a fund or a portfolio. The idea underlying the approach of Cohen et al. (2005) is to consider that the collective choices made by these managers, together with an independent assessment of their individual quality, reveal the quality of the assets that they hold. Using the same notation as before, the value of their peer group holding-based performance measure at time t, denoted by $\delta_{P,t}^{(h)}$, is defined as follows:

$$\delta_{P,t}^{(h)} = \sum_{i=1}^{N} w_{P,i,t}\delta_{i,t}^{(h)} \tag{8-43}$$

where $\delta_{i,t}^{(h)} \equiv \sum_{q=1}^{Q}(v_{q,i,t} \times \mu_q)$ indicates the quality of asset i estimated through portfolio holdings in the peer group, in which $v_{q,i,t} \equiv \frac{w_{q,i,t}}{\sum_{q=1}^{Q} w_{q,i,t}}$ is the proportion of asset i held by manager q among the peer group, and μ_q is the intrinsic performance of that same manager q. The authors mention that μ_q can be defined, for instance, as Jensen's alpha ($\mu_q \equiv \alpha_q$), Grinblatt and Titman's (1993) self-benchmarked performance measure ($\mu_q \equiv \text{SBP}_q$), or the measures developed by Daniel et al. (1997) and discussed in the previous sub-section. The aggregate portfolio performance is obtained by averaging the periodical ones:

$$\delta_P^{(h)} = \frac{1}{T}\sum_{t=1}^{T}\delta_{P,t}^{(h)} = \frac{1}{T}\sum_{t=1}^{T}\sum_{i=1}^{N} w_{P,i,t}\delta_{i,t}^{(h)} \tag{8-44}$$

The rationale underlying the formula is rather intuitive. The average asset quality indicator $\bar{\delta}_i = \frac{1}{T}\sum_{t=1}^{T}\delta_{i,t}^{(h)}$ is indeed computed as the weighted intrinsic performance of each manager, in which each weight corresponds to their holding in the asset. Its value is high if the better managers (those with a high μ_q) also decide to allocate a higher weight in this asset (reflected in a higher value of $v_{q,i,t}$). The performance of the manager of portfolio P is thus the weighted average of the qualities of the assets in which they have decided to invest.

8.4.3.2 The peer group trading-based performance measure

With the time series of returns and weights of all portfolio managers, Cohen et al. (2005) are also able to determine the share of the change in weights invested in each asset that results from a voluntary trade, as opposed to the pure market effect. For the manager of portfolio P, the voluntary change in weight (i.e., the net trade) of asset i at time t is $\Delta w_{P,i,t} \equiv w_{P,i,t} - w_{P,i,t-1}\frac{1+R_{i,t}}{1+R_{P,t}}$. If $\Delta w_{P,i,t} > 0$, this means that the manager has chosen to increase their position in the asset, while a negative value corresponds to a divestment.

The signs of trades are important indicators of market timing. If a manager has decided to reduce the size of a position, it is necessary to check whether the corresponding asset was of good or poor quality at that moment. In the same spirit as in formula (8-43), the peer group trading-based performance measure at time t, denoted by $\delta_{P,t}^{(\Delta h)}$, is defined as follows:

$$\delta_{P,t}^{(\Delta h)} = \sum_{i \in N_{P,t}^{+}} x_{P,i,t}^{+}\delta_{i,t}^{(\Delta h)} - \sum_{i \in N_{P,t}^{-}} x_{P,i,t}^{-}\delta_{i,t}^{(\Delta h)} \tag{8-45}$$

where $N_{P,t}^{+} = \{i : \Delta w_{P,i,t} > 0\}$ and $N_{P,t}^{-} = \{i : \Delta w_{P,i,t} > 0\}$ are the sets of stocks for which the manager has decided to increase and decrease their position, respectively; and $x_{P,i,t}^{+} \equiv \frac{\Delta w_{P,i,t}}{\sum_{i \in N_{P,t}^{+}} \Delta w_{P,i,t}}$ and $x_{P,i,t}^{-} \equiv \frac{\Delta w_{P,i,t}}{\sum_{i \in N_{P,t}^{-}} \Delta w_{P,i,t}}$ are the fractions of the purchase (resp. sale) of stock i in the total purchases (resp. sales) made by the manager at time t. Similarly to the previous formula, $\delta_{i,t}^{(\Delta h)}$ represents the quality of asset i reflected in the peer group's voluntary trading decisions. It is now defined as $\delta_{i,t}^{(\Delta h)} \equiv \sum_{q \in Q_{i,t}^{+}}(y_{q,i,t}^{+} \times \mu_q) - \sum_{q \in Q_{i,t}^{-}}(y_{q,i,t}^{-} \times \mu_q)$, where $Q_{i,t}^{+} = \{q : \Delta w_{q,i,t} > 0\}$ and $Q_{i,t}^{-} = \{q : \Delta w_{q,i,t} < 0\}$ denote the sets of managers who have decided to increase and decrease their position in asset i, respectively; and $y_{q,i,t}^{+} \equiv \frac{\Delta w_{q,i,t}}{\sum_{q \in Q_{i,t}^{+}} \Delta w_{q,i,t}}$ and $y_{q,i,t}^{-} \equiv \frac{\Delta w_{q,i,t}}{\sum_{q \in Q_{i,t}^{-}} \Delta w_{q,i,t}}$ are the fractions of the purchase (resp. sale) of asset i made by manager q in the total purchases (resp. sales) made by all managers at time t.

The structure of the expression for $\delta_{P,t}^{(\Delta h)}$ disentangles the situations in which the manager decides to buy securities whose quality, at the time of the trade, is considered good and the divestments in low-quality assets. As before, the global portfolio performance equals

$$\delta_{P}^{(\Delta h)} = \frac{1}{T}\sum_{t=1}^{T}\delta_{P,t}^{(\Delta h)} = \frac{1}{T}\sum_{t=1}^{T}\left[\sum_{i \in N_{P,t}^{+}} x_{P,i,t}^{+}\delta_{i,t}^{(\Delta h)} - \sum_{i \in N_{P,t}^{-}} x_{P,i,t}^{-}\delta_{i,t}^{(\Delta h)}\right] \tag{8-46}$$

It is important to note that the indicators proposed by Cohen et al. (2005) are mostly qualitative and remote from each other. They are neither meant to add-up to anything meaningful – each equation stands on its own – nor to be interpreted as any kind of abnormal return. Indeed, it is perfectly possible that a manager achieves outstanding values for both $\delta_{P,t}^{(h)}$ and $\delta_{P,t}^{(\Delta h)}$ while simultaneously posting a very bad rate of return for the same period. This approach is thus mostly useful in order to assess the persistence of the portfolio manager's performance over time, as discussed in Chapter 17.

8.4.4 Measuring performance with a return-based benchmark

If data on the portfolio manager's asset holdings and trades is accurate, Equation (8-37) reflects the reality of the dynamic evolution of their decisions. This is valuable information because it is not contaminated by any kind of bias that may affect the statistical treatment of data. However, whereas portfolio holdings provide exact information about the portfolio manager's decisions, they do not as such indicate the risk factors to which they have decided to be exposed. In that sense, return-based analysis, in the spirit of the multifactor models analyzed in Chapter 7, can be seen as a complement, rather than a mere substitute, to holding-based portfolio analysis. We present here two approaches that have been proposed to reconcile these two sources of information.

8.4.4.1 The two-stage nonlinear regression approach

How to make a clever and harmonious use of holding- and return-based analyses in order to uncover the manager's market timing behavior? In the context of the single-factor model, Jiang, Yao, and Yu (2007) propose to merge these approaches in a two-stage procedure.[14]

First, they use the holding-based decomposition of portfolio returns in order to obtain its dynamic exposures to the risk factor:

$$R_{P,t} = \sum_{i=1}^{N} w_{P,i,t}(\alpha_{i,t} + \beta_{i,t}(R_{M,t} - R_F) + \varepsilon_{i,t}) \tag{8-47}$$

where $\alpha_{i,t}$ and $\beta_{i,t}$ represent the alpha and beta of asset i with respect to the market index using returns up to time t (with a time window going back to a starting point $t - l$). Thus, the estimated holding/return-based beta of the portfolio is defined as $\widehat{\beta}_{P,t} \equiv \sum_{i=1}^{N} w_{P,i,t}\beta_{i,t}$.

In the second stage, the authors verify whether the behavior of this time-varying beta corresponds to the one underlying the Henriksson and Merton (1981) or Treynor and Mazuy (1966) model as in Equations (8-27a) and (8-27b), respectively. This is performed by regressing

[14]Their analysis can easily be extended in a multifactor setup. It has also been adapted to the context of fixed-income portfolios, as discussed in Section 12.2.2 of Chapter 12.

the estimated portfolio betas obtained in the first stage on the variables corresponding to the structure of the expected dependence of these betas to market returns:

$$\widehat{\beta}_{P,t} = \beta_P^{(\text{hm})} - \gamma_P^{(\text{hm})} 1_{\{R_f > R_{M,t}\}} + \eta_P^{(\text{hm})} \tag{8-48a}$$

$$\widehat{\beta}_{P,t} = \beta_P^{(\text{tm})} + \gamma_P^{(\text{tm})} \times [R_{M,t} - R_f] + \eta_P^{(\text{tm})} \tag{8-48b}$$

where, for each regression, the intercept (beta) and the slope (gamma) represent the estimated values of the corresponding betas and gammas of the HM and TM models.

The rule is then simple: If no regression is significant, there is no evidence of market timing as measured with the HM or TM structure; otherwise, choose the model with the largest R^2 and compute the combined holding-based performance measure of the portfolio, called $\pi_P^{(h+\text{hm})}$ or $\pi_P^{(h+\text{tm})}$ depending on the specification chosen (HM or TM), according to one of the formulas recommended in the first two sections, namely, by using the cumulative alpha retrieved from Equation (8-47) and adding the adjustment for the gamma computed in Equation (8-48a) or (8-48b):

$$\pi_P^{(h+\cdot\cdot)} = \frac{1}{T}\sum_{t=1}^{T}\sum_{i=1}^{N} w_{P,i,t}\alpha_{i,t} + f(\gamma_P^{(\cdot\cdot)}) \tag{8-49}$$

where "··" stands for hm or tm, depending on the model chosen, and $f(\gamma_P^{(\cdot\cdot)})$ is one of the adjustments proposed in the first two sections.

Alternatively, with the betas obtained from the first stage, one of the performance measures developed in Section 8.3 may be used. This would be the case, for instance, when there is a strong suspicion that the manager has practiced some form of market timing but neither the HM nor the TM specifications is conclusive, which means that another, more flexible model for the behavior of the beta should be adopted instead.

8.4.4.2 The double-adjusted alpha approach

In the more general context of a multifactor model, such as the ones examined in Chapter 7, an alternative approach is to let the abnormal return (measured with the multifactor alpha) depend on the portfolio characteristics that are related to the factors (thus using essentially the same information as the one used for the factor construction) within a cross-section of comparable portfolios. This procedure is thus primarily applicable in order to assess the performance of mutual funds within a specific universe.

Busse, Jiang, and Tang (2021) propose a two-stage approach in which they estimate the multifactor alpha through a rolling regression and then regress this alpha on the characteristics of the fund's holdings in order to isolate the manager's performance obtained after controlling for that dimension. Formally, the procedure leading to the double-adjusted performance measure for a given period τ, which we denote by $\alpha\alpha_P^{(\tau)}$ by reference to the two-pass approach, is obtained by starting from the rolling regression alpha $\alpha_P^{MF(\tau)}$ retrieved from Equation (8-28). Then, the alpha of each fund i is cross-sectionally regressed against the fund's characteristics, which uses information contained in its holdings, over the N funds in the sample:

$$\alpha_i^{MF(\tau)} = a_\tau + \sum_{k=1}^{K} c^{(\tau)} x_{i,k}^{(\tau-1)} + \eta_i^{(\tau)} \tag{8-50}$$

where $x_{i,k}^{(\tau-1)} \equiv (X_{i,k}^{(\tau-1)} - \overline{X}_k^{(\tau-1)})$ in which $X_{i,k}^{(\tau-1)}$ represents fund i's characteristic related to factor k during the previous period, and $\overline{X}_k^{(\tau-1)} = \frac{1}{N}\sum_{i=1}^{N} X_{i,k}^{(\tau-1)}$ is the cross-sectional average of these characteristics. For instance, if the factor represents the size premium, then $X_{i,k}^{(\tau)}$ can be the value-weighted average of the market capitalizations of the fund's components during the time period.

On the basis of the estimated coefficients of regression (8-50), we obtain the fund's performance with the following formula:

$$\alpha\alpha_P^{(\tau)} = \alpha_P^{MF(\tau)} - \sum_{k=1}^{K} \hat{c}^{(\tau)} x_{P,k}^{(\tau-1)} \tag{8-51}$$

The authors interpret the second term of the right-hand side as the fund's characteristic-driven performance, which controls for its composition. Thus, $\alpha\alpha_P^{(\tau)}$ provides a cleaner version of the fund manager's skills. Naturally, it is possible to aggregate this measure over time. This can be used, for instance, for the purpose of assessing the capacity of the fund manager to sustain their level of performance over time (see Chapter 17 for a discussion of this issue).

The CX-T example (continued)

We slightly change the assumptions of the previous examples and consider now that the betas of Fund CX-C presented in Table 8-14 indeed represent the fund's investment in another fund, namely, Fund CX-A, the rest being invested in the risk-free asset. We also consider that the market beta of CX-A at each point in time has been obtained thanks to the TM model, whose coefficients can be found in Table 8-9. This means that, for Fund CX-A, Equation (8-27b) is calibrated as $\beta_{CX\text{-}A,t} = 0.80 + 10.18 \times [R_{M,t} - R_f]$. The market beta of fund CX-C at each point in time t is thus equal to $\hat{\beta}_{CX\text{-}C,t} = w_{CX\text{-}C,CX\text{-}A,t} \times \beta_{CX\text{-}A,t}$.

The TM alpha of fund CX-A is assumed to be constant and equal to $\alpha_{CX\text{-}A,t} = \alpha_{CX\text{-}A} =$ 0.22%. Thus, the alpha of CX-C is $\alpha_{CX\text{-}C} = \frac{1}{24}\sum_{t=1}^{T} w_{CX\text{-}C,CX\text{-}A,t}\alpha_{CX\text{-}A,t} = \frac{0.22\%}{24}\sum_{t=1}^{T} w_{CX\text{-}C,CX\text{-}A,t}$ = 0.11%.

(continued)

(continued)

Performing a linear regression of the time series of the $\widehat{\beta}_{CX\text{-}C,t}$ on either the binary variable $1_{\{R_f > R_{M,t}\}}$ (i.e., a series that takes a value of 1 is the market excess return is positive and 0 otherwise) for the HM model, or on $[R_{M,t} - R_f]$ for the TM model, provides the results reported in Table 8-17.

TABLE 8-17 CX-T example – Regression outputs for the time-varying betas of Fund CX-C.

Regression outputs	HM	TM
$Beta_{TM}$	0.50	0.40
St. dev. $beta_{TM}$	0.03	0.02
$Gamma_{TM}$	−0.24	6.26
St. dev. $gamma_{TM}$	0.06	1.14
R^2	45.19%	57.56%

There is an obvious dominance of the Treynor–Mazuy model in that instance. We apply the variance-based performance adjustment for this model: $f(\gamma_{CX\text{-}C}^{(tm)}) = \gamma_{CX\text{-}C}^{(tm)} \times \sigma_M^2 = 6.26 \times (2.11\%)^2 = 0.28\%$. Thus, the holding/return-based performance measure for Fund CX-C is finally equal to its alpha plus the adjustment: $\pi_{CX\text{-}C}^{(H+tm)} = 0.11\% + 0.28\% = 0.39\%$.

8.5 A ROADMAP FOR MARKET TIMING PERFORMANCE APPRAISAL

Throughout this chapter, we have consistently assumed that (i) a potential market timing skill by the portfolio manager could be identified and that (ii) an estimation of its impact on performance could be made through one of the approaches listed before. Fulfilling both assumptions is not that straightforward. Regarding the first one, it is possible that either the manager's market timing skill is diagnosed by mistake or that this skill fails to be uncovered in spite of its existence. The second assumption entails that it is possible to find a way among the numerous techniques described earlier in this chapter – notwithstanding the ones that have not been treated because of their complexity or lower popularity in the field. In this concluding section, we return to these two assumptions and provide some insights in order to overcome the associated difficulties.

8.5.1 Flawed evidence about market timing

8.5.1.1 Failing to detect actual market timing

Unless there is a clear qualitative indication about not only *that*, but also *how* a portfolio manager has successfully anticipated market movements, such information has to be inferred from the data. For instance, some managers communicate to their investors their own forecasts, and it is easy to check *ex post* whether they were right, wrong, or simply randomizing the market. When portfolio holdings and trades are available, it is also reasonable to consider that market timing skills can be flushed out from a deep dive into the granular data. However, when only portfolio or fund returns are available with a certain frequency, there are many situations that may lead to a failure to detect the market timing skill of the manager, in spite of its genuine presence. The most common reasons are as follows:

- *A wrong choice of factor(s)*: Model misspecification is one of the worst enemies of return-based statistical analysis. This is particularly valid regarding the detection of potential market timing, because it entails (i) identifying the factor that the manager tries to time and (ii) determining the structure of the dependence between factor time-varying exposures and their subsequent returns. Thus, it is not sufficient to select one or several factors to which the portfolio returns would display a linear sensitivity; it is also required to spot those – not necessarily the same ones – for which the beta varies over time in a nonlinear way. This latter challenge involves search methods that are at the same time more sophisticated and prone to estimation errors than traditional linear regressions.
- *Failure to identify the structure of market timing*: As stated above, uncovering those factors for which there is evidence of market timing is one thing; measuring the dependence between exposures and factor realizations is another one. For instance, the discussion of flexible methods in the context of the HM or TM approaches shows that the measurement of performance is impacted by the identification of the right shape of the time-varying beta. Once again, if the observer has access to additional information (portfolio holdings, qualitative insights, manager's forecasts), the estimation is made easier. In the absence of such precisions, it is mostly a matter of using the right statistical approach and tools.
- *Lower frequency of observations than the one of decisions*: Perhaps the least obvious reasons for failing to identify market timing in spite of its presence are related to the frequency of observations. If the manager's timing decisions are made more frequently (e.g., on a daily or a weekly basis) than the basis for the observations of portfolio returns (e.g., monthly), the effects of timing might not arise as such. Rather, the abnormal return posted by the successful manager could be simply ignored – because frequent timing decisions introduce noise at the level of the sample that hampers statistical inference – or wrongly attributed to an asset selection skill. This issue has been emphasized in numerous studies (see, e.g., Bollen and Busse, 2001), and it pleads for the adoption of data with a frequency that could reasonably correspond to the intensity of the portfolio manager's activity.

8.5.1.2 Mistakenly detecting market timing

Even though the opposite phenomenon – uncovering evidence of market timing in spite of its absence – may seem less intuitive and likely, there are numerous instances that could lead to its appearance. Some are merely the result of unwanted measurement problems, but some others can also appear because of the manager's willingness to window-dress the outcome of their action.[15] The major sources of illusory market timing are as follows:

- *Artificial influence of investment flows*: As initially shown by Edelen (1999), there is a positive association between market returns and investment flows to mutual funds. These inflows raise the proportion of cash in the funds' asset allocation at the moment of the reception of the funds. This, in turn, may result in negative biases in the market timing coefficient when measured with the HM or the TM model.
- *Option-like characteristics of positions*: Some individual assets held within a portfolio, without being actively traded, can be characterized by a positive coskewness with market returns. As shown by Jagannathan and Korajczyk (1986), this may influence the market timing coefficients without reflecting an associated portfolio management skill.
- *Confusion with a conditional specification*: As discussed in Chapter 7, a portfolio manager may condition their factor exposures upon the realization of lagged instrumental variables. The resulting betas become time varying as a result of the variability of the instruments. If the model lacks the suited conditional structure, a residual variability can be identified and confused with evidence for market timing. Nevertheless, the existence of conditional betas that depend on public and lagged information is not analogous to pure time-varying betas, which are forward-looking by nature.
- *Artificial return smoothing*: The phenomenon of stale prices, which is quite pervasive for portfolios with illiquid assets such as private equity, real estate, or some hedge fund strategies, is a well-known issue for statistical analysis. In short, the difficulty of obtaining a marked-to-market valuation of some of the portfolio's assets obliges – or allows – its manager to use model-based estimates that produce a smooth pattern of consecutive prices. This reduces the variance and induces an artificial positive serial correlation of portfolio returns.[16] Because it is perfectly possible to orientate the smoothing pattern in the direction chosen by the manager – a phenomenon known as "managed pricing" – there are cases in which they can also provide the illusion of market timing whereas it is purely artificial.
- *Convex (or concave) portfolio strategies*: The Henriksson and Merton (1981) and Treynor and Mazuy (1966) models clearly show it: replicating a portfolio return pattern that resembles market timing is rather easy for a passive manager who would systematically invest in long or short option strategies. Hopefully, the adjustment methods proposed in

[15]This issue is discussed in more detail in Chapter 18.
[16]We explain how this issue can be overcome in Chapter 12.

Sections 8.1 and 8.2 should enable the analyst to conclude about zero abnormal performance when the convexity (or concavity) of the payoff structure is properly accounted for. However, this could lead to the wrong conclusion that the portfolio has not outperformed because the positive market timing skill would be simply offset by a negative asset selection skill, whereas there would be simply nothing to be truly detected.

8.5.2 Measuring the performance of a market timer: A decision tree approach

Consider that, when confronted with a set of historical information about a given portfolio, the analyst is aware of the potential pitfalls discussed in subsection 8.5.1. Their next challenge is to determine how the suspected market timing skill of the portfolio manager should be assessed through a relevant performance measurement approach.

Throughout the chapter, many performance measures have been proposed without any explicit hierarchy between them. This situation often occurs in the field of portfolio performance, with many competing measures aiming to address the same types of management skills. In this particular case, however, we believe that there is some structure to be grasped in order to find one's way that leads to the choice of the right measure (or set of measures to choose among) depending on the situation and the available information. The presence of such a structure is the reason why we propose a decision tree approach. Following its nodes and branches, the objective is to land onto a favored performance measurement approach, with its associated formula(s), in each instance. Of course, the exercise has its own weaknesses: With the material of this chapter, there are potentially many ways to construct such a decision-making tool. We believe that the merits of attempting to provide this decision tree largely overcome its drawbacks.

Our decision tree is developed in Figure 8-13. For clarity of exposition, we have excluded from the analysis the numerous declinations of the models in their conditional versions. In most cases, it is necessary to go through the conditional versions of the statistical return-based models in order to obtain a full and accurate picture of the portfolio return generating process and its associated performance measures.

The root node of the decision tree reflects the most sensitive information in order to assess the presence of a market timing behavior by the portfolio manager: Do we have access to their detailed holdings over time or not. In the affirmative, the material developed in Section 8.4 fully applies to the analysis of their performance. Otherwise, there are two questions to answer before selecting an approach to appraise performance: (i) can we reasonably gauge that the portfolio manager has attempted to time the market? and (ii) can we revoke the presence of statistical biases causing a spurious impression of market timing? Then, if both answers are positive, the tree splits into the directions of either a simple (nonlinear regression-based) approach discussed in Sections 8.1 and 8.2 or a more sophisticated technique discussed in Section 8.3. When a hybrid approach is used, mixing the use of individual portfolio holdings and a return-based analysis of the corresponding assets as in the model of Equations (8-48a) or (8-48b), the tree becomes recombinant.

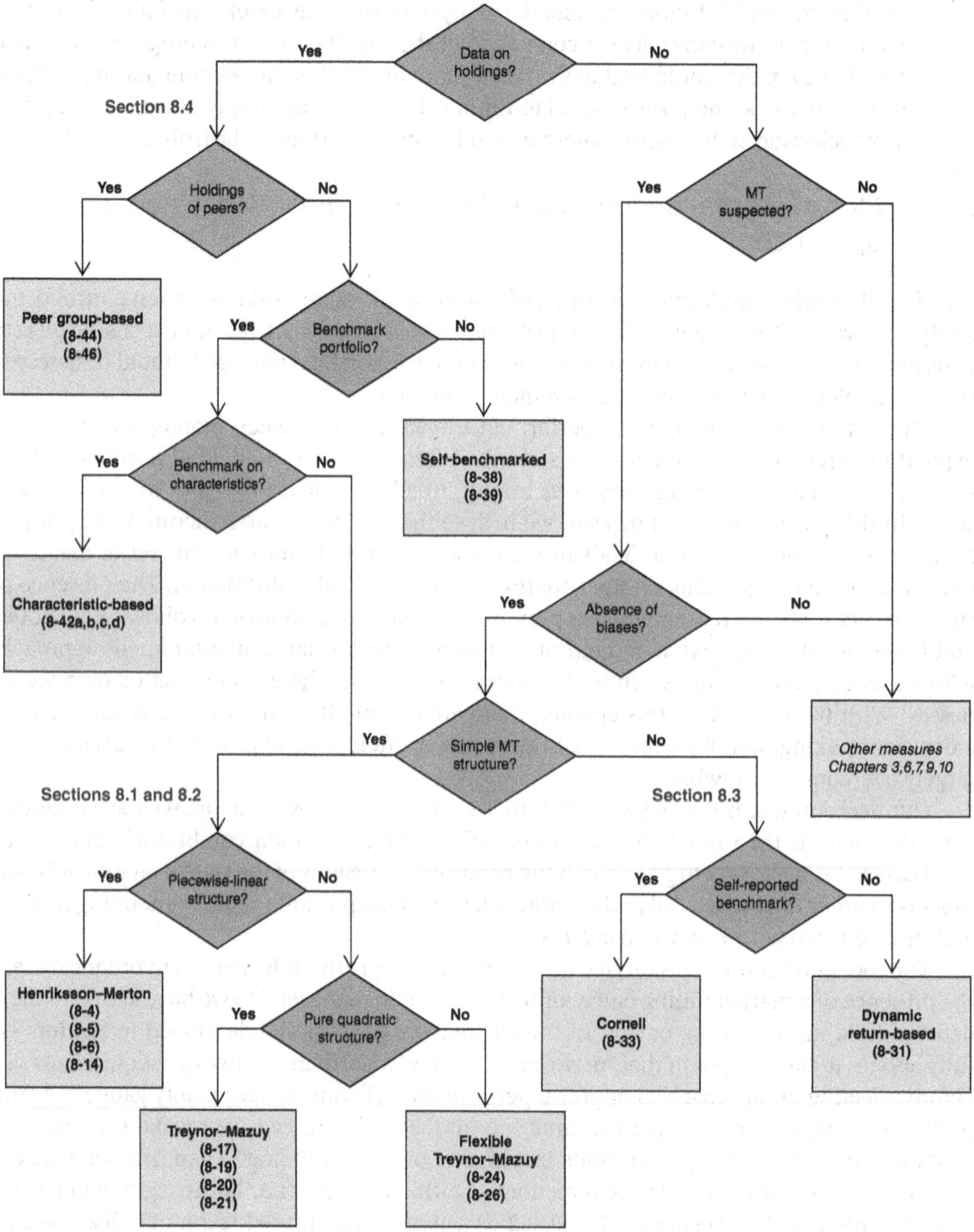

FIGURE 8-13 A decision tree to choose the adequate performance measure in the presence of market timing.

The CX-T example (continued)

Since detailed information is known about Fund CX-C, its performance should be measured according to the techniques examined in Section 8.4. Applying the HM and TM models to the other two funds has resulted in many regression outputs. We can summarize them with their associated R^2 as shown in Table 8-18.

TABLE 8-18 CX-T example – R^2 from the different nonlinear market timing regressions.

R^2	CX-A	CX-B
Linear	67.8%	52.9%
Original HM	78.4%	69.7%
Optimized HM	79.2%	**73.9%**
Original TM	76.8%	72.3%
Mixed TM–HM	**80.5%**	73.1%

Fund CX-A is worthy of further investigation. The best fitting model appears to be the mixed model of Equation (8-25). Its geometric comparison with the HM and TM specifications is shown in Figure 8-14.

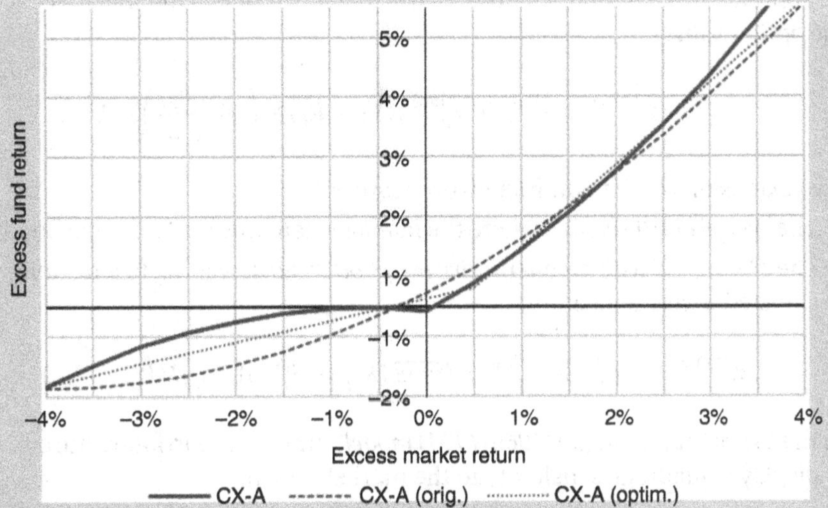

FIGURE 8-14 CX-T example – Fitted regression curves for fund CX-A.

(continued)

(continued)

The actual market timing behavior of this manager is different: concave (negative market timer) in the region of losses, and convex and rather aggressive market timer in the region of gains. None of the pure HM or TM versions of the models is able to uncover this asymmetric timing behavior.

Applying the decision tree to this fund points to the application of Equation (8-26) with the data of Table 8-13. The resulting value of the adjusted performance of the manager is given by $\pi_{\text{CX-A}}^{(\text{tm+hm})} = 0.54\%$.

Key Takeaways and Equations

- In the *Henriksson and Merton (1981) (HM) model*, the excess portfolio return is supposed to display a piecewise-linear sensitivity to the market return:

$$R_{P,t} - R_f = \alpha_P^{(\text{hm})} + \beta_P^{(\text{hm})}[R_{M,t} - R_f] + \gamma_P^{(\text{hm})}\max[R_f - R_{M,t}, 0] + \varepsilon_{P,t} \quad (8\text{-}1)$$

The portfolio performance adjusted for market timing is obtained by reflecting the value of the put option replicated by the portfolio manager. This put option can be approximated in three different ways, the purest one being the direct account for the option value:

$$\pi_P^{(\text{hm},o)} = \alpha_P^{(\text{hm})} + \gamma_P^{(\text{hm})} \times (1 + R_f) \times \left(2\Phi\left(\frac{\sigma_M}{2}\right) - 1\right) \quad (8\text{-}4)$$

- Two extensions of the HM framework feature:
  - The *Weigel (1991) model*, where the manager can time the stock and bond markets.
  - The *HM model with an alternative threshold return*, leading to a flexible version of adjusted performance:

$$\pi_P^{(\text{hm},a)L} = \alpha_P^{(\text{hm})} + \gamma_P^{(\text{hm})} \times (\overline{\max}[R_{M,t} - R_L^*, 0] - q_M^{L+}(\overline{R}_M - R_L^*)) \quad (8\text{-}14)$$

- In the *Treynor and Mazuy (1966) (TM) model*, the excess portfolio return is supposed to display a quadratic sensitivity to the market return:

$$R_{P,t} - R_f = \alpha_P^{(\text{tm})} + \beta_P^{(\text{tm})}[R_{M,t} - R_f] + \gamma_P^{(\text{tm})}[R_{M,t} - R_f]^2 + \varepsilon_{P,t} \quad (8\text{-}15)$$

The portfolio performance adjusted for market timing is obtained by reflecting the value of the delta and convexity of the option replicated by the portfolio manager. These option features can be approximated in four different ways, the purest one being the direct account for the option value:

$$\pi_P^{(tm,o)} = \alpha_P^{(tm)} + \beta_P^{(tm)}\left(\frac{1}{\Delta^{\tau^*\kappa^*}} - 1\right)R_f - \frac{\beta_P^{(tm)}}{\Delta^{\tau^*\kappa^*}}\Theta^{\tau^*\kappa^*} \tag{8-17}$$

- Two extensions of the TM framework feature:
  - The *cubic TM model*, in which the coefficient of the cubic market return might signal that the regression is misspecified.
  - The *mixed TM–HM model* where the manager may adopt different nonlinear market sensitivities in different market environments, with associated performance:

$$\pi_P^{(tm+hm)} = \alpha_P^{(tm+hm)} + \beta_{P+}^{(tm+hm)}\left(\overline{\max}\,[R_{M,t} - R_f, 0] - q_M^+(\overline{R}_M - R_f)\right)$$
$$+\gamma_P^{(tm+hm)} \times \overline{[R_{M,t} - R_f]^2} + q_M^+\gamma_{P+}^{(tm+hm)}\overline{\max}[R_{M,t} - R_f, 0]^2 \tag{8-26}$$

- When betas are estimated dynamically over time, either through a rolling windows regression or with more sophisticated estimation techniques such as the *Kalman filter*, the difference between the average portfolio return and that of the regression-based benchmark is given by

$$\overline{R}_P - \overline{R}_B = \overline{\alpha}_P^{MF} + \frac{1}{T}\sum_{t=1}^{T}\sum_{k=1}^{K}(\beta_{P,k,t} - \overline{\beta}_{P,k})F_{k,t} \tag{8-31}$$

When the benchmark is self-reported by the portfolio, the *Cornell (1979) performance measure* can be applied for sufficiently large sample sizes:

$$GC_P = \overline{\alpha}_P^{MF} + \text{plim}\left(\frac{1}{T}\sum_{t=1}^{T}(\beta_{P,t} - \overline{\beta}_P)R_{B,t}\right) \tag{8-33}$$

- In order to assess the manager's ability to time the market, Grinblatt and Titman (1989a, 1989b) define the *positive period weighting measure* of a portfolio as

$$PPWM_P = \sum_{t=1}^{T}\dot{w}_t(R_{P,t} - R_f) \tag{8-34}$$

(continued)

(continued)

where, for some reference passive portfolio, its positive period weighting measure level is null: $\text{PPWM}_B = \sum_{t=1}^{T} \dot{w}_t(R_{B,t} - R_f) = 0$.

- The knowledge of individual portfolio holdings over time consists of the ability to split the portfolio return into its contributions at any time:

$$R_{P,t} = \sum_{i=1}^{N} w_{P,i,t} R_{i,t} \tag{8-37}$$

- In this context, there are four approaches to isolate market timing in portfolio performance:
  - The *self-benchmarked performance measure* of Grinblatt and Titman (1993) is defined as

$$\text{SBP}_P \equiv \frac{I}{T-l} \sum_{t=l+1}^{T} \text{SBP}_{P,t} = \frac{I}{T-l} \sum_{t=l+1}^{T} \sum_{i=1}^{N} (w_{P,i,t} - w_{P,i,t-l}) R_{i,t} \tag{8-38}$$

  - The *performance measure is based on a characteristic-based benchmark* of Daniel, Grinblatt, Titman, and Wermers (1997), who decompose total portfolio return into three components: the "average style" measure $\text{AS}_{P,t}$, the "characteristic selectivity" measure $\text{CS}_{P,t}$, and the "characteristic timing" measure $\text{CT}_{P,t}$:

$$R_{P,t} = \text{AS}_{P,t} + \text{CS}_{P,t} + \text{CT}_{P,t} \tag{8-42a}$$

$$\text{AS}_{P,t} = \sum_{i=1}^{N} w_{P,i,t-l} R_{i,t}^{b_{t-l-1}} \tag{8-42b}$$

$$\text{CS}_{P,t} = \sum_{i=1}^{N} w_{P,i,t} (R_{i,t} - R_{i,t}^{b_{t-1}}) \tag{8-42c}$$

$$\text{CT}_{P,t} = \sum_{i=1}^{N} (w_{P,i,t} R_{i,t}^{b_{t-1}} - w_{P,i,t-l} R_{i,t}^{b_{t-l-1}}) \tag{8-42d}$$

  - The *peer group holding-based performance measure and its associated peer group trading-based performance measure* proposed by Cohen, Coval, and Pástor (2005) are based on measures of quality of each asset held through information about other portfolio managers' holdings and trades:

$$\delta_P^{(h)} = \frac{1}{T} \sum_{t=1}^{T} \delta_{P,t}^{(h)} = \frac{1}{T} \sum_{t=1}^{T} \sum_{i=1}^{N} w_{P,i,t} \delta_{i,t}^{(h)} \tag{8-44}$$

$$\delta_P^{(\Delta h)} = \frac{1}{T}\sum_{t=1}^{T}\delta_{P,t}^{(\Delta h)} = \frac{1}{T}\sum_{t=1}^{T}\left[\sum_{i\in N_{P,t}^{+}} x_{P,i,t}^{+}\delta_{i,t}^{(\Delta H)} - \sum_{i\in N_{P,t}^{-}} x_{P,i,t}^{-}\delta_{i,t}^{(\Delta H)}\right] \tag{8-46}$$

- Finally, it is possible to measure *performance with a return-based benchmark* by specifying

$$R_{P,t} = \sum_{i=1}^{N} w_{P,i,t}(\alpha_{i,t} + \beta_{i,t}(R_{M,t} - R_F) + \varepsilon_{i,t}) \tag{8-47}$$

In that case, the analysis and performance measurement can revert back to the HM or the TM model if the resulting portfolio time-varying beta adopts the structure assumed in the respective models, which leads to a *combined holding-based HM (or TM) performance measure:*

$$\pi_P^{(H+\cdot\cdot)} = \frac{I}{T}\sum_{t=1}^{T}\sum_{i=1}^{N} w_{P,i,t}\alpha_{i,t} + f(\gamma_P^{(\cdot\cdot)}) \tag{8-49}$$

where "··" stands for hm or tm.

- Before choosing a performance measure that explicitly addresses the market timing skill of the manager, it is necessary to make sure to avoid three types of biases: (i) *failing to detect actual market timing*, through a wrong choice of factor(s), (ii) *failure to identify the structure of market timing*, or a lower frequency of observations than the one of decisions, and (iii) *mistakenly detecting market timing* because of an artificial influence of investment flows, option-like characteristics of positions, confusion with a conditional specification, artificial return smoothing, or convex (or concave) portfolio strategies.
- Because there are so many ways to measure performance with market timing, we propose a *decision tree approach* that should enable the analyst to adequately manage this issue in various contexts discussed in this chapter.

REFERENCES

Admati, A., Bhattacharya, S., Pfleiderer, P., and S. Ross (1986), On timing and selectivity. *The Journal of Finance*, Vol. 41, pp. 715–732.

Bauer, R., Otten, R., and A. Tourani-Rad (2006), New Zealand mutual funds: Measuring performance and persistence in performance. *Accounting and Finance*, Vol. 46, pp. 237–363.

Bollen, N. P. B., and J. A. Busse (2001), On the timing ability of mutual fund managers. *The Journal of Finance*, Vol. 56, pp. 1075–1094.

Bollen, N. P. B., and J. A. Busse (2004), Short-term persistence in mutual fund performance. *The Review of Financial Studies*, Vol. 18, pp. 569–597.

Busse, J. A. (1999), Volatility timing in mutual funds: Evidence from daily returns. *The Review of Financial Studies*, Vol. 12, pp. 1009–1041.

Busse, J. A., Jiang, L., and Y. Tang (2021), Double-adjusted mutual fund performance. *The Review of Asset Pricing Studies*, Vol. 11, pp. 169–208.

Chan, L. K. C., Chen H.-L., and J. Lakonishok (2002), On mutual fund investment styles. *The Review of Financial Studies*, Vol. 15, pp. 1407–1437.

Chen, Y., and B. Liang (2007), Do market timing hedge funds time the market? *Journal of Financial and Quantitative Analysis*, Vol. 42, pp. 827–856.

Cohen, R., Coval, J., and L. Pástor (2005), Judging fund managers by the company they keep. *The Journal of Finance*, Vol. 60, pp. 1057–1096.

Coles, J. L., Daniel, N. D., and F. Nardari (2006), Does the choice of model or benchmark affect inference in measuring mutual fund performance? Working Paper, Arizona State University.

Cornell, B. (1979), Asymmetric information and portfolio performance management. *Journal of Financial Economics*, Vol. 7, pp. 381–390.

Cumby, R. E., and J. D. Glen (1990), Evaluating the performance of international mutual funds. *The Journal of Finance*, Vol. 45, pp. 497–521.

Daniel, K., Grinblatt, M., Titman, S., and R. Wermers (1997), Measuring mutual fund performance with characteristic-based benchmarks. *The Journal of Finance*, Vol. 52, pp. 1035–1058.

Edelen, R. (1999), Investor flows and the assessed performance of open-ended mutual funds. *Journal of Financial Economics*, Vol. 53, pp. 439–466.

Ferson, W. E., and R. Schadt (1996), Measuring fund strategy and performance in changing economic conditions. *The Journal of Finance*, Vol. 51, pp. 425–462.

Goetzmann, W., Ingersoll, J., Spiegel, M., and I. Welch (2007), Portfolio performance manipulation and manipulation-proof performance measures. *The Review of Financial Studies*, Vol. 20, pp. 1503–1546.

Grinblatt, M., and S. Titman (1989a), Portfolio performance evaluation: Old issues and new insights. *The Review of Financial Studies*, Vol. 2, pp. 393–421.

Grinblatt, M., and S. Titman (1989b), Mutual fund performance: An analysis of quarterly portfolio holdings. *Journal of Business*, Vol. 62, pp. 393–416.

Grinblatt, M., and S. Titman (1993), Performance measurement without benchmarks: An examination of mutual fund returns. *Journal of Business*, Vol. 66, pp. 47–68.

Grinblatt, M., and Titman, S. (1994), A study of monthly mutual fund returns and performance evaluation techniques. *Journal of Financial and Quantitative Analysis*, Vol. 29, pp. 419–444.

Henriksson, R. D. (1984), Market timing and mutual fund performance: An empirical investigation. *Journal of Business*, Vol. 57, pp. 73–96.

Henriksson, R. D., and R. Merton (1981), On market timing and investment performance. II. Statistical procedures for evaluating forecasting skills. *Journal of Business*, Vol. 54, pp. 513–533.

Hübner, G. (2016), Option replication and the performance of a market timer. *Studies in Economics and Finance*, Vol. 33, pp. 2–25.

Jagannathan, R., and R. A. Korajczyk (1986), Assessing the market timing performance of managed portfolios. *Journal of Business*, Vol. 59, pp. 217–235.

Jiang, G. J., Yao, T., and T. Yu (2007), Do mutual funds time the market? Evidence from portfolio holdings. *Journal of Financial Economics*, Vol. 86, pp. 724–758.

Lehmann, B., and D. Modest (1987), Mutual fund performance evaluation: A comparison of benchmarks and benchmark comparisons. *The Journal of Finance*, Vol. 42, pp. 233–265.

Mamaysky, H., Spiegel, M., and H. Zhang (2008), The causes and consequences of recent financial market bubbles. *The Review of Financial Studies*, Vol. 21, pp. 233–264.

Merton, R. C. (1981), On market timing and investment performance. I. An equilibrium theory of value for market forecasts. *Journal of Business*, Vol. 54, pp. 363–406.

Roll, R. (1977), A critique of the asset pricing theory's tests. Part I: On past and potential testability of the theory. *Journal of Financial Economics*, Vol. 4, pp. 125–176.

Treynor, J. L., and K. K. Mazuy (1966), Can mutual funds outguess the market? *Harvard Business Review*, Vol. 44, pp. 131–136.

Weigel E. J. (1991), The performance of tactical asset allocation. *Financial Analysts Journal*, Vol. 47 (5), pp. 63–70.

Wermers, R. (2006), Performance evaluation with portfolio holdings information. *North American Journal of Economics and Finance*, Vol. 17, pp. 207–230.

CHAPTER 9

Preference-based Performance for the Standard Investor

INTRODUCTION

Most, if not all, of the ways to measure and appraise performance discussed until now have adopted the perspective of the portfolio manager. In this context, they apply a "one-size-fits-all" approach by considering that the investors – thus the customers – are fully homogeneous and informed. They can, without any particular difficulty, grasp everything about the portfolio's risk and return characteristics and optimally allocate their investments accordingly. In reality, even when they try to behave rationally (which is what we assume here), investors are heterogeneous and many of them, especially individual ones, cannot proactively shape the allocation of their assets in order to accommodate the specific characteristics of their portfolios. To explicitly address the needs of those "standard" investors, it is necessary to account for their preferences in the management charter of their portfolios and to measure performance accordingly. This is the subject matter of this chapter.

We start with the "standard" rational investor's decision-making framework by characterizing the structure of the von Neumann–Morgenstern utility functions and their associated properties. The major ones (negative exponential, power, and quadratic) are discussed, and their implications regarding performance measurement are introduced. Within the Standard Portfolio Theory (SPT) framework, this gives birth to the famous *Quadratic score* as a special case of the definition of expected utility (EU) as a combination of the moments of the portfolio returns. In addition to this very classical performance measure that considers portfolio performance in isolation, we also examine the situation in which the investor has the choice between a specific portfolio and an otherwise passive allocation between the market portfolio and the risk-free asset fitting their preferences. We propose two performance measures depending on how the investor's risk profile is captured: The *Quadratic alpha* if we know the risk-aversion coefficient and the *Target volatility alpha* if we know the target risk level.

It is also possible to move away from the SPT world. Within the family of hyperbolic absolute risk-aversion (HARA) utility functions, we also introduce parametric versions that feature the higher moments of the distribution of returns. We choose two special cases that can prove to be very effective: the linear-exponential utility, which enables us to extend the Quadratic score with skewness and kurtosis, and the flexible three-parameter utility that encompasses most cases of HARA functions. There are also some interesting sample-based versions including the *Power-based certainty equivalent*, of which a special case is the Morningstar Risk-Adjusted Return ("MRAR") used by Morningstar to rank portfolios, and the *Power-based compensative rebate*, a relative inefficiency measure. Finally, we show that even the Sharpe ratio can be affected when the investor's preferences are accounted for. We introduce the notion of the *utility-consistent Sharpe ratio*, which involves a correction for higher moments depending on which shape of the utility function is chosen.

This chapter should be viewed as the first one of a diptych. Considering that all investors are entirely rational is convenient but not realistic. When their behavioral traits are taken into account, there are also a variety of ways to appraise portfolio performance, as discussed in Chapter 10.

The HiMeLo Example – Part I

HiMeLo Wealth Management provides its customers with three types of discretionary portfolio management mandates, proposed according to their associated risk profiles. The trailing volatility level of each portfolio is controlled so as to match the target risk of their three kinds of customers: They are set to $\sigma_{\text{Lo}}^{\text{target}} = 4\%$, $\sigma_{\text{Me}}^{\text{target}} = 8\%$, and $\sigma_{\text{Hi}}^{\text{target}} = 12\%$, for the low-, medium-, and high-risk model portfolios, respectively. The monthly realized rates of return and their summary statistics are reported in Table 9-1.

TABLE 9-1 HiMeLo example – Monthly rates of return and summary statistics.

Month	Low	Medium	High
Jan	0.48%	−3.28%	0.74%
Feb	2.08%	5.94%	9.98%
Mar	−0.73%	−1.33%	−2.58%
Apr	−0.46%	−0.03%	−1.11%

TABLE 9-1 *(continued)*

Month	Low	Medium	High
May	0.35%	0.33%	0.30%
Jun	1.36%	0.59%	0.87%
Jul	0.27%	0.68%	−0.29%
Aug	0.97%	1.42%	1.99%
Sep	1.47%	1.45%	1.06%
Oct	0.36%	0.12%	0.00%
Nov	−2.62%	−1.99%	−5.07%
Dec	0.30%	1.38%	0.99%
Mean return	3.83%	5.29%	6.87%
Standard deviation	4.22%	7.85%	12.22%
Skewness	−1.13	0.92	1.54
Excess kurtosis	2.34	2.88	5.09

The risk–return properties of the three portfolios and the risk-free asset (whose level is a constant 1.44% for the period) are represented in the graph shown in Figure 9-1.

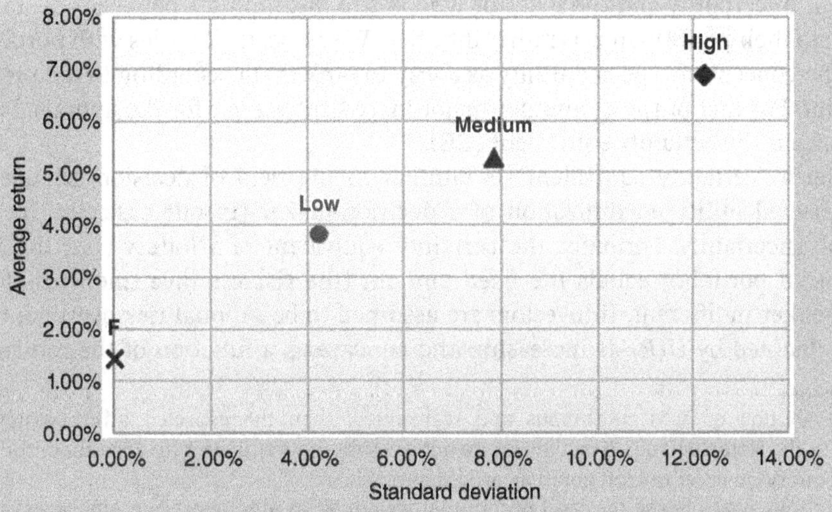

FIGURE 9-1 HiMeLo example – Risk–return properties of the three model portfolios.

9.1 THE STRUCTURE OF THE RATIONAL INVESTOR'S PREFERENCES

The core of the preference-based performance measurement approach lies in the inclusion of the investor's risk profile, typically characterized by an estimate of their level of risk aversion, into the assessment of portfolio performance. In this section, we review the basics of the von Neumann–Morgenstern (1953) expected utility framework and discuss its usefulness for portfolio performance appraisal.

9.1.1 Utility functions and certainty equivalents

When an individual is confronted with various uncertain prospects or "lotteries" with random consumption outcomes, they are led to express a choice. This choice reveals their preferences. If lottery X is chosen instead of Y, then they prefer X over Y or, expressed symbolically, $X \succ Y$. If they are indifferent, then we write $X \sim Y$. The von Neumann–Morgenstern utility function is nothing but a way to translate this ordinal relation into a cardinal inequality of the form

$$X \succ (\text{resp. } \prec, \sim)\ Y \Longleftrightarrow \mathrm{E}(U(X)) > (\text{resp. } <, =)\ \mathrm{E}(U(Y)) \tag{9-1}$$

where $\mathrm{E}(U(X)) = \sum_{i=1}^{N} \mathrm{Pr}_i U(X_i)$ is the expected utility of the realizations of lottery X across all N states of the world according to their respective probabilities Pr_i (the same holds for lottery Y).[1]

The parallelism between the situation of the individual who has to express a choice in a situation of uncertainty and the investor who has to discriminate between several portfolios according to their performance is rather intuitive. We associate lotteries with portfolio returns and use the concept of expected utility as a way to rank them according to the preferences of the investor. For that purpose, another major ingredient we use for the appraisal of portfolio performance is the certainty equivalent (CE).

The term "certainty equivalent" is familiar in the field of decision sciences. It refers to the expected utility maximization of a decision-maker (in our case, the investor) in a context of uncertainty. Formally, the certainty equivalent of a lottery (i.e., the investment in a financial portfolio) equals the fixed amount (the riskless investment) that leaves the decision-maker indifferent. If investors are assumed to be rational risk averters, their utility function, denoted by $U(R)$, is increasing and concave as a function of the return R.[2] Then,

---

[1]If the distribution of X is continuous and real-valued, then the expected utility writes $\mathrm{E}(U(X)) = \int_{-\infty}^{+\infty} U(x) f(x) \mathrm{d}x$. Note that, in this section, we do not use subscripts either for the investor or for the portfolio (unless necessary) in order to keep notation as light as possible.

[2]Utility functions typically use the level of terminal wealth W as argument. In a one-period model, using wealth or returns is equivalent as $W = W_0(1 + R)$ for an initial wealth level W_0. Thus, our choice makes no difference and certainly eases exposition. Using wealth and returns would lead to different properties of utility functions in multiperiod models, but this is beyond the scope of this chapter.

the notion of certainty equivalent CE(R) that exhibits no risk is such that CE(R) $\sim R$ or, equivalently,

$$U(\mathrm{CE}(R)) = \mathrm{E}(U(R)) \tag{9-2}$$

This idea can be represented graphically in Figure 9-2.

The graph plots the utility functions $U_A(R)$ and $U_B(R)$ of two different investors A and B. Both curves are increasing and concave functions of the portfolio return R, whose realizations can only take two values R^+ and R^- with equal probabilities (50%) during the investment horizon.

The image of each possible realization of the portfolio return indicates the intensity of the investor's associated satisfaction. We have normalized the functions in such a way that their cardinal values are equal for both R^+ and R^-. In the von Neumann–Morgenstern framework, the expected utility (i.e., the average of the utilities, reported on the vertical axis in our example) reflects the investor's global satisfaction with the portfolio. The concavity of the utility function entails that both investors are risk averse. This can be understood by noting that they would obtain a higher satisfaction from the expected portfolio return than the average one that they actually extract: $U_j(\mathrm{E}(R)) > \mathrm{E}(U_j(R))$ for $j = A, B$. Nevertheless, the curvature of $U_A(R)$ is the most pronounced, indicating that A is a more risk-averse investor than B.

What is the meaning of the certainty equivalent in this context? We report on the graph $\mathrm{CE}_A(R)$ and $\mathrm{CE}_B(R)$ as the projections of the expected utility on the horizontal axis according to each of the utility functions. These are the values of a riskless rate of return that would provide exactly the same level of satisfaction as the portfolio to the investor. Thus, this is a fixed rate

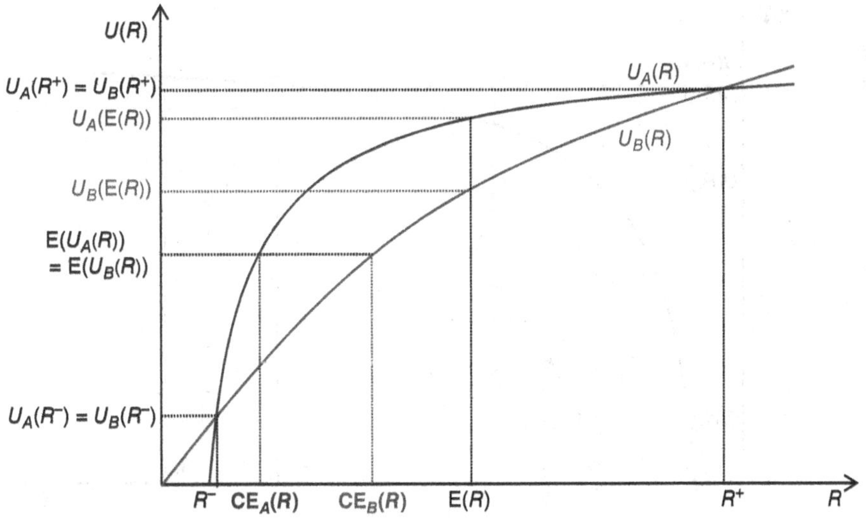

FIGURE 9-2 Certainty equivalents for two utility functions.

of return that makes them exactly indifferent to the risky portfolio; this is the reason why it is usually called a "certainty equivalent". Investor *B*, who is less risk averse, has a higher CE than that of *A*. Hence, one has to offer a higher riskless rate of return to induce them to give up the risky investment.

The certainty equivalent is important in the context of performance appraisal because it can be viewed as a normalized surplus offered by a portfolio. Consider now the example in which investor *A* is confronted with three portfolios *P*, *Q*, and *F*, the latter one being a fixed-income instrument.

The graph in Figure 9-3 shows that certainty equivalents represent a useful basis for comparison for portfolios that can presumably be very different. Portfolios *P* and *Q* are designed so as to share the same expected return (i.e., $\frac{R_P^+ + R_P^-}{2} = \frac{R_Q^+ + R_Q^-}{2}$), but *P* is riskier than *Q* as its returns are more distant from their common expectation (i.e., $R_P^- < R_Q^-$ and $R_P^+ > R_Q^+$). The consequence of the investor's risk aversion is that they prefer *Q* over *P*: $E(U(R_Q)) > E(U(R_P))$. Since the utility function is increasing, this translates into the same rankings of their projections: $CE(R_Q) > CE(R_P)$. Thus, the ordering of the investor's preferences is faithfully represented by the ranking of the associated certainty equivalents. Furthermore, since the fixed-income asset is riskless, it follows that $CE(R_F) = R_f$. The risk-free rate represents an anchor for the comparison of the investor's satisfaction level. As $CE(R_Q) > R_f$, portfolio *Q* delivers a surplus of expected utility over the risk-free investment, $s(R_Q) = CE(R_Q) - R_f > 0$. Similarly, the utility surplus provided by portfolio *P* is negative. From an *ex post* perspective, the certainty

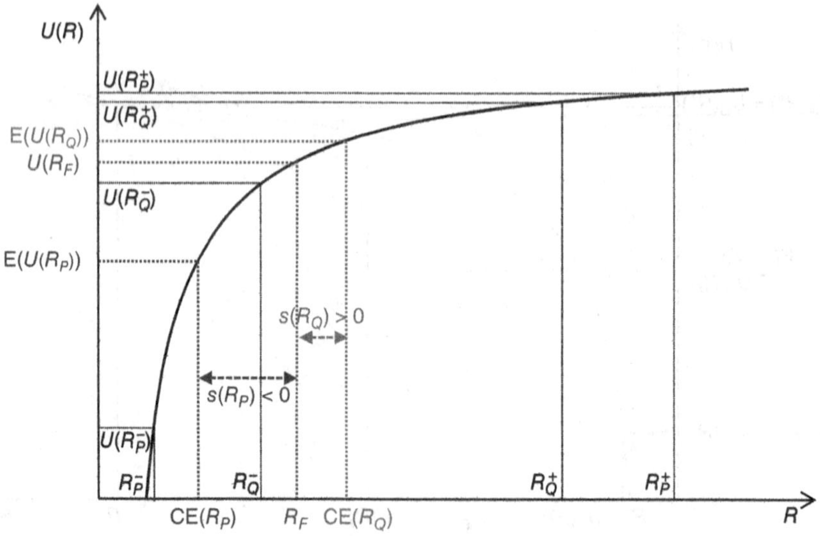

FIGURE 9-3 Certainty equivalents for different portfolios and the risk-free asset.

equivalent measures the intensity of the satisfaction perceived by the investor with the actual behavior of their portfolio over the period of observations.

Getting back to the characterization of the investor's preferences, we consider that the utility function of the investor is known and applied to the sample of T consecutive returns of the portfolio, namely $\{R_1, \ldots, R_T\}$. Applying the previous reasoning, and if the returns are serially independent,[3] the *ex post* certainty equivalent of the portfolio can be written as

$$\mathrm{CE}(R) = U^{-1}\left(\frac{1}{T}\sum_{t=1}^{T} U(R_t)\right) \tag{9-3}$$

where $U^{-1}(\cdot)$ stands for the inverse of the utility function such that $U^{-1}(U(x)) = x$. This expression reflects the risk-adjusted performance of the portfolio *from the point of view of the investor*. Thus, unlike most performance measures discussed so far, it is necessarily investor specific as it requires the knowledge of the utility function that applies to their profile.

If the utility function is strictly increasing, Equation (9-3) also entails that either the EU or the CE can be indifferently used as portfolio performance measures.

9.1.2 Properties of utility functions

9.1.2.1 Attitudes toward risk

The application of certainty equivalents relies on the desirable properties of the utility function of a rational risk-averse individual, namely that it should (at least) be increasing and concave. This implies that, considering $U(R)$ as the investor's utility function, $U'(R) > 0$ and $U''(R) < 0$.

There are also other important considerations regarding the properties of this function. They relate to the Arrow (1964)–Pratt (1964) coefficients of absolute and relative risk aversion:

$$\mathrm{ARA}(R) = -\frac{U''(R)}{U'(R)} \tag{9-4a}$$

$$\mathrm{RRA}(R) = -\frac{R \times U''(R)}{U'(R)} \tag{9-4b}$$

If an investor exhibits constant absolute risk aversion (CARA), in the context of portfolio choice, this entails that they allocate a constant *amount* in risky assets, regardless of their wealth. If they exhibit constant relative risk aversion (CRRA), in the context of portfolio choice, then they allocate a constant *proportion* in risky assets, regardless of they wealth.

[3] The situation in which the distribution of returns exhibits some time dependence, such as GARCH effects or autocorrelation, would be dealt with through a parametric approach that is directly discussed in the next sections.

In general, it is commonly accepted that most investors are characterized by a decreasing absolute risk aversion (DARA) and either a decreasing or constant relative risk aversion (DRRA or CRRA). Note that the notion of risk tolerance is simply the inverse of the absolute risk aversion.

9.1.2.2 Standard forms of utility functions

Most utility functions used in practice belong to the class of HARA, whose common feature is that their ARA is a hyperbolic function of returns (i.e., its shape is "one divided by a linear function of R"). The generic form of a HARA utility function can be written as follows:

$$U(R) = \frac{\eta}{1-\eta}\left(\frac{\lambda R}{\eta} + \phi\right)^{1-\eta} \tag{9-5}$$

where parameters λ, η, and ϕ are investor-specific and determine the risk-aversion properties of the utility function.

Several types of utility functions belonging to this class are remarkable, either for their properties regarding risk aversion or for other reasons related to their tractability.[4]

- The *negative exponential* utility function ($\phi = 1, \lambda > 0, \eta \to \infty$):

$$U(R) = -e^{-\gamma R} \tag{9-6}$$

  where $\gamma > 0$. This function exhibits constant absolute risk aversion (CARA) because $\text{ARA}(R) = \gamma$. Note that this entails an increasing relative risk aversion (IRRA). This is not a very realistic utility function, but it can be useful for modeling purposes, considering that the investor has a wealth level normalized to one.
- The *power* utility function (also known as the *isoelastic* utility function) ($\phi = 1, \lambda = \eta$, $\eta > 0$):

$$U(R) = \frac{(1+R)^{1-\gamma}}{1-\gamma} \tag{9-7}$$

  where $\gamma \neq 1$. This function exhibits CRRA because $\text{RRA}(R) = \gamma$. It is more realistic than the negative exponential while remaining relatively simple as it distinguishes investors on only one parameter.

  Note that the *logarithmic* utility function $U(R) = \log(1 + R)$ stands as a limiting case of the power utility function for $\gamma = 1$. It also entails CRRA with $\text{RRA}(R) = 1$. It is sometimes used for economic modeling purposes but is seldom used in the context of portfolio management as it would correspond to an overly aggressive investor type (very low risk aversion).

---

[4]We report the simplest and most classical versions of these utility functions. This is the reason why the functional forms do not necessarily match with the corresponding simplifications of Equation (9-5).

- The *quadratic* utility function ($\eta = -1$):

$$U(R) = R - \frac{1}{2}\gamma(R - \mathrm{E}(R))^2 \tag{9-8}$$

where $\gamma > 0$ and $\gamma R < 1$.[5] Applying Equation (9-4a) yields $\mathrm{ARA}(R) = \frac{\gamma}{1-\gamma R}$. This function exhibits increasing absolute risk aversion (IARA) and, consequently, also an increasing relative risk aversion. This behavior is not at all realistic, but it is the simplest utility function that is fully consistent with the mean–variance framework if the returns are not normally distributed. Note that if R is riskless (= a constant), then $U(R) = R$.

From a theoretical standpoint, the power utility function stands out as the one in this list that is closest to the anticipated behavior of most investors. The properties of the three major utility functions are summarized in Table 9-2.

The grayed cells represent impossible outcomes, while the two cells framed in bold are the most desirable ones. However, even though the power utility function dominates the other two, the actual behavior of those utility functions does not differ very largely for reasonable parameter values. We report in the graph shown in Figure 9-4 the values of the three utility functions for returns ranging between 0 and 20% by scaling the functions so that $U(0\%) = 0$ and $U(20\%) = 1$.

We have chosen $\gamma = 10$ for the negative exponential and power functions, and $\gamma = 4.7$ for the quadratic one. The behaviors and the functions, both their slope and curvature, remain very close to each other. Thus, given the difficulty inherent in the assessment of an investor's risk-aversion coefficient in practice, the choice among these three specifications does not

TABLE 9-2 Summary of the properties of the remarkable utility functions.

Absolute risk aversion	Relative risk aversion		
	Decreasing (DRRA)	Constant (CRRA)	Increasing (IRRA)
Decreasing (DARA)		Power $U(R) = \frac{(1+R)^{1-\gamma}}{1-\gamma}$	
Constant (CARA)			**Negative exponential** $U(R) = -e^{-\gamma R}$
Increasing (IARA)			**Quadratic** $U(R) = R - \frac{1}{2}\gamma(R - \mathrm{E}(R))^2$

[5] For high levels of return, the utility function starts to decrease. This phenomenon is called "satiation." This is not a reasonable property, and this is one of the many drawbacks of the quadratic utility function.

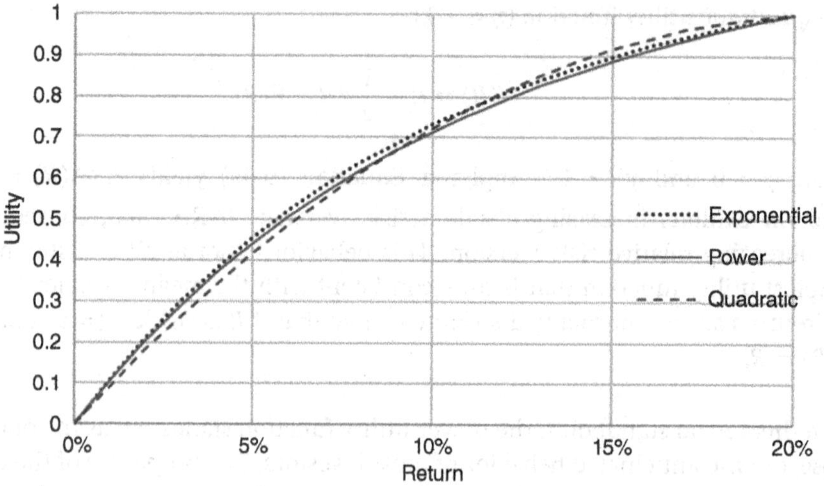

FIGURE 9-4 Representation of the negative exponential, power, and quadratic utility functions.

make a large difference for most real-life applications. As emphasized by Kallberg and Ziemba (1983), what really matters is the adequate calibration of the risk-aversion parameter that corresponds to the investor type.

9.2 PREFERENCE-BASED PERFORMANCE IN THE STANDARD PORTFOLIO THEORY

The field of performance measurement all began with the classical measures examined in Chapter 3 and more particularly with the Sharpe ratio developed in the SPT framework. On several occasions, however, we have shed light on its merits, its particularly strong theoretical grounding, but also its limitations – specifically, its heavy reliance on homemade leverage. In Chapter 4, we show that the Sharpe ratio is a tool that enables the risk-averse, rational "mean–variance" investor to select their utility-maximizing portfolio, but at the same time, in Section 5.1.2 of Chapter 5, we outline the fact that practical limitations may hinder investors to freely position themselves along the reward-to-volatility line of their portfolio, whose slope is precisely its Sharpe ratio. In the same chapter, we propose a certainty equivalent criterion (Equation (5-2)) that reflects the level of satisfaction obtained from a portfolio. Interestingly, this criterion might rank portfolios with different risk levels that diverge from the ordering obtained with the Sharpe ratio. This concretely means that taking the investor's preferences into account may produce results that are different from the outcomes of the application of a classical performance measure.

Under the SPT framework, the expected utility approach to performance appraisal can be rolled out in two major ways. The perspective depends on how the investor is supposed to be characterized regarding their risk profile. The investor's preferences can be directly assessed using the risk-aversion coefficient of their utility function. This approach yields the famous "Quadratic score"[6] that only depends on the average and variance of portfolio returns. However, as it is relatively standard in wealth management practices, these preferences over risk can be alternatively approximated using a "volatility budget" that is easier to explain and estimate. In that case, we have to develop a consistent way to measure performance. These two approaches are discussed sequentially below.

9.2.1 Quadratic performance measures

Beyond the observation of returns, assessing the portfolio performance in the eyes of a particular investor entails the knowledge of their attitude toward risk. For expected utility theory to be applicable in the mean–variance context, one has to ensure that investors agree upon the use of the variance (or, equivalently, standard deviation) of returns as an adequate measure of portfolio risk. This is automatically the case if returns are normally distributed, but this assumption is hard to justify in practice.

Alternatively, we can posit that the investor's preferences obey the quadratic utility function specified in Equation (9-8).[7] The risk-aversion coefficient that characterizes this function assigns a penalty to the square of the portfolio's excess returns.

9.2.1.1 The Quadratic score

We first consider the portfolio in isolation, as if there were no passive investment that the investor could adopt and leverage with the risk-free asset. Computing the expectation of the quadratic utility function, after a few transformations, we reach the *Quadratic score* or "Q-score" $Q_P^j \equiv Q_P(\gamma_j)$. This preference-based performance measure is the *ex post* expected utility of the returns on portfolio P as considered by investor j:

$$Q_P^j = \mathrm{E}[U_j(R_P)] = \overline{R}_P - \frac{1}{2}\gamma_j\sigma_P^2 \tag{9-9}$$

where $\overline{R}_P$ and σ_P^2 stand for the mean and variance of the portfolio returns, respectively, and γ_j represents the investor's risk-aversion coefficient.

---

[6]We prefer introducing this new name rather than using the terms "Sharpe score" or "Sharpe alpha," as called by Plantinga and de Groot (2002), in order to avoid any confusion with the Sharpe ratio.

[7]Markowitz (2014) claims that the assumption of normally distributed returns or a quadratic utility function is a sufficient, but not a necessary condition in order to apply the SPT. If investors agree upon the fact that the mean–variance efficient frontier is a satisfactory proxy for their set of efficient portfolios, one can still use all the properties of mean–variance optimization. We will depart from the SPT with other specifications of investors' preferences.

Because the Q-score is a fixed amount, $E[U_j(Q_P(\gamma_j))] = U_j\left(\overline{R}_P - \frac{1}{2}\gamma_j\sigma_P^2\right) = \overline{R}_P - \frac{1}{2}\gamma_j\sigma_P^2$, it can also be interpreted as the certainty equivalent of the portfolio. This performance measure assigns different certainty equivalent scores for the same portfolio but for different investors. Thus, unlike the Sharpe ratio, it may result in different portfolio rankings depending on the degree of risk aversion of the investor considered and may thus contradict the diagnosis produced by the Sharpe ratio itself regarding portfolio performance. Furthermore, Equation (9-9) does not feature the risk-free rate. Thus, even though it can be used as a benchmark in order to compare a portfolio's expected utility, the riskless asset does not play any particular role in this context. If one wants to establish a basis for comparison, the utility surplus of the portfolio provides the expression for the *excess Quadratic score* or "xQ-score":

$$xQ_P^j = \overline{R}_P - R_f - \frac{1}{2}\gamma_j\sigma_P^2 \tag{9-10}$$

In the familiar risk–return framework in which risk is measured through volatility, it is possible to graphically represent all the portfolios (be them accessible or not) that exhibit exactly the same expected utility for a given investor through their indifference curves. Their associated indifference curves exhibit a quadratic function form of the type:

$$\overline{R}_P = k + \frac{1}{2}\gamma_j\sigma_P^2 \tag{9-11}$$

where k is a constant representing the intercept of the curve and reflects the certainty equivalent of every portfolio that lies on the curve. The higher the value of this constant k is, the higher the expected utility. Interestingly, for a given investor, the investment curves are always parallel and cannot intersect. In order to visually compare two different portfolios, it suffices to check which one is located on the highest indifference curve.

Another interesting property of Equation (9-11) is that its level of convexity only depends on the investor's risk-aversion coefficient γ_j. Thus, the indifference curves of more risk-averse investors (with a high value of γ_j) are more convex. Graphically, this translated S into "steeper" curves than for less risk-averse investors, whose indifference curves tend to be "flatter." This is reflected in the graph shown in Figure 9-5, inspired by Figure 5-3 of Chapter 5.

Portfolios L and H display two very different risk levels. According to their Sharpe ratios, L dominates H, but, as indicated before, the risk-free rate does not intervene in the computation of the Q-scores. We consider two investors, denoted by a and d, with different risk profiles. For the more aggressive investor a with risk-aversion coefficient γ_a, the associated indifference curves are relatively flat. This investor assigns the higher Quadratic score to portfolio H: $Q_H(\gamma_a) > Q_L(\gamma_a)$. This translates into their indifference curve going through the coordinates of H lying above those that go through L. On the contrary, for the defensive investor d, the bowing of the indifference curves is much more pronounced. Their Q-score of portfolio L exceeds that of H: $Q_H(\gamma_d) < Q_L(\gamma_d)$.

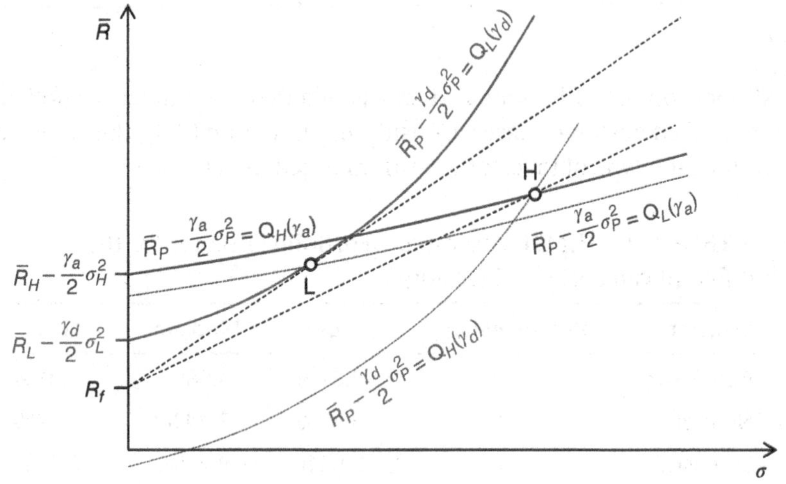

FIGURE 9-5 Quadratic scores and indifference curves for two different investors.

The Quadratic score is not only useful to appraise the performance of portfolios exhibiting different risk levels when the investor does not have the possibility to use leverage. It is also an indispensable tool in the normative portfolio choice framework. As discussed in Section 4.2.1 of Chapter 4, it is because a risk-averse investor tries to maximize their expected utility through their portfolio choice that the use of total risk is justified in this context. Nevertheless, this performance measure has a number of drawbacks and weaknesses. It requires the knowledge of the investor's risk-aversion level, which is a difficult task to estimate. More critically, it ignores (or at least neglects) the non-Gaussian character of the distribution of most asset returns and relies on a utility function that does not practically fit what we know about the investors' actual structure of preferences, as we will see later. Furthermore, if the Q-score is derived from the quadratic utility function, one has to be aware that this function involves the unrealistic (i) increasing absolute and relative risk aversion and (ii) possibility of satiation for too high rates of return.

All in all, despite its drawbacks, the Quadratic score is a useful crude estimate of portfolio performance when a simplified structure of investor risk profiles is considered (indeed, Figure 9-4 shows how closely the competing utility functions reflect investors' preferences), but it might be sufficient to account for investors' heterogeneity regarding their attitudes toward risk.

HiMeLo example (continued)

HiMeLo Wealth Management has segmented their private clientele into three categories (defensive, neutral, and aggressive) according to their levels of risk-aversion coefficients. The representative customer's risk aversion in each category is the following: $\gamma_a = 2, \gamma_n = 6$, and $\gamma_d = 10$.

(continued)

(continued)

The first question asked by management is whether the model portfolios adequately address their targeted customer bases. Considering Equation (9-9), the Quadratic scores of the portfolios for each type of investor are summarized in Table 9-3.

TABLE 9-3 HiMeLo example – Portfolio Q-scores for the different categories of investors.

Investor	Risk aversion γ_j	Low	Medium	High
Aggressive	2	3.66%	4.68%	**5.38%**
Neutral	6	3.30%	**3.44%**	2.39%
Defensive	10	**2.94%**	2.21%	−0.59%

For each row, the value reported in bold corresponds to the highest Q-score. Portfolio positioning appears to be effective, as each of them provides the highest Q-score for the corresponding targeted investor: aggressive for the High portfolio, neutral for the Medium portfolio, and defensive for the Low portfolio. The only close values are reported for the neutral investors, who might hesitate between the Low and Medium portfolios whose Q-scores are close to each other as shown in Figure 9-6.

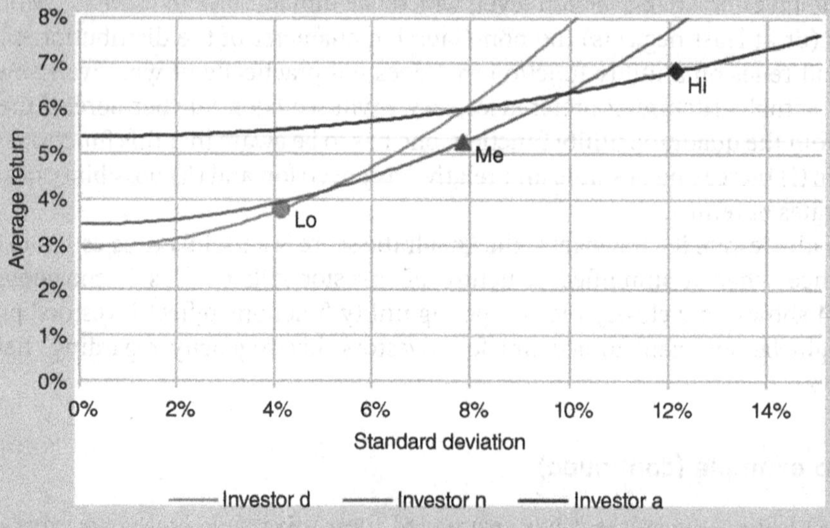

FIGURE 9-6 HiMeLo example – Selected portfolios and their associated indifference curves.

The nature of information contained in the indifference curves goes beyond the preference-adjusted performance appraisal of the three model portfolios. They also point to the volatility zones for which each investor is likely to express their preference for a leveraged portfolio according to its reward-to-volatility relation. The defensive investor would favor portfolios with a volatility that does not exceed 5%; the neutral investor would probably prefer a volatility ranging between 5 and 10%, and the aggressive investor would want a risk higher than 10%. This can represent a useful tool for the classification of allocation funds or portfolios according to their homogeneity. We come back to this issue later in the example.

9.2.1.2 The Quadratic alpha

Instead of considering the portfolio as a single investable asset, the investor may examine an otherwise optimal investment in the market portfolio M together with the risk-free asset as a credible alternative. Since this portfolio must be chosen so as to maximize their expected utility, we know from Section 4.2.1 of Chapter 4 (Equation (4-3)) that this portfolio yields a realized utility equal to $R_f + \frac{1}{2\gamma_j}\text{SR}_M^2$, where SR_M is the Sharpe ratio of the market portfolio. However, this portfolio is not directly comparable with P because they do not necessarily have the same level of volatility. In order to properly assess the added value of the actively managed portfolio over the passive one, it is necessary to compute the average return of a portfolio with the same risk as P, but that lies on the same indifference curve as the optimized passive investment. This is performed by using Equation (9-11), replacing k with $R_f + \frac{1}{2\gamma_j}\text{SR}_M^2$, which leads to what we can call the *Quadratic alpha* or "Q-alpha," denoted by $\text{Q}\alpha_P^j$:

$$\text{Q}\alpha_P^j = \overline{R}_P - R_f - \frac{1}{2}\gamma_j\sigma_P^2 - \frac{1}{2\gamma_j}\text{SR}_M^2 \tag{9-12}$$

The difference with the excess Q-score of Equation (9-10) resides in the presence of a second penalty term $\frac{1}{2\gamma_j}\text{SR}_M^2$ that further reduces portfolio performance: $\text{Q}\alpha_P^j = \text{xQ}_P^j - \frac{1}{2\gamma_j}\text{SR}_M^2$. This is a logical outcome of the fact that we impose a supplementary challenge to portfolio P: it must not only beat the riskless asset but also outperform the best possible passive investment, which is shown in Figure 9-7.

The figure illustrates the situation of an investor who has the choice between, on one hand, the actively managed portfolio P and, on the other hand, the market portfolio optimally combined with the riskless asset, with coordinates M^*. This optimal combination yields a utility surplus of $\frac{1}{2\gamma_j}\text{SR}_M^2$, represented as a vertical distance on the return axis. The distance between the return of P and the leveraged version of M^*, represented by M' on the graph, is the same as the distance between the intercepts of their two parallel indifference curves.

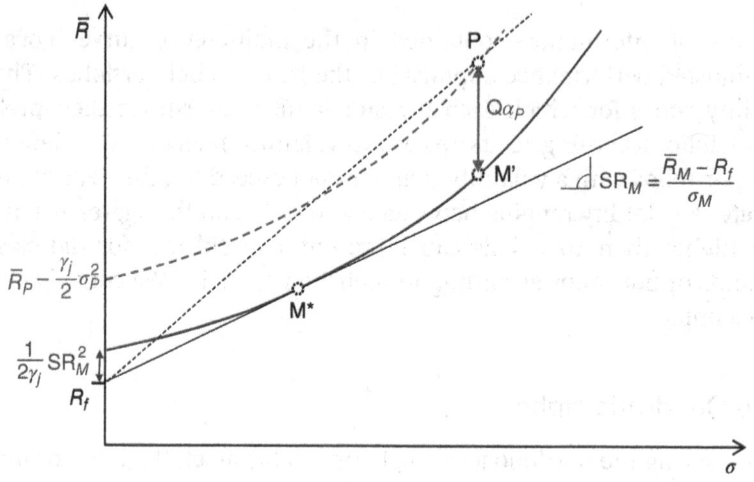

FIGURE 9-7 Graphical representation of the Quadratic alpha.

An interesting property of the Quadratic alpha is that it remains the same irrespective of whether the reference point for volatility is taken as the active portfolio (as in the figure) or the optimized passive portfolio M^*. This comes from the fact that the indifference curves are parallel, and thus the vertical distance between them is always the same whichever level of risk is chosen.

This illustration also reveals why preventing the investor from using leverage with an actively managed portfolio such as P results in a potential loss of utility for the investor. If the straight line joining the risk-free rate R_f to the coordinates of P is not exactly tangent with the indifference curve, this means that it is possible to do even better by changing the risk of the portfolio through a combination with the risk-free asset. This is the reason why the Quadratic alpha defined here is lower than the Total risk alpha introduced in Chapter 6.

Finally, it remains to be noted that the portfolio rankings obtained with the Q-score, the excess Q-score and the Q-alpha are the same for a given investor, as these performance measures differ from each other with a constant amount that does not depend on the portfolios' characteristics.

HiMeLo example (continued)

Because of its customer segmentation, HiMeLo is concerned about whether the portfolio management offering that is well positioned for the current clientele remains acceptable for investors who would have compared the actively managed funds with a standard ETF on the World stock index. The mean return and volatility of that ETF were equal to $\overline{R}_M = 9\%$ and

$\sigma_M = 20\%$ during the same period. It can be combined with an investment in the risk-free asset whose rate of return remains fixed at 1.44%.

Applying the risk-aversion coefficients of the three types of investors allows us to revise the performance measures of Table 9-3 accordingly to obtain the Quadratic alphas as shown in Table 9-4.

TABLE 9-4 HiMeLo example – Portfolio Q-alphas for different categories of investors.

Investor	Risk aversion γ_j	Market Q-score	Low	Medium	High
Aggressive	2	5.01%	−1.36%	−0.34%	**0.37%**
Neutral	6	2.63%	0.67%	**0.81%**	−0.24%
Defensive	10	2.15%	**0.79%**	0.06%	−2.75%

Fortunately, for the company, all three portfolios targeting the associated investor profiles maintain a positive performance. Economically, the figures in bold mean that the added value of the actively managed portfolios is positive, but all-in-all lower than 1%. Graphically, this can be seen in Figure 9-8 that can be matched with Figure 9-6.

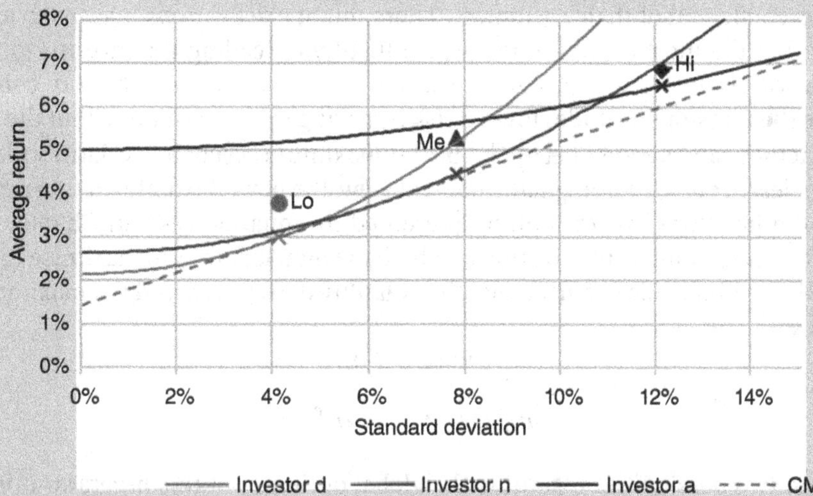

FIGURE 9-8 HiMeLo example – Selected portfolios and the indifference curves for the market portfolio.

The three symbols are at the same place as in Figure 9-6, and the indifference curves are parallel but lower. The dashed straight line represents the *ex post* Capital Market Line

(continued)

(continued)

(CML), to which the three curves are tangent. The Quadratic alpha is equal to the distance between each symbol and the corresponding cross on the indifference curve.

Note that the tangency point of the indifference curve is very close to the associated cross for the Low portfolio (investor d) and the Medium portfolio (investor n), but it appears to correspond to a much higher volatility level for the High portfolio (investor a). This can be verified by comparing the Q-alpha, which accounts for the difference in risks between the active portfolio and the optimal one on the CML, with the Total risk alpha defined (in Equation (6-65) in Chapter 6) as the distance between the portfolio return and the corresponding coordinates on the CML, i.e., $T\alpha_P = \overline{R}_P - R_f - \frac{\sigma_P}{\sigma_M}(\overline{R}_M - R_f)$. For the three portfolios, they are respectively equal to $T\alpha_{\text{Lo}} = 3.83\% - 1.44\% - \frac{4.22\%}{20\%}(9\% - 1.44\%) = 0.80\%$, $T\alpha_{\text{Me}} = 0.89\%$, and $T\alpha_{\text{Hi}} = 0.81\%$. These values are close to the Q-alphas for the Low and Medium, but not at all for the High portfolio, thereby confirming the visual impression from the graph.

9.2.2 The Target volatility alpha

In practice, very few professional wealth or asset managers attempt to explicitly compute the risk-aversion coefficient of their customers. There might exist various reasons to explain this observation, but the most obvious one is the difficulty of leading the investor to reveal this information with standard risk profiling techniques. Instead, it is much more convenient to characterize the investor's attitudes toward risk by asking them questions about the maximum volatility that they can tolerate.[8] Let $\sigma_P^{(j)\max}$ be this maximum acceptable volatility for investor j.

Nevertheless, from a very pragmatic point of view, the portfolio optimization program that maximizes the investor's expected utility presented in Equation (2-7) in Chapter 2 must be replaced with a constrained optimization in which the manager tries to maximize the expected return of the portfolio while ensuring that the volatility does not exceed the maximum acceptable volatility:

$$\max_P \mathrm{E}(R_P) \tag{9-13a}$$

$$\text{subject to}: \sigma_P \leq \sigma^{(j)\max} \tag{9-13b}$$

There are two possibilities regarding the global optimum of this program. It is either an interior solution, in which case the constraint is not binding – or it is a corner solution, in

[8]There are many ways of explaining the notion of "risk" that makes sense to an investor, such as "*how much can you afford to lose on your portfolio during the worst of ten years*?" or "*what is the maximum probability of losing money on your portfolio over one year that you can bear?*," but eventually the challenge of the portfolio manager is to translate the answer into a maximum level of the volatility of portfolio returns.

which case the constraint is binding. However, since, from an *ex ante* perspective, the expected return of the portfolio is an increasing function of its volatility, the only way to maximize it is to set $\sigma_P = \sigma^{(j)\max}$ and adopt the corner solution. This means that $\sigma^{(j)\max}$ represents the investor's desired portfolio volatility, in short $\sigma^{(j)}$, that replaces the risk-aversion coefficient in the characterization of their preferences.[9]

For this investor, the optimal passive portfolio has a return of $R^*(\sigma^{(j)}) = \frac{\sigma_P^{(j)}}{\sigma_M}\overline{R}_M + \left(1 - \frac{\sigma^{(j)}}{\sigma_M}\right)R_f$. The coordinates of this portfolio $(\sigma^{(j)}, R^*(\sigma^{(j)}))$ correspond to the tangency point of their indifference curve, whose equation is $\overline{R}_x = k + \frac{1}{2}\gamma_j\sigma_x^2$, with the CML. It entails that $\left.\frac{d\left(k+\frac{1}{2}\gamma_j\sigma_x^2\right)}{d\sigma_x}\right|_{\sigma_x=\sigma^{(j)}} = SR_M$, i.e., the Sharpe ratio of the market portfolio, which is also the slope of the CML. Solving this identity leads to the identification of the investor's risk-aversion coefficient $\gamma_j = \frac{SR_M}{\sigma^{(j)}}$ and the associated Q-score $Q_P^{(j)} = R_f + \frac{1}{2}SR_M\sigma^{(j)}$. For this investor, the required return of the actual portfolio P is equal to the one that lies on the same indifference curve, namely $R_f + \frac{1}{2}SR_M\left(\sigma^{(j)} + \frac{\sigma_P^2}{\sigma^{(j)}}\right)$. The associated performance is thus equal to the mean portfolio return minus this expression for the required return. This defines the *Target volatility alpha* or "V-alpha" of investor j, denoted by $V\alpha_P^j$:

$$V\alpha_P^j = \overline{R}_P - R_f - \frac{1}{2}SR_M\left(\sigma^{(j)} + \frac{\sigma_P^2}{\sigma^{(j)}}\right) \tag{9-14}$$

The structure of Equation (9-14) is similar to that of the xQ-score but with a different penalty for risk. This comes from the fact that the manager imposes on the investor to adopt another portfolio than their optimal one. Note that, despite its practical usefulness, the V-alpha has never, to the best of our knowledge, been proposed as an alternative preference-based performance measure in the literature. We can represent this measure graphically in Figure 9-9 that looks close to that of Figure 9-7.

The main difference with Figure 9-7 resides in the intercept of the indifference curve of the optimal passive portfolio, in which there is no need to specify the investor's risk-aversion coefficient anymore. The Target volatility alpha and the Quadratic alpha can thus be used interchangeably, depending on how the investor's attitudes toward risk are estimated.

The use of the V-alpha also has an interesting implication for the comparison of portfolios with different levels of risk and return. Naturally, their measure of performance directly gives their ordering. However, consider now that there is some uncertainty about the target level of volatility chosen by some investors, who may topple on one side or the other. From

[9]This is exactly the viewpoint adopted by Fama (1972) to characterize the investor's perspective in his performance decomposition framework, described in Chapter 13.

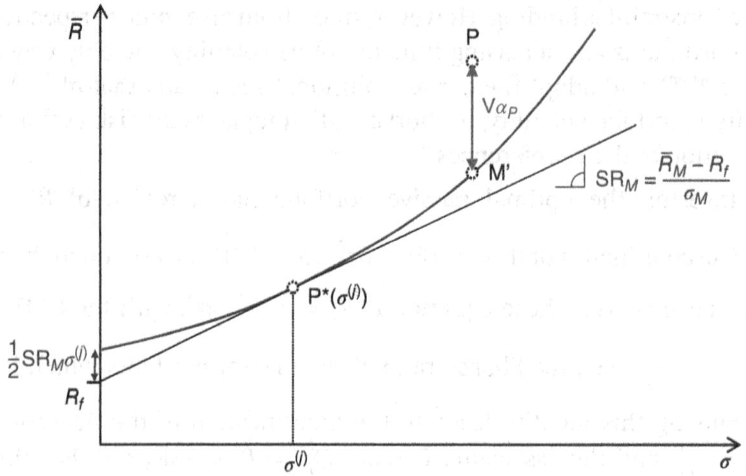

FIGURE 9-9 Graphical representation of the Target volatility alpha.

formula (9-14), the switching level of target volatility that characterizes an investor's indifference between portfolios P and Q, which we denote by $\sigma^{(J)}_{P\sim Q}$, is given by the following equation:

$$\sigma^{(J)}_{P\sim Q} = \frac{1}{2}\mathrm{SR}_M \frac{\sigma_P^2 - \sigma_P^2}{\overline{R}_P - \overline{R}_Q} \tag{9-15}$$

This expression can prove to be very useful for customer segmentation purposes, as it provides an estimation of the "gray zone" in which the investor is more likely to hesitate between two portfolios with different risks and returns.

HiMeLo example (continued)

Searching for a new clientele, the company has streamlined its investor profiling system. This time, each prospect is asked what is the maximum volatility that they can afford within they global allocation portfolio. The outcome that arises from the process is that we have "equity" investors (e) who can accept a volatility of 15%, "balanced" ones (b) with a target volatility of 9%, and "stable" investors (s) who do not want any risk higher than 3%. Using these targets in Equation (9-14) and applying the risk-aversion coefficients of the three types of investors allows us to revise the performance measures of Table 9-3 accordingly to obtain the Target volatility alphas as shown in Table 9-5.

TABLE 9-5 HiMeLo example – Portfolio V-alphas for the new categories of investors.

Investor	Target volatility $\sigma^{(J)}$	Low	Medium	High
Equity	15.00%	−0.67%	0.24%	**0.71%**
Balanced	9.00%	0.32%	**0.86%**	0.60%
Stable	3.00%	**0.71%**	−0.59%	−4.54%

Because of the very distinct levels of target risk chosen by the investors, the performance levels of the three portfolios are very different. Since we deal with target volatilities that are represented graphically in Figure 9-10 (unlike risk-aversion coefficients), we can represent in the risk–return graph the switching volatilities between the Low and Medium portfolios, on the one hand, and the Medium and High portfolios, on the other hand.

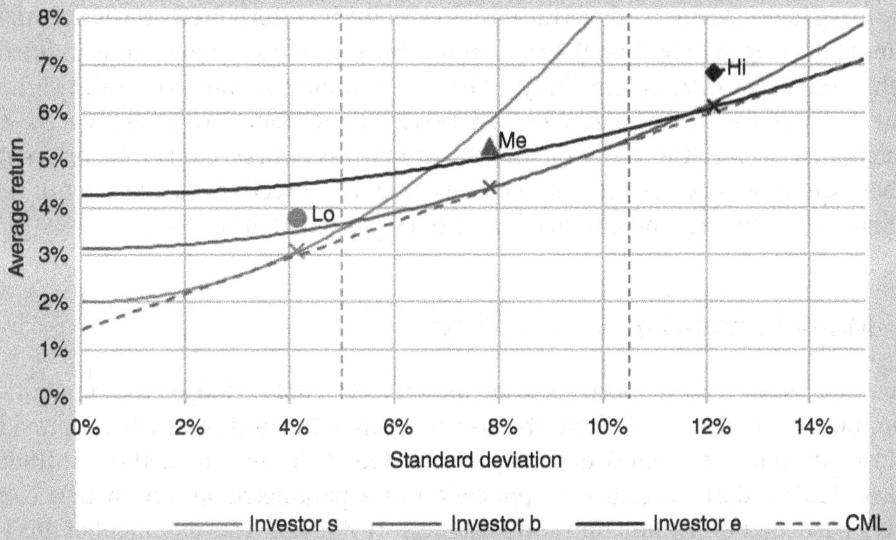

FIGURE 9-10 HiMeLo example – Selected portfolios and the indifference curves with target volatility portfolios.

The distances between the three portfolios and their counterparts using the indifference curves, which correspond to the V-alphas, are almost the highest possible ones (they are close to their Total risk alphas calculated above), indicating that the portfolio positioning is largely adequate for these investor types.

(continued)

(continued)

Using Equation (9-15), we have also computed the two switching volatility levels that are equal to $\sigma^{(j)}_{Hi\sim Me} = \frac{1}{2} \times 0.38 \frac{12.22\%^2 - 7.85\%^2}{6.87\% - 5.29\%} = 10.50\%$ and $\sigma^{(j)}_{Me\sim Lo} = \frac{1}{2} \times 0.38 \frac{7.85\%^2 - 4.22\%^2}{5.29\% - 3.83\%} = 5.68\%$. If the company wants to enhance the dichotomization of the portfolios, it should probably work on the risk of the Low portfolio that stands relatively close to the switching volatility with the Medium fund.

9.3 PERFORMANCE MEASUREMENT WITH STANDARD UTILITY FUNCTIONS

In Section 9.1, we discussed the properties of standard utility functions that belong to the HARA class. One takeaway from this analysis is the lack of realism of the quadratic utility function regarding how it accommodates the structure of the investor's preferences over risk. Thus, the material developed in Section 9.2 loses in representativeness what it gains in tractability.

In this section, we develop three ways to handle a number of interesting utility functions in the context of performance measurement. We first introduce the generalization of the expected utility computation with the use of moments (variance, skewness, etc.) of the return distribution. Then, we show how performance can be computed directly by using the full sample of data. Finally, we introduce the notion of a utility-consistent Sharpe ratio.

9.3.1 Moment-based expected utility

The Quadratic score can be derived from the straight application of the quadratic utility function, but it can also result from the use of many other utility functions provided that the returns are (close to being) normally distributed. This second method, introduced by Samuelson (1970), derives from the application of a parametric approach that consists of selecting a particular utility function and applying a Taylor series development of this function around the portfolio's expected return. This leads to the following generic equation:

$$U_j(R_P) \simeq \sum_{i=0}^{n} (i!)^{-1} U_j^{(i)}(\text{E}(R_P)) \times [R_P - \text{E}(R_P)]^i \tag{9-16}$$

where $i! \equiv i \times (i-1) \times \cdots \times 2 \times 1$ is the factorial operator, and $U_j^{(i)}(\text{E}(R_P))$ is the ith derivative of the utility function taken at value $\text{E}(R_P)$. Since there is a residual beyond order n considered to be of negligible magnitude, the equality is only approximate.

A large number of applications have been proposed starting from expression (9-16). The most generic form of expected utility performance is derived by Billio, Maillet, and Pelizzon (2022) under the following expression:

$$E[U_j(R_P)] \simeq \sum_{i=1}^{n} \pi_{i,j,P} \times m_{P,i} \tag{9-17}$$

where $m_{P,i} \equiv E[R_P - E(R_P)]^i$ is the ith moment of the distribution of the returns of portfolio P and $\pi_{i,j,P}$ is the sensitivity of investor j to this ith moment.[10] Note that $\pi_{i,j,P}$ depends on the first moment (mean), regardless of i.

The authors define the first part of expression (9-17) as the Generalized Utility-based N-moment measure (GUN), which stands as a proxy for the investor's expected utility and can be considered an adequate generalized preference-based performance measure. Normalizing $\pi_{1,j,P}$ to one (as we can rescale utility functions) and considering the *ex post* realized portfolio returns, we can express this performance measure as

$$GUN_P^j = \overline{R}_P + \sum_{i=2}^{n} \pi_{i,j,P} \times \hat{m}_{P,i} \tag{9-18}$$

where $\hat{m}_{P,i} = \hat{E}(R_P - \overline{R}_P)^i$ is the sample moment of order i of the portfolio returns.

Equation (9-18) makes intuitive sense for $n = 4$, i.e., if the investor cares about the first four moments of the distribution of returns. The interpretations of the sensitivities are also interesting. Coefficient $\pi_{1,j,P}$ (normalized to one) is called "greediness." $\pi_{2,j,P} < 0$ is the investor's "risk aversion" (see Section 9.1), $\pi_{3,j,P} > 0$ is her "prudence," and $\pi_{4,j,P} < 0$ is her "temperance."

Based on the structure of Equation (9-18), Billio et al. (2022) study how some familiar utility functions (power, exponential, and quadratic) can be translated under this parametric approach. We propose below two utility functions that are particularly interesting in the field of performance measurement.

9.3.1.1 Performance with linear-exponential utility

The utility function featuring a mixture of linear and exponential components, called in short "linex," is particularly interesting in the parametric context. Bell (1988; 1995) has shown that it ticks a number of boxes regarding desirable properties of utility functions: It displays decreasing risk aversion at all wealth levels, obeys the "one-switch rule" (i.e., it makes sure that there is only one wealth level that leads the investor to switch from less risky to riskier assets), and

[10] For this equation to make sense, the first moment is non-centered (expected return) and all the other moments are centered (variance, etc.).

approaches risk neutrality for small gambles when the investor becomes extremely rich. The linex utility function has the form

$$U_j(R_P) = R_P - b_j e^{-c_j R_P} \tag{9-19}$$

where b_j and c_j are two investor-specific parameters that characterize their preferences. They can be interpreted as follows: parameter b_j indicates the investor's risk aversion, whereas c_j measures their risk perception, i.e., the degree to which their concern about risk is due to extreme downside outcomes rather than mere volatility risk. After applying the Taylor series expansion (9-16) and using some rescaling of the parameters, the investor's expected utility, which we call here the *four-moment Quadratic score* or $4mQ_P^j$, can be written as follows:

$$4mQ_P^j = \overline{R}_P - \frac{1}{2}\gamma_j\sigma_P^2\left[1 - \frac{1}{3}(\psi_j\sigma_P)\mu_{P,3} + \frac{1}{12}(\psi_j\sigma_P)^2 e\mu_{P,4}\right] \tag{9-20}$$

where the sample skewness $\mu_{P,3}$ and excess kurtosis $e\mu_{P,4}$ are obtained according to Equations (5-13a) and (5-13b) in Chapter 5, and γ_j and ψ_j are interpreted as the investor's normalized risk aversion and risk-perception coefficients, respectively.

With Equation (9-20), the meaning of γ_j and ψ_j becomes very intuitive. The content of the parenthesis represents the investor's *variance multiplier*, which stands as the deviation of the investor's assessment of portfolio risk from the pure variance. If $\psi_j = 0$, they are a pure mean–variance investor. Then the whole expression exactly collapses to Equation (9-9) or, put simply, $4mQ_P^j = Q_P^j$. Consequently, γ_j can be seen as a pure risk-aversion coefficient. The higher the value taken by ψ_j, the greater the relative importance of the third (skewness) and fourth (kurtosis) moments in the risk assessment. This corresponds to an increasing fear of extreme risks, whose impact on skewness and kurtosis is relatively greater than on the variance. Compared with the mean–variance investor, the investor displaying a higher ψ_j will assign a utility bonus to portfolios with a positive skewness and, to a certain extent, a low or negative excess kurtosis.

There is a caveat to the straightforward interpretations of the parameters, however. The absolute value of the risk assessment (the expression between parentheses) changes with the value of ψ_j. In turn, this risk level influences the corresponding value of γ_j. Thus, for two investors with different risk perceptions but with the same level of risk aversion, the differences in their ψ_j will impact their γ_j. In order to obtain the same risk penalty (the second term of Equation (9-20)) for both investors, it is necessary to ensure that the product $\gamma_j\left[1 - \frac{1}{3}(\psi_j\sigma_P)\mu_{P,3} + \frac{1}{12}(\psi_j\sigma_P)^2 e\mu_{P,4}\right]$ is equal. We illustrate in Table 9-6 the necessary adjustment that must be applied to γ_j in order to leave a portfolio's risk penalty invariant for different levels of ψ_j (considering a value of $\sigma_P = 10\%$). We use the same four portfolio characteristics as in Table 6-17 of Chapter 6.

TABLE 9-6 Multiplier of the Gaussian risk-aversion coefficient γ_j for different risk-perception coefficients ψ_j.

Skewness $\mu_{P,3}$	Excess kurtosis $e\mu_{P,4}$	Risk perception ψ_j				
		0	1	2	5	10
0	**0**	1.00	1.00	1.00	1.00	1.00
−0.5	**0**	1.00	0.98	0.97	0.92	0.86
0	**6.9**	1.00	1.00	0.99	0.93	0.78
−0.5	**6.9**	1.00	0.98	0.96	0.87	0.69

The table shows that, in general, the worse the skewness (more negative) and the kurtosis (more positive), the bigger the adaptation that is necessary in order to assign the same expected utility of a given portfolio for two investors with different risk perceptions.

A key consideration regarding Equation (9-20) is the challenge of assessing the relevant values of γ_j and ψ_j for an investor. In general, we recommend a sequential profiling approach, as it would be difficult to estimate both parameters simultaneously. An effective method is to start with the determination of ψ_j by letting the investor choose between portfolios exhibiting the same mean return but various trade-offs between variance, on the one hand, and skewness and kurtosis, on the other hand. If an investor tends to prefer portfolios with lower variance but less favorable third and fourth moments, their risk-perception coefficient is likely to be low. Another investor who accepts a higher variance in order to reduce their exposure to extreme risks will have a higher risk-perception coefficient. Once a reasonable value of ψ_j is set, we can use the certainty equivalent approach in the traditional way (just like in the quadratic utility case) in order to assess the risk-aversion coefficient γ_j.

HiMeLo example (continued)

Based on the use of the linex function, HiMeLo Wealth Management has made a more granular segmentation of their private clientele (Figure 9-11), which now belongs to five categories according to a "cross-based profiling matrix" (we report the product $\psi_j\sigma_P$ in order to directly use the portfolio's skewness and kurtosis in the assessment of portfolio performance according to Equation (9-20)).

(continued)

(continued)

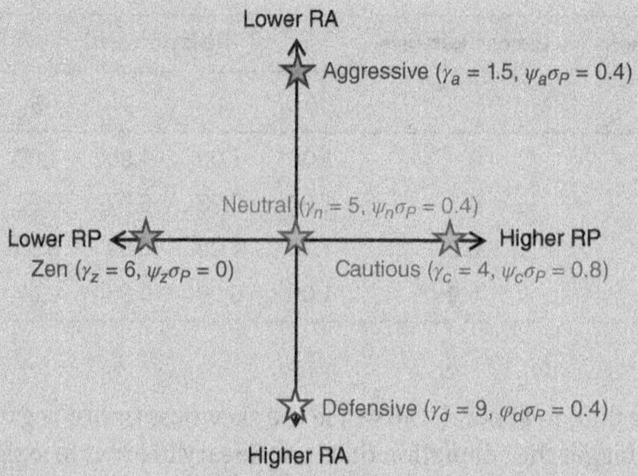

FIGURE 9-11 HiMeLo example – Segmentation in a two-dimensional profile matrix.

The two new investor profiles are the "Zen" one, which is characterized by an insensitivity to higher moments ($\psi_z\sigma_P = 0$) and the "Cautious" one, with a very high risk-perception coefficient. The other three profiles are similar to the original ones, with an adjustment in order to make them sensitive to higher moments by setting the risk-perception coefficient to 0.4 and by slightly adjusting the risk-aversion coefficient according to the increase in the variance multiplier.

In order to quantify the expected utility of the three portfolios offered by the company, we again use the data of Table 9-1, this time with the addition of the portfolios' skewness and excess kurtosis that are necessary in order to implement the formula of the four-moment Quadratic score. The results are summarized in Table 9-7.

TABLE 9-7 HiMeLo example – Portfolio four-moment Q-scores for the different categories of investors.

Investor	Risk aversion γ_j	Risk perception $\psi_j\sigma_P$	Low	Medium	High
Aggressive	1.5	0.4	3.68%	4.87%	**5.90%**
Neutral	5	0.4	3.31%	**3.88%**	3.65%
Defensive	9	0.4	**2.89%**	2.75%	1.08%
Cautious	4	0.8	3.33%	4.17%	**4.30%**
Zen	6	0	3.30%	**3.44%**	2.39%

According to their performance measures, the three portfolios still target the right categories of investors. Compared to the other two portfolios, the Low portfolio's performance deteriorates, mostly because of its negative skewness ($\mu_{Lo,3} = -1.13$), while the Medium and High portfolios have a favorable (positive) third moment of their distribution.

Because their risk-perception coefficient is nil, the Zen investor is the same as the one previously diagnosed as "Neutral" (Table 9-3), and therefore the performances are identical. The Cautious one has a strong distaste for extreme risks ($\psi_c \sigma_P = 0.8$), and therefore is likely to favor a portfolio displaying a positive asymmetry in returns. This is the case for the High portfolio ($\mu_{Hi,3} = +1.54$). Thus, whereas the investor has a moderate risk-aversion coefficient, the protective aspect of the riskiest portfolio is appealing to them. The firm should probably complete their portfolio offering with a less risky, but highly right-skewed portfolio (like a protective put) in order to further enhance their preference-adjusted performance.

9.3.1.2 Performance with flexible three-parameter utility

Instead of focusing on the traditional HARA utility functions depending on a single parameter described in Section 9.1, it is more insightful to go one step beyond the linex function analyzed here above. The flexible three-parameter (FTP) utility function proposed by Conniffe (2007) probably represents the most general formulation to date of a utility function that can exhibit all kinds of behaviors regarding absolute and relative risk aversions. The function is expressed as follows:

$$U_j(R_P) = \frac{1}{\xi_j}\left\{1 - \left[1 - \kappa_j \xi_j \left(\frac{R_P^{1-\phi_j} - 1}{1 - \phi_j}\right)\right]^{\frac{1}{\kappa_j}}\right\} \tag{9-21}$$

where ξ_j, κ_j, and ϕ_j are the three parameters that characterize the magnitude and shape of the risk-aversion measure.[11] In general, κ_j can be positive or negative, but Conniffe (2007) considers that both ξ_j and ϕ_j should be positive. From Equation (9-21), we draw the absolute risk-aversion coefficient:

$$\text{ARA}_j(R_P) = \frac{(1 - \kappa_j)\xi_j R_P^{\phi_j}}{1 - \kappa_j \xi_j \left(\frac{R_P^{1-\phi_j} - 1}{1-\phi_j}\right)} + \frac{\phi_j}{R_P} \tag{9-22}$$

[11] There are a number of parameter restrictions that are necessary for the utility function to work.

and

$$\mathrm{RRA}_j(R_P) = \mathrm{ARA}_j(R_P) \times R_P.$$

We can use this utility function as the generic HARA formulation in the parametric approach (up to the fourth moment) by creating the associated FTP Quadratic score or $3\mathrm{pQ}_P^j$:

$$3\mathrm{pQ}_P^j = U_j(\overline{R}_P) - \frac{U_j''(\overline{R}_P)}{2}\sigma_P^2 + \frac{U_j'''(\overline{R}_P)}{6}\widehat{m}_{P,3} - \frac{U_j''''(\overline{R}_P)}{24}\widehat{m}_{P,4} \tag{9-23}$$

where $U_j''(\overline{R}_P) = -\overline{R}_P^{\phi_j}\left[1 - \kappa_j \xi_j \left(\frac{\overline{R}_P^{1-\phi_j} - 1}{1-\phi_j}\right)\right]^{\frac{1}{\kappa_j}-1} \times \mathrm{ARA}_j(\overline{R}_P)$ and the other higher order derivatives also have an analytical form (too long to be reported here). In a portfolio allocation framework, Hübner and Lejeune (2022) propose to use the following ranges for the three FTP parameters: $\kappa_j \in [-2, +2]$, $\xi_j \in [0.25, 10]$, and $\phi_j \in [-0.05, +1.5]$. Some combinations result in implausible values, but most of them yield reasonable outcomes.

9.3.2 Sample-based expected utility

The formulas for the expected utility and certainty equivalent proposed in Equations (9-1) and (9-3), respectively, can prove to be extremely useful for the creation of performance measures that do not rely on any parametric specification. These expressions essentially "let the data speak" by literally applying the expected utility framework to a sample of observed returns, substituting probabilities by realized frequencies.

Beyond the fact that this procedure fully uses all information available about the investment, it has the advantage of allowing a comparison with any other type of portfolio, be it a rollover investment in a fixed-income asset at each time period, which plays the role as the riskless reference portfolio, or another actively managed portfolio with a totally different set of sample returns. These two possibilities lead to preference-based performance measures that consider another portfolio's realized return as an anchor.

9.3.2.1 Statistical certainty equivalents

Because we deal with realized portfolio returns over potentially long periods, the challenge here is to simultaneously account for the compounding effect and the presence of the fixed-income asset, which might not remain constant for the period, as an opportunity cost of the portfolio investment. For that purpose, we need to use the geometric excess return that will enter the certainty equivalent formula (9-3). It is defined as follows:

$$r_{P,t}^{g} = \frac{1 + R_{P,t}}{1 + R_{f,t}} - 1 = \frac{R_{P,t} - R_{f,t}}{1 + R_{f,t}} \tag{9-24}$$

We use this formula in order to generically define the historical preference-adjusted performance of a portfolio as the certainty equivalent of its geometric excess return, CE_P^j:

$$CE_P^j = U_j^{-1}\left(\frac{1}{T}\sum_{t=1}^{T} U_j(1 + r_{P,t}^{g})\right) - 1 \tag{9-25}$$

In principle, any utility function can lend itself to being used with this formula. Two of them, both discussed by Billio et al. (2022), are worth mentioning here as they echo discussions that will be carried out in later chapters. The first one is the power utility function presented in Equation (9-7). Considering a frequency of n observations per year ($n = 12$ for monthly, $n = 52$ for weekly), the associated *Power-based certainty equivalent* $pwCE_P^j$ is written as

$$pwCE_P^j = \left[\frac{1}{T}\sum_{t=1}^{T} (1 + r_{P,t}^{g})^{-\gamma_j}\right]^{-\frac{n}{\gamma_j}} - 1 \tag{9-26}$$

This expression serves as the basis for the Morningstar mutual fund ranking system discussed in Chapter 15, with a specific calibration of $\gamma_j = 2$ and $n = 12$. It is then called the Morningstar Risk-Adjusted Return or "MRAR" (see Morningstar, 2002).

The second utility function whose calibration with historical data makes much sense is the one proposed by Goetzmann, Ingersoll, Spiegel, and Welch (2007) in order to avoid performance manipulation issues. The *manipulation-proof certainty equivalent* $mpCE_P^j$ has the following form:[12]

$$mpCE_P^j = -\frac{n}{\gamma_j}\log\left[\frac{1}{T}\sum_{t=1}^{T} (1 + r_{P,t}^{g})^{-\gamma_j}\right] \tag{9-27}$$

This function looks very similar to Equation (9-26), as $mpCE_P^j = \log(1 + pwCE_j)$. It clearly involves a power utility function. Nevertheless, as underlined by the authors, it addresses a different motivation: Rather than attempting to characterize a "representative investor," it tries to address a set of axioms that prevent the performance measure from

[12] For the sake of consistency in notations, we use the same definition of the risk-aversion coefficient γ_j for both formulas (9-26) and (9-27). In the notation of Goetzmann et al. (2007), they use a parameter $\rho_j \equiv \gamma_j - 1$.

being manipulated, intentionally or not, by using uninformed portfolio management strategies providing the illusion of superior performance. This issue will be studied in detail in Chapter 18.

HiMeLo example (continued)

Instead of implementing the Quadratic score using the sample mean and variance of returns, the company decides to test a historical estimation of the power utility function. Using the data of Table 9-1, three investor profiles, with associated risk-aversion coefficients $\gamma_a = 2$, $\gamma_n = 5$, and $\gamma_d = 8$, are used for the computation of Equation (9-26) (the coefficients slightly differ from those used in Table 9-4 because we do not use the same utility function). The outcomes are summarized in Table 9-8.

TABLE 9-8 HiMeLo example – Portfolio power certainty equivalents for different categories of investors.

Investor	Risk aversion γ_j	Low	Medium	High
Aggressive	2	2.16%	3.06%	**3.55%**
Neutral	5	1.91%	**2.25%**	1.71%
Defensive	8	**1.64%**	1.45%	0.03%

The portfolios that target each type of investor still reach their objective: High for aggressive one, Medium for neutral, and Low for defensive. Thus, from a historical perspective, all portfolios fulfill their role and deliver the highest preference-based performance for their associated category of investors.

Compared with Table 9-3 (parametric Q-score), there is a clear improvement to be noted for the Medium and High ones. This can be explained by their favorable asymmetry of returns, reflected in their positive skewness. To verify this, we compute the certainty equivalents of all portfolios using the quadratic utility function (Equation (9-8)) with excess returns, and compare the results with the excess Quadratic score xQ (i.e., the utility surplus of the Q-score over the risk-free rate of 1.44%). The outcome of this analysis for the Neutral investor is summarized in Figure 9-12.

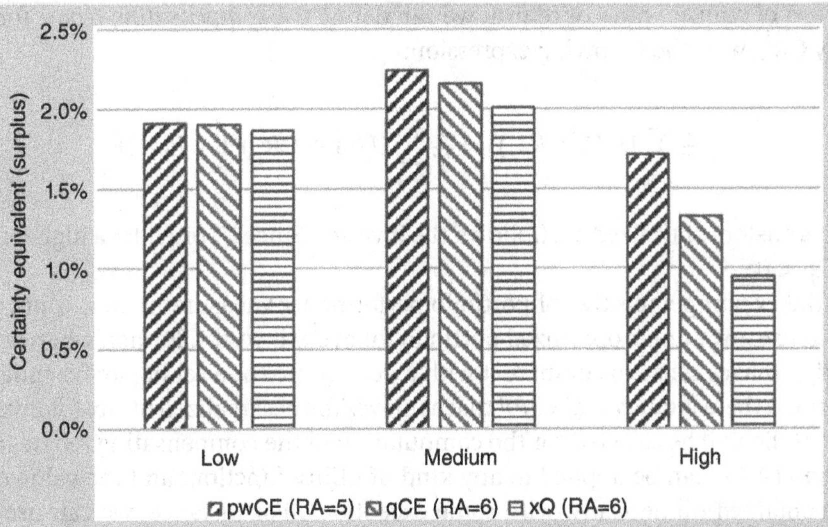

FIGURE 9-12 HiMeLo example – Utility surplus with three approaches for the Neutral investor.

The excess Q-score obtained analytically with Equation (9-10) for the Medium and High portfolios (right bars) is worse than their historical counterparts (middle bars), especially for the High one whose skewness is the most positive. With that particular portfolio, we can clearly see how the extreme returns influence the power utility function compared with the quadratic one.

9.3.2.2 The compensating rebate investment

The economic notion of compensating variation, initially proposed by Hicks (1939), was introduced in the context of optimal portfolio management by de Palma and Prigent (2009). It refers to the implied additional initial investment that an investor with a given level of risk aversion γ_j must invest in portfolio P in order to reach the same expected utility as with another portfolio P^* that has been optimally designed so as to maximize their satisfaction.[13] Similarly, we can characterize the reduction in the investment made in P^* that can make it indifferent to P. The bigger this haircut (in absolute value), the lower the portfolio quality. When adapted

[13]In a similar vein, de Palma and Prigent (2009) introduce an alternative notion of relative satisfaction as the ratio of the portfolio's expected utility to the one of the optimal portfolio. In the context of performance measurement, this notion is less useful as it yields a scalar number whose interpretation is less intuitive than the one discussed here.

to the context of realized rates of return, we can define the *compensating rebate* for investor j, denoted by CR_P^j, with the following expression:

$$\frac{1}{T}\sum_{t=1}^{T} U_j((1+R_{P,t})) = \frac{1}{T}\sum_{t=1}^{T} U_j((1+CR_P^j)(1+R_{P*,t})) \tag{9-28}$$

where P^* is a custom optimized portfolio for the investor. Since P^* provides a higher satisfaction than P, $CR_P^j < 0$.

From the *ex post* perspective of portfolio performance measurement, it is not possible to identify and use any *ex ante* optimized portfolio for every investor. Rather, when portfolio P is considered, it makes sense to compare it with a peer group (or a set of passive indexes). From this peer group, there is one member P^{*j} that achieves the best realized utility for investor j. This specific portfolio will be selected for the computation of the compensating rebate investment.

Equation (9-28) can be applied to any kind of utility function, and the value of CR_P^j will usually be obtained numerically, with some exceptions. For instance, we can use the power utility function again. If we consider that there are K competing portfolios in the peer group, then we obtain the *Power-based compensating rebate*:

$$\text{pwCR}_P^j = \left[\frac{\sum_{t=1}^{T}(1+R_{P,t})^{-\gamma_j}}{\sum_{t=1}^{T}(1+R_{P*j,t})^{-\gamma_j}}\right]^{-\frac{n}{\gamma_j}} - 1 \leq 0 \tag{9-29}$$

where $\sum_{t=1}^{T}(1+R_{P*j,t})^{-\gamma_j} = \min_{P_1,\ldots,P_K} \sum_{t=1}^{T}(1+R_{P_i,t})^{-\gamma_j}$ is the portfolio achieving the largest realized utility for investor j.

A portfolio whose realized utility is closer to the best one P^{*j} achieves a less negative performance. In a sense, the realized compensating rebate investment is a measure of "relative inefficiency." The value that is observed for each portfolio corresponds to a kind of sunk cost, expressed as a yearly rate of return, borne by the investor who has selected the wrong investment for their profile. This formulation ensures that better portfolios obtain higher (less negative) performance.

The compensating rebate approach has the advantage of producing rankings that perfectly correspond to the set of portfolios that compose the group. Unlike the certainty equivalent, there is no role played by the risk-free rate. This avoids the need for choosing and estimating this rate, a procedure that can sometimes lend itself to some arbitrary or difficult choices (see Chapter 5 for a discussion of this issue).

HiMeLo example (continued)

We apply the same set of investor profiles as in the preceding case for the power utility function, namely three profiles, with $\gamma_a = 2$, $\gamma_n = 5$, and $\gamma_d = 8$. The outcomes are summarized in Table 9-9.

TABLE 9-9 HiMeLo example – Portfolio power compensating rebates for different categories of investors.

Investor	Risk aversion γ_j	Low	Medium	High
Aggressive	2	−1.34%	−0.47%	**0.00%**
Neutral	5	−0.33%	**0.00%**	−0.52%
Defensive	8	**0.00%**	−0.19%	−1.59%

This time, the computation of each portfolio's performance is made relative to the most satisfactory one for each investor profile. The best performer is thus assigned a rebate of 0%. The risk-free rate plays no particular role.

9.3.3 The utility-consistent Sharpe ratio

We know from Chapter 5 that, because of the importance of the skewness and kurtosis of portfolio returns, the Sharpe ratio may not adequately reflect risk-adjusted performance. The first section of Chapter 6 proposes a number of adjustments of the measure in order to account for the non-Gaussian character of returns. Most of these adjustments do not explicitly relate to investors' preferences, and therefore lend themselves to an arbitrary calibration. Nevertheless, it is remarkable to note that, under the mean–variance framework, the normative portfolio optimization problem of the rational utility-maximizing investor, which corresponds to Equation (4-1) of Chapter 4, leads to a simple connection between the expected utility (which, as a reminder, is also a certainty equivalent in the case of the Q-score) and the Sharpe ratio. Starting from the solution of the portfolio optimization problem of Equation (4-3), we write the *utility-consistent Sharpe ratio* uSR_P^{*j} as

$$\text{uSR}_P^{*j} = \sqrt{2\gamma_j(U_j^{\max} - R_f)} \tag{9-30}$$

where $U_j^{\max} \equiv \sup \text{E}(U_j(R_P))$ is the expected utility obtained from the best possible allocation between the risk-free asset and portfolio P for an investor whose risk-aversion coefficient is γ_j.

This is the idea developed by Hodges (1998) who further simplifies the problem by considering the negative exponential utility function of Equation (9-6). This leads to a version of Equation (9-30) that is independent of the risk-aversion coefficient γ_j. This logic is pursued by Pézier (2012) in the context of several calibrations of HARA utility functions of Equation (9-5) and non-Gaussian distributions of returns. He obtains different numerical approximations of the utility-consistent Sharpe ratio $\text{uSR}_P^{\left(\frac{1}{\eta}\right)}$ as a function of the ratio $\frac{1}{\eta}$ (appearing in Equation (9-5)) as

$$\text{uSR}_P^{(0)} = \text{SR}_P \times \left(1 + \frac{\mu_{P,3}}{6}\text{SR}_P - \frac{e\mu_{P,4}}{24}\text{SR}_P^2\right) \text{ for } \frac{1}{\eta} = 0 \text{ (negative exponential)} \tag{9-31a}$$

$$\text{uSR}_P^{(0.5)} = \text{SR}_P \times \left(1 + \frac{\mu_{P,3}}{4}\text{SR}_P - \frac{e\mu_{P,4}}{8}\text{SR}_P^2\right) \text{ for } \frac{1}{\eta} = 0.5 \text{ (hyperbolic)} \tag{9-31b}$$

$$\text{uSR}_P^{(1)} = \text{SR}_P \times \left(1 + \frac{\mu_{P,3}}{3}\text{SR}_P - \frac{(2e\mu_{P,4} + 1)}{8}\text{SR}_P^2\right) \text{ for } \frac{1}{\eta} = 1 \text{(logarithmic)} \tag{9-31c}$$

$$\text{uSR}_P^{(2)} = \text{SR}_P \times \left(1 + \frac{\mu_{P,3}}{2}\text{SR}_P - \frac{(5e\mu_{P,4} + 6)}{8}\text{SR}_P^2\right) \text{ for } \frac{1}{\eta} = 2 \text{ (square root)} \tag{9-31d}$$

Note that the formulation of Equation (9-31a) corresponds to the adjusted Sharpe ratio defined in Equation (6-18) in Chapter 6.

Because of the normative character of this performance measure, it is always independent from the investor's risk aversion. It only depends on the shape of the utility function considered (represented by the value of η). In practice, this performance measure (and its various avatars) does not provide the actual certainty equivalent of a portfolio but reflects the utility extracted from its best possible combination with the risk-free investment for a certain type of investor. Instead of directly providing the certainty equivalent of this optimal portfolio, the formula is inverted in order to deliver the corresponding variant of the Sharpe ratio.[14]

HiMeLo example (continued)

The company needs to check whether investors with different types of utility functions would still rank the three portfolios in the same order under the assumption that they would have the opportunity to leverage them optimally. For that usage, the various utility-consistent Sharpe ratios are computed with the associated skewness and kurtosis coefficients. The results are summarized in Table 9-10.

[14] Zakamouline and Koekebakker (2009) go one step further by specifying a specific probability distribution for portfolio returns, namely the Normal Inverse Gaussian (NIG). They derive an analytical formula for the utility-consistent Sharpe ratio, called "Adjusted for Skewness and Kurtosis Sharpe ratio" (ASKSR) that depends on the four parameters of the NIG distribution.

TABLE 9-10 HiMeLo example – Utility-consistent Sharpe ratios.

Utility specification	Low	Medium	High
Original SR	*0.57*	*0.49*	*0.44*
Negative exponential	0.49	0.51	0.48
Hyperbolic	0.42	0.50	0.46
Logarithmic	0.32	0.46	0.42
Square root	−0.02	0.30	0.25

Because of its negative skewness, the Low portfolio's utility-consistent Sharpe ratio deteriorates as the value of η decreases. This contrasts with the performance of the Medium and High portfolios, which initially increases (positive skewness effect) and then decreases (high kurtosis effect). These results also emphasize the limitations of these approximations, as a positive skewness associated with a large kurtosis is unequivocally favorable and should enhance performance for many types of risk-averse investors.

Key Takeaways and Equations

- In general, the performance of a portfolio adjusted for the rational investor's preferences is obtained by computing its realized expected utility or its associated *certainty equivalent*, defined as

$$\mathrm{CE}(R) = U^{-1}\left(\frac{1}{T}\sum_{t=1}^{T} U(R_t)\right) \tag{9-3}$$

- The attitude toward risk of an investor is generally assessed through the Arrow (1964)–Pratt (1964) *coefficients of absolute and relative risk aversion*:

$$\mathrm{ARA}(R) = -\frac{U''(R)}{U'(R)} \tag{9-4a}$$

$$\mathrm{RRA}(R) = -\frac{R \times U''(R)}{U'(R)} \tag{9-4b}$$

(continued)

(continued)

- The major types of *HARA* utility functions used in this context are as follows:
  - The negative exponential utility function:

$$U(R) = -e^{-\gamma R} \tag{9-6}$$

  - The power utility function:

$$U(R) = \frac{(1+R)^{1-\gamma}}{1-\gamma} \tag{9-7}$$

  whose special case is the logarithmic utility function $U(R) = \log(1+R)$ for $\gamma = 1$.
  - The quadratic utility function:

$$U(R) = R - \frac{1}{2}\gamma(R - \mathrm{E}(R))^2 \tag{9-8}$$

  The power utility function is the most realistic one as it involves CRRA and DARA.
- Defining performance as an expected utility, the *Quadratic score*, or Q-score, is the measure that is compatible with the SPT framework, using the sample mean and variance of returns:

$$Q_P^j = \mathrm{E}[U_j(R_P)] = \overline{R}_P - \frac{1}{2}\gamma_j\sigma_P^2 \tag{9-9}$$

- When the investor takes into account the optimal passive investment as an alternative to the actively managed portfolio, there are two ways to measure its performance as an additional expected utility:
  - If the investor's profile is characterized by their level of risk aversion γ_j, performance is measured with the *Quadratic alpha* or Q-alpha:

$$\mathrm{Q}\alpha_P^j = \overline{R}_P - R_f - \frac{1}{2}\gamma_j\sigma_P^2 - \frac{1}{2\gamma_j}\mathrm{SR}_M^2 \tag{9-12}$$

  - If the investor's profile is characterized by their target level of portfolio volatility $\sigma^{(j)}$, performance is measured with the *Target volatility alpha* or V-alpha:

$$\mathrm{V}\alpha_P^j = \overline{R}_P - R_f - \frac{1}{2}\mathrm{SR}_M\left(\sigma^{(j)} + \frac{\sigma_P^2}{\sigma^{(j)}}\right) \tag{9-14}$$

- The Q-score is a special case of the most generic form of expected utility performance that expresses expected utility as a weighted sum of the moments of the return distribution. It is defined as

$$\mathrm{E}[U_j(R_P)] \simeq \sum_{i=1}^{N} \pi_{i,j,P} \times m_{P,i} \tag{9-17}$$

- This approach leads to two particular cases:
  - The *four-moment Quadratic score* corresponding to the linear-exponential utility:

$$4\mathrm{mQ}_P^j = \overline{R}_P - \frac{1}{2}\gamma_j \sigma_P^2 \left[1 - \frac{1}{3}(\psi_j \sigma_P)\mu_{P,3} + \frac{1}{12}(\psi_j \sigma_P)^2 e\mu_{P,4}\right] \tag{9-20}$$

  - The *FTP Quadratic score* corresponding to the three-parameter utility function:

$$3\mathrm{pQ}_P^j = U_j(\overline{R}_P) - \frac{U_j''(\overline{R}_P)}{2}\sigma_P^2 + \frac{U_j'''(\overline{R}_P)}{6}\widehat{m}_{P,3} - \frac{U_j''''(\overline{R}_P)}{24}\widehat{m}_{P,4} \tag{9-23}$$

- It is also possible to measure performance directly from the sample of returns with a *certainty equivalent excess return* of the form

$$\mathrm{CE}_P^j = U_j^{-1}\left(\frac{1}{T}\sum_{t=1}^{T} U_j(1 + r_{P,t}^g)\right) - 1 \tag{9-25}$$

  The most popular of such approaches is the use of the power utility function:

$$\mathrm{pwCE}_P^j = \left[\frac{1}{T}\sum_{t=1}^{T}(1 + r_{P,t}^g)^{-\gamma_j}\right]^{-\frac{n}{\gamma_j}} - 1 \tag{9-26}$$

  The particular case in which $\gamma_j = 2$ corresponds to the MRAR.
- When the portfolio is matched with a peer group, it is possible to measure performance as a *compensating rebate*, interpreted as a kind of sunk cost, expressed as a yearly rate of return, borne by the investor who has selected the wrong investment for their profile:

$$\frac{1}{T}\sum_{t=1}^{T} U_j((1 + R_{P,t})) = \frac{1}{T}\sum_{t=1}^{T} U_j((1 + \mathrm{CR}_P^j)(1 + R_{P*,t})) \tag{9-28}$$

(continued)

(continued)

With the power utility function, portfolio performance is written as

$$\mathrm{pwCR}_P^j = \left[\frac{\sum_{t=1}^{T}(1+R_{P,t})^{-\gamma_j}}{\sum_{t=1}^{T}(1+R_{P*j,t})^{-\gamma_j}}\right]^{-\frac{n}{\gamma_j}} - 1 \leq 0 \quad (9\text{-}29)$$

- From a normative point of view, it is possible to draw a utility-consistent version of the Sharpe ratio that, under certain assumptions about the shape of the HARA utility function, looks like adjusted versions of the Sharpe ratio encountered in Chapter 6:

$$\mathrm{uSR}_P^{(0)} = \mathrm{SR}_P \times \left(1 + \frac{\mu_{P,3}}{6}\mathrm{SR}_P - \frac{e\mu_{P,4}}{24}\mathrm{SR}_P^2\right) \text{ for } \frac{1}{\eta} = 0 \text{ (negative exponential)} \quad (9\text{-}31a)$$

$$\mathrm{uSR}_P^{(0.5)} = \mathrm{SR}_P \times \left(1 + \frac{\mu_{P,3}}{4}\mathrm{SR}_P - \frac{e\mu_{P,4}}{8}\mathrm{SR}_P^2\right) \text{ for } \frac{1}{\eta} = 0.5 \text{ (hyperbolic)} \quad (9\text{-}31b)$$

$$\mathrm{uSR}_P^{(1)} = \mathrm{SR}_P \times \left(1 + \frac{\mu_{P,3}}{3}\mathrm{SR}_P - \frac{(2e\mu_{P,4}+1)}{8}\mathrm{SR}_P^2\right) \text{ for } \frac{1}{\eta} = 1 \text{ (logarithmic)} \quad (9\text{-}31c)$$

$$\mathrm{uSR}_P^{(2)} = \mathrm{SR}_P \times \left(1 + \frac{\mu_{P,3}}{2}\mathrm{SR}_P - \frac{(5e\mu_{P,4}+6)}{8}\mathrm{SR}_P^2\right) \text{ for } \frac{1}{\eta} = 2 \text{ (square root)} \quad (9\text{-}31d)$$

REFERENCES

Arrow, K. (1964), The role of securities in the optimal allocation of risk-bearing. *Review of Economic Studies*, Vol. 31, pp. 91–96.

Bell, D. E. (1988), One-switch utility functions and a measure of risk. *Management Science*, Vol. 34, pp. 1416–1424.

Bell, D. E. (1995), Risk, return, and utility. *Management Science*, Vol. 41, pp. 23–30.

Billio, M., Maillet, B., and L. Pelizzon (2022), A meta-measure of performance related to both investors and investments characteristics. *Annals of Operations Research*, Vol. 313, pp. 1405–1447.

Conniffe, D. (2007), The flexible three parameter utility function. *Annals of Economics and Finance*, Vol. 8, pp. 57–63.

de Palma, A., and J.-L. Prigent (2009), Standardized versus customized portfolio: A compensating variation approach. *Annals of Operations Research*, Vol. 165, pp. 161–185.

Fama, E. (1972), Components of investment performance. *The Journal of Finance*, Vol. 17, pp. 551–567.

Hicks, J. R. (1939), *Value and Capital: An Inquiry into Some Fundamental Principles of Economic Theory*. Clarendon Press.

Hodges, S. (1998), A generalization of the Sharpe ratio and its applications to valuation bounds and risk measures. Working Paper, Financial Options Research Centre, University of Warwick.

Hübner, G., and T. Lejeune (2022), Portfolio choice and mental accounts: A comparison with traditional approaches. *Finance*, Vol. 43, pp. 95–121.

Goetzmann, W., Ingersoll, J., Spiegel, M., and I. Welch (2007), Portfolio performance manipulation and manipulation-proof performance measures. *The Review of Financial Studies*, Vol. 20, pp. 1503–1546.

Kallberg, J. G., and W. T. Ziemba (1983), Comparison of alternative utility functions in portfolio selection problems. *Management Science*, Vol. 29, pp. 1257–1276.

Markowitz, H. (2014), Mean–variance approximations to expected utility. *European Journal of Operational Research*, Vol. 234, pp. 346–355.

Morningstar (2002), The new Morningstar rating™ methodology. *Report #22/04/02*, Morningstar Research Centre.

Pézier, J. (2012), Rationalisation of investment preference criteria. *Journal of Investment Strategies*, Vol. 1 (3), pp. 3–65.

Plantinga, A., and S. de Groot, (2002), Risk-adjusted performance measures and implied risk attitudes. *Journal of Performance Measurement*, Vol. 6 (2), pp. 9–20.

Pratt, J. W. (1964), Risk aversion in the small and in the large. *Econometrica*, Vol. 32, pp. 122–136.

Samuelson, P. (1970), The fundamental approximation theorem of portfolio analysis in terms of means, variances and higher moments. *Review of Economic Studies*, Vol. 37, pp. 537–542.

von Neumann, J., and O. Morgenstern (1953), *Theory of Games and Economic Behavior*. Princeton University Press.

Zakamouline, V., and S. Koekebakker (2009), Portfolio performance evaluation with generalized Sharpe ratios: Beyond the mean and variance. *Journal of Banking & Finance*, Vol. 33, pp. 1242–1254.

CHAPTER 10

Preference-based Performance for the Behavioral Investor

INTRODUCTION

Moving away from rational expected utility theory, the behavioral finance approach is also rich in insights regarding preference-based performance measurement. In that context, *behavioral utility* hinges on the presence of a reservation rate that separates gains from losses and the existence of loss aversion in the investor's mindset. In this chapter, we show how performance measures have been adapted to this framework. In particular, the famous *Prospect Theory* (PT), which belongs to this family, has also led to some insightful performance measures. Referring back to Chapter 9, which is dedicated to performance measurement assuming that the investor behaves rationally, the importance of adjustments that must be brought in order to accommodate behavioral biases can be fairly light, as is the *Semi-quadratic score*, also known as the Fouse index.

The greater the complexity in the investor's behavior is accounted for, the more sophisticated the performance measure becomes. This leads to developing measures, such as the *Prospect Theory score* or, in the case of the characterization of optimal portfolios, the Prospect Theory Sharpe ratio, also known as the *Farinelli–Tibiletti ratio*. Some popular performance measures derive from it, like the *Omega*, but we show that it is important to understand the meaning of their calibration.

Besides theoretically well-justified ways to assess portfolio performance in the context of behavioral finance, we have also listed in this chapter a number of "*gains-over-losses*" measures. The reader will find in this list some well-known measures, such as the Rachev ratio, the Batting averages, the Capture ratios, or the Percentage gain ratios but also less popular ones with potentially interesting implications.

Finally, we investigate the field of mental accounts and its implications for goal-based investing (GBI). This topic implies that performance is assessed through the probability of reaching the investor's objective. The classical measure in this context is the *Stutzer convergence index*. Furthermore, we show how to appraise portfolio performance in the more general situation of the presence of tolerance levels for losses and gain/loss asymmetry. We accordingly define a measure that we believe to be very insightful, namely the *Global Goal-based performance*, that can be parametrized in various ways. This particular setup is not yet largely discussed in the literature, but we believe that it is worth studying it given its practical relevance.

Compared with classical performance measures or even those that correspond to the profile of a rational risk-averse investor, some of the formulas reported in this chapter may seem relatively complicated. This is not a voluntary attempt to create black boxes, rather it is the correct and rigorous way to respond to one of the major insights brought by behavioral finance in the context of the investor's decision-making behavior. Individuals are genuinely complex, they differ from each other in many dimensions, and this translates into many parameters that are necessary to define.

The HiMeLo example – part II

We again use the HiMeLo Wealth Management discretionary portfolio management mandates. The dataset is the same as in Table 9-1 of Chapter 9, which is reproduced as Table 10-1.

TABLE 10-1 HiMeLo example – Monthly rates of return and summary statistics (same as Table 9-1).

Month	Low	Medium	High
Jan	0.48%	−3.28%	0.74%
Feb	2.08%	5.94%	9.98%
Mar	−0.73%	−1.33%	−2.58%
Apr	−0.46%	−0.03%	−1.11%
May	0.35%	0.33%	0.30%
Jun	1.36%	0.59%	0.87%
Jul	0.27%	0.68%	−0.29%
Aug	0.97%	1.42%	1.99%
Sep	1.47%	1.45%	1.06%
Oct	0.36%	0.12%	0.00%
Nov	−2.62%	−1.99%	−5.07%
Dec	0.30%	1.38%	0.99%
Mean return	3.83%	5.29%	6.87%
Standard deviation	4.22%	7.85%	12.22%
Skewness	−1.13	0.92	1.54
Excess kurtosis	2.34	2.88	5.09

The company is aware that it might be necessary to account for a more sophisticated approach for the risk profiling of investors than merely trying to capture their risk-aversion coefficient or volatility budget. The new challenge, as discussed throughout the chapter, is to verify to what extent the current portfolio mix can satisfactorily address the reality of customer behavior with regard to their investment decisions.

10.1 THE STRUCTURE OF THE BEHAVIORAL INVESTOR'S PREFERENCES

Investors do not always behave rationally. Their decisions are often influenced by some psychological or sociological traits that lead them to depart from what would be expected in standard expected utility theory. This is also the case for their portfolio choices. If one wants to design performance measures that reflect the actual investors' preferences, these biases have to be understood and accounted for. Thus, the field of behavioral finance extends utility theory in different ways and has led to many associated developments in performance measurement. They are examined in detail in this section.

10.1.1 Reference point and loss aversion

If one still wants to work within the expected utility framework, how does the investor's psychological traits affect the translation of their preferences? A first answer is given by Markowitz (1959) himself. He suggests that, since investors are probably more concerned about downside risk than upside potential, it is more appropriate to use the notion of "semivariance" than the mere variance of returns when returns are not normally distributed. Semivariance is just the square of downside volatility defined in Section 6.2.3 of Chapter 6 and is, among others, the risk ingredient of the Sortino ratio (Chapter 6, Equation (6-29)). Starting from this point of view, Fishburn (1977) proposes to represent the investor's preferences by means of a utility function that is split into two parts: it behaves linearly (and thus entails risk neutrality) on the upside and is concave (power utility function) on the downside.

Even though Fishburn's (1977) specification is unlikely to fit most investors' attitudes toward gains and losses, it paves the way to what constitutes the dual core of the behavioral approach to expected utility: (i) the existence of a reservation rate $\underline{R}$ that separates the region of perceived gains from the region of perceived losses and (ii) the identification of two distinct segments of utility functions, called $U^+(R)$ and $U^-(R)$, that are increasing in R, but whose shapes differ in the regions of gains and losses. Thus, in general, we can represent the structure of the preferences of the "behavioral investor" with the following generic equation:

$$U_{\underline{R}}(R) = \begin{cases} U^+(R) \text{ if } R \geq \underline{R} \\ U^-(R) \text{ if } R \leq \underline{R} \end{cases} \tag{10-1}$$

where $U^+(\underline{R}) = U^-(\underline{R})$, i.e., the function is continuous at $\underline{R}$. As already discussed in Chapter 6 (in the context of the Roy ratio), the reservation rate $\underline{R}$, which is investor specific, influences

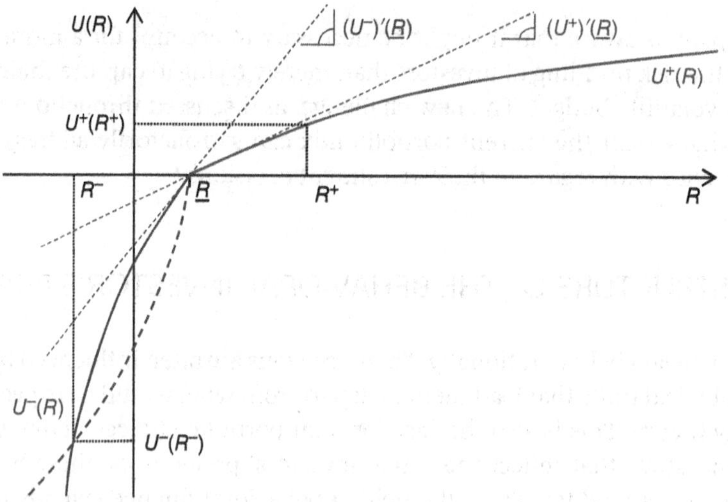

FIGURE 10-1 Behavioral type of utility function.

portfolio choice. Everything else being equal, a higher reservation rate makes it more likely to end up in the region of losses. Thus, the investor who sets the bar high exposes themselves to being more often disappointed. In order to mitigate this feeling, they are more likely to opt for a riskier allocation, delivering a higher expected return, and therefore raising the probability of experiencing a gain relative to the reservation rate.

The generic structure of the behavioral utility function can be represented by the graph shown in Figure 10-1.

The reservation rate $\underline{R}$ is the rate of return that marks the border between gains and losses for the investor. It is thus specific to each individual. This threshold return is represented as positive on the graph, but it can be null or even negative.[1] At this particular point, the utility function is still continuous but not differentiable. We observe a kink, which corresponds to the fact that the structure of the investor preferences when they perceive to make a gain (to the right of $\underline{R}$) is structurally different from the one when they perceive to make a loss (to the right of $\underline{R}$). The existence of this kink is the key feature that distinguishes the behavioral from the standard investor. Note that, even though the shape of the upper segment of the utility function is supposed to be concave, nothing prevents the investor from being risk seeking in the region of losses. This is represented by the dashed convex line on the left side of the graph.

The slope of the utility function on the downside, represented as $U^-(R)$, appears to be steeper than that on the upside $U^+(R)$. Thus, the disappointment of a given loss (for instance, $R^- = \underline{R} - \Delta R$ on the graph) is stronger than the feeling of satisfaction felt for a corresponding similar gain (e.g., $R^+ = \underline{R} + \Delta R$ on the graph). This phenomenon leads to the notion of loss

[1]Some specific examples of the values that $\underline{R}$ can take are presented in Section 6.2.1 of Chapter 6.

aversion, which appears when the ratio of the derivatives of $U^-(R)$ and $U^+(R)$, denoted by $(U^-)'(R)$ and $(U^+)'(R)$, respectively, is greater than one at $\underline{R}$: $\text{LA}(\underline{R}) = \frac{\lim_{R \nearrow \underline{R}} (U^-)'(\underline{R})}{\lim_{R \searrow \underline{R}} (U^+)'(\underline{R})} > 1$. This can be clearly verified by the difference in slopes of the tangent lines (thin dashed lines) on the graph. This ratio $\text{LA}(\underline{R})$ is defined by Köbberling and Wakker (2005) as the investor loss-aversion index. As previously mentioned, even though the graph presents a downside utility function exhibiting risk aversion ($(U^-)''(R) < 0$), it is also possible that the investor becomes risk loving in the region of losses, as shown below.

Setting the reservation rate $\underline{R}$ for the investor, we can define their absolute loss-aversion coefficient for any level of return $R > \underline{R}$ in the following way:

$$\text{ALA}_{\underline{R}}(R) = \frac{(U^-)'(2\underline{R} - R)}{(U^+)'(R)} \tag{10-2}$$

which is nothing other than a generalization of Kahnemann and Tversky's (1979) definition of loss aversion for any functional forms of utility functions $U^-(R)$ and $U^+(R)$ and the level of the reservation rate $\underline{R}$.[2] For instance, setting $\underline{R} = 2\%$, the investor's absolute loss-aversion coefficient at a return of $R = 10\%$ is equal to $\text{ALA}_{2\%}(10\%) = \frac{(U^-)'(-6\%)}{(U^+)'(+10\%)}$. Coming back to Figure 10-1, the investor's loss-aversion coefficient at R^+ is the ratio of the slopes of the tangency line of U^- taken at R^- and the one of the tangency line of U^+ taken at R^+. Note that, for the special case $\underline{R} = 0$, we simply obtain $\text{ALA}_{0\%}(R) = \frac{(U^-)'(-R)}{(U^+)'(R)}$. The same formula holds if the utility function is defined in terms of excess returns over the reservation rate instead of total returns.

Considering the simplest type of utility function considered in Chapter 9, namely the quadratic version, the behavioral version compatible with Equation (10-1) would be the piecewise-quadratic utility function of the form

$$U_{\underline{R},\lambda,\gamma}(R) = \begin{cases} R - \underline{R} - \frac{1}{2}\gamma^+(R - \underline{R})^2 \text{ if } R > \underline{R} \\ -\lambda\left(\underline{R} - R - \frac{1}{2}\gamma^-(\underline{R} - R)^2\right) \text{ if } R < \underline{R} \end{cases} \tag{10-3}$$

where γ^+ is the coefficient of risk aversion in the region of gains, γ^- is the coefficient of risk aversion in the region of losses, and λ is the loss-aversion coefficient.

10.1.2 The Prospect Theory framework

In their Nobel prize-winning contribution, Kahneman and Tversky (1979) question the following three major tenets of expected utility theory: (i) the application of expectation

[2]If $R < \underline{R}$, the formula becomes $= -\frac{(U^-)'R}{(U^+)'(2\underline{R}-R)}$ without any change in the interpretation of the coefficient.

(Equation (9-1) of Chapter 9) using objective probabilities, (ii) the symmetric treatment of gains and losses compared to any specific reference point, and (iii) the concavity of the utility function that is implied by risk aversion. Using mostly controlled experiments, they show how these three axioms are often violated in practice because of several behavioral effects.

The authors develop their "Prospect Theory" (and the variant "Cumulative Prospect Theory" (CPT) later on) by starting with the behavioral utility framework of Figure 10-1. Regarding the three axioms of expected utility theory, they suggest the replacement of the objective probabilities of outcomes that underlie Equation (9-1) in Chapter 9, and in particular the formula $E(U(R)) = \sum_{i=1}^{N} \Pr_i U(R_i)$, by an alternative specification that takes the following generic form (adapted to our framework of portfolio returns):

$$V(R) = \sum_{i=1}^{N} \pi(\Pr_i) U_{\underline{R}}(R_i) \tag{10-4}$$

where $V(R)$ is the investor's value function, $\pi(\Pr_i)$ is a subjective probability weighting function or "decision weight" that overweighs events that are close to impossibility ($\pi(\Pr_i) > \Pr_i$ for small $\Pr_i$) and underweighs the other events ($\pi(\Pr_i) > \Pr_i$ for medium or high $\Pr_i$),[3] and $U_{\underline{R}}(R)$ is the investor's utility function defined as a function of the reservation rate $\underline{R}$, which plays the role of a pivotal point between gains and losses. Under the PT, this utility function is concave in the area of gains and convex (risk loving) in the area or losses, i.e., Equation (10-1) takes the following form:

$$U_{\underline{R}}(R) = \begin{cases} U^{+}(R) \text{ with } (U^{+})''(R) < 0 \text{ if } R > \underline{R} \\ U^{-}(R) \text{ with } (U^{-})''(R) > 0 \text{ if } R < \underline{R} \\ U^{+}(\underline{R}) = U^{-}(\underline{R}) \text{ with } (U^{+})'(\underline{R}) < (U^{-})'(\underline{R}) \end{cases} \tag{10-5}$$

In order to use the PT framework in an analytically tractable format, it has become standard to adopt Tversky and Kahneman's (1992) proposed parametrization of the value function (leaving aside the issue of the weighting function) through the following dual power utility function:

$$U_{\underline{R},\lambda,\gamma}(R) = \begin{cases} (R - \underline{R})^{\gamma^{+}} \text{ if } R > \underline{R} \\ -\lambda(\underline{R} - R)^{\gamma^{-}} \text{ if } R < \underline{R} \end{cases} \tag{10-6}$$

where $0 < \gamma^{+} < 1$ is the coefficient of risk aversion in the region of gains (with constant RRA), $0 < \gamma^{-} < 1$ is the coefficient of risk lovingness in the region of losses, and λ is the loss-aversion coefficient.[4] In the special case of $\gamma^{+} = \gamma^{-}$, the utility functions are symmetric, and we have

[3]The CPT of Tversky and Kahneman (1992) replaces the weighting function of probabilities with the one of cumulative probabilities, thereby making the theory compatible with stochastic dominance criteria.

[4]For simplicity, we adopt the notation that has become conventional in the behavioral finance context instead of the standard formula for the power utility function used in Chapter 9.

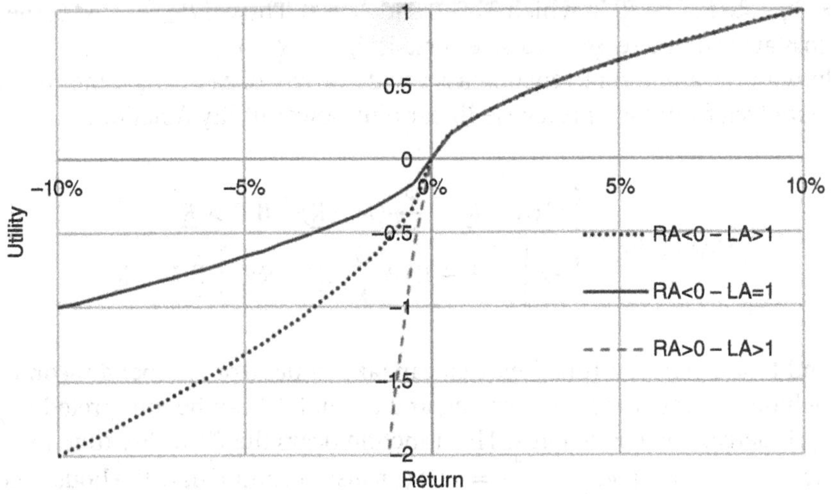

FIGURE 10-2 Shapes of the dual power utility function in Prospect Theory.

a constant absolute loss aversion: $ALA_{\lambda}(R) = \lambda$. The various situations that can be modeled according to the dual power utility function of Equation (10-6) are represented in Figure 10-2.

For the three specifications represented on the graph, we have chosen the same value of $\gamma^{+} = 0.6$ (and rescaled the utility function so that $U(10\%) = 1$) and set $\underline{R} = 0\%$. On the negative returns side, the investor can be risk averse (RA > 0), which is the case if $\gamma^{-} > 1$ (it is equal to 1.4 on the cases represented on the graph), or they can be risk loving (RA < 0), which is the case if $\gamma^{-} < 1$ (equal to 0.6 on the cases represented on the graph). When the investor is loss averse (LA > 1), the negative part of their utility function decreases faster. The case where $\gamma^{-} = \gamma^{+}$ and $\lambda = 2$ (continuous line) reveals a perfectly symmetric "S-shape" of the utility function. In the Prospect Theory, the typical utility function corresponds to the dotted line (RA < 0 and LA > 1).

In their experimental study, Tversky and Kahneman (1992) use $\lambda = 2.25$ for a representative investor, but there is a wide range of plausible values provided that $\lambda > 1$. Note that, because of the minus sign for the utility function in the region of losses, a value of γ^{-} lower than 1 entails that the function is convex and the investor is risk seeking. If one wants to represent a risk-averse investor, then it corresponds to $\gamma^{-} > 1$.

A very useful extension of the PT framework is proposed by Barberis, Huang, and Santos (2001). They bring in the notion of the "house-money effect," according to which an investor's loss aversion varies over time according to whether they have recently recorded gains or losses. This dynamic version of the Prospect Theory leads to the following specification:

$$U_{\underline{R},\lambda,\gamma}(R_t) = \begin{cases} (R_t - \underline{R})^{\gamma^{+}} \text{ if } R_t > \underline{R} \\ -\lambda_t(\underline{R} - R_t)^{\gamma^{-}} \text{ if } R_t < \underline{R} \end{cases} \tag{10-7}$$

where $\lambda_t = \lambda_0 - \lambda_1(R_{t-1} - \underline{R})$ in which $\lambda_0 > 0$ and $\lambda_1 > 0$. Thus, if $R_{t-1} - \underline{R} < 0$, the level of the investor's loss aversion increases and vice versa if $R_{t-1} - \underline{R} > 0$.

Finally, with the ambition to encompass a wide variety of cases, Zakamouline (2014) proposes a generalized form for a piecewise-linear plus power utility function:

$$U_{\underline{R},\lambda,\psi,\gamma}(R) = \begin{cases} 1^+(R-\underline{R}) + \dfrac{\psi^+}{\gamma^+}(R-\underline{R})^{\gamma^+} & \text{if } R > \underline{R} \\ -\lambda\left[1^-(\underline{R}-R) + \dfrac{\psi^-}{\gamma^-}(\underline{R}-R)^{\gamma^-}\right] & \text{if } R < \underline{R} \end{cases} \tag{10-8}$$

where 1^+ and 1^- are indicator functions that can take values 0 or 1, depending on whether one wants to include a linear component or not, and ψ^+ and ψ^- can be interpreted as upside and downside risk-perception coefficients. This function bears the PT utility function as a special case in which $1^+ = 1^- = 0$ and $\frac{\psi^+}{\gamma^+} = \frac{\psi^-}{\gamma^-} = 1$. It can also accommodate the house-money effect.

10.2 PERFORMANCE MEASUREMENT WITH BEHAVIORAL UTILITY

10.2.1 Behavioral performance scores

Besides the particular functional form of a behavioral utility function that features two segments, the estimation of the investor's expected utility and certainty equivalents obey similar rules to those governing the utility of a "fully rational" standard investor depicted in Chapter 9.

Taking this simplification into account, the generic form of the behavioral utility function of Equation (10-1) leads to a utility score of a given portfolio P that takes the form

$$\mathrm{E}[U_j(R_P)] = \frac{1}{T}\sum_{t=1}^{T}[1_{\{R_P \geq \underline{R}_j\}}U_j^+(R_P) + 1_{\{R_P < \underline{R}_j\}}U_j^-(R_P)] \tag{10-9}$$

where $1_{\{R_P \geq \underline{R}_j\}}$ is a binary variable that takes a value of 1 if $R_P \geq \underline{R}_j$ and 0 otherwise. Whatever the functional forms adopted for $U_j^+(R_P)$ and $U_j^-(R_P)$, Equation (10-9) can always be implemented using the sample returns, leading to a performance measure that reflects the investor's perceived expected utility of the portfolio during the sample period. Nevertheless, there are some useful analytical simplifications.[5]

[5] In all applications that follow, it is possible to replace the investor-specific reservation rate $\underline{R}_j$ with the return of a benchmark portfolio $R_{B,t}$ that is independent from any particular investor. In that case, the interpretation of the performance measure is closer to the one of the Information ratio than to the original Sharpe ratio.

10.2.1.1 The behavioral-quadratic score

In the case of the piecewise-quadratic utility function of Equation (10-3), Zakamouline and Koekebakker (2009) provide the expression for the associated portfolio performance, which we call the *behavioral-Quadratic score* or, in short, the "bQ-score" bQ_P^j:

$$bQ_P^j = \overline{R}_P - (\lambda_j - 1)d\overline{R}_P(\underline{R}_j) - \frac{1}{2}(\lambda_j\gamma_j^- \times d\sigma_P^2(\underline{R}_j) + \gamma_j^+ \times u\sigma_P^2(\underline{R}_j)) \quad (10\text{-}10)$$

where $d\overline{R}_P(\underline{R}_j) = \frac{1}{T}\sum_{t=1}^{T}\max(\underline{R}_j - R_{P,t}, 0)$, $d\sigma_P^2(\underline{R}_j) = \frac{1}{T}\sum_{t=1}^{T}(\max(\underline{R}_j - R_{P,t}, 0))^2$, and $u\sigma_P^2(\underline{R}_j) = \frac{1}{T}\sum_{t=1}^{T}(\max(R_{P,t} - \underline{R}_j, 0))^2$ are the downside mean, the downside variance, and the upside variance of the portfolio returns relative to the reservation rate $\underline{R}_j$, respectively.[6]

The Q-score presented in Chapter 9 represents a special case of the bQ-score in which $\underline{R}_j = \overline{R}_P$, $\lambda_j = 1$ and $\gamma_j^+ = \gamma_j^- = \gamma_j$. Furthermore, setting $\lambda_j = 1$ and $\gamma_j^+ = 0$, the performance measure corresponds to the mean–semivariance utility score suggested by Markowitz (1959). This particular specification has become popular under the name of the "Fouse index" as proposed by Sortino and Price (1994) but for consistency we call it the *Semi-Quadratic score* sQ_P^j:

$$sQ_P^j = \overline{R}_P - \frac{1}{2}\gamma_j d\sigma_P^2(\underline{R}_j) \quad (10\text{-}11)$$

Unlike the performance measures developed in the context of rational expected utility maximization, the bQ-score uses the partial moments of the distribution of returns. Using a reservation rate $\underline{R}$ as a pivotal point, the lower partial and upper partial moments of order k are respectively defined as[7]

$$\text{LPM}_{k,P}(\underline{R}) = \text{E}[(\underline{R} - R_{P,t})^k | R_{P,t} \leq \underline{R}] \quad (10\text{-}12\text{a})$$

$$\text{UPM}_{k,P}(\underline{R}) = \text{E}[(R_{P,t} - \underline{R})^k | R_{P,t} > \underline{R}] \quad (10\text{-}12\text{b})$$

and their sample estimators are, respectively,

$$dm_{k,P}(\underline{R}) = \sqrt[k]{\frac{1}{T}\sum_{t=1}^{T}(\max(\underline{R} - R_{P,t}, 0))^k} \quad (10\text{-}13\text{a})$$

$$um_{k,P}(\underline{R}) = \sqrt[k]{\frac{1}{T}\sum_{t=1}^{T}(\max(R_{P,t} - \underline{R}, 0))^k} \quad (10\text{-}13\text{b})$$

[6]Unlike the sample estimators of the moments (variance, skewness etc.), it is not necessary to divide the sum by $T - 1$ to obtain an unbiased estimate because we use a constant reservation rate instead of the sample mean.
[7]Note that formula (10-12a) is the same as Equation (6-25) used to generically define downside risk in Chapter 6.

HiMeLo example (continued)

Instead of using a segmentation based on risk aversion, the company wishes to consider investors' heterogeneity on the basis of their loss-aversion level, corresponding to coefficient λ in the behavioral framework. The company defines the "cold-blooded" investor c, the "median" investor m, and the "emotional" investor e corresponding to a low, average, and high loss-aversion coefficient, respectively. For each investor, the reservation rate is set to $\underline{R}_j = 0$.

In order to test this possibility, the piecewise-quadratic utility function is adopted, and the bQ-score of each portfolio is computed according to a single risk-aversion coefficient for all investors, amounting to $\gamma_j^+ = \gamma_j^- = 2$ for all j.

The three levels of loss aversion considered are $\lambda_c = 1.1$, $\lambda_m = 1.3$, and $\lambda_e = 1.5$. Applying Equation (10-10) for the bQ-score of each portfolio, we obtain Table 10-2.

TABLE 10-2 HiMeLo example – Behavioral quadratic scores for different categories of investors.

Investor	Loss aversion λ_j	Low	Medium	High
Cold-blooded	1.1	3.27%	4.02%	**4.52%**
Median	1.3	2.49%	**2.66%**	2.64%
Emotional	1.5	**1.72%**	1.30%	0.77%

The Medium portfolio does not easily dominate the other two for the Median investor: this result contrasts with the corresponding one in Table 9-3 of Chapter 9 for a simple but counterintuitive reason: Because of its positive skewness, this portfolio provides a lower incentive to take risks in the loss zone, which is something that risk-loving investors dislike. Note also that the utility scores obtained with the behavioral version of the quadratic utility function are much lower than the original Q-scores of Table 9-3.

10.2.1.2 The Prospect Theory score

The dual power utility function proposed by Kahneman and Tversky (1979) in the context of the Prospect Theory lends itself very well to the definition of a behavioral utility score. In particular, from an *a posteriori* perspective, the use of observed rates of return (whose frequencies of observation are identical and equal to $\frac{1}{T}$) makes the application of a subjective weighting function largely irrelevant. The application of Equation (10-6) with the sample estimators of the partial moments leads to the *PT score*:

$$\mathrm{PT}^j_P = um_{\gamma_j^+,P}(\underline{R}_j) - \lambda_j dm_{\gamma_j^-,P}(\underline{R}_j) \tag{10-14}$$

Within the framework of expected utility maximization, Melnikoff (1998) proposes focusing on the loss-aversion coefficient, considered the most important feature of the behavioral finance framework, and getting rid of the difficulty of estimating the risk-aversion parameters by setting them at $\gamma_j^+ = \gamma_j^- = 1$. For the same reason, the reservation rate is set equal to the risk-free rate. In that case, Equation (10-14) simplifies further as the *lambda-PT score*:

$$\lambda\mathrm{PT}^j_P = \overline{R}_P - (\lambda_j - 1)d\overline{R}_P(R_f) \tag{10-15}$$

Finally, the score corresponding to the piecewise-linear plus power utility function is written as

$$\mathrm{ZPT}^j_P = 1_j^+\ u\overline{R}_P(\underline{R}_j) + \frac{\psi_j^+}{\gamma_j^+} um_{\gamma_j^+,P}(\underline{R}_j) - \lambda_j\left(1_j^-\ d\overline{R}_P(\underline{R}_j) + \frac{\psi_j^-}{\gamma_j^-} dm_{\gamma_j^-,P}(\underline{R}_j)\right) \tag{10-16}$$

This generalized performance score entails the calibration of seven investor-specific parameters. Even though this looks like a very sophisticated process, it can be performed sequentially.

HiMeLo example (continued)

If one attempts to make the same portfolio positioning exercise as before with the dual power utility function of the original Prospect Theory framework, setting $\gamma^+ = \gamma^- = 0.6$ as the calibration proposed by the authors, it is necessary to lower the potential values of λ in order to obtain the adequate discrimination of portfolios (Table 10-3).

TABLE 10-3 HiMeLo example – Prospect Theory scores for different categories of investors.

Investor	Loss aversion λ_j	Low	Medium	High
Cold-blooded	1	4.33%	4.68%	**4.81%**
Median	1.2	4.06%	**4.15%**	4.07%
Emotional	1.4	**3.79%**	3.61%	3.32%

(*continued*)

(continued)

Another interesting approach to discriminate investors is to fix a constant value of λ for all investors and to focus on something that is much more convenient to assess, namely their specific reservation rate $\underline{R}_j$. For the three selected portfolios, if one sets $\lambda = 1.12$ and $\gamma^+ = \gamma^- = 0.6$, it is instructive to review the evolution of their PT-scores as a function of the reservation rate $\underline{R}_j$, which is represented in Figure 10-3.

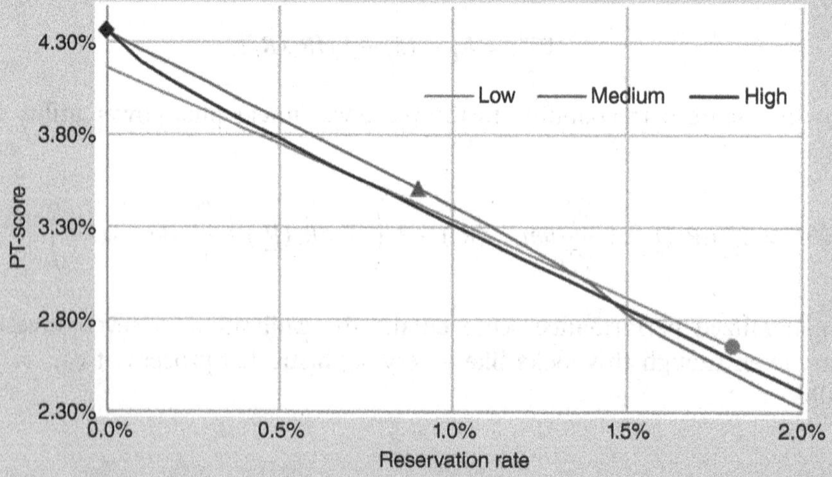

FIGURE 10-3 HiMeLo example – PT-scores of the three portfolios as a function of the reservation rate.

The three lines plot the PT-score of the corresponding portfolios as a function of the reservation rate. Contrary to what could be expected from the interpretation of $\underline{R}$, the relative standing of the portfolios with lower risk increases as the reservation rate increases. If one sets $\underline{R}_j = 0\%$, the High portfolio dominates (diamond symbol on the graph). For intermediate levels, the Medium portfolio dominates (as for $\underline{R}_j = 0.8\%$ corresponding to the triangle). For high reservation rates, the Low portfolio outperforms (like for $\underline{R}_j = 1.8\%$ corresponding to the circle). Again, this phenomenon is due to the assumption that the investor becomes risk seeking in the region of losses.

The HiMeLo example above suggests that the behavioral finance framework has to be used with great caution in order to assess portfolio performance as the reversal of investors' preferences in the region of losses may lead to very counterintuitive results. In particular, assuming that investors might want to gamble when they incur losses (typically not too large) can be understandable from an *ex ante* perspective, i.e., when they make their investment decisions. When the situation is considered *a posteriori*, it is much harder to justify this type of assumption. Observing realized losses, the investor might regret their risk-seeking behavior and revise the structure of their preferences in order to assess portfolio performance. This is the reason why, in the next section, some ratios that have been proposed in this context implicitly assume that the investor is risk averse in the region of gains *and* losses.

10.2.2 Normative behavioral performance ratios

A drawback of the behavioral approach to the measurement of expected utility is the inflation of the number of investor-specific parameters. From the single risk-aversion coefficient used in the original Q-score, one has to assess four parameters (reservation rate, risk aversion for gains and for losses, and loss aversion) for the behavioral version of the Q-score presented in Equation (10-10). This large increase in complexity explains why, in practice, behavioral ratios – which are more parsimonious in parameters – are preferred over behavioral scores.

10.2.2.1 The behavioral Sharpe ratio

Recall that the Sharpe ratio and its associated utility-consistent version of Section 9.3.3 of Chapter 9 associate the performance of a given portfolio with its capacity to maximize the expected utility of an investor within an optimal allocation framework (i.e., by holding the portfolio in combination with the risk-free asset). In order to derive those kinds of performance measures, it is necessary to know the *structure* of the investor's preferences over risk, but not their *individual parameter value.*

In the behavioral context, this distinction is revealed to be a precious asset. Zakamouline and Koekebakker (2009) apply the same approach as the one underlying the derivation of the utility-consistent Sharpe ratio, but with the piecewise-quadratic utility function of Equation (10-7). They obtain an expression that could be interpreted as a *Behavioral Sharpe ratio* bSR_P^j:

$$\text{bSR}_P^j = \frac{\overline{R}_P - \underline{R}_j - (\lambda_j - 1)d\overline{R}_P(\underline{R}_j)}{\sqrt{\lambda_j \theta_j d\sigma_P^2(\underline{R}_j) + u\sigma_P^2(\underline{R}_j)}} \tag{10-17}$$

where $\theta_j = \frac{\gamma_j^-}{\gamma_j^+}$ is the ratio of the investor's downside to upside risk-aversion coefficients.

As such, there is still limited parsimony compared to the behavioral Q-score: there is only one parameter less to be estimated. However, the saving can become more substantial when either γ_j^+ or γ_j^- is set equal to zero, corresponding to risk neutrality for gains or for losses, respectively. Then, the authors show that the performance measure can be simplified as

$$\text{bSR}_P^{j-} = \frac{\overline{R}_P - \underline{R}_j - (\lambda_j - 1)d\overline{R}_P(\underline{R}_j)}{d\sigma_P(\underline{R}_j)} \text{ if } \gamma_j^+ = 0 \tag{10-18a}$$

$$\mathrm{bSR}_P^{j+} = \frac{\overline{R}_P - \underline{R}_j - (\lambda_j - 1)d\overline{R}_P(\underline{R}_j)}{u\sigma_P(\underline{R}_j)} \text{ if } \gamma_j^- = 0 \tag{10-18b}$$

where $d\sigma_P(\underline{R}_j) \equiv dm_{2,P}(\underline{R}_j) = \sqrt{\frac{1}{T}\sum_{t=1}^{T}(\max(\underline{R}_j - R_{P,t}, 0))^2}$ and $u\sigma_P(\underline{R}_j) \equiv um_{2,P}(\underline{R}_j) = \sqrt{\frac{1}{T}\sum_{t=1}^{T}(\max(R_{P,t} - \underline{R}_j, 0))^2}$ are the downside and upside volatility of the returns, respectively.

Thus, if either of the risk-aversion coefficients is set to 0, it is not necessary to estimate the other one. Only the reservation rate and the loss-aversion coefficient need to be known. Note that, if returns are assumed to be i.i.d., the yearly version of each of the ratios is, as in the case of the Sharpe ratio, equal to the periodic ratio multiplied by the square root of time.

Out of this set of equations, it is relatively straightforward to recognize three famous special cases by gradually restricting the investor-specific parameter values:

- If $\lambda_j = 1$, $\gamma_j^+ = \gamma_j^- > 0$, and $\underline{R}_j = R_f$, i.e., only one parameter reflects the investor's attitudes toward risk, Equation (10-17) collapses to the Sharpe ratio.
- If $\lambda_j = 1$ and $\gamma_j^+ = \gamma_j^- > 0$, Equation (10-17) collapses to the Roy ratio as represented in Equation (6-19) of Chapter 6.
- If $\lambda_j = 1$ and $\gamma_j^+ = 0$, Equation (10-18a) collapses to the Sortino ratio as represented in Equation (6-29) of Chapter 6.

Remarkably, restricting the values of the behavioral parameters led to the justification of performance measures that were originally introduced as largely heuristic ratios and that were relatively disconnected from the behavioral finance framework. It also means that what is the most important distinctive feature of the behavioral utility framework compared to the rational one is the presence of a loss-aversion coefficient λ_j that is larger than 1.

HiMeLo example (continued)

As in the previous application of the bQ-score, the company adopts a calibration $\gamma_j^+ = \gamma_j^- = 2$ for all j, leading to a single value of $\theta_j = 1$, and focuses on the two sensible behavioral parameters, namely the loss-aversion level λ that can vary from 1 to 1.5, and the reservation rate that can vary from 0 to 2.5%. Applying formula (10-17) to the various specifications leads to Table 10-4.

TABLE 10-4 HiMeLo example – Behavioral Sharpe ratios for different behavioral parameters.

Reservation rate $\underline{R}_j$	Loss aversion λ_j	Low	Medium	High
0%	1	**0.92**	0.69	0.58
	1.25	**0.65**	0.46	0.38
	1.5	**0.42**	0.24	0.19
1.25%	1	**0.63**	0.53	0.48
	1.25	**0.36**	0.29	0.26
	1.5	**0.11**	0.06	0.07
2.5%	1	0.33	0.37	**0.37**
	1.25	0.05	0.11	**0.15**
	1.5	−0.19	−0.12	**−0.05**

As could be expected from the results of Table 10-4, the Medium portfolio does not easily match behavioral profiles. It does not dominate the other two portfolios for any of the specifications.

The table also shows that the behavioral Sharpe ratio does not lend itself to comparisons across behavioral parameter values. Modifying either the reservation rate or the loss-aversion coefficient radically changes the average level of the bSR for all portfolios. In the table, only horizontal comparisons make sense. This issue applies to any performance measure built on investor-specific parameters.

10.2.2.2 The Prospect Theory Sharpe ratio

The simplification of the measurement of performance can also be substantial in the context of the Prospect Theory. Under the traditional specification of the dual power utility function of Equation (10-6), the outcome of the optimization exercise leads to a *Prospect Theory Sharpe ratio* PTSR_P^{j*}, a performance measure initially proposed by Farinelli and Tibiletti (2008), which is usually called the *Farinelli–Tibiletti ratio* F-T_P^j:

$$\text{F-T}_P^j \equiv \text{PTSR}_P^{j*} = \frac{um_{\gamma_j^+,P}(\underline{R}_j)}{dm_{\gamma_j^-,P}(\underline{R}_j)} \equiv \frac{\sqrt[\alpha_j]{\frac{1}{T}\sum_{t=1}^{T}(\max(R_{P,t}-\underline{R}_j,0))^{\alpha_j}}}{\sqrt[\beta_j]{\frac{1}{T}\sum_{t=1}^{T}(\max(\underline{R}_j-R_{P,t},0))^{\beta_j}}} \tag{10-19}$$

where $\alpha_j \equiv \gamma_j^+$ is the risk-aversion coefficient in the area of gains, and $\beta_j \equiv \gamma_j^-$ is the risk-aversion coefficient in the area of losses. The formulation on the right-hand side of Equation (10-19) corresponds to the traditional presentation of the F-T ratio, but we can immediately see that it corresponds to a ratio of partial moments.

In the spirit of Kahneman and Tversky's (1979) Prospect Theory, one expects to observe $0 < \alpha_j \leq 1$ (risk aversion in the region of gains) and $0 < \beta_j \leq 1$ (risk-seeking behavior in the area of losses). Nevertheless, as we will see in the next section, many heuristic performance measures that derive from the F-T ratio do not respect these conditions.

The striking feature of this (simple) ratio is the removal of the loss-aversion coefficient λ_j thanks to the simple structure of the dual power utility function. Essentially, this is the same phenomenon as the one that leads the transition from the Q-score (which features the investor's risk aversion) to the Sharpe ratio (which is independent from the risk aversion). However, when the house-money effect of Barberis et al. (2001) is taken into account, Gemmill, Hwang, and Salmon (2006) show that the lambda remains in the equation. The dynamic version of the F-T ratio becomes

$$\text{dF-T}_P^j = \frac{um_{\gamma_j^+,P}(\underline{R}_j)}{\widetilde{dm}_{\gamma_j^-,P}(\underline{R}_j)} = \frac{\sqrt[\alpha_j]{\frac{1}{T}\sum_{t=1}^{T}(\max(R_{P,t} - \underline{R}_j, 0))^{\alpha_j}}}{\sqrt[\beta_j]{\frac{1}{T}\sum_{t=1}^{T}\frac{\lambda_{jt}}{\lambda_j}(\max(\underline{R}_j - R_{P,t}, 0))^{\beta_j}}} \tag{10-20}$$

where $\lambda_{jt} = \lambda_{j0} - \lambda_{j1}(R_{P,t-1} - \underline{R}_j)$ is the time-varying loss-aversion coefficient.[8] In practice, λ_{j0} should be close to the loss-aversion level λ_j estimated in the PT framework, and λ_{j1} would realistically be such that only a very positive lagged return would lead the time-varying loss aversion to approach the neutral value of 1. For instance, $\lambda_{j1} \approx \frac{(\lambda_{j0}-1)}{2\sigma_P}$ might be a realistic value.

Taking the general case of the piecewise-linear plus power utility function of Zakamouline (2014) represented in Equation (10-8), there is no tractable (analytical) possibility to obtain a performance ratio unless one imposes the condition that $\gamma_j^+ = \gamma_j^- \equiv \gamma_j$, i.e., the power functions are identical on the upside and the downside. In that case, using the same approach as before, the author shows that the generic performance measure obtained under this framework can be expressed in a very similar fashion as the behavioral Sharpe ratio of Equation (10-17). The *z-Sharpe ratio* zSR_P^j is written as

$$\text{zSR}_P^j = \frac{\overline{R}_P - \underline{R}_j - (\lambda_j - 1)d\overline{R}_P(\underline{R}_j)}{\sqrt[\gamma_j]{\lambda_j \zeta_j dm_{\gamma_j,P}(\underline{R}_j) + um_{\gamma_j,P}(\underline{R}_j)}} \tag{10-21}$$

[8] Gemmill et al. (2006) consider this performance measure in the context of a benchmarked portfolio, which means that they develop a version of the Information ratio. This enables them to extract λ_{jt} from the root expression in the denominator. We stick here to a version of their measure that is conceptually closer to the Farinelli–Tibiletti ratio.

where $\zeta_j = \frac{\psi_j^-}{\psi_j^+}$ is the ratio of the investor's downside to upside risk-perception coefficients of the power function, which in this case play the role of upside and downside risk-aversion indicators, respectively. Because it entails that the risk-aversion parameters are identical in the areas of gains and losses, the zSR_p^j cannot nest the F-T ratio as a special case. Nevertheless, several well-known heuristic performance ratios discussed below can be viewed as special cases of this performance measure.

HiMeLo example (continued)

The Farinelli–Tibiletti ratio only requires three investor-specific inputs, whose estimations are considered realistic by management: the reservation rate $\underline{R}_j$, the risk aversion in the area of gains α_j, and the one in the area of losses β_j. It is decided that 12 different sets of parameters are tested. For each combination, the portfolio achieving the best F-T ratio is normalized at 100% and the other two portfolios are matched on a relative basis. The results are summarized in Table 10-5.

TABLE 10-5 HiMeLo example – Relative levels of the F-T ratios for different parameter combinations.

Res. rate	R.A. losses	R.A. gains		
		$\alpha_j = 0.6$	$\alpha_j = 0.9$	$\alpha_j = 1.2$
$\underline{R}_j = 0\%$	$\beta_j = 1.5$	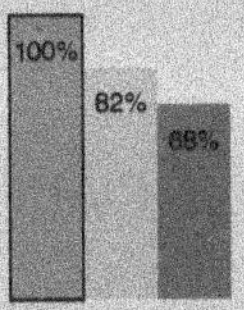	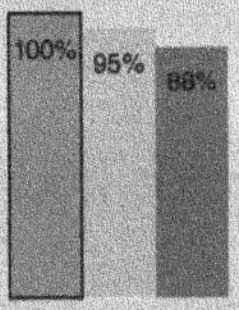	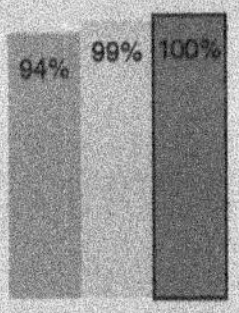
	$\beta_j = 3.0$	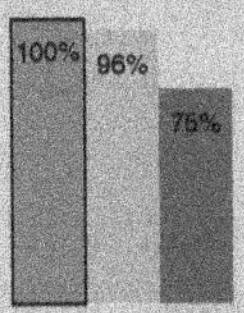	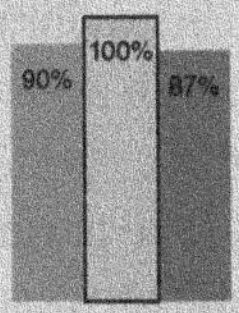	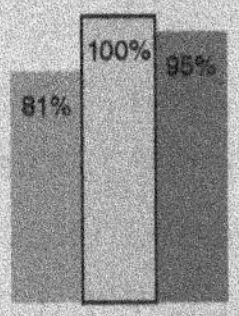
$\underline{R}_j = 3\%$	$\beta_j = 1.5$	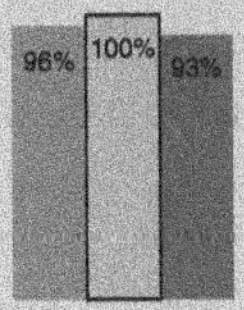	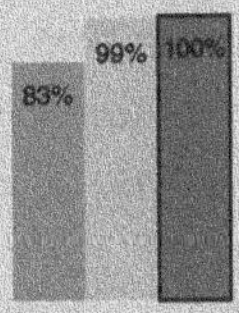	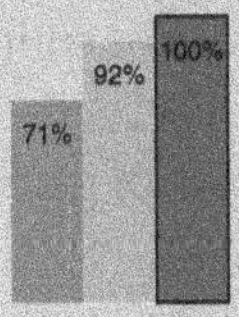
	$\beta_j = 3.0$	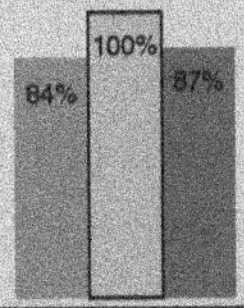	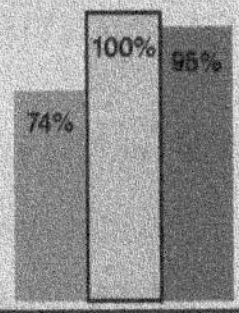	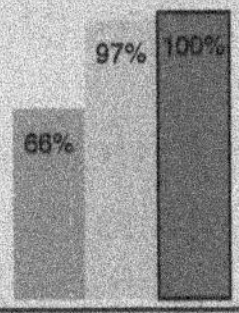

(continued)

(continued)

For each set of parameters, the best performing fund's histogram is framed in bold. Several statements can be made regarding the portfolio offering:

- There is no really dominant dimension that allows discrimination between investors alone.
- When the reservation rate is low, the best portfolio tends to have low risk;
- When risk aversion in gains is high (=high alpha), the best portfolio tends to have low risk.
- When risk aversion in losses is high (=high beta), the best portfolio tends to have low risk.
- Nevertheless, there is an exception: for a low reservation rate and average risk aversion in gains, an increase in risk aversion in losses leads to the choice of a riskier portfolio (from the Low to the Medium one).

This latter finding shows that, in the presence of non-Gaussian returns, the application of the Farinelli–Tibiletti ratio could lead to portfolio rankings that are not necessarily in line with the intuition. As in the case of any performance measure that relies on a multiple set of parameters that are not portfolio specific, but rather customer specific, the actual values of the ratios based on sample data must be used and interpreted with great caution.

10.3 PERFORMANCE AS RATIOS OF GAINS OVER LOSSES

Once the straightjacket of (behavioral) utility theory is left aside, it is tempting to experiment performance measures that adopt an analogous approach of "gain-to-loss ratios" without constraining the parameters to reflect the investor's attitudes toward risk or losses. These performance measures might still be parented with the behavioral framework, but they do not rest on a straightforward mapping between a realistic utility function and the associated portfolio performance. We split them into two categories: the first one gathers measures that adopt the shape of the Farinelli–Tibiletti ratio with specific parameters, and the second one pools various heuristic types of gain–loss ratios.

10.3.1 Ratios of partial moments

Because the Farinelli–Tibiletti ratio of Equation (10-19) stems from a particular normative application of the Prospect Theory framework, its use can be justified on the basis of a particular structure of investors' preferences. Several specific calibrations of the reservation rate, alpha, and beta parameters of the formula have been proposed over time, some of which are nowadays very popular in the practice of performance measurement.

For the sake of clarity, we can simply write $\text{F-T}_P^j \equiv \text{F-T}_P(\alpha_j, \beta_j, \underline{R}_j)$ and compare the various measures proposed in the literature with this generic form. Even though some ratios are also discussed in Chapter 6, we find it appropriate to re-examine them under the lens of the behavioral finance framework.

- The *original Prospect Theory ratio:*

$$\text{oPTR}_P^j \equiv \text{F-T}_P(0.6, 0.6, \underline{R}_j) = \sqrt[0.6]{\frac{\frac{1}{T}\sum_{t=1}^{T}(\max(R_{P,t} - \underline{R}_j, 0))^{0.6}}{\frac{1}{T}\sum_{t=1}^{T}(\max(\underline{R}_j - R_{P,t}, 0))^{0.6}}} \tag{10-22}$$

This ratio corresponds to the experimental calibration of the dual power utility functions that has become standard in the PT literature. It assigns an equal weight to the upside and the downside deviations from the reservation rate, which is a view that is consistent with the fact that investors are risk averse in gains and risk seeking in losses.

In the spirit of Gemmill et al. (2006) we can adapt this measure to the house-money effect. Adopting again the original PT calibration $\lambda_0 = 2.25$ and using (for instance) a reasonable value of $\lambda_1 = \frac{(\lambda_0 - 1)}{2\sigma_P} = \frac{0.625}{\sigma_P}$, we can design a dynamic version of the *original Prospect Theory ratio* defined as

$$\text{doPTR}_P^j \equiv \text{dF-T}_P(0.6, 0.6, \underline{R}_j)$$

$$= \sqrt[0.6]{\frac{\frac{1}{T}\sum_{t=1}^{T}(\max(R_{P,t} - \underline{R}_j, 0))^{0.6}}{\frac{1}{\bar{\lambda}_P T}\sum_{t=1}^{T}\left(2.25 - \frac{0.625}{\sigma_P}\right)(R_{P,t-1} - \underline{R}_j)(\max(\underline{R}_j - R_{P,t}, 0))^{0.6}}} \tag{10-23}$$

where $\bar{\lambda}_P = \frac{1}{T}\sum_{t=1}^{T}\left(2.25 - \frac{0.625}{\sigma_P}\right)(R_{P,t-1} - \underline{R}_j)$ is the average loss aversion of the investor over the sample time window.

Even though there is no explicit mention of this performance ratio in the literature, it is certainly worth being seriously considered as it encompasses all the key features of Prospect Theory. The main difficulty lies in the calibration of the PT parameters (including the house-money effect). This would be worth being used in very sophisticated wealth management applications that use behavioral finance for instance.

- The *Omega* (Keating and Shadwick, 2002):

$$\Omega_P^j \equiv \text{F-T}_P(1, 1, \underline{R}_j) = \frac{u\bar{R}_P(\underline{R}_j)}{d\bar{R}_P(\underline{R}_j)} \tag{10-24}$$

The Omega is nothing other than the ratio of the upside mean over the downside mean return. It is appealing as it seems to simply contrast a pure gain to a pure loss. As shown by Bertrand and Prigent (2011), this very popular ratio corresponds to the ratio of a call option over a put option on the portfolio. As discussed in Chapter 6, the Omega is connected with the Omega-Sharpe ratio defined in Equation (6-26) by the relation $\Omega_P^j = \Omega SR_P^j + 1$.

In spite of its simplicity and intuitiveness, the Omega does not obey a realistic set of properties regarding investors' preferences. Its use involves the assumption of a piecewise-linear Prospect Theory, which means that the investor displays risk neutrality both in the areas of gains and losses. Caporin, Costola, Jannin, and Maillet (2018) show that, both theoretically and empirically, the Omega performance measure ranks funds and portfolios in an inappropriate manner.

The special case in which $\underline{R}_j = R_f$ is called the *Gain–loss ratio* (Bernardo and Ledoit, 2000).

- The *Upside Potential Ratio* (Sortino, van der Meer, and Plantinga, 1999):

$$\text{UPR}_P^j \equiv \text{F-T}_P(1, 2, \underline{R}_j) = \frac{u\overline{R}_P(\underline{R}_j)}{d\sigma_P(\underline{R}_j)} \tag{10-25}$$

This performance measure is meant to penalize large downside deviations from the reservation rate (the denominator) to a larger extent than it rewards upside deviations (the numerator). It corresponds to a utility function that exhibits risk neutrality in the area of gains ($\alpha_j = 1$) and risk aversion in the area of losses ($\beta_j = 2$). Thus, this performance measure is conceptually closer to Fishburn's (1977) early specification discussed in Section 10.3.1 than to the Prospect Theory of Kahneman and Tversky (1979).

Note that the famous Sortino ratio (Equation (6-29) of Chapter 6) is directly connected with this ratio by the relation $\text{SorR}_P^j = \frac{\overline{R}_P - \underline{R}_j}{d\sigma_P(\underline{R}_j)} = \text{UPR}_P^j - \frac{d\overline{R}_P(\underline{R}_j)}{d\sigma_P(\underline{R}_j)}$.

- The *Variability Skewness* (Bacon, 2021):

$$\text{VSk}_P^j \equiv \text{F-T}_P(2, 2, \underline{R}_j) = \frac{u\sigma_P(\underline{R}_j)}{d\sigma_P(\underline{R}_j)} \tag{10-26}$$

This ratio has the merit of providing an indication of the portfolio return's asymmetry, depending on whether its value exceeds one (positive skewness) or not (negative skewness). We are moving further away from the behavioral setup as this value would correspond to an opposite structure of the investor's preferences (risk seeking in gains, risk averse in losses).

- The *modified Kappa ratio*:

$$\text{m}\kappa\text{R}_P^j \equiv \text{F-T}_P(1, 3, \underline{R}_j) = \frac{u\overline{R}_P(\underline{R}_j)}{dm_{3,P}(\underline{R}_j)} \tag{10-27}$$

TABLE 10-6 Special cases of the Farinelli–Tibiletti ratio.

Region of losses		Region of gains		
		Risk aversion $\alpha_j = 0.6$	Risk neutrality $\alpha_j = 1$	Risk lovingness $\alpha_j = 2$
Risk lovingness	$\beta_j = 0.6$	**Original P-T** $oPTR_P^j$		
Risk neutrality	$\beta_j = 1$		**Omega** Ω_P^j	
Risk aversion	$\beta_j = 2$		**Upside potential** UPR_P^j	**Variability skewness** VSk_P^j
	$\beta_j = 3$		**Modified kappa** $m\kappa R_P^j$	

This performance measure echoes the Kappa ratio of Kaplan and Knowles (2004) that was encountered in Chapter 6 (Equation (6-30)) through the relation $m\kappa R_P^j = \kappa R_P^j + \frac{d\bar{R}_P(\underline{R}_j)}{dm_{3,P}(\underline{R}_j)}$. Equation (10-27) mostly builds on a version in which the investor is very risk averse in the region of losses. By raising (the absolute value of) negative deviations to a cubic power, this ratio penalizes the downside risk even further compared to the ones that focus on the first or second lower partial moments. In that respect, that measure approaches the spirit of the ratios based on extreme risk.

Table 10-6 summarizes the linkage between the F-T ratio and the various measures discussed in this subsection.

None of the popular performance measures really correspond to the spirit of the Prospect Theory, which explains our attempt to fill this gap with the original PT ratio. However, the fact that all the performance measures reported in Table 10-6 involve very different assumptions regarding the investor's risk-aversion coefficients is not an issue *per se*, and we do not wish to make any value judgment regarding their use, except perhaps with the word of caution related to the use of the Omega, whose weaknesses have been largely documented in the literature.

HiMeLo example (continued)

We pursue the implementation of the F-T ratio by applying the calibrations of alpha and beta proposed in Table 10-6. We again use two values of the reservation rate $\underline{R}_j = 0\%$ and $\underline{R}_j = 3\%$. The results are displayed in Table 10-7.

(continued)

(continued)

TABLE 10-7 HiMeLo example – Relative levels of the ratios of partial moments.

		R.A. gains		
Res. rate	**R.A. losses**	$\alpha_j = 0.6$	$\alpha_j = 1$	$\alpha_j = 2$
$\underline{R}_j = 0\%$	$\beta_j = 0.6$	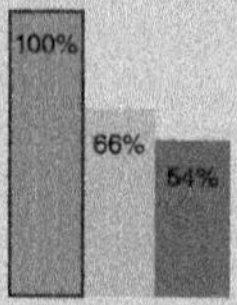		
	$\beta_j = 1.0$		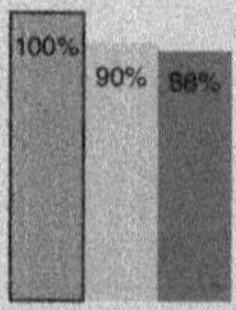	
	$\beta_j = 2.0$		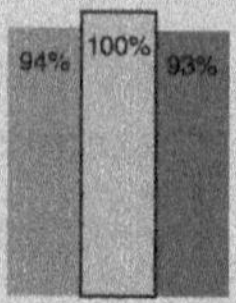	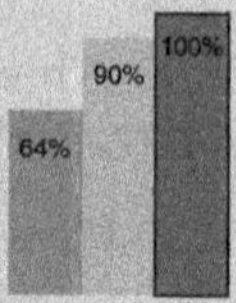
	$\beta_j = 3.0$		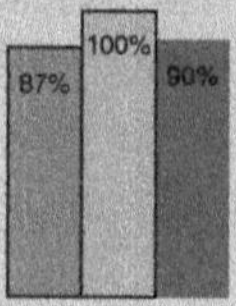	
$\underline{R}_j = 3\%$	$\beta_j = 0.6$	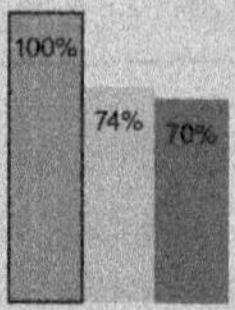		
	$\beta_j = 1.0$		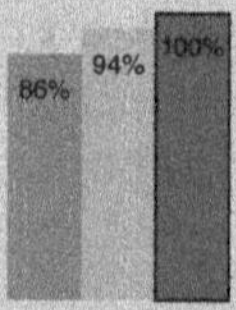	
	$\beta_j = 2.0$		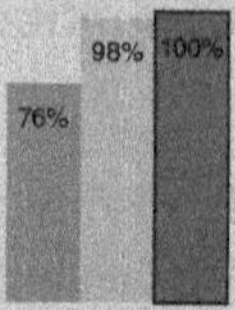	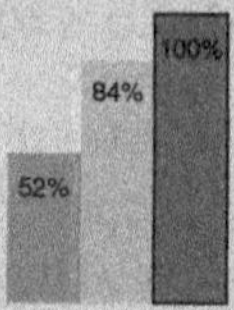
	$\beta_j = 3.0$		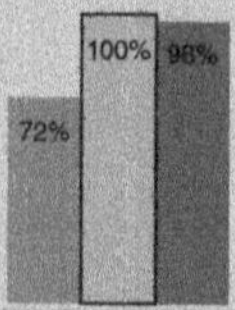	

From a relative performance perspective, the rankings are mostly discriminant for values of alpha that are either low ($\alpha_j = 0.6$) or high ($\alpha_j = 2$).

The Low portfolio only emerges for the low level of the reservation ratio or a high risk aversion in the area of gains. Because of its unfavorable left asymmetry, it is quickly dominated when the risk aversion in the area of losses increases. On the other hand, the ranking of the High portfolio largely improves when the reservation rate rises. The Medium portfolio dominates the other two when the investor is risk-neutral in gains and risk averse in losses. In this case, the portfolio simultaneously benefits from a lower risk than the High fund and a more favorable left tail than the Low one. This underlines how difficult it is to adequately interpret the various versions of the F-T ratio based on higher exponents.

10.3.2 Heuristic versions of gain–loss ratios

One of the major drawbacks of the F-T ratio precisely resides in its excessive parsimony. Despite the fact that one of the key tenets of the whole behavioral finance framework is the existence of loss-aversion behavior, this dimension is totally absent from the ratios of partial moments (with the exception of the dynamic F-T ratio, but with a substantial associated estimation issue). This is the reason why many measures have been proposed in order to approach as much as possible the spirit of the behavioral framework, without necessarily relying on solid theoretical underpinnings.

10.3.2.1 Ratios of adjusted gains over adjusted losses

We list here three main performance measures that belong to the family of gain–loss ratios and that call upon the principles of behavioral finance, namely the Prospect ratio, the Prospect-CVaR ratio, and the Rachev ratio.

- The *Prospect ratio* (Watanabe, 2014):

$$\text{ProR}_P^j = \frac{u\overline{R}_P(\underline{R}_j) - \lambda_j d\overline{R}_P(\underline{R}_j) - \underline{R}_j}{d\sigma_P(\underline{R}_j)} \tag{10-28}$$

This ratio addresses the key feature of the Prospect Theory, namely the existence of loss aversion, within the scope of a gain–loss ratio. The author discards the issue of differential risk-aversion levels and focuses on the importance of the loss-aversion λ_j and its impact on the gain–loss ratio.

The principle of the ratio is intuitive. Starting from the Sortino ratio, the modification lies in the "magnification" of losses, represented by the term $d\overline{R}_P(\underline{R}_j)$, through the impact of the loss-aversion parameter λ_j.[9]

- The *Prospect-CVaR ratio* (Zakamouline, 2010):

$$\text{PCVaRR}_P^{j,x} = \frac{um_{\gamma_j^+,P}(\underline{R}_j)}{\text{hCVaR}_{\gamma_j^-,P}^{(1-x)}} \equiv \frac{\sqrt[\alpha_j]{\frac{1}{T}\sum_{t=1}^{T}(\max(R_{P,t}-\underline{R}_j,0))^{\alpha_j}}}{\sqrt[\beta_j]{\frac{1}{T-n_x}\sum_{s=1}^{T-n_x}(R_{P,n_x}-R_{P,s})^{\beta_j}}} \tag{10-29}$$

where, as before, $\gamma_j^+ = \alpha_j$ and $\gamma_j^- = \beta_j$, and R_{P,n_x} is the return that is ranked at the n_xth place in the list of the portfolio returns ordered from the highest to the lowest one, i.e., $n_x = \lceil T(1-x)\rceil$ in which $\lceil\cdot\rceil$ stands for the ceiling (lowest integer greater than or equal to) of the argument, and $R_{P,s}$ is the sth return that is lower than R_{P,n_x} for $s = 1, \ldots, T-n_x$. For instance, if we use monthly data for a period of ten years ($T = 12 \times 10 = 120$) and the confidence level is $(1-x) = 95\%$, $n_x = \lceil 120 \times 0.95\rceil = 114$, i.e., R_{P,n_x} is the return ranked 114th or the seventh one from the minimum, and we sum at the denominator the return differences between R_{P,n_x} and the six lowest observations of the sample.[10] We define $\text{hCVaR}_{\beta_j,P}^{(1-x)} \equiv \sqrt[\beta_j]{\frac{1}{T-n_x}\sum_{i=1}^{T-n_x}(R_{P,n_x}-R_{P,i})^{\beta_j}}$ as the moment of order β_j of the CVaR, and note that it is equal to the historical CVaR of the portfolio for the special case $\beta_j = 1$.

This ratio (which is also called the "Z-ratio" by Bacon, 2021) is a mixture of the F-T ratio, through the use of two different exponents on the numerator and denominator, and the implementation of extreme risk in performance, through the computation of a power of the most extreme return deviations on the denominator. It can be interpreted as if there were two reservation rates: the one corresponding to the cutoff point between gains and losses $\underline{R}_j$ on the numerator, and the one that distinguishes "normal" and "extreme" losses (corresponding to the portfolio Value-at-Risk) R_{P,n_x} on the denominator.[11]

---

[9]Watanabe (2014) proposes further to adjust the downside volatility on the numerator by adding the downside skewness and the downside kurtosis, but these adjustments are arbitrary and not discussed here.

[10]We have already encountered this notion, which is related to the historical conditional Value-at-Risk, in Section 6.2.5 of Chapter 6 dedicated to extreme risk.

[11]There is a second version where the numerator uses the extreme gains and the denominator uses the lower partial moment, but we believe that its interpretation is not straightforward (see Bacon, 2021, for a further discussion).

- The *Generalized Rachev ratio* (Biglova, Ortobelli, Rachev, and Stoyanov, 2004):

$$\mathrm{GRacR}_P^{j,x,y} = \frac{\mathrm{hCGaR}_{\gamma_j^+,P}^{(1-y)}}{\mathrm{hCVaR}_{\gamma_j^-,P}^{(1-x)}} \equiv \frac{\sqrt[\alpha_j]{\frac{1}{n_y}\sum_{i=1}^{n_y}(R_{P,i}-R_{P,n_y})^{\alpha_j}}}{\sqrt[\beta_j]{\frac{1}{T-n_x}\sum_{i=1}^{T-n_x}(R_{P,n_x}-R_{P,i})^{\beta_j}}} \tag{10-30}$$

where R_{P,n_y} is the return that is ranked at the n_yth place in the list of the portfolio returns ordered from the highest to the lowest one, i.e., $n_y = \lfloor Ty + 1 \rfloor$ in which $\lfloor \cdot \rfloor$ stands for the floor (least integer lower than or equal to) of the argument, and $R_{P,i}$ is the ith return that is higher than R_{P,n_y} for $i = 1, \ldots, n_y$. For instance, if we use monthly data for a period of ten years ($T = 12 \times 10 = 120$) and the confidence level is $(1 - y) = 95\%$, $n_x = \lceil 120 \times 0.05 + 1 \rceil = 7$, i.e., R_{P,n_y} is the return ranked 7th or the seventh one from the maximum, and we sum at the denominator the return differences between R_{P,n_y} and the six highest observations of the sample. Similarly to the previous ratio, we define $\mathrm{hCGaR}_{\alpha_j,P}^{(1-y)} \equiv \sqrt[\alpha_j]{\frac{1}{n_y}\sum_{i=1}^{n_y}(R_{P,i}-R_{P,n_y})^{\alpha_j}}$ as the moment of order α_j of the conditional Gain-at-Risk.

The Generalized Rachev ratio mixes the structure of the Farinelli–Tibiletti ratio with a focus on extreme events only. Pursuing the same type of interpretation as before, this performance measure represents a version of the F-T ratio in which there are two distinct reservation rates, namely R_{P,n_y} on the upside and R_{P,n_x} on the downside. This involves that none of the portfolio returns that belong to the "body" of the distribution (i.e., between the Gain-at-Risk (GaR) and the Value-at-Risk (VaR)) is accounted for in performance appraisal. As noted by the authors, this ratio of "extreme gains over extreme losses" is suitable only for fat-tailed distributions. It has to be manipulated and interpreted with great caution since it neglects the largest part of the returns. We advocate considering it as a complement to more traditional performance measures and to ensure choosing not too extreme values of the confidence levels $(1 - x)$ and $(1 - y)$ in order to retain a sufficient number of observations in the computation.

Note that when $\alpha_j = \beta_j = 1$, Formula (10-30) simplifies to the simple *Rachev ratio* or $\mathrm{RacR}_P^{x,y}$:

$$\mathrm{RacR}_P^{x,y} = \frac{\mathrm{hCGaR}_P^{(1-y)}}{\mathrm{hCVaR}_P^{(1-x)}} \equiv \frac{\frac{1}{n_y}\sum_{i=1}^{n_y}(R_{P,i}-R_{P,n_y})}{\frac{1}{T-n_x}\sum_{i=1}^{T-n_x}(R_{P,n_x}-R_{P,i})} \tag{10-31}$$

In that case, the link with behavioral finance is entirely lost as the investor is supposed to exhibit risk neutrality in both the gain and loss area – notwithstanding their risk attitudes between these two zones, which are ignored.

- The *Up/Down Rachev ratio* (Ortobelli, Biglova, Rachev, and Stoyanov, 2010):

$$\text{udRacR}_P^j = \frac{\overline{\text{du}}_P(\underline{R}_j)}{\overline{\text{dd}}_P(\underline{R}_j)} \tag{10-32}$$

where $\overline{\text{dd}}_P(\underline{R}_j) = \frac{1}{T}\sum_{t=1}^{T} \text{dd}_{P,t}(\underline{R}_j)$ and $\overline{\text{du}}_P(\underline{R}_j) = \frac{1}{T}\sum_{t=1}^{T} \text{du}_{P,t}(\underline{R}_j)$ are the average portfolio drawdowns and drawups of the portfolio's excess return over the reservation rate. These notions are defined respectively as $\text{dd}_{P,t}(\underline{R}_j) = \frac{\max\limits_{\tau=1,\dots,t}(V_{P,\tau}-(1+\underline{R}_j)^{\tau})-(V_{P,t}-(1+\underline{R}_j)^{t})}{\max\limits_{\tau=1,\dots,t}(V_{P,\tau}-(1+\underline{R}_j)^{\tau})}$ and $\text{du}_{P,t}(\underline{R}_j) = \frac{(V_{P,t}-(1+\underline{R}_j)^{t})-\min\limits_{\tau=1,\dots,t}(V_{P,\tau}-(1+\underline{R}_j)^{\tau})}{\min\limits_{\tau=1,\dots,t}(V_{P,\tau}-(1+\underline{R}_j)^{\tau})}$, where $V_{P,\tau}$ is the net asset value of the portfolio at time τ.

The notion of drawdown was already encountered in Section 6.2.4 of Chapter 6. In the current instance, it is considered relative to the investor-specific reservation rate and contrasted with the notion of drawup that is the reflection of a feeling of gain.

Note that the same authors also propose a *Max Up/Down Rachev ratio* based on the maximum drawdown and drawup instead of their average:

$$\text{MudRacR}_P^j = \frac{\text{du}_{P,\max}(\underline{R}_j)}{\text{dd}_{P,\max}(\underline{R}_j)} \tag{10-33}$$

where $\text{dd}_{P,\max}(\underline{R}_j) = \max\limits_t(\text{dd}_{P,t}(\underline{R}_j))$ and $\text{du}_{P,\max}(\underline{R}_j) = \max\limits_t(\text{du}_{P,t}(\underline{R}_j))$.

HiMeLo example (continued)

We focus on the Prospect ratio (Equation (10-28)) as this is the performance measure that explicitly features the investor's loss-aversion coefficient λ_j.

In order to discriminate portfolios, it is not interesting to let λ_j vary as in the case of the behavioral quadratic score shown in Table 10-2. Rather, the discriminating dimension becomes the reservation rate $\underline{R}_j$ that makes the difference, in the same spirit as the Roy ratio introduced in Chapter 6. We thus define three categories of investors: the demanding one with $\underline{R}_d = 2\%$, the tempered one with $\underline{R}_t = 1\%$, and the sober one with $\underline{R}_s = 0\%$. They all share the same loss-aversion coefficient of $\lambda_d = \lambda_t = \lambda_s = 1.1$. Applying Equation (10-28) for the Prospect ratio of each portfolio, we obtain Table 10-8.

The outcome of this analysis matches the previous ones obtained from the behavioral quadratic scores (Table 10-2) and the Prospect Theory scores (Table 10-3), especially regarding the difficult positioning of the Medium portfolio.

There is a key difference though, as the investor segmentation relies here on the reservation rate, whereas it was more effective to distinguish investors on the basis of their

TABLE 10-8 HiMeLo example – Prospect ratios for different categories of investors.

Investor	Reservation rate $\underline{R}_j$	Low	Medium	High
Demanding	2%	0.135	0.170	**0.184**
Tempered	1%	0.244	**0.247**	0.239
Sober	0%	**0.362**	0.329	0.296

loss-aversion coefficient before. As a check, we propose in Figure 10-4 the evolution of the Prospect ratios as a function of the loss-aversion coefficient for the three different values of the reservation rate reported above, namely, $\underline{R}_d = 2\%$, $\underline{R}_t = 1\%$, and $\underline{R}_s = 0\%$.

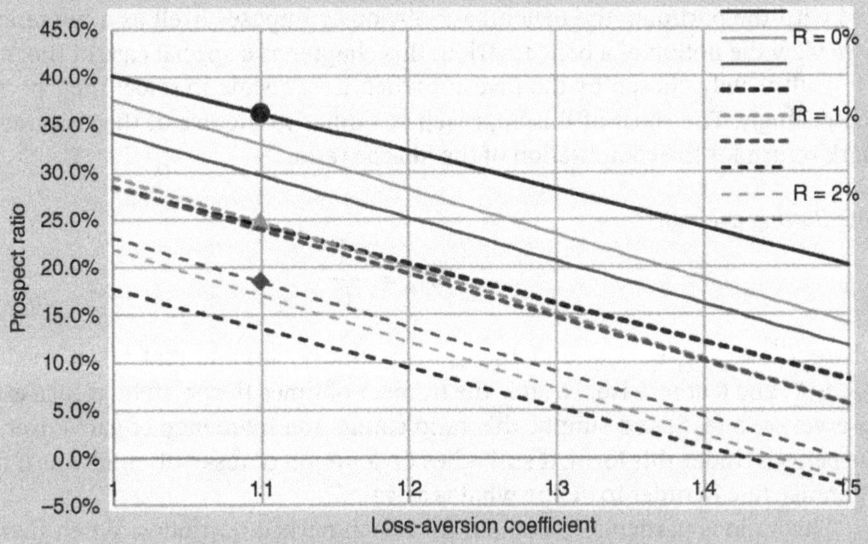

FIGURE 10-4 HiMeLo example – Prospect ratios of the three portfolios as a function of loss aversion.

For each value of the reservation rate, the Prospect ratio is a decreasing value of the loss-aversion coefficient. This is a natural consequence of the increasing penalty that is associated with the downside mean as lambda increases. However, for low ($\underline{R}_j = 0\%$ – continuous lines) or high ($\underline{R}_j = 2\%$ – thin dotted lines) values of the reservation rate, the lines do not cross. The only discriminant dimension in the ratio is therefore the level of $\underline{R}_j$ itself. We have reported on the graph the coordinates corresponding to the dominant portfolios outlined in Table 10-8, each of them being vertically aligned with the loss-aversion coefficient of $\lambda_j = 1.1$.

10.3.2.2 Ratios based on frequencies of gains and losses

Until this point in the chapter, a common feature of all performance measures that we have examined is the necessity to estimate a variety of investor-specific parameters. A number of performance measures approach the notions of "gains" and "losses" in a much less sophisticated fashion, without having to make substantial assumptions about the investor's preferences, while attempting to deliver measures whose appraisal would approximate quite decently the way most investors would rank portfolios according to their preferences. Thus, in spite of their simplicity, they have the merit of providing a crude but insightful picture of portfolio performance.

In order to alleviate the issue of measuring investor preferences further, some of the measures examined in this subsection replace the investor-specific reservation rate $\underline{R}_j$ with a much more objective notion of the "portfolio benchmark" $R_{B,t}$. When it exists and has been officially associated with the portfolio, the benchmark obviously imposes itself as a reference. Nevertheless, we view the notion of a benchmark in this chapter as a special case of the reservation rate, as it is ultimately chosen by the investor when they decide to select their portfolio and treat it accordingly. The spirit of this approach is similar to the use of the risk-free rate as a benchmark return for the computation of the Sharpe ratio.

- The *Batting average:*[12]

$$\mathrm{BA}_P^j = \frac{T_P^{+j}}{T} \tag{10-34}$$

where $T_P^{+j} \equiv \sum_{t=1}^{T} 1_{\{R_{P,t} > \underline{R}_j\}}$ and $1_{\{R_{P,t} > \underline{R}_j\}}$ is a binary variable that takes a value of 1 if $R_{P,t} > \underline{R}_j$ and 0 otherwise, i.e., it is the number of times the portfolio return exceeds the reservation rate. Stated simply, this ratio counts the frequency of gains over the sample period. Under this form, it still relies on a notion of reservation rate as it requires a reference rate in order to define what is a "gain."

This ratio is particularly popular for benchmarked portfolios. When there exists a benchmark B whose returns are $R_{B,t}$, then it is straightforward to define a periodic gain by simply looking at the portfolio's excess return $R_{P,t} - R_{B,t}$. It is thus no longer necessary to define a reservation rate, and the *benchmark-based Batting average* is defined as

$$\mathrm{bBA}_P = \frac{T_{(P-B)}^{+}}{T} \tag{10-35}$$

where $T_{(P-B)}^{+} \equiv \sum_{t=1}^{T} 1_{\{R_{P,t} > R_{B,t}\}}$ and $1_{\{R_{P,t} > R_{B,t}\}}$ is a binary variable that takes a value of 1 if $R_{P,t} > R_{B,t}$ and 0 otherwise, reflecting the number of times the portfolio differential return is positive.

---

[12] This name comes from the world of baseball. It refers to the frequency of successful hits by a player while at bat.

- The *Percentage gain ratio*:

$$\text{PerR}_P^j = \frac{T_P^{+j}}{T_B^{+j}} \tag{10-36}$$

where $T_B^{+j} \equiv \sum_{t=1}^{T} 1_{\{R_{B,t} > \underline{R}_j\}}$ is the number of times the benchmark return exceeds the reservation rate.

This ratio has the advantage of providing a clear cutoff value equal to $\text{PerR}_P^j = 1$ between good and bad performance. Even though it is particularly relevant to consider an investor-specific reservation rate, it is often merely presented as a pure ratio of portfolio over benchmark positive returns, i.e., with a reservation rate of 0, as in Bacon (2021).

A similar perspective is provided by two avatars, the *Up percentage ratio* and the *Down percentage ratio*:

$$\text{uPerR}_P = \frac{T_P^{+B\&B^+}}{T_B^{+}} \tag{10-37a}$$

$$\text{dPerR}_P = \frac{T_P^{+B\&B^-}}{T_B^{-}} \tag{10-37b}$$

where $T_B^{+} \equiv \sum_{t=1}^{T} 1_{\{R_{B,t}>0\}}$ (resp. $T_B^{-} \equiv \sum_{t=1}^{T} 1_{\{R_{B,t}<0\}}$) is the number of times the benchmark return is positive (resp. negative), and $T_P^{+B\&B^+} \equiv \sum_{t=1}^{T} 1_{\{R_{P,t}>R_{B,t}\}} \times 1_{\{R_{B,t}>0\}}$ (respectively $T_P^{+B\&B^-} \equiv \sum_{t=1}^{T} 1_{\{R_{P,t}>R_{B,t}\}} \times 1_{\{R_{B,t}<0\}}$) is the number of times the portfolio return exceeds its benchmark when its return is positive (respectively negative).

These ratios aim at determining the portfolio manager's ability to outperform in different market environments and do not depend on any reservation rate. These measures are not meant to capture portfolio performance over the whole spectrum of returns and should not be used in isolation. Furthermore, they appear to be more useful for investment firms to evaluate their portfolio managers than for investors to appraise the portfolio achievements.[13]

- The *Capture ratios* (Morningstar, 2011):

$$\text{uCapR}_P = \frac{\sum_{t=1}^{T} R_{P,t} \times 1_{\{R_{B,t}>0\}}}{\sum_{t=1}^{T} R_{B,t} \times 1_{\{R_{B,t}>0\}}} \tag{10-38a}$$

$$\text{dCapR}_P = \frac{\sum_{t=1}^{T} R_{P,t} \times 1_{\{R_{B,t}<0\}}}{\sum_{t=1}^{T} R_{B,t} \times 1_{\{R_{B,t}<0\}}} \tag{10-38b}$$

[13] We refer to Chapter 18 for the discussion of agency issues between the different stakeholders.

$$\text{CapR}_P \equiv \frac{\text{uCapR}_P}{\text{dCapR}_P} = \frac{\left(\sum_{t=1}^{T} R_{P,t} \times 1_{\{R_{B,t}>0\}}\right)\left(\sum_{t=1}^{T} R_{B,t} \times 1_{\{R_{B,t}<0\}}\right)}{\left(\sum_{t=1}^{T} R_{B,t} \times 1_{\{R_{B,t}>0\}}\right)\left(\sum_{t=1}^{T} R_{P,t} \times 1_{\{R_{B,t}<0\}}\right)} \tag{10-39}$$

The Upside, Downside, and Up/Down Capture ratios, respectively uCapR_P, dCapR_P, and CapR_P, aim at detecting the ability of portfolio managers to outperform their benchmark when they are in the gains or losses territories. Taken in isolation, the ratios uCapR_P and dCapR_P naturally deliver an incomplete picture of portfolio performance and should rather be considered indicators of relative risk. The Up/Down Capture ratio (or, in short, the Capture ratio) CapR_P provides the full picture. As noted by Bacon (2021), it provides an indication of the convexity of the profile of excess returns over the benchmark. A ratio greater than one indicates positive asymmetry.

These Capture ratio indicators, since they were introduced by Morningstar in 2011, have been shown by Marlo and Stark (2019) to reveal some persistence in performance and are often used by investors (both individual and institutional ones) in their fund allocation decisions.

- The *Inverse d-ratio* (Lavinio, 1999):

$$\text{id}_P^j = \frac{T_P^{+j}\, u\bar{R}_P(\underline{R}_j)}{T_P^{-j}\, d\bar{R}_P(\underline{R}_j)} \equiv \frac{T_P^{+j} \times \sum_{t=1}^{T} \max(R_{P,t} - \underline{R}_j, 0)}{T_P^{-j} \times \sum_{t=1}^{T} \max(\underline{R}_j - R_{P,t}, 0)} \tag{10-40}$$

where $T_P^{-j} \equiv \sum_{t=1}^{T} 1_{\{R_{P,t}<\underline{R}_j\}}$ is the number of times the portfolio return is lower than the reservation rate.

We choose to present this ratio as the inverse of the original d-ratio, whose level is negatively related to performance. This ratio is very close to the Omega (Equation (10-24)) except that, for the inverse d-ratio, the sums of gains and losses are divided by their respective number of occurrences and not by the total number of observations as with the Omega. Note that the ratio was originally developed with a reservation rate of 0.

- The *Gain-to-Pain ratio* (Schwager, 2012):

$$\text{GtPR}_P^j = \frac{\bar{R}_P - \underline{R}_j}{d\bar{R}_P(\underline{R}_j)} \equiv \frac{\sum_{t=1}^{T}(R_{P,t} - \underline{R}_j)}{\sum_{t=1}^{T} \max(\underline{R}_j - R_{P,t}, 0)} \tag{10-41}$$

where we can also write the denominator as $\sum_{t=1}^{T} 1_{\{R_{P,t}<\underline{R}_j\}}(\underline{R}_j - R_{P,t})$.

This ratio aims at determining whether the sum of all the losses (the "pain") experienced over the sample period is compensated by the cumulative return ("gain").[14] According to the author, this is a way to focus on the downside volatility through a measure that is very intuitive. The threshold for a good GtPR is equal to 1, and excellent when it exceeds 1.5 (with monthly returns).

Even though it is not the purpose of this measure, it relates to the investor's loss aversion. Because of its structure of summing up all the cumulative losses (denominator) and contrasting them with the overall gain (numerator), it can be roughly interpreted as the maximum level of the loss-aversion coefficient that makes the investor satisfied with the portfolio. For instance, if $GtPR_P^j = 1.2$, it would mean that an investor with a loss-aversion coefficient that is lower than or equal to 1.2 would have felt more satisfaction than disappointment with the portfolio.

HiMeLo example (continued)

We examine the behavior of the three benchmark-free performance measures based on frequencies as a function of the reservation rate (expressed in monthly frequency for the sake of consistency). The results are reported in Figure 10-5.

The top graph represents the Batting average (Equation (10-34)), the middle one represents the Inverse d-ratio (Equation (10-40)), and the bottom one represents the Gain-to-Pain ratio (Equation (10-41)). It is immediately visible that the Inverse d-ratio behaves very closely to the Batting average, although with a greater contrast between portfolios when the reservation rate is low. The rate level for which the investor switches between the Low and the High portfolio is very close in both cases (as expected, the Medium one is almost never preferred). Because of its better discriminating power, the Inverse d-ratio should probably be favored.

The Gain-to-Pain ratio exhibits a different behavior. In the case of all three portfolios, this ratio never exceeds 1 except for the Low portfolio when $\underline{R}_j = 0\%$. Even though this measure is simple and its interpretation is straightforward, it turns out that even decently managed portfolios may have a hard time delivering a total return that exceeds their cumulative losses. This performance measure must be analyzed with caution.

(continued)

[14]Note that the ratio was initially designed with a reservation rate $\underline{R}_j = 0$.

(continued)

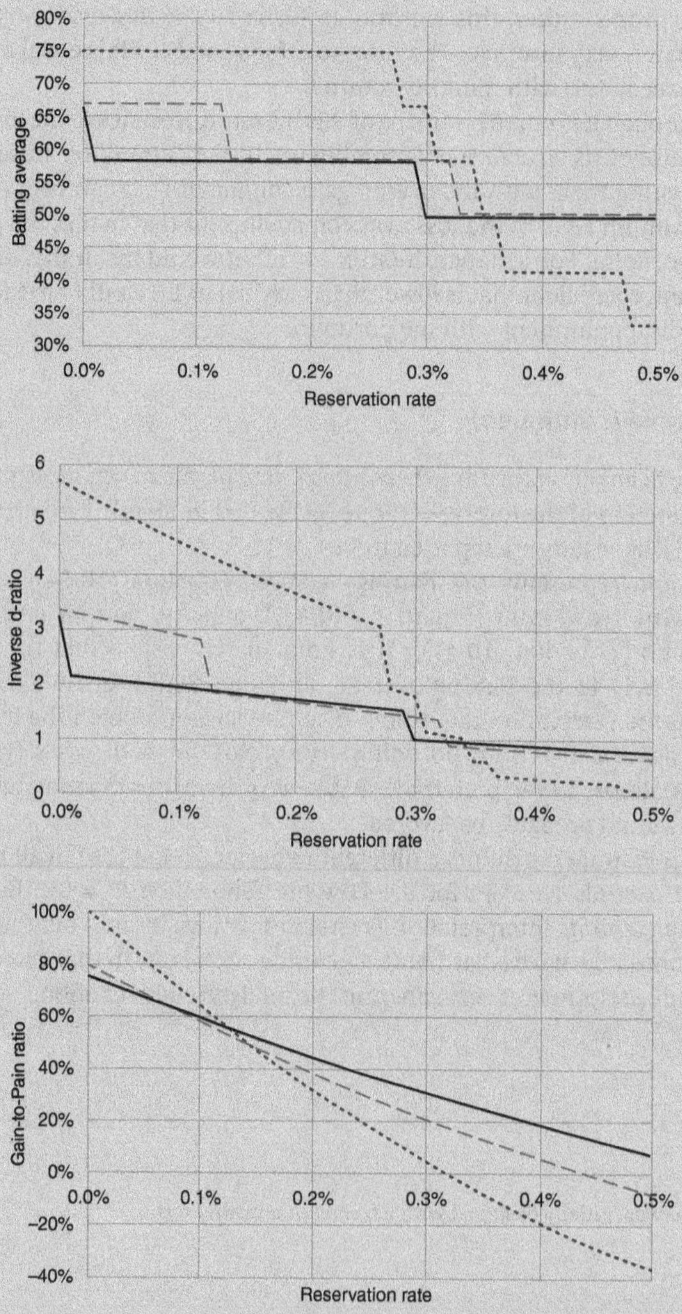

FIGURE 10-5 HiMeLo example – Frequency-based performance of the three portfolios as a function of the reservation rate.

10.4 MENTAL ACCOUNTING AND PORTFOLIO PERFORMANCE

Evidencing the distinction between gains and losses and emphasizing the notions of loss aversion, the reversal of risk preferences in the area of losses or the replacement of probabilities with subjective decision weights are not the only takeaways of behavioral finance applicable to portfolio management. Another consequence of the influence of the investors' psychological traits on their portfolio decisions is their organization of wealth in a distinct set of "mental accounts," a concept originally introduced by Thaler (1985; 1999). Each of these accounts is mentally organized in a waterproof ledger so that the decisions associated with any one of them are ring-fenced and do not impact the other ones. With regard to financial investments, individuals assign specific goals, such as "keeping some precautionary liquidity cushion," "preparing my retirement," or "accumulating wealth in order to buy a secondary house," for instance. They associate a specific investment horizon and dedicated utility function to each of these accounts, which may differ from one account to another.

The mental accounting (MA) framework was adapted to the issue of optimal portfolio choice by Das, Markowitz, Scheid, and Statman (2010). Investors seek to maximize the expected return of each account while controlling for risk, measured by the probability of failing to achieve a certain threshold level of return. Consequently, the authors present the investor's optimal portfolio choice problem as the following optimization program for account j, considering that we deal with continuously compounded returns defined as $R_P^c = \log(1 + R_P)$ so as to use their additivity property:

$$\max_P \mathrm{E}(R_P^c) \tag{10-42a}$$

$$\text{subject to: } \Pr[R_P^{c,H_j} \le \underline{R}_j^c H_j] \le \omega_j \tag{10-42b}$$

where $R_P^{c,H_j} = \sum_{t=1}^{H_j} R_{P,t}^c$ is the portfolio's cumulative continuously compounded return over H_j periods, which corresponds to the investment horizon of account j, $\underline{R}_j^c$ is the continuously compounded reservation rate associated with this account, and ω_j is the tolerance probability for not achieving this minimum threshold return. The investor can have as many distinct mental accounts as necessary in order to properly partition their investment objectives.

Under this specification, the notion of risk refers to the threat of not reaching the investor's return objective, reflected in the probability associated with this event. Instead of constraining the portfolio volatility (or any other pre-specified risk measure such as the Value-at-Risk (VaR) or the downside deviation) not to exceed a certain level, the investor wants the shortfall probability to be under control. For instance, if we set $H_j = 60$ months (5 years), $\underline{R}_j^c = 0.5\%$ (6% per year), and $\omega_j = 5\%$ (tolerance for a 5% probability of shortfall), the optimal portfolio is the one that delivers the highest expected rate of return while ensuring that the investor has a 95% chance of obtaining at least a cumulative return of 30% at the end of the period.

Starting from this basic formulation, we can identify two approaches for the measurement of portfolio performance adapted to the mental accounting framework. The first one belongs to the field of normative measures by determining the optimal convergence criterion for a specific investor type. The second one directly refers to the Goal-Based Investment (GBI) framework and determines performance according to the set of the investor's objectives.

10.4.1 Measuring performance with optimal convergence criteria

As in the previous sections, the investor's characteristics that underlie portfolio choice in the MA framework are numerous and potentially difficult to estimate. For a given account, they feature the reservation rate $\underline{R}_j^c$, the investment horizon H_j, and the tolerance probability ω_j. Measuring performance based on the speed of convergence of a portfolio toward its return objective represents a way to overcome this issue by allowing a more parsimonious parametrization.

10.4.1.1 The Stutzer convergence index

When the portfolio manager is confronted with a situation analogous to that of Equations (10-42a) and (10-42b), Stutzer (2000) tries to adopt a behavioral point of view. He argues that this manager will select a portfolio that will make the probability of its return in excess of the reservation rate to be negative decay to 0% at the fastest possible rate. The advantage of such an approach is to replace the investor-specific horizon with a portfolio-specific convergence rate criterion. Furthermore, instead of considering the perspective of a motley group of customers, it is only necessary to assess the manager's risk aversion. If the manager has a power utility function as in Equation (9-7) of Chapter 9, the decay rate optimization criterion, also known as the *Stutzer convergence index* D_P^j, is written as

$$D_P^j = \max_{\gamma^*}\left(-\log\frac{1}{T}\sum_{t=1}^{T} e^{\gamma^*(R_{P,t}^c-\underline{R}_j^c)}\right) \tag{10-43}$$

where $\gamma^* < 0$ is the implied negative value of the risk-aversion coefficient parameter that maximizes the decay rate of the probability that the portfolio return falls short of its reservation rate. In the special case of normally distributed returns, Stutzer (2003) further shows that the Gaussian version of the performance measure has the following form:

$$gD_P^j = \frac{1}{2}\left(\frac{\overline{R}_P^c - \underline{R}_j^c}{\sigma_P^c}\right)^2 \tag{10-44}$$

where $\overline{R}_P^c = \frac{1}{T}\sum_{t=1}^{H_j} R_{P,t}^c$ and $\sigma_P^c \equiv \sigma(R_P^c) = \sqrt{\frac{1}{T-1}\sum_{t=1}^{H_j}(R_{P,t}^c - \overline{R}_P^c)^2}$ are the mean and standard deviation of the portfolio's continuously compounded returns, respectively.

The expression between parenthesis in Equation (10-44) looks very similar to the Sharpe ratio, however with two differences: (i) the reservation rate replaces the risk-free interest rate and (ii) it is expressed in terms of continuous rather than simple compound returns because we stand in a multiperiod perspective for which compounding then matters. We can interpret this expression as a continuous-time version of the Roy ratio introduced in Equation (6-19) of Chapter 6, i.e., $\text{RoyR}_P^c = \frac{\overline{R}_P^c - \underline{R}_j^c}{\sigma_P^c}$. Provided that it is positive, this ratio can be substituted with gD_P^j as it provides the exact same portfolio rankings.

10.4.1.2 The Convergence score

Because it focuses on the probability of meeting an objective, the Stutzer convergence index focuses on the percentile of the distribution of returns rather than on its expectation. In doing so, it neglects the extent of the potential portfolio loss if the target return is not met. For a loss-averse investor, this might obviously represent important missing information.

In an attempt to merge the properties of the Stutzer convergence index and the Kappa of Kaplan and Knowles (2004), Kaplan (2005, cited by Cogneau and Hübner, 2009)[15] proposes a convergence index, called *Lambda*, which is consistent with the use of the Fishburn (1977) utility function:

$$\Lambda_P^j = \max_{\gamma^*} \left\{ \gamma^*(\overline{R}_P^c - \underline{R}_j^c) - \frac{1}{T} \sum_{t=1}^{T} [\mathrm{e}^{-\max(-\gamma^*(R_{P,t}^c - \underline{R}_j^c),0)} - \max(-\gamma^*(R_{P,t}^c - \underline{R}_j^c), 0) - 1] \right\} \quad (10\text{-}45)$$

where the second term represents the loss penalty function.

HiMeLo example (continued)

Adopting a similar classification procedure as in the preceding case (a demanding, a tempered, and a sober investor), we consider this time a stronger discrimination of investor types by setting the (continuously compounded) reservation rates equal to $\underline{R}_d^c = 4\%$, $\underline{R}_t^c = 2\%$, and $\underline{R}_s^c = 0\%$.

Performing, for each investor type, the optimization program proposed in Equations (10-42a) and (10-42b) leads to the results shown in Table 10-9 for the decay rates.

(continued)

[15] Unfortunately, the technical paper of Kaplan (2005) that introduces this measure is not publicly available anymore.

(continued)

TABLE 10-9 HiMeLo example – Stutzer convergence index for different categories of investors.

Investor	Reservation rate $\underline{R}_j^c$	Low	Medium	High
Demanding	4%	0.000% (0.0)	0.125% (−2.3)	**0.259%** **(−2.2)**
Tempered	2%	0.825% (−10.6)	**0.827%** **(−6.1)**	0.763% (−3.9)
Sober	0%	**3.463%** **(−20.8)**	2.182% (−10.1)	1.555% (−5.6)

In each cell, we report the associated opposite risk-aversion coefficient between parentheses. For the demanding investor, the reservation rate $\underline{R}_d^c = 4\%$ is greater than the continuous mean return of the Low portfolio, which is equal to 3.83%. This is the reason why the only acceptable attitude for the asset manager is to be risk neutral ($\gamma = 0$) with an associated null decay rate. In addition, the Low portfolio appears to dominate the other ones for a large set of realistic values of the reservation rate. It is only when $\underline{R}_j^c$ reaches the neighborhood of 2% that it becomes dominated by the Medium one. The High portfolio would only be chosen for very high (i.e., aggressive) values of $\underline{R}_j^c$, which underlines that this convergence criterion does not necessarily overlap other classical performance measures that tend to favor riskier portfolios.

10.4.2 Measuring performance for goal-based portfolios

The mental accounting framework naturally leads to the "goal-based investing" approach, according to which, within each account, the investor tries to design a portfolio that aims at achieving specific objectives. We can translate the basic version of the goal-based investment criterion by considering a simplified dual program of mental accounts presented in Equations (10-42a) and (10-42b) in which the constraint on the expected return of the portfolio is directly integrated into the risk minimization objective:

$$\min_P \Pr[R_P^{c,H_j} \leq \tau_j H_j] \tag{10-46}$$

where τ_j is the continuously compounded target rate of return of the portfolio. Under this specification, the investor does not need to specify a minimum expected return as a constraint because all that matters is the result that they want to achieve, and their assessment of risk is the likelihood that the portfolio will not reach this objective. Furthermore, the probability of failing to reach the target return, defined as ω_j in Equation (10-42b), does not show up either because it is precisely the probability that the investor seeks to minimize.

For a portfolio that has specifically been created and managed for that purpose, evaluating its performance at the end of the investment horizon is straightforward. Since the portfolio lifetime exactly matches the investment horizon, one essentially studies the whole population of returns that had to be accounted for in the assessment of the shortfall probability: either the realized portfolio return has exceeded the target or not. However, in general, we have to deal with sampled return distributions. The series of realized returns of a given portfolio usually starts at a moment that differs from the investor's goal-setting time and ends at a different moment as well. In particular, this is always the case when analyzing live mutual funds because, by definition, their lifetime extends beyond the moment of performance evaluation.

Confronted with a sampled distribution of returns, the investor has to assess the likelihood of achieving their goal through its statistical properties. In this case, the *Goal-based performance* of the portfolio corresponding to the expression (10-46), denoted by GBP^j_P, is defined as the *ex post* estimated probability of reaching the investor's objective (which is the complement of the shortfall probability):

$$\text{GBP}^j_P = 1 - \widehat{\Pr}[\overline{R}^{c,H_j}_P \leq \tau_j] \tag{10-47}$$

where $\overline{R}^{c,H_j}_P = \frac{1}{H_j}\sum_1^{H_j} R^c_{P,t}$ is the mean portfolio return over the investment horizon, and $\widehat{\Pr}[\cdot]$ refers to the probability of obtaining the argument inferred from the sample.

From the rather simplistic starting point of the risk minimization objective (10-46), it is necessary to bring some additional realism. The practical translation of GBI in wealth management was originally proposed by Brunel (2003). He identifies four types of buckets for accounts: liquidity, income, capital preservation, and growth. Within each bucket, a sub-portfolio can be assigned not only with many different objectives regarding their destination, but also their main characteristics from a risk and return point of view.

Brunel (2003) also shows that, under this process, some people may be more affected by losses than others, and even the same person can react differently to gains and losses from one account to another. This translates into asymmetric investor-specific responses to downside risk and upside potential. Applying this principle leads to the following representation proposed by Hübner and Lejeune (2021), called the horizon-asymmetry mental accounting (HAMA) framework:[16]

[16]We have slightly transformed their notation to ensure the consistency of the formulation with the rest of the section. All rates of return are continuously compounded.

$$\max_P \mathrm{E}(R_P^c) \tag{10-48a}$$

$$\text{subject to: } \Pr[\overline{R}_P^{c,H_j} \leq \mathrm{E}(R_P^c) - \delta_j] - \eta_j \Pr[\overline{R}_P^{c,H_j} \geq \mathrm{E}(R_P^c) + \delta_j] \leq \omega_j \tag{10-48b}$$

where δ_j is a tolerance level of the shortfall that can be incurred below the expected return before the investor considers the outcome as a "loss," and η_j is a gain/loss asymmetry trade-off coefficient that rewards gains beyond a certain level.[17] The difference in probabilities in the constraint inequality (10-48b) can be interpreted as the shortfall probability (first term) adjusted for the surplus probability (second term) or, in short, the asymmetry-adjusted shortfall probability.

The logic of the optimization program can best be understood if returns are Gaussian and i.i.d. (independent and identically distributed). Let the periodic returns have a volatility equal to σ_P^c. Over one period, the probability that the return (which is equal to its mean) falls below $\mathrm{E}(R_P^c) - \delta_j$ is equal to $\Phi\left(-\frac{\delta_j}{\sigma_P^c}\right)$, where $\Phi(x) \equiv \Pr[Z \leq x]$ with $Z \rightsquigarrow \mathcal{N}(0,1)$, i.e., it represents the probability that a standard normal random variable is lower than or equal to x. Over H_j periods, the volatility of the mean return mechanically shrinks to $\frac{\sigma_P^c}{\sqrt{H_j}}$. Thus, with that horizon, the shortfall probability becomes $\Phi\left(-\frac{\sqrt{H_j}\times\delta_j}{\sigma_P^c}\right)$, which takes a much lower value. Under the standard assumption that portfolio risk increases with expected return, the investor can thus afford to adopt a riskier portfolio as their horizon increases, which is a very intuitive result.

Furthermore, the presence of a second (negative) term in Equation (10-48b) gives a reward to the right tail of the returns distribution. Confronted with the same portfolio, an investor with a higher value of η_j will mitigate the shortfall probability to a larger extent, thereby affording a higher risk and obtaining a higher expected return as a result of the optimization.[18]

Starting with the probability distribution of the returns of a given portfolio, Figure 10-6 illustrates the logic underlying the organization of mental accounts that results from the HAMA framework.

The upper part of the figure represents the initial situation of an investor who contemplates an investment whose probability density function of returns is represented by the wide dashed curve. If they adopt an investment horizon H_0, the resulting distribution of the mean return corresponds to the continuous, narrower curve. This investor has a tolerance of δ_0 around the expected portfolio return so that there is a probability of $x_0\%$ falling in the left tail (shortfall) and $y_0\%$ landing in the right tail (surplus). The gain/loss asymmetry trade-off coefficient is $\eta_0 < 1$, whose impact is visually represented by the less dense hatching of the right tail than of the left tail. Unfortunately for this investor, they observe that the asymmetry-adjusted shortfall probability is too high, i.e., $x_0\% - \eta_0 \times y_0\% > \omega_0$. Thus, the portfolio is too risky for this account.

[17]For the sake of parsimony, we define the same tolerance level for the upside potential and the shortfall risk.
[18]An application of this optimization program is examined in Chapter 16 in the context of the design of structured products.

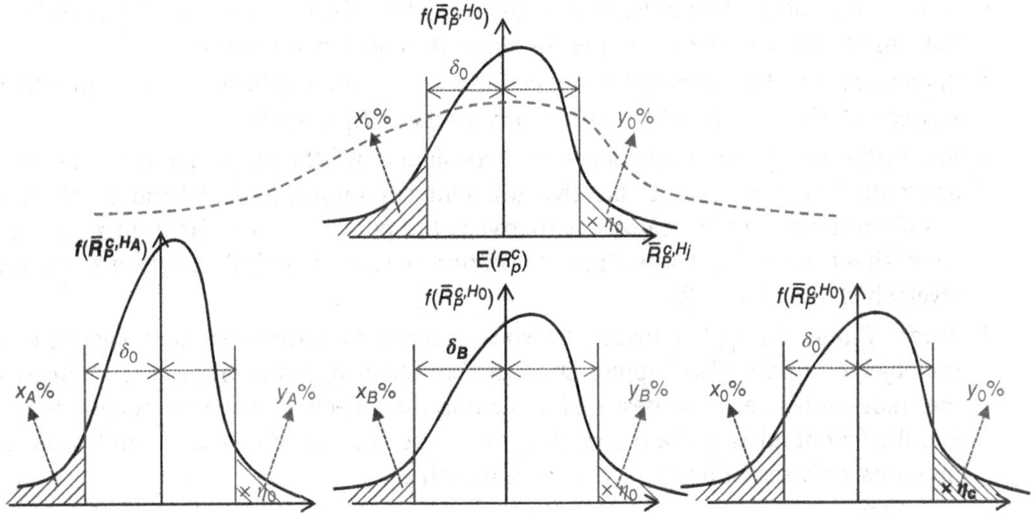

FIGURE 10-6 Mechanism of the horizon-asymmetry mental accounting (HAMA) framework.

How can this situation be resolved by keeping the same portfolio? The answers lie in the three charts on the lower part of the figure. The left one corresponds to the situation arising when the investment horizon increases. The density function becomes narrower, leading to a lower shortfall probability ($x_A\% < x_0\%$), which is less than offset by a corresponding lower surplus probability ($y_A\% < y_0\%$). Combining these two effects, the asymmetry-adjusted shortfall probability respects the constraint, i.e., $x_A\% - \eta_0 \times y_A\% \leq \omega_0$. The middle graph shows the impact of adopting a larger tolerance level $\delta_B > \delta_0$, which leads to a wider range of acceptable mean returns, and makes the resulting asymmetry-adjusted shortfall probability acceptable again: $x_B\% - \eta_0 \times y_B\% \leq \omega_0$. Finally, the right graph shows the impact of an upward revision of the gain/loss asymmetry coefficient $\eta_C > \eta_0$. Without changing either the horizon or the tolerance, this adjustment is sufficient to satisfy the constraint: $x_0\% - \eta_C \times y_0\% \leq \omega_0$.

There is a clear connection of this probability-based setup with the Prospect Theory framework studied in Section 10.1. The investment horizon directly impacts the riskiness of the portfolio and is mostly related to the investor's risk aversion. The tolerance level drives the investor's reservation rate because we can define it as $\underline{R}_j \equiv E(R_p^c) - \delta_j$. Finally, the gain/loss asymmetry tradeoff can be viewed as a proxy for the investor's level of loss aversion. Because of the flexibility of the HAMA framework, Hübner and Lejeune (2021) show not only that it can produce similar optimal portfolio allocations to those delivered by most utility functions, but also that it can result in realistic portfolio allocations that utility functions are unable to justify with reasonable parameter values.

In the context of GBI under this general HAMA framework, the challenge is to find a formulation that allows a transition from the optimization program of Equations (10-48a) and (10-48b) to a convergence criterion in the spirit of Equation (10-46). For each account, we consider that the investor's profile is characterized by four parameters (some of which are already encountered in the HAMA framework):

1. *Horizon* H_j: This is the moment (in periods) at which the investor wishes to cash-in the outcome of the investment in order to satisfy its associated purpose.
2. *Target return* τ_j: For each dollar invested in the account, the investor wants to achieve a target terminal wealth of V_j, which induces that $\tau_j H_j = \log V_j$.
3. *Reservation rate* $\underline{R}_j$: The investor agrees to consider that if the realized return falls within a certain distance below the objective, this shortfall is not substantial and the objective is still considered to be realized. Otherwise, the portfolio is too far from τ_j, and the shortfall is perceived as a loss. From this notion, we can identify the investor's tolerance level which is $\nu_j \equiv \tau_j - \underline{R}_j$.
4. *Trade-off intensity* η_j: The investor wishes to achieve a return that is at least equal to the objective and is also happier above it. Parameter η_j characterizes the intensity of the trade-off between the desire of exceeding the objective above the tolerance level and the fear of missing the reservation rate. In general, for risk-averse and loss-averse investors, only the values of $\eta_j < 1$ are reasonable.

Under the HAMA framework, the target rate of return τ_j merges with the best expected return that can be achieved by the optimized portfolio. Furthermore, as in the original GBI formulation statement, the maximum acceptable shortfall probability ω_j is bypassed as the objective is now to minimize it. Bringing all this together, it leads to the following goal-based optimization program:

$$\min_{P}(\Pr[\overline{R}_P^{c,H_j} \leq \tau_j - \nu_j] - \eta_j \Pr[\overline{R}_P^{c,H_j} \geq \tau_j + \nu_j]) \tag{10-49}$$

In terms of the assessment of realized portfolio performance, the measure of the *Global Goal-based performance*, denoted by GGBP_P^j, is the adjusted probability of reaching the investor's objective:

$$\text{GGBP}_P^j = \frac{1}{1+\eta_j}(1 - \widehat{\Pr}[\overline{R}_P^{c,H_j} \leq \tau_j - \nu_j] + \eta_j \widehat{\Pr}[\overline{R}_P^{c,H_j} \geq \tau_j + \nu_j]) \tag{10-50}$$

Note that, by normalizing the expression through the division by $1 + \eta_j$, the possible values of Equation (10-50) are bounded between 0 and 1.

10.4.3 Goal-based performance estimation methods

Since Equation (10-50) represents a generalized expression of the basic formula (10-47) for goal-based investment performance, we thus focus on the former version, knowing that it can be simplified. We distinguish two main approaches for the measurement of this performance indicator: historical and parametric.

10.4.3.1 Historical goal-based performance

When the approach is applied in the context of existing portfolios whose performance is to be appraised *a posteriori*, the raw material for the evaluation is the sample of observed periodical total returns. The key of the estimation procedure is the investor's investment horizon H_j. It corresponds to the length of the time window that extends between the initial investment and the final divestment. Naturally, the investor does not know in advance what would be the most appropriate timing for initiating the investment, and therefore the entry (and thus exit) time is random. In this specific context, in which the history of a portfolio returns could be anything from very small to very large compared with the investment horizon, we can list three types of treatment of historical data, depending on whether the sample period is large enough compared to the investment horizon.

1. The *pure historical estimation.*

   Consider that $H_j = nT_j$, where $\frac{1}{n}$ is the return measurement interval and T_j is the number of consecutive returns that are necessary to cover the investment horizon.[19] If we have $T >> T_j$ observations, we can draw a large number of overlapping sub-samples of consecutive returns. Since the investor's entry and exit points would in reality happen in a random way, there are $T - T_j + 1$ consecutive subsamples that exactly match the investment horizon with an average portfolio return equal to $\overline{R}_{P,k}^{c,H_j}$ for $k = 1, \ldots, T - T_j + 1$. The associated pure historical estimation of the performance measure, called hGGBP_P^j, simply estimates the frequencies with which the sample means fall to the left and to the right of the tolerance interval around the target rate of return. The measure is written as

$$\text{hGGBP}_P^j = \frac{1}{1+\eta_j}\left(1 - \frac{T_P^{-j}}{T - T_j + 1} + \eta_j \frac{T_P^{+j}}{T - T_j + 1}\right) \tag{10-51}$$

   where $T_P^{-j} = \sum_{k=1}^{T-T_j+1} 1_{\{\overline{R}_{P,k}^{c,H_j} \leq \tau_j - \nu_j\}}$ and $T_P^{+j} = \sum_{k=1}^{T-T_j+1} 1_{\{\overline{R}_{P,k}^{c,H_j} \geq \tau_j + \nu_j\}}$ represent the number of times a final shortfall and a final surplus are observed across all subsamples, respectively.

2. The *extended historical estimation.*

   If one considers that T covers a complete financial cycle, it is possible to increase the number of subsamples by duplicating the sample and connecting the final observation with the initial one. This method, called the circular block method, creates an additional $T_j - 1$ number of subsamples with consecutive returns, so that there is a total of T subsamples for which the average return can be drawn.

[19]For simplicity, we consider that T_j is an integer number. Otherwise, we simply set $T_j = \lceil nH_j \rceil$ in which $\lceil \cdot \rceil$ stands for the ceiling (lowest integer greater than or equal to) of the argument.

The extended historical estimation of the performance measure, called $h^*GGBP^j_P$, is written as

$$h^*GGBP^j_P = \frac{1}{1+\eta_j}\left(1 - \frac{T_P^{*-j}}{T} + \eta_j \frac{T_P^{*+j}}{T}\right) \quad (10\text{-}52)$$

where $T_P^{*-j} = \sum_{k=1}^{T} 1_{\{\overline{R}_{P,k}^{c,H_j} \leq \tau_j - \nu_j\}}$ and $T_P^{*+j} = \sum_{k=1}^{T} 1_{\{\overline{R}_{P,k}^{c,H_j} \geq \tau_j + \nu_j\}}$.

3. The *resampled historical estimation*.

When the investment horizon increases, the number of usable subsamples for the pure historical estimation shrinks and eventually falls to zero when $T = T_j$. Beyond that level, i.e., if $T < T_j$, neither the pure nor the extended historical estimation procedures are even applicable. One then has to use bootstrapping techniques in order to generate a sufficiently large number S of strings of T_j observations. For each simulated sample, we denote by $\overline{R}_{P,s}^{c,H_j}$ the continuously compounded arithmetic average return. We obtain

$$\widehat{h}GGBP^j_P = \frac{1}{1+\eta_j}\left(1 - \frac{S_P^{-j}}{S} + \eta_j \frac{S_P^{+j}}{S}\right) \quad (10\text{-}53)$$

where $S_P^{-j} = \sum_{s=1}^{S} 1_{\{\overline{R}_{P,s}^{c,H_j} \leq \tau_j - \nu_j\}}$ and $S_P^{+j} = \sum_{s=1}^{S} 1_{\{\overline{R}_{P,s}^{c,H_j} \geq \tau_j + \nu_j\}}$.

The key difference between Equations (10-52) and (10-53) is naturally that S can be arbitrarily large, while T is bound to be equal to the size of the sample. Furthermore, as the extended sample introduces an artificial link between the last and the first observations that could be at odds with the real time-dependence structure of the data, the latter characteristic can be explicitly used in the procedure through an adequate block-bootstrap methodology.

The three approaches described above are represented in Figure 10-7.

The left chart illustrates the pure historical approach. The column on the left represents the original sample, while the other columns correspond to the subsamples extracted from it. Each subsample simply corresponds to a string of consecutive observations of length T_j, and a total of $T - T_j + 1$ samples can be drawn. This approach's main advantage is to leave the data intact and to exactly correspond to the estimation of frequencies underlying the probabilistic character of the performance measure. It is suitable when the frequency of observations is high and the horizon is much shorter than the sample period. For instance, if $T = 520$ (10 years of weekly data) and $T_j = 104$ (an investment horizon of 2 years), this procedure produces $T - T_j + 1 = 417$ usable consecutive overlapping subsamples.

The chart in the middle of the figure shows how the extended historical estimation procedure, using the circular block method, completes the original sample in order to obtain exactly T subsamples of returns spanning T_j observations. For instance, in the previous example, an additional number of $T_j - 1 = 103$ new subsamples are appended to the original set.

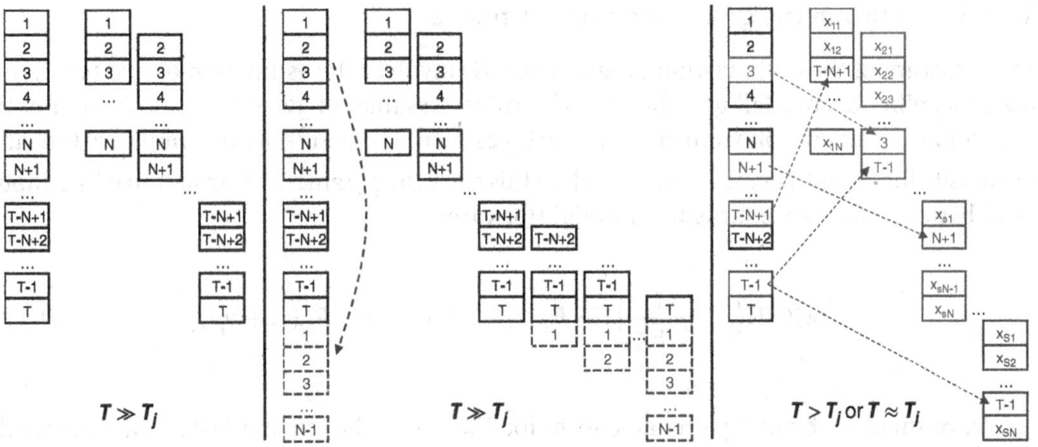

FIGURE 10-7 Illustrations of the three types of historical estimation procedures (***N*** **=** $\boldsymbol{T_j}$ in the boxes).

Beyond the increase in the number of blocks, the procedure has the advantage of using each observation the exact same number of times, which fully addresses the issue of using overlapping subsamples of data. The main drawback is the unnatural connection made between the end and the beginning of the original sample in order to produce additional artificial observations.

The right chart illustrates how the resampled estimation works, with the application of a bootstrapping approach by randomly drawing returns from the original sample (with replacement) in order to construct a potentially unlimited series of S subsamples. This is the only workable approach when T is not high enough compared with T_j. For instance, if only five years of monthly returns ($T = 60$) are available, it is practically impossible to obtain a reasonable set of subsamples, regardless of the value of T_j. The procedure breaks any potential time-series dependence in the data, a drawback that can be mitigated by selecting blocks of consecutive returns rather than isolated ones, as illustrated in the figure.[20]

It remains to be noted that the effectiveness of any historical procedure, even the resampled estimation one, becomes very limited when the investment horizon T_j increases compared with T. In the HiMeLo example treated throughout the chapter, for instance, we have only one year of monthly data ($T = 12$) to work with. It would make no sense to attempt to use the data points directly in order to assess the adjusted probability of reaching the investor's objective that underlies the estimation of the Global Goal-based performance measure. This is why it may make sense to use parametric estimation approaches.

[20]There are a number of constraints to be respected on the block resampling procedure to preserve the original properties of the time series (e.g., higher order moments, autocorrelation structure, unconditional distribution of changes). See Coroneo, Nyholm, and Vidova-Koleva (2011) for a complete discussion.

10.4.3.2 Parametric goal-based performance

The structure of the optimization program (10-49) involves the estimation of two tail events: the probability of shortfall and the one of surplus. Assume, in general, a distribution of the continuous mean portfolio returns up to the investment horizon H_j with cumulative probability density function $F_{\mathcal{D}}(x) \equiv \Pr[\overline{R}_P^{c,H_j} \leq x]$. In this case, the parametric translation of the Global Goal-based performance measure is straightforward:

$$\text{pGGBP}_P^j = \frac{1}{1+\eta_j}[1 - F_{\mathcal{D}}(\tau_j - \nu_j) + \eta_j\,(1 - F_{\mathcal{D}}(\tau_j + \nu_j))] \tag{10-54}$$

Nevertheless, obtaining a reliable form for $F_{\mathcal{D}}(x)$ is a challenging task, as it involves the characterization of the distribution of mean returns. Unless the periodic portfolio returns exhibit no serial correlation and are drawn from a stable distribution (such as the Gaussian one), it is not possible to infer the functional form of the distribution of the mean from the distribution of the individual returns. Thus, this particular route is difficult to follow. Instead, it is possible to start from the Gaussian distribution assumption and to address the impact of asymmetry and fat-tailedness through relatively mild assumptions, as discussed below.

1. The *parametric Gaussian estimation.*

   Consider the case with independent and identically distributed (i.i.d.) periodical returns following a Gaussian probability law: $R_{P,t}^c \rightsquigarrow \mathcal{N}(\mu_P, \sigma_P^2)$, where $\mu_P \equiv \mathrm{E}(R_P^c)$.[21] Since returns are i.i.d., $\overline{R}_P^{c,H_j} \rightsquigarrow \mathcal{N}\left(\mu_P, \frac{\sigma_P^2}{T_j}\right)$, where, as before, $T_j = \frac{H_j}{\Delta t}$ and Δt is the return measurement interval. We focus on the estimate of the first moment which is $\widehat{\mu}_P = \overline{R}_P^c$.[22] Then $\widehat{\Pr}[\overline{R}_P^{c,H_j} \leq \tau_j - \nu_j] = \Phi\left(\frac{(\tau_j - \nu_j - \overline{R}_P^c)\sqrt{T_j}}{\sigma_P}\right)$ and $\widehat{\Pr}[\overline{R}_P^{H_j} \geq \tau_j + \nu_j] = \Phi\left(\frac{(\overline{R}_P^c - \tau_j - \nu_j)\sqrt{T_j}}{\sigma_P}\right)$, where $\Phi(\cdot)$ denotes the cumulative density function of the standard normal distribution. This leaves:

$$\text{gGGBP}_P^j = \frac{1}{1+\eta_j}\left[1 - \Phi\left(\frac{(\tau_j - \nu_j - \overline{R}_P^c)\sqrt{T_j}}{\sigma_P}\right) + \eta_j\,\Phi\left(\frac{(\overline{R}_P^c - \tau_j - \nu_j)\sqrt{T_j}}{\sigma_P}\right)\right] \tag{10-55}$$

   This expression becomes very simple if $\tau_j = \overline{R}_P^c$. Then, the two percentiles are symmetrically located around the mean and we obtain the symmetric Global Goal-based

[21] In this section, we have removed superscript "c" from the symbols of the moments of the continuously compounded portfolio returns to avoid any heavier notation.
[22] It is considered here for simplicity that the standard deviation is known.

performance measure:

$$\text{sGGBP}_P^j = \frac{1}{1+\eta_j}\left[1-(1-\eta_j)\,\Phi\left(\frac{-\nu_j\sqrt{T_j}}{\sigma_P}\right)\right] \tag{10-56}$$

This will simply assign a higher performance to portfolios with lower risk. However, even in the Gaussian case, taking into account the upside potential of the distribution of returns may matter if the expected portfolio return differs from the investor's objective.

2. The *semi-parametric Cornish–Fisher estimation*.

The Cornish–Fisher expansion has already been encountered in several sections of Chapter 6. It can prove to be particularly useful in the current context.

Consider that $R_{P,t}^c \rightsquigarrow \mathcal{D}(\mu_P, \sigma_P^2, m_{P,3}, m_{P,4})$, where $\mathcal{D}$ is a probability distribution with third- and fourth-centered moments equal to $m_{P,3}$ and $m_{P,4}$, respectively. In general, if returns are i.i.d., the distribution $\mathcal{D}'$ of the average return $\overline{R}_P^{c,H_j} \rightsquigarrow \mathcal{D}'\left(\mu_P, \frac{\sigma_P^2}{T_j}, \frac{m_{P,3}}{T_j^2}, \frac{m_{P,4}}{T_j^3} + \frac{(3(T_j-1)\sigma_P^4}{T_j^3}\right)$ differs from $\mathcal{D}$.[23] Nevertheless, if T_j is sufficiently large, then from the Central Limit Theorem we can assume that this distribution $\mathcal{D}'$ converges sufficiently toward the Gaussian distribution so that the Cornish–Fisher approximation of the percentiles of the distribution can be applied. Adapting the formula of Equation (10-55) with the modified volatility defined in Equation (6-13) of Chapter 6, we reach the modified Global Goal-based performance, or $mGGBP_P^{j,1-x}$:

$$\text{mGGBP}_P^{j,1-x} = \frac{1}{1+\eta_j}\left[1-\Phi\left(\frac{(\tau_j-\nu_j-\overline{R}_P^c)\sqrt{T_j}}{m\sigma_P^{(x-)}}\right)+\eta_j\,\Phi\left(\frac{(\overline{R}_P^c-\tau_j-\nu_j)\sqrt{T_j}}{m\sigma_P^{(x+)}}\right)\right] \tag{10-57}$$

in which $m\sigma_P^{(x-)} = \sigma_P \times \frac{z_{x-,P}^*}{z_x}$ and $m\sigma_P^{(x+)} = \sigma_P \times \frac{z_{x+,P}^*}{z_x}$ are defined as the modified volatilities for surplus and shortfall, respectively, and their associated volatility multipliers are given by

$$z_{x-,P}^* = z_x + (z_x^2-1)\frac{\mu_{P,3}}{6\sqrt{T_j}} + (z_x^3-3z_x)\frac{e\mu_{P,4}}{24T_j} - (2z_x^3-5z_x)\frac{\mu_{P,3}^2}{36T_j} \tag{10-58a}$$

$$z_{x+,P}^* = z_x - (z_x^2-1)\frac{\mu_{P,3}}{6\sqrt{T_j}} + (z_x^3-3z_x)\frac{e\mu_{P,4}}{24T_j} - (2z_x^3-5z_x)\frac{\mu_{P,3}^2}{36T_j} \tag{10-58b}$$

where $\mu_{P,3} \equiv \frac{m_{P,3}}{\sigma_P^3}$ and $e\mu_{P,4} \equiv \frac{m_{P,4}}{\sigma_P^4} - 3$ are the skewness and excess kurtosis of the continuous portfolio returns, respectively.

[23] Indeed, in this case, all the moments of the mean return are mechanically determined as a function of T_j.

TABLE 10-10 Cornish–Fisher multipliers for the shortfall and surplus modified volatilities.

	C-F with $\mu_{P,3} = 0, e\mu_{P,4} = 6.9$		C-F with $\mu_{P,3} = -0.5, e\mu_{P,4} = 6.9$	
Horizon T_j	$z^*_{x-,P}$	$z^*_{x+,P}$	$z^*_{x-,P}$	$z^*_{x+,P}$
1	−2.43	−2.43	−2.63	−2.16
12	−2.00	−2.00	−2.06	−1.93
36	−1.97	−1.97	−2.01	−1.93
60	−1.97	−1.97	−2.00	−1.94
120	−1.96	−1.96	−1.99	−1.94

The structures of the Gaussian and modified versions of the performance measures are very similar. They only differ thanks to the volatilities and their associated multipliers. The difference between $z^*_{x-,P}$ and $z^*_{x+,P}$ resides in the sign of the skewness term. In $z^*_{x-,P}$, it is positive, whereas it is negative for $z^*_{x+,P}$. Thus, if the skewness is negative, the modified volatility $m\sigma_P^{(x-)}$ increases, thereby penalizing the shortfall probability, while it leads to a decrease in $m\sigma_P^{(x+)}$ which also penalizes the surplus probability. The confidence level $1 - x$ chosen for the estimation of the volatility multipliers reflects the importance given to higher moments in the estimation.[24]

For very long horizons, the impact of the skewness and kurtosis on the mean tends to vanish, but it can be material when T_j is not too large. Table 10-10, using the same skewness and kurtosis inputs as in Table 6-15 of Chapter 6, illustrates the impact of the increase in investment horizon on the volatility adjustments. For that purpose, we choose a confidence level of $1 - x = 97.5\%$ which corresponds to a value of $z_{2.5\%} = -1.96$.

HiMeLo example (continued)

At first, in order to implement the GBI framework, it is necessary to transform the data of Table 10-1 into continuously compounded returns by using the formula $R^c_{P,t} = \log(1 + R_{P,t})$. We consider that the company's typical investors have two types of horizons: a short-term horizon of one year ($T_j = 12$) and a medium-term horizon of five years ($T_j = 60$). In order

[24]As a reminder, the choice of the confidence level $1 - x$ should be made carefully (see Section 6.1.3 of Chapter 6 for a discussion).

to compute the Cornish–Fisher volatility multipliers, we implement formulas (10-58a) and (10-58b) using a confidence level of $1 - x = 97.5\%$, which corresponds to a Gaussian value of $z_{2.5\%} = -1.96$. The relevant summary statistics are provided in Table 10-11.

TABLE 10-11 HiMeLo example – Summary statistics and multipliers of the continuously compounded returns.

	Low	Medium	High
Mean return	3.75%	5.00%	6.19%
Standard deviation	4.23%	7.75%	11.90%
Skewness	−1.17	0.82	1.37
Excess kurtosis	2.45	2.67	4.70
Shortfall multiplier ($T_j = 12$)	−2.12	−1.86	−1.78
Shortfall multiplier ($T_j = 60$)	−2.03	−1.91	−1.88
Surplus multiplier ($T_j = 12$)	−1.80	−2.08	−2.15
Surplus multiplier ($T_j = 60$)	−1.89	−2.01	−2.04

We consider three levels of target returns: $\tau_j = 2\%, 4\%, 6\%$, associated with a single tolerance level of $\nu_j = 2\%$ for all investors. Finally, we use three possible levels of the gain/loss trade-off coefficient $\eta_j = 0, \eta_j = 0.4$ and $\eta_j = 0.8$. The modified Global Goal-based performance measures are reported in Table 10-12 (each histogram corresponds to the estimated probability according to formula (10-57)).

The adjusted probabilities of achieving the investment goal decrease with the level of η_j because of the impact of the normalization factor $\frac{1}{1+\eta_j}$ in the formula. Thanks to this factor, the discrimination level between the portfolios is greater as the gain/loss trade-off increases as well. Because of the relatively high target returns at $\tau_j = 4\%$ and $\tau_j = 6\%$, the expected return of the High portfolio tends to dominate the adverse impact of its risk. This is also the case for low target returns ($\tau_j = 2\%$) if the investment horizon is sufficiently large. Only for the most conservative goal (low target, low horizon, low trade-off coefficient), do the other portfolios provide a higher probability of achieving the objective.

(continued)

(continued)

TABLE 10-12 HiMeLo example – Modified Global Goal-based performance of the three portfolios.

		Gain/Loss trade-off		
Horizon	**Target return**	$\eta_j = 0.0$	$\eta_j = 0.4$	$\eta_j = 0.8$
$T_j = 12$	$\tau_j = 2\%$	100%, 99%, 98%	83%, 90%, 90%	74%, 85%, 86%
	$\tau_j = 4\%$	91%, 92%, 91%	65%, 75%, 80%	51%, 66%, 74%
	$\tau_j = 6\%$	42%, 68%, 76%	30%, 52%, 63%	24%, 42%, 56%
$T_j = 60$	$\tau_j = 2\%$	100%, 100%, 100%	80%, 95%, 98%	70%, 93%, 96%
	$\tau_j = 4\%$	100%, 100%, 100%	71%, 76%, 87%	55%, 63%, 80%
	$\tau_j = 6\%$	33%, 85%, 93%	23%, 61%, 70%	18%, 47%, 56%

Key Takeaways and Equations

- In the behavioral utility framework, the utility function is split into two parts on either side of the reservation rate, and the utility function is steeper in the area of losses, which corresponds to loss-averse investor behavior. The most popular form of such utility function is the *dual power utility function* proposed in the Prospect Theory framework:

$$U_{\underline{R},\lambda,\gamma}(R) = \begin{cases} (R - \underline{R})^{\gamma^+} \text{ if } R > \underline{R} \\ -\lambda(\underline{R} - R)^{\gamma^-} \text{ if } R < \underline{R} \end{cases} \tag{10-6}$$

- The generic form of the behavioral utility score is written as

$$\mathrm{E}[U_j(R_P)] = \frac{1}{T}\sum_{t=1}^{T}[1_{\{R_P \geq \underline{R}_j\}}U_j^+(R_P) + 1_{\{R_P < \underline{R}_j\}}U_j^-(R_P)] \tag{10-9}$$

- From this formulation, the major performance measures are as follows:
  - The *behavioral-Quadratic score*:

$$\mathrm{bQ}_P^j = \overline{R}_P - (\lambda_j - 1)d\overline{R}_P(\underline{R}_j) - \frac{1}{2}(\lambda_j\gamma_j^- \times d\sigma_P^2(\underline{R}_j) + \gamma_j^+ \times u\sigma_P^2(\underline{R}_j)) \tag{10-10}$$

  - The *Prospect Theory score*:

$$\mathrm{PT}_P^j = um_{\gamma_j^+,P}(\underline{R}_j) - \lambda_j dm_{\gamma_j^-,P}(\underline{R}_j) \tag{10-14}$$

- Normative performance measures can also be derived from the behavioral finance. The generic forms of these kinds of measures are as follows:
  - The *behavioral Sharpe ratio*:

$$\mathrm{bSR}_P^j = \frac{\overline{R}_P - \underline{R}_j - (\lambda_j - 1)d\overline{R}_P(\underline{R}_j)}{\sqrt{\lambda_j\theta_j d\sigma_P^2(\underline{R}_j) + u\sigma_P^2(\underline{R}_j)}} \tag{10-17}$$

  - The *Prospect Theory Sharpe ratio*, also known as the *Farinelli–Tibiletti ratio*:

$$\text{F-T}_P^j = \mathrm{PTSR}_P^{j*} = \frac{um_{\gamma_j^+,P}(\underline{R}_j)}{dm_{\gamma_j^-,P}(\underline{R}_j)} \equiv \frac{\sqrt[\alpha_j]{\frac{1}{T}\sum_{t=1}^{T}(\max(R_{P,t} - \underline{R}_j, 0))^{\alpha_j}}}{\sqrt[\beta_j]{\frac{1}{T}\sum_{t=1}^{T}(\max(\underline{R}_j - R_{P,t}, 0))^{\beta_j}}} \tag{10-19}$$

- For the sake of clarity, we can simply write $\text{F-T}_P^j \equiv \text{F-T}_P(\alpha_j, \beta_j, \underline{R}_j)$. This ratio has a number of interesting specific parametrizations:
  - The original Prospect Theory ratio: $\mathrm{oPTR}_P^j \equiv \text{F-T}_P(0.6, 0.6, \underline{R}_j)$.

(continued)

(continued)

- The Omega: $\Omega_P^j \equiv \text{F-T}_P(1,1,\underline{R}_j)$.
- The Upside Potential Ratio: $\text{UPR}_P^j \equiv \text{F-T}_P(1,2,\underline{R}_j)$.
- The Variability Skewness: $\text{VSk}_P^j \equiv \text{F-T}_P(2,2,\underline{R}_j)$.
- The modified Kappa ratio: $\text{m}\kappa\text{R}_P^j \equiv \text{F-T}_P(1,3,\underline{R}_j)$.

- There exist some heuristic variations of performance measures based on behavioral finance either based on ad hoc variations of the Prospect Theory or on frequencies of gains and losses.
  - Noticeable ratios of adjusted gains over adjusted losses are the *Prospect ratio*:

$$\text{ProR}_P^j = \frac{u\bar{R}_P(\underline{R}_j) - \lambda_j d\bar{R}_P(\underline{R}_j) - \underline{R}_j}{d\sigma_P(\underline{R}_j)} \tag{10-28}$$

the *Generalized Rachev ratio*:

$$\text{GRacR}_P^{j,x,y} = \frac{\text{hCGaR}_{\gamma_j^+,P}^{(1-y)}}{\text{hCVaR}_{\gamma_j^-,P}^{(1-x)}} \equiv \frac{\sqrt[\alpha_j]{\frac{1}{n_y}\sum_{i=1}^{n_y}(R_{P,i} - R_{P,n_y})^{\alpha_j}}}{\sqrt[\beta_j]{\frac{1}{T-n_x}\sum_{i=1}^{T-n_x}(R_{P,n_x} - R_{P,i})^{\beta_j}}} \tag{10-30}$$

and the *Up/Down Rachev ratio*:

$$\text{udRacR}_P^j = \frac{\overline{\text{du}}_P(\underline{R}_j)}{\overline{\text{dd}}_P(\underline{R}_j)} \tag{10-32}$$

  - Noticeable measures of the frequencies of gains over losses are the *Batting average*:

$$\text{BA}_P^j = \frac{T_P^{+j}}{T} \tag{10-34}$$

and the *Capture ratio*:

$$\text{CapR}_P \equiv \frac{\text{UCR}_P}{\text{DCR}_P} = \frac{\left(\sum_{t=1}^{T} R_{P,t} \times 1_{\{R_{B,t}>0\}}\right)\left(\sum_{t=1}^{T} R_{B,t} \times 1_{\{R_{B,t}<0\}}\right)}{\left(\sum_{t=1}^{T} R_{B,t} \times 1_{\{R_{B,t}>0\}}\right)\left(\sum_{t=1}^{T} R_{P,t} \times 1_{\{R_{B,t}<0\}}\right)} \tag{10-39}$$

- It is also possible to measure portfolio performance in the MA framework. Considering the original setup, the performance of a portfolio managed for a given account is given by the *Stutzer convergence index*:

$$D_P^j = \max_{\gamma^*}\left(-\log \frac{1}{T}\sum_{t=1}^{T} e^{\gamma^*(R_{P,t}^c - \underline{R}_j^c)}\right) \quad (10\text{-}43)$$

- When the framework (MA) is adapted to the context of GBI, the most general form of the performance measure is given by the *Global Goal-based performance*:

$$\text{GGBP}_P^j = \frac{1}{1+\eta_j}(1 - \widehat{\Pr}[\overline{R}_P^{c,H_j} \leq \tau_j - \nu_j] + \eta_j\, \widehat{\Pr}[\overline{R}_P^{c,H_j} \geq \tau_j + \nu_j]) \quad (10\text{-}50)$$

- The implementation of the GGBP requires us either to use and transform historical data or to use a parametric approach. Using the Cornish–Fisher expansion in the context of the Gaussian distribution of returns, the corresponding formula becomes

$$\text{mGGBP}_P^{j,1-x} = \frac{1}{1+\eta_j}\left[1 - \Phi\left(\frac{(\tau_j - \nu_j - \overline{R}_P^c)\sqrt{T_j}}{m\sigma_P^{(x-)}}\right) + \eta_j\, \Phi\left(\frac{(\overline{R}_P^c - \tau_j - \nu_j)\sqrt{T_j}}{m\sigma_P^{(x+)}}\right)\right] \quad (10\text{-}57)$$

REFERENCES

Bacon, C. R. (2021), *Practical Risk-Adjusted Performance Measurement, 2nd Edition*. Wiley, Wiley Finance Series.

Barberis, N., Huang, M., and T. Santos (2001), Prospect theory and asset prices. *Quarterly Journal of Economics*, Vol. 116, pp. 1–53.

Bernardo, A. E., and O. Ledoit (2000), Gain, loss and asset pricing. *Journal of Political Economy*, Vol. 108, pp. 144–172.

Bertrand, P., and J.-L. Prigent (2011). Omega performance measure and portfolio insurance. *Journal of Banking & Finance*, Vol. 35, pp. 1811–1823.

Biglova, A., Ortobelli, S., Rachev, S. T., and S. Stoyanov (2004), Different approaches to risk estimation in portfolio theory. *The Journal of Portfolio Management*, Vol. 31 (1), pp. 103–112.

Brunel, J. L. P. (2003), Revisiting the asset allocation challenge through a behavioral finance lens. *Journal of Wealth Management*, Vol. 6, pp. 10–20.

Caporin M., Costola, M., Jannin, G., and B. Maillet (2018), On the (ab)use of Omega? *Journal of Empirical Finance*, Vol. 46, pp. 11–33.

Cogneau, P., and G. Hübner (2009), The (more than) 100 ways to measure portfolio performance: Part 2: Special measures and comparison. *Journal of Performance Measurement*, Vol. 14 (1), pp. 56–69.

Coroneo, L., Nyholm, K., and R. Vidova-Koleva (2011), How arbitrage-free is the Nelson and Siegel model? *Journal of Empirical Finance*, Vol. 18, pp. 393–407.

Das, S., Markowitz, H., Scheid, J., and M. Statman (2010), Portfolio optimization with mental accounts. *Journal of Financial and Quantitative Analysis*, Vol. 45, pp. 311–334.

Farinelli, S., and L. Tibiletti (2008), Sharpe thinking in asset ranking with one-sided measures. *European Journal of Operational Research*, Vol. 185, pp. 1542–1547.

Fishburn, P. C. (1977), Mean-risk analysis with risk associated with below-target returns. *American Economic Review*, Vol. 67, pp. 116–126.

Gemmill, G., Hwang, S., and M. Salmon (2006), Performance measurement with loss aversion. *Journal of Asset Management*, Vol. 7 (3–4), pp. 190–207.

Hübner, G., and T. Lejeune (2021), Mental accounts with horizon and asymmetry preferences. *Economic Modelling*, Vol. 103, # 105615.

Kahneman, D., and A. Tversky (1979), Prospect theory: An analysis of decision under risk. *Econometrica*, Vol. 47, pp. 263–291.

Kaplan, P. D. (2005), A unified approach to risk-adjusted performance. Unpublished mimeo, Morningstar Inc.

Kaplan, P. D., and J. A. Knowles (2004), Kappa: A generalized downside risk-adjusted performance measure. *Journal of Performance Measurement*, Vol. 8 (3), pp. 42–54.

Keating, C., and W. Shadwick (2002), A universal performance measure. *Journal of Performance Measurement*, Vol. 6 (3), pp. 59–84.

Köbberling, V., and P. P. Wakker (2005), An index of loss aversion. *Journal of Economic Theory*, Vol. 122, pp. 1110–1131.

Lavinio, S. (1999). *The Hedge Fund Handbook*. McGraw-Hill.

Markowitz, H. (1959), *Portfolio Selection*. Efficient Diversification of Investments. John Wiley.

Marlo, T., and J. R. Stark (2019), Capture ratios: Seizing market gains, avoiding losses, and attracting investors' funds. *Journal of Investing*, Vol. 29 (1), pp. 80–94.

Melnikoff, M. (1998), Investment performance analysis for investors. *The Journal of Portfolio Management*, Vol. 25 (1), pp. 95–107.

Morningstar (2011), Introducing upside and downside capture ratios. *Morningstar The Short Answer*.

Ortobelli, S., Biglova, A., Rachev, S. T., and S. Stoyanov (2010), Portfolio selection based on a simulated copula. *Journal of Applied Functional Analysis*, Vol. 5 (2), pp. 177–193.

Schwager, J. D. (2012), *Market Wizards: Interviews with Top Traders*. John Wiley & Sons.

Sortino, F. A., and L. N. Price (1994), Performance measurement in a downside risk framework. *Journal of Investing*, Vol. 3 (3), pp. 510–564.

Sortino, F. A., van der Meer, R., and A. Plantinga (1999), The Dutch triangle. *The Journal of Portfolio Management*, Vol. 26 (1), pp. 50–58.

Stutzer, M. (2000), A portfolio performance index. *Financial Analysts Journal*, Vol. 56 (3), pp. 52–61.

Stutzer, M. (2003), Portfolio choice with endogenous utility: A large deviations approach. *Journal of Econometrics*, Vol. 116, pp. 365–386.

Thaler, R. H. (1985), Mental accounting and consumer choice. *Marketing Science*, Vol. 4, pp. 199–214.

Thaler, R. H. (1999), Mental accounting matters. *Journal of Behavioral Decision Making*, Vol. 12, pp. 183–206.

Tversky, A., and D. Kahneman (1992), Advances in prospect theory: Cumulative representation of uncertainty. *Journal of Risk and Uncertainty*, Vol. 5, pp. 297–323.

Watanabe, Y. (2014), New prospect ratio: Application to hedge funds with higher order moments. *Journal of Performance Measurement*, Vol. 19 (1), pp. 41–53.

Zakamouline, V. (2010), On the consistent use of VaR in portfolio performance evaluation: A cautionary note. *The Journal of Portfolio Management*, Vol. 37 (1), pp. 92–104.

Zakamouline, V. (2014), Portfolio performance evaluation with loss aversion. *Quantitative Finance*, Vol. 14, pp. 699–710.

Zakamouline, V., and S. Koekebakker (2009), A generalisation of the mean–variance analysis. *European Financial Management*, Vol. 15, pp. 934–970.

PART III - *Analyze*

ANALYZING AND MONITORING PERFORMANCE

The first half of the book is devoted to the presentation of different ways to measure performance and the justification of their relevance for appraising the efficiency of the portfolio management process. In total, we identify more than 100 ways to assess portfolio performance. Picking and applying one or a few of them is just not enough to complete a fully consistent portfolio management process. Beyond the pure measurement of past performance ("what performance did the portfolio achieve?"), a well-designed framework entails the understanding of this performance generation ("how did the portfolio achieve that performance?"). From such a framework meaningful lessons can be learnt to further strengthen the portfolio management process.

The first challenge addressed in this "analyze" part is to clarify the selection criteria for the choice of performance measures. Because the large set of measures studied in Parts I and II might create a sense of plethora, we devote **Chapter 11** to the systematic review of the measures and their underlying dimensions (analytical and statistical). The outcome of this chapter is a dashboard that, we hope, sheds more light on the necessary considerations underlying the selection of one or several measures for the analysis of performance.

Another key feature of this part of the book is the design of adapted performance measurement frameworks for the analysis of specific asset classes. In **Chapter 12**, we study how to tackle three major categories of investments, namely fixed-income securities, hedge funds, and private equity. We discuss how their own specificities must be accounted for regarding how to analyze the quality of the portfolio management process.

The last two chapters are devoted to the heart of performance analysis, namely the contribution and attribution approaches. **Chapter 13** introduces the challenges raised by the ambition of carrying out a granular analysis of performance. We start with the fundamentals of performance decomposition in the risk–return space. This helps the understanding and interpreting of the components of performance. It also paves the way for a meaningful decomposition of the major ratio-based performance measures, namely the Sharpe and Information ratios.

We complete the performance decomposition process with **Chapter 14** that is entirely devoted to performance attribution analysis. We introduce the classical Brinson-Hood-Beebower approach and its most important extensions in the fields of multiple periods and asset classes. Even though this chapter is not meant to encompass a fully detailed treatment of the matter, we focus on two key contemporaneous topics, namely statistical attribution and the treatment of the ESG dimension in performance attribution, which are particularly helpful in the analysis of the determinants of performance.

CHAPTER 11

Navigating the Maze of Portfolio Performance

INTRODUCTION

The aim of the first part of this book is to explore the universe of performance measurement in a comprehensive and structured way. The intended outcome is a wide and relatively detailed overview of many different, yet defendable ways to appraise the performance of an actively managed portfolio. The reader who would have gone through all this material may legitimately feel overwhelmed with the quantity of information. Furthermore, as the chapters do not follow a hierarchical structure, there has not been any indication to date about the criteria that the user of the full library of performance measures should implement in order to select one or several of them from the shelf. In sum, we have developed a kind of maze and have explored many of its corners, but we have not yet delivered the map to navigate it.

In this chapter, we have the ambition to provide some directions in order to ease the reader's journey through this maze. This does not mean that our goal is to be normative about the performance measure selection process. Many measures have been proposed with acceptable justifications and practical advantages, and our job is neither to praise nor to despise them. Rather, the objective here is to provide a set of methods, developed by ourselves or by some authors who have undertaken a similar task, in order to make an educated choice about how to appraise portfolio performance and the meaning associated with this decision.

We start by building our own *summary list* of the most important and/or interesting performance measures that we have discussed so far. Even though this list is necessarily subjective, it is also sufficiently comprehensive (116 formulas) to be considered representative of the field. Because we want this to be a practical tool, we roll out this list in two ways: by order of appearance in the book and by alphabetical order, with a lexicon of the symbols used in the equations.

The next step is the presentation of three alternative approaches that can be used (and have actually been proposed by different authors) to navigate the maze. The first one is a taxonomy that takes the form of a *decision tree* structure, aiming to assist the user in the final choice of a performance measure. The second one is a pair of *analytical sorting procedures* that associate performance to some logical dimensions. The third one is a set of *statistical techniques* (correlation analysis, principal components analysis (PCA), and cluster analysis) that extract information from the portfolio rankings produced with alternative performance measures. The outcomes of these types of analyses, as performed by different authors, display variations but generally lead to relatively similar dimensions that underlie the universe of performance measures.

Finally, to close the loop, we dare ourselves to dive into the list and extract a logical structure from it. Unsurprisingly, the output of this analysis is in line with the structure of the previous chapters. We develop a dashboard that is relatively synthetic (one page) and based on clear partitioning mechanisms that, we hope, will be helpful in the selection process of a performance measure.

11.1 THE SPECTRUM OF PERFORMANCE MEASUREMENT

11.1.1 The purpose of the exercise

A total of six chapters (Chapters 3 and 6–10) have been devoted to the presentation, discussion, and implementation of a wide variety of performance measures. The list of all these measures is not, and will never be exhaustive, for three main reasons. First, we have deliberately left out some existing measures or particular calibrated versions. There are various reasons for this. Some can be obviously redundant with others that are more popular or better shaped. We can also consider, in a subjective but assumed opinion, that some measures are anecdotal and of too limited use. There are also a number of very complex measures, either by design or because of the difficulty of implementing them, that we believe are too long to deal with in a limited space compared to their applicability. We apologize to the authors of these measures and are open to reconsider their presentation in a forthcoming edition. Second, we may have ignored some very impactful performance measures because, in spite of our efforts to cover this specialized literature, we have simply not found them. With all possible honesty, we believe that we have covered all the most influential or important ones, but we would be pleased to identify any new insightful way to appraise portfolio performance that would be at the same time important and pragmatic. Third, it is simply impossible to be exhaustive at a given point in time (the writing of this book) in a constantly evolving domain such as this one. There are still many ways to assess portfolio performance yet to be invented, published, and disseminated. This is an inherent limitation of this kind of exercise.

In the meantime, we have been very pleased to introduce, discuss, and justify some new measures of performance that, to the best of our knowledge, have not been published elsewhere. Each time we have done that, we have had a justification that we thought to be reasonable. Some new measures are thus added to an already large array of existing ones because of this book.

In total, we count 116 different performance measures discussed so far, scattered and numbered throughout the preceding chapters, namely, 7 in Chapter 3, 47 in Chapter 6, 9 in Chapter 7, 16 in Chapter 8, 9 in Chapter 9, and 28 in Chapter 10. In this current pivotal chapter, our purpose is to bridge the "appraisal" part of the book with the "analysis" one. The intent is to provide the reader with a toolkit that consists of three consecutive steps: (i) gather and summarize, in a complete table, the performance measures that we have considered, together with a glossary of the symbols featured in each of those measures; (ii) examine different approaches that have been proposed by different authors in order to either choose one or several of these formulas, or to understand how they should be interpreted in case they are used to appraise portfolio performance; and (iii) provide our own summary table with a structured approach to objectivize the choice of one or several performance measures. The outcome should be interpreted as different dashboards, corresponding to their authors' sensitivities (including ours), aiming at designing a cartography of the maze of performance measures. Each reader can choose to rely on their preferred one or simply to use them as different compasses in order to forge their own opinion about which (type of) measure should be employed in different circumstances.

11.1.2 The complete list of performance measures

We report, in Tables 11-1 and 11-2, the list of the 116 measures displayed exactly as they appear in the corresponding chapters. Table 11-1 reports them in their order of appearance in the text, while Table 11-2 reports them in alphabetic order. Thus, there is no hierarchical treatment of the formulas at this stage – this is discussed in the next sections. In Table 11-1, the first column refers to the equation number in the text (the first figure is the chapter number and the second one is the number of the equation within the chapter), while the last column refers to the alphabetical ordering number, from 001 to 116, assigned to each of them in Table 11-2. This is the other way around in Table 11-2: The first column refers to the alphabetical ordering number, from 001 to 116, and the last column indicates the reference number of the equation.

In both tables, the second column provides the name of each measure as we have called them. The subscript P corresponds to the portfolio, while, when applicable, the superscript j corresponds to the investor. Other subscripts or superscripts are explained in the glossary tables. If a particularly famous name is attached to some of them, it is also reported between parentheses. The third column displays the measure's corresponding symbol, whereas the fourth column provides the formula.

It is necessary to use a very wide array of symbols in order to identify the parameters that appear in these performance measures, but many of them are found numerous times across the formulas. It would be counterproductive to explain in detail each of these symbols specifically for each measure. Therefore, we provide two glossary tables, with similar structures, in order to explain them. Table 11-3 contains all symbols starting with a letter from the Roman alphabet, while Table 11-4 contains all symbols starting with a letter from the Greek alphabet. The symbols are listed by alphabetical order of initials in the first column. A short definition is provided in the second column. The third and fourth columns list the references of all performance measures that use the symbol (perhaps sometimes with a slight modification) in Tables 11-1 and 11-2. Some rows correspond to performance measures that are used as inputs of other performance measures. For instance, aSR_P, the adjusted Sharpe ratio, which is a measure ordered under reference (6-18) and number 009, is used in the performance measures with references (6-71) (Adjusted risk-adjusted performance), (6-72) (Adjusted relative risk-adjusted performance), and (6-73) (Adjusted total risk alpha).

Detailed explanations of each performance measure are proposed in the corresponding chapter. To avoid redundancies, we do not reinterpret the measures here and ask the interested reader to refer to the relevant chapters in order to obtain the sought-after clarifications.

TABLE 11-1 The complete list of performance measures (by order of appearance).

Ref	Name	Symbol	Formula	#
(3-1)	Peer group comparison return	PG_P	$\overline{R}_P - \overline{R}_G$	067
(3-3)	Sharpe ratio	SR_P	$\frac{\overline{R}_P - R_f}{\sigma_P}$	094
(3-10)	Treynor ratio	TR_P	$\frac{\overline{R}_P - R_f}{\beta_P}$	109
(3-11)	Jensen's alpha	α_P	$\overline{R}_P - [R_f + \beta_P(\overline{R}_M - R_f)]$	043
(3-13)	Modified Jensen's alpha	$m\alpha_P$	$\frac{\alpha_P}{\beta_P}$	051
(3-22)	Information ratio	IR_P	$\frac{\overline{R}_{(P-B)}}{\sigma_{(P-B)}}$	041
(3-24)	Appraisal ratio	AR_P	$\frac{\alpha_P}{\sigma_{\varepsilon P}}$	013
(6-2)	Geometric Sharpe ratio	SR_P^g	$\frac{e^{H(\overline{R}_P+\sigma_P^2/2)} - e^{HR_f^c}}{e^{H(\overline{R}_P+\sigma_P^2/2)}\sqrt{e^{H\sigma_P^2} - 1}} \times \sqrt{\frac{n}{H}}$	036
(6-3)	Average Sharpe ratio	$\overline{SR}_P$	$\frac{H-T}{H-1}SR_P^g + \frac{T-1}{H-1}SR_P$	015
(6-4)	Revised Sharpe ratio	rSR_P	$\frac{\overline{R}_P - \overline{R}_f}{\sigma_{(P-f)}}$	084
(6-15)	Efficiency measure	eSR_P	$\frac{\overline{R}_P - \overline{R}_f}{\overline{R}_P^* - \overline{R}_f}$	028
(6-17)	Normalized Sharpe ratio	nSR_P	$\frac{\alpha_P + \beta_P(\overline{R}_{IM} - R_{If})}{\sqrt{\beta_P^2\sigma_{IM}^2 + \sigma_{\varepsilon P}^2}}$	061
(6-18)	Adjusted Sharpe ratio	aSR_P	$SR_P \times \left(1 + \frac{\mu_{P,3}}{6}SR_P - \frac{e\mu_{P,4}}{24}SR_P^2\right)$	009
(6-19)	Roy ratio	$RoyR_P$	$\frac{\overline{R}_P - \underline{R}}{\sigma_P}$	091
(6-21)	MAD ratio	$MADR_P$	$\frac{\overline{R}_P - R_f}{MAD_P}$	046

TABLE 11-1 *(continued)*

Ref	Name	Symbol	Formula	#
(6-22)	Minimax ratio	mMR_P	$\frac{\overline{R}_P - R_f}{mM_P}$	048
(6-23)	Gini ratio	GiR_P	$\frac{\overline{R}_P - R_f}{Gi(R_P - R_f)}$	039
(6-24)	Range ratio	RgR_P	$\frac{\overline{R}_P - R_f}{hRg_P}$	082
(6-26)	Omega–Sharpe ratio	ΩSR_P	$\frac{\overline{R}_P - \underline{R}}{d\overline{R}_P(\underline{R})}$	063
(6-27)	Reward to half-volatility	RHV_P	$\frac{\overline{R}_P - R_f}{h\sigma_P}$	086
(6-28)	Reward to semi-volatility	RSV_P	$\frac{\overline{R}_P - R_f}{s\sigma_P}$	088
(6-29)	Sortino ratio	$SorR_P$	$\frac{\overline{R}_P - \underline{R}}{d\sigma_P(\underline{R})}$	099
(6-30)	Kappa ratio	κR_P	$\frac{\overline{R}_P - \underline{R}}{dm_{3,P}(\underline{R})}$	044
(6-32)	Calmar ratio	$CalR_P$	$\frac{\overline{R}_P - R_f}{dd_{P,max}}$	020
(6-33)	Sterling ratio	$SteR_P$	$\frac{\overline{R}_P - R_f}{\overline{dd}_{P,signif}}$	102
(6-34)	Sterling–Calmar ratio	$StCaR_P$	$\frac{\overline{R}_P - R_f}{\overline{dd}_{P,max}}$	103
(6-35)	Sharper ratio (a.k.a. Burke ratio)	ShR_P	$\frac{\overline{R}_P - R_f}{\sigma_{dd_{P,signif}}}$	095
(6-36)	Pain ratio	PR_P	$\frac{\overline{R}_P - R_f}{\overline{dd}_P}$	066
(6-37)	Ulcer ratio	UR_P	$\frac{\overline{R}_P - R_f}{\sigma_{dd_P}}$	110
(6-44)	Reward to VaR	VR_P^{1-x}	$\frac{\overline{R}_P - R_f}{hVaR_P^{(1-x)}}$	089
(6-45)	Reward to CVaR	CVR_P^{1-x}	$\frac{\overline{R}_P - R_f}{hCVaR_P^{(1-x)}}$	085

TABLE 11-1 *(continued)*

Ref	Name	Symbol	Formula	#
(6-46)	Tail ratio	TVR_P^{1-x}	$\frac{\overline{R}_P - R_f}{hTVaR_P^{(1-x)}}$	106
(6-47)	Modified Sharpe ratio	mVR_P^{1-x}	$\frac{\overline{R}_P - R_f}{mVaR_P^{(1-x)}}$	055
(6-48)	Modified reward to CVaR	$mCVR_P^{1-x}$	$\frac{\overline{R}_P - R_f}{mCVaR_P^{(1-x)}}$	054
(6-52)	Alternative Treynor ratio	aTR_P	$\frac{\overline{R}_P - R_f}{\sigma_{\rho P}}$	012
(6-53)	Alternative modified Jensen's alpha	$am\alpha_P$	$\frac{\alpha_P}{\sigma_{\rho P}}$	011
(6-55)	Geometric Information ratio	gIR_P	$\frac{\overline{R}^g_{(P-B)}}{\sigma^g_{(P-B)}}$	035
(6-56)	Adjusted Information ratio	aIR_P	$IR_P \times \left(1 + \frac{\mu_{(P-B),3}}{6} IR_P - \frac{e\mu_{(P-B),4}}{24} IR_P^2\right)$	005
(6-57)	Downside Information ratio	dIR_P	$\frac{\overline{R}_{(P-B)}}{d\sigma_P(\overline{R}_B)}$	026
(6-59)	Active Calmar ratio	aCR_P	$\frac{\overline{R}_{(P-B)}}{add_{P,max}}$	002
(6-60)	Active Pain ratio	aPR_P	$\frac{\overline{R}_{(P-B)}}{\overline{add}_P}$	003
(6-61)	Active Ulcer ratio	aUR_P	$\frac{\overline{R}_{(P-B)}}{\sigma_{add_P}}$	004
(6-62)	Reward to relative VaR	aVR_P^{1-x}	$\frac{\overline{R}_{(P-B)}}{VaR^{(1-x)}_{(P-B)}}$	087
(6-63)	Risk-adjusted performance (a.k.a. M-squared)	M_P^2	$R_f + \frac{\sigma_M}{\sigma_P}(\overline{R}_P - R_f)$	090
(6-64)	Relative risk-adjusted performance	$RRAP_P$	$\frac{\sigma_M}{\sigma_P}(\overline{R}_P - R_f) - (\overline{R}_M - R_f)$	083
(6-65)	Total risk alpha	$T\alpha_P$	$(\overline{R}_P - R_f) - \frac{\sigma_P}{\sigma_M}(\overline{R}_M - R_f)$	108
(6-67)	G-H one	$GH1_P$	$\overline{R}_P - [w_M^* \overline{R}_M + (1 - w_M^*)\overline{R}_f]$	037

TABLE 11-1 *(continued)*

Ref	Name	Symbol	Formula	#
(6-68)	G-H two	$GH2_P$	$[w_P^*\overline{R}_P + (1 - w_P^*)\overline{R}_f] - \overline{R}_M$	038
(6-71)	Adjusted risk-adjusted performance	$aRAP_P$	$\overline{R}_P + aSR_P \times (\sigma_M - \sigma_P)$	007
(6-72)	Adjusted relative risk-adjusted performance	$aRRAP_P$	$(\overline{R}_P - \overline{R}_M) + aSR_P \times (\sigma_M - \sigma_P)$	006
(6-73)	Adjusted total risk alpha	$aT\alpha_P$	$\overline{R}_P - R_f - aSR_M \times \sigma_P$	010
(6-75)	Normalized excess return	nER_P	$\dfrac{\overline{R}_P - R_f}{\sigma^2_{\varepsilon P/P}}$	060
(6-76)	Specific excess return	sER_P	$(\overline{R}_P - R_f)(1 - \sigma^2_{\varepsilon P/P})$	100
(6-77)	Normalized alpha	$n\alpha_P$	$\dfrac{\alpha_P}{\frac{\sigma_P}{\sigma_M}(1 - \rho_{PM})} \times (\overline{R}_M - R_f)$	059
(7-11)	Multifactor alpha	α_P^{MF}	$\overline{R}_P - \left[\overline{R}_f + \sum_{k=1}^{K} \beta_{P,k}(\overline{F}_k - \overline{R}_f)\right]$	056
(7-12)	Modified multifactor alpha	$m\alpha_P^{MF}$	$\alpha_P^{MF} \dfrac{\overline{R}_B - \overline{R}_f - \alpha_B^{MF}}{\overline{R}_P - \overline{R}_f - \alpha_P^{MF}}$	053
(7-14)	Absolute modified multifactor alpha	$m\alpha_P^{MF,abs}$	$\dfrac{\alpha_P^{MF}}{\beta_P^*}$	001
(7-19)	Multifactor relative risk-adjusted performance	$RRAP_P^{MF}$	$\dfrac{\sigma_B}{\sigma_P}(\overline{R}_P - R_f) - \dfrac{\sigma_B}{\sigma_{B^{MF}}}(\overline{R}_B^{MF} - R_f)$	058
(7-20)	Split risk–return performance	$SRRP_P$	$\alpha_P^{MF} - MRP \times (\sigma_P - \sigma_{B^{MF}})$	101
(7-21)	Multifactor pure Information ratio	IR_P^{pure}	$\dfrac{\alpha_P^{MF}}{\sigma_{\varepsilon P}}$	057
(7-24)	Single-factor modified alpha	$m\alpha_P^{1F}$	$\alpha_P \dfrac{\beta_B}{\beta_P}$	098
(7-32)	Conditional multifactor alpha	α_P^{cMF}	$\alpha_{P,0}^{MF} + \mathbf{A}_P^{T}\overline{\mathbf{z}}$	024
(7-35)	CAPM stochastic discount factor alpha	$\alpha_P^{SDF,CAPM}$	$\alpha_P(\overline{R}_m - R_f)$	021
(8-4)	Option-based adjusted HM alpha	$\pi_P^{(hm,o)}$	$\alpha_P^{(hm)} + \gamma_P^{(hm)} \times (1 + R_f) \times \left(2\Phi\left(\frac{\sigma_M}{2}\right) - 1\right)$	064

TABLE 11-1 *(continued)*

Ref	Name	Symbol	Formula	#
(8-5)	Approximate HM alpha	$\pi_P^{(hm,a)}$	$\alpha_P^{(hm)} + \gamma_P^{(hm)} \times (\overline{max}[R_{M,t} - R_f, 0] - q_M^+(\overline{R}_M - R_f))$	014
(8-6)	Simplified HM alpha	$\pi_P^{(hm,s)}$	$\alpha_P^{(hm)} + \gamma_P^{(hm)} \times \overline{max}[R_{M,t} - R_f, 0]$	096
(8-7)	Modified HM adjusted alpha	$m\pi_P^{(hm)}$	$\dfrac{\alpha_P^{(hm)} + \gamma_P^{(hm)} \times g_M}{\beta_P^{(hm)} - (1 - q_M^+)\gamma_P^{(hm)}}$	050
(8-14)	Flexible approximate HM alpha	$\pi_P^{(hm,a),L}$	$\alpha_P^{(hm)} + \gamma_P^{(hm)} \times (\overline{max}[R_{M,t} - R_L^*, 0] - q_M^{L+}(\overline{R}_M - R_L^*))$	030
(8-17)	Option-based adjusted TM alpha	$\pi_P^{(tm,o)}$	$\alpha_P^{(tm)} + \beta_P^{(tm)}\left(\dfrac{1}{\Delta^{\tau^*\kappa^*}} - 1\right)R_f - \dfrac{\beta_P^{(tm)}}{\Delta^{\tau^*\kappa^*}}\Theta^{\tau^*\kappa^*}$	065
(8-19)	Quadratic TM alpha	$\pi_P^{(tm,q)}$	$\alpha_P^{(tm)} + \gamma_P^{(tm)} \times (1 + R_f)^2 \times (e^{\sigma_M^2} - 1)$	080
(8-20)	Variance-based TM alpha	$\pi_P^{(tm,v)}$	$\alpha_P^{(tm)} + \gamma_P^{(tm)} \times \sigma_M^2$	115
(8-21)	Simplified TM alpha	$\pi_P^{(tm,s)}$	$\alpha_P^{(tm)} + \gamma_P^{(tm)} \times \overline{[R_M - R_f]^2}$	097
(8-33)	Cornell measure	GC_P	$\overline{\alpha}_P^{MF} + \text{plim}\left(\dfrac{1}{T}\sum_{t=1}^{T}(\beta_{P,t} - \overline{\beta}_P)R_{B,t}\right)$	025
(8-34)	Positive period weighting measure	$PPWM_P$	$\sum_{t=1}^{T} w_t(R_{P,t} - R_f)$	071
(8-38)	Self-benchmarked performance	SBP_P	$\dfrac{1}{T-l}\sum_{t=l+1}^{T}\sum_{i=1}^{N}(w_{P,i,t} - w_{P,i,t-l})R_{i,t}$	092
(8-41)	Adjusted self-benchmarked performance	$aSBP_P$	$SBP_P - \sum_{k=1}^{K} b_{P,k}\overline{F}_k$	008
(8-44)	Peer group holding-based performance	$\delta_P^{(h)}$	$\dfrac{1}{T}\sum_{t=1}^{T}\sum_{i=1}^{N} w_{P,i,t}\delta_{i,t}^{(h)}$	068
(8-46)	Peer group trading-based performance	$\delta_P^{(\Delta h)}$	$\dfrac{1}{T}\sum_{t=1}^{T}\left[\sum_{i\in N_{P,t}^+} x_{P,i,t}^+\delta_{i,t}^{(\Delta h)} - \sum_{i\in N_{P,t}^-} x_{P,i,t}^-\delta_{i,t}^{(\Delta h)}\right]$	069
(8-49)	Combined holding-based performance	$\pi_P^{(h+..)}$	$\dfrac{1}{T}\sum_{t=1}^{T}\sum_{i=1}^{N} w_{P,i,t}\alpha_{i,t} + f(\gamma_P^{(..)})$	023
(9-9)	Quadratic score	Q_P^j	$\overline{R}_P - \dfrac{1}{2}\gamma_j\sigma_P^2$	079

TABLE 11-1 *(continued)*

Ref	Name	Symbol	Formula	#
(9-10)	Excess quadratic score	xQ^j_P	$\overline{R}_P - R_f - \frac{1}{2}\gamma_j\sigma^2_P$	029
(9-12)	Quadratic alpha	$Q\alpha^j_P$	$\overline{R}_P - R_f - \frac{1}{2}\gamma_j\sigma^2_P - \frac{1}{2\gamma_j}SR^2_M$	078
(9-14)	Target volatility alpha	$V\alpha^j_P$	$\overline{R}_P - R_f - \frac{1}{2}SR_M\left(\sigma^{(j)} + \frac{\sigma^2_P}{\sigma^{(j)}}\right)$	107
(9-20)	Four-moment quadratic score	$4mQ^j_P$	$\overline{R}_P - \frac{1}{2}\gamma_j\sigma^2_P\left(1 - \frac{1}{3}(\psi_j\sigma_P)\mu_{P,3} + \frac{1}{12}(\psi_j\sigma_P)^2 e\mu_{P,4}\right)$	031
(9-26)	Power-based certainty equivalent	$pwCE^j_P$	$\left[\frac{1}{T}\sum_{t=1}^{T}(1 + r^g_{P,t})^{-\gamma_j}\right]^{-\frac{n}{\gamma_j}} - 1$	072
(9-27)	Manipulation-proof certainty equivalent	$mpCE^j_P$	$-\frac{n}{\gamma_j}\log\left[\frac{1}{T}\sum_{t=1}^{T}(1 + r^g_{P,t})^{-\gamma_j}\right]$	047
(9-29)	Power-based compensating rebate	$pwCR^j_P$	$\left[\frac{\sum_{t=1}^{T}(1 + R_{P,t})^{-\gamma_j}}{\sum_{t=1}^{T}(1 + R_{P*j,t})^{-\gamma_j}}\right]^{-\frac{n}{\gamma_j}} - 1$	073
(9-30)	Utility-consistent Sharpe ratio	uSR^{*j}_P	$\sqrt{2\gamma_j(U^{max}_j - R_f)}$	113
(10-10)	Behavioral-quadratic score	bQ^j_P	$\overline{R}_P - (\lambda_j - 1)d\overline{R}_P(\underline{R}_j) - \frac{1}{2}(\lambda_j\gamma^-_j \times d\sigma^2_P(\underline{R}_j) + \gamma^+_j \times u\sigma^2_P(\underline{R}_j))$	017
(10-11)	Semi-quadratic score	sQ^j_P	$\overline{R}_P - \frac{1}{2}\gamma_j d\sigma^2_P(\underline{R}_j)$	093
(10-14)	PT score	PT^j_P	$um_{\gamma^+_j,P}(\underline{R}_j) - \lambda_j dm_{\gamma^-_j,P}(\underline{R}_j)$	077
(10-15)	Lambda-PT score	λPT^j_P	$\overline{R}_P - (\lambda_j - 1)d\overline{R}_P(R_f)$	045
(10-17)	Behavioral Sharpe ratio	bSR^j_P	$\frac{\overline{R}_P - \underline{R}_j - (\lambda_j - 1)d\overline{R}_P(\underline{R}_j)}{\sqrt{\lambda_j\theta_j d\sigma^2_P(\underline{R}_j) + u\sigma^2_P(\underline{R}_j)}}$	018
(10-19)	Prospect Theory Sharpe ratio (a.k.a. Farinelli–Tibiletti ratio)	$F - T^j_P$	$\frac{um_{\gamma^+_j,P}(\underline{R}_j)}{dm_{\gamma^-_j,P}(\underline{R}_j)}$	076
(10-20)	Dynamic Farinelli–Tibiletti ratio	$dF - T^j_P$	$\frac{um_{\gamma^+_j,P}(\underline{R}_j)}{\widetilde{dm}_{\gamma^-_j,P}(\underline{R}_j)}$	027

TABLE 11-1 *(continued)*

Ref	Name	Symbol	Formula	#
(10-21)	Z-Sharpe ratio	zSR_P^j	$\dfrac{\overline{R}_P - \underline{R}_j - (\lambda_j - 1)d\overline{R}_P(\underline{R}_j)}{\sqrt[\gamma_j]{\lambda_j \zeta_j dm_{\gamma_j,P}(\underline{R}_j) + um_{\gamma_j,P}(\underline{R}_j)}}$	116
(10-24)	Omega ratio	Ω_P^j	$\dfrac{u\overline{R}_P(\underline{R}_j)}{d\overline{R}_P(\underline{R}_j)}$	062
(10-25)	Upside potential ratio	UPR_P^j	$\dfrac{u\overline{R}_P(\underline{R}_j)}{d\sigma_P(\underline{R}_j)}$	112
(10-26)	Variability skewness	VSk_P^j	$\dfrac{u\sigma_P(\underline{R}_j)}{d\sigma_P(\underline{R}_j)}$	114
(10-27)	Modified kappa ratio	$m\kappa R_P^j$	$\dfrac{u\overline{R}_P(\underline{R}_j)}{dm_{3,P}(\underline{R}_j)}$	052
(10-28)	Prospect ratio	$ProR_P^j$	$\dfrac{u\overline{R}_P(\underline{R}_j) - \lambda_j d\overline{R}_P(\underline{R}_j) - \underline{R}_j}{d\sigma_P(\underline{R}_j)}$	075
(10-29)	Prospect-CVaR ratio	$PCVaRR_P^{j,x}$	$\dfrac{um_{\gamma_j^+,P}(\underline{R}_j)}{hCVaR_{\gamma_j^-,P}^{(1-x)}}$	074
(10-30)	Generalized Rachev ratio	$GRacR_P^{j,x,y}$	$\dfrac{hCGaR_{\gamma_j^+,P}^{(1-y)}}{hCVaR_{\gamma_j^-,P}^{(1-x)}}$	034
(10-31)	Rachev ratio	$RacR_P^{x,y}$	$\dfrac{hCGaR_P^{(1-y)}}{hCVaR_P^{(1-x)}}$	081
(10-32)	Up/Down Rachev ratio	$udRacR_P^j$	$\dfrac{\overline{du}_P(\underline{R}_j)}{\overline{dd}_P(\underline{R}_j)}$	111
(10-34)	Batting average	BA_P^j	$\dfrac{T_P^{+j}}{T}$	016
(10-35)	Benchmark-based batting average	bBA_P	$\dfrac{T_{(P-B)}^{+}}{T}$	019
(10-36)	Percentage gain ratio	$PerR_P^j$	$\dfrac{T_P^{+j}}{T_B^{+j}}$	070
(10-39)	Capture ratio	$CapR_P$	$\dfrac{uCapR_P}{dCapR_P}$	022
(10-40)	Inverse d-ratio	id_P^j	$\dfrac{T_P^{+j} u\overline{R}_P(\underline{R}_j)}{T_P^{-j} d\overline{R}_P(\underline{R}_j)}$	042

TABLE 11-1 *(continued)*

Ref	Name	Symbol	Formula	#
(10-41)	Gain-to-pain ratio	$GtPR_P^j$	$\frac{\overline{R}_P - \underline{R}_j}{d\overline{R}_P(\underline{R}_j)}$	032
(10-43)	Stutzer convergence index	D_P^j	$\max_{\gamma^*}\left(-\log \frac{1}{T}\sum_{t=1}^{T} e^{\gamma^*(R_{P,t}^c - \underline{R}_j^c)}\right)$	104
(10-51)	Historical Global Goal-based performance	$hGGBP_P^j$	$\frac{1}{1+\eta_j}\left(1 - \frac{T_P^{-j}}{T - T_j + 1} + \eta_j \frac{T_P^{+j}}{T - T_j + 1}\right)$	040
(10-55)	Gaussian Global Goal-based performance	$gGGBP_P^j$	$\frac{1}{1+\eta_j}\left[1 - \Phi\left(\frac{(\tau_j - \nu_j - \overline{R}_P^c)\sqrt{T_j}}{\sigma_P}\right) + \eta_j \Phi\left(\frac{(\overline{R}_P^c - \tau_j - \nu_j)\sqrt{T_j}}{\sigma_P}\right)\right]$	033
(10-56)	Symmetric Global Goal-based performance	$sGGBP_P^j$	$\frac{1}{1+\eta_j}\left[1 - (1 - \eta_j)\, \Phi\left(\frac{-\nu_j\sqrt{T_j}}{\sigma_P}\right)\right]$	105
(10-57)	Modified Global Goal-based performance	$mGGBP_P^{j,1-x}$	$\frac{1}{1+\eta_j}\left[1 - \Phi\left(\frac{(\tau_j - \nu_j - \overline{R}_P^c)\sqrt{T_j}}{m\sigma_P^{(x-)}}\right) + \eta_j \Phi\left(\frac{(\overline{R}_P^c - \tau_j - \nu_j)\sqrt{T_j}}{m\sigma_P^{(x+)}}\right)\right]$	049

TABLE 11-2 The complete list of performance measures (by alphabetical order).

#	Name	Symbol	Formula	Ref
001	Absolute modified multifactor alpha	$m\alpha_P^{MF,abs}$	$\frac{\alpha_P^{MF}}{\beta_P^*}$	(7-14)
002	Active Calmar ratio	aCR_P	$\frac{\overline{R}_{(P-B)}}{add_{P,max}}$	(6-59)
003	Active Pain ratio	aPR_P	$\frac{\overline{R}_{(P-B)}}{\overline{add}_P}$	(6-60)
004	Active Ulcer ratio	aUR_P	$\frac{\overline{R}_{(P-B)}}{\sigma_{addP}}$	(6-61)
005	Adjusted Information ratio	aIR_P	$IR_P \times \left(1 + \frac{\mu_{(P-B),3}}{6} IR_P - \frac{e\mu_{(P-B),4}}{24} IR_P^2\right)$	(6-56)
006	Adjusted relative risk-adjusted performance	$aRRAP_P$	$(\overline{R}_P - \overline{R}_M) + aSR_P \times (\sigma_M - \sigma_P)$	(6-72)
007	Adjusted risk-adjusted performance	$aRAP_P$	$\overline{R}_P + aSR_P \times (\sigma_M - \sigma_P)$	(6-71)
008	Adjusted self-benchmarked performance	$aSBP_P$	$SBP_P - \sum_{k=1}^{K} b_{P,k}\overline{F}_k$	(8-41)
009	Adjusted Sharpe ratio	aSR_P	$SR_P \times \left(1 + \frac{\mu_{P,3}}{6} SR_P - \frac{e\mu_{P,4}}{24} SR_P^2\right)$	(6-18)
010	Adjusted total risk alpha	$aT\alpha_P$	$\overline{R}_P - R_f - aSR_M \times \sigma_P$	(6-73)
011	Alternative modified Jensen's alpha	$am\alpha_P$	$\frac{\alpha_P}{\sigma_{\rho P}}$	(6-53)
012	Alternative Treynor ratio	aTR_P	$\frac{\overline{R}_P - R_f}{\sigma_{\rho P}}$	(6-52)
013	Appraisal ratio	AR_P	$\frac{\alpha_P}{\sigma_{\varepsilon P}}$	(3-24)
014	Approximate HM alpha	$\pi_P^{(hm,a)}$	$\alpha_P^{(hm)} + \gamma_P^{(hm)} \times (\overline{\max[R_{M,t} - R_f, 0]} - q_M^+(\overline{R}_M - R_f))$	(8-5)
015	Average Sharpe ratio	$\overline{SR}_P$	$\frac{H-T}{H-1} SR_P^g + \frac{T-1}{H-1} SR_P$	(6-3)
016	Batting average	BA_P^j	$\frac{T_P^{+j}}{T}$	(10-34)

TABLE 11-2 *(continued)*

#	Name	Symbol	Formula	Ref
017	Behavioral quadratic score	bQ_P^j	$\overline{R}_P - (\lambda_j - 1)d\overline{R}_P(\underline{R}_j) - \frac{1}{2}(\lambda_j\gamma_j^- \times d\sigma_P^2(\underline{R}_j) + \gamma_j^+ \times u\sigma_P^2(\underline{R}_j))$	(10-10)
018	Behavioral Sharpe ratio	bSR_P^j	$\frac{\overline{R}_P - \underline{R}_j - (\lambda_j - 1)d\overline{R}_P(\underline{R}_j)}{\sqrt{\lambda_j\theta_j d\sigma_P^2(\underline{R}_j) + u\sigma_P^2(\underline{R}_j)}}$	(10-17)
019	Benchmark-based batting average	bBA_P	$\frac{T_{(P-B)}^+}{T}$	(10-35)
020	Calmar ratio	$CalR_P$	$\frac{\overline{R}_P - R_f}{dd_{P,max}}$	(6-32)
021	CAPM stochastic discount factor alpha	$\alpha_P^{SDF,CAPM}$	$\alpha_P(\overline{R}_m - R_f)$	(7-35)
022	Capture ratio	$CapR_P$	$\frac{uCapR_P}{dCapR_P}$	(10-37)
023	Combined holding-based performance	$\pi_P^{(h+\cdots)}$	$\frac{1}{T}\sum_{t=1}^{T}\sum_{i=1}^{N} w_{P,i,t}\alpha_{i,t} + f(\gamma_P^{(\cdots)})$	(8-49)
024	Conditional multifactor alpha	α_P^{cMF}	$\alpha_{P,0}^{MF} + \mathbf{A}_P^T\overline{\mathbf{z}}$	(7-32)
025	Cornell measure	GC_P	$\overline{\alpha}_P^{MF} + \text{plim}\left(\frac{1}{T}\sum_{t=1}^{T}(\beta_{P,t} - \overline{\beta}_P)R_{B,t}\right)$	(8-33)
026	Downside Information ratio	dIR_P	$\frac{\overline{R}_{(P-B)}}{d\sigma_P(\overline{R}_B)}$	(6-57)
027	Dynamic Farinelli–Tibiletti ratio	$dF - T_P^j$	$\frac{um_{\gamma_j^+,P}(\underline{R}_j)}{\widetilde{dm}_{\gamma_j^-,P}(\underline{R}_j)}$	(10-20)
028	Efficiency measure	eSR_P	$\frac{\overline{R}_P - \overline{R}_f}{\overline{R}_P^* - \overline{R}_f}$	(6-15)
029	Excess quadratic score	xQ_P^j	$\overline{R}_P - R_f - \frac{1}{2}\gamma_j\sigma_P^2$	(9-10)
030	Flexible approximate HM alpha	$\pi_P^{(hm,a),L}$	$\alpha_P^{(hm)} + \gamma_P^{(hm)} \times (\overline{\max}[R_{M,t} - R_L^*, 0] - q_M^{L+}(\overline{R}_M - R_L^*))$	(8-14)
031	Four-moment quadratic score	$4mQ_P^j$	$\overline{R}_P - \frac{1}{2}\gamma_j\sigma_P^2\left(1 - \frac{1}{3}(\psi_j\sigma_P)\mu_{P,3} + \frac{1}{12}(\psi_j\sigma_P)^2 e\mu_{P,4}\right)$	(9-20)

TABLE 11-2 *(continued)*

#	Name	Symbol	Formula	Ref
032	Gaussian Global Goal-based performance	gGGBP_P^j	$\frac{1}{1+\eta_j}\left[1-\Phi\left(\frac{(\tau_j-\nu_j-\overline{R}_P^c)\sqrt{T_j}}{\sigma_P}\right)+\eta_j\,\Phi\left(\frac{(\overline{R}_P^c-\tau_j-\nu_j)\sqrt{T_j}}{\sigma_P}\right)\right]$	(10-55)
033	Gain-to-pain ratio	GtPR_P^j	$\frac{\overline{R}_P-\underline{R}_j}{d\overline{R}_P(\underline{R}_j)}$	(10-41)
034	Generalized Rachev ratio	$\text{GRacR}_P^{j,x,y}$	$\frac{\text{hCGaR}_{\gamma_j^+,P}^{(1-y)}}{\text{hCVaR}_{\gamma_j^-,P}^{(1-x)}}$	(10-30)
035	Geometric Information ratio	gIR_P	$\frac{\overline{R}_{(P-B)}^g}{\sigma_{(P-B)}^g}$	(6-55)
036	Geometric Sharpe ratio	SR_P^g	$\frac{e^{H(\overline{R}_P,+\sigma_P^2/2)}-e^{HR_f^c}}{e^{H(\overline{R}_P,+\sigma_P^2/2)}\sqrt{e^{H\sigma_P^2}-1}}\times\sqrt{\frac{n}{H}}$	(6-2)
037	G-H one	GH1_P	$\overline{R}_P-[w_M^*\overline{R}_M+(1-w_M^*)\overline{R}_f]$	(6-67)
038	G-H two	GH2_P	$[w_P^*\overline{R}_P+(1-w_P^*)\overline{R}_f]-\overline{R}_M$	(6-68)
039	Gini ratio	GiR_P	$\frac{\overline{R}_P-R_f}{\text{Gi}(R_P-R_f)}$	(6-23)
040	Historical Global Goal-based performance	hGGBP_P^j	$\frac{1}{1+\eta_j}\left(1-\frac{T_P^{-j}}{T-T_j+1}+\eta_j\frac{T_P^{+j}}{T-T_j+1}\right)$	(10-51)
041	Information ratio	IR_P	$\frac{\overline{R}_{(P-B)}}{\sigma_{(P-B)}}$	(3-22)
042	Inverse d-ratio	id_P^j	$\frac{T_P^{+j}u\overline{R}_P(\underline{R}_j)}{T_P^{-j}d\overline{R}_P(\underline{R}_j)}$	(10-40)
043	Jensen's alpha	α_P	$\overline{R}_P-[R_f+\beta_P(\overline{R}_M-R_f)]$	(3-11)
044	Kappa ratio	κR_P	$\frac{\overline{R}_P-\underline{R}}{dm_{3,P}(\underline{R})}$	(6-30)
045	Lambda-PT score	λPT_P^j	$\overline{R}_P-(\lambda_j-1)d\overline{R}_P(R_f)$	(10-15)
046	MAD ratio	MADR_P	$\frac{\overline{R}_P-R_f}{\text{MAD}_P}$	(6-21)

TABLE 11-2 *(continued)*

#	Name	Symbol	Formula	Ref
047	Manipulation-proof certainty equivalent	$mpCE_P^j$	$-\frac{n}{\gamma_j}\log\left[\frac{1}{T}\sum_{t=1}^{T}(1+r_{P,t}^{g})^{-\gamma_j}\right]$	(9-27)
048	Minimax ratio	mMR_P	$\frac{\overline{R}_P - R_f}{mM_P}$	(6-22)
049	Modified Global Goal-based performance	$mGGBP_P^{j,1-x}$	$\frac{1}{1+\eta_j}\left[1-\Phi\left(\frac{(\tau_j-\nu_j-\overline{R}_P^c)\sqrt{T_j}}{m\sigma_P^{(x-)}}\right)+\eta_j\,\Phi\left(\frac{(\overline{R}_P^c-\tau_j-\nu_j)\sqrt{T_j}}{m\sigma_P^{(x+)}}\right)\right]$	(10-57)
050	Modified HM adjusted alpha	$m\pi_P^{(hm)}$	$\frac{\alpha_P^{(hm)}+\gamma_P^{(hm)}\times g_M}{\beta_P^{(hm)}-(1-q_M^{+})\gamma_P^{(hm)}}$	(8-7)
051	Modified Jensen's alpha	$m\alpha_P$	$\frac{\alpha_P}{\beta_P}$	(3-13)
052	Modified kappa ratio	$m\kappa R_P^j$	$\frac{u\overline{R}_P(\underline{R}_j)}{dm_{3,P}(\underline{R}_j)}$	(10-27)
053	Modified multifactor alpha	$m\alpha_P^{MF}$	$\alpha_P^{MF}\frac{\overline{R}_B-\overline{R}_f-\alpha_B^{MF}}{\overline{R}_P-\overline{R}_f-\alpha_P^{MF}}$	(7-12)
054	Modified reward to CVaR	$mCVR_P^{1-x}$	$\frac{\overline{R}_P - R_f}{mCVaR_P^{(1-x)}}$	(6-48)
055	Modified Sharpe ratio	mVR_P^{1-x}	$\frac{\overline{R}_P - R_f}{mVaR_P^{(1-x)}}$	(6-47)
056	Multifactor alpha	α_P^{MF}	$\overline{R}_P-\left[\overline{R}_f+\sum_{k=1}^{K}\beta_{P,k}(\overline{F}_k-\overline{R}_f)\right]$	(7-11)
057	Multifactor pure Information ratio	IR_P^{pure}	$\frac{\alpha_P^{MF}}{\sigma_{\varepsilon P}}$	(7-21)
058	Multifactor relative risk-adjusted performance	$RRAP_P^{MF}$	$\frac{\sigma_B}{\sigma_P}(\overline{R}_P-R_f)-\frac{\sigma_B}{\sigma_{BMF}}(\overline{R}_B^{MF}-R_f)$	(7-19)
059	Normalized alpha	$n\alpha_P$	$\frac{\alpha_P}{\frac{\sigma_P}{\sigma_M}(1-\rho_{PM})}\times(\overline{R}_M-R_f)$	(6-77)
060	Normalized excess return	nER_P	$\frac{\overline{R}_P - R_f}{\sigma_{\varepsilon P/P}^2}$	(6-75)

TABLE 11-2 *(continued)*

#	Name	Symbol	Formula	Ref
061	Normalized Sharpe ratio	nSR_P	$\frac{\alpha_P + \beta_P(\overline{R}_{IM} - R_{If})}{\sqrt{\beta_P^2\sigma_{IM}^2 + \sigma_{\varepsilon P}^2}}$	(6-17)
062	Omega ratio	Ω_P^j	$\frac{u\overline{R}_P(\underline{R}_j)}{d\overline{R}_P(\underline{R}_j)}$	(10-24)
063	Omega-Sharpe ratio	ΩSR_P	$\frac{\overline{R}_P - \underline{R}}{d\overline{R}_P(\underline{R})}$	(6-26)
064	Option-based adjusted HM alpha	$\pi_P^{(hm,o)}$	$\alpha_P^{(hm)} + \gamma_P^{(hm)} \times (1 + R_f) \times \left(2\Phi\left(\frac{\sigma_M}{2}\right) - 1\right)$	(8-4)
065	Option-based adjusted TM alpha	$\pi_P^{(tm,o)}$	$\alpha_P^{(tm)} + \beta_P^{(tm)}\left(\frac{1}{\Delta^{\tau^*\kappa^*}} - 1\right)R_f - \frac{\beta_P^{(tm)}}{\Delta^{\tau^*\kappa^*}}\Theta^{\tau^*\kappa^*}$	(8-17)
066	Pain ratio	PR_P	$\frac{\overline{R}_P - R_f}{\overline{dd}_P}$	(6-36)
067	Peer group comparison return	PG_P	$\overline{R}_P - \overline{R}_G$	(3-1)
068	Peer group holding-based performance	$\delta_P^{(h)}$	$\frac{1}{T}\sum_{t=1}^{T}\sum_{i=1}^{N} w_{P,i,t}\delta_{i,t}^{(h)}$	(8-44)
069	Peer group trading-based performance	$\delta_P^{(\Delta h)}$	$\frac{1}{T}\sum_{t=1}^{T}\left[\sum_{i\in N_{P,t}^+} x_{P,i,t}^+\delta_{i,t}^{(\Delta h)} - \sum_{i\in N_{P,t}^-} x_{P,i,t}^-\delta_{i,t}^{(\Delta h)}\right]$	(8-46)
070	Percentage gain ratio	$PerR_P^j$	$\frac{T_P^{+j}}{T_B^{+j}}$	(10-36)
071	Positive period weighting measure	$PPWM_P$	$\sum_{t=1}^{T} w_t(R_{P,t} - R_f)$	(8-34)
072	Power-based certainty equivalent	$pwCE_P^j$	$\left[\frac{1}{T}\sum_{t=1}^{T}(1 + r_{P,t}^g)^{-\gamma_j}\right]^{-\frac{n}{\gamma_j}} - 1$	(9-26)
073	Power-based compensating rebate	$pwCR_P^j$	$\left[\frac{\sum_{t=1}^{T}(1 + R_{P,t})^{-\gamma_j}}{\sum_{t=1}^{T}(1 + R_{P*j,t})^{-\gamma_j}}\right]^{-\frac{n}{\gamma_j}} - 1$	(9-29)

TABLE 11-2 *(continued)*

#	Name	Symbol	Formula	Ref
074	Prospect-CVaR ratio	$PCVaRR_P^{j,x}$	$\frac{um_{\gamma_j^+,P}(\underline{R}_j)}{hCVaR_{\gamma_j^-,P}^{(1-x)}}$	(10-29)
075	Prospect ratio	$ProR_P^j$	$\frac{u\overline{R}_P(\underline{R}_j) - \lambda_j d\overline{R}_P(\underline{R}_j) - \underline{R}_j}{d\sigma_P(\underline{R}_j)}$	(10-28)
076	Prospect Theory Sharpe ratio (a.k.a. Farinelli–Tibiletti ratio)	$F-T_P^j$	$\frac{um_{\gamma_j^+,P}(\underline{R}_j)}{dm_{\gamma_j^-,P}(\underline{R}_j)}$	(10-19)
077	PT score	PT_P^j	$um_{\gamma_j^+,P}(\underline{R}_j) - \lambda_j dm_{\gamma_j^-,P}(\underline{R}_j)$	(10-14)
078	Quadratic alpha	$Q\alpha_P^j$	$\overline{R}_P - R_f - \frac{1}{2}\gamma_j\sigma_P^2 - \frac{1}{2\gamma_j}SR_M^2$	(9-12)
079	Quadratic score	Q_P^j	$\overline{R}_P - \frac{1}{2}\gamma_j\sigma_P^2$	(9-9)
080	Quadratic TM alpha	$\pi_P^{(tm,q)}$	$\alpha_P^{(tm)} + \gamma_P^{(tm)} \times (1+R_f)^2 \times (e^{\sigma_M^2} - 1)$	(8-19)
081	Rachev ratio	$RacR_P^{x,y}$	$\frac{hCGaR_P^{(1-y)}}{hCVaR_P^{(1-x)}}$	(10-31)
082	Range ratio	RgR_P	$\frac{\overline{R}_P - R_f}{hRg_P}$	(6-24)
083	Relative risk-adjusted performance	$RRAP_P$	$\frac{\sigma_M}{\sigma_P}(\overline{R}_P - R_f) - (\overline{R}_M - R_f)$	(6-64)
084	Revised Sharpe ratio	rSR_P	$\frac{\overline{R}_P - \overline{R}_f}{\sigma_{(P-f)}}$	(6-4)
085	Reward to CVaR	CVR_P^{1-x}	$\frac{\overline{R}_P - R_f}{hCVaR_P^{(1-x)}}$	(6-45)
086	Reward to half-volatility	RHV_P	$\frac{\overline{R}_P - R_f}{h\sigma_P}$	(6-27)
087	Reward to relative VaR	aVR_P^{1-x}	$\frac{\overline{R}_{(P-B)}}{VaR_{(P-B)}^{(1-x)}}$	(6-62)
088	Reward to semi-volatility	RSV_P	$\frac{\overline{R}_P - R_f}{s\sigma_P}$	(6-28)
089	Reward to VaR	VR_P^{1-x}	$\frac{\overline{R}_P - R_f}{hVaR_P^{(1-x)}}$	(6-44)
090	Risk-adjusted performance (a.k.a. M-squared)	M_P^2	$R_f + \frac{\sigma_M}{\sigma_P}(\overline{R}_P - R_f)$	(6-63)

TABLE 11-2 *(continued)*

#	Name	Symbol	Formula	Ref
091	Roy ratio	$RoyR_P$	$\frac{\overline{R}_P - \underline{R}}{\sigma_P}$	(6-19)
092	Self-benchmarked performance	SBP_P	$\frac{1}{T-l}\sum_{t=l+1}^{T}\sum_{i=1}^{N}(w_{P,i,t} - w_{P,i,t-l})R_{i,t}$	(8-38)
093	Semi-quadratic score	sQ_P^j	$\overline{R}_P - \frac{1}{2}\gamma_j d\sigma_P^2(\underline{R}_j)$	(10-11)
094	Sharpe ratio	SR_P	$\frac{\overline{R}_P - R_f}{\sigma_P}$	(3-3)
095	Sharper ratio (a.k.a. Burke ratio)	ShR_P	$\frac{\overline{R}_P - R_f}{\sigma_{dd_{P,signif}}}$	(6-35)
096	Simplified HM alpha	$\pi_P^{(hm,s)}$	$\alpha_P^{(hm)} + \gamma_P^{(hm)} \times \overline{\max}[R_{M,t} - R_f, 0]$	(8-6)
097	Simplified TM alpha	$\pi_P^{(tm,s)}$	$\alpha_P^{(tm)} + \gamma_P^{(tm)} \times \overline{[R_M - R_f]^2}$	(8-21)
098	Single-factor modified alpha	$m\alpha_P^{1F}$	$\alpha_P \frac{\beta_B}{\beta_P}$	(7-24)
099	Sortino ratio	$SorR_P$	$\frac{\overline{R}_P - \underline{R}}{d\sigma_P(\underline{R})}$	(6-29)
100	Specific excess return	sER_P	$(\overline{R}_P - R_f)(1 - \sigma^2_{\varepsilon P/P})$	(6-76)
101	Split risk–return performance	$SRRP_P$	$\alpha_P^{MF} - MRP \times (\sigma_P - \sigma_{BMF})$	(7-20)
102	Sterling ratio	$SteR_P$	$\frac{\overline{R}_P - R_f}{\overline{dd}_{P,signif}}$	(6-33)
103	Sterling–Calmar ratio	$StCaR_P$	$\frac{\overline{R}_P - R_f}{\overline{dd}_{P,max}}$	(6-34)
104	Stutzer convergence index	D_P^j	$\max_{\gamma^*}\left(-\log\frac{1}{T}\sum_{t=1}^{T} e^{\gamma^*(R_{P,t}^c - \underline{R}_j^c)}\right)$	(10-44)
105	Symmetric Global Goal-based performance	$sGGBP_P^j$	$\frac{1}{1+\eta_j}\left[1 - (1-\eta_j)\,\Phi\left(\frac{-\nu_j\sqrt{T_j}}{\sigma_P}\right)\right]$	(10-56)
106	Tail ratio	TVR_P^{1-x}	$\frac{\overline{R}_P - R_f}{hTVaR_P^{(1-x)}}$	(6-46)
107	Target volatility alpha	$V\alpha_P^j$	$\overline{R}_P - R_f - \frac{1}{2}SR_M\left(\sigma^{(j)} + \frac{\sigma_P^2}{\sigma^{(j)}}\right)$	(9-14)
108	Total risk alpha	$T\alpha_P$	$(\overline{R}_P - R_f) - \frac{\sigma_P}{\sigma_M}(\overline{R}_M - R_f)$	(6-65)

TABLE 11-2 *(continued)*

#	Name	Symbol	Formula	Ref
109	Treynor ratio	TR_P	$\frac{\overline{R}_P - R_f}{\beta_P}$	(3-10)
110	Ulcer ratio	UR_P	$\frac{\overline{R}_P - R_f}{\sigma_{dd_P}}$	(6-37)
111	Up/Down Rachev ratio	$udRacR_P^j$	$\frac{\overline{du}_P(\underline{R}_j)}{\overline{dd}_P(\underline{R}_j)}$	(10-32)
112	Upside potential ratio	UPR_P^j	$\frac{u\overline{R}_P(\underline{R}_j)}{d\sigma_P(\underline{R}_j)}$	(10-25)
113	Utility-consistent Sharpe ratio	uSR_P^{*j}	$\sqrt{2\gamma_j(U_j^{max} - R_f)}$	(9-30)
114	Variability skewness	VSk_P^j	$\frac{u\sigma_P(\underline{R}_j)}{d\sigma_P(\underline{R}_j)}$	(10-26)
115	Variance-based TM alpha	$\pi_P^{(tm,v)}$	$\alpha_P^{(tm)} + \gamma_P^{(tm)} \times \sigma_M^2$	(8-20)
116	Z-Sharpe ratio	zSR_P^j	$\frac{\overline{R}_P - \underline{R}_j - (\lambda_j - 1)d\overline{R}_P(\underline{R}_j)}{\sqrt[\gamma_j]{\lambda_j\zeta_j dm_{\gamma_j,P}(\underline{R}_j) + um_{\gamma_j,P}(\underline{R}_j)}}$	(10-21)

TABLE 11-3 Glossary of symbols used in the formulas (Roman alphabet).

Symbol	Definition	References (chapters)	Numbers (list)
$\overline{add}_P$	Average active portfolio drawdown	(6-60)	003
$add_{P,max}$	Maximum active portfolio drawdown	(6-59)	002
aSR_M	Market adjusted Sharpe ratio	(6-73)	010
aSR_P	Portfolio adjusted Sharpe ratio ((6-18) - 009)	(6-71), (6-72), (6-73)	006, 007, 010
$\mathbf{A}_P^T$	Vector of portfolio sensitivities to the conditioning instruments	(7-32)	024
$b_{P,k}$	Coefficient of the kth factor of the regression of the self-benchmarked portfolio performance	(8-41)	008
$dCapR_P$	Downside portfolio capture ratio	(10-39)	022
$\overline{dd}_P$	Average portfolio drawdown	(6-36)	066
$dd_{P,max}$	Maximum drawdown of the portfolio returns	(6-32)	020
$\overline{dd}_{P,max}$	Average of the maximum sub-period drawdowns	(6-34)	103
$\overline{dd}_{P,signif}$	Average of the most significant drawdowns	(6-33)	102
$dm_{3,P}(\underline{R}_j)$	Downside third centered moment of the portfolio returns (for investor j)	(6-30), (10-27)	044, 052
$dm_{\gamma_j,P}(\underline{R}_j)$	Downside centered moment of order γ_j of the portfolio returns (for investor j)	(10-21)	116
$dm_{\gamma_j^-,P}(\underline{R}_j)$	Downside centered moment of order γ_j^- of the portfolio returns (for investor j)	(10-14), (10-19)	076, 077
$\widetilde{dm}_{\gamma_j^-,P}(\underline{R}_j)$	Downside centered moment of order γ_j^- of the portfolio returns with time-varying loss aversion (for investor j)	(10-20)	027

TABLE 11-3 *(continued)*

Symbol	Definition	References (chapters)	Numbers (list)
$d\overline{R}_P(\underline{R}_j)$	Downside mean portfolio return (for investor *j*)	(6-26), (10-10), (10-17), (10-21), (10-24), (10-28), (10-40), (10-41)	017, 018, 032, 042, 062, 063, 075, 116
$d\overline{R}_P(R_f)$	Downside mean excess portfolio return	(10-15)	045
$d\sigma_P(\overline{R}_B)$	Downside tracking error	(6-57)	026
$d\sigma_P(\underline{R})$	Downside volatility of the portfolio returns (for investor *j*)	(6-29), (10-25), (10-26), (10-28)	075, 099, 112, 114
$d\sigma_P^2(\underline{R}_j)$	Downside variance of the portfolio returns (for investor *j*)	(10-10), (10-11), (10-17)	017, 018, 093
$e\mu_{P,4}$	Excess kurtosis of the portfolio returns	(6-18), (9-20)	009, 031
$e\mu_{(P-B),4}$	Excess kurtosis of the differential returns	(6-56)	005
$f(\gamma_P^{(..)})$	Adjustment for convexity where ".." stands for *hm* or *tm* depending on the model chosen	(8-49)	023
$\overline{F}_k$	Average return of factor *k*	(7-11), (8-41)	008, 056
$\text{Gini}(R_P - R_f)$	Gini's rescaled mean difference of the portfolio excess returns	(6-23)	039
g_M	Market remuneration per unit of HM gamma	(8-7)	050
H	Holding horizon	(6-2)	015
$\text{hCGaR}_P^{(1-y)}$	Historical portfolio conditional Gain-at-Risk	(10-31)	081
$\text{hCGaR}_{\gamma_j^+,P}^{(1-y)}$	Moment of order γ_j^+ of the portfolio historical conditional Gain-at-Risk	(10-30)	034
$\text{hCVaR}_P^{(1-x)}$	Historical portfolio conditional Value-at-Risk	(6-45), (10-31)	081, 085
$\text{hCVaR}_{\gamma_j^-,P}^{(1-x)}$	Moment of order γ_j^- of the portfolio historical conditional Value-at-Risk	(10-29), (10-30)	034, 074

TABLE 11-3 *(continued)*

Symbol	Definition	References (chapters)	Numbers (list)
$h\sigma_P$	Half-volatility of portfolio returns	(6-27)	086
hRg_P	Half-range of the portfolio returns	(6-24)	082
$hTVaR_P^{(1-x)}$	Historical portfolio tail Value-at-Risk	(6-46)	106
$hVaR_P^{(1-x)}$	Historical portfolio excess Value-at-Risk	(6-44)	089
IR_P	Portfolio Information ratio ((3-22) - 041)	(6-56)	005
MAD_P	Mean absolute deviation of portfolio returns	(6-21)	046
$\overline{\max}[X, 0]$	Average value of the maximum between X and 0	(8-5), (8-6), (8-14)	014, 030, 096
$mCVaR_P^{(1-x)}$	Modified portfolio conditional Value-at-Risk	(6-48)	054
mM_P	Maximum of the negative portfolio returns	(6-22)	048
$m\sigma_P^{(x-)}$	Modified portfolio volatility for shortfall	(10-57)	049
$m\sigma_P^{(x+)}$	Modified portfolio volatility for surplus	(10-57)	049
MRP	Market risk premium	(7-20)	101
$mVaR_P^{(1-x)}$	Modified portfolio excess Value-at-Risk	(6-47)	055
n	Frequency of return computations per year	(6-2), (9-26), (9-27), (9-29)	036, 047, 072, 073
N	Number of assets in the portfolio	(8-38), (8-44), (8-46), (8-49)	023, 068, 069, 092
$N_{P,t}^{+}$	Set of assets for which the portfolio manager has decided to increase their position at time t	(8-46)	069
$N_{P,t}^{-}$	Set of assets for which the portfolio manager has decided to decrease their position at time t	(8-46)	069

TABLE 11-3 *(continued)*

Symbol	Definition	References (chapters)	Numbers (list)
plim(X)	Probability limit of X	(8-33)	025
q_M^+	Observed frequency of positive excess market returns	(8-5), (8-7)	014, 050
q_M^{L+}	Observed frequency of market returns that exceed the threshold R_L^*	(8-14)	030
$\underline{R}$ or $\underline{R}_j$	Reservation rate (for investor j)	(6-19), (6-26), (6-29), (6-30), (10-17), (10-21), (10-28), (10-41)	018, 032, 044, 063, 075, 091, 099, 116
$\underline{R}_j^c$	Continuously compounded reservation rate (for investor j)	(10-43)	104
$\overline{R}_B$	Average benchmark return	(7-12)	053
$R_{B,t}$	Benchmark return at time t	(8-33)	025
$\overline{R}_B^{MF}$	Average multifactor benchmark return	(7-19)	058
R_f	Risk-free rate	(3-3), (3-10), (3-11), (6-21), (6-22), (6-23), (6-24), (6-27), (6-28), (6-32), (6-33), (6-34), (6-35), (6-36), (6-37), (6-44), (6-45), (6-46), (6-47), (6-48), (6-52), (6-63), (6-64), (6-65), (6-75), (6-76), (6-73), (6-77), (7-19), (7-35), (8-4), (8-5), (8-6), (8-17), (8-19), (8-34), (9-10), (9-12), (9-14), (9-30)	010, 012, 014, 020, 021, 029, 039, 043, 046, 048, 054, 055, 058, 064, 066, 059, 060, 064, 071, 078, 080, 082, 083, 085, 086, 088, 089, 090, 094, 095, 096, 100, 102, 103, 106, 107, 108, 109, 110, 113
$\overline{R}_f$	Average fixed-income return	(6-4), (6-15), (6-67), (6-68), (7-11), (7-12)	028, 037, 038, 053, 056, 084
R_f^c	Continuously compounded risk-free rate	(6-2)	036
R_{lf}	Long-term risk-free rate	(6-17)	061
$\overline{R}_G$	Average peer group return	(3-1)	067
$R_{i,t}$	Return of asset i at time t	(8-38)	093
R_L^*	Strike price of the put option that maximizes the R^2 of the HM regression	(8-14)	030
$\overline{R}_{lM}$	Average long-term market return	(6-17)	061

TABLE 11-3 *(continued)*

Symbol	Definition	References (chapters)	Numbers (list)
$\overline{R}_M$	Average market return	(3-11), (6-64), (6-65), (6-67), (6-68), (6-72), (6-77), (7-35), (8-5), (8-14)	006, 014, 021, 030, 037, 038, 043, 059, 083, 108
$R_{M,t}$	Market return at time t	(8-5), (8-6), (8-14)	014, 030, 096
$\overline{[R_M - R_f]^2}$	Average squared market excess return	(8-21)	098
$\overline{R}_P$	Average portfolio return	(3-1), (3-3), (3-11), (6-2), (6-4), (6-15), (6-19), (6-21), (6-22), (6-23), (6-24), (6-26), (6-27), (6-28), (6-29), (6-30), (6-32), (6-33), (6-34), (6-35), (6-36), (6-37), (6-44), (6-45), (6-46), (6-47), (6-48), (6-52), (6-63), (6-64), (6-65), (6-67), (6-68), (6-71), (6-72), (6-73), (6-75), (6-76), (7-11), (7-12), (7-19), (9-9), (9-10), (9-12), (9-14), (9-20), (10-10), (10-11), (10-15), (10-17), (10-21), (10-41)	006, 007, 010, 012, 017, 018, 020, 028, 029, 031, 032, 036, 037, 038, 039, 043, 044, 045, 046, 048, 053, 054, 055, 056, 058, 060, 063, 066, 067, 072, 078, 079, 082, 083, 084, 085, 086, 088, 089, 090, 091, 093, 095, 099, 100, 102, 103, 106, 108, 109, 110, 116
$\overline{R}_P^{\,c}$	Average continuously compounded portfolio return	(10-43), (10-55), (10-57)	033, 049, 104
$\overline{R}_P^{\,*}$	Average return of the mean–variance efficient portfolio	(6-15)	028
$\overline{R}_{(P-B)}$	Average differential return (a.k.a. Portfolio Tracking difference)	(3-22), (6-57), (6-59), (6-60), (6-61), (6-62)	002, 003, 004, 026, 041, 087
$\overline{R}_{(P-B)}^{\,g}$	Average geometric differential returns	(6-55)	011
$r_{P,t}^{g}$	Geometric portfolio excess returns at time t	(9-26), (9-27)	047, 072
$R_{P,t}$	Portfolio return at time t	(8-34), (9-29)	071, 073
$R_{P*j,t}$	Custom optimized portfolio return at time t for investor j	(9-29)	073

TABLE 11-3 *(continued)*

Symbol	Definition	References (chapters)	Numbers (list)
SBP_P	Portfolio self-benchmarked performance ((8-38) - 093)	(8-41)	008
SR_M	Market Sharpe ratio	(9-12), (9-14)	078, 107
SR_P	Portfolio Sharpe ratio ((3-3) - 095)	(6-3), (6-17)	062, 015
SR_P^g	Portfolio Geometric Sharpe ratio ((6-2) - 036)	(6-3)	015
$s\sigma_P$	Semi-volatility of portfolio returns	(6-28)	088
T	Number of observations in the sample	(6-3), (8-33), (8-44), (8-46), (8-49), (9-26), (9-27), (9-29), (10-34), (10-43), (10-35), (10-51)	015, 016, 019, 023, 025, 040, 047, 068, 069, 072, 073, 104
T_j	Number of observations that matches the investment horizon of investor j	(10-51), (10-55), (10-56), (10-57)	033, 040, 049, 105
T_P^{-j}	Number of times the portfolio return is lower than the reservation rate (for investor j)	(10-40), (10-51)	040, 042
T_B^{+j}	Number of times the benchmark return exceeds the reservation rate (for investor j)	(10-36)	070
T_P^{+j}	Number of times the portfolio return exceeds the reservation rate (for investor j)	(10-34), (10-36), (10-40), (10-51)	016, 040, 042, 070
$T_{(P-B)}^{+}$	Number of times the portfolio differential return is positive	(10-35)	019
$uCapR_P$	Upside portfolio capture ratio	(10-39)	022
$um_{\gamma_j,P}(\underline{R}_j)$	Upside centered moment of order γ_j of the portfolio returns (for investor j)	(10-21)	116

TABLE 11-3 *(continued)*

Symbol	Definition	References (chapters)	Numbers (list)
$um_{\gamma_j^+,P}(\underline{R}_j)$	Upside centered moment of order γ_j^+ of the portfolio returns (for investor *j*)	(10-14), (10-19), (10-20), (10-29)	027, 074, 076, 077
$u\bar{R}_P(\underline{R}_j)$	Upside mean portfolio return (for investor *j*)	(10-24), (10-25), (10-27), (10-28)	052, 062, 075, 112
$u\sigma_P(\underline{R}_j)$	Upside volatility of the portfolio returns (for investor *j*)	(10-25), (10-26)	112, 114
$u\sigma_P^2(\underline{R}_j)$	Upside variance of the portfolio returns (for investor *j*)	(10-10), (10-17)]	017, 018
U_j^{max}	Expected utility obtained from the best possible allocation for investor *j*	(9-30)	113
$VaR_{(P-B)}^{(1-x)}$	Active portfolio excess Value-at-Risk	(6-62)	087
x (and *y*)	Confidence level	(6-44), (6-45), (6-46), (6-47), (6-48), (6-62), (10-29), (10-30), (10-57)	034, 049, 054, 055, 074, 085, 087, 089, 106
$x_{P,i,t}^+$	Fraction of the purchase of stock *i* in the total purchases made by the manager at time *t*	(8-46)	069
$x_{P,i,t}^-$	Fraction of the sale of stock *i* in the total sales made by the manager at time *t*	(8-46)	069
w_M^*	Target market weight	(6-67)	037
w_P^*	Target portfolio weight	(6-68)	038
$w_{P,i,t}$	Weight of asset *i* in the portfolio at time *t*	(8-38), (8-44), (8-49)	023, 068, 092
$\dot{w}_t$	Neutral weight assigned to the return at time *t*	(8-34)	071
$\bar{\mathbf{z}}$	Vector of the average values of the conditioning instruments	(7-32)	024

TABLE 11-4 Glossary of symbols used in the formulas (Greek alphabet).

Symbol	Definition	References (chapters)	Numbers (list)
α_B^{MF}	Benchmark multifactor alpha	(7-12)	053
$\alpha_{i,t}$	Alpha of asset *i* using returns up to time *t*	(8-49)	023
α_P	Portfolio Jensen's alpha ((3-11) - 043)	(3-11), (3-24), (6-17), (6-53), (6-77), (7-24), (7-35)	011, 013, 021, 043, 059, 061, 098
$\alpha_P^{(hm)}$	Henriksson–Merton (HM) portfolio regression intercept	(8-4), (8-5), (8-6), (8-7), (8-14)	014, 030, 050, 064, 096
$\alpha_{P,0}^{MF}$	Portfolio unconditional multifactor alpha	(7-32)	024
α_P^{MF}	Portfolio multifactor alpha ((7-11) - 057)	(7-12), (7-14), (7-20), (7-21), (8-33)	001, 025, 053, 057, 101
$\alpha_P^{(tm)}$	Treynor–Mazuy (TM) portfolio regression intercept	(8-17), (8-19), (8-20), (8-21)	065, 080, 097, 115
β_B	Benchmark market (=single factor) beta	(7-24)	098
β_P	Portfolio market (=single factor) beta	(3-10), (3-11), (3-13), (6-17), (7-24)	043, 051, 061, 098, 109
$\overline{\beta}_P$	Average time-varying portfolio market beta	(8-33)	025
$\beta_P^{(hm)}$	Henriksson–Merton (HM) portfolio market beta	(8-7)	050
β_P^*	Portfolio representative beta	(7-14)	001
$\beta_{P,k}$	Portfolio beta with respect to factor *k*	(7-11)	056
$\beta_P^{(tm)}$	Treynor–Mazuy (TM) portfolio market beta	(8-17)	065
$\beta_{P,t}$	Time-varying portfolio market beta at time *t*	(8-33)	025
$\delta_{i,t}^{(\Delta h)}$	Quality of asset *i* estimated through portfolio tradings in the peer group at time *t*	(8-46)	069
$\delta_{i,t}^{(h)}$	Quality of asset *i* estimated through portfolio holdings in the peer group at time *t*	(8-44)	068
$\Delta^{\tau^*\kappa^*}$	Delta of the cheapest replicating option with maturity τ^* and moneyness κ^*	(8-17)	065

TABLE 11-4 *(continued)*

Symbol	Definition	References (chapters)	Numbers (list)
γ^*	Implied negative risk aversion level that maximizes the decay rate	(10-43)	104
γ_j	Risk-aversion coefficient of investor j	(9-9), (9-10), (9-12), (9-20), (9-26), (9-27), (9-29), (9-30), (10-11), (10-21)	029, 031, 047, 072, 073, 078, 079, 093, 113, 116
γ_j^-	Downside risk-aversion coefficient of investor j	(10-10)	017
γ_j^+	Upside risk-aversion coefficient of investor j	(10-10)	017
$\gamma_P^{(hm)}$	Henriksson–Merton (HM) portfolio market timing coefficient	(8-4), (8-5), (8-6), (8-7), (8-14)	014, 030, 050, 064, 096
$\gamma_P^{(tm)}$	Treynor–Mazuy (TM) portfolio market timing coefficient	(8-19), (8-20), (8-21)	080, 097, 115
ζ_j	Ratio of downside to upside risk-perception coefficients of investor j	(10-21)	116
η_j	Trade-off intensity between gains and losses for investor j	(10-51), (10-55), (10-56), (10-57)	032, 040, 049, 105
θ_j	Ratio of downside to upside risk-aversion coefficients of investor j	(10-17)	018
$\Theta^{\tau^*\kappa^*}$	Theta of the cheapest replicating option with maturity τ^* and moneyness κ^*	(8-17)	065
λ_j	Loss-aversion coefficient of investor j	(10-10), (10-14), (10-15), (10-17), (10-21), (10-28)	017, 018, 045, 075, 077, 116
$\mu_{P,3}$	Skewness of the portfolio returns	(6-18), (9-20)	009, 031
$\mu_{(P-B),3}$	Skewness of the differential returns	(6-56)	005
ν_j	Tolerance level above and below the target rate of return for investor j	(10-55), (10-56), (10-57)	033, 049, 105

TABLE 11-4 *(continued)*

Symbol	Definition	References (chapters)	Numbers (list)
ρ_{PM}	Correlation between the portfolio and market returns	(6-77)	059
σ_{add_P}	Standard deviation of the active portfolio drawdowns	(6-61)	004
σ_B	Standard deviation of benchmark returns	(7-19)	058
σ_{BMF}	Standard deviation of multifactor benchmark returns	(7-19), (7-20)	058, 101
σ_{dd_P}	Standard deviation of the portfolio drawdowns	(6-37)	110
$\sigma_{dd_{P,signif}}$	Standard deviation of the most significant portfolio drawdowns	(6-35)	095
σ_{ε_P}	Standard deviation of portfolio residual returns	(3-24), (7-21)	013, 057
$\sigma^2_{\varepsilon_P}$	Variance of portfolio residual returns	(6-17)	061
$\sigma^2_{\varepsilon_P/P}$	Idiosyncratic fraction of the variance of portfolio returns	(6-75), (6-76)	060, 100
$\sigma^{(j)}$	Target standard deviation of returns for investor *j*	(9-14)	107
σ_M	Standard deviation of market returns	(6-63), (6-64), (6-65), (6-71), (6-72), (6-77), (8-4)	006, 007, 059, 064, 083, 090, 108
σ^2_M	Variance of market returns	(8-19), (8-20)	080, 115
$\sigma_{(P-B)}$	Standard deviation of the differential returns (a.k.a. Portfolio Tracking error)	(3-22)	041
$\sigma^g_{(P-B)}$	Standard deviation of the geometric differential returns	(6-55)	035
$\sigma_{(P-f)}$	Standard deviation of portfolio excess returns over the fixed-income asset	(6-4)	084
σ_P	Standard deviation of portfolio returns	(3-3), (6-19), (6-63), (6-64), (6-65), (6-71), (6-72), (6-73), (6-77), (7-19), (7-20), (9-20), (10-55), (10-56)	006, 007, 010, 031, 033, 058, 059, 083, 090, 091, 094, 101, 105, 108

TABLE 11-4 *(continued)*

Symbol	Definition	References (chapters)	Numbers (list)
σ_P^2	Variance of portfolio returns	(6-2), (9-9), (9-10), (9-12), (9-14), (9-20)	029, 031, 036, 078, 079, 107
$\sigma_{\rho P}$	Systematic volatility of portfolio returns	(6-52), (6-53)	011, 012
τ_j	Continuously compounded target rate of return of the portfolio for investor *j*	(10-55), (10-56)	033, 049
ψ_j	Risk-perception coefficient of investor *j*	(9-20)	031
$\Phi(x)$	Cumulative probability that a standard normal random variable is lower than or equal to *x*	(8-4), (10-55), (10-56), (10-57)	033, 049, 064, 105

11.1.3 The need for navigation tools

The measures listed in Tables 11-1 and 11-2 are presented without any order other than their appearance in previous chapters or mere alphabetical order, respectively. This raw material is thus unprocessed. The tables raise, in our opinion, two important questions. The first and most important one addresses the very usefulness of what we are about to do: *Does it make sense to keep this many measures?* After all, many practitioners, by choice or perhaps by ignorance, use only a handful or maybe even just one or two measures to appraise performance. Furthermore, based on a limited number of measures, Eling and Schuhmacher (2007) and Eling (2008) conclude that the choice of alternative performance measures from the Sharpe ratio does not really alter the rankings, either in the hedge funds or in the mutual funds universe. Nevertheless, there are very good reasons to consider a vast array of measures choosing from. Let us briefly develop three of them:

1. The families of performance measures listed in Table 11-1 are very heterogeneous. Even if there are many variations of performance measures that look very similar (especially among those measures developed in Chapter 6, which is the main focus of the aforementioned critical articles), it is likely that portfolio rankings produced with measures belonging to different families will produce contrasted classifications. This conjecture has been confirmed by several studies, such as Haas Ornelas, Silva Junior, and Barros Fernandes (2012) or Adcock, Areal, Céu Cortez, Oliveira, and Silva (2020), which use a set of performance measures that cover a broader spectrum.
2. It is necessary to use the most appropriate performance measure, either from the manager's or from the investor's perspective depending on the purpose, either for evaluation or communication. Even if two measures may produce very similar outcomes, the situation might require choosing one of them simply because there could be situations

in which these two measures would produce very different results. Making an *ex ante* choice is necessary in order to avoid being suspected of any manipulation *ex post.*

3. Having a variety of performance measures at one's disposal, with different types of skills being appraised, is potentially useful for different applications than simply ranking managers or portfolios. In particular, as discussed in Chapter 17, past performance can be an interesting indication of future performance, provided that a sufficiently thorough analysis is carried out. The list in Table 11-1 contains valuable information that needs to be retrieved. Narrowing this list in a blind fashion might lead to a loss that would impoverish the analysis.

We are thus tempted to provide a positive answer to this first question, keeping in mind that it would be recommendable to prune the list by eliminating some potentially superfluous measures – but certainly not almost all of them – for further analyses. Then, the second reasonable question is: *How can we perform a meaningful discrimination between these measures?* This is the purpose of the following sections, which focus on logical and empirical approaches that can be carried out in order to answer this question.

11.2 ARIADNE'S STRING TAXONOMY

Even though the twin articles of Cogneau and Hübner (2009a; 2009b) (hereafter C-H) do not explicitly refer to the name of Ariadne, we find it appropriate to associate their approach with the mythological Greek character who helped Theseus escape the labyrinth of Minos thanks to a breadcrumb system, "Ariadne's string," that she had given to him. The authors' ambition is to encompass as much as possible the universe of portfolio performance measurement by sorting 102 of them (after removing redundancies) in a decision tree. The manager, analyst, or investor is led to determine which type of performance measure should be adopted on the basis of a set of consecutive branches and leaves.

We rework their approach in two steps. The first one corresponds to the broad partitioning of the universe of measures in homogeneous blocks. The second one proposes a deep dive into each block and associates their listed measures with those reported in Table 11-1.

11.2.1 The global decision tree

The first level of partitioning of performance measures proposed by Cogneau and Hübner (2009a) is represented in Figure 11-1.

Compared with Exhibit 1 of Cogneau and Hübner (2009a), we add to their tree the types of questions associated with each decision node in order to reach the final block in which the desired performance measure will be chosen.

The approach consists of two main stages. The initial stage aims at isolating performance measures that have been developed for two types of specific situations. The first one relates to

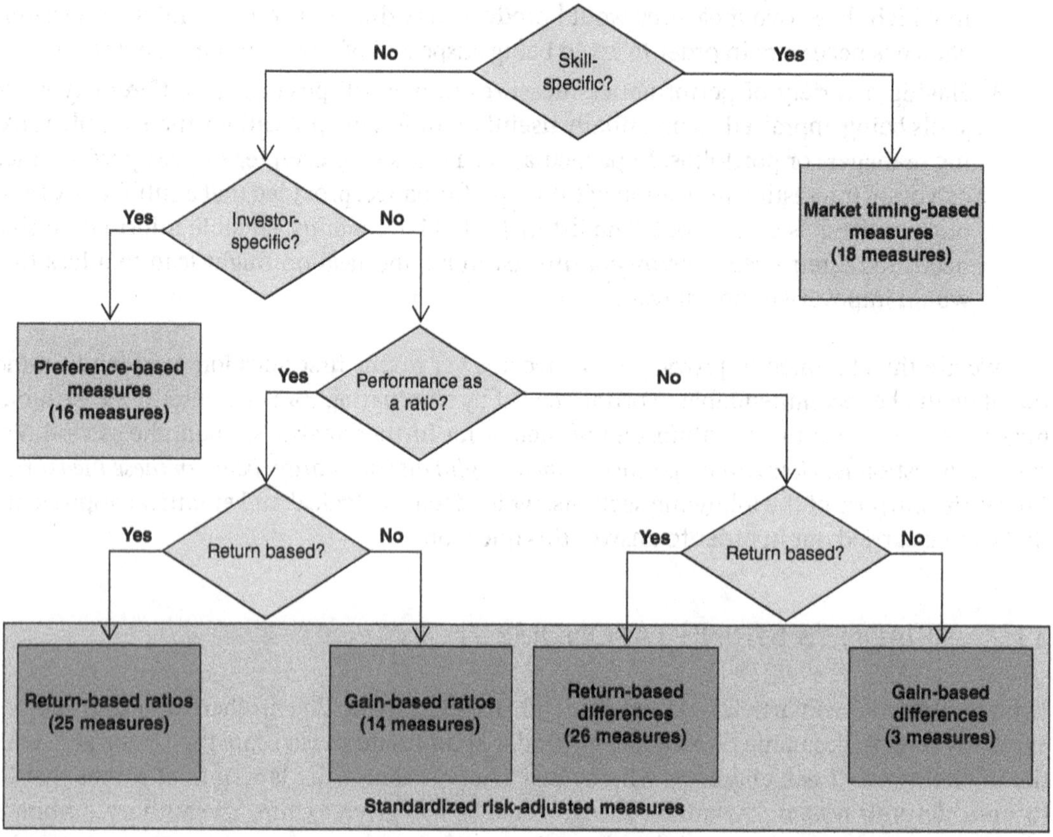

FIGURE 11-1 The global decision tree for performance measurement. *Source*: Adapted from Cogneau and Hübner (2009a), Exhibit 1.

the type of skill on which the measurement focus is set. If the appraisal of performance is not supposed to be holistic but rather concentrated on the manager's market timing abilities, there is no need to go further down the tree. Likewise, investor-specific performance measurement represents a particular challenge. As discussed in the next subsections, it is worth mentioning that the set of measures attributed to these two categories does not exactly embrace the ones discussed in Chapter 8 (for market timing) and Chapters 9 and 10 (for preference-based).

Once the special cases are adequately accounted for, we remain with a broad set of standardized risk-adjusted performance measures that features the majority of candidates (68 remaining measures). The split is performed according to two dimensions whose intersections leave relatively homogeneous categories. The first one focuses on the way performance is translated (a ratio or a difference). The second one addresses how value creation is assessed (a return or a gain). The tree presents this rather artificially as a sequence of decisions, but there is indeed no hierarchy in the way these dimensions must be handled.

11.2.2 The sub-partitioning per category

Figure 11-1 features three categories of measures. Each of them is, in turn, organized in a logical fashion. We examine them hereunder through a graphical representation of the partitioning approach and a summary table that bridges the cited measures with our list in Section 11.1.

11.2.2.1 Market-timing-based measures

The organization of market-timing-based measures is represented in Figure 11-2.

The expression "Original measures" in Figure 11-2 has to be understood as those obtained using the piecewise-linear or quadratic regressions of Henriksson and Merton (1981) (acronym HM) and Treynor and Mazuy (1966) (acronym TM), respectively, which are discussed in detail in Chapter 8.

This organization is less hierarchical than the decision tree that we introduced in Figure 8-12 of Chapter 8, which features 17 measures. We present a summary in Table 11-5, which makes the connections between the C-H categories and the measures discussed within Table 11-1 or elsewhere in the book.[1]

The results in Table 11-5 show that our list in Table 11-1 mostly covers the original regression-based measures of HM and TM and the so-called period-based measures. The sub-categories corresponding to the extensions of the original measures feature some specific

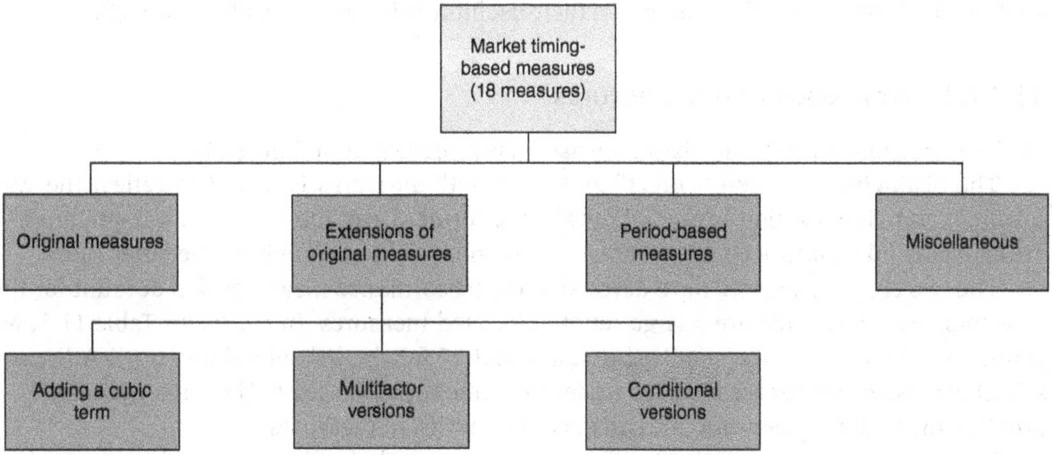

FIGURE 11-2 The sub-partitioning of the market-timing-based measures. *Source*: Adapted from Cogneau and Hübner (2009b), Exhibit 5.

[1]The number of measures referenced in the tables may differ from the ones reported in the figures because several formulas in one list may correspond to a measure listed only once in the other list.

TABLE 11-5 Matching analysis for the market-timing-based measures.

C-H category	C-H sub-category	References in list	Other references
Original measures		(8-4), (8-5), (8-6), (8-7), (8-14), (8-17), (8-19), (8-20), (8-21)	(8-12)
Extensions of original measures	**Adding a cubic term**	N/A	(8-24)
	Multifactor versions	N/A	(8-9), (8-22)
	Conditional versions	N/A	(8-10), (8-23)
Period-based measures		(8-33), (8-34), (8-38), (8-41), (8-44), (8-46), (8-49)	N/A
Miscellaneous		N/A	N/A

formulas that are discussed in Chapter 8, but that we view as too generic to be included in Table 11-1. Nevertheless, they can prove their usefulness in various contexts as well.[2]

11.2.2.2 Preference-based measures

The organization of preference-based measures is represented in Figure 11-3.

The distinction between "Direct" and "Indirect" measures is meant to reflect the way investor's individualization is carried out. In the former case, the investor's risk preferences are explicitly taken into account, whereas this is an implied parameter in the latter case.

The two chapters that we have devoted to the performance measures that account for the investors' preferences feature a large set of associated measures. In the list in Table 11-1, we count 36 of them (9 for the standard investor and 27 for the behavioral investor). A limited subset of these measures are reported under the same header in the C-H taxonomy. Table 11-6 provides the matching between the category and our listed measures.

Under the "Utility function-based" category, we mostly find two types of measures: certainty equivalents and utility-consistent Sharpe ratios. Within the "Prospect Theory-based" category, the focus is narrowed down to ratios featuring the loss-aversion coefficient. In the

[2]The C-H "Miscellaneous" category only features two measures, involving a complex estimation procedure, and we have discarded them from our analysis. The interested reader can refer to Cogneau and Hübner (2009b) for details.

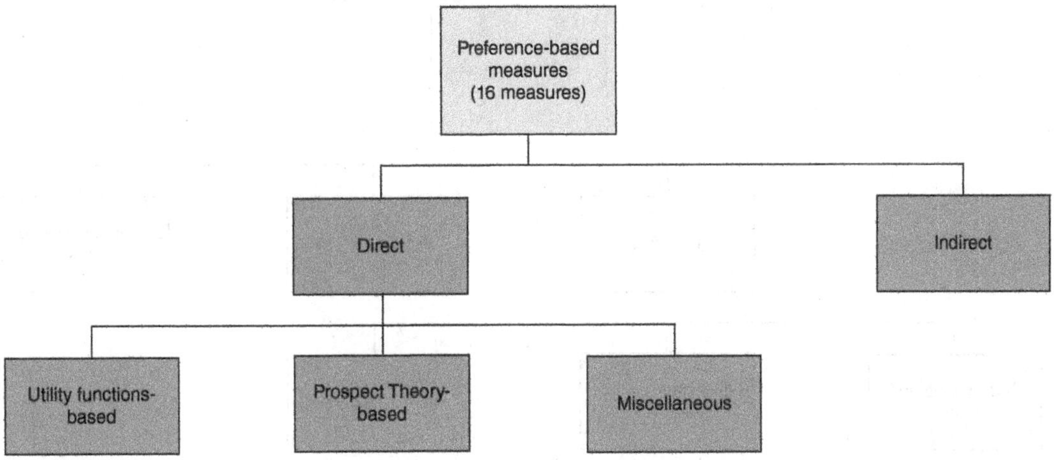

FIGURE 11-3 The sub-partitioning of the preference-based measures. *Source*: Adapted from Cogneau and Hübner (2009b), Exhibit 4.

TABLE 11-6 Matching analysis for the preference-based ratios.

C-H category	C-H sub-category	References in list	Other references
Direct	**Utility functions-based**	(9-26), (9-27), (9-29), (9-30), (10-43)	(10-45)
	Prospect Theory-based	(10-17), (10-21), (10-28)	N/A
	Miscellaneous	(10-51), (10-55), (10-56), (10-57)	(4-4), (6-78)
Indirect		(8-44), (8-46)	(8-42a-d)

"Miscellaneous" category, we find it appropriate to include the family of goal-based investing performance measures (Equations (10-49), (10-53), (10-54), and (10-55)). Finally, the "Indirect" measures are mostly related to the investor's sensitivity to market timing and therefore feature some measures discussed in Chapter 8, which are already mentioned in Table 11-5.

11.2.2.3 Standardized risk-adjusted ratios

This is a vast category featuring a large set of measures. The C-H classification approach obeys the same logic as that proposed in Chapter 4, namely by segregating performance measures on the basis of their associated type of risk (total, systematic, or specific). We summarize the C-H scheme in Figure 11-4.

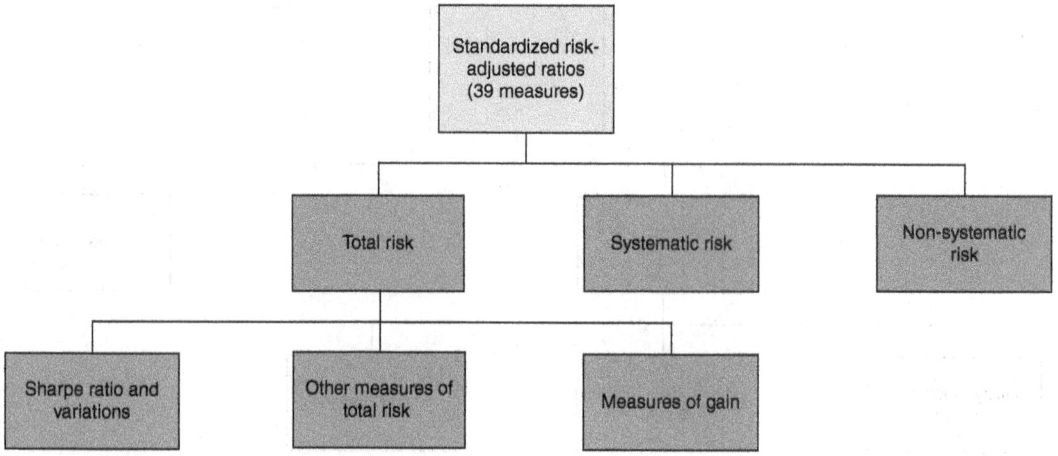

FIGURE 11-4 The sub-partitioning of the standardized risk-adjusted ratios. *Source*: Adapted from Cogneau and Hübner (2009a), Exhibit 2.

The category mostly mixes performance measures labeled as extensions of the classical measures (Chapter 6) with some measures that have been developed in the context of behavioral finance and examined in Chapter 10. Table 11-7 summarizes the correspondences with our list.

The major difference to be noted between the C-H taxonomy and our classification of performance measures relates to measures of gain. As evidenced in Chapter 10, a number of such measures derive from the behavioral finance framework and are justified according to Prospect Theory.

11.2.2.4 Standardized risk-adjusted differences

Unlike in the previous subsection, the logic underlying the inventory of performance measures representing standardized risk-adjusted differences (i.e., incremental return) is not driven by the measurement of risk but rather by the level of sophistication of the return-generating process underlying the estimation of abnormal return. The organization of the associated measures is represented in Figure 11-5.

This category features many more performance measures than those that we propose in similar groups. This is mostly related to the fact that Cogneau and Hübner (2009a) sometimes associate the same type of performance measures with several different models, thereby multiplying the number of ways to assess performance. Table 11-8 summarizes the correspondences.

From our point of view, this category displays the largest heterogeneity across the performance measures. Concerning the "Incremental returns vs benchmark of risk-free rate" category, we mostly find total risk-based differential returns in the spirit of the *M*-squared (Equation (6-63)). Under the category "Incremental returns vs market," we only refer to four

TABLE 11-7 Matching analysis for the standardized risk-adjusted ratios.

C-H category	C-H sub-category	References in list	Other references
Total risk	**Sharpe ratio and variations**	(3-3), (6-2), (6-3), (6-4), (6-15), (6-17), (6-18), (6-19)	(5-35a), (6-7)
	Other measures of total risk	(6-21), (6-22), (6-23), (6-24), (6-26), (6-27), (6-28), (6-29), (6-30), (6-37), (6-44), (6-45), (6-47), (6-48)	N/A
	Measures of gain	(6-32), (6-33), (6-34), (6-35), (6-36), (10-19), (10-20), (10-24), (10-25), (10-26), (10-27), (10-29), (10-30), (10-31), (10-32), (10-40), (10-41)	(10-33), (10-35a)
Systematic risk		(3-10), (3-13), (6-52), (6-53), (7-12), (7-14), (7-24)	N/A
Non-systematic risk		(3-22), (3-24), (6-55), (6-56), (6-57), (6-59), (6-60), (6-61), (6-62), (6-75), (6-77), (7-21)	(5-35b)

measures in our list in Table 11-1, compared with a total of 17 measures in the C-H taxonomy. Finally, under the "Difference between gain and shortfall aversion" category, we find performance measures that belong to the class of certainty equivalents, in the spirit of the Quadratic score (Equation (9-9) in Table 11-1). They can be designed on the basis of the preferences of the standard investor (Chapter 9) or the behavioral one (Chapter 10). This category obviously intersects the group of preference-based measures listed in Table 11-6, but the authors have chosen to prioritize their characteristic of an incremental return.

11.2.3 Discussion

Even though the number of measures reported in both the C-H and our lists is close to each other, we note some significant differences in the selections, with the noticeable exception of market-timing-based performance measures that generally encompass the same dimensions.

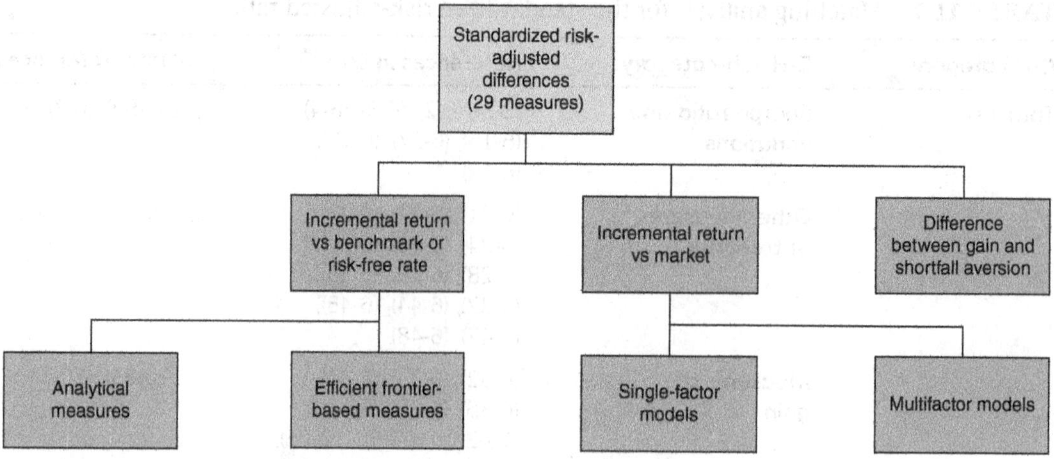

FIGURE 11-5 The sub-partitioning of the standardized risk-adjusted differences. *Source*: Adapted from Cogneau and Hübner (2009a), Exhibit 3.

TABLE 11-8 Matching analysis for the standardized risk-adjusted differences.

C-H category	C-H sub-category	References in list	Other references
Incremental return vs benchmark or risk-free rate	**Analytical measures**	(3-1), (6-63), (6-64), (6-71), (6-72), (6-73), (6-76), (7-19), (7-20)	N/A
	Efficient frontier-based measures	(6-67), (6-68)	N/A
Incremental return vs market	**Single-factor models**	(3-11), (6-65), (7-35)	(3-18), (5-20), (5-28)
	Multifactor models	(7-11), (7-32)	N/A
Difference between gain and shortfall aversion		(9-9), (9-10), (9-12), (9-14), (9-20), (10-10), (10-11), (10-14), (10-15)	N/A

There are only a limited number (18) of measures reported in the C-H taxonomy that we have covered in earlier chapters but not included in our list. Furthermore, we have discarded 24 measures listed in the taxonomy, either because we considered them too complex or arbitrary (14 measures) or because they refer to particular applications of the same generic measure (the alpha) for different applications (10 measures).

On the other hand, we list as many as 47 performance measures reported in Table 11-1, which were not considered by Cogneau and Hübner (2009a; 2009b). There are various reasons for this. The first and most obvious one is that the literature has evolved since the publication of their study and some new measures have arisen. Nevertheless, this is not the scenario in the majority of cases. Another explanation is our focus on two areas: variations of risk-adjusted ratios presented in Chapter 6 and the development of many preference-based performance measures proposed in Chapters 9 and 10. Finally, there is a category of very popular performance measures based on frequencies of gains and losses, such as the Batting average (Equation (10-34)) and similar ratios, which were ignored by the authors.

The main source of disagreement between the lists matched in this section relates to the use of preference-based measures. Whereas Cogneau and Hübner (2009b) adopt a restrictive interpretation for this category, we contend that every time the investor-specific preferences regarding risk or losses appear in a formula, they become *ipso facto* individualized. This is the reason that the listed measures developed in Chapters 9 and (in particular) Chapter 10 are scattered across different categories.

This discussion certainly calls for an attempt to reconcile the categories through a mapping procedure. This is what we propose at the end of this chapter, when other ways to navigate the maze of performance measures are reviewed and analyzed.

11.3 ANALYTICAL SORTING APPROACHES

Several authors have attempted to provide analytical guidance to navigate the maze of performance measures through their publications. Two such roadmaps, which aim to handle a large set of performance measures through a parsimonious set of classification rules, are investigated here: the classification of Caporin, Jannin, Lisi, and Maillet (2014) and the periodic table of Bacon (2021).

11.3.1 The logical typology in four families

Caporin et al. (2014) perform a detailed survey of 32 performance measures (supplemented by the evocation of many more but without details). Their universe is narrower than the previously studied ones, but they present sufficient commonalities to allow the authors to associate them with four families of performance measures on the basis of objective, analytical criteria:

1. Relative measures, expressed as risk-adjusted ratios.
2. Absolute measures, expressed as a reward over a reference portfolio or asset.
3. Density-based measures that rely on the distributional characteristics of the return distribution.
4. Utility-based measures that are explicitly designed to match the investor's risk preferences.

Unlike the taxonomy of Cogneau and Hübner (2009a; 2009b), the measures are not organized in a decision tree system. They are not hierarchized either. The major contribution of the four-family (henceforth 4F) approach is to propose a framework in which each measure belonging to a given family can be characterized by a single generic equation with an adequate set of parameter values. Although this obviously limits the applicability of the approach to those formulas that respect the functional form, it provides an objective segregation rule between families (inter-family heterogeneity), while it allows an easy comparison of the measures that belong to the same category (intra-family homogeneity), in the spirit of a rating system.

11.3.1.1 Measures of relative performance

The common feature of the measures of relative performance is their structure as a ratio. The generic formula associated with this performance measure, denoted PM_P, is

$$PM_P = \frac{\mathcal{P}(R_P - \tau_1)}{\mathcal{R}(R_P - \tau_2) \times c_P} \tag{11-1}$$

where $\mathcal{P}(\cdot)$ is a function of the portfolio return and $\mathcal{R}(\cdot)$ is a risk measure associated with the portfolio. Parameters τ_1 and τ_2 are threshold levels (that can be equal to zero), and c_P is a correction factor.

The authors of the survey list many measures that belong to this category but relate each of them to what they consider to be the most important ones. A summary of their discussions is provided in Table 11-9. Note that we do not exactly follow their order of presentation to ease comparability with our own list.

This table (and the subsequent ones) reports the measures listed with their equations in Caporin et al. (2014) with their ingredients. The grayed ones are not included in our list. The last column lists the connected references in our list (sometimes also mentioned in the survey), i.e., those measures that simultaneously (i) match the functional form associated with the 4F measure and (ii) share the same type of interpretation.

The authors list three measures that we have not discussed before. The double Sharpe ratio (DSR) of Vinod and Morey (2001) and the Sharpe ratio for skewness alone (ASSR) of Zakamouline and Koekebakker (2009) differ from the Sharpe ratio through the adjustment factor c_P. For the DSR, it is equal to the inverse of the standard deviation of the Sharpe ratio

TABLE 11-9 Matching analysis for the family of measures of relative performance.

Sub-family	4F Measure	Functions			Correspondences	
		$\mathcal{P}(R_P - \tau_1)$	$\mathcal{R}(R_P - \tau_2)$	c_P	Reference	Connected
Total risk ratios	SR_P	$\overline{R}_P - R_f$	σ_P	1	(3-3)	(6-2), (6-4), (6-15), (6-17), (6-18), (6-19)
	DSR_P	$\overline{R}_P - R_f$	σ_P	$(\sigma_{SR_P})^{-1}$	N/A	
	$ASSR_P$	$\overline{R}_P - R_f$	σ_P	$f(SR_P, \mu_{P,3}, \gamma_j, \gamma_j^{(3)})$	N/A	
	GiR_P	$\overline{R}_P - R_f$	$Gi(R_P - R_f)$	1	(6-23)	(6-21), (6-22), (6-24), (6-30)
	$L - P_P$	$\tilde{R}_P$	$nVaR_P^{(1-x)} + nGaR_P^{(1-x)}$	1	N/A	
	$SorR_P$	$\overline{R}_P - \underline{R}$	$d\sigma_P(\underline{R})$	1	(6-29)	(6-26), (6-27), (6-28), (10-41)
	UR_P	$\overline{R}_P - R_f$	σ_{ddP}	1	(6-37)	(6-32), (6-33), (6-34), (6-35), (6-36)
	VR_P^{1-x}	$\overline{R}_P - R_f$	$hVaR_P^{(1-x)}$	1	(6-44)	(6-45), (6-46), (6-47), (6-48)
Systematic risk ratios	TR_P	$\overline{R}_P - R_f$	β_P	1	(3-10)	(3-13), (6-52), (6-53), (7-12), (7-14), (8-7)
Specific risk ratios	IR_P	$\overline{R}_P - \overline{R}_B$	$\sigma_{(P-B)}$	1	(3-22)	(6-55), (6-56), (6-57), (6-59), (6-60), (6-61), (6-62), (6-75), (7-21)
	AR_P	α_P	$\sigma_{\varepsilon P}$	1	(3-24)	

itself. For the ASSR, it is a function of the Sharpe ratio, the skewness of portfolio returns ($\mu_{P,3}$), the investor's risk aversion (γ_j), and the investor's preference for skewness ($\gamma_j^{(3)}$).[3] Another measure, called the L-Performance measure (L-P) introduced by Darolles, Gouriéroux, and Jasiak (2009), is equal to the ratio of the median portfolio return ($\tilde{R}_P$) divided by the range of the percentile of the distribution between the confidence levels of x and $1 - x$, represented

[3]The detailed derivation and interpretation of these ratios can be found in the respective papers.

by the sum of the Value-at-Risk and its opposite, the Gain-at-Risk, obtained with numerical simulations, respectively denoted by $\text{nVaR}_P^{(1-x)}$ and $\text{nGaR}_P^{(1-x)}$.[4] This measure has a similar meaning to the Gini ratio, although obtained with some manipulations.

With a few exceptions, all the variations listed in the last column are discussed in Chapter 6 of the current book. Only some extensions to multifactor models (Chapter 7) or specific versions of measures developed under the scope of behavioral finance (Chapter 10) can also be considered a part of this family.

The focus on the functional form as a ratio that characterizes this first family of measures clearly leads us to skip considerations related to the type of risk considered (total, systematic, or specific) or to the measurement unit of the output (a scalar number of a value in percentage). In other words, a large fraction of the issues discussed in Chapter 4 are sacrificed on the altar of the analytical point of view. In order to reconcile the 4F view with the one defended in that chapter, we propose grouping the measures into three sub-families represented in the first column of the table.

11.3.1.2 Measures of absolute performance

The family of measures producing an absolute performance level always delivers an output in percentage points. The second important characteristic of these measures is that, instead of controlling for the portfolio risk directly, they refer to the comparable performance of a theoretically equivalent portfolio. The generic equation that supports these two features is written as

$$\text{PM}_P = \Pi(\mathcal{P}(R_P - \tau_1), \mathcal{P}^{\text{th}}(R_P - \tau_2 | \Omega)) \tag{11-2}$$

where $\Pi(\cdot)$ is the function that matches the two arguments in order to produce the performance output, and $\mathcal{P}^{\text{th}}(\cdot|\Omega)$ is a function of the return of some theoretically comparable portfolio conditional on some information represented by the information set Ω.

The generic form of Equation (11-2) is often much simpler as the function $\Pi(\cdot)$ is generally simply defined as the difference of the two arguments:

$$\text{PM}_P = \mathcal{P}(R_P - \tau_1) - \mathcal{P}^{\text{th}}(R_P - \tau_2 | \Omega) \tag{11-3}$$

The vast majority of absolute performance measures respect Equation (11-3). Similar to subsection 11.3.1.1, Table 11-10 examines the main measures belonging to this family and their functional form.

The zero beta alpha (ZB-α) of Black (1972) is the only measure examined by Caporin et al. (2014) in this category that is excluded from our list. For all the other ones, we have transformed the original equation in order to display them in terms of a difference between the portfolio return (usually in excess of the risk-free rate) and that of a reference portfolio.

[4] For more detailed explanations about these notions, we refer the reader to Section 6.2.5 of Chapter 6.

TABLE 11-10 Matching analysis for the family of measures of absolute performance.

Sub-family	4F Measure	Functions		Correspondences	
		$\mathcal{P}(R_P - \tau_1)$	$\mathcal{P}^{th}(R_P - \tau_2 \mid \Omega)$	Reference	Connected
Systematic risk differences	α_P	$\overline{R}_P - R_f$	$\beta_P(\overline{R}_M - R_f)$	(3-11)	(3-1), (7-35)
	$ZB - \alpha_P$	$\overline{R}_P - R_Z$	$\beta_P(\overline{R}_M - R_Z)$	N/A	
	α_P^{MF}	$\overline{R}_P - \overline{R}_f$	$\sum_{k=1}^{K} \beta_{P,k}(\overline{F}_k - \overline{R}_f)$	(7-11)	(7-20), (7-24)
	α_P^{cMF}	$\overline{R}_P - \overline{R}_f$	$\sum_{k=1}^{K} \beta_{i,k,0}(\overline{F}_k - \overline{R}_f) + \sum_{k=1}^{K}\sum_{l=1}^{L} \beta_{i,k,l}[\overline{z_{l,t-1} \times (F_{k,t} - R_f)}]$	(7-32)	
Total risk differences	$RRAP_P$[5]	$\frac{\sigma_M}{\sigma_P}(\overline{R}_P - R_f)$	$(\overline{R}_M - R_f)$	(6-64)	(6-63), (6-67), (6-68), (6-71), (6-72), (6-73), (7-19)
	$T\alpha_P$	$\overline{R}_P - R_f$	$\frac{\sigma_P}{\sigma_M}(\overline{R}_M - R_f)$	(6-65)	
Specific risk differences	$n\alpha_P$	$\frac{(\overline{R}_M - R_f)}{\frac{\sigma_P}{\sigma_M}(1-\rho_{PM})}(\overline{R}_P - R_f)$	$\frac{(\overline{R}_M - R_f)}{\frac{\sigma_P}{\sigma_M}(1-\rho_{PM})}\beta_P(\overline{R}_M - R_f)$	(6-77)	(6-76)
Timing-based differences	$\pi_P^{(hm,s)}$	$\overline{R}_P - R_f$	$\beta_P^{(hm)}(\overline{R}_M - R_f)$	(8-6)	(8-4), (8-5), (8-14), (8-17), (8-19), (8-20)
	$\pi_P^{(tm,s)}$	$\overline{R}_P - R_f$	$\beta_P^{(tm)}(\overline{R}_M - R_f)$	(8-21)	
	$PPWM_P$	$\sum_{t=1}^{T} w_t R_{P,t}$	$\sum_{t=1}^{T} w_t R_f$	(8-34)	(8-33), (8-38), (8-41), (8-44), (8-46), (8-49)

[5]Even though the authors discuss the M^2 (equation (6-63)), we find it more suitable to report the Relative risk-adjusted performance as this measure better corresponds to the difference between two rates of return.

The structure of the table clearly suggests the partitioning into four sub-families. The first one comprises Jensen's alpha and its multifactor avatars. These measures only use the portfolio betas as a reflection of their systematic risk exposures. The second and third sub-families adopt total and specific risk adjustments to the portfolio excess return. Finally, the authors associate portfolio excess returns adjusted for the market timing effects with a fourth sub-family. It is interesting to note that, for the Henriksson and Merton and Treynor and Mazuy models, the terms that reflect market timing, respectively equal to $\gamma_P^{(hm)} \times \overline{\max[R_{M,t} - R_f, 0]}$ and $\gamma_P^{(tm)}\overline{[R_{M,t} - R_f]^2}$ in Equations (8-6) and (8-21), are neither part of the excess return nor of the theoretical portfolio return: They are part of the abnormal return of the portfolio, and the sign of the adjustment depends on the one of the gamma coefficient.

11.3.1.3 Density-based measures

The family of density-based measures explicitly uses the characteristics of the observed distribution of portfolio returns. It can be seen as an extension of the first family, insofar as the numerator of the associated performance measures only uses the first moment (mean) of the returns distribution. The generic formula for this family is

$$PM_P = \frac{\mathcal{P}^+(R_P)}{\mathcal{P}^-(R_P)} \tag{11-4}$$

where $\mathcal{P}^+(R_P)$ represents a characteristic of the right (positive) side of the distribution of portfolios returns, associated with a notion of "gain," whereas $\mathcal{P}^-(R_P)$ represents a characteristic of the left (negative) side of the same distribution, and reflects a feeling of "loss."

The authors identify that the majority of performance measures belonging to this group share a similar structure: (i) They display one or several levels of a *threshold* (between gains and losses) that is associated with a reservation rate and (ii) they display two *intensification constants* (one for the numerator and one for the denominator) reflecting the investor's attitudes toward gains and losses. However, they do not include any explicit parameter reflecting the investor's risk aversion or related concept.[6] The measures associated with this family are presented in Table 11-11.

Because of its associated constraints, this family is relatively narrow and only features performance measures developed in the context of the behavioral investor. There is only one measure absent from our list, namely Bernardo and Ledoit's (2000) gain–loss ratio (G-L_P), which is only a special case of the Omega. Note that none of the measures listed here features an investor's specific coefficient, be it of risk aversion (gamma), loss aversion (lambda), or others.

[6]To some extent, this exclusion can be viewed as an artificial one since the "normalization constant" sometimes represents the investor's level of risk aversion, as in the Prospect Theory framework discussed in Chapter 10.

TABLE 11-11 Matching analysis for the family of density-based measures.

Sub-family	4F Measure	Functions		Correspondences	
		$\mathcal{P}^+(R_P)$	$\mathcal{P}^-(R_P)$	Reference	Connected
Prospect theory-based gain/loss ratios	Ω_P^j	$u\bar{R}_P(\underline{R}_j)$	$d\bar{R}_P(\underline{R}_j)$	(10-24)	(10-26), (10-27)
	G-L_P	$u\bar{R}_P(R_f)$	$d\bar{R}_P(R_f)$	N/A	
	UPR_P^j	$u\bar{R}_P(\underline{R}_j)$	$d\sigma_P(\underline{R}_j)$	(10-25)	
	F-T_P^j	$um_{\gamma_j^+,P}(\underline{R}_j)$	$dm_{\gamma_j^-,P}(\underline{R}_j)$	(10-19)	
	dF-T_P^j	$um_{\gamma_j^+,P}(\underline{R}_j)$	$\widetilde{dm}_{\gamma_j^-,P}(\underline{R}_j)$	(10-20)	
Heuristic gain/loss ratios	$\text{GRacR}_P^{j,x,y}$	$\text{hCGaR}_{\gamma_j^+,P}^{(1-y)}$	$\text{hCVaR}_{\gamma_j^-,P}^{(1-x)}$	(10-30)	(10-29), (10-32), (10-40), (10-41)
	$\text{RacR}_P^{x,y}$	$\text{hCGaR}_P^{(1-y)}$	$\text{hCGaR}_P^{(1-y)}$	(10-31)	

As discussed in Chapter 10, the measures listed are segregated in two sub-families, depending on whether they obey the theoretical developments underpinning the Prospect Theory framework.

11.3.1.4 Utility-based measures

This last family identifies performance measures that explicitly refer to the investor's preferences over risk through one or several individualized parameters. It does not segregate the ones that belong to the standard (Chapter 9) or behavioral (Chapter 10) approach of the investor's utility. The generic formula is written as follows:

$$\text{PM}_P = \mathcal{G}(\text{E}[U_j(R_P - \tau_1)]) \tag{11-5}$$

where $U_j(R_P - \tau_1)$ is the utility function of investor j, and $\mathcal{G}(\cdot)$ is a specific function that relates the investor's expected utility to portfolio performance.

The measures belonging to this fourth family are reported in Table 11-12.[7]

The number of performance measures listed within this family is very limited compared to our own list. We can nevertheless distinguish three logical approaches in order to assess performance from the point of view of the individual investor's preferences: the pure certainty equivalent calculated with the full sample of data, the synthetic utility score that uses the moments of the distribution, and the probability score associated with goal-based investing.

[7]The authors include the Doubt ratio of Brown, Kang, In, and Lee (2010), but we rather view this measure as a heuristic test for performance manipulation and discuss it in Chapter 18.

TABLE 11-12 Matching analysis for the family of utility-based measures.

Sub-family	4F Measure	Function $\mathcal{G}(\mathrm{E}[U_j(R_P - \tau_1)])$	Correspondences Reference	Connected
Sample-based certainty equivalents	pwCE_P^j	$\left[\frac{1}{T}\sum_{t=1}^{T}(1+r_{P,t}^g)^{-\gamma_j}\right]^{-\frac{n}{\gamma_j}} - 1$	(9-26)	(9-29), (9-30)
	mpCE_P^j	$-\frac{n}{\gamma_j}\log\left[\frac{1}{T}\sum_{t=1}^{T}(1+r_{P,t}^g)^{-\gamma_j}\right]$	(9-27)	
Synthetic utility scores	$\lambda\mathrm{PT}_P^j$	$\overline{R}_P - (\lambda_j - 1)d\overline{R}_P(R_f)$	(10-15)	(9-9), (9-10), (9-12), (9-14), (9-20), (10-10), (10-11), (10-14)
Goal-based probabilities	D_P^j	$\max_\theta\left(-\log\frac{1}{T}\sum_{t=1}^{T}e^{\theta(R_{P,t}^C - \underline{R}_j^C)}\right)$	(10-43)	(10-51), (10-55), (10-56), (10-57)

11.3.1.5 Discussion

We note that a series of performance measures are excluded from these families, even though they are well documented and relatively popular. These measures, all developed in Chapter 10, belong to two categories:

1. *Pure frequency-based measures*: They are simpler than the ones reported in the third family (density-based measures) and probably less precise, but they are fairly pragmatic. The most popular one is the Batting average (Equation (10-34)), and they also feature Equations (10-35), (10-36), (10-39), and (10-40) in Table 11-1.
2. *Hybrid density/utility-based performance measures*: They represent the intersection between the third (density-based measures) and the fourth (utility-based measures) families because they simultaneously adopt the form of a gain-to-loss ratio and feature an investor-specific coefficient. There are three such associated measures: the Behavioral Sharpe ratio (Equation (10-17)), the Z-Sharpe ratio (Equation (10-21)), and the Prospect ratio (Equation (10-28)).

11.3.2 The organization of performance measures in a periodic table

In order to provide a structured way to classify performance measures, Bacon (2021), inspired by an idea put forward by Feibel, provides a tabular solution whose logical organization is similar to the famous periodic table of chemical atomic elements of Mendeleev. The great merit of this approach is to impose a logical two-dimensional tabular structure on the list of performance measures and therefore to facilitate the selection of an appropriate formula based on objective criteria. This comes with a cost, however, as the table only accommodates a limited set of measures. Thus, any formula that does not fulfill the conditions for being part of the grid is either discarded or put in a "miscellaneous measures" category.

11.3.2.1 The design of the periodic table

The core of Bacon's (2021) periodic table is a 6x6 matrix with an additional column for risk-adjusted returns. The logical construction of the table is driven by two sets of risk categorizations.

The seven columns are organized according to the way risk-adjusted performance is appraised. They are described as follows:

1. *Absolute*: The portfolio return is used in a stand-alone fashion.
2. *Relative*: The portfolio return is matched with that of a benchmark portfolio.
3. *Downside*: The partial moments are used, with the associated notion of downside risk.
4. *Gain–loss*: Metrics associated with the notions of upside and downside are matched with a ratio.
5. *Prospect*: The investor's preferences are integrated in the measure (using Prospect Theory or a comparable approach).
6. *Drawdown*: The notion of risk is associated with portfolio drawdown.
7. *Risk-adjusted return*: The performance takes the form of a return adjusted with a risk penalty.

The six rows feature the descriptive statistics that are used in order to assess the riskiness of the portfolio returns. They are ranked by the author's perceived decreasing order of importance:

(a) *First moment* (estimated with an average or a range);
(b) *Second moment* (associated with the variance);
(c) *Third moment* (associated with skewness);
(d) *Fourth moment* (associated with kurtosis);
(e) *Systematic risk* (associated with a covariance);
(f) *Extreme risk* (associated with a tail risk measure such as the Value-at-Risk).

The author proposes an additional category, outside the matrix, for the miscellaneous measures.

11.3.2.2 Presentation of the periodic table

In Table 11-13, we reproduce the content of Table 12.1 of Bacon (2021) with our associated reference, when it exists, that allows a comparison between his classification and the list of performance measures in Table 11-1.[8]

We proceed with the analysis by the order of columns. For each performance measure, we refer to the cross-coordinates for each measure (for instance, the Sharpe ratio SR_P corresponds to coordinate b1).

1. *Absolute*: Total risk-based measures start and derive from the Sharpe ratio (coordinate b1), with the exception of the Treynor ratio (e1). We miss in our list the Skew-adjusted Sharpe ratio $S\text{-}aSR_P$ (c1) proposed by Bacon (2021), which is just the same measure as the adjusted Sharpe ratio aSR_P (d1) without the adjustment for the kurtosis in Equation (6-18).
2. *Relative*: This column gathers the Information ratio (b2) and some of its avatars. Interestingly, Bacon (2021) includes the benchmark-based batting average bBA_P (a2) as the first component. Whereas we view this measure as a heuristic behavioral gain/loss measure, the author favors the "relative risk" attribute of this measure. In addition, as in the previous case, we miss the Skew-adjusted Information ratio $S\text{-}aIR_P$ (c2) proposed by Bacon (2021) which is again the same as the adjusted Information ratio aIR_P (d2) without the kurtosis effect.
3. *Downside*: This is a relatively homogeneous category for which all associated measures are examined in Chapter 6. The first missing formula is the Sortino–Satchell ratio of order four, denoted $S\text{-}S^4R_P$ (d3). This ratio, discussed at length by Kaplan and Knowles (2004), is a generalization of the Kappa ratio κR_P (c3) up to any exponent at the denominator, and the formula for cell (d3) simply raises it to the power four. Regarding the Reward-to-Duration ratio RtD_P (e3), we discuss this type of measure together with performance measures for fixed-income instruments in Chapter 12.
4. *Gain–loss*: This purely behavioral category gathers variations in the Farinelli–Tibiletti (c4 and d4) ratio with various parameters. A noticeable exception – and to some extent an outlier in this category – is the Timing ratio $TimR_P$ (e4) proposed by Bacon (2021), which is defined as $TimR_P = \dfrac{\beta_P^{(hm)}}{\beta_P^{(hm)} - \gamma_P^{(hm)}}$, where $\beta_P^{(hm)}$ and $\gamma_P^{(hm)}$ are the sensitivity coefficients in the Henriksson–Merton model of Equation (8-1) in Chapter 8. Even though this ratio is an interesting way to simply characterize the convex pattern of the portfolio returns, we view it as too incomplete to represent portfolio performance as it does not take the intercept ($\alpha_P^{(hm)}$) into account.

[8]We do not report here the list of miscellaneous performance measures, which do not obey any particular logical structure, that are included in the original table, in order to avoid useless complexity in the discussion.

TABLE 11-13 Matching analysis for the periodic table of performance measures.

	1. Absolute		2. Relative		3. Downside		4. Gain–loss		5. Prospect		6. Drawdown		7. Risk-adjusted return	
	Name	Ref.	Name	Ref.	Name	Ref.	Name	Ref.	Name	Ref.	Name	Ref.	Name	Ref.
(a) **1st moment**	$MADR_P$	(6-21)	bBA_P	(10-35)	ΩSR_P	(6-26)	Ω^j_P	(10-24)	$\Omega\text{-}P^j_P$	N/A	$SteR_P$	(6-33)	PG_P	(3-1)
(b) **2nd moment**	SR_P	(3-3)	IR_P	(3-22)	$SorR_P$	(6-29)	VSk^j_P	(10-26)	$ProR^j_P$	(10-28)	ShR_P	(6-35)	M^2_P	(6-63)
(c) **3rd moment**	$S\text{-}aSR_P$	N/A	$S\text{-}aIR_P$	N/A	$\varkappa R_P$	(6-30)	$F\text{-}T^j_P$	(10-19)[9]	$S\text{-}ProR^j_P$	N/A	$CalR_P$	(6-32)	$S\text{-}aRAP_P$	N/A
(d) **4th moment**	aSR_P	(6-18)	aIR_P	(6-56)	$S\text{-}S^4R_P$	N/A	$F\text{-}T^j_P$	(10-19)	$nProR^j_P$	N/A	PR_P	(6-36)	$aRAP_P$	(6-71)
(e) **Systematic**	TR_P	(3-10)	AR_P	(3-24)	RtD_P	N/A	$TimR_P$	N/A	zSR^j_P	(10-21)	UR_P	(6-37)	α_P	(3-11)
(f) **Extreme**	VR^{1-x}_P	(6-44)	aVR^{1-x}_P	(6-62)	CVR^{1-x}_P	(6-45)	$RacR^{x,y}_P$	(10-31)	$GRacR^{j,x,y}_P$	(10-30)	$RcDR_P$	N/A	$V\text{-}aRAP_P$	N/A

Source: Adapted from Bacon (2021), Table 12.1.

[9] The Farinelli–Tibiletti ratio (equation (10-19)) is parametrized differently for the third and fourth moments. In the case of the third moment, Bacon (2021) calls it the gain–loss skewness.

5. *Prospect*: Compared with the previous category, this one explicitly accounts for the investor's attitudes toward risk (especially the loss-aversion coefficient) in the appraisal of performance. Several measures developed under this umbrella are not included in our list. These are the Omega-Prospect ratio $\Omega\text{-}P_P^j$ (a5), the Skew-adjusted Prospect ratio S-ProR_P^j (c5), and the New Prospect ratio nProR_P^j (d5) proposed by Watanabe (2014). They are all variants of the original Prospect ratio ProR_P^j (b5) with *ad hoc* adjustments that cannot be theoretically justified in light of the utility function underlying the Prospect Theory framework.
6. *Drawdown*: The performance measures displayed in the table span the ones proposed in Section 6.2.4 of Chapter 6. What is missing is the Return to conditional drawdown RcDR_P (f6), defined by Bacon (2021) as the ratio of the portfolio excess return over the conditional Drawdown-at-Risk (i.e., the average of the drawdowns that exceed a certain percentile). In a sense, this is the extreme risk measure of a metric (the drawdown), which itself focuses on tail events.[10]
7. *Risk-adjusted returns*: The measures listed here mostly refer to Jensen's alpha (e7) for systematic risk and the M^2 (also called risk-adjusted performance) (b7) for total risk. The interpretation of the Skew-adjusted M^2, i.e., S-aRAP_P (c7), and the reasons for the non-inclusion in our list are similar to those provided in items 1 and 2. The last measure called "M^2 for VaR" V-aRAP_P (f7) uses a VaR adjustment for the M^2.

11.3.2.3 Discussion

Besides this column-by-column analysis that underlines the additional measures compared with our list, we can underline the consequences of the differences in the conceptions between the table and our list.

The periodic table represents a set of "compulsory figures," whereas the list in Table 11-1 is the outcome of a "freestyle" exercise. The advantages of one mirror the drawbacks of the other. To comply with the logical construction of the table, it might be necessary to include some performance measures that may not be theoretically justifiable or inserted with a shoehorn. Furthermore, by imposing a strict matrix structure, Bacon (2021) severely restricts the set of performance measures to one per cell, i.e., 42 measures. The other interesting formulas (he lists 14 of them, some of which not being really meant to assess risk-adjusted performance) must be classified as "miscellaneous." Such constraints do not hold in the case of the list, which simply itemizes the most relevant measures (from a subjective point of view) resulting from a lengthy discussion throughout six chapters. We are free to include or exclude any measure,

[10] Bacon (2021) acknowledges that the Sterling ratio produces very similar results without the associated complexity.

and the final outcome is a list that obeys a looser structure and whose content can freely evolve over time.

An important consideration is what each census of performance measure really misses. The periodic table reveals some loopholes in the list, mostly related to the focus on the third moment (skewness). They are perfectly assumed by the authors of this book – otherwise they would have been added in the writing. On the other hand, the table does not account for a number of dimensions that are dealt with in Table 11-1: performance for multifactor models (Chapter 7), market timing (Chapter 8), the standard investor (Chapter 9), and goal-based investing (Chapter 10). The creator of the periodic table is aware of most of these measures and many others, as evidenced in Bacon's (2021) book, and features some of them in the miscellaneous category. The table is evolutionary, and some of its future instances will probably let some new measures in.

Like its famous chemical counterpart, the periodic table of performance is a powerful synthetic tool. Its user can draw off-the-shelf formulas whose correspondence with the nature (column) and order (row) of risk is perfectly controlled for. This easy and transparent structure is absent from the list in Table 11-1. In the last section of this chapter, we attempt to sort it out and propose some solutions in order to approach the readability of the periodic table structure.

11.4 STATISTICAL SORTING APPROACHES

Beyond the analytical attempts to sort the universe of performance measures in a logical way, is there any method that would provide an objective classification of performance measures, with only a very limited intervention of judgment calls? In order to answer this question, let us go back to the original criticism regarding the redundancy of many performance measures. It stems from a statistical correlation analysis of the actual performances of mutual funds and hedge funds, with a selected (and relatively narrow) set of measures. In this section, we propose to extend this type of analysis, both with the universe of selected measures and with the statistical tools employed.

11.4.1 Correlation-based evidence

It is fair to consider that the criticisms made by Eling and Schuhmacher (2007) and Eling (2008) are at least to some extent founded. Considering our list of 116 performance measures, extending it with the additional 26 ones proposed by Cogneau and Hübner (2009a; 2009b) (even though a number of them can be viewed as particular calibrations of some general formulations), and completing this list with five new ones from Caporin et al. (2014) and 11 others from Bacon (2021), we reach a total of 157 potentially different measures. To this, we can add an almost infinite number of different calibrations for many of them (the investor-specific ones, those that depend on a confidence level, and those that use a form of reservation rate). This

TABLE 11-14 Structure of the two-by-two fund ranking comparisons.

Fund	Value with measure X (V_i^X)	Rank with measure X (S_i^X)	Value with measure Y (V_i^Y)	Rank with measure Y (S_i^Y)
A	0.51%	14	0.19	17
B	0.33%	19	0.26	13
⋮	⋮	⋮	⋮	⋮

plethora of ways to appraise the performance of a single portfolio is obviously excessive, at least from a statistical point of view. That is, be they fully justifiable from a theoretical or practical point of view, if they produce (almost) exactly the same portfolio rankings all the time, they are simply homothetic versions of each other. If a manager, an analyst, or an investor wants to have a "library" of performance measures at their disposal with the objective of selecting the most appropriate one depending on the circumstance, this person should ensure that the inventory of measures has discarded all the redundant ones so that the choice is really discriminant.

The fastest, "quick and dirty" way to identify potential redundancies between performance measures is to perform a correlation analysis, as proposed by Caporin and Lisi (2011) and Cogneau and Hübner (2015). A similar procedure, although driven by a different objective, is depicted in Section 4.4.2 of Chapter 4, with a modified starting point. Consider a basis of N portfolios of funds for which two performance measures have been computed during the same period of time. In a similar vein as in Table 4-13 of Chapter 4, we can compare the rankings produced with the competing measures as shown in Table 11-14 (with illustrative figures).

A clear issue with the use of two very different performance measures is the difference in their respective measurement unit or simply the scale of the outcome that they produce. This makes a direct comparison of the outcomes (V_i^X and V_i^Y) potentially meaningless. As a potential solution, the analysis is applied to the ranks instead of the values. There are many ways to carry out a comparative analysis of the portfolio ranks. In his paper devoted to the study of performance measures themselves, Hübner (2007) applies two of them: Spearman's rank correlation coefficient defined as

$$\rho_{XY}^{\Sigma} = \frac{\text{Cov}(S_i^X, S_i^Y)}{\sigma(S_i^X)\sigma(S_i^Y)} \tag{11-6}$$

and Cohen's kappa, which is a measure of the agreement of judgments made by different raters. It is based on the 2×2 contingency table, in which the portfolios are considered "winners" if their rank is above the median and "losers" otherwise:

$$\rho_{XY}^{\kappa} = \frac{2}{N}\left[\sum_{i=1}^{N} 1_{\left\{S_i^X < \frac{N}{2} \& S_i^Y < \frac{N}{2}\right\}} + \sum_{i=1}^{N} 1_{\left\{S_i^X > \frac{N}{2} \& S_i^Y > \frac{N}{2}\right\}}\right] - 1 \tag{11-7}$$

A third useful and popular approach to assess the degree of rank correlation between the two lists is given by Kendall's tau. Its basis is a comparison between pairs of funds whose relative orders are similar across both ranking systems with the pairs of funds whose rankings are reversed. The formula is written as follows:

$$\rho_{XY}^{\tau} = \frac{2}{N(N-1)}\left[\sum_{i=1}^{N}\sum_{j=1,j\neq i}^{N}\left(1_{\{S_i^X<S_j^X \& S_i^Y<S_j^Y\}} + 1_{\{S_i^X>S_j^X \& S_i^Y>S_j^Y\}}\right) - \sum_{i=1}^{N}\sum_{j=1,j\neq i}^{N}\left(1_{\{S_i^X<S_j^X \& S_i^Y>S_j^Y\}} + 1_{\{S_i^X>S_j^X \& S_i^Y<S_j^Y\}}\right)\right] \quad (11\text{-}8)$$

To our knowledge, the most comprehensive attempt to apply one of these techniques in order to reduce the universe of performance measures was made by Cogneau and Hübner (2015), who started from their own (updated) taxonomy discussed in Section 11.2. They use a sample of 1624 mutual funds distributed worldwide, whose performance is estimated using weekly returns on a yearly basis from 1995 to 2010 according to 147 performance measures (either with different formulas or with different parameter calibrations). For each time window, the 147 × 147 matrix of Kendall's tau is estimated according to Equation (11-8), and all these matrices are averaged over time. For each pair, the authors discard one performance measure if their correlation exceeds 85%. The choice of the withdrawn measure is based on a judgment call by taking care to keep the most theoretically justifiable measure or calibration.[11]

The outcome of their analysis is a list of 56 measures (thus a reduction by 62% of the original set), which can be summarized in Table 11-15.[12]

The table displays seven categories that largely correspond to the logical taxonomy performed by the same authors in 2009. Some are much more populated than others, but this statement alone says nothing about their relative importance. Fortunately, all seven categories proposed by the authors feature at least one measure that appears in our list in Table 11-1.

There are four new measures that are retained by the authors. The Israelsen's Roy ratio (iRoyR), which involves the same correction made to negative Sharpe ratios (Equation (5-35a) in Chapter 5), is a variant of the Roy ratio. We have already discussed the logical flaw underlying this measure; nevertheless, because of the complete reversal of ranks for negative values, it is not surprising that its correlation with "reasonable" measures can be low. The same criticism

[11]Alternatively, the decision to consider two measures are equivalent can be made according to statistical inference. The null hypothesis is then $H_0 : \rho_{XY}^{\cdot} = 1$ where the superscript $. = \Sigma, \kappa, \tau$ and the rejection criterion is based on a one-sided test (see Hübner, 2007, for a discussion). A similar approach is adopted by Caporin and Lisi (2011) for their selection procedure and they end up with a critical value of $\rho_{XY}^{\cdot} = 0.822$.

[12]The specific parameter values can be found in Cogneau and Hübner (2015), Appendix 1. The procedure distinguishes between the coefficients of the HM and TM market timing models, which explains the existence of two associated categories. For the purpose of our discussion, they should be considered together.

TABLE 11-15 List of the measures retained by Cogneau and Hübner (2015).

Class	Count	Proportion	References in list	Other references
Market timing alphas	7	12.5%	(8-6), (8-17)	(8-1), (8-9), (8-10), (8-15) (2x)
Market timing gammas	8	14.3%		(8-1), (8-9) (3x), (8-10), (8-15) (3x)
Return-based ratios	15	26.8%	(3-13), (6-29), (6-33), (6-45) (2x), (6-47), (6-52), (6-75), (6-77), (7-12)	(5-35b), iRoyR (2x), S+SK, SorR+SK
Gain-based ratios	11	19.6%	(10-19), (10-25), (10-31) (6x), (10-32) (2x)	(10-33)
Return-based differences	9	16.1%	(3-11), (6-63), (6-64), (6-76) (2x), (7-11) (2x),[13] (7-20), (7-32)	
Preference-based	5	8.9%	(10-28), (10-43) (2x)	P+SK (2x)
Gain-based differences	1	1.8%	(10-11)	

Source: Adapted from Cogneau and Hübner (2015), Table 3.

holds for the Sharpe ratio, the Sortino ratio and the Prospect ratio augmented with skewness and kurtosis (respectively S+SK, SorR+SK, and P+SK) of Watanabe (2006). Because the adjustments are purely *ad hoc*, they introduce some noise in the estimation of performance and reduce the rank correlations in a spurious way. Thus, compared with our list, the additional measures retained with this correlation analysis do not appear to bring much added value; rather, they introduce a potential source of unwelcome noise in performance appraisal.

This agnostic approach discards some famous performance measures, such as the Sharpe ratio (3-3), the Treynor ratio (3-10), and the Information ratio (3-22). It selects many return-based ratios and differences but only one gain-based difference. This is an interesting first cleansing exercise, but it says nothing about whether the remaining measures (i) are the best possible mix in order to address all the dimensions of performance and (ii) can be grouped and/or hierarchized by their order of importance in order to discriminate portfolio managers.

[13]Specifically, the multifactor models, the Fama–French three-factor model and the style analysis framework (see Chapter 7).

11.4.2 Principal components analysis

With a rank correlation matrix retrieved from the fund rankings, a natural next step is to identify the presence of a factor structure that underlies these correlations. The classical approach for achieving this objective is the principal components analysis (PCA), which is already briefly discussed in Section 7.1.2 of Chapter 7 in the context of the arbitrage pricing theory (APT). We adapt and develop further the exposition.

The starting point of the analysis is the rank correlation matrix that we call $\mathbf{\Omega}$. The dimension of this square matrix is equal to the number of competing performance measures N. As in the APT case, the outcome of the analysis expresses this matrix as

$$\mathbf{\Omega} \approx \mathbf{B\Lambda B}^{\mathrm{T}} + \mathbf{\Theta} \tag{11-9}$$

where $\mathbf{B}$ is an $N \times K$ matrix of the first K eigenvectors (ranked by decreasing levels of their corresponding eigenvalues) of the original matrix $\mathbf{\Omega}$, $\mathbf{\Lambda}$ is the variance–covariance matrix of the common factors of the drivers of performance, and $\mathbf{\Theta}$ is a diagonal matrix of the residual (unexplained) components of the performance measures $\sigma^2_{\varepsilon i}$. Each individual coefficient b_{ij}, $i = 1, \ldots, N$ and $j = 1, \ldots, K$ of matrix $\mathbf{B}$ is interpreted here as the intensity of the link between performance measure i and the underlying dimension j.

In order to make economic sense of the PCA outcome and determine the optimal dimension of the $\mathbf{\Lambda}$ matrix, it is necessary to make two choices. The first one is the methodological way to rotate the $N \times N$ matrix of the eigenvectors of the original matrix $\mathbf{\Omega}$ resulting from the factor analysis so as to obtain an equivalent system in which the coefficients are more contrasted from one vector to another. In other words, the goal is to obtain, for the largest set of measures, one or several values of b_{ij} that are very high, and all other values b_{ik}, $k \neq j$ that are very low. Several methods can be used, such as the orthogonal (Varimax) rotation, and also more sophisticated methods, such as Quartimax, Equimax.

The second choice is to determine an objective criterion for the reduction from N to K, i.e., the selection procedure of the number of eigenvectors with the highest associated eigenvalues after the rotation. This can be a visual criterion (stop when there is a substantial gap between two adjacent values) or a quantitative criterion (minimum threshold for the eigenvalue, target level of explained variance, ...).

Pursuing their initial efforts to identify the structure underlying the determinants of portfolio performance, Cogneau and Hübner (2020) perform this type of analysis with the samc sample of their previous paper on a set of 36 performance measures, selected after a rank correlation analysis similar to the one discussed above but with a stricter set of rules. They apply the PCA to the rank correlation matrix and perform a Varimax rotation. The outcome of this analysis is represented in Figure 11-6.

This combined graph represents a traditional way of visualizing the outcome of a PCA. It summarizes the most important results of the analysis. The left axis reflects the percentage of

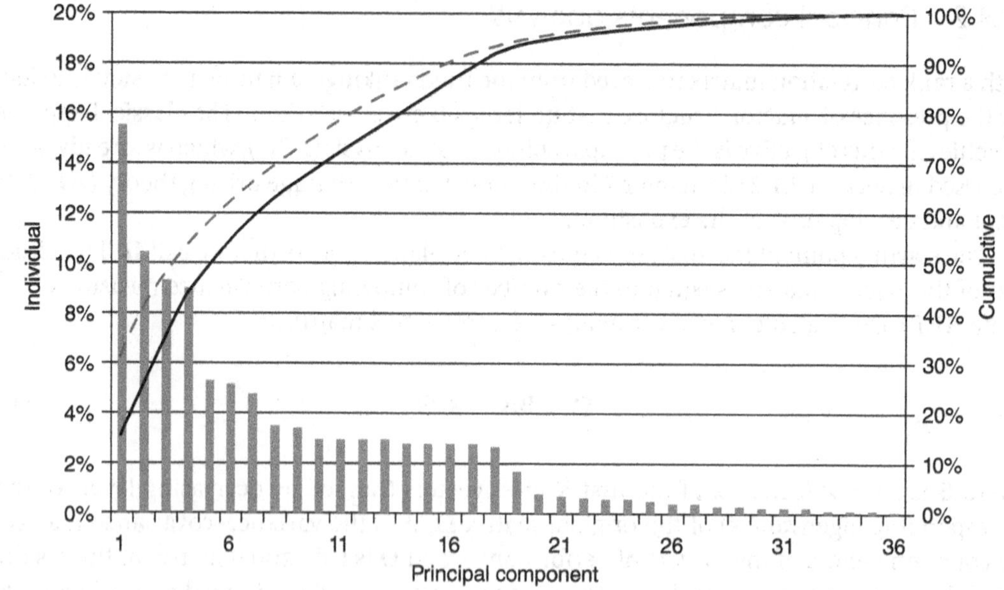

FIGURE 11-6 Outcome of the principal components analysis (PCA) on 36 performance measures. *Source:* Cogneau and Hübner (2020), Figure 2.

variance explained by each individual eigenvector. They are represented by the histograms, ranked by decreasing height. The right axis reflects the cumulative proportion of the total variance of the rankings explained by the original (dashed line) and rotated (continuous line) principal components.

Considering that the Varimax rotation does not too seriously reduce the explanatory power of the first set of components in comparison with the enhancement in their respective interpretations, the next question is where to draw the bar. Visually, it can be after the fourth or the seventh component. The authors propose to use the first 18 ones for their further analysis of performance persistence. Altogether, they explain 90% of the total variance of the rankings. The first seven factors, on which we will focus here, explain almost 60% of the variance. This means that the rest, i.e., more than 80% of the principal components (29/36), only explain about 40% of the variability in the classifications made with the sample of mutual funds. It is thus logical to focus on these seven factors.

Table 11-16 reports the performance measures (i) whose sensitivity to these seven factors is the most important,[14] and (ii) whose interpretation remains relatively homogeneous for each component.

[14]Cogneau and Hübner (2020) set the threshold at a sensitivity coefficient level above 0.75.

TABLE 11-16 Main performance measures associated with the first seven principal components.

Factor	Measures	References	Interpretation	Potential other candidates
f1	$udRacR_P^j$	(10-32)	Preference-related measures – trajectory-based	(10-51), (10-55), (10-56), (10-57)
	$MudRacR_P^j$	(10-33)		
	D_P^j	(10-43)		
f2	$T\alpha_P$	(6-65)	Abnormal return – total of "full" risk-adjusted	(6-67), (6-73), (8-19), (8-20), (8-21)
	$\pi_P^{(tm,o)}$	(8-17)		
f3	$\gamma_P^{(hm)}$	Part of (8-4)	Market timing – convexity	N/A
	$\gamma_P^{(tm)}$	Part of (8-17)		
f4	$RRAP_P$	(6-64)	Excess return – total or specific risk-adjusted	(6-63), (6-68), (6-71), (6-72)
	sER_P	(6-76)		
f5	$F-T_P^j$	(10-19)	Preference-related ratios – partial moments	(10-20), (10-26), (10-27)
	UPR_P^j	(10-25)		
f6	α_P	(3-11)	Abnormal return – unadjusted	(7-11), (7-24), (7-32), (7-35)
	$\alpha_P^{(tm)}$	Part of (8-23)		
f7	$RacR_P^{x,y}$	(10-31)	Preference-related ratios – extreme risk	(10-30)

Source: Adapted from Cogneau and Hübner (2020), Table III.

The fourth column of Table 11-16 provides our own interpretation of the measures associated with the main principal components, i.e., the most important ones from a statistical point of view.[15]

[15]For the sake of completeness, the other 11 important principal components all feature one single representative performance measure. The major measures that appear there are the alternative Treynor ratio (Equation (6-52)), the normalized alpha (Equation (6-77)), the modified multifactor alpha (Equation (7-12)), and the split risk–return performance (Equation (7-20)). See Cogneau and Hübner (2020) for the full discussion.

The first set of measures is the most peculiar one. It associates the Up/Down Rachev measures (Equation (10-32) and (10-33)) with the convergence criterion of Stutzer (Equation (10-43)). These measures have the common feature of being driven by the trajectory of the portfolio value, either through the drawups/drawdowns or through the empirical probability of reaching a target return. The second factor gathers measures of risk-adjusted alphas (thus "abnormal returns") but not with systematic risk like with Jensen's alpha.[16] The third dimension is related to the convexity adjustment in the regression-based market timing models. It does not *per se* correspond to a performance measure but rather to one of its components. The fourth factor refers to an excess return (over the risk-free rate) with some adjustment for total or specific but not systematic risk. The fifth and seventh dimensions are the only ones based on ratios. They use the partial moments (fifth) or the extreme risk (seventh) in order to perform the risk adjustment. The only "classical" measure that explicitly appears is Jensen's alpha (sixth PC), standing here as an unadjusted measure of abnormal return.

This table underlines the fact that appraising performance is not an easy task. Rankings based on the simplest or most classical measures might not convey the full picture about managers' skills. More importantly, performance is far from being a unidimensional notion. It is probably useful to combine several approaches in order to fully cover the full set of possibilities to discriminate the ability of portfolio managers to create value for their investors. Statistical classification approaches might provide a different picture from normative rankings. The set of components or measures that best discriminate managers does not necessarily correspond to the types of skills that the analyst or investor is looking for.

11.4.3 Cluster analysis

Another statistical approach that uses the portfolio rankings produced with different performance measures consists of attempting to find similarities between the classifications obtained with some measures and dissimilarities with others. The objective of this procedure, called "cluster analysis," is not to extract common factors that would explain the differences in rankings, with a hierarchy between them, such as the PCA. Rather, it modestly aims at creating groups, or "clusters," of performance measures that all produce analogous rankings within the groups (intra-homogeneity), and dissimilar rankings between the groups (inter-heterogeneity). There is no need to eliminate highly correlated measures because they would naturally belong to the same group, without polluting the rest of the analysis.

There are various techniques to carry out a cluster analysis, whose common feature is to use a notion of distance between the objects (here the performance measures) and form the clusters so as to minimize the distances within the groups and maximize the distances between the groups. In the same paper as before, Cogneau and Hübner (2020) perform a cluster analysis on the eigenvalues of the rankings, using a squared distance criterion, on their original set of 147 measures. They end up with the dendrogram shown in Figure 11-7.

[16]We refer to the notion of "full" risk as an indicator of the adjustment for convexity in the HM or TM model.

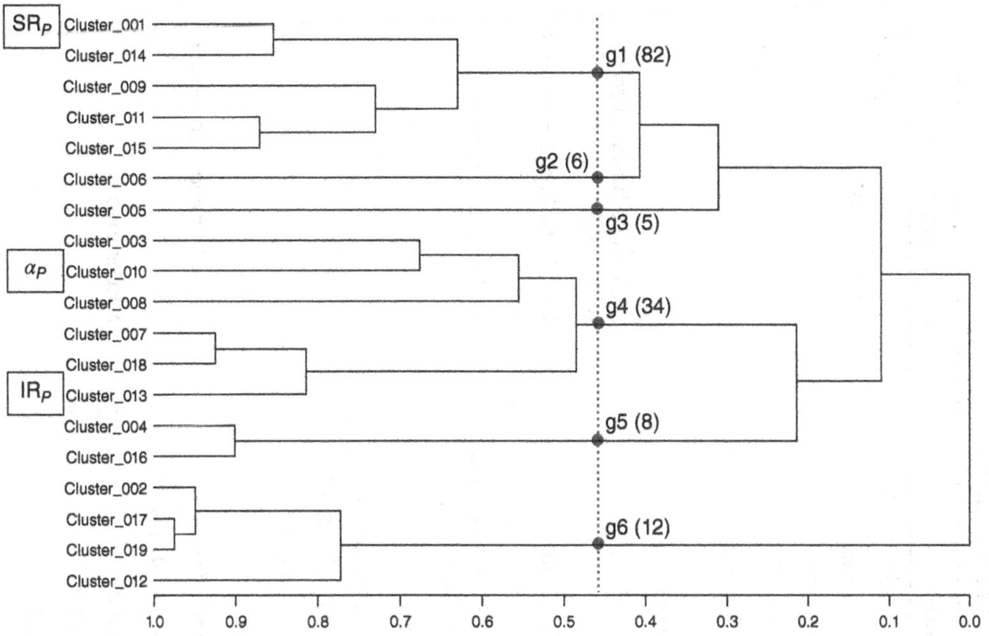

FIGURE 11-7 Dendrogram of the cluster analysis on 147 performance measures. *Source*: Adapted from Cogneau and Hübner (2020), Figure 3.

Figure 11-7 shows the dendrogram that summarizes the results of the cluster analysis. There are 19 identified clusters, ordered by increasing level of segregation. The first cluster features 54 measures (including the Sharpe ratio), whereas the last one only comprises one measure: the normalized alpha (Equation (6-77)). The graph reads from left to right, where two clusters merge at each step. To the left of the chart, we have reported the location of the three most popular classical measures: the Sharpe ratio (cluster 1), Jensen's alpha (cluster 10), and the Information ratio (cluster 13).

We find it interesting to cut the chart near to its middle. This is represented by the vertical dashed line, featuring intersections (dots) that correspond to six clusters. The parentheses report the number of measures included in each of these clusters. The interpretation of these clusters – resulting from a judgment-free statistical exercise – can be related to the properties of the majority of the measures included in them, which is summarized Table 11-17.

The very first cluster (C01 in Table 11-17) features 54 measures, all related to the Sharpe ratio. This large number of similar performance measures provides some support to the studies that do not consider it necessary to use more than one single measure, provided that they all belong to the same family. There is also a second group that is relatively wide (g4), featuring 34 measures, mostly characterized by the use of abnormal performance (with the exception of the Information ratio). Some preference-based measures are isolated from the rest in g2 and g3.

TABLE 11-17 Main performance measures associated with the first six clusters.

Group	# Clusters	# Measures	Main measures	Interpretation
g1	5	82	C01: SR (3-3), SorR (6-29), CalR (6-32)	Standardized risk-adjusted ratios – total risk
			C14: ProR (10-29)	
			C09: mCVR (6-48)	
			C11: udRacR (10-32), D (10-43)	
			C15: mVR (6-47)	
g2	1	6	C06: sQ (10-11)	Preference-based absolute performance
g3	1	5	C05: gRacR (10-30)	Gain-based ratio – extreme risk
g4	6	34	C03: M^2 (6-63), sER (6-76), Q (9-12), pwCE (9-26)	Absolute performance
			C10: α (3-11)	
			C08: TR (3-10), mα (3-11)	
			C07: α^{MF} (7-11), $\alpha^{(tm)}$ (8-17)	
			C18: $\gamma^{(hm)}$ part of (8-5)	
			C13: IR (3-22)	
g5	2	8	C04: $\gamma^{(hm)}$ part of (8-5)	Market timing – convexity
			C16: $\gamma^{(tm)}$ part of (8-16)	
g6	4	12	C02: UPR (10-25)	Miscellaneous
			C17: HM-α (N/A)	
			C19: nα (6-77)	
			C12: SRRP (7-20)	

Source: Adapted from Cogneau and Hübner (2020), Figure 3.

All in all, the resulting groups encompass some segregating dimensions already met before. Nevertheless, the limits of the exercise can also be clearly seen from the identification of the most important measures, whose association with different groups does not seem to obey any clear logic. It would be perhaps useful to reproduce this kind of exercise with another set of measures and/or funds in order to confirm (or not) the results from this study.

11.5 DASHBOARD

In this final section, we attempt to synthesize the takeaways of different approaches used to sort performance measures in a meaningful order. The starting point remains the structure of the list in Table 11-1, which itself reflects the organization of the chapters devoted to the presentation of the various ways to appraise portfolio performance.

Table 11-18 proposes a logical organization of the listed performance measures. Even though it is not structured as a decision tree, its reads in a relatively close way. The choice of a cell (i.e., a given row and a given column) corresponds to a decision path for the selection of one or several closely connected performance measures. We exclude the timing-based measures as this corresponds to the first bifurcation of the decision tree presented in Figure 11-1 and a specific tree for these measures was already presented in Chapter 8.

At the row level, we use three levels of disaggregation based on the nature of the input/output relation underlying the measurement of performance. The first one distinguishes the "standardized" measures that do not make any difference from one investor to another versus the "individualized" measures that explicitly use an investor-specific parameter related to their attitudes toward risk or losses – with the exception of the reservation rate – in the determination of performance. From the perspective of the structure of this book, the former category gathers formulas presented in Chapters 3–7, whereas the latter category features measures discussed in Chapters 9 and 10.

The nature of the second horizontal disaggregation level depends on the first one. For standardized measures, we adopt the same criterion as the one discussed in Chapter 4, namely the nature of the risk that is at stake for the control of the input in performance: total, systematic, or specific. For individualized measures, we use the natural segregation between the "standard" investor (Chapter 9) and the "behavioral" one (Chapter 10).

For the third level, the most discriminant dimension differs from one category to another. Regarding total and specific risk, we find it appropriate to distinguish the measures based on a symmetric notion of risk (volatility or similar, that account for both sides of the distribution of returns around the mean) from those that only care about downside risk (partial moments, drawdowns, or tail risks). For systematic risk, the natural segregation from our point of view comes from the number of risk factors (one or several) that are used for the determination of risk exposures. Regarding preference-based (individualized) measures, the split is performed according to the greatest segregating dimension in each of the corresponding chapters. For

TABLE 11-18 Synthetic dashboard to guide the choice of a performance measure.

First level	Second level	Third level	Ratio (scalar)		Difference (percentage)		Other output	
			References	Interpretation	References	Interpretation	References	Interpretation
Standardized	**Total risk**	**Symmetric risk**	(3-3) (6-2) to (6-24)	Excess return per unit of volatility or equivalent	(6-63) to (6-72)	Abnormal return after controlling for volatility or equivalent		
		Downside risk	(6-26) to (6-48)	Excess return per unit of downside-oriented total risk				
	Systematic risk	**Single factor**	(6-52) to (6-53)	Abnormal return per unit of systematic volatility	(3-1) (3-10) to (3-13) (7-24)	Abnormal return after controlling for systematic risk	(7-35)	No-arbitrage-based adjusted alpha (in % squared)
		Multifactor			(7-11) to (7-20) (7-32)	Abnormal return after controlling for multiple systematic risk exposures		
	Specific risk	**Symmetric risk**	(3-22) to (3-24) (6-55) to (6-56) (7-21)	Abnormal return per unit of specific volatility	(6-75) to (6-77)	Abnormal return after controlling for specific risk		
		Downside risk	(6-57) to (6-62)	Excess return per unit of downside-oriented specific risk				

TABLE 11-18 *(continued)*

First level	Second level	Third level	Ratio (scalar)		Difference (percentage)		Other output	
			References	Interpretation	References	Interpretation	References	Interpretation
Individualized	**Standard Investor**	**Synthetic**			(9-9) to (9-20)	Return adequately penalized for volatility	(9-30)	Score for the best possible investor's profile (in sqrt of %)
		Sample-based			(9-26) to (9-29)	Certainty equivalent for an individualized investor profile		
	Behavioral Investor	**Prospect Theory**	(10-17) to (10-30)	Individualized perceived gain per unit of perceived loss	(10-10) to (10-15)	Return penalized for individualized perceived loss		
		Heuristic	(10-31) to (10-32)	Intuitive notion of gain per unit of loss			(10-34) to (10-40)	Indicator of manager's ability to outperform (frequency or ratio)
		Goal-Based					(10-43) to (10-57)	Probability of reaching the investor's goal

the standard investor, we can clearly identify the "synthetic" measures that are based on distribution characteristics (mean, volatility) and the "sample-based" measures that compute a certainty equivalent on the basis of the full set of data. For the behavioral investor, the organization of the measures suggests the coexistence of measures that are explicitly related to some theoretical version of the Prospect Theory, with others that are obviously connected to behavioral finance but mostly from a heuristic perspective, whereas the third set of measures are related to goal-based investing.

At the column level, we focus on the measurement unit, irrespective of the nature of what is measured. This corresponds to the discussion performed in Chapter 4 regarding the distinction to be made between performance measures that yield some synthetic scalar figure through a ratio and those that deliver an excess or "abnormal" rate of return in percentage compared with some reference. Because there exist some measures whose output can neither be classified as a ratio nor a difference, we propose a third category with "other output."

For every non-empty intersection, we provide the list of references for all measures that can be associated with the corresponding dimensions, together with a short interpretation. Each of the 116 measures listed in Table 11-1 can be located in a unique cell of Table 11-18. Their repartition largely corresponds to the way they have been presented before.

The classical performance measures and their various revisited versions of Chapter 6 appear at the first horizontal level and in the first two vertical categories. Most of these measures appear as ratios, but some of them, using versions of total and specific risk, also produce an excess return in percentage. The performance measures discussed in Chapter 7 all use a version of systematic risk, with the exception of the multifactor pure Information ratio (Equation (7-21)) that uses the residual of a multifactor regression and therefore belongs to the specific risk category. Given the nature of the model used to generate that measure, it is not possible to associate it with another chapter.

Regarding the individualized performance measures, the horizontal classification perfectly fits the organization of the related chapters. It is easy to relate each of them to a ratio, a difference, or a probability, except for the (normative) utility-consistent Sharpe ratio (Equation (9-30)) whose measurement unit is highly unusual.

Some cells remain empty within the first two column categories. Given the intuitive superiority of measures of differences over ratios, especially for communication purposes, this is not a serious issue for the "ratio" dimension. It might indeed be interesting to develop some new measures leading to a differential return when a measure of downside (total or specific) risk is adopted or for heuristic or goal-based behavioral approaches. Maybe such measures exist and are convincing, in which case we will be delighted to complete this table.

In conclusion, the logical organization of performance measures examined so far is closely connected with the Ariadne's string taxonomy presented in Section 11.2. What does this new exercise bring? First, we believe that some dimensions that were not present in Cogneau and Hübner's (2009a; 2009b) census have been added and located in the table. Second, we have attempted to include some interesting features of the two analytical approaches examined in

Section 11.3, namely some objective criteria for the distinction of families of measures proposed by Caporin et al. (2014), and the same type of matrix organization as the one proposed by Bacon (2021), even though the natures of the dimensions that he proposes are different from ours. Finally, we try to make some sense – although to a limited extent – of the data-driven dimensions of performance highlighted with various statistical sorting approaches discussed in Section 11.4. All in all, given the complexity of the field of performance appraisal, we hope that the dashboard proposed in the current section can provide some help for investors, analysts, or managers in order to find one's way in this complicated but exciting maze.

Key Takeaways and Equations

- The six preceding chapters dedicated to the presentation and discussion of performance measures result in our own census of 116 different performance measures, which are listed in Table 11-1 by order of references and in Table 11-2 by alphabetical order.
- A legitimate question is whether some or perhaps even all these measures are largely redundant. If not, then it is necessary to adopt some clear criteria in order to sort them in a meaningful fashion and be able to select the most adequate ones given the purpose and the circumstances of performance appraisal.
- We list three types of approaches to achieve this task:
  - A *decision tree approach* in which the choice of the performance measure results from successive answers to unequivocal questions about the dimensions that are favored in the analysis.
  - An *analytical approach* in which measures are organized in a logical way according to one or several dimensions.
  - A *statistical approach* in which the comparison of portfolio rankings obtained with different measures allows the analyst to detect similarities or dissimilarities between them in a systematic and judgment-free way.
- The decision tree approach proposed by Cogneau and Hübner (2009a; 2009b) performs a large taxonomy of more than 100 measures. It involves four decisions that lead the way through the universe of performance measures: (i) Do we attempt to assess a timing skill? (ii) Do we accommodate the investor's preferences? (iii) Do we measure performance as a ratio? (iv) Do we use a notion of return? The answers to these four questions allow a substantial reduction in the amount of formulas to choose from.

(*continued*)

(continued)

- The main sources of disagreement between the taxonomy and our organization of the measures are the classification of some behavioral preference-based measures and the negligence of several heuristic or goal-based measures in their universe.
- We distinguish two variants of the analytical approach: the *logical typology* in four families of Caporin et al. (2014) and the matrix organization in a *periodic table* by Bacon (2021).
- Each of the four families of Caporin et al. (2014) adopts a particular analytical structure that is common to all associated performance measures:
  - Measures of relative performance have the form

$$\mathrm{PM}_P = \frac{\mathcal{P}(R_P - \tau_1)}{\mathcal{R}(R_P - \tau_2) \times c_P} \tag{11-1}$$

  - Measures of absolute performance generally have the form

$$\mathrm{PM}_P = \mathcal{P}(R_P - \tau_1) - \mathcal{P}^{\mathrm{th}}(R_P - \tau_2|\Omega) \tag{11-3}$$

  - Density-based measures have the form

$$\mathrm{PM}_P = \frac{\mathcal{P}^{+}(R_P)}{\mathcal{P}^{-}(R_P)} \tag{11-4}$$

  - Utility-based measures have the form

$$\mathrm{PM}_P = \mathcal{G}(\mathrm{E}[U_j(R_P - \tau_1)]) \tag{11-5}$$

  Within each of these families, we can distinguish up to four sub-families. However, this sorting approach does not easily accommodate the pure frequency-based measures and the hybrid density/utility-based performance measures.
- The periodic table adopts a 6×7 matrix structure in which the columns are organized according to the way risk-adjusted performance is appraised, and the rows feature the descriptive statistics that are used in order to assess the riskiness of the portfolio returns. The measures that do not fit this structure are classified as "miscellaneous." Even though the number of measures displayed in this table is necessarily limited, its structure reveals some sources of discrepancies with the list in Table 11-1, either because it proposes some measures that do not correspond to the criteria of the table or because the table must feature some measures that are discarded from the list.
- Statistical sorting approaches aim at detecting commonalities between performance measures through the analysis of the portfolio rankings they produce. We list three methods associated with this objective:

- *Correlation analysis*, in which the correlations between rankings allow the detection of redundancies.
- *Principal components analysis* (PCA) that identifies common sources of variations that underlie the variance–covariance matrix of the rankings.
- *Cluster analysis* that pools performance measures in homogeneous groups while simultaneously ensuring that the groups are sufficiently diverse.

- For correlation analysis, we use a rank correlation measure in order to identify those measures that deliver too similar rankings and are considered redundant. A good candidate is Kendall's tau:

$$\rho_{XY}^{\tau} = \frac{2}{N(N-1)}\left[\sum_{i=1}^{N}\sum_{j=1,\, j\neq i}^{N}\left(1_{\{S_i^X<S_j^X \& S_i^Y<S_j^Y\}} + 1_{\{S_i^X>S_j^X \& S_i^Y>S_j^Y\}}\right) - \sum_{i=1}^{N}\sum_{j=1,\, j\neq i}^{N}\left(1_{\{S_i^X<S_j^X \& S_i^Y>S_j^Y\}} + 1_{\{S_i^X>S_j^X \& S_i^Y<S_j^Y\}}\right)\right] \tag{11-8}$$

From a basis of 147 measures, Cogneau and Hübner (2015) manage to reduce the universe to a list of 56 measures with limited redundancies. This list spans all dimensions of performance.

- The application of a PCA to a set of 36 measures whose redundancies have already been removed leads to the identification of seven components that explain almost 60% of the variance of the rankings. Interpreting these components leads to the identification of similar dimensions.
- With cluster analysis, similar types of conclusions can be drawn, but it turns out that the group of standardized risk-adjusted ratios features many measures deemed similar, which might explain why studies that compare these types of ratios could conclude that they are largely redundant.
- Based on all this evidence, we propose a dashboard through a double-entry table in order to provide some guidance for the selection of a performance measure (excluding those aiming to assess market timing, as discussed in detail in Chapter 8) as a function of several criteria.
  - For the nature of the measure, we propose three levels of selection. The first one is the choice between a standardized or an individualized way to appraise portfolio performance. The second one relates to the type of risk considered (for standardized measures) and to the type of investor considered (for individualized measures). The third one brings more granularity.
  - For the measurement unit, we distinguish measures using a ratio (scalar), a difference (percentage), or another output.

(continued)

(continued)

The matrix form enables us to locate all the performance measures listed in Table 11-1.

REFERENCES

Adcock, C., Areal, N., Céu Cortez, M., Oliveira, B., and F. Silva (2020), Does the choice of fund performance measure matter? *Investment Analysts Journal*, Vol. 49 (1), pp. 53–77.

Bacon, C. R. (2021), *Practical Risk-Adjusted Performance Measurement, 2nd Edition.* Wiley.

Bernardo, A. E., and O. Ledoit (2000), Gain, loss and asset pricing. *Journal of Political Economy*, Vol. 108, pp. 144–172.

Black, F. (1972), Capital market equilibrium with restricted borrowing, *Journal of Business*, Vol. 45, pp. 444–455.

Brown, S. J., Kang, M., In, F. H., and G. Lee (2010), Resisting the manipulation of performance metrics: an empirical analysis of the manipulation-proof performance measure. Working Paper, Monash University.

Caporin, M., and F. Lisi (2011), Comparing and selecting performance measures using rank correlations. *Economics: The Open-Access, Open-Assessment E-Journal*, Vol. 5 (1), 2011-10.

Caporin, M., Jannin, G. M., Lisi, F., and B. B. Maillet (2014), A survey of the four families of performance measures. *Journal of Economic Surveys*, Vol. 28, pp. 917–942.

Cogneau, P., and G. Hübner (2009a), The (more than) 100 ways to measure portfolio performance: Part 1: Standardized risk-adjusted measures. *Journal of Performance Measurement*, Vol. 13 (4), pp. 56–71.

Cogneau, P., and G. Hübner (2009b), The (more than) 100 ways to measure portfolio performance: Part 2: Special measures and comparison. *Journal of Performance Measurement*, Vol. 14 (1), pp. 56–69.

Cogneau, P., and G. Hübner (2015), The prediction of fund failure through performance diagnostics. *Journal of Banking & Finance*, Vol. 50, pp. 224–241.

Cogneau, P., and G. Hübner (2020), International mutual funds performance and persistence across the universe of performance measures. *Finance*, Vol. 41, pp. 97–176,

Darolles, S., Gouriéroux, C., and J. Jasiak (2009), L-performance with an application to hedge funds. *Journal of Empirical Finance*, Vol. 16, pp. 671–685.

Eling, M. (2008), Does the measure matters in the mutual fund industry? *Financial Analysts Journal*, Vol. 64 (3), pp. 54–66.

Eling, M., and F. Schuhmacher (2007), Does the choice of performance measure influence the evaluation of hedge funds? *Journal of Banking & Finance*, Vol. 31, pp. 2632–2647.

Haas Ornelas, J. R., Silva Junior, A. F., and J. L. Barros Fernandes (2012), Yes, the choice of performance measure does matter for ranking of U.S. mutual funds. *International Journal of Finance & Economics*, Vol. 17, pp. 61–72.

Henriksson, R. D. and R. Merton (1981), On market timing and investment performance. II. Statistical procedures for evaluating forecasting skills. *Journal of Business*, Vol. 54, pp. 513–533.

Hübner, G. (2007), How do performance measures perform? *The Journal of Portfolio Management*, Vol. 33 (Summer), pp. 64–74.

Kaplan, P. D., and J. A. Knowles (2004), Kappa: A generalized downside risk-adjusted performance measure. *Journal of Performance Measurement*, Vol. 8 (3), pp. 42–54.

Treynor, J. L., and K. K. Mazuy (1966), Can mutual funds outguess the market? *Harvard Business Review*, Vol. 44, pp. 131–136.

Vinod, H. D., and M. R. Morey (2001), A double Sharpe ratio. *Advances in Investment Analysis and Portfolio Management*, Vol. 8, pp. 57–65.

Watanabe, Y (2006), Is Sharpe ratio still effective? *Journal of Performance Measurement*, Vol. 11 (1), pp. 55–66.

Watanabe, Y. (2014), New prospect ratio: Application to hedge funds with higher order moments. *Journal of Performance Measurement*, Vol. 19 (1), pp. 41–53.

Zakamouline, V., and S. Koekebakker (2009), Portfolio performance evaluation with generalized Sharpe ratios: Beyond the mean and variance. *Journal of Banking & Finance*, Vol. 33, pp. 1242–1254.

CHAPTER 12

Performance Design for Specific Asset Classes

INTRODUCTION

The list of performance measures presented and discussed in Chapter 11 has been aimed at exhaustiveness. This does not preclude, however, the provision of some adaptations in order to enhance the quality of the assessment of performance. This necessity appears, in our view, in two kinds of contexts: (i) for investments in some specific asset classes whose behavior deserves particular caution in preparing the data and explaining the returns, and (ii) for portfolio strategies that require the use of performance-related tools in order to make adequate investment decisions. The first category (specific asset classes) is the subject of the current chapter, whereas the second one (specific investment strategies), which mostly involves a decision-making process, is the focus of Chapter 16.

From a high-level perspective, there are two types of asset classes for which the material developed so far can reasonably be deemed insufficient or unsatisfactory. The first one is the whole universe of *fixed-income investments*, generally associated with bonds and other types of debt instruments. Bond returns are usually less volatile than those of stocks, but they might also be more difficult to analyze because of a variety of factors that influence them and their nonstationary behavior. Even though we cannot really state that dedicated performance measures have been purposively developed for this asset class, we investigate how some of the classical measures, usually developed in other contexts, have been adapted to bonds. In particular, the performance analysis framework heavily hinges on the definition of the portfolio benchmark. We examine, in turn, the cases of *statistical*, *self-defined*, *characteristic-based*, and *mixed benchmarks*.

The second broad asset class that deserves a thorough investigation in this chapter is a very heterogeneous one. It encompasses different types of *alternative investments*. One of the key characteristics that many of them have in common is their lack of underlying liquidity.

This raises a well-known issue in asset management, namely the presence of *stale pricing* that contaminates returns data. Before measuring the performance of alternative funds, we show why dealing with this phenomenon is important and how adequate statistical responses can be put in place.

The last sections of this chapter are devoted to two interesting, but complicated alternative asset classes. For the first one, namely *hedge funds* (HFs), we particularly focus on two delicate issues. These are the presence of biases in the returns data, whose neglection could largely alter the quality of performance analysis, and the necessity of adding specific risk factors in multifactor regressions to deal with the sophistication of the managers' investment strategies. For the second asset class, *private equity* (PE), the most fundamental issue is how to define and correctly measure the periodic return of the investment. When this is completed, the second challenge is to connect these returns with market data in order to obtain a measure of abnormal return, which is the typical way of assessing their performance. As a final topic, we further investigate the consequence of *managed pricing*, which appears when the fund manager voluntarily introduces some bias in the returns.

The DFSO Example – Part I

The Deep Forest Science Organization (DFSO) is a not-for-profit organization dedicated to the investigation of innovative artificial intelligence applications in science. In the context of its activities, it has to manage, via a dedicated investment office, a significant amount of endowment capital in order to distribute regular research (doctoral and postdoctoral) fellowships and to subsidize various targeted organizations. Because most of the committed outflows are fixed (and growing at the nominal inflation rate), the endowment portfolio is managed according to the principles of a defined benefit obligation (DBO) fund. In particular, the structure of the fund's liabilities has a present value that mostly depends on the nominal interest rate, but the funding ratio (i.e., total assets/total liabilities) is below 100%. Consequently, the investment management unit of the DFSO endowment fund cannot simply afford to invest all assets in a passively managed bond portfolio. Instead, it has to find the best possible strategic asset allocation in terms of risk–return trade-off while keeping tail risk strictly under control.

After a careful examination of the diversification properties and the potential rate of return of different asset classes, the CIO office has come up with the structure of asset allocation as shown in Table 12-1, expressed by wide asset classes and considering the allocation bounds (min and max).

The challenge identified by management is to provide a true and fair view of the actual performance of each portfolio segment, taking into account the issues raised by the asset class under consideration. The scope of the analysis is the latest calendar year, with the use of monthly data for each instrument.

TABLE 12-1 DFSO example – Minimum, target, and maximum allocations per asset class.

Asset class	Min	Target	Max
Equities	10%	**20%**	30%
Fixed income	20%	**30%**	40%
Real assets	15%	**20%**	25%
Private equity	4%	**8%**	12%
Hedge funds	8%	**12%**	16%
Commodities and managed futures	2%	**4%**	6%
Cash	2%	**6%**	10%

12.1 FIXED-INCOME PORTFOLIO RETURNS

Many performance measures have been developed and adjusted for various purposes. There are some specificities associated with fixed-income instruments (bonds and other similar securities involving a promised steady stream of income) that require some substantial adaptations of the appraisal of the performance of portfolios featuring these securities. Such adaptations are necessary for a number of reasons, the most important of which are listed below:[1,2]

- Bonds almost never deliver a constant risk–return trade-off because of the "pull-to-par" phenomenon, a force that makes their price converge to their face value and their risk decrease as they approach maturity.
- Bonds are at the same time very similar to each other (when they share the same characteristics) and very diverse throughout the range of various available fixed-income instruments.
- A bond price explicitly depends on its yield to maturity, which itself fluctuates according to (largely exogenous) interest rate and spread movements.
- The perspective of a bond investor substantially differs from that of a stock investor. Whereas the latter usually challenges the observed price through some valuation

[1]For simplicity of exposition, we use the terms "bonds" and "fixed-income instruments" interchangeably within this section. Furthermore, we use symbol D (debt) in the mathematical notations in order not to confuse it with the benchmark B used throughout the book, including in this section.

[2]This list of selected features is partially inspired from the discussions of Campisi (2000) and Bacon (2019).

exercise, the former mostly considers that the bond price reflects its value and chooses it in order to gain exposure to some market-wide factors, such as the yield curve, credit spreads, and currencies. This makes the dimension of "asset selection" less relevant for bonds than for stocks.

- Precise and undisputable benchmarking is more difficult for bonds than for stocks given the diversity of instruments, the illiquid character of many individual bonds, and the lower availability of public references.

In this section, we discuss various components of bond returns in order to understand what portfolio managers should primarily consider in their investment decisions. This enables us, in the next section, to examine the specific performance measurement approaches that are usually implemented, depending on whether one solely relies on the portfolio returns or whether the detailed information about the individual bond holdings are included in the analysis.

12.1.1 The components of bond returns

Bonds and other fixed-income securities are traditional financial instruments, together with equities, but with a very different behavior. Considering the plain-vanilla fixed coupon bond without any optional feature, its price–yield relationship (net of accrued interest) is written as[3]

$$D_t = \sum_{i=1}^{N} \frac{C}{(1+y_{D,t})^{t_i}} + \frac{100}{(1+y_{D,t})^{t_N}} \equiv \sum_{i=1}^{N} \frac{\mathrm{CF}_{t_i}}{(1+y_{D,t})^{t_i}} \tag{12-1}$$

where D_t is the current bond (debt) price, C is the constant coupon (in %), t_N is the bond's final maturity, and $y_{D,t}$ is the yield-to-maturity. The second expression represents the generic view of the bond price as the sum of its discounted cash flows, where $\mathrm{CF}_{t_i} = C$ for $s = 1, \ldots, N-1$ and $\mathrm{CF}_{t_N} = C + 100$.

In this equation, the random variable on the right-hand side is $y_{D,t}$, which fluctuates according to systematic (market-wide) as well as idiosyncratic (issuer-specific) risk factors. The bond price changes according to both deterministic and random sources of variations. Understanding them helps design a proper framework to assess the performance of a bond portfolio manager.

Leaving the issue of currency selection aside,[4] we can summarize the relevant dimensions for the bond return decomposition through the chart shown in Figure 12-1, inspired by the review of Bacon (2019) and mixing the waterfall analyses of Campisi (2000) and Lord (1997).

From this tree, we can express the bond return $R_{D,t}$ as the sum of a deterministic term $dR_{D,t}$ and a stochastic (random) term $yR_{D,t}$. The categories shown in Figure 12-1 are further described below.

[3]Given the purpose of this section, we do not find it necessary to deepen the discussion of bond pricing mechanisms.

[4]The issue of currency selection is explicitly dealt with in Chapter 14, in the context of fixed-income attribution.

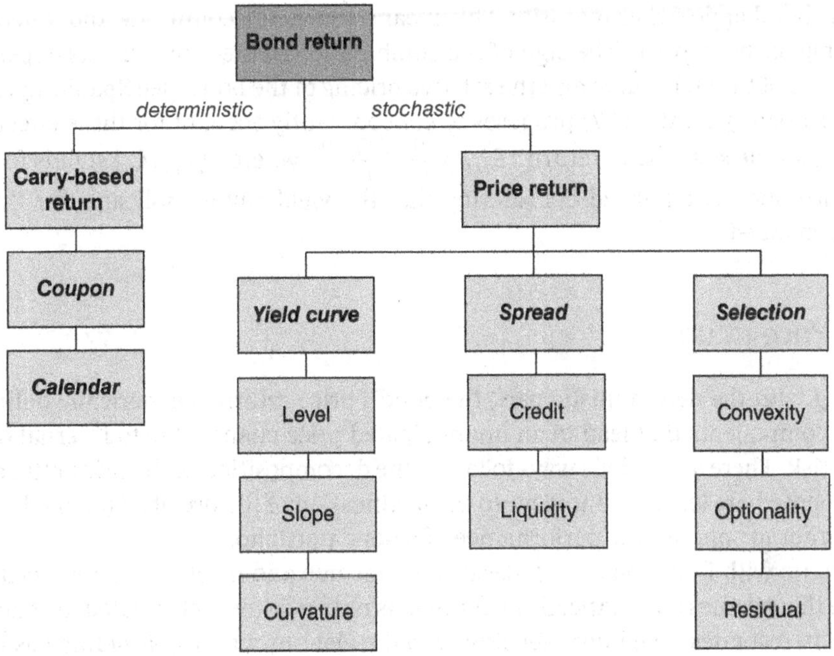

FIGURE 12-1 Summary of the components of bond returns.

12.1.2 Carry-based return

The return obtained by merely carrying the bond is the purely deterministic part of the periodic bond return $dR_{D,t}$. It corresponds to the sum of the accrued coupon effect $cR_{D,t}$ and the mechanical convergence of the bond price toward its face value consecutive to the passage of time $\tau R_{D,t}$.

(a) *Coupon return*: As its name indicates, a fixed-income instrument produces income in the form of a coupon. The current yield, measured as $cR_{D,t} = \frac{C}{D_t} \times \Delta t$, where C is the coupon rate, D_t is the current price of the bond, and where Δt refers to the passage of time, is the measure proposed by Campisi (2000) for this dimension.

(b) *Calendar return:* Unless the bond is priced exactly at par, its price differs from the face value (or, more generally, the redemption price at maturity). As time goes by, there is a natural phenomenon of amortization of the premium or discount called the "pull-to-par." From a static perspective, it features two distinct effects: (i) accretion (resp. decline) of the discount (resp. premium) over time and (ii) roll down (resp. roll up) of the yield curve as the bond is repriced according to a yield corresponding to a shorter maturity. If the yield curve is upward sloping, the bond yield decreases as the bond approaches maturity. This means a lower discount rate and, *ceteris paribus*, a higher bond price. The sign of the combination of these two effects depends on the shape of the yield curve and the relative pricing of the bond (see Spaulding, 2003, for a discussion). Lord (1997) proposes to concomitantly account for these effects through the simple static bond return $\tau R_{D,t} = \frac{D_{t+1}\{YC_t\}-D_t}{D_t}$, where $D_{t+1}\{YC_t\}$ stands for the bond price one period ahead considering that the yield curve applicable for this bond is unchanged.

12.1.3 Price return

Contrasting with the deterministic part, the bond's price return is generically defined as the sum of all components that lead to an unanticipated price change due to internal or external sources of risk. There are various ways to tackle the decomposition of the price return. The one that we propose here leads, in our view, to the justification of the use of an adapted multifactor model in order to appraise the performance of a bond portfolio.

It all starts with Equation (12-1). Besides the income and mechanical appreciation of the bond price that accrues automatically over time, its return is inversely related to changes in the reference interest rates. The linear sensitivity to the yield-to-maturity is defined as the bond's modified duration. According to the first-order Taylor series development of the bond price variation around its yield, we can write

$$yR_{D,t} \approx -\text{Dur}_{D,t} \times \Delta y_{D,t} \tag{12-2}$$

where $yR_{D,t}$ represents the price return of the bond, $\text{Dur}_{D,t}$ is its modified duration, and $\Delta y_{D,t}$ is the change in the bond's yield.

Because it is derived from infinitesimal calculus, this relation is only (approximately) valid for a small time interval. Furthermore, it ignores the higher order or optional terms, which is discussed later. Despite these limitations, its usefulness resides in expressing the bond's price return as the product of a linear, constant sensitivity coefficient with the change in yield that summarizes all sources of randomness in the price. The decomposition of $\Delta y_{D,t}$ provides different sources of risks that influence the stochastic evolution of the bond's price. They can be represented with a summation of three terms:

$$\Delta y_{D,t} = \Delta y_{D,t}^{(r)} + \Delta y_{D,t}^{(s)} + \Delta y_{D,t}^{(o)} \tag{12-3}$$

where $\Delta y_{D,t}^{(r)}$, $\Delta y_{D,t}^{(s)}$, and $\Delta y_{D,t}^{(o)}$ are the yield curve component, the spread component, and the selection component of the change in the bond yield, respectively. These components are briefly examined below.

(a) *Yield-curve-sensitive return*: The first component of the bond-specific yield $y_{D,t}$ is the market interest rate, materialized by its term structure, also called the yield curve that we denote by $\{YC_t\}$. In its purest form, this curve represents the function connecting the maturity of a cash flow paid by the reference borrower (typically the government) with its associated discount rate.

Even though the yield curve is a continuous function of the maturity, it is customary to consider that its evolution over time can be adequately represented by means of three elements. The most important one reflects its general level (i.e., the value of some reference rate on the curve), the second one reflects its slope (i.e., the difference between a reference long-term and short-term rate), and the third one reflects its curvature (i.e., the difference between the slopes taken at two different segments of the curve). The yield-to-maturity of any riskless bond would mostly depend on the evolution of these three factors. Consequently, we can represent the variation of the pure interest rate component of the bond yield, denoted by $\Delta y_{D,t}^{(r)}$, in the following way:

$$\Delta y_{D,t}^{(r)} = b_{D,\text{Level},t} \times f_{\text{Level}}\{YC_t\} + b_{D,\text{Slope},t} \times f_{\text{Slope}}\{YC_t\} + b_{D,\text{Curv},t} \times f_{\text{Curv}}\{YC_t\} \quad (12\text{-}4)$$

where $f_{\text{Level}}\{YC_t\}$, $f_{\text{Slope}}\{YC_t\}$, and $f_{\text{Curv}}\{YC_t\}$ are factors that reflect the variations in the level, slope, and curvature of the yield curve, respectively. These factors can be proxied by "key rates" of the yield curve, by linear combinations of different points on this curve that bear a similar interpretation, or by more sophisticated expressions resulting from the fitting of a parametric function on the observed term structure.

(b) *Spread-sensitive return*: The second component of the yield corresponds to the reward for different risks perceived by the bondholders. These mostly feature credit and liquidity risks and are translated into spreads whose levels indicate the add-ons required by bond investors according to the market conditions. In a similar vein to Equation (12-4), we can thus express the spread component of the bond yield, denoted by $\Delta y_{D,t}^{(s)}$, as

$$\Delta y_{D,t}^{(s)} = b_{D,\text{Cre},t} \times f_{\text{Cre}}\{CSC_t\} + b_{D,\text{Liq},t} \times f_{\text{Liq}}\{LSC_t\} \quad (12\text{-}5)$$

where $f_{\text{Cre}}\{CSC_t\}$ and $f_{\text{Liq}}\{LSC_t\}$ are factors that relate to the credit spread curve and the liquidity spread curve, respectively. Usually, they correspond to the yield differential between two different bonds with the same maturity by exhibiting different credit ratings and liquidity levels.

(c) *Selection-related return*: The third component of yield gathers some effects that are specific to the instrument itself and that have an impact on its required return. Two such effects can be clearly identified: the bond's convexity premium, which results from the second term of the Taylor series development,[5] and the optionality premium that is related to the presence of long (e.g., convertibility and putability) or short (e.g., callability) options embedded in the bond contract. The final effect can be viewed as idiosyncratic or related to trading or pricing mechanisms. Consequently, we can write the last component $\Delta y_{D,t}^{(o)}$ as

$$\Delta y_{D,t}^{(o)} = b_{D,\text{Conv},t} \times f_{\text{Conv}}((\Delta y_{D,t})^2) + b_{D,\text{Opt},t} \times f_{\text{Opt}}\{O_{D,1,t}, \ldots, O_{D,n,t}\} + \Delta y_{D,t}^{(\text{resid})} \quad (12\text{-}6)$$

where $f_{\text{Conv}}((\Delta y_{D,t})^2)$ is the factor that relates to the convexity adjustment (which depends on the change in the squared bond yield) and $f_{\text{Opt}}\{O_{D,1,t}, \ldots, O_{D,n,t}\}$ is the optionality factor, whose remuneration depends on the n embedded options denoted by $O_{D,1,t}, \ldots, O_{D,n,t}$. Finally, $\Delta y_{D,t}^{(\text{resid})}$ stands for the change in the bond yield that is not explained by any other effect and can be viewed as an idiosyncratic term.

As a result of the substitution of Equation (12-3) with the contents of Equations (12-4) to (12-6) and the integration of this expression in Equation (12-2), we come up with a synthetic expression that gathers all effects for the total bond return:

$$R_{D,t} = dR_{D,t} + \sum_{k=1}^{7} \beta_{D,k,t} F_{k,t} + \varepsilon_{D,t} \quad (12\text{-}7)$$

where $\beta_{D,k,t} = -\text{Dur}_{D,t} \times b_{D,k,t}$ is the factor sensitivity coefficient for the seven occurrences of k (namely, Level, Slope, Curv, Cre, Liq, Conv, and Opt) appearing in Equations (12-4) to (12-6), and $F_{k,t} = f_k(\cdot)$ are the realizations of the corresponding factors.

The structure of expression (12-7) can be shrunk or extended, depending on whether some factors are considered insufficient or superfluous. Furthermore, it is important to note that the coefficients are time dependent simply because the bond characteristics (and in particular the bond's modified duration, which is common to all of them) change with the passage of time. Thus, we are confronted with a highly dynamic and sophisticated expression. Nevertheless, it has two main merits: (i) being linear and (ii) resembling a multifactor model of the kind encountered in Chapter 7. This is the basis for the adaptation of performance measurement methods in the context of fixed income (see the next subsection) as well as for the implementation of specific bond attribution models that is further analyzed in Section 14.3.2 of Chapter 14.

It remains to be noted that some factors are more important than others in Equation (12-7). Establishing priorities, we can reasonably consider that the first two factors of the yield curve and the spread dimensions, namely, the level of the curve and the credit spread, are those

[5] From a rigorous point of view, we should include a second convexity term in Equation (12-2), but it is more convenient, for expositional purposes, to include this effect in the decomposition of a single variable Δy_D. Eventually, both ways to include a convexity element yield the same result regarding the global bond return decomposition.

that matter most. This is empirically confirmed by Cici and Gibson (2012). The corresponding coefficients $b_{D,\text{Level},t}$ and $b_{D,\text{Cre},t}$ are usually proxied by the bond duration and spread sensitivity, respectively.

DFSO example (continued)

The fixed-income portfolio of the endowment fund is invested in direct lines (individual bonds) and actively managed. Considering the two main sources of portfolio returns, the following high-level decomposition is used as input for further performance measurement:

$$R_{P,t} = \sum_{i=1}^{N} w_{P,i,t} R_{i,t} = dR_{P,t} - \text{Dur}_{P,t} \times \Delta y_{P,t}$$

where $dR_{P,t}$, $\text{Dur}_{P,t}$, and $\Delta y_{P,t}$ are the deterministic (carry-based) return, the modified duration, and the change in yield measure at the portfolio level, respectively. Their monthly values are reported in Table 12-2.

TABLE 12-2 DFSO example – Decomposition of the monthly bond portfolio returns.

	Return $R_{P,t}$	Carry $dR_{P,t}$	Duration $\text{Dur}_{P,t}$	Δ yield $\Delta y_{P,t}$
Jan	−1.16%	0.24%	6.54	0.21%
Feb	2.67%	0.22%	6.48	−0.38%
Mar	0.89%	0.23%	6.33	−0.10%
Apr	−1.62%	0.24%	6.48	0.29%
May	−0.73%	0.25%	6.69	0.15%
Jun	0.82%	0.23%	6.5	−0.09%
Jul	1.21%	0.23%	6.32	−0.16%
Aug	1.40%	0.21%	6.12	−0.19%
Sep	−0.60%	0.25%	6.68	0.13%
Oct	1.69%	0.26%	6.91	−0.21%
Nov	0.98%	0.23%	6.64	−0.11%
Dec	0.23%	0.24%	6.53	0.00%
Average	**0.48%**	**0.24%**	**6.52**	**−0.04%**

(continued)

(continued)

Table 12-2 serves as the basis for further statistical analysis and the design of adapted performance measures.

12.2 PERFORMANCE FRAMEWORK FOR FIXED-INCOME PORTFOLIOS

Given the bond return specificities examined in the previous section, it becomes necessary to adapt the performance analysis framework in order to accommodate them. We identify two main directions, depending on whether the focus is on the statistical analysis of bond portfolio returns or whether the holdings and trades are explicitly accounted for. In either case, the key consideration to be addressed is the type of benchmark against which performance is appraised.

12.2.1 Return-based fixed-income portfolio performance

Based on the analysis of a single bond, we can turn to a portfolio that aggregates several exposures. We distinguish two return-based approaches to measure and analyze performance, depending on the type of chosen reference: either a statistical or a self-defined benchmark.

12.2.1.1 Performance with a statistical benchmark

The structure of Equation (12-7), which naturally emerges as the consequence of the decomposition of the bond return in its various components, shares the features of a time-varying factor model. However, it applies to one single bond, whereas we are primarily interested in estimating the performance of a global fixed-income portfolio. The extension from one asset to a whole portfolio has three main practical implications.

First, even though each bond held within the portfolio has its own sensitivity coefficients with respect to the risk factors, the manager usually makes sure to hold a certain average exposure to the dimensions of interest (typically interest rate level and credit spread being first considered) that are kept under control. In other words, the portfolio rebalancing decisions are made so that, at the portfolio level, the exposures remain relatively steady. Consequently, if P is a portfolio containing bonds $i = 1, \ldots, N$, we can simplify the situation by assuming

$$\beta_{P,k,t} = \sum_{i=1}^{N} w_{i,t}\beta_{i,k,t} \approx \beta_{P,k} \tag{12-8}$$

where $w_{i,t}$ is the weight of bond i at time t in the portfolio.

The second extension points toward a greater complexity at the portfolio level. Many bond portfolio managers diversify their portfolios according to issuer types (government, corporate, and institutions), currencies, and regions. Whereas Equation (12-7) is meant to apply at the individual bond level, the diversity of bond exposures could lead to identification of different risk factors that refer to the same source of risk. For instance, since yield curves do not behave in the same way for different currencies, an international portfolio is likely to depend on several yield-related factors.

The last important difference resides in the identification of a duration-based reference rate, denominated in the domestic currency of the portfolio's target investor, that is required for the purpose of appraising performance. This can be, but is not necessarily, the portfolio's benchmark return, which is typically a composite one, and is discussed later. This reference rate, simply denoted by $R_{f,t}^{(B)}$, serves as a proxy for the reference bond rate or return, i.e., the one that the investor expects to obtain if the portfolio is passively managed according to their own benchmark conditions. Note that this rate can be positive or negative, depending on the remuneration of the various bond risks. These variations induce some modifications to Equation (12-7) in order to adapt it to the portfolio level. In its generic form, the expression becomes

$$R_{P,t} - R_{f,t}^{(B)} = \alpha_P^{\mathrm{MF}} + \sum_{k=1}^{K} \beta_{P,k} F_{k,t} + \varepsilon_{P,t} \tag{12-9}$$

where α_P^{MF} is the multifactor alpha of the bond portfolio corresponding to the K relevant factors:

$$\alpha_P^{\mathrm{MF}} = \overline{R}_P - \overline{R}_f^{(B)} - \sum_{k=1}^{K} \beta_{P,k} \overline{F}_k \tag{12-10}$$

Equation (12-10) corresponds, with minor variations, to Equation (7-11) of Chapter 7, which provides a general definition of the multifactor alpha. This means that all performance measures developed within that context can also apply to a bond portfolio and, *a fortiori*, to a hybrid (mixture of stocks and bonds) fund or portfolio. The key difference with Chapter 7, however, resides in (i) the identification of the benchmark interest rate and (ii) the choice of the factors.

Regarding the benchmark interest rate, it is also possible to consider a short-term average money-market rate $R_{f,t}$ whose average is $\overline{R}_f$ and to apply the same specification as Equation (12-9) to the portfolio benchmark whose return is $R_{f,t}^{(B)}$, leading to the twin regressions:

$$R_{P,t} - R_{f,t} = \tilde{\alpha}_P^{\mathrm{MF}} + \sum_{k=1}^{K} \tilde{\beta}_{P,k} F_{k,t} + \varepsilon_{P,t} \tag{12-11a}$$

$$R_{f,t}^{(B)} - R_{f,t} = \tilde{\alpha}_B^{\mathrm{MF}} + \sum_{k=1}^{K} \tilde{\beta}_{B,k} F_{k,t} + \varepsilon_{B,t} \tag{12-11b}$$

where $\tilde{\alpha}_P^{MF}$ and $\tilde{\alpha}_B^{MF}$ are the multifactor alpha of the portfolio and benchmark with respect to the short-term rate.

Under this variation, we can come up with a more precise measurement of the bond portfolio performance by using the modified multifactor alpha (Equation (7-12) of Chapter 7) in excess of the benchmark multifactor alpha:

$$m\alpha_P^{MF} = \tilde{\alpha}_P^{MF} \frac{\overline{R}_f^{(B)} - \overline{R}_f - \tilde{\alpha}_B^{MF}}{\overline{R}_P - \overline{R}_f - \tilde{\alpha}_P^{MF}} - \tilde{\alpha}_B^{MF} \tag{12-12}$$

Note that Equation (12-12) only makes sense if both the numerator and denominator of the ratio have the same sign, i.e., we can identify a common excess return for both the portfolio and benchmark.

Regarding the choice of factors, Blake, Elton, and Gruber (1993), the first authors who have empirically investigated the question of bond mutual funds, tested several specifications and already concluded that it was necessary to include at least three factors: a general bond index, a term-structure index, and a credit index. Since the release of this seminal study, many other specifications and factors have been proposed (see Bai, Bali, and Wen, 2019, for a comprehensive review), but the red wire has remained the same: For pure bond funds, the identification of factors mostly corresponds to the waterfall of Figure 12-1, whereas hybrid funds require a mixture of equity- and bond-related factors, especially the three factors identified by Blake et al. (1993).

Alternatively to market-based factors, bond investor preferences appear to matter as well. They significantly differ from their equity investor counterparts. Bai et al. (2019) show that downside risk matters to bond investors to a substantial extent and that a corresponding risk factor deserves to be included in the factor model. Moving further along this line, Bai, Bali, and Wen (2016) find that variance, skewness, and kurtosis risk factors may serve as a complement to the traditional factors used in the model. Interestingly, bond investors generally display some aversion to positive skewness, as evidenced by François, Heck, Hübner, and Lejeune (2022).

Finally, it must be noted that bond portfolio rankings based on multifactor alphas seem to have some limits. In a recent puzzling study featuring a great number of alternative specifications, Dang, Hollstein, and Prokopczuk (2022) document that bond fund customers almost solely base their investment or divestment decisions on the observed Sharpe ratios, despite the moderate relevance of this performance measure in the context of fixed-income mutual funds.

DFSO example (continued)

Starting from the data of Table 12-2, a more refined analysis of the source of yield variations is carried out. Two factors are selected for that purpose: the change in the level of the one-year sovereign interest rate $\Delta 1y_t$ and the change in the spread between 10-year BBB and AAA corporate bond yield, Δs_t. Considering time-varying sensitivity coefficients (related to the change in the weights of the different bonds within the portfolio over time), the corresponding regression equation then looks like $\Delta y_{P,t} = b_{y_P,r,t} \times \Delta 1y_t + b_{y_P,s,t} \times \Delta s_t + \eta_{P,t}$, where the last term is the unexplained variation of the yield.

Implementing a two-factor model with constant betas as in Equation (12-9) involves the identification of the benchmark rate $R_{f,t}^{(B)}$. We simply consider that it has a constant carry-based return of 0.23%/month, a duration of five years, and its yield betas are equal to 1.1 with respect to the one-year rate and 0.2 with respect to the credit spread. Thus, we obtain $R_{f,t}^{(B)} = 0.23\% - 5.5 \times \Delta 1y_t - 1 \times \Delta s_t$.

The outcome of this first-level analysis is represented in Table 12-3.

TABLE 12-3 DFSO example – Bond portfolio yield sensitivities.

	Δ yield $\Delta y_{P,t}$	Sensi. rate $b_{y_P,r,t}$	Δ rate $\Delta 1y_t$	Sensi. spread $b_{y_P,s,t}$	Δ spread Δs_t	Residual $\eta_{P,t}$	Bench. rate $R_{f,t}^{(B)}$
Jan	0.21%	1.16	0.17%	0.34	0.19%	−0.05%	*−0.90%*
Feb	−0.38%	1.13	−0.12%	0.33	−0.16%	−0.19%	*1.05%*
Mar	−0.10%	1.05	0.04%	0.31	−0.02%	−0.14%	*0.03%*
Apr	0.29%	1.15	0.12%	0.37	0.19%	0.08%	*−0.62%*
May	0.15%	1.23	−0.13%	0.39	0.25%	0.21%	*0.70%*
Jun	−0.09%	1.17	−0.12%	0.41	−0.20%	0.13%	*1.09%*
Jul	−0.16%	1.11	−0.01%	0.38	−0.28%	−0.04%	*0.57%*
Aug	−0.19%	1.02	0.06%	0.34	−0.15%	−0.20%	*0.05%*
Sep	0.13%	1.26	−0.11%	0.31	0.36%	0.15%	*0.48%*
Oct	−0.21%	1.36	−0.32%	0.35	0.15%	0.18%	*1.84%*
Nov	−0.11%	1.2	0.14%	0.36	0.08%	−0.31%	*−0.62%*
Dec	0.00%	1.15	0.13%	0.35	−0.12%	−0.11%	*−0.37%*
Average	**−0.04%**	**1.17**	**−0.01%**	**0.35**	**0.02%**	**−0.02%**	**0.27%**

To compute the multifactor alpha, the explained variable depends on the specification: It is (i) the monthly bond portfolio return in excess of the benchmark rate in Equation (12-9), (ii) the monthly bond portfolio return in excess of the short-term rate in Equation (12-11a), or (iii) the monthly benchmark portfolio return in excess of the

(continued)

(continued)

short-term rate in Equation (12-11b). Each of them is regressed against the variables previously identified, namely, $\Delta 1y_t$ and Δs_t. The output is given in Table 12-4.

TABLE 12-4 DFSO example – Multifactor regression results.

	MF alpha			Beta rate			Beta spread		
	α_P^{MF}	$\tilde{\alpha}_P^{MF}$	$\tilde{\alpha}_B^{MF}$	$\beta_{P,r}$	$\tilde{\beta}_{P,r}$	$\tilde{\beta}_{B,r}$	$\beta_{P,s}$	$\tilde{\beta}_{P,s}$	$\tilde{\beta}_{B,s}$
Estimate	0.31%	0.39%	0.08%	1.51	−3.99	−5.50	−3.36	−4.36	−1.00
St. dev.	0.24%	0.24%	0.00%	1.69	1.69	0.00	1.22	1.22	0.00
t-stat	1.27	1.60	N.A.	0.89	−2.36	N.A.	−2.75	−3.57	N.A.

The portfolio multifactor alpha computed with its duration-based benchmark is 0.31% per month, corresponding to a yearly 3.69%. The other two specifications leave an additional abnormal return of 0.08% for both the portfolio and the benchmark. The computation of the modified multifactor alpha is irrelevant because the required portfolio return $\overline{R}_P - \overline{R}_f - \alpha_P^{MF}$ is negative.

12.2.1.2 Performance with a self-defined benchmark

Despite the fact that benchmark indexes are relatively scarce and difficult to closely associate with bond portfolios, their use is common in the fund industry and is justified for two reasons. From an empirical perspective, Gebhardt, Hvidkjaer, and Swaminathan (2005) found that the bulk of the expected return obtained by bond portfolios results from systematic risk exposures. Bai, Bali, and Wen (2021) further document that idiosyncratic risk appears not to be priced on the bond market. Thus, only systematic risk appears to matter. On the other hand, as Spaulding (2003) puts it, neither sector selection nor security selection makes any real difference from a practical point of view. The active portfolio manager's job is mostly to anticipate what will be the evolution of the yield curve (both level and slope), the spread curve, and the creditworthiness of different issuer types or geographical zones. All these dimensions are primarily measured through the divergence from the portfolio benchmark.

What can we take away from this discussion? If the fund or portfolio has a self-identified benchmark, it makes full sense to appraise the quality of the active management decisions through a measure of deviation with respect to that benchmark, represented by the tracking difference $\overline{R}_P - \overline{R}_B \equiv \overline{R}_{(P-B)}$, also referred to as the (self-benchmarked) portfolio alpha.

In this context, the simplest type of benchmark portfolio that would be considered is a pure (modified) duration-based bond index, denominated in the currency of reference, and considered exempt from credit risk. This basic case corresponds to a situation in which (i) the factor return corresponding to the level of the yield curve is the return of this index, denoted by $R_{f,t}^{(B)}$, (ii) the beta of the portfolio with this factor is unity ($\beta_{P,\text{Level}} = 1$), and (iii) the exposure to every factor other than the interest rate level is discarded ($\beta_{P,k} = 0\ \forall k \neq \text{Level}$). Starting from Equation (12-9), the return of the portfolio is then simply written as

$$R_{P,t} - R_{f,t}^{(B)} = \alpha_P^{\text{Dur}} + \varepsilon_{P,t} \tag{12-13}$$

where α_P^{Dur} is the duration-based self-benchmarked performance or, in short, the *Duration alpha*, which is defined as

$$\alpha_P^{\text{Dur}} = \overline{R}_{(P-B)} = \overline{R}_P - \overline{R}_f^{(B)} \tag{12-14}$$

In spite of its apparent simplicity, expression (12-14) corresponds to the reality of a number of managers whose compass is the target duration of their portfolio. It is also very useful for two reasons: It makes it possible to adapt the classical performance measures developed in Chapter 3 in the context of fixed income portfolios, and it allows an analysis of performance in the same spirit as Fama's decomposition, which is generically discussed in Chapter 13.

First, we can use the analogy between the Duration alpha of Equation (12-14) and the classical Jensen's alpha developed in the context of generic mutual funds. The modified duration, in its quality of a sensitivity coefficient shown in Equation (12-2), plays the role of an absolute systematic risk exposure. The benchmark has a duration of Dur_B and an average return of $\overline{R}_f^{(B)}$. This corresponds to a duration excess return equal to $\lambda_B^{\text{Dur}} = \overline{R}_f^{(B)} - \overline{R}_f$, with $\overline{R}_f$ being the short-term rate with a (nearly) zero duration. This is the market remuneration for maturity risk within any bond portfolio sharing the same benchmark. The slope of the "bond market line," which reflects how the market has rewarded duration risk, is simply equal to $\frac{\overline{R}_f^{(B)} - \overline{R}_f}{\text{Dur}_B}$, i.e., the benchmark excess return per unit of duration.[6] If we consider the portfolio's own duration, denoted by Dur_P, we can (still by analogy with the Standard Portfolio Theory framework) define the portfolio's *Duration beta* as $\beta_P^{\text{Dur}} \equiv \frac{\text{Dur}_P}{\text{Dur}_B}$. This enables us to define the *Duration Treynor ratio* (TR_P^{Dur}) and the *Duration modified alpha* ($\text{m}\alpha_P^{\text{Dur}}$) in a straightforward fashion:[7]

$$\text{TR}_P^{\text{Dur}} = \frac{\overline{R}_P - \overline{R}_f}{\beta_P^{\text{Dur}}} \tag{12-15}$$

$$\text{m}\alpha_P^{\text{Dur}} = \frac{\alpha_P^{\text{Dur}}}{\beta_P^{\text{Dur}}} \tag{12-16}$$

[6]Note that, in this self-benchmarked framework, there is no difference between systematic and total risk as the durations of the portfolio and the benchmark are taken with respect to the same interest rate. This entails that their duration-based returns are perfectly correlated. Thus, the benchmark excess return per unit of duration is the counterpart of both the slope of the Capital Market Line (CML) and the Security Market Line (SML).

[7]Bacon (2021) similarly defines the Reward to Duration without reference to the benchmark as $\text{RtD}_P = \frac{\overline{R}_P - \overline{R}_f}{\text{Dur}_P}$.

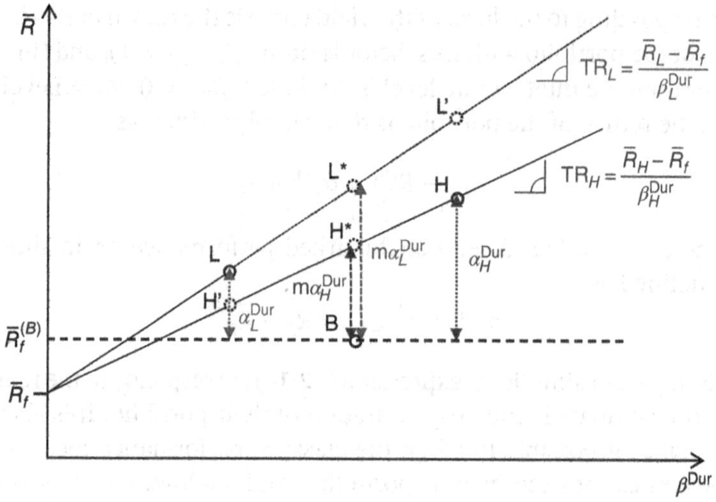

FIGURE 12-2 Graphical representation of the duration-based classical performance measures.

To assess the implications of duration-based classical performance assessment, consider Figure 12-2, which is an adapted version of Figure 3-7 of Chapter 3.

The graph of Figure 12-2 generally bears the same interpretation as that of Figure 3-7 of Chapter 3, with some slight differences. The managers of portfolios *L* and *H* have decided to adopt a lower and larger duration than the one of their common benchmark *B*, respectively. Even though they both have obtained a positive abnormal return, their performance is appraised differently. The Duration alpha of *L* appears to be lower than that of *H*. This is graphically reflected by the distance between the coordinates of the portfolios and their image on the horizontal line whose distance from the short-term rate is $\lambda_B^{\text{Dur}} = \overline{R}_f^{(B)} - \overline{R}_f$, which is positive in this case (due to a decrease in the level of interest rates). Nevertheless, by extending their portfolio duration, the manager of *H* has taken a greater risk than that of *L*. This is because any change in interest rate (positive or negative) has a larger homothetic impact on their resulting portfolio return. To make sense of this, consider that the average interest rate change during the period is positive. It entails that $\lambda_B^{\text{Dur}} < 0$, i.e., all slopes become negative on the graph. Everything else remaining equal, the performance of *H* would become more negative than that of *L*. Making a parallel with the notion of homemade leverage, it makes sense to compare these two portfolios by combining each of them with short-term borrowing or lending at the spot riskless rate $\overline{R}_f$ in order to neutralize their duration risk. Their performance would then be assessed through their Duration modified alpha, with in this case $m\alpha_H^{\text{Dur}} < m\alpha_L^{\text{Dur}}$.

However, the analogy of Figure 12-2 with the classical performance measures has some limitations. Part of the outperformance of portfolio *H* over that of *L* reflected in a higher Duration alpha $\alpha_H^{\text{Dur}} > \alpha_L^{\text{Dur}}$ must find its root into some other positive contributions to performance than duration risk. The manager of *H* might have obtained a better remuneration for credit or

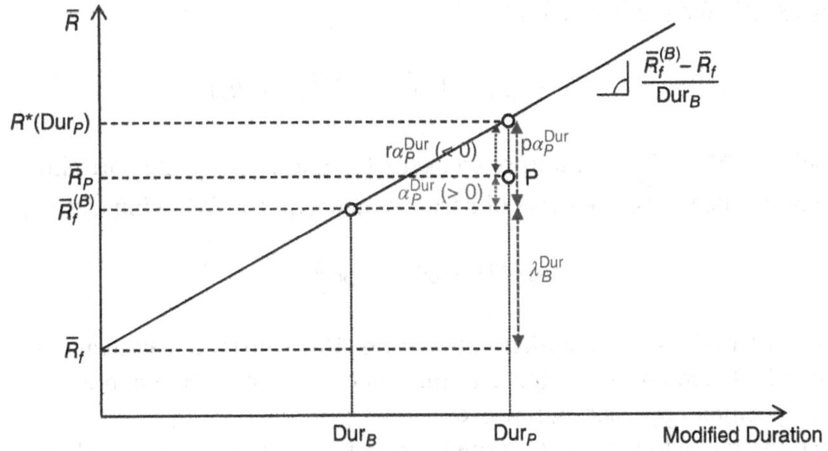

FIGURE 12-3 Wagner and Tito's (1977) decomposition of the average bond portfolio return.

liquidity risk, or simply selected better bonds. It would be unfair to attribute this unequivocal better performance to only higher leverage. In this context, the second usefulness of this simple self-benchmarked framework is to allow an analysis of performance in the same spirit as Fama's decomposition, which is generically discussed in Chapter 13. The key difference between bond and equity portfolios in that respect is that, in the former case, it is only systematic risk that matters. The duration-based analysis of Wagner and Tito (1977), which resembles but simplifies that of Fama, thus makes full sense here. It is represented in Figure 12-3, adapted from the authors' paper.

The chart shows how the final average portfolio return, denoted by $\overline{R}_P$ on the graph, can be represented as the sum of risk- and performance-based components.

The impact of the management effect on the portfolio is reflected in its total performance α_P^{Dur}, which is positive on the graph. Nevertheless, the decomposition of this abnormal return reveals two opposite effects. On the one hand, the manager's choice to increase the portfolio duration compared with the benchmark ($\mathrm{Dur}_P > \mathrm{Dur}_B$) mechanically leads to a higher return $R^*(\mathrm{Dur}_P) = \overline{R}_f + \frac{\mathrm{Dur}_P}{\mathrm{Dur}_B}(\overline{R}_f^{(B)} - \overline{R}_f)$ because of a good choice of active portfolio risk (a higher duration with a positive reward). This active risk management choice delivered a positive excess return $p\alpha_P^{\mathrm{Dur}} = R^*(\mathrm{Dur}_P) - \overline{R}_f^{(B)} > 0$. This value, called the "diversification premium" within the classical Fama's decomposition framework, can be interpreted as the *pure duration alpha*, which reflects the manager's market timing skill. On the other hand, for the same level of duration, the manager delivered an actual return that is lower than the one required according to the chosen duration level. This difference is equal to the *residual duration alpha* $r\alpha_P^{\mathrm{Dur}} = \overline{R}_P - R^*(\mathrm{Dur}_P)$, which takes a negative value in our illustration. At the same time, this measure echoes the Jensen's alpha, when systematic risk is considered, and the Total alpha defined, in the context of traditional equity-based portfolios, in Equation (6-65) of Chapter 6, by adopting exactly the same structure:

$$r\alpha_P^{\text{Dur}} = (\overline{R}_P - \overline{R}_f) - \beta_P^{\text{Dur}}(\overline{R}_f^{(B)} - \overline{R}_f) \tag{12-17}$$

where, as before, $\beta_P^{\text{Dur}} \equiv \frac{\text{Dur}_P}{\text{Dur}_B}$ is interpreted as the Duration beta of the portfolio.

We can reconcile the components of performance with the following identity:

$$r\alpha_P^{\text{Dur}} = \alpha_P^{\text{Dur}} - p\alpha_P^{\text{Dur}} \tag{12-18}$$

Equation (12-18) looks very similar to Equation (13-4) retrieved from Fama's original analytic framework. There are two important differences between the bond and equity performance decomposition approaches, however.

The first one refers to the fact that the bond portfolio manager freely chooses to adopt a higher or lower duration than that of their benchmark, depending on whether they anticipate a decrease (higher duration) or a decrease (lower duration) in the level of interest rates. This contrasts with the active portfolio choice of the equity manager, who must accept some positive idiosyncratic risk to try to beat their benchmark, and therefore whose Total risk alpha will always be lower than their Jensen's alpha (see Equation (13-6) in Chapter 13).

The second difference resides in the duration excess return λ_B^{Dur}. In the context of the CAPM, it corresponds to the market excess return, which is expected to be positive. With regard to bond markets, the story slightly differs because the duration excess return (not to be confused with the term premium in the context of the yield curve, which is also expected to be positive in the long run) depends on the observed change in interest rates during the period of reference. This change can be indifferently positive or negative, irrespective of the change in the yield curve because, in short, it merely results from the application of Equation (12-2) to the case of the benchmark.

The combination of the manager's active duration choice $\text{Dur}_P - \text{Dur}_B$ together with the remuneration of duration risk through the duration excess return λ_B^{Dur} leads to the scenarios reported in Table 12-5. They represent the quintessence of the bond portfolio manager's main challenge.

TABLE 12-5 Combined impact of active duration and duration excess return on the pure duration alpha.

Active duration	Duration excess return	
	$\lambda_B^{\text{Dur}} < 0$	$\lambda_B^{\text{Dur}} > 0$
$\text{Dur}_P - \text{Dur}_B < 0$	$p\alpha_P^{\text{Dur}} > 0$	$p\alpha_P^{\text{Dur}} < 0$
$\text{Dur}_P - \text{Dur}_B > 0$	$p\alpha_P^{\text{Dur}} < 0$	$p\alpha_P^{\text{Dur}} > 0$

The pure duration alpha as a performance measure has the advantage of directly isolating the outcome of the manager's duration bet. Lengthening the portfolio duration pays off when interest rates fall, which leads to a positive duration excess return because of the negative sign of the right-hand side of Equation (12-2). This outcome, represented in the bottom right corner of the table, corresponds to the situation depicted in Figure 12-3. The other reported cases reflect how the manager's anticipation of interest rate movements translates into the portfolio's abnormal return.

Whereas Figure 12-3 provides a way to split the bond portfolio performance into a pure interest rate component and a "residual" that reflects the manager's selection abilities, the very same approach can be adopted for other important active decisions made by the portfolio manager. In particular, consider the case of a portfolio whose major divergence with respect to its benchmark is not related to duration but to credit exposures. This is the case when the manager decides to tilt the portfolio toward safer or riskier issuers. Replacing the duration excess return with the credit spread excess return in Figure 12-2 leads to the same type of analysis, but with the credit spread sensitivity on the horizontal axis. The slope of the oblique line becomes the spread excess return of the benchmark. Then, along the same logic as before, we can define the *residual credit alpha* $\mathrm{r}\alpha_P^{\mathrm{Cre}}$ with an expression analogous to that of Equation (12-17):

$$\mathrm{r}\alpha_P^{\mathrm{Cre}} \equiv \overline{R}_P - R^*(\beta_P^{\mathrm{Cre}}) = (\overline{R}_P - \overline{R}_f) - \frac{\beta_P^{\mathrm{Cre}}}{\beta_B^{\mathrm{Cre}}}(\overline{R}_f^{(B)} - \overline{R}_f) \tag{12-19}$$

where β_P^{Cre} and β_B^{Cre} are the sensitivity coefficients of the portfolio and the benchmark with respect to the change in the credit spread, respectively.

The same logic can be applied to the other types of portfolio sensitivities, even though the primary focus is generally less likely to be made on the other components of the bond portfolio returns.

DFSO example (continued)

The benchmark is considered both from the perspective of duration and credit spread exposures. Using the information previously collected, we first compute the bond portfolio pure sensitivities with respect to the reference variables $\Delta 1y_t$ and Δs_t through the formulas $\mathrm{Dur}_{P,t}^{\Delta 1y} = \mathrm{Dur}_{P,t} \times b_{y_P,r,t}$ and $\mathrm{Cre}_{P,t}^{\Delta 1y} = \mathrm{Dur}_{P,t} \times b_{y_P,s,t}$. The corresponding sensitivities for the benchmark are known to be equal to $\mathrm{Dur}_{B,t}^{\Delta 1y} = \overline{\mathrm{Dur}_B^{\Delta 1y}} = 5.5$ and $\mathrm{Cre}_{B,t}^{\Delta 1y} = \overline{\mathrm{Cre}_B^{\Delta 1y}} = 1.0$. From this information, we obtain the portfolio duration beta equal to $\beta_P^{\mathrm{Dur}} \equiv \frac{\overline{\mathrm{Dur}_P^{\Delta 1y}}}{\overline{\mathrm{Dur}_B^{\Delta 1y}}} = \frac{7.62}{5.5} = 1.38$ and $\beta_P^{\mathrm{Cre}} \equiv \frac{\overline{\mathrm{Cre}_P^{\Delta 1y}}}{\overline{\mathrm{Cre}_B^{\Delta 1y}}} = \frac{2.30}{1.0} = 2.30$.

(*continued*)

(continued)

The computation of the self-defined benchmark-based performance measures is summarized in Table 12-6.

TABLE 12-6 DFSO example – Performance measures with self-defined benchmark.

Performance measure	Duration	Credit
Alpha	2.49%	2.49%
Treynor ratio	2.87%	1.73%
Modified alpha	1.79%	1.08%
Residual alpha	1.91%	0.54%
Pure alpha	0.58%	1.95%

The first three rows correspond to Figure 12-2. The Duration and Credit alphas are identical because they are simply equal to the average differential return between the portfolio and the benchmark. Because the Treynor ratio and the modified alpha are computed against the short-term rate of 1.80%, they could be larger than the alpha. This is the case for the Duration Treynor ratio.

The last two rows refer to Figure 12-3. By definition, the sum of the pure alpha and the residual alpha must be equal to the alpha, regardless of the dimension chosen (duration or credit). Nevertheless, because the portfolio's credit beta is much larger than the duration beta, the split between the performance attributed to superior factor timing (pure alpha) and the residual (residual alpha) substantially differs. This is reflected in Figure 12-4, showing the outcome of the analysis of Figure 12-3 according to the duration and credit dimensions.

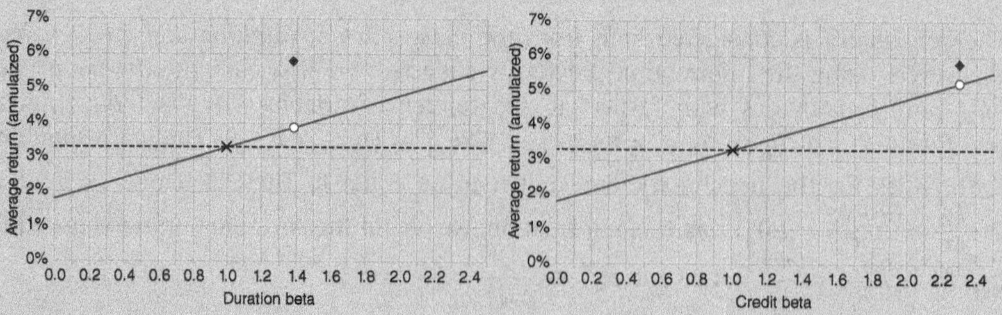

FIGURE 12-4 DFSO example – Performance decomposition according to duration and credit risks.

In both graphs, the cross represents the benchmark whose beta is normalized to one. The circle on the bond market line reflects the reward for factor risk. Its distance with respect to the horizontal dashed line provides the pure alpha. The diamond represents the coordinates of the portfolio. Its distance with respect to the circle is equal to the residual alpha. The comparison between the right and left figures shows the difference in perspective: According to duration risk (left), most of the performance is due to selection skills. The analysis with credit risk reveals that most of the performance comes from the manager's ability to capture the credit spread.

12.2.2 Holding-based Fixed-income Portfolio Performance

Since it is generally accepted that most of the origin of the bond portfolio performance comes from the evidence (or not) of superior market timing skills, we should logically turn to the types of performance measures developed in that particular context, namely those discussed in Chapter 8. In particular, given the nature of a bond portfolio, the knowledge of the full history of the portfolio's holdings proves to be insightful. Indeed, because bonds are generally very homogeneous investment vehicles regarding their market sensitivities, dedicated portfolio managers have the tendency to hold more concentrated portfolios than their equity counterparts, as evidenced by Qin and Wang (2021). Thus, studying the portfolio managers' holding choices is likely to reveal how they try to outperform their benchmarks.

12.2.2.1 Performance with a characteristic-based benchmark

The first route is adopted by Cici and Gibson (2012), who implement a similar methodology to that of Daniel, Grinblatt, Titman, and Wermers (1997) in order to decompose the portfolio return into three components. These are the required return (the "average style" measure $AS_{P,t}$), the manager's selectivity (the "bond selection" measure $BS_{P,t}$),[8] and the manager's timing (the "characteristic timing" measure $CT_{P,t}$). The structure proposed by the author is the same as the one met in Equations (8-42b) to (8-42d) of Chapter 8, reproduced here:

$$AS_{P,t} = \sum_{i=1}^{N} w_{P,i,t-l} R_{i,t}^{b_{t-l-1}} \tag{12-20a}$$

$$BS_{P,t} = \sum_{i=1}^{N} w_{P,i,t} (R_{i,t} - R_{i,t}^{b_{t-1}}) \tag{12-20b}$$

$$CT_{P,t} = \sum_{i=1}^{N} (w_{P,i,t} R_{i,t}^{b_{t-1}} - w_{P,i,t-l} R_{i,t}^{b_{t-l-1}}) \tag{12-20c}$$

[8]In the original paper by Daniel et al. (1997), this notion is called the "characteristic selectivity."

where $w_{P,i,t-j}$ is the weight of bond i in the portfolio at time $t-j$ and $R_{i,t}^{b_{t-j}}$ is the corresponding return of a (value-weighted) control portfolio of bonds sharing the same characteristics as bond i. The authors use quarterly data and take $l = 4$, i.e., they look at one year-lagging weights and returns to implement their measures.

In order to construct the control portfolios, the authors have to choose the most relevant dimensions. Following the conclusions of Gebhardt et al. (2005), they naturally select duration and credit spreads to select the matching bonds.

Cici and Gibson (2012) go one step beyond the analysis of Daniel et al. (1997). Because they observe holdings at infrequent times (on a quarterly basis), they realize that the sum of the three components does not necessarily add up to the total observed gross portfolio return. They adopt the Wermers (2000) approach to identify the drivers of this difference and use the notion of *Net Return gap* $\text{nrg}_{P,t}$ as defined in Kacperczyk, Sialm, and Zheng (2008), in order to design the selectivity-based source of portfolio performance. This measure is defined as

$$\text{nrg}_{P,t} = \tilde{R}_{P,t} - \sum_{i=1}^{N} w_{P,i,t} R_{i,t} - c_{P,t} \tag{12-21}$$

where $\tilde{R}_{P,t}$ stands for the gross return of the portfolio, and $c_{P,t}$ represents the sum of costs and fees (relative to the last net asset value) to be deducted in order to obtain the net return.[9]

12.2.2.2 Performance with a mixed holding/regression-based benchmark

A second approach, still related to the market timing measures developed in Section 8.4 of Chapter 8, uses a method adapted from Jiang, Yao, and Yu (2007) that mixes a factor model to explain the returns and the Treynor and Mazuy (TM) and/or the Henriksson and Merton (HM) model to detect performance. In the context of bond portfolios, Huang and Wang (2014) propose replacing the CAPM's market excess return by a factor equivalent to the periodic duration excess return $\lambda_{B,t}^{\text{Dur}} = R_{f,t}^{(B)} - R_{f,t}$ encountered in the previous subsection. Considering a single-factor model, they propose applying the same sequence as Jiang et al. (2007) in order to determine the convexity coefficients:

1. Use the holding-based decomposition of portfolio returns in order to obtain its dynamic exposures to the risk factor (similar to Equation (8-47) of Chapter 8):

$$R_{P,t} = \sum_{i=1}^{N} w_{P,i,t}(\alpha_{i,t}^{\text{Dur}} + \beta_{i,t}^{\text{Dur}}(R_{f,t}^{(B)} - R_{f,t}) + \varepsilon_{i,t}) \tag{12-22}$$

[9] This indicator is found to be a good predictor of future portfolio performance, as discussed in Chapter 17.

where $\alpha_{i,t}^{\text{Dur}}$ and $\beta_{i,t}^{\text{Dur}}$ represent the Duration alpha and Duration beta of bond i with respect to the duration excess return using returns up to time t (with a time window going back to a starting point $t - l$).

2. Aggregate the individual duration betas to obtain the estimated one of the whole portfolios at time t as $\widehat{\beta}_{P,t}^{\text{Dur}} \equiv \sum_{i=1}^{N} w_{P,i,t}\beta_{i,t}^{\text{Dur}}$.
3. Regress the estimated portfolio duration betas on the variables corresponding to the structure of the expected dependence of these duration betas on duration excess returns similar to Equations (8-48a) and (8-48b) of Chapter 8:

$$\widehat{\beta}_{P,t}^{\text{Dur}} = \beta_P^{\text{Dur(hm)}} - \gamma_P^{\text{Dur(hm)}} 1_{\{R_{f,t} > R_{f,t}^{(B)}\}} + \eta_P^{\text{Dur(hm)}} \quad \text{(12-23a)}$$

$$\widehat{\beta}_{P,t}^{\text{Dur}} = \beta_P^{\text{Dur(tm)}} + \gamma_P^{\text{Dur(tm)}} \times [R_{f,t}^{(B)} - R_{f,t}] + \eta_P^{\text{Dur(hm)}} \quad \text{(12-23b)}$$

where, for each regression, the intercept (beta) and the slope (gamma) represent the estimated values of the corresponding betas and gammas of the HM and TM models.

The determination of timing-adjusted performance for the bond portfolio is then obtained through the following generic equation:

$$\pi_P^{(h+\cdot\cdot)} = \frac{1}{T}\sum_{t=1}^{T}\sum_{i=1}^{N} w_{P,i,t}\alpha_{i,t}^{\text{Dur}} + f(\gamma_P^{\text{Dur}(\cdot\cdot)}) \quad \text{(12-24)}$$

where "‥" stands for hm or tm, depending on the model chosen, and $f(\gamma_P^{\text{Dur}(\cdot\cdot)})$ is one of the adjustments proposed in Sections 8.1 and 8.2 of Chapter 8.

12.3 ILLIQUID ALTERNATIVE INVESTMENT PORTFOLIO RETURNS

Even though many performance measures have been developed and adjusted for a wide spectrum of purposes, there are some particularities associated with several classes of alternative investments that deserve a specific treatment.

As explained by Anson (2006), the notion of "alternative investment" is difficult to define precisely. At the same time, this encompasses "alternative strategies" that use sophisticated techniques to manage portfolios that mostly comprise traditional financial instruments such as listed stocks and bonds, and "alternative assets" that involve asset classes that do not belong, *stricto sensu*, to the traditional ones mentioned above. The frontier is sometimes hard to delineate, and fueling this debate is certainly not the purpose of this chapter. Rather, we will focus on two aspects. The first one is a common attribute to many (yet not all) alternative investment portfolios, namely, their relative lack of liquidity and the potential consequences regarding performance appraisal. The second one refers to specificities related to two types of portfolios that (unambiguously) belong to the alternative investments category, namely, hedge funds (a major "alternative strategy") and private equity (a major "alternative asset").

12.3.1 The issue of illiquidity

With the exception of some specific investments or strategies (such as Global Macro or Managed Futures – also known as Commodity Trading Advisors or CTAs – hedge fund strategies), a natural common characteristic of many alternative investments is their lack of liquidity. This can be inherent to the assets held within the portfolio that are infrequently valued, as is the case for many private equity, real estate (RE), or collectibles funds, or linked with the potential difficulties of unfolding sophisticated trading strategies involving leverage, short sales, or derivatives, as in many arbitrage-based hedge fund strategies. Even if the portfolio's liquidity seems to be guaranteed at face value, some specific circumstances – such as massive redemptions from investors – might lead to an effective lack of liquidity at the investor's level, especially when the situation is most critical.

Concretely, this lack of liquidity leads to a phenomenon generally known as "stale pricing." Reported prices reflect a mixture of present and past information. An intuitive illustration comes from the world of venture capital. For a given fund, the portfolio of invested companies is usually fully valued (using in-depth discounted cash flow valuation, for instance) at yearly or, at most, semi-annual frequencies. However, many investors, especially institutional ones, require an estimate of the value of their positions at more frequent (e.g., monthly) intervals. How can these standpoints be reconciled? The fund manager is led to use proxies (market comparisons, probing, extrapolations, ...) to "fill the gaps," with less reliability of the results, but more importantly, with the tendency to align estimated prices with previous observations. This usually results in artificial smoothing of the series of prices (and thus of returns), usually in an unwanted fashion.[10]

The presence of stale prices creates positive serial correlation in the observed time series of returns. Why is this an issue? After all, if returns have a predictable component, this is potentially good news for the investor. Imagine that the next month's return is made up with the average of this month's return and a purely unpredictable component (which corresponds to an autocorrelation coefficient of 50%). Then, if you observe a positive return now, simply buy more of this fund, because it is likely that the next return will be positive as well. This would simply be a breach in the informationally efficient market hypothesis, and smart investors could take advantage of it. Unfortunately, in almost all cases, this is impossible due to the

[10] On some occasions, the manager may be tempted to seize this opportunity to deliberately change the fund's valuation in order to artificially inflate or deflate the returns. This situation, typical of private equity, is known as "managed pricing" and will be dealt with in Section 12.5.3. There are also other reasons for this phenomenon of stale pricing, like time-varying leverage or the impact of incentive fees, as discussed by Getmansky, Lo, and Makarov (2004).

subscription/redemption rules and other rebalancing constraints applicable to these illiquid funds. From the moment of the decision to buy or sell shares of these funds to the actual recording of the transaction, much more than one month usually elapses, which makes it impossible to apply this "hop in, hop out" strategy. In short, artificial return smoothing pollutes true portfolio returns, it is not exploitable, and it must be corrected in order to have a true and fair view of the risk–return properties of an illiquid portfolio.

A first approach is to directly account for the presence of serial correlation in the design of performance measures, without attempting to recover the series of true, "unpolluted" returns. This is the way adopted by Lo (2002), through his autocorrelation-adjusted Sharpe ratio, and already examined in Equations (6-6) and (6-7) of Chapter 6. This is sufficient for the purpose of measuring performance with the Sharpe ratio, but its drawback is that it does not allow any further exploitation of the data.

A second, more ambitious approach is to directly remove the effects of smoothing from the observed returns. The corrected series can then be freely used for any destination: computing performance measures, explaining the returns through factor analysis, making predictions, etc. We review two methods aiming to fill this objective below.[11]

12.3.2 Statistical adjustment methods

12.3.2.1 Direct adjustment for autocorrelation

Historically, the issue of artificial smoothing was first recognized in the field of real estate funds by Geltner (1991). He proposes a simple adjustment method for the removal of the first-order autocorrelation of returns, which has been subsequently adopted in the early hedge fund literature.

Consider that the observed smoothed portfolio return, denoted by $\tilde{R}_{P,t}$, follows an autoregressive process of order 1 or, in short, an AR(1), which is fully due to smoothing. This process is written as

$$\tilde{R}_{P,t} = \rho_0 + \rho_1 \tilde{R}_{P,t-1} + \varepsilon_{P,t} \tag{12-25}$$

where ρ_0 is a constant and ρ_1 represents the coefficient of the first lag of the process.

Under this assumption, the observed return can be expressed as a weighted average between the lagged observed return and the true unsmoothed portfolio return $R_{P,t}$, free from autocorrelation:

$$\tilde{R}_{P,t} = (1 - \rho_1) R_{P,t} + \rho_1 \tilde{R}_{P,t-1} \tag{12-26}$$

[11] The consequence of these methods is the removal of *all* observed autocorrelation. This hinges on the assumption that it is entirely due to artificial smoothing. If, for whatever reason, a fraction of this autocorrelation can be exploited with an adequate trading strategy, the unsmoothing procedures would lead to an "overcorrection" of the phenomenon and deliver a biased picture of the true pattern of the portfolio returns.

and we simply solve this equation to obtain the unknown true return:

$$R_{P,t} = \frac{\tilde{R}_{P,t} - \rho_1 \tilde{R}_{P,t-1}}{1 - \rho_1} \tag{12-27}$$

where, at a starting point, the oldest observation is considered equal to the true one $(R_{P,1} \equiv \tilde{R}_{P,1})$.

This method works well only if the first-order autocorrelation is significant, whereas the higher order coefficients are nil.[12] Okunev and White (2003) (henceforth OW) show how to generalize the procedure in the case of an AR(L) process of a similar type as that of Equation (6-5) of Chapter 6:

$$\tilde{R}_{P,t} = \rho_0 + \sum_{l=1}^{L} \rho_l \tilde{R}_{P,t-l} + \varepsilon_{P,t} \tag{12-28}$$

where ρ_l represents the coefficient of the lth lag of the process.

Following Equation (12-26), the authors wish to express the observed return as a weighted average. Nevertheless, the averaging coefficient is to be determined in a more complex way:

$$\tilde{R}_{P,t} = (1 - \phi_0) R_{P,t} + \sum_{l=1}^{L} \phi_l \tilde{R}_{P,t-l} \tag{12-29}$$

where $\phi_0 + \sum_{l=1}^{L} \phi_l = 1$, i.e., the equation reflects a weighted average.

Note that we are not interested in the identification of these weighting coefficients: All that matters is to retrieve $R_{P,t}$, but how to obtain this unsmoothed return? The authors show that the mere application of Equation (12-27) does not even remove the first-order autocorrelation. Rather, it is necessary to work progressively to gradually "purify" the time series of returns from the smoothing contamination. They first define the first-order adjusted return $R_{P,t}^{(1)}$ with a structure similar to Equation (12-27):

$$R_{P,t}^{(1)} = \frac{\tilde{R}_{P,t} - c_1 \tilde{R}_{P,t-1}}{1 - c_1} \tag{12-30}$$

where $c_1 = \frac{1+\rho_2 \pm \sqrt{(1+\rho_2)^2 - 4\rho_1^2}}{2\rho_1}$ is a parameter that enables us to remove the first-order autocorrelation in the observed returns.

The adjusted process $R_{P,0}^{(1)}, \ldots, R_{P,T}^{(1)}$ is, by construction, free from first-order autocorrelation but not from higher order ones. These remaining autocorrelation coefficients are still to be

[12]Some other unsmoothing approaches that refine the original Geltner (1991) one are discussed in detail by Marcato and Key (2007).

neutralized. The second-order adjustment is then obtained as

$$R_{P,t}^{(2)} = \frac{R_{P,t}^{(1)} - c_2 R_{P,t-2}^{(1)}}{1 - c_2} \tag{12-31}$$

where $c_2 = \frac{1+\rho_4^{(1)} \pm \sqrt{(1+\rho_4^{(1)})^2 - 4(\rho_2^{(1)})^2}}{2\rho_2^{(1)}}$ in which $\rho_2^{(1)}$ and $\rho_4^{(1)}$ are the second- and fourth-order autocorrelation coefficients of the series of adjusted returns $R_{P,t}^{(1)}$.

The OW procedure presents the advantage of not altering the mean return. It only changes the risk parameters (variance, higher moments). Its drawback is that it only deals with purely autoregressive processes. For practical purposes, Cavenaile, Coën, and Hübner (2011) show that, when the method is applied to hedge fund returns, it is usually sufficient to stop after the second iteration. Thus, one can associate the "true" unsmoothed return with the one obtained after the second adjustment: $R_{P,t} \equiv R_{P,t}^{(2)}$. As for the Geltner (1991) case, it is necessary to consider the oldest two observations to be equal to the true ones ($R_{P,1} \equiv \tilde{R}_{P,1}$ and $R_{P,2} \equiv \tilde{R}_{P,2}$).

12.3.2.2 Structural adjustment for smoothing

The leading unsmoothing method in the hedge fund world nowadays was originally proposed by Getmansky, Lo, and Makarov (2004) (henceforth GLM). They reverse the adjustment problem by not starting from the serial correlation of the returns but rather by the target structure that connects the true returns with the observed ones. Instead of Equation (12-29), which results from an autoregressive process, they posit that the actual relationship is written as

$$\tilde{R}_{P,t} = \sum_{l=0}^{L} \theta_l R_{P,t-l} \tag{12-32}$$

where $\sum_{l=0}^{L} \theta_l = 1$, i.e., the observed portfolio return is a weighted average of the true returns up to the lag of order L. It is also generally assumed that $\theta_l \geq 0 \; \forall l$.

Once the coefficients θ_l are known, the true series of returns is obtained by reverting Equation (12-32):

$$R_{P,t} = \frac{\tilde{R}_{P,t} - \sum_{l=1}^{L} \theta_l R_{P,t-l}}{\theta_0} \tag{12-33}$$

This equation is solved recursively by considering the L oldest observations from the sample being equal to the true ones ($R_{P,t} \equiv \tilde{R}_{P,t}$ for $t = 1, \ldots, L$), and computing the true return from observation $L+1$ up to observation T.

There are some cases where the smoothing coefficients θ_l obey a deterministic structure. The authors list three of them: $\theta_l = \frac{1}{L+1}$ (constant weight), $\theta_l = \frac{2(L-l+1)}{(L+1)(L+2)}$ (linearly declining weight), or $\theta_l = \frac{\delta^l(1-\delta)}{1-\delta^{L+1}}$ for some constant $\delta < 1$ (exponentially declining weight). In such circumstances, it is necessary to identify (i) the number of lags involved in the process and (ii) the corresponding linkage between the coefficients. This can be done by testing the various specifications and minimizing a fitting error criterion such as the root-mean-squared error (RMSE).

More generally, Getmansky et al. (2004) show that the structure of Equation (12-32) induces that the demeaned observed returns $x_{P,t} \equiv \tilde{R}_{P,t} - \overline{\tilde{R}}_P$ follow a moving average process of order L or, in short, MA(L). There are two ways of estimating the coefficients θ_l: on a stand-alone basis or in the context of a linear factor model used to explain the real returns. The latter approach calls for a regression-based analysis. The first estimation method, which has been widely adopted in the literature, is generally performed using a maximum likelihood criterion. For such a specification, the classical method used is the "innovations algorithm" proposed by Brockwell and Davis (1991) and proposed in standard statistical packages.

Like the OW procedure, the GLM approach leaves the mean of the process invariant, with a slight bias related to the necessity to use of using the first L observations to start the process. Practically, as shown by Cavenaile et al. (2011), the choice between OW and GLM makes relatively little difference if a low number of lags ($L = 1$ or 2) is chosen, with OW being slightly more conservative. If there is evidence of a higher order of relevant lags ($L \geq 3$), as is generally the case for series with a heavy seasonality like in the real estate universe, the GLM procedure is much more practical to apply. This is probably the reason why it has become a standard approach in many empirical studies.

DFSO example (continued)

The management of three classes of alternative investments, hedge funds, real estate, and private equity, has been delegated to an external asset management company. The mandate given is to reap as much as possible the illiquidity premium through the mix of investments. The external managers have warned DFSO that they could only feed indicative monthly returns by making a number of assumptions. For the hedge fund positions, the manager can refresh 50% of the portfolio value every month. For the sake of reporting, it is agreed that the remaining 50% of the returns will be based on an exponential moving average of the previous returns according the GLM model. For the RE investments, the external manager puts in its best efforts to provide marked-to-market valuations of the properties on a regular basis, but has to make price extrapolations for a significant part of the portfolio on a monthly basis. Consequently, there is a fair amount of unintended price smoothing, but it is up to DFSO to find out the unsmoothing scheme in order to recover the series of actual returns.

The three original series of excess returns are reported in Table 12-7, together with the excess return of the global stock market index.

TABLE 12-7 DFSO example – Observed excess returns for hedge funds, real estate, private equity, and the market index.

	Hedge funds (HF)	Real estate (RE)	Private equity (PE)	Market
Jan	0.36%	0.52%	0.54%	1.22%
Feb	2.71%	1.56%	2.56%	3.69%
Mar	0.28%	1.86%	0.26%	−0.35%
Apr	−0.41%	0.81%	−0.85%	−1.09%
May	−0.14%	0.42%	0.11%	0.36%
Jun	−0.61%	0.81%	−0.28%	0.33%
Jul	0.77%	0.13%	1.20%	2.66%
Aug	1.25%	0.41%	3.59%	2.42%
Sep	−0.16%	−0.43%	−0.99%	−0.65%
Oct	1.81%	0.14%	2.05%	3.01%
Nov	1.95%	0.27%	3.06%	−2.69%
Dec	0.72%	0.58%	−0.63%	−1.65%
Average	**0.71%**	**0.59%**	**0.89%**	**0.61%**
St. dev.	**1.04%**	**0.62%**	**1.58%**	**2.01%**

The information about the construction of HF returns allows us to recover the deterministic calibration of the GLM parameters from Equation (12-32). Since 50% of the return is contemporaneous to the observation, we obtain that $\theta_0 = 0.5 = \frac{\delta^0(1-\delta)}{1-\delta^{L+1}}$. Setting $L = 3$ leaves $\delta = 0.544$ and, consequently, $\theta_1 = 0.272, \theta_2 = 0.148$, and $\theta_3 = 0.080$. With these parameters, we can use Equation (12-33) to recover the unsmoothed series.

Regarding the RE returns, the story underlying the manager's computation method suggests the calibration of an autoregressive process. The regression on the first lagged returns (AR(1)) on the last 11 returns (the first observation is lost) leaves an estimate of $\hat{\rho}_1 = 0.502$, which is statistically significant at the 95% confidence level. The calibration of an AR(2) on 10 observations provides $\hat{\rho}_1 = 0.553$ (significant) and $\hat{\rho}_2 = -0.067$ (insignificant). We thus stick to a first-order autocorrelation process and use the original Geltner (1991) unsmoothing method. The application of Equation (12-27) yields the time series of unsmoothed returns.

The private equity returns call for a specific treatment to be dealt with later.

The reconstructed series are represented in Table 12-8.

(continued)

(continued)

TABLE 12-8 DFSO example – Unsmoothed returns for hedge funds and real estate.

	Hedge funds (HF)	Real estate (RE)
Jan	0.36%	0.52%
Feb	2.71%	2.61%
Mar	0.28%	2.16%
Apr	−1.83%	−0.25%
May	0.20%	0.03%
Jun	−0.83%	1.21%
Jul	2.23%	−0.55%
Aug	1.50%	0.68%
Sep	−1.66%	−1.28%
Oct	3.72%	0.71%
Nov	2.13%	0.40%
Dec	−0.55%	0.89%
Average	**0.69%**	**0.59%**
St. dev.	**1.77%**	**1.08%**

The grayed cells correspond to the unmodified figures. These must be kept invariant in order to start the recursive computation formulas. For all the other values, the cells are filled according to the GLM formula (HF) and the OW formula (RE). For instance, the August HF return is obtained by applying the formula $R_{\text{HF,Aug}} = \frac{\tilde{R}_{\text{HF,Aug}} - 0.272 R_{\text{HF,Jul}} - 0.148 R_{\text{HF,Jun}} - 0.08 R_{\text{HF,May}}}{0.5}$. For the real estate portfolio, we have $R_{\text{RE,Aug}} = \frac{\tilde{R}_{\text{HF,Aug}} - 0.502 \tilde{R}_{\text{HF,Jul}}}{1 - 0.502}$.

The comparison of Tables 12-7 and 12-8 confirms the stated properties of both adjustment methods: Unsmoothing the series leaves the mean return almost unaffected, whereas it increases the volatility and therefore reduces all risk-adjusted performance measures. This can be visually confirmed with the patterns of cumulative observed and unsmoothed returns, as shown in in the graph in Figure 12-5.

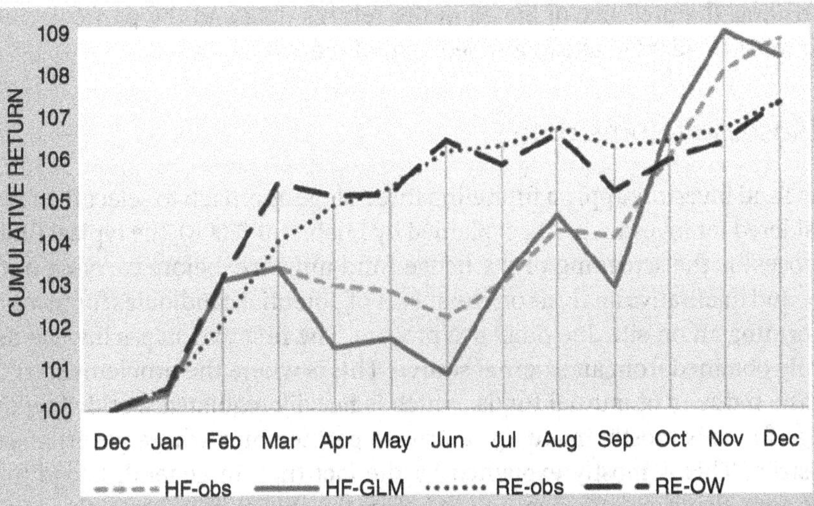

FIGURE 12-5 DFSO example – Comparison of cumulative observed and unsmoothed returns.

Even though the start and finish are almost equivalent for the observed (light dashed/dotted) and unsmoothed lines, their journeys differ. The oscillating pattern is more pronounced for the real estate portfolio, which is typical of the unsmoothing of an AR(1) process. The difference is more complex to interpret for the Hedge Fund portfolio. This explains why the GLM procedure, which is relatively easy to implement and flexible enough to accommodate various patterns, is usually preferred for empirical applications.

12.4 PERFORMANCE FRAMEWORK FOR HEDGE FUNDS

Obtaining a faithful appraisal of the performance of a hedge fund is a challenge that was identified relatively late in the history of finance (at the end of the twentieth century), but whose importance has been widely recognized since then. As Aragon and Ferson (2007) point out, the generous fee structure (management + performance) of hedge funds tends to attract the best active portfolio managers, many of whom being able to deliver good performance. Furthermore, the variety and relative opacity of their investment strategies make these funds prone to be affected by agency issues, as discussed in Chapter 18.

Many measures discussed in Chapter 6, some of them being famous like the Sortino ratio, have been developed with an eye on the assessment of hedge fund performance. The purpose of this section is not to redo this exercise. Rather, we aim to answer the following question: *What are the specificities of the hedge fund industry that deserve particular attention in the context of the design of a performance measurement framework*? Beyond the illiquidity issue – a common feature of many alternative asset classes examined in Section 12.3 – we can identify two other main dimensions: the presence of biases in the returns data and the particularities of factor models that must be adapted to explain hedge fund returns.

12.4.1 Biases in returns data

Many hedge fund investors apply a funneling three-stage approach to select the few funds that will be considered for investment. As explained by Lhabitant (2006), the typical first step in the selection process is the screening of the hedge fund universe, before carrying out an off-site quantitative and qualitative analysis on the subset of potential candidates for investments, and finally performing an on-site due diligence process. The first two stages involve dealing with data generally obtained from an external source. This is where the problems start to appear.

Unlike the industry of mutual funds, which is heavily regulated worldwide, the community of hedge funds is mostly made up of private partnerships whose governance is usually not overly strict. This is mostly explained by the fact that, in general, hedge funds do not make public advertising and offering, and therefore the challenge of protecting retail investors is not relevant for them. One of the consequences of this looser framework is the difficulty of obtaining comparable and reliable data about hedge fund returns and characteristics on a comprehensive basis. Hedge fund managers freely choose to disclose data or not, and they also choose to which organization they disclose these data. Therefore, there is no unique, standardized database about hedge fund returns but rather a (nowadays fortunately limited) number of sources of information that are updated on a regular basis.

The lack of centralization and standardization of hedge fund data, a phenomenon called "data fragmentation," is likely to generate a number of biases in the computation of their risk and return properties, causing misleading insights regarding their true performance. Specifically, three types of biases are likely to substantially influence the quality of the analysis:

1. *Survivorship bias*: This issue, previously encountered in Section 6.3 of Chapter 6, involves the overrepresentation of surviving funds in commercial databases. Because defunct funds (i.e., those funds that have disappeared somewhere during the time window spanned by the database) might have recorded lower average returns than the surviving ones, this might create a positive bias in the data. The issue, already present but well understood in the mutual funds universe, is aggravated with hedge funds because of the intrinsic incompleteness of commercial vendors' databases.[13] Furthermore, the attrition rate within the hedge fund world can be very large, especially within smaller and younger funds, as shown for instance in the aftermath of the

[13]This was particularly the case in the pre-1994 period, because data vendors used to discard the whole returns history of a fund as soon as it ceased reporting. The post-1994 period is hopefully less problematic (see Capocci and Hübner, 2004, for a discussion).

2008 global financial crisis. There were various attempts to quantify the magnitude of the bias in average returns, but most authors reach an estimate of 2–3% annually.

2. *Backfilling bias*: Since information disclosure is voluntary, many fund managers do not immediately report their returns at the moment of their creation. Thus, at the moment they start to report, they already have a track record behind them. Then, they have the option to freely choose to backfill their returns or not. This creates a potential upward bias because the managers who choose to backfill their past returns would typically do so if they can show a nice history, i.e., if their past returns show an advantageous pattern. As indicated by Titman and Tiu (2011), this issue can be especially troublesome in the case of a single manager who has launched multiple funds. This manager would be tempted to only report the returns of the most successful ones.
3. *Self-selection bias*: Why would a manager choose to report to a database? And then, to which one? Two explanations coexist: *The best funds do not need to advertise*, which would apply to the highest quality fund managers who do not want and do not need to open their fund and share their secrets, and *the worst funds do not want to advertise*, and they would not do so because they are not forced to. In practice, it is difficult to identify which of these opposite effects dominate simply because they are per essence unobservable, and thus not quantifiable.

The conjunction of these types of issues is very well illustrated by Lhabitant (2006), who shows how a single database of hedge funds can suffer from the discretionary reporting options in Figure 12-6.

Are there solutions to overcome these issues? There is a consensus to consider that two actions help mitigate their effects. The first one is to use the largest possible set of databases. In a vast meta-analysis, Joenväärä, Kauppila, Kosowski, and Tolonen (2021) use seven commercial databases and show that none of them feature more than 50% of the total number of reporting hedge funds in history. They propose a methodology to merge information contained in these databases in order to avoid double counts and to correct reporting mistakes. Importantly, they indeed find that the biases can be substantially mitigated after conducting this exercise. The message is that relying on a single data vendor is likely to lead to an overestimation of hedge fund performance and persistence (as discussed in Chapter 17).

The second solution, specifically aiming to reduce the backfilling bias, is to avoid relying on early returns data for any single hedge fund. The oldest returns are the most likely to be artificially entered in the database in order to magnify the fund's history, but it is not possible to identify with a snapshot of the database consultation which of the funds have done this manipulation. Provided that the database is rich and diverse enough, the cleanest solution is to simply erase several months of returns for every fund. Some useful data might be discarded, but this is the price to pay for getting rid of the problem. This, again, calls for having originally as much data as possible.

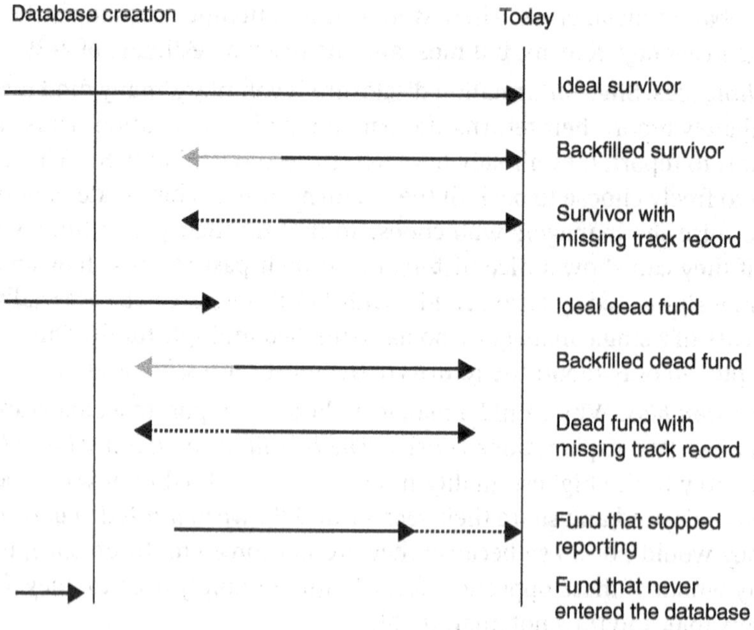

FIGURE 12-6 Illustration of the potential issues with hedge fund databases. *Source*: Lhabitant (2006), Figure 21.1.

12.4.2 Unconventional factor exposures

For many decades after the birth of the first hedge fund in 1949, this asset class has remained obscure to many researchers. The first comprehensive study published by Fung and Hsieh (1997) shed light on many unexplored aspects. One of them, which directly affects the way hedge fund performance is measured, drew a lot of attention: the nonlinearity of the relation between their returns and those of risk factors traditionally used in mutual fund studies. What the authors called the "trading strategy factors," i.e., the reflection of how the manager gets exposure to the relevant risk factors, appeared to be critical in order to understand how hedge fund returns must be explained with external market variables.

The first scientific response to this discovery was the creation of new factors built to capture the trading behavior of hedge fund managers through their associated returns. The underlying reasoning is intuitive. The flexibility of the mandate given to hedge fund managers allows them to use gearing, derivatives, and short sales in many markets in order to curb their sensitivities in a convex or concave way. It is possible to use one of the market timing models discussed in Chapter 8, but this might lead to overly restrictive specifications. The most straightforward way to tackle this behavior is to include the returns of index-based derivatives as risk factors and to estimate the sensitivity of the portfolio to these special factors.

The purpose of this section is not to enter the details of the many techniques that have been developed in this context, but two of them have quickly stood out: the Fung and Hsieh (2004) and the Agarwal and Naik (2004) models. They share a common structure: These are linear multifactor models, in the spirit of those examined in Chapter 7, but they make a distinction between spot market-based factors, such as equity and bond returns, and option market-based factors:

$$R_{P,t} - R_{f,t} = \alpha_P^{MF} + \sum_{k=1}^{K} \beta_{P,k} F_{k,t} + \sum_{d=K+1}^{K+D} \beta_{P,d} O_{d,t} + \varepsilon_{P,t} \quad (12\text{-}34)$$

where $\beta_{P,d}$ for $d = K + 1, \ldots, K + D$ is the portfolio sensitivity with respect to the returns of option-based strategy $O_{d,t}$ at time t.

Fung and Hsieh (2004) propose three such factors that replicate the returns of lookback straddles. These are portfolios involving simultaneous positions of the same sign in lookback call and put options. They are meant to replicate the successful outcome of a trend-following strategy (entering the market when an upward or downward price movement starts and leaving it at the end of the trend). Agarwal and Naik (2004) use the returns of at-the-money and out-of-the-money (OTM) index calls and puts as their option-based variables.

Even though the enrichment of the set of explanatory factors is useful, it does not appear to be sufficient in order to track the hedge fund managers' behaviors. Hence, as a complement to these new families of variables, variations in model specifications are also regularly proposed in order to let betas vary over time. These include conditional asset pricing specifications (Patton and Ramadorai, 2013), changepoint regression techniques (Bollen and Whaley, 2009), or the use of Kalman filters to estimate time-varying sensitivity coefficients, as explained in Chapter 8. For as sophisticated as they may be, it appears that most of these econometric models cannot fully address the frequency and intensity with which hedge funds change their factor exposures and leverage. Furthermore, the large heterogeneity among hedge fund managers makes the faithful application of a single model illusory. Thus, as Ardia, Barras, Gagliardini, and Scaillet (2023) explain, hedge fund models are doomed to be more or less misspecified, and their estimation is particularly arduous.

As a consequence of these difficulties, the fund's alpha and betas are estimated with bias and noise. Ardia et al. (2023) use a large cross-section of funds to study their properties at the population level. Furthermore, the residual term $\varepsilon_{P,t}$ of Equation (12-34) is likely to contain useful, but unrecognized information about the fund's performance. In that particular context, Karehnke and de Roon (2020) propose an adjustment of the regression alpha that corrects for the fund's co-skewness with the market that is not reflected in the model's specification. Their measure, called the *Prudent alpha* α_P^{pr}, can be adapted in the context of the "best possible" multifactor model, in the spirit of Equation (12-34), in order to define its multifactor counterpart:[14]

$$\alpha_P^{pr(MF)} = \alpha_P + \gamma_{Sk}^{*} \, \text{Cov}(\varepsilon_{P,t}, R_{B,t}^{*2}) \quad (12\text{-}35)$$

[14] Karehnke and de Roon (2020) define their prudent alpha with reference to the Jensen's alpha α_P and the residual term directly computed by regressing the fund's returns on those of its benchmark.

where γ^*_{Sk} is the representative investor's preference for skewness, and $R^{*2}_{B,t}$ is the squared return of the optimal benchmark portfolio for the investor, i.e., the one that maximizes their expected utility.

The identification of the benchmark is an arduous task because it requires the assessment of the investor's risk-aversion coefficient and the identification of the utility-maximizing portfolio according to this coefficient. For the constant relative risk-aversion investor,[15] the authors determine that $\gamma^*_{Sk} = \frac{\gamma^*(\gamma^*+1)}{2\overline{R}^{*2}_B}$, and they test values of the risk-aversion coefficients $\gamma^* = 4$ and $\gamma^* = 10$, with little difference in the results.

DFSO example (continued)

The external hedge fund manager usually adopts a classical long–short equity strategy, but it appears that the weights of the long and short legs of the portfolio vary over time. As a first attempt to explain the portfolio performance, a simple market model is calibrated on the reference market index whose returns are reported in Table 12-7. The linear regression equation is the following (standard errors between parentheses):

$$R_{\text{HF},t} = \underset{(0.44\%)}{0.36\%} + \underset{(0.22)}{0.54}\, R_{M,t} + \underset{(1.47\%)}{\varepsilon_{\text{HF},t}}$$

The R^2 of this model is 37.8%, which casts doubt on the overall relevance of the specification.

Given the manager's strategy, it is decided to implement a simple version of the Agarwal and Naik (2004) approach by including the returns of two synthetic OTM index options (one call and one put) with a maturity of one month (thus expiring at the moment of the return computation). To implement this model, the initial price of each synthetic option is obtained using the Black–Scholes pricing formula with the index price normalized to one ($S_t = 1$), volatility $\sigma = 12\%$, interest rate $R_f = 2.5\%$, maturity one month ($T - t = 1/12$), and strike price of $K_{\text{Call}} = 1.005$ for the call and $K_{\text{Put}} = 0.995$ for the put. This leads to initial option values being constant for each month equal to $\text{Call}_t \equiv \text{Call} = 1.24\%$ and $\text{Put}_t \equiv \text{Put} = 1.05\%$. Then, for each monthly observation, the returns of the corresponding options are computed as $R_{\text{Call},t} = \frac{\max(1+R_{M,t}-K_{\text{Call}},0)-\text{Call}}{\text{Call}}$ and $R_{\text{Put},t} = \frac{\max(K_{\text{Put}}-1-R_{M,t},0)-\text{Put}}{\text{Put}}$. The application of these formulas leads to the following series of monthly option returns as shown in Table 12-9.

[15] See Chapter 9 for a discussion.

TABLE 12-9 DFSO example – Returns of synthetic OTM call and put options.

	OTM call	OTM put
Jan	−100%	−42%
Feb	−100%	157%
Mar	−100%	−100%
Apr	−44%	−100%
May	−100%	−100%
Jun	−100%	−100%
Jul	−100%	74%
Aug	−100%	54%
Sep	−86%	−100%
Oct	−100%	102%
Nov	108%	−100%
Dec	9%	−100%
Average	**−67.69%**	**−29.63%**
St. dev.	**64.72%**	**97.48%**

For this particular time series, the average return of each option is negative, but this does not mean that it would be so in the long run, and it actually does not matter for the application foreseen here.

Using these new time series together with the index returns in an "augmented" regression corresponding to Equation (12-34) yields the following outcome:

$$\underset{}{R_{HF,t}} = \underset{(0.48\%)}{1.67\%} + \underset{(1.00)}{1.53}\, R_{M,t} - \underset{(0.015)}{0.006}\, R_{Call,t} + \underset{(0.015)}{0.031}\, R_{Put,t} + \underset{(0.94\%)}{\varepsilon_{HF,t}}$$

Compared with the previous specification, the R^2 of this model augmented with option-based returns more than doubles to 79.5%. The positive and significant exposure to the put option returns suggests that the manager is successful in protecting the left tail of the returns distribution. This translates into a strong and statistically significant multifactor alpha that contrasts with the noisy intercept of the single-factor regression above.

To compare the fitting performances of the linear and augmented models, Figure 12-7 plots the observed (unsmoothed) returns of the hedge fund segment together with the fitted returns obtained by applying both tested regressions.

(continued)

(continued)

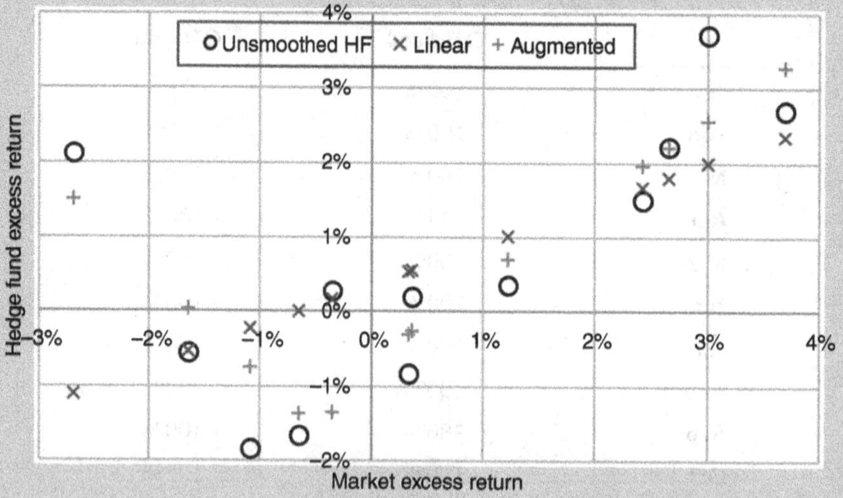

FIGURE 12-7 DFSO example – Observed and fitted hedge fund portfolio returns.

The key difference between the linear fit (crosses) and the option-augmented fit (pluses) is located on the left of the picture. Only the augmented model approaches the very positive observed return, represented by a circle, obtained by the manager. The poorest predicted returns occur when the market return is slightly negative: The OTM put option is worthless, and the strategy delivers negative returns. Again, the coordinates of the pluses provide a better reflection of this phenomenon than a linear specification.

12.5 PERFORMANCE FRAMEWORK FOR PRIVATE EQUITY

The term "private equity" is here considered a generic word that encompasses different kinds of private market investment strategies in equity or equity-linked products. These feature venture capital, leveraged buyouts, mezzanine financing and distressed debt investing. By their nature of private market investments, these kinds of portfolios are obviously subject to the illiquidity issues described in Section 12.3. Nevertheless, there are additional relevant considerations to reliably assess the performance of investments made in these vehicles.[16]

[16]We do not wish to address here the question of the outperformance or underperformance of PE investments compared to public equity markets, which is the subject of an ample literature with contrasted findings (see Gohil and Vyas, 2016, for a review).

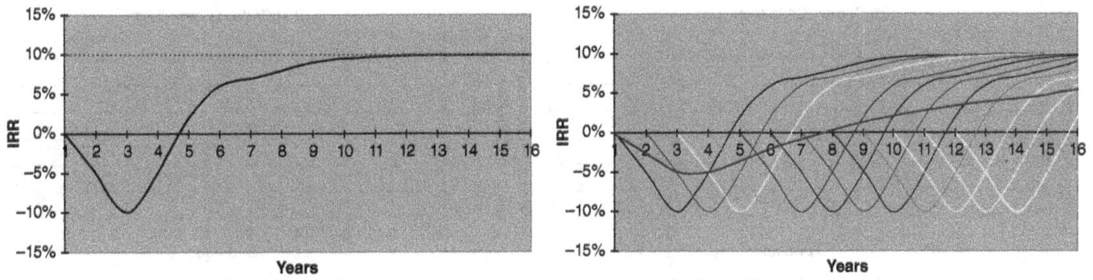

FIGURE 12-8 Illustration of the logic underlying vintage year diversification.

From a portfolio perspective, private equity allocations are seldom considered isolated investments in a single fund. The main reasons for this necessity to diversify are twofold, both related to the inherent constraints of these long-term commitments.

First, the pattern of internal rates of returns (IRRs) (discussed in Section 12.5.1) recorded within a fund at a given point in time does not obey a stationary process at all. A fund typically declines in value during the first years of its lifetime (this period is sometimes called the "valley of tears"), and then positive returns appear only gradually. This situation, mostly due to the early payment of most costs and fees and to the valuation policy of numerous funds, creates a hockey stick or "J-curve" pattern.

Second, the investor's commitment to a fund locks them in for a rather long period (depending on the type of underlying strategy). This exposes them to the risk of entering at the wrong moment, i.e., when valuations are too high and subsequent economic conditions are poor. These two reasons call for a "vintage year diversification" allocation strategy by entering different funds (possibly following different strategies) at different creation dates or "vintage years." This logic is illustrated in Figure 12-8.

The left chart represents the hockey stick pattern of the IRR of a single fund, whereas the right chart shows how a diversification strategy across vintage years leads to a softening of the J-curve.

Because of these specificities, it is important not only to have adequate tools to assess the performance of each single fund but also to adapt the analysis to a diversified fund-of-fund type of allocation.

12.5.1 Fund cash flows and performance

Unlike traditional funds or portfolios, the amount committed to a private equity fund almost never matches the actual investment. An investor who wishes to commit $10 million to a fund will not immediately witness an actual investment of the same amount because the capital calls are made on a "pay as you invest" basis, i.e., the amounts are gradually released at the same rhythm as the fund's investments are made. Furthermore, under the same logic, cash flows are repaid to investors at the same pace as divestments are made by the fund. Unfortunately,

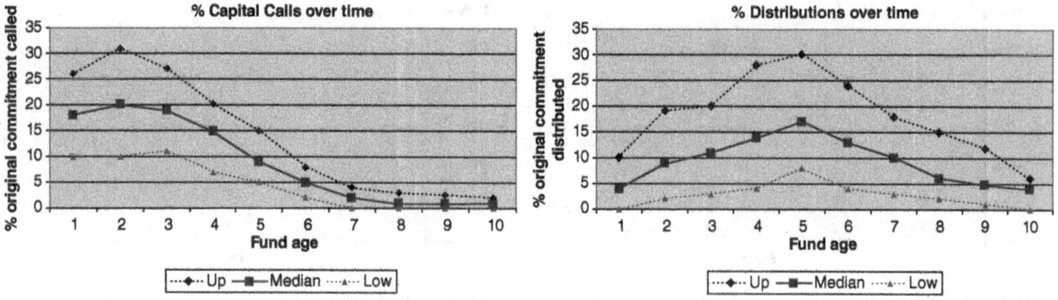

FIGURE 12-9 Expected evolution of capital calls and distributions over time.

it is not possible to predict with precision the schedule of capital calls and distributions over time. This is illustrated in the chart shown in Figure 12-9, summarizing LBO data gathered by Meredith, De Brito, and De Figueiredo (2006).

On each graph, the solid line reports the yearly average cash flow as a proportion of committed capital, while the dotted lines reflect the (approximate) confidence bounds. The left chart shows a relatively smooth pattern of capital calls over time, peaking in the second year, and steadily decaying until year seven when it becomes very close to zero. On the right graph, it appears that the distributions mostly take place in the middle of the fund's lifetime.[17] Both patterns show relatively wide confidence intervals around the mean proportions, indicating how difficult it is to anticipate the schedule of cash flows at the fund's origination date.

12.5.1.1 Unadjusted fund performance

Calculating the fund's performance before its final closure date in this context is challenging because the amounts at stake fluctuate randomly over time. Considering cash outflows (capital calls) as an input to performance measurement, a basic indicator, the *Total value to paid-in ratio* ($TVPI_P$) can be designed, which is calculated as

$$TVPI_P = \frac{\sum_{t=1}^{T} CIF_{P,t} + NAV_{P,T}}{\sum_{t=1}^{T} COF_{P,t}} \qquad (12\text{-}36)$$

where $CIF_{P,t}$ and $COF_{P,t}$ are the cash inflows (income) and outflows (expense) allocated to the investor at time t until the present moment T, and $NAV_{P,T}$ is the fund's latest net asset value.

This ratio can be further broken down into two additive components: the distribution to paid-in ratio $DPI_P = \frac{\sum_{t=1}^{T} CIF_{P,t}}{\sum_{t=1}^{T} COF_{P,t}}$, which measures the cumulative investment returned relative

[17]Most funds studied in the sample have a lifetime ranging between ten and twelve years, but it also depends on the category of PE investment.

to invested capital, and the residual value to paid-in ratio $RVPI_P = \frac{NAV_{P,T}}{\sum_{t=1}^{T} COF_{P,t}}$, which measures the part of invested capital still tied-up in the fund.

One has to bear in mind, as Meyer and Mathonet (2005) note, that this measure does not account for the time value of money and the riskiness associated with the investment, beyond the particular schedule of the inflows and outflows. This is why more sophisticated approaches have been proposed, adjusting for either of the two components.

The most straightforward approach to tackle the time value of money issue is to use the IRR recorded within a fund at a given point in time, which corresponds to the following formula:

$$\sum_{t=1}^{T} \frac{(CIF_{P,t} - COF_{P,t})}{(1 + IRR_{P,T})^t} + \frac{NAV_{P,T}}{(1 + IRR_{P,T})^T} = 0 \tag{12-37}$$

The internal rate of return computed at time T, denoted by $IRR_{P,T}$, reflects the investor's realized rate of return clinched at this very point in time. It is only at the final liquidation of the fund that the final return is known to the investor. Unfortunately, it does not obey a stationary process at all because of the J-curve effect discussed above.[18] Furthermore, it is totally self-centered and therefore does not reflect the riskiness of the fund. At the fund level, a commonly accepted solution is to include some kind of benchmarking in order to indirectly deal with this issue through the family of market-adjusted fund performance indicators.

As a consequence of the uncertainty surrounding the schedule of commitments and distributions illustrated in Figure 12-9, the use of IRR as a performance measure may leave a biased picture about a PE fund's actual performance over its lifetime, especially during its first couple of years. Figure 12-10, taken in September 2012, shows the proportion of PE funds belonging to different categories that shift from one quartile to another as a function of its age. If performance were perfectly predictable, this fraction would remain very close to zero. Nevertheless, the graph shows that a relatively steady ranking can only be observed when the fund approaches its liquidation time (ca. 10 years), after the bulk of its cash inflows and outflows have been recorded. This evidence calls for a more adequate way of estimating performance, especially during the fund's building period (first four years of existence).

12.5.1.2 Market-adjusted fund performance

How to compute an IRR that is more meaningful than that of Equation (12-37)? A popular solution, which is well known in the field of corporate finance, is to design a version of the modified internal rate of return (MIRR) method. Instead of directly discounting the cash flows

[18] Indeed, the notion of IRR based on the traditional net present value equation with the fund's observed past cash flows and current net asset value is misleading, because it neglects the cash inflows and outflows from new investments that are not included in the current fund's portfolio. Meyer and Mathonet (2005) recommend the use of qualitative analysis in order to obtain an estimate of these cash flows, but this is a highly difficult exercise.

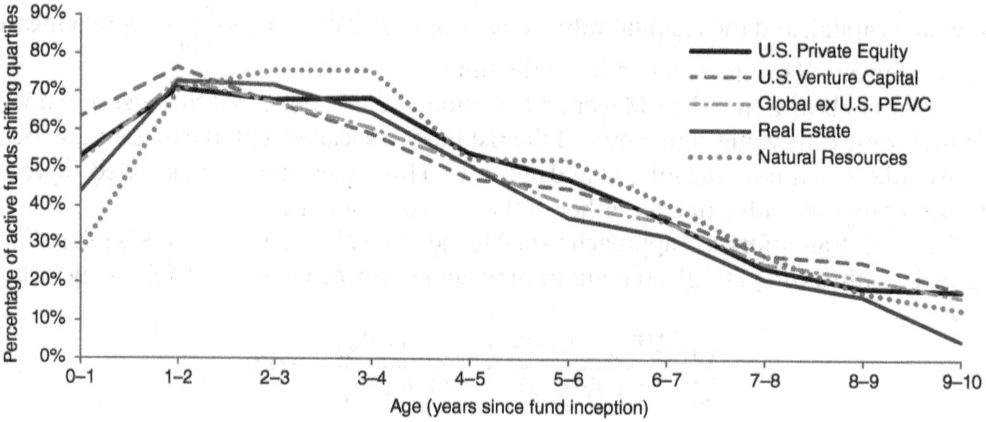

FIGURE 12-10 Proportion of funds that shift performance quartiles as a function of their age. *Source*: Cambridge Associates LLC. Retrieved at `https://www.cambridgeassociates.com/insight/a-framework-for-benchmarking/`

at the moment when they occur, the MIRR procedure uses a two-step approach. First, capitalize these cash flows at a compounding rate reflecting a relevant cost of capital, computed using market-based indexes, up to a certain common date. Then, discount the sum of these compounded cash flows at a rate setting the investment NPV to zero. This rate corresponds to the investment's profitability. This approach, generically called "public market equivalents" (PMEs), has two advantages over the original IRR formula: (i) It enables the analyst to set the cost of capital at a meaningful and contemporaneous level and (ii) it is less noisy than the IRR because it pulls all cash flows as well as the fund's NAV ahead in time until a common date, thereby ensuring a better harmonization of the procedure.

The origin of the family of PME models comes from the intuitive formula proposed by Long and Nickels (1996). Their so-called index comparison method $ICM_{P,T}$ of a fund is given by

$$\frac{\sum_{t=1}^{T}\left[(CIF_{P,t} - COF_{P,t}) \times \frac{B_T}{B_t}\right]}{(1 + ICM_{P,T})^T} = 0 \qquad (12\text{-}38)$$

where $MIRR_{P,T} \equiv ICM_{P,T}$ is the fund's modified internal rate of return, considering a benchmark total return index whose value is B_t at time t and B_T at T coinciding with fund's maturity (which explains the absence of a NAV component). The ICM is commonly called the LN-PME measure, in contrast with subsequent variations and extensions.[19]

[19]We refer the reader to Gredil, Griffiths, and Stucke (2023) for a review of these extensions. Korteweg and Nagel (2016) propose a generalized PME by averaging the values across funds in order to infer a stochastic discount factor (SDF)-implied benchmark from the fund universe itself.

The expression of Equation (12-38) looks relatively close to that of (12-37) that determines the IRR. They would actually be equivalent if we set $NAV_{P,T} = 0$ and $\frac{B_T}{B_t} = (1 + ICM_{P,T})^{T-t}$, which would correspond to the self-benchmarked case. Usually, a market-wide stock index is chosen as a proxy. It allows the net cash flow $CIF_{P,t} - COF_{P,t}$ of a given period to be put into perspective regarding the prevailing market conditions. If B_t is high, the implied cost of capital is low, and the compounding factor $\frac{B_T}{B_t}$ is moderate. The numerator of Equation (12-38) is interpreted as the fund's net future value or the PME net asset value:

$$NFV_{P,T} \equiv NAV_{P,T}^{(PME)} \equiv \sum_{t=1}^{T} \left[(CIF_{P,t} - COF_{P,t}) \times \frac{B_T}{B_t} \right] \tag{12-39}$$

The LN-PME measure provides an estimate of a fund's performance through the return per dollar committed to the fund. A popular alternative to this PME measure is provided by Kaplan and Schoar (2005) (KS), whose ratio provides an appraisal of performance per dollar invested (i.e., as if the whole commitment was released at the fund's inception). Their $KS\text{-}PME_{P,T}$ is written as

$$KS\text{-}PME_{P,T} = \frac{\sum_{t=1}^{T} \left(CIF_{P,t} \times \frac{B_T}{B_t} \right) + NAV_{P,T}}{\sum_{t=1}^{T} \left(COF_{P,t} \times \frac{B_T}{B_t} \right)} = \frac{\sum_{t=1}^{T} \left(CIF_{P,t} \times \frac{B_0}{B_t} \right) + NAV_{P,T} \times \frac{B_0}{B_T}}{\sum_{t=1}^{T} \left(COF_{P,t} \times \frac{B_0}{B_t} \right)} \tag{12-40}$$

This expression simply compares the terminal value of all incomes (inflows), including the latest residual NAV, with that of expenses (outflows). We can alternatively express the KS measure as a ratio of discounted inflows to outflows, as in the second expression in which both elements of the fraction are multiplied by a factor $\frac{B_0}{B_T}$.

When the residual NAV of the fund – thus not corresponding to a cash flow – is included, the ICM retrieved from Equation (12-38) also corresponds to the definition of the *Direct alpha*, denoted by $D\alpha_P$, introduced by Gredil, Griffiths, and Stucke (2023):

$$\frac{\sum_{t=1}^{T} \left[(CIF_{P,t} - COF_{P,t}) \times \frac{B_T}{B_t} \right] + NAV_{P,T}}{(1 + D\alpha_{P,T})^T} = 0 \tag{12-41}$$

These two versions of the PME approach can actually be reconciled easily. On the one hand, according to Equation (12-41), the fund has outperformed the market if $D\alpha_{P,T} > \overline{R}_B \equiv \left(\frac{B_T}{B_0} \right)^{\frac{1}{T}} - 1$, i.e., if the modified internal rate of return has exceeded the average benchmark return. On the other hand, according to Equation (12-40), the fund has outperformed the market if $KS\text{-}PME_{P,T} > 1$. Furthermore, the notion of PME can be intuitively associated with the determination of an abnormal return. Given the Direct alpha measure defined before, we can define the *incremental Direct alpha* or $\text{iD}\alpha_P$ by going one step beyond the proposal made by Gredil et al. (2023) as

$$\text{iD}\alpha_P = \text{D}\alpha_{P,T} - \overline{R}_B = (\text{KS-PME}_{P,T})^{\frac{1}{H_{P,B}}} - \overline{R}_B - 1 \qquad (12\text{-}42)$$

where $H_{P,B} = \frac{\log \text{KS-PME}_{P,T}}{\log(1+\text{D}\alpha_{P,T})}$ is the benchmark-adjusted duration of the fund, which corresponds to an average lifetime of the cash inflows and outflows. The incremental Direct alpha can really be considered as the average abnormal return posted by the fund over its lifetime, in line with the interpretation of the original Jensen's alpha. This is a similar line to the one proposed by Phalippou and Gottschalg (2009) and subsequently marketed under the name of PERACS alphas, with differences in implementation.

The notions of PME and Direct alpha developed here are much less sensitive to the schedule of the fund's capital calls and distributions than the original IRR approach. Nevertheless, they share the potential drawback of not considering any adjustment for the fund's systematic risk. This means that the fund's beta is supposed to be equal to one, whichever the type of fund, with respect to its benchmark. As claimed by Sorensen and Jagannathan (2015), this simplification can be reasonably justified at the fund's level. Nevertheless, the issue can become relevant in the case of a portfolio of relatively heterogeneous investments in PE funds. This is what we discuss below.

12.5.2 Abnormal returns of private equity portfolios

The challenge of the investor who engages in a private equity allocation is to go beyond the analysis of a single fund for the determination of their global portfolio performance. The major difficulty, compared with a portfolio of publicly traded securities, is that a number of intermediaries intervene in the investment process. As shown by Anson (2006), this creates potential distortions in the portfolio valuation process that must be adequately addressed for performance appraisal.

Because of the usually high correlation between private equity and public equity markets, it is generally attempted to assess performance by an analogy with a stock portfolio. Furthermore, the typical investor in private equity is supposed to be sufficiently diversified so as to afford the exposure to idiosyncratic risk inherent in the concentration of positions in PE funds.[20] Nevertheless, the complexity and specificity of each investment makes it hazardous to consider fitting a sophisticated multifactor regression model in the spirit of hedge funds, as in Equation (12-34) above. Therefore, the preferred approach for the assessment of performance is to identify the portfolio's abnormal return on the basis of a single-factor model, generically associated with Jensen's alpha in the context of the CAPM, or a simple *passe-partout* version

[20] We will investigate the particular case of the undiversified investor in Section 16.3 of Chapter 16.

of a multifactor model with, at most, one or two additional risk factors, such as size, value, or liquidity premiums.[21]

Consider the generic single-factor model as the base model, leading to the computation of an adapted version of Jensen's alpha, denoted by α_P^{PE}, as in Equation (3-11) of Chapter 3:

$$\alpha_P^{PE} = \overline{R}_P^{PE} - [\overline{R}_f^{PE} + \beta_P^{PE}(\overline{R}_B^{PE} - \overline{R}_f^{PE})] \tag{12-43}$$

where, compared with the original market model, $\overline{R}_B^{PE}$ is the average benchmark portfolio return that can possibly differ from the market index $\overline{R}_M$.

In Equation (12–43), all parameters and variables have superscript PE because of the absolute necessity to adapt the model's ingredients to the particular problems associated with private equity. We focus here on the difficulties associated with the correct estimation of these ingredients and summarize some of the answers that have been provided by different authors.[22]

(a) *Portfolio return* $R_{P,t}^{PE}$: The issue of self-reporting at the fund level, prone to a number of estimation biases (voluntary or not), calls for some solutions in order to obtain a faithful estimate. The most logical solution, proposed by Gompers and Lerner (1997), is to mark to market (MtM) each participation. This means that, instead of relying on the published or reported NAV, it is necessary to perform a full valuation of the securities issued by the invested companies. The authors show, on the basis of a case study, that this yields a substantial increase in the significance of the regression. Driessen, Lin, and Phalippou (2012) propose another procedure based on a two-step implicit assessment of the return, which we denote by $\widehat{R}_{P,t}^{PE}$. Their approach, which relies on fund-level investments and dividends (i.e., cash inflows and outflows), is much less resource-consuming than the MtM. It essentially aims at replacing a fund's IRR in Equation (12-37) by the estimated portfolio return using the CAPM equation in which every fund has the same average industry alpha and beta at the moment of observation:

$$(1 + \text{IRR}_{P,T})^T = \prod_{t=1}^{T}(1 + \widehat{R}_{P,t}^{PE}) = \prod_{t=1}^{T}(1 + \alpha + R_f^{PE} + \beta(R_{B,t}^{PE} - R_f^{PE})) \tag{12-44}$$

The determination of the industry alpha α and beta β is performed through the minimization of a distance function on the cross-section of all PE portfolios. Once this is known, the identification of $\widehat{R}_{P,t}^{PE}$ at the fund's level depends on its particular schedule of cash flows.

[21] This is the approach proposed by Gompers and Lerner (1997) who adopt the Fama–French three-factor model introduced in Chapter 2.

[22] We insist here on the fact that the abundance of the literature on the subject does not realistically allow us to be exhaustive. Rather, we wish to highlight the directions that can be taken in order to tackle the estimation issues.

(b) *Risk-free rate* $\widehat{R}_f^{PE}$: Because PE investments are long-term strategies, the logic underlying the choice of the risk-free rate associated with this asset class is to match the horizon of the investor's cash flows with that of a riskless bond. This is in line with the determination of Black's zero beta portfolio discussed in Chapter 2. Hence, the input for the risk-free rate in Equation (12-43) should be the yield of a government bond (or any alternative considered to be default risk free) whose duration matches that of the fund's cash flows. Since these are not known in advance, an estimation must be made. For a standard PE fund, the duration at inception is somewhere between six and eight years. However, regarding the estimation of the fund's alpha and beta parameters through a linear regression, the focus should be on the maximization of the explanatory power of the model. For practical purposes, a much shorter rate should be chosen.[23]

(c) *Benchmark return* $R_{B,t}^{PE}$: There are two main possibilities to associate a benchmark with the portfolio of the PE funds. The simplest one is to adopt the standard one-factor model assumption by choosing a proxy that most closely matches the investment characteristics. The dominant approach is to use a broad stock index of the same region or country as the underlying portfolio, especially when a multifactor model is used. In general, as shown by Phalippou (2013) in the case of LBO funds, using a small-cap index provides more accurate estimates. This is consistent with the much lower average company size in PE portfolios compared to listed stocks.

However, when the funds underlying the PE portfolio are very heterogeneous, this solution of a single market-based benchmark might not be accurate. A more elaborate approach, proposed by Meyer and Mathonet (2005), is the use of a commitment-weighted benchmark. Concretely, considering that each component fund $i = 1, \dots, N$ has its own benchmark with return $R_{B_i,t}$, then the global benchmark return is defined as $R_{B,t}^{PE} = \sum_{i=1}^{N} w_{i,t} R_{B_i,t}$, where the commitment weights are defined as $w_{i,t} = \frac{c_{i,t}}{\sum_{i=1}^{N} c_{i,t}}$ for $c_{i,t}$ being the actual commitment invested in each fund.

(d) β_P^{PE}: In the standard single-factor equation format that Equation (12-43) underlies, the portfolio beta would be obtained using market data by the standard formula $\beta_P^{PE} = \frac{Cov(R_P^{PE}, R_B^{PE})}{(\sigma_B^{PE})^2} \equiv \rho_{PB}^{PE} \frac{\sigma_P^{PE}}{\sigma_B^{PE}}$, where ρ_{PB}^{PE} stands for the correlation coefficient between the portfolio and benchmark returns, while σ_P^{PE} and σ_B^{PE} are the volatilities of the portfolio and benchmark returns, respectively. This appears to be a simple formula to implement, but its ingredients are difficult to estimate, especially regarding the correlation coefficient that is unobservable. There are essentially three solutions to this problem: (i) the use of quoted comparable companies, (ii) the adoption of alternative relative risk measures, and (iii) the determination of bottom-up betas. This is indeed a standard problem in corporate finance, and each approach has its own pros and cons.[24]

[23]See Chapter 6 for a complete discussion of these matters.

[24]A completely different approach is provided by Driessen et al. (2012), already discussed above, but there are also other innovative ways proposed in the specialized literature.

12.5.3 Dealing with managed pricing

The estimation of Equation (12-43) through regression analysis involves the use of reliable time series for the periodic portfolio returns. In Section 12.3, we have examined some statistical techniques that might provide more comfort with the use of "unsmoothed" historical returns. Unfortunately, the phenomenon of "managed pricing," which is often suspected in the private equity industry, requires specific efforts that go beyond the simple removal of autocorrelation or moving average effects.

Private equity managers have much, if not complete, discretion to mark the value of their investments. Due to this lack of external control, they might be tempted, at times, to price illiquid participations in a way that is most convenient regarding their own objectives. Gompers (1996) shows that some fund managers, when they are in the fundraising process, tend to price their portfolios quite aggressively and may neglect to sufficiently mark down their most disappointing investments. Anson (2006) also notes that it can be the other way around: They apply conservative pricing to protect their reputation, in which case they will tend to mark down faster and wait before marking up to avoid raising expectations. Thus, managed pricing involves, as in the case of stale pricing, a dependence of current prices over previous ones, but in a way determined artificially by the portfolio manager. Nevertheless, the structure of this dependence is not straightforward and must be uncovered on a case by case basis.

In order to identify the existence of managed pricing, Anson (2006) proposes adapting to the PE industry a methodology that was originally developed by Asness, Krail, and Liew (2001) in the context of hedge funds. The starting point of the analysis is a treatment for stale prices that differs from the OW and the GLM techniques depicted in Section 12.3.1 by directly altering the single-factor regression equation with the lagged benchmark return. The proposed specification goes up to the third lag:[25]

$$R_{P,t}^{\mathrm{PE}} - R_{f,t}^{\mathrm{PE}} = \alpha_P^{\mathrm{PE}} + \beta_P^{(0)\mathrm{PE}}(R_{B,t}^{\mathrm{PE}} - R_{f,t}^{\mathrm{PE}}) + \sum_{l=1}^{3} \beta_P^{(l)\mathrm{PE}}(R_{B,t-l}^{\mathrm{PE}} - R_{f,t-l}^{\mathrm{PE}}) + \varepsilon_{P,t} \qquad \text{(12-45)}$$

where $\beta_P^{(l)\mathrm{PE}}$ is the sensitivity coefficient of the excess return of the PE portfolio to the lth lag of the benchmark excess return.

This procedure, totally agnostic to the presence of managed pricing, delivers an alpha that has the same interpretation as in Equation (12-9). Nevertheless, assuming that the benchmark return does not exhibit any serial correlation, the "true" beta of the portfolio would then be equal to the sum of the estimated betas: $\check{\beta}_P^{\mathrm{PE}} = \sum_{l=0}^{3} \beta_P^{(l)\mathrm{PE}}$. There is evidence of smoothing if $\check{\beta}_P^{\mathrm{PE}} > \beta_P^{\mathrm{PE}}$ obtained with the simple regression with no lag. If this is the case and the average risk premium is positive, then it also means that the resulting performance measure adjusted

[25]This can be particularly useful when one uses quarterly data in order to capture seasonal patterns. In practice, the choice of the number of lags to be considered is a matter of finding the best specification.

for stale prices, denoted by $\check{\alpha}_P^{PE}$, is approximately equal to[26]

$$\check{\alpha}_P^{PE} \approx \alpha_P^{PE} - (\check{\beta}_P^{PE} - \beta_P^{PE})(\overline{R}_B^{PE} - \overline{R}_f^{PE}) < \alpha_P^{PE} \tag{12-46}$$

Equation (12-46) entails that, in the usual case where stale prices induce an increase in the adjusted beta, the correction also reduces the abnormal return of the portfolio.

This technique is inspired by the Dimson beta presented in Equation (5-22) of Chapter 5. In the published research in the hedge fund field, it has not become as popular as the GLM procedure. However, unlike the other unsmoothing techniques that only focus on the portfolio returns, this one, being regression-based, can be adapted to uncover managed pricing practices. To do so, we start from Equation (12-45) and introduce a dummy (binary) variable whose value depends on the sign of the realized market return. Anson (2006) proposes two alternative specifications, but it is more practical to use a single regression of the form

$$R_{P,t}^{PE} - R_{f,t}^{PE} = \alpha_P^{PE} + \sum_{l=0}^{3} \beta_P^{-(l)PE}(R_{B,t-l}^{PE} - R_{f,t-l}^{PE}) + \sum_{l=0}^{3} \gamma_P^{(l)PE} 1_{\{R_{B,t}^{PE} > R_{f,t}^{PE}\}}(R_{B,t-l}^{PE} - R_{f,t-l}^{PE}) + \varepsilon_{P,t} \tag{12-47}$$

where $1_{\{R_{B,t}^{PE} > R_{f,t}^{PE}\}}$ is a binary variable that takes a value of 1 if $R_{B,t}^{PE} > R_{f,t}^{PE}$ and 0 otherwise.

The purpose of this equation is to let the fund beta depend on the current market conditions. If the observed risk premium is positive, then the beta for each market excess return is equal to $\beta_P^{+(l)PE} = \beta_P^{-(l)PE} + \gamma_P^{(l)PE}$. On the contrary, when the excess market return is negative, the dummy variable $1_{\{R_{B,t}^{PE} > R_{f,t}^{PE}\}}$ is null and each beta is simply equal to $\beta_P^{-(l)PE}$. This specification allows us to test both kinds of managed pricing behaviors. The aggressive pricing behavior would in general lead to a situation in which $\beta_P^{+PE} \equiv \sum_{l=0}^{3} \beta_P^{+(l)PE} > \sum_{l=0}^{3} \beta_P^{-(l)PE} \equiv \beta_P^{-PE}$, and conversely conservative pricing entails that $\beta_P^{+PE} < \beta_P^{-PE}$.

In a similar vein as in Equation (12-46), the alpha corrected for managed pricing $\check{\alpha}_P^{PE}$ can be computed as

$$\check{\alpha}_P^{PE} \approx \alpha_P^{PE} - \left(\sum_{l=0}^{3} \beta_P^{-(l)PE} - \beta_P^{PE}\right)(\overline{R}_B^{PE} - \overline{R}_f^{PE}) - \sum_{l=0}^{3} \gamma_P^{(l)PE} \overline{1_{\{R_{B,t}^{PE} > R_{f,t}^{PE}\}}(R_{B,t-l}^{PE} - R_{f,t-l}^{PE})} \tag{12-48}$$

where $\overline{1_{\{R_{B,t}^{PE} > R_{f,t}^{PE}\}}(R_{B,t-l}^{PE} - R_{f,t-l}^{PE})} = \frac{1}{T}\sum_{t=1}^{T} 1_{\{R_{B,t}^{PE} > R_{f,t}^{PE}\}}(R_{B,t-l}^{PE} - R_{f,t-l}^{PE})$ is the average lagged risk premium of order l conditional on the fact that the current risk premium is positive. Note that, unlike the case of simple stale pricing, there is no indication here that the corrected alpha should be *a priori* higher or lower than the one resulting from the simple CAPM regression.

[26]The rounding difference is due to the fact that the average lagged risk premium slightly differs from the total average risk premium due to the omission of one observation per lag. It becomes negligible for large sample sizes.

DFSO example (continued)

DFSO has a single investment in a portfolio of buyout funds run by a single general partner, whose returns are reported in Table 12-7. The management of DFSO suspects that the internal valuation rules of the PE fund do not foresee a full revaluation of the investments at the same frequency as the one used for reporting (monthly returns). Worse still, it appears that the fund returns are relatively high each time the stock market has posted strong returns over the preceding month. The pattern of these good returns raises some questions. This is the reason why DFSO's CIO has decided to use the Anson (2006) approach to detect the presence of aggressive managed pricing policies.

The single-factor regression of the raw PE returns on the market provides the following results (standard errors between parentheses):

$$\underset{}{R_{\mathrm{PE},t}} = \underset{(0.48\%)}{0.72\%} + \underset{(0.23)}{0.37}\, R_{M,t} + \underset{(1.55\%)}{\varepsilon_{\mathrm{PE},t}}$$

The R^2 of this model is 21.6%, with a positive but insignificant alpha. This low explanatory power calls for further tests.

Because the sample features only 12 observations, it is decided to adopt the simplest specification, namely, the use of one lag in regressions (12-45) and (12-47). The outcome of the joint analysis of stale and managed pricing provides the following estimation results:

$$R_{\mathrm{PE},t} = \underset{(0.49\%)}{0.43\%} + \underset{(0.22)}{0.38}\, R_{M,t} + \underset{(0.23)}{0.35}\, R_{M,t-1} + \underset{(1.45\%)}{\varepsilon_{\mathrm{PE},t}}$$

$$R_{\mathrm{PE},t} = \underset{(0.61\%)}{-1.01\%} - \underset{(0.44)}{0.89}\, R_{M,t} + \underset{(0.19)}{0.29}\, R_{M,t-1} + \underset{(0.65)}{1.88}\, 1_{\{R_{M,t}>0\}} R_{M,t} + \underset{(0.42)}{0.18}\, 1_{\{R_{M,t}>0\}} R_{M,t-1} + \underset{(1.03\%)}{\varepsilon_{\mathrm{PE},t}}$$

The R^2 are equal to 39% for the first regression (stale pricing) and 76.9% for the second one (managed pricing). Thus, the evidence of asymmetry in the fund's response to market returns, both the simultaneous and lagged ones, appears to be convincing. This goes along with a degradation of the alpha, becoming negative in the most complete specification.

Table 12-10 reports the upward and downward betas ($\beta_P^{+\mathrm{PE}}$ and $\beta_P^{-\mathrm{PE}}$) according to all three specifications.

The estimated beta almost doubles when stale prices are taken into account, but there is no asymmetry. When the managed pricing behavior is taken into account, the evidence of aggressive pricing behavior becomes clear, with the downward beta becoming negative.

(continued)

(*continued*)

TABLE 12-10 DFSO example – Upward and downward betas for the three specifications.

Beta	Single factor	Stale pricing	Managed pricing
β_P^{+PE}	0.37	0.73	1.46
β_P^{-PE}	0.37	0.73	−0.60

Finally, the fitting quality of the adjusted regressions for stale and managed prices is represented in Figure 12-11, in a graph similar to that of Figure 12-7.

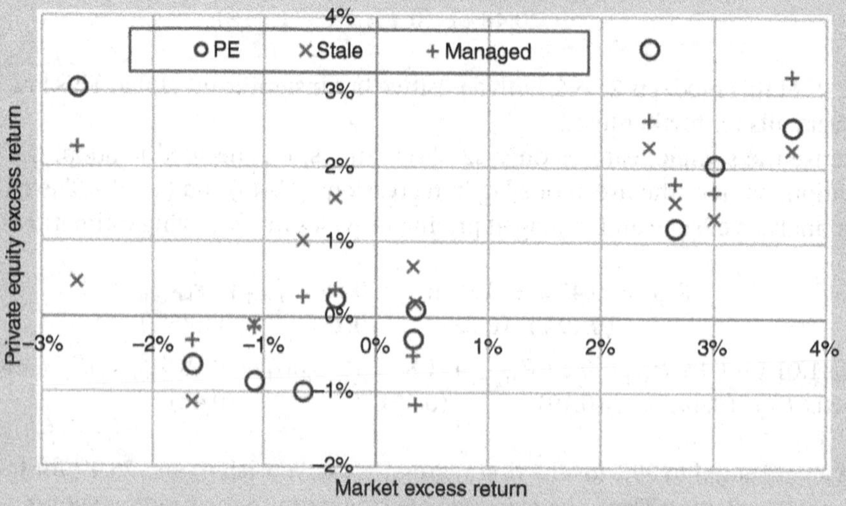

FIGURE 12-11 DFSO example – Observed and fitted private equity portfolio returns.

The circles correspond to the reported PE returns. A linear fit could be accurate except for the extreme left observation, which is very high despite the worst simultaneous market return. In general, the quality of the fit with the stale prices regression (crosses) is relatively good except for that particular observation, for which this specification fails to reflect the very positive portfolio outcome. In comparison, dealing with managed pricing (pluses) leads to a very accurate picture of the dependence structure between the fund's and the market returns. Note as well that this dependence structure is neither linear nor V-shaped as in Figure 12-7. The specification of Equation (12-47) is indeed much more nonlinear than that of the option-based approach used in the context of hedge funds.

Key Takeaways and Equations

- The return of fixed-income instruments (bonds) can be decomposed into a deterministic part (the "carry-based return") and a stochastic part (the "priced return"). This second component is split into three parts: the interest rate yield curve, the credit spread, and a part that can be attributed to the selection decisions of the bond portfolio manager. Altogether, accounting for these effects would lead to a generic seven-factor return model with time-varying coefficients:

$$R_{D,t} = \mathrm{d}R_{D,t} + \sum_{k=1}^{7} \beta_{D,k,t} F_{k,t} + \varepsilon_{D,t} \tag{12-7}$$

- When it is considered at the bond portfolio level, using a benchmark rate of return as a reference, the performance is generally estimated using the *multifactor alpha with constant betas*:

$$\alpha_P^{\mathrm{MF}} = \overline{R}_P - \overline{R}_f^{(B)} - \sum_{k=1}^{K} \beta_{P,k} \overline{F}_k \tag{12-10}$$

As an alternative, one can use an average money-market rate as a common reference for both the active and benchmark portfolio returns, which allows the use of the modified multifactor alpha:

$$\mathrm{m}\alpha_P^{\mathrm{MF}} = \tilde{\alpha}_P^{\mathrm{MF}} \frac{\overline{R}_f^{(B)} - \overline{R}_f - \tilde{\alpha}_B^{\mathrm{MF}}}{\overline{R}_P - \overline{R}_f - \tilde{\alpha}_P^{\mathrm{MF}}} - \tilde{\alpha}_B^{\mathrm{MF}} \tag{12-12}$$

- In the self-benchmarked case, such as a duration-based one, portfolio performance is simply defined as the difference between the average portfolio and benchmark returns:

$$\alpha_P^{\mathrm{Dur}} = \overline{R}_{(P-B)} = \overline{R}_P - \overline{R}_f^{(B)} \tag{12-14}$$

- From this perspective, one can isolate a pure duration component, called the *pure duration alpha*, from the *residual duration alpha* due to other drivers than the duration:

$$\mathrm{r}\alpha_P^{\mathrm{Dur}} = (\overline{R}_P - \overline{R}_f) - \beta_P^{\mathrm{Dur}}(\overline{R}_f^{(B)} - \overline{R}_f) \tag{12-17}$$

(continued)

(continued)

The same type of analysis can be performed with other dimensions. If credit risk is privileged, then we can define the ***residual credit alpha*** in an analogous way:

$$r\alpha_P^{\text{Cre}} \equiv \overline{R}_P - R^*(\beta_P^{\text{Cre}}) = (\overline{R}_P - \overline{R}_f) - \frac{\beta_P^{\text{Cre}}}{\beta_B^{\text{Cre}}}(\overline{R}_f^{(B)} - \overline{R}_f) \tag{12-19}$$

- If the bond portfolio has a holding-based benchmark, two main approaches have been proposed: (i) decomposing the portfolio return into the required return, the manager's selectivity, and the manager's timing, as in the model of Daniel, Grinblatt, Titman, and Wermers (1997), and (ii) mixing a factor model to explain the returns and the Treynor and Mazuy and/or the Henriksson and Merton model to detect performance as in Jiang, Yao, and Yu (2007).
- Before trying to measure the performance of portfolios featuring alternative investments, such as real estate, hedge funds, or private equity, it is important to deal with the phenomenon of ***stale prices*** that often appear with illiquid investments. This issue generates a spurious serial dependence structure in observed portfolio returns that must be corrected to more faithfully reflect the actual changes in portfolio values.
- There are two main statistical methods whose purpose is to deal with this issue:
  - The direct adjustment for autocorrelation fits an autoregressive process on the series of returns. In its simplest form of an AR(1) process, the unsmoothed periodic return is expressed as

$$R_{P,t} = \frac{\tilde{R}_{P,t} - \rho_1 \tilde{R}_{P,t-1}}{1 - \rho_1} \tag{12-27}$$

  - The structural adjustment for smoothing proposed by Getmansky, Lo, and Makarov (2004) posits a form of moving average process for the returns. The reconstructed series of unsmoothed returns is obtained with the following formula:

$$R_{P,t} = \frac{\tilde{R}_{P,t} - \sum_{l=1}^{L} \theta_l R_{P,t-l}}{\theta_0} \tag{12-33}$$

- When specifically dealing with hedge fund returns, an important issue to tackle is the presence of biases in the returns data and the necessity to deliver an adequate treatment. The major biases belong to three categories: (i) ***survivorship bias***, due to the relative absence of defunct funds in the data obtained from the vendor; (ii) ***backfilling bias***, which appears when funds add past returns data when they start reporting to the database; and (iii) ***self-selection bias***, whose root is the fund's voluntary decision to start reporting data for marketing reasons.

- The computation of a hedge fund's abnormal return through the multifactor alpha usually requires a sophistication of the regression model. The standard approach is to include a number of *option-based factors* in order to address the flexibility of the fund managers' strategies and their use of leverage:

$$R_{P,t} - R_{f,t} = \alpha_P^{\mathrm{MF}} + \sum_{k=1}^{K} \beta_{P,k} F_{k,t} + \sum_{d=K+1}^{K+D} \beta_{P,d} O_{d,t} + \varepsilon_{P,t} \qquad (12\text{-}34)$$

Because of the uncertainty surrounding the identification of the best possible model specification for each fund, its performance can be adjusted with a correction that accounts for the investor's preference for skewness through the notion of *prudent alpha*:

$$\alpha_P^{\mathrm{pr(MF)}} = \alpha_P + \gamma_{Sk}^{*} \, \mathrm{Cov}(\varepsilon_{P,t}, R_{B,t}^{*2}) \qquad (12\text{-}35)$$

- A simplified performance measure, which does not reflect the fund's risk or time value of money, is given by the *Total value to paid-in ratio*:

$$\mathrm{TVPI}_P = \frac{\sum_{t=1}^{T} \mathrm{CIF}_{P,t} + \mathrm{NAV}_{P,T}}{\sum_{t=1}^{T} \mathrm{COF}_{P,t}} \qquad (12\text{-}37)$$

- The determination of rates of return for a private equity portfolio is usually performed through the determination of its *Kaplan–Schoar public market equivalent* (KS-PME):

$$\text{KS-PME}_{P,T} = \frac{\sum_{t=1}^{T} \left(\mathrm{CIF}_{P,t} \times \frac{B_T}{B_t}\right) + \mathrm{NAV}_{P,T}}{\sum_{t=1}^{T} \left(\mathrm{COF}_{P,t} \times \frac{B_T}{B_t}\right)} = \frac{\sum_{t=1}^{T} \left(\mathrm{CIF}_{P,t} \times \frac{B_0}{B_t}\right) + \mathrm{NAV}_{P,T} \times \frac{B_0}{B_T}}{\sum_{t=1}^{T} \left(\mathrm{COF}_{P,t} \times \frac{B_0}{B_t}\right)} \qquad (12\text{-}40)$$

Another version of this measure is given by the *incremental Direct alpha*, providing a market-adjusted abnormal rate of return:

$$\mathrm{iD}\alpha_P = \mathrm{D}\alpha_{P,T} - \overline{R}_B = (\text{KS-PME}_{P,T})^{\frac{1}{H_{P,B}}} - \overline{R}_B - 1 \qquad (12\text{-}42)$$

- To determine the abnormal return of a portfolio of PE funds, a version of Jensen's alpha is often used:

$$\alpha_P^{\mathrm{PE}} = \overline{R}_P^{\mathrm{PE}} - [\overline{R}_f^{\mathrm{PE}} + \beta_P^{\mathrm{PE}}(\overline{R}_B^{\mathrm{PE}} - \overline{R}_f^{\mathrm{PE}})] \qquad (12\text{-}43)$$

but all ingredients of the formula have to be adjusted to the portfolio specificities.

(continued)

(continued)

- Beyond the stale price issue that contaminates all illiquid asset classes, private equity fund returns may also suffer from *managed pricing*, i.e., the propensity of managers to artificially adjust the fund returns according to the evolution of the stock market. To detect and correct this issue, a solution is the use of a regression framework with lagged benchmark returns and asymmetric betas:

$$R_{P,t}^{PE} - R_{f,t}^{PE} = \alpha_P^{PE} + \sum_{l=0}^{3} \beta_P^{-(l)PE}(R_{B,t-l}^{PE} - R_{f,t-l}^{PE}) + \sum_{l=0}^{3} \gamma_P^{(l)PE} 1_{\{R_{B,t}^{PE} > R_{f,t}^{PE}\}}(R_{B,t-l}^{PE} - R_{f,t-l}^{PE}) + \varepsilon_{P,t} \tag{12-47}$$

- There is evidence of aggressive pricing if $\beta_P^{+PE} \equiv \sum_{l=0}^{3} \beta_P^{+(l)PE} > \sum_{l=0}^{3} \beta_P^{-(l)PE} \equiv \beta_P^{-PE}$ or conservative pricing if $\beta_P^{+PE} < \beta_P^{-PE}$.

REFERENCES

Agarwal, V., and N. Y. Naik (2004), Risks and portfolio decisions involving hedge funds. *The Review of Financial Studies*, Vol. 17, pp. 63–98.

Anson, M. J. P. (2006), *Handbook of Alternative Assets, 2nd Edition.* Wiley, Wiley Finance Series.

Aragon, G. O., and W. E. Ferson (2007), Portfolio performance evaluation. *Foundations and Trends in Finance*, Vol. 2, pp. 83–190.

Ardia, D., Barras, L., Gagliardini, P., and O. Scaillet (2023), Is it alpha or beta? Decomposing hedge fund returns when models are misspecified. *Journal of Financial Economics*, forthcoming.

Asness, C., Krail, R., and J. Liew (2001), Do hedge funds hedge? *The Journal of Portfolio Management*, Vol. 28 (Fall), pp. 6–19.

Bacon, C. R. (2019), *Performance Attribution. History and Progress.* CFA Research Foundation.

Bacon, C. R. (2021), *Practical Risk-Adjusted Performance Measurement, 2nd Edition.* Wiley, Wiley Finance Series.

Bai, J., Bali, T. G., and Q. Wen (2016), *Do the distributional characteristics of corporate bonds predict their future returns?* Working Paper.

Bai, J., Bali, T. G., and Q. Wen (2019), Common risk factors in the cross-section of corporate bond returns. *Journal of Financial Economics*, Vol. 131, pp. 619–642.

Bai, J., Bali, T. G., and Q. Wen (2021), Is there a risk–return tradeoff in the corporate bond market? Time-series and cross-sectional evidence. *Journal of Financial Economics*, Vol. 142, pp. 1017–1037.

Blake, C., Elton, E., and M. Gruber (1993), The performance of bond mutual funds. *Journal of Business*, Vol. 66, pp. 371–403.

Bollen, N. P. B., and R. E. Whaley (2009), Hedge fund risk dynamics: Implications for performance appraisal. *The Journal of Finance*, Vol. 64, pp. 985–1035.

Brockwell, P., and R. Davis (1991), *Time Series: Theory and Methods, 2nd Edition*. Springer.

Campisi, S. (2000), Primer on fixed income performance attribution. *Journal of Performance Measurement*, Vol. 4 (4), pp. 14–25.

Capocci, D., and G. Hübner (2004), Analysis of hedge fund performance. *Journal of Empirical Finance*, Vol. 11, pp. 55–89.

Cavenaile, L., Coën, A., and G. Hübner (2011), The impact of illiquidity and higher moments of hedge fund returns on their risk-adjusted performance and diversification potential. *Journal of Alternative Investments*, Vol. 13 (4), pp. 9–29.

Cici, G., and S. Gibson (2012), The performance of corporate bond mutual funds: Evidence based on security-level data. *Journal of Financial and Quantitative Analysis*, Vol. 47, pp. 159–178.

Dang, T. D., Hollstein, F., and M. Prokopczuk (2022), How do corporate bond investors measure performance? Evidence from mutual fund flows. *Journal of Banking & Finance*, Vol. 142, 106553.

Daniel, K., Grinblatt, M., Titman, S., and R. Wermers (1997), Measuring mutual fund performance with characteristic-based benchmarks. *The Journal of Finance*, Vol. 52, pp. 1035–1058.

Driessen, J., Lin, T.-C., and L. Phalippou (2012), A new method to estimate risk and return of nontraded assets from cash flows: The case of private equity funds. *Journal of Financial and Quantitative Analysis*, Vol. 47, pp. 511–535.

François, P., Heck, S., Hübner, G., and T. Lejeune (2022), Comoment risk in corporate bond yields and returns. *Journal of Financial Research*, Vol. 45, pp. 471–512.

Fung, W., and D. A. Hsieh (1997), Empirical characteristics of dynamic trading strategies: The case of hedge funds. *The Review of Financial Studies*, Vol. 10, pp. 275–302.

Fung, W., and D. A. Hsieh (2004), Hedge fund benchmarks: A risk-based approach. *Financial Analysts Journal*, Vol. 60 (5), pp. 65–80.

Gebhardt, W. R., Hvidkjaer, S., and B. Swaminathan (2005), The cross-section of expected corporate bond returns: Betas or characteristics? *Journal of Financial Economics*, Vol. 75, pp. 85–114.

Geltner D. (1991), Smoothing in appraisal-based returns. *Journal of Real Estate Finance and Economics*, Vol. 4, pp. 327–334.

Getmansky, M., Lo, A. W., and I. Makarov (2004), An econometric model of serial correlation and illiquidity in hedge fund returns. *Journal of Financial Economics*, Vol. 74, pp. 529–610.

Gohil, R. K., and V. Vyas (2016), Private equity performance: A literature review. *The Journal of Private Equity*, Vol. 19 (3), pp. 76–88.

Gompers, P. (1996), Grandstanding in the venture capital industry. *Journal of Financial Economics*, Vol. 42, pp. 136–156.

Gompers, P., and J. Lerner (1997), Risk and reward in private equity investments: The challenge of performance assessment. *Journal of Private Equity*, Vol. 1 (2), pp. 5–12.

Gredil, O. R., Griffiths, B., and R. Stucke (2023), Benchmarking private equity: The direct alpha method. *Journal of Corporate Finance*, Vol. 81, 102360.

Huang, J.-Z., and Y. Wang (2014), Timing ability of government bond fund managers: Evidence from portfolio holdings. *Management Science*, Vol. 60, pp. 2091–2109.

Jiang, G.J., Yao, T., and T. Yu (2007), Do mutual funds time the market? Evidence from portfolio holdings. *Journal of Financial Economics*, Vol. 86, pp. 724–758.

Joenväärä, J., Kauppila, M., Kosowski, R., and P. Tolonen (2021), Hedge fund performance: Are stylized facts sensitive to which database one uses? *Critical Finance Review*, Vol. 10, pp. 271–327.

Kacperczyk, M., Sialm, C., and L. Zheng (2008), Unobserved actions of mutual funds. *The Review of Financial Studies, Vo.* 21, pp. 2379–2416.

Kaplan, S., and A. Schoar (2005), Private equity performance: Returns, persistence, and capital flows. *The Journal of Finance*, Vol. 60, pp. 1791–1823.

Karehnke, P., and F. de Roon (2020), Spanning tests for assets with option-like payoffs: The case of hedge funds. *Management Science*, Vol. 66, pp. 5969–5989.

Korteweg, A., and S. Nagel (2016), Risk-adjusting the returns to venture capital. *The Journal of Finance*, Vol. 71, pp. 1437–1470.

Lhabitant, F.-S. (2006), *Handbook of Hedge Funds.* Wiley, Wiley Finance Series.

Lo, A.W. (2002), The statistics of Sharpe ratios. *Financial Analysts Journal*, Vol. 58 (4), pp. 36–52.

Long, A. M., and C. J. Nickels (1996), *A private investment benchmark.* Working Paper.

Lord, T. J. (1997), The attribution of portfolio and index returns in fixed income. *Journal of Performance Measurement*, Vol. 2 (1), pp. 45–57.

Marcato, G., and T. Key (2007), Smoothing and implications for asset allocation choices. *The Journal of Portfolio Management*, Vol. 33 (5), pp. 85–98.

Meredith, R., De Brito, N., and R. De Figueiredo (2006), Portfolio management with illiquid investments. *Citigroup Alternative Investments*, (June), pp. 26–31.

Meyer, T., and P.-Y. Mathonet (2005), *Beyond the J Curve: Managing a Portfolio of Venture Capital and Private Equity Funds.* Wiley.

Okunev, J., and D. White (2003), *Hedge fund risk factors and Value-at-Risk of credit trading strategies.* Working Paper.

Patton, A. J., and T. Ramadorai (2013), On the high-frequency dynamics of hedge fund risk exposures. *The Journal of Finance*, Vol. 68, pp. 597–635.

Phalippou, L. (2013), Performance of buyout funds revisited? *Review of Finance*, Vol. 18, pp. 189–218.

Phalippou, L., and O. Gottschalg (2009), The performance of private equity funds. *The Review of Financial Studies*, Vol. 22, pp. 1747–1776.

Qin, N., and Y. Wang (2021), Does portfolio concentration affect performance? Evidence from corporate bond mutual funds. *Journal of Banking & Finance*, Vol. 123, 106033.

Sorensen, M., and R. Jagannathan (2015), The public market equivalent and private equity performance. *Financial Analysts Journal*, Vol. 71 (4), pp. 43–50.

Spaulding, D. (2003), *Investment Performance Attribution*. McGraw-Hill.

Titman, S., and C. Tiu (2011), Do the best hedge funds hedge? *The Review of Financial Studies*, Vol. 24, pp. 123–168.

Wagner, W. H, and D. A. Tito (1977). Definitive new measures of bond performance and risk. *Pension World*, Vol. 13, pp. 10–12.

Wermers, R. (2000), Mutual fund performance: An empirical decomposition into stock-picking talent, style, transaction costs, and expenses. *The Journal of Finance*, Vol. 55, pp. 1655–1695.

CHAPTER 13

The Granular Analysis of Performance

INTRODUCTION

As a preliminary step toward the classical performance attribution methods, it is necessary to understand the principles of the granular analysis of portfolio performance. *Performance decomposition* represents the first level of such an analysis. This approach, introduced by Fama (1972), can be seen as the historical root of the attribution framework. It enables the analyst to identify the contributors to the portfolio's required returns and emphasizes what remains as a true abnormal return after all the risk premiums are taken into account. Thanks to Fama's (1972) approach, we examine in the first section how the precursors of market timing and security selection components of performance can be isolated.

Attributing performance to its relevant drivers is a codified exercise. It must obey a certain number of principles. It first entails that the *contributors to the portfolio return* are properly identified. It also requires the identification of the various levels of decision-making in the portfolio management process, from the strategic asset allocation to the individual security selection levels. Furthermore, there are a certain number of rules to respect when building a *performance attribution framework*. However, attempting to make full use of granular information can pay off in the end. From an *ex ante* perspective, we show that such information can be useful in order to forecast the (intended) sources of active portfolio returns.

Endowed with detailed information about portfolio and benchmark holdings and returns, it is possible to perform a meaningful granular analysis in the spirit of the attribution process at the level of risk-adjusted performance measures. We examine the most popular ones, namely, the *Sharpe ratio contribution and attribution*, as well as the *Information ratio attribution*. Even though risk cannot be decomposed linearly in a straightforward manner, it is still possible to isolate and analyze the notions of active risk and component Sharpe (or Information) ratio at the level of each individual portfolio constituent.

This chapter is a natural introduction to Chapter 14, which is devoted to the development of "classical" performance attribution models, mostly focusing on the portfolio's excess return over its benchmark. Considered altogether, both the current and next chapters are neither meant to replace a full dedicated book on performance attribution, such as some famous ones, nor to encompass the full spectrum of practitioners' papers published on this topic. Rather, our ambition with this material is to provide some guidance to "get started" in this domain and to identify the adequate issues and resources in order to build, maintain, and understand a performance attribution system.

The VAS Example – Part I

One year ago, the Chief Investment Officer (CIO) of VAS Asset Management launched three start-up funds, each one endowed with a $100 million seed cash investment, and run by newly appointed promising managers. Their mandate was clear: outperform a well-defined passive benchmark portfolio with the same weighting of 50% equities, 40% bonds, and 10% cash. After one year, a deep dive would be carried out with the most detailed possible granular analysis in order not only to detect the extent of the outperformance but also to analyze its drivers. Now that the CIO has one year of available data, the time has come to perform this comprehensive examination of each fund's performance.

Benchmark returns, considering the risk-free rate set at 1.80% per year (0.15% per month) for cash, and the World ACWI index (the proxy for the market portfolio, in gray) are reported in Table 13-1.

TABLE 13-1 VAS example – Monthly rates of return of the benchmark and market.

Month	Stocks (50%)	Bonds (40%)	Cash (10%)	Benchmark (100%)	Market
Jan	0.61%	0.07%	0.15%	**0.35%**	−3.66%
Feb	2.13%	0.25%	0.15%	**1.18%**	4.69%
Mar	4.22%	0.09%	0.15%	**2.16%**	−1.08%
Apr	0.38%	−0.29%	0.15%	**0.09%**	0.51%
May	−7.52%	0.02%	0.15%	**−3.74%**	−7.76%
Jun	3.23%	−0.71%	0.15%	**1.35%**	8.00%
Jul	−8.99%	0.10%	0.15%	**−4.44%**	−3.26%
Aug	7.09%	1.42%	0.15%	**4.13%**	8.40%
Sep	5.18%	1.35%	0.15%	**3.15%**	4.66%
Oct	2.20%	1.43%	0.15%	**1.69%**	1.14%
Nov	4.49%	0.53%	0.15%	**2.47%**	3.79%
Dec	−4.86%	−0.42%	0.15%	**−2.58%**	−7.37%

For each of the funds, denominated "Verso" (**V**), "Alloco" (**A**), and "Selecto" (**S**), we have gathered the monthly return and weight (average for each month) of each asset class in Tables 13-2 to 13-4.

TABLE 13-2 VAS example – Monthly rates of return of the Verso fund.

Month	Returns			*Weights*			Verso
	Stocks	Bonds	Cash	*Stocks*	*Bonds*	*Cash*	
Jan	1.27%	0.39%	0.36%	*55.7%*	*43.1%*	*1.2%*	**0.88%**
Feb	3.58%	0.46%	0.25%	*54.2%*	*42.7%*	*3.1%*	**2.14%**
Mar	4.91%	0.15%	0.32%	*52.9%*	*40.6%*	*6.5%*	**2.68%**
Apr	1.96%	−0.25%	0.18%	*51.6%*	*39.7%*	*8.7%*	**0.93%**
May	−5.54%	0.01%	0.19%	*50.4%*	*40.4%*	*9.2%*	**−2.77%**
Jun	3.96%	−0.85%	0.11%	*49.7%*	*39.6%*	*10.7%*	**1.64%**
Jul	−9.05%	−0.02%	0.02%	*48.5%*	*39.4%*	*12.1%*	**−4.39%**
Aug	6.56%	1.23%	−0.06%	*48.7%*	*37.2%*	*14.1%*	**3.64%**
Sep	5.02%	1.11%	0.03%	*47.2%*	*38.9%*	*13.9%*	**2.81%**
Oct	1.96%	0.97%	0.09%	*48.9%*	*36.5%*	*14.6%*	**1.33%**
Nov	3.25%	0.69%	0.12%	*50.2%*	*37.3%*	*12.5%*	**1.90%**
Dec	−5.87%	−0.45%	0.15%	*48.1%*	*41.0%*	*10.9%*	**−2.99%**

TABLE 13-3 VAS example – Monthly rates of return of the Alloco fund.

Month	Returns			*Weights*			Alloco
	Stocks	Bonds	Cash	*Stocks*	*Bonds*	*Cash*	
Jan	0.72%	0.09%	0.15%	*51.5%*	*37.6%*	*10.9%*	**0.42%**
Feb	2.03%	0.22%	0.15%	*57.2%*	*39.7%*	*3.1%*	**1.25%**
Mar	3.97%	0.14%	0.15%	*53.6%*	*38.4%*	*8.0%*	**2.19%**
Apr	0.64%	−0.37%	0.15%	*51.6%*	*36.2%*	*12.2%*	**0.21%**
May	−6.50%	0.14%	0.15%	*43.2%*	*35.4%*	*21.4%*	**−2.73%**
Jun	2.58%	−0.82%	0.15%	*47.1%*	*38.9%*	*14.0%*	**0.92%**
Jul	−8.42%	0.01%	0.15%	*44.3%*	*42.6%*	*13.1%*	**−3.71%**
Aug	6.32%	1.65%	0.15%	*49.9%*	*45.9%*	*4.2%*	**3.92%**

(continued)

(*continued*)

TABLE 13-3 (*continued*)

Month	Returns			Weights			Alloco
	Stocks	Bonds	Cash	*Stocks*	*Bonds*	*Cash*	
Sep	5.09%	1.28%	0.15%	*56.6%*	*42.5%*	*0.9%*	**3.43%**
Oct	1.89%	1.49%	0.15%	*54.3%*	*44.8%*	*0.9%*	**1.70%**
Nov	4.23%	0.37%	0.15%	*50.3%*	*41.8%*	*7.9%*	**2.29%**
Dec	−4.36%	−0.54%	0.15%	*44.0%*	*38.5%*	*17.5%*	**−2.10%**

TABLE 13-4 VAS example – Monthly rates of return of the Selecto fund.

Month	Returns			Weights			Selecto
	Stocks	Bonds	Cash	*Stocks*	*Bonds*	*Cash*	
Jan	0.87%	0.14%	0.15%	*50.4%*	*40.9%*	*8.7%*	**0.51%**
Feb	2.59%	0.34%	0.15%	*49.2%*	*41.5%*	*9.3%*	**1.43%**
Mar	4.06%	0.19%	0.15%	*47.5%*	*39.8%*	*12.7%*	**2.02%**
Apr	0.96%	−0.34%	0.15%	*49.2%*	*38.1%*	*12.7%*	**0.36%**
May	−6.23%	0.05%	0.15%	*50.2%*	*40.1%*	*9.7%*	**−3.09%**
Jun	4.30%	−1.01%	0.15%	*52.3%*	*40.5%*	*7.2%*	**1.85%**
Jul	−8.63%	0.31%	0.15%	*50.6%*	*40.0%*	*9.4%*	**−4.23%**
Aug	6.61%	1.63%	0.15%	*48.9%*	*41.6%*	*9.5%*	**3.92%**
Sep	4.23%	1.11%	0.15%	*49.2%*	*40.2%*	*10.6%*	**2.54%**
Oct	2.85%	1.87%	0.15%	*50.7%*	*39.5%*	*9.8%*	**2.20%**
Nov	5.02%	0.43%	0.15%	*51.6%*	*38.7%*	*9.7%*	**2.77%**
Dec	−4.20%	−0.72%	0.15%	*52.6%*	*40.9%*	*6.5%*	**−2.49%**

The summary statistics of the funds, benchmark, and market are reported in Table 13-5.

TABLE 13-5 VAS example – Main return, risk, and performance indicators.

	Verso	Alloco	Selecto	Benchmark	Market
Mean return	7.80%	7.80%	7.80%	5.80%	8.06%
Standard deviation	8.96%	8.30%	8.92%	9.43%	18.93%
Sharpe ratio	0.67	0.72	0.67	0.42	0.33
Jensen's alpha	2.00%	2.00%	2.00%		
Information ratio	1.02	1.48	1.74		

At first sight, the risk–return properties of the three funds do not enable the CIO to decisively discriminate them on the basis of their main performance indicators. The cumulative returns of the funds provide further insight into their profiles, as shown in Figure 13-1.

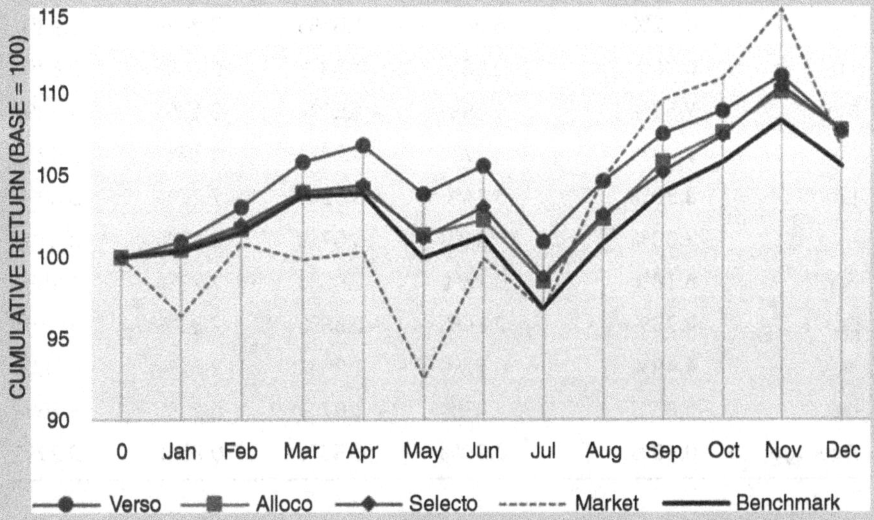

FIGURE 13-1 VAS example – Cumulative rates of return.

Whereas Verso seems to initially outperform the benchmark, with a gradual erosion over time, the other two portfolios (Alloco and Selecto) are much harder to distinguish from each other. In particular, it is difficult from the observation of this chart to guess what type of

(continued)

(continued)

skill has led the three fund managers to generate a cumulative alpha of 2% over the elapsed 12-month period.

We further investigate the composition of the equity part of the benchmark and portfolios. For the benchmark, the investment in equities is split into four sectors: Technology (Tec) with a constant weight of 37%, Financials (Fin) with a weight of 17%, Cyclicals (Cyc) with a weight of 24%, and Defensive (Def) with a weight of 22%. The detailed returns per sector are reported in Table 13-6.

TABLE 13-6 VAS example – Monthly returns of the equity sectors for the benchmark.

Month	Returns				
	Benchmark stocks	**Tec**	**Fin**	**Cyc**	**Def**
Jan	**0.61%**	0.81%	0.69%	0.62%	0.20%
Feb	**2.13%**	2.69%	3.22%	1.56%	0.97%
Mar	**4.22%**	6.98%	1.65%	3.84%	1.98%
Apr	**0.38%**	−0.56%	1.53%	0.75%	0.67%
May	**−7.52%**	−9.65%	−4.50%	−9.12%	−4.53%
Jun	**3.23%**	5.37%	0.24%	4.12%	0.97%
Jul	**−8.99%**	−13.44%	−6.12%	−7.20%	−5.68%
Aug	**7.09%**	10.34%	6.67%	8.32%	0.61%
Sep	**5.18%**	6.75%	2.96%	7.29%	1.95%
Oct	**2.20%**	2.16%	−0.88%	2.33%	4.51%
Nov	**4.49%**	6.32%	1.99%	2.62%	5.38%
Dec	**−4.86%**	−7.03%	−1.07%	−5.21%	−3.76%
Average	**0.68%**	**0.90%**	**0.53%**	**0.83%**	**0.27%**

Here, we focus on the comparison between the Alloco and Selecto funds. The monthly returns and weights of each of the sectors are provided in Tables 13-7 and 13-8.

TABLE 13-7 VAS example – Monthly returns and weights of the equity sectors for the Alloco fund.

Month	Returns					Weights			
	Alloco Stocks	Tec	Fin	Cyc	Def	Tec	Fin	Cyc	Def
Jan	**0.72%**	0.77%	0.66%	0.91%	0.43%	*38.9%*	*16.8%*	*24.8%*	*19.5%*
Feb	**2.03%**	2.26%	3.09%	1.65%	0.91%	*40.1%*	*18.9%*	*22.4%*	*18.6%*
Mar	**3.97%**	6.04%	2.06%	3.67%	0.63%	*42.0%*	*16.2%*	*27.5%*	*14.3%*
Apr	**0.64%**	−0.70%	1.95%	0.95%	1.05%	*28.3%*	*12.1%*	*22.8%*	*36.8%*
May	**−6.50%**	−10.36%	−4.43%	−9.32%	−4.00%	*22.6%*	*19.7%*	*18.4%*	*39.3%*
Jun	**2.58%**	4.56%	−0.52%	3.21%	0.03%	*38.6%*	*15.7%*	*27.9%*	*17.8%*
Jul	**−8.42%**	−13.91%	−6.58%	−6.66%	−5.39%	*29.1%*	*18.9%*	*25.6%*	*26.4%*
Aug	**6.32%**	8.69%	6.01%	7.07%	0.11%	*39.0%*	*17.5%*	*26.3%*	*17.2%*
Sep	**5.09%**	6.20%	2.66%	7.00%	1.48%	*39.9%*	*15.3%*	*28.0%*	*16.8%*
Oct	**1.89%**	1.97%	−0.99%	2.02%	3.09%	*40.2%*	*12.6%*	*22.0%*	*25.2%*
Nov	**4.23%**	7.18%	1.08%	1.29%	3.35%	*42.7%*	*13.9%*	*21.3%*	*22.1%*
Dec	**−4.36%**	−6.83%	−1.17%	−5.99%	−1.97%	*32.0%*	*18.9%*	*24.5%*	*24.6%*
Average	**0.68%**	**0.49%**	**0.32%**	**0.48%**	**−0.02%**	**36.1%**	**16.3%**	**24.3%**	**23.2%**

TABLE 13-8 VAS example – Monthly returns and weights of the equity sectors for the Selecto fund.

Month	Returns					Weights			
	Selecto Stocks	Tec	Fin	Cyc	Def	Tec	Fin	Cyc	Def
Jan	**0.87%**	0.89%	1.11%	0.84%	0.67%	*36.2%*	*17.9%*	*24.6%*	*21.3%*
Feb	**2.59%**	3.04%	3.75%	1.93%	1.72%	*37.8%*	*15.9%*	*23.2%*	*23.1%*
Mar	**4.06%**	7.23%	1.24%	4.02%	1.01%	*36.3%*	*15.7%*	*25.1%*	*22.9%*
Apr	**0.96%**	0.58%	1.88%	0.86%	1.01%	*37.2%*	*16.9%*	*24.8%*	*21.1%*
May	**−6.23%**	−8.55%	−3.20%	−7.56%	−3.15%	*38.1%*	*17.6%*	*23.0%*	*21.3%*
Jun	**4.30%**	6.44%	1.56%	5.22%	2.07%	*36.2%*	*17.9%*	*23.5%*	*22.4%*
Jul	**−8.63%**	−14.14%	−5.23%	−6.02%	−4.46%	*37.9%*	*18.2%*	*23.1%*	*20.8%*
Aug	**6.61%**	9.86%	5.63%	6.98%	1.38%	*36.8%*	*17.2%*	*24.6%*	*21.4%*

(continued)

(continued)

TABLE 13-8 *(continued)*

Month	Returns					Weights			
	Selecto Stocks	Tec	Fin	Cyc	Def	Tec	Fin	Cyc	Def
Sep	**4.23%**	6.52%	2.02%	6.52%	−0.26%	36.2%	16.1%	24.6%	23.1%
Oct	**2.85%**	2.94%	−0.06%	2.89%	4.78%	37.5%	16.4%	23.6%	22.5%
Nov	**5.02%**	6.99%	2.50%	2.93%	5.87%	37.0%	17.4%	23.1%	22.5%
Dec	**−4.20%**	−6.52%	0.01%	−4.22%	−3.62%	36.6%	17.3%	24.6%	21.5%
Average	**1.04%**	**1.27%**	**0.93%**	**1.20%**	**0.59%**	**37.0%**	**17.0%**	**24.0%**	**22.0%**

13.1 THE FUNDAMENTALS OF PERFORMANCE DECOMPOSITION

Decomposing portfolio performance in order to uncover its roots has been a major challenge for investors, managers, and analysts for many decades, and has nowadays reached a high degree of maturity, as explained by Bacon (2023) in his comprehensive book largely devoted to this topic. The fundamental starting point of performance attribution can be traced back to Fama's (1972) article, whose aim was to partition an active portfolio realized return into interpretable components.

13.1.1 Fama's (1972) performance decomposition framework

The analysis is entirely carried out in the context of the Capital Asset Pricing Model (CAPM) on an *ex post* basis (even though it also features the *ex ante* expected returns of financial assets). It consists of a decomposition of the realized (cumulative or average) portfolio return $\overline{R}_P$ into additive fragments, each one corresponding to an interpretable premium.

For the purpose of the performance decomposition, the risk measure chosen in our presentation is the volatility of returns, and thus we stand in the mean–volatility framework.[1] The benchmark for the investor is a combination of the market portfolio and the risk-free asset, but the logic underlying the analysis can be adapted to any investor-specific passive benchmark. Fama (1972) distinguishes three risk levels displayed by the portfolio that matter for the investor:

[1]The analysis made by Fama (1972) focuses on the beta, but the outcome is equivalent.

1. *Total risk*: This corresponds to the volatility of realized returns $\sigma_P \equiv \sigma(R_P)$ that the investor eventually bears by holding the portfolio.
2. *Actual systematic risk*: The portfolio beta $\beta_P \equiv \frac{\text{Cov}(R_P,R_M)}{\sigma_M^2} = \frac{\rho_{PM}\sigma_P}{\sigma_M}$ characterizes the systematic part of portfolio risk in the context of the CAPM. In our chosen risk–return framework, in which the market risk premium is itself normalized by its volatility, this translates into a systematic portfolio volatility equal to $\sigma_{\rho P} \equiv \beta_P\sigma_M = \rho_{PM}\sigma_P$. Note that, since $\rho_{PM} \leq 1$ by definition, $\sigma_{\rho P} \leq \sigma_P$ thanks to the effect of portfolio diversification.[2]
3. *Target investor risk*: Irrespective of what (total or systematic) risk level the portfolio manager has achieved, the investor *j* assigns themselves an objective regarding the target risk level, denoted by $\sigma_P^{(j)}$, as discussed in Section 9.2.2 of Chapter 9.[3] We generalize Fama's (1972) original point of view by not specifying whether this target is defined in terms of total or systematic risk. In corollary, there is no particular constraint on its value relative to the other measures of risk so that it can be lower, higher than, or equal to total risk or actual systematic risk.

Each risk level corresponds to an associated required rate of return. Because we are in the CAPM context, it is obtained by applying the market reward-to-volatility ratio with *ex post* data:

$$R^*(x) = R_f + x\left[\frac{\overline{R}_M - R_f}{\sigma_M}\right] \tag{13-1}$$

where $R^*(x)$ is the required average rate of return, and x is the associated volatility risk level for $x = \sigma_P, \sigma_{\rho P}, \sigma_P^{(j)}$. Consequently, the required return $R^*(\sigma_P)$ features three additive components:

$$R^*(\sigma_P) = R_f + \lambda_P + \delta_P \tag{13-2}$$

where $\lambda_P = R^*(\sigma_{\rho P}) - R_f$ is the risk premium and $\delta_P = R^*(\sigma_P) - R^*(\sigma_{\rho P})$ is the diversification premium. The first premium reflects the market-driven reward compensating the portfolio for its systematic risk. The second premium represents the necessary remuneration that the manager should obtain in exchange for their active choice to diverge from the market portfolio and bear some specific risk that could be diversified away. Furthermore, the risk premium can be broken down into two components:

$$\lambda_P = \lambda_P^{(j)} + \lambda_P^{(m)} \tag{13-3}$$

where $\lambda_P^{(j)} = R^*(\sigma_P^{(j)}) - R_f$ reflects the investor's risk premium, i.e., the remuneration that the investor wants in order to compensate for the risk taken; and $\lambda_P^{(j)} = R^*(\sigma_{\rho P}) - R^*(\sigma_P^{(j)})$ is the

[2]The systematic portfolio volatility has already been encountered in Section 6.3.1 of Chapter 6 with the alternative Treynor ratio and the alternative modified Jensen's alpha.
[3]We used notation $\sigma^{(j)}$ in Chapter 9, but we add subscript P in the current chapter to ease the exposition.

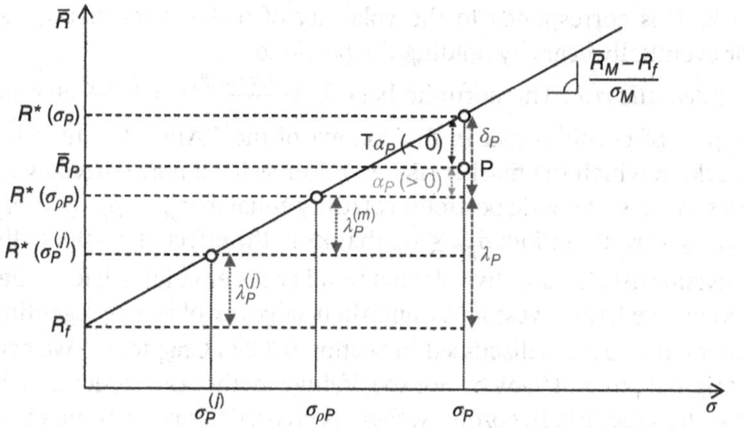

FIGURE 13-2 Fama's (1972) decomposition of the average portfolio return.

manager's risk premium, i.e., the return differential that is required from the manager to compensate for the difference between their target risk level and the systematic one of the portfolio. The application of Equations (13-1) to (13-3) leads to Figure 13-2.

The chart shows how various components sum up together to achieve the final portfolio return. Only one premium featured in Equation (13-2) is necessarily positive: the diversification premium δ_P because the specific that it compensates for cannot be negative. Everything in the risk premium can be positive or negative: the total risk premium λ_P because the correlation coefficient ρ_{PM} can be negative if the manager is a short seller; the investor's risk premium $\lambda_P^{(j)}$ for the same reason; and the manager's risk premium $\lambda_P^{(m)}$ if the investor has opted for a higher risk level than the manager. They are all represented as positive on the graph.

The coordinates of the portfolio are represented by point P in the figure. In the situation shown in the illustration, its mean return $\overline{R}_P$ locates somewhere between the required return based on systematic risk $R^*(\sigma_{\rho P})$ and that based on total risk $R^*(\sigma_P)$, but any other situation is possible. As indicated with the double arrows to the left of the coordinates, the differences between the mean portfolio return and the two levels of required returns represent two well-known performance measures: $\overline{R}_P - R^*(\sigma_{\rho P}) = \alpha_P$, i.e., Jensen's alpha (Chapter 3, formula (3-11)), and $\overline{R}_P - R^*(\sigma_P) = \mathrm{T}\alpha_P$, i.e., the Total risk alpha (Chapter 6, formula (6-65)), which is also called "net selectivity" by Fama. In the figure, the former is positive, and the latter is negative. These two performance measures are reconciled thanks to the following formula:

$$\mathrm{T}\alpha_P = \alpha_P - \delta_P \tag{13-4}$$

and, since $\delta_P > 0$ by definition, this also means that $\mathrm{T}\alpha_P < \alpha_P$. It is easier for a manager to produce a positive alpha than a positive Total risk alpha because the latter performance measure includes the cost of the portfolio's limited diversification that goes along with its active risk.

13.1.2 Interpreting performance decomposition

13.1.2.1 Accounting for the investor's point of view

In Fama's (1972) article, the performance decomposition framework is viewed as a sort of toolkit. The author does not commit further toward a case-by-case analysis of the meaning of the identified components. We can go a bit further, notably in light of the discussion of which performance measure should be used in the spirit of Chapter 4. Indeed, the point of view of the investor is of paramount importance in order to adequately interpret the components of portfolio performance. There are two types of questions to take into account: (i) *Does the investor care about systematic or total risk?* and (ii) *If the investor cares about total risk, is their target the expression of their risk preferences or not?* Depending on the answers, the components of performance should be interpreted in radically different fashions:

1. *The investor only cares about systematic risk*: In that case, the manager's risk premium is a pure reflection of their active systematic risk compared with the level chosen by the investor. $\lambda_P^{(m)}$ represents the necessary compensation for the shift in portfolio risk imposed by the manager on the investor, $R^*(\sigma_{pP})$ is the required return, and the adequate way to assess the added value brought by the actively managed portfolio to the investor is Jensen's alpha α_P, which is positive in Figure 13-2. The total risk alpha (and the total diversification premium) can be discarded from the analysis.
2. *The investor only cares about total risk without indicating their risk aversion*: We stand in the situation in which the portfolio's investment is made in conjunction with other financial assets, with the aim of maximizing the aggregate Sharpe ratio. Systematic risk does not really matter, so the manager's risk premium is irrelevant. All that matters is the portfolio's total risk σ_P, and the diversification risk premium is a true component of the required rate of return, which is equal to $R^*(\sigma_P)$. The relevant performance measure is the Total risk alpha $T\alpha_P$, which is negative in Figure 13-2.
3. *The investor only cares about total risk and wishes their risk aversion to be accounted for*: The decomposition is only partially relevant. The risk–return trade-off of the portfolio chosen by the investor is supposed to maximize their expected utility. This means that the coordinates $\left(\sigma_P^{(j)}, R^*\left(\sigma_P^{(j)}\right)\right)$ correspond to the tangency point of their indifference curve, whose equation is $\overline{R}_x = k + \frac{1}{2}\gamma_j\sigma_x^2$, with the CML. In that case, we have to use the Target volatility alpha of investor j already defined in Equation (9-14) of Chapter 9.

$$V\alpha_P^j = (\overline{R}_P - R_f) - \frac{1}{2}\text{SR}_M\left(\sigma_P^{(j)} + \frac{\sigma_P^2}{\sigma_P^{(j)}}\right) \tag{13-5}$$

Note that, because the optimal indifference curve is necessarily above the SML, the required portfolio return $R^*(\sigma_P;\gamma_j)$ in the third case is higher than $R^*(\sigma_P)$, and thus we have

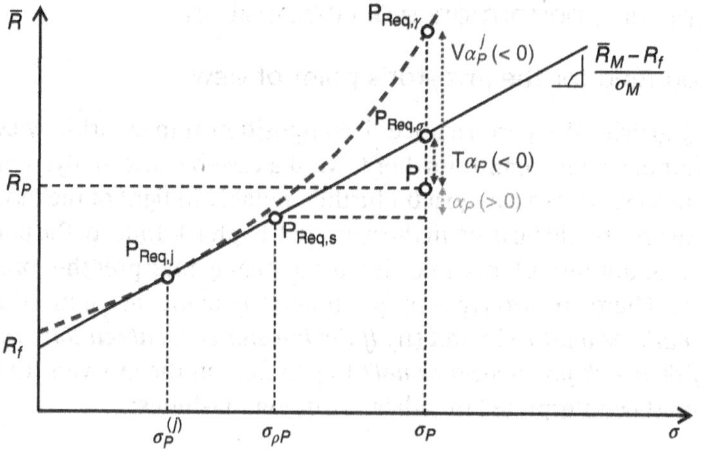

FIGURE 13-3 Relevant performance measures for the three points of view of an investor.

a final ordering of the three performance measures that are relevant for the three cases examined:

$$V\alpha_P^j < T\alpha_P < \alpha_P \quad (13\text{-}6)$$

where α_P is the relevant performance measure in case 1, $T\alpha_P$ is relevant in case 2, and $V\alpha_P^j$ is relevant in case 3. These three cases are represented in Figure 13-3.

The VAS example (continued)

VAS Asset Management actively commercializes its funds to customers whose volatility budget is supposed to be 5% on average, and whose own benchmark should probably be close to the market portfolio represented in Table 13-1. Obviously, this year's financial market conditions have been more volatile than initially expected. Considering this type of information, the CIO wishes to ascertain how the company's representative customer would assess the performance generated by the three funds.

First, we consider that the representative investor j has a target volatility of $\sigma_P^{(j)} = 5\%$. Considering that $R_f = 1.80\%$ and the Sharpe ratio of the market portfolio is $SR_M \equiv \frac{\bar{R}_M - R_f}{\sigma_M} = 0.35$ from Table 13-5, we obtain that $R^*(\sigma_P^{(j)}) = 1.80\% + 0.35 \times 5\% = 3.53\%$, which is valid for all three portfolios **V**, **A**, and **S**. This indicates that the investor's level of risk aversion is equal to $\gamma_j = \frac{SR_M}{\sigma_P^{(j)}} = \frac{0.35}{0.05} = 6.91$.

Second, considering the data presented in Tables 13-1 to 13-4, we obtain the following correlation levels: $\rho_{VM} = 0.79$, $\rho_{AM} = 0.78$, and $\rho_{SM} = 0.82$. This leads to the characterization of the funds' relevant risk levels and performance components as shown in Table 13-9.

TABLE 13-9 VAS example – Fama's (1972) performance decomposition.

		Verso	Alloco	Selecto
Risk	Target risk $\sigma_P^{(j)}$	5%	5%	5%
	Systematic risk σ_{pP}	6.76%	6.20%	6.97%
	Total risk σ_P	8.57%	7.95%	8.54%
Premium	Investor's premium $\lambda_P^{(j)}$	1.73%	1.73%	1.73%
	Manager's premium $\lambda_P^{(m)}$	0.61%	0.41%	0.68%
	Diversification δ_P	0.62%	0.60%	0.54%
Performance	Jensen's alpha α_P	3.66%	3.86%	3.59%
	Total risk alpha $T\alpha_P$	3.03%	3.25%	3.05%
	Target volatility alpha $V\alpha_P^j$	2.59%	2.95%	2.61%

All three funds generate a positive performance, regardless of the indicator. Nevertheless, there are notable differences. Even though Alloco and Selecto deliver a very similar performance level, the former beats the latter by circa 0.30%. Furthermore, the relative ranking of Verso and Selecto switches depending on whether the Jensen's alpha (based on systematic risk) or the other metrics are used. This is due to the difference in their correlations with the market portfolio.

We zoom in on the Verso fund in order to obtain a graphical interpretation of the results. Figure 13-4 reports the major insights retrieved from Table 13-9 regarding that fund.

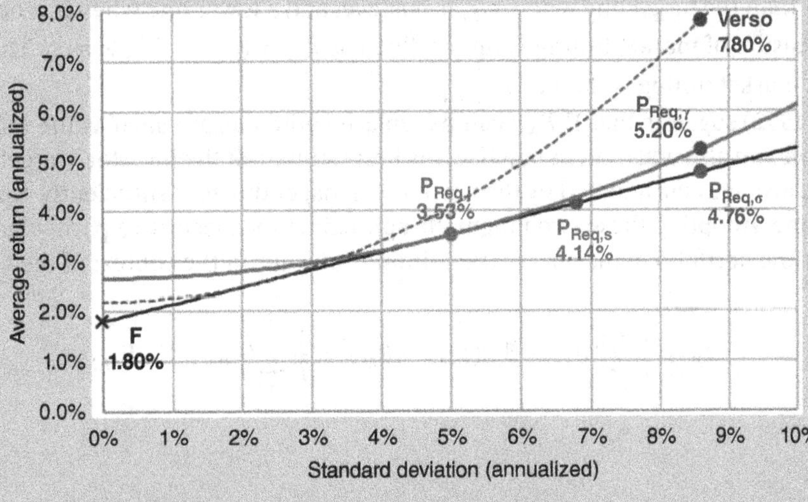

FIGURE 13-4 VAS example – Fama's (1972) performance decomposition for the Verso fund.

(continued)

(*continued*)

Because of the relatively moderate Sharpe ratio of the chosen market portfolio, various required returns do not substantially differ from each other.

The picture would be very different if, for instance, the target investor's risk level had been equal to 4% instead of 5%. In that case, the required return would have shifted to a level of 5.66%, and the Target volatility alpha would have shrunk to 2.13%. The fund would be attractive (i.e., deliver a positive performance) for investors whose risk budget is larger than or equal to 2.3%. The indifference curve for this investor, reaching the coordinates of the portfolio, is represented by the dashed gray line.

13.1.2.2 Aggregating performance decomposition over time

Fama (1972) lists some further ways to partition performance by introducing a potential difference between the *ex ante* expected returns and the *ex post* realized one. An insightful use of such a partitioning choice is provided by Kon (1983). He uses Fama's (1972) definition of market timing by first considering his decomposition over a single period of time. If the investor cares about the portfolio's systematic risk, then we can set $\sigma_P^{(j)} = (\rho_{PM}\sigma_P)^{(j)}$ and, since the market portfolio risk σ_M is a given, this means that this investor has a target beta $\beta_P^{(j)}$. Furthermore, if the portfolio manager has chosen another level of systematic risk at a given point in time t, this means that their beta is also different from the investor's target one: $\beta_{P,t} \neq \beta_P^{(j)}$. The reason for this choice can be the manager's anticipation that the market portfolio return during the same period would differ from its expected one. We can denote this difference by $\pi_{M,t} = R_{M,t} - \mathrm{E}(R_M)$. If the manager has made the right choice, this means that they have a higher beta than the target one when $\pi_{M,t}$ is positive, and a lower one when it is negative. The periodic measure of market timing is thus defined as $\tau_{P,t} = (\beta_{P,t} - \beta_P^{(j)}) \times \pi_{M,t}$. The aggregate measure of market timing is then $\tau_P \equiv \frac{1}{T}\sum_{t=1}^{T} \tau_{P,t}$.

Fama (1972) suggests that $\mathrm{E}(R_M)$ can be replaced with a proxy such as the sample mean. Moreover, we can also add that, in practice, the best estimate of the investor's target beta might often be the average beta adopted by the portfolio manager during a sufficiently representative period of time. Adopting these two pragmatic approximations leads to a particularly intuitive formula for the portfolio manager's market timing behavior in the context of the CAPM:

$$\tau_P = \frac{1}{T}\sum_{t=1}^{T}(\beta_{P,t} - \overline{\beta}_P)(R_{M,t} - \overline{R}_M) = \frac{1}{T}\sum_{t=1}^{T}(\beta_{P,t} - \overline{\beta}_P)R_{M,t} \tag{13-7}$$

where $\overline{\beta}_P = \frac{1}{T}\sum_{t=1}^{T}\beta_{P,t}$ is the estimate of $\beta_P^{(j)}$ and $\overline{R}_M = \frac{1}{T}\sum_{t=1}^{T}R_{M,t}$ is the estimate of $E(R_M)$. The last equality results from the fact that $\frac{1}{T}\sum_{t=1}^{T}(\beta_{P,t} - \overline{\beta}_P)\overline{R}_M = \frac{1}{T}\sum_{t=1}^{T}\beta_{P,t}\overline{R}_M - \frac{1}{T}\sum_{t=1}^{T}\overline{\beta}_P\overline{R}_M = 0$.

This expression looks very familiar. It corresponds to the Cornell performance measure of market timing defined in Equation (8-33) of Chapter 8. The only difference resides in the definition of the benchmark portfolio, which is the self-reported one in the Cornell measure and is defined as the market portfolio in the current context. It is not surprising to anticipate that this measure serves as the basis for the identification of the market timing component of a portfolio's abnormal return that underlies the traditional performance attribution framework examined in Chapter 14.

The VAS example (continued)

Using the data about the three funds' and the market return, the corresponding betas are the following: $\beta_V = 0.79 \times \frac{8.57\%}{18.12\%} = 0.37$, $\beta_A = 0.78 \times \frac{7.95\%}{18.12\%} = 0.34$, and $\beta_S = 0.82 \times \frac{8.54\%}{18.12\%} = 0.38$.

In order to obtain the monthly exposure to the market, which is necessary for the computation of τ_P in Equation (13-7), we assume that the beta evolves in parallel with the relative allocation to equities of each fund. Thus, for instance, $\beta_{V,Jan} \approx \frac{55.7\%}{50.5\%} \times 0.37 = 0.41$,

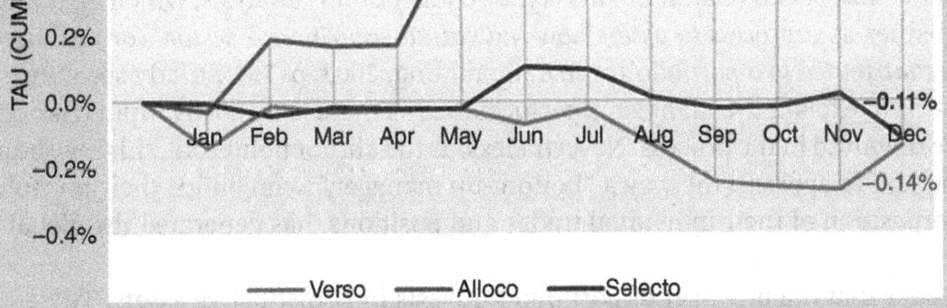

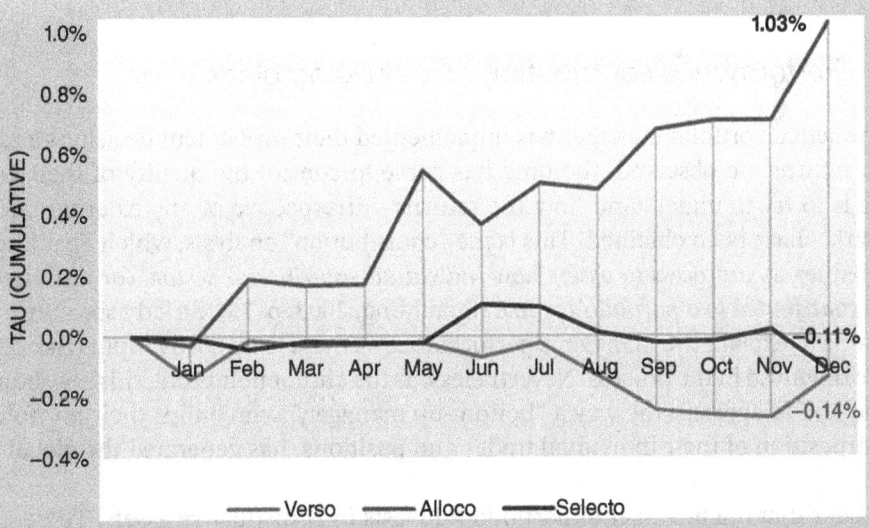

FIGURE 13-5 VAS example – Evolution of the market timing of each fund over time.

(continued)

(continued)

where 50.5% stands for the average allocation to equities of the fund during the year. The graph presented in Figure 13-5 reports the cumulative evolution of the market timing measure over time for each fund. The final value corresponds to the annualized value of τ_P.

Obviously, fund Alloco stands out as the most successful market timer, with a steady increase in its measure of performance over time. This also means that, because the other two funds reach similar aggregate performance levels, their manager must have other merits. This is verified later.

13.2 ATTRIBUTING PERFORMANCE

When we reviewed the various ways of appraising a manager's market timing skills in Chapter 8, it stood clear that the most precise and granular approach was based on the full knowledge of the portfolio holdings and trades over time, as discussed in Section 8.4 of that chapter. Attribution analysis represents a systematic, fully observation-based (as opposed to statistics-based) way to process information in order to retrieve the impact of the manager's investment decisions in the generation of superior returns. In the current section, we introduce the principles of this type of analysis. Then, we discuss an *ex ante* modeling approach that lends support to performing a meaningful *ex post* analysis.

13.2.1 Performance contribution as a building block

When the active portfolio manager has implemented their investment decisions and realized portfolio returns are observed, the time has come to control the quality of their work. The first step is to try to understand how the returns – irrespective of any external reference or benchmark – have been obtained. This is the "contribution" analysis, which Spaulding (2003) simply defines as *a process to assess how individual securities or sectors (or any sub-portfolio element) contributed to a portfolio's return* (Spaulding, 2003, p. 15). Strictly speaking, this does not allow us to explain the manager's performance as there is no costly input (risk or external reference) involved in the process. Nevertheless, as the author points out, this may be an appropriate method to appraise the way a "bottom-up manager," who builds their portfolio mostly as a superposition of their individual trades and positions, has generated the global portfolio return.

Consider that the manager of portfolio P invests in N distinctive assets. These can range from individual securities (direct lines) to broad asset classes such as "stocks" or "bonds." For each of these assets, we have the corresponding investment weight $w_{P,i,t}$ at the beginning of the period t and total rate of return $R_{i,t}$ for $i = 1, \ldots, N$ at each observed point in time

$t = 1, \ldots, T$ so that the periodic portfolio return is the weighted average of the asset returns $R_{P,t} = \sum_{i=1}^{N} w_{P,i,t} R_{i,t}$.[4]

At each point in time, the contribution of asset i to the total portfolio performance, denoted by $c_i(R_{P,t})$, is simply the product of the asset weight with the asset return:

$$c_i(R_{P,t}) = w_{P,i,t} R_{i,t} \tag{13-8}$$

Usually, the weight and return are also presented separately in order to better understand where the contribution of the asset mostly originates from, especially when this contribution is large. It is also possible to perform the contribution analysis as a percentage of the total return. Nevertheless, the interpretation becomes tedious when returns are negative.

There are some basic rules that must be respected in order for the contribution analysis to make sense. Spaulding (2003) lists three such rules that we can describe as follows: (i) the sum of the contribution effects must always be equal to the portfolio return at any point in time, i.e., $R_{P,t} = \sum_{i=1}^{N} c_i(R_{P,t})$; (ii) the weight of each asset at time t should exclude any market effect during the time interval (i.e., weights should be expressed as relative market values at the beginning of the period); and (iii) the cash position, if any, is included as one of the N assets. The third condition ensures that the global portfolio is partitioned, including any (positive or negative) cash balance.

In addition to these principles, the question arises whether it is necessary to account for any cash flow (in or out) that happens during the time interval between time t and $t + 1$.[5]

The averaging of performance contributions over time can also be instructive.[6] It is defined as

$$c_i(\overline{R}_P) = \frac{1}{T} \sum_{t=1}^{T} w_{P,i,t} R_{i,t} \tag{13-9}$$

This extension serves two main purposes: (i) examining its trending behavior over the time window (this can be done through moving averages as well) and (ii) obtaining a less noisy version of the way each asset has participated in the production of the aggregate portfolio return.

[4]We identify P in the subscript of the weight as this will be an important discriminating dimension when a benchmark is accounted for. This notation ensures consistency with the one adopted for attribution analysis.

[5]We can deal with this issue in a generic way through defining the cash flow-adjusted weight $\tilde{w}_{P,i,t} = \frac{w_{P,i,t} + \text{wCF}_{P,i,t}}{\sum_{i=1}^{N} (w_{P,i,t} + \text{wCF}_{P,i,t})}$ where $\text{wCF}_{P,i,t}$ represents the weighted cash flow of asset i during the period. This is the basis of "money-weighted attribution" (Spaulding and Campisi, 2007). However, there is a debate as to whether one has to consider that the management of the cash flows is made internally, at the manager's level, or externally, at the investor's level. In general, for attribution analysis, the focus is on the manager and thus the use of time-weighted returns (excluding cash flows) appears to be preferable.

[6]This is not to be confused with multiperiod contribution, which involves a compounding effect. This is discussed in detail (in the context of attribution analysis) in Chapter 14.

The VAS example (continued)

We do not need the benchmark's characteristics in order to perform the contribution analysis for each of the three funds. From the information contained in Tables 13-1 to 13-3, we can compute the month-by-month contribution of the three asset classes (stocks, bonds and cash) to the overall return of the three funds. This information is summarized in Figures 13-6 to 13-8.

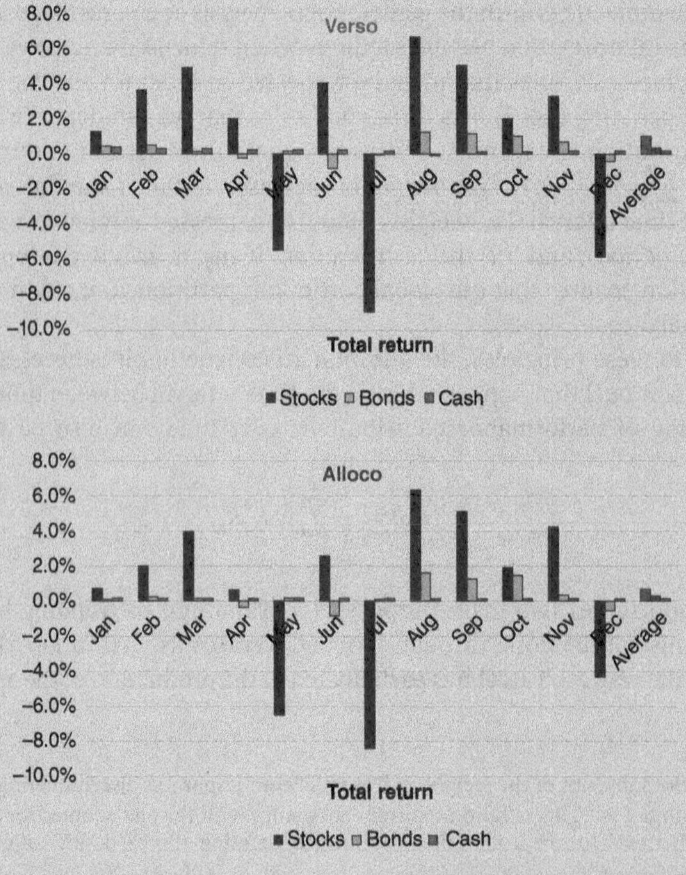

FIGURE 13-6 VAS example – Monthly performance contribution per asset class (total returns).

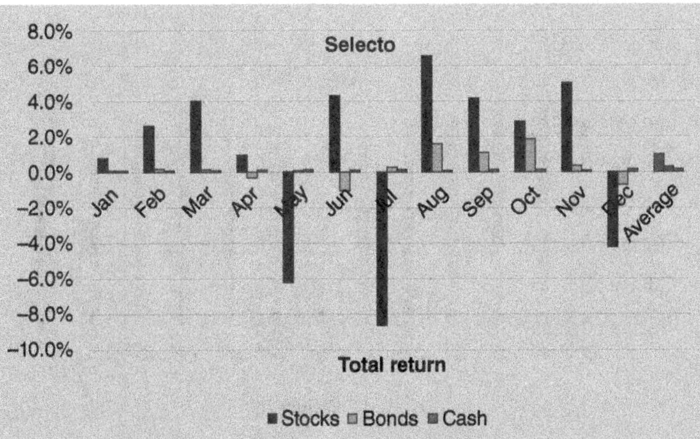

FIGURE 13.6 (*Continued*)

Matching the information of the three sets of charts mainly reveals that the *Verso* fund outperforms its peers during the first half of the period thanks to the superior contribution of the equity investments, which is overweighed by the portfolio manager during the first part of the year (Figure 13-7). The Alloco fund generally has lower asset class returns than the Selecto fund (Figure 13-6), but the manager's allocation decisions are much more dynamic (Figure 13-7) and adequate, which leads to a global average return that is in line with the peers.

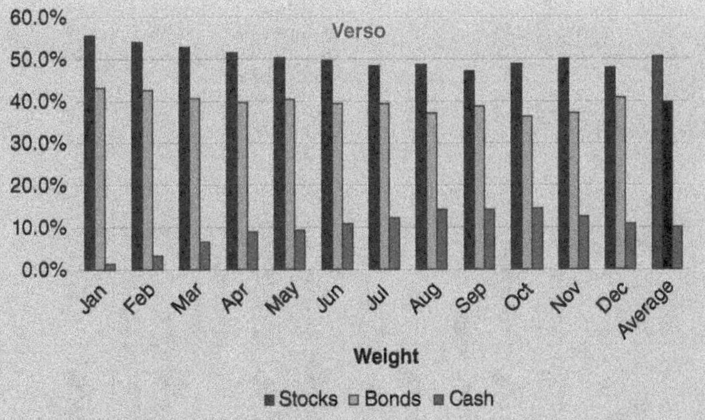

FIGURE 13-7 VAS example – Monthly performance contribution per asset class (weights).

(continued)

(continued)

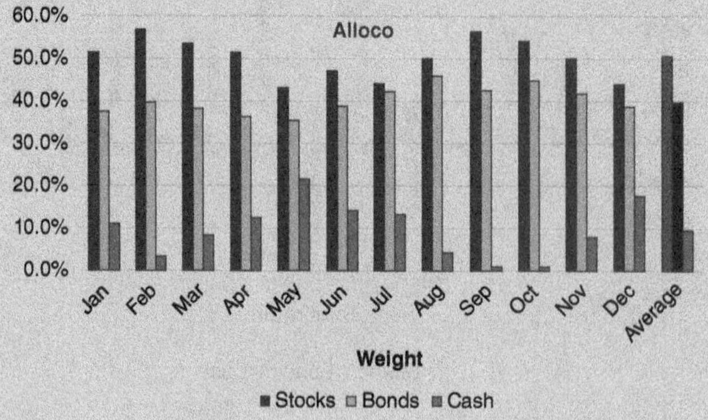

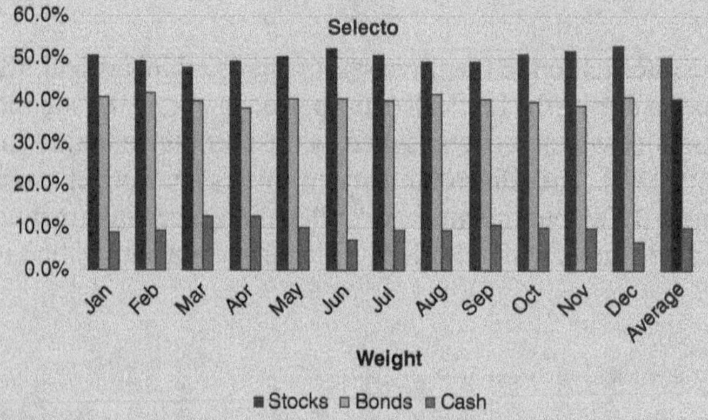

FIGURE 13.7 *(Continued)*

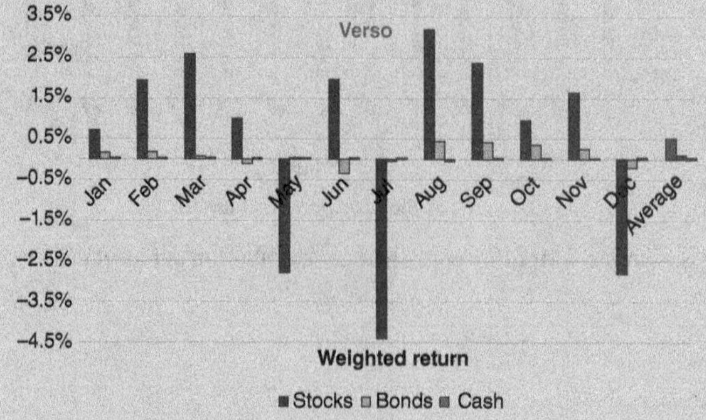

FIGURE 13-8 VAS example – Monthly performance contribution per asset class (weighted returns).

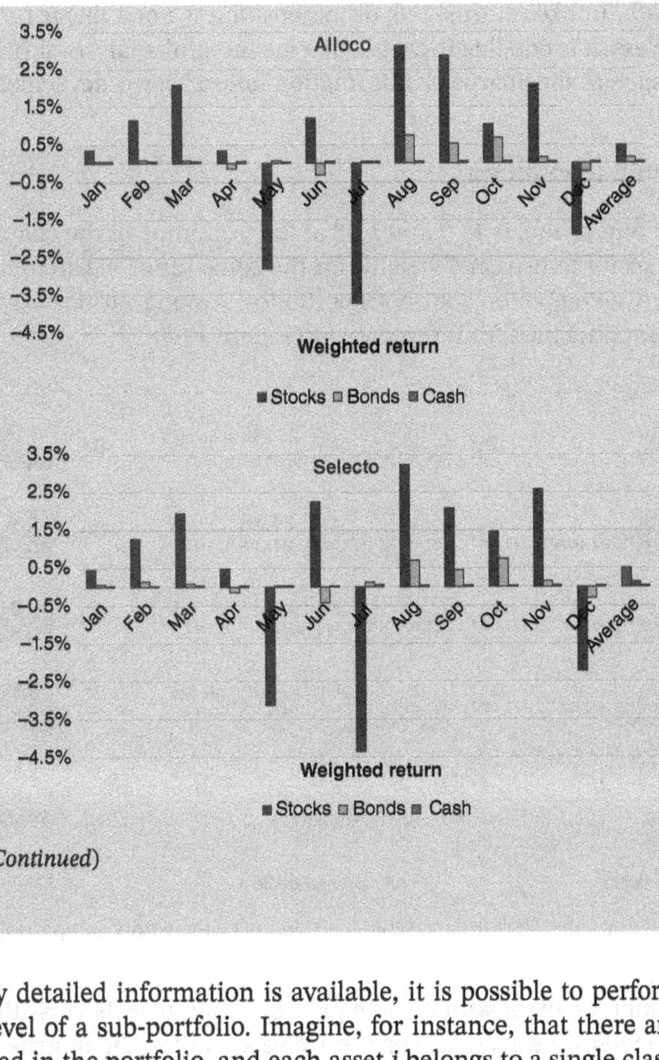

FIGURE 13.8 (*Continued*)

If sufficiently detailed information is available, it is possible to perform the exact same analysis at the level of a sub-portfolio. Imagine, for instance, that there are K distinct asset classes represented in the portfolio, and each asset i belongs to a single class, so that we have a two-layered partition of the portfolio. Then, as before, the contribution of the return of the kth asset class to the global portfolio is written as $c_k(R_{P,t}) = w_{P,k,t}R_{P,k,t}$, while the contribution of the ith asset to the return of its own asset class k is written as

$$c_i(R_{P,k,t}) = \frac{w_{P,i,t}}{\sum_{i \in k} w_{P,i,t}} R_{i,t} \tag{13-10}$$

where $\sum_{i \in k} w_{P,i,t}$ is the sum of the weights of all assets that belong to the kth asset class.

Performance contribution analysis is not necessarily as mechanical as it may seem. An interesting development of this concept integrates portfolio risk in the process. This extension is not trivial because, unlike returns, risk decomposition is not a linear function of portfolio weights. Nevertheless, it is possible to carry out a meaningful analysis of risk-adjusted performance measures such as the Sharpe or Information ratios. This is developed in Section 13.3.

The VAS example (continued)

With the information of Tables 13-7 and 13-8 at the beginning of the chapter, we can compare the average sector returns and weights for the Alloco and Selecto funds, as well as the product of these two components for both portfolios. Among various ways to present this information, we propose the layout presented in Figure 13-9.

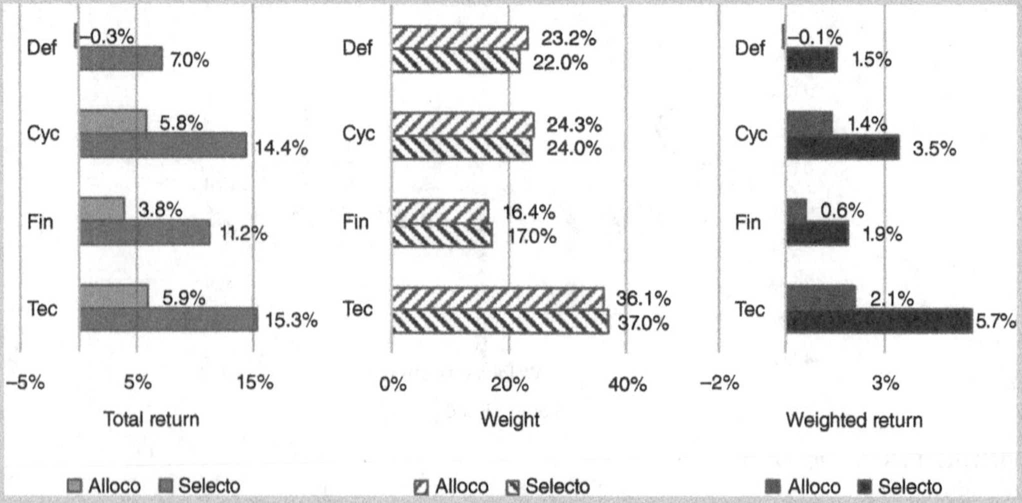

FIGURE 13-9 VAS example – Performance contribution inside the equity sub-portfolios for Alloco and Selecto.

The contribution analysis within the equity portfolio reveals very different behavior for both funds: whereas the average weights are very similar, the returns achieved by the manager of the Selecto fund are substantially greater than those of the Alloco fund. One can wonder how it is possible that, despite such a difference, both portfolio managers eventually reach almost exactly the same average aggregate rate of return. The answer lies in the timing behavior of the Alloco fund that appears in Figure 13-8. This very same dynamic behavior is reproduced within the equity asset class, as indicated in the second part of Table 13-8.

All this contribution analysis leaves a taste of *trop peu*. What we clearly miss is a common basis for comparison. In our example, it is obviously possible to design such a comparative framework thanks to the presence of a common benchmark portfolio. This is essentially where attribution analysis differs from and complements the benchmark-free contribution analysis.

13.2.2 What is performance attribution?

To define performance attribution, it is wise to give the word to two renowned specialists in this field. Generally speaking, attribution is *"the act of determining the contributors or causes of a result or effect"* (Spaulding, 2003, p. 2). Thus, there is a clear link with the contribution analysis examined above, but it is not enough as we miss the "transformation" of inputs into outputs that precisely generates performance. In the context of portfolio management, Bacon (2023) defines performance attribution as: "... *a technique used to quantify the excess return of a portfolio against its benchmark into the active decisions of the investment decision process"* (Bacon, 2023, p. 239). It represents the *a posteriori* way to rationalize the motivations of a manager to engage in active portfolio management by diverging from their benchmark.

As Bacon (2023) explains, performance attribution analysis serves at least four main purposes:

1. To enable the analyst to quantify the consequences of the decisions made by the portfolio manager. It is necessary to have a tool that links these decisions to their exact and unambiguous effects on the portfolio rate of return in order to demonstrate the presence or absence of added value in the actual outcome.
2. To help portfolio managers themselves to gain a quantitative understanding of the drivers of their performance relative to their benchmark. They can better detect sweet spots and pain points and engage in a critical diagnosis of their management process.
3. To objectivize and make transparent the dialogue between the portfolio manager and their client. Once the benchmark is clear to all parties, the output of performance attribution does not lie, and it is in principle impossible to escape the unforgiven report of the analysis.
4. To assist senior management in their assessment of the outcome of the portfolio management process within their firm, in order not only to detect outliers or specific skills but also to provide a basis for incentive management or the setting of quantifiable objectives.

13.2.2.1 The levels of attribution analysis

Addressing the different levels of attribution analysis entails the understanding of the types of decisions made by an active portfolio manager that may have an influence on how they can positively diverge from their benchmark. The first attempt to disentangle the different categories of such decisions in the broad context of pension funds (which is an interesting laboratory due to the complexity of the asset and liability management process) is due to Holbrook (1977). He defines three main steps in the decision-making process: policy, strategy, and selection. He introduces the notion of performance attribution by considering that the influence of each type of decision on performance must be evaluated separately, in order to adequately inform investors about the reasons for the outperformance or underperformance and enable them to take corrective action on that basis.

In order to match the typical contemporaneous approach of modern pension funds, we propose to slightly adjust Holbrook's (1977) categorization by considering four levels of decisions: (i) policy, (ii) strategic, (iii) tactical (which can be split into two layers depending on the granularity), and (iv) selection.[7] The waterfall is illustrated in Figure 13-10.

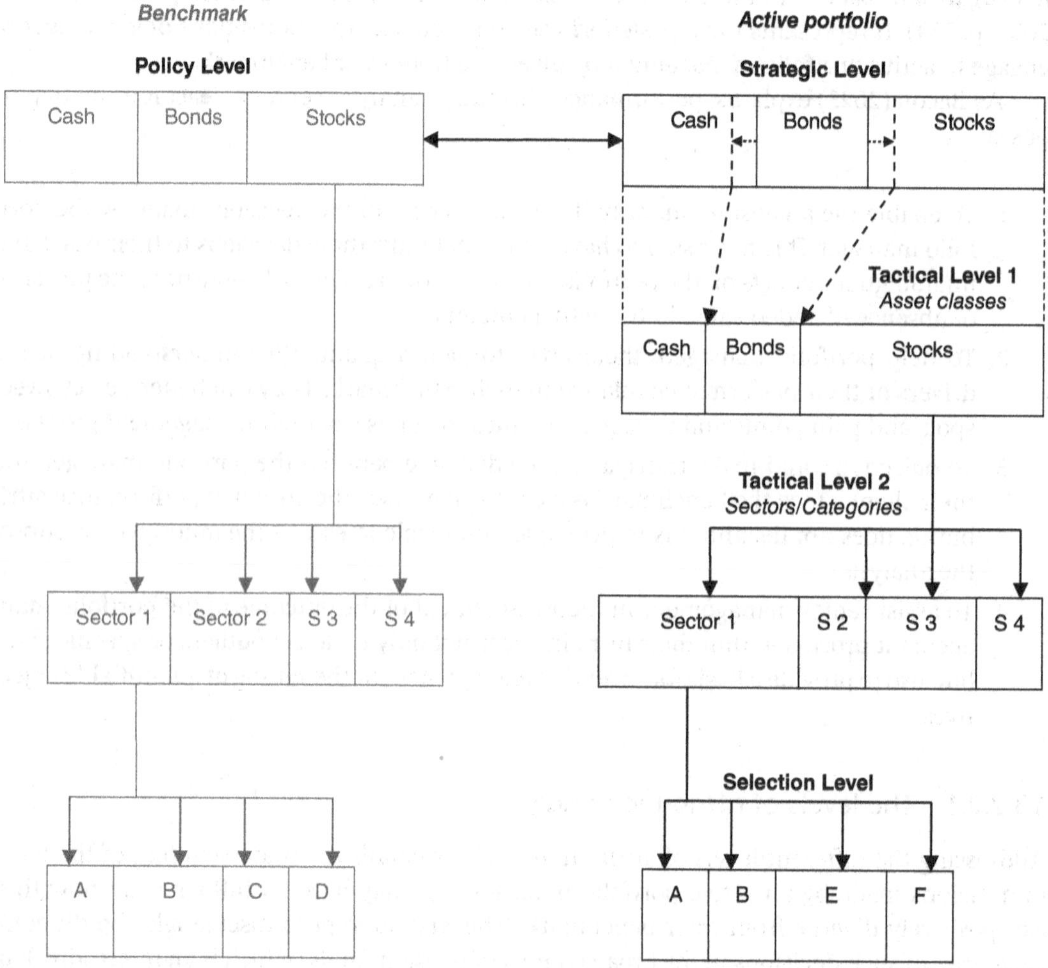

FIGURE 13-10 Waterfall of the decision-making process in active portfolio management.

[7]There are other possible categorizations of the investment decision-making process, but we are confident that this one makes full sense from a practical point of view and is used, explicitly or not, by many asset managers.

The four levels of investment decisions that should be considered in the performance attribution analysis can be briefly described as follows:

(i) *The policy level*: It corresponds to the commitment made by the portfolio manager to adopt a long-term target allocation between broad asset classes (equities, fixed income, real assets, alternative investments, cash, ...), which corresponds to their assessment of the most appropriate composition in order to optimize the risk–return properties of the investment. It usually results from either a contractual commitment (for mutual funds or discretionary portfolios) or a long-term forecasting study (for institutional asset managers such as pension funds or insurance companies). The output of this decision is the definition of the long run benchmark portfolio that serves as the reference point for the assessment of performance.

In the figure, we represent a simple illustration of three-asset class allocation between stocks, bonds, and cash. The size of each block reflects the relative weight of the corresponding asset class.

(ii) *The strategic level*: Within the context of a multi-year management process, it considers the target asset allocation for the medium term. This is not *per se* an active portfolio management decision, as it reflects the correction that should be brought to the policy portfolio in order to address the risk and return properties of various asset classes over a foreseeable future (generally one to three years, but can be longer if there is no well-defined policy portfolio). If the benchmark is not defined through the policy portfolio, then this strategic asset allocation replaces it and corresponds to the reference that the manager aims to outperform with their active decisions.

On the chart, these decisions are reflected with the change in the respective sizes represented by shifts in the block sizes.

(iii) *The tactical level*: At this level, the manager may choose to diverge from the target asset allocation defined at the upper echelon. The purpose of these decisions is to take advantage of differences in expected returns or risk levels, with the explicit goal of outperforming the benchmark. Usually, a tolerance level is specified, either in terms of allocation bounds or active risk (tracking error (TE) or any other metric), or both.

Tactical decisions may apply at the highest level to the broad asset classes considered in the strategic asset allocation. Going downstream, there are also potential tactical decisions made within asset classes. This can take place, for instance, by diverging from the sector allocations of the equity part of the benchmark portfolio. However, any other criterion (geographical, currency-based, per type of issuer, etc.) can be adopted when relevant.

From the perspective of the analysis of performance, it is difficult to distinguish active tactical bets that result from a voluntary decision to move away from the strategic allocation from passive drifts that are simply the consequence of different behaviors of the asset classes in which the manager has invested. In the second case, the manager may not have been fully conscious that the actual allocation has moved away from the benchmark weights. Be it conscious (active) or not (passive), an observed divergence between the actual and the strategic asset allocation has consequences that have to be borne by the manager. Thus, the nature of a tactical change in the allocation must be fully accounted for in the analysis of performance, whatever its cause.

In the figure, we represent two layers of tactical decisions. The upper one represents the traditional first level of active allocation decisions on the basis of asset classes. On the lower one, we focus on the equity portfolio, and the manager decides to change the relative weights of the sectors represented in the benchmark index (whose composition is given on the left part of the figure). Note that, for this purpose, we normalize the equity sub-portfolio to a weight of 100% in order to properly focus on the changes in allocations adopted within this portfolio, irrespective of the tactical decisions made at the upper level.

(iv) *The selection level*: This is the lowest level of active portfolio management decisions. It involves the identification of the individual securities to invest in, as well as the actual amount of each investment. When it is applied to equities, this process is usually called "stock picking." The logic of such decisions is driven toward taking advantage of a mispricing of some assets compared to others. The active choice made by the manager is to overweight or underweight some specific securities in comparison with their weight in the benchmark. There is no timing issue involved here, as the purpose is far from trying to anticipate wide market movements.

The logic of this waterfall corresponds to a classical top-down asset management process, in which each lower level has to comply with the choices made upstream. Note that, in the case of a bottom-up portfolio management process, the tactical bets mostly arise as a collateral effect of the choice of the securities involved in the portfolio. Nevertheless, despite the fact that the global allocation might simply result from the superposition of the manager's atomistic portfolio construction choices, they cannot ignore its consequences and are always free to take action in order to get closer to the benchmark's allocation. On the other side of the spectrum, some fund or portfolio managers may decide to neglect the possibility of investing in direct lines (because of lack of expertise, interest, or mandate), and the waterfall would then truncate somewhere in the middle part of the chart. In this case, the last level of tactical decisions would then be considered as the selection stage.

What is the formal outcome of such a model? We have: (i) on top of the process, a *benchmark portfolio* (the policy or the strategic allocation, depending on the perspective) whose weights are supposed to reflect the absence of any active management decision by the manager; (ii) at each intermediary layer, deviations from the benchmark that are attributed to *market timing decisions* (a.k.a. allocation decisions), whichever its degree of granularity; and (iii) at the bottom of the process, individual investment choices that reflect the *security selection decisions* by the manager.

We can characterize three basic building blocks in order to perform the performance attribution analysis at a given point in time t:

- The individual asset return $R_{i,t}$;
- The individual asset weight within the portfolio $w_{P,i,t}$;
- The individual asset weight within the benchmark $w_{B,i,t}$.

This is the necessary and usually sufficient material needed to carry out most of the types of attribution analyses introduced in the next section. Starting from the individual positions, it is possible to progressively aggregate information to retrieve the benchmark and portfolio weights and returns for every group of assets, up to the most global allocation level that corresponds to the highest level of the active management decisions.

Finally, it is worth mentioning the two golden rules that must be satisfied at all times in a performance attribution system (Spaulding, 2003): (i) it should represent the active decision of the portfolio manager and (ii) it should ensure that the sum of the effects is equal to the portfolio excess return.

The VAS example (continued)

We take the Alloco fund, whose tactical bets are the most pronounced, as an illustration of the process. Considering the decisions made by the manager at the beginning of May, we can build a waterfall decision-making process similar to that of Figure 13-10 as shown in Figure 13-11.

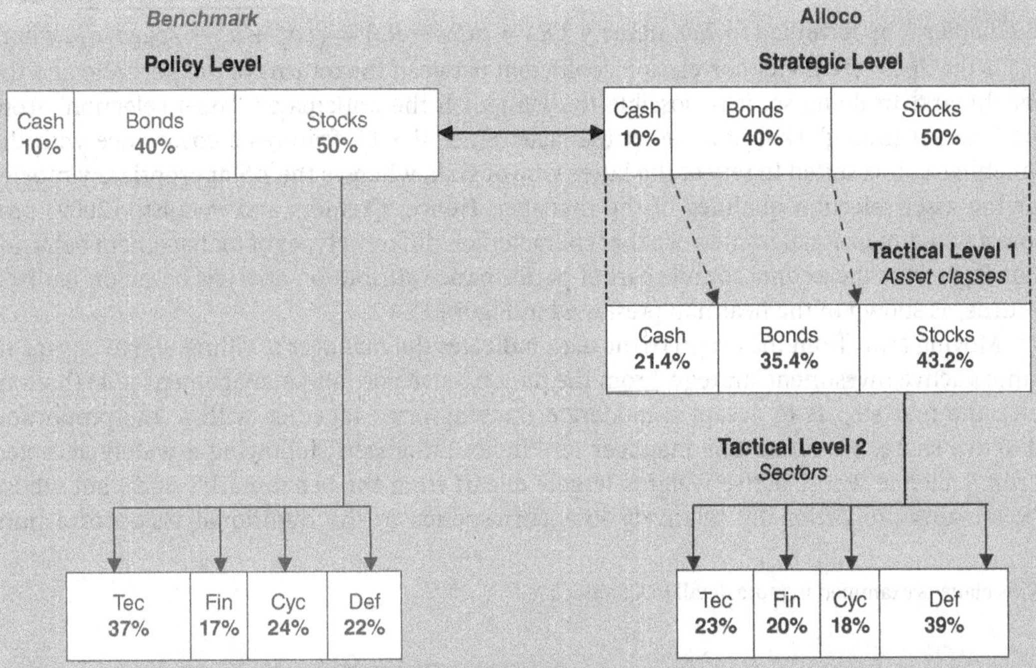

FIGURE 13-11 VAS example – Waterfall of the decision-making process for the Alloco fund (May).

13.2.2.2 Anticipating the drivers of performance

The importance of performance attribution does not limit itself to an *ex post* assessment of the effectiveness of a manager's investment decisions. It can also be viewed as a predictive tool. In particular, the portfolio's active trading decisions – before even turning to the full decomposition of a portfolio's excess return over its benchmark – are by themselves an indicator of the manager's ability to produce and reproduce abnormal returns over time. Without being by itself a performance measure, the portfolio's *Active share* defined by Cremers and Petajisto (2009), denoted by $AS_{P,t}$, seems to demonstrate its usefulness as an indicator of future performance in the field of mutual funds.[8] Its formula simply stands as

$$AS_{P,t} = \frac{1}{2}\sum_{i=1}^{N}\left|w_{P,i,t} - w_{B,i,t}\right| \tag{13-11}$$

where $w_{P,i,t}$ and $w_{B,i,t}$ denote the weights of asset i for $i = 1, \ldots, N$ in the actively managed portfolio and its benchmark, respectively. Because they mostly adopt an *ex ante* perspective, the authors do not explicitly aggregate this measure over time. Nevertheless, we can also recover the same type of expression for any period of reference T as the *Average Active share* aAS_P:

$$aAS_P = \frac{1}{2T}\sum_{t=1}^{T}\sum_{i=1}^{N}\left|w_{P,i,t} - w_{B,i,t}\right| \tag{13-12}$$

The authors consider this measure in conjunction with the notion of *Tracking error* defined in Chapter 3 by formula (13-21), namely $TE_P = \sigma(R_P - R_B) = \sqrt{\sigma_P^2 + \sigma_B^2 - 2\rho_{PB}\sigma_P\sigma_B}$, where ρ_{PB} is the linear (Pearson) correlation coefficient between the returns of the portfolio and the benchmark. In doing so, it is possible to distinguish the anticipated "asset selection" from the "market timing" skill of an asset manager. Since the TE features a covariance with the benchmark, it is suited to reflect the latter type of skill, whereas the AS appropriately proxies for the asset selection qualities of the manager. Hence, Cremers and Petajisto (2009) propose a two-dimensional framework that characterizes different types of management behavior that represents the *ex ante* counterpart of performance attribution analysis based on realized returns, as shown in the heatmap presented in Figure 13-12.

Moving away from the origin of the axes indicates the manager's willingness to engage in a more active investment strategy. From the pure passive portfolio management style (bottom left), the first step is to accept a moderate tracking error together with a low proportion of active share. We name this manager an "Index Enhancer," following a widely accepted term. Someone whose active weights largely depart from the benchmark's ones, but whose TE remains proportionally relatively low, corresponds to the traditional vision of a pure

[8]This claim is examined in more detail in Chapter 17.

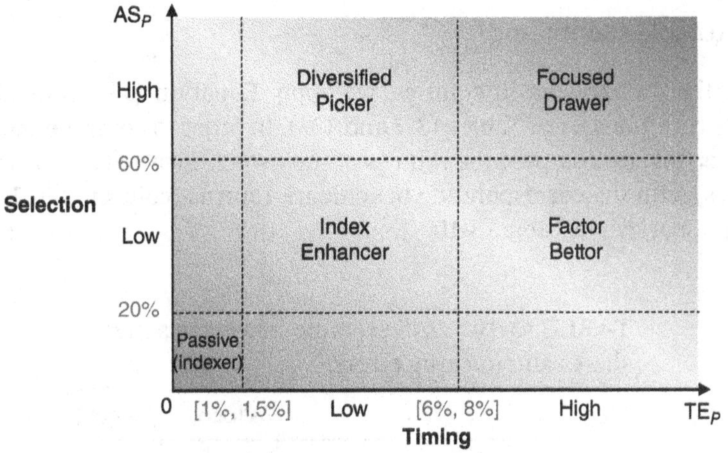

FIGURE 13-12 Heatmap of the *ex ante* active manager's anticipated skills. *Source:* Cremers and Petajisto (2009), Figure 1 – wording and figures added by the authors.

"Diversified Picker," who sticks to the mandate of closely following the risk factors underlying the benchmark, but whose major efforts are dedicated to picking the right assets. For these managers, a large fraction of the active risk is diversifiable, which explains the shift between the AS and TE measures. On the other hand, the manager who accepts a high tracking error but whose active weights do not follow the same trends is a "Factor Bettor," who mostly tries to anticipate wider market movements affecting the risk premiums and attempts to capture them. The last case remains, with the manager who simultaneously opts for a high TE and a high AS. According to Cremers and Petajisto (2009), such a manager simultaneously decides to engage in active individual asset selection (large active share) and bets on the remuneration of risk factors (large tracking error). This "Focused Drawer" is at the same time an active asset selector and market timer. Note that, according to the data of their Table 1, this category of extremely active fund managers would feature a relatively low proportion of the number of funds and their aggregate assets under management, i.e., circa 10–20%.

In their study focusing on equity fund managers, the authors consider that an AS lower than 20% (whose TE never exceeds 2%) cannot be distinguished from a pure index fund.[9] The "Low" active share category spans values from 20% to 60%. Beyond that proportion, managers are considered to be "High" on the active share criterion. Regarding the tracking error, the cutoff points are not clear in the study, but the "Low" range appears to span TE values from 1%/1.5% to somewhere between 6% and 8%. These values are indicative and specific to their sample, of course, but they reflect the way the asset management industry can be partitioned according to this pair of indicators.

[9]During the period of their study, the proportion of exchange traded funds (ETFs) of the aggregate mutual fund market was extremely low.

The VAS example (continued)

Focusing on the investments in equities, we apply Equation (13-12) on the Alloco and Selecto funds with the data of Tables 13-7 and 13-8. In order to compute the funds' respective tracking errors, we compare the returns of their stock-invested sub-portfolios (column 2 in the tables) with the corresponding benchmark returns (column 2 in Table 13-1). The results are summarized in Table 13-10.

TABLE 13-10 VAS example – Average active shares and tracking errors.

	Alloco	Selecto
Average active share aAS_P	7.8%	1.4%
Tracking error TE_P	1.8%	2.2%

The outcome of this table looks surprising in light of the interpretation of Cremers and Petajisto (2009). From the evolution of their holdings, it becomes clear that the manager of Alloco put most of the emphasis on market timing, whereas Selecto appears mostly as a good asset selector. Nonetheless, the values of aAS and TE suggest the opposite diagnosis. The interpretation lies in the fact that we are studying an intermediate portfolio layer: neither at the level of asset classes (this is the superior level) nor at the stage of individual security selection. The strong sector allocation activity of the Alloco fund is perceived as a security selection behavior although it still remains at the level of market timing. Because it generates a substantially higher (and different) return on its equity portfolio than the benchmark, the manager of the Selecto fund has a higher tracking error in spite of a very moderate timing behavior.

This example shows, at the same time, the limits of the *ex ante* approach and the need for a detailed and well-substantiated analysis of the influence of the actual weights and returns on the aggregate fund performance.

13.3 DECOMPOSING RISK-ADJUSTED PERFORMANCE RATIOS

In general, the granular analysis of performance rests on measures of risk-adjusted returns, like the generic alpha (measure of excess return of the portfolio over its benchmark, be it the original Jensen's one-factor alpha or the multifactor version studied in other chapters).

Section 13.2 has paved the way to a systematic performance decomposition framework known as "attribution analysis" using excess return, studied in detail in Chapter 14. Nevertheless, the same principles (identifying performance components, then applying the analysis on excess returns) can be transposed to other major performance measures, such as the Sharpe ratio and the Information ratio. These applications are examined below.

13.3.1 Granular analysis of the Sharpe ratio

Many consumers of financial information do not have access to or simply do not wish to use detailed holdings and/or transactions data at the most granular sub-portfolio level. A fund-of-fund manager, for instance, will generally not bother to fully look through all funds within their investment universe for every single point in time. Many non-professional investors can simply not afford to obtain and use the most detailed set of information about all components of their portfolio. Rather, they know the risk–return characteristics of their global portfolio and of their building blocks over a certain period – not necessarily with high frequencies, without feeling it necessary to go much further. However, at that level, applying attribution analysis techniques will probably be perceived as highly useful, and the first candidate for this purpose is naturally the Sharpe ratio. Steiner (2011) provides the keys to make sense of this analysis.

13.3.1.1 Contributions to the Sharpe ratio

As a first step of the analysis, Steiner (2011) proposes decomposing the Sharpe ratio of a portfolio of assets into a set of meaningful components. Consider, as usual, a portfolio P composed of N assets whose average weight in the portfolio during the reference period is w_i, for $i = 1, \ldots, N$. Its Sharpe ratio is, as per Chapter 3, defined as

$$\mathrm{SR}_P = \frac{\overline{R}_P - R_f}{\sigma_P} \tag{13-13}$$

where $\overline{R}_P$ and σ_P represent the mean and standard deviation of the portfolio returns, respectively, and R_f is the rate of return of the riskless asset, which is considered constant over the period.

The decomposition of the numerator is straightforward because of the linearity of the mean, i.e., $\overline{R}_P - R_f = \sum_{i=1}^{N} w_i(\overline{R}_i - R_f)$. Since the sum is distributive, we can then simply rewrite Equation (13-13) by multiplying the numerator and denominator of each term of the summation by the same factor $\rho_{iP}\sigma_i$, where σ_i is the volatility of asset i and ρ_{iP} is the correlation coefficient between the returns of asset i and those of the overall portfolio P.[10] The outcome of this simple adjustment enables us to obtain a meaningful decomposition:

$$\mathrm{SR}_P = \sum_{i=1}^{N} \underbrace{\frac{w_i \rho_{iP} \sigma_i}{\sigma_P}}_{\text{risk weight}} \times \underbrace{\frac{1}{\rho_{iP}} \frac{\overline{R}_i - R_f}{\sigma_i}}_{\text{component SR}} \tag{13-14}$$

As shown by Steiner (2011), this expression can be split into two parts:

- The *risk weight* $w_i' = \frac{w_i \rho_{iP} \sigma_i}{\sigma_P}$. To make sense of it, note that overall portfolio volatility can be partitioned according to its sum of marginal risk contributions through the following expression: $\sigma_P = \sum_{i=1}^{N} w_i \frac{\partial \sigma_P}{\partial w_i} = \sum_{i=1}^{N} w_i \rho_{iP} \sigma_i$. Thus, $\sum_{i=1}^{N} w_i' = 1$ and we can interpret w_i' as the relative contribution of asset i to the overall portfolio risk.
- The *component Sharpe ratio* $c_i(\mathrm{SR}_P)$, which is the product of the diversification effect $\frac{1}{\rho_{iP}}$ and the individual Sharpe ratio $\frac{\overline{R}_i - R_f}{\sigma_i}$. The less correlated the asset is with the portfolio, the greater its contribution of the Sharpe ratio. If ρ_{iP} is negative, the same reasoning holds as the risk weight is negative and thus a lower correlation increases the overall Sharpe ratio contribution.

Equation (13-14) represents an insightful way to partition the global portfolio Sharpe ratio. Because we can express it as $\mathrm{SR}_P = \sum_{i=1}^{N} w_i' \times c_i(\mathrm{SR}_P)$, it is possible to identify, for each sub-portfolio, what is its exact proportion of the global performance $p_i(\mathrm{SR}_P) = \frac{w_i' c_i(\mathrm{SR}_P)}{\mathrm{SR}_P}$ and compare it with its corresponding asset weight w_i. Those assets for which $p_i(\mathrm{SR}_P) > w_i$ are positive contributors to performance. The manager of the global portfolio should have reinforced this position in order to enhance the overall performance. If they believe that the risk–return properties that they have observed in the past are likely to be good predictors for the future, then this becomes a useful tool for the decision-making process regarding the allocation of the portfolio's resources between the different components, which is illustrated in Figure 13-13.

In this figure that represents the analysis for a portfolio with three sub-funds A, B, and C, it appears that Fund A has a smaller weight in the portfolio than its proportion in the global Sharpe ratio, i.e., $p_A(\mathrm{SR}_P) > w_A$. The manager can consider a reinforcement of the allocation in that fund at the expense of the one of Fund B whose contribution is below average. Increasing the weight of asset A will (i) reduce the weights of all other assets (if the change is done incrementally by reducing all assets proportionally); (ii) increase, in proportion to its weight times its standard deviation, the contribution of A to the overall Sharpe ratio; and (iii) slightly decrease the contribution of all other assets to the overall Sharpe ratio. This phenomenon is

---

[10]We can simply compute it as $\rho_{iP} = \frac{\mathrm{Cov}(R_i, R_P)}{\sigma_i \sigma_P} = \frac{\mathrm{Cov}\left(R_i, \sum_{i=1}^{N} w_i R_i\right)}{\sigma_i \sigma_P} = \frac{w_i \sigma_i^2 + \sum_{j \neq i} w_j \mathrm{Cov}(R_i, R_j)}{\sigma_i \sigma_P}$.

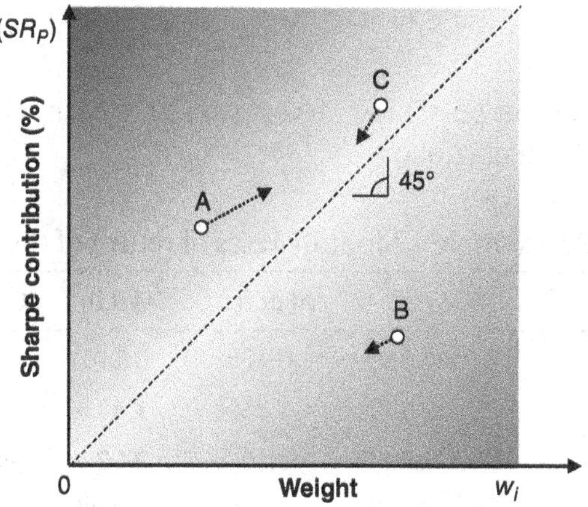

FIGURE 13-13 Heatmap of the Sharpe ratio contributors.

represented by the dotted arrows on the graph, which all converge to a corner of the graph (up-right for an increase, down-left for a decrease) with an intensity that is proportional to their volatility and the change in weight. Because of the diversification benefit of combining the assets with each other, it also suggests that the gradual portfolio rebalancing process (without necessarily trying to optimize the global Sharpe ratio, which can be done analytically but could involve negative weights) has to be done in a progressive way, starting with the most impactful changes, and gradually fine-tuning the portfolio composition.

The VAS example (continued)

The CIO is particularly interested in a fund of fund that has been bundled by one of the firm's experienced asset managers. It combines the three internal funds with an external one, called Complemo, whose performance seems to be outstanding. The monthly returns of this fund and their benchmark are reported in Table 13-11, mirroring the other funds' returns, together with their means, standard deviations, correlations with benchmark, and Sharpe ratios.

The current composition of the fund of funds is almost equally weighted between the four funds, with $w_{\mathbf{Verso}} = 22\%$, $w_{\mathbf{Alloco}} = 24\%$, $w_{\mathbf{Selecto}} = 28\%$, and $w_{\mathbf{Complemo}} = 26\%$. Using information from Table 13-11, we retrieve all necessary information in order to perform the decomposition of the Sharpe ratio for the global portfolio, which is summarized in Table 13-12.

Because of its low correlation with the global portfolio, the Complemo fund provides a very strong diversification effect. This reduces its risk weight and increases its component

(continued)

(continued)

Sharpe ratio. The other three portfolios are very similar to each other and thus have a strong correlation with the global portfolio.

TABLE 13-11 VAS example – Monthly rates of return of the four selected funds.

Month	Verso	Alloco	Selecto	Complemo	Benchmark
Jan	0.88%	0.42%	0.51%	0.12%	0.35%
Feb	2.14%	1.25%	1.43%	−0.36%	1.18%
Mar	2.68%	2.19%	2.02%	−0.56%	2.16%
Apr	0.93%	0.21%	0.36%	1.69%	0.09%
May	−2.77%	−2.73%	−3.09%	0.23%	−3.74%
Jun	1.64%	0.92%	1.85%	−1.06%	1.35%
Jul	−4.39%	−3.71%	−4.23%	0.11%	−4.44%
Aug	3.64%	3.92%	3.92%	5.32%	4.13%
Sep	2.81%	3.43%	2.54%	−0.96%	3.15%
Oct	1.33%	1.70%	2.20%	4.70%	1.69%
Nov	1.90%	2.29%	2.77%	−1.69%	2.47%
Dec	−2.99%	−2.10%	−2.49%	1.20%	−2.58%
Mean return	**7.80%**	**7.80%**	**7.80%**	**8.74%**	**5.80%**
Standard deviation	**8.96%**	**8.30%**	**8.92%**	**7.66%**	**9.43%**
Correlation w/ benchmark	**97.65%**	**99.54%**	**99.29%**	**16.86%**	
Sharpe ratio	**0.670**	**0.723**	**0.672**	**0.906**	**0.424**

TABLE 13-12 VAS example – Building blocks for the Sharpe ratio contribution – current allocation.

	Verso	Alloco	Selecto	Complemo	Portfolio
Weight	22%	24%	28%	26%	100%
Correlation with portfolio	93.68%	95.70%	96.14%	42.92%	100%
Risk weight	26.34%	27.21%	34.26%	12.19%	100%
Component SR	0.715	0.755	0.699	2.112	0.891
Proportion of global SR	**21.13%**	**23.07%**	**26.89%**	**28.91%**	**100%**

Using the same analysis, the CIO attempts to determine the contributions to the overall Sharpe ratio when a weight of 1% is removed from the allocation to the first three funds, while the weight of Complemo increases by 3%. The outcome is shown in Table 13-13, which shares the same structure as Table 13-12.

TABLE 13-13 VAS example – Building blocks for the Sharpe ratio contribution – alternative allocation.

	Verso	Alloco	Selecto	Complemo	Portfolio
Weight	21%	23%	27%	29%	100%
Correlation with portfolio	92.27%	94.55%	95.01%	46.58%	100%
Risk weight	25.28%	26.30%	33.34%	15.07%	100%
Component SR	0.726	0.764	0.708	1.946	0.914
Proportion of global SR	**20.08%**	**22.01%**	**25.82%**	**32.10%**	**100%**

The global Sharpe ratio has greatly improved thanks to the reallocations, even slightly exceeding that of the best fund (Complemo). It clearly follows from the exercise that the weight of this new fund should be reinforced further. We can graphically follow the evolution of the proportion that each fund accounts for in the global Sharpe ratio, as shown in Figure 13-14.

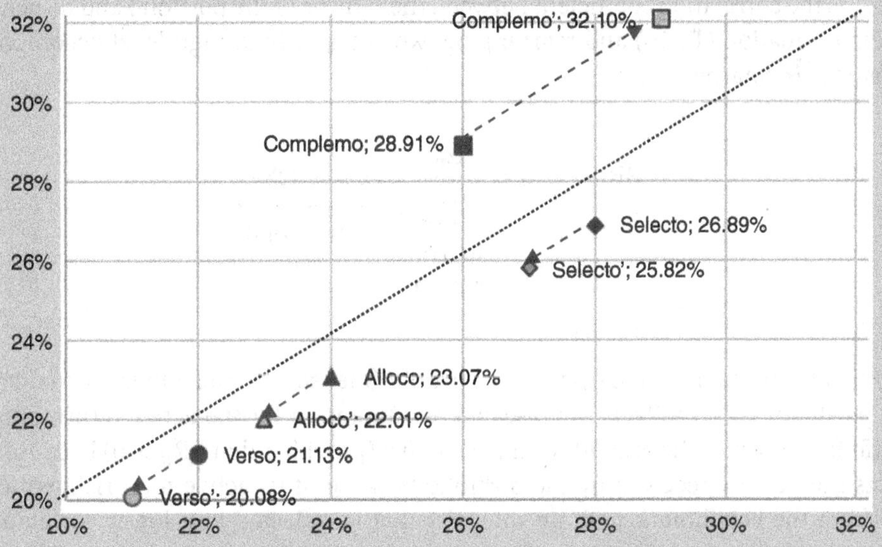

FIGURE 13-14 VAS example – Evolution of the proportions of the global Sharpe ratio.

13.3.1.2 Sharpe ratio attribution

For the second step of Steiner's (2011) analysis, we have to involve the benchmark and its own Sharpe ratio. We saw in Chapter 3 how to statistically test the significance of the difference between the Sharpe ratios of two portfolios. Sharpe ratio attribution serves a different purpose: we want to identify the responsibility of each of the components for the observed difference. The outcome could be radically different from that of the previous subsection because the correlations that matter are mostly those with the benchmark instead of those with the portfolio itself.

The objective proposed by Steiner (2011) is to explain the difference between the Sharpe ratios of the portfolio and the benchmark, defined as

$$\mathrm{SR}_P - \mathrm{SR}_B = \frac{\overline{R}_P - R_f}{\sigma_P} - \frac{\overline{R}_B - R_f}{\sigma_B} \tag{13-15}$$

The link between the portfolio and the benchmark can be generically represented through the traditional single-factor regression output, namely:

$$\overline{R}_P - R_f = \alpha_P + \beta_P(\overline{R}_B - R_f) = \alpha_P + \rho_{PB}\sigma_P \mathrm{SR}_B \tag{13-16}$$

where ρ_{PB} is the correlation coefficient between the returns of the portfolio and its benchmark. By dividing Equation (13-16) and rearranging, we obtain a first, high-level decomposition of the difference in Sharpe ratios:

$$\mathrm{SR}_P - \mathrm{SR}_B = \underbrace{\frac{\alpha_P}{\sigma_P}}_{\substack{\text{active}\\ \text{return}}} + \underbrace{(\rho_{\mathrm{PB}} - 1)\mathrm{SR}_B}_{\substack{\text{active total}\\ \text{risk}}} \tag{13-17}$$

The first term has the same sign as the portfolio's Jensen's alpha, but it is penalized by the level of portfolio risk. It reflects the rescaled remuneration for the active return obtained by the portfolio manager. The second term is negative (provided that $\mathrm{SR}_B > 0$) because $\rho_{\mathrm{PB}} \leq 1$. It reflects the penalty received by the portfolio because of its active total risk, which drives it away from the benchmark with an intensity that is reflected in a lower correlation. This structure – a split between the reward for active return and the penalty for active total risk – is the one sought after for the complete look through of the fund's performance.

The portfolio alpha can be partitioned linearly: $\alpha_P = \sum_{i=1}^{N} w_i \alpha_i$. The portfolio correlation with the benchmark can also be decomposed linearly by noting that $\rho_{PB} = \beta_P \frac{\sigma_B}{\sigma_P} = \sum_{i=1}^{N} w_i \beta_i \frac{\sigma_B}{\sigma_P} = \sum_{i=1}^{N} w_i \rho_{iB} \frac{\sigma_i}{\sigma_P}$. Thus, both the active return and active risk of Equation (13-17) can be expressed as a function of each asset:

$$SR_P - SR_B = \sum_{i=1}^{N} \left[w_i' \times \frac{1}{\rho_{iP}} \frac{\alpha_i}{\sigma_i} + w_i \times \left(\rho_{iB} \frac{\sigma_i}{\sigma_P} - 1 \right) SR_B \right] \tag{13-18}$$

where, as before, $w_i' = \frac{w_i \rho_{iP} \sigma_i}{\sigma_P}$ is the risk weight and, by analogy, $\frac{1}{\rho_{iP}} \frac{\alpha_i}{\sigma_i}$ is the component active return, while $\rho_{iB} \frac{\sigma_i}{\sigma_P} - 1$ can be interpreted as the component specific risk of asset i.

Because both active risk and active return can be expressed as a weighted sum of the respective components due to each asset, a full portfolio diagnosis of the drivers of the Sharpe ratio difference is possible. This allows the analyst to go one step beyond the mere Sharpe ratio decomposition.

The VAS example (continued)

The current and alternative fund-of-funds allocations examined in Tables 13-12 and 13-13 are further investigated regarding the attribution of the differences in Sharpe ratios with the benchmark. For the current allocation, the difference in Sharpe ratios is equal to $SR_{cur} - SR_B = 0.891 - 0.424 = 0.467$, whereas the alternative allocation delivers a delta of $SR_{alt} - SR_B = 0.914 - 0.424 = 0.490$.

The application of the attribution formula of Equation (13-18) leaves the results graphically represented in Figure 13-15.

The passage from the current to the alternative allocation leads to an increase of 0.023 in the portfolio Sharpe ratio. The almost single contributor to the increase is Complemo, whose active return contribution increases from 0.237 to 0.270 (+0.033) but whose active risk decreases from −0.090 to −0.100 (−0.01). An interesting phenomenon occurs with the other three funds. Their component specific risk is very positive thanks to their high volatility and very high correlation with the benchmark. Even though the global active risk is negative, only Complemo has a negative component-specific risk.

(continued)

(continued)

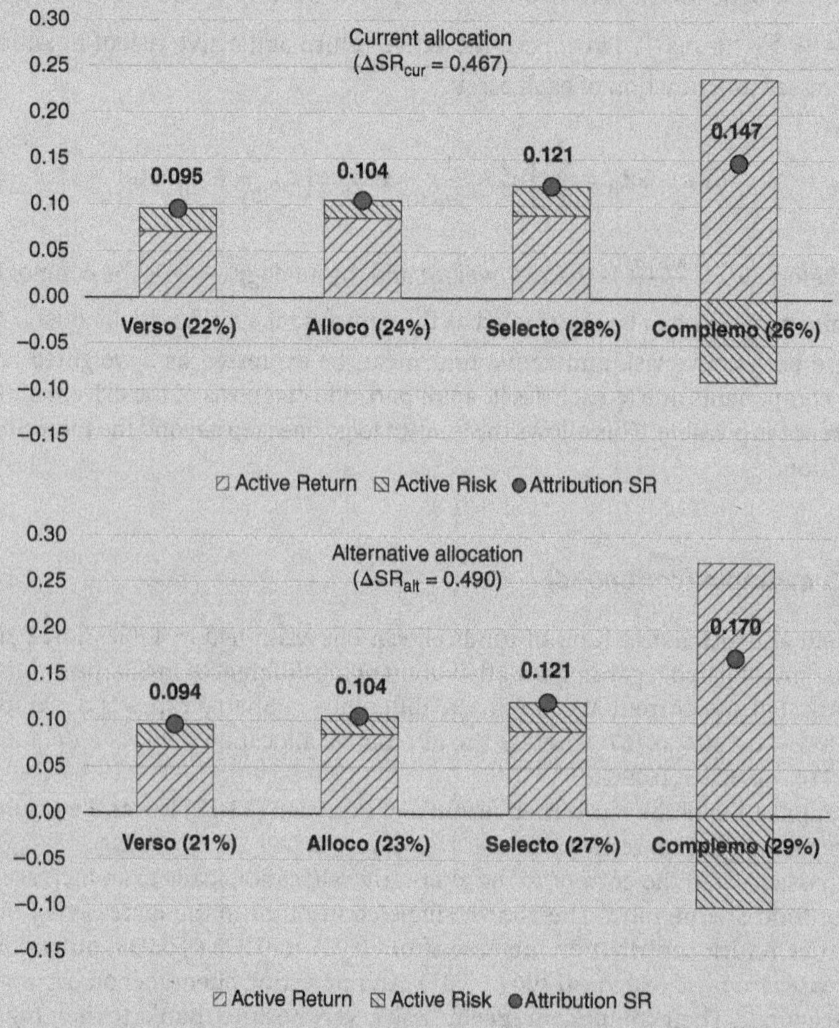

FIGURE 13-15 VAS example – Fund-by-fund attribution of the difference in Sharpe ratios.

13.3.2 Granular analysis of the Information ratio

The existence of a benchmark portfolio, be it self-reported or analytical (as discussed in Chapter 7), naturally calls for the granular investigation of the performance measure that is more specifically designed for this case, namely the Information ratio. We proceed in two steps. First, we develop the principles of IR attribution analysis and then examine how this analysis must be adapted in the case where the self-reported and analytical benchmarks differ.[11]

13.3.2.1 Global Information ratio attribution

The principles of IR attribution analysis proposed, among others, by Menchero (2006/2007), look extremely similar to the Sharpe ratio contribution analysis presented in Section 13.3.1.1.

Indeed, remembering that the portfolio volatility $\sigma_P \equiv \sigma(R_P)$ is nothing more than a special case of the Tracking error $\text{TE}_P \equiv \sigma(R_P - R_B)$, where the benchmark is set to be the risk-free asset, i.e., $R_B = R_f$, the Sharpe ratio can also be viewed as a specific instance of the Information ratio. Since the IR is already a risk-adjusted measure of a differential return, it already includes the benchmark return, and thus the IR contribution analysis is equivalent to its attribution analysis.

Adapting Equation (13-14) to this new context leads to the following expression:

$$\text{IR}_P = \sum_{i=1}^{N} \underbrace{\frac{w_i \rho_{\text{TE}_i\text{TE}_P} \text{TE}_i}{\text{TE}_P}}_{\text{active risk weight}} \times \underbrace{\frac{1}{\rho_{\text{TE}_i\text{TE}_P}} \frac{\overline{R}_i - \overline{R}_B}{\text{TE}_i}}_{\text{component IR}} \tag{13-19}$$

where $\rho_{\text{TE}_i\text{TE}_P} = \frac{\text{Cov}(R_i - R_B, R_P - R_B)}{\text{TE}_i \text{TE}_P}$ is the correlation between the asset and the portfolio's excess returns, and $\frac{\overline{R}_i - \overline{R}_B}{\text{TE}_i}$ is the Information ratio associated with each portfolio component i. We can therefore define the notion of "active risk weight" $aw_i^{\prime} = \frac{w_i \rho_{\text{TE}_i\text{TE}_P} \text{TE}_i}{\text{TE}_P}$, whose behavior may substantially differ from the risk weight $w_i^{\prime}$ identified in the context of the decomposition of the Sharpe ratio.

The VAS example (continued)

The contrast between the very high correlation coefficients of the three original funds with their benchmark and the relatively low correlation observed with Complemo suggests that the analysis of the Information ratio would deliver very different results from the ones regarding the Sharpe ratio. Table 13-14 shows, for the current allocation, the difference in dispersion of the (total) risk weights reported in Table 13-12 and the active risk weights obtained by applying formula (13-19).

(continued)

[11]The implementation of classical attribution methods to the case of the IR is discussed in Chapter 14.

(continued)

TABLE 13-14 VAS example – Total risk weights versus active risk weights.

	Verso	Alloco	Selecto	Complemo
Weight w_i	**22%**	**24%**	**28%**	**26%**
Correlation with portfolio returns ρ_{iP}	93.68%	95.70%	96.14%	42.92%
(Total) risk weight w'_i	**26.34%**	**27.21%**	**34.26%**	**12.19%**
Correlation with portfolio differential returns $\rho_{TE_i TE_P}$	26.88%	69.12%	51.92%	97.75%
Active risk weight aw'_i	**3.62%**	**6.99%**	**5.22%**	**84.18%**

The phenomenon that explains the strong difference between the total and active risk weights is quite simple. Because of its singular behavior, Complemo has a strong influence on the variability of the excess return of the portfolio over its benchmark. In other words, its returns largely explain the global tracking difference. This translates into a very high value of $\rho_{TE_i TE_P}$ and, in turn, a high active risk weight.

Under the current allocation, the portfolio Information ratio is equal to $IR_P = \frac{2.25\%}{3.35\%} = 0.670$, whereas it reaches a value of $IR_P = \frac{2.25\%}{3.66\%} = 0.622$ under the alternative allocation. The only reason for this degradation is the increase in the tracking error induced by the higher weight given to Complemo, whose specific risk is larger than those of the other funds. This can be visually checked in Figure 13-16, which represents the split of the total IR under both allocations with pie charts.

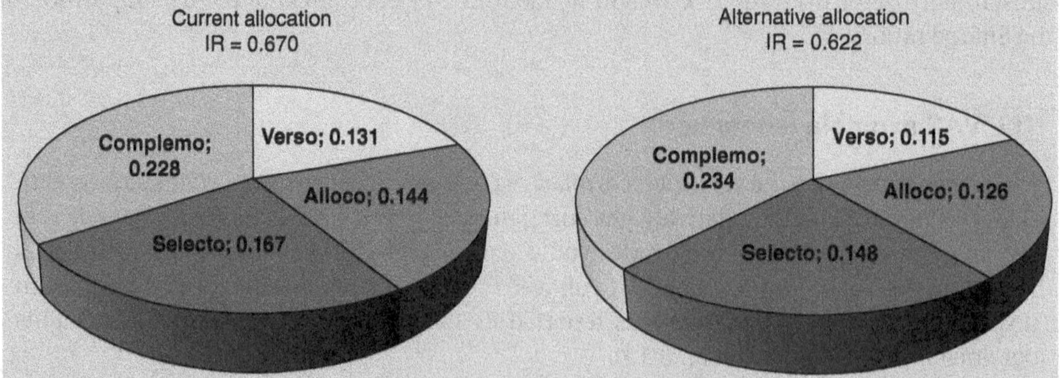

FIGURE 13-16 VAS example – Pie charts of the Information ratio attribution.

The increase in the Complemo weight allows the manager to inflate the contribution of that particular fund to the total IR, but this comes at the expense of a more than proportional drop in the contributions of the other three funds, with a negative overall effect on the performance. This contrasts with the results of the Sharpe ratio attribution analysis, which showed an improvement brought by the alternative allocation on that dimension.

13.3.2.2 Factor-based Information ratio attribution

Building on the principles of the Information ratio attribution, Menchero and Poduri (2008) propose a useful extension to risk-adjusted performance attribution in a multifactor setup. Their framework allows the decomposition of the portfolio return in three parts: the one that corresponds to the self-reported (that they call 'custom') benchmark returns, the one that corresponds to the incremental return obtained by the analytical benchmark, and the idiosyncratic part.

The starting point of the analysis is the expression of the portfolio excess return over its benchmark denoted by $r_{P,t} \equiv R_{P,t} - R_{B,t}$ through an expression that resembles the generic Equation (7-3) of the multifactor model presented in Chapter 7, adapting the notation to our purposes:

$$r_{P,t} = \sum_{k=1}^{K} \beta_{P,k} F_{k,t} + \beta_{P,0,t} \tag{13-20}$$

where each $\beta_{P,k}$ represents the sensitivity of the excess return $r_{P,t}$ to the kth analytical factor return denoted by $F_{k,t}$, and $\beta_{P,0,t} = \beta_{P,0} + \varepsilon_{P,t}$ is the portfolio's idiosyncratic excess return, which is equal to the sum of the constant idiosyncratic abnormal return $\beta_{P,0}$ and a pure noise term $\varepsilon_{P,t}$ with $\mathrm{E}(\varepsilon_{P,t}) = 0$ and $\mathrm{Cov}(\varepsilon_{P,t}, F_{k,t}) = 0\ \forall k$. Drilling down the portfolio at the level of its individual components, we can further characterize $\beta_{P,k} = \sum_{i=1}^{N} w_i \beta_{i,k}$ and $\beta_{P,0,t} = \sum_{i=1}^{N} w_i(\beta_{i,0} + \varepsilon_{i,t})$.

Since $r_{P,t}$ is an excess return, we can represent the portfolio's Information ratio as $\mathrm{IR}_P = \frac{\bar{r}_P}{\sigma(r_P)}$. Our objective is thus to properly decompose this expression into meaningful granular components. However, expression (13-20) represents the outcome of a statistical multifactor model. The choice of the factors is driven by the quest for the best set of explanatory variables and the most representative return-generating process. It does not necessarily use the same types of factors and/or the same sensitivity coefficients as for the determination of the self-reported benchmark. Knowing that the excess return (left-hand side of expression (13-20)) is invariant to the choice of factors, the alternative factor model that applies to the "real life" expression of the return-generating process should be written as

$$r_{P,t} = \sum_{l=1}^{L} b_{P,l} I_{l,t} + b_{P,0,t} \tag{13-21}$$

where each $b_{P,l} = \sum_{i=1}^{N} w_i b_{i,l}$ represents the sensitivity of the excess return $r_{P,t}$ to the lth custom index return denoted by $I_{l,t}$, and, as before, $b_{P,0,t} = b_{P,0} + \eta_{P,t} = \sum_{i=1}^{N} w_i(b_{i,0} + \eta_{i,t})$ is the portfolio's idiosyncratic excess return with this new universe of factors.

The model of Equation (13-21) would in general be less powerful than Equation (13-20) in explaining the systematic part of the returns, but it is not the objective. Rather, it aims at providing the most meaningful insight regarding the portfolio manager's active decisions on the factors that are economically relevant according to their mandate.

Reconciling these two multifactor models in an attribution framework is not as trivial as it may seem. A tempting solution would indeed be to merge them and consider a set of $K + L$ factors (removing the identical ones, if any) and re-estimating the model. Because both specifications are supposed to be substitutes to each other, the level of collinearity of the variables would make the estimation difficult. Furthermore, there is a hierarchy in the models: even though Equation (13-20) might be more accurate, the one that matters for the analyst and the investor is unequivocally the specification of Equation (13-21). It is thus necessary to use the information of the analytical model without damaging the picture delivered by the custom factor model.

The solution proposed by Menchero and Poduri (2008) is indeed to merge the two models, but only after having orthogonalized the analytical factors with the custom ones. By properly regressing each analytical factor $F_{k,t}$ on the whole set of custom indexes $I_{l,t}$, we ensure that the residual of the regression, denoted by $\tilde{F}_{k,t}$, becomes uncorrelated with each index, i.e., $\text{Cov}(I_{l,t}, \tilde{F}_{k,t}) = 0$. After this operation, the extended model has to be re-estimated again and adopts the following final structure:

$$r_{P,t} = \sum_{l=1}^{L} b_{P,l} I_{l,t} + \sum_{k=1}^{K} \tilde{\beta}_{P,k} \tilde{F}_{k,t} + \tilde{b}_{P,0,t} \tag{13-22}$$

where $\tilde{\beta}_{P,k} = \sum_{i=1}^{N} w_i \tilde{\beta}_{i,k}$ represents the sensitivity of the excess return $r_{P,t}$ to the kth orthogonalized analytical factor return and $\tilde{b}_{P,0,t} = \tilde{b}_{P,0} + \nu_{P,t} = \sum_{i=1}^{N} w_i(\tilde{b}_{i,0} + \nu_{i,t})$ has the same structure as before. Additionally, it is necessary to constrain the parameters so that $\sum_{i=1}^{N} b_{i,l}\tilde{\beta}_{i,k} = 0\ \forall k, l$ in order to ensure the zero correlation of the residual returns.

By construction, the correlations between the three blocks of Equation (13-22) are all set to zero. Thanks to this property, we can now safely apply the same principles as before for the decomposition of the Information ratio:

$$\text{IR}_P = aw_P^{(b)}\text{IR}_P^{(b)} + aw_P^{(\tilde{\beta})}\text{IR}_P^{(\tilde{\beta})} + aw_P^{(\tilde{b})}\text{IR}_P^{(\tilde{b})} \tag{13-23}$$

where $aw_P^{(b)}$, $aw_P^{(\tilde{\beta})}$, and $aw_P^{(\tilde{b})}$ are the portfolio's active risk weights of the custom factors, the orthogonalized analytical factors, and the idiosyncratic component, respectively, defined as

$$aw_P^{(b)} = \sum_{l=1}^{L} aw_P^{(b_l)} = \sum_{l=1}^{L} \frac{\sum_{i=1}^{N} w_i b_{i,l} \sigma_{I_l} \rho_{I_l r_P}}{\sigma_{r_P}} \tag{13-24a}$$

$$aw_P^{(\tilde{\beta})} = \sum_{k=1}^{K} aw_P^{(\tilde{\beta}_k)} = \sum_{k=1}^{K} \frac{\sum_{i=1}^{N} w_i \tilde{\beta}_{i,k} \sigma_{\tilde{F}_k} \rho_{\tilde{F}_k r_P}}{\sigma_{r_P}} \tag{13-24b}$$

$$aw_P^{(\tilde{b})} = \sum_{i=1}^{N} aw_i^{(\tilde{b}_i)} = \sum_{i=1}^{N} w_i \frac{\sigma_{\nu_i} \rho_{\nu_i r_P}}{\sigma_{r_P}} \tag{13-24c}$$

and $\mathrm{IR}_P^{(b)}$, $\mathrm{IR}_P^{(\tilde{\beta})}$, and $\mathrm{IR}_P^{(\tilde{b})}$ are the portfolio's component Information ratios of the custom factors, the orthogonalized analytical factors, and the idiosyncratic component, respectively, defined as

$$\mathrm{IR}_P^{(b)} = \frac{1}{aw_P^{(b)}} \sum_{l=1}^{L} aw_P^{(b_l)} \mathrm{IR}_P^{(b_l)} \tag{13-25a}$$

$$\mathrm{IR}_P^{(\tilde{\beta})} = \frac{1}{aw_P^{(\tilde{\beta})}} \sum_{k=1}^{K} aw_P^{(\tilde{\beta}_k)} \mathrm{IR}_P^{(\tilde{\beta}_k)} \tag{13-25b}$$

$$\mathrm{IR}_P^{(\tilde{b})} = \frac{1}{aw_P^{(\tilde{b})}} \sum_{i=1}^{N} aw_i^{(\tilde{b}_i)} \mathrm{IR}_P^{(\tilde{b}_i)} \tag{13-25c}$$

in which, for each equation, each individual component Information ratio is simply defined as $\mathrm{IR}_P^{(x)} = \frac{1}{\rho_{r_x r_P}} \frac{\bar{r}_x}{\sigma_{r_x}}$ for $r_{x,t} = b_{P,l} I_{l,t}$ (custom factors), $r_{x,t} = \tilde{\beta}_{P,k} \tilde{F}_{k,t}$ (orthogonalized analytical factors), and $r_{x,t} = \tilde{b}_{P,0,t}$ (idiosyncratic component). The full granular analysis per asset results from breaking up the portfolio factor betas as the weighted sum for each asset beta.

It is also worth noting that the simplified version of the Menchero and Poduri (2008) analysis with $K = 1$ and $L = 1$ can make sense as well. In that case, the formulas become largely streamlined. The portfolio excess return is written as follows:

$$r_{P,t} = b_P I_t + \tilde{\beta}_P \tilde{F}_t + \tilde{b}_{P,0,t} \tag{13-26}$$

where $b_P = \sum_{i=1}^{N} w_i b_i$, $\tilde{\beta}_P = \sum_{i=1}^{N} w_i \tilde{\beta}_i$ and $\tilde{b}_{P,0,t} = \sum_{i=1}^{N} w_i(\tilde{b}_{i,0} + \nu_{i,t})$. Note that the constraint $\sum_{i=1}^{N} b_i \tilde{\beta}_i = 0$ still holds.

The decomposition of the Information ratio of Equation (13-23) can be performed immediately at the individual asset level, without having to aggregate the effects per factor:

$$aw_P^{(b)} = \frac{\sum_{i=1}^{N} w_i b_i \sigma_I \rho_{Ir_P}}{\sigma_{r_P}}; aw_P^{(\tilde{\beta})} = \frac{\sum_{i=1}^{N} w_i \tilde{\beta}_i \sigma_{\tilde{F}} \rho_{\tilde{F}r_P}}{\sigma_{r_P}}; aw_P^{(\tilde{b})} = \frac{\sum_{i=1}^{N} w_i \sigma_{v_i} \rho_{v_i r_P}}{\sigma_{r_P}} \quad (13\text{-}27)$$

Finally, the component Information ratios can also be immediately expressed for each individual security:

$$IR_P^{(b)} = \frac{1}{aw_P^{(b)}} \sum_{i=1}^{N} aw_i^{(b)} IR_P^{(b_i)} \quad (13\text{-}28a)$$

$$IR_P^{(\tilde{\beta})} = \frac{1}{aw_P^{(\tilde{\beta})}} \sum_{i=1}^{N} aw_i^{(\tilde{\beta})} IR_P^{(\tilde{\beta}_i)} \quad (13\text{-}28b)$$

$$IR_P^{(\tilde{b})} = \frac{1}{aw_P^{(\tilde{b})}} \sum_{i=1}^{N} aw_i^{(\tilde{b})} IR_P^{(\tilde{b}_i)} \quad (13\text{-}28c)$$

where, in the same spirit as before, $IR_P^{(x_i)} = \frac{1}{\rho_{r_{x_i} r_P}} \frac{\bar{r}_{x_i}}{\sigma_{r_{x_i}}}$ for $r_{x_i,t} = w_i b_i I_t$ (custom factor), $r_{x_i,t} = w_i \tilde{\beta}_i \tilde{F}_t$ (orthogonalized analytical factor), and $r_{x_i,t} = w_i(\tilde{b}_{i,0} + v_{i,t})$ (idiosyncratic component).

Naturally, in the absence of a statistical factor analysis, the simple use of the custom factor analysis removes one dimension of the analysis and leaves the very same set of formulas but without the term using the orthogonalized factor loadings $\tilde{\beta}$.

In a nutshell, this whole procedure serves one major goal: to use as much information as possible for the full understanding of the three dimensions of a manager's observed abnormal return. The procedure that includes the analytical factors in the analysis might seem overly sophisticated, but it allows the analyst to distinguish between, on the one hand, the manager's ability to reap the premium returns that are not included in the self-reported factors, which is mostly the outcome of an allocation decision (timing), and, on the other hand, the superior selection of securities in the portfolio that reveals a selection skill. Thus, even at the seemingly complicated level of a risk-adjusted differential return, it is possible to implement a meaningful attribution analysis.

Key Takeaways and Equations

- The origin of performance attribution can be traced back to Fama's (1972) *decomposition framework* in the context of the Capital Asset Pricing Model. He distinguishes three levels of risk that matter for the investor:
  - Total risk $\sigma_P \equiv \sigma(R_P)$;
  - Actual systematic risk $\sigma_{\rho P} \equiv \beta_P \sigma_M = \rho_{PM} \sigma_P$;

- Target investor risk $\sigma_P^{(j)}$.

For each of these risk types, the *ex post* required return is obtained by applying the CAPM, and the global portfolio required return can be split into three additive components:

$$R^*(\sigma_P) = R_f + \lambda_P + \delta_P \tag{13-2}$$

where $\lambda_P = R^*(\sigma_{\rho P}) - R_f$ is the risk premium and $\delta_P = R^*(\sigma_{\rho P}) - R^*(\sigma_{\rho P})$ is the diversification premium.

- The relevant portfolio performance measure depends on the point of view of the investor. If they care about systematic risk, it should be *Jensen's alpha* α_P; if they care about total risk, without indicating their risk aversion, it should be the *Total risk alpha* $\mathrm{T}\alpha_P$; and if they care about total risk and wish their risk aversion to be accounted for, it should be the *Target volatility alpha* $\mathrm{V}\alpha_P^j$. The ordering of these three performance measures is always the same:

$$\mathrm{V}\alpha_P^j < \mathrm{T}\alpha_P < \alpha_P \tag{13-6}$$

- It is further possible to isolate the market timing behavior of the portfolio manager by a formula that looks close to the Cornell performance measure:

$$\tau_P = \frac{1}{T}\sum_{t=1}^{T}(\beta_{P,t} - \overline{\beta}_P)(R_{M,t} - \overline{R}_M) = \frac{1}{T}\sum_{t=1}^{T}(\beta_{P,t} - \overline{\beta}_P)R_{M,t} \tag{13-7}$$

- In order to set up a performance attribution method, it is first necessary to apply the *performance contribution analysis*, which consists of isolating the contributors to the portfolio return defined as

$$c_i(R_{P,t}) = w_{P,i,t}R_{i,t} \tag{13-8}$$

Similarly, the contribution of an asset to the return of its own asset class k to the global portfolio return is defined as

$$c_i(R_{P,k,t}) = \frac{w_{P,i,t}}{\sum_{i\in k} w_{P,i,t}}R_{i,t} \tag{13-10}$$

- The purpose of performance attribution analysis is fourfold: (i) to quantify the consequences of the decisions made by the portfolio manager, (ii) to gain a quantitative understanding of the drivers of the manager's performance relative to their benchmark, (iii) to make transparent the dialogue between the portfolio manager and their client, and (iv) to provide senior management with a basis for incentive management or the setting of quantifiable objectives.

(continued)

(continued)

- The most intuitive way to distinguish the levels of portfolio management decisions for which attribution analysis can be performed is to consider four levels: (i) policy, (ii) strategic, (iii) tactical (which can be split into two layers depending on the granularity), and (iv) selection.
- An attribution model should feature three main components: a *benchmark portfolio*, deviations attributed to *market timing decisions*, and deviations attributed to *security selection decisions*. In order to obtain these components, three building blocks are required:
  - The individual asset return $R_{i,t}$;
  - The individual asset weight within the portfolio $w_{P,i,t}$;
  - The individual asset weight within the benchmark $w_{B,i,t}$;
- From an *ex ante* perspective, the notions of *Average Active share* defined as

$$\text{aAS}_P = \frac{1}{2T}\sum_{t=1}^{T}\sum_{i=1}^{N}\left|w_{P,i,t} - w_{B,i,t}\right| \tag{13-12}$$

  and *Tracking error* TE_P are potential predictors of the selectivity skill and market timing skill of a portfolio manager, respectively. Cremers and Petajisto (2009) propose a two-dimensional framework that characterizes different archetypes of management behavior depending on the values of these two indicators. We name them "Index Enhancer" (low aAS_P and low TE_P), "Diversified Picker" (high aAS_P and low TE_P), "Factor Bettor" (low aAS_P and high TE_P), and "Focused Drawer" (high aAS_P and high TE_P).
- It is possible to perform a meaningful granular analysis on the Sharpe ratio in order to isolate the influence of its constituents on the overall performance.
  - The first stage of the process consists of performing the *Sharpe ratio contribution analysis*. Its outcome delivers the following decomposition:

$$\text{SR}_P = \sum_{i=1}^{N}\underbrace{\frac{w_i\rho_{iP}\sigma_i}{\sigma_P}}_{\text{risk weight}} \times \underbrace{\frac{1}{\rho_{iP}}\frac{\overline{R}_i - R_f}{\sigma_i}}_{\text{component SR}} \tag{13-14}$$

  - The second stage consists of examining the difference between the Sharpe ratios of the portfolio and its benchmark through the *Sharpe ratio attribution analysis*. Its most granular output is

$$\text{SR}_P - \text{SR}_B = \sum_{i=1}^{N}\left[w_i' \times \frac{1}{\rho_{iP}}\frac{\alpha_i}{\sigma_i} + w_i \times \left(\rho_{iB}\frac{\sigma_i}{\sigma_P} - 1\right)\text{SR}_B\right] \tag{13-18}$$

- The same principle can also be applied to the *Information ratio attribution analysis.* In that case, the contribution analysis is sufficient as the IR is already expressed as a measure of risk-adjusted performance over the benchmark:

$$\mathrm{IR}_P = \sum_{i=1}^{N} \underbrace{\frac{w_i \rho_{\mathrm{TE}_i \mathrm{TE}_P} \mathrm{TE}_i}{\mathrm{TE}_P}}_{\text{active risk weight}} \times \underbrace{\frac{1}{\rho_{\mathrm{TE}_i \mathrm{TE}_P}} \frac{\overline{R}_i - \overline{R}_B}{\mathrm{TE}_i}}_{\text{component IR}} \tag{13-19}$$

- In the case of a multifactor modeling approach, the IR attribution analysis must be adapted in order to account for the potential difference between the statistical factor analysis and the self-reported (custom) factor analysis. After orthogonalizing the first set of factors with the second ones, the excess return of the portfolio over its benchmark $r_{P,t} \equiv R_{P,t} - R_{B,t}$ can be represented as follows:

$$r_{P,t} = \sum_{l=1}^{L} b_{P,l} I_{l,t} + \sum_{k=1}^{K} \tilde{\beta}_{P,k} \tilde{F}_{k,t} + \tilde{b}_{P,0,t} \tag{13-22}$$

In that case, the portfolio IR can be split into three parts, and the attribution analysis can be performed using the same principles as before:

$$\mathrm{IR}_P = \mathrm{aw}_P^{(b)} \mathrm{IR}_P^{(b)} + \mathrm{aw}_P^{(\tilde{\beta})} \mathrm{IR}_P^{(\tilde{\beta})} + \mathrm{aw}_P^{(\tilde{b})} \mathrm{IR}_P^{(\tilde{b})} \tag{13-23}$$

- In the special case of a single-factor model, the formulation of the excess return can be simplified to

$$r_{P,t} = b_P I_t + \tilde{\beta}_P \tilde{F}_t + \tilde{b}_{P,0,t} \tag{13-26}$$

and the same analysis as Equation (13-23) can be carried out with the active weights defined as

$$\mathrm{aw}_P^{(b)} = \frac{\sum_{i=1}^{N} w_i b_i \sigma_I \rho_{I r_P}}{\sigma_{r_P}}; \mathrm{aw}_P^{(\tilde{\beta})} = \frac{\sum_{i=1}^{N} w_i \tilde{\beta}_i \sigma_{\tilde{F}} \rho_{\tilde{F} r_P}}{\sigma_{r_P}} \mathrm{aw}_P^{(\tilde{b})} = \frac{\sum_{i=1}^{N} w_i \sigma_{v_i} \rho_{v_i r_P}}{\sigma_{r_P}} \tag{13-27}$$

REFERENCES

Bacon, C. R. (2023), *Practical Portfolio Performance Measurement and Attribution, 3rd Edition*. John Wiley & Sons.

Cremers, K. J. M., and A. Petajisto (2009), How active is your fund manager? A new measure that predicts performance. *The Review of Financial Studies*, Vol. 22, pp. 3329–3365.

Fama, E. (1972), Components of investment performance. *The Journal of Finance*, Vol. 17, pp. 551–567.

Holbrook, J. P. (1977), Investment performance of pension funds. *Journal of the Institute of Actuaries*, Vol. 104, pp. 15–91.

Kon, S. T. (1983), The market-timing performance of mutual fund managers. *Journal of Business*, Vol. 56, pp. 323–347.

Menchero, J. G. (2006/2007), Risk-adjusted performance attribution. *Journal of Performance Measurement*, Vol. 11 (2), pp. 22–28.

Menchero, J. G., and V. Poduri (2008), Custom factor attribution. *Financial Analysts Journal*, Vol. 64 (2), pp. 81–92.

Spaulding, D. (2003), *Investment Performance Attribution*. McGraw-Hill.

Spaulding, D., and S. Campisi (2007), The case for money-weighted attribution. *Journal of Performance Measurement*, Vol. 11 (Performance Attribution Supplement), pp. 8–20.

Steiner, A. (2011), Sharpe ratio contribution and attribution analysis. Research Note, Andreas Steiner Consulting GmbH.

CHAPTER 14

Performance Attribution Methods

INTRODUCTION

Whereas Chapter 13 paved the way for setting up a systematic approach for the granular analysis of performance, we are now in the process of developing pragmatic and scalable methods for performance attribution. The building block for this type of analysis is the single-period attribution model of *Brinson, Hood, and Beebower* (BHB) and, even more precisely, that of *Brinson and Fachler* (BF). The principles of both systems are the partitioning of a portfolio's excess return over its benchmark into an Allocation effect and a Selection effect, completed with an Interaction effect that can be studied in isolation or attached to one of the major effects. Even at this basic level, we do not deny some issues that need to be overcome. They are related to the main inputs of the attribution process, namely, the returns and weights of the portfolio and benchmark's constituents, as well as some challenges of the investment decision process that require adequate specific answers. The specific challenges of *environmental–social–governance (ESG) screening* and *asset selection processes* can be adequately addressed through an adaptation of the attribution procedure.

Endowed with the principles of attribution, we can investigate more complex situations that require appropriate adjustments. The first of those challenges is the extension of the attribution system to multiperiod returns. The compounding effect is not trivial and requires a treatment that respects the principles of attribution and makes economic sense. We discuss two important (but by far not the only) solutions, namely, *logarithmic smoothing* and *geometric attribution*. This is a very crowded area with practical systems proposed by commercial vendors, and our discussion sheds light on the limitations of a section that cannot pretend to be exhaustive on the matter.

There are also interesting challenges related to specific portfolio types. We devote a section to the discussion of three such situations: global multicurrency portfolios, fixed-income investments, and derivatives (mostly as overlays). The adaptation of the traditional BHB or BF attribution is not straightforward in any of these cases, but it is still possible to isolate meaningful effects and to perform a decomposition of excess returns using weights and returns, as in the original setup.

Risk should not necessarily be ignored in performance attribution. The last section reconciles to a large extent the content of this chapter with Chapter 13, which primarily focused on risk-based analysis. We discuss a relatively simple, but effective extension of the analysis through *factor-based attribution*, which allows us to mix holding and return-based analysis in a single method. We close the loop started in Chapter 13 with Fama's (1972) performance decomposition by showing how systematic and total risk can be explicitly introduced in the *risk-based performance attribution* system, with possibly finer interpretations of the effects.

As a final note to this Introduction, we acknowledge that attribution analysis can be seen as a *chasse gardée* of the practitioners' world. We have to be modest with this reality, but not shy. This chapter really aims to provide an overview of the methods and challenges that we view as most representative and deliver workable insights into this matter. Interested readers can always access more specialized resources *ad libitum*.

The VAS Example – part II

We reuse the same example as in Chapter 13. For each of the funds, denominated "Verso" (**V**), "Alloco" (**A**), and "Selecto" (**S**) and their common benchmark **B**, we reproduce the data in Tables 14-1 to 14-7.

TABLE 14-1 VAS example – Monthly rates of return of the benchmark and market.

Month	Stocks (50%)	Bonds (40%)	Cash (10%)	Benchmark (100%)	Market
Jan	0.61%	0.07%	0.15%	**0.35%**	−3.66%
Feb	2.13%	0.25%	0.15%	**1.18%**	4.69%
Mar	4.22%	0.09%	0.15%	**2.16%**	−1.08%
Apr	0.38%	−0.29%	0.15%	**0.09%**	0.51%
May	−7.52%	0.02%	0.15%	**−3.74%**	−7.76%
Jun	3.23%	−0.71%	0.15%	**1.35%**	8.00%
Jul	−8.99%	0.10%	0.15%	**−4.44%**	−3.26%
Aug	7.09%	1.42%	0.15%	**4.13%**	8.40%
Sep	5.18%	1.35%	0.15%	**3.15%**	4.66%
Oct	2.20%	1.43%	0.15%	**1.69%**	1.14%
Nov	4.49%	0.53%	0.15%	**2.47%**	3.79%
Dec	−4.86%	−0.42%	0.15%	**−2.58%**	−7.37%

TABLE 14-2 VAS example – Monthly rates of return of the Verso fund.

Month	Returns			Weights			Verso
	Stocks	Bonds	Cash	*Stocks*	*Bonds*	*Cash*	
Jan	1.27%	0.39%	0.36%	*55.7%*	*43.1%*	*1.2%*	**0.88%**
Feb	3.58%	0.46%	0.25%	*54.2%*	*42.7%*	*3.1%*	**2.14%**
Mar	4.91%	0.15%	0.32%	*52.9%*	*40.6%*	*6.5%*	**2.68%**
Apr	1.96%	−0.25%	0.18%	*51.6%*	*39.7%*	*8.7%*	**0.93%**
May	−5.54%	0.01%	0.19%	*50.4%*	*40.4%*	*9.2%*	**−2.77%**
Jun	3.96%	−0.85%	0.11%	*49.7%*	*39.6%*	*10.7%*	**1.64%**
Jul	−9.05%	−0.02%	0.02%	*48.5%*	*39.4%*	*12.1%*	**−4.39%**
Aug	6.56%	1.23%	−0.06%	*48.7%*	*37.2%*	*14.1%*	**3.64%**
Sep	5.02%	1.11%	0.03%	*47.2%*	*38.9%*	*13.9%*	**2.81%**
Oct	1.96%	0.97%	0.09%	*48.9%*	*36.5%*	*14.6%*	**1.33%**
Nov	3.25%	0.69%	0.12%	*50.2%*	*37.3%*	*12.5%*	**1.90%**
Dec	−5.87%	−0.45%	0.15%	*48.1%*	*41.0%*	*10.9%*	**−2.99%**

TABLE 14-3 VAS example – Monthly rates of return of the Alloco fund.

Month	Returns			Weights			Alloco
	Stocks	Bonds	Cash	*Stocks*	*Bonds*	*Cash*	
Jan	0.72%	0.09%	0.15%	*51.5%*	*37.6%*	*10.9%*	**0.42%**
Feb	2.03%	0.22%	0.15%	*57.2%*	*39.7%*	*3.1%*	**1.25%**
Mar	3.97%	0.14%	0.15%	*53.6%*	*38.4%*	*8.0%*	**2.19%**
Apr	0.64%	−0.37%	0.15%	*51.6%*	*36.2%*	*12.2%*	**0.21%**
May	−6.50%	0.14%	0.15%	*43.2%*	*35.4%*	*21.4%*	**−2.73%**
Jun	2.58%	−0.82%	0.15%	*47.1%*	*38.9%*	*14.0%*	**0.92%**
Jul	−8.42%	0.01%	0.15%	*44.3%*	*42.6%*	*13.1%*	**−3.71%**
Aug	6.32%	1.65%	0.15%	*49.9%*	*45.9%*	*4.2%*	**3.92%**
Sep	5.09%	1.28%	0.15%	*56.6%*	*42.5%*	*0.9%*	**3.43%**
Oct	1.89%	1.49%	0.15%	*54.3%*	*44.8%*	*0.9%*	**1.70%**
Nov	4.23%	0.37%	0.15%	*50.3%*	*41.8%*	*7.9%*	**2.29%**
Dec	−4.36%	−0.54%	0.15%	*44.0%*	*38.5%*	*17.5%*	**−2.10%**

(continued)

(continued)

TABLE 14-4 VAS example – Monthly rates of return of the Selecto fund.

Month	Returns			*Weights*			Selecto
	Stocks	Bonds	Cash	*Stocks*	*Bonds*	*Cash*	
Jan	0.87%	0.14%	0.15%	*50.4%*	*40.9%*	*8.7%*	**0.51%**
Feb	2.59%	0.34%	0.15%	*49.2%*	*41.5%*	*9.3%*	**1.43%**
Mar	4.06%	0.19%	0.15%	*47.5%*	*39.8%*	*12.7%*	**2.02%**
Apr	0.96%	−0.34%	0.15%	*49.2%*	*38.1%*	*12.7%*	**0.36%**
May	−6.23%	0.05%	0.15%	*50.2%*	*40.1%*	*9.7%*	**−3.09%**
Jun	4.30%	−1.01%	0.15%	*52.3%*	*40.5%*	*7.2%*	**1.85%**
Jul	−8.63%	0.31%	0.15%	*50.6%*	*40.0%*	*9.4%*	**−4.23%**
Aug	6.61%	1.63%	0.15%	*48.9%*	*41.6%*	*9.5%*	**3.92%**
Sep	4.23%	1.11%	0.15%	*49.2%*	*40.2%*	*10.6%*	**2.54%**
Oct	2.85%	1.87%	0.15%	*50.7%*	*39.5%*	*9.8%*	**2.20%**
Nov	5.02%	0.43%	0.15%	*51.6%*	*38.7%*	*9.7%*	**2.77%**
Dec	−4.20%	−0.72%	0.15%	*52.6%*	*40.9%*	*6.5%*	**−2.49%**

TABLE 14-5 VAS example – Monthly returns of the equity sectors for the benchmark.

Month	Returns				
	Benchmark Stocks	Tec (37%)	Fin (17%)	Cyc (24%)	Def (22%)
Jan	**0.61%**	0.81%	0.69%	0.62%	0.20%
Feb	**2.13%**	2.69%	3.22%	1.56%	0.97%
Mar	**4.22%**	6.98%	1.65%	3.84%	1.98%
Apr	**0.38%**	−0.56%	1.53%	0.75%	0.67%
May	**−7.52%**	−9.65%	−4.50%	−9.12%	−4.53%
Jun	**3.23%**	5.37%	0.24%	4.12%	0.97%
Jul	**−8.99%**	−13.44%	−6.12%	−7.20%	−5.68%
Aug	**7.09%**	10.34%	6.67%	8.32%	0.61%
Sep	**5.18%**	6.75%	2.96%	7.29%	1.95%
Oct	**2.20%**	2.16%	−0.88%	2.33%	4.51%
Nov	**4.49%**	6.32%	1.99%	2.62%	5.38%
Dec	**−4.86%**	−7.03%	−1.07%	−5.21%	−3.76%
Average	**0.68%**	**0.90%**	**0.53%**	**0.83%**	**0.27%**

TABLE 14-6 VAS example – Monthly returns and weights of the equity sectors for the Alloco fund.

Month	Returns					Weights			
	Alloco Stocks	Tec	Fin	Cyc	Def	Tec	Fin	Cyc	Def
Jan	**0.72%**	0.77%	0.66%	0.91%	0.43%	*38.9%*	*16.8%*	*24.8%*	*19.5%*
Feb	**2.03%**	2.26%	3.09%	1.65%	0.91%	*40.1%*	*18.9%*	*22.4%*	*18.6%*
Mar	**3.97%**	6.04%	2.06%	3.67%	0.63%	*42.0%*	*16.2%*	*27.5%*	*14.3%*
Apr	**0.64%**	−0.70%	1.95%	0.95%	1.05%	*28.3%*	*12.1%*	*22.8%*	*36.8%*
May	**−6.50%**	−10.36%	−4.43%	−9.32%	−4.00%	*22.6%*	*19.7%*	*18.4%*	*39.3%*
Jun	**2.58%**	4.56%	−0.52%	3.21%	0.03%	*38.6%*	*15.7%*	*27.9%*	*17.8%*
Jul	**−8.42%**	−13.91%	−6.58%	−6.66%	−5.39%	*29.1%*	*18.9%*	*25.6%*	*26.4%*
Aug	**6.32%**	8.69%	6.01%	7.07%	0.11%	*39.0%*	*17.5%*	*26.3%*	*17.2%*
Sep	**5.09%**	6.20%	2.66%	7.00%	1.48%	*39.9%*	*15.3%*	*28.0%*	*16.8%*
Oct	**1.89%**	1.97%	−0.99%	2.02%	3.09%	*40.2%*	*12.6%*	*22.0%*	*25.2%*
Nov	**4.23%**	7.18%	1.08%	1.29%	3.35%	*42.7%*	*13.9%*	*21.3%*	*22.1%*
Dec	**−4.36%**	−6.83%	−1.17%	−5.99%	−1.97%	*32.0%*	*18.9%*	*24.5%*	*24.6%*
Average	**0.68%**	**0.49%**	**0.32%**	**0.48%**	**−0.02%**	***36.1%***	***16.3%***	***24.3%***	***23.2%***

TABLE 14-7 VAS example – Monthly returns and weights of the equity sectors for the Selecto fund.

Month	Returns					Weights			
	Selecto Stocks	Tec	Fin	Cyc	Def	Tec	Fin	Cyc	Def
Jan	**0.87%**	0.89%	1.11%	0.84%	0.67%	*36.2%*	*17.9%*	*24.6%*	*21.3%*
Feb	**2.59%**	3.04%	3.75%	1.93%	1.72%	*37.8%*	*15.9%*	*23.2%*	*23.1%*
Mar	**4.06%**	7.23%	1.24%	4.02%	1.01%	*36.3%*	*15.7%*	*25.1%*	*22.9%*
Apr	**0.96%**	0.58%	1.88%	0.86%	1.01%	*37.2%*	*16.9%*	*24.8%*	*21.1%*
May	**−6.23%**	−8.55%	−3.20%	−7.56%	−3.15%	*38.1%*	*17.6%*	*23.0%*	*21.3%*
Jun	**4.30%**	6.44%	1.56%	5.22%	2.07%	*36.2%*	*17.9%*	*23.5%*	*22.4%*
Jul	**−8.63%**	−14.14%	−5.23%	−6.02%	−4.46%	*37.9%*	*18.2%*	*23.1%*	*20.8%*
Aug	**6.61%**	9.86%	5.63%	6.98%	1.38%	*36.8%*	*17.2%*	*24.6%*	*21.4%*
Sep	**4.23%**	6.52%	2.02%	6.52%	−0.26%	*36.2%*	*16.1%*	*24.6%*	*23.1%*
Oct	**2.85%**	2.94%	−0.06%	2.89%	4.78%	*37.5%*	*16.4%*	*23.6%*	*22.5%*
Nov	**5.02%**	6.99%	2.50%	2.93%	5.87%	*37.0%*	*17.4%*	*23.1%*	*22.5%*
Dec	**−4.20%**	−6.52%	0.01%	−4.22%	−3.62%	*36.6%*	*17.3%*	*24.6%*	*21.5%*
Average	**1.04%**	**1.27%**	**0.93%**	**1.20%**	**0.59%**	***37.0%***	***17.0%***	***24.0%***	***22.0%***

(continued)

(continued)

These tables are analogous to Tables 13-1 to 13-4 and 13-6 to 13-8 of Chapter 13.

In addition to investigating the sources of differences between Alloco and Selecto, the CIO wishes to understand why the Verso fund has witnessed two contrasting semesters, with a first part of the year in which the manager largely outperformed the benchmark and with a disappointing second semester that led the fund's global performance to revert back to its peers' returns.

14.1 ATTRIBUTION ANALYSIS FOR A SINGLE PERIOD

14.1.1 The Brinson, Hood, and Beebower attribution model

While the roots of performance attribution analysis can be traced back to Fama's (1972) work discussed in Chapter 13, the formalization of the granular analysis of portfolio performance and its interpretation in terms of timing and selection (and second order drivers) was first performed in a systematic manner by Brinson, Hood, and Beebower (1986) (henceforth BHB).[1] The classical way to carry out performance attribution analysis is thus generally known as the "BHB attribution" model or sometimes the "Brinson attribution" model.

We develop this approach using our own notation for the sake of consistency and clarity. We posit that there are in total N individual assets in the universe (be they included in the portfolio, the benchmark, or both), each denoted by i ($i = 1, 2, \ldots, N$). As discussed in Section 13.2 of Chapter 13, the raw material that we used for the subsequent analyses was made of three building blocks, all observed at a given point in time t:

- The individual asset return $R_{i,t}$;
- The individual asset weight within the portfolio $w_{P,i,t}$;
- The individual asset weight within the benchmark $w_{B,i,t}$.

For the attribution analysis to make sense, it is necessary to consider the lowest level of aggregation of assets for which there exists a difference in return between the portfolio and the benchmark. For that purpose, we consider that there are K distinct categories, called "segments," represented in the portfolio, and each asset i belongs to a single segment k ($k = 1, 2, \ldots, K$).

[1] These authors did not invent attribution analysis though. Bacon (2019) documents that the same types of formulas were already in use during the 1970s.

We can then characterize the benchmark and portfolio returns with the following generic equations:

$$R_{B,t} = \sum_{k=1}^{K} w_{B,k,t} R_{B,k,t} \tag{14-1a}$$

$$R_{P,t} = \sum_{k=1}^{K} w_{P,k,t} R_{P,k,t} \tag{14-1b}$$

where $w_{P,k,t} = \sum_{i \in k} w_{P,i,t}$ and $w_{B,k,t} = \sum_{i \in k} w_{B,i,t}$ are the weights of segment k in the portfolio and benchmark, respectively, and $R_{P,k,t} = \frac{\sum_{i \in k} w_{P,i,t} R_{i,t}}{w_{P,k,t}}$ and $R_{B,k,t} = \frac{\sum_{i \in k} w_{B,i,t} R_{i,t}}{w_{B,k,t}}$ are their returns, respectively.

The goal of the analysis is to explain the determinants of the excess return, i.e., the difference between expressions (14-1b) and (14-1a):

$$R_{P,t} - R_{B,t} = \sum_{k=1}^{K} w_{P,k,t} R_{P,k,t} - \sum_{k=1}^{K} w_{B,k,t} R_{B,k,t} \tag{14-2}$$

Of course, if the detail of the information does not reach the level of individual securities (for instance, with a pure top-down portfolio view), one can directly start with the lowest granularity: It is important here to have a (potentially) different level of the return for the portfolio and the benchmark associated with their investment in segment k, which is obviously not the case at the level of individual assets whose rate of return is independent of the portfolio to which it belongs.

14.1.1.1 The portfolio attribution effects

BHB decompose the arithmetic portfolio returns for a given period t in four "quadrants" whose interpretation can be related to the policy (passive) returns, asset allocation, and asset selection, as shown in Table 14-8.

The returns obtained in quadrants II and III are often termed the "notional allocation" (NA) return $R_{P,t}^{(\text{all})} \equiv R_{P(\text{NA}),t}$ and the "notional selection" (NS) return $R_{P,t}^{(\text{sel})} \equiv R_{P(\text{NS}),t}$. From these quadrants, we can decompose the portfolio's excess return into three parts:

$$R_{P,t} - R_{B,t} \equiv \mathbf{IV} - \mathbf{I} = \mathcal{T}_{P,t} + \mathcal{S}_{P,t} + \mathcal{I}_{P,t} \tag{14-3}$$

TABLE 14-8 The BHB quadrants.

		Selection	
		Passive	Active
Allocation	Passive	**Quadrant I** *Benchmark* $R_{B,t} = \sum_{k=1}^{K} w_{B,k,t} R_{B,k,t}$	**Quadrant III** *Benchmark and selection* $R_{P,t}^{(sel)} = \sum_{k=1}^{K} w_{B,k,t} R_{P,k,t}$
	Active	**Quadrant II** *Benchmark and allocation* $R_{P,t}^{(all)} = \sum_{k=1}^{K} w_{P,k,t} R_{B,k,t}$	**Quadrant IV** *Portfolio* $R_{P,t} = \sum_{k=1}^{K} w_{P,k,t} R_{P,k,t}$

Source: Adapted from Brinson et al. (1986), Table 1.

where the three components of the right-hand side are the "Allocation" (also called "Timing" in the context of the BHB model) $\mathcal{T}_{P,t}$, "Selection" $\mathcal{S}_{P,t}$, and "Other" $\mathcal{I}_{P,t}$ effects (which are further characterized in a later stage) defined by

$$\mathcal{T}_{P,t} \equiv \mathbf{II} - \mathbf{I} = \sum_{k=1}^{K} (w_{P,k,t} - w_{B,k,t}) R_{B,k,t} \tag{14-4a}$$

$$\mathcal{S}_{P,t} \equiv \mathbf{III} - \mathbf{I} = \sum_{k=1}^{K} w_{B,k,t} (R_{P,k,t} - R_{B,k,t}) \tag{14-4b}$$

$$\mathcal{I}_{P,t} \equiv \mathbf{IV} - \mathbf{II} - \mathbf{III} + \mathbf{I} = \sum_{k=1}^{K} (w_{P,k,t} - w_{B,k,t})(R_{P,k,t} - R_{B,k,t}) \tag{14-4c}$$

The first two components can be interpreted as follows. The *Allocation effect* $\mathcal{T}_{P,t}$ represents the marginal impact of the manager's choice to move away from the benchmark weights in each segment, while controlling for the selection of assets by only considering the benchmark returns. Under the same logic, the *Selection effect* $\mathcal{S}_{P,t}$ represents the marginal impact of the manager's choice of the assets composing each segment, while controlling the timing of the investments by only considering the benchmark weights. The third component $\mathcal{I}_{P,t}$ is the cross-product of the selection and timing effects. This can be seen as an *Interaction effect*. For a given segment k, it is positive when the factors are either both positive or both negative. The first case corresponds to a situation where the manager overweighs a segment in which they have superior selection skills. The second one reflects the situation where the manager underweights a segment in which they have an inferior selection ability. Thus, the Interaction component reflects some kind of "lucidity," whereby the manager recognizes where they do better or worse than a passive portfolio and affect their resources accordingly.[2] Note that, since $\sum_{k=1}^{K}(w_{P,k,t} - w_{B,k,t}) = 0$, there must be positive and negative values for the first factor, but there is no guarantee about the sign of $(R_{P,k,t} - R_{B,k,t})$.

In order to understand the drivers of an active manager's performance, it is very useful to express each effect in percentage. Taking the portfolio return as the basis generally leads to observing that, on average, most of its return can be attributed to the strategic allocation decisions. Adopting the excess return instead reveals the importance of each effect in the generation of the global performance.

The VAS example (continued)

We apply the BHB attribution analysis on the three funds at the first tactical level (asset classes). The outcome for the average return is summarized in Table 14-9 (we leave cash out as its effect is immaterial).

TABLE 14-9 VAS example – Outcome of the BHB attribution analysis at the level of asset classes.

		Allocation $\mathcal{T}_P$	Selection $\mathcal{S}_P$	Interaction $\mathcal{I}_P$	Total	Global $R_P - R_B$
Verso	Stocks	0.02%	0.16%	0.02%	**0.19%**	0.17%
	Bonds	−0.01%	−0.01%	0.00%	**−0.02%**	
Alloco	Stocks	0.17%	0.00%	−0.01%	**0.15%**	0.17%
	Bonds	0.02%	−0.01%	0.00%	**0.01%**	
Selecto	Stocks	−0.02%	0.18%	0.01%	**0.16%**	0.17%
	Bonds	0.00%	0.01%	0.00%	**0.01%**	

(continued)

[2]Instead of considering it as a separate effect, some professionals propose assigning the Interaction effect to the Selection effect, defined then as the "gross Selection effect" $\mathcal{S}'_{P,t} = \sum_{k=1}^{K} w_{P,k,t}(R_{P,k,t} - R_{B,k,t})$, i.e., where $w_{P,k,t}$ replaces $w_{B,k,t}$. This approach is consistent with a process in which the Interaction effect is not the direct outcome of specific investment decisions but rather derives from a natural top-down portfolio management approach where asset allocation decisions are made first and then followed logically by security selection whose portfolio weights are given (see Bacon, 2023). This point of view is confirmed by Christopherson, Carino, and Ferson (2009), who suggest that the association of the Interaction effect with either Allocation or Selection depends on the focus of the analysis.

(continued)

The results for the allocation in stocks reveal very different skills, as shown in Figure 14-1.

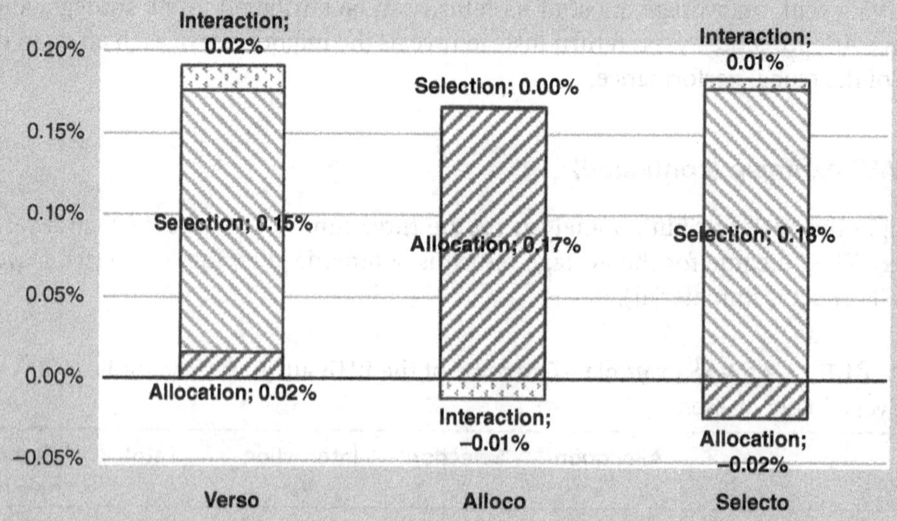

FIGURE 14-1 VAS example – Contribution of different effects to the average excess return.

Even though all three fund managers have delivered exactly the same average return, the granular analysis of their performance drivers unequivocally reveals that two managers (Verso and Selecto) outperform their benchmark because of superior selection skills, while the one for the the Alloco fund is mainly successful at anticipating market movements. In all three cases, the Interaction effect is low, as could be expected from its secondary nature.

14.1.1.2 Detailed attribution analysis per segment

Digging into each individual segment, we can reconcile the notions of performance attribution with the performance contribution introduced in Section 13.2 of Chapter 13 through the following expression:

$$c_k(R_{P,t}) - c_k(R_{B,t}) = c_k(\mathcal{T}_{P,t}) + c_k(\mathcal{S}_{P,t}) + c_k(\mathcal{I}_{P,t}) \tag{14-5}$$

where $c_k(R_{P,t}) = w_{P,k,t}R_{P,k,t}$ and $c_k(R_{B,t}) = w_{B,k,t}R_{B,k,t}$ are the contributions of segment k to the portfolio and benchmark returns, respectively, and $c_k(\mathcal{T}_{P,t}) = (w_{P,k,t} - w_{B,k,t})R_{B,k,t}$, $c_k(\mathcal{S}_{P,t}) = w_{B,k,t}(R_{P,k,t} - R_{B,k,t})$, and $c_k(\mathcal{I}_{P,t}) = (w_{P,k,t} - w_{B,k,t})(R_{P,k,t} - R_{B,k,t})$ are the contributions of segment k to the Allocation, Selection and Interaction effects, respectively.

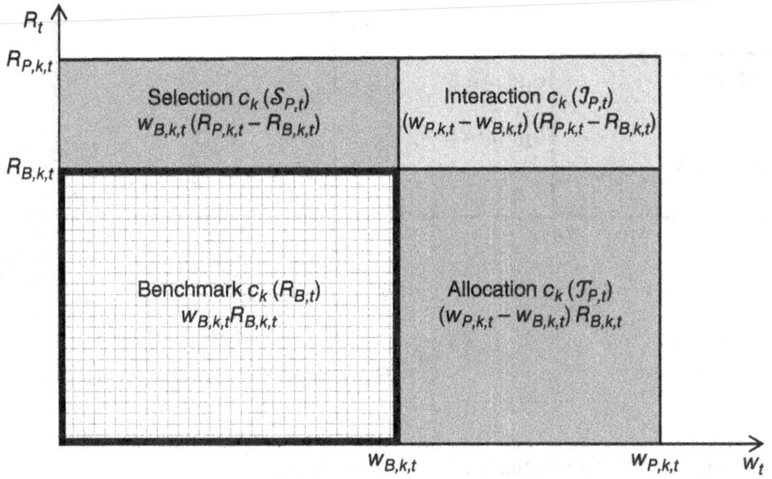

FIGURE 14-2 Geometric interpretation of the components of performance in the BHB model. *Source*: Adapted from Bacon (2023), Figure 6.2.

In order to obtain an intuitive and visual understanding of the drivers of the global impact of each skill at the total portfolio level, Bacon (2023) suggests a segment-per-segment geometric interpretation of the three components of excess return together with the benchmark return. Schematically, it consists of representing the weighted return as the surface of a rectangle whose bases are the weight and the return of the segment. This translates into the graph shown in Figure 14-2.

In order to make interpretation easier, the rectangle representing the component return of the benchmark is framed with a thicker line. We have represented the situation in which every component is positive. This is naturally the easiest case, but it is also possible to represent negative areas through hatching or another shade. Even though this chart is meant to illustrate how total return can be decomposed, its utility extends beyond a visual impression. Thanks to the fact that both dimensions (weight and return) differ from one segment to another, it is possible to organize a complete geometric overview of the performance by placing the graphs side by side while keeping the same respective scales (provided that there are not too many such categories). In Figure 14-3, we illustrate how this can be displayed in the generic case of two asset classes.

In the example, the overall benchmark return is zero: There is an equal weight on both categories ($w_{B,1,t} = w_{B,2,t} = 50\%$), and the positive return contribution of the first segment is perfectly offset by that of the second segment, i.e., $c_1(R_{B,t}) = -c_2(R_{B,t})$. Consequently, the areas of the rectangles representing the benchmark contribution returns are equal. Moreover, since the sum of the weights of the portfolio must add up to one, it necessarily follows that $w_{P,1,t} - w_{B,1,t} = w_{B,1,t} - w_{P,2,t}$. This explains that the bases of the rectangles featuring the Allocation and Interaction effects are equal on both parts of the figure.

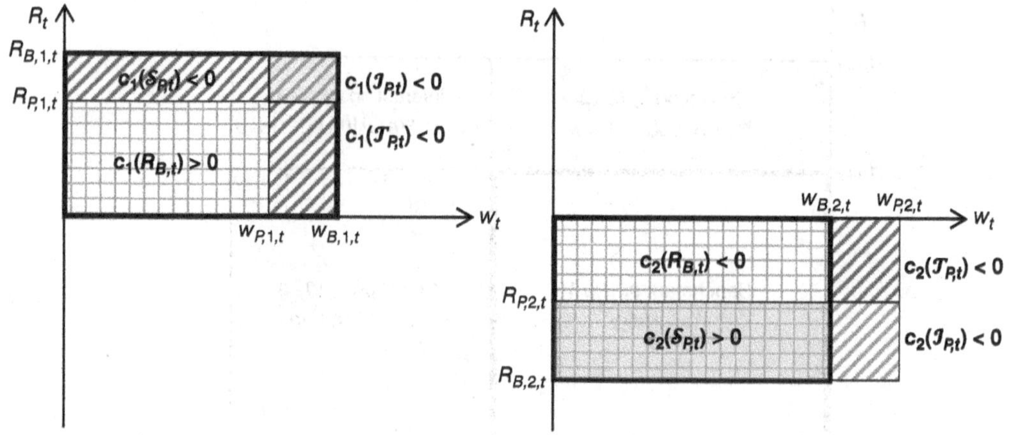

FIGURE 14-3 Geometric attribution analysis with two segments.

For the first segment, we have $w_{P,1,t} < w_{B,1,t}$ and $R_{P,1,t} < R_{B,1,t}$. Thus, both the Allocation and the Selection effects are negative. Their respective rectangles reduce the size of the benchmark one, which is a bad outcome since returns are positive. Nevertheless, the Interaction effect is positive because it results from the product of two negative factors. Geometrically, this can be understood from the fact that the area of this rectangle has been deducted twice from the benchmark: once with the Allocation effect and once with the Selection effect. In order to avoid double counting, it has to be restored once.

For the second segment, the story is largely different. Because the benchmark return is negative, the decision to overweigh this asset class was a bad one, leading to a negative Allocation effect. On the other hand, the return of this segment in the portfolio is less negative than for the benchmark, indicating a positive Selection effect. Because of the conflicting outcomes of the two first-order attribution effects, the Interaction effect is negative. Note that, instead of putting side by side different segments for a single portfolio, it is also possible to compare different portfolios on the same segment. This is helpful in distinguishing between managers on their skills while perfectly controlling for the conditions of the challenge.

The principles of attribution analysis involve two dichotomous comparisons (weights and returns) made simultaneously. It can thus be applied to a single type of decision at a time. Referring back to the waterfall of the investment decision-making process presented in Figure 13-10 of Chapter 13, the attribution analysis can be performed at the strategic level (considering the policy portfolio as the benchmark), at the asset class level (considering the strategic allocation as the benchmark), and then at any other inferior level for which information is known about the benchmark composition.

In the case of a subordinated analysis, the link between different levels must be determined through the Selection effect computed upstream from the analysis. Consider that we want to perform the analysis at the level of asset class k, which is itself composed of another set of L

categories. The excess return of the portfolio for this asset class is equal to $R_{P,k,t} - R_{B,k,t}$, which is equivalent to the contribution to the Selection effect divided by the weight of the asset class in the benchmark, i.e., $\frac{c_k(\mathcal{S}_{P,t})}{w_{B,k,t}}$. Thus, we obtain the following decomposition:

$$R_{P,k,t} - R_{B,k,t} \equiv \frac{c_k(\mathcal{S}_{P,t})}{w_{B,k,t}} = \mathcal{T}_{P,k,t} + \mathcal{S}_{P,k,t} + \mathcal{I}_{P,k,t} \tag{14-6}$$

where, analogously as before, $\mathcal{T}_{P,k,t} = \sum_{l=1}^{L}(w'_{P,l,t} - w'_{B,l,t})R_{B,l,t}$, $\mathcal{S}_{P,k,t} = \sum_{l=1}^{L} w'_{B,l,t}(R_{P,l,t} - R_{B,l,t})$, and $\mathcal{I}_{P,k,t} = \sum_{l=1}^{L}(w'_{P,l,t} - w'_{B,l,t})(R_{P,l,t} - R_{B,l,t})$ are the Allocation, Selection, and Interaction effects associated with the asset class, respectively, and $w'_{P,l,t} = \frac{w_{P,l,t}}{w_{P,k,t}}$ and $w'_{B,l,t} = \frac{w_{B,l,t}}{w_{B,k,t}}$ are the normalized weights (ensuring that they add up to one).

With regard to asset classes with a certain degree of complexity, like fixed-income securities or multicurrency portfolios, the generic analysis must be adapted, as discussed in the next section.

The VAS example (continued)

Focusing on the equity asset class, the data of Tables 14-6 and 14-7 allow us to perform a second BHB attribution analysis on the stock sub-portfolios for the Alloco and Selecto funds on the four sectors represented in the benchmark. Running the same analysis as before yields Table 14-10.

TABLE 14-10 VAS example – Outcome of the BHB attribution analysis at the level of equity sectors.

		Allocation	Selection	Interaction	Total	Global
Alloco	Tec	0.35%	−0.15%	0.01%	**0.21%**	**0.00%**
	Fin	−0.03%	−0.04%	0.00%	**−0.06%**	
	Cyc	0.08%	−0.08%	0.00%	**0.00%**	
	Def	−0.10%	−0.07%	0.03%	**−0.14%**	
	Total	**0.30%**	**−0.33%**	**0.03%**	**0.00%**	
Selecto	Tec	−0.03%	0.14%	0.00%	**0.11%**	**0.36%**
	Fin	−0.01%	0.07%	0.00%	**0.06%**	
	Cyc	0.02%	0.09%	0.00%	**0.10%**	
	Def	0.02%	0.07%	0.00%	**0.08%**	
	Total	**−0.01%**	**0.37%**	**0.00%**	**0.36%**	

(continued)

(continued)

The diagnosis appears to be very different from the global analysis regarding the generation of outperformance by the two fund managers. For the Alloco fund, the Allocation effect emerges again, but the excess return is more than offset by a poor Selection effect. The global impact of active management is nil. For the Selecto fund, a very positive Selection effect is recorded, but it is not annihilated by any poor timing. We can reconcile the value of the last column of the table with the global analysis of Table 14-9 by noting that the excess returns of the equity asset classes are equal to $\frac{c_{\text{Stock}}(\mathcal{S}_{\text{Alloco}})}{w_{B,\text{Stock}}} = \frac{0.00\%}{50\%} = 0.00\%$ and $\frac{c_{\text{Stock}}(\mathcal{S}_{\text{Selecto}})}{w_{B,\text{Stock}}} = \frac{0.18\%}{50\%} = 0.36\%$, respectively. This shows that the takeaways obtained with a certain degree of analysis do not necessarily percolate to the other levels.

Finally, it is interesting to apply Bacon's (2023) geometric analysis in a synoptic manner in order to grasp the nature and magnitude of different effects at a given point in time. We apply this for the Technology (Tec) sector in May with the information of Tables 14-6 and 14-7. The data that are relevant for the analysis are summarized in Table 14-11.

TABLE 14-11 VAS example – Weights and returns for the Technology sector (May).

	Alloco	Selecto	Benchmark
Weight	22.6%	38.1%	37%
Return	−10.4%	−8.55%	−9.65%
Allocation	1.39%	−0.11%	
Selection	−0.26%	0.41%	
Interaction	0.10%	0.01%	
Total	**1.23%**	**0.31%**	

Geometrically, this is represented by Figure 14-4.

We truncated the axes in order to focus on the regions of interest. The benchmark weight and return are identical on both graphs, but the visual impression is very different. On the left graph, the importance of the good timing of the Alloco manager clearly appears with a large surface. The interaction term is positive because the manager was lucid enough

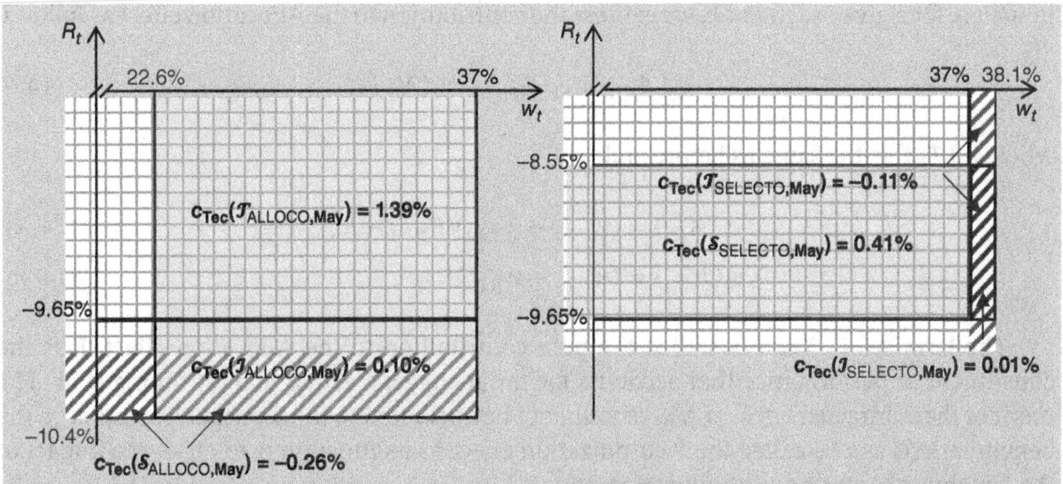

FIGURE 14-4 VAS example – Components of performance for the Technology sector (May).

to underweigh this sector by 22.6% − 37% = −14.4% in a moment when they obtained a worse return than the benchmark by −10.4% − 9.65% = −0.75%. On the right graph, there is almost no Allocation effect, but the Selecto fund manager has successfully picked the stocks belonging to this sector so as to outperform the benchmark by 1.10%, which leads to a Selection effect of 0.41% once this extra return is multiplied by the benchmark weight of 37%.

14.1.2 Refining market timing: The Brinson and Fachler model

The approach proposed by Brinson and Fachler (1985), henceforth BF, is perhaps less popular than the BHB model, but it addresses an additional dimension that makes it more precise and accurate for the assessment of a manager's genuine ability to outperform their benchmark. Specifically, besides a different wording, the key difference between the BF and the BHB frameworks resides within the identification of the market timing skill.

Recall that, in the BHB model, the Allocation effect is represented through Equation (14-4a) by the expression $\mathcal{T}_{P,t} = \sum_{k=1}^{K}(w_{P,k,t} - w_{B,k,t})R_{B,k,t}$. The second factor $R_{B,k,t}$ representing the return of segment k inside the benchmark is indeed the combination of two distinct elements: (i) the benchmark return $R_{B,t}$ and (ii) the excess return of the particular segment k over its benchmark, namely $R_{B,k,t} - R_{B,t}$. The manager only shows some merit when they overallocate the portfolio when the second element is positive, regardless of the sign and magnitude of $R_{B,k,t}$ in isolation.

In the BF model, we rewrite Equation (14-3) as

$$R_{P,t} - R_{B,t} = \mathcal{A}_{P,t} + \mathcal{S}_{P,t} + \mathcal{I}_{P,t} \tag{14-7}$$

in which, for a given segment k, we express the contribution to the Allocation effect as follows:

$$c_k(\mathcal{A}_{P,t}) = c_k(\mathcal{T}_{P,t}) - c_k(\mathcal{N}_{P,t}) \quad (14\text{-}8)$$

where $c_k(\mathcal{T}_{P,t})$ is the same as before and

$$c_k(\mathcal{A}_{P,t}) = (w_{P,k,t} - w_{B,k,t})(R_{B,k,t} - R_{B,t}) \quad (14\text{-}9a)$$

$$c_k(\mathcal{N}_{P,t}) = (w_{P,k,t} - w_{B,k,t})R_{B,t} \quad (14\text{-}9b)$$

The term $c_k(\mathcal{A}_{P,t})$ can be called the pure contribution to the Allocation effect. It is the constituent of performance that accounts for the manager's actual market timing skill. The merit of the subtracted term $c_k(\mathcal{N}_{P,t})$ should not be attributed to the manager but rather to the benchmark. It can be called the Neutralization effect as its function is to offset the impact of the benchmark return on the allocation impact.

By construction, $\mathcal{N}_{P,t} = \sum_{k=1}^{K} c_k(\mathcal{N}_{P,t}) = \sum_{k=1}^{K}(w_{P,k,t} - w_{B,k,t})R_{B,t} = 0$, and thus the global Allocation effect is the same in both the BHB and BF models at the portfolio level: $\mathcal{T}_{P,t} = \mathcal{A}_{P,t} = \sum_{k=1}^{K}(w_{P,k,t} - w_{B,k,t})(R_{B,k,t} - R_{B,t})$. This means that the disaggregation of total performance at the highest level is the same in the BHB and BF analyses. Only the constituents of performance differ at the segment level.

In a similar vein as Figure 14-2, Bacon (2023) proposes a geometric interpretation of the components of performance in the BF model, as shown in Figure 14-5, in which the rectangles representing the Allocation and Benchmark effects are both split into two parts.

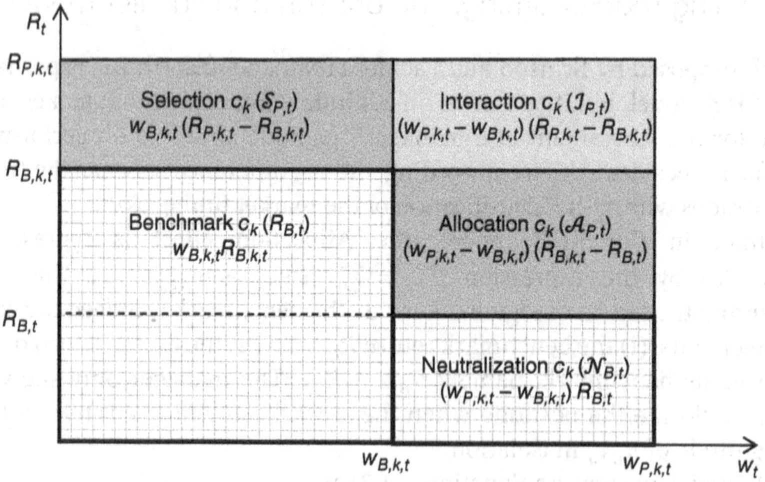

FIGURE 14-5 Geometric interpretation of the components of performance in the BF model. *Source:* Adapted from Bacon (2023), Figure 6.3.

The VAS example (continued)

Considering the allocation in equities, we note that the average return of this asset class at the benchmark level is equal to 0.68%. Replacing $c_k(\mathcal{T}_{P,t})$ with $c_k(\mathcal{A}_{P,t})$ in the computation of the Allocation effect produces the comparative results as shown in Table 14-12.

TABLE 14-12 VAS example – Difference between the Allocation effects in the BHB and BF models.

		BHB	BF
Alloco	Tec	0.35%	0.36%
	Fin	−0.03%	−0.02%
	Cyc	0.08%	0.08%
	Def	−0.10%	−0.11%
	Total	**0.30%**	**0.30%**
Selecto	Tec	−0.03%	−0.03%
	Fin	−0.01%	−0.01%
	Cyc	0.02%	0.02%
	Def	0.02%	0.02%
	Total	**−0.01%**	**−0.01%**

The differences are very small and negligible for the Selecto fund given the very low intensity of active allocation decisions of its manager. In the case of Alloco, the Allocation effect is higher with the BF model for the Technology and Financial sectors simply because the manager has overallocated the weights in the form sector whose average return exceeds the benchmark (0.90% for Tec), whereas they have underallocated to the Financial sector whose return was lower than the benchmark (0.53% for Fin).

14.1.3 Practical issues to consider

Even when attribution analysis is performed at the straight level of single-period returns, a number of questions have to be addressed, as discussed by Spaulding (2003) and Bacon (2023). It is not the purpose of this chapter to dig deep into this topic – we leave it to specific books dedicated to performance attribution – but we believe that it is worthwhile to briefly discuss the most important types of issues to consider.

14.1.3.1 The returns

Attribution analysis requires two types of inputs: returns and weights. Regarding the former, different choices have to be made, and their implications must be well understood:

- *Choosing the frequency of computation.*
  Having returns and weights available at a high frequency of computation, particularly on a daily basis, does not necessarily mean that this is the best possible unit of analysis. There are indeed clear advantages of using the highest possible frequency when the data and infrastructure are of blameless quality, and this can prove to be useful when the portfolio management style itself involves trading decisions that match a daily measurement interval or when there is uncertainty about the behavior of the risk factors used in the analysis. There are however substantial drawbacks that should not be overlooked. As DiBartolomeo (2003) explains, microstructure effects, mostly driven by infrequent trading and liquidity issues, may cast doubt on the statistical properties of daily returns. The best is sometimes the enemy of good, and a careful cost–benefit analysis is recommended before deciding to use data at the highest possible frequency. Furthermore, as Bacon (2023) suggests, the use of daily calculation is recommended when it is doable, but it does not make sense to perform daily analysis as performance attribution is mostly concerned with understanding the drivers of performance for long horizons.
- *Defining returns appropriately.*
  Time-weighted or money-weighted returns? As discussed in Chapter 13, it is generally considered that time-weighted returns, whose aim is to neutralize intermediate cash flows in the computation provide a better match with the way a portfolio is often actually managed. Since the focus is on the manager and not the investor, whenever the inflows and outflows are managed internally within the portfolio, this is doubtlessly the preferred option. Nevertheless, there are situations in which money-weighted returns should be used. This is the case for illiquid asset classes such as private equity or real estate, for which commitments and distributions do not specifically depend on the manager's own decisions. As Spaulding and Campisi (2007) put it, the principle is clear: As soon as cash flows materially influence the investment process, they should be included in the analysis, and money-weighted returns are recommended in that case. It is also important to recall that, whichever method is used, the golden rules of attribution analysis must be respected at all times, and in particular, the sum of the effects is equal to the portfolio's excess return.

14.1.3.2 The weights

Some specific cases must be dealt with in a way to ensure the sound application of attribution analysis with adequate asset or segment weights.

- *Treating leverage.*
Even when the portfolio management process is not particularly sophisticated, some investment decisions may affect exposures to risk factors so that the simple multiplication of asset weights with their associated returns no longer reflects the correct performance. These situations, called "risk positioning" by Brinson, Singer, and Beebower (1991), arise when the portfolio manager uses different forms of leverage in order to alter their exposures. The desired leverage effect can typically be obtained in three manners: through derivatives, gearing, or short sales.
Attribution with derivatives is discussed in Section 14.3. The other two forms of leverage, namely borrowing money in order to increase the portfolio's risk exposures[3] and borrowing assets in order to sell them short (as in some long/short or market neutral hedge fund strategies), lead to a situation in which the ratio (sum of total positive exposures/total portfolio value) is greater than one. If this is the case, the general principle is to (i) assign a negative weight to the positions that generate leverage and (ii) multiply them by the actual return of the asset. This guarantees that a short position (in cash or any other asset) that multiplies a positive return generates a loss at the portfolio level. The procedure must ensure that $\sum_{w_i>0} w_i + \sum_{w_i<0} w_i = 1$.
- *Caring about off-benchmark positions.*
Because the benchmark is usually specified as a basket of indexes, there are sometimes portfolio holdings that, to any extent, do not match any benchmark components. These are called "off-benchmark decisions." Since the portfolio weight and return of these assets, which we respectively call $w_{P,k_0,t}$ and $R_{P,k_0,t}$, both differ from zero, they must be accounted for in the attribution system but necessarily with a corresponding nil benchmark segment weight: $w_{B,k_0,t} = 0$.
The solution is given by assigning a corresponding benchmark return $R_{B,k_0,t}$ that differs from zero. Bacon (2023) distinguishes three calibrations of the benchmark return, depending on what kind of effect is to be identified (in the BF model): (i) if it appears only in the Selection effect, then $R_{B,k_0,t} = R_{B,t}$ (overall benchmark return); (ii) if it appears only in the Allocation effect, then $R_{B,k_0,t} = R_{P,k_0,t}$ (equal portfolio and benchmark segment returns); and (iii) if it appears in both the Selection and Allocation effects, then $R_{B,k_0,t}$ is chosen as a passive index return whose characteristics closely match those of the portfolio segment. Since the benchmark segment weight equals zero, none of these choices alters the global outcome of the attribution analysis.

[3]The opposite situation, in which the manager decides to hold a cash position in order to decrease their exposure, is called "damping" by Bacon (2023). It falls, according to us, under the broad scope of cash investments and obeys the classical attribution principles.

14.1.3.3 The portfolio management perspective

Another set of decisions to be carefully weighed when preparing the attribution analysis is to ensure that the system adequately catches the intentions of the portfolio managers when making their decisions. Among the many considerations that can be relevant, we point out two of them.

- *Adapting the system to the investment decision process: top-down or bottom-up.* The major perspective adopted by classical attribution analysis is the top-down process depicted in Chapter 13, starting with the strategic allocation decisions and then drilling down inside the segments in order to generate extra returns from tactical decisions up to the individual security selection process.

  Alternatively, some portfolio managers may adopt the bottom-up logic, building up their portfolios as the superposition of individual decisions regarding the selection of securities. Since the portfolio's global allocation can be viewed as a by-product of these decisions, trying to assess the full-fledged attribution through the BHB or BF approach is meaningless: there is simply no dedicated asset allocation process through active portfolio management decisions. Here again, an adaptation of the framework discussed by Bacon (2023) is useful. The process starts at the individual security level. For every asset i, it is first checked whether it appears in the benchmark or not. In the former case, we have $R_{P,i,t} = R_{B,i,t}$ but $w_{P,i,t} \neq w_{B,i,t}$. In the latter case, $w_{P,i,t} > 0$ and $w_{B,i,t} = 0$. Furthermore, there are also assets that appear in the benchmark but not in the portfolio, which means that $w_{B,i,t} > 0$ and $w_{P,i,t} = 0$. Second, for the same asset, there are potentially differences in returns between the position held in the portfolio because of transactions made during the period. In that case, it is acknowledged that $R_{P,i,t} \neq R_{B,i,t}$. This set of rules is summarized in Table 14-13.

  Putting all these elements together, the attribution analysis considers each asset as its own segment, i.e., $K = N$, and the BHB or BF attribution system works similarly as before.

TABLE 14-13 Summary of weights and returns for bottom-up portfolio management.

Asset in portfolio	Timing effect	Weights	Returns
P and *B*	No	$w_{P,i,t} \neq w_{B,i,t} \neq 0$	$R_{P,i,t} = R_{B,i,t} \neq 0$
	Yes	$w_{P,i,t} \neq w_{B,i,t} \neq 0$	$R_{P,i,t} \neq R_{B,i,t} \neq 0$
P only	N/A	$w_{P,i,t} \neq 0, w_{B,i,t} = 0$	$R_{P,i,t} \neq 0, R_{B,i,t} = 0$
B only	N/A	$w_{P,i,t} = 0, w_{B,i,t} \neq 0$	$R_{P,i,t} = 0, R_{B,i,t} \neq 0$

- *Partitioning the investment universe adequately.*
  The choice of the segments, both for the portfolio and the benchmark, is another important decision to make. The general principles are very intuitive:
  1. The segments represent a partition for both the portfolio and the benchmark. This is consistent with the golden rules expressed in Chapter 13. The overlap between the segment types of the portfolio and the benchmark should be maximized (e.g., both portfolios should preferably use the same segments).
  2. The partitioning by asset class must be consistent with the investment decision process. At the global level, it should match the types of asset classes for which a strategic asset allocation is made.
  3. The order to the sub-partitioning (by asset class) must be consistent with the order of priority in the tactical decisions. For equities, the choice must typically be made between geography, sector, or factor-based criteria. Nothing prevents a waterfall, but it should always respect a hierarchical approach within the same attribution analysis. Nothing prevents either parallel analyses on different criteria, provided that the additional complexity of the interpretation is justified.
  4. Preferably, the benchmark choice should be adapted to the portfolio management process, and not conversely. In particular, the benchmark constituents should encompass as much as possible the set of securities that compose the investment universe for the manager.

14.1.4 The ESG dimension in attribution analysis

Many investors increasingly care about the ESG characteristics of their portfolio. This dimension creates a number of issues to consider. First, the scores awarded to companies and their associated rankings largely differ across the spectrum of data vendors and consultants that have specialized in the field. Second, the E, S, and G attributes of a given firm or organization may largely diverge from each other, which potentially calls for a detailed granular analysis of the global score in order to determine the exact contribution of each sub-dimension of a portfolio's ESG attributes to its performance. Third, there is still debate regarding the magnitude and sign of the return premium that can be associated with ESG characteristics.[4]

Regarding performance attribution, the ESG dimension is not neutral to many investors. A natural question to be asked in this context would be how to isolate the pure ESG-related active returns from the traditional BHB or BF framework. The contribution of Grégoire (2019) provides an answer to this concern.

[4]These considerations are analyzed in greater depth in Section 16.4 of Chapter 16, which is entirely dedicated to the links between ESG and financial performance.

14.1.4.1 ESG-restricted attribution

What distinguishes most portfolios with an explicit ESG focus from those that are indifferent to this dimension is a sort of restriction on the investment universe. Restrictive investment constraints can be of various kinds (exclusion policies, best-in-class selection, choice of a particular thematic, ...), but they all end up reducing the investable assets to ESG-compatible securities. The objective of the particular ESG attribution analysis is to disentangle the impact of these restrictions (which occur upstream of the actual investment decisions) from the pure active portfolio management process.

According to this view, the focus is set on the benchmark composition. Instead of directly focusing on $R_{B,t} = \sum_{k=1}^{K} w_{B,k,t} R_{B,k,t}$ as in Equation (14-1b), Grégoire (2019) defines an intermediate portfolio return, called $R_{\text{ESG},t}$, that summarizes the information contained in the ESG-related set of restrictions. This benchmark represents a subset of the initial one in terms of composition (because of the excluded securities) but must be neutral in terms of segment allocations.

Formally, for each asset i belonging to segment k, the author defines its weight in the ESG portfolio by using the following formula:

$$w_{\text{ESG},i,t} = \begin{cases} \tilde{w}_{B,i,t} \times \varphi_{k,t} \text{ if } i \in \text{ESG}_t \\ 0 \text{ if } i \notin \text{ESG}_t \end{cases} \tag{14-10}$$

where ESG_t is the set of all eligible securities in the benchmark, $\tilde{w}_{B,i,t} = \frac{w_{B,i,t}}{\sum_{j \in \text{ESG}_t} w_{B,j,t}}$ is the weight of the asset in the restricted universe of eligible assets in the benchmark, and $\varphi_{k,t} = \frac{w_{B,k,t}}{\tilde{w}_{B,k,t}}$ in which $\tilde{w}_{B,k,t} = \frac{\sum_{j \in \text{ESG}_t \& j \in k} w_{B,j,t}}{\sum_{j \in \text{ESG}_t} w_{B,j,t}}$ is a normalization coefficient that ensures the neutrality of the segment allocation between the original and the ESG-restricted benchmarks. For instance, consider an investment universe that is composed of five assets (1–5) belonging to three segments A (for assets 1 and 2), B (for assets 3 and 4) and C (for asset 5). Their associated benchmark weights are $w_{B,1,t} = 20\%$, $w_{B,2,t} = 10\%$, $w_{B,3,t} = 10\%$, $w_{B,4,t} = 20\%$, and $w_{B,5,t} = 40\%$. The fourth one is excluded from the ESG-restricted benchmark. The application of the formula of Equation (14-10) provides the output summarized in Table 14-14.

As the table shows, the weight of each segment (50% for A, 30% for B, and 20% for C) remains unaffected by the procedure. Since the fourth asset is discarded from the ESG-adjusted benchmark (shaded row in the table), not only its weight is distributed across the remaining ones, but the segment-related normalization reshuffles the other assets' weights so as to keep the segment allocation unchanged.

The next step of the attribution process is to distinguish the performance that can be attributed to the pure active decisions from the one that results from the shrinkage of the investment universe in order to comply with the ESG-related constraints through the following equation:

$$R_{P,t} - R_{B,t} = (R_{P,t} - R_{\text{ESG},t}) + (R_{\text{ESG},t} - R_{B,t}) \tag{14-11}$$

TABLE 14-14 Illustration of the computation of ESG-adjusted benchmark weights.

Segment	Asset	$w_{B,i,t}$	ESG-adjusted weight $\tilde{w}_{B,i,t}$	Normalization $\varphi_{k,t}$	ESG weight $w_{ESG,i,t}$
A	1	20%	$\frac{20\%}{80\%} = 25\%$	$\frac{30\%}{37.5\%} = 0.80$	25% × 0.80 = 20%
	2	10%	$\frac{10\%}{80\%} = 12.5\%$	$\frac{30\%}{37.5\%} = 0.80$	12.5% × 0.80 = 10%
B	3	10%	$\frac{10\%}{80\%} = 12.5\%$	$\frac{30\%}{12.5\%} = 2.40$	12.5% × 2.40 = 30%
	4	20%	0%	0	0%
C	5	40%	$\frac{40\%}{80\%} = 50\%$	$\frac{40\%}{50\%} = 0.80$	50% × 0.80 = 40%

The identifiable effects can be expressed as follows:

$$R_{P,t} - R_{B,t} = \mathcal{A}_{P,t} + \mathcal{S}_{P,t} + \mathcal{I}_{P,t} + \mathcal{S}^{ESG}_{P,t} \tag{14-12}$$

where the first three terms (Allocation, Selection, and Interaction effects) are similar to those of Equation (14-7), replacing the benchmark by the ESG portfolio.

The fourth effect, the ESG–Selection effect, is specifically linked to the restrictions involved in the ESG policy. Since, by construction, we have that $w_{B,k,t} = w_{ESG,k,t}$ at the segment level, the only effect left is indeed related to securities selection:

$$\mathcal{S}^{ESG}_{P,t} = \sum_{k=1}^{K} w_{B,k,t}(R_{ESG,k,t} - R_{B,k,t}) \tag{14-13}$$

At a more granular level (within the segments), it is nevertheless possible to perform a full attribution analysis because the individual ESG weights $w_{ESG,i,t}$ differ from the original ones in the benchmark $w_{B,i,t}$ for all segments that involve restrictions. Thus, pursuing the same logic, the within-segment attribution analysis leads to the identification of a pure Allocation effect: $c_k(R_{ESG,t}) - c_k(R_{B,t}) = c_k(\mathcal{A}_{ESG,t})$ where

$$c_k(\mathcal{A}_{ESG,t}) = \sum_{j \in k}(w_{ESG,j,t} - w_{B,j,t})R_{j,t} \tag{14-14}$$

For instance, in Table 14-14, it is clear that the individual weights for segments A and C are unchanged, whereas the weight of asset 4 (from 20% to 0%) is entirely redistributed to asset 3 (from 10% to 30%) within the same segment B. Nonetheless, each security's return is the same in the ESG portfolio and the benchmark. Thus, the decision to discard asset 4 is profitable if $R_{3,t} > R_{4,t}$.

The outcome of the analysis will provide insight regarding the financial attractiveness of the decision to restrict the investment universe to only ESG-eligible securities. If the effect is globally positive, this means that this decision has paid off, i.e., that the market has somehow remunerated ESG-friendly policies. Otherwise, this entails that the restriction of the investment universe penalizes the global portfolio. In principle, both scenarios are possible, as discussed in Section 16.4 of Chapter 16.

14.1.4.2 The effect of negative screening

The example of Table 14-14 works provided that every segment is represented in the ESG benchmark portfolio. Otherwise, as explained by Grégoire (2019), an additional adjustment has to be made in order to restrict the original benchmark to those segments that are not excluded from the portfolio.

The procedure that he proposes is split into two steps. The first one involves the creation of an artificial "Negative Screening" (NS) portfolio that links the ESG-restricted and the benchmark portfolios. This portfolio uses the information about the excluded segments, but not about the excluded assets within each segment. Considering again the individual securities, their weights are simply recomputed so that the non-excluded segments keep the same relative weights with respect to each other in the resulting portfolio through the equation

$$w_{\text{NS},i,t} = \begin{cases} \breve{w}_{B,i,t} \text{ if } k_i \in \text{NS}_t \\ 0 \text{ if } k_i \notin \text{NS}_t \end{cases} \tag{14-15}$$

where $\breve{w}_{B,i,t} = \frac{w_{B,i,t}}{\sum_{k_j \in \text{NS}_t} w_{B,j,t}}$ is the weight of the asset in the restricted universe of the segments retained after the screening process.

The second step is to create the ESG portfolio with only those sectors that are retained using the same procedure as before but replacing the original weights $w_{B,i,t}$ with the screening-adjusted ones $\breve{w}_{B,i,t}$ in Equation (14-10). We illustrate the two-step process, using the same data as Table 14-14, but this time excluding segment C from the eligible universe in the screening process. The outcome is summarized in Table 14-15.

The introduction of the negative screening step induces a proportional shift of the weights of all assets in the non-rejected segments (A and B), including the assets that will subsequently be discarded (asset 4). This is the reason why the ESG-adjusted weights $\tilde{w}_{B,i,t}$ differ from those of Table 14-14. Compared with the previous situation, the NS portfolio still features asset 4, whereas the ESG portfolio shrinks to the three assets that are retained in the actively managed portfolio.

TABLE 14-15 Illustration of the computation of the NS and ESG benchmark weights.

Segment	Asset	$w_{B,i,t}$	NS-adjusted weight $w_{NS,i,t}$	ESG-adjusted weight $\tilde{w}_{B,i,t}$	Normalization $\phi_{k,t}$	ESG weight $w_{ESG,i,t}$
A	1	20%	$\frac{20\%}{60\%} = 33.3\%$	$\frac{33.3\%}{66.7\%} = 50\%$	$\frac{50\%}{75\%} = 0.67$	$50\% \times 0.67 = 33.3\%$
	2	10%	$\frac{10\%}{60\%} = 16.7\%$	$\frac{16.7\%}{66.7\%} = 25\%$	$\frac{50\%}{75\%} = 0.67$	$25\% \times 0.67 = 16.7\%$
B	3	10%	$\frac{10\%}{60\%} = 16.7\%$	$\frac{16.7\%}{66.7\%} = 25\%$	$\frac{50\%}{25\%} = 2.00$	$25\% \times 2.00 = 50\%$
	4	20%	$\frac{20\%}{60\%} = 33.3\%$	0%	0	0%
C	5	40%	0%	0%	0	0%

The performance attribution equation also features an additional step, with the differential returns that are ordered by the inverse order of the decision-making process:

$$R_{P,t} - R_{B,t} = (R_{P,t} - R_{ESG,t}) + (R_{ESG,t} - R_{NS,t}) + (R_{NS,t} - R_{B,t}) \quad (14\text{-}16)$$

The NS portfolio plays the role of the benchmark for the ESG one. The comparison of the Negative Screening and benchmark portfolios (last term) induces the emphasis of an additional effect:

$$R_{P,t} - R_{B,t} = \mathcal{A}_{P,t} + \mathcal{S}_{P,t} + \mathcal{I}_{P,t} + \mathcal{S}^{ESG}_{P,t} + \mathcal{A}^{NS}_{P,t} \quad (14\text{-}17)$$

This time, the new effect involves only allocation decisions because the segment returns have not been modified, i.e., $R_{B,k,t} = R_{NS,k,t}$. The Screening–Allocation effect is written as

$$\mathcal{A}^{NS}_{P,t} = \sum_{k=1}^{K} (w_{NS,k,t} - w_{B,k,t}) R_{B,k,t} \quad (14\text{-}18)$$

where $w_{NS,k,t} = \sum_{j \in k} \tilde{w}_{B,i,t}$ represents the weight of segment k in the Negative Screening portfolio.

The remarks made before regarding the restrictions of the ESG universe of assets apply to the negative screening decisions as well. The sign of the effect will depend on whether the discarded sectors deliver superior or inferior returns in comparison with the remaining ones after the screening process.

14.2 MULTIPERIOD ATTRIBUTION ANALYSIS

In the example that we have developed so far, we have taken the average return of the benchmark and the funds. This can be justified if the objective of the analysis is to assess the average source of each effect on the outperformance of a portfolio manager during a single time period. The approach is interesting because the average excess return of a portfolio over its benchmark, which is also known as its "abnormal return," has a famous name: the alpha. It is thus acceptable to apply the following formula as a statistical aggregation of Equation (14-3):

$$\overline{R}_P - \overline{R}_B \equiv \alpha_P = \overline{\mathcal{T}}_P + \overline{\mathcal{S}}_P + \overline{\mathcal{I}}_P \tag{14-19}$$

where $\overline{\mathcal{T}}_P = \frac{1}{T}\sum_{t=1}^{T} \mathcal{T}_{P,t}$, $\overline{\mathcal{S}}_P = \frac{1}{T}\sum_{t=1}^{T} \mathcal{S}_{P,t}$, and $\overline{\mathcal{I}}_P = \frac{1}{T}\sum_{t=1}^{T} \mathcal{I}_{P,t}$ are the average Allocation, Selection, and Interaction effects, respectively.

In that approach, the sample is specifically used as a tool for statistical analysis. Each periodic observation is considered as a single draw from this sample, and the purpose is to check whether there is a reproduction of the effects in a statistically significant manner with the associated traditional inference tools (see Chapter 3 for a discussion).

The meaning of this statistical analysis should not be confused with a dedicated multiperiod attribution analysis whose purpose is to examine the drivers of performance for a horizon longer than one period. The results of the analysis with single-period arithmetic returns cannot simply be added up to obtain the multiperiod one because we would miss the compounding effect. In other words, the issue can be written as

$$R_{P,0\to T} - R_{B,0\to T} \neq (R_{P,1} - R_{B,1}) + (R_{P,2} - R_{B,2}) + \ldots + (R_{P,T} - R_{B,T}) \tag{14-20}$$

where $R_{P,0\to T}$ and $R_{B,0\to T}$ are the cumulative (i.e., total) return of the portfolio and the benchmark, respectively, over the sample period.

The issue of linking single-period returns so as to find a relation similar to Equation (14-20) that avoids the disturbing inequality sign is far from being simple. A tempting solution would be to use continuously compounded (i.e., logarithmic) returns. They have the additive property: the multiperiod return of a portfolio is indeed equal to the sum of the periodic returns. However, this is still not that simple, since adding up the logarithmic version of each effect in discrete time would miss a fair deal of the cross-product return. Thus, the sum of the effects does not match the total excess return.

There have been many attempts to solve the issue of correctly attributing multiperiod excess returns.[5] Bacon (2023) puts them in two categories: "smoothing" methods that distribute the residuals of Equation (14-20) in a structured way across the effects, and pure "linking" methods that compound the effects over time but create a path-dependence. In what follows, we develop two elegant and workable versions of such methods: logarithmic smoothing coefficient attribution, and geometric attribution.

[5]For an insightful discussion and a comprehensive list of related papers, see Bacon (2019).

14.2.1 The logarithmic smoothing coefficient attribution method

If we could observe the portfolio return on infinitesimal time variations, it would write at any time t as the instantaneous rate of return $R^{\Delta}_{P,t} \equiv \lim_{\Delta t \to 0} R_{P,t+\Delta t}$. Applying the same principle for the benchmark gives $R^{\Delta}_{B,t}$. Since these are single-period returns, we can apply Equation (14-3):

$$R^{\Delta}_{P,t} - R^{\Delta}_{B,t} = \mathcal{T}^{\Delta}_{P,t} + \mathcal{S}^{\Delta}_{P,t} + \mathcal{I}^{\Delta}_{P,t} \tag{14-21}$$

where $\mathcal{T}^{\Delta}_{P,t}$, $\mathcal{S}^{\Delta}_{P,t}$, and $\mathcal{I}^{\Delta}_{P,t}$ are the instantaneous Allocation, Selection and Interaction effects, respectively. To obtain these cumulative effects over time, we take the integrals on both sides:

$$\int_0^T (R^{\Delta}_{P,t} - R^{\Delta}_{B,t})\mathrm{d}t = \int_0^T \mathcal{T}^{\Delta}_{P,t}\mathrm{d}t + \int_0^T \mathcal{S}^{\Delta}_{P,t}\mathrm{d}t + \int_0^T \mathcal{I}^{\Delta}_{P,t}\mathrm{d}t \tag{14-22}$$

which provides what Christopherson et al. (2009) call an "idealized attribution system." In practice, it is necessary to simplify this expression as, instead of dealing with instantaneous returns, we have to make do with only returns observed with a certain frequency. For the left-hand side of the equation, there is no real issue: we can simply write $\int_0^T R^{\Delta}_{P,t}\mathrm{d}t \equiv R^c_{P,0\to T} = \log(1 + R_{P,0\to T})$ and $\int_0^T R^{\Delta}_{B,t}\mathrm{d}t \equiv R^c_{B,0\to T} = \log(1 + R_{B,0\to T})$. However, on the right-hand side, we have to use the approximation $\int_0^T \mathcal{T}^{\Delta}_{P,t}\mathrm{d}t + \int_0^T \mathcal{S}^{\Delta}_{P,t}\mathrm{d}t + \int_0^T \mathcal{I}^{\Delta}_{P,t}\mathrm{d}t \approx \sum_{t=1}^T \mathcal{T}^c_{P,t} + \sum_{t=1}^T \mathcal{S}^c_{P,t} + \sum_{t=1}^T \mathcal{I}^c_{P,t}$, where the terms are the continuously compounded values of the effects ($\mathcal{T}^c_{P,t} = \log(1 + \mathcal{T}_{P,t})$, etc.) so that we obtain an approximate relation of the kind:

$$R^c_{P,0\to T} - R^c_{B,0\to T} \approx \sum_{t=1}^T \mathcal{T}^c_{P,t} + \sum_{t=1}^T \mathcal{S}^c_{P,t} + \sum_{t=1}^T \mathcal{I}^c_{P,t} \tag{14-23}$$

This relation leaves a residual equal to the difference between the actual sum in Equation (14-21) and the approximated one of (14-23). According to the second principle of attribution discussed in Chapter 13, this should not occur. Cariño (1999) suggests a method to distribute the residual proportionately.[6] He then obtains the multiperiod arithmetic effects by the following system:

$$R_{P,0\to T} - R_{B,0\to T} = \tilde{\mathcal{T}}_P + \tilde{\mathcal{S}}_P + \tilde{\mathcal{I}}_P \tag{14-24}$$

in which $\tilde{\mathcal{T}}_P$, $\tilde{\mathcal{S}}_P$ and $\tilde{\mathcal{I}}_P$ are the aggregate effects. They are defined by

$$\tilde{\mathcal{T}}_P = \sum_{t=1}^T \frac{l_{P,t}}{l_{P,T}} \mathcal{T}_{P,t},\ \tilde{\mathcal{S}}_P = \sum_{t=1}^T \frac{l_{P,t}}{l_{P,T}} \mathcal{S}_{P,t} \text{ and } \tilde{\mathcal{I}}_P = \sum_{t=1}^T \frac{l_{P,t}}{l_{P,T}} \mathcal{I}_{P,t} \tag{14-25}$$

[6]The other very popular multiperiod attribution approaches are found in Menchero (2000), who provides an optimized distribution method for the residual (smoothing), and Frongello (2002) who compounds attribution effects through time (linking).

where $l_{P,t} = \frac{\log(1+R_{P,t})-\log(1+R_{B,t})}{R_{P,t}-R_{B,t}}$ or $l_{P,t} = \frac{1}{1+R_{P,t}}$ if $R_{P,t} = R_{B,t}$, and, likewise, we have $l_{P,T} = \frac{\log(1+R_{P,0\to T})-\log(1+R_{B,0\to T})}{R_{P,0\to T}-R_{B,0\to T}}$ or $l_{P,T} = \frac{1}{1+R_{P,0\to T}}$ if $R_{P,1\to T} = R_{B,1\to T}$. The expression $\frac{l_{P,t}}{l_{P,T}}$ is called the linking coefficient. It serves as a reconciliation device between discretely compounded returns used for the single-period attribution and the continuously compounded returns that should be used in an additive fashion in multiperiod attribution.

The VAS example (continued)

Thanks to the logarithmic smoothing contribution method, it is possible to examine the evolution of each of the effects for the three funds. For that purpose, it is first necessary to compute the linking coefficients, as shown in Table 14-16.

TABLE 14-16 VAS example – Linking coefficients.

	Verso	Alloco	Selecto
Jan	0.994	0.996	0.996
Feb	0.984	0.988	0.987
Mar	0.976	0.979	0.980
Apr	0.995	0.998	0.998
May	1.034	1.033	1.035
Jun	0.985	0.989	0.984
Jul	1.046	1.042	1.045
Aug	0.963	0.961	0.961
Sep	0.971	0.968	0.972
Oct	0.985	0.983	0.981
Nov	0.979	0.977	0.974
Dec	1.029	1.024	1.026
Global	**0.938**	**0.938**	**0.938**

For each month, we report the corresponding $l_{P,t}$. The last row represents the global link $l_{P,T}$ for each fund. For instance, the linking coefficient for the Verso fund in January is equal to $\frac{l_{V,\text{Jan}}}{l_{V,\text{Global}}} = \frac{0.994}{0.938} = 1.0595$. The table shows how strongly extreme values, such as those in July or August, are affected by the passage from discrete to continuous compounding. It is also interesting to note that, because the global link is systematically lower than the monthly links, the linking coefficients are all greater than one. This means that the strength of the arithmetic effect is reinforced with the passage to multiperiod attribution. Thanks to this information, we can compute the cumulative effects for all funds by using Equation (14-24).

Because the aggregate effect is the exact sum of the individual ones, the data in Table 14-17 can be considered a faithful representation of the evolution of each of the portfolios' cumulative excess returns. Interestingly, they do not add up to the same amount for the three funds, thereby contradicting the information from Table 13-5 of Chapter 13 showing that the funds share the same arithmetic alpha of 2.00%. The compounded alpha is not only greater but it also differs from one fund to the other.

TABLE 14-17 VAS example – Cumulative effects.

	Verso	Alloco	Selecto
Jan	0.56%	0.08%	0.17%
Feb	1.57%	0.15%	0.43%
Mar	2.11%	0.19%	0.29%
Apr	3.00%	0.32%	0.58%
May	4.07%	1.44%	1.29%
Jun	4.38%	0.98%	1.82%
Jul	4.43%	1.80%	2.06%
Aug	3.93%	1.58%	1.85%
Sep	3.58%	1.87%	1.22%
Oct	3.20%	1.88%	1.76%
Nov	2.61%	1.70%	2.07%
Dec	2.16%	2.22%	2.17%

The evolution of the global effect over time is also instructive. As expected, it mostly stems from the management of the equities compartment. Studying in detail the cumulative effects for the three portfolios leads to Figure 14-6.

(continued)

(continued)

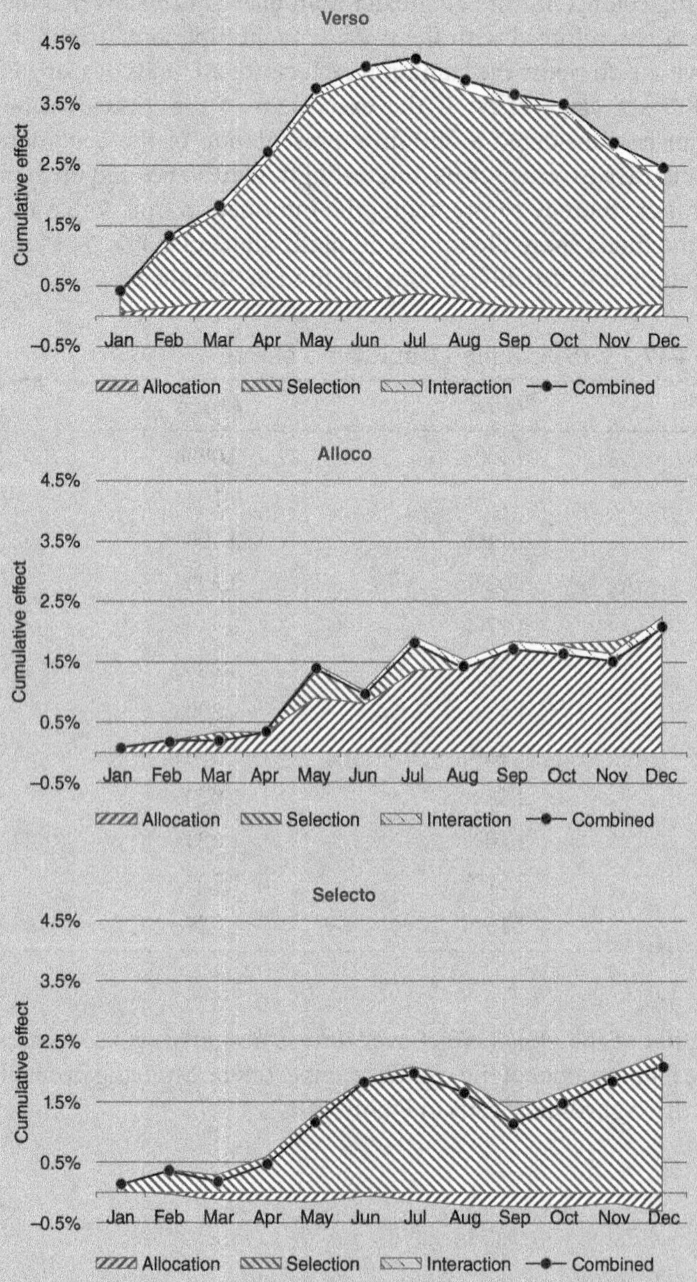

FIGURE 14-6 VAS example – Cumulative evolution of the three effects for the equity compartments.

Only month-by-month information could have revealed what stands clear from the graphs: The Verso fund clearly has two distinct phases, with a great outperformance during the first half of the year and a progressive negative performance during the second half. Almost all the effect is a wrong selection (probably not on individual securities, but rather on sector, regional, or factor allocation that turned partly wrong). The middle and bottom graphs also confirm that the generation of extra returns by Alloco and Selecto are mostly due to Allocation and Selection effects, respectively.

14.2.2 The geometric attribution method

The phenomenon that is responsible for the disturbing inequality of Equation (14-20) is the use of arithmetic periodic returns. Bacon (2002) argues that geometric returns, in spite of their lack of additivity, have a number of advantages in attribution analysis. They are compoundable (thus leaving no residual), convertible across currencies, and proportionate. Recall how we expressed the excess geometric return in Chapter 6, namely, $r^g_{P-j,t} \equiv \frac{1+R_{P,t}}{1+R_{j,t}} - 1$ for any reference portfolio j. This is the starting point of the geometric attribution method introduced by Burnie, Knowles, and Teder (1998) (henceforth BKT) and refined by Weber (2018) in order to introduce the geometric Interaction effect. This model builds on the Brinson–Fachler model described in Section 14.1.2.

The original BKT attribution model features only an Allocation and a gross Selection effect (the latter one including the Interaction effect). The perspective is thus largely driven by a top-down approach. Adapting the generic formula (14-7), we obtain

$$r^g_{P-B,t} \equiv \frac{1+R_{P,t}}{1+R_{B,t}} - 1 = (1+\mathcal{A}^g_{P,t})(1+\mathcal{S}'^g_{P,t}) - 1 \tag{14-26}$$

where $\mathcal{A}^g_{P,t}$ and $\mathcal{S}'^g_{P,t}$ are the geometric Allocation and gross Selection effects, respectively, which are defined by

$$\mathcal{A}^g_{P,t} = \frac{1+R_{P(\mathrm{NA}),t}}{1+R_{B,t}} - 1 \tag{14-27a}$$

$$\mathcal{S}'^g_{P,t} = \frac{1+R_{P,t}}{1+R_{P(\mathrm{NA}),t}} - 1 \tag{14-27b}$$

where, as stated before in our interpretation of Table 14-8, $R_{P(\mathrm{NA}),t} = \sum_{k=1}^{K} w_{P,k,t} R_{B,k,t}$ is the return of the notional allocation portfolio.

Burnie et al. (1998) show further how to aggregate the segment-per-segment effects to the global one in an additive way: $\mathcal{A}^g_{P,t} = \sum_{k=1}^{K} c_k(\mathcal{A}^g_{P,t})$ and $\mathcal{S}'^g_{P,t} = \sum_{k=1}^{K} c_k(\mathcal{S}'^g_{P,t})$, in which the individual contributions are defined as

$$c_k(\mathcal{A}^g_{P,t}) = \frac{(w_{P,k,t} - w_{B,k,t})(R_{B,k,t} - R_{B,t})}{1 + R_{B,t}} \tag{14-28a}$$

$$c_k(\mathcal{S}'^g_{P,t}) = \frac{w_{P,k,t}(R_{P,k,t} - R_{B,k,t})}{1 + R_{P(NA),t}} \tag{14-28b}$$

In order to make the original BKT method fully comparable with the Brinson and Fachler analysis, Weber (2018) shows how to extract the geometric Interaction effect from the gross Selection effect:

$$r^g_{P-B,t} = (1 + \mathcal{A}^g_{P,t})(1 + \mathcal{S}^g_{P,t})(1 + \mathcal{I}^g_{P,t}) - 1 \tag{14-29}$$

where $\mathcal{A}^g_{P,t}$ is unchanged and where the geometric (net) Selection effect $\mathcal{S}^g_{P,t}$ and Interaction effect $\mathcal{I}^g_{P,t}$ are given by

$$\mathcal{S}^g_{P,t} = \frac{1 + R_{P(NS),t}}{1 + R_{B,t}} - 1 \tag{14-30a}$$

$$\mathcal{I}^g_{P,t} = \frac{(1 + R_{P,t})(1 + R_{B,t})}{(1 + R_{P(NA),t})(1 + R_{P(NS),t})} - 1 \tag{14-30b}$$

in which, as before, $R_{P(NS),t} = \sum_{k=1}^{K} w_{B,k,t} R_{P,k,t}$ is the return of the notional selection portfolio.

Because the Selection effect has been "purified" from the Interaction effect, the contribution at the segment level is also neater than in expression (14-27b). The price to pay is the creation of a version of the contribution of the Interaction effect that does not recombine at the portfolio level. We have to define a "cross-segment Interaction term" as the difference between the full effect and the sum of the contributions:

$$c_k(\mathcal{S}^g_{P,t}) = \frac{w_{B,k,t}(R_{P,k,t} - R_{B,k,t})}{1 + R_{P(NA),t}} \tag{14-31a}$$

$$c_k(\mathcal{I}^g_{P,t}) = \frac{(w_{P,k,t} - w_{B,k,t})(R_{P,k,t} - R_{B,k,t})}{(1 + R_{P(NA),t})(1 + R_{P(NS),t})} \tag{14-31b}$$

$$c_{CS}(\mathcal{I}^g_{P,t}) \equiv \mathcal{I}^g_{P,t} - \sum_{k=1}^{K} c_k(\mathcal{I}^g_{P,t}) = \frac{R_{P,t}R_{B,t} - R_{P(NA),t}R_{P(NS),t}}{(1 + R_{P(NA),t})(1 + R_{P(NS),t})} \tag{14-31c}$$

Bacon (2019, p.19) notes that "*Because geometric excess returns compound through time and because geometric allocation effects and geometric selection effects compound together within each period, geometric allocation and geometric selection must also compound through time.*"

Although this was apparently not the intent of Burnie et al. (1998), the use of geometric attribution allows a multiperiod analysis by simply compounding the effects over time, through the formula (see Weber, 2018, for the generalization of the model):

$$r^g_{P-B,0\to T} = \prod_{t=1}^{T}(1 + \mathcal{A}^g_{P,t})(1 + \mathcal{S}^g_{P,t})(1 + \mathcal{I}^g_{P,t}) - 1 \tag{14-32}$$

Similarly, for the effects, we have $\mathcal{A}^g_{P,0\to T} = \prod_{t=1}^{T}(1 + \mathcal{A}^g_{P,t}) - 1$, $\mathcal{S}^g_{P,0\to T} = \prod_{t=1}^{T}(1 + \mathcal{S}^g_{P,t}) - 1$, and $\mathcal{I}^g_{P,0\to T} = \prod_{t=1}^{T}(1 + \mathcal{I}^g_{P,t}) - 1$.

The VAS example (continued)

We concentrate on the active management of the equities segment with the comparison of the cumulative effects of Alloco and Selecto. The added value of the geometric attribution model is that we can safely look at the cumulative effects in a retrospective way, as the effects will exactly correspond to what would have been obtained at the very same moment of the observation. Graphically, the representation of the three effects (and their combined one) for the two funds using the extended BKT model of Weber (2018) gives the visual impression shown in Figure 14-7.

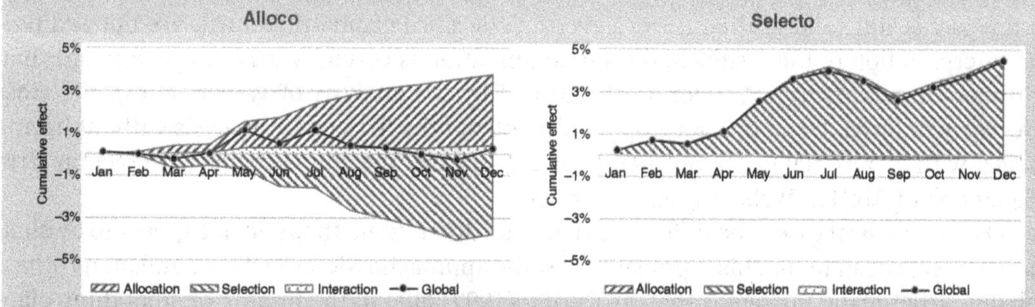

FIGURE 14-7 VAS example – Cumulative evolution of the three effects within the equity segment.

We already knew that the Alloco fund had delivered almost no excess return overall within the equities segment. The graph shows that the manager had originally performed decently, with a cumulative effect reaching about 1% in the middle of the year. The degradation of performance mostly occurred during the second semester, with selection decisions that more than offset the steadily positive allocation effect over time. For Selecto, the story is almost linear, with no or very limited Allocation and Interaction effects.

14.2.3 A short discussion

There are many other ways of implementing a multiperiod attribution analysis (see Fischer and Wermers, 2013, for a complete taxonomy), but we believe that the two methods discussed in this section are relatively simple and representative of their own category. Even though they serve the same purpose of delivering results that can be used in a multiperiod analysis, they are not fully equivalent.

The logarithmic linking approach has the great merit of preserving the additive property of returns. Because of this characteristic, it entails no particular difficulty when aggregating or disaggregating various effects at any level since everything can be summed up in space and in time. It eases to a great extent the interpretation and the presentation of results. This advantage comes with a cost however. The residual of Equation (14-23) has to be distributed according to a linking coefficient that takes into account the whole sample period through the global link function $l_{P,T}$. It is thus impossible to reconcile the outcome of the *ex post* analysis on a certain time window, for which all periods are necessary, with a shorter sub-period that would only use part of the data.

By contrast, a major advantage related to the use of the geometric attribution method is the independence of the effects over time, without the necessity to make strong assumptions on residuals. This is not only useful for the analysis of sub-periods within a whole sample time window (like quarterly attribution within a full year, for instance); it also means that the attribution analysis can be built up over time, in an incremental manner. The values obtained for any specific period t will remain the same ahead of that period, so that the analysis made in the past is still valid in the future. Nevertheless, since geometric returns are not additive, the interpretation of the results and their combination is certainly less straightforward than with continuous returns. Moreover, as outlined by the analysis of Weber (2018), the cross effects are not trivial, and it is not easy to fully roll out the BHB or BF analysis without having to deal with a "residual of the residuals," as captured by the cross-segment Interaction term (Equation (14-31c)) in Weber's (2018) analysis.

Overall, in most cases, the differences between different methods do not appear to be qualitatively very substantial. This is probably why the approaches described here and many others cohabit. What really matters is that, as Cariño (1999) puts it, the linking or smoothing algorithm meets three characteristics: (i) generality (it supports any additive single-period pattern), (ii) familiarity (same interpretation for multiperiod and single-period results), and (iii) the absence of residuals (no distortion of the results because of an unexplained effect).

14.3 EXTENDING THE SCOPE OF ATTRIBUTION ANALYSIS

Attribution analysis is at the same time powerful and flexible, but it must be manipulated with caution. The principles of the BHB or the BF attribution frameworks can, and indeed even must, be adapted when the actively managed portfolio displays specific features. We discuss here two such cases: the global portfolio, for which the currency exposures must be dealt with, and the fixed-income portfolio (or segment thereof) that requires an adequate treatment of its components. We also address issues related to portfolio overlays with derivative instruments such as futures or options.

14.3.1 Attribution for a global portfolio

What is the main issue, unreported in the Brinson analysis and its refinements, that arises when the portfolio is managed globally from a geographical perspective? The unambiguous answer is the impact of currency movements. In the classical performance attribution analysis, the perspective adopted is that of the investor, who observes returns in their home currency. This works finely if neither the portfolio nor the benchmark has a direct foreign currency exposure. However, difficulties emerge when several currencies are at stake in the portfolio.

The issue of currency exposures was initially raised by Allen (1991). He claims that the attribution system should quantify the specific impact of each managerial decision on the portfolio by neutralizing all other ones. In the case of a multicurrency portfolio, the manager can decide to adopt some active risk regarding the hedging (or not) of specific currencies in a different way from the expectations of the investor, i.e., the exposure of the benchmark. This type of decision has to be accounted for in performance attribution. Two major models take care about this issue: the simple extension of Brinson–Fachler by Ankrim and Hensel (1994) and the more sophisticated version of Karnosky and Singer (1994).[7]

14.3.1.1 The arithmetic multicurrency version of Ankrim and Hensel (1994)

As stated by Ankrim and Hensel (1994), the BHB or BF attribution framework is distorted with three problems when currency exposures are introduced: (i) the effects of currency appreciation/depreciation in returns is not separated from the allocation or selection decisions in returns; (ii) the influence of currency hedging decisions on home currency returns is not identified; and (iii) the difference between the investor's hedging choice and the benchmark currency exposure is not accounted for.

To understand the nature of the problem, it is necessary to split the return of a foreign currency X, denoted by $R_{X,t} = \frac{X_{t+1}-X_t}{X_t}$, into two very distinctive components that depend on the delivery price of the forward contract F of that same currency:

$$R_{X,t} = R_{E,t} + R_{F,t} \tag{14-33}$$

where $R_{E,t} = \frac{X_{t+1}-F_{t+1}}{X_t}$ is the "currency surprise," i.e., the rate of change of the currency that is not explained by its forward price, and $R_{F,t} = \frac{F_{t+1}-X_t}{X_t}$ is the "forward premium," i.e., the relative gain or loss on the currency that is provided thanks to the exposure to the forward contract.

[7]We harmonize notations as much as possible, thereby largely departing from the papers' original ones.

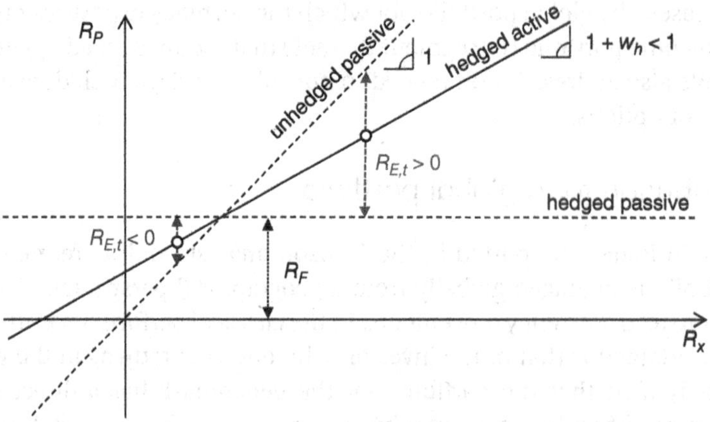

FIGURE 14-8 Decomposition of currency return between the deterministic and random parts.
Source: Adapted from Ankrim and Hensel (1994), Figure A.

Whereas $R_{E,t}$ is random, $R_{F,t}$ is purely deterministic at time t, and therefore should not be associated with a component of the manager's performance. To illustrate this, consider an investor whose home currency is the US Dollar (USD). The current exchange rate of the Euro (EUR) is at parity: $X_t = 1$. The forward price of the EUR for a delivery one period ahead is $F_{t+1} = 1.05$. This corresponds to an appreciation of the currency: $R_{F,t} = \frac{1.05-1.00}{1.00} = 5\%$. If the EUR actually prices at $X_{t+1} = 1.02$ at that moment, $R_{E,t} = \frac{1.02-1.05}{1.00} = -3\%$, and the application of Equation (14-33) tells us that the total return of 2% on the currency should be split between a deterministic part of +5% and a pure random part of −3%.

What is the impact of the manager's decisions regarding currency hedging on the portfolio's excess return? Consider that they decide to adopt a short proportion of $w_h < 0$ of the portfolio's market value on the forward contracts. The impact of this hedge can be understood with the graph shown in Figure 14-8.

The figure shows the outcome of a portfolio management choice consisting of leaving a currency exposure fully unhedged or partially hedging it for a fraction w_h of the exposure. The unhedged return – aside from any other effect – is represented by the oblique straight line with a unit slope. The return of the fully hedged position is a constant, represented by the constant dashed line. Imagine that, in the first case, the currency return is positive but lower than the forward premium. Even though the portfolio has a positive return, the currency surprise is negative. Considering the situation on the right of the graph, the currency return is higher than the forward premium, and therefore the manager should be rewarded for a positive decision not to hedge the risk. Deciding to hedge with a ratio w_h induces a reduction in the magnitude of the surprise that is proportional to the intensity of the hedge.

Taking this decomposition of the currency return into account, Ankrim and Hensel (1994), henceforth AH, propose an attribution framework that directly extends the BF one. It starts with the following expression for the portfolio return expressed as a function of its $k = 1, \ldots, K$ currency segments, which expands Equation (14-1b):

$$R_{P,t} = \sum_{k=1}^{K} w_{P,k,t} R^{L}_{P,k,t} + \sum_{k=1}^{K} w_{P,k,t} R_{E_k,t} + \sum_{k=1}^{K} w_{P,k,t} R_{F_k,t} + \sum_{k=1}^{K} w_{P,h_k,t} R_{h_k,t} \tag{14-34}$$

where $R^{L}_{P,k,t} \approx R_{P,k,t} - R_{X_k,t} - \frac{w_{P,h_k,t}}{w_{P,k,t}} R_{h_k,t}$ is the return of segment k expressed in the currency of that segment ("Local"),[8] $R_{X_k,t} = R_{E_k,t} + R_{F_k,t}$ in which $R_{E_k,t}$ and $R_{F_k,t}$ are the corresponding currency surprises and forward premiums, respectively, and $R_{h_k,t} = \frac{F_{k,t+1} - X_{k,t+1}}{X_{k,t+1}} = \frac{R_{E_k,t}}{1 + R_{F_k,t}}$ is the forward return.

The last term of the equation reflects the weighted contribution of the forward returns through the hedging decisions. It represents the (random) relative gain or loss from the position taken in the forward contract. The final segment portfolio returns $R_{P,k,t}$ for the investor (in their home currency) are thus not represented in the expression because they are broken down into portfolio and currency effects.

We can represent the benchmark return in exactly the same way, but with the associated weights, knowing that there is no difference in the components of the currency returns:

$$R_{B,t} = \sum_{k=1}^{K} w_{B,k,t} R^{L}_{B,k,t} + \sum_{k=1}^{K} w_{B,k,t} R_{E_k,t} + \sum_{k=1}^{K} w_{B,k,t} R_{F_k,t} + \sum_{k=1}^{K} w_{B,h_k,t} R_{h_k,t} \tag{14-35}$$

In that case, the value taken by each currency hedging coefficient $w_{B,h_k,t}$ depends on whether the corresponding returns are fully, partially, or not hedged within the benchmark.

In the AH model, we rewrite Equation (14-7) in this context as the sum of five distinct terms:

$$R_{P,t} - R_{B,t} = \mathcal{A}^{L}_{P,t} + \mathcal{S}^{L}_{P,t} + \mathcal{I}^{L}_{P,t} + \mathcal{A}^{X}_{P,t} + \mathcal{A}^{F}_{P,t} \tag{14-36}$$

where the first three 'pure' effects are very similar as before, but with constituents that are all expressed in their corresponding currency returns:

$$\mathcal{A}^{L}_{P,t} = \sum_{k=1}^{K} (w_{P,k,t} - w_{B,k,t})(R^{L}_{B,k,t} - R^{L}_{B,t}) \tag{14-37a}$$

$$\mathcal{S}^{L}_{P,t} = \sum_{k=1}^{K} w_{B,k,t}(R^{L}_{P,k,t} - R^{L}_{B,k,t}) \tag{14-37b}$$

[8] This expression ignores the compounding effect, as it should in principle feature the cross-product between the two rates, i.e., (excluding hedging for simplicity) $R_{P,k,t} = R^{u}_{P,k,t} + R_{X_k,t} + R^{u}_{P,k,t} R_{X_k,t}$. This issue will be addressed later.

$$\mathcal{I}^{\mathrm{L}}_{P,t} = \sum_{k=1}^{K}(w_{P,k,t} - w_{B,k,t})(R^{\mathrm{L}}_{P,k,t} - R^{\mathrm{L}}_{B,k,t}) \tag{14-37c}$$

where $R^{\mathrm{L}}_{B,t} = \sum_{k=1}^{K} w_{B,k,t} R^{\mathrm{L}}_{B,k,t}$ is the benchmark return expressed in the currency of denomination of each segment.

The full currency impact is represented by two new effects that can both be interpreted as indications of timing: the Currency Allocation effect $\mathcal{A}^{\mathrm{X}}_{P,t}$ and the Forward Allocation effect $\mathcal{A}^{\mathrm{F}}_{P,t}$:

$$\mathcal{A}^{\mathrm{X}}_{P,t} = \sum_{k=1}^{K}(w_{P,k,t} - w_{B,k,t})(R_{E_k,t} - R_{E,t}) + \sum_{k=1}^{K}(w_{P,h_k,t} - w_{B,h_k,t})R_{h_k,t} \tag{14-38a}$$

$$\mathcal{A}^{\mathrm{F}}_{P,t} = \sum_{k=1}^{K}(w_{P,k,t} - w_{B,k,t})(R_{F_k,t} - R_{F,t}) \tag{14-38b}$$

where $R_{E,t} = \sum_{k=1}^{K} w_{B,k,t} R_{E_k,t}$ and $R_{F,t} = \sum_{k=1}^{K} w_{B,k,t} R_{F_k,t}$ are the weighted average currency surprise and forward premium, respectively.

Note that since $R_{F_k,t}$ is deterministic, so is $R_{F,t}$. This means that $\mathcal{A}^{\mathrm{F}}_{P,t}$ is not random but is fully known at the moment of the allocation. This is thus not a determinant of portfolio performance but rather the mechanical consequence of the currency allocation decisions. Bacon (2023) suggests that this effect should be integrated into the pure Allocation effect in order to have a comprehensive view of the manager's market timing skill.

In general, the impact of the forward premium is small when the interest differential between the home and the segment currencies is limited. It may become material for regions in which interest rates are high, such as some emerging countries affected by a high level of inflation.

The VAS example (continued)

The CIO is puzzled with the pattern of excess returns of the Verso fund, which increased in the first half and decreased in the second half of the year, and wishes to investigate the characteristics of this portfolio further. It turns out that the portfolio manager has substantially diverged from the geographical allocation of the benchmark, taking important regional foreign exchange (FX) bets, especially in the equity segment in which the portfolio invests in the USD, EUR, and UK Sterling (GBP). The domestic currency of the fund is USD. Whereas the benchmark regional index returns are expressed in USD (no hedging), the manager has systematically decided to hedge 50% of the exposure to the fund's foreign currencies (EUR and GBP).

We set the focus on two months for which the difference in returns between the fund and the benchmark returns have a similar magnitude but an opposite sign: February ($R_{V,\text{Stock,Feb}} - R_{B,\text{Stock,Feb}} = 3.58\% - 2.13\% = 1.45\%$) and November ($R_{V,\text{Stock,Nov}} - R_{B,\text{Stock,Nov}} = 3.25\% - 4.49\% = -1.24\%$). The complete data regarding these two dates are represented in Table 14-18.

TABLE 14-18 VAS example – Fund, benchmark, and currency data for the Verso fund (February and November) in the AH model.

Portfolio	Parameter	Symbol	February			November		
			USD	EUR	GBP	USD	EUR	GBP
Verso	Return	$R_{V,k,t}$	3.45%	3.27%	4.33%	3.45%	3.32%	2.87%
	Weight	$w_{V,k,t}$	43.8%	34.4%	21.8%	41.3%	31.4%	27.3%
	Hedge ratio	$w_{V,h_k,t}$		−17.2%	−10.9%		−15.7%	−13.7%
Benchmark	Return	$R_{B,k,t}$	2.48%	1.21%	3.36%	3.86%	5.29%	4.44%
	Weight	$w_{B,k,t}$	47.0%	38.0%	15.0%	47.0%	38.0%	15.0%
Currency	Surprise	$R_{E_k,t}$		−3.30%	−3.54%		6.69%	3.72%
	Forward	$R_{F_k,t}$		−0.12%	−1.33%		−0.17%	−1.47%

We do not report the hedge ratio for the benchmark as the currencies are not hedged there.

From Table 14-18, the application of the BF attribution model from Equations (14-7) to (14-9b) is straightforward and leads to the graph shown in Figure 14-9, summarizing the sum of contributions of each currency segment.

It appears that the fund's excess return is mostly attributed to a selection effect in that analysis because of the very contrasted returns between the fund and the benchmark within the currency segments.

However, the detailed data in the table show significant currency movements during these two months. They were adverse in February and advantageous in November. As a first qualitative insight, we can guess that the global currency effect has been positive for Verso in February (compared with the benchmark) thanks to its hedging policy, whereas it is opposite for November.

The AH analysis should further substantiate this impression with the detailed analysis per segment, as shown in Table 14-19.

(continued)

(continued)

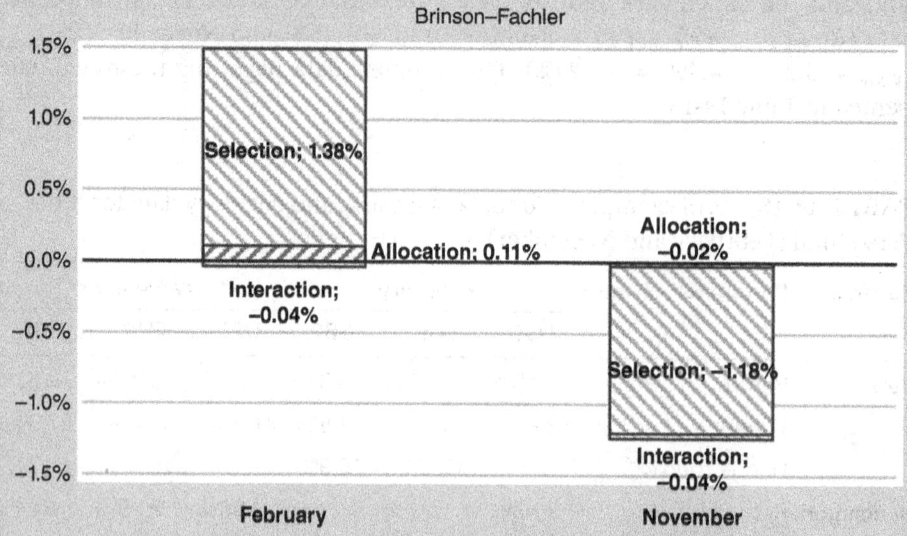

FIGURE 14-9 VAS example – Brinson–Fachler global effects for the Verso fund (February and November).

TABLE 14-19 VAS example – Ankrim–Hensel analysis for the Verso fund (February and November).

Effect	February				November			
	USD	EUR	GBP	Global	USD	EUR	GBP	Global
Pure allocation	0.05%	−0.02%	0.28%	**0.31%**	−0.12%	0.19%	0.06%	**0.13%**
Pure selection	0.46%	0.16%	−0.12%	**0.49%**	−0.19%	0.52%	0.05%	**0.38%**
Pure interaction	−0.03%	−0.01%	−0.06%	**−0.10%**	0.02%	−0.09%	0.04%	**−0.03%**
Currency allocation	−0.06%	0.62%	0.27%	**0.84%**	0.18%	−1.29%	−0.44%	**−1.55%**
Forward allocation	−0.01%	0.00%	−0.07%	**−0.09%**	−0.02%	−0.01%	−0.15%	**−0.17%**

Now that currency impacts are taken into account, the magnitude of the pure effects appear much more stable from February to November. The FX-related effects, by contrast, capture a very large part of the fluctuations. It is worth mentioning that, even though the USD is the domestic currency of the fund – and thus does not expose it to FX risk – the application of a BF-type of analysis can emphasize a potential Allocation effect because of the manager's choice to over-allocate or underallocate the portfolio in that currency when it outperforms or underperforms the average currency returns. In February, the USD was appreciated relative to the other currencies, and thus the manager's decision to underweight the dollar was incorrect.

The graphical translation of the global results in Table 14-18 confirms the diagnosis (Figure 14-10): The key effect that drives the attribution analysis is related to currency allocation, while the pure Allocation and Selection effects of the manager are consistently positive.

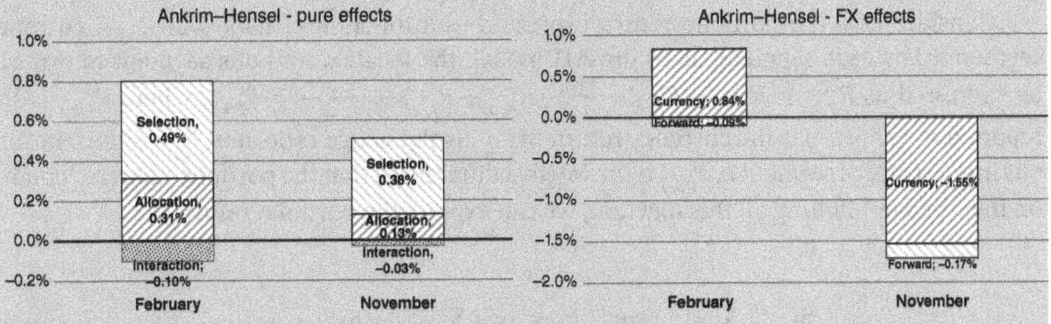

FIGURE 14-10 VAS example – Ankrim–Hensel global effects for the Verso fund (February and November).

14.3.1.2 The multicurrency version of Karnosky and Singer (1994) with continuous returns

The model proposed by Karnosky and Singer (1994) (henceforth KS) is contemporaneous to that of Ankrim and Hensel (1994). It adopts a slightly different stance by (i) using continuously compounded returns (instead of simple returns as in AH), (ii) considering the no-arbitrage pricing mechanism in order to embed the forward premium in the returns, and (iii) recognizing that the manager's currency hedging decision indeed represents a carry trade strategy in which they adopt a short position in the foreign currency and a corresponding and equivalent long position in the domestic one. This leads to a more comprehensive model, integrating hedging policies directly in returns, without having to approximate the effects (no cross-effects left out of the analysis) and relying on arbitrage principles (which, for instance, can easily accommodate cross-currency hedging decisions). We present a simplified but instructive version here.

In the KS model, we consider that each rate of return is continuously compounded (they all bear superscript "c"). The model introduces two main modifications with respect to the AH model. First, thanks to the use of continuous rates, it makes sense to model that FX forward contracts are correctly priced. This allows us to express the return of the forward hedge contract $R^c_{h,t}$ as follows:

$$R^c_{h,t} = R^c_{X,t} + R^c_{fX,t} - R^c_{fD,t} \tag{14-39}$$

where $R^c_{h,t} = \log(1 + R_{h,t})$ is the continuously compounded (i.e., continuous) forward return, $R^c_{X,t} = \log(1 + R_{X,t})$ is the continuous currency return, and $R^c_{fX,t}$ and $R^c_{fD,t}$ are the continuous interest rates in the foreign and domestic currencies X and D, respectively.

Second, we can consider the hedging decisions of the portfolio manager as two simultaneous carry trades: a short position in the foreign currency deposit and a long position in the domestic currency deposit. This means that, for every forward contract with a weight $w_{P,X,t}$, we have the exact opposite weight in the domestic currency $w_{P,D,t} = -w_{P,X,t}$. Thanks to this (legitimate) twist, the hedging weights always sum up to 0.

Consider now the portfolio return expressed as a function of its $k = 1, \ldots, K$ currency segments. For each segment, as in the AH model, the local continuous segment return can be expressed as $R^{cL}_{P,k,t} = R^c_{P,k,t} - R^c_{X_k,t} - \frac{w_{P,h_k,t}}{w_{P,k,t}}(R^c_{X_k,t} + R^c_{f_k,t}) - \frac{w_{P,k,t}+w_{P,h_k,t}}{w_{P,k,t}}\delta^c_{P,k,t}$, where $R^c_{P,k,t}$ is the reported return, $R^c_{X_k,t}$ is the currency return, $w_{P,h_k,t}$ is the hedge ratio, and $R^c_{f_k,t}$ is the continuous interest rate of segment k. $\delta^c_{P,k,t}$ is the interest differential that the portfolio manager obtains on their hedge.[9] Putting all this together, we can express the portfolio return as

$$R^c_{P,t} = \sum_{k=1}^{K} w_{P,k,t}(R^{cL}_{P,k,t} - R^c_{f_k,t}) + \sum_{k=1}^{K} w'_{P,k,t}(R^c_{X_k,t} + R^c_{Pf_k,t}) \qquad (14\text{-}40)$$

where $w'_{P,k,t} = w_{P,k,t} + w_{P,h_k,t}$ is the hedge-corrected weight of the portfolio in currency segment k with $\sum_{k=1}^{K} w_{P,h_k,t} = 0$ and thus $\sum_{k=1}^{K} w'_{P,k,t} = 1$, and $R^c_{Pf_k,t} = R^c_{f_k,t} + \delta^c_{P,k,t}$ stands for the continuous interest rate that can be obtained by the manager in that segment. The expression $R^{cL}_{P,k,t} - R^c_{f_k,t}$ is also referred to as the portfolio risk premium.

We have exactly the same structure for the continuous benchmark return:

$$R^c_{B,t} = \sum_{k=1}^{K} w_{B,k,t}(R^{cL}_{B,k,t} - R^c_{f_k,t}) + \sum_{k=1}^{K} w'_{B,k,t}(R^c_{X_k,t} + R^c_{f_k,t}) \qquad (14\text{-}41)$$

where $R^{cL}_{B,k,t} - R^c_{f_k,t}$ is the benchmark risk premium and $w'_{B,k,t} = w_{B,k,t} + w_{B,h_k,t}$ is the hedge-corrected weight of the benchmark in currency segment k, with $\sum_{k=1}^{K} w'_{B,k,t} = 1$.

The authors point out the additive structures of Equations (14-40) and (14-41) with two very distinct components. The first part of each equation is the market allocation return, whereas the second one is the currency allocation return.

---

[9] Even though this appears not to be explicitly mentioned in their paper, it is possible that the manager obtains a different rate than the benchmark on the hedging policy. This possibility explains why quadrants CI and CIII as well as quadrants CII and CIV might differ in Table 14-20.

Matching these two expressions in the BF model and splitting them into the first part (pure effects) and the second part (currency effects) enable us to obtain the desired effects as usual:

$$R^c_{P,t} - R^c_{B,t} = \underbrace{\mathcal{A}^{cL}_{P,t} + \mathcal{S}^{cL}_{P,t} + \mathcal{I}^{cL}_{P,t}}_{\text{Market effects}} + \underbrace{\mathcal{A}^{cX}_{P,t} + \mathcal{S}^{cX}_{P,t} + \mathcal{I}^{cX}_{P,t}}_{\text{Currency effects}} \tag{14-42}$$

where the first three "pure" market effects are very similar as before, but with constituents that are all expressed in their corresponding currency returns:

$$\mathcal{A}^{cL}_{P,t} = \sum_{k=1}^{K} (w_{P,k,t} - w_{B,k,t})((R^{cL}_{B,k,t} - R^c_{f_k,t}) - (R^{cL}_{B,t} - R^c_{f,t})) \tag{14-43a}$$

$$\mathcal{S}^{cL}_{P,t} = \sum_{k=1}^{K} w_{B,k,t}(R^{cL}_{P,k,t} - R^{cL}_{B,k,t}) \tag{14-43b}$$

$$\mathcal{I}^{cL}_{P,t} = \sum_{k=1}^{K} (w_{P,k,t} - w_{B,k,t})(R^{cL}_{P,k,t} - R^{cL}_{B,k,t}) \tag{14-43c}$$

where $R^{cL}_{B,t} - R^c_{f,t} = \sum_{k=1}^{K} w_{B,k,t}(R^{cL}_{B,k,t} - R^c_{f_k,t})$ is the weighted average benchmark risk premium across each segment.

The full currency impact is also represented by three effects. As shown in Table 14-20, the structure is similar to that of the market effects:

$$\mathcal{A}^{cX}_{P,t} = \sum_{k=1}^{K} (w'_{P,k,t} - w'_{B,k,t})((R^c_{X_k,t} + R^c_{f_k,t}) - (R^c_{B,X,t} + R^c_{f,t})) \tag{14-44a}$$

$$\mathcal{S}^{cX}_{P,t} = \sum_{k=1}^{K} w'_{B,k,t}(R^c_{P,f_k,t} - R^c_{f_k,t}) \tag{14-44b}$$

$$\mathcal{I}^{cX}_{P,t} = \sum_{k=1}^{K} (w'_{P,k,t} - w'_{B,k,t})(R^c_{P,f_k,t} - R^c_{f_k,t}) \tag{14-44c}$$

where $R^c_{B,X,t} + R^c_{f,t} = \sum_{k=1}^{K} (w'_{P,k,t} - w'_{B,k,t})(R^c_{X_k,t} + R^c_{f_k,t})$ is the weighted average benchmark total currency return across each segment.

It is worth noting that if $R^c_{P,f_k,t} = R^c_{f_k,t}$, i.e., the portfolio manager obtains no different interest rate conditions than the benchmark, then both the Currency Selection and Currency Interaction effects are set to zero. In that case, only the Currency Allocation effect remains. This effect can actually be broken down further by remembering that $w'_{P,k,t} = w_{P,k,t} + w_{P,h_k,t}$ and $w'_{B,k,t} = w_{B,k,t} + w_{B,h_k,t}$. Splitting the market exposure and the hedging weights leads to a similar type of decomposition as in the AH framework.

TABLE 14-20 The KS quadrants.

		Security selection				Hedge selection	
		Passive	Active			Passive	Active
Market allocation	**Passive**	**(M)Quadrant I** *Benchmark* $\sum_{k=1}^{K} w_{B,k,t}(R^{cL}_{B,k,t} - R^{c}_{f_k,t})$	**(M)Quadrant III** *Benchmark and selection* $\sum_{k=1}^{K} w_{B,k,t}(R^{cL}_{P,k,t} - R^{c}_{f_k,t})$	Currency allocation	**Passive**	**(C)Quadrant I** *Benchmark* $\sum_{k=1}^{K} w'_{B,k,t}(R^{c}_{X_k,t} + R^{c}_{f_k,t})$	**(C)Quadrant III** *Benchmark and selection* $\sum_{k=1}^{K} w'_{B,k,t}(R^{c}_{X_k,t} + R^{c}_{P,f_k,t})$
	Active	**(M)Quadrant II** *Benchmark and allocation* $\sum_{k=1}^{K} w_{P,k,t}(R^{cL}_{B,k,t} - R^{c}_{f_k,t})$	**(M)Quadrant IV** *Portfolio* $\sum_{k=1}^{K} w_{P,k,t}(R^{cL}_{P,k,t} - R^{c}_{f_k,t})$		**Active**	**(C)Quadrant II** *Benchmark and allocation* $\sum_{k=1}^{K} w'_{P,k,t}(R^{c}_{X_k,t} + R^{c}_{f_k,t})$	**(C)Quadrant IV** *Portfolio* $\sum_{k=1}^{K} w'_{P,k,t}(R^{c}_{X_k,t} + R^{c}_{P,f_k,t})$

Source: Adapted from Karnosky and Singer (1994), Figure 4.

The VAS example (continued)

As an alternative to the AH attribution model, the CIO wishes to isolate the exact effects – without arithmetic approximations – of the market exposures and the currency exposures of Verso. The perspective is the same, with a focus on the February and November returns of the fund and the benchmark. In particular, they want to check whether the impact of the fund's adverse financing conditions in February should be taken into account, with the necessity to pay a significant spread on the hedging operations.

Expressing all returns in their continuously compounded versions, we obtain $R^c_{V,Stock,Feb} - R^c_{B,Stock,Feb} = 1.41\%$ and $R^c_{V,Stock,Nov} - R^c_{B,Stock,Nov} = -1.19\%$. The relevant data for the KS analysis are summarized in Table 14-21.

TABLE 14-21 VAS example – Fund, benchmark, and currency data for the Verso fund (February and November) in the KS model.

Portfolio	Parameter	Symbol	February			November		
			USD	EUR	GBP	USD	EUR	GBP
Verso	Return	$R^c_{V,k,t}$	3.39%	3.22%	4.24%	3.39%	3.27%	2.83%
	Weight	$w_{V,k,t}$	43.8%	34.4%	21.8%	41.3%	31.4%	27.3%
	Hedge ratio	$w_{V,h_k,t}$	28.1%	−17.2%	−10.9%	29.4%	−15.7%	−13.7%
	Delta	$\delta^c_{V,k,t}$	0.00%	0.00%	0.00%	0.00%	−0.31%	−0.36%
Benchmark	Return	$R^c_{B,k,t}$	2.45%	1.20%	3.33%	3.79%	5.15%	4.35%
	Weight	$w_{B,k,t}$	47.0%	38.0%	15.0%	47.0%	38.0%	15.0%
Currency	Return	$R^c_{X_k,t}$	0.00%	−3.48%	−4.99%	0.00%	6.32%	2.23%
	Risk-free	$R^c_{f_k,t}$	2.42%	2.54%	3.76%	2.90%	3.07%	4.38%

Beyond the passage from simple to continuous returns, the key differences between Table 14-21 and Table 14-18 are (i) the presence of a non-zero hedge ratio for the domestic currency (USD), which exactly offsets the hedge ratios for the other currencies (zero aggregate hedge ratio), and (ii) the presence of a "Delta," which is the funding cost (−) or benefit (+) that the fund enjoys for its funding policy. If this delta is set to zero, as in February, this means that $R^c_{V,f_k,Feb} = R^c_{f_k,Feb}$ and thus both $\mathcal{S}^{cX}_{V,Feb} = 0$ and $\mathcal{J}^{cX}_{V,Feb} = 0$.

The KS analysis provides the detailed results per segment as shown in Table 14-22.

(continued)

(continued)

TABLE 14-22 VAS example – Karnosky–Singer analysis for the Verso fund (February and November).

Effect	February				November			
	USD	EUR	GBP	Global	USD	EUR	GBP	Global
Market allocation	0.05%	−0.02%	0.21%	**0.23%**	−0.14%	0.18%	−0.09%	**−0.05%**
Market selection	−0.29%	0.59%	0.04%	**0.34%**	−1.15%	1.12%	0.29%	**0.26%**
Market interaction	0.02%	−0.06%	0.02%	**−0.02%**	0.14%	−0.20%	0.24%	**0.19%**
Currency allocation	1.78%	−0.79%	−0.14%	**0.85%**	0.79%	−2.19%	−0.10%	**−1.50%**
Currency selection	0.00%	0.00%	0.00%	**0.00%**	0.00%	−0.12%	−0.05%	**−0.17%**
Currency interaction	0.00%	0.00%	0.00%	**0.00%**	0.00%	0.07%	0.00%	**0.07%**

The diagnosis is slightly different in this case because of the presence of an additional funding cost that reinforces the negative currency effect in November, which is reflected in Figure 14-11.

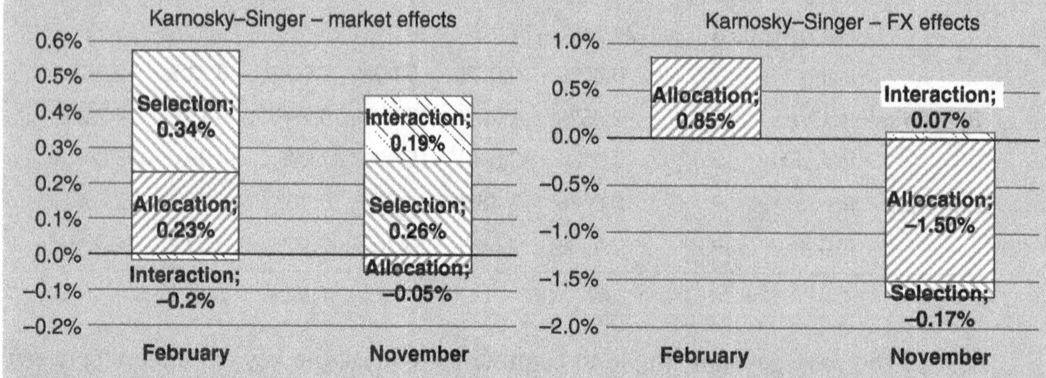

FIGURE 14-11 VAS example – Karnosky–Singer global effects for the Verso fund (February and November).

14.3.2 Attribution for fixed-income investments

Every type of attribution analysis developed thus far has been primarily conceived for portfolios dominated by stock investments. Even though most allocation funds or portfolios feature a significant proportion of bonds or other fixed-income instruments, they are then considered a standard asset class for the sake of the computation of the overall effects. This is logical if one wants to adopt a standard methodology for the inter-segment analysis.

Nevertheless, fixed-income instruments display their own very specific characteristics that distinguish them from stocks. Performing a BHB or a BF analysis within a segment featuring a homogeneous set of bonds would ignore most of them and might lead to erroneous conclusions. It is advisable to adapt the attribution model for that specific asset class. We have already discussed in Section 12.1 of Chapter 12 the specificities of a fixed-income portfolio that motivate why performance measurement and attribution analysis must be adapted. We now dig into a model that bridges what we have previously examined with the reality of a bond portfolio.

14.3.2.1 The fixed-income attribution approach

Campisi (2000) mentions five relevant differences with equities for performance analysis. In short, these are (i) a finite maturity, (ii) a fixed return with no or limited upside, (iii) a less active and liquid secondary market, (iv) market yields as a common driver of price change, and (v) a smaller degree of heterogeneity, all bonds being relatively similar in nature and behavior.

Two major consequences can be drawn from these statements. First, in the context of an actively managed fixed-income portfolio, allocation decisions matter much more than individual bond selection. Unlike for stocks, individual bond mispricing appears less often and is probably less substantial. This does not deny the talent of a manager who is able to pick individual bonds whose return will surprise the market, for instance, because of a wrong consensus about their credit quality or mispriced embedded options, but it is often a second-order source of returns for most portfolios. Therefore, most fixed-income attribution systems consider the selection effect as a residual one, after all other relevant performance drivers have been taken into account.

Second, the relevant dimensions of the allocation effects have to be identified *ex ante* and are likely to be numerous and complex. This is where fixed-income attribution models mostly differ from each other, depending on the way they choose to partition the sources of potential outperformance that they consider to be relevant (bearing in mind that the unexplained part of the returns after accounting for all the hypothesized effects will be attributed to asset selection).

In order to avoid redundancies, we refer the reader to Section 12.1 in Chapter 12 for a discussion of the sources of returns associated with a bond portfolio. Essentially, attribution models adapt the expression of various effects to various dimensions encompassed in this framework. The earlier ones, focusing purely on the fixed-income part of the portfolio, are proposed by Lord (1997) and Campisi (2000). There have been many other methods proposed in the specialized literature.

Probably, the most convenient way to synthetically present the specificities of fixed-income portfolios for attribution purposes is to adapt a classical BF model to the specificities of the fixed-income world, as proposed by Feibel (2003). His model features three components of active returns for a given portfolio: (i) the choice of the portfolio's (modified) duration $\mathrm{Dur}_{P,t}$;[10] (ii) the choice of the allocation per 'sector' segment (treasuries, corporates, mortgage, cash…); and (iii) the selection of specific issuers within each segment with various techniques. Dimensions (ii) and (iii) refer to the familiar Allocation and Selection effects, whereas the effect associated with the first one appears to be specific. In order to isolate it, we can simply define the portfolio's yield curve return $yR_{P,t}$ as

$$yR_{P,t} = -\sum_{k=1}^{K} w_{P,k,t}\mathrm{Dur}_{P,k,t}\Delta y_{k,t} = \sum_{k=1}^{K} w_{P,k,t} yR_{P,k,t} \tag{14-45}$$

where $\mathrm{Dur}_{P,k,t}$ is the weighted average modified duration of the bonds belonging to segment k, and $\Delta y_{k,t}$ is the weighted average change of the bonds' yields to maturity in the same segment. The same equation as (14-45) holds for the benchmark. The expression $yR_{P,k,t} \equiv -\mathrm{Dur}_{P,k,t}\Delta y_{k,t}$ stands for the yield curve return of segment k, exactly as in Equation (12-2) of Chapter 12.

It results that once the yield curve return of the portfolio is isolated for every segment, we can define the residual return as 'anything else' than the pure impact of the yield curve: $rR_{P,k,t} \equiv R_{P,k,t} - yR_{P,k,t}$. Finally, we rewrite Equation (14-3) by distributing the returns of the portfolio and the benchmark:

$$R_{P,t} - R_{B,t} = \sum_{k=1}^{K} w_{P,k,t}(yR_{P,k,t} + rR_{P,k,t}) - \sum_{k=1}^{K} w_{B,k,t}(yR_{B,k,t} + rR_{B,k,t}) \tag{14-46}$$

and the BHB or BF model can be run on this equation, splitting the Selection effect into two parts:

$$\mathcal{S}_{P,t} = \mathcal{D}_{P,t} + \mathcal{R}_{P,t} \tag{14-47}$$

where the Duration effect $\mathcal{D}_{P,t}$ and the Residual effect $\mathcal{R}_{P,t}$ are respectively defined as

$$\mathcal{D}_{P,t} = \sum_{k=1}^{K} w_{B,k,t}(yR_{P,k,t} - yR_{B,k,t}) \tag{14-48a}$$

$$\mathcal{R}_{P,t} = \sum_{k=1}^{K} w_{B,k,t}(rR_{P,k,t} - rR_{B,k,t}) \tag{14-48b}$$

For as simplistic as it seems, this extension could be sufficient for many purposes, especially when the analysis is done on a multi-asset portfolio whose fixed-income segment is not dominant and managed in a relatively classical fashion. Interestingly, this approach can be combined with a multicurrency attribution model. This is essentially the scope of the

[10] The notation of this chapter (generic debt contract, duration, yield, etc.) is consistent with that of Chapter 12.

Van Breukelen (2000) model that combines a version of the Feibel (2003) extension with the Karnosky and Singer (1994) model developed in Section 14.3.2.

The VAS example (continued)

For the Verso fund, further analysis is also needed on the fixed-income part. The manager has fully hedged all currency exposures, and the portfolio weights are not *per se* very different from the benchmark, but the differential in returns remains puzzling, with the same downward trend over the course of the year. It is decided to look at the details of the portfolio exposures to different categories represented in the Bond segment. These are made of three sectors based on the type of issuer: Government, Corporates, and High Yield (all types of issuers below Investment Grade). The benchmark is split according to the same rule in three sub-indexes, each with its own duration that is recorded every month.

For the equity part, the analysis focuses on two remarkable months: January and October. The excess returns that have to be explained are the following: January ($R_{V,Bond,Jan} - R_{B,Bond,Jan} = 0.39\% - 0.07\% = 0.32\%$) and October ($R_{V,Bond,Oct} - R_{B,Bond,Oct} = 0.35\% - 0.57\% = -0.22\%$). The data for the fund and the benchmark that are used for the simple fixed-income attribution method of Feibel (2003) are presented in Table 14-23.

TABLE 14-23 VAS example – Fund, benchmark, and yield data for the Verso fund (January and October) in the Feibel (2003) model.

Portfolio	Parameter	Symbol	*January*			*October*		
			Gov	Corp	HY	Gov	Corp	HY
Verso	Return	$R_{V,k,t}$	0.64%	0.42%	−0.06%	0.37%	0.42%	0.22%
	Weight	$w_{V,k,t}$	37.9%	38.4%	23.7%	38.9%	41.0%	20.1%
	Duration	$Dur_{V,k,t}$	6.2	6.7	3.2	5.4	6.2	3.9
Benchmark	Return	$R_{B,k,t}$	0.25%	0.17%	−0.49%	0.35%	0.47%	1.22%
	Weight	$w_{B,k,t}$	40.0%	40.0%	20.0%	40.0%	40.0%	20.0%
	Duration	$Dur_{B,k,t}$	4.6	4.9	4.9	4.4	4.5	4.3
Yield	Change	$\Delta y_{k,t}$	−0.12%	−0.07%	0.14%	−0.25%	−0.34%	0.27%

The outcome of the analysis regarding the Allocation and Interaction effects is fairly negligible for both periods. The picture delivered by the Duration and Residual effects are different. Figure 14-12 reports the breakup of these two effects per issuer type for both dates.

(*continued*)

(continued)

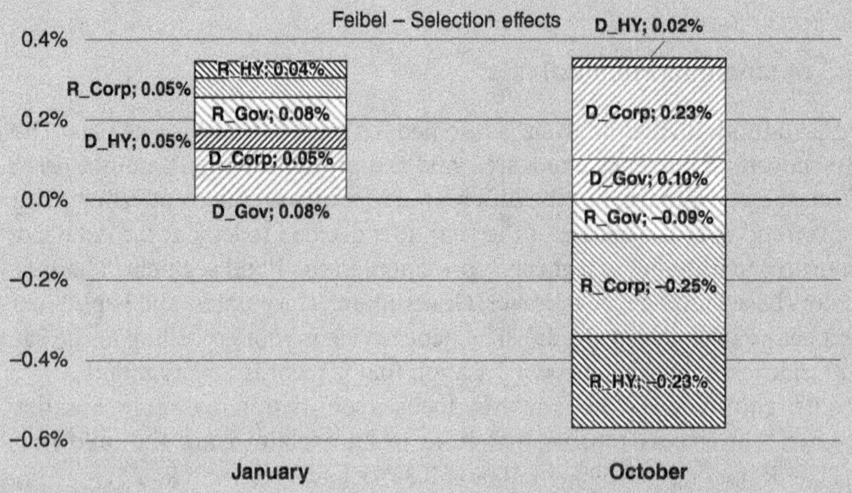

FIGURE 14-12 VAS example – Duration and Residual effects for the Verso fund (January and October).

Whereas the effects for all sub-segments are (moderately) positive in January, adding up to an overall value of $\mathcal{S}_{V,Jan} = 0.34\%$, the results are very contrasted in October: a positive Duration effect amounts to $\mathcal{D}_{V,Oct} = 0.35\%$, but a strongly negative Residual effect of $\mathcal{R}_{V,Oct} = -0.57\%$, which mostly explains in itself the negative excess return. This is where the analysis shows its limits because it is impossible to investigate further why this unexplained "residual" yields this negative outcome across all types of issuers, as shown in Figure 14-12.

14.3.2.2 The sector-based version of Campisi (2011)

Even though it coexists with many competing fixed-income attribution models, the Campisi (2011) sector-based attribution framework has the merit of intuitively and pragmatically extending the basic model while encompassing the main dimensions of the return of a fixed-income portfolio, namely by splitting total return into four parts:

$$R_{P,t} = \sum_{k=1}^{K} w_{P,k,t}(cR_{P,k,t} + yR_{P,k,t} + sR_{P,k,t} + rR_{P,k,t}) \tag{14-49}$$

where, for each segment k, $cR_{P,k,t} = \frac{1}{w_{P,k,t}} \sum_{i \in k} w_{P,i,t} \frac{c_i \Delta t}{D_{i,t}}$ is the income (or "carry") return in which, for every bond with price $D_{i,t}$, $c_i \Delta t$ is the exact accrued interest during the period; $yR_{P,k,t}$ is the yield curve return defined above; $sR_{P,k,t}$ is the spread return; and $rR_{P,k,t}$ is the selection return. They are respectively computed as follows:

$$cR_{P,k,t} = \sum_{i\in k} \frac{w_{P,i,t}}{w_{P,k,t}} \frac{c_i \Delta t}{D_{i,t}} \tag{14-50a}$$

$$yR_{P,k,t} = -\text{Dur}_{P,k,t} \Delta y_{k,t} \tag{14-50b}$$

$$sR_{P,k,t} = -\text{Dur}_{P,k,t} \Delta s_{k,t} \tag{14-50c}$$

$$rR_{P,k,t} = R_{P,k,t} - cR_{P,k,t} - yR_{P,k,t} - sR_{P,k,t} \tag{14-50d}$$

where $D_{i,t}$ is the individual price of bond i, $c_i \Delta t$ is the exact accrued interest during the period, and

$$\Delta s_{k,t} = -\frac{R_{B,k,t} - cR_{B,k,t} - yR_{B,k,t}}{\text{Dur}_{B,k,t}} \tag{14-51}$$

is the implied change of the sector spread of the segment retrieved from the benchmark.

The selection return $rR_{P,k,t}$ is computed as the residual term after all the other effects are accounted for. By construction, it is zero for the benchmark: $rR_{B,k,t} = 0$ because its own spread return is itself defined as a residual term.

Overall, the final excess return can be written as the sum of four components:

$$R_{P,t} - R_{B,t} = \mathcal{C}_{P,t} + \mathcal{Y}_{P,t} + \mathcal{Z}_{P,t} + \mathcal{R}_{P,t} \tag{14-52}$$

where the Carry excess return $\mathcal{C}_{P,t}$, the Yield curve excess return $\mathcal{Y}_{P,t}$, the Spread excess return $\mathcal{Z}_{P,t}$, and the Residual return $\mathcal{R}_{P,t}$, altogether defined as

$$\mathcal{C}_{P,t} = \sum_{k=1}^{K} w_{P,k,t} cR_{P,k,t} - \sum_{k=1}^{K} w_{B,k,t} cR_{B,k,t} \tag{14-53a}$$

$$\mathcal{Y}_{P,t} = \sum_{k=1}^{K} w_{P,k,t} yR_{P,k,t} - \sum_{k=1}^{K} w_{B,k,t} yR_{B,k,t} \tag{14-53b}$$

$$\mathcal{Z}_{P,t} = \sum_{k=1}^{K} w_{P,k,t} sR_{P,k,t} - \sum_{k=1}^{K} w_{B,k,t} sR_{B,k,t} \tag{14-53c}$$

$$\mathcal{R}_{P,t} = \sum_{k=1}^{K} w_{P,k,t} rR_{P,k,t} \tag{14-53d}$$

The Carry excess return represents the "Static effect," which is perfectly predictable and thus purely deterministic. The Yield curve excess return represents the "Systematic effect": It is the one whose driver comes from interest rate market movements. The Spread excess return represents the pure "Tactical effect": It is a source of return in which the manager can

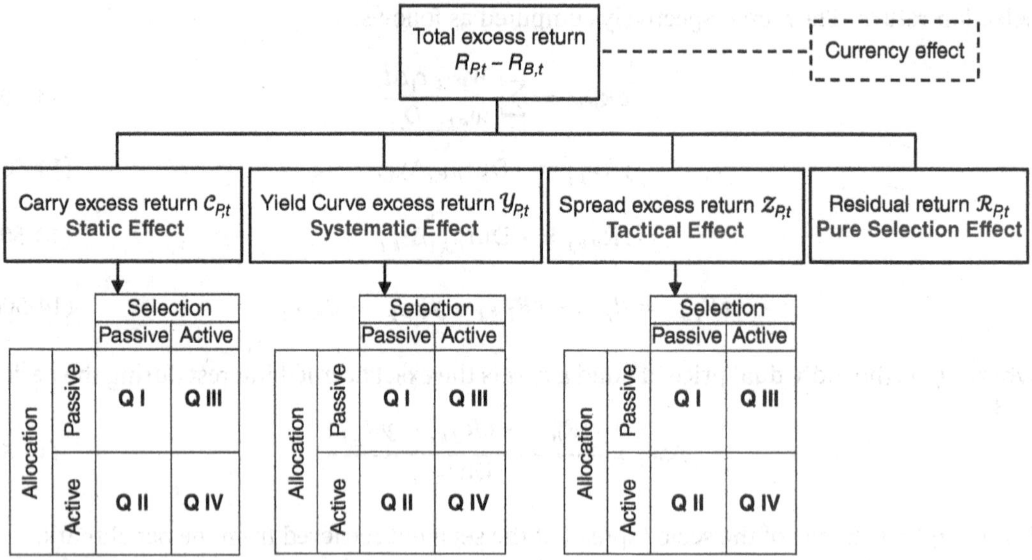

FIGURE 14-13 Excess return decomposition approach in sector-based fixed-income attribution. *Source*: Adapted from Campisi (2011), Figure 1.

simultaneously activate an allocation and a selection skill. Finally, the Residual return is a pure bond picking effect. Its sign drives the last source of performance.

For each identified dimension, it is in principle possible to isolate the classical effects (Allocation, Selection, Interaction). Note that the method can accommodate currency effects as an overlay, even though it is not the focus of the procedure. This is summarized in the chart shown in Figure 14-13.

This method has the great merit of soliciting a limited set of data while at the same time identifying the major components of bond excess returns. This can be seen as a useful trade-off between the adaptations made necessary by this type of portfolio and the intuitiveness and tractability, which is at the core of standard attribution analysis. As highlighted by the author, the results are highly likely to be close to the true representation of the determinants of a bond manager's excess returns.

The VAS example (continued)

It is possible to further investigate the properties of the Bond portfolio thanks to the Campisi (2011) model. The data from Table 14-23 are still valid, but they can be further completed with two new pieces of information: (i) the income gathered with the accrued coupon (and other price effects) and (ii) the change in implied credit spread obtained from the reverse engineering of the benchmark sector returns. The additional set of information is summarized in Table 14-24.

TABLE 14-24 VAS example – Additional bond data for the Verso fund (January and October).

Portfolio	Parameter	Symbol	*January*			*October*		
			Gov	Corp	HY	Gov	Corp	HY
Verso	Carry (sum)	$cR_{V,k,t}$	0.14%	0.17%	0.30%	0.13%	0.15%	0.28%
Benchmark	Carry (sum)	$cR_{B,k,t}$	0.15%	0.18%	0.28%	0.17%	0.19%	0.32%
Spread	(implied) Change	$\Delta s_{k,t}$	0.10%	0.07%	0.02%	0.21%	0.28%	−0.48%

The last row of the table does not come out of the blue; rather, it directly follows from the rest of the data. For instance, for the first cell, we can apply Equation (14-51) and obtain $\Delta s_{\text{Gov,Jan}} = -\frac{0.25\%-0.15\%-0.55\%}{4.6} = 0.10\%$. The application of the Campisi (2011) attribution method of Equation (14-52) yields the detailed results per issuer type for both dates as shown in Table 14-25.

TABLE 14-25 VAS example – Campisi (2011) analysis for the Verso fund (January and October).

Effect	*January*				*October*			
	Gov	Corp	HY	Global	Gov	Corp	HY	Global
Carry	−0.01%	−0.01%	0.01%	**0.00%**	−0.01%	−0.02%	−0.01%	**−0.04%**
Yield curve	0.06%	0.04%	0.03%	**0.14%**	0.09%	0.25%	0.02%	**0.36%**
Spread	−0.05%	−0.04%	0.00%	**−0.09%**	−0.07%	−0.21%	−0.04%	**−0.31%**
Residual	0.14%	0.10%	0.03%	**0.27%**	0.00%	−0.05%	−0.18%	**−0.23%**

These results are summarized in a graph shown in Figure 14-14, which shows a much more precise picture regarding the effects.

Compared with Figure 14-13, this new decomposition explains what lies behind the "residual" effect: the contribution from the Spread effect is negative, indicating wrong tactical bets on the credit side (mostly on the governmental and corporate issuers, where the manager got the spread changes wrong with their choices of durations). The very positive residual effect in January was due to a good selection of investment grade issuers in January, but the negative value in October was mostly attributed to the high yield segment.

(continued)

(continued)

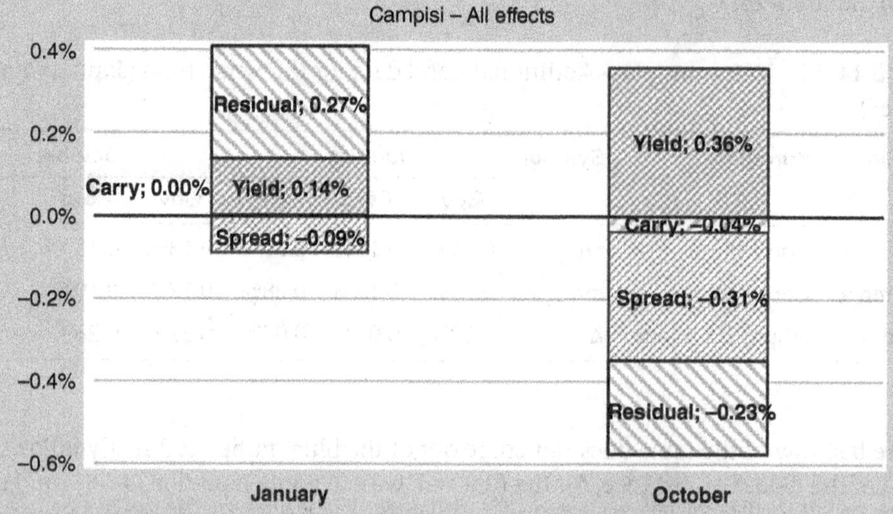

FIGURE 14-14 VAS example - Carry, Yield Curve, Spread, and Residual effects for the Verso fund (January and October).

14.3.3 Derivatives overlays

Using derivative contracts in the management process essentially leads to a situation where the portfolio's actual exposure to an asset return differs from its holdings because of the synthetic position. The general principle of the inclusion of derivatives in an attribution system is to find what Bacon (2023) calls a "notional asset." This is a replicating strategy with spot positions (and their associated weights) whose cost matches the value of the contract and whose periodic rate of return matches that of the contract, i.e.,

$$\sum_{d_i} w_{P,d_i,t} = w_{P,d,t} \tag{14-54a}$$

$$\sum_{d_i} w_{P,d_i,t} R_{d_i,t} = \tilde{w}_{P,d,t} R_{d,t} \tag{14-54b}$$

where $d_i = 1, \ldots, D$ stands for each asset that is necessary to invest in (long or short positions), with a weight of $w_{P,d_i,t}$ and a return of $R_{d_i,t}$, in order to replicate the derivative whose weight in the portfolio is $w_{P,d,t}$, whose exposure is $\tilde{w}_{P,d,t}$, and whose return is $R_{d,t}$.

The merit of the system is to express the outcome of the derivative overlay, represented by $\tilde{w}_{P,d,t} R_{d,t}$, as a weighted sum of asset returns $R_{d_i,t}$ that can be assigned to portfolio segments and therefore be readily usable for attribution analysis.

The simplest form of this decomposition, with standard derivatives, involves a notional asset featuring two positions: one in a traded asset (the underlying of the derivative) and the other in a fixed-income security, possibly bearing a different interest rate from the other cash positions held within the portfolio. Thus, we have $w_{P,d_1,t} = w_{P,d_S,t}$ for some assets S and $w_{P,d_2,t} = w_{P,d_{\text{Cash}},t}$, as shown below. If asset S is already held within the portfolio with an initial weight of $w_{P,S,t}$, then the global (hedged) weight after adjustment for derivatives becomes $w'_{P,S,t} = w_{P,S,t} + w_{P,d_S,t}$, whereas the part invested in cash joins the portfolio's cash segment.

14.3.3.1 Futures contracts

With financial futures, or similar "delta one" (i.e., linearly sensitive) derivative contracts, the weight $w_{P,F,t} = 0$, whereas the exposure $\tilde{w}_{P,F,t} = \frac{\#_F \times Q_F \times F_t}{P_t} \neq 0$, where $\#_F$ is the number of contracts, Q_F is the contract multiplier, F_t is the unit futures price, and P_t is the total portfolio value.

Finding the notional asset consists of splitting the exposure to the underlying of the contract into two components (weights) of equal size but opposite signs, replicating the equivalent carry trade strategy. The first weight $w_{P,F_S,t}$ (asset) multiplies the return of the underlying of the contract, while the second one $w_{P,F_{\text{Cash}},t}$ (cash) carries the market interest rate. $w_{P,F_S,t} > 0$ if the position is long on the underlying, and $w_{P,F_S,t} < 0$ otherwise. Of course, if the derivative's cost of carry differs from the market interest rate because of any financial income or cost or convenience yield, the return of the cash component should reflect it, such that equality (14-54b) is always respected:

$$w_{P,F_S,t} = -w_{P,F_{\text{Cash}},t} = \tilde{w}_{P,F,t} \tag{14-55a}$$

$$w_{P,F_S,t}R_{S,t} + w_{P,F_{\text{Cash}},t}R_{f^*,t} = \tilde{w}_{P,F,t}R_{F,t} \tag{14-55b}$$

where $R_{f^*,t}$ is the return of the risk-free asset that allows Equation (14-55b) to be satisfied.

For instance, consider a portfolio whose holding in a stock index S amounts to 10% of the total portfolio size ($w_{P,S,t} = 10\%$) with a return of $R_{S,t} = 1\%$. The manager has decided to hedge half of the exposure with a futures contract, whose return equals 0.995 times that of the index (because of the cost of carry). Thus, we have $\tilde{w}_{P,F,t} = -5\%$ and $R_{F,t} = 0.995\%$. The notional asset is composed of a short position in the index of $w_{P,F_S,t} = -5\%$ and a long position in cash of $w_{P,F_{\text{Cash}},t} = 5\%$ and their corresponding returns are $R_{F_S,t} = R_{S,t} = 1\%$ and $R_{F_{\text{Cash}},t} = R_{f^*,t} = 0.005\%$. The hedged portfolio weight in the index becomes $w'_{P,S,t} = 10\% + (-5\%) = 5\%$.

14.3.3.2 Options

If options or more sophisticated derivatives are used, the same principle remains applicable, but the replicating strategy must be identified with arbitrage reasoning and updated regularly. Furthermore, the derivative generally has a non-zero weight in the portfolio that must be accounted for. Note that the weight and exposure are here the same: $\tilde{w}_{P,d,t} = w_{P,d,t}$. In the case of plain-vanilla call or put options, the way the notional asset is determined by Stannard (1996). We slightly deviate from his path in order to correspond to the same principles as above. The sequence can be summarized with the following steps: (i) assess the asset weight in the notional asset as the option's economic exposure to the underlying asset S using its delta: $w_{P,O_S,t} = \frac{\#_O \times \Delta_{O,t} \times S_t}{P_t}$, where $\#_O$ is the number of options, $\Delta_{O,t}$ is the option delta, S_t is the underlying price, and P_t is the total portfolio value; (ii) compute the cash weight invested in the notional asset $w_{P,O_{Cash},t}$ by difference so that

$$w_{P,O_S,t} + w_{P,O_{Cash},t} = w_{P,O,t} \tag{14-56a}$$

$$w_{P,O_S,t}R_{S,t} + w_{P,O_{Cash},t}R_{f^*,t} = w_{P,O,t}R_{O,t} \tag{14-56b}$$

Equation (14-56b) is nothing more than the equivalent of the arbitrage relation that links the option price (and return) with the one of its replicating portfolio using the underlying (first term) and the risk-free asset (second term). In practice, $R_{f^*,t}$ is obtained endogenously to solve the equality by incorporating the hedging inefficiencies.[11]

Consider a similar example as before. To protect their returns, for each unit of the index held in the portfolio, the manager has purchased a put option on the same underlying (i.e., $\#_S = \#_O$), for a total amount $w_{P,O,t} = \tilde{w}_{P,O,t} = 0.2\%$ compared to the total portfolio value. Whereas the asset return is $R_{S,t} = 1\%$, the return of the option position is $R_{O,t} = -34.8\%$, which means that the return of the hedge is $w_{P,O,t}R_{O,t} = 0.2\% \times (-34.8\%) = -0.696\%$. The option has a delta of $\Delta_{O,t} = -0.7$. Because $w_{P,S,t} = \frac{\#_S \times S_t}{P_t} = 10\% = \frac{\#_O \times S_t}{P_t}$, we obtain the first weight as $w_{P,O_S,t} = -0.7 \times w_{P,S,t} = -7\%$, and thus the second weight equals $w_{P,O_{Cash},t} = w_{P,O,t} - w_{P,O_S,t} = 0.2\% - (-7\%) = 7.2\%$. Applying Equation (14-56b) leads to $w_{P,O_S,t}R_{S,t} + w_{P,O_{Cash},t}R_{f^*,t} = (-7\%) \times 1\% + 7.2\% \times R_{f^*,t} = -0.696\%$, which means that the cash position has generated $R_{f^*,t} = 0.056\%$. The hedged portfolio weight is $w'_{P,S,t} = 10\% + (-7\%) = 3\%$.

14.4 STATISTICAL PERFORMANCE ATTRIBUTION

The idea of isolating allocation, selection and (possibly) interaction effects in realized portfolio performance does not limit itself to the treatment of holding-based returns. It is also possible to apply the same principles in the context of a statistical analysis of portfolio returns, with potentially very meaningful results. We discuss two important types of such approaches, namely first the use of statistical factors as an alternative basis to portfolio holdings and second the explicit account for risk in the attribution framework.

[11] Fischer and Wermers (2013) propose a finer approach in which the other relevant option sensitivities are separated from the synthetic cash position. We refer the interested reader to their discussion.

14.4.1 Factor-based attribution analysis

The original Brinson attribution analysis builds on asset weights and returns. Nevertheless, the same principles can be applied if one complements the beginning-of-period portfolio holdings with the statistical estimates of factor exposures in the spirit of the multifactor analysis discussed in Chapter 7.[12]

We consider again a portfolio and its benchmark with their respective individual weights and returns. The additional information used for the attribution analysis is the application of a common multifactor model with L distinct factors that explains the common sources of returns and leaves only a residual term unexplained.[13] The combination of these two sets of information enables us to write the portfolio excess return in the following way:

$$R_{P,t} - R_{B,t} = \sum_{l=1}^{L} (\beta_{P,l,t} - \beta_{B,l,t}) F_{l,t} + (\beta_{P,0,t} - \beta_{B,0,t}) \tag{14-57}$$

where each $\beta_{P,l,t} = \sum_{i=1}^{N} w_{P,i,t}\beta_{i,l}$ represents the sensitivity of the portfolio return $R_{P,t}$ to the lth analytical factor return denoted by $F_{l,t}$ and $\beta_{P,0,t} = \sum_{i=1}^{N} w_{P,i,t}(\beta_{i,0} + \varepsilon_{i,t})$ is the weighted sum of each asset's constant idiosyncratic abnormal return $\beta_{i,0}$ and a pure noise term $\varepsilon_{i,t}$. The same interpretations hold for the benchmark portfolio.

From the perspective of the BHB attribution framework, the right-hand side of Equation (14-57) readily proposes the decomposition that is sought for. The first term seems to exactly match the shape of the Allocation effect of Equation (14-4a), by simply replacing the weights with the betas and the benchmark segment returns with the factor returns. The second term thus summarizes the Selection and Interaction effects altogether.

The analysis becomes more insightful when individual assets are aggregated by segments. Since the factors betas are additive in a linear multifactor model, we can then rewrite the model in the following way:

$$R_{P,t} - R_{B,t} = \sum_{l=1}^{L} (\beta_{P,l,t} - \beta_{B,l,t}) F_{l,t} + \sum_{k=1}^{K} w_{P,k,t}\delta_{P,k,t} - \sum_{k=1}^{K} w_{B,k,t}\delta_{B,k,t} \tag{14-58}$$

where, as before, $w_{P,k,t} = \sum_{i \in k} w_{P,i,t}$ and $w_{B,k,t} = \sum_{i \in k} w_{B,i,t}$ are the weights of segment k in the portfolio and benchmark, respectively, and $\delta_{P,k,t} = \frac{\sum_{i \in k} w_{P,i,t}(\beta_{i,0}+\varepsilon_{i,t})}{w_{P,k,t}}$ and $\delta_{B,k,t} = \frac{\sum_{i \in k} w_{B,i,t}(\beta_{i,0}+\varepsilon_{i,t})}{w_{B,k,t}}$ are their idiosyncratic returns.

---

[12]If the asset weights are unknown or considered to be constant, the situation is considerably simplified and can be viewed as a special case of the analysis carried out here.

[13]In order to avoid any confusion with the notation used everywhere else in this chapter, we enumerate the factors $l = 1, \dots, L$ whereas letter k is used in the other chapters of this book.

The only step left is to merge both parts of the formula, in the same spirit as for the factor-based Information ratio attribution analysis examined in Section 13.3.2 of Chapter 13, but this time with a different purpose: instead of focusing on the risk decomposition, we now acknowledge that there is a combination of $L+K$ benchmark weights. The first L ones are the systematic factor exposures for the whole allocation and leave neither any selection nor interaction effect. The remaining K ones are the sector weights that multiply the idiosyncratic returns that are left unexplained by the common factors. Adopting the same notation as for the BF model, we can disentangle the three effects as follows:

$$\mathcal{A}_{P,t} = \sum_{l=1}^{L}(\beta_{P,l,t} - \beta_{B,l,t})F_{l,t} + \sum_{k=1}^{K}(w_{P,k,t} - w_{B,k,t})(\delta_{B,k,t} - \delta_{B,t}) \tag{14-59a}$$

$$\mathcal{S}_{P,t} = \sum_{k=1}^{K} w_{B,k,t}(\delta_{P,k,t} - \delta_{B,k,t}) \tag{14-59b}$$

$$\mathcal{I}_{P,t} = \sum_{k=1}^{K}(w_{P,k,t} - w_{B,k,t})(\delta_{P,k,t} - \delta_{B,k,t}) \tag{14-59c}$$

where $\delta_{B,t} = \sum_{k=1}^{K} w_{B,k,t}\delta_{B,k,t}$ is the average benchmark idiosyncratic return across the segments.[14]

The added value of performing a multifactor analysis on top of the knowledge of the asset holdings stands out. Explaining the Allocation effect is particularly interesting, as we may distinguish two subcomponents: the Factor effect and the Idiosyncratic effect.

The Factor effect $\mathcal{F}_{P,t} \equiv \sum_{l=1}^{L}(\beta_{P,l,t} - \beta_{B,l,t})F_{l,t}$ represents the factor bets taken by the manager, in the spirit of various possibilities to explain portfolio returns discussed in detail in Chapter 7. The Idiosyncratic effect $\mathcal{U}_{P,t} \equiv \sum_{k=1}^{K}(w_{P,k,t} - w_{B,k,t})(\delta_{B,k,t} - \delta_{B,t})$ reflects the remaining segment bets that already control for the systematic risk of the assets. The other two effects explicitly focus on pure selectivity, getting rid of any asset's hidden factor exposure that would be mistakenly confused with a specific abnormal return.

When the individual or sector weights are unknown, it is not possible to reach that level of detail. Nevertheless, the split between the systematic and idiosyncratic parts of the returns presented in Equation (14-58) remains valid and can already provide useful information.

The VAS example (continued)

Instead of applying the pure Brinson–Fachler analysis for the three funds on their holdings, the management decides to complement the analysis with a single-factor model by using the

[14] It is not possible to deduce the average factor return because the betas do not necessarily sum up to 1.

market returns reported in Table 14-1. The estimation of the single-factor beta is performed by ordinary least-squares regression for each of the segments and then aggregated with each periodic weight in order to obtain the global market beta for each portfolio: $\beta_{X,t} = w_{X,\text{Stock},t} \times \beta_{\text{Stock}_X} + w_{X,\text{Bond},t} \times \beta_{\text{Bond}_X} + w_{X,\text{Cash},t} \times \beta_{\text{Cash}_X}$, where X = V, A, S, and B. This provides the series of coefficients as shown in Table 14-26.

Because of its constant allocation between the segments, the benchmark's beta is a constant. Not surprisingly given its manager's style, the Alloco fund has the largest variation in betas.

On the basis of this information, we can isolate the Factor effect for each of the funds and perform the BF attribution analysis on the idiosyncratic effects according to Equations (14-59a) to (14-59c). The results for the average effects are summarized in Table 14-27.

TABLE 14-26 VAS example – Aggregate single-factor betas.

Month	Verso	Alloco	Selecto	Benchmark
Jan	0.425	0.369	0.383	0.402
Feb	0.414	0.409	0.374	0.402
Mar	0.403	0.384	0.361	0.402
Apr	0.393	0.369	0.373	0.402
May	0.385	0.312	0.381	0.402
Jun	0.379	0.340	0.396	0.402
Jul	0.370	0.323	0.384	0.402
Aug	0.371	0.363	0.372	0.402
Sep	0.360	0.407	0.374	0.402
Oct	0.372	0.392	0.384	0.402
Nov	0.382	0.363	0.390	0.402
Dec	0.368	0.319	0.398	0.402
Average	**0.385**	**0.363**	**0.381**	**0.402**
Standard deviation	**0.020**	**0.033**	**0.011**	**0.000**

Compared with the results of the original BHB attribution analysis presented in Table 14-9, the new Factor effect reveals little difference for the Verso and Selecto funds. However, the situation is totally different for Alloco. Most of the outperformance formerly attributed to the allocation to equities (0.17% per month in Table 14-9) has faded away.

(continued)

(continued)

Part of it has been absorbed by the common Factor effect, and, surprisingly, a substantial fraction of the Idiosyncratic effect is attributed to the allocation in cash (0.04% per month, which makes up to almost 0.5% per year). Thus, accounting for the systematic risk factor bet of the manager of this fund drastically changes the picture regarding the source of its outperformance, as shown in Figure 14-15.

TABLE 14-27 VAS example – Outcome of the Factor-based attribution analysis.

		Allocation $\mathcal{A}_P$		Selection $\mathcal{S}_P$	Interaction $\mathcal{I}_P$	Total	Global $R_P - R_B$
		Factor $\mathcal{F}_P$	Idiosyncratic $\mathcal{U}_P$				
Verso	Stocks	**−0.02%**	0.01%	0.17%	0.01%	**0.19%**	**0.17%**
	Bonds		0.00%	−0.01%	0.00%	**−0.01%**	
	Cash		0.01%	0.00%	0.00%	**0.01%**	
Alloco	Stocks	**0.06%**	0.03%	0.03%	0.00%	**0.06%**	**0.17%**
	Bonds		0.01%	−0.01%	0.00%	**0.00%**	
	Cash		0.04%	0.00%	0.00%	**0.04%**	
Selecto	Stocks	**−0.02%**	−0.01%	0.19%	0.01%	**0.19%**	**0.17%**
	Bonds		0.00%	0.01%	0.00%	**0.01%**	
	Cash		−0.01%	0.00%	0.00%	**−0.01%**	

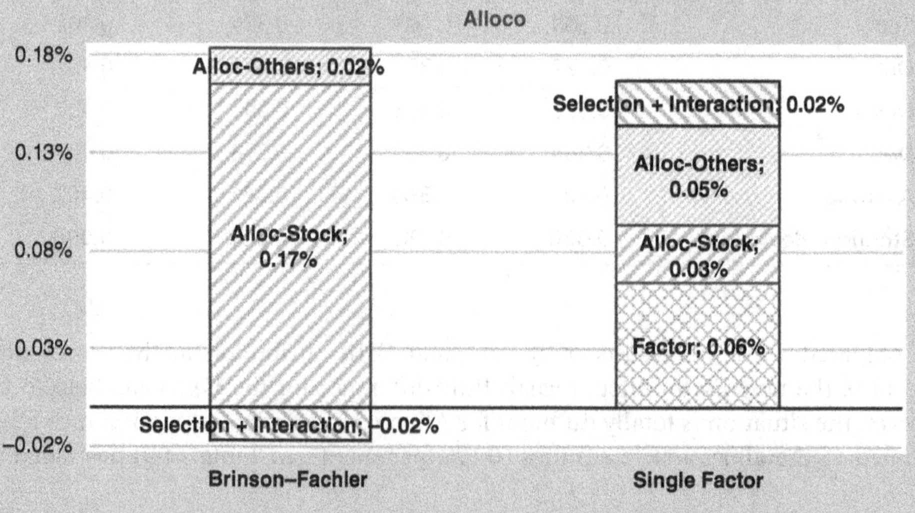

FIGURE 14-15 VAS example – Attribution effects with the BF and the single-factor approaches.

The diagnosis suggested by the breakup of Alloco's excess return reveals the true nature of its manager's decision-making process. The main source of performance is a superior anticipation of the market rate of return. Besides these active directional exposures, the manager also succeeds in forecasting each segment's own excess return. The picture delivered by the classical BF attribution without isolating the systematic part of the returns appears to be, in this particular case, largely misleading.

14.4.2 Risk-adjusted attribution

In Section 13.3 of Chapter 13, we discussed how to decompose some of the major risk-adjusted performance measures, such as the Sharpe ratio or the Information ratio. Even though portfolio risk cannot be decomposed in a linear fashion, there exist methods enabling the analyst to allocate fractions of risk that are relevant for each portfolio component. It is thus not surprising to observe that the traditional Brinson analysis framework can be adapted in order to accommodate the partition of portfolio risk in various effects.[15]

The challenge here is to implement an attribution method that controls for differences in risks between the portfolio (and its segments) and the benchmark. As a comprehensive attempt to reconcile performance attribution analysis with the classical risk–return framework proposed in the Standard Portfolio Theory, Fisher and D'Alessandro (2019) show how to attribute performance in the Fama (1972) decomposition framework, discussed in the first section of Chapter 13.[16]

As the starting point of the analysis, we consider an adapted version of Figure 13-2 of Chapter 13 in which risk is represented by the portfolio beta instead of volatility. Since we work in the scope of performance attribution, the portfolio is benchmarked: We also report the coordinates of this benchmark B that replaces, in a sense, the market portfolio. Thus, in this setup, $\beta_B = 1$. Consequently, the investor's target risk level in Fama's (1972) framework is replaced with this unit benchmark beta. Finally, for the sake of clarity, we represent the portfolio with a rate of return that exceeds all required returns. This leads to Figure 14-16.

Because we use the raw beta as a measure of risk, the coefficient that reflects the portfolio's total risk is obtained by $\beta_P^{\mathrm{F}} = \frac{\sigma_P}{\sigma_B} = \frac{\beta_P}{\rho_{PB}}$, where we assume that the correlation coefficient ρ_{PB} is positive, which should reasonably be the case for a benchmarked portfolio. The authors call β_P^{F} "Fama's beta," but we prefer to call it the "Total risk beta" for consistency. The required portfolio return is $R^*(\beta_P^{\mathrm{F}})$ if one cares about total risk; otherwise, it is equal to $R^*(\beta_P)$ with systematic risk. As a reminder, $\lambda_P^{(m)}$ is the manager's risk premium, and δ_P represents the diversification premium.

---

[15]In the particular case of a portfolio that is mean–variance efficient subject to a tracking error constraint (i.e., lying on the "tracking error variance efficient frontier"), Bertrand (2005) shows that the Information ratios of the Allocation, Selection and Interaction effects are the same and equal to the IR of the global portfolio.

[16]Alternative approaches have been proposed, like Spaulding (2016) who proposes to attribute the M^2.

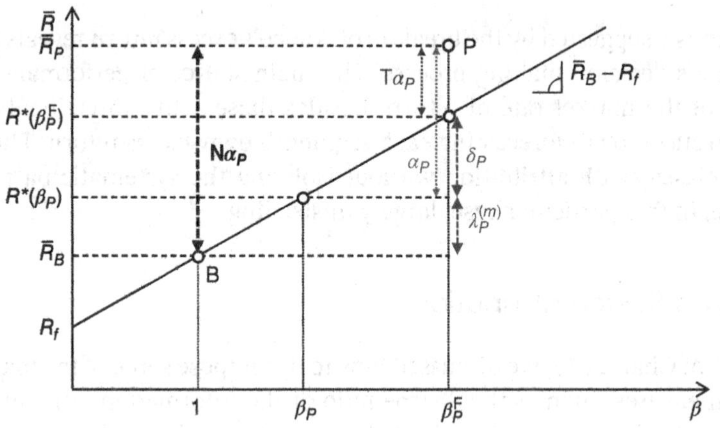

FIGURE 14-16 Adapted decomposition of the average portfolio return with beta as risk measure.

From a basic attribution point of view, the performance of the portfolio is the so-called "Nominal alpha" $N\alpha_P = \overline{R}_P - \overline{R}_B$. However, taking risk into account reveals another picture. The total portfolio's required return is equal to $R_B + \lambda_P^{(m)} + \delta_P$. Jensen's alpha α_P is the adequate measure of performance if the investor cares about systematic risk, whereas the Total risk alpha $T\alpha_P$, also called "net selectivity" by Fama (1972), should be used if the investor cares about total risk.[17]

The disturbing feature of Figure 14-16 is that all the required rates of return are not aligned vertically, i.e., they correspond to different levels of risk. Fisher and D'Alessandro (2019) suggest a different approach in which all rates of return are plotted successively above the portfolio raw beta of β_P and the benchmark beta of 1. We can summarize the procedure in two steps:

1. Draw an "implied SML" that links the risk-free rate with the coordinates of a point whose risk is the raw beta but whose required return is the one obtained with total risk, $R^*(\beta_P^F)$. The slope of this line is thus equal to $\frac{R^*(\beta_P^F)-R_f}{\beta_P} = \frac{\beta_P^F(\overline{R}_B-R_f)}{\beta_P} = \frac{\overline{R}_B-R_f}{\rho_{PB}}$. The denominator addresses the increase in the risk premium due to the portfolio's active risk: the higher the departure from the benchmark is, the lower the correlation and the larger the premium.
2. From the coordinates of a point P' whose return is the actual one of the portfolio and whose risk is its beta – thus on the same line as the one in step one – draw two lines: (i) one that is parallel to the implied SML (slope $\frac{\overline{R}_B-R_f}{\rho_{PB}}$) and (ii) another one that is parallel to the original SML (slope $\overline{R}_B - R_f$). The images of a beta of 1 – corresponding to the

[17]See Chapter 13 for a complete discussion.

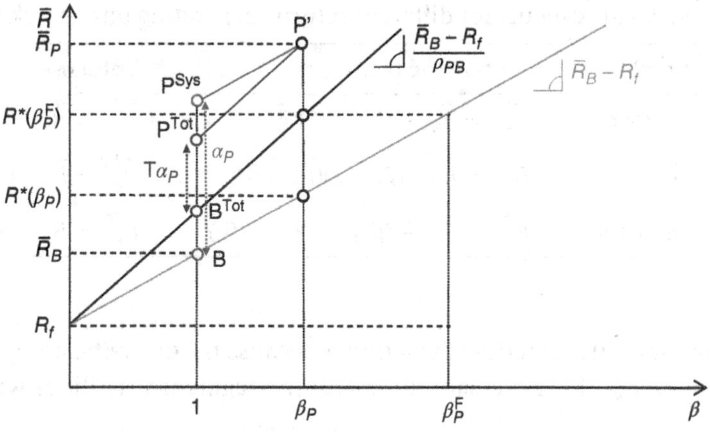

FIGURE 14-17 Rescaled risk-adjusted portfolio returns.

benchmark risk – on these two lines reflect the total risk-adjusted return of the portfolio (for the implied SML) and the beta risk-adjusted return (for the original SML).

This procedure is summarized in the graph shown in Figure 14-17, which can be matched with Figure 14-16.

The graph clearly suggests that there are two possible levels for the risk-adjusted analysis. The first one, which considers systematic risk only, preserves Jensen's alpha as the measure of performance. It is equal to the vertical distance between the coordinates of the benchmark B and the raw beta risk-adjusted portfolio P^{Sys}. The second one relies on total risk. The performance measure is still the Total risk alpha, which is equal to the distance between P^{Tot} and B^{Tot}, the latter one being the coordinate of a point with a beta of 1 on the implied SML and with a return of $R_f + \frac{\bar{R}_B - R_f}{\rho_{PB}}$.

Since the procedure "simply" translates the performance measures to the left of the graph, what is its added value for performance attribution then? The answer resides in the granular treatment of the portfolio and benchmark segment returns. Originally, in the BHB analysis, the excess return is broken up according to Equation (14-2), with the segment weights and returns. As shown in Figure 14-17, there is a necessity to adjust these returns for the differential risk levels. The same types of adjustments must be made at the segment level, with the generic formula:

$$\overline{R}^{X}_{i,k} = \overline{R}_{i,k} - (\beta^{X}_{i,k} - 1)(\overline{R}_B - R_f) \tag{14-60}$$

where $i = P, B$ and $X =$ F or nil, depending on whether we take the total risk beta or the raw one.

If the weights are constant during the estimation period, the weighted sum of component raw betas is equal to the global portfolio beta, i.e., $\beta_P = \sum_{k=1}^{K} w_{P,k}\beta_{P,k}$. Unfortunately, this is not

TABLE 14-28 Risk adjustments for different returns depending on the risk type considered.

	Level	Systematic risk	Total risk
Benchmark	Segment	$\overline{R}_{B,k}^{Sys} = \overline{R}_{B,k} - (\beta_{B,k} - 1)(\overline{R}_B - R_f)$	$\overline{R}_{B,k}^{Tot} = \overline{R}_{B,k} - (\beta_{B,k} - 1)(\overline{R}_B - R_f)$
Portfolio	Global	$\overline{R}_P^{Sys} = \overline{R}_P - (\beta_P - 1)(\overline{R}_B - R_f)$	$\overline{R}_P^{Tot} = \overline{R}_P - (\beta_P^F - 1)(\overline{R}_B - R_f)$
	Segment	$\overline{R}_{P,k}^{Sys} = \overline{R}_{P,k} - (\beta_{P,k} - 1)(\overline{R}_B - R_f)$	$\overline{R}_{P,k}^{Tot} = \overline{R}_{P,k} - (\beta_{P,k}^F - 1)(\overline{R}_B - R_f)$

the case with the simple use of ratios of volatilities because the diversification effect entails that $\sum_{k=1}^{K} w_{P,k} \frac{\sigma_{P,k}}{\sigma_B} > \frac{\sigma_P}{\sigma_B} \equiv \beta_P^{F}$. It is necessary to replace the segment volatilities with the marginal risk contributions $\frac{\partial \sigma_P}{\partial w_k} = \rho_{kP}\sigma_{P,k}$ so that the total risk beta for each segment k is defined as

$$\beta_{P,k}^{F} = \frac{\rho_{kP}\sigma_{P,k}}{\sigma_B} = \beta_{P,k}\frac{\rho_{kP}}{\rho_{kB}} \tag{14-61}$$

which ensures that $\sum_{k=1}^{K} w_{P,k}\beta_{P,k}^{F} = \sum_{k=1}^{K} w_{P,k}\frac{\rho_{kP}\sigma_{P,k}}{\sigma_B} = \frac{\sigma_P}{\sigma_B} = \beta_P^{F}$ (apparently, this necessary adjustment is not explicitly discussed by Fisher and D'Alessandro, 2019). Applying the same principle to the benchmark betas would lead to $\beta_{B,k}^{F} = \beta_{B,k}\frac{\rho_{kB}}{\rho_{kB}} = \beta_{B,k}$. Thus, the benchmark segment betas are the same regardless of the selected risk dimension.

Equation (14-61) shows that the beta adjustment at the segment level results from a trade-off between the impact of its correlation with the benchmark on active risk (lower correlation leads to an increase in beta) and the beneficial influence that a low correlation with the portfolio has on its intrinsic diversifying behavior (low correlation leads to a decrease in beta).

In Table 14-28, we summarize the formulas for the risk adjustments depending on whether systematic risk (β_P) or total risk (β_P^{F}) is the relevant metric for the investor.

Thus, for a given portfolio, the attribution analysis can be carried out at three parallel levels: Nominal alpha (no adjustment), Jensen's alpha (systematic risk adjustment), or Total risk alpha (total risk adjustment). The formulas reported in Table 14-28 provide the inputs for each of the risk-adjusted analyses. Of course, performing these types of adjustments may lead to a radically different picture from the unadjusted returns.

The price to pay for the possibility of differentiating the level of analysis is the impossibility of applying it for multiperiodical returns in a straightforward manner since the additivity of the betas only works if the weights are constant over the period. Thus, if one wants to dive into periodic returns, it is necessary to re-compute the betas for every single period. A convenient approach for the estimation of periodic betas is to set the weights of every segment to be constant and equal to the current periodic weight $w_{P,k,T}$. The reconstructed periodic portfolio return is simply equal to the weighted average of the periodic segment return in a kind of "clean portfolio backtesting":

$$R'_{P,t} = \sum_{k=1}^{K} w_{P,k,T} R_{P,k,t} \tag{14-62}$$

where $t = 0, \ldots, T$ is the estimation window for the beta and volatilities. The portfolio and segment betas are then estimated for the current date T and their additivity is preserved. As the benchmark's segment weights are constant, this issue does not apply in this case.

Performing a full-fledged attribution analysis for the three levels of the Fama's (1972) decomposition framework reconciles the rather theoretical vision of portfolios in a risk–return world that underlies the CAPM with the very practical objectives of the Brinson attribution analysis. Hence, this final section closes the loop of the granular analysis of performance that started in Chapter 13.

The VAS example (continued)

We focus on the equity segment of the Alloco fund in May. From Table 14-6, we obtain the weights of different sectors as $w_{A,Tec,May} = 22.6\%$, $w_{A,Fin,May} = 19.7\%$, $w_{A,Cyc,May} = 18.4\%$, and $w_{A,Def,May} = 39.3\%$. Our first task is to rebuild a virtual sample of global portfolio returns using these weights and the segment returns of Table 14-6, as shown in Table 14-29.

TABLE 14-29 VAS example – Rebuilt sample of segment returns on the basis of the weights of May.

Month	Alloco stocks (initial)	Alloco stocks (rebuilt)
Jan	0.72%	0.64%
Feb	2.03%	1.78%
Mar	3.97%	2.69%
Apr	0.64%	0.81%
May	−6.50%	−6.50%
Jun	2.58%	1.53%
Jul	−8.42%	−7.78%
Aug	6.32%	4.49%
Sep	5.09%	3.80%
Oct	1.89%	1.84%
Nov	4.23%	3.39%
Dec	−4.36%	−3.65%

(continued)

(continued)

For instance, the January return is obtained by $R_{A,Jan} = \sum_k w_{A,k,May} R_{A,k,Jan} = 22.6\% \times 0.77\% + 19.7\% \times 0.66\% + 18.4\% \times 0.91\% + 39.3\% \times 0.43\% = 0.64\%$. Thanks to the new set of returns, we can compute the raw betas and total risk betas for the fund as well as the benchmark, as shown in Table 14-30.

TABLE 14-30 VAS example – Computation of the raw and total risk betas for the Alloco fund.

		Global	Tec	Fin	Sys	Def
Benchmark	Volatility	5.14%	7.36%	3.43%	5.42%	3.38%
	Correlation with benchmark	100.00%	99.52%	90.18%	97.45%	85.53%
	Beta	**1.000**	**1.425**	**0.602**	**1.028**	**0.562**
Alloco	Volatility	4.03%	7.25%	3.39%	5.20%	2.60%
	Correlation with benchmark	99.19%	99.48%	88.22%	95.92%	84.30%
	Correlation with fund	100.00%	98.62%	89.40%	94.74%	89.23%
	Raw beta	**0.778**	**1.402**	**0.582**	**0.970**	**0.426**
	Total risk beta	**0.784**	**1.390**	**0.590**	**0.958**	**0.451**

In May, because its allocation is largely tilted toward the Defensive (Def) sector, the global Equity segment of the Alloco fund has a relatively low raw beta. Since the correlation of the rebuilt series of returns with the benchmark is close to one, the raw and total risk betas are very close to each other. For the sectors, the picture is very heterogeneous regarding their betas, ranging from less than 0.5 to more than 1.4. The correction from the raw to the total risk beta is not very pronounced because (again) of the fact that the fund and benchmark are very similar, leading to a limited loss of diversification. Interestingly, at the sector level, the diversifying character of two of them (Tec and Sys) leads to a decrease in beta from the raw to the total risk version. This shows how important it is to account for both the loss of portfolio diversification driven by ρ_{kB}, on the one hand, and the diversifying power of a particular segment within the portfolio reflected by ρ_{kP}, on the other hand.

The application of the BF attribution model on the risk-adjusted returns delivers, as expected, very different results for the Nominal alpha, on the one hand, and the Jensen's and Total risk alphas, on the other hand. The breakdown per sector confirms this claim, as shown in Figure 14-18.

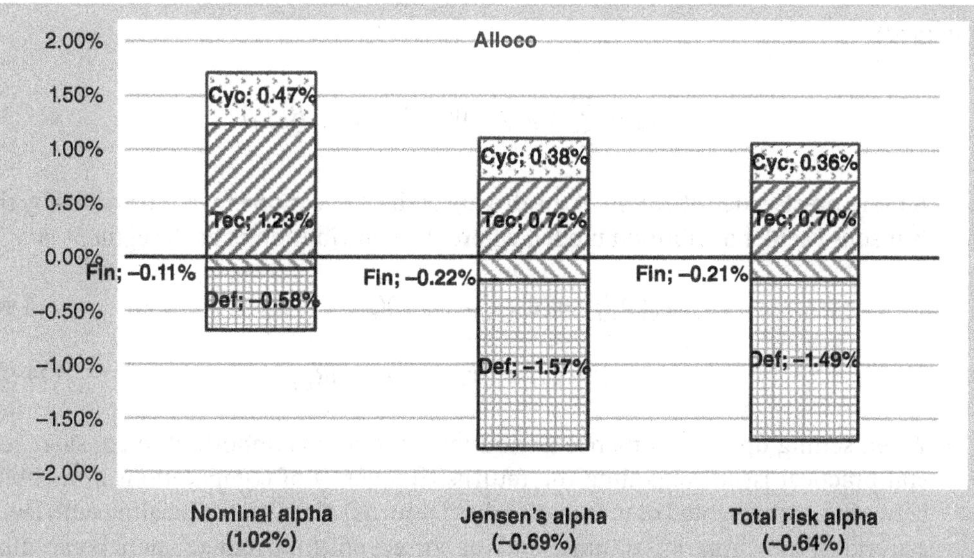

FIGURE 14-18 VAS example – Risk-adjusted attribution by sector for the Alloco fund (May).

Key Takeaways and Equations

- The general objective of performance attribution analysis is to explain the determinants of the excess return

$$R_{P,t} - R_{B,t} = \sum_{k=1}^{K} w_{P,k,t} R_{P,k,t} - \sum_{k=1}^{K} w_{B,k,t} R_{B,k,t} \tag{14-2}$$

- The classical Brinson–Hood–Beebower attribution model leads to a decomposition of performance in three parts: the Allocation (also called Timing in BHB) effect $\mathcal{T}_{P,t}$, the Selection effect $\mathcal{S}_{P,t}$, and the Interaction effect $\mathcal{I}_{P,t}$ defined as

$$\mathcal{T}_{P,t} = \sum_{k=1}^{K} (w_{P,k,t} - w_{B,k,t}) R_{B,k,t} \tag{14-4a}$$

$$\mathcal{S}_{P,t} = \sum_{k=1}^{K} w_{B,k,t} (R_{P,k,t} - R_{B,k,t}) \tag{14-4b}$$

(continued)

(continued)

$$\mathcal{I}_{P,t} = \sum_{k=1}^{K} (w_{P,k,t} - w_{B,k,t})(R_{P,k,t} - R_{B,k,t}) \tag{14-4c}$$

- A more precise identification of the drivers of the Allocation effect is provided by the Brinson–Fachler attribution model, where the contribution of each segment is

$$c_k(\mathcal{A}_{P,t}) = (w_{P,k,t} - w_{B,k,t})(R_{B,k,t} - R_{B,t}) \tag{14-9a}$$

$$c_k(\mathcal{N}_{P,t}) = (w_{P,k,t} - w_{B,k,t})R_{B,t} \tag{14-9b}$$

- When setting up a performance attribution system, it is important to consider several practical issues regarding the returns (frequency of computations and choice between time-weighted or money-weighted returns), the weights (dealing with leverage and off-benchmark positions), and the correct portfolio management perspective (top-down or bottom-up, partitioning).
- The inclusion of ESG-related restrictions in an attribution system involves (i) dealing with the restriction of the set of benchmark assets to only those that are ESG-eligible and (ii) accounting for the negative screening process that leads to discarding some segments from the investable universe. The resulting outcome of the system is written as

$$R_{P,t} - R_{B,t} = \mathcal{A}_{P,t} + \mathcal{S}_{P,t} + \mathcal{I}_{P,t} + \mathcal{S}_{P,t}^{\text{ESG}} + \mathcal{A}_{P,t}^{\text{NS}} \tag{14-17}$$

where $\mathcal{S}_{P,t}^{\text{ESG}}$ is the ESG–Selection effect and $\mathcal{A}_{P,t}^{\text{NS}}$ is the Screening–Allocation effect.
- When attribution analysis is performed for multiple periods, the issue of compounding returns makes it impossible to merely add up the effects obtained with the single-period analysis. The solutions are either "smoothing methods," in which the residual of the compounding process is distributed across periods, or "linking methods," which compound all effects over time. Two of the most popular methods are as follows:
  - The logarithmic smoothing coefficient attribution method that distributes the residual of the compounding process in a proportional manner, leading to

$$R_{P,0\to T} - R_{B,0\to T} = \tilde{\mathcal{I}}_P + \tilde{\mathcal{S}}_P + \tilde{\mathcal{I}}_P \tag{14-24}$$

  - The geometric attribution method that performs the attribution analysis on the geometric excess returns:

$$r_{P-B,0\to T}^{g} = \prod_{t=1}^{T} (1 + \mathcal{A}_{P,t}^{g})(1 + \mathcal{S}_{P,t}^{g})(1 + \mathcal{I}_{P,t}^{g}) - 1 \tag{14-32}$$

- For a globally managed portfolio, the issue of foreign currency exposures and hedging has to be addressed carefully.
  - As a simple extension of the BF attribution framework, the Ankrim and Hensel (1994) model adds two currency-related effects, the Currency Allocation effect $\mathcal{A}^{X}_{P,t}$ and the Forward Allocation effect $\mathcal{A}^{F}_{P,t}$:

$$\mathcal{A}^{X}_{P,t} = \sum_{k=1}^{K}(w_{P,k,t} - w_{B,k,t})(R_{E_k,t} - R_{E,t}) + \sum_{k=1}^{K}(w_{P,h_k,t} - w_{B,h_k,t})R_{h_k,t} \tag{14-38a}$$

$$\mathcal{A}^{F}_{P,t} = \sum_{k=1}^{K}(w_{P,k,t} - w_{B,k,t})(R_{F_k,t} - R_{F,t}) \tag{14-38b}$$

  - The version of Karnosky and Singer (1994) uses the additive property of continuous returns. It also distinguishes the pure market effects from the currency-related effects with the same type of distinction between the drivers of performance:

$$R^{c}_{P,t} - R^{c}_{B,t} = \underbrace{\mathcal{A}^{cL}_{P,t} + \mathcal{S}^{cL}_{P,t} + \mathcal{I}^{cL}_{P,t}}_{\text{Market effects}} + \underbrace{\mathcal{A}^{cX}_{P,t} + \mathcal{S}^{cX}_{P,t} + \mathcal{I}^{cX}_{P,t}}_{\text{Currency effects}} \tag{14-42}$$

- For fixed-income portfolios or segments, it is necessary to distinguish different types of effects. A simple extension of the BF model splits the Selection effect into a Duration effect and a Residual effect:

$$\mathcal{D}_{P,t} = \sum_{k=1}^{K} w_{B,k,t}(yR_{P,k,t} - yR_{B,k,t}) \tag{14-48a}$$

$$\mathcal{R}_{P,t} = \sum_{k=1}^{K} w_{B,k,t}(rR_{P,k,t} - rR_{B,k,t}) \tag{14-48b}$$

- The sector-based attribution method splits the total portfolio return into four parts. Its final excess return can be written as the sum of four components: the Carry excess return $\mathcal{C}_{P,t}$ that represents the "Static effect," the Yield curve excess return $\mathcal{Y}_{P,t}$ that represents the "Systematic effect," the Spread excess return $\mathcal{Z}_{P,t}$ that represents the pure "Tactical effect," and the Residual return $\mathcal{R}_{P,t}$ that is a pure bond picking effect, altogether defined as

$$\mathcal{C}_{P,t} = \sum_{k=1}^{K} w_{P,k,t}cR_{P,k,t} - \sum_{k=1}^{K} w_{B,k,t}cR_{B,k,t} \tag{14-53a}$$

(continued)

(continued)

$$\mathcal{Y}_{P,t} = \sum_{k=1}^{K} w_{P,k,t} yR_{P,k,t} - \sum_{k=1}^{K} w_{B,k,t} yR_{B,k,t} \quad \text{(14-53b)}$$

$$\mathcal{Z}_{P,t} = \sum_{k=1}^{K} w_{P,k,t} sR_{P,k,t} - \sum_{k=1}^{K} w_{B,k,t} sR_{B,k,t} \quad \text{(14-53c)}$$

$$\mathcal{R}_{P,t} = \sum_{k=1}^{K} w_{P,k,t} rR_{P,k,t} \quad \text{(14-53d)}$$

- If the portfolio manager uses derivatives overlays for hedging purposes, the attribution principle is to find a "notional asset," a replicating strategy with spot positions whose cost matches the value of the contract and whose periodic rate of return matches that of the contract. The weights of this notional asset solve a simple set of equations.
  - In the case of futures:

$$w_{P,F_S,t} = -w_{P,F_{\text{Cash}},t} = \tilde{w}_{P,F,t} \quad \text{(14-55a)}$$

$$w_{P,F_S,t} R_{S,t} + w_{P,F_{\text{Cash}},t} R_{f^*,t} = \tilde{w}_{P,F,t} R_{F,t} \quad \text{(14-55b)}$$

  - In the case of options:

$$w_{P,O_S,t} + w_{P,O_{\text{Cash}},t} = w_{P,O,t} \quad \text{(14-56a)}$$

$$w_{P,O_S,t} R_{S,t} + w_{P,O_{\text{Cash}},t} R_{f^*,t} = w_{P,O,t} R_{O,t} \quad \text{(14-56b)}$$

- Factor-based attribution is a technique that allows us to isolate the influence of a set of common sources of risk on the performance. The excess return is written as

$$R_{P,t} - R_{B,t} = \sum_{l=1}^{L} (\beta_{P,l,t} - \beta_{B,l,t}) F_{l,t} + \sum_{k=1}^{K} w_{P,k,t} \delta_{P,k,t} - \sum_{k=1}^{K} w_{B,k,t} \delta_{B,k,t} \quad \text{(14-58)}$$

  This leads to a refined characterization of the Allocation effect that features a systematic and a specific component:

$$\mathcal{A}_{P,t} = \sum_{l=1}^{L} (\beta_{P,l,t} - \beta_{B,l,t}) F_{l,t} + \sum_{k=1}^{K} (w_{P,k,t} - w_{B,k,t})(\delta_{B,k,t} - \delta_{B,t}) \quad \text{(14-59a)}$$

$$\mathcal{S}_{P,t} = \sum_{k=1}^{K} w_{B,k,t} (\delta_{P,k,t} - \delta_{B,k,t}) \quad \text{(14-59b)}$$

$$\mathcal{I}_{P,t} = \sum_{k=1}^{K} (w_{P,k,t} - w_{B,k,t})(\delta_{P,k,t} - \delta_{B,k,t}) \quad \text{(14-59c)}$$

- In the context of Fama's (1972) performance decomposition, it is also possible to perform a risk-adjusted version of attribution analysis by rescaling the portfolio and benchmark returns according to their systematic or total risk beta. Before applying portfolio attribution, it is necessary to redefine the periodic portfolio returns according to the last portfolio weight:

$$R'_{P,t} = \sum_{k=1}^{K} w_{P,k,T} R_{P,k,t} \quad (14\text{-}62)$$

REFERENCES

Allen, G. C. (1991), Performance attribution for global equity portfolios. *The Journal of Portfolio Management*, Vol. 18 (1), pp. 59–65.

Ankrim, E. M., and C. R. Hensel (1994), Multicurrency performance attribution. *Financial Analysts Journal*, Vol. 50 (2), pp. 29–35.

Bacon, C. R. (2002), Excess returns – arithmetic or geometric? *Journal of Performance Measurement*, Vol. 6 (3), pp. 23–31.

Bacon, C. R. (2019), *Performance Attribution. History and Progress*. CFA Research Foundation.

Bacon, C. R. (2023), *Practical Portfolio Performance Measurement and Attribution, 3rd Edition*. John Wiley & Sons.

Bertrand, P. (2005), A note on portfolio performance attribution: Taking risk into account. *Journal of Asset Management*, Vol. 5, pp. 428–435.

Brinson, G. P., and N. Fachler (1985), Measuring non-U.S. equity portfolio performance. *The Journal of Portfolio Management*, Vol. 11 (3), pp. 73–76.

Brinson, G. P., Hood, L. R. Jr., and G. L. Beebower (1986), Determinants of portfolio performance. *Financial Analysts Journal*, Vol. 42 (4), pp. 39–44.

Brinson, G. P., Singer, B. D., and G. L. Beebower (1991), Determinants of portfolio performance II: An update. *Financial Analysts Journal*, Vol. 47 (3), pp. 40–48.

Burnie, J. S., Knowles, J. A., and T. J. Teder (1998), Arithmetic and geometric attribution. *Journal of Performance Measurement*, Vol. 3 (1), pp. 59–68.

Campisi, S. (2000), Primer on fixed income performance attribution. *Journal of Performance Measurement*, Vol. 4 (4), pp. 14–25.

Campisi, S. (2011), A sector based approach to fixed income performance attribution. *Journal of Performance Measurement*, Vol. 15 (3), pp. 23–42.

Cariño, D. (1999), Combining attribution effects over time. *Journal of Performance Measurement*, Vol. 3 (4), pp. 5–14.

Christopherson, J. A., Cariño, D. R., and W. E. Ferson (2009), *Portfolio Performance Measurement and Benchmarking*. McGraw-Hill.

DiBartolomeo, D. (2003), Just because we can doesn't mean we should: Why daily observation frequency in performance attribution is not better. *Journal of Performance Measurement*, Vol. 7 (3), pp. 30–36.

Fama, E. (1972), Components of investment performance. *The Journal of Finance*, Vol. 17, pp. 551–567.

Feibel, B. J. (2003), *Investment Performance Measurement*. John Wiley & Sons, Wiley Finance, The Frank J. Fabozzi Series.

Fischer, B. R., and R. Wermers (2013), *Performance Evaluation and Attribution of Security Portfolios*. Academic Press.

Fisher, J. D., and J. D'Alessandro (2019), Risk-adjusted attribution analysis of real estate portfolios. *The Journal of Portfolio Management*, Vol. 45 (7), pp. 80–94.

Frongello, A. S. B. (2002), Linking single period attribution results. *Journal of Performance Measurement*, Vol. 6 (3), pp. 10–22.

Grégoire, P. (2019), Measuring the contributions of SRI/ESG investment strategies. *Journal of Performance Measurement*, Vol. 24 (1), pp. 8–18.

Karnosky, D. S., and B. D. Singer (1994), *Global Asset Management and Performance Attribution*. Research Foundation of the Institute of Chartered Financial Analysts, Charlottesville, VA.

Lord, T. J. (1997), The attribution of portfolio and index returns in fixed income. *Journal of Performance Measurement*, Vol. 2 (1), pp. 45–57.

Menchero, J. G. (2000), An optimized approach to linking attribution effects over time. *Journal of Performance Measurement*, Vol. 5 (1), pp. 36–42.

Spaulding, D. (2003), *Investment Performance Attribution*. McGraw-Hill.

Spaulding, D. (2016), Risk-adjusted performance attribution: Why it makes sense and how to do it. *Journal of Performance Measurement*, Vol. 20 (4), pp. 42–56.

Spaulding, D., and S. Campisi (2007), The case for money-weighted attribution. *Journal of Performance Measurement*, Vol. 11 (Performance Attribution Supplement), pp. 8–20.

Stannard, J. C. (1996), Measuring investment returns of portfolios containing futures and options. *Journal of Performance Measurement*, Vol. 1 (1), pp. 27–33.

Van Breukelen, G. (2000), Fixed income attribution. *Journal of Performance Measurement*, Vol. 4 (4), pp. 61–68.

Weber, A. (2018), Geometric attribution and the interaction effect. *Journal of Performance Measurement*, Vol. 22 (4), pp. 6–19.

PART IV - *Act*

USING PERFORMANCE FOR DECISION-MAKING

The ultimate step in the portfolio management process is the feedback loop leading to potential sanctions, rewards, or simply improvements in the decision chain. Portfolio performance appraisal and analysis play a key role in this cyclical approach. It clinches, in an objective way, how the investment decisions have led to satisfactory results regarding the efficient use of the inputs, and in particular the risk taken by the manager. In this last part, we investigate how performance-related topics may help in this context. Our perspective addresses four dimensions, each deployed in a dedicated chapter, sharing a common denominator: they examine the conditions under which an investor, analyst, or manager can faithfully use performance information in their decision-making process.

The first topic, tackled in **Chapter 15**, refers to the quality of the disclosure and usage of performance-related information. There are two major dimensions discussed in this chapter. The first one is the communication of performance from the producer to the user. The challenges are not similar depending on whether it concerns individual or collective investment vehicles. We examine the conditions under which the quality of disclosure is adequate and usable in order to form well-educated decisions. The second dimension addresses performance diagnostics and analytics. The objective is to fully understand the quality of the investment process relative to the investor's needs, be they associated with their risk profile or the comparison with peers.

Chapter 16 addresses the core of this part of the book, namely the direct use of performance for specific investment decisions. We show that the investor's maximization of their optimization criterion frequently involves the inclusion of risk and return dimensions through their translation in a performance measure. The domains of application include the choice of an investment universe, the design of specific strategies, or different types of investor needs.

Within this chapter, we also examine the interactions between financial and non-financial (ESG) criteria through the lens of performance optimization.

We devote **Chapter 17** to a topic that is not often addressed in detail in similar books, but that we view as very important: the link between performance and predictability in the quality of the portfolio management process. This is indeed one of the key challenges for the decision-maker: how to make sure that the past investment experience delivers useful forecasting insights regarding the future. We do not only examine the notion of performance persistence, but we also go beyond this dimension by considering various ways to link the past with the future with the help of portfolio performance.

As a final contribution, **Chapter 18** addresses the many issues related to the use of performance for decision-making. We first analyze the agency issues between the stakeholders and the role played by performance in the governance of their relationships. This enables us to discuss the normative framework for the design of a performance measurement process. The chapter also reviews a number of problems related to the identification of manager skills.

CHAPTER 15

Disclosing and Verifying Portfolio Performance

INTRODUCTION

The first necessary step in the investment decision-making process is to ensure that all relevant information is available and of sufficient quality. Then, with good material, it is important to make adequate use of this information in order to apply well-grounded portfolio selection criteria. This chapter is devoted to the communication channels available for investment firms to disclose their performance and for investors to conduct in-depth and/or comparative analyses of funds and portfolios.

We begin with a review of the *Global Investment Performance Standards* (GIPS). Promoted by the CFA Institute, these standards have become the major compliance reference for disclosing fund performance globally over the past two decades.

Beyond these principles, the main challenge for both the producer and the consumer of financial investments is to communicate effectively. This concerns both pooled funds and individually managed portfolios. For the first category, performance disclosure is a heavily constrained process. We show how the design of the two main communication documents, the *prospectus* and the *factsheet*, can – or cannot – convey information in the most effective fashion, in a way that lends itself to insightful performance analysis from the side of the investor. Regarding personal portfolio performance disclosure, the key document is the *periodic performance report*. It can be more detailed than the factsheet, and there are some additional principles that we discuss in order to maximize its usefulness for decision-making purposes.

Finally, *fund rating agencies* (FRAs) are important actors in the world of fund performance communication. They provide us with a market scan and a screening process of a large universe of funds. In the last section, we discuss the main methodological choices that they adopt in order to offer a view on the funds' relative performances. It is important, for the investor, to understand what they cover and what they do not. Additionally, for those who want to dig deeper into the matter, we examine some of the main portfolio analysis approaches, namely, *portfolio diagnostics* and *portfolio optimization*. Even though the issue of portfolio optimization generally goes beyond the use of performance indicators, it appears that the distinction between financial and non-financial performance indicators, and the investor preferences associated with these dimensions, is an important driver of portfolio choice. This final topic paves the way for the discussion of environmental, social, and governance (ESG)-related issues that are discussed in Chapter 16.

15.1 THE GLOBAL INVESTMENT PERFORMANCE STANDARDS

With the development of a worldwide asset management industry, the need to define best practices in reporting and communicating with investors has gradually emerged. The GIPS, which we review in this section, today stand as the internationally recognized standards for asset management firms. The GIPS initiative was launched in 1995 and was initially sponsored by the Association for Investment Management and Research that later became the CFA Institute. After the first publication in 1999, several updates of the GIPS editions have been released over the past two decades. The latest version, issued in June 2019, is sponsored by more than 40 countries across the world. A note by Deloitte (2020) reports that among the top 100 worldwide asset management firms, 85 (representing more than 60% of assets under management globally) claimed compliance with GIPS as of December 2015.

The goal of this section is to provide a brief survey of the GIPS to highlight their objectives, structure, and implementation. For more details, we refer interested readers to in-depth study of the GIPS presented in Chapter 16 of Fischer and Wermers (2012), Chapter 7 of Bacon (2023), or the official documentation published by the CFA Institute (2019).

15.1.1 Objectives

According to BCG (2022), the size of the global asset management industry was estimated as $112 trillion in 2021. Even if North America still represents the major market (with a 33% of market share and a steady growth rate of around 10% per year), several regions exhibit comparable if not superior market growth rates (12% for Latin America and 18% for Asia-Pacific). Given the increasing level of international competition, it has become very profitable for all the actors in the asset management industry to rely on widely accepted performance standards.

For asset management firms, compliance with the GIPS conveys a signal of professional rigor and credibility to existing and prospective clients. The internal review process helps these firms reinforce their professionalism and control their risks. The GIPS also have international implications: Adherence to global standards fosters competition on a level playing field despite disparities in investment practices and regulation across countries and regions. For investors, the dissemination of common reporting and communication standards is a key factor in establishing trust in the investment mandate. It also increases the quality of performance assessment using reliable information and data.

The benefits of compliance with the GIPS among hedge funds have recently been measured by Foster, Ngo, and Pyles (2021). They find that hedge funds more likely to comply are smaller and have stronger internal control procedures. They also have less experienced managers, and their accounts are less often labeled in the US currency. All in all, these findings suggest that GIPS compliance helps certify the good quality of small and risky funds. The authors further find evidence of lower fees charged by these GIPS-compliant funds.

15.1.2 Performance report

Compliance with the GIPS relies on the definition and publication of policies and procedures (P&Ps) that explain adherence to the standards. Distinct GIPS P&P reports are made for *composites* (a strategy sold to segregated clients) and for *pooled funds* (a participation in a specific fund sold to various clients). As far as pooled funds are concerned, distribution can be either limited (when participation is sold in a one-on-one meeting) or broad (when there is no direct relation between the firm and the investor).[1]

The GIPS performance report is structured around synthetic quantitative information accompanied by several disclosures including a statement of compliance, a definition of the firm, a description of the composite, and details about the methodology.

15.1.2.1 Statement of compliance

The GIPS reports disclosed by an investment firm must begin with a statement of compliance. This is a strong commitment as it applies to the *entire* firm, i.e., compliance is meant at all levels (accounts, funds, portfolios, investment strategies, ...). Once stated, compliance must be documented. To this end, the firm must establish and publish policies and procedures. Among the many provisions, the maintenance of funds, and the calculation, presentation, and distribution of performance stand out as the major stakes.

As is typically the case with compliance, commitment to the GIPS is not static. It is also an engagement to follow and adapt to changes in regulation and standards. In this regard, best practices for asset management are in constant evolution. Expert verifiers regularly publish their views on the latest compliance issues that deserve special attention (see, e.g., Spaulding, 2017; Spaulding, Simpson, Reeves, Rossi, and Barnette, 2018). Compliance with the GIPS can be verified by an independent firm. This verification is conducted on a voluntary basis, and the investment firm can choose the verifying entity.

[1] In the 2020 GIPS standards, pooled fund reports to broad distribution are optional.

15.1.2.2 Definition of the firm

The statement of compliance is typically followed by a definition of the firm. This helps the investor determine the boundaries of assets and strategies. This is usually accompanied by a brief history of the company. The period of ongoing verification can be mentioned (GIPS requirements must have been followed for at least five years to claim compliance). Defining the firm also gives their owners the opportunity to clearly state their strategy and competitive positioning.

15.1.2.3 Description of the composite or the pooled fund

According to the GIPS, the presentation of the investment firm's business is organized around the distinct notions of pooled funds and composites. The former (for instance, mutual funds, pension funds, or unit investment trusts) are marketed products and are therefore subject to some form of standardization and regulation. They are also known as collective portfolio management (CPM) vehicles. Composites, by contrast, are associated with a specific investment mandate or strategy offered to segregated accounts. Their definition is much more idiosyncratic to the firm. Thus, for a clear assessment of the firm's business, it becomes essential for the investor to understand how composites are structured and maintained. In the next sections, we study how to effectively communicate in the case of pooled funds (Section 15.2) and composites (Section 15.3).

Even if the notion of a composite revolves around the investment strategy, other dimensions such as the asset class, the investment style, the use of derivatives, or the resort to leverage complete the definition of the composite. An important provision of the GIPS is that all fee-paying, discretionary portfolios must be included in at least one composite. Discretion in this context is meant as representativeness of the strategy. The GIPS-compliant firm must have an established policy that determines whether a portfolio is discretionary or not. Spaulding et al. (2018) discuss some considerations to take into account, such as the practice of call before trading, restrictions on sectors or certain securities, or credit limits.

Among the possible criteria for creating a composite, Fischer and Wermers (2012) list the following:

- Similar geographical asset classes
- Similar strategies
- Weighting range of asset classes, in the case of balanced portfolios
- Same benchmark
- Similar use of derivatives
- Similar use of currency hedging instruments
- Comparable risk classes
- Comparable investment approach (e.g., active, low tracking error, and passive)
- Similar investment objectives (e.g., achievement of a minimum return target)

Once a composite has been objectively defined and described, the GIPS set some conditions to correctly maintain it over time. The general rule is that the inclusion of every portfolio into composites should be clearly established from the start. Transfers from one composite to another remain exceptional and should be carefully motivated. If the firm launches new strategies, then new corresponding composites must be created. More generally, the P&Ps define the criteria for creating new composites. Moreover, for enhanced transparency, terminated composites must nevertheless be disclosed five years after they ended.

15.1.3 Information content

15.1.3.1 Quantitative data

Tables 15-1 and 15-2 display the typical quantitative information contained in GIPS reports for pooled funds and composites, respectively. Each item in these tables is then discussed in more detail. These two tables contain 10 years of data, which is the minimal reporting period. For investment firms with only 5–10 years of compliance, the whole period must be reported.

Since a composite contains several portfolios that are all managed according to a common investment strategy, the composite return is calculated as the asset-weighted average of all the portfolios in the composite.

1. Return calculation

The investment firm has the possibility of reporting either time-weighted returns or money-weighted returns. The former method is strongly encouraged. In fact, money-weighted returns can be reported only if the firm can prove that it has control over external cash flows

TABLE 15-1 Sample GIPS pooled fund report.

Name of the firm
Name of the pooled fund
Reporting period: 1 January 2013 to 31 December 2023

Year	Gross return (%)	Net return (%)	Benchmark return (%)	Three-year return Fund (%)	Three-year return Benchmark (%)	Three-year st. dev. Fund (%)	Three-year st. dev. Benchmark (%)	Fund assets ($ M)	Firm assets ($ M)
2023	5.12	4.88	4.43	6.17	5.74	10.92	11.24	224	1648
2022	6.25	5.90	4.82	8.20	7.13	14.55	13.89	232	1591
...	...	...	...	...	...	...	...	...	...
2014	2.15	1.81	2.26	5.38	4.66	12.78	12.75	179	1393

Source: Adapted from CFA Institute (2019).

TABLE 15-2 Sample GIPS composite report.

Name of the firm
Name of the composite
Reporting period: 1 January 2013 to 31 December 2023

Year	Gross return (%)	Net return (%)	Benchmark return (%)	Three-year st. dev. Composite (%)	Three-year st. dev. Benchmark (%)	Number of portfolios	Internal dispersion (%)	Composite assets ($ M)	Firm assets ($ M)
2023	4.05	3.12	3.02	12.12	11.80	32	3.1	656	2203
2022	−0.88	−1.64	−0.50	11.89	10.55	37	4.2	592	1989
...	...	...	...	...	...	...	...	...	...
2014	7.55	6.61	6.32	13.28	14.11	35	2.7	551	1677

Source: Adapted from CFA Institute (2019).

and if the portfolio (in the composite or in the pooled fund) either has a closed-end feature, has a fixed life or a fixed commitment, or contains a large portion of illiquid assets.

Let H denote the horizon for calculating the return (typically a year). The horizon is divided into n subperiods (typically months for GIPS compliance). Consider a portfolio P with value $V_{P,h}$ at the end of subperiod h, receiving a net cash flow (inflows minus outflows) CF_h during subperiod h. Assuming that each subperiod h has a length d_h (expressed in years), annualized time-weighted returns are geometric average returns computed as follows:

$$\mathrm{TWR}_{P,[0,T]} = \left(\prod_{h=1}^{n} (1 + R_{P,h})^{d_h}\right)^{1/H} - 1 \tag{15-1}$$

where the return for subperiod h is defined as

$$R_{P,h} = \frac{V_{P,h} - (V_{P,h-1} + \mathrm{CF}_{P,h})}{V_{P,h-1} + \mathrm{CF}_{P,h}} \tag{15-2}$$

The GIPS favor time-weighted returns because this calculation method controls the biases caused by uncontrolled inflows and outflows (such as deposits and withdrawals) and makes comparisons across funds easier.

An alternative return computation, also accepted by the GIPS, is the modified Dietz method. It is similar to the formula for time-weighted returns except that the denominator for subperiod returns is based on the average capital. That is,

$$R_{P,h} = \frac{V_{P,h} - (V_{P,h-1} + \mathrm{CF}_{P,h})}{V_{P,h-1} + \overline{\mathrm{CF}}_{P,h}} \tag{15-3}$$

TABLE 15-3 Inflows and outflows of a fictitious portfolio.

Date	Initial value	Inflow	Outflow	Terminal value
31 Jan				100
1 Feb	100			
12 Feb		8		
18 Feb			5	
28 Feb				104
1 Mar	104			
5 Mar		6		
20 Mar			7	
31 Mar				105

where $\overline{\text{CF}}_{P,h}$ is the sum of all flows weighted by the fraction of time between the occurrence date and the end of the subperiod.

To illustrate the difference between the two methods, consider the evolution of a portfolio value depicted in Table 15-3.

Suppose that subperiod returns are calculated every month. According to the "true" time-weighted method, these subperiod returns are given by $R_{P,\text{Feb}} = \frac{104-(100+8-5)}{100+8-5} = 0.971\%$ and $R_{P,\text{Mar}} = \frac{105-(104+6-7)}{104+6-7} = 1.961\%$. The annualized time-weighted return over the period is

$$\text{TWR}_{P,\text{Feb}-\text{Mar}} = ((1 + 0.971\%)(1 + 1.961\%))^{365/59} - 1 = 19.712\%.$$

According to the modified Dietz method, the subperiod returns are given by (assuming flows occur at the end of the day) $R_{P,\text{Feb}} = \frac{104-(100+8-5)}{100+8\times\frac{16}{28}-5\times\frac{10}{28}} = 0.973\%$ and $R_{P,\text{Mar}} = \frac{105-(104+6-7)}{104+6\times\frac{26}{31}-7\times\frac{11}{31}} = 1.877\%$. The resulting annualized time-weighted return over the period is given by

$$\text{TWR}_{P,\text{Feb}-\text{Mar}} = ((1 + 0.973\%)(1 + 1.877\%))^{365/59} - 1 = 19.118\%.$$

Ignoring inflows, outflows, and their timing, the portfolio performance over two months would have been evaluated at

$$\text{TWR}_{P,\text{Feb}-\text{Mar}} = (1 + 5\%)^{365/59} - 1 = 35.234\%.$$

As shown in this simple example, the rigorous application of the GIPS prevent the manipulation of performance. The key for a reliable return calculation is the correct identification of "significant" cash flows. Compliance with the GIPS requires that the investment firm display a significant cash flow policy, i.e., a set of rules that characterizes what must be considered a significant cash flow for each composite and for which periods. Imposing transparency on the cash flows and their timing helps objectively determine subperiods over which time-weighted returns are calculated.

For some illiquid asset classes (such as private equity or infrastructure), it is extremely difficult to re-evaluate the value of the portfolio on a high-frequency periodic basis. In those cases, it is possible to report money-weighted returns, which are computed like internal rates of returns. For GIPS compliance, portfolios must be reevaluated at least annually.

2. Benchmarking

According to the GIPS, the investment firm must justify its choice of benchmark for every pooled fund or composite (see Tables 15-1 and 15-2). The benchmark for a composite must be related to the corresponding investment strategy. If substantial differences exist between the strategy represented by the benchmark and the composite's investment mandate, the firm must disclose and explain them. Similarly, if the firm opts for no benchmarking, it must provide a motivation for this.

3. Return dispersion

As shown in Tables 15-1 and 15-2, pooled funds and composites must also report a measure of return dispersion. Although the GIPS allow alternative measures such as high–low return range or interquartile range, the equally weighted standard deviation is the most commonly reported dispersion metric, which is defined as

$$\sigma_P = \sqrt{\frac{\sum_{i=1}^{N} (R_i - \overline{R})^2}{N}} \qquad (15\text{-}4)$$

where N is the number of portfolios in the pooled fund or the composite, and $\overline{R}$ is the average return over the reporting period. The standard deviation is calculated on monthly returns over a three-year period and reported on an annualized basis.

4. Internal dispersion

Table 15-2 also indicates that GIPS composite reports must mention the number of portfolios and internal dispersion (compulsory for five portfolios or more). The latter measures performance heterogeneity across portfolios within a composite. It can be expressed as a range or as a standard deviation. Internal dispersion should be as low as possible to reflect the consistency of the investment strategy that defines the composite. This information is not applicable to pooled funds. It is usually replaced with more data on the historical performance of the fund and its benchmark, as shown in Table 15-1.

5. Size metrics

Finally, the last two columns of Tables 15-1 and 15-2 show the size of the pooled funds or the composites and the size of the firm. By gauging the relative importance of the fund or the composite (and their associated strategies), this information allows us to check the coherence of the firm's self-definition and management objectives. It is also a way for investors to assess whether the pooled fund or the composite should be considered core business (with corresponding expectations in terms of allocated resources).

15.1.3.2 Other relevant information

The other relevant information to be included in the performance report is the presentation of risks, the fee disclosure, and the statements about availability of information.

1. Presentation of risks

As mentioned previously, the risk associated with performance is presented through the form of a return dispersion metric (standard deviation is recommended) and a measure of internal dispersion. Beyond these quantitative indicators, the GIPS require that the investment firm disclose any use of leverage, derivatives, and short positions. If the use is substantial, the firm must also mention its frequency and the types of instruments involved.

The GIPS further contain a general requirement to disclose "*all significant events that would help a prospective client interpret the compliance presentation.*" The wording of that requirement is general on purpose. It is meant to encompass a wide variety of situations that investors should be aware of. Examples include changes in the management team, in the legal framework, or in the company ownership structure.

Finally, it is recommended that the investment firm comment on the additional sources of risk that composites might be exposed to. These include, but are not limited to, credit, counterparty, or liquidity risks.

2. Fee disclosure

GIPS-compliant firms can report gross-of-fees returns, net-of-fees returns, or both (as shown in Tables 15-1 and 15-2). For a clean appreciation of managerial skills, investors should have access to returns before fees.

The GIPS require disclosure of a fine decomposition of fees. There are three broad categories: investment management fees, trading expenses, and administrative fees. In many situations, the latter category can be considered as being out of the manager's control. The existence of performance-based fees must be disclosed, if applicable.

3. Availability of information

The methodology for producing the GIPS report must be made available upon request, and that availability must be explicitly mentioned. If compliance with the GIPS has been verified by an external party, the verification report should also be available upon request.

15.2 COMMUNICATING FUND PERFORMANCE EFFECTIVELY

Because they target multiple investors, CPM vehicles, commonly referred to as "pooled funds" in the GIPS universe (in short, we call them simply "funds" here), are subject to a series of constraints regarding the quality and quantity of information that they convey to the market. First of all, if the investment firm that commercializes a given fund claims to be *GIPS compliant*, it has to respect the associated guidelines explained in Section 15.1, in particular regarding the measurement of periodic returns. Second, fund managers cannot generally afford to fully personalize their communication.[2] This entails that complex investor-specific information, such as risk aversion, loss aversion, reservation rate, or mental account information, cannot be reasonably estimated. This does not preclude the use of some assumptions related to the investor's risk profile, such as risk tolerance (maximum risk budget) or investment horizon. As a consequence, risk-adjusted performance-related information disclosed to fund investors or prospects must be rather *generic*. Furthermore, there must be a certain level of *standardization* – the fund cannot afford to provide many specific types of disclosures that would create informational imbalances between people investing in the same vehicle – as well as *investor protection*, from a regulatory, contractual, or compliance-based standpoint. Finally, it is necessary to maintain a certain level of *concision* in the transmission of information. In this context, fund managers and investors face a common challenge but with different perspectives.

Consider first the fund managers' situation. We start from the principle that they wish to disclose transparent and intelligible information in order to provide a "fair and true view" of the outcome of their investment decisions. Within the constrained framework described above, they must primarily (i) provide all compulsory (from both the legal and compliance perspectives) information about the fund; (ii) let investors precisely understand what the fund is exactly doing; and (iii) deliver the necessary quantitative elements (return, risk, and/or performance) that are needed to frame each investor's own unbiased opinion about the fund's performance.

The investor's point of view is that of a consumer of pre-packaged information. Depending on their degree of sophistication, the requirements may differ. The unsophisticated retail fund customer needs to quickly understand, in an unequivocal way, whether the fund has delivered an adequate level of performance without any further calculation. At the other end of the spectrum, very knowledgeable investors or analysts must have all necessary risk and return data available in order to design themselves their own key performance indicators, be it to monitor a particular fund or to realize a meaningful comparative analysis across different instruments.

[2]Some exceptions exist, especially when the portfolio managed for an individual or a homogeneous group (family, investment club, . . .) has been established under the structure of a fund for practical or estate planning motivations. In that case, we may reasonably consider that the personalization objective prevails over the technical structure, and the case falls under the "personal portfolio management" situation that is analyzed in Section 15.3.

All these standpoints must be satisfied, as much as possible, within a limited set of deliverables. Sections 15.2.1 and 15.2.2 investigate the consequences of this issue in the design and interpretation of fund-specific informational documents. The focus is on the appraisal of portfolio performance. This entails that we do not position ourselves regarding the appropriateness of the choices made on other dimensions regarding either compulsory and voluntary information or document design.

15.2.1 Performance-related prospectus information

The "pre-contractual information" terminology refers to all documents that are distributed to the prospect investor up to the moment when they make the actual decision to invest – or not – in the collective investment vehicle. This is where the regulatory provisions are the most stringent, especially when the fund targets non-professional customers.

There are substantial regional differences regarding the requirements set by the competent authorities about the type, format, and content of the information made available to investors. In general, for a given fund, these requirements apply at two main levels: the compulsory layout and the approval of the content. This typically involves two kinds of documents. The first and longest one is the *statutory (complete) prospectus*. It provides the full description of the fund regarding its structure, investment objective and policies, valuation, remuneration structure (fees and commissions, and expenses), shareholder information (subscription and redemption, policies, eligible operations, and tax consequences), services, etc. Depending on the jurisdiction, some additional structured information must be provided as well, for instance, on the ESG policies and commitments for regulated European mutual funds. The prospectus comprises at least several dozen pages, but it can extend to hundreds when the fund is complex and/or represents an umbrella fund featuring several compartments.

Even though the prospectus must be made available to all investors, they usually do not wish to spend hours peeling its content. This is the reason why fund sponsors must also provide a *condensed prospectus* (CP) that gathers the key information about the fund. It takes the form of a heavily standardized short document, usually less than 10 pages long, whose name changes from one region to another (e.g., the "Summary Prospectus" in the USA, regulated by the US Securities and Exchange Commission (SEC); the two- or three-page "Key Information Document" in the European Union,[3] regulated by the European Securities and Markets Authority (ESMA); or the four-page "Product Highlight Sheet" in Singapore, regulated by the Monetary Authority of Singapore). This document is meant to be a complement to the prospectus, and investors are supposed to read both before committing to their investment decisions. Nevertheless, most investors would primarily rely on their analysis of the CP to make their choice.

[3] This document replaces the KIID (Key Investor Information Document) that was prevailing for mutual funds (UCITS) until 2022.

What's in it regarding the measurement of fund performance? The information contained in the CP is necessarily limited regarding statistical data because of the necessity to remain simple and pedagogical when addressing a retail investor who is not supposed to be highly educated in asset and portfolio management. Furthermore, it is a "static" document, which is updated with a moderate frequency, and thus its information must be valid for a long period.

Nonetheless, despite these limitations inherent to the nature of the document, there is very useful information about (at least) six topics. We list them below and provide some hints regarding the insights that could be gathered in the context of the appraisal and analysis of the fund's performance.

1. Investment strategy and policies

The most important financial information regarding the fund is naturally what it intends to do with the money made available by its investors. The manager must first disclose whether the fund is actively seeking to outperform the market or not (e.g., trackers, which are studied in Chapter 16). If they adopt an active risk management perspective, then the manager must at least communicate (i) what is the aim of the fund (in a few synthetic sentences); (ii) which asset classes constitute the investment universe; and (iii) in which geographical zones they focus on. Then, depending on the strategic focus, relevant additional information can be provided concerning investment style and exposures to risk factors, trading and holding approaches, hedging or protection policies, etc.

How to use this information? For the reader, it helps in choosing and designing the performance measure that will prove to be most suitable for the investor. We list below some of the directions in which the analysis may proceed.

- Understanding the portfolio manager's strategy provides guidance regarding the *choice of a classical performance measure* according to the principles set forth in Chapter 4. For instance, if the fund presents itself as a holistic investment with a target allocation level, the Sharpe ratio (or its avatars) appears to be appropriate. If the fund is very thematic (e.g., stocks only with a clear geographical focus), then a measure based on systematic risk (Treynor ratio and modified Jensen's alpha) would in principle be favored. When the fund aims at complementing a traditional, well-diversified portfolio, then the Information ratio is more suitable.
- Details about the fund's asset class universe, regional focus, style factors, etc., represent indications that may drive the *identification of risk factors in a multifactor model*, with the intent to develop a performance measurement approach discussed in Chapter 7. The identification of relevant factors may lead to the creation of a return-based benchmark. Even if the fund has a self-reported benchmark, this type of statistical analysis could reinforce the understanding of the fund's genuine risk exposures and challenge the determination of abnormal returns reported directly by the fund. Furthermore, using the same detailed information, it makes it possible to *determine a peer group* – possibly

different from those used in a generic fashion by fund rating agencies (see the next section) – on which several types of analyses can be carried out (see Section 3.1 of Chapter 3).

- If the fund manager clearly announces that their strategy involves the possibility of actively trading in different market segments that are in the scope of the investment universe, this might be a case for suspecting *the existence (or not) of market timing skills*. Be it the case, then one should carefully consider the adoption of a technique for assessing the extent to which this activity is successful through a measurement approach developed in Chapter 8.
- The fund's indications regarding risk management policies and use of various types of instruments (derivatives, gearing, short sales, and buying on margin) provide useful technical information on the *possible nonlinearities in returns*. The measurement of performance could be adapted or calibrated in order to avoid the pitfalls associated with these nonlinearities. For instance, this hints into the need to measure higher moments (skewness and kurtosis) in order to correct the classical performance measures as in Chapter 6.

2. Returns

This is where the requirements vary the most because the provision of expected returns is a particularly delicate matter. In most cases (as in the US approach, and in general according to the GIPS norms), the fund should report its past yearly returns up to a certain horizon (e.g., 10 years). In some other situations (as in the EU), a very structured range of historical scenarios, with their qualitative interpretation, is provided. Some CPs simply do not provide any past or future indications about rates of return.

How to use this information? There is realistically little to do with this information. The US Summary Report delivers the past mean return, but it has to be matched with a risk estimate in order to be usable. Interestingly, the same document provides the minimum and maximum quarterly returns, which allow the computation of a simplified version of Young's (1998) minimax ratio (Equation (6-22) of Chapter 6).

3. Risk

Under different systems, a high-level description of various types of risks borne by the investor must be provided. The CP should disclose a complete inventory of the risk types that the fund incurs, with associated narratives. This includes, but is not restricted to, the market risk exposure of the fund.

How to use this information? This, *per se*, is only useful for performance measurement to the extent that market risk is concerned. However, there are pieces of information, for instance in the Key Information Document (KID) for regulated mutual funds domiciled in the EU, that can be directly interpreted in the context of performance measurement. We focus on two of them:

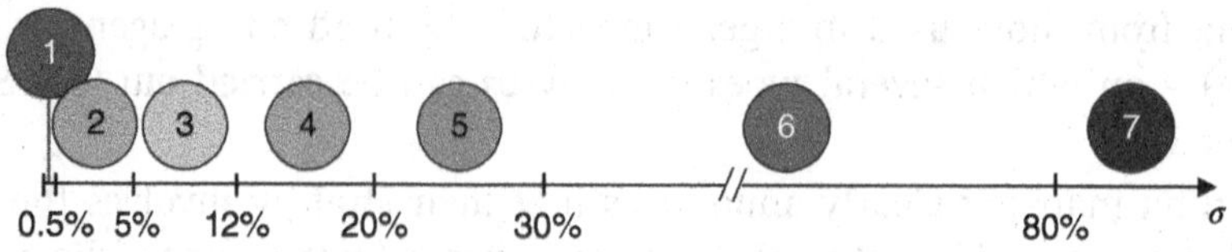

FIGURE 15-1 Representation of the volatility intervals in the Key Information Document.

- The KID provides an assessment of the number of years that the investor should consider holding the fund ("recommended holding periods"). It serves as the basis for the return scenarios mentioned above. This information can be used as an *assessment of the investment horizon* in the context of the implementation of goal-based investment measures, as discussed in Section 10.4 of Chapter 10.
- Also included in the EU-related KID, a potentially useful item – but to be handled with care – is the *Synthetic Risk Indicator* (SRI). It reports the volatility interval in which the investor can reasonably expect the fund's riskiness to locate over the recommended holding period. Given the potential complexity of some fund structures (life-cycle funds, structured funds, . . .), it is in general necessary to implement a simulation procedure to obtain the desired volatility estimate.[4] The mapping of the resulting seven SRI values in their respective volatility intervals is summarized in Figure 15-1.

Figure 15-1 shows that the volatility intervals are not of equal lengths. In particular, levels 6 and 7 correspond to risk levels that are seldom met in practice. This can indeed be explained by (i) the characteristics of some sophisticated or highly leveraged regulated products (such as leveraged ETFs) and (ii) the credit riskiness of some issuers of collective investment vehicles that "piles up" over their market risk.

Note that, because of the inclusion of credit risk (the risk of non-repayment in full of the issuer of the product), the SRI value cannot always be identified with pure volatility risk. Nevertheless, for most mutual funds, this is a relatively reliable indicator. This information is of potentially great value for two main purposes. The first one is the *decision about homemade leverage*. Indeed, a number of performance measures – starting from the most popular one, the Sharpe ratio – rely on the investor's knowledge of the fund risk level in order to decide upon their lending or borrowing intensity to reach their desired level of risk. The second one refers to the *discussion about the investor's desired risk level* in Chapter 9. Knowing in which category

[4]See European Securities and Markets Authority (2017) for the complete roadmap. It includes both market and credit risks, featuring a sophisticated methodology that uses the Cornish-Fisher expansion discussion in Chapter 6. It replaces a former Synthetic Risk and Return Indicator that was only focusing on market risk (see European Securities and Markets Authority, 2010) and whose Gaussian mapping onto a volatility equivalent (from 0 to >25%) could lead to a biased assessment of the true portfolio risk (see Hübner, 2012, for a discussion).

a fund belongs is helpful to identify the associated investor's target risk or risk-aversion coefficient. This, in turn, allows us to implement relevant investor-specific total risk performance measures.

4. Benchmark

When it exists, the self-defined benchmark is most often explicitly communicated in the CP. In contrast, when applicable, the document must also disclose the absence thereof. This happens when the fund announces a total return or an absolute return strategy, for instance. In that case, it attempts to deliver a rate of return whose realization does not explicitly depend on a classical risk factor or index. In such situations, the benchmark is supposed to be a version of the market interest rate.

How to use this information? The disclosure of the fund's benchmark is obviously a precious piece of information. We view three main associated uses regarding performance measurement:

- Every performance *measure built upon the fund's self-defined benchmark* is directly applicable. They are developed in Chapters 3 and 6 in various sections. Note that it also makes it easier to implement *regression-based analysis of market timing* (because the index that is to be outperformed is known) in the spirit of Sections 8.1 and 8.2 of Chapter 8.
- Once the benchmark of a fund is known, it becomes easier to identify the other funds that share the same reference in order to *constitute the peer group* and perform in-depth comparisons, as in Section 3.1 of Chapter 3.
- Any benchmark could be challenged. Since, as indicated above, the fund must also disclose its strategy, it is possible to *match an analytical (return-based) benchmark* to determine the extent to which the self-defined one faithfully reflects the risk factors that the portfolio is actually tracking.

5. Costs and fees

An estimation, that is as accurate as possible, of various costs and fees charged to the investor, for various asset classes (if any) and under different relevant scenarios (in the case of variable fees), must be provided in all regulated CPs.

How to use this information? Performance measures are in general computed with the net-of-fees returns as an input. Nevertheless, the investor should not confuse fund performance with the manager's actual skill. As discussed in Chapter 18, the gross returns best reflect this latter dimension. Thus, data about costs and fees are useful in order to reconstruct the exact picture about the manager's capacity to outperform. It also eases the comparison of different fund managers by controlling their various expense ratios.

6. Sustainability

Because many investors care about non-financial sustainability criteria, especially regarding the environmental, social, and governance (ESG) dimensions of the fund's investment policy, it has become compulsory in many regulatory systems to include relevant information on this aspect. The CP must clearly disclose the intensity of the efforts deployed in these matters. The outcome ranges from "no consideration of ESG criteria" up to "not only does the fund care about these criteria, but seeks to reach substantial objectives regarding sustainability through its investments."[5]

How to use this information? A fund's commitment to sustainability involves two major consequences: (i) the limitation of the investment universe by discarding asset segments or individual securities that do not match the fund's investment policy and (ii) the sensitivity of the fund's rate of return to ESG-related factors. Depending on the fund's statements regarding the importance of sustainability criteria, the investor should consider performance measures that explicitly account for this non-financial dimension, as discussed in Chapter 16.

15.2.2 Performance-related factsheet information

Whereas various versions of the prospectus and the associated advertising material delivered to the prospect investor are heavily regulated and supervised, the formalism of post-contractual disclosure is much less strict. This is where the design of the periodical documents made available to the investor can prove to be particularly insightful or, on the contrary, disappointing regarding the assessment of performance.

In order to communicate with investors, funds mostly deliver long or short types of *factsheets* at regular time intervals. The major requirements are linked to the content (information must be correct and complete, compliant with the GIPS requirements if applicable) but not to the form. There are, however, a few topics that should preferably be covered in the factsheet to convey the type of information that the investor might legitimately seek to obtain. The order and level of detail may differ, but these correspond to three broad categories: (i) fund-related information; (ii) portfolio information; and (iii) risk, return, and performance information.

The first topic (fund-related information) essentially covers elements already examined at the prospectus level.

The topic of portfolio information is likely to bring important new insights compared to the statutory or the condensed prospectus, because the factsheet must reflect contemporaneous information that evolves over time. Typically, the rubric contains the top ten holdings with their respective weights, the allocation per asset class or sub-asset class (depending on the type of portfolio), and (if applicable) by currencies. Due to limited space constraints, the breakdown

[5]Probably the most structured regulatory approach regarding this dimension is the EU Sustainable Finance Disclosure Regulation (SFDR) that imposes a classification of mutual funds into Article 6 (no claim on sustainability), Article 8 (claim on sustainable investments but no claim of intended sustainability objective), or Article 9 (claim of intended sustainability objective) (see European Parliament and Council, 2019).

cannot be exhaustive, but it is considered to be sufficient to identify how the portfolio is being managed and what the key risks are. Although the informative content of this topic can be substantial, it cannot really be used in order to implement a portfolio performance measure discussed so far.

The last topic is the most important for our purpose. The factsheet always reports numerical and graphical information about the return of the fund and, if it exists, its self-defined benchmark. There are two types of data that can be gathered. We call them *insight-driven* and *evidence-driven information* as far as performance measurement is concerned.

15.2.2.1 Insight versus evidence-driven information

Insight-driven information represents factual elements that are reported in the form of tables and graphs and whose objective is to provide the investor with easily interpretable data into the fund's realized return. Their common feature is that they are not meant to be used in any formula that would deliver an estimate of the fund's risk-adjusted performance (beyond a differential return). This category covers two "must-have" factsheet components: usually (i) a graph showing the fund's and the benchmark's yearly returns (with histograms) or, alternatively, cumulative returns (with curves); and (ii) a table representing the cumulative year-to-date, one-year, three-year, five-year, and since inception fund and benchmark cumulative returns. While they can be readily understood by almost any investor (which is clearly an important advantage), these cannot be used as such for performance measurement, with the exception of the self-benchmarked Jensen's alpha when the data are in tabular form.

Evidence-driven information, by contrast, is always numerical. It either directly discloses a performance measure or allows its computation in conjunction with other elements present in the factsheet. Thus, besides data on returns, evidence-driven information also features risk, to the extent that they can be matched with corresponding returns, and performance figures. Given the assumption that all data reflect a fair and true view, the investor or analyst can rely on this information and use it as a faithful basis to form an educated opinion. The difference in point of view between insight-driven and evidence-driven information is illustrated in Table 15-4.

We have gathered monthly returns for a fund and its benchmark over the same period of five years and nine months (69 observations), starting in January 2018. This information is used, without any manipulation, to fill in the fund factsheet according to the concurrent logics.

The left part displays a typical set of insight-driven information, with total returns reported over different time periods (all ending at the present time). With some algebra, it is possible to retrieve two statistically useful estimates, namely, average returns (by differentiating the total returns over different periods, taking care of the compounding effect) or a rough estimate of the yearly standard deviation. This represents very light material for the purpose of assessing the performance of the fund and its benchmark. Note that the same impression as the table could

TABLE 15-4 Illustration of insight-driven and evidence-driven identical information.

Insight-driven information			*Evidence-driven information*						
Period	**Fund**	**Benchmark**	**Year**	**Portfolio**	**Q1**	**Q2**	**Q3**	**Q4**	**Total**
YTD	7.33%	5.55%	**2023**	**Fund**	4.50%	3.69%	−0.94%		**7.33%**
1 Year	9.54%	7.08%		**Benchmark**	3.88%	3.08%	−1.43%		**5.55%**
2 Years	5.31%	0.49%	**2022**	**Fund**	−2.24%	−6.08%	−0.47%	2.06%	**−6.74%**
3 Years	21.47%	16.49%		**Benchmark**	−2.83%	−6.66%	−1.07%	1.45%	**−8.97%**
4 Years	22.63%	15.21%	**2021**	**Fund**	4.67%	3.92%	0.78%	5.20%	**15.32%**
5 Years	29.80%	21.62%		**Benchmark**	4.76%	2.80%	0.87%	4.58%	**13.61%**
Inception	31.84%	23.81%	**2020**	**Fund**	−12.33%	8.84%	2.44%	5.22%	**2.85%**
				Benchmark	−13.38%	8.14%	2.53%	6.72%	**2.49%**
			2019	**Fund**	7.24%	2.07%	2.97%	3.29%	**16.42%**
				Benchmark	7.97%	1.93%	2.61%	2.98%	**16.30%**
			2018	**Fund**	−1.62%	1.51%	1.70%	−6.09%	**−4.62%**
				Benchmark	−2.21%	2.39%	1.67%	−6.52%	**−4.84%**

have been conveyed with a graph but with no usable quantitative information for performance measurement.

The right part of the table shows how the same raw data can be used to report evidence-driven information. The layout is heavier – it occupies more space – and is undoubtedly less attractive. This is why it should preferably be used in conjunction with a graph. However, the data are directly usable because they constitute a sample of 23 return observations for both the fund and the benchmark. Based on this, the reader of the factsheet can compute measures based on systematic, total, and residual risk. Table 15-5 compares the summary statistics of the original time series (69 monthly observations) with those of the quarterly data (23 observations) retrieved from Table 15-4.

Moving from monthly to quarterly arithmetic returns has an impact on the first four moments, but the magnitude of the changes is similar for both the fund and the benchmark. Consequently, systematic risk (beta) and residual risk (Tracking error for the Information ratio and residual standard deviation for the Appraisal ratio) are altered only to a limited extent (up to a 10% variation). Statistical inference is weaker when fewer datapoints are used, but still applicable, especially if the same frequency is used for the comparison with other funds and portfolios. It is also worth noting that extreme events and large drawdowns, as in the first quarter of 2020, do appear when evidence-driven information is disclosed, whereas they can be hidden when more condensed insight-based information is preferred.

TABLE 15-5 Summary statistics with monthly and quarterly returns.

	Fund		Benchmark	
	Monthly	*Quarterly*	*Monthly*	*Quarterly*
Mean	5.18%	5.27%	4.12%	4.22%
St. dev.	8.53%	9.45%	8.95%	9.95%
Skewness	−0.94	−1.22	−0.86	−1.21
Excess kurtosis	3.22	2.09	3.07	2.10
Beta	0.94	0.94		
Tracking error	1.36%	1.23%		
Residual st. dev.	1.26%	1.09%		

15.2.2.2 The informative factsheet

It is obvious that, with limited available space and many important dimensions to cover, combined with the necessity of an attractive design, a fund factsheet cannot only focus on evidence-driven information in the "return, risk, and performance" section. There must be some visual element that catches the eye and allows the investor to quickly gauge whether the fund's profile appears to be satisfactory or not. Thus, the designer of the factsheet should carefully choose their battles. "Hard" information that leads to a rigorous performance assessment must be crisp, precise, and focused. Only when this objective is achieved, does the factsheet fulfill its role of a truly informative document beyond the marketing gimmicks. This is what we call the "informative factsheet."

How can we provide any advice regarding the design of such a factsheet? From a pure performance point of view, we can provide some suggestions. Here are, according to us, some useful principles that should be followed in the design and implementation of the document:

1. *Focus*: Any risk or performance measure must be useful for the investor's decision-making process. Given the space constraints, and the limited attention time that most investors will assign to checking the factsheet, potentially superfluous information should be avoided, even though it could be theoretically interesting to consider it in a longer document.

   Example: If the fund has a clear self-defined thematic benchmark like "European equities," sophisticated total risk-based performance measures like the Sortino ratio do not bring any significant insight on top of the Sharpe ratio because total risk is not the most relevant measure to the investor.[6]

[6]See Chapter 4 for a discussion of the issue of the selection of classical performance measures.

2. *Parsimony*: Fewer but well-targeted performance measures are more effective than many disconnected ones. The fund manager must disclose specific risk and performance measures and explain them to the investors.

   Example: If the fund announces no benchmark, then the factsheet should provide at least the Sharpe ratio. Additional measures should be meant (i) to complete the Sharpe ratio by adjusting for relevant risk or return alternatives (see Chapter 6) and/or (ii) to deliver an alternative picture with a nonparametric approach, as in Section 10.3 of Chapter 10. However, if the fund has a narrow benchmark, even the Sharpe ratio is questionable: The fund should favor systematic risk-based performance measures, such as the Treynor ratio or the modified Jensen's alpha (but not both as they are redundant), and possibly extend it to a multifactor version (Chapter 7) or a measure that reflects market timing (Chapter 8), if this dimension is relevant.
3. *Consistency*: The reported risk, return, and performance values should be reconciled whenever possible. There should be no discrepancy regarding the inputs that are used in the process.

   Example: If the Jensen's alpha, the beta, and the tracking error are simultaneously provided, these inputs correspond to neither the calculation of the Information ratio (because the Jensen's alpha obtained with the application of the beta is not equal to the tracking difference) nor the Appraisal ratio (because the tracking error is not equal to the standard deviation of the residual of the market model).
4. *No ambiguity*: The glossary (either as a document appendix or an online resource) should be unambiguous and complete. This should not necessarily reach the level of detail of the statistical computation models, but it should cover the definitions of the financial terms used as well as the key components of the ratios.

   Example: If the Sharpe ratio is provided, the nature of the risk-free rate should be provided, as well as the length of the time window used for its computation.
5. *Comparability*: Graphs can give a visual impression, but are not as precise as factual figures. Their merit is to reflect some dynamic behavior of the fund and its benchmark. Their use for performance appraisal is conditioned on the fact that all performance-relevant information has been communicated effectively, and they bring additional insight that can be tracked over time. Similarly, information retrieved from an external fund rating agency (as studied in Section 15.4) provides an independent assessment of the fund's quality.

   Example: If the factsheet tracks a rolling alpha, computed over a sliding window of fixed length, the contemporaneous value of this performance indicator is less meaningful than a graph showing the evolution of this measure over time, with possibly green- and red-colored areas depending on whether the value is in the positive or negative territory.

15.3 COMMUNICATING PERSONAL PORTFOLIO PERFORMANCE EFFECTIVELY

Whereas the communication of pooled fund performance-related information is heavily corseted by regulatory and compliance-related (including the GIPS) constraints, these do not strictly apply to personal portfolio management vehicles. Indeed, the portfolio manager is tied by contractual arrangements and ad hoc agreements with their customer, as well as by the commitments of the composite to which the portfolio belongs (see Section 15.1). However, they are not obliged to obey any particular formalism regarding the length or the compulsory elements featured in the periodic performance reports delivered to the final customer. Consequently, the questions about the layout and content of the document change. They are much less of: *How can I squeeze relevant information about performance into a condensed and standardized format?*, but more of: *How can I provide comprehensive and structured information about performance that allows my customer to fully understand how I have added value with active portfolio management?* Well-equipped portfolio managers have access to very sophisticated functionalities of their portfolio management system, including analytics and reporting. Furthermore, many market data providers offer ancillary services enabling finance professionals to carry out a wide range of comparative and historical analyses. The manager's challenge is thus not to access high-quality information, but to translate and transmit its most relevant ingredients to her customers.

For many organizations that are active in personal portfolio management (private banks, wealth management houses, and independent financial advisors), it is necessary to adopt a structure that is scalable (in order not to incur costs that inflate with the number of customers) but, at the same time, allows an individualized communication and interpretation. We distinguish the construction of a report for a single portfolio and one providing a consolidated view of several portfolios managed on behalf of the same household or family unit.

15.3.1 Information for a single portfolio

We categorize the type of information and what constitutes, in our view, the desirable content regarding performance-related elements in the periodic report delivered to the investor. Some reports do not disclose them all, especially the peer group, because this might put the manager at risk of being diagnosed as an underperformer, either temporarily or permanently. Nevertheless, demanding investors should be aware that, in order to obtain "value-for-money," they need a full transparency over how their money has been managed and how the manager has delivered their promises.

15.3.1.1 Factual information

The elements of factual information that are necessary to carry out a comprehensive performance analysis are summarized in Table 15-6.[7]

15.3.1.2 The informative periodical portfolio report

Regardless of whether the data represented in Table 15-6 are made available or not, the periodic customer performance report may disclose some performance estimates and propose different types of analysis. We believe that the five principles set forth in Section 15.2.2.2 are also applicable here, but they must be completed in order to produce a high value-added personalized document. We list three types of requirements that the personal portfolio periodic report should preferably fulfill in order to deliver top-notch quality of information regarding portfolio performance.

6. *Suitability*: This notion is central in the investor's "duty of care," and at the heart of regulatory requirements regarding portfolio advice (e.g., in the Markets in Financial Instruments Directive in the EU). Disclosing at least one classical performance measure is a must-have, but the precise knowledge of the investor's needs is a precious asset here. We refer to Chapter 4 for the identification of the proper risk type that corresponds to the customer profile or the portfolio destination. Nevertheless, it is possible to go further in two directions: (i) bringing refinements to the performance estimation in the spirit of Chapter 6 or (ii) integrating investor-specific risk-aversion information (Chapter 9) or behavioral criteria (Chapter 10) into the report.

   Example: If the portfolio is managed according to a goal-based investment approach described in Section 10.4 of Chapter 10, the report should disclose, along with the parameters used for the definition of the investor's mental account, the probability of achieving the objective with the current portfolio value.
7. *Transparency*: Evidence presented in Table 15-6 shows that the investor could have access to detailed information on absolutely all returns, holdings, and even trades. Of course, if everything is available – which is hardly the case in practice – they can perform their own analysis. However, as an alternative (or sometimes as an additional disclosure), the fund manager can also provide the full performance contribution (Chapter 13) and attribution (Chapter 14) of performance. The customer should expect that, if all granular data are not reported in the document, they are at least endowed with the

[7] For portfolio and benchmark holdings, subscript t denotes the beginning of the reporting period and $t + 1$ denotes the end of the period, i.e., the present time.

TABLE 15-6 Key ingredients of the periodical portfolio report.

Category	Element	Comments
Assets under management	$V_{P,t+1}$, $V_{P,t}$	Not only the net asset value (NAV) of the portfolio must be known at the beginning and the end of each period (with an exact reconciliation from one period to another) but also the portfolio exposures (in a percentage of the NAV) if gearing techniques or derivative instruments are used in order to modify the portfolio gross leverage.
Returns	$\{R_{P,t}\}$	The periodical portfolio returns, properly accounting for inflows and outflows,[8] is a must-have. The exact figures must be known by the investor in order to process whatever return-based performance measure they deem appropriate but also with a view on the potential consolidation of several portfolios (which the portfolio manager does not necessarily know).
Segments	$w_{P,k,t+1}$, $w_{P,k,t}$, $R_{P,k,t}$, $w_{P,h_k,t+1}$, $w_{P,h_k,t}$	The partitioning of the global portfolio into relevant segments with their associated returns should be clear and consistent over time. This is valid at the level of asset classes but also any subsegment that makes sense for the portfolio. The segment weights (either assets or exposures) must sum up to one.[9] The gross and net currency exposures have to be provided as well in order to determine the currency hedge ratios $w_{P,h_k,t}$.[10]
Holdings and trades	$w_{P,i,t+1}$, $w_{P,i,t}$, $\Delta w_{P,i,t}$	The full transparency of the portfolio holdings and trades has to be known by the investor, in order to properly track the generators of performance. The report should distinguish active trades $\Delta w_{P,i,t}$ (purchases and sales) from "corporate events," such as splits or dividends in shares, that modify holdings without any intervention of the portfolio manager.
Benchmark	$\{R_{B,t}\}$, $w_{B,k,t+1}$, $w_{B,k,t}$, $R_{B,k,t}$	If a benchmark has been identified and agreed upon between the investor and the manager, it is compulsory to deliver periodic benchmark returns, segment weights, and segment returns in a coherent manner. From an *ex ante* perspective, the parties should agree on the return computation rules: before or after costs and fees (i.e., neutralization of costs), before or after tax, in domestic currency or after hedge, etc. These rules must be applied consistently over time.
Peers	$R_{PG1,t}, \ldots, R_{PGN,t}$	The cherry on the cake is the *a priori* identification of a peer group, whose composition is in principle frozen and transparent, and whose observed periodic performance is tracked and shared with the investor. As for the benchmark, the parties should agree on the return computation rules. This peer group is particularly useful when no benchmark has been identified or agreed upon, because no portfolio manager can seriously claim that there is no other competitor around.

[8]See Section 15.1 for a discussion on how cash flows must be accounted for.
[9]Note that the weight at the beginning of the reporting period is not necessary included in the report since it must correspond to the weight at the end of the former reporting period.
[10]See Section 14.3.1 of Chapter 14 for a discussion of how to use this information.

performance attribution analysis (with the whole history) that is consistent with the generation of performance.

Example: If the portfolio manager actively uses derivatives overlays in order to hedge equity, interest rate, or currency risks, the outcome of their trades should be visible through an adapted attribution system as in Section 14.3.1 (for currency hedging) and/or Section 14.3.3 (for derivatives) of Chapter 14.

8. *Dynamic monitoring*: The investor–manager relationship is meant to be a durable one. The manager's commitment to superior performance must be closely monitored in order to allow for constructive feedback and, if applicable, changes in the mandate. Thus, the analytics regarding risk, return, and performance have to be presented in a dynamic fashion, with each period bringing an incremental observation. This is valid for attribution analysis, rolling-window tracking of risk and performance, or progression toward a goal-based target.

   Example: Considering a goal-based investment strategy as in item 6, it is worth constructing a graphical interface showing the evolution of probability cones. This allows a comparison of the earlier assessment of the potential future returns until a given horizon with an updated picture, knowing what has been the portfolio trajectory since then. Figure 15.2 illustrates how the analysis can take place with a pre-determined final horizon H, bearing in mind that a similar analysis can be carried out with a sliding horizon (i.e., the distance between the present and the final investment dates is constant).

   In Figure 15-2, we illustrate the case of a portfolio whose investment horizon is set to H years and displaying slightly negatively skewed and leptokurtic returns. The initial isodensity curves corresponding to confidence levels of 95%, 75%, 50% (median), 25%, and 5% are represented with the light dotted curves. These were computed at portfolio inception time 0. At the current time t, the portfolio value has evolved until a rather disappointing level V_t, below the median. The new probability cones (solid lines) draw the shaded area. If the investor has a minimum final portfolio value V_H^- in mind, the new situation clearly shows a degradation of the probability of achieving it. The situation is even worse if the same investor assigns a bonus to any outcome above V_H^+ because the graph shows that the upside probability has shrunk as well.

15.3.2 Consolidation of information for several portfolios

The challenge of consolidation of several portfolios differs to a large extent from the delivery of performance for a single one. The main difference resides in the treatment of heterogeneity found between the reports, on which the investor or the analyst has little, if any, control.

The first challenge is to recombine different portfolios in order to obtain the full picture regarding risk and returns. If the data gathered in Table 15-6 are complete, they can basically be reproduced at the consolidated level. Considering this portfolio as the investor's global asset

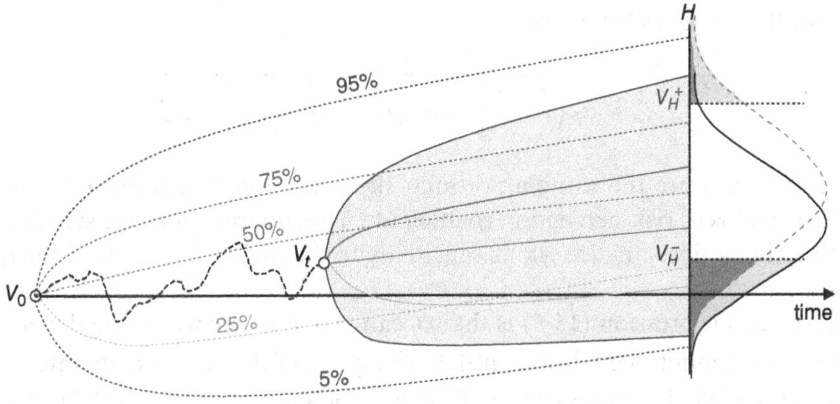

FIGURE 15-2 Illustration of the use of probability cones in the portfolio monitoring report.

allocation, all analytical procedures can be carried out at that level. One has to bear in mind, though, that total risk (volatility or any other substitute) is the relevant dimension for performance measurement.

If the global portfolio has been constituted according to a bottom-up logic, with thematic sub-portfolios being managed in order to capture abnormal returns on market segments that do not overlap (such as asset classes, geographical zones, styles, . . .), then it makes no particular sense to compare their performance. However, if the perspective is rather to let different managers compete with each other within the umbrella of the global portfolio – as it is the case for a number of wealthy investors who do not wish to "put all their eggs in the same basket," then a comparative analysis is relevant.

There are many possible ways to analyze the performance of a group of portfolio managers. We focus on this issue in the next section, where we discuss various approaches for rating portfolios. However, in the context of portfolio consolidation, one graphical analysis stands out: the dynamic risk–return framework. This is already the approach followed in Section 3.1 of Chapter 3 in order to compare the peer group members for an actively managed portfolio (Figure 3-3). This time, however, the viewpoint is different because we stand in a dynamic perspective, with the idea of monitoring the whole set of portfolios from one period to another.

Because we are not necessarily trying to accommodate the traditional mean–volatility framework underlying the Standard Portfolio Theory (SPT), nothing prevents the analyst from using an alternative measure of risk. It can be one of those discussed in Chapter 6 (Value-at-Risk, drawdown, lower partial moments, adjusted volatility, etc.). In this context, it would be even more interesting to capture the investor's preferences over risks and to use, for instance, a measure of risk associated with the linear-exponential utility function discussed in Section 9.3.1 of Chapter 9. In that case, using Equation (9-20), we can define the investor-specific risk measure $\mathcal{R}_P^j$ as

$$\mathcal{R}_P^j = \sigma_P \sqrt{1 - \frac{1}{3}(\psi_j \sigma_P)\mu_{P,3} + \frac{1}{12}(\psi_j \sigma_P)^2 e\mu_{P,4}} \quad (15\text{-}5)$$

where $\mu_{P,3}$ and $e\mu_{P,4}$ are the sample portfolio skewness and excess kurtosis, and ψ_j is the investor's (normalized) risk-perception coefficient.[8] The square root factor stands for a volatility multiplier that reflects the investor's sensitivity to the higher moments of the distribution of returns.

The issue with expression (15-5) is that ψ_j can take any positive value depending on the investor's risk perception, which may inflate the value of $\mathcal{R}_P^j$ and blur its interpretation. In order to accommodate the expression for $\mathcal{R}_P^j$ in a framework similar to the SPT, Plunus, Gillet, and Hübner (2015) define the Equivalent Risky Allocation (ERA) of the portfolio for investor j, which is denoted by ERA_P^j as a simple ratio:

$$\text{ERA}_P^j = \frac{\mathcal{R}_P^j}{\mathcal{R}_B^j} \quad (15\text{-}6)$$

where $\mathcal{R}_B^j$ represents the risk measure associated with the global investor benchmark B, considered to be the one achieving the desired risk level according to the suitability criterion.

We illustrate how this approach can be deployed with the risk–return graph shown in Figure 15-3.

The graph shows the evolution of the realized risk and return of a universe featuring five sub-portfolios, aggregated into a global one, and associated with a benchmark considered suitable for the investor. The arrows point to the movements in this two-dimensional space from the previous reference period to the current time. This synoptic view allows us to visualize not only the risk–return trade-off of each portfolio, but also to what extent the risk mandate set by the investor has been respected. This analysis can also be completed by a similar one with differential returns (horizontal axis: Tracking error – vertical axis: Tracking difference), with a similar visual interface.

15.4 FUND RATINGS AND PORTFOLIO ANALYTICS

People who want to make investment decisions have the choice between many vehicles: thousands of different actively managed funds, passive index trackers, direct investments or, for the wealthiest ones, hiring professional portfolio managers. Because the material that must be processed is huge and unstructured, some guidance is usually appreciated. To help in the

[8] See Section 9.3.1 of Chapter 9 for more detailed explanations.

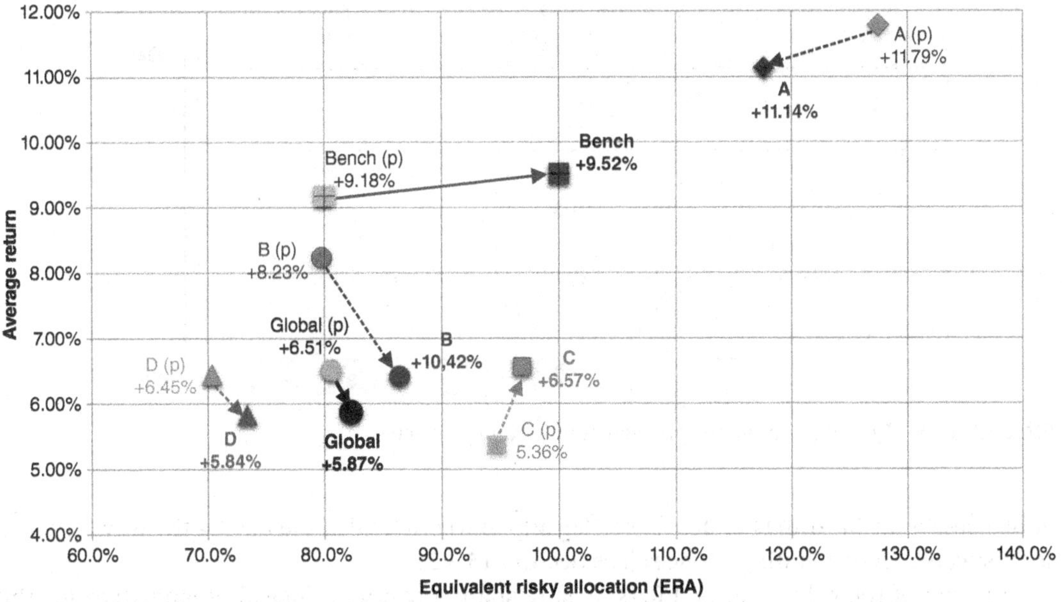

FIGURE 15-3 Illustration of the investor-specific dynamic risk–return framework.

screening process, some companies provide a regularly updated set of fund ratings on the basis of proprietary or publicly disclosed criteria. These are the "fund rating agencies" (FRAs). Alternatively, a number of firms allow an in-depth comparative study of portfolios, through their portfolio analysis systems.

15.4.1 Fund rating agencies

Fund rating agencies (FRAs) are meant to provide investors and analysts with the necessary information in order to screen funds and select the one they want to invest in. Their approach slightly differs from that of credit rating agencies (CRAs). The aim of a CRA is to create homogeneous groups that gather bond issuers sharing a similar probability of default or expected default loss. They do not apply any hierarchy within each group. In contrast, FRAs consider groups as a tool to gather funds sharing similar non-performance related characteristics with the objective of classifying them within the group according to some performance-related criteria.

The global fund rating market is largely dominated by one actor, Morningstar Inc., through its "Star Rating" attributed to mutual funds. The methodology is transparent, and the access to the rankings is free. Probably because this service has turned into a commodity, some large competitors, such as S&P Capital IQ, have decided to withdraw from this market. Nevertheless, several actors remain, either addressing a niche market with high added-value rating systems

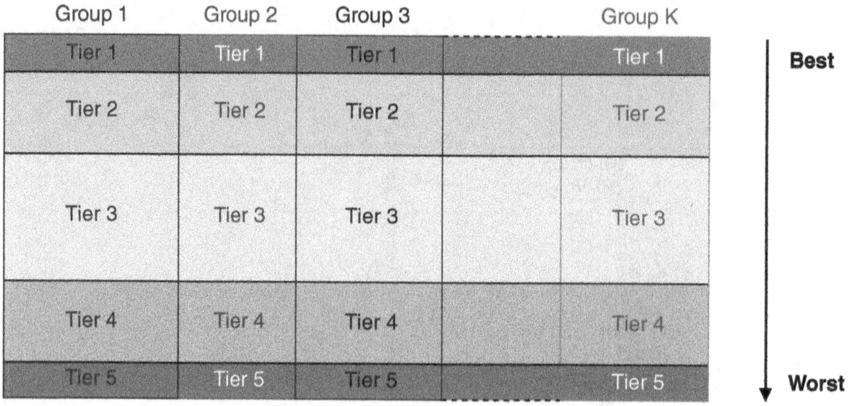

FIGURE 15-4 Typical partitioning approach of fund rating agencies.

or by using it (as Morningstar does) as a flagship marketing attribute paving the way for more sophisticated fee-generating services (see Section 15.4.2).

In spite of their differences, FRAs usually share a common logical organization for the delivery of their ratings across a universe of funds. It is summarized in Figure 15-4.

Figure 15-4 shows how the rating of a universe of funds is carried out by most FRAs. They start by partitioning this universe into *K* groups of funds of various sizes that are meant to be as different from each other as possible, but inside which the funds are as similar as possible. This is where Morningstar applies its "Style Box" methodology. Then, within each group, the funds are ranked according to a certain methodology from the best to the worst one. The ratings, typically on a five-notch scale, are attributed to the funds according to their percentile. In the figure, the top 10% belong to the Tier 1 group (highest ranking); the next 22.5% are in Tier 2; the next 35% are in Tier 3; the next 22.5% are in Tier 4; and the bottom 10% are in Tier 5. This is the scale adopted by Morningstar for its "Star Rating" system, from five stars (Tier 1) to one star (Tier 5). Other cutoff points can be applied, for instance, using quintiles as in the Lipper Leaders scale from Refinitiv.

It is impossible – and by the way probably useless – to address all market actors within the scope of this book. They are too numerous, their number and identity fluctuate over time, and it is not our purpose to describe their offering. Nevertheless, we can attempt here to identify the relevant dimensions underlying their approaches. As it is the undisputable market leader, we often refer to Morningstar as the base case, but also quote other systems when applicable.

15.4.1.1 Product-driven versus investor-driven ratings

Historically, fund rating systems have been primarily product-driven by construction. This means that they focus on the intrinsic quality of the fund management process, without particular consideration for its adequacy with the specific profile of various investors. Consider, for instance, an outstanding all-equity fund with an excellent management and other qualitative features, which is able to consistently beat its benchmark. Within its homogeneous group of funds sharing a similar strategy, this fund will presumably belong to the Tier 1 funds. Nevertheless, if a highly risk-averse investor contemplates an investment in this fund, they would probably not appreciate it. Of course, one may argue that they could use the familiar "home-made leverage" process in order to change the risk level of the fund. This means that it is the investor's responsibility to adapt their portfolio allocation to the characteristics of the product, and not the opposite.

The challenge of a customer-centric approach is to accommodate the heterogeneity of investors' attitudes toward risk at the level of ratings. For this purpose, it would first be necessary to adopt a performance measurement approach that explicitly accounts for their profile, in the spirit of the formulas developed in Chapters 9 and 10. This step is actually taken by Morningstar, whose chosen measure is the Power-based certainty equivalent, called pwCE_P^j, presented in Equation (9-26) of Chapter 9. In this context, the formula is called the Morningstar Risk-Adjusted Return or "MRAR":

$$\text{MRAR}_P^j \equiv \text{pwCE}_P^j = \left[\frac{1}{T}\sum_{t=1}^{T}(1 + r_{P,t}^g)^{-\gamma_j}\right]^{-\frac{n}{\gamma_j}} - 1 \tag{15-7}$$

where $r_{P,t}^g = \frac{1+R_{P,t}}{1+R_{f,t}} - 1$ is the fund's geometric excess return.

The formula of Equation (15-7) leaves room for addressing different investor profiles. However, the FRA chooses a "one-size-fits-all" approach using the specific calibration of $\gamma_j = 2$ and $n = 12$. The basis for the attribution of the Star Ratings is thus

$$\text{MRAR}_P(2) = \left[\frac{1}{T}\sum_{t=1}^{T}(1 + r_{P,t}^g)^{-2}\right]^{-6} - 1 \tag{15-8}$$

where $T = 36, 60$, or 120 depending on the length of the time window used to compute the rating.

If investors' heterogeneity is not reflected in the formula, then how is it done through the partitioning approach of Figure 15-4? We identify two main answers (not necessarily mutually exclusive) to this question:

1. By grouping funds in a way that is consistent with segregated investor profiles. This is typically the case with groups containing "allocation funds" with different equity proportions or target volatilities. Thus, the investor who wishes to choose a fund whose strategic asset allocation corresponds to their own profile simply focuses on the group that contains the adequate funds and selects one of the best performing funds within this group. This is the solution adopted by Morningstar in its partitioning, which allows

several "allocation" groups to coexist with many other group types that do not obey any investor profiling logic.

2. By applying, for each fund, multiple performance indicators whose combination may address the needs of various types of investors. Refinitiv's Lipper Leaders Rating System, for example, delivers five different ratings for a particular fund. The first three criteria address investor risk profiling dimensions: total return, consistent return (in relation to risk aversion), and preservation (in relation to loss aversion). The last two refer to investors' concerns for taxes and expenses. The choice of a fund results from the application of multidimensional selection criteria that might differ from one person to another.[9]

15.4.1.2 Backward-looking versus forward-looking ratings

The challenge of ranking funds on the basis of their observed performance is twofold. First, it helps to understand how portfolio managers have fared compared to each other, with the logic of rewarding or penalizing managers, or checking whether the trust put by the investor has paid off to them. However, this is generally not their first motivation for reviewing the ratings. Second and most importantly, the purpose is to select funds with the hope of outperforming the market in the future. Consider, for instance, a rating system that would be systematically wrong: Tier 5 funds would always outperform, and Tier 1 funds would always underperform. The investor, aware of this negative predictive capacity, could use the rating information to select the worst ranked funds, not for their past performance, but for their future performance. This would be a well-functioning predictive system, but not in the way it was intended to.

The implementation of fund rating methodologies with a view on performance prediction complexifies the process. As we discuss later in Chapter 17, past performance could be considered a potential predictor of future performance (in which case we refer to the notion of "performance persistence"), but (i) this is not true for any performance measure and (ii) the predictability is not limited to past performance, and presumably not to simple easily observable metrics, but can be extended to other attributes. This double limitation makes the readability of ratings that focus on performance predictability more tedious. Nevertheless, some standpoints can be emphasized regarding the forward-looking characteristics of fund ratings. We distinguish three of them:

- *Some rating systems might not be intrinsically forward-looking, but trigger effects that indirectly create some persistence.* This is particularly true for the leading one – the Morningstar Star Rating. The position of a fund within the rating scheme has a significant impact on fund flows. Extensive research has shown that four- and five-star funds attract net inflows, whereas lower starred funds experience substantial outflows.[10] However,

[9]See Refinitiv (n.d.) for the methodological explanation.
[10]See Otero-González, Leite, Durán-Santomil, and Domingues (2022) for some recent evidence.

this is not necessarily only due to the simple "dumb money" phenomenon uncovered by Chevalier and Ellison (1997), which might generate some ephemeral and only artificial outperformance. Huang, Li, and Weng (2020) show that becoming well-rated may also enhance the fund's reputation in a virtuous cycle, in which those funds have managed to find better information in order to obtain an upgrade, thereby creating persistence in a kind of self-fulfilling prophecy.

- *Some rating systems present themselves as intrinsically and only forward-looking by design.* The purpose is thus not to reflect a simple past performance measure that would be intuitively grasped by the investor (such as Jensen's alpha). Rather, a potentially complex composite measure is used to rank funds on the basis of their future potential. This is, among others, the approach followed by the FE Fundinfo Crown Ratings, which aggregates information on abnormal returns, volatility, and time-consistency of performance. The price to pay is the almost complete neglection of investor-specific criteria. Another view is to let backward-looking and forward-looking ratings coexist for the same set of funds and "let the investor decide." This explains why Morningstar, in addition to its historically successful Star Rating system, has more recently developed a parallel "Medalist Rating" methodology (Morningstar, 2023). This system is based on the aggregation of information on three pillars: the management ("People"), the strategy and execution ("Process"), and the organization ("Parent"). The fund universe is split according to a different approach from the Star Ratings, based on the similarities in their "alpha potential estimate". Because the associated scores are assessed by internal analysts, the genesis of the Medalist Ratings is less intuitive and transparent than the Star Ratings. These rating systems serve wholly different purposes, and they are not meant to be substitutes for each other.
- *Some rating systems combine backward- and forward-looking dimensions in an attempt to capture persistence in performance.* The perspective is directly inspired by the persistence analysis methods discussed in Chapter 17. The rating is based on a mix of backward-looking performance – in order to provide the investor with an assessment of how the manager has delivered superior results through its actual activities – with an estimation of their capacity to sustain their outperformance in the near or distant future. In the fund rating ecosystem, a popular method adopted to bridge present and future performance is the use of the Hurst exponent as an indicator of "absolute persistence," as introduced in Section 17.2.3 of Chapter 17. This is the case, for instance, of the Europerformance rating system. Others, such as Quantalys, use a parametric market timing approach in the spirit of the Henriksson and Merton (1981) model presented in Section 8.1 of Chapter 8.

15.4.1.3 The coexistence of financial and non-financial dimensions

Some FRAs have found it necessary to not only report but also rank funds according to non-financial performance criteria, in response to the growing investors' demand for that type of information in the management of mutual funds. These criteria mostly involve environmental, social and governance dimensions. The FRAs that consider these aspects of performance usually provide a complement set of ratings, such as the four-scale ESG Commitment Level by Morningstar. The interested investors can then integrate this information in their fund selection process.

Unlike the examples shown in subsections 15.4.1.1 and 15.4.1.2 regarding investor-driven and forward-looking viewpoints, it has not – to the best of our knowledge – become possible to fully integrate the non-financial dimension of sustainability into the purely financial performance ratings. As discussed in Chapter 16, ESG preferences do not muddle with the investor's pure financial profile (risk aversion, loss aversion, return objective, ...). Rather, sustainability preferences seem to exist on their own and must be mirrored with financial preferences in order to reflect the complexity of the investor's decision-making criteria. We discuss this issue in the next subsection.

15.4.2 Portfolio analysis systems

Because they have to broadly communicate on collective investment vehicles (whether active or passive), fund rating agencies are constrained by a necessary standardization of information in their ratings. For premium users however, they can provide a much more in-depth and customized analysis. This possibility is indeed not restricted to companies that publish fund ratings: any agent that has access to portfolio data can commit to provide investors with performance analytics that may help them in their decision-making process. This is also not restricted to mutual funds. Any portfolio, real or virtual, can be processed according to similar methods. We investigate two interesting applications related to portfolio analysis systems: portfolio diagnostics and portfolio optimization using performance indicators.

15.4.2.1 Portfolio diagnostics

Portfolio diagnostics represents the natural extension of performance ratings to the individual investment unit. The standpoint is analogous to the objective of a medical diagnosis. Considering a given, specific portfolio, the objective is to assess its quality through the examination of a number of "symptoms" retrieved from the data. The logic of the analysis can be twofold: a comparative and an intrinsic logic. We focus here on the first approach, as the second one has been largely addressed in the two previous sections and will also be discussed in the scope of portfolio optimization.

Comparative diagnostics essentially convey the same type of information as that of ratings, with some noticeable differences:

- The peer group can be freely determined according to any kind of clustering criterion. This includes product or investor profile similarities. Thus, the analysis can be organized according to the specific needs of the investor or to the comparison of managers who compete with each other.

- The portfolio under review can be of a different nature from the matching ones. It is possible, for instance, to create a virtual portfolio and to compare it with a universe of well-established mutual funds. Active and passive portfolios can be compared to each other as well.
- It is not necessary to know the full return history of a portfolio over a given time window to perform the analysis. If the portfolio holdings are known, a synthetic return history can be drawn and used as the basis for the comparison. This approach can serve as a building block for portfolio optimization purposes.
- Several competing ranking systems can be simultaneously applied to a single selected universe. This can prove to be useful not only to compare different portfolios from a financial vs non-financial (ESG-type) performance but also to challenge different performance measures. Indeed, the flexibility of the framework allows us to change benchmarks, risk types, estimation methods, and investor-specific parameters in order to determine which portfolio would be best for which type of investor.

A genuine investor-driven analysis incorporating pure performance metrics can be accommodated in a much more integrated fashion than the ones described in Section 15.4.1.1. As an insightful application of such an approach, consider a set of portfolios or funds that has been extracted from a given universe. The objective is not to make a partition out of it: this issue is indeed irrelevant for each particular instance of the comparative analysis. Next, a number of different investor profiles are determined. This can be done by using different volatility targets or risk-aversion parameters (Chapter 9), loss-aversion parameters or reservation rates (Section 10.2 of Chapter 10) or mental account parameters (Section 10.4 of Chapter 10). For each pre-specified profile, the portfolios are ranked in the same spirit as in Figure 15-4. The process is illustrated in Figure 15-5.

The chart illustrates how the system can fully address investors' heterogeneity in a comprehensive way. Drawing from a portfolio universe, any group of funds or portfolios can be created. They do not necessarily partition the universe, and they can even overlap, as suggested by the ovals at the top of the figure. Once selected, the group is then analyzed for each customer profile (A and B in the chart). Within each sample, a ranking scheme is processed along the same types of principles as in Figure 15-4, leading to a tiering system (five ratings, from Tier 1 to Tier 5 in the example).

The key property brought by the flexibility in the approach is the possibility to have different rankings for the same group of funds but for different profiles. Consider portfolio P that simultaneously belongs to Group 1 and Group 2, both analyzed for two investor profiles. For Profile A, it is ranked as a Tier 2 investment within Group 1 and a Tier 3 investment within Group 2. For Profile B, however, it is ranked as a Tier 4 investment within Group 1 and a

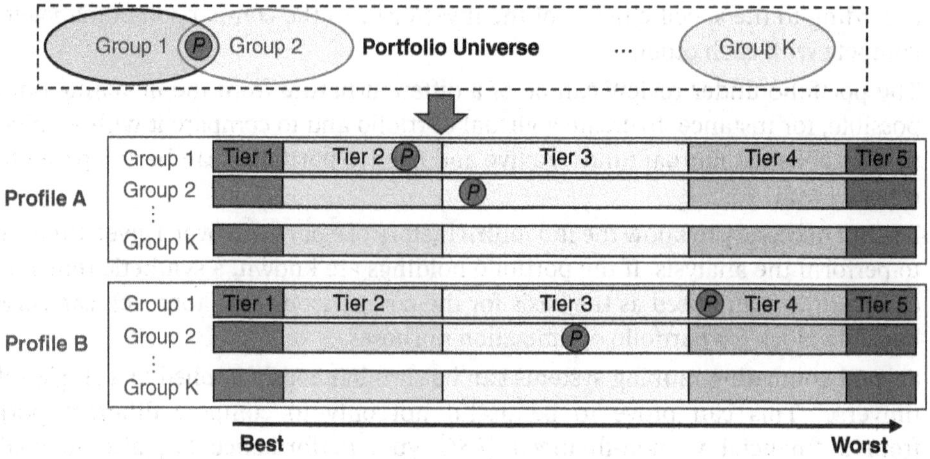

FIGURE 15-5 Partitioning approach of a flexible portfolio diagnostic system.

Tier 3 investment within Group 2. The non-monotonicity from one profile to another can be explained by three main reasons: (i) variations in portfolio risk levels can result in differences regarding suitability to investor risk profiles; (ii) variations in risk-adjusted performance levels can result in differences in the investors' assessment of portfolio desirability; and (iii) variations in group compositions can affect a portfolio's relative positioning within each of the groups. The outcome of these three drivers can lead to a picture such as the one illustrated on the graph.

This framework lends itself particularly well to associating well-performing portfolios with a wide variety of investor types. An even more customer-centric approach is to directly associate portfolios with their best-suited profile. Consider again Figure 15-5, but this time directly focusing on the positioning of portfolio *P* within a single group, say Group 1. If one merges information about the profile and performance, then it becomes clear that this portfolio should be associated with Profile A investors and not proposed to the ones corresponding to Profile B.

This point of view opens up many possibilities. Of course, the traditional approach would be to characterize investors on the basis of their target volatility or risk aversion in a pure mean–variance framework. A good portfolio would be at the same time one whose risk level corresponds to the investor's appetite and whose risk-adjusted performance looks promising. However, it is possible to go far beyond this limitative vision of the investor's risk preferences by introducing behavioral aspects. For instance, consider that the investor's utility function corresponds to Bell's (1988; 1995) linear-exponential ("linex") specification introduced in Section 9.3.1 of Chapter 9. The investor's investment criterion is to maximize the four-moment Quadratic score $4mQ_p^j$, presented in Equation (9-20) of Chapter 9, which can be conveniently written as

$$4\text{mQ}_P^j = \overline{R}_P - \frac{1}{2}\gamma_j(\mathcal{R}_P^j)^2 \tag{15-9}$$

where $\mathcal{R}_P^j = \sigma_P\sqrt{1 - \frac{1}{3}(\psi_j\sigma_P)\mu_{P,3} + \frac{1}{12}(\psi_j\sigma_P)^2 e\mu_{P,4}}$, as in Equation (15-5), is the risk of portfolio P as perceived by investor j, and γ_j and ψ_j are interpreted as the investor's normalized risk-aversion and risk-perception coefficients, respectively.

There are two intricated dimensions that are relevant to the investor in Equation (15-9): the portfolio riskiness according to their point of view and the way this riskiness is being rewarded by the mean return. Putting all this together could lead to a substantially enhanced diagnostic quality. Figure 15-6 illustrates how this can be performed in practice.

The discs in the figure represent five investor profiles defined according to the risk-aversion (vertical axis) and risk-perception (horizontal axis) dimensions. A higher investor's risk-aversion coefficient γ_j plots lower on the graph, while a higher risk-perception coefficient ψ_j (greater sensitivity to negative skewness and higher kurtosis) plots to the left. Each chain is associated with a portfolio, whose positioning evolves over time according to the arrows. The coordinates of the chain in the plane correspond to the best possible match between the portfolio risk $\mathcal{R}_P^j$ and the investor's profile whose parameters are γ_j and ψ_j. We call this the portfolio's "reverse profile." For instance, for the upper left portfolio (three horizontal dots), its reverse profile matches an "aggressive" investor with a high

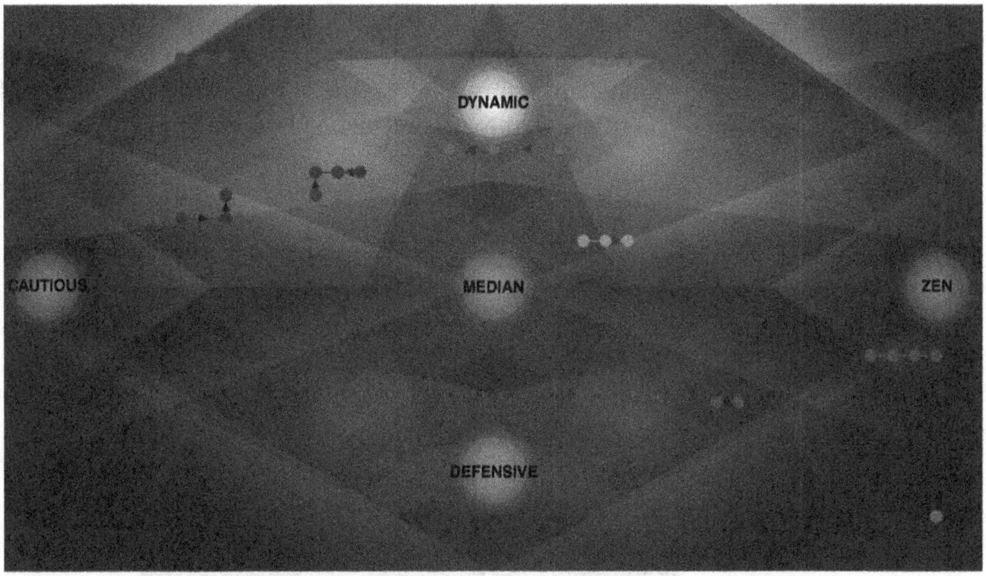

FIGURE 15-6 Illustration of portfolio diagnostics with the use of the linex function.
Source: www.sopiad.com

risk-perception coefficient ("cautious"). The portfolio performance adjusted to this profile is reflected by the shading intensity. Through this type of interface, the user (advisor or investor) can thus simultaneously determine the suitability and desirability of any set of portfolios, be them real or virtual portfolios.

15.4.2.2 Portfolio optimization using performance indicators

The next natural step after diagnosing a disease is to cure it. From a portfolio management perspective, this is the portfolio optimization phase. To what extent does it relate to past performance? Ultimately, the answer hinges on the notion of performance predictability that we have already mentioned and that will be the focus of Chapter 17. If a number of indicators – possibly including past performance – can be used as predictors of future risk and return, it can be useful to select those assets with the highest potential and to combine them in order to obtain the best forecasted subsequent performance. Starting from Figure 15-6, for instance, the challenge would be to simultaneously obtain the chain that is closest to the target investor profile (suitability) and that is likely to deliver the highest performance (desirability).

There is not much more that we can bring to this issue of portfolio optimization from the performance standpoint, except from one dimension: the interplay between financial and non-financial performance criteria. In the context of the determination of the investor's optimal portfolio, it is important to gauge not only their traditional risk profile (as a basis for the calibration of their expected utility) but also what we generically call their ESG-related preferences. Then, we can summarize the essence of the investor's problem through the chart shown in Figure 15-7.

The two-dimensional framework represents the level of the portfolio's ESG excellence on the horizontal axis and its financial performance on the vertical axis. The chart reflects the nature of the investor's potential dilemma. It all depends upon a key question: *Will*

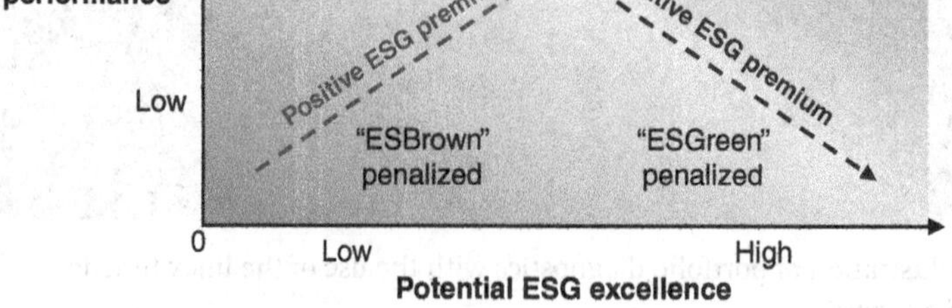

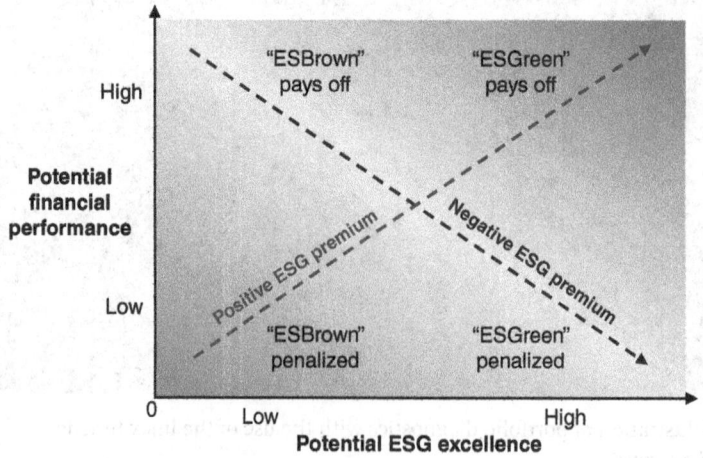

FIGURE 15-7 Heatmap of the interaction between ESG and financial performance.

it pay off to be ESG excellent? If the answer is positive, this means that there is a positive ESG-related premium (upward-trending arrow on the graph). Then, the optimization problem is relatively straightforward. Regardless of their ESG-related preferences (and thus required portfolio characteristics on that dimension), the investor can afford to only make investment decisions on the basis of financial performance criteria. The badly performing ESG portfolios (for which we use the neologism "Esbrown") will have the tendency to underperform the "Esgreen" portfolios. This is a virtuous circle. If, on the other hand, the ESG premium is negative (downward-trending arrow on the graph), the situation considerably complexifies. The investor's trade-off between ESG and financial requirements influences the portfolio composition. Esbrown portfolios, everything else being equal, outperform Esgreen portfolios. A trade-off between both sets of criteria is indispensable.

The key issue here is the future ESG premium related to the optimization criteria. There are two questions to consider. First, is the notion of "ESG excellence," measured retrospectively, related to already excellent investments (i.e., the greener ones) or to those that have the best potential to become excellent because they are in a fast transition phase? Second, how will the market remunerate this excellence in the future, regardless of the past? In Chapter 16, we analyze this issue as it does not entail any simple and straightforward answers.

Key Takeaways and Equations

- The Global Investment Performance Standards are the global reference standards put forward by the CFA Institute with regard to performance reporting in the asset management industry. Compliance with the GIPS relies on the definition and publication of policies and procedures that explain adherence to the standards.
- The GIPS performance reports must be created for every composite and every pooled fund identified within the investment firm. These reports contain *synthetic quantitative performance metrics* along with *qualitative information*, such as a definition of the firm, a description of composites, and details about the methodology.
- Among the standardized items disseminated by the GIPS are the return calculation (with priority given to time-weighted returns), the return dispersion (with priority given to the standard deviation), and the internal dispersion of a composite.
- The issue of communicating fund performance in an effective manner is driven by a number of requirements. Information must be generic, standardized, compliant with investor protection, and concise. It is mostly disclosed at two levels: pre-contractual information through the *prospectus* (complete and condensed) and post-contractual information through the *factsheet*.

(continued)

(continued)

- To form an investment decision, the investor mostly relies on information contained in the condensed prospectus, whose design is usually heavily constrained by regulatory and compliance rules. Insights regarding performance-related matters can be gathered around six topics: (i) investment strategy and policies, (ii) returns, (iii) risk, (iv) benchmark, (v) costs and fees, and (vi) sustainability.
- The fund factsheet features two kinds of performance-related elements: insight-driven and evidence-driven information. Only the latter type can be directly exploited to appraise fund performance. In relation to its effective usage, we define five properties of the *informative factsheet*:
  1. Focus
  2. Parsimony
  3. Consistency
  4. No ambiguity
  5. Comparability
- Compared to mutual funds, the communication of personal portfolio performance is less constrained by formal requirements. We distinguish two kinds of challenges regarding information disclosure: the case of a single portfolio and the case of consolidation for several portfolios.
- The periodical report for a single portfolio should provide a sufficient set of information that can be exploited for the assessment and analysis of performance. In addition to the five requirements of the factsheet, we add three more properties of the *informative periodical report*:
  6. Suitability
  7. Transparency
  8. Dynamic monitoring
- The consolidation of performance-related information for several portfolios raises the challenge of obtaining a synoptic view of their observed risk–return properties. In order to enhance their comparability, a useful tool is to use the Equivalent Risky Allocation risk measure for a given investor profile:

$$\text{ERA}_P^j = \frac{\mathcal{R}_P^j}{\mathcal{R}_B^j} \tag{15-6}$$

where $\mathcal{R}_P^j$ is the investor-specific risk measure.

- Fund rating agencies provide some useful information to help investors screen the universe of mutual funds through their partitioning into different homogeneous groups. Their aim is different from credit rating agencies, as FRAs attempt to rank funds within the group they belong to, usually by splitting funds according to their performance percentile. The leading agency, Morningstar Inc., assigns ratings on the basis of the MRAR formula, which is the Power-based certainty equivalent with a risk-aversion coefficient of 2 and a monthly frequency:

$$\text{MRAR}_P(2) = \left[\frac{1}{T}\sum_{t=1}^{T}(1 + r_{P,t}^{g})^{-2}\right]^{-6} - 1 \tag{15-8}$$

- Rating systems that coexist have different properties regarding three dimensions:
  - *Investor centricity*: Some FRAs address it using specific target groups of funds, while others derive multidimensional rating scales whose combinations address customer heterogeneity.
  - *Forward-looking orientation*: Some systems are deliberately designed to maximize the predictability of observed ratings regarding future potential performance.
  - *Non-financial criteria*: Because of the specificity of ESG-related criteria, some FRAs propose ratings for sustainability in parallel with the pure financial ones.
- Portfolio analysis systems allow us to study funds in greater detail than simple ratings. They accommodate more precise information regarding peer group compositions, portfolio types, return history, or performance measures themselves. The flexibility of portfolio diagnostics allows the creation of multiple portfolio rankings corresponding to different investor profiles.
- The major challenge of portfolio optimization systems regarding the use of performance metrics is the coexistence of financial and non-financial (ESG) criteria. If the investor cares about ESG, a trade-off must be found if the return premium associated with this dimension is negative, which is an empirical issue.

REFERENCES

Bacon, C. R. (2023), *Practical Portfolio Performance Measurement and Attribution*. John Wiley & Sons.

Bell, D. E. (1988), One-switch utility functions and a measure of risk. *Management Science*, Vol. 34, pp. 1416–1424.

Bell, D. E. (1995), Risk, return, and utility. *Management Science*, Vol. 41, pp. 23–30.

BCG (2022), Global asset management 2022, 20th Edition. Technical report.

CFA Institute (2019), Global investment performance standards (GIPS) for firms 2020. Technical report.

Chevalier, J., and G. Ellison (1997), Risk taking by mutual funds as a response to incentives. *Journal of Political Economy*, Vol. 105, pp. 1167–1200.

Deloitte (2020), Understanding the new GIPS 2020 standards. Technical report.

European Parliament and Council (2019), Regulation (EU) 2019/2088 of the European Parliament and of the Council of 27 November 2019 on sustainability-related disclosures in the financial services sector. *Official Journal of the European Union*, Vol. 317, pp. 1–16.

European Securities and Markets Authority (2010), CESR's guidelines on the methodology for the calculation of the synthetic risk and reward indicator in the Key Investor Information Document. *ESMA Document*, # JC-2017-49. Available at: https://www.esma.europa.eu/sites/default/files/library/2015/11/10_673.pdf

European Securities and Markets Authority (2017), PRIIPs – Flow diagram for the risk and reward calculations in the PRIIPs KID. *CESR Document*, #10-673. Available at: https://www.esma.europa.eu/sites/default/files/library/jc_2017_49_priips_flow_diagram_risk_reward_rev.pdf

Fischer, B. R., and R. Wermers (2012), *Performance Evaluation and Attribution of Security Portfolios*. Academic Press.

Foster, L., Ngo, T., and M. K. Pyles (2021), GIPS and hedge funds: Is compliance a certification agent? *The Journal of Alternative Investments*, Vol. 24 (2), pp. 124–136.

Henriksson, R. D., and R. Merton (1981), On market timing and investment performance. II. Statistical procedures for evaluating forecasting skills. *Journal of Business*, Vol. 54, pp. 513–533.

Huang, C., Li, F., and X. Weng (2020), Star ratings and the incentives of mutual funds. *The Journal of Finance*, Vol. 75, pp. 1715–1765.

Hübner, G. (2012), Is the KIID sufficient to associate portfolios to investor profiles? *Bankers, Markets & Investors*, Vol. 118 (May–June), pp. 14–21.

Morningstar (2023), Morningstar Medalist Rating™ methodology. Technical document, Morningstar research.

Otero-González, L., Leite, P., Durán-Santomil, P., and R. Domingues (2022), Morningstar Star Ratings and the performance, risk and flows of European bond mutual funds. *International Review of Economics and Finance*, Vol. 82, pp. 479–496.

Plunus, S., Gillet, R., and G. Hübner (2015), Equivalent risky allocation: The new ERA of risk measurement for heterogeneous investors. *American Journal of Industrial and Business Management*, Vol. 5, pp. 351–365.

Refinitiv (n.d.), Lipper Leaders from Refinitiv. An introduction to the Lipper Leaders Rating system. Technical document.

Spaulding, D. (2017), What the CCO needs to know about performance measurement. *Journal of Performance Measurement*, Vol. 21 (3), pp. 30–35.

Spaulding, D. D., Simpson, J. D., Reeves, A., Rossi, D. D., and J. Barnette (2018), Best practices for GIPS policies & procedures. *Journal of Performance Measurement*, Vol. 22 (4), pp. 26–33.

Young, M. R. (1998), A minimax portfolio selection rule with linear programming solution. *Management Science*, Vol. 44, pp. 673–683.

CHAPTER 16

Applications of Performance in Investment Decisions

INTRODUCTION

Performance measures have been primarily developed with the aims of monitoring and controlling actively managed portfolios. The richness of their universe, however, can also prove to be useful in the scope of the decision-making process. The purpose of this chapter, which is at the heart of the "Act" word in the book's subtitle, is to show how an investor or a manager can usefully borrow from the performance concepts in order to instruct their decision mechanisms.

We analyze here how performance measurement approaches are helpful in three different decision-making contexts: the selection of an investment universe, the design of a particular portfolio strategy, and the adequacy of a portfolio to the specific investor's needs.

The issue examined in the first section is fundamental. It relates to the decision to add a homogeneous set of financial assets for consideration in the investment process. If the investor's portfolio features stocks and bonds, is it interesting to add alternative investments? If the portfolio is invested domestically, should one also consider international assets? Answering these kinds of questions is not straightforward because extending the universe of eligible investments involves time and costs, and the game is worth the candle only if the improvement is substantial enough. Starting from the efficient frontier, we introduce the notions of *intersection* and *spanning* and their associated statistical testing approaches, as well as the *Gibbons, Ross, and Shanken test* of the difference in Sharpe ratios.

The second section directs the spotlight on two types of investment strategies. The first one, the core–satellite strategy, involves a combination of passive and active investment components. We show how the *portable alpha* technique can be implemented in this context. The other application focuses on structured products, whose sophistication deserves a dedicated treatment. We distinguish between the analysis of periodic returns, for which *stochastic dominance criteria* are adapted, and the examination of terminal payoffs, which lend themselves to the analysis of their alignment with the investor's *mental account satisfaction*.

In the third section, we examine the situations of three specific categories of investors: institutional, pure indexing, and undiversified ones. Their portfolio choice is driven by very different considerations. Institutional investors usually primarily care about the divergence of their portfolio compared with a benchmark. We emphasize how the *value added of an active portfolio* is related to the Information ratio. For pure indexers, whose goal is to select the best possible tracker of an index, we rebut the Information ratio in favor of an *efficiency indicator*. Finally, we study the situation of investors who have to accept a significant underdiversification of their portfolio to access a specific investment. For this category of people, such as buy-to-let real estate investors or entrepreneurs, whose situations are seldom addressed in the performance literature, we emphasize how versions of the *Quadratic alpha* can be used in the decision-making process.

Last but not least, the fourth section of this chapter addresses a very timely issue, namely the inclusion of environmental, social, and governance (ESG) criteria in the portfolio selection process. This non-financial dimension, which is in constant evolution regarding the reliability of the scoring process of financial assets, introduces a potential trade-off between financial risk–return concerns, on the one hand, and ESG excellence, on the other hand. We present an adapted framework derived from the original Standard Portfolio Theory (SPT) and outline the existence of an *ESG risk premium* and the derivation of an *ESG market portfolio*. We further emphasize how traditional performance measures, such as the Sharpe ratio, Jensen's alpha, and multifactor alpha, are affected by the financial consequences of the ESG tastes of investors. This topic is in constant evolution, with theory still at its infancy and many controversial empirical findings: This last section should be considered as a step in the development of performance-related tools that will certainly gain maturity in the forthcoming years.

The DFSO Example – Part II

The strategic asset allocation of the endowment fund of the Deep Forest Science Organization (DFSO), whose performance has been examined in Chapter 12, features a second layer of subclasses for which target investment weights are also foreseen. The management of the fund is committed to provide an in-depth diagnosis and analysis of the portfolio management approach attached to each of these subclasses, which are summarized in Table 16-1.

For each subclass, when relevant (private equity and hedge funds are excluded from the exercise), the CIO has decided to consider different possible options regarding the associated management approach: active without a specific benchmark, active with a well-identified benchmark, or passive. There are also a few additional choices to make regarding the associated vehicles (bricks and mortar versus paper real estate, product structure for commodities, ...). Management is eager to use the relevant tools in order to make an educated choice regarding various possibilities offered in each circumstance.

TABLE 16-1 DFSO example – Portfolio management approach per subclass of assets.

Asset class	Subclass	Management approach	Target
Equities	Equities USA	Active (optimized) + ESG	7.5%
	Equities Europe	Active + ESG	7.5%
	Equities RoW	Passive (ETF)	5%
Bonds	Bonds USA	Active	20%
	Bonds Europe	Passive (ETF)	10%
Real estate	Real estate USA	Active (physical)	15%
	Real estate RoW	Passive (ETF)	5%
Alternatives	*Private equity*	*(out of scope)*	8%
	Hedge funds	*(out of scope)*	12%
	Commodities and managed futures	Structured product	4%
Cash	Cash invest	Short-duration ETF	4%
	Cash cushion	Bank account	2%

In addition, the Board of DFSO has expressed its willingness to hold a certain fraction of the portfolio in high-grade ESG assets, as rated per the agency chosen after a careful due diligence. These considerations concern the US and European equities subclasses of the Equities portfolio.

Different sections of this chapter provide guidance regarding the criteria that can prove to be relevant in the investment decision-making process.

16.1 USING PERFORMANCE TO DETERMINE THE INVESTMENT UNIVERSE

Measuring portfolio performance is not only a device to appraise the achievements of a manager or to assess the outcome of an investment. It can also serve as a tool fulfilling the purpose of a decision-making process. In this respect, it switches from a controlling mechanism to a helpful contribution to the execution of portfolio management decisions. In what follows, we discuss how the use of classical performance measures, and in particular the Sharpe ratio, can become useful in deciding whether a universe of assets should be extended or not.

When a portfolio manager has to allocate assets, there are three main ways (not necessarily mutually exclusive) to perform it. The first one is to apply pure qualitative criteria, fed by expertise and/or experience. The second one consists of the implementation of heuristic rules, such as equally weighted or risk-weighted allocations. The third and most ambitious approach is the use of portfolio optimization techniques. These are arduous and hazardous to implement because they rely on risk and return forecasts that necessarily extrapolate contemporaneous or past information. Nevertheless, despite the difficulty of the task, it is recommended to try to make the best possible use of available information in order to enhance the quality of the management of investors' assets.

In the context of the familiar mean–variance framework, it is tempting to use past periodic asset returns as a major input for portfolio optimization. In that case, we have already examined in Section 4.3.4 of Chapter 4 different ways to use the Information ratio in order to come up with decision rules related to the selection of individual portfolios or the weights allocated to individual assets in a core–satellite approach to asset allocation.

Another point of view, which is the subject of the current section, is the decision to add – or not – an asset class (or category) to a universe of existing assets. Consider, for instance, an asset manager whose current portfolio composition mixes traditional asset classes (stocks and bonds) because these are those for which they can count on in-house expertise. Their customers are generally satisfied with the returns they receive, but they are somewhat frustrated by the manager's lack of openness toward some alternative asset classes (hedge funds, private equity, commodities, ...) that could enhance their risk–return portfolio trade-off. The kind of question that the asset manager should ask is: *Is it worth including a new category of assets in my investment universe, considering the research and monitoring efforts that it would require?* The answer lies in the comparative analysis of optimal portfolio compositions and uses some of the classical performance measures – specifically, Jensen's alpha and the Sharpe ratio – for this purpose.

16.1.1 The notions of intersection and spanning of efficient frontiers

In what follows, we consider that risk is measured with the volatility (or, equivalently, the variance) of returns, as in the Standard Portfolio Theory (SPT) introduced in Chapter 2, and extensively exploited for the design of performance measures. Under that framework, the notion of a mean–variance efficient frontier is central. If the investor has access to K risky financial assets, they can create Pareto-efficient portfolios that cannot be simultaneously dominated by any other one on both the risk and return dimensions. In the volatility–expectation space, the set of all these portfolios constitutes the upper segment of a hyperbola (concave, increasing curve), as shown in Chapter 2.

The question raised in the beginning of this section amounts to considering the introduction of a new set of N risky financial assets as a potential complement of the initial ones. Obviously, with this enhanced investment opportunity set featuring $K + N$ financial securities, the portfolio manager cannot do worse (in terms of diversification and risk–return trade-off) than with the original universe. The challenge is to determine whether the improvement of the efficient frontier is sufficiently important to warrant the effort of expanding the universe.

In this situation, three types of phenomena can occur, which we rank from the least to the most advantageous. The first one is the total absence of improvement whatsoever. The augmented frontier (using all the $K + N$ assets) stays the same as the original one (with the initial K assets) because the newly added assets are redundant and do not provide any diversification benefit. The second case is a partial improvement but not for all risk levels. The new frontier is connected with the old one through one common efficient portfolio for a given level of volatility but lies above the original curve for all other ones. In the third case, the frontier built with the larger set "levitates" above the initial one, without any connecting point between the two. As explained by de Roon and Nijman (2001) in their survey paper, the first two cases correspond to a situation of spanning (equal frontiers) and intersection (one common point between the two frontiers), respectively. The logic of the analysis is summarized in Figure 16-1, in which risk is measured by volatility (σ) and wealth increase is represented by the expected return (μ).

The original frontier is represented by the upper segment of the dashed lower curve. If the augmented frontier spans it, this means that both frontiers are indistinguishable from each other. We have represented it as a continuous curve that fits the shape of the original one. The second situation (intersection) is reflected by the continuous curve that seems to enlarge the initial one, with a single connecting point corresponding to portfolio I. Note that, at this point, both frontiers have the same tangency. The intercept of their tangency line, represented by μ_{Z_I}, can be interpreted as the expected return of the portfolio with a beta equal to zero with respect to I (as in Black's, 1972, version of the CAPM). The room for improvement is limited

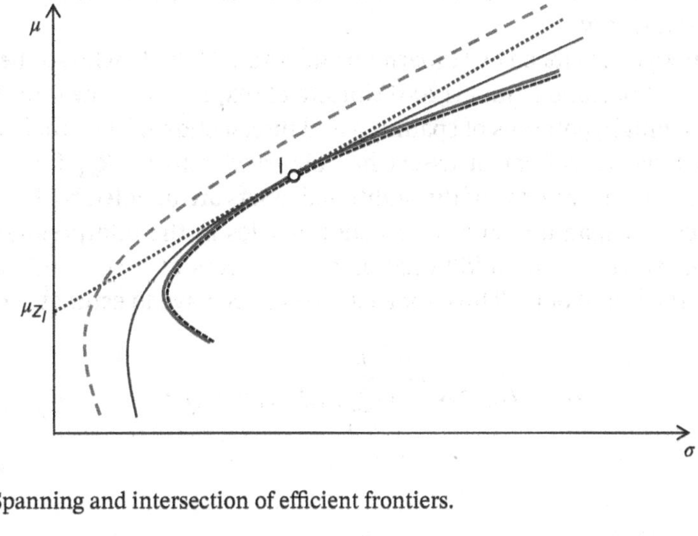

FIGURE 16-1 Spanning and intersection of efficient frontiers.

but can be sufficient to obtain a better risk–return trade-off for some risk levels. Finally, the most favorable situation is represented by the long-dashed curve whose efficient portfolios all dominate the ones on the original frontier.

Figure 16-1 provides an *ex ante* picture. From this point of view, it suffices to observe a slight distance between the original and the augmented efficient frontiers to conclude about the diversification potential of the new set of assets. However, in practice, nobody knows for sure the true expected return and risk of financial securities. Rather, we have to make the best possible use of sampled returns in order to infer risk and return estimates. This raises the question of the significance of the difference between the shapes and coordinates of the estimated efficient frontiers. Furthermore, the analysis has not yet considered the presence of a riskless asset, whose combination with efficient portfolios leads to allocations with coordinates aligning on a straight line. These two considerations call for the application of adequate testing procedures, which involve the manipulation of well-established performance measures, as discussed below.

16.1.2 Testing the improvement of the investment universe

16.1.2.1 Improving an efficient frontier with new assets

Starting with a sample of historical returns, the challenge of the portfolio manager is to check whether a new series can improve the existing efficient frontier based on historical returns. Since we deal with a statistical problem, the key consideration is to assess whether the enhanced efficient frontier significantly improves the one obtained with the initial set. From the perspective of portfolio management, this problem is equivalent to checking, with the available data, whether the existing universe of assets – leading to an estimated efficient frontier – would benefit from the inclusion of an additional, hopefully not perfectly correlated, new asset class or category.

This problem was introduced by Huberman and Kandel (1987), who studied all three cases discussed above. De Roon and Nijman (2001) intuitively explain how the multifactor alpha can be used to test the null hypotheses of spanning and intersection of the efficient frontiers.

Consider that the initial set of assets has observed returns $R_{k,t}$ for $k = 1, \ldots, K$ and $t = 1, \ldots, T$. Similarly, the returns of the additional assets are denoted by $R_{i,t}$ for $i = 1, \ldots, N$. The key to the tests of spanning and intersection resides in the interpretation of a multiple regression of the returns of the additional assets in excess of a constant return R_Z (to be defined later) on the initial ones. Thus, for each asset i, we have to estimate equation

$$R_{i,t} - R_Z = \alpha_i^{(Z)} + \sum_{k=1}^{K} \beta_{i,k}(R_{k,t} - R_Z) + \varepsilon_{i,t} \qquad (16\text{-}1)$$

where we can define $\alpha_i^{(Z)}$ as the *generalized multifactor alpha*,[1] which is equal to

$$\alpha_i^{(Z)} = \overline{R}_i - R_Z - \sum_{k=1}^{K} \beta_{i,k}(\overline{R}_k - R_Z) \tag{16-2}$$

Note that we can only estimate this regression for $K < T$, i.e., the number of observations should be large enough compared with the number of initial assets.

Because we repeat the regression of Equation (16-1) N times, there are $N \times K$ estimated coefficients $\beta_{i,k}$, and there are N intercepts $\alpha_i^{(Z)}$. For what follows, it is convenient to use matrix notation, and we define matrix $\mathbf{B} = \begin{pmatrix} \beta_{1,1} & \cdots & \beta_{1,K} \\ \vdots & \ddots & \vdots \\ \beta_{N,1} & \cdots & \beta_{N,K} \end{pmatrix}$ and vector $\mathbf{A}^{(Z)} = \begin{pmatrix} \alpha_1^{(Z)} \\ \vdots \\ \alpha_N^{(Z)} \end{pmatrix}$ accordingly.

To understand the logic of the interception test, consider the situation of portfolio I in Figure 16-1. Because the two frontiers intersect at this point, their tangency lines and corresponding zero-beta expected return (the intercept) μ_{Z_I} are the same. Thus, there is no portfolio made up with a combination of the new set of assets and the zero-beta portfolio that outperforms the optimal portfolio with the initial set of assets. Using realized returns, this would entail that if portfolio I is known together with its associated zero-beta return $\overline{R}_{Z_I}$, then the vector of alphas is not significantly different from a vector of zeros:

$$\mathbf{A}^{(Z_I)} = \mathbf{0} \equiv \begin{pmatrix} 0 \\ \vdots \\ 0 \end{pmatrix} \tag{16-3}$$

where $\mathbf{A}^{(Z_I)}$ is the vector of alphas with the intercept $R_Z = \overline{R}_{Z_I}$.

Following a similar reasoning, the hypothesis of spanning entails that both the initial and enhanced efficient frontiers intersect at every point, corresponding to all possible values of R_Z. Thus, the condition for the spanning null hypothesis to hold is

$$\mathbf{A}^{(Z)} = \mathbf{0} \ \forall R_Z \tag{16-4}$$

Even though Equations (16-3) and (16-4) appear relatively straightforward, their translation into test statistics is less straightforward. Under the assumption that returns are stationary and ergodic, it is possible to use a Wald test statistic for both hypotheses.[2]

[1] De Roon and Nijman (2001) use the name "*generalized Jensen's alpha*," but we prefer to use the term *multifactor* in order to remain consistent with the terminology adopted before.

[2] See de Roon and Nijman (2001) for a description of how to construct these estimates.

An interesting case arises when a single asset Q is considered for the enhanced frontier. Testing for intersection amounts to determining whether this new asset is mean–variance efficient on the existing frontier. The trick here is to reverse the problem: consider this single asset as the original universe ($K = 1$) and apply Equations (16-1) to (16-4) on all other assets, interpreted here as the new candidates for expanding the (single asset) universe. In that particular case, we use a single-factor model in which each beta is equal to $\beta_i = \frac{\text{Cov}(R_i,R_Q)}{\sigma_Q^2}$ and the intercept is the generalized Jensen's alpha $\alpha_i^{(Z)} = \overline{R}_i - R_Z - \beta_i(\overline{R}_Q - R_Z)$. Under the assumption of a Gaussian distribution of returns, Equation (16-4) can be tested using Hotelling's T^2 test, which is a multivariate generalization of the univariate Student *t*-test.

Comparing these intersection and spanning conditions reveals that the second hypothesis is much stronger than the first one. Hence, rejecting the null hypothesis of spanning (an infinity of interception points) should happen more often than rejecting the hypothesis of a single interception point. There is, however, a difficulty associated with Equation (16-3), as it supposes that the zero-beta rate $\overline{R}_{Z_I}$ is known. In practice, assessing where the interception could happen is difficult, and it might be necessary to explore different possible values for the zero-beta rate in order to reach the one for which the empirical distance between the original and enhanced efficient frontiers is the lowest.

For all these reasons, it can appear more convenient to simplify the problem by (i) focusing on the intersection hypothesis, which is at the same time more realistic and more difficult to reject, and (ii) restricting the problem to the use of the risk-free rate as a single possible value for the zero-beta rate, which is consistent with the traditional version of the CAPM. This is what the next subsection examines.

16.1.2.2 Improving the optimal Sharpe ratio with new assets

Introducing the constant risk-free interest rate R_f into the reasoning opens up the possibility to think in terms of Sharpe ratios. Instead of looking for intersecting portfolios as in Figure 16-1, Gibbons, Ross, and Shanken (1989) (henceforth GRS) propose to consider the properties of the optimal portfolios of the original and enhanced frontiers and, in particular, to compare their Sharpe ratios. If they differ substantially enough, then – regardless of whether we consider the issue from a spanning or intersection perspective – we can safely conclude that every possible combination of the "enhanced optimal portfolio" with return $R^*_{K+N,t}$ with the risk-free rate significantly outperforms the combinations of the "original optimal portfolio" $R^*_{K,t}$ with the same risk-free rate.

The respective Sharpe ratios of the original and enhanced optimal portfolios are defined as $\text{SR}^*_K = \frac{\overline{R}^*_K - R_f}{\sigma^*_K}$ and $\text{SR}^*_{K+N} = \frac{\overline{R}^*_{K+N} - R_f}{\sigma^*_{K+N}}$, respectively. Because the enhanced set is richer (and provided that excess returns are not simultaneously negative for all assets), it must be that

$SR_K^* \le SR_{K+N}^*$. The GRS test amounts to an assessment of the significance of this difference through the following expression:

$$\hat{F}^{(N,T-N-1)}_{SR_K^*=SR_{K+N}^*} = \frac{T(T-N-1)}{N(T-2)} \times \frac{SR_{K+N}^{*\,2} - SR_K^{*\,2}}{1 + SR_K^{*\,2}} \tag{16-5}$$

which follows (under the null hypothesis of no improvement in the Sharpe ratio) a Fisher F-distribution with degrees of freedom N and $T-N-1$. For large values of T, this distribution converges to a chi-square distribution with N degrees of freedom.

As the authors mention, the second fraction of this expression $W \equiv \frac{SR_{K+N}^{*\,2} - SR_K^{*\,2}}{1 + SR_K^{*\,2}}$ itself follows a Wishart distribution. This ratio also enables us to obtain a very intuitive geometric interpretation of the GRS test. Gibbons et al. (1989) re-express this equation as follows:

$$W = \left[\frac{\sqrt{1 + SR_{K+N}^{*\,2}}}{\sqrt{1 + SR_K^{*\,2}}}\right]^2 - 1 \tag{16-6}$$

where the argument of the square brackets is a ratio of Euclidian distances between two coordinates in the mean–volatility space. The larger this ratio is, the larger the relative distance, and the stronger the improvement brought by the new set of assets. This intuition is illustrated in Figure 16-2, inspired by Figure 1a in Gibbons et al. (1989).

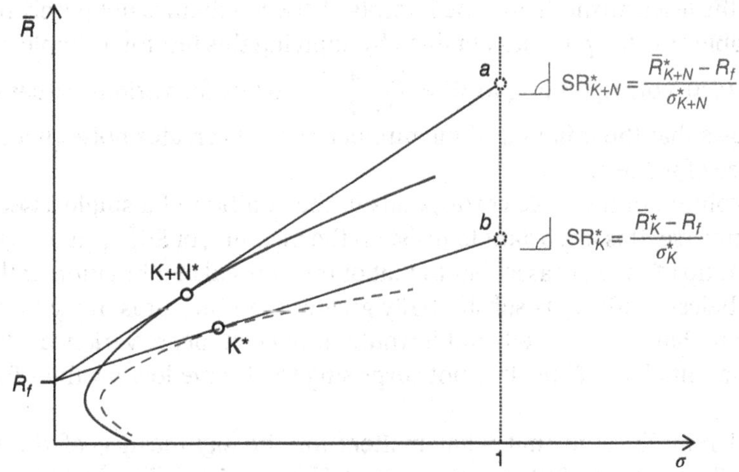

FIGURE 16-2 Graphical representation of the Gibbons et al. (1989) test.

As in Figure 16-1, we have represented the original and enhanced efficient frontiers, corresponding to the initial and augmented universes of assets. The original frontier, which is represented with a thin dashed curve, is not very important. Portfolio K^*, which is the tangency portfolio to the original Capital Market Line (CML) drawn from the risk-free rate R_f, is the only one that counts by now. With the addition of N new assets, a superior frontier is drawn above the original one, with a new tangency portfolio $K+N^*$ and a new CML with a larger slope. The GRS test amounts to comparing the slopes of the new vs. old CML. The translation of Equation (16-6) leads to the comparison between the distance of the segment $[R_f, a]$ (the numerator) and the segment $[R_f, b]$ (the denominator). This ratio of distances depends on the difference between the slopes, i.e., the original and enhanced Sharpe ratios.

As the figure shows, the reasoning considers, as in subsection 16.1.2.1, that the original frontier is constituted of a single asset, being the tangency portfolio ($K = 1$), and that we consider adding $N > 1$ additional assets to this single one. Thus, the number of securities used in order to construct the original frontier is irrelevant to the application of the test. This is essentially the perspective adopted by Lhabitant (2006) in his discussion. However, practically, it can be convenient to view the problem in the opposite way. If one additional asset (or asset class), i.e., $N = 1$, is considered as an addition to an existing optimal allocation featuring $K > 1$ asset classes, the test amounts to determining whether this single additional asset is mean–variance efficient and thus improves the investment opportunity set. The larger the initial universe is, the better the initial tangency portfolio, and the more difficult it is for the additional asset to improve it.

Because of the fraction appearing in the first factor of the expression, the significance of the test in Equation (16-5) increases with the number of observations (T) and decreases with the number of assets (N). Nevertheless, these two numbers also affect the number of degrees of freedom of the test statistic. Thus, the interplay between them is not purely mechanical. We illustrate in Table 16-2 the p-values obtained by applying this test for a simple case $SR_K^* = 0.25$ and $SR_{K+N}^* = 0.40$, corresponding to $W = \frac{0.4^2-0.25^2}{1+0.25^2} = 0.092$ for various values of T and N. In general, it shows that the inflation of the number of assets creates noise that rapidly reduces the significance of the test.

The first column of the table corresponds to the addition of a single asset or portfolio to the existing universe. It is important to insist on the meaning of SR_{K+1}^*. It does not correspond to the Sharpe ratio of the new asset but to that of the optimal combination of the old and new assets. Nevertheless, if SR_{K+1}^* is substantially greater than SR_K^*, it is likely that the new asset has an excellent Sharpe ratio itself, and it would have been mean–variance efficient if it were included in the initial set. Thus, it is not surprising to observe low p-values for $N = 1$ in our illustration.

As a final remark, note that what matters for the significance of the test is not the difference in Sharpe ratios but in the squared Sharpe ratios. For instance, if we had set $SR_K^* = 0.35$ and $SR_{K+N}^* = 0.50$ (i.e., the same difference in Sharpe ratios as in the example), the p-value for $T = 90$ and $N = 5$ would have fallen to 9.4% (compared to 17.6% in the table). Thus, it is more difficult to improve the Sharpe ratio when the original one is already high.

TABLE 16-2 *p*-values of the Fisher test for various combinations of T and N.

	Number of additional assets (N)							
T	1	2	5	10	25	50	75	100
12	31.9%	62.5%	97.9%	100.0%				
24	15.2%	36.7%	86.9%	99.9%	100.0%			
60	2.2%	7.5%	41.2%	90.4%	100.0%	100.0%		
90	0.5%	2.0%	17.6%	68.4%	99.7%	100.0%	100.0%	
120	0.1%	0.5%	6.7%	43.4%	97.5%	100.0%	100.0%	100.0%
240	0.0%	0.0%	0.1%	2.4%	44.8%	100.0%	100.0%	100.0%
360	0.0%	0.0%	0.0%	0.1%	5.9%	99.1%	100.0%	100.0%

DFSO example (continued)

Two segments of the equity portfolio of DFSO are managed internally: the domestic (US) equities and the Rest-of-World (RoW) equities. The CIO wishes to establish whether it would make sense to add new assets to the existing portfolios from a risk–return point of view.

The US equity portfolio is actively managed using quantitative optimization on a set of 50 large cap stocks. The resulting portfolio has obtained, over the past five years, an average return of $\overline{R}_{US} = 7.56\%$ with a volatility of $\sigma_{US} = 11.89\%$ on a yearly basis. For the RoW segment, DFSO uses an Exchange Traded Fund (ETF), which is supposed to give an exposure to the South-East Asian market (including China). The return and risk of this portfolio have been equal to $\overline{R}_{RoW} = 8.20\%$ and $\sigma_{RoW} = 13.70\%$, respectively.

For the US portfolio, the weakness identified is the lack of exposure to small cap stocks. Instead of trying to gather the expertise to actively manage such a portfolio, the CIO investigates the use of a US small cap ETF on the Russell 2000 index. Regarding the RoW portfolio, the management is aware that it would be interesting to expand the investment opportunity set to other regions of the world (South America, Oceania, Eastern Europe, Middle East, and Africa) through a set of five dedicated ETFs.

After retrieving monthly data from a five-year time window (same length and frequency as the reported results) and constructing the enhanced efficient frontiers using the existing portfolio and the new candidate ETFs, we obtain the summary outcome presented in Table 16-3, using a flat average interest rate of 4%.

(continued)

(*continued*)

TABLE 16-3 DFSO example – Risk and return statistics of the optimal portfolios.

	US equities		RoW equities	
	Initial	Augmented	Initial	Augmented
Number	50	50+1	1	1+5
Mean	6.56%	8.41%	8.20%	10.79%
Volatility	11.89%	11.52%	13.70%	12.51%
Sharpe ratio	**0.22**	**0.38**	**0.31**	**0.54**

The Sharpe ratio improvement appears to be more pronounced for the RoW portfolio, with a simultaneous substantial enhancement in return and reduction in risk. This is visually confirmed with the graph shown in Figure 16-3, showing the four versions of the CML.

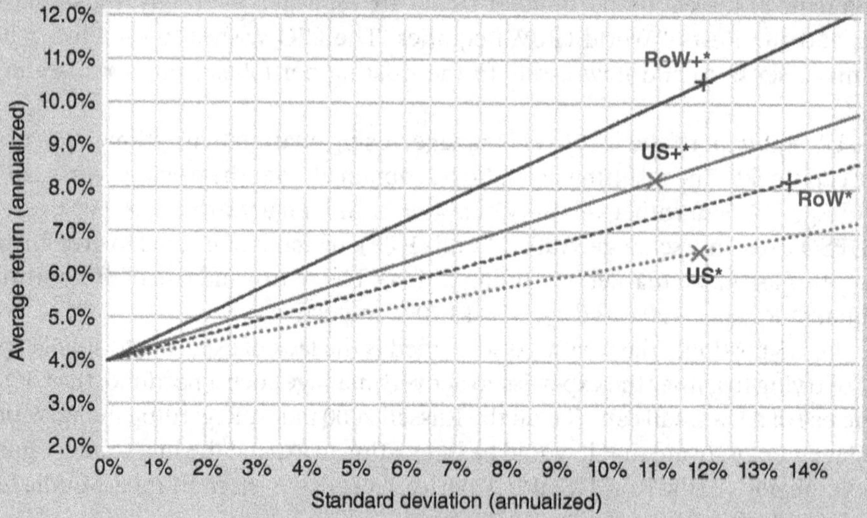

FIGURE 16-3 DFSO example – Risk and return properties of the optimal portfolios.

The dotted lines represent the Capital Market Lines for the initial allocations, whereas the solid lines report the outcome for the enhanced optimal allocations.

With the data of Table 16-3, we apply the GRS test, bearing in mind that the number of assets brought in the augmented universe plays an important role in the estimation of the *F*-statistic and the degrees of freedom.

Since $T = 60$ observations are available, the difference between the numbers of added securities in both cases has a material impact. Improving the US portfolio's Sharpe ratio with only one ETF results in a large and very significant value of the F-statistic. On the other hand, even though the increase in the Sharpe ratio for the RoW single ETF portfolio is economically substantial, the statistical significance remains weak, with a p-value barely below 10% (Table 16-4).

TABLE 16-4 DFSO example – Outcome of the GRS test for US equities and RoW equities.

	US equities	RoW equities
W	0.10	0.18
$\hat{F}$	5.74	2.05
Degrees of freedom	1-58	5-54
p-value	**1.98%**	**8.63%**

16.2 USING PERFORMANCE FOR PORTFOLIO STRATEGY DESIGN

In this section, we examine how performance measurement tools can be helpful in the determination or the improvement of some specific portfolio management strategies. The first application focuses on the application of a core–satellite allocation approach. The contribution of performance analysis, tilted toward measures of abnormal return, introduces the notion of "portable alpha" in order to disentangle the risk exposure decisions from the ability to capture the abnormal return of an actively managed portfolio. In a second application, we show how probabilistic and behavioral approaches to performance can help design a structured product that is suitable for an investor.

16.2.1 Enhancing returns in a core–satellite allocation

Many managers are confronted with the challenge of simultaneously keeping up with the risk profile of their portfolio and delivering an extra return, after fees, to their investors. Failing to reconcile either of these objectives would weaken the customer's trust in the quality of the portfolio management process. A portfolio that would considerably shift its risk exposures for the purpose of "capturing some alpha" and a portfolio that would give up on any quest for abnormal return for the sake of replicating a passive but well-mastered benchmark would both lead to some feeling of disappointment.

This difficulty is particularly relevant in the context of core–satellite strategies. This approach aims at bringing the best of both worlds: the parsimonious cost structure and

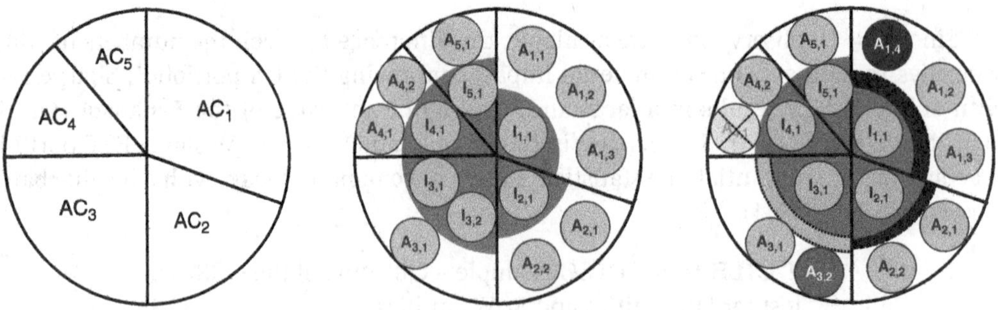

FIGURE 16-4 Schematic representation of the core–satellite portfolio management process.

predictability of risk exposures of passive investments, through the "core" of the portfolio, and the potential for outperformance brought by active portfolio management through the "satellite." Their combination should also ensure that the global core–satellite allocation perfectly matches the investor's risk profile at all times while delivering an extra return without compromising the portfolio's diversification benefits.

The core–satellite portfolio construction process can generally be described through a three-stage process, as illustrated in Figure 16-4 (inspired by Vanguard, 2017).

Figure 16-4 shows how to schematically, from left to right, represent a core–satellite portfolio allocation and management process. The first step (left chart) corresponds to the preparation stage. A target asset allocation is set, defining the weight to be invested in each asset class, which in this example are numbered from 1 to 5. The size of each slice of the pie reflects the proportion of the corresponding asset class. Once this strategic asset allocation process is made, each asset class is split into two parts, represented in the middle chart. The inner part represents the core, whose weight is proportional to the shaded area. This sub-portfolio is primarily invested in index funds or ETFs ($I_{x,y}$) whose aim is to passively replicate one or more indices that are representative of the asset class. The outer part, the satellite, is allocated between actively managed portfolios ($A_{x,y}$) whose portfolios are invested in the same types of assets, but with a mandate to generate extra returns over the indices. The right chart shows how this core–satellite allocation can dynamically evolve over time.[3] The manager can decide to increase or decrease the mix between the core and the satellite within each asset class (inflation or deflation of the shaded area). They can also consider that some actively managed funds can be replaced (e.g., from $A_{1,1}$ to $A_{1,4}$), added in place of a passive investment (e.g., from $I_{3,2}$ to $A_{3,2}$), or removed (e.g., fund $A_{4,1}$).

We are interested in this latter aspect of the core–satellite strategy. The decision to modify the allocation in one or several actively managed funds, even if it remains within a specific

[3]The possibilities are not limited to this example: for instance, the manager can decide to tactically change the asset allocation (this case is discussed in Chapter 14) or to change the set of index funds used in order to fulfill the core of the strategy. We do not represent this graphically in order to ease the interpretation of the figure.

category (i.e., an asset class in Figure 16-4), triggers waterfalling consequences regarding the portfolio's risk exposures. The new betas with respect to some risk factors are very likely to be different from the former ones. This, in turn, might endanger the risk profile of the global portfolio. Thus, if nothing is done in order to preserve this equilibrium, the manager could fall from Charybdis to Scylla: By attempting to improve the portfolio's abnormal return, they would drive it away from its investor suitability purpose.

The natural solution to this apparent attempt to square the circle comes from the world of financial risk management. When confronted with the necessity to mitigate a source of risk without altering the economic exposure, the risk manager will often consider the use of derivatives. Even though it is done with a different purpose, the technique of portability of alpha obeys the same type of logic. As Kung and Pohlman (2004) summarize, "*portable alpha enables investors to budget risk and enhance alpha (potentially) without dramatically changing asset allocation.*"

This idea is not new – it was initially introduced by Treynor and Black (1973) in the context of portfolio management and has been used for many years by some prominent asset management companies. However, the wider recognition of the benefits of this technique happened simultaneously with the increased interest in hedge fund strategies, and especially the Long/Short and Market Neutral strategies, because of the low correlation of their abnormal return (broadly defined as either their alpha or the return generated by their alternative betas) with those of traditional asset classes such as stocks and bonds.

Consider the situation of a core–satellite allocation as in Figure 16-4, in which we focus on the third asset class for the sake of simplicity.[4] The manager of the global portfolio P wishes to replace an index fund or equivalent with an actively managed fund. Their respective periodic returns $R_{I,t}$ and $R_{A,t}$ correspond to the classical multifactor equation:

$$R_{I,t} = R_f + \sum_{k=1}^{K} \beta_{I,k}(R_{k,t} - R_f) + \varepsilon_{I,t} \tag{16-7a}$$

$$R_{A,t} = \alpha_A + R_f + \sum_{k=1}^{K} \beta_{A,k}(R_{k,t} - R_f) + \varepsilon_{A,t} \tag{16-7b}$$

where we set $\alpha_I = 0$ in Equation (16-7a) even though, in the case of an ETF or an index fund, it is usually slightly negative (see Section 16.2.2).

According to the portfolio manager's anticipation, $\alpha_A > 0$ but, as it is the case in general, $\beta_{A,k} \neq \beta_{I,k}$. The challenge is thus to capture as much as possible this abnormal return. Nevertheless, there are two important types of limitations that the manager has to take into account:

1. *Investment constraints*: The manager cannot invest more than a certain amount in the actively managed fund for various potential reasons: (i) concentration constraints,

[4]Other cases, involving the replacement or the removal of an actively managed fund, are similar in their reasoning and produce the same types of rules of the portability of alpha.

limiting the exposure to a single asset, to a homogeneous group of assets (i.e., same sector) or to a certain type of risk (i.e., same currency); (ii) control ratio constraints, which preclude the portfolio manager from owning more than a certain percentage of the total net asset value of a given fund; (iii) liquidity constraints, which are related to the contribution of the invested fund's illiquidity to the one of the overall portfolio; or (iv) funding constraints, which are related to the funding that is necessary to manage the risks involved with the portable alpha strategy induced by the investment itself. Taking all these constraints into account, we also have to take as a given that the maximum weight invested in active fund A is w_A, which corresponds to a divestment of $-\Delta w_I$ in the index fund.[5]

2. *Risk budgeting*: The initial portfolio composition was supposed to display satisfactory risk exposures, materialized by the factor betas. This means that each lost beta $-\Delta w_I \beta_{I,k}$ should be recovered in full through an adequate investment strategy. Since this is not possible with the active fund alone ($w_A \beta_{A,k} = \Delta w_I \beta_{A,k} \neq w_I \beta_{I,k}$), an additional set of investments have to be contemplated in order to fulfill this objective.

Taking these two elements into account, the portable alpha strategy will typically involve the use of an overlay of K derivative contracts ($d = 1, \ldots, K$), each one with a notional amount expressed as a proportion to the total portfolio value, denoted by x_d, and whose return is $R_{d,t} = R_f + \sum_{k=1}^{K} \beta_{d,k}(R_{k,t} - R_f) + \varepsilon_{d,t}$. To be effective in this context, their required characteristics are in general that (i) they are zero-cost strategies at inception (thus $w_d = 0$, such as futures or swaps), only involving a margin requirement; (ii) they all provide some exposure to at least one of the K risk factors; (iii) their aggregate exposure to any risk factor beyond the K initial ones is negligible; and (iv) none of them is perfectly correlated with any combination of the other ones. If these four conditions are met, then the notional amount to be committed to each contract x_d consists of the solution of the following system of equations:

$$\sum_{d=1}^{K} x_d \beta_{d,k} = w_A(\beta_{I,k} - \beta_{A,k}) \text{ for } k = 1, \ldots, K \tag{16-8}$$

Representing problem (16-8) in matrix form with $\mathbf{X}_d = \begin{pmatrix} x_1 \\ \vdots \\ x_K \end{pmatrix}$ being the (unknown) $K \times 1$ vector of notional amounts, $\mathbf{B} = \begin{pmatrix} \beta_{1,1} & \cdots & \beta_{1,K} \\ \cdots & \ddots & \vdots \\ \beta_{K,1} & \cdots & \beta_{K,K} \end{pmatrix}$ being the $K \times K$ matrix of risk exposures of

[5]We neglect here the potential cash investment that the manager has to consider simultaneously with the purchase of the active fund, assuming that the current portfolio's cash position is sufficient to cover the liquidity needs. Otherwise, we would have that $\Delta w_I = w_A + w_{\text{cash}}$ and we would pursue the same reasoning with slightly more complex maths.

the derivatives contracts, and $\mathbf{Y} = \begin{pmatrix} \beta_{I,1} - \beta_{A,1} \\ \vdots \\ \beta_{I,K} - \beta_{A,K} \end{pmatrix}$ being the $K \times 1$ vector of differential betas between the index and the active fund, the unique solution to this system is obtained with standard matrix algebra as

$$\mathbf{X}_d = w_A \mathbf{B}^{-1} \mathbf{Y} \tag{16-9}$$

where $\mathbf{B}^{-1}$ is the inverse of matrix $\mathbf{B}$ such that $\mathbf{B}^{-1}\mathbf{B} = \mathbf{I}_K$. Matrix $\mathbf{B}$ is supposed to be invertible because the derivatives are not redundant in their factor exposures.

Once the derivatives are identified and the exposures are known, then the return of the new portfolio P', defined as $R_{P',t} = R_{P,t} - w_A R_{I,t} + w_A R_{A,t} + \sum_{d=1}^{K} x_d R_{d,t}$, has restored the original exposure with respect to each factor:

$$\beta_{P',k} - \beta_{P,k} = w_A(\beta_{I,k} - \beta_{A,k}) + \sum_{d=1}^{K} x_d \beta_{d,k} = 0 \text{ for } k = 1, \ldots, K \tag{16-10}$$

which leads to the following simplified expression:

$$R_{P',t} = R_{P,t} + w_A \alpha_A + \varepsilon_{P',t} \tag{16-11}$$

where $\varepsilon_{P',t} = \varepsilon_{P,t} - w_A \varepsilon_{I,t} + w_A \varepsilon_{A,t} + \sum_{d=1}^{K} x_d \varepsilon_{d,t}$ is the resulting idiosyncratic risk that is uncorrelated with the K systematic risk factors.

Expression (16-11) materializes the notion of portable alpha. If it is properly executed, it entails that the portfolio manager can be free to choose whatever active fund they find promising, capture this fund's alpha, and manage risk exposures in such a way that the risk profile of the portfolio is fully preserved.

In practice, the number of risk exposures that are simultaneously considered remains limited to one or two exposures. In that case, the solution of the problem presented in Equation (16-9) is considerably simplified. Consider $K = 2$, as in the DFSO example below. Then, the matrix of coefficients $\mathbf{B} = \begin{pmatrix} \beta_{1,1} & \beta_{1,2} \\ \beta_{2,1} & \beta_{2,2} \end{pmatrix}$ is a (2×2)-dimensional one, and the solution is expressed as

$$x_1 = w_A \frac{\beta_{2,2}(\beta_{I,1} - \beta_{A,1}) - \beta_{2,1}(\beta_{I,2} - \beta_{A,2})}{\beta_{1,1}\beta_{2,2} - \beta_{2,1}\beta_{1,2}} \tag{16-12a}$$

$$x_2 = w_A \frac{\beta_{1,1}(\beta_{I,2} - \beta_{A,2}) - \beta_{1,2}(\beta_{I,1} - \beta_{A,1})}{\beta_{1,1}\beta_{2,2} - \beta_{2,1}\beta_{1,2}} \tag{16-12b}$$

The two-dimensional case would be particularly adapted to fixed-income portfolios. As explained in Section 12.1 of Chapter 12, such portfolios are naturally exposed to several well-identified sources of risk, the first two of which are maturity and credit factors. In the vast

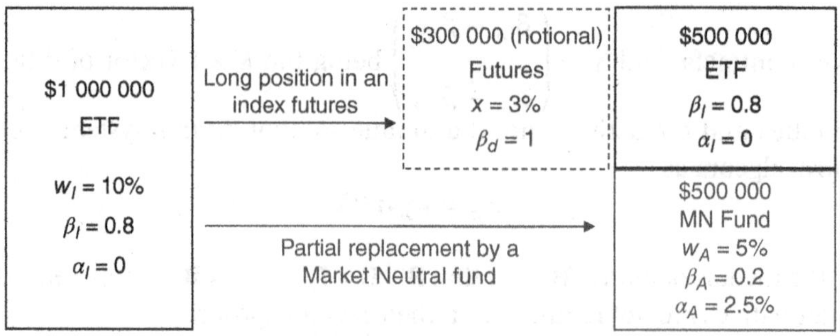

FIGURE 16-5 Illustration of the portable alpha mechanism.

majority of practical cases involving equities, only one significant risk factor is considered, which means that only one futures contract is necessary, with a notional x and a beta β_d. Applying the same principle as before, the notional investment in the derivatives contract is simply equal to

$$x = w_A \frac{(\beta_I - \beta_A)}{\beta_d} \qquad (16\text{-}13)$$

The single-factor case is illustrated in the chart shown in Figure 16-5, which provides a visual representation of the portable alpha mechanism.

In this example, the global core–satellite portfolio has a net asset value of V_0 = \$10 million. The initial passive investment in an ETF, whose beta with respect to the risk factor is $\beta_I = 0.8$, amounts to \$1 million. The manager has identified a promising Market Neutral fund with a very low beta ($\beta_A = 0.2$) but a promising alpha ($\alpha_A = 2.5\%$). They wish to capture this outperformance while respecting two constraints: (i) the global portfolio beta should remain unchanged and (ii) the maximum concentration amount in an active fund is 5%. Applying the portable alpha technique, the solution is to sell $-\Delta w_I \times V_0 = -5\% \times \$10$ million = \$500 000 of the ETF to subscribe to the fund for the same amount $w_A \times V_0 = 5\% \times \$10$ million = \$500 000, and to adopt a long position in a futures contract written on the same index as the risk factor, with a beta $\beta_d = 1$, with a notional that is equal to $x \times V_0 = 5\% \frac{(0.8-0.2)}{1} \times \$10$ million = \$300 000. Overall, the global portfolio under focus (i) keeps a beta of 0.8 and (ii) captures an alpha of 2.5% on half of the position. This reconciles the joint objective of holding risk under control while enjoying the benefits of the good actively managed fund that has been identified.

It is worth noting that the portable alpha technique generally involves a substantial use of cash and should be funded accordingly. Holding long positions in index and active funds, as in the example of Figure 16-5, freezes a corresponding capital investment. Holding a position in futures contracts implies that the fund manager must be ready to not only commit the initial margin necessary to enter the position but also to respond to the margin calls in case of a deterioration of the derivatives exposure (i.e., a long position and the underlying index price falls). It is possible, as Kung and Pohlman (2004) explain, to create unfunded portable alpha strategies by essentially replacing the passive investment strategy with a pure cash position. Under this situation, the cash generates interest income and can be used to sustain the margin requirements underlying the futures contract.

DFSO example (continued)

The fixed-income allocation of DFSO is split into two parts: the US Bond portfolio (20%) and the European Bond portfolio (10%). The former is internally managed actively, whereas the latter is entirely invested in a single Euro Corporate Bond ETF with an intermediate duration and an investment grade quality, which corresponds to the management's desired levels of exposures based on the following multifactor regression used for the European fixed-income portfolio:

$$R_{P,t} - R_{f,t} = \alpha_P + \beta_P^{\text{Dur}}(R_{\text{Dur},t} - R_{f,t}) + \beta_P^{\text{Cre}}(R_{\text{Cre},t} - R_{f,t}) + \varepsilon_{P,t}$$

After a thorough screening of Euro-focused bond mutual funds and a successful due diligence, the DFSO research team has come up with a candidate for investment. It is a short-duration fund mostly investing in distressed near-maturity corporate debt. Considering the same factor model that is used to estimate the ETF's factor exposures, this fund delivers a two-factor alpha that is close to 3%.

Given the total size of the fund, it is decided not to exceed a weight of 2.5% of the total DFSO portfolio for this investment, to be done through a corresponding divestment from the ETF. Furthermore, the management unit wishes not to alter the European Bond portfolio's existing exposures to the duration and spread factors following this operation. For this purpose, two futures contracts have been identified: the Euro-Bund futures contract written on the German government bond with a residual lifetime between 8.5 and 10.5 years, and the short-term Euro-BTP futures contract written on the Italian's Buoni del Tesoro Poliennali (BTP) with a residual lifetime between 2 and 3.25 years. The former contract has a large duration beta, whereas the second one has a reasonable spread beta, and both are considered sufficiently liquid.

The regression estimates for the funds and derivative contracts are represented in Table 16-5.

Table 16-5 reveals that the replacement of part of the initial ETF with an equivalent position in the active fund would reduce the duration risk, but increase the credit spread exposures. The futures contracts seem to fulfill their role: The Euro-Bund Futures has a large duration beta, whereas the Short-Term Euro BTP Futures is largely exposed to the credit spread factor.

(continued)

(continued)

TABLE 16-5 DFSO example – Regression estimates for the bond funds and futures.

	Funds		Futures	
	Euro Corp Bond ETF	Active Fund	Euro-Bund Futures	Short-Term Euro BTP Futures
Beta rate	0.89	0.42	1.09	0.31
Beta credit spread	0.56	1.96	0.06	0.85
Alpha	−0.18%	2.97%	0.00%	0.00%

Considering an active weight of $w_A = -\Delta w_I = 2.5\%$, we apply the formula of Equations (16-12a) and (16-12b) in order to obtain the initial commitments to the futures contracts:

$$x_{\text{Bund}} = 2.5\%\frac{0.85(0.89 - 0.42) - 0.31(0.56 - 1.96)}{1.09 \times 0.85 - 0.31 \times 0.06} = 2.30\%$$

and

$$x_{\text{BTP}} = 2.5\%\frac{1.09(0.56 - 1.96) - 0.06(0.89 - 0.42)}{1.09 \times 0.85 - 0.31 \times 0.06} = -4.28\%$$

Thus, if, for instance, the amount invested in the active fund is \$50 million, then it is necessary to take a long position of $\frac{2.30\%}{2.50\%} \times \$50$ million = \$1 150 000 in the Bund contract and a short position of $\frac{-4.28\%}{2.50\%} \times \$50$ million = −\$2 140 000 in the BTP contract. The resulting alpha captured by this strategy is equal to $2.5\% \times (-0.18\% + 2.97\%) = 2.5\% \times 3.15\% = 0.079\%$. This appears negligible at the global portfolio level but reveals an economically substantial contribution for the European fixed-income segment.

16.2.2 Designing suitable structured products

Many investors are tempted to invest in structured financial products. These are sophisticated portfolio management strategies that bundle together several spot and/or derivative (usually optional) positions in order to provide the customer with a specific payoff pattern through a single investment vehicle. These products usually have a finite maturity. Their complexity ranges from a "simple" portfolio of a long-only investment associated with a single option, like a protective put (asset + put option), to very complex associations of exotic derivatives with a payoff structure meant to appeal to the customer who purchases this product instead of a traditional "buy-and-hold strategy."

The question of the retrospective performance appraisal with historical data of such vehicles has a limited scope and interest. Traditional performance measures such as the Sharpe ratio or Jensen's alpha, for instance, are definitely not suited to them. More sophisticated performance measures based on extreme or downside risk, like many of those developed in Chapter 6, miss an important dimension underlying the design of these products: They have been specifically created so as to fulfill the investor's wishes (as perceived by the structurer), and therefore the whole distribution of their returns is important. Focusing on the left tail of the returns distribution would deliver an incomplete picture of their performance. Indeed, what can be considered the most suitable way to assess a structured product's performance is to measure the satisfaction level obtained by the investor whose preferences for risk and returns are known. This can be done for the standard or the behavioral investor, as investigated in Chapters 9 and 10, respectively.

When the issue shifts from the past performance of an existing product to the design of a new one, the landscape changes radically. The challenge for the creator of this product is to determine whether the structuring mechanism would correspond to the investor's expectations. The assessment must be made across all possible scenarios. For that purpose, relying on the historical returns of an otherwise similar vehicle barely helps. Because it represents only one among a wide set of realizations, it is unlikely to faithfully represent how the same kind of portfolio would behave in the future. It is therefore necessary to simulate many possible trajectories, in a realistic fashion, and determine the distribution of those trajectories that would maximize *ex ante* the investor's expected utility. We examine two situations below. The first one corresponds to a structured product with very long or infinite maturity, for which the pattern of periodic returns is highly relevant for the investor. The second one involves a vehicle with a contractual finite maturity. In that case, the terminal product payoff matters most. In both cases, we examine the generic case of a portfolio involving the combination of long and/or short positions in traditional financial securities (through physical holding or replication with swaps and futures), together with long and/or short positions in option contracts or synthetic replicating strategies.

16.2.2.1 The stochastic dominance criterion for periodic returns

The first category of structured products that we examine corresponds to a portfolio aiming to dynamically renew the long/short and optional characteristics at regular intervals. The key to the reasoning is to provide the investor with a substitute for a traditional portfolio that features, beyond financial assets such as stocks and bonds, the exposure to option-based strategies that provide a convex or a concave pattern of returns. These classical products include, for instance, stop-loss strategies, funds that provide a capital protection that is reset every quarter of a year, or portfolios involving a constant combination of long and optional positions in some traded index. There is no self-liquidating product maturity, but a continuous renewal of the desired optional qualities of the portfolio.

Structuring a financial product of this kind usually involves at least four important choices: (i) the selection of the assets composing the long and short positions – typically an index or a basket of securities; (ii) the type of optional properties associated with the product (long or short options, calls and/or puts, plain-vanilla or exotic, moneyness and maturities, exact or approximate optional behavior, ...); (iii) the underlying of the option contracts or synthetic replicating positions – usually the same set or a subset of the chosen assets; and (iv) the frequency at which the optional characteristics are to be reset.

Some of these products are designed "on demand," following a request of some specific customer, whereas others are offered to a large public. In this latter case, the ideal way to design a structured financial product would be to identify a representative customer, with a standard or a behavioral utility function as in Chapters 9 and 10, and to try to design the optimal instrument for this particular customer. However, in the forward-looking approach underlying product design, this can prove to be a very difficult task for at least two reasons. First, there is no guarantee that the client who will purchase this product will match the utility-based assumptions that were used to conceive it. Consider the standard quadratic utility function, for instance. If the product has been optimized with a risk-aversion coefficient of $\gamma_j = 6$, whereas it turns out that most of the clientele's profile corresponds to $\gamma_j = 12$, the product would be deemed unsuitable for them. Second, it is very hard to claim that a product's features are optimal for a certain investor profile unless all alternative product design possibilities have been tested for the same profile.

Thus, attempting to exactly match a product with a specific profile might seem overly ambitious. More modestly, the design characteristics chosen for a particular portfolio will be pragmatically made according to some decision rule. A well-known probabilistic approach called the *stochastic dominance (SD) criterion*, based on the characteristics of the distribution of the returns, represents a very useful candidate because it applies to a wide category of investor profiles without the necessity to calibrate their respective utility functions.

The intuition behind the SD criterion within the context of portfolio choice can be understood as follows. Consider two portfolios P and Q for which the full distribution function of their periodic returns is known. Then, we can determine that if the statement *Portfolio P stochastically dominates portfolio Q* is true, this implies that *every* investor whose risk profile corresponds to some standard characteristics such as preference for higher wealth, risk aversion for all levels of wealth, or both (depending on the order of the stochastic dominance), will prefer portfolio P over Q. If a given investor j corresponding to this standard risk profile observes that P stochastically dominates Q, they will unequivocally choose portfolio P. The converse is not true, however: the fact that the very same investor prefers some portfolio S over portfolio P does not imply that S stochastically dominates P. Thus, the notion of stochastic dominance is stronger than the notion of preference.

The following example illustrates these notions. Every month, portfolio P delivers the same return as portfolio Q plus an extra 1%, regardless of the market circumstances. Without any doubt, every investor who prefers more over less (thus with an increasing utility function) will prefer P over Q, irrespective of their level of risk aversion. Next, consider portfolio S that provides on average a slightly higher return than P plus an extra Gaussian random return with a zero expectation. It is thus riskier than P but has a higher expected return. The investors who display a large risk aversion will prefer portfolio P, whereas the investors with a very low risk aversion or who are even risk neutral will prefer S, even though both types of investors prefer more over less. Considering the same order for the stochastic dominance criterion, we can conclude that P dominates Q, but we can neither conclude that P dominates S nor that S dominates P.

From a distributional perspective, the SD criterion is translated as follows. For two portfolios P and Q, the investor observes $f_P(r)$ and $f_Q(r)$, with $f_i(r)dr \equiv \Pr[r < R_{i,t} \leq r + dr]$, being the probability density functions (in short pdf) associated with the returns of P and Q.[6] Consequently, the investor also knows $F_P(r) = \int_{-\infty}^{r} f_P(x)dx$ and $F_Q(r) = \int_{-\infty}^{r} f_Q(x)dx$, with $F_i(r) \equiv \Pr[R_{i,t} \leq r]$ being the cumulative density functions (in short cdf). The first-order stochastic dominance (FSD) of P over Q is defined as

$$P \text{ FSD } Q \Longleftrightarrow F_P(r) \leq F_Q(r)\ \forall r \in \chi \text{ and } \exists r^* \in \chi:\ F_P(r^*) < F_Q(r^*) \tag{16-14}$$

where χ is the union of the supports of the distributions of the returns of P and Q, i.e., the set of all values of the possible returns for at least one of these two portfolios.

Likewise, the second-order stochastic dominance (SSD) is defined as[7]

$$P \text{ SSD } Q \Longleftrightarrow \int_{-\infty}^{r} F_P(x)dx \leq \int_{-\infty}^{r} F_Q(x)dx\ \forall r \in \chi \text{ and } \exists r^* \in \chi:\ \int_{-\infty}^{r^*} F_P(x)dx < \int_{-\infty}^{r^*} F_Q(x)dx \tag{16-15}$$

From an expected utility perspective, the fact that P FSD Q implies that any rational investor who prefers more over less, i.e., with an increasing utility function, will prefer P over Q. The fact that P SSD Q implies that any rational risk-averse investor, i.e., with a concave utility function, will prefer P over Q. The intuition underlying both notions of FSD and SSD can be best understood graphically as illustrated in Figure 16-6.

Both charts represent the shape of the cumulative density functions of two portfolios P and Q. Being defined as the probability that the return is lower than or equal to the value on the horizontal axis, these functions are always increasing and comprised between 0 and 1.

The left graph illustrates the first-order stochastic dominance. The cdf of the returns of P is lower than that of Q for all possible values of the return r. Visually, this corresponds to a function $F_P(r)$ that always lies below the other one $F_Q(r)$. It means that, regardless of the

[6]For simplicity, we assume here that the support of their distribution, i.e., the set of all possible values for the returns, is continuous. If this support is discrete, i.e., only a finite set of values can be observed, the reasoning is similar but the notation changes from integrals to summation symbols.

[7]The stochastic dominance criterion can be extended to any order K. It involves computing K successive integrals of the cdf. In practice, the analysis rarely goes beyond $K = 3$, corresponding to the third-order stochastic dominance.

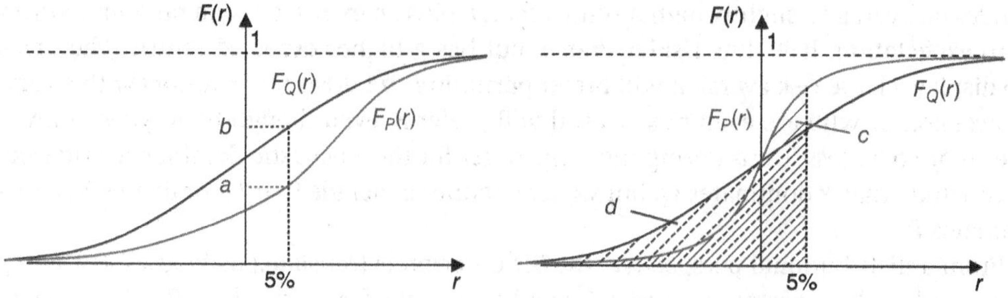

FIGURE 16-6 First- and second-order stochastic dominance.

level of return considered, there is always a higher probability that the return of portfolio Q will be lower than this threshold than that of P. We show this on the graph with $r = 5\%$. For this return, the probabilities of falling short of this target are equal to a for portfolio P and b for portfolio Q. Since $a < b$, there is a lower chance of being disappointed by an investment in P than in Q. This reasoning holds for any level of target return. Thus, every rational decision maker who prefers more over less will unequivocally prefer P over Q. This is what P FSD Q implies.

The right chart is slightly more complicated but conveys the same type of idea. The cdf of the returns of P appears to be more concentrated around the middle of the graph than that of Q. This essentially means that there is a higher probability of observing a large deviation from the middle with portfolio Q than with P. This visual impression is translated into the difference between the areas under both curves for every level of return. The fact that this area is always larger for Q than for P induces that there is always a larger expected downside deviation for the former than for the latter portfolio. We show it again on the graph with $r = 5\%$. The cumulative area under $F_Q(r)$ up to that point (represented with the dashed oblique lines) is larger than that under $F_P(r)$. Visually, this translates into the inequality of areas $c < d$. This exactly corresponds to the condition stated in Equation (16-15). It entails that Q is riskier than P, which means that any risk-averse investor will prefer P over Q. This is what P SSD Q implies.

Applying the notion of stochastic dominance in the field of portfolio management involves dealing with samples of returns rather than the whole population. This implies not only that we cannot observe the exact cdf of the returns distribution for sure but also that phenomena such as serial correlation or moving average of returns, which often occur for some portfolios (see Chapter 12) may contaminate statistical inference. This issue has been studied by Linton, Maasoumi, and Whang (2005), who propose a procedure in order to meaningfully test, using an adaptation of the Kolmogorov–Smirnov adjustment test, the presence of stochastic dominance in a general situation where there are more than two portfolios being challenged. Their approach is applied by Annaert, Van Osselaer, and Verstraete (2009) in the context of various configurations of the portfolio insurance strategy, a structured product that essentially combines a long investment in an asset (usually an index) together with a put option or a similar strategy on the same asset.

We consider the design of a structured product that involves N possible variations, which in our case will be the portfolios. The sources of these variations can be the option moneyness or maturity if an option is traded, the floor and multiplication coefficient if the constant proportion portfolio insurance (CPPI) technique is applied, the frequency of rebalancing, etc. For each of them, a backtest or a bootstrapped simulation of the periodic portfolio returns is obtained and denoted by $R_{i,t}$ for $i = 1, \ldots, N$ (the set of portfolios) and $t = 1, \ldots, T$ (the sample window). The issue that we face is the following: *If the investor is rational and risk averse, which configuration should we choose for this product?* The procedure that Annaert et al. (2009) propose consists of three steps (we only consider the FSD and SSD cases).

1. For each portfolio i, compute the following test statistic:

$$\hat{\tau}_T^{(1)}(i) = \min_{j \neq i} \sup_{r \in \chi} \sqrt{T}(\hat{F}_i(r) - \hat{F}_j(r)) \tag{16-16a}$$

$$\hat{\tau}_T^{(2)}(i) = \min_{j \neq i} \sup_{r \in \chi} \sqrt{T}\left(\int_{-\infty}^{r} \hat{F}_i(x)dx - \int_{-\infty}^{r} \hat{F}_j(x)dx\right) \tag{16-16b}$$

where $\hat{F}_.(r) = \frac{1}{T}\sum_{t=1}^{T} 1_{\{R_{.,t} \leq r\}}$, in which $1_{\{R_{.,t} \leq r\}}$ is a binary function that takes a value of 1 if $R_{.,t} \leq r$ and 0 otherwise, stands for the proportion of the observed returns that are smaller than or equal to r.

Equation (16-16a) aims to measure the greatest negative distance between the cdf of each portfolio and the best remaining ones. Looking at Figure 16-6, it is equivalent to looking at all the cdfs and, for each one, finding the value of r for which even the best remaining portfolio has its return cdf above all the others. This gives an indication about whether this portfolio FSD all the other ones (if $\hat{\tau}_T^{(1)}(i)$ is negative) and to what extent (considering how negative it is). The is the same logic behind Equations (16-16b) regarding SSD.

2. Divide the sample into $T - b + 1$ sub-samples of consecutive return observations, each having an equal size b. We complete this set of sub-samples by artificially connecting the last observation with the first one so that an additional number of $b - 1$ sub-samples of artificially connected observations can be drawn. This creates a total number of $(T - b + 1) + (b - 1) = T$ sub-samples.[8] Kläver (2005) suggests a value of $b = 10\sqrt{T}$, which obviously makes sense when T is sufficiently large. For each sub-sample $s = 1, \ldots, T$, recompute Equations (16-16a) and (16-16b) to obtain $\hat{\tau}_s^{(1)}(i)$ and $\hat{\tau}_s^{(2)}(i)$.
3. Obtain the p-value of the test of stochastic dominance for each portfolio by the following formula:

$$\hat{p}_T^{(1)}(i) = \frac{1}{T}\sum_{s=1}^{T} 1_{\left\{\hat{\tau}_s^{(1)}(i) > \hat{\tau}_T^{(1)}(i)\right\}} \text{ and } \hat{p}_T^{(2)}(i) = \frac{1}{T}\sum_{s=1}^{T} 1_{\left\{\hat{\tau}_s^{(2)}(i) > \hat{\tau}_T^{(2)}(i)\right\}} \tag{16-17}$$

[8]This technique, called the circular block method, has already been discussed in Section 10.4.3 of Chapter 10. It is illustrated in the middle chart of Figure 10-7.

If none of these p-values is sufficiently low (e.g., below 5%), then we cannot reject the hypothesis that there is no portfolio that stochastically dominates all the others. If this is the case for all tested levels of SD (limited here to FSD and SSD), the portfolios are considered to be SD efficient.

Note that this procedure can be adapted to test whether a portfolio would be dominated by the other ones. The logic is reversed: for each portfolio, we check whether the worst of the remaining ones stochastically dominates it. If this is the case, the dominated portfolio would be ejected from the efficient set.

Interestingly, the notion of stochastic dominance can also be transposed into the Prospect Theory framework discussed in Section 10.1 of Chapter 10. Levy and Wiener (1998) define the notion of Prospect Stochastic Dominance (PSD) as follows:

$$P \text{ PSD } Q \Leftrightarrow \int_{r^-}^{r^+} F_P(x)dx \leq \int_{r^-}^{r^+} F_Q(x)dx \; \forall r^+ > \underline{R}, r^- < \underline{R} \in \chi$$

$$\text{and } \exists r^{+*} > \underline{R}, r^{-*} < \underline{R} \in \chi: \int_{r^{-*}}^{r^{+*}} F_P(x)dx < \int_{r^{-*}}^{r^{+*}} F_Q(x)dx \qquad (16\text{-}18)$$

where $\underline{R}$ is the reservation rate that separates the investor's perception of gains versus losses.

The stochastic dominance criterion appears to be very useful in the exploratory work of trying to determine whether a structured product fulfills its role as a "one-size-fits-all" portfolio. Finding out that one portfolio dominates all the others, or even (more modestly) that a given configuration achieves reasonably low p-values in Equation (16-17) can prove to be very helpful in order to make decisions – compared with the very severe approach of pure statistical testing. For instance, comparing the option-based portfolio insurance with the constant proportion portfolio insurance (CPPI) strategies using the SD criterion, Maalej and Prigent (2016) find that the latter structuring method third-order stochastically dominates the former one. Thus, if one is confronted with the challenge of constructing this kind of product, their choice would naturally lean toward the CPPI that provides more comfort about its ability to please a wide array of investors.

16.2.2.2 The mental account satisfaction criterion for terminal payoffs

Another very important category of structured products consists of those whose terminal payoff is ultimately all that matters to the investor. Consider a fund that provides capital protection to the investor at some prespecified horizon H. Before that moment, nothing precludes the net asset value of this fund from being lower than the invested capital because this is not the fund's commitment. Moreover, since capital protection is warranted exactly at time H, this property vanishes after that moment, which corresponds to the product's maturity. Thus, unlike the previous subsection for which we were investigating the portfolio's journey, only its destination really matters here.

It is obvious that the *ex ante* analysis of a structured product of that kind should not be performed by merely examining the statistical properties of the series of periodic returns. Rather, a thorough understanding of the distribution of the possible portfolio payoffs at its maturity H is necessary in order to instruct the decision-maker. The frequency at which this payoff is observed for a specific product is extremely low: It occurs only once, precisely at the product's maturity. Thus, the first challenge is to construct a sufficiently large sample of potential horizon payoffs. The two main approaches for such a task are Monte Carlo (i.e., numerical) simulations and bootstrapping (i.e., resampling) techniques. The former method has been introduced in Section 3.3.2 of Chapter 3 and can be adapted to the context of any structured product, whereas the latter method is discussed in Section 10.4.3 of Chapter 10.

Consider a similar setup as in the previous subsection: A set of N possible configurations are put in competition. The basis for comparing their merits is the distribution of their payoff at a common horizon H (expressed as a multiple of the compound period, i.e., if the horizon is 10 years and returns are computed on a monthly basis, then $H = 10 \times 12 = 120$). If the product matures before this moment at $h < H$ (for instance when there is an early redemption feature), then a common assumption must be made in order to let this payoff evolve from h to H, for instance by investing the redemption amount at the prevailing interest rate (which must be simulated as well). By multiplying the number of simulations or resamplings, we obtain an inventory of S instances of the final product payoff for each of the N assets.

In this context, the use of a traditional utility function in order to determine the investor's expected satisfaction extracted from each of the products tested is a real possibility. This raises however a problem of consistency. It lies in the reconciliation of the functions examined in Chapters 9 and 10 with the purpose of product structuring. With the exception of some behavioral utility functions, most of the standard ones would rank linear portfolios (i.e., long- or short-only) above those that feature options. Why would one need to craft a sophisticated product if the investor would ultimately prefer a simple one? Furthermore, the use of parametric functions, which assign a specific utility value to each and every final payoff, bumps on the same set of arguments as in the previous subsection: How to characterize the target investor knowing that the actual group of customers is likely to be heterogeneous? How to make sure that the chosen product will actually be the optimal one, given that it is almost impossible to identify it explicitly?

A workable and adapted solution is provided by the mental accounts setup discussed in Section 10.4 of Chapter 10. This approach lays the fundamentals of goal-based investing, which essentially corresponds to the investor's problem here. However, the objective in this case is not to determine whether a given portfolio has fulfilled the investor's objective or not, but to decide about the best possible design of the structured product. The interest of the simulation exercise lies in the multiplication of the number of periodic returns (H) by the number of simulated paths (S). If their product is sufficiently large, then we can reasonably assess that the mean periodic return over all scenarios, defined as $\overline{\overline{R}}_P^{c,H}$, approaches the expected return of the structured product over the considered horizon:

$$E(R_P^c) \approx \overline{\overline{R}}_P^{c,H} = \frac{1}{S}\sum_{s=1}^{S} \overline{R}_{P,s}^{c,H} = \frac{1}{S \times H}\sum_{s=1}^{S}\sum_{\tau=1}^{H} R_{P,s,\tau}^{c} \tag{16-19}$$

where $R_{P,s,\tau}^c$ is the portfolio continuously compounded return (in order to ensure their additivity) under scenario $s = 1, \ldots, S$ at time $\tau = 1, \ldots, H$.

Because we have this rich information about the estimation of the portfolio's expected return through the "double average" $\overline{\overline{R}}_P^{c,H}$, we can indeed use a decision criterion based on a constrained optimization, which is the essence of the mental account framework, rather than "simply" checking whether each of the products tested meets the investor's goal, which is all we can do when we have only one trajectory as in the case of past performance.

For this purpose, we find it more convenient to start from the general formulation of the horizon-asymmetry mental accounting (HAMA) problem proposed by Hübner and Lejeune (2021) and reproduced below:[9]

$$\max_P E(R_P^c) \tag{16-20a}$$

$$\text{subject to: } \Pr[\overline{R}_{P,s}^{c,H} \leq E(R_P^c) - \delta] - \eta \times \Pr[\overline{R}_{P,s}^{c,H} \geq E(R_P^c) + \delta] \leq \omega \tag{16-20b}$$

where Pr[ ] refers to the probability of obtaining the argument inferred from the sample, δ is a tolerance level of the shortfall that can be incurred below the expected return before the investor considers the outcome as a "loss," ω is the tolerance probability for not achieving the minimum threshold return, and $0 \leq \eta \leq 1$ is a gain/loss asymmetry trade-off coefficient that rewards gains beyond a certain level.

The decision-making process that is consistent with the optimization program above is

$$\max_P \overline{\overline{R}}_P^{c,H} \tag{16-21a}$$

$$\text{subject to: } \frac{S_P^-}{S} - \eta\,\frac{S_P^+}{S} \leq \omega \tag{16-21b}$$

where $S_P^- = \sum_{s=1}^{S} 1_{\left\{\overline{R}_{P,s}^{c,H} \leq \overline{\overline{R}}_P^{c,H} - \delta\right\}}$ and $S_P^+ = \sum_{s=1}^{S} 1_{\left\{\overline{R}_{P,s}^{c,H} \geq \overline{\overline{R}}_P^{c,H} + \delta\right\}}$ represent the number of times a final shortfall and a final surplus are observed across all scenarios, respectively.

[9]These are analogous to Equations (10-48a) and (10-48b) of Chapter 10. We have removed subscript j from the original formulas to ease exposition.

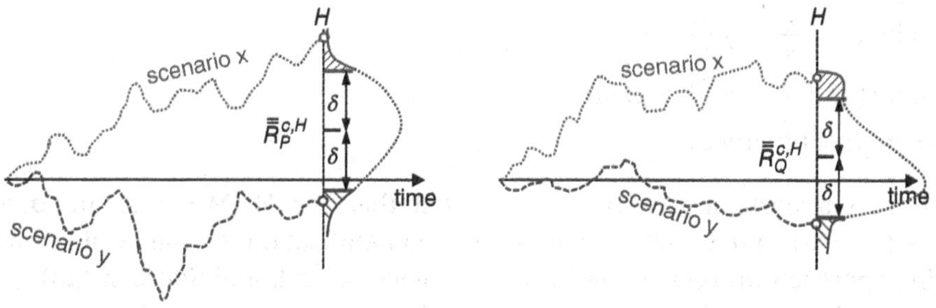

FIGURE 16-7 Application of the HAMA framework to the design of a structured product.

Concretely, it suffices to rank all structured products in descending order, and retain the first one for which condition (16-21b) is respected. The rationale of the procedure is illustrated in Figure 16-7, which takes the example of two competing configurations of a structured product for a given category of investors.

Figure 16-7 shows how to apply the optimization program in order to choose between two structured products P (left graph) and Q (right graph). For both portfolios, the same scenarios are drawn (the sample paths of two of them being shown), leading to an empirical distribution of their terminal payoff that is reflected through the density curves that stretch vertically on the far right of each chart. The first reveals a behavior that is quite similar to a traditional portfolio, whereas the second one displays a positive asymmetry but seems to truncate the gains after a certain level.

To compare these portfolios, we consider a single representative mental account. Within this account, the investor considers that the realized average return falls short of the objective if it is farther than a distance of $\delta\%$ below the expectation, but they are positively surprised if the return is $\delta\%$ above the expectation. Furthermore (not represented on the graph), they have a trade-off coefficient between positive and negative surprises of η and a tolerance probability ω.

By taking average returns across all scenarios, we can approach their expected returns by using formula (16-19). Their respective estimates $E(R_P^c) \approx \bar{\bar{R}}_P^{c,H}$ and $E(R_Q^c) \approx \bar{\bar{R}}_Q^{c,H}$ are represented on the graph as the means of both distributions. Consequently, the zones corresponding to gains and losses are delimited by taking a distance of $+\delta$ and $-\delta$. It can immediately be seen that this favors portfolio Q, whose average return is lower. Thus, whereas its risk profile is more conservative than P, its assessment is favored by a lower expected return. On the other hand, since the horizon is long enough, the higher expected return of P drags up the cumulative returns of this product. This explains why the situation depicted in scenario y is not that dramatic.

The decision criterion is eventually quite straightforward: we count the number of scenarios S_i^- that fall below the lower threshold $\bar{\bar{R}}_i^{c,H} - \delta$ for $i = P, Q$ (like scenario y for both portfolios), and we do the same for the number of scenarios S_i^+ that exceed the upper threshold $\bar{\bar{R}}_i^{c,H} + \delta$. The chosen portfolio will be

- Product P if $\frac{S_P^-}{S} - \eta \frac{S_P^+}{S} \leq \omega$;
- Product Q if $\frac{S_P^-}{S} - \eta \frac{S_P^+}{S} > \omega$ but $\frac{S_Q^-}{S} - \eta \frac{S_Q^+}{S} \leq \omega$;
- No product otherwise.

As a final remark, it remains to be noted that the HAMA program presented in Equations (16-20a) and (16-20b) represents a generalization of the well-known mental accounting approach introduced by Das, Markowitz, Scheid, and Statman (2010). Setting η equal to 0 leads back to their original framework. The objective remains the same (maximizing the expected return), but the constraint becomes the control of the shortfall probability that must remain below the investor's tolerance probability ω.

DFSO example (continued)

Regarding the allocation of 4% in commodities and managed futures, the Board of DFSO is concerned about the impact of inflation and geopolitical events on the portfolio. It has been asked to the fund's management unit to consider an investment in a structured product with a limited downside risk over an investment horizon of 10 years, but leaving a substantial upside potential. Consequently, the CIO has obtained three competitive proposals, called X, Y, and Z, for the structuring of a product using a common underlying commodity index designed to fit the investment objective. For each of them, a complete simulation study of the potential final payoffs (including reinvestment of the interim cash flows, if applicable) has been carried out using exactly the same assumptions and 50 000 simulated draws using the exact same scenarios for all three cases. The outcome is provided in Table 16-6.

The first column of Table 16-6 reports the lower bound of the mean continuously compounded yearly return of the product. The last row reports the average of all these mean returns across all scenarios. The histograms resulting from the simulation exercise are reported in Figure 16-8. They show substantial differences in the patterns of the products' payoffs (Figure 16-8).

Product X displays the payoff distribution that is closest to a Gaussian one but with a negative skewness. Product Y clearly truncates the left tail of the distribution (no outcome below −8%) with a positive skewness, but the mode of the distribution is the lowest among the three products. Finally, Product Z displays a relatively concentrated distribution but has a "secondary cluster" of returns that are very negative (below −10%), typical of a product featuring the sale of a deep-out-of-the-money put option.

In order to assess the fund's risk appetite, it is decided to adopt the horizon-asymmetry mental accounting (HAMA) approach with the following parameter values: $\delta = 6\%$ (which

TABLE 16-6 DFSO example – Outcomes of the numerical scenarios for the three structured products.

Lower bound	X	Y	Z
−20%	12	0	0
−18%	25	0	0
−16%	141	0	898
−14%	286	0	1254
−12%	399	0	789
−10%	489	0	256
−8%	697	1285	365
−6%	869	1967	496
−4%	1222	2659	852
−2%	1896	5325	1868
0%	2866	6588	2699
2%	4201	6233	3567
4%	5962	4598	4820
6%	6921	3899	6226
8%	6639	3366	6714
10%	5509	3011	6988
12%	4278	2774	6521
14%	3310	2456	3234
16%	2169	1852	1664
18%	1108	1424	557
20%	685	991	211
22%	210	722	21
24%	85	662	0
26%	17	151	0
28%	4	37	0
30%	0	0	0
Sum	**50 000**	**50 000**	**50 000**
Average $\bar{\bar{R}}_i^{c,10}$	**7.5%**	**6.0%**	**7.0%**

(continued)

(continued)

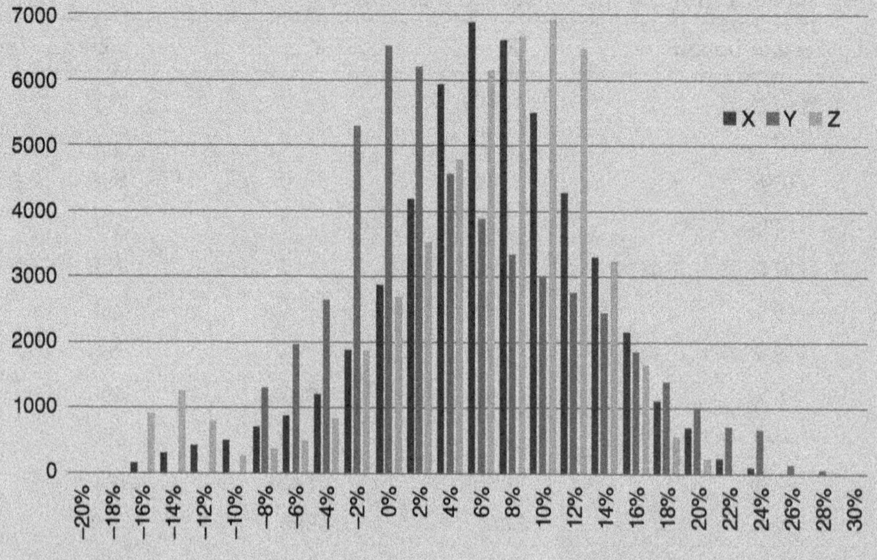

FIGURE 16-8 DFSO example – Histograms of the scenario outcomes for the three structured products.

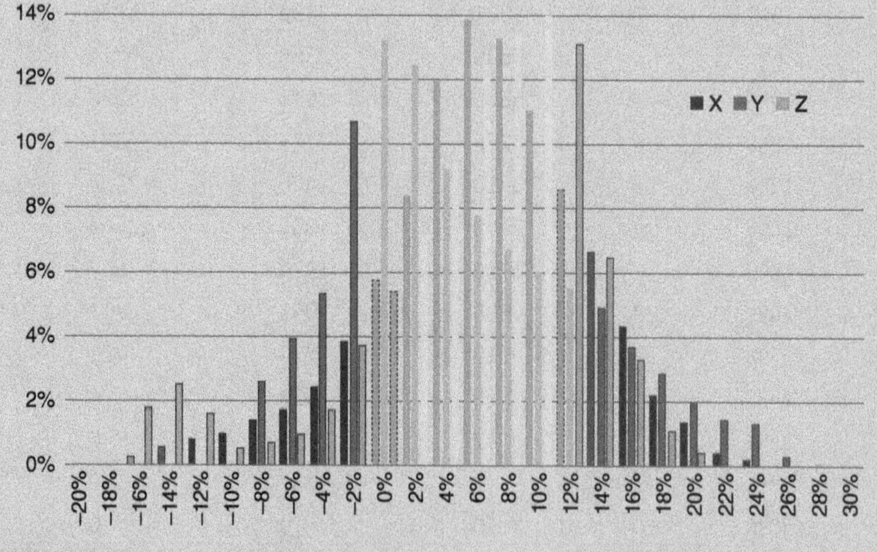

FIGURE 16-9 DFSO example – Repartition of the histograms under the HAMA framework.

corresponds to the largest distance such that the lower bound is negative for none of the three products), $\eta = 0.7$, reflecting a material appetite for gains, and $\omega = 10\%$, corresponding to a tolerance of a shortfall (adjusted for the potential upside) occurring once every 10 years. Applying these parameters leads to the graph shown in Figure 16-9, reflecting the same kinds of histograms (but this time with the observed frequencies) and highlighting the critical zones (beyond tolerance).

The situations where the product delivers a return that is short from its associated lower bound or above its upper bound are represented with darker histograms. The intervals are different for the three products: they are equal to [1.5%, 13.5%] for X, [0.0%, 12.0%] for Y, and [1.0%, 13.0%] for Z because of the differences in their means. Discarding the center of the distributions reveals a very unfavorable pattern for product Y. Applying condition (16-21b) to each product leads to $\frac{S_i^-}{S} - \eta \frac{S_i^+}{S} = 12\%$ for X, 20% for Y, and 10% for Z. Since only this latter product respects the Board's risk appetite, this one should be chosen. Had the asymmetry trade-off coefficient been higher, for instance $\eta = 0.85$, then the constraint would be met for X as $\frac{S_X^-}{S} - 0.85 \frac{S_X^+}{S} = 9.4\%$ and this product would have been chosen given its higher average return. On the contrary, with $\eta = 0$ (only consideration for losses), none of the products would respect the constraint, and they should all be discarded for being too aggressive.

16.3 USING PERFORMANCE TO SERVE INVESTOR NEEDS

The third set of applications of performance usage in the asset management process relates to the particular needs of certain types of investors. To instruct their decisions, they should be equipped with some objective criteria that will help them to avoid making mistakes. The focus is thus on the identity of the investor, rather than on the intrinsic portfolio characteristics. In the next subsections, we tackle three archetypes of economic actors. The first one is the institutional investor, whose problem is often related to the presence of a well-defined benchmark that the manager is supposed to outperform. The second one is the passive investor. This person also considers a benchmark, but their objective is mostly to replicate its return behavior with the lowest risk and costs. The third one is the "structurally undiversified" investor, such as the entrepreneur or real estate investor, who has to consider a relevant cost of capital to appraise the quality of a venture.

16.3.1 Institutional investors

In Section 3.4.2 of Chapter 3, we discussed the *ex post* perspective of the benchmarked investor. The performance criterion that naturally addresses this investor's situation is the Information ratio IR_P. After the portfolio return has been recorded, its level of IR_P is known, and Grinold and Kahn (1995) propose a heuristic scale to translate numerical values of the Information ratio into qualitative assessments of the manager's success in active management.

From an *ex ante* perspective, the same authors posit that the mandate that ought to be given to an active portfolio manager depends on the investor's level of residual risk aversion, which they denote by λ_R. From their experience, reasonable values for λ_R range from 0.05 (low risk aversion) to 0.15 (high risk aversion).

In an analogy to the CAPM,[10] the investor wishes to maximize the value added from active portfolio management, which is defined as the expected active return diminished by a penalty for active risk. To do so, they have access to a portfolio manager who can reach, but not exceed, a certain level of the Information ratio (IR) (the "budget constraint"). As a reminder, the IR is written as (as in Equation (3-22) of Chapter 3)

$$IR_P = \frac{TD_P}{TE_P} = \frac{\overline{R}_{(P-B)}}{\sigma_{(P-B)}} \tag{16-22}$$

where the numerator is the benchmark B tracking difference $TD_P = \overline{R}_P - \overline{R}_B \equiv \overline{R}_{(P-B)}$ and the denominator is the tracking error $TE_P = \sigma(R_P - R_B) \equiv \sigma_{(P-B)}$, i.e., the volatility of its differential return.

The objective function maximizes the value added (VA_P) and takes the following form:

$$\max_{\sigma_{(P-B)}} VA_P = TD_P - \lambda_R \sigma^2_{(P-B)} \text{ subject to } TD_P = IR_P \sigma_{(P-B)} \tag{16-23}$$

The outcome of this optimization exercise is given by $\sigma^*_{(P-B)} = \frac{IR_P}{2\lambda_R}$, and the maximum level of value added that can be obtained by the investor, denoted by VA^*_P, is the following:

$$VA^*_P = \frac{IR^2_P}{4\lambda_R} \tag{16-24}$$

Thus, the authors emphasize a quadratic relation between the level of a manager's expected Information ratio and the maximum reward that can be expected by their client. Consistent with this discussion, Grinold and Kahn (1995) assert that the threshold for an *ex post* "good" IR before fees is 0.5. When it exceeds 0.75, it is considered "very good," and an IR equal to or greater than 1.0 is considered "exceptional." These levels translate into a maximum potential gain from active management that depends on the interaction between the investor's residual risk-aversion level λ_R and the manager's potential Information ratio IR_P, which is summarized in Table 16-7.

Hence, the add-on that the investor could hope to achieve in their risk-adjusted return would be, in the best possible case, capped to an expectation of 5%. An investor who is very risk averse and who is exclusively confronted with a "good" asset manager can only expect a

[10]The subsequent optimization program presented in Equation (16-22) is similar to the objective function of an investor with a quadratic utility function in the context of the mean–variance framework (see Chapter 2). This reasoning was initially proposed by Treynor and Black (1973) in the context of the Appraisal ratio, for which the benchmark is identified as being a leveraged version of the market portfolio.

TABLE 16-7 Potential value added as a function of residual risk aversion and Information ratio.

IR_p (before fees)	Residual risk aversion λ_R		
	Aggressive (0.05)	Moderate (0.10)	Restrained (0.15)
Exceptional (1.0)	5.00%	2.50%	1.67%
Very good (0.75)	2.81%	1.41%	0.94%
Good (0.50)	1.25%	0.63%	0.42%

Source: Grinold and Kahn (1995), Table 5.4.

modest surplus, even before paying the fees associated with active portfolio management. This point clearly emphasizes why only investors who display a quite significant tolerance for risk should seriously consider a delegation to very active portfolio managers.

Nevertheless, this analysis has its drawbacks as well. A hidden weakness of the Information ratio is its economic dependence upon the return of its benchmark. The value of active risk, i.e., the voluntary divergence from the benchmark, ultimately hinges on the level of this divergence. Even though this value does not explicitly derive from Equation (16-22), the optimal weight in the active portfolio w_P^* increases when the expected benchmark return decreases.[11] Consequently, the contribution of the active portfolio in the global Sharpe ratio of a core–satellite portfolio also increases unambiguously; hence, the value added of an active portfolio for a rational investor. Therefore, its incremental performance is not only reflected in its Information ratio but also depends on the prevailing market conditions, specifically the market risk premium. This proposition is indeed fairly intuitive. When the market is "supportive" and generously rewards the risk taken, departing from the market portfolio is less attractive. An alpha of 1% when the market delivers 10% does not at all mean the same as when the market only delivers 2%. This type of information, which is crucial to assess the value of active risk, is absent from the Information ratio.

16.3.2 Pure index investors

Benchmarks are not only important for institutional investors. Those who look for the replication of an index also have a reference portfolio in mind. The key difference is that, through their investment, they do not seek to outperform it but only to gain access to it at the best possible conditions. They will do so through index funds, Exchange Traded Funds (ETFs) or

[11]This can be seen by considering Equation (4-5) in Chapter 4 in the context of the Appraisal ratio: the structure of w_P^* positively depends on the expected market return through its component x_P.

derivative contracts. We focus here on investors who wish to have a long-only, durable exposure to an index, mostly through direct investments in trackers,[12] and call them here the pure index investors or, in short, pure indexers.

Two remarks have to be made at this stage, to understand the forthcoming content. First, the notion of "best possible conditions" encompasses, but is not restricted to, the direct costs and fees of the replication materialized by the total expense ratio. There are also some other key dimensions that determine the attractiveness of an ETF. The major one is its liquidity, which is of paramount importance to some categories of investors, especially regarding market depth (maximum size of a trade that does not move the price) and width (bid-ask spread risk). Another consideration is the type of index replication, either full physical, optimized, or synthetic, that generates different types of risks and costs.

Second, being a pure index investor does not necessarily mean being a passive one, even though passive investors belong to this category. There are numerous reasons why someone would like to replicate an index: in the scope of a core–satellite allocation (see Chapter 12), in order to implement market timing strategies (see Chapter 8), or even simply because the index itself results from an active portfolio management strategy that has been translated into a benchmark portfolio.

16.3.2.1 Limitations of the Information ratio

In principle, the Information ratio IR_P represents the most natural criterion for the selection of an ETF (denoted by P) to mimic a benchmark index B. It corresponds to the case of a passive complement (the index) from which the portfolio manager diverges, incurring a deviation risk for the investor.

A first issue raised by the Information ratio is its inability to encompass all dimensions related to the risks and costs of the tracker discussed at the beginning of this section. The substance of the IR is a match of the tracking error with the tracking difference. There is no space for outside elements if they do not appear at the numerator or the denominator of Equation (16-22). Nonetheless, this issue can be overcome by adapting the Information ratio if necessary but at the expense of weakening its interpretability.

On top of the aforementioned considerations, there is a third major issue related to the sign of this performance measure. The periodic differential return of this vehicle is structurally negative because of the costs and fees. This means that the ETF's tracking difference $TD_P < 0$. In addition, the tracking error is always positive by definition. Consequently, in general, $IR_P < 0$ for any tracker. Thus, selecting an ETF involves choosing among all portfolios whose performance is intrinsically negative. This, in principle, does not represent any hindrance regarding the validity of this ratio. As discussed in Section 5.5.2 of Chapter 5, the interpretation of Information or Sharpe ratios is not fundamentally altered when they are negative. Nevertheless,

[12]The use of derivatives in the context of portable alpha strategies, for instance, is discussed in Section 16.2.1. In what follows, we focus on the most natural vehicle that is in use nowadays, namely ETFs, but the analysis is also valid for index funds.

TABLE 16-8 Illustration of the difficulty of using the Information ratio for trackers.

ETF	TD_P	TE_P	IR_P	$\lvert IR_P \rvert$
X	−0.10%	0.25%	−0.40	0.40
Y	−0.10%	0.20%	−0.50	0.50
Z	−0.08%	0.20%	−0.40	0.40

the structural negativity of the IR is a problem here. Indeed, the particular objectives of the ETF investor are sometimes not adequately addressed by the use of the Information ratio as a decision criterion. Generally, the investor is much more concerned about the absolute dispersion of the tracking difference than about the level of the tracking error relative to this tracking difference. To grasp this, note that we are not strictly speaking about the situation depicted in Section 4.3.4 of Chapter 4, namely the case of a passive complement, that justifies the use of the Information ratio. The issue here is to replace the index, which is not or hardly investable, with a close substitute. There is no discussion about their relative weights: this is a one-for-one exchange. Consequently, the potential magnitude of the deviation (abnormal return) has a much greater importance than the ratio of the average deviation over its volatility. The simple example presented in Table 16-8 sheds light on this statement.

This numerical example illustrates the fallacy of only relying on a ratio in these circumstances. Consider first ETFs X and Y. Since they have the exact same tracking difference, the discriminant dimension is their tracking error. The fact that X is riskier is clearly a weakness because it signals that this ETF does a poorer job in tracking its index. Thus, no pure indexer would reasonably prefer this tracker, even though its Information ratio is greater than that of Y.

From this reasoning, one could be tempted to say: "*Why not simply compare trackers on the basis of the absolute value of their Information ratio?*", as in the last column of the table. The ordering of preferences would be consistent with the performance estimates. Unfortunately, this does not hold. This is shown by comparing ETFs Y and Z. This time, they have the same volatility of differential returns: only their tracking difference matters. Since Z is cheaper than Y, the result of the comparison is again unambiguous: every pure index investor would favor Z. This is in line with the use of the Information ratio, but not with its absolute value.

A second limitation of the use of the Information ratio in the context of trackers, underlined by Hassine and Roncalli (2013), appears when they are considered in a more global portfolio allocation process featuring active and passive funds altogether, as in the core–satellite allocation process. The substitution of a benchmark by a tracker with a negative tracking difference invalidates the pure application of homemade leverage, which is crucial for the Information ratio to correctly compare active portfolios with different tracking errors. The imperfect replication of the index indeed changes the rules of the game to the detriment of

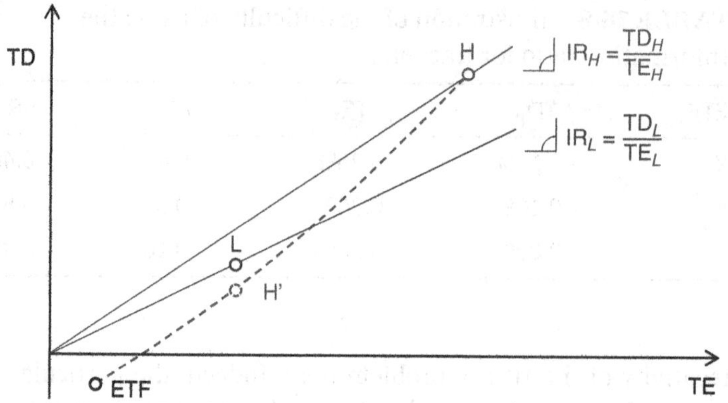

FIGURE 16-10 Information ratios with the use of trackers for homemade leverage. *Source:* Adapted from Hassine and Roncalli (2013), Figure 6.

the strategy that uses the tracker in the replication exercise. This potential issue is illustrated in Figure 16-10, which replicates Figure 3-10 of Chapter 3.

The graph shows how the use of a tracker instead of the index itself potentially distorts the portfolio diagnosis. From the perspective of Information ratios alone, benchmarked portfolio H dominates L since its tracking difference is large enough to compensate a larger tracking error. This is materialized by the slope of the lines drawn from the origin of the axes. Nevertheless, if the investor has a certain budget of tracking error – as would be the case of an institutional investor, discussed in Section 16.3.1 – then they are obliged to combine fund H with a tracker. It is represented on the graph by a point whose coordinates are close to the origin but with a positive TE and a negative TD. The combination of the ETF with portfolio H leads to a set of attainable portfolios represented by the dashed curve. Portfolio H', which is on this curve, has the same tracking error as L but is clearly dominated with a more negative tracking difference.

16.3.2.2 The efficiency indicator for trackers

Overall, the Information ratio does not seem to be a very effective criterion supporting the choice of a tracker for the pure indexer. It is not comprehensive enough to cover all relevant aspects for the investor, and its application might lead to wrong decisions both for the choice of a tracker and for the assessment of benchmarked portfolios using trackers. So, how to combine the information content of the tracking difference, the tracking error, and of all other relevant risk and return considerations in a single indicator summarizing the attractiveness of a tracker?

The conceptual solution proposed by Hassine and Roncalli (2013) is an efficiency indicator that uses the Value-at-Risk (VaR). This notion, which we have already examined in Section 6.2.5 of Chapter 6, represents the worst level of loss that will be recorded with a certain level of confidence $1 - x$. However, there is a key difference between the usage made in

Chapter 6 and the one proposed here. In the context of the design of a performance measure, we use the VaR as a measure of portfolio risk that is meant to replace the volatility of portfolio returns, for instance in the case of the Sharpe ratio. In the current context, the VaR itself represents the indicator of the tracker's efficiency by simultaneously encompassing its tracking difference and tracking error in a single expression. This is the reason why, unlike Equations (6-44) to (6-48) of Chapter 6 which use an excess VaR (or its closely related notion of excess conditional VaR), the measure proposed by the authors is the absolute VaR. The tracking efficiency indicator with the confidence level $1-x$, denoted by $\text{TEI}_P^{(1-x)}$, is generally written as follows:

$$\text{TEI}_P^{(1-x)} = -\arg\left(\Pr\left[R_{(P-B),t} - \text{bas}_{P,t} \leq \text{TEI}_P^{(1-x)}\right] = x\%\right) \tag{16-25}$$

where $\text{bas}_{P,t}$ is the tracker's bid-ask spread (in percentage points) prevailing at time t.

From this expression, considering a constant bid-ask spread, Hassine and Roncalli (2013) provide a Gaussian version of the indicator if we assume, as for the justification of the Information ratio, that the differential return $R_{(P-B),t}$ follows a normal distribution:

$$\text{gTEI}_P^{(1-x)} = \overline{R}_{(P-B)} - \text{bas}_P - z_{1-x} \times \sigma_{(P-B)} \tag{16-26}$$

where z_{1-x} is the $(1-x)$th percentile of the standard normal distribution (i.e., corresponding to $Z \rightsquigarrow \mathcal{N}(0,1)$), also called the VaR multiplier. Note that the $\text{gTEI}_P^{(1-x)}$ is usually negative.

The expression (16-26) displays the desirable properties regarding the previous discussion: It is positively related to the tracking difference and negatively related to the tracking error, and it takes into account the associated costs. For instance, if we set a confidence level $1-x = 95\%$ with an associated VaR multiplier of $z_{1-x} = 1.645$ (see Table 6-14 of Chapter 6 for different multiplier values) and set a flat $\text{bas}_P = 0.025\%$, the efficiency indicators for the three illustrative ETFs of Table 16-8 are respectively equal to $\text{gTEI}_X^{(95\%)} = -0.10\% - 0.025\% - 1.645 \times 0.25\% = -0.536\%$, $\text{gTEI}_Y^{(95\%)} = -0.454\%$, and $\text{gTEI}_Z^{(95\%)} = -0.434\%$. This corresponds to the rational ranking $Z > Y > X$ that we obtained using common sense arguments.

The idea of using a VaR measure as in Equation (16-25) opens up two interesting directions, which are not mutually exclusive, for decision-makers. The first one is to use this efficiency indicator in an optimization program, as if it were a pure risk measure. The pure index investor might choose to use it as an objective, e.g., max $\text{TEI}_P^{(1-x)}$ subject to $\text{AUM}_P \geq \text{AUM}_{\min}$ if one wants to select an ETF with a sufficiently large level of assets under management (AUM). However, the efficiency indicator can also be used as a constraint, bearing in mind that what ultimately matters economically is the tracking difference net of costs: max $\overline{R}_{(P-B)} - \text{bas}_P$ subject to $\text{TEI}_P^{(1-x)} \geq \text{TEI}_{\min}$.[13]

[13]Using expression (16-26), this example trivially reduces to a simple constraint of a cap on the tracking error. However, it makes full sense if one works with a more sophisticated assumption than the Gaussian distribution.

The second direction goes toward a more realistic modeling of the distribution of differential returns. Some ETFs drawn on very illiquid indexes, for instance, exhibit a moderate level of tracking error but occasionally move away from their target in a dramatic fashion. This would translate into very undesirable negative skewness and high kurtosis of the distribution of their differential returns. Adopting an analogous perspective as in Section 6.5.2 of Chapter 6, we can design some useful variations of the original efficiency indicator. We propose below three types of extensions, bearing in mind that they can themselves lead to more sophisticated versions. The first one is the generalized Gaussian efficiency indicator $\text{ggTEI}_P^{(1-x)}$, which takes into account the potential variability of the bid-ask spread and its correlation with the other variables. The second one is the modified efficiency indicator $\text{mTEI}_P^{(1-x)}$, which results from the application of the Cornish-Fisher expansion including skewness and kurtosis introduced in Section 6.1.3 of Chapter 6. Finally, the modified conditional efficiency indicator $\text{mCTEI}_P^{(1-x)}$ replaces the VaR with the (absolute) Conditional Value-at-Risk, introduced in Equation (6-39) of Chapter 6. The corresponding formulas are reported below:

$$\text{ggTEI}_P^{(1-x)} = \overline{R}_{(P-B)} - \overline{\text{bas}_P} - z_{1-x} \times \sigma_{(P-\text{bas}-B)} \tag{16-27}$$

where $\sigma_{(P-\text{bas}-B)} = \sqrt{\sigma_P^2 + \sigma_{\text{bas}}^2 + \sigma_B^2 - 2\rho_{P\text{bas}}\sigma_P\sigma_{\text{bas}} - 2\rho_{PB}\sigma_P\sigma_B + 2\rho_{\text{bas}B}\sigma_{\text{bas}}\sigma_B}$ is the tracking error of the net-of-spread tracker return;

$$\text{mTEI}_P^{(1-x)} = \overline{R}_{(P-B)} - \text{bas}_P + z_{x,P}^* \times \sigma_{(P-B)} \tag{16-28a}$$

$$z_{x,P}^* = z_x + (z_x^2 - 1)\frac{\mu_{(P-B),3}}{6} + (z_x^3 - 3z_x)\frac{e\mu_{(P-B),4}}{24} - (2z_x^3 - 5z_x)\frac{\mu_{(P-B),3}^2}{36} \tag{16-28b}$$

where $\mu_{(P-B),3}$ and $e\mu_{(P-B),4} \equiv \mu_{(P-B),4} - 3$ are the skewness and excess kurtosis of the excess portfolio returns, respectively; and

$$\text{mCTEI}_P^{(1-x)} = \overline{R}_{(P-B)} - \text{bas}_P - q_{x,P}^* \times \sigma_{(P-B)} \tag{16-29a}$$

$$q_{x,P}^* = q_x \times \left(1 + z_x\frac{\mu_{(P-B),3}}{6} + (z_x^2 - 1)\frac{e\mu_{(P-B),4}}{24} - (2z_x^2 - 1)\frac{\mu_{(P-B),3}^2}{36}\right) \tag{16-29b}$$

where $q_x = \frac{1}{x}\varphi(z_x) > 0$ in which $\varphi(z_x) \equiv \frac{e^{-z_x^2/2}}{\sqrt{2\pi}}$ is the value of the density function of the standard normal distribution taken at percentile z_x.

DFSO example (continued)

The allocation in cash and equivalent (i.e., ultrashort maturity fixed-income instruments) only features a precautionary amount of 2% of the total portfolio value kept on a bank's balance sheet for internal compliance reasons. For the rest, it is decided to invest in an ETF that replicates a short-term money market index. After a complete screening (type of replication, AUM, and volumes), a shortlist of three candidates was retained. Their relevant summary statistics are displayed in Table 16-9.

TABLE 16-9 DFSO example – Summary statistics for the three ultrashort bond ETFs.

	A	B	C
Tracking difference	−0.050%	−0.065%	−0.036%
Tracking error	0.024%	0.019%	0.016%
Bid-ask spread	0.010%	0.020%	0.030%
Skewness	−0.27	−0.44	−1.45
Excess kurtosis	3.75	1.66	9.89

The internal risk appetite framework has been designed according to an extreme risk approach for the management of cash, which is perfectly in line with the use of an efficiency index. The confidence level chosen is $1 - x = 97.5\%$. The CIO wishes to obtain several indicators before making the choice, with a particular care for the measure's economic relevance for the fund.

Applying various formulas of Equations (16-26), (16-28a), and (16-29a) for the TEI provides the results presented in Table 16-10.

TABLE 16-10 DFSO example – Performance indicators for the three ETFs.

	A	B	C
Information ratio	**−2.08**	−3.42	−2.25
$gTEI_P^{(1-x)}$	−0.107%	−0.122%	**−0.097%**
$mTEI_P^{(1-x)}$	−0.116%	−0.128%	**−0.114%**
$mCTEI_P^{(1-x)}$	−0.145%	**−0.143%**	−0.150%

We have shown in bold the results corresponding to the most favorable indicator for each row.

As already mentioned before, the use of the Information ratio in this context does not lend itself to a clear-cut interpretation. Tracker A has the best IR but is unambiguously

(continued)

(continued)

dominated by tracker C on both the TD and the TE. This clearly shows when the Gaussian TEI is used. The correction for skewness and kurtosis through the modified VaR estimate (with the $\text{mTEI}_P^{(1-x)}$) does not alter the ranking. It is only when the conditional VaR is used, that the favorable higher moments of tracker B are shown. Because of its thinner tail than its competitors (through a better kurtosis) and a lower tracking error than tracker A, it is tracker B that is eventually the most attractive. The interpretation goes as follows: with ETF B, there is a 97.5% chance to lose up to 12.8 basis points compared to the benchmark ($\text{mTEI}_P^{(1-x)}$), but if this happens, the average loss peaks at 14.3 basis points ($\text{mCTEI}_P^{(1-x)}$), which is the lowest among the three funds.

16.3.3 Undiversified investors

In spite of its practical relevance for many people, the question of how to assess the performance of an investment made by someone who is forced to remain undiversified, such as an individual real estate investor or an entrepreneur, remains a relatively neglected issue. Many orthodox economists would be tempted to waive this concern by stating that these types of investors are simply acting in an irrational way (after all, diversifying your portfolio is the first principle that is taught in an introductory finance course), and therefore there is no need to appraise the performance of their venture through a traditional risk–return type of metric.

This contemptuous attitude would be short-sighted, however. It is fair to say that measuring the past performance of such investments with the traditional sample-based statistical estimation is doomed to failure because of the lack of data at the individual asset level. Indeed, the actual outcome of the investment is largely binary: it has succeeded – sometimes beyond expectations, or it has failed – sometimes with a complete write-off. The *ex post* assessment of the actual risk borne during the investment lifetime is contaminated by this final result. Nevertheless, contemplating a significant undertaking that does not match the basic diversification standards does not necessarily mean that the investor acts irrationally. Consider, for instance, a scientist who manages to patent a great invention. This proprietary asset is potentially very valuable, but it requires significant cash investments to scale it up. If the business plan is convincing, this person should probably seriously consider selling most of (if not all) their financial assets to undertake the project, together with financial partners, at the clear sacrifice of the diversification of their market risk exposures. Is this a stupid move? It can be, but surely not always, as witnessed by the great success of many entrepreneurs. The point we want to make in this subsection is that this decision is worth being analyzed in a cold-blooded fashion, and performance measurement techniques can be helpful in such a context.

We assume that the investor has done their homework in a rigorous fashion: They have designed a convincing business plan, with "what if" scenario and sensitivity analyses that have enabled them to identify, regarding the investment in project P, the relevant risk and return estimates to substantiate their decision-making process. These ingredients are at least equal to three:

- The project's average yearly return across scenarios, denoted by $\overline{R}_P$;[14]
- The project returns' anticipated intrinsic standard deviation, denoted by σ_P;
- The correlation between the project and the market returns, denoted by ρ_{PM}.

This list suggests that this person's world is similar to that underlying the Standard Portfolio Theory. However, the undiversified investor denoted by j, in this context, is someone who is characterized by three specific features:

1. They hold a proprietary access to an asset, i.e., in their absence, it is not accessible to all other financial investors (this entails that $\overline{R}_P$ is high compared with σ_P).
2. In comparison with their net worth, the asset requires a personal cash commitment that is not compatible with their optimal diversification objectives and sometimes even requires the intervention of an external financial agent (i.e., they must invest a substantial proportion w_P of their own net worth).
3. The asset return exhibits a substantial specific risk that does not make it an obvious substitute for the market portfolio (i.e., ρ_{PM} is low).

Here, we make a distinction between two archetypes of situations. The first one is the "mild" case in which the investor is forced to make a significant cash outflow to purchase an asset but still has the possibility to combine it with a financial portfolio and to use some form of leverage. We call the involved persons the "buy-to-let real estate investors." The second one is more extreme: it involves a drastic choice between remaining invested with financial assets and putting a very large stake in the venture, possibly with the backing of other investors. This category is what we call "entrepreneurs."

16.3.3.1 Buy-to-let real estate investors

Many people and households whose personal net worth is sufficient are tempted to engage in direct real estate investments for purely financial motives, with the intention of extracting lease or rent income, or even to resell it with a capital gain. Usually, the unit size of the investment, including the purchase price, expenses, and refurbishment, exceeds the disposable amount that is not yet committed to financial assets. Thus, it is necessary to either (i) sell financial assets, (ii) borrow from a financial institution, or (iii) both. This strategy is called "buy-to-let"

[14]In this particular setup, the mean return is not computed from a sample of past returns but from the distribution of the future estimated rates of return. We can thus view $\overline{R}_P$ as the investor's proxy for the expected return $E(R_P)$.

and indeed generally involves leveraging a down payment with a bank loan, but also changing the investor's global asset allocation.

The typical problem of investor j who engages in a buy-to-let transaction is that they must commit at least a fraction $\breve{w}_P$ of their net worth in the project (with potentially $\breve{w}_P > 1$) in order to achieve an acceptable Loan-to-Value ratio (LTV). The question we ask is: "*What is the surplus that this project is supposed to bring with respect to the investor's required return?*" This surplus, which is similar to a measure of abnormal return, is provided by a performance measurement technique.

A common approach to this type of issue is called the *opportunity cost of capital*, initially developed in the context of entrepreneurial finance by Kerins, Kiholm Smith, and Smith (2004). These authors consider that the investor's wealth is split between the high-risk project (fixed weight $\breve{w}_P$) and the market portfolio, with a residual weight of $1 - \breve{w}_P$. Once this portfolio is determined, it is compared with a pure financial portfolio (with the market and the risk-free rate) exhibiting the same risk level. The project opportunity cost of capital, i.e., its required return R_P^{req}, is the one that makes these two portfolios equally profitable, which translates into

$$\breve{w}_P R_P^{\text{req}} + (1 - \breve{w}_P)\overline{R}_M = R_f + \frac{\sigma_j}{\sigma_M}(\overline{R}_M - R_f) \tag{16-30}$$

where $\sigma_j = \sqrt{\breve{w}_P^2\sigma_P^2 + (1 - \breve{w}_P)^2\sigma_M^2 + 2\breve{w}_P(1 - \breve{w}_P)\rho_{PM}\sigma_P\sigma_M}$ is the volatility of the investor's portfolio containing the project.

The project surplus is simply equal to the difference between its estimated average return and the opportunity cost R_P^{req}. Rearranging this equation yields the project's opportunity-based alpha for the investor, denoted by $o\alpha_P^j$:

$$o\alpha_P^j \equiv \overline{R}_P - R_P^{\text{req}} = \overline{R}_P - \overline{R}_M - \frac{1}{\breve{w}_P}\left(\frac{\sigma_j}{\sigma_M} - 1\right)(\overline{R}_M - R_f) \tag{16-31}$$

The expected surplus mostly depends on the factor $\frac{1}{\breve{w}_P}\left(\frac{\sigma_j}{\sigma_M} - 1\right)$. If the parenthesis is positive, it inflates the opportunity cost of capital, and the project's attractiveness is positively related to the weight $\breve{w}_P$ that the investor should commit. However, this is not very intuitive, as usually this commitment is viewed as a constraint.

This framework is only applicable when $\breve{w}_P < 1$ since the investor would be short-selling the market portfolio otherwise. Furthermore, the opportunity cost approach neglects two important elements: (i) the investor has access to both the market portfolio and the risk-free asset for the rest of their wealth and (ii) their feelings regarding the level of risk that they have to bear with the project are intimately linked to their risk profile, usually reflected in their risk-aversion coefficient.

The perspective proposed by Garvey (2001), which we call the *constrained certainty equivalent approach*, includes both features. Even though it was also developed in the context of entrepreneurial finance, it is particularly well suited to the buy-to-let investor's situation. Here, we consider a real estate investment with relatively low intrinsic risk σ_P but requiring a high proportional commitment $\check{w}_P$, so that the rescaled risk for the investor, equal to $\check{w}_P\sigma_P$ is relatively large. For instance, imagine that $\sigma_P = 5\%$, which is relatively defensive, but $\check{w}_P = 250\%$ because the property is onerous compared to the investor's current wealth. From their own point of view, the project's risk is equal to $\check{w}_P\sigma_P = 5\% \times 250\% = 12.5\%$. For that purpose, the investor can take a mortgage loan from the bank with a rate R_f.[15] If they wish, they can still hold a proportion of their wealth invested in the market portfolio (and potentially also use it as an additional collateral in a Lombard credit approach). The investor only cares about the expectation and the variance of the returns distribution, thus trying to maximize their Quadratic score as in Equation (9-9) of Chapter 9, with a risk-aversion coefficient of γ_j.

Garvey (2001) shows that if $\check{w}_P$ is fixed and the investor is free to allocate their wealth between the market portfolio with weight w_M and the riskless rate with weight $1 - w_M - \check{w}_P$, the portfolio P^* that maximizes their expected utility provides a constrained Quadratic score cQ^j_{P*} equal to

$$cQ^j_{P*} = R_f + \check{w}_P(\overline{R}_P - R_f) + w^*_M(\overline{R}_M - R_f) - \frac{1}{2}\gamma_j\sigma^2_{P*} \tag{16-32}$$

where $w^*_M = \frac{\overline{R}_M - R_f}{\gamma_j\sigma^2_M} - \check{w}_P\beta_P$ is the optimal weight in the market portfolio, $\beta_P = \frac{\rho_{PM}\sigma_P}{\sigma_M}$ is the project beta, and $\sigma^2_{P*} = \check{w}^2_P\sigma^2_P + w^*_M\sigma^2_M(w^*_M + 2\check{w}_P\beta_P)$ is the variance of the optimal portfolio return.

The next step is to match the expected utility obtained in Equation (16-32) with the optimal expected utility in the absence of the project, which is equal to $Q^{j,\text{req}}_P = R_f + \frac{1}{2\gamma_j}\text{SR}^2_M$, in which SR_M is the Sharpe ratio of the market portfolio (see Equation (4-3) of Chapter 4). The difference between these two Q-scores provides the constrained Quadratic alpha, or $cQ\alpha^j_P$, that reflects the investor's decision criterion to invest or not in the project:

$$cQ\alpha^j_P = cQ^j_{P*} - Q^{j,\text{req}}_P = \check{w}_P\alpha_P + \frac{1}{2\gamma_j}\text{SR}^2_M - \frac{1}{2}\gamma_j\sigma^2_{P*} \tag{16-33}$$

where $\alpha_P = \overline{R}_P - R_f - \beta_P(\overline{R}_P - R_f)$ is the Jensen's alpha of the project.

There are three ingredients to this expression. The first one represents the project's attractiveness, represented by the rescaled alpha. To obtain it, the project beta can be assessed, for instance, using market comparable REITs. An investment with low risk or low correlation with the market will be more attractive from this point of view. The second one reflects the additional gain obtained by having the opportunity to optimize the weight invested in the market portfolio. Finally, the risk penalty corresponds to the risk of the global portfolio. The project is attractive to the investor provided that $cQ\alpha^j_P > 0$, i.e., the expected utility of the constrained

[15] Logically, the borrowing rate R_b would be higher than the risk-free rate R_f. The model can be adapted at the cost of additional complexity without changing the key result; it would simply make the project slightly less attractive.

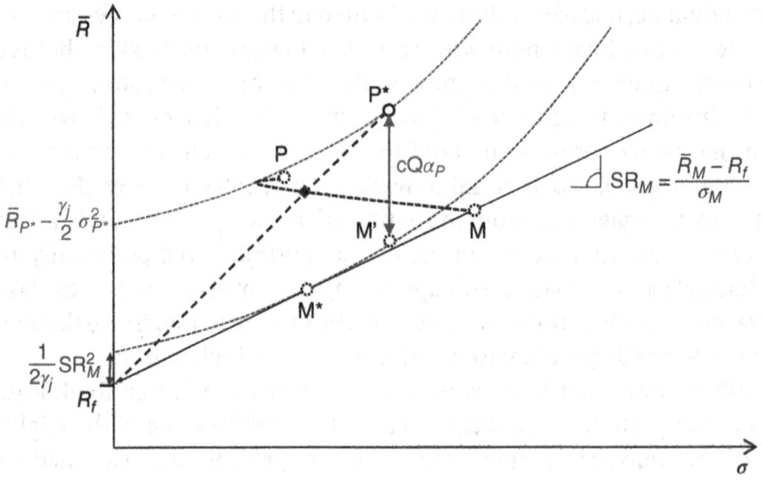

FIGURE 16-11 Graphical representation of the constrained Quadratic alpha.

portfolio featuring the project exceeds that of the otherwise optimized allocation in financial assets. It is worth noting that this performance measure can be greater than Jensen's alpha thanks to the scaling effect of the constrained investment weight $\check{w}_P$.

The logic of the constrained Quadratic alpha approach is illustrated in the graph shown in Figure 16-11.

The three investable assets are the project *P* (constrained by a minimum weight), the market portfolio *M*, and the risk-free asset whose return is R_f. In the absence of the project, the optimal allocation for investor *j* corresponds to portfolio M^* that is tangent to their indifference curve (as in Figure 9-7 of Chapter 9). In order to reach a global utility maximization, the investor first combines the risky portfolios *P* and *M* to reach the coordinates represented by the black diamond on the graph. Usually, this portfolio will be closer to *P* since the global position, including the market, is then leveraged with the riskless asset in order to respect the investment constraint, leading to portfolio P^*. The constrained Quadratic alpha simply represents the difference between the certainty equivalents of M^* and P^*, represented graphically as the vertical distance between the indifference curves.

It is important to insist about the difference in perspectives between the measures developed in Chapter 9, such as the Quadratic alpha, and the one presented here. In the former case, the performance measures are viewed as an aid to appraise the realized output of a portfolio manager from the point of view of a risk-averse investor. They can be used prospectively for portfolio selection provided that the investor accepts that the sample statistics are faithful representations of the future risk and expected return. In the current case, we are definitely forward-looking, and the performance measure is explicitly used as a criterion in a decision-making process.

To the best of our knowledge, there has been no documented similar measure developed in the context of low-risk/large-scale projects, but this approach can be used in a variety of decision-making processes, in infrastructure or timberland projects for instance, even for institutional investors.

DFSO example (continued)

Regarding DFSO's allocation to real estate, the portfolio is split into two parts: the US Real estate (US-RE) segment (15% of the global portfolio) and the rest of the world segment (5%) through an ETF.

The US RE segment is currently invested in a well-diversified portfolio of REITs for 10% of the global portfolio (thus $\frac{2}{3}$ of the segment weight), whereas the remaining 5% is kept on term accounts considering the perceived current riskiness of the real estate market. This decision is motivated by the fact that the management considers the following estimates for risk and return: $\sigma_{US-RE} = 15\%$ and $E(R_{US-RE}) = 10\%$. With a risk-free rate set at $R_f = 4\%$, the implied risk aversion for DFSO in this segment can be retrieved by the reverse engineering of the weight invested in REITs, considered to be the market portfolio in this segment: $w_{US-RE} = \frac{E(R_{US-RE})-R_f}{\gamma_j \sigma^2_{US-RE}}$; thus, $\gamma_j = \frac{E(R_{US-RE})-R_f}{w_{US-RE} \times \sigma^2_{US-RE}} = \frac{10\%-4\%}{\frac{2}{3} \times (15\%)^2} = 4$. This is the risk-aversion level that is assumed for the decision-making process.

TABLE 16-11 DFSO example – Summary statistics for the three physical RE projects.

	20th Street	4th Avenue	Broadway
Weight (in % of segment)	160%	200%	180%
Expected return	8.0%	8.5%	9.0%
Volatility	5%	7%	6%
Correlation with US-RE	0.4	0.2	0.6
Beta	0.13	0.09	0.24
Alpha	3.20%	3.94%	3.56%

After careful investigations, it is decided to replace, if possible, the paper real estate by a physical investment in a potentially large-scale (investment outlays up to twice the amount available) but a very profitable project. Three candidates have been identified: one on 20th Street in city A, one on 4th Avenue in city B, and one on Broadway in city C. Many simulations have been conducted regarding the lease rates, vacancy rates, inflation, terminal selling price, etc. together with a connection of each scenario with economic and financial conditions. The output of this long rigorous process is compiled in the summary statistics presented in Table 16-11.

(*continued*)

(continued)

At first sight, the second project (4th Avenue) displays the best potential, with a low beta and a high alpha. Nevertheless, given the parameter differences between the three properties, it is decided to carry out the analysis of Equation (16-33). The outcome is provided in Table 16-12.

TABLE 16-12 DFSO example – Performance indicators for the three physical RE projects.

	20th Street	4th Avenue	Broadway
Weight in US-RE	45.3%	48.0%	23.5%
Weight in risk-free investment	−105.3%	−148.0%	−103.5%
Global portfolio volatility	12.4%	17.0%	13.2%
Constrained Q-score	10.04%	10.12%	10.92%
Constrained Q-alpha	4.04%	4.12%	4.92%

It becomes apparent that the third project should be adopted in spite of its higher correlation with the market portfolio (and thus lower diversifying potential). To further understand the drivers of performance, it is useful to decompose the constrained Quadratic alpha into its three components (Figure 16-12).

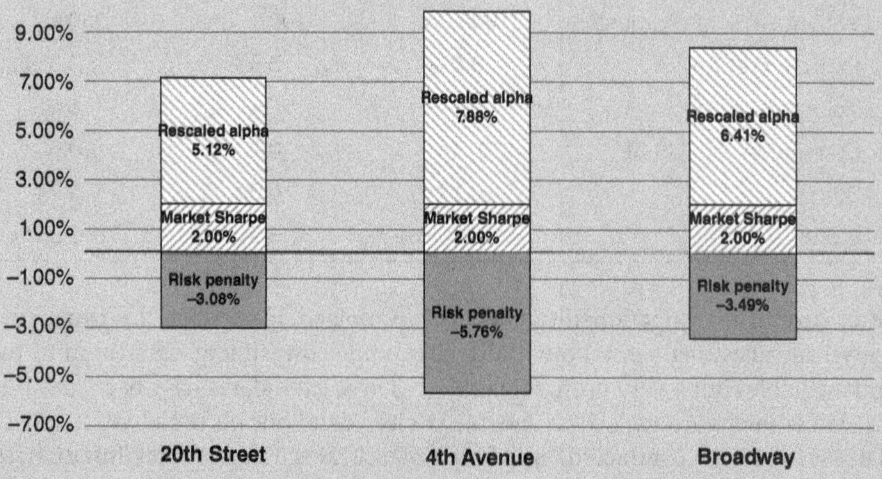

FIGURE 16-12 DFSO example – Decomposition of the constrained Quadratic alpha.

The 4th Avenue project involves a substantially larger gearing (up to 1.5 of the available amount of equity) and results in a significantly riskier global portfolio. This latter element penalizes its constrained Q-score. In contrast, the Broadway project's alpha more than compensates for the risk penalty, which explains why it also dominates the relatively safe 20th Street project.

16.3.3.2 Entrepreneurs

The entrepreneur is confronted with the decision to allocate a large share of their wealth in a single venture.[16] There are two main reasons why their situation differs from the one studied above. The first one is the nature of the project to invest in. First, a venture project generally involves a substantial risk level. Instead of increasing it through a form of leverage as in the real estate project, the decision-maker will be tempted to reduce their risk exposure by finding someone who shares the risk but also the economic rights attached to it. Second, the intervention of the risk-free investment is much less relevant here, both from a lending and a borrowing perspective. The entrepreneur will not naturally be in a position to invest a fraction of their wealth in a fixed-income investment, but they will also have a hard time – obviously with some exceptions – convincing a bank to obtain a substantial loan (at the personal, not the corporate level) in order to undertake the venture.

The starting point of the analysis is rather similar to the buy-to-let real estate investor case. There is still a project with an intrinsic risk level σ_P and anticipated mean return $\overline{R}_P$, which is presumably very high. Its size is K times (a large multiple) the entrepreneur's net worth. Thus, from their perspective, the project has a risk of $K\sigma_P$ and a return of $K\overline{R}_P$. Consequently, even though they have a private access to it, they often cannot afford to invest in the venture alone and would probably accept sharing its benefits in order to decrease their exposure.

From this perspective, Alperovych, François, and Hübner (2023) propose an approach in which the entrepreneur addresses a venture capitalist (VC) who offers to take a stake in the project at the expense of a capture of a fraction of the project's equity. There is no hard constraint on the fraction of their wealth that they have to dedicate to the venture. Rather, the determination of this weight results from an optimization process and is denoted by w_P^*.

The contract between the venture capitalist and the entrepreneur entails that, for an investment of w_P^* in the project, the entrepreneur obtains an equity ownership of $\delta \frac{w_P^*}{K}$, with δ being the dilution factor. For instance, if $K = 2$ (the project costs twice the entrepreneur's own wealth), $w_P^* = 0.5$ and $\delta = 1.2$, this means that the entrepreneur invests $\frac{w_P^*}{K} = 25\%$ of

[16] For the purpose of this subsection, the nature or stage of the entrepreneurial project does not matter. We solely focus on the financial determinants of the decision, excluding any other operational or qualitative consideration.

the total initial value of the project but obtains $\delta \frac{w_P^*}{K} = 30\%$ of the equity. Depending on the relative bargaining powers of the parties, δ can be above or below one as a result of the negotiations.[17]

In the framework proposed by Alperovych et al. (2023), setting a dilution factor of δ is equivalent to a situation in which the VC investor lets the entrepreneur simultaneously (i) invest themselves w_P^* in the project and (ii) lend or borrow the difference with their net worth $1 - w_P^*$ at a flat transfer rate, denoted by τ (if $w_P^* < 1$, then τ is a lending rate, whereas it is a borrowing rate if $w_P^* > 1$). This rate is connected with the dilution rate by the relation

$$\delta = 1 + \frac{1 - w_P^*}{w_P^*} \frac{\tau - R_f}{\overline{R}_P} \tag{16-34}$$

We use the same utility maximization approach as in the previous subsection, but this time the entrepreneur contracts with the venture capitalist, and there are only two assets to invest in: The project and an account that is remunerated at the transfer rate τ. The portfolio P^* that maximizes their expected utility provides a venture-based Quadratic score $\text{v}Q_{P*}^j$ equal to

$$\text{v}Q_{P*}^j = \tau + w_P^*(\overline{R}_P - \tau) - \frac{1}{2}\gamma_j w_P^{*2}\sigma_P^2 = (1 - w_P^*)\tau + w_P^*\left(\overline{R}_P - \frac{1}{2}(\overline{R}_M - R_f)\right) \tag{16-35}$$

where $w_P^* = \frac{\overline{R}_M - R_f}{\gamma_j \sigma_P^2}$ is the optimal weight invested in the project, which depends neither on the level of the transfer rate, because it results from the joint optimization of the entrepreneur's and the venture capitalist's expected utilities, nor on the project size K except as an upper bound for w_P^*.[18]

Equation (16-35) shows that the score is an optimally weighted average of the transfer rate and the project return penalized by half the market risk premium. As in the real estate case, the entrepreneur's optimal expected utility in the absence of the project is equal to $Q_P^{j,\text{req}} = R_f + \frac{1}{2\gamma_j}\text{SR}_M^2$. The difference between the Q-scores provides the venture Quadratic alpha or $\text{v}Q\alpha_P^j$:

$$\text{v}Q\alpha_P^j = \text{v}Q_{P*}^j - Q_P^{j,\text{req}} = (1 - w_P^*)\tau + w_P^*\left(\overline{R}_P - \frac{1}{2}(\overline{R}_M - R_f)\right) - \left(R_f + \frac{1}{2\gamma_j}\text{SR}_M^2\right) \tag{16-36}$$

[17] Considering that K corresponds to the project's post-money valuation, it can be much larger than the initial cost, because the pre-money valuation is positive. A dilution factor lower than one is not anomalous; it simply means that the VC investor captures part of the project's added value.

[18] In this setup, the VC investor is supposed to be well-diversified and to have access to the market rates $\overline{R}_M$ and R_f, which explains the presence of these two variables in the formula for w_P^*. Alperovych et al. (2023) also consider the more general case where the VC has access to different rates.

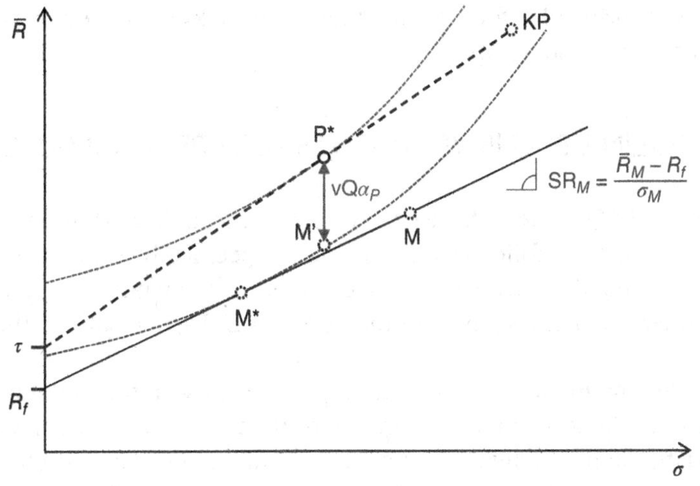

FIGURE 16-13 Graphical representation of the venture Quadratic alpha.

The investment in the project with the partnership of the venture capitalist is attractive to the entrepreneur provided that $vQ\alpha_P^j > 0$, i.e., the expected utility of the VC-backed project exceeds that of the otherwise optimized allocation in financial assets.

The mechanism of the venture Quadratic alpha determination is illustrated in the graph shown in Figure 16-13.

The availability of the VC contract is equivalent to allowing the entrepreneur to locate their optimal portfolio on a straight line originating from intercept τ, the transfer rate, and that reaches the point corresponding to the portfolio coordinates multiplied by its size, denoted by KP. This is represented by the thick dashed line. The optimal allocation leads to the choice of portfolio P^*, which is located at the tangency point with the entrepreneur's indifference curve. Interestingly, the authors prove that if the performance is positive (i.e., the new indifference curve is above the one with financial assets), it is always greater than the stand-alone investment. Thus, the entrepreneur always has the incentive to search for a venture capitalist who will offer an acceptable dilution rather than undertake the project on their own. It stands clear on the graph, on which the original optimal financial portfolio is denoted by M^*, that this is the case here.

The only specific ingredients that are necessary in order to implement this decision criterion are the project's risk and return characteristics, the investor's risk-aversion coefficient, and the dilution factor of the contract (equivalent to the transfer rate). Unlike the previous case (Equation (16-33)), the project beta with respect to the market does not intervene. Moreover, the project size K is not directly relevant (it only affects the VC's decision to propose a certain level of the dilution factor in the contract) as the entrepreneur is only concerned about their own stake in the project. Thus, this framework appears to be reasonably parsimonious and could provide useful principles for a rational decision-making process in an otherwise very emotional field of entrepreneurship.

16.4 RECONCILING ESG INVESTMENTS AND PERFORMANCE

There is no doubt that ESG criteria have become of significant importance for a growing number of investors in their portfolio selection process. Specifically, they include non-financial considerations regarding the ESG performance of issuing companies or organizations in their analysis of investment vehicles, such as mutual funds or ETFs, that contain their equity or debt securities.

Since the 1970s, many studies have attempted to answer the general question of the outperformance or underperformance of mutual funds according to their ESG characteristics. On the one hand, the standard diversification argument entails that restricting the universe of assets to only those that exhibit positive ESG externalities shrinks the investment possibilities and exposes the investor to unnecessary (and thus unrewarded) idiosyncratic risk, leading to structural underperformance. On the other hand, given the growing awareness of the need for more sustainable finance, those companies that have recognized this need earlier than others might earn a quality premium from their preparedness, leading to a long-run outperformance. The vast literature on the subject is essentially inconclusive. The purpose of this section is neither to take sides nor to discuss this phenomenon from an empirical perspective[19] but to investigate the consequences of ESG considerations regarding the investor's performance criteria in their decision-making process.

16.4.1 The ESG-extended Standard Portfolio Theory

The original Standard Portfolio Theory (SPT) introduced in Chapter 2 represents a purely financial framework in which economic agents behave rationally by maximizing their expected utility of future wealth. To do so, they only consider the expected return and risk of financial assets in their allocation decisions. This approach leaves in principle no space for non-financial considerations, which are left out of the optimal portfolio allocation program. Nevertheless, the framework has proven to be flexible enough to accommodate modifications toward more realism. This is the approach adopted by Pástor, Stambaugh, and Taylor (2021) (henceforth PST) in order to include the investors' ESG concerns in an extended version of the SPT.

The core idea of the PST equilibrium model is to simultaneously endow (i) financial assets with an "ESG characteristic" through a score that distinguishes them from each other and (ii) investors with a structure of ESG preferences through an individual coefficient that directly relates to the ESG characteristic. "Esbrown" (for ESG-Brown) assets (those with a

[19] We refer the interested reader to the comprehensive treatment of sustainable investments by Roncalli (2023).

low ESG score) will be strongly disliked by agents with an intense preference for ESG but will leave ESG-insensitive investors indifferent. "Esgreen" (for ESG-Green) assets, by contrast, will appeal to ESG-sensitive investors. From this rather intuitive way to introduce the ESG dimension into the SPT framework, the authors derive insightful results that allow us to better understand its impact in portfolio management and in the appraisal of performance.

We use a similar formulation as in Section 2.1 of Chapter 2 and use matrix notation. There are N risky assets ($i = 1, \dots, N$) with returns $R_{i,t}$. Regarding financial variables, as before, $\boldsymbol{\mu}$ denotes the vector of risky asset expected returns with dimension $N \times 1$, $\mathbf{1}$ denotes the unit vector of dimension $N \times 1$, and the $N \times N$ variance covariance matrix is $\mathbf{V}$. R_f is the risk-free rate. Investors have a risk-aversion parameter of γ that penalizes the variance of the portfolio returns in their expected utility maximization.[20]

On the financial securities side, the authors introduce an $N \times 1$ vector of observable "ESG characteristics," denoted by $\mathbf{g}$, that summarizes the quality of each asset regarding the externalities that they produce. Assets for which $g_i > 0$ or $g_i < 0$ are the "esgreen" (positive social impact) and the "esbrown" (negative social impact) ones. On the investor side, a second driver of preferences is introduced through an "ESG taste" coefficient $\delta \geq 0$. It reflects the magnitude of the nonpecuniary benefits that the agent extracts from the ESG characteristics of the firms they invest in.

Applying the same utility maximization technique as in Chapter 2, we obtain a very similar expression to Equation (2-7):

$$\max_P [\mathrm{E}(R_P) + \delta g_P] - \frac{\gamma}{2}\sigma^2(R_P) \tag{16-37}$$

The novelty resides in the portfolio weighted nonpecuniary benefit $g_P = \mathbf{w}_P{}^{\mathrm{T}}\, \mathbf{g}$, where $\mathbf{w}_P$ is the allocation vector of dimension $N \times 1$ containing all the weights assigned to each risky asset in the portfolio. Solving this problem, the formulation of the optimal allocation vector $\mathbf{w}$ is given by Pástor et al. (2021) as

$$\mathbf{w} = \frac{1}{\gamma}\mathbf{V}^{-1}\left(\boldsymbol{\mu} - R_f\mathbf{1} + \frac{\delta}{\gamma}\mathbf{g}\right) \tag{16-38}$$

Using the same logic as for the derivation of the CAPM, the key insight obtained by the authors relates to the market portfolio and the determination of the required return of each individual asset or portfolio. We first consider that γ and δ represent the risk aversion and ESG taste of the representative investor, i.e., the average value across all economic agents. Their ratio $\frac{\delta}{\gamma}$ is referred to as the market "esbrown aversion" for brevity. Isolating the vector of expected excess returns $\boldsymbol{\mu} - R_f\mathbf{1}$ from the equation and pre-multiplying it by the optimal allocation vector gives the financial market equity premium $\mu_{\mathrm{FM}} - R_f$ which is equal to

$$\mu_{\mathrm{FM}} - R_f \equiv \mathbf{w}^{\mathrm{T}}(\boldsymbol{\mu} - R_f\mathbf{1}) = \gamma\sigma^2_{\mathrm{FM}} - \frac{\delta}{\gamma}g_{\mathrm{FM}} \tag{16-39}$$

where $g_{\mathrm{FM}} \equiv \mathbf{w}^{\mathrm{T}}\mathbf{g}$ is the "esgreenness" of the financial market portfolio.

[20] As in Chapter 2, we do not directly introduce subscript j for the investor in order to simplify the exposition.

The first term of this expression corresponds to the original relationship between the risk and expected return of the market portfolio in the original SPT. The second term is new. Since we can reasonably assume that both δ and γ are positive, its sign entirely depends on that of the financial market's esgreenness g_{FM}, which is the value-weighted average of all firms' ESG characteristics. If the financial market portfolio is "esgreen," $g_{FM} > 0$ and the financial market risk premium is lower than in the absence of ESG preferences. Thus, everything else being equal, a stock market that becomes more sustainable sacrifices financial returns as a compensation for ESG benefits and vice versa if the financial market is esbrown. Naturally, if the average market risk aversion depends on the market's esgreenness, this relationship may not hold.

In what follows, we assume that $g_{FM} = 0$. This means that, on average, esgreen firms counterbalance esbrown ones or, more pragmatically, the ESG score of each firm is considered relative to the standard on the financial market.[21] Furthermore, this implies that an "esgreen-neutral" market portfolio earns exactly the same expected return as in the absence of heterogeneous ESG preferences.

16.4.2 Classical performance measures with ESG tastes

Given the modifications brought by the insertion of ESG preferences into the Standard Portfolio Theory, it is likely that the performance measures associated with this framework will be impacted as well. Indeed, Pástor et al. (2021) outline some implications for the Sharpe ratios, alphas, and betas, and for assets and portfolios. Since their framework essentially considers the negative influence of ESG financial performance (via the trade-off between financial and non-financial sources of utility), these implications are unsurprisingly unfavorable. Nevertheless, in the following discussion, we open up the field to other, potentially more positive dimensions.

16.4.2.1 The Sharpe ratio

First, regarding the Sharpe ratio, the consequences are particularly important. As discussed in the next subsection, rational investors hold not only one but two risky portfolios at equilibrium. This means that the "market portfolio" is not alone. To maximize their expected utility, the investor must complement their optimal allocation in the "financial market portfolio" obtained above, with the aim of maximizing their risk–return trade-off, with another one in the "ESG market portfolio," with the aim of maximizing their ESG score–financial loss trade-off. For a given investor j who is characterized by coefficients γ_j and δ_j, their resulting

[21] Obviously, none of these two justifications are necessarily meant to hold in practice. Compared to an absolute ESG norm, it is perfectly possible that the global industry falls short of this criterion (esbrown market portfolio) or exceeds it (esgreen market portfolio).

global equilibrium portfolio $P^{(j)}$ has the following expected return and variance:

$$\mathrm{E}(R_{P(j)}) \equiv \mu_{P(j)} = \mu_{\mathrm{FM}} - \delta_{(j-\mathrm{FM})}\left(\frac{\delta}{\gamma^3}\varphi_G\right) \tag{16-40}$$

$$\sigma^2(R_{P(j)}) \equiv \sigma^2_{P(j)} = \sigma^2_{\mathrm{FM}} + \delta^2_{(j-\mathrm{FM})}\left(\frac{1}{\gamma^4}\varphi_G\right) \tag{16-41}$$

where $\delta_{(j-\mathrm{FM})} \equiv \delta_j - \delta$ is the investor's differential ESG taste compared with the market average, and $\varphi_G \equiv \mathbf{g}^{\mathrm{T}}\mathbf{V}^{-1}\mathbf{g}$ stands for an ESG-weighted precision coefficient, which is positive.

The investor's ESG taste influences both the return and risk that they obtain. If they are more demanding than the market regarding the non-financial performance of their portfolio, i.e., $\delta_{(j-\mathrm{FM})} > 0$, then they have to accept a lower rate of return. Investors whose ESG taste is lower than that of the market benefit from a higher expected return. Because of the intervention of $\delta^2_{(j-\mathrm{FM})}$ in the expression (16-41), a larger divergence between the investor's and the market-wide ESG taste, whichever its sign, results in a higher variance than that of the financial market portfolio.

Combining these two equations leads to the formulation for the ESG-adjusted reward-to-variability ratio, denoted by RVR^j_P, which can be viewed as its *ex ante* (anticipated) Sharpe ratio of the optimal portfolio for the investor:

$$\mathrm{RVR}^j_P = \frac{\mu_{\mathrm{FM}} - R_f - \delta_{(j-\mathrm{FM})}\left(\frac{\delta}{\gamma^3}\varphi_G\right)}{\sqrt{\sigma^2_{\mathrm{FM}} + \delta^2_{(j-\mathrm{FM})}\left(\frac{1}{\gamma^4}\varphi_G\right)}} \tag{16-42}$$

The graph presented in Figure 16-14 illustrates the sensitivity of the reward-to-variability ratio as a function of the investor's differential ESG taste for various combinations of the ESG parameter values. We take as initial calibration the following values: $\mu_{\mathrm{FM}} - R_f = 6\%$, $\sigma_{\mathrm{FM}} = 15\%$, which corresponds to a market RVR of 0.4 (the circle on the graph), and $\gamma = 2$ (the simulations show that a higher risk-aversion coefficient leads to a much lower sensitivity of the ratio).

The "ESG-demanding investor," with a positive differential ESG taste $\delta_{(j-\mathrm{FM})}$, condemns themselves to sacrificing their financial remuneration, as shown by the decreasing pattern of the curves on the right of the graph. This phenomenon is reinforced when the ESG scores are rather concentrated (larger value of φ_G), which makes the investor's requirement more difficult to fulfill. Looking at the left side of the chart, corresponding to who we call the "ESG-lax investor" with $\delta_{(j-\mathrm{FM})} < 0$, we note the contradictory effects of the increase in risk premium on the one hand and the increase in volatility on the other hand. Eventually, the second effect rapidly dominates. In other words, someone who wishes to take advantage of the "esbrown premium" that rewards the poorly performing firms regarding sustainable criteria only benefits from it for small deviations from the market standard. As the negative preference

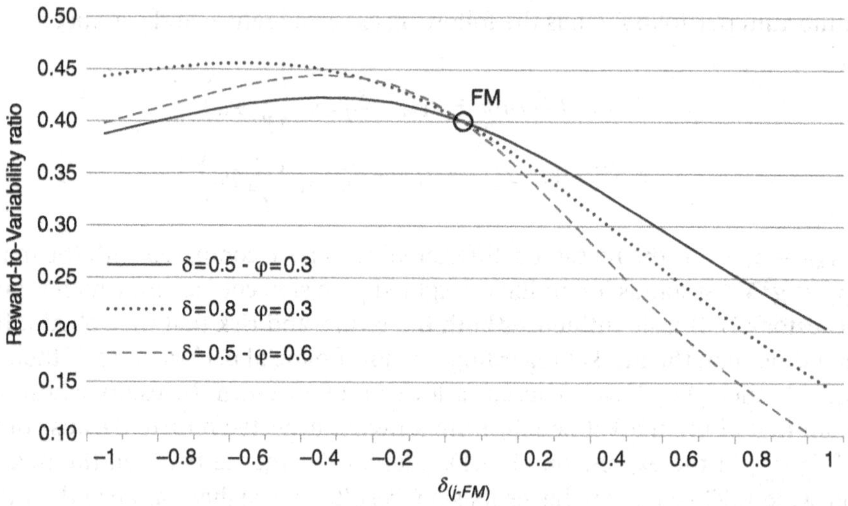

FIGURE 16-14 Illustration of the RVR of the optimal investor portfolio as a function of ESG tastes.

for ESG becomes stronger, the portfolio starts to lack diversification and the potential Sharpe ratio is affected.

The PST framework paves the way for the adaptation of SPT to ESG investment criteria and proposes many additional results that we will discuss later. The approach of Pedersen, Fitzgibbons, and Pomorski (2021) (henceforth PFP) brings additional insight regarding the use of Sharpe ratios for portfolio choice. They follow essentially the same route and reach similar theoretical results, including the shape of Figure 16-14, but they bring in three important modifications.

The first one concerns the financial market portfolio FM. Since the authors reason in terms of (absolute) ESG scores, they acknowledge that the esgreenness of this portfolio is not zero. They posit that $g_{FM} > 0$. This makes the original PST framework more difficult to handle.

The second one relates to the positive externalities brought by excellence in ESG-related indicators on corporate operating performance. This positive causal relationship between ESG and financial performance, without which there would be no financial incentive to invest in esgreen firms whatsoever, appears to be well-justified as demonstrated by Giese, Lee, Melas, Nagy, and Nishikawa (2019) among others. The knowledge of this causality obviously represents very useful information for the investment decision-making process. Agents who have this information can express return expectations conditionally of this information, whereas uninformed agents have to rely on unconditional (i.e., blind) expectations.

As a third modification, the PFP framework introduces three categories of investors instead of two in the PST framework. The "Type-M" (subscript m) is the ESG-motivated investor. In short, they are equivalent to the ESG-demanding one with $\delta_{(m-\mathrm{FM})} > 0$ and are well aware of the link between ESG score and corporate performance. The other two exhibit no specific ESG-related preference. The "Type-A" (subscript a) investor is aware of the added value of ESG characteristics but would only invest in above-average ESG stocks if they receive a financial incentive in terms of risk or expected return. The "Type-U" (subscript u) investor shares the same financial utility function as the Type-A one, but is unaware of any advantage of ESG investing. Since this investor ignores the information, they cannot recognize any risk or return element attached to the ESG characteristics of their portfolio. Even though, from an *ex ante* perspective, we could say that $\delta_{(a-\text{FM})} = \delta_{(u-\text{FM})} = 0$, both types of investors may end up holding portfolios tilted toward below-average ESG characteristics compared to the financial market portfolio, becoming *de facto* ESG-lax investors.

We present the discussion in the context of the use of performance measures for decision-making. The first major incremental result of the PFP model relates to the optimal portfolio choice as a function of the investor's risk aversion γ^j and ESG taste δ^j. Obviously, this only makes sense for Type-M investors. From a financial point of view, their problem is to maximize their expected utility while satisfying the constraint of achieving a minimum level of portfolio's esgreenness, which we denote by $g^j \equiv \delta^j \tilde{g}$ for some constant $\tilde{g}$.[22] A more demanding investor has a larger δ^j and thus a tighter constraint. This formulation has the advantage of separating the financial and non-financial dimensions, one being taken as the objective and the other one as a constraint. The solution is written as

$$\max_P \left[\frac{(\text{SR}_P^{(j)})^2}{2\gamma^j} + g_P \right] \tag{16-43}$$

where $\text{SR}_P^{(j)} = \max_P \text{SR}_P$ subject to $g_P \geq g^j$. Note that the value of γ^j is irrelevant here, as the investor is always free to use homemade leverage to change the global portfolio volatility, as in the original version of the SPT.

Note also that the financial market portfolio displays the unconstrained maximum Sharpe ratio SR_{FM} and has an esgreenness level of $g_{\text{FM}} > 0$. Two situations can arise from this optimization problem:

1. The investor's minimum esgreenness $g^j \leq g_{\text{FM}}$. Then, the constraint is not binding, and the investor chooses the financial market portfolio with Sharpe ratio SR_{FM}. Note that this is necessarily the case of the Type-A investor because $g^a = 0$: $\text{SR}_P^{(a)} = \text{SR}_{\text{FM}}$.
2. The investor's minimum esgreenness $g^j > g_{\text{FM}}$. Then, the constraint is binding, and the investor chooses a portfolio whose Sharpe ratio is lower than the market. This is the case for the most demanding Type-M investors: $\text{SR}_P^{(m)} < \text{SR}_{\text{FM}}$.

Furthermore, the Type-U investor, being unaware of the pros and cons of ESG criteria, also tries to maximize their Sharpe ratio (without ESG constraints) but might not select the best

[22] We keep and adapt the same notation as before (and thus diverge from the one of Pedersen et al., 2021) for the sake of consistency throughout the section.

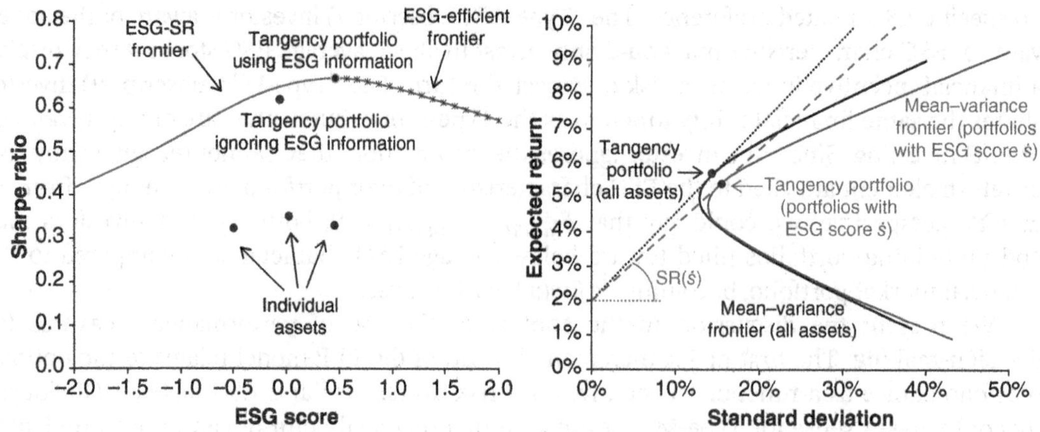

FIGURE 16-15 Illustrations of the ESG-efficient frontier and the ESG-restricted mean–variance efficient frontier. Source: Pedersen et al. (2021), Figure 1, Panels A (left chart) and B (right chart).

allocation because they neglect any potential ESG-risk premium that may favor some stocks and disadvantage others. Thus, in all generality, $SR_P^{(u)} \leq SR_{FM}$.

This first major result of the PFP framework is summarized in Figure 16-15, retrieved from their article.

The left chart illustrates the outcome of the constrained optimization of Equation (16-43). The horizontal axis represents the portfolio ESG scores (i.e., their esgreenness). The upper envelope plots the best possible Sharpe ratios for each ESG level. The top level is achieved by the financial market portfolio whose performance is SR_{FM}. Nobody who has a lower constraint on portfolio esgreenness, including Type-A investors, has an incentive to choose a worse one, but Type-U investors might actually miss this portfolio and locate below the curve, as indicated on the graph. However, investors who want a better ESG score must agree to give away some financial performance to achieve their desired ESG level. Their optimal Sharpe ratios align on the curve to the right of the financial market portfolio. This is what the authors call the "ESG-efficient frontier." This concept is illustrated on the right chart, which uses the familiar volatility-expected return axes. It shows how a Type-M investor with a high minimum acceptable esgreenness g^j (noted s^j on the graph) restricts their investment possibilities. The tangency portfolio for this investor has a lower Sharpe ratio than the market ($SR_P^{(m)} < SR_{FM}$).

How can this *ex ante* theoretical result be translated into an *ex post* performance measurement perspective? If investors are aware of their ESG profile when selecting their portfolio and actually apply the constrained optimization program of Equation (16-43), their challenge is to appraise the actual performance achieved by their portfolio in a synthetic way. It is relatively fair to say that the related financial literature is still in its infancy at the moment of writing this book.

An intuitive and appealing but *ad hoc* construct whose interpretation is globally consistent with the ESG-motivated investor's expected utility maximization is provided by Horan, Dimson, Emery, and Blay (2022). They introduce what they call the R-cube measure as a weighted sum of the original Sharpe ratio and an ESG-based performance metric. Their $R_P^{(j)3}$ measure is written as (still using our consistent notation)

$$R_P^{(j)3} = SR_P + \lambda^j \frac{g_P - g_B}{\sigma(g_B)} \tag{16-44}$$

where λ^j is the ESG intensity scaling factor, g_B is the ESG score (esgreenness) of a benchmark portfolio, and $\sigma(g_B)$ is defined as the volatility of ESG scores across the benchmark components. Horan et al. (2022) suggest that the choice of the benchmark type is left at the discretion of the use of this measure.

Unlike the traditional Sharpe ratio, the ESG-related performance component does not normalize the outperformance $g_P - g_B$ by an estimate of portfolio risk, but rather by a dispersion measure at the benchmark level that is meant to normalize the numerator by some sort of scaling coefficient. Accordingly, the authors call the ratio $\frac{g_P - g_B}{\sigma(g_B)}$ the Normalized ESG quotient of the portfolio. It tells how many standard deviations is the portfolio's esgreenness above (or below) the benchmark.

The measure is investor-specific through the coefficient λ^j. It involves a clear trade-off between financial and non-financial performance. This is why λ^j is interpreted as a scaling factor. It is obviously connected with the ESG taste coefficient δ^j, but it also mixes information about the investor's risk aversion. It is thus a hybrid construct tailored to the needs of the *ad hoc* measure.

The flexibility of the R-cube measure is welcome in order to assess periodical changes in the ESG portfolio properties. The intent is to address the potential window-dressing behavior ("greenwashing") of the portfolio manager, who might be tempted to clinch the composition of the portfolio at different reporting times but to trade without consideration of ESG criteria during interim periods. In its simplest form, the R-cube change, denoted by $\Delta R_P^{(j)3}$, is written as

$$\Delta R_P^{(j)3} = SR_P + \lambda_\Delta^j \frac{\Delta g_P - \Delta g_B}{\sigma(\Delta g_B)} \tag{16-45}$$

where λ_Δ^j reflects the investor's intensity factor for ESG change, and $\Delta g_P = \sum_{i=1}^N \overline{w}_i \frac{g_{i,t} - g_{i,t-1}}{g_{i,t-1}}$ is the weighted average change in esgreenness of the assets $i = 1, \ldots, N$ held in the portfolio during the period (the same holds for the benchmark).[23]

16.4.2.2 The alpha and beta

What does this extended framework imply in terms of asset betas and alphas using a single factor, namely the financial market portfolio? Intuitively, since the equilibrium relationships emphasized in the previous subsection involve a financial market portfolio that does not

[23]The formula becomes more sophisticated, but has an analogous form, if one wishes to measure precisely the changes in portfolio holdings during the period.

satisfy all investors, they are likely to hold other risky assets in order to fulfill their ESG tastes. Thus, the two-fund separation theorem does not hold: a third portfolio must contribute to the investor's optimal asset allocation.

Reverting to the PST framework, Pástor et al. (2021) obtain the equivalent to the Security Market Line by combining Equations (16-38) and (16-39) in the same spirit as in the original CAPM. Applying it to any security i or portfolio P, they obtain the following ESG-SML equation:

$$\mu_i = R_f + \beta_{i,\mathrm{FM}}(\mu_{\mathrm{FM}} - R_f) - \frac{\delta}{\gamma} g_i \tag{16-46}$$

where $\beta_{i,\mathrm{FM}} = \rho_{i\mathrm{FM}} \frac{\sigma_i}{\sigma_{\mathrm{FM}}}$ remains unchanged compared to the original one, considering that the financial market portfolio is the same in both frameworks.

Equation (16-46) clearly suggests that the expected asset return with ESG preferences differs from the original one by the last term $-\frac{\delta}{\gamma} g_i$, which only depends on the sign of g_i because $\frac{\delta}{\gamma} > 0$ at the market level. Thus, esgreen firms ($g_i > 0$) earn a lower premium, whereas esbrown firms ($g_i < 0$) earn a higher return.

The story is not so straightforward under the model modification brought by Pedersen et al. (2021). In their PFP model, they clearly distinguish between the unconditional (=uninformed) and conditional (informed) expected returns at the firm level. The authors consider three "extreme" situations in the financial market, each of which corresponds to one single type of investor that would dominate the trades and holdings:

- If Type-U (uninformed) investors dominate, then only Type-A and Type-M investors screen ESG criteria, but the ESG-related abnormal performance does not show up in prices. The better the ESG score of a company is, the greater the return that its stock will deliver, unrelated to its systematic risk. The conditional expected returns are written as

$$\mu_i|(\mathbf{g}, u) = R_f + \beta_{i,\mathrm{FM}}(\mu_{\mathrm{FM}} - R_f) + \pi_u g_{(i-\mathrm{FM})} \tag{16-47}$$

  where $\mu_i|(\mathbf{g}, u) \equiv \mathrm{E}(R_i|(\mathbf{g}, u))$ is the expected return of stock i conditional on the knowledge of esgreenness information $\mathbf{g}$ and the dominance of Type-U investors, and $\pi_u > 0$ is the market remuneration associated with the differential esgreenness of the stock denoted by $g_{(i-\mathrm{FM})} = g_i - g_{\mathrm{FM}}$.
- If Type-M (motivated) investors dominate, then everybody is well informed about the link between ESG criteria and performance (which is factored into equilibrium prices), but the most important group of investors is willing to sacrifice expected returns for esgreener stocks. We essentially return to the base case of the PST framework. The conditional expected returns are written as

$$\mu_i|(\mathbf{g}, m) = R_f + \beta^C_{i,\mathrm{FM}}(\mu_{\mathrm{FM}}|(\mathbf{g}, m) - R_f) - \pi_m g_{(i-\mathrm{FM})} \tag{16-48}$$

where $\mu_i|(\mathbf{g}, m) \equiv E(R_i|(\mathbf{g}, m))$ is the expected return of stock i conditional on the knowledge of esgreenness information $\mathbf{g}$ and the dominance of Type-M investors, the same holds for $\mu_{FM}|(\mathbf{g}, m)$, $\beta^C_{i,FM}$ is the beta of stock i conditional on esgreenness information,[24] and $\pi_m > 0$ is the market remuneration associated with the differential esgreenness of the stock.

- If Type-A (aware) investors dominate, then everybody is well informed about the link between ESG criteria and performance (which is factored into equilibrium prices), but investors only want to maximize their expected utility without constraints on ESG criteria. This case corresponds to the standard CAPM one for conditional returns:

$$\mu_i|(\mathbf{g}, a) = R_f + \beta^C_{i,FM}(\mu_{FM}|(\mathbf{g}, a) - R_f) \tag{16-49}$$

What Equations (16-47) to (16-49) tell altogether is that (i) for the informed investor (Type-M or Type-A), the beta of a stock or portfolio with respect to the financial market portfolio is not affected by its esgreenness; (ii) the conditional expected return has the same shape as in Equation (16-46), with an additional esgreenness term on top of the CAPM formula; and (iii) the sign of this additional term depends on who "makes the law" on the market. If investors are mostly aware (Type-A) or motivated (Type-M), asset prices adjust to the information content associated with esgreenness, and there is no ESG-related premium (Type-A) or a negative one (Type-M). If investors are unaware (Type-U), prices ignore the information content of stock esgreenness, and the best ones on this criterion earn a positive premium.

The consequences of the nuanced predictions of the PSP regarding the estimation of Jensen's alpha are important. When the traditional market model $R_{P,t} - R_f = \alpha_P^{CAPM} + \beta_{P,M}(R_{M,t} - R_f) + \varepsilon_{i,t}$ is estimated without consideration of any ESG effect, the application of the above equations produces the following outcome, using the notation π_{ESG} to reflect the ESG market premium:

$$\alpha_P^{True} = \alpha_P^{CAPM} - \pi_{ESG} \times g_{(P-FM)} \tag{16-50}$$

where α_P^{True} stands for the "true" alpha that takes into account the ESG characteristics of the firm, $\pi_{ESG} > 0$ if the market is dominated by Type-U investors, $\pi_{ESG} < 0$ if the market is dominated by Type-M investors (also in the PST framework, in which case $\pi_{ESG} = \frac{\delta}{\gamma}$), and $\pi_{ESG} = 0$ if the market is dominated by Type-A investors. Factor $g_{(P-FM)}$ reflects the portfolio's esgreenness indicator relative to the market.

We can interpret Equation (16-50) as follows: Jensen's alpha will overstate the true portfolio performance of esgreen firms when $\pi_{ESG} > 0$, i.e., the market "rewards" esgreener firms with a positive risk premium. In the PST case, in which greener firms earn a lower return, $\alpha_P^{True} > \alpha_P^{CAPM}$: the alpha measured in the traditional way underestimates the true

[24] This beta is not computationally different from the standard beta, but simply uses the conditional returns (taking into account the ESG-related outperformance) as an input.

TABLE 16-13 Summary of the signs of the ESG premium and its constituents in different markets and periods.

		North America	Eurozone	Europe ex-EMU	Japan	Global Developed
2010–2013	ESG	−−	−	0	+	0
	E	−	0	+	−	0
	S	−	−	0	−	−
	G	−	0	+	0	+
2014–2017	ESG	++	++	0	−	+
	E	++	++	−	+	++
	S	+	+	0	0	+
	G	+	++	0	+	++

Source: Bennani et al. (2018).

performance of an esgreen portfolio. Note that since the estimation of the (conditional) beta remains unchanged, the same conclusions hold for the Treynor ratio and the modified Jensen's alpha (i.e., replace α_P^{CAPM} by α_P^{True} in the computations).

According to Pedersen et al. (2021), the relatively general and inconclusive result of Equation (16-50) appears to match empirical evidence across regions and periods. This is also confirmed by the results obtained by the comprehensive study of Bennani et al. (2018) whose summary of major results regarding the sign of the ESG premium and its constituents is reproduced in Table 16-13.

The results are most contrasted on the North American (USA and Canada) markets, for which the authors evidence a very contrasted influence on stock esgreenness on their risk-adjusted returns. The evolution from one period to another is generally clear, with a market that turns from mostly unaware (Type-U) to motivated (Type-M). More recent evidence also suggests that the dominance of motivated investors has been further reinforced, but it experienced a strong pushback at the moment of the burst of the war in Ukraine and the subsequent renewed interest in fossil energy sources.

The time dependence of the ESG premium also shows important implications on the stationarity of the return distribution related to esgreenness characteristics. The truth of a past period is not that of the future one: This is particularly relevant in the context of ESG investing, as outlined by Pástor, Stambaugh, and Taylor (2022) in their study of green returns.

16.4.2.3 The influence of ESG ratings uncertainty and heterogeneity

The theoretical models developed earlier in this section overlook a very practical issue in which many users of ESG data are usually very aware of ESG uncertainty. The plethora of data vendors, variety of criteria, differences in approaches, measurement difficulties, and lack of historical data altogether lead to a much lower perceived confidence in the association between a firm's reported ESG score and its actual quality regarding its sustainable character. By extending the PST framework in the presence of ESG uncertainty, Avramov, Cheng, Lioui, and Tarelli (2022) emphasize the presence of two conflicting forces: (i) uncertainty reduces the strength of the ESG premium, leading to a lower magnitude of the associated premium; and (ii) uncertainty increases the riskiness of portfolios, leading to a higher level of the market risk premium. These conflicting forces show that the sign of the aggregate impact of preference for esgreenness on the financial market risk premium $\mu_{\text{FM}} - R_f$ can be either positive or negative, depending on which effect dominates. A similar conclusion is reached for the Sharpe ratio and Jensen's alpha, whose behavior is inconclusive as well. This entails, in particular, that *the risk premium of a green stock could exceed that of a brown stock in the presence of ESG uncertainty* (Avramov et al., 2022, p. 646).

Beyond the uncertainty surrounding the interpretation of observed ESG scores, the fact that this is an aggregation of three very different sets of indicators also creates difficulties related to their heterogeneity. An interesting takeaway of Table 16-13 is the sometimes very nuanced diagnosis resulting from the decomposition of the ESG score into its environmental (E), social (S), and governance (G) components. In general, the sensitivity of stock returns to their environmental score is more pronounced than for the other two families of indicators.

Indeed, there is no reason why investors would necessarily display the same intensity of preferences for the three types of indicators. Furthermore, the dispersion of firm scores on the three dimensions may be very high, leading to different intensities of the associated criteria. These represent very intuitive explanations regarding the potential differences between the excess returns of firms displaying different scores for the E, S, and G components. However, studies such as Choi, Gao, and Jiang (2020) and Engle, Giglio, Kelly, Lee, and Stroebel (2020) also come up with an additional objective justification regarding the E-score in particular, namely the ability of green stock to hedge climate-related risk. This means that a greener stock has the ability to protect the investor against the consequences of climate-related adverse events by concomitantly providing higher financial returns.

Pástor et al. (2021) introduce the climate dimension in their framework through a climate random variable C_t for which investors have a positive preference $c > 0$. For each firm i, the residual term of the CAPM regression has a certain "climate beta" β_{iC} with respect to this variable. Then, the authors show that formula (16-46) for the expected return of a security becomes

$$\mu_i = R_f + \beta_{i,\text{FM}}(\mu_{\text{FM}} - R_f) - \frac{\delta}{\gamma} g_i + \beta_{i,C}[c(1 - \rho^2_{\text{FMC}})] \tag{16-51}$$

where ρ_{FMC} is the correlation coefficient between the market returns and the climate variable.

Furthermore, in the special case in which the ESG score g_i represents a perfect hedge ($\beta_{i,C} = -\xi g_i$ for a constant $\xi > 0$), formula (16-51) simplifies further. In that particular case of a perfect climate hedge (CH), we can write the alpha (Equation (16-50)) as

$$\alpha_P^{\text{True}} = \alpha_P^{\text{CAPM}} - \pi_{\text{ESG+CH}} \times g_{(P-\text{FM})} \tag{16-52}$$

where $\pi_{ESG+CH} = \pi_{ESG} - c(1 - \rho^2_{FMC})\xi$. Since all elements of the last term are positive, the alpha measured under the traditional CAPM approach displays an additional upward bias compared with the true one for climate-friendly stocks or portfolios.

16.4.3 ESG risk premium and performance

So far, we have uncovered the existence of a risk premium associated with the firm's ESG characteristics, the fact that this premium is generalized across the market, and the possibility that it varies over time. These three findings in the literature suggest something familiar: the existence of a risk factor, complementing the financial market risk premium, in a multifactor model. This factor might be subsumed by existing ones, such as the "Quality" factor discussed in Chapter 7, but more research is probably needed at this stage to reach a definite conclusion.

The underpinning for the use of a multifactor model is given by Pástor et al. (2021) as an aftermath of their theoretical framework. Because an investor j expresses their preference for esgreenness, holding the financial market portfolio alone at equilibrium and leveraging it with the riskless asset (which is not necessarily green) will in general not satisfy the non-financial part of their utility function. Thus, the authors justify a three-factor separation theorem: to obtain full satisfaction, the investor simultaneously holds (i) the financial market portfolio, (ii) the riskless asset, and (iii) the ESG market portfolio.

This latter portfolio, denoted by GM, has the following characteristics: (i) it has a positive esgreenness, i.e., $g_{GM} > 0$ as long as there is an appetite for it ($\delta > 0$); (ii) it has a zero beta with respect to the financial market portfolio $\beta_{GM,FM} = 0$; and (iii) its excess return is equal to its CAPM alpha and is equal to $\alpha^{CAPM}_{GM} = \mu_{GM} - R_f = \pi_{ESG} \times g_{(P-FM)}$. Avramov et al. (2022) further obtain that a similar result holds if the market esgreenness is different from zero ($g_{GM} \neq 0$) and explain that the equilibrium choice of the ESG market portfolio is the one that maximizes the Sharpe ratio across all possibilities:

$$\text{GM} = \arg\max_{P} \frac{\mu_P - R_f}{\sigma_P} \text{ subject to } \beta_{P,FM} = 0 \tag{16-53}$$

Then, the two-factor ESG alpha α^{M+G}_P of a portfolio P is simply obtained as the intercept of a multifactor regression of the portfolio excess returns on those of the Financial and ESG market portfolios:

$$\alpha^{M+G}_P = \overline{R}_P - R_f - \beta_{P,FM}(\overline{R}_{FM} - R_f) - \beta_{P,GM}(\overline{R}_{GM} - R_f) \tag{16-54}$$

where $\beta_{P,FM} = \rho_{PFM}\frac{\sigma_P}{\sigma_{FM}}$ and $\beta_{P,GM} = \rho_{PGM}\frac{\sigma_P}{\sigma_{GM}}$ are the two factors that are uncorrelated.

Figure 16-16 graphically interprets the performance that is generated within a three-dimensional framework.

Figure 16-16 mirrors Figure 7-3 of Chapter 7, which illustrates the multifactor alpha, with the difference being that the axes are orthogonal (90° angle in the chart). The bold straight

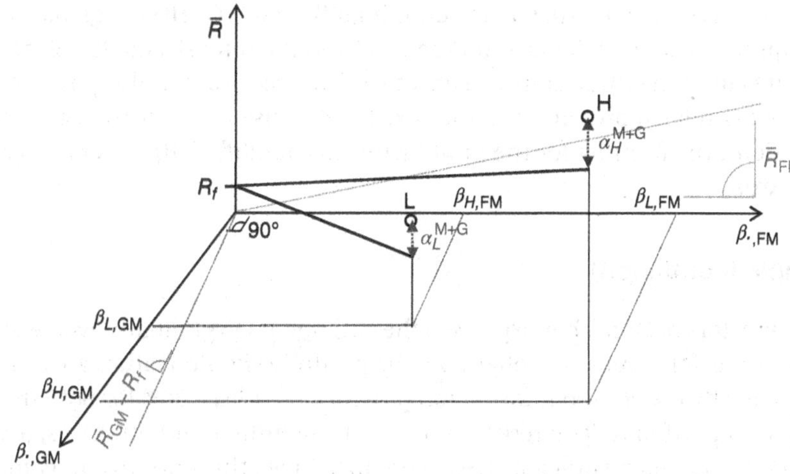

FIGURE 16-16 Graphical representation of the two-factor ESG alpha.

lines originating from the risk-free rate correspond to the expected returns for two portfolios H and L. Because the same causes produce the same effects, the same criticisms as those raised in Chapter 7 relative to the use of the two-factor alpha to assess performance apply here as well. The graph suggests that $0 < \alpha_L^{\text{M+G}} < \alpha_H^{\text{M+G}}$, i.e., portfolio H has outperformed portfolio L. Nevertheless, not only their betas are different (H has a larger beta than L for both dimensions), but also they are not proportional to each other. Thus, simply comparing their alphas makes little sense in that context.

Fortunately, the PST framework allows a rather simple application of the concept of multifactor modified alpha described in Section 7.2.1 of Chapter 7. The risk factors are orthogonal by construction, and the representative investor on the market would hold in equilibrium a fraction w_{FM}^* in the Financial market portfolio and $w_{\text{GM}}^* = 1 - w_{\text{FM}}^*$ in the ESG market portfolio, whose values depend on the esgreenness of the Financial market portfolio. Thus, we know what is the global market benchmark B and its sensitivities because $\beta_{B,\text{FM}} = w_{\text{FM}}^*$ and $\beta_{B,\text{GM}} = 1 - w_{\text{FM}}^*$. Applying formula (7-12) in Chapter 7, the two-factor ESG-modified alpha $\text{m}\alpha_P^{\text{M+G}}$ is

$$\text{m}\alpha_P^{\text{M+G}} = \alpha_P^{\text{M+G}} \times \frac{w_{\text{FM}}^* (\overline{R}_{\text{FM}} - R_f) + (1 - w_{\text{FM}}^*)\, \pi_{\text{ESG}}\, g_{(P-\text{FM})}}{\beta_{P,\text{FM}} (\overline{R}_{\text{FM}} - R_f) + \beta_{P,\text{GM}}\, \pi_{\text{ESG}}\, g_{(P-\text{FM})}} \tag{16-55}$$

The graphical interpretation is analogous to the one shown in Figure 7-4 of Chapter 7, with the two factors being identified as the excess return of the Financial and ESG market portfolios.

In practice, many construction methods can be implemented for the creation of an empirical ESG factor. Pástor et al. (2021) suggest a esgreenness-weighted average of market-adjusted returns. Pástor et al. (2022) construct a "Green-minus-Brown" (GMB) hedge portfolio in the spirit of the empirical factors of Fama and French. Given the remarks made before about the relevance of segregating the three constituents of the ESG scores, it is also possible to isolate specific E-, S-, and G-related premiums, if they exist.[25] Because it is very robust to these alternative specifications, the formula for the multifactor ESG modified alpha remains applicable in all these contexts.

DFSO example (continued)

The Board of Directors of DFSO has expressed the willingness to gradually evolve toward an esgreener equity portfolio. As a first objective, the portfolio should feature an average ESG score, as computed by the chosen information provider, of at least 30% for both the US and European Equities portfolios. The research team has identified, in both cases, a portfolio with zero market beta and a sufficient ESG score to achieve this objective in combination with the current financial market portfolio for both markets. The relevant data are reported in Table 16-14 (the risk-free rate is 4% in the USA and 3% in Europe).

TABLE 16-14 DFSO example – Financial and ESG statistics for the Financial and ESG market portfolios.

		US equities		European equities	
		Fin. market	ESG market	Fin. market	ESG market
Financial indicators	Mean	8.41%	2.80%	7.46%	0.60%
	Volatility	11.52%	11.25%	12.87%	10.74%
	FM beta	1	0	1	0
ESG indicators	Esgreenness	10%	50%	20%	50%
	ESG risk premium	0%	−3%	0%	−8%
	Dispersion (σ_g)	32%	41%	34%	28%
Performance	Sharpe ratio	0.38	−0.11	0.35	−0.22
	FM alpha	0.00%	−1.20%	0.00%	−2.40%

Starting from this information, the portfolio manager's objective is to maximize the aggregate Sharpe ratio while satisfying the constraint (30% ESG score for the global portfolio). This implies that $w_{FM(US)} = 50\%$ for the US Equities market and $w_{FM(Eur)} = 66.7\%$

[25] Indeed, it is perfectly possible that $\pi_{ESG} = 0$ as in Equation (16-49), with no remuneration of ESG characteristics.

for European equities. One must also report to the Board the consequences of this ESG requirement on the global portfolio alpha and the R^3 as a new synthetic performance measure with $\lambda^j = 0.10$. The outcome of the analysis is summarized in Table 16-15.

TABLE 16-15 DFSO example – Performance measures for the aggregate portfolios.

	ESG-US equities	ESG-Eur. equities
Sharpe ratio	0.20	0.23
FM alpha	−0.60%	−0.80%
R^3	0.32	0.32

The Board can judge whether the requirement to hold a minimum percentage of ESG assets is affordable given the risk–return objectives. The R^3 can be used as a monitoring tool in that context.

Key Takeaways and Equations

- When a new set of risky financial assets is considered as a potential complement of the initial one, the challenge is to determine whether the improvement of the efficient frontier is sufficiently important to warrant the effort of expanding the universe. There are three types of outcomes:
  - The total absence of improvement whatsoever ("spanning");
  - A partial improvement, but not for all risk levels ("intersection");
  - The new frontier "levitates" above the initial one, without any connecting point.
- The *tests for spanning and intersection* focus on the value of the generalized multi-factor alpha:

$$\alpha_i^{(Z)} = \overline{R}_i - R_Z - \sum_{k=1}^{K} \beta_{i,k}(\overline{R}_k - R_Z) \qquad (16\text{-}2)$$

(continued)

(continued)

- The hypothesis of intersection is not rejected if

$$\mathbf{A}^{(Z_I)} = \mathbf{0} \equiv \begin{pmatrix} 0 \\ \vdots \\ 0 \end{pmatrix} \tag{16-3}$$

- The hypothesis of spanning is not rejected if

$$\mathbf{A}^{(Z)} = \mathbf{0}\ \forall R_Z \tag{16-4}$$

- When a riskless asset is introduced, the Gibbons, Ross, and Shanken (1989) test focuses on the *improvement of the optimal Sharpe ratio*:

$$\widehat{F}^{(N,T-N-1)}_{\mathrm{SR}_K^*=\mathrm{SR}_{K+N}^*} = \frac{T(T-N-1)}{N(T-2)} \times \frac{\mathrm{SR}_{K+N}^{*\,2} - \mathrm{SR}_K^{*\,2}}{1+\mathrm{SR}_K^{*\,2}} \tag{16-5}$$

- We examine two situations in which performance analysis can be useful for portfolio strategy design: core–satellite allocation and the design of structured products.
- For the implementation of a core–satellite allocation strategy, an important challenge is to implement a *portable alpha strategy*. It involves adding up the alpha of a satellite portfolio to the return profile of the core:

$$R_{P',t} = R_{P,t} + w_A\alpha_A + \varepsilon_{P',t} \tag{16-11}$$

- For the implementation of a suitable structured product, two approaches are presented:
  - The *stochastic dominance criterion* is most adapted to the situation of periodic returns. The choice of a product instead of another one involves comparing the cumulative density functions of their returns distributions. The first-order and second-order stochastic dominance criteria are written as

$$P\ \mathrm{FSD}\ Q \Leftrightarrow F_P(r) \le F_Q(r)\ \forall r \in \chi \text{ and } \exists r^* \in \chi\text{: } F_P(r^*) < F_Q(r^*) \tag{16-14}$$

$$P\ \mathrm{SSD}\ Q \Leftrightarrow \int_{-\infty}^{r} F_P(x)\mathrm{d}x \le \int_{-\infty}^{r} F_Q(x)\mathrm{d}x\ \forall r \in \chi \text{ and } \exists r^* \in \chi\text{:}$$
$$\int_{-\infty}^{r^*} F_P(x)\mathrm{d}x < \int_{-\infty}^{r^*} F_Q(x)\mathrm{d}x \tag{16-15}$$

- The *mental account satisfaction criterion* involves finding the product whose terminal payoff distribution maximizes the expected periodic return while satisfying the constraint attached to the investor's mental account:

$$\max_P \overline{\overline{R}}_P^{c,H} \tag{16-21a}$$

$$\text{subject to: } \frac{S_P^-}{S} - \eta \frac{S_P^+}{S} \leq \omega \tag{16-21b}$$

- Regarding the use of performance to serve investor needs, we examine three archetypes: institutional investors, pure index investors, and undiversified investors.
- Institutional investors are mostly concerned with the *value added of their active portfolio* compared to its associated benchmark linked with their residual level of risk aversion λ_R. Its maximum level is given by

$$\text{VA}_P^* = \frac{\text{IR}_P^2}{4\lambda_R} \tag{16-24}$$

- Pure index investors are concerned with the selection of the most efficient index tracking vehicle. The Information ratio is not suitable for this purpose. The performance measure associated with the choice of a tracker is given by a *tracking efficiency indicator*. In the Gaussian case, it is given by

$$\text{gTEI}_P^{(1-x)} = \overline{R}_{(P-B)} - \text{bas}_P - z_{1-x} \times \sigma_{(P-B)} \tag{16-26}$$

- Undiversified investors, who must accept investing a substantial fraction of their net worth in a single asset, are classified into two categories: buy-to-let real estate investors and entrepreneurs. Some investment selection criteria can be designed according to the SPT framework.
- For buy-to-let real estate investors who need to use leverage to purchase an asset, their selection criterion should be based on the *constrained Quadratic alpha*:

$$\text{cQ}\alpha_P^j = \text{cQ}_{P*}^j - Q_P^{j,\text{req}} = \check{w}_P \alpha_P + \frac{1}{2\gamma_j}\text{SR}_M^2 - \frac{1}{2}\gamma_j \sigma_{P*}^2 \tag{16-33}$$

- For entrepreneurs who need to contract with an external venture capitalist, their selection criterion should be based on the *venture Quadratic alpha*:

$$\text{vQ}\alpha_P^j = \text{vQ}_{P*}^j - Q_P^{j,\text{req}} = (1 - w_P^*)\tau + w_P^*\left(\overline{R}_P - \frac{1}{2}(\overline{R}_M - R_f)\right) - \left(R_f + \frac{1}{2\gamma_j}\text{SR}_M^2\right) \tag{16-36}$$

(continued)

(*continued*)

- Reconciling environmental, social, and governance investments and performance involves integrating non-financial criteria, namely "esgreenness" g_P, in the portfolio selection decision process. A version of the SPT extended to ESG investing leads to a general formulation of the financial market equity premium expressed as

$$\mu_{FM} - R_f \equiv \mathbf{w}^T(\boldsymbol{\mu} - R_f\mathbf{1}) = \gamma\sigma_{FM}^2 - \frac{\delta}{\gamma}g_{FM} \tag{16-39}$$

- The optimal portfolio choice depends on the Sharpe ratio through the following expression:

$$\max_P \left[\frac{(\mathrm{SR}_P^{(j)})^2}{2\gamma^j} + g_P\right] \tag{16-43}$$

where $\mathrm{SR}_P^{(j)} = \max_P \mathrm{SR}_P$ subject to $g_P \geq g^j$.

- An extension of this framework to different types of investors leads to an expression for the *ESG-adjusted alpha* of a portfolio as

$$\alpha_P^{\mathrm{True}} = \alpha_P^{\mathrm{CAPM}} - \pi_{\mathrm{ESG}} \times g_{(P-FM)} \tag{16-50}$$

in which the sign of π_{ESG} depends on the investor type that dominates on the market: positive for Type-U (unaware), null for Type-A (aware), and positive for Type-M (motivated).

- The existence of ESG investment criteria leads to the implementation of a new ESG factor that justifies the use of a *two-factor ESG alpha*:

$$\alpha_P^{\mathrm{M+G}} = \overline{R}_P - R_f - \beta_{P,\mathrm{FM}}(\overline{R}_{\mathrm{FM}} - R_f) - \beta_{P,\mathrm{GM}}(\overline{R}_{\mathrm{GM}} - R_f) \tag{16-54}$$

- Because the financial and ESG betas of portfolios are not directly comparable, we advocate the use of a two-factor ESG-modified alpha:

$$m\alpha_P^{\mathrm{M+G}} = \alpha_P^{\mathrm{M+G}} \times \frac{w_{\mathrm{FM}}^*(\overline{R}_{\mathrm{FM}} - R_f) + (1 - w_{\mathrm{FM}}^*)\,\pi_{\mathrm{ESG}}\,g_{(P-FM)}}{\beta_{P,\mathrm{FM}}(\overline{R}_{\mathrm{FM}} - R_f) + \beta_{P,\mathrm{GM}}\,\pi_{\mathrm{ESG}}\,g_{(P-FM)}} \tag{16-55}$$

REFERENCES

Alperovych, Y., P. François, and G. Hübner (2023), A portfolio approach to venture capital financing. Working Paper.

Annaert, J., Van Osselaer, S., and B. Verstraete (2009), Performance evaluation of portfolio insurance strategies using stochastic dominance criteria. *Journal of Banking & Finance*, Vol. 33, pp. 272–280.

Avramov, D., Cheng, S., Lioui, A., and A. Tarelli (2022), Sustainable investing with ESG rating uncertainty. *Journal of Financial Economics*, Vol. 145, pp. 642–664.

Bennani, L., Le Guenedal, T., Lepetit, F., Ly, L., Mortier, V., Roncalli, T., and T. Sekine (2018), How ESG investing has impacted the asset pricing in the equity market. Working Paper.

Black, F. (1972), Equilibrium without restricted borrowing. *Journal of Business*, Vol. 45, pp. 444–454.

Choi, D., Gao, Z., and W. Jiang (2020), Attention to global warming. *The Review of Financial Studies*, Vol. 33, pp. 1112–1145.

Das, S., Markowitz, H., Scheid, J., and M. Statman (2010), Portfolio optimization with mental accounts. *Journal of Financial and Quantitative Analysis*, Vol. 45, pp. 311–334.

de Roon, F., and T. E. Nijman (2001), Testing for mean–variance spanning: A survey. *Journal of Empirical Finance*, Vol. 8, pp. 111–155.

Engle, R., Giglio, S., Kelly B., Lee, H., and J. Stroebel (2020), Hedging climate risk news. *The Review of Financial Studies*, Vol. 33, pp. 1184–1216.

Garvey, G. T. (2001), What is an acceptable rate of return for an undiversified investor? Working Paper, Peter F. Drucker Graduate School of Management, Claremont Graduate University.

Gibbons, M., Ross, S., and J. Shanken (1989), A test of the efficiency of a given portfolio. *Econometrica*, Vol. 57, pp. 1121–1152.

Giese, G., Lee, L.-E., Melas, D., Nagy, Z., and L. Nishikawa (2019), Foundations of ESG investing: How ESG affects equity valuation, risk, and performance. *The Journal of Portfolio Management*, Vol. 45 (5), pp. 69–83.

Grinold, R. C., and R. N. Kahn (1995), *Active Portfolio Management*. Irwin.

Hassine, M., and T. Roncalli (2013), Measuring performance of exchange-traded funds. *Journal of Index Investing*, Vol. 4 (3), pp. 57–85.

Horan, S., Dimson, E., Emery, C., and K. Blay (2022), ESG investment performance evaluation: An integrated approach. *Journal of Investment Management*, Vol. 20 (4), pp. 17–34.

Huberman, G., and S. Kandel (1987), Mean variance spanning. *The Journal of Finance*, Vol. 42, pp. 873–888.

Hübner, G., and T. Lejeune (2021), Mental accounts with horizon and asymmetry preferences. *Economic Modelling*, Vol. 103, #105615.

Kerins, F., Kiholm Smith, J., and R. Smith (2004), Opportunity cost of capital for venture capital investors and entrepreneurs. *Journal of Financial and Quantitative Analysis*, Vol. 39, pp. 385–405.

Kläver, H. (2005), Testing for stochastic dominance using circular block methods. Working Paper, Graduate School of Risk Management, University of Köln.

Kung, E., and L. Pohlman (2004), Portable alpha philosophy, process and performance. *The Journal of Portfolio Management*, Vol. 30 (3), pp. 78–87.

Levy, H., and Z. Wiener (1998), Stochastic dominance and prospect dominance with subjective weighting functions. *Journal of Risk and Uncertainty*, Vol. 16, pp. 147–163.

Lhabitant, F.-S. (2006), *Handbook of Hedge Funds*. Wiley, Wiley Finance Series.

Linton, O., Maasoumi, E., and Y.-J. Whang (2005), Consistent testing for stochastic dominance under general sampling schemes. *Review of Economic Studies*, Vol. 72, pp. 735–765.

Maalej, H., and J.-L. Prigent (2016), On the stochastic dominance of portfolio insurance strategies. *Journal of Mathematical Finance*, Vol. 6, pp. 14–27.

Pástor, L., Stambaugh, R. F., and L. A. Taylor (2021), Sustainable investing in equilibrium. *Journal of Financial Economics*, Vol. 142, pp. 550–571.

Pástor, L., Stambaugh, R. F., and L. A. Taylor (2022), Dissecting green returns. *Journal of Financial Economics*, Vol. 146, pp. 403–424.

Pedersen, L. H., Fitzgibbons, S., and L. Pomorski (2021), Responsible investing: The ESG-efficient frontier. *Journal of Financial Economics*, Vol. 142, pp. 572–597.

Roncalli, T. (2023). *Handbook of Sustainable Finance*. Available at `http://www.thierry-roncalli.com/SustainableFinance.html`

Treynor, J. L., and F. Black (1973), How to use security analysis to improve portfolio selection. *Journal of Business*, Vol. 46, pp. 66–86.

Vanguard (2017), *Vanguard's Guide to Core–Satellite Investing*. Available at https://static.vgcontent.info/crp/intl/auw/docs/resources/adviser/GuideToCoreSatelliteInvesting.pdf

CHAPTER 17

Performance and Predictability

INTRODUCTION

Measuring portfolio performance would be of limited use if it was not also a tool to predict the future. After all, if an active portfolio manager has been found to outperform (the market or their competitors), this might indicate the presence of superior skills that would enable them to reproduce the same achievements after the observation date. Obviously, evidencing some connection between past realization of some variables and future indicators of portfolio management quality is a major challenge. Every investor, analyst, or even manager would consider this a valuable piece of information.

However, before reaching this objective, many methodological choices have to be made. It would not be wise to go ahead first in some exploratory studies without having in mind what kind of relationship could be emphasized. Is this going to be a pure performance persistence study (past performance predicts future performance) or something wider than that? Is performance an input, an output, or both? What other variables should be considered? Are we considering the portfolio in isolation or within a group of competitors? These elements should be dealt with early in the process in order to design an adequate analytical framework. Furthermore, it is important to avoid falling into different types of traps in different stages of the process (data gathering, model implementation, and interpretation of results). All these elements are discussed in the first, nontechnical section, before we dig into the main types of models.

Absolute persistence in performance consists of the identification of portfolio-specific abilities to sustain a certain level of performance over time. It is the least researched area in this field. However, it is a very important issue for the investor. We discuss how to apply this type of analysis within two unconventional frameworks, namely the rolling windows and the persistence horizon approaches. A technically more challenging, but very powerful method is the estimation of the *Hurst exponent* of a portfolio, which indicates the long-run memory of its observed performance.

Within the context of *relative persistence*, to which the bulk of empirical studies belong, the objective is more easily attainable, but equally challenging: distinguishing the "persistently good" and, possibly, the "persistently bad" managers compared to the rest of a homogeneous group. This is essentially a ranking-based approach, for which we can distinguish two main types of applications. The *recursive portfolio analysis* uses an ordinal method to classify funds according to their past performance and then studies the subsequent performance of portfolios based on these rankings. The *matched ranking analysis* is fully ordinal: it looks at portfolio rankings before and after the moment of the observation and establishes the possible connection between the two. The use of *contingency tables* belongs to this approach.

There have been many scientific research papers devoted to the topic of relative persistence. The purpose of this chapter is not to carry out another extensive literature review. Rather, we concentrate on the workable takeaways that can be retrieved from this research. We hope that this will optimize the usefulness of our discussion.

The PrediLab Analytics Example

The management of the GTN Asset Management Company, whose flagship funds were examined in Chapters 4 and 5, has appointed the experts of PrediLab Analytics, a consultancy company that specializes in persistence analysis, to perform a deep dive exercise on the Thematic fund, and in particular on the predictability of a series of indicators with the help of selected performance metrics.

The consultant is endowed with the detailed risk and return data of 10 comparable funds, including the Thematic one, as well as the market index **M** and the risk-free asset **F** (set at a constant value of 1.44%) during two consecutive time periods.

Over the first time period, the market has obtained a mean return $\overline{R}_{M,1} = 7.39\%$ and volatility $\sigma_{M,1} = 8.83\%$. The risk and return characteristics of the 10 considered funds as well as their correlation with the market return are summarized in Table 17-1 (equivalent to the data of Table 4-14 of Chapter 4).

TABLE 17-1 Predilab example – Means, volatilities, and correlations for the peer group during period 1.

Fund	Mean	St. dev.	Correlation (M)
Thematic	4.72%	6.41%	0.48
B1	4.51%	5.75%	0.63
B2	5.12%	7.65%	0.45
B3	4.11%	3.96%	0.61
B4	6.28%	6.23%	0.90
B5	7.01%	8.21%	0.79
B6	3.99%	4.52%	0.85
B7	3.52%	3.79%	0.53
B8	4.39%	5.43%	0.51
B9	4.22%	5.90%	0.75

The following period at the same time exhibits more volatility and a lower risk premium. For the market index, the mean return $\overline{R}_{M,2} = 4.21\%$ and volatility $\sigma_{M,2} = 11.15\%$. The risk-free rate equals 2.40% per year (Table 17-2).

TABLE 17-2 Predilab example – Means, volatilities, and correlations for the peer group during period 2.

Fund	Mean	St. dev.	Correlation (M)
Thematic	4.09%	7.72%	0.39
B1	3.46%	6.73%	0.45
B2	3.69%	9.23%	0.29
B3	7.63%	8.54%	0.55
B4	5.36%	10.95%	0.86
B5	2.85%	5.51%	0.39
B6	6.01%	8.99%	0.50
B7	3.20%	6.07%	0.35
B8	5.61%	5.02%	0.25
B9	3.31%	4.21%	0.34

These joint tables serve as the basis for further analyses. More detailed information is released progressively throughout the chapter.

17.1 WHAT DOES PREDICTABILITY ENCOMPASS?

Why measure performance? There are two main reasons: a backward-looking one and a forward-looking one. The backward-looking perspective aims at controlling the quality of the portfolio management process. It belongs to the traditional "preparation–execution–control" managerial cycle examined in Chapter 1 and represents the cornerstone of the control stage. The chapters devoted to performance measurement are largely in line with this point of view. The forward-looking perspective is more ambitious but also hazardous. If past performance is a predictor of the future one, then it is possible to design investment strategies aiming to capture the benefits induced by the signal and deliver extra returns. Conversely, if there is no connection between the past and future performance whatsoever, i.e., reproducing past good or bad returns is purely a matter of luck, then the whole exercise is worthless and just represents a waste of time and resources.

Evidencing the existence or the absence of any link between past and future performance has been a major concern since the advent of the CAPM, and more particularly Jensen's (1968) claim that mutual fund managers apparently did not generate positive abnormal returns on average. The initial thunderbolt in this field came from the study of Carhart (1997). He associated the apparent empirical evidence of persistence in performance (called in this context the "hot hands" effect) with the portfolio's sensitivity to momentum effect discussed in Chapter 7 and showed not only that positive persistence could not be found, but also that the only convincing evidence was that of "negative persistence" among the worst managers.

Since the publication of Carhart's (1997) study, an important stream of literature has been devoted to the identification of performance persistence in the mutual and alternative investment fund industries, and the investigation of its potential causes. Our aim in this chapter is nevertheless not to produce an exhaustive literature review of the research outputs in this field. Rather, in this section, we identify the "what," the "why," and the "how" of performance predictability analysis.

17.1.1 The potential links between performance and predictability

The classical approach about predictability mentioned above is rather restrictive, as it only considers past and future performance, with the exclusion of any other type of indicator. It is necessary to enlarge this perspective because the potential links between performance and predictability are likely to be a complex nexus of relations.

The common denominator of all these connections involves two elements: (i) the use of one or several performance measures involving a specific portfolio under analysis (denoted as *P*) and (ii) a functional relation between past observations made on some random variables, on the one hand, and the future anticipated realizations of random variables (that can be similar or different), on the other hand.

Indeed, one can consider a variety of setups in which these two conditions would be fulfilled. We distinguish the following four generic situations, ordered from the simplest to the most sophisticated case.

1. *Intrinsic pure performance prediction* only focuses on a specific portfolio's past and future performance measures. This is the simplest case in which one tries to predict the future performance of a portfolio using one or several past observations of performance measures (the same as the one to be forecasted or different ones) using a mapping function. This type of model can be represented as

$$\Pi(m_{P,t\rightarrow}) = \Lambda(\mathcal{M}_{P,\rightarrow t-1}) \quad (17\text{-}1)$$

where $\Pi(m_{P,t\rightarrow})$ is a prediction function (e.g., the expectation or the sign) of a performance measure m for portfolio P for a period of time starting at the present time t and denoted by "$t \rightarrow$," $\Lambda(\cdot)$ is the forecasting function, and $\mathcal{M}_{P,\rightarrow t-1}$ is a vector of performance measures associated with the same portfolio P for a period of time ending at the past time $t-1$ and denoted by "$\rightarrow t-1$." A simple example of this kind of model would be a linear regression of the current performance on its lagged value.

2. *Multiple pure performance prediction* adopts the same stance as before but simultaneously deals with several comparable portfolios, both for the predictors and for the forecasts. Its corresponding equation is written as

$$\Pi(m_{P,t\rightarrow}, m_{\{\nsim P\},t\rightarrow}) = \Lambda(\mathcal{M}_{P,\rightarrow t-1}, \mathcal{M}_{\{\nsim P\},\rightarrow t-1}) \quad (17\text{-}2)$$

where $\{\nsim P\}$ stands for the set of portfolios that are simultaneously examined, but excluding P. A typical application of this approach is the intertemporal comparison of portfolio rankings before and after the current observation date.

3. *Generalized performance prediction* opens up the set of potential performance predictors to other types of portfolio-specific variables that are deemed relevant. The model can focus on intrinsic or multiple performance prediction. In its most generic form, the equation is written as

$$\Pi(m_{P,t\rightarrow}) = \Lambda(\mathcal{M}_{P,\rightarrow t-1}, \mathcal{Q}_{P,\rightarrow t-1}) \quad (17\text{-}3a)$$

$$\Pi(m_{P,t\rightarrow}, m_{\{\nsim P\},t\rightarrow}) = \Lambda(\mathcal{M}_{P,\rightarrow t-1}, \mathcal{M}_{\{\nsim P\},\rightarrow t-1}, \mathcal{Q}_{P,\rightarrow t-1}, \mathcal{Q}_{\{\nsim P\},\rightarrow t-1}) \quad (17\text{-}3b)$$

where $\mathcal{Q}_{P,\rightarrow t-1}$ and $\mathcal{Q}_{\{\nsim P\},\rightarrow t-1}$ are vectors of variables other than performance measures associated with portfolio P and its complement $\{\nsim P\}$ for a period of time ending at the past time $t-1$. This approach can be viewed as an extension of the previous one, in which the analysis is enhanced by the use of any indicator that proves to be effective in predicting portfolio performance.

4. *Generic prediction using performance* uses performance measures (possibly among other predictors) in order to forecast another type of portfolio-specific indicator.

$$\Pi(\mathcal{q}_{P,t\to}) = \Lambda(\mathcal{M}_{P,\to t-1}, \mathcal{Q}_{P,\to t-1}) \tag{17-4a}$$

$$\Pi(\mathcal{q}_{P,t\to}, \mathcal{q}_{\{\sim P\},t\to}) = \Lambda(\mathcal{M}_{P,\to t-1}, \mathcal{M}_{\{\sim P\},\to t-1}, \mathcal{Q}_{P,\to t-1}, \mathcal{Q}_{\{\sim P\},\to t-1}) \tag{17-4b}$$

where $\mathcal{q}_{P,t\to}$ and $\mathcal{q}_{\{\sim P\},t\to}$ are variables other than performance measures associated with portfolio P and its complement $\{\sim P\}$ for a period of time starting at the present time t. The most studied of these types of variables in the literature is the flow of funds entering or leaving the portfolio, especially in the case of mutual funds.

This list represents the starting point of many ways to implement a model for predictability analysis involving performance measures.

17.1.2 Why would predictability exist or not?

The debate initiated by Jensen (1968) about whether professional asset managers are able to deliver net-of-fees positive abnormal returns to the benefit of their investors has obvious implications for the study of predictability. If Jensen's claim – subsequently confirmed by many other studies – is correct, then finding evidence of superior performance by an active portfolio manager would be the result of pure luck, and finding persistence in this performance would be even more lucky. To illustrate this, consider the null hypothesis regarding a specific performance measure of the kind: "The portfolio manager does not deliver any abnormal performance" with a confidence level of 95%. If this hypothesis holds true and the statistical test is well specified, about 5% (one minus the confidence level) will be diagnosed as delivering positive performance. However, if we take a subsequent, non-overlapping time period and replicate the same test on the same group of managers, there will be another 5% of the managers who will have statistically beaten the market by chance. What, then, is the proportion of the whole group of managers who have posted significant performance *twice*? Because this is a pure random outcome and hazard has no memory, this proportion would be 5% × 5% = 0.25%. Out of a population of 1000 managers, this would only spot two or three of them. Thus, to believe in performance persistence, one has to first accept the idea that some managers are indeed able to distinguish themselves through their outperformance or underperformance.

The whole question about the use of portfolio performance in the assessment of some sort of predictability therefore seems to hinge on the assumption that realized performance is not a pure element of noise. Nevertheless, the reality is not that straightforward. We have to distinguish three ways to use performance in this context: whether performance is used as an input, an output, or both an input and an output.

17.1.2.1 Performance as an input

If investors choose an actively managed portfolio, they must usually be convinced that its manager has some kind of skill enabling them to outperform the market or their peers. Starting from this statement, it is understandable to consider that portfolio performance could serve as the basis for the prediction of various variables that depend on the investor's response to information about past performance.

Inflows and outflows represent a first set of natural candidates as predicted variables. In the world of mutual funds, it has been documented for many years (see, e.g., Chevalier and Ellison, 1997) that many investors "chase performance" and tend to invest in past winning funds, creating a phenomenon of a "dumb money" effect in the case of absence of any particular skill among the managers. An alternative, rational explanation of the link between fund flows and past performance is provided by Berk and Green (2004). They show that, if some fund managers actually display the necessary skills to outperform the market, investors who recognize it will flow massive new cash to the best funds. These inflows will hamper their potential to outperform and, if the market is sufficiently competitive, will pull the performance back to that of their peers. In a sense, the predictability shifts from future performance to cash flows. Both types of explanations induce a positive relation between past performance and future flows. This, in turn, might induce the predictable character of other related types of variables.

The first category of indicators affected by past performance refers to attributes linked to the behavior of portfolio managers themselves. Since the most successful ones tend to attract additional funds, they can adjust their fee levels upward. On the other hand, the underperforming funds are likely to experience outflows that can lead to a higher management turnover due to the disappointment of their investment firms.

The second category is directly related to portfolio characteristics. As an outcome of superior or inferior past performance, some managers may decide to modify the systematic risk exposures (style shift) or the total risk level of their portfolios. This can be particularly anticipated in the case of underperforming funds, whose managers could respond by gambling on a risk-based recovery in a typical principal–agent conflict.[1] Another output of past performance is the probability of a fund's survival on a stand-alone basis. The consequence of a disappointing performance, either through outflows or the fragility of the manager's tenure, might indeed simply be the decision to close the fund, either through liquidation or a merger with another fund. While this event does not *per se* represent a substantial loss for the investor, it sometimes comes at a significant cost that may affect their net return.

All these potential relationships between past performance and future variables yield potentially testable implications. Some have been investigated in the scientific literature, while others have not. In addition, one may also think about other output variables that are worth further analysis.

[1]This type of situation is examined in depth in Chapter 18.

17.1.2.2 Performance as an output

In general, when performance measures are involved as an output, predictability is called "persistence." The use of this term can be explained by the fact that the ability to consistently reproduce superior or inferior performance levels over consecutive time periods is intimately tied to the portfolio manager's skill. It is thus natural to associate performance predictability with their capacity to persistently outperform the market or their peers.

The vast majority of research produced in the field of persistence focuses on ways to forecast future performance with whichever indicator, based on public information (i.e., available to investors), that is considered relevant. Besides past performance itself (discussed below), several types of indicators have been considered, either because of theoretical or empirical reasons.[2] They can be categorized as follows, bearing in mind that this list is not meant to be exhaustive and that this type of research has a strong exploratory character:

1. *The fund*: Some of the characteristics of a fund can serve as predictors of its future performance. As explained by Boyson (2007), the Berk and Green (2004) model implies that the *size* and *age* of a fund can be used as predictors of future performance. The rationale for this dependence is the potentially faster adjustment of performance metrics to variations in fund flows for young and small funds. For these kinds of funds, we can expect a stronger dependence of future performance on past performance, i.e., a greater negative persistence in performance.[3] Additionally, a fund's *expense ratio* may also influence the investors' reactions to superior or inferior performance: they would probably forgive more easily a disappointing return if the fund is relatively cheap than if it costly. Unsurprisingly, Bu and Lacey (2009) find a positive relation between this variable and the probability of a fund's termination. Finally, the initial argument of Berk and Green (2004) can actually be reverted: *Cash flows* entering or leaving a fund also serve as a predictor of future performance. This is shown, among others, by Kosowski, Naik, and Teo (2007) in the context of hedge funds, whose dependence between flows and subsequent performance appears to be particularly pronounced.
2. *The manager*: It is natural to focus on the fund manager as a potential determinant of future performance. After all, this person and their team are the main, if not only people, responsible for the outcome of the active portfolio manager. Several studies, cited by Cremers et al. (2019), have emphasized the link between the lead manager's *education* and their fund's future performance. Consistent with agency theory, we can also expect a positive link between *stake* (ownership proportion) held by the manager in the fund and its subsequent capacity to outperform. This relative importance of having "skin in the game" is confirmed, among others, by Cremers, Driessen, Maenhout, and Weinbaum (2009) and Khorana, Servaes, and Wedge (2007).

[2] See Cremers, Fulkerson, and Riley (2019) for a recent comprehensive literature review.

[3] This explanation entails that variables such as fund age and size should be used in conjunction with past performance, also used as an input.

3. *The market*: The relative impact of the manager's skills can differ depending on the prevailing conditions in financial markets. As shown by Kacperczyk, van Nieuwerburgh, and Veldkamp (2014), asset selection and market timing skills, which represent the two main drivers of a manager's ability to outperform the market, may produce different outcomes according to prevailing *market cycles* (bear and bull markets). Other stock market characteristics, such as their level of *liquidity* or *volatility*, may affect the capacity of managers to successfully implement their skills.
4. *The industry*: Because most of the persistence in portfolio performance is measured relative to a homogeneous group, the structure of the competition within this group might play a substantial role in predictability. First of all, the *nature* of the assets in which fund managers invest is important. For asset classes in which illiquidity levels and barriers to entry are important, such as private equity (Kaplan and Schoar, 2005) or high-yield fixed income (Huij and Derwall, 2008), persistence is more likely to be found than in markets that tend to integrate information efficiently into prices. Second, the *competitiveness* of the industry matters. As shown by Hoberg, Kumar, and Prabhala (2018), managers who face less competition within their category typically achieve a performance level that is more consistent over time. Finally, Darolles, Gagliardini, and Gouriéroux (2014) show that the *interdependences* between managers (through frailty or contagion effects) may also have adverse effects on their future performance, including fund termination probabilities.
5. *The holdings and trades*: This dimension is probably the most heavily tested type of input regarding the determinants of performance persistence.

   Regarding fund holdings, the notion of *active share* (i.e., a measure of the distance between the portfolio's and the benchmark's holdings) proposed by Cremers and Petajisto (2009) and already discussed in Chapter 13 (Equation (13-11)) appears to be an important potential predictor of future performance. The rationale is that managers who dare to move away from the assets' benchmark weights have the ability to outperform their peers, even though this finding has been largely challenged.[4] According to Kacperczyk, Sialm, and Zheng (2005) and more recently confirmed by Goldman, Sun, and Zhou (2016), another important predictor of future performance appears to be the *concentration* of the portfolio's holdings, with the idea that more focused managers achieve better and more consistent performance levels over time.

   The way fund managers trade their positions is another potential major predictor. As theoretically shown and empirically confirmed by Pástor, Stambaugh, and Taylor (2017), portfolio *turnover* stands as a predictor of future performance. Moreover, Kacperczyk, Sialm, and Zheng (2008) show how active management can be proxied by the *return gap*, which represents the difference between the actual portfolio returns and the theoretical ones considering the portfolio's reported holdings. Consistent with

[4] See Cremers et al. (2019) for a discussion.

the findings made with the active share, the authors show that the return gap is a good persistence indicator.

6. *The exposures*: As a final set of candidates in our list, the portfolio's risk exposures, measured through the sensitivities to common factors, may also signal how the manager is likely to subsequently generate outperformance. The general principle is similar to those underlying holdings and trades indicators: Proxies for active management represent predictors of future performance, especially if the manager is good at identifying breaches in the hypothesis of informationally efficient markets. This all began with the Carhart (1997) study, which identified the momentum factor as a key premium on which active managers could position themselves to generate abnormal returns. In the same spirit, Amihud and Goyenko (2013) evidence that the *statistical significance* of a multifactor regression of the fund's returns, represented by its R^2, is a negative indicator of persistence: The lower this significance is, the greater the subsequent ability to outperform. Another type of indicator is the *style choice* made by the portfolio manager depending on market conditions. For instance, Massa and Yadav (2015) show that the exposure to "high-sentiment stock" (i.e., stocks that are prone to investor speculative bets) negatively affects the manager's persistence. Finally, some *risk indicators* can themselves be relevant to forecast future performance. For instance, Riley and Yan (2022) emphasize the negative relationship between a fund's maximum drawdown (as defined in Chapter 6) and its consecutive performance.

The items contained in this list represent the dimensions that have been shown to have a potentially significant influence on future performance. The literature is constantly evolving in this area. This shows how rich and intense the question of the drivers of performance persistence has been and still is in the field of active portfolio management.

17.1.2.3 Performance as input and output

The first obvious potential driver of future portfolio performance is the realized one. This is indeed the natural consequence of the assumed existence of superior abilities displayed by some managers: They should be able to prove that the one-period performance is not the outcome of pure luck but rather reproduces itself over time. Furthermore, there is an indirect effect. If any indicator listed above is a potential predictor of future performance, then in turn its materialization should itself allow further performance prediction. This also explains why, in some studies, performance measures may simultaneously be used with other variables in order to maximize the predictive feature of the model.

Using performance measures both as inputs and outputs has two major advantages. It makes the interpretation and communication of the results substantially easier by addressing a direct connection between the past and future results of the portfolio management process. It also allows a wider view of the possible dependence structure of performance over time.

In particular, as emphasized by Droms (2006), the presence of *negative* persistence (i.e., persistence mostly identified among the worst performers), which appears to be easier to detect than positive performance, is made possible with this approach.

Nevertheless, even though prior performance stands as the most obvious input for persistence studies, evidencing predictability in practice is a major challenge. There are three main reasons for this difficulty.[5] First, as discussed in Chapter 11, there exists a multitude of performance measures that encompass many possible dimensions. This diversity might lead to picking the wrong set of performance measures compared to the real ones on which managers compete with each other and/or with the market. Finding no evidence of persistence could reveal, instead of the absence of continuity in the performance, simply an incorrect selection of performance measures. This is the reason why some studies, like in Cogneau and Hübner (2015; 2020), use composite measures to overcome this issue.

Second, there exists a substantial danger of confusing performance with something else, thereby either missing the link or, on the contrary, uncovering some false impression of persistence. The first phenomenon occurs when the performance measure is misspecified and encompasses something else that is indeed persistent. This is a typical issue when multifactor models are used in order to measure performance, as it is the case in many studies. If a relevant risk factor has been ignored, part of the abnormal return may be attributed to outperformance instead of the exposure to a risk premium. Provided that this premium is usually positive (for instance, in the case of remuneration for extreme but rare risks), this will be translated into a diagnosis of persistence. The second phenomenon might occur because of the noise that is inherent to the estimation of performance. Some methods have been developed in order to minimize this estimation error, as will be discussed in Section 17.1.4.

Finally, contamination issues may alter the link between the measure of performance and the real value of the manager's skill. This may happen when the return to the investor differs from the one generated by the manager, typically because of various costs and fees. As Barras, Scaillet, and Wermers (2010) show, the proportion of outperforming managers before fees is substantially larger when net-of-fee returns are used to estimate performance. Not surprisingly, Cuthbertson, Nitzsche, and O'Sullivan (2022) find that adjusting for the fees reinforces the diagnosis of persistence when it is present.

17.1.3 Types of persistence analyses

Following Jensen's (1968) and Carhart's (1997) studies, much of the research published in the field of active portfolio management has fueled a substantial skepticism regarding the ability of managers to "beat the market," especially when the analysis is carried out on returns net of management fees and other expenses. On the other hand, as Berk and Green (2004) also point out, it is possible to have a situation in which managers simultaneously exceed (or fall short of) their passive benchmark whereas they do not manage to distinguish from each other

[5]These issues will be discussed in detail in Section 17.1.4.

because of the competitiveness of the fund market. These two types of reasoning – skepticism over managers' skills and market competition – both justify why the literature is split into two types of studies, respectively termed absolute and relative persistence analysis, with a strong dominance of the second category.

17.1.3.1 Absolute persistence analysis

The natural extension of portfolio performance measurement over a single period of time is the comparison of this observation with another one, made during a subsequent period, with a view to establishing a relationship between the two. Absolute persistence refers to the study of the nature and materiality of this relationship, which excludes observations made on other portfolios of funds. This encompasses the cases of Equations (17-1), (17-3a) and (17-4a).

In its simplest form, the prediction function Π takes the form of the expectation operator, and the forecasting function Λ is a linear combination of its arguments. Taking Equation (17-3a) as the generic case, this would translate into:

$$\mathrm{E}(m_{P,t\rightarrow}) = \lambda_0 + \sum_k \lambda_k m_{P,k,\rightarrow t-1} + \sum_l \varphi_l q_{P,l,\rightarrow t-1} \tag{17-5}$$

where $\mathrm{E}(m_{P,t\rightarrow})$ stands for the expected level of future performance of portfolio P, λ_0 is the intercept, λ_k is the forecasting coefficient associated with the kth performance measure, and φ_l is the forecasting coefficient associated with the lth other indicator used in the model. This is nevertheless not the only approach that can be used in order to assess absolute portfolio performance, as discussed in detail in the next section.

17.1.3.2 Relative persistence analysis

Unlike the absolute persistence approach, the relative version of the analysis does not explicitly aim at predicting the link between past and future performance of a portfolio. Rather, the stance is a comparative one. Considering a group of portfolio managers that share a homogeneous type of mandate, the objective of the analysis is to determine how effectively they make their investment decisions relative to each other. This is done through the analysis of the consequences of these decisions, namely their associated portfolio performance. The extent to which each manager outperforms a passive reference (either a benchmark portfolio or a theoretical hurdle) is therefore not the focus. The relative persistence approach is consistent with Equations (17-2), (17-3b), and (17-4b).

Because of the comparative focus, the most popular way to handle a relative persistence model is to examine portfolio rankings observed over different time periods. The existence of relative persistence would entail that the future rank of a fund could be at least partly predicted with its previous one. Applying this to Equation (17-2) would lead to the following expression:

$$E(\mathrm{Rk}(m_{1,t\rightarrow}), \ldots, \mathrm{Rk}(m_{P,t\rightarrow}), \ldots, \mathrm{Rk}(m_{N,t\rightarrow}))$$
$$= g(\mathrm{Rk}(m_{1,\rightarrow t-1}), \ldots, \mathrm{Rk}(m_{P,\rightarrow t-1}), \ldots, \mathrm{Rk}(m_{N,\rightarrow t-1})) \quad (17\text{-}6)$$

where $\mathrm{Rk}(m_{i,\cdot})$ denotes the rank of portfolio i according to the performance measure over the period considered, and $g(\cdot)$ is the rank forecasting function.

Equation (17-6) simply entails that the ranking obtained in the past is the best estimator for the ranking in the future. Obviously, as presented here, this model looks overly simplistic as well as presumably too ambitious. If one could simply afford to observe the classification of portfolios or mutual funds according to a simple criterion in order to infer the whole future ordering of managers, this would represent invaluable but fairly unrealistic information. However, there are some investment categories, mostly involving illiquid assets and strong limitations like private equity (see Chapter 12), for which such a situation could occur. More realistically, two kinds of modifications of the formula could ease the exercise: either the refinement of the ranking system used for prediction, or the use of a weaker prediction function than the complete ranking expectation. These potential solutions are developed further in Sections 17.3 and 17.4.

17.1.3.3 A discussion

The absolute and relative types of persistence studies do not represent competing approaches. They both coexist because they mostly bring complementary insights into predictability. The dimensions according to which both types of analysis differ are summarized in Table 17-3.

Absolute persistence deals with each specific portfolio. By conditioning future risk-adjusted performance (or any other relevant metric) on past observations, it is possible to identify whether a given portfolio or fund exhibits some level of persistence, whereas it might not exist for other portfolios. The estimation procedure can also be precisely tailored to the specificities of the portfolio, even though many models use a cross-section of similar funds in order to enhance the significance of the relation. Whenever the output of the model lends

TABLE 17-3 Summary of differences between absolute and relative persistence studies.

	Absolute persistence	Relative persistence
Output	Cardinal	Ordinal
Focus	Individual portfolio	Peer group
Modeling approach	Parametric – one-dimensional	Nonparametric – multidimensional
Key stakeholder	Investor	Manager

itself to clear interpretations, it is also possible to clearly segregate "positive," "absent," and "negative" persistence without ambiguity.

From a modeling point of view, there are also key differences between both approaches. Typically, absolute persistence is estimated parametrically in a single-dimensional space. This usually takes the form of a regression model. On the other hand, as relative persistence hinges on a comparison of ordinal measures, the range of techniques that can be used exhibits a greater variety. This also includes the diversity in the validation mechanisms, for which non-parametric estimation approaches sometimes require less classical statistical inference.

Furthermore, because of their nature, most absolute persistence studies allow a meaningful comparison of the portfolio performance with an external reference, which can be of any kind (passive or active benchmark), or even in absolute terms. This is of primary importance to investors, who usually care much more about the capacity of a portfolio manager to deliver positive returns (compared with the market or in stand-alone) than whether they are better or worse than their peers. By contrast, relative persistence analysis usually adopts the point of view of the manager and their stakeholders, including fund selectors, by limiting the universe to a homogeneous group of peers.

PrediLab example (continued)

As a first level of investigation, the analysts of PrediLab are studying the predictability of the funds' Jensen's alphas. From the data of Table 17-1, the outcome of the estimation yields the summary as shown in Table 17-4.

TABLE 17-4 Predilab example – Jensen's alphas for periods 1 and 2.

Fund	Period 1		Period 2	
	Alpha	Rank	Alpha	Rank
Thematic	1.21%	2	0.99%	5
B1	0.63%	8	0.24%	8
B2	1.36%	1	0.77%	6
B3	1.04%	6	4.23%	1
B4	1.06%	5	1.40%	4
B5	1.20%	3	−0.25%	10
B6	−0.04%	9	2.71%	3
B7	0.73%	7	0.16%	9
B8	1.08%	4	2.75%	2
B9	−0.20%	10	0.29%	7

The perspectives taken in this first analysis are twofold. At first, a simple linear regression analysis is performed on the estimated alphas. The outcome of Equation (17-5) is as follows:

$$E(\alpha_{P,2}) = 1.27\% + 0.074 \times \alpha_{P,1}$$

and the regression R^2 equals 0.076%, which corresponds to a correlation coefficient of $\rho(\alpha_{P,1}, \alpha_{P,2}) = \sqrt{0.076\%} = 2.75\%$. This is an almost flat regression line, as shown in Figure 17-1.

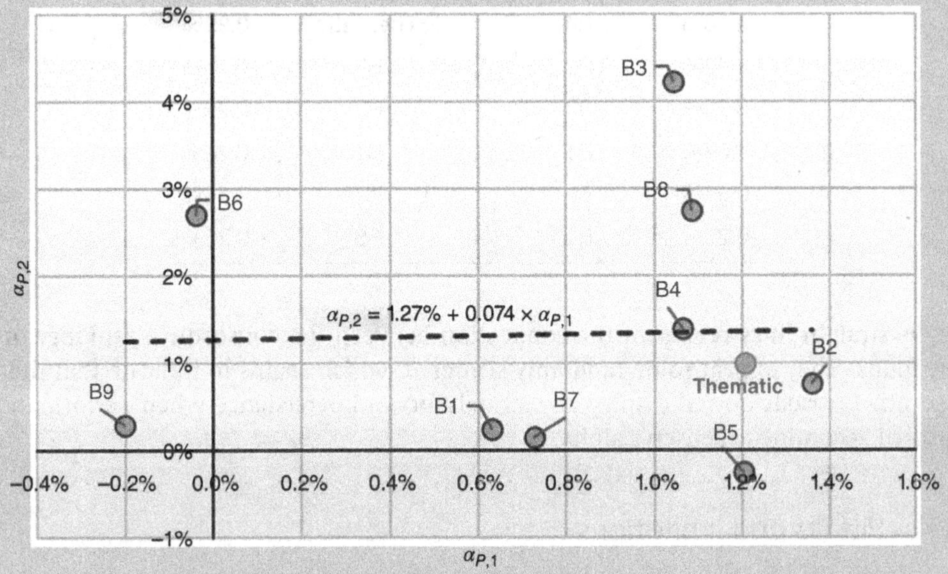

FIGURE 17-1 Predilab example – Dependence between Jensen's alphas in period 2 vs period 1.

Regarding the fund rankings, the most straightforward implementation of the persistence analysis is to consider the rank correlation. The Spearman rank correlation coefficient equals 2.75%, which means that the ranks are almost uncorrelated from one period to another. This is best represented by Table 17-5.

(continued)

(continued)

TABLE 17-5 Predilab example – Match of consecutive rankings with Jensen's alpha.

$\alpha_{P,1}$	Fund	Fund	$\alpha_{P,2}$
1.36%	B2	B3	4.23%
1.21%	**Thematic**	B8	2.75%
1.20%	B5	B6	2.71%
1.08%	B8	B4	1.40%
1.06%	B4	**Thematic**	**0.99%**
1.04%	B3	B2	0.77%
0.73%	B7	B9	0.29%
0.63%	B1	B1	0.24%
−0.04%	B6	B7	0.16%
−0.20%	B9	B5	−0.25%

The straight lines represent the connection between the consecutive rankings of the same funds. They appear to be randomly scattered, which seems to indicate that the two consecutive periods do not display any straightforward persistence when performance is measured according to Jensen's alpha.

17.1.4 Pitfalls and limitations

Studying any sort of predictability in the returns of financial portfolios, and in particular the persistence of an actively managed fund's performance, is an exercise that is prone to many types of mistakes. They indeed go both ways, leading to either under- or overestimation of the phenomenon. On the one hand, it is sometimes very difficult to uncover where this persistence indeed hides. A wrong setup, an inconsistent approach, or a test that is not powerful enough could easily miss out on the identification of the genuine effect. On the other hand, the temptation to find something interesting about return predictability, which really represents the "grail quest" of many asset managers or financial investors, might contaminate (voluntarily or not) the rigor and quality of the analysis. We go through a series of elements that one should take into account in order to avoid, as much as possible, these pitfalls.

The discussion is split into three parts, corresponding to the stages of the analysis: the preparation of the data, the execution of the persistence model, and the interpretation of the resulting outputs.

17.1.4.1 Preparing the data

Appraising performance for a single portfolio is a task that is already relatively challenging. This is a topic that we addressed in an entire chapter (Chapter 5). Studying persistence involves two sources of additional complexity, namely the need to extend the sample to multiple horizons (this is the essence of the exercise) and, very often, to a group of comparable funds that are studied in a simultaneous fashion.

The first issue that probably comes to mind is the potential effect of the survivorship bias. Examining a cross-section of funds whose returns are available during a full time period involves dealing only with those funds that have survived until the end date. Because they have been more likely to yield better returns than their defunct peers, there is a significant risk of overestimating the average performance of the whole group by only selecting the survivors.[6]

The issue of survivorship bias has non-trivial consequences in the context of persistence analysis. The studies of Brown, Goetzmann, Ibbotson, and Ross (1992) and Elton, Gruber, and Blake (1996) both show that, because of their average past outperformance, focusing on surviving funds only might lead to having the illusion of subsequent persistence in performance. This intuitive connection between past and future biases would call for using only survivorship bias-free data, i.e., the full universe of live and defunct funds. However, Linnainmaa (2013) then emphasizes the potential importance of the "reverse survivorship bias." Since some funds may have disappeared due to bad luck or other circumstances that have nothing to do with their managers' skills, these funds would not be likely to underperform in the subsequent period, had they still existed. Thus, measuring the cross-section of observed performance across all funds would *understate* the true one. The author suggests a correction mechanism that corrects this bias, which can be material.

Second, the selection of the group of funds on which persistence is assessed is a delicate matter. Hoberg et al. (2018) define the notion of "customized rivals" for characterizing what the peer group should ideally look like in order to study (mostly relative) performance persistence. This peer group is made up of the funds that are in competition with each other, thereby making sense of the notion of relative persistence. Even if, for practical matters, it might not be workable to apply the spatial methodology proposed by the authors, it is necessary to consider the fact that grouping funds according to the dimension on which the persistence study is based, namely competition, is a cardinal principle. This also means that, since this criterion may differ from the one (classically adopted) of the common self-reported benchmark, it might be necessary to adapt the performance measurement tools to the fact that funds may actually be comparable regarding persistence, while at the same time largely differing with respect to their benchmark or factor exposures.

[6]The importance and economic significance of this bias has been discussed in Section 5.3.1 of Chapter 5.

17.1.4.2 Implementing the model

The presence of style bias is an implementation problem with potentially strong consequences for the quality of the persistence diagnosis. This bias consists of ignoring the influence of a risk factor on past and future returns. In Carhart's (1997) famous study, it is precisely this bias that is at stake. He finds that failure to account for the momentum effect leaves a wrong impression of persistence in mutual fund performance. Just like the measurement of abnormal return such as Jensen's alpha can be altered by the presence of a relevant factor neglected in the computation of "normal return," this also impacts the analysis of performance persistence based on these abnormal returns – which constitute the bulk of empirical studies in this field, as we will see later. Sometimes, this style bias is particularly difficult to detect. This happens when managers dynamically change their factor exposures over time. Failing to detect these style drifts, for instance by imposing the very same return generating process for every fund, would result in a flawed picture of performance persistence. As shown by Mamaysky, Spiegel, and Zhang (2007), if such a bias is suspected (for instance, if the group of funds is not perfectly homogeneous and/or if managers are very likely to change their style exposures over time), it is necessary to refine the estimation techniques and to use fund-specific empirical calibrations.

In a related fashion, the existence of uncertainties about the right model to use among multiple plausible ones, or about the calibration of the chosen model, may blur the estimation of persistence in performance. Furthermore, even if the model appears to be valid, there is a strong likelihood that the funds with the most extreme good or bad performance – generally those whose persistence is the most closely examined – obtain their results due to some noise rather than skill.

The main issue here is that the outcome of the initial performance estimation is contaminated by undesired effects that, in turn, alter the effectiveness of the persistence methodology. A number of solutions have been proposed in order to mitigate these effects. Two of them have become standard, namely the bootstrapping methodology of Fama and French (2010) and the Bayesian performance estimation approach of Baks, Metrick, and Wachter (2001). The former consists of simulating a large set of return histories in order to reduce the noise element in the estimation as much as possible. The latter uses the properties of Bayes' rule in order to improve the performance estimation by introducing realistic prior beliefs rather than using only the plain-vanilla "frequentist" estimation of the multifactor alpha depicted in Chapter 7.

17.1.4.3 Interpreting the results

Imagine that the estimation of both the input and the output of the persistence study are blameless. Reaching the conclusion about persistence in performance, or absence thereof, relies on a sound interpretation of available statistical evidence. All types of studies must be carried out with great caution in order not to provide an illusion of persistence that actually would not exist, or vice versa.

First of all, one has to be extremely careful about the use of statistical inference in this context, especially with the interpretation of what is "statistically significant" in hypothesis testing. Barras et al. (2010) emphasize that the proper distinction between skill and luck would generally lead to a much lower proportion of funds that genuinely beat the market. Harvey, Liu, and Zhu (2016) plead for very severe statistical tests underlying the validation of multifactor models. Their approach, with stricter criteria than traditional inference, can often be adapted to the issue of persistence estimation. Furthermore, testing the existence of persistence is not the same as merely testing performance. Essentially, it involves two periods, one for the estimation and the other for the validation. One has to be very cautious about the empirical conditions of the study, especially the potential contamination of the validation sample with an artificial dependence on the estimation one.

Time-related elements play a role as well. The horizon matters for persistence: Bollen and Busse (2001; 2005) show that the evidence of persistence is much more pronounced in the short term than over longer periods for mutual funds. Findings of persistence may also be sensitive to the period tested. The time window over which the study is conducted may also deliver contrasting results. As mentioned in their comprehensive literature review, Cremers et al. (2019) state that "*Studies that ignore the impact of market conditions make managers as a whole appear less skilled than they are.*" Not only will evidence of persistence usually be different when markets are bullish or bearish, volatile or calm, and with high or low liquidity, but it also seems to decay over time due to an increase in the informational efficiency of prices (Conrad, Wahal, and Xiang, 2015) or competition among managers (Pástor et al., 2017). Thus, the truth of one study may not still be valid for another, more recent market environment.

The comprehensive discussion of all potential issues that must be addressed in order to faithfully detect any predictability in portfolio would require a complete literature review, which is not the purpose of this subsection. Its intent is, more modestly, to raise some caveats that one has to bear in mind before attempting to answer the question of the determinants of future portfolio performance, through one or several of the methodologies discussed in the next three sections.

17.2 ABSOLUTE PERSISTENCE

Is a fund or portfolio manager able to beat the market in a consistent manner? For an investor who chooses to trust an active portfolio manager, this is a key question. Its answer requires the estimation of a dependence structure between realized (past) and forthcoming (future) performance.

There are two ways to tackle this problem: either through making a full use of the portfolio's historical information considered in isolation or by extending the sample size with a cross-section of comparable portfolios. Portfolio-specific persistence corresponds to the first category of analysis, whereas cross-sectional persistence belongs to the second one.

Consider a single portfolio P for which we have a sample of T observations. These can be the returns, or any other variable, provided that it varies over time in a random fashion (therefore excluding static or deterministic variables such as the manager's education level or age, for instance). The aim of portfolio-specific persistence analysis is to stick to this sample in order to derive some predictability of performance. The goal of the procedure is twofold. First, it aims at evidencing a substantial average level of performance achieved by the portfolio. Second, it checks whether this level is sustained over time and does not behave erratically.

We examine hereafter three methods of assessing persistence at the portfolio level: the relatively straightforward rolling windows approach, a parametric approach to assess the persistence horizon, and a semi-parametric approach that consists of the estimation of the Hurst exponent, an indicator that reflects the capacity of the portfolio manager to exhibit long-run persistence.

17.2.1 The rolling windows approach

Partitioning the sample into a set of disjoint sub-samples in order to estimate relevant statistical indicators (like performance measures themselves) generally leads to a too large reduction in the number of observations. One has to accept letting sub-samples overlap to a certain extent. This idea has already been exploited in Section 8.3.1 of Chapter 8, in which the full sample of size T is split into sub-samples of equal size $L < T$, the first one featuring the first L observations $\{R_{P,1}, \ldots, R_{P,L}\}$, the second one using the same sample but dropping the first observation and adding the first next consecutive one $\{R_{P,2}, \ldots, R_{P,L+1}\}$, and so on until the last sub-sample featuring the last L observations $\{R_{P,T-L+1}, \ldots, R_{P,T}\}$. The same procedure is applied to all variables, such as the factor returns or specific indicators considered relevant for the analysis.

For each of the sub-samples denoted by $\tau = 1, \ldots, T - L + 1$, the performance of the portfolio whose persistence is under review is estimated, leading to its period-specific value $m_P^{(\tau)}$ (this is a generic symbol that can be whatever performance measure is considered relevant). There are various ways to exploit the series of $m_P^{(\tau)}$, but one has to bear in mind the heavy overlap of the underlying data.

The first challenge is to determine whether the performance achieved by the portfolio is economically as well as statistically significant. The basis for this analysis is a set of $T - L + 1$ draws of the portfolio performance, whose average is $\overline{m}_P$ and standard deviation is σ_{m_P}. It would be tempting to use a simple Student t-statistic against the average performance of a corresponding passive portfolio, denoted by m^*, i.e., using the formula $\frac{\overline{m}_P - m^*}{\sigma_{m_P}/\sqrt{T-L}}$ to perform the statistical inference. Such an approach can be applied if the observations are supposed to be independent of each other, which is not the case here as there is a strong correlation between the estimates made on the overlapping samples.

In this context, a simple approach is proposed by Fays, Hübner, and Lambert (2022) with the case of a trading strategy tested over a long horizon. As a basic indicator of the long-run stability of portfolio performance, they suggest computing the proportion of the periodic estimates of performance that are significantly different from the reference value.[7] The frequency indicator is then obtained by

$$f_x(m_P^{(\tau)} > m^*(\tau)) = \frac{1}{T-L+1} \sum_{\tau=1}^{T-L+1} 1_{\{p(m_P^{(\tau)})<x\}} \tag{17-7}$$

where $m^*(\tau)$ is the reference value of the performance measure for period τ, and $1_{\{p(m_P^{(\tau)})<x\}}$ is an indicator function that takes the value of 1 if the p-value of the test statistic associated with the periodic performance, denoted by $p(m_P^{(\tau)})$, is lower than the rejection probability (confidence level) x and 0 otherwise. Note that if $m^*(\tau) = m^*$, the reference value is a constant, as in the case of the alpha for which the reference value is $m^* = 0$.

The function $f_x(m_P^{(\tau)} > m^*(\tau))$ simply provides the estimated probability that someone who would invest at a random point in time in portfolio P and who would hold during τ time periods would have significantly outperformed the reference value. For instance, for a period of 10 years with weekly data, we would have $T = 52 \times 10 = 520$ observations. Consider sub-samples of $L = 104$ (two years). The number of overlapping periods is then equal to $T - L + 1 = 417$. If, among these sub-samples, there are 265 cases in which the portfolio outperformed with a confidence level of $1 - x = 95\%$, this means that an investor who would have decided to buy this portfolio at a completely random point in time would have had $f_{95\%}(m_P^{(\tau)} > m^*(\tau)) = \frac{265}{417} = 63.5\%$ of chances to significantly outperform the market.

The indicator of Equation (17-7) is not severe enough, however. Provided that there would be a few outliers scattered throughout the sample, an artificially high number of sub-samples containing these observations might strongly impact the frequency measure and deliver a wrong picture. Fays et al. (2022) suggest using the family-wise error rate already introduced in Section 7.1.3 of Chapter 7. Their idea is to use an analogy with the assessment of multiple trading strategies proposed by Harvey and Liu (2014). The investor's point of view, when they decide to adopt a portfolio at a random point in time with a holding horizon of L periods, is similar to that of someone who would simultaneously test the same investment strategy at τ different points in time. In order to ensure a consistent selection process, they propose reinforcing the selection criterion by lowering the rejection probability in the spirit of the Holm criterion but adapted to the structure of the sample. At first, it is necessary to order the performance estimates, renamed $m_p(k)$, $k = 1, \ldots, T - L + 1$ from the best (highest) one with index

[7] For the classical performance measures (Sharpe ratio, Jensen's alpha, modified Jensen's alpha, Information ratio, and Appraisal ratio), the most popular tests of significance are examined in Chapter 3.

1, i.e., $m_p(1) = \arg\max_{m_P^{(\tau)}}(m_P^{(\tau)} - m^*(\tau))$, to the worst (lowest) one with index $T - L + 1$, i.e., $m_p(T - L + 1) = \arg\min_{m_P^{(\tau)}}(m_P^{(\tau)} - m^*(\tau))$. Then, the new criterion is written as

$$f_x(m_P^{(\tau)} \gg m^*(\tau)) = \frac{1}{T-L+1} \sum_{k=1}^{T-L+1} 1_{\{p(m_P(k))<x_k\}} \tag{17-8}$$

where the authors propose $x_k = \frac{(T-L+2-k)}{(T-L+1)\times\sum_{i=1}^{k}\frac{1}{i}} \times x$. This expression for x_k ensures that the rejection criterion becomes more severe as we go down the list. For instance, imagine that $T = 60$, $L = 24$, and $x = 5\%$. The rejection level for the first (largest) observation is $x_1 = \frac{(60-24+2-1)}{(60-24+1)\times\frac{1}{1}} \times 5\% = 5\%$. For the second largest one, it becomes $x_2 = \frac{(60-24+2-2)}{(60-24+1)\times\left(\frac{1}{1}+\frac{1}{2}\right)} \times 5\% = 3.24\%$, for the third one it is equal to $x_3 = \frac{(60-24+2-3)}{(60-24+1)\times\left(\frac{1}{1}+\frac{1}{2}+\frac{1}{3}\right)} \times 5\% = 2.58\%$, and so on.

If periodic superior performance is confirmed during a long time window, the second challenge is to determine whether it is erratic or not. It would be useless to detect excellent performance once every three periods, for instance, while the portfolio returns are disappointing the rest of the time. Thus, provided that the portfolio performance is good overall, its continuity needs to be warranted. Still using rolling windows, Fays et al. (2022) simply propose assessing the presence of a linear time trend with the regression

$$m_P^{(\tau)} - m^*(\tau) = a_P + b_P\tau + \varepsilon_{P,\tau} \tag{17-9}$$

The presence of performance persistence is confirmed if the lower values of the confidence bounds of the regression are always positive, i.e., if the absence of outperformance $(m_P^{(\tau)} - m^*(\tau) = 0)$ would only be observed by chance. This would very likely be the case if a_P (the intercept) is significantly positive, b_P (the linear trend) is insignificant or significantly positive, and if the regression itself is significant. If another type of trending behavior is suspected, an alternative specification (e.g., a quadratic one) can be foreseen. The same principles apply regarding the analysis of the confidence interval.

As an illustration, Fays et al. (2022) test a strategy featuring a systematic calendar trade on long–short portfolios of small vs large stocks (i.e., "size" portfolios) at different times of the year (long in January, neutral until September, short in the last quarter (Q4)), using both the original Fama and French (FF) stock sorting criteria and their own proposed one, called DSN. They compare this strategy with another one in which the portfolio is only long the size portfolio in January and invested in cash otherwise. They use the Sharpe ratio ($m_P^{(\tau)} \equiv \text{SR}_P^{(\tau)}$) on five-year rolling windows from 1968 until 2019. Their main results are summarized in Figure 17-2.

The left part of the figure represents the evolution of the five-year Sharpe ratios for the long–short (L/S) strategies using the FF size factor. There is a clear decaying trend for both

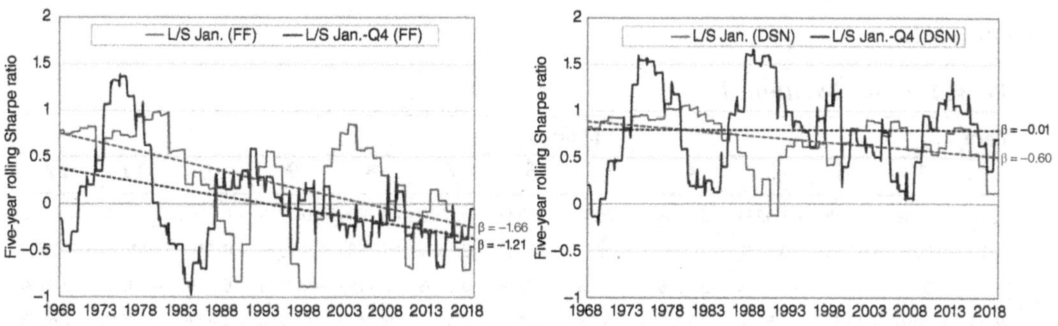

FIGURE 17-2 Illustration of trending analysis for five-year rolling Sharpe ratios. *Source*: Fays et al. (2022), Figure 4.

strategies, which entails that even if the initial performance was positive, it has not stood the test of time. The right graph, in contrast, shows no trend for the "L/S Jan.-Q4" strategy Sharpe ratio, with a high average of 0.79. The authors show that less than 30% of observations are lower than 0.5.

PrediLab example (continued)

Because the persistence analysis using the funds' alphas does not seem to provide satisfactory results, the analyst decides to use the modified Jensen's alpha $m\alpha_P = \frac{\alpha_P}{\beta_P}$ instead.

When applied to the series of returns for the Thematic fund, the time series of beta-rescaled excess returns over the market-based benchmark, which we simply denote by $mR_{(P-B),t} \equiv \frac{R_{P,t}-[R_f+\beta_P[R_{M,t}-R_f]]}{\beta_P}$, leaves the monthly data over 10 years ($T = 10 \times 12 = 120$) that are reported, in matrix form, in Table 17-6.

TABLE 17-6 Predilab example – Modified excess returns over the benchmark for the Thematic fund.

Year	Month											
	1	2	3	4	5	6	7	8	9	10	11	12
2013	1.29%	1.28%	−0.01%	−0.51%	−2.27%	0.16%	0.45%	0.44%	0.20%	−0.29%	0.50%	2.65%
2014	2.35%	2.65%	0.24%	0.36%	0.59%	−0.05%	−1.73%	0.21%	−0.66%	0.69%	0.75%	0.39%
2015	1.04%	0.46%	0.16%	3.47%	−1.81%	−1.50%	0.26%	0.28%	0.05%	−0.89%	0.94%	−0.28%
2016	0.01%	−0.01%	2.87%	−1.04%	1.41%	0.39%	−0.15%	−0.07%	−1.20%	0.21%	−1.37%	−1.21%
2017	0.48%	7.32%	−0.91%	0.39%	0.52%	−0.51%	0.43%	0.40%	−0.22%	0.20%	−0.38%	−1.94%

(*continued*)

(continued)

TABLE 17-6 (continued)

Year	Month											
	1	2	3	4	5	6	7	8	9	10	11	12
2018	0.33%	−0.48%	−1.02%	0.61%	0.70%	−0.45%	−0.10%	−0.28%	−0.18%	−0.23%	−0.87%	−0.32%
2019	0.62%	−0.56%	0.36%	−0.35%	0.73%	2.18%	−0.14%	−0.24%	0.77%	−0.31%	−0.11%	1.28%
2020	0.32%	−0.42%	−0.43%	−0.23%	−0.20%	0.32%	0.53%	0.27%	−0.06%	−0.42%	−0.46%	0.91%
2021	0.48%	−0.14%	1.52%	−0.24%	−0.26%	−0.11%	0.98%	3.74%	0.02%	−1.87%	−0.26%	1.55%
2022	0.42%	0.16%	0.56%	0.36%	−1.07%	−0.84%	1.55%	−0.58%	3.12%	−0.76%	−0.52%	2.74%

The yearly average of the series, which corresponds to the fund's modified alpha, is equal to $m\alpha_{\text{Thematic}} = 3\%$. The annualized standard deviation is equal to 4.32%. Regarding the significance of the overall performance, it can be roughly estimated with the $\boldsymbol{t}$-statistic of the mean return being equal to $\hat{\boldsymbol{t}}_{m\alpha_p=0} = \frac{0.25\%}{1.25\%}\sqrt{119} = 2.20$, thus quite convincingly high.[8]

The evolution of the cumulative returns is displayed in Figure 17-3.

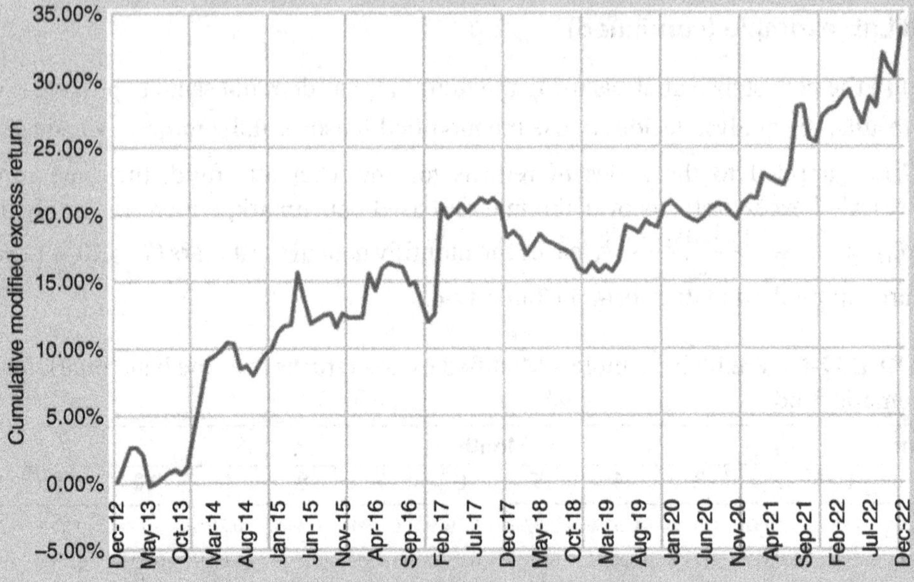

FIGURE 17-3 Predilab example – Cumulative modified excess returns for the Thematic fund.

[8]Remember however that the Student $\boldsymbol{t}$-statistic is not appropriate for the modified Jensen's alpha (see Section 3.3 of Chapter 3). Nevertheless, as a rough estimate, this can give an insightful first indication.

The visual inspection of Figure 17-3 delivers an encouraging impression. It is decided to dig further into this series in order to detect some possible persistence in the generation of the fund's outperformance using the rolling windows approach.

The evolution of the modified Jensen's alpha over time is examined using three-year rolling windows, for a total of $120 - 36 + 1 = 85$ observations. According to Equation (17-7), the frequency of outperformance (with $m^*(\tau) \equiv \mathrm{m}\alpha^* = 0$) is tested against three probability levels $x = 10\%, 20\%$, and 50%, whose corresponding t-statistics with 84 degrees of freedom are $t_{84,1-x} = 1.66, 1.29$, and 0, respectively. The resulting outcomes are as follows: $f_{10\%}(\mathrm{m}\alpha_P^{(\tau)} > 0) = 12.9\%$, $f_{20\%}(\mathrm{m}\alpha_P^{(\tau)} > 0) = 30.6\%$, and $f_{50\%}(\mathrm{m}\alpha_P^{(\tau)} > 0) = 89.4\%$. Thus, we cannot conclude that there is strong evidence for a frequent outperformance (only roughly 10% of the time), but there is a 90% chance of obtaining a positive abnormal return for an investor who invests at a random moment in time for a period of three years.

The visual inspection of the rolling modified alphas sheds more light on these findings. It is summarized in Figure 17-4.

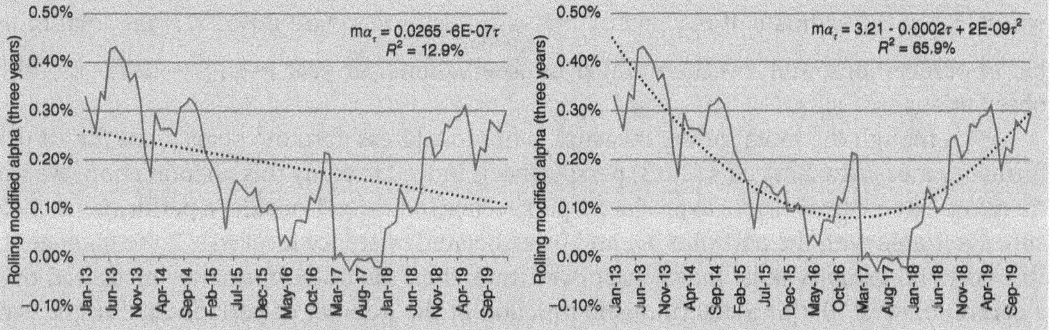

FIGURE 17-4 Predilab example – Rolling window modified alphas for the Thematic fund.

Both graphs represent the same time series of the three-year rolling modified alphas, but the left graph fits a linear relation whereas the right graph fits a quadratic one. It appears clearly that the mild downward linear trend does not fit the data well, with a small R^2 of 12.9%. Rather, the portfolio has experienced a strong start, another strong end, and a relative lack of performance in the middle of the studied time period. The quadratic fit is very good ($R^2 = 65.9\%$) and only gets close to zero at its minimum level (in 2016).

17.2.2 The persistence horizon approach

17.2.2.1 The original K-Ratio

Another potential solution to the issue of absolute persistence is provided by adapting Kestner's (1996) *K-Ratio*, denoted by K-R_P, initially developed in the context of quantitative trading strategies and refined later by the same author (Kestner, 2013).[9] The computation method of the original K-R_P consists of a two-step procedure. In the first step, the cumulative portfolio abnormal return (thus not considering rolling windows but aggregating portfolio excess returns over its benchmark B over time) is regressed against time in the spirit of Equation (17-9):[10]

$$\sum_{s=1}^{t}(R_{P,s} - R_{B,s}) = b_{P,0} + b_{P,1}t + \varepsilon_{P,t} \quad (17\text{-}10)$$

where $t = 1, \ldots, T$ in order to encompass the whole measurement period.

In the second step, the t-statistic of the regression slope is divided by the number of observations and normalized by the square root of the number of yearly observations to obtain the value of K-R_P:

$$\text{K-R}_P = \frac{\widehat{b}_{P,1}}{\sigma_{\widehat{b}_{P,1}}} \times \frac{\sqrt{n}}{T} \quad (17\text{-}11)$$

where $\widehat{b}_{P,1}$ is the estimate of $b_{P,1}$ and $\sigma_{\widehat{b}_{P,1}} = \frac{\sigma_\varepsilon}{\sqrt{T-1}\sigma_t}$ is its standard error, T is the total number of observations, and n is the number of observations per year (e.g., $n = 12$ for monthly observations).

Even though the intent of the measure is not to address absolute persistence for all performance measures, Kestner's (2013) perspective is indeed to study this phenomenon. We can therefore extend the measure to produce a persistence indicator. Consider a performance measure associated with the portfolio m_p and its associated reference level m^*. If the manager of this portfolio exhibits skills that persist over time, then the outperformance measured over a certain interval $[0, t]$ is a deterministic function of the number of periods used in the estimation: $m_{p,[0,t]} - m^*_{[0,t]} = (m_p - m^*)f(t)$, for some function of time $f(t)$. For instance, this function is $f(t) = t$ for measures of abnormal returns such as the alpha (single factor or multifactor) and $f(t) = \sqrt{t}$ for the Sharpe and Information ratios. Thus, we start with a generalized version of Equation (17-9):

$$m_{p,[0,t]} - m^*_{[0,t]} = g_{P,H}f(t) + \varepsilon_{P,t} \quad (17\text{-}12)$$

where $t = 1, \ldots, H$. This is a regression without an intercept as the starting point of the process is necessarily the origin of the axes. The measurement horizon $h \leq H \leq T$ varies in order to encompass different time windows. The lower bound h ensures that the value of H is not too low in order to have enough data points available for the regression.

[9]There have been various versions of this ratio. We report the last one proposed by the author.

[10]In the case of geometric returns, we can take the product of compound returns or the sum of the continuously compounded version, *ad libitum*.

17.2.2.2 The extended K-Ratio

Unlike the scope of the original performance measure, the purpose of the measurement is to detect up to what horizon the outperformance persists. We thus define the *extended K-Ratio* for horizon H, denoted by eK-R$_P(H)$, as the normalized slope coefficient of the regression:

$$\text{eK-R}_P(H) = \frac{\widehat{g}_{P,H}}{\sigma_{\widehat{g}_{P,H}}} \tag{17-13}$$

where $\widehat{g}_{P,H} = \frac{\sum_{t=1}^{H} f(t)(m_{p,[0,t]} - m^*_{[0,t]})}{\sum_{t=1}^{H}(f(t))^2}$ is the estimate of $g_{P,H}$ and $\sigma_{\widehat{g}_{P,H}} = \frac{\sigma_\varepsilon}{\sqrt{H-1}\sigma_{f(t)}}$ is its standard error. For the cases of the Jensen's or multifactor alpha ($f(t) = t$) or the Sharpe ratio ($f(t) = \sqrt{t}$), for instance, we can simplify the estimate of $g_{P,H}$ respectively as $\widehat{g}_{P,H} = \frac{\sum_{t=1}^{H} t\times\alpha_{p,[0,t]}}{\sum_{t=1}^{H} t^2}$ and $\widehat{g}_{P,H} = \frac{2\sum_{t=1}^{H}\sqrt{t}(\text{SR}_{p,[0,t]} - \text{SR}^*_{[0,t]})}{H(H+1)}$.

The expression eK-R$_P(H)$ can readily be interpreted as a t-statistic for the trending coefficient. It tends to increase with the number of observations and decrease with the variance of the error term. If the performance measure follows a constant trend during a certain time period, the values of $\widehat{g}_{P,H}$ and eK-R$_P(H)$ will both increase. However, as soon as the trend vanishes or reverts, the slope $\widehat{g}_{P,H}$ will quickly decrease and its standard deviation $\sigma_{\widehat{g}_{P,H}}$ will sharply increase, leading eK-R$_P(H)$ to collapse.

The persistence horizon for the portfolio performance with a $1-x$ confidence level, denoted by $H^*_{m_p,x}$, is the maximum length of the investment horizon for which the extended K-Ratio is statistically significant:

$$H^*_{m_p,x} = \sup_{H\leq T}\left(\text{eK-R}_P(H) \geq t_{(H-1);1-\frac{x}{2}}\right) \tag{17-14}$$

where $t_{(H-1);1-\frac{x}{2}}$ is the $\left(1-\frac{x}{2}\right)$th percentile of the Student t-distribution with $H-1$ degrees of freedom. If $H^*_{m_p,x} = T$, then there is no evidence of loss in persistence during the whole period. Naturally, if the initial performance indicator is negative, Equation (17-14) must be adapted with the opposite signs.

The logic underlying this persistence indicator, using the Sharpe ratio as an example, is illustrated in Figure 17-5.

The performance measure that is examined is the cumulative difference between the portfolio Sharpe ratio and a reference value SR* (scale of the right axis on the graph). The evolution of this difference is represented by the thin dotted line, initially trending up, reaching its maximum roughly at the middle of the chart, then going down. Naturally, it would be convenient to conclude that the superior portfolio performance has persisted until this peak. However, this is difficult in practice because (i) immediately after this peak, the observed deviation might

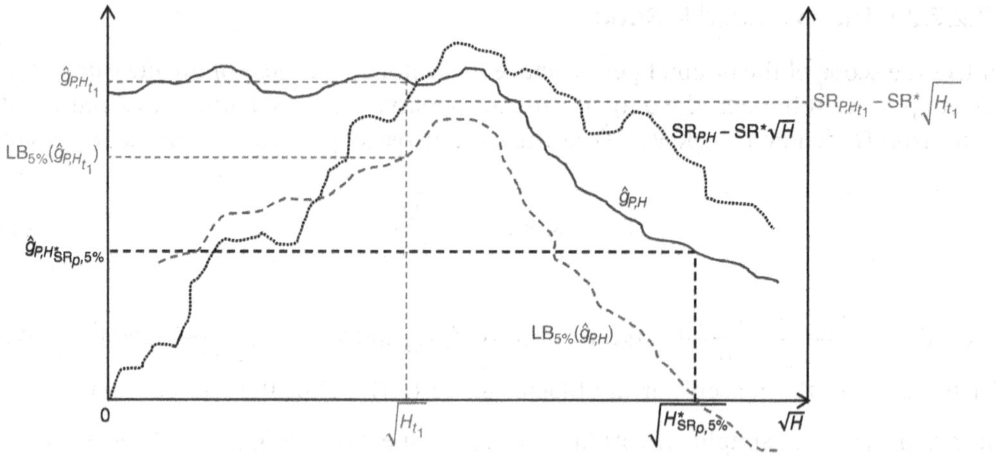

FIGURE 17-5 Graphical illustration of the persistence horizon with the Sharpe ratio.

be due to bad luck rather than the exhaustion of the quality of the strategy, and (ii) since the analyst has no crystal ball, they cannot immediately guess that the curve would move downward so sharply before observing it.

The outcome of regression Equation (17-12) is represented by the thick continuous line (scale of the left axis of the graph). As long as the trend is clear and steady, the slope coefficient does not change much. When performance starts to deteriorate, the coefficient falls accordingly, evidencing the break. We also illustrate, with the dashed line, a plausible behavior of the associated lower confidence bound (at a confidence level of $1 - x = 95\%$) for the slope coefficient, denoted by $\mathrm{LB}_{5\%}(\hat{g}_{P,H})$. It only starts to make sense to compute it after a minimum number of observations. Initially, as the regression is performed on only a few data points, the confidence interval for $\hat{g}_{P,H}$ is relatively wide. However, as the trend strengthens and the number of observations rises, the interval narrows and the lower bound increases. For instance, at horizon H_{t_1}, the positive evolution of the Sharpe ratio has become quite reliable and the quality of the estimate $\hat{g}_{P,H_{t_1}}$ is high. However, once the performance starts to fall, not only does the slope coefficient decrease, but its standard deviation $\sigma_{\hat{g}_{P,H}}$ also increases, leading the extended K-Ratio of Equation (17-13) to plummet. The horizon at which $\text{eK-R}_P(H^*_{\mathrm{SR}_p,5\%}) = t_{(H^*_{\mathrm{SR}_p,5\%}-1);97.5\%}$ corresponds to the point at which the lower bound of the confidence interval hits the horizontal axis, i.e., the t-statistic represented by the extended K-Ratio at horizon $H^*_{\mathrm{SR}_p,5\%}$, is no longer statistically significant.

It remains to be noted that the persistence horizon indicator does not really correspond to the traditional setup of statistical inference, in which a confidence level is typically set at a high level ($1 - x \geq 90\%$) because the analyst wants to strictly control the "Type-I error", i.e., the probability of rejecting a null hypothesis of no outperformance if it is true. In the current case, we are more in the spirit of a "Type-II error" environment, in which the null hypothesis is the presence of persistence. In practice, a much lower confidence level can therefore be chosen.

PrediLab example (continued)

Starting from the pattern of Figure 17-3, we estimate the linear regression without the intercept corresponding to Equation (17-12) for every horizon. The outcome is displayed in Figure 17-6.

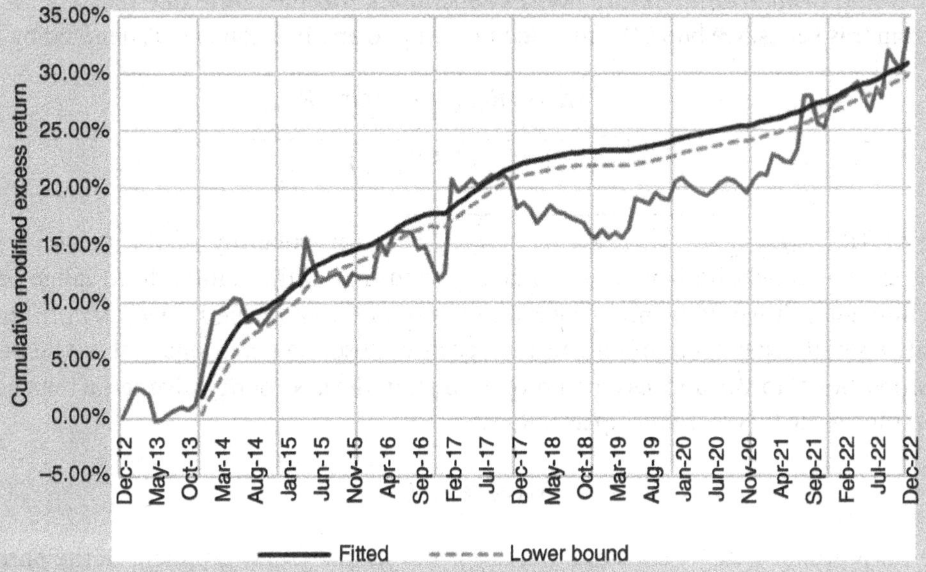

FIGURE 17-6 Predilab example – Cumulative modified excess returns for the Thematic fund.

The graph reveals a very stable pattern for the time trend, with a lower bound (considering a confidence level of 95%) that remains very close, in spite of the relative drop observed in the middle of the period. Thus, this analysis shows clear evidence of absolute persistence in the series.

17.2.3 The Hurst exponent

Our objective is to determine whether a portfolio manager who achieves a superior performance during an initial time interval is able to keep up with the same achievement over a long period of time. Since performance persistence is mostly a matter of the memory of the portfolio performance generation, it makes sense to call upon physical sciences that have many applications of similar issues. An elegant approach that can be applied to persistence analysis is provided by Hurst (1951) in his study of the optimal dam sizing of the Nile River. Mandelbrot (2004) subsequently showed how his work could be applied to study the long-term properties of financial time series.

When applied in the field of performance, the *Hurst exponent* of a portfolio P, denoted by $\mathcal{H}_P$, reflects the propension of the time series of its abnormal returns to revert back to a long-run mean or, conversely, to head to a particular direction. In a sense, the Hurst exponent is the long-term counterpart to the notion of autocorrelation (high Hurst = positive autocorrelation; low Hurst = negative autocorrelation).

In order to obtain an estimate of the Hurst exponent, it is necessary to prepare the data. Consider the portfolio excess return over its benchmark B as the raw material: $R_{(P-B),t} \equiv R_{P,t} - R_{B,t}$. From this series, we build the rescaled range up to any horizon $\theta \leq T$, denoted by $\Lambda_P(\theta)$:

$$\Lambda_P(\theta) = \frac{\max\limits_{t=1,\ldots,\theta} R_{(P-B),t} - \min\limits_{t=1,\ldots,\theta} R_{(P-B),t}}{\sigma^{(\theta)}(R_{(P-B)})} \tag{17-15}$$

where $\sigma^{(\theta)}(R_{(P-B)}) = \sqrt{\frac{1}{\theta-1}\sum_{t=1}^{\theta}(R_{(P-B),t} - \overline{R}_{(P-B)})^2}$ is the volatility of the portfolio excess returns estimated over horizon θ. It can be expected that, if the standardized range behaves as a white noise, it would be proportional to the square root of the horizon $\sqrt{\theta}$. In the case of positive serial dependence of returns (i.e., positive absolute persistence), it would be more than proportional to $\sqrt{\theta}$, and less than proportional in the case of negative serial dependence. We can thus write this relationship as follows:

$$\Lambda_P(\theta) \approx c \times \theta^{\mathcal{H}_P} \tag{17-16}$$

where c is a proportionality constant and $\mathcal{H}_P$ is the simple Hurst exponent of the portfolio's excess returns.[11]

The estimation of the Hurst exponent uses a log-linearization of Equation (17-16) on which a linear regression is performed:

$$\log \Lambda_P(\theta) = \log c + \mathcal{H}_P \log \theta + \varepsilon_{P,\theta} \tag{17-17}$$

Equation (17-17) can be estimated with a simple least-squared regression, provided that the sample respects two conditions: (i) it is sufficiently large (since the relation is valid asymptotically, it requires a large value of T, certainly greater than 50 data points), and (ii) its design allows the use of standard estimation techniques.

The second condition raises a potential issue. It would be tempting to simply use rolling windows or to build up the sample by picking the first two observations ($\theta = 2$), then the first three ($\theta = 3$), then the first four, and so on. However, this would simultaneously create problems of heteroscedasticity and overlap of variables. Partitioning the data in sub-samples of equal sizes does not lead to any variability of θ, whereas using non-overlapping periods of

[11] There exists a generalized version of the Hurst exponent whose discussion goes beyond the scope of this chapter.

unequal sizes leaves the heteroscedasticity problem unsolved. The standard solution is thus to apply the following algorithm:[12]

- Partition the sample into $k = 1,2,3, \ldots, T/2$ non-overlapping sub-samples of equal size (if there is a remainder in the division, the remaining observations are distributed across the sub-samples). For each partition, the corresponding sub-samples each have a size of $\theta_i = T/k$ for $i = 1, \ldots, k$;
- For every partition of size T/k, compute the rescaled range associated with each sub-sample $\Lambda_P(\theta_i)$ according to Equation (17-15);
- Average the standardized ranges across the sub-samples in order to obtain the representative rescaled range: $\widehat{\Lambda}_P(T/k) = \frac{1}{k}\sum_{i=1}^{k} \Lambda_P(\theta_i)$;
- Perform the linear regression of Equation (17-17) with the series of representative rescaled ranges and their corresponding lengths: $\log \widehat{\Lambda}_P(T/k) = \log c + \mathcal{H}_P \log T/k + \varepsilon_{P,T/k}$. This regression features $T/2$ observations.

When the Hurst exponent is estimated, it remains to be determined whether it corresponds to a persistent performance trajectory or not. Evidence of positive persistence corresponds to $\mathcal{H}_P > 0.5$, whereas persistence is negative (i.e., performance tends to switch signs) if $\mathcal{H}_P < 0.5$. This case is known as "anti-persistence." Regarding significance, there are sophisticated bootstrapping approaches to derive numerical values for the confidence interval, but a heuristic rule gives reasonable results, yet tilted toward too often rejecting the null hypothesis of the absence of persistence (i.e., too narrow a confidence interval around the value 0.5):

$$\widehat{Z}_{\mathcal{H}_P=0.5} = (\mathcal{H}_P - 0.5)\sqrt{T} \tag{17-18}$$

where Z follows a standard normal distribution with expectation of 0 and variance of 1.

In practice, it is necessary to either choose a very high confidence level in order to come up with a faithful rejection rule (for instance, $x = 99\%$) or to perform a more precise assessment of the confidence interval around the base value $\mathcal{H}_P = 0.5$ as in Weron (2002).

Finally, when can we conclude that a portfolio exhibits a virtuous combination of performance and persistence? An answer is given in the methodology note of the Europerformance (2006) style rating, which nowadays is held by the SIX Telekurs Group. This rating methodology assigns the highest rating (five stars) to funds that simultaneously obtain evidence of positive performance and persistence. Generalizing the reasoning, we can come up with the summary as shown in Table 17-7.

[12]Bear in mind that this approach produces a rather noisy estimation if the sample size is limited. Furthermore, the Hurst exponent is biased because $\overline{\Lambda}_P(\theta) \neq E(\Lambda_P(\theta)) = \frac{\theta-\frac{1}{2}}{\theta}\frac{\Gamma((\theta-1)/2)}{\sqrt{\pi}\Gamma(\theta/2)}\sum_{i=1}^{\theta}\sqrt{\frac{\theta-i}{i}}$, where $\Gamma(\cdot)$ is the Euler function (i.e., a version of the factorial for any real positive number) in the base Gaussian (i.e., white noise) case and for small samples. As shown by Weron (2002), ignoring this bias typically leads to an overestimation of the Hurst exponent.

TABLE 17-7 Combined impact of the absolute performance and persistence on portfolio quality.

Absolute performance	Absolute persistence		
	$\mathcal{H}_P < 0.5$	$\mathcal{H}_P = 0.5$	$\mathcal{H}_P > 0.5$
$\overline{R}_{(P-B)} < 0$	(+)	(−)	−
$\overline{R}_{(P-B)} = 0$	?	=	?
$\overline{R}_{(P-B)} > 0$	(−)	(+)	+

The signs between parentheses indicate a weaker effect. Since the indicator of absolute persistence reflects the tendency of performance to reproduce itself ($\mathcal{H}_P > 0.5$) or to reverse ($\mathcal{H}_P < 0.5$) over time, it is the combination of performance *and* persistence that signals the anticipated portfolio performance. The only unequivocal situations consist of positive or negative performance combined with positive persistence: the investor knows that the good or bad results are likely to reproduce themselves (upper and lower right cells). Absent the evidence of persistence, a good or bad performance is a much less reliable indicator for the future. Interestingly, the combination of good performance and anti-persistence ($\mathcal{H}_P < 0.5$) can be worrisome (lower left cell), as the investor could fear that the future outcome of the portfolio will be opposite to the positive one observed until the present moment. The same reasoning holds for negative performance and anti-persistence, which can be seen as a good sign (upper left cell). In the case of the absence of performance, the persistence analysis is inconclusive.

PrediLab example (continued)

We apply the algorithm on the basis of the 120 observations of Table 17-6. The original sample is split into sub-samples for all the divisors of 120, namely 120, 60, 40, 30, 24, 20, 15, 12, 10, 8, 6, 5, 4, 3, and 2 observations (15 values of θ). The outcome of the procedure is reported in Table 17-8.

TABLE 17-8 Predilab example – Rescaled ranges obtained from the sample partitions.

k	$\theta = T/k$	$\hat{\Lambda}_P(T/k)$
60	2	0.707
40	3	1.116
30	4	1.471
24	5	1.734
20	6	2.043

TABLE 17-8 *(continued)*

k	$\theta = T/k$	$\hat{\Lambda}_P(T/k)$
15	8	2.455
12	10	2.928
10	12	3.084
8	15	3.584
6	20	4.343
5	24	4.476
4	30	5.024
3	40	5.218
2	60	6.228
	120	10.413

Taking the natural logarithms of these values and fitting a linear regression according to Equation (17-17) yields the graph shown in Figure 17-7.

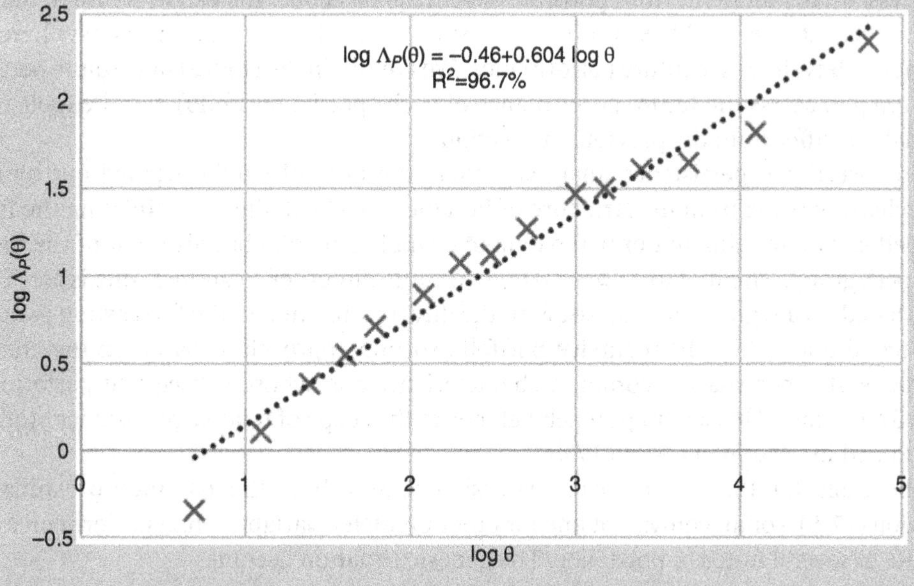

FIGURE 17-7 Predilab example – Linear regression for the Hurst exponent.

(continued)

(continued)

The value of the Hurst exponent is thus equal to $\mathcal{H}_{\text{Thematic}} = 0.604$. Since there are 120 observations, we obtain $\hat{Z}_{\mathcal{H}_{\text{Thematic}}=0.5} = 0.104 \times \sqrt{120} = 1.14$, which is insufficient to conclude that the fund's performance exhibits a significant long-run persistence.

The difference between the diagnoses obtained with the persistence horizon and the Hurst exponent approach mostly lies in the long-run character of the latter method. Its validity hinges on a sufficiently long history of the time series, which is not the case here.

17.2.4 Cross-sectional performance persistence

For an investor who focuses on a single portfolio, considering it in isolation and measuring its performance over two or even several more time intervals would be an ideal setup. Nevertheless, for analysts or researchers, it is necessary to broaden the scope of the analysis, either for the selection of one or several funds among a group of actively managed portfolios, or for the understanding of the factors that drive the persistence of performance.

Indeed, when rich data are available for a cross-section of comparable portfolios, another perspective than the in-depth analysis of a single portfolio becomes possible and can prove to be insightful regarding the predictability analysis using performance measures. The objective is essentially different from portfolio-specific persistence. Instead of trying to determine whether persistence would exist or not for a single portfolio, the analysis focuses here on the common determinants of future performance. We are still in the context of absolute persistence (i.e., trying to assess the future performance of each specific portfolio), but the tools used for the analysis differ from the previous subsections.

Cross-sectional persistence analysis gathers the bulk of studies carried out by finance researchers. Starting from the structure of Equation (17-5), it aims at estimating the forecasting coefficients by using not only the data of a single portfolio but also that of the members of its peer group. The literature has taken two routes in order to address this issue. The first one is based on a regression analysis, with the direct estimation of the forecasting parameters. The second one, called the recursive portfolio sorting approach, is based on the creation of subgroups of funds sharing common characteristics and whose subsequent performance is tracked over time. This latter approach belongs to the scope of relative persistence studies and is examined in Sections 17.3 and 17.4.

The basis for the multivariate regression approach is the parametric estimation of Equation (17-5) – or an equivalent one for other predicted variables than performance – using the data of several funds or portfolios. The generic equation becomes

$$m_{i,\tau} = \lambda_0 + \sum_k \lambda_k m_{i,k,\tau-1} + \sum_l \varphi_l q_{i,l,\tau-1} + \nu_{i,\tau} \tag{17-19}$$

where $i = 1, \ldots, N$ is the number of funds and $\tau = 1, \ldots, \mathbf{T}$ is the number of time periods used in the analysis.[13]

The most common form of Equation (17-19) resorts to the multifactor alpha on both sides of the equation ($m_{i,\tau} = \alpha_{i,\tau}^{\text{MF}}$ and $m_{i,k,\tau-1} \equiv m_{i,\tau-1} = \alpha_{i,\tau}^{\text{MF}}$), as originally introduced by Grinblatt and Titman (1992) with an eight-factor model. This means that the estimation method uses a two-pass regression framework in the spirit of the Fama and MacBeth (1973) methodology. The first pass uses the multifactor model in order to obtain the performance measure for different time periods, similar to Equation (7-3) of Chapter 7:

$$R_{i,s} = \alpha_{i,\tau-1}^{\text{MF}} + \sum_{k=1}^{K} \beta_{i,k,\tau-1} F_{k,s} + \varepsilon_{i,s} \quad (17\text{-}20)$$

$$R_{i,t} = \alpha_{i,\tau}^{\text{MF}} + \sum_{k=1}^{K} \beta_{i,k,\tau} F_{k,t} + \varepsilon_{i,t} \quad (17\text{-}21)$$

where $s \leq \tau - 1$ and $\tau - 1 < t \leq \tau$ correspond to the time intervals used for the estimation of multifactor alpha for time periods $\tau - 1$ and τ. Each $\beta_{i,k,\tau-1}$ and $\beta_{i,k,\tau}$ represents the factor beta of fund i estimated for time periods $\tau - 1$ and τ, respectively, with $F_{k,s}$ and $F_{k,t}$ standing for the realization of their corresponding factor returns.[14]

Once the lagged and current alphas are estimated on the basis of Equations (17-20) and (17-21), the second pass consists of the estimation of the prediction equation:

$$\widehat{\alpha}_{i,\tau}^{\text{MF}} = \lambda_{0,\tau} + \lambda_{1,\tau} \widehat{\alpha}_{i,\tau-1}^{\text{MF}} + \nu_{i,\tau} \quad (17\text{-}22)$$

where $\widehat{\alpha}_{i,\tau-1}^{\text{MF}}$ and $\widehat{\alpha}_{i,\tau}^{\text{MF}}$ are the estimated coefficients of regressions (17-20) and (17-21), respectively, and $\lambda_{1,\tau}$ is the persistence coefficient for time period τ. Its significance means that the performance is persistent (if positive) or anti-persistent (if negative).

The estimation of Equation (17-22) can be performed in a rolling window analysis (reproduced independently for each time period τ) or in a panel framework (the time windows are pooled together, resulting in a $\mathbf{T} \times N$ sample size with a unique parameter estimation).

There are a number of possible variations that are meant to improve the estimation of Equation (17-22). We list a few of them below, which are not mutually exclusive:

1. *Replacing lagged estimated performance* with another, closely related regressor that enhances the quality of the predictive model:

$$\widehat{\alpha}_{i,\tau}^{\text{MF}} = \lambda_{0,\tau} + \lambda_{1,\tau} f(\widehat{\alpha}_{i,\tau-1}^{\text{MF}}) + \nu_{i,\tau} \quad (17\text{-}23)$$

---

[13] Since there are T observations overall, we need to partition the sample in order to avoid overlaps in the time periods used for the estimation, thus $\mathbf{T} < T$.

[14] For the sake of clarity, we do not include the interest rate in this very general specification. It is meant to be included in the factor returns.

where $f(\widehat{\alpha}_{i,\tau-1}^{MF})$ is a function of the estimated alpha. It can be a refined or more precise estimate of the same performance measure, i.e., $f(\widehat{\alpha}_{i,\tau-1}^{MF}) = \widehat{\widehat{\alpha}}_{i,\tau-1}^{MF}$, for instance, using bootstrapping techniques (as in, e.g., Kosowski, Timmermann, White, and Wermers, 2006) or Bayesian estimation procedures (as in, e.g., Busse and Irvine, 2006), or more simply by adding back the costs and fees in order to obtain the "gross return alphas." The function can also link the alpha to the corresponding percentile ($p\%$) or decile ($d\%$) of the fund's rank among its peers, i.e., $f(\widehat{\alpha}_{i,\tau-1}^{MF}) = p\%_{i,T-i}$.

2. *Combining lagged estimated performance* with other performance indicators in order to create a single composite performance measure:

$$\widehat{\alpha}_{i,\tau}^{MF} = \lambda_{0,\tau} + \lambda_{1,\tau} c(\widehat{\alpha}_{i,\tau-1}^{MF}, m_{i,1,\tau-1}, \ldots, m_{i,K,\tau-1}) + \nu_{i,\tau} \tag{17-24}$$

   where $c(\cdot)$ is some composite function of the estimated alpha and K other performance measures. This is the approach followed among others by Cogneau and Hübner (2020), who create linear combinations of different standardized performance measures.

3. *Completing lagged estimated performance* with other variables of interest, such as the ones examined in Section 17.1.2.2:

$$\widehat{\alpha}_{i,\tau}^{MF} = \lambda_{0,\tau} + \lambda_{1,\tau}\widehat{\alpha}_{i,\tau-1}^{MF} + \sum_l \varphi_l q_{i,l,\tau-1} + \nu_{i,\tau} \tag{17-25}$$

   where φ_l is the forecasting coefficient associated with the lth indicator. This is exactly the structure of Equation (17-5).

4. *Completing current predicted performance* with other variables of interest, in order to isolate the predictive character of lagged performance:

$$\widehat{\alpha}_{i,\tau}^{MF} = \lambda_{0,\tau} + \lambda_{1,\tau}\widehat{\alpha}_{i,\tau-1}^{MF} + \sum_l \phi_l q_{i,l,\tau} + \nu_{i,\tau} \tag{17-26}$$

   where ϕ_l is the coefficient associated with the lth contemporaneous characteristic associated with fund i. This equation fully corresponds to the spirit of the Fama–MacBeth procedure, in which each $q_{i,l,\tau}$ could be, for instance, the factor beta of fund i estimated for the current time period τ, i.e., $q_{i,l,\tau} = \beta_{i,l,\tau}$ for $l = 1, \ldots, K$.

When the estimation is done and considered to be reliable, it is then possible to use the fitted value of regression (17-22) or any of its variations in order to produce an expected performance value at the fund's level, conditionally on the information known up to time $\tau - 1$.

$$E_{\tau-1}(\widehat{\alpha}_{i,\tau}^{MF}) = \lambda_{0,\tau} + \lambda_{1,\tau}\widehat{\alpha}_{i,\tau-1}^{MF} \tag{17-27}$$

This equation applies to any time period τ if the estimation is done using rolling windows. Naturally, when the estimation is done using the whole panel data, it uses the full history of the sample. In that case, the only application of Equation (17-27) for performance prediction is *a posteriori*, namely $\tau - 1 = T$.

The examples shown above, using the multifactor alpha as both input and output of the persistence studies, can be adapted to the case of any other performance measure. In particular, the measures of abnormal return listed in Chapter 11 lend themselves particularly well to this type of exercise.

Overall, these alternative ways of testing performance persistence follow the same objective: to maximize the explanatory power of the parametric regression. The challenge is thus to obtain the highest possible predictive character of the lagged variables while at the same time avoiding spurious effects (biases) that would contaminate the results.

PrediLab example (continued)

Instead of using the funds' Jensen's alphas, whose predictability appears to be poor according to Figure 17-1, the analyst decides to use the modified Jensen's alpha ($m\alpha_P$), whose results gathered during the absolute performance analysis are encouraging. Furthermore, the company has collected the Active shares (AS_P) of each of the ten funds, as defined in Chapter 13. These inputs are summarized in Table 17-9.

TABLE 17-9 Predilab example – Modified Jensen's alphas and active shares.

Fund	Period 1		Period 2
	Modified alpha	Active share	Modified alpha
Thematic	3.47%	43%	2.55%
B1	1.54%	25%	0.53%
B2	3.49%	77%	2.64%
B3	3.81%	66%	7.67%
B4	1.68%	36%	1.62%
B5	1.64%	13%	−0.64%
B6	−0.09%	89%	5.41%
B7	3.20%	9%	0.45%
B8	3.46%	67%	10.92%
B9	−0.40%	35%	0.87%

(continued)

(continued)

The analysis carried out with univariate regressions over a single time window reveals interesting results: the coefficient of determination (R^2) using the modified Jensen's alpha equals 12.9%, whereas it is 52.0% for the Active share. Their respective outputs are represented in Figure 17-8.

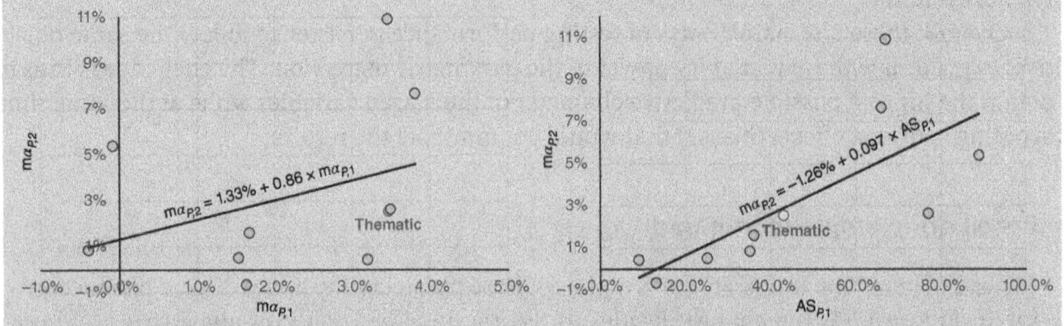

FIGURE 17-8 Predilab example – Univariate regression results on modified Jensen's alphas.

Since the two predictors have a moderate correlation coefficient $\rho(m\alpha_{P,1}, AS_{P,1}) = 6.9\%$, they can both be used in a multivariate regression, rather than being used in isolation as displayed in Figure 17-8. The resulting estimated relation, whose $R^2 = 61.6\%$, is

$$\widehat{m\alpha}_{P,2} = -2.75\% + 0.75\,\widehat{m\alpha}_{P,1} + 0.094\,\mathrm{AS}_{P,1} + \nu_{P,2}$$

Since the predicting variables for the thematic fund equal $\widehat{m\alpha}_{T,1} = 3.47\%$ and $\mathrm{AS}_{T,1} = 43\%$, the expected performance of this fund using data known at time 1 is equal to $\mathrm{E}_1(\widehat{m\alpha}_{T,2}) = -2.75\% + 0.75 \times 3.47\% + 0.094 \times 43\% = 3.88\%$. Paradoxically, the fit would have been better for this particular fund using the Active share alone, but it would have been worse (on average) for the other funds in the sample.

17.3 RELATIVE PERSISTENCE WITH RECURSIVE PORTFOLIOS

Is a fund or portfolio manager able to beat their peers in a consistent manner? This question, which mirrors the one initially opening the previous section, is a key matter for an analyst that must provide advice or make a selection among a homogeneous group of funds but also for investment firms themselves in their quest of identifying and keeping the best possible managers within their category. Furthermore, given the difficulty of identifying accurate benchmarks for many portfolios, it can prove to be more convenient, but also more reliable, to assess a portfolio's performance relative to its well-identified group of competitors for a number of purposes, including research. These are all reasons why relative persistence studies are numerous but also, to a large extent, insightful.

In this section, we cover the first main approach proposed to capture the existence of performance persistence among a group of comparable portfolios, namely the recursive portfolio method, which mixes ordinal and cardinal techniques. The second approach, covered in Section 17.4, gathers the various applications of the matched ranking method. It explicitly adopts portfolio rankings as both the input and output of the analysis.

17.3.1 Creating quantile portfolios

The regression-based approach presented in Section 17.2.4 involves a fully parametric estimation, usually considered to be linear, of the link between the predicting and the predicted variables. This is a strong assumption. Such a setup might not faithfully reflect the dependence structure between past and future performance. The recursive portfolio sorting approach, introduced by Hendricks, Patel, and Zeckhauser (1993) and popularized by Carhart (1997), provides an answer to this challenge.

The starting point of the method is similar to the logic underlying the first-pass regression of Equation (17-20), which corresponds here to the portfolio formation period. For each of the N_{t-1} assets in the sample at time $t-1$, a performance measure, chosen for its potential predictive character, is estimated using a number h of observations. Thus, we have a common input $m_{i,\rightarrow t-1}$ for $i = 1, \ldots, N_{t-1}$. Unlike the multivariate regression approach, the time periods used for the analysis do not need to be non-overlapping. Thus, the full sample size of T observations can be used without limitation. Since the first h observations must be used in order to compute the first performance measure, we have usable data for $t = h+1, h+2, \ldots, T$.

The key difference occurs in the second stage. Every asset, on the basis of its ranking at time $t-1$, is assigned to an equally-weighted "quantile portfolio" that comprises only those assets that belong to the same quantile (quartile, quintile, decile, …) at the same moment.

$$R_{q_{t-1},t} = \frac{1}{n_{q_{t-1}}} \sum_{i \in q_{t-1}} R_{i,t} \tag{17-28}$$

where $q_{t-1} = 1, \ldots, Q$ ($Q = 4$ for quartiles, $Q = 5$ for quintiles, $Q = 10$ for deciles, etc.) is the quantile of size $n_{q_{t-1}}$, with $\sum_{q_{t-1}=1}^{Q} n_{q_{t-1}} = N_{t-1}$, based on the ranking made on performance measure $m_{i,\rightarrow t-1}$. For instance, if there are 100 funds and $\text{Rk}(m_{i,\rightarrow t-1}) = 43$, then $q_{t-1} = 5$ for this portfolio i.

Because the rankings may change from one period to the next, the procedure must be repeated for each point in time. Thus, the composition of the quantile portfolios evolves over time. If an asset disappears between the estimation period $t-1$ and the subsequent measurement period t, a realistic rule must be applied, such as the equal reallocation of the remaining assets across the quantile portfolio. The procedure is illustrated in the chart shown in Figure 17-9.

The upper and lower parts of Figure 17-9 represent the logical flow of the recursive portfolio sorting methodology at two points in time t and $t+1$. Consider the upper part. We start with a panel of N_{t-1} portfolios, for each of which we use the h lagged observations. With this data set, we compute the associated performance measure m and rank the funds accordingly through the ranking list $\boldsymbol{S}_{(\to t-1)}$, from the best (denoted by $m^{\#1}_{\to t-1}$) to the worst one (denoted by $m^{\#N_{t-1}}_{\to t-1}$), which corresponds to the column in the middle of the chart. The list $\boldsymbol{S}_{(\to t-1)}$ is then sliced according to the number of quantiles chosen, whose cutoffs are represented by the thick horizontal lines. With the selected stocks for each quantile, the corresponding quantile portfolio return is computed for the consecutive time period t. The exact same process is applied to the next period, which corresponds to the lower part of the figure, and so on with the subsequent periods.

We outline the case of portfolio i, represented in bold. Its performance computed at time $t-1$ sets it at the second rank ($m^{\#2}_{\to t-1}$). Thus, for period t, this fund contributes to the return of the first quantile portfolio with return $R_{1,t}$. The next period, however, the performance of

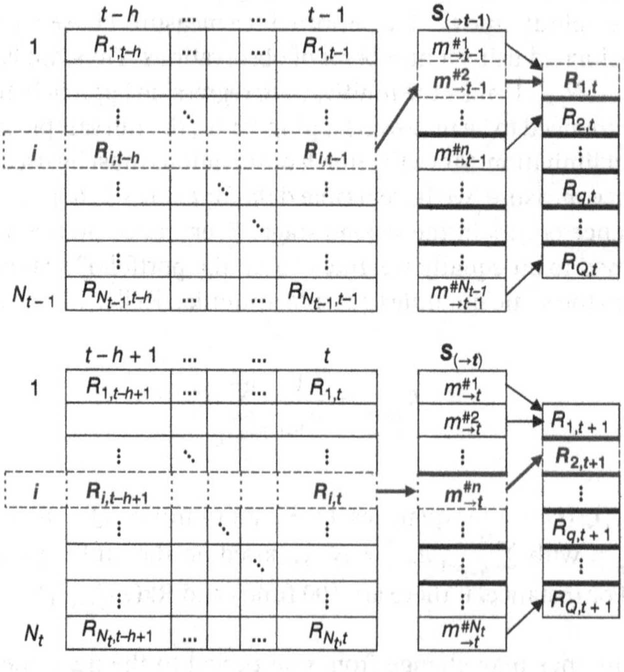

FIGURE 17-9 Illustration of the recursive portfolio sorting methodology.

the very same portfolio has deteriorated, leading to put it at rank n ($m^{\#n}_{\rightarrow t}$) in the new list $\boldsymbol{S}_{(\rightarrow t)}$. Since the fund no longer belongs to the first quantile portfolio, its subsequent return at time $t+1$ contributes to the second quantile portfolio, whose return is denoted by $R_{2,t+1}$ on the chart.

Eventually, we have material consisting of Q portfolios, whose composition at each point in time only depends on information about performance measure m observed until that moment. If this measure is a good predictor of future performance or any other indicator, then the behavior of the quantile portfolios should display notable differences from one quantile to another.

Note that, as a variation of the procedure, the rebalancing of the quantile portfolio composition can be done with a lower frequency than one time period. This means that the value of the performance measure is frozen from the initial portfolio formation until the next rebalancing date. Quite often, to avoid intra-year seasonality issues, the rebalancing frequency is chosen to be one year in many studies.

17.3.2 The performance of quantile portfolios

Fitting a regression line in the spirit of Equation (17-19) is not possible, because of the lack of direct causality between the original fund returns and the quantile portfolios. Nevertheless, there are various ways to exploit the time series of the newly created portfolios $R_{q_{t-1},t}$. Two of them fall under the scope of performance persistence: the global performance of the actual quantile portfolios and the performance of quantile portfolios with constant allocations.[15]

17.3.2.1 Global performance of the actual quantile portfolios

The most straightforward type of analysis is to directly look at the series of returns of the quantile portfolios over different horizons in order to estimate an associated performance measure. The objective is to determine whether the ranking criterion used in the portfolio formation phase represents an allocation strategy that can deliver superior returns. Since the quantile portfolios are supposed to behave jointly but always with different assets, relatively standard statistical inference techniques can be applied. In particular, studying the difference between the extreme quantile portfolios usually provides the largest probability of finding evidence of persistence. A common test is to merely compute the difference between their average returns:

$$\hat{t}_{\overline{R}_1-\overline{R}_Q=0} = \frac{\sqrt{\theta-1}(\overline{R}_1-\overline{R}_Q)}{\sigma(R_1-R_Q)} \tag{17-29}$$

where θ is the horizon of the test (up to $T-h$) and $\overline{R}_q = \frac{1}{\theta}\sum_{t=h+1}^{h+\theta} R_{q,t}$ for $q=1$ and $q=Q$.

[15] Since the recursive portfolio sorting approach also serves as a basis for survivorship probability estimation and contingency tables, the corresponding discussions will be performed in the next section.

Some performance measures can be used as well. Taking again the case of the multifactor alpha, a commonly applied analysis is the **t**-test of differences:

$$\hat{t}_{\alpha_1^{MF}-\alpha_Q^{MF}=0} = \frac{\sqrt{\theta-1}(\overline{aR}_1 - \overline{aR}_Q)}{\sigma(aR_1 - aR_Q)} \tag{17-30}$$

where $aR_{q,t} = R_{q,t} - \sum_{k=1}^{K} \beta_{q,k} F_{k,t}$ is the abnormal return of quantile portfolio q (for $q = 1$ and $q = Q$) obtained using the same multifactor model for both portfolios.

It is also possible to directly study a single performance measure applied to a hedge portfolio (long the first quantile and short the last one), whose return is denoted by $R_{(1-Q),t} \equiv R_{1,t} - R_{Q,t}$, when inference is based on less standard assumptions. For instance, if an analyst wants to take skewness and kurtosis into account, they may use Equation (3-8) of Chapter 3 to build a confidence interval around the observed Sharpe ratio $\text{SR}_{(1-Q)}$:

$$\text{SR}_{(1-Q)} \pm z_{1-\frac{x}{2}} \times \sqrt{\frac{1}{\theta}\left(1 + (\mu_{(1-Q),4} - 1)\frac{\text{SR}^2_{(1-Q)}}{4} - \mu_{(1-Q),3}\text{SR}_{(1-Q)}\right)} \tag{17-31}$$

where $\mu_{(1-Q),3} \equiv \frac{\text{E}(R_{(1-Q)} - \overline{R}_{(1-Q)})^3}{\sigma^3_{(1-Q)}}$ and $\mu_{(1-Q),4} \equiv \frac{\text{E}(R_{(1-Q)} - \overline{R}_{(1-Q)})^4}{\sigma^4_{(1-Q)}}$ are, respectively, the skewness and kurtosis of the hedge portfolio estimated over horizon θ.

17.3.2.2 Performance of the quantile portfolios with constant allocation

Another perspective is to study the capacity of the formation criterion to construct portfolios whose subsequent performance persists over time. In the previous case, each of the Q quantile portfolio is rebalanced every period and remains unique. Here, the idea is to consider the composition of each quantile portfolio at a given point in time t, to freeze this composition, and to study this portfolio's evolution after time t. The question is not so much *whether* persistence exists, but *how long* it may last.

Specifically, for each quantile portfolio corresponding to quantile q and time t, its cumulative return is calculated θ periods ahead as $R_{q,t\to t+\theta} \equiv R_{q,\theta,t}$ with constant weights, with the special case $R_{q,t\to t+1} = R_{q,t}$ if $\theta = 1$. This procedure can be reproduced for every period t from $h+1$ (because we need the first h periods to form the first set of quantile portfolios) until $T - \theta$ (because we need the last θ to measure the cumulative returns).

Unlike in the previous case, the calendar portfolios do not reflect a single investment strategy (with the portfolio composition being rebalanced every period) but a multitude of specific strategies with a common root, namely a criterion set at time $t-1$ in order to make an initial allocation at time t. Exploiting this material entails a limited comparability of the portfolio properties over time. The Sharpe ratios of two calendar portfolios starting at different dates, for example, cannot be compared with each other because they correspond to two potentially very different financial market conditions in terms of mean returns and volatilities. Thus, the analysis is restricted to total, excess, or abnormal returns whose average across portfolios can be insightful.

In general, tests of average differences are performed in a similar fashion as in Equations (17-29) or (17-30) but with a slightly different definition of the average return

$$\hat{t}_{\overline{R}_{1,\theta}-\overline{R}_{Q,\theta}=0} = \frac{\sqrt{T-\theta-h-2}(\overline{R}_{1,\theta}-\overline{R}_{Q,\theta})}{\sigma(R_{1,\theta}-R_{Q,\theta})} \tag{17-32}$$

where $\overline{R}_{q,\theta} = \frac{1}{T-\theta-h-1}\sum_{t=h+1}^{T-\theta} R_{q,\theta,t}$ for $q = 1$ and $q = Q$.

$$\hat{t}_{\alpha_{1,\theta}^{MF}-\alpha_{Q,\theta}^{MF}=0} = \frac{\sqrt{T-\theta-h-2}(\overline{aR}_{1,\theta}-\overline{aR}_{Q,\theta})}{\sigma(aR_{1,\theta}-aR_{Q,\theta})} \tag{17-33}$$

where $aR_{q,\theta,t} = R_{q,\theta,t} - \sum_{k=1}^{K}\beta_{q,k}F_{k,\theta,t}$ is the abnormal return of quantile calendar portfolio q (for $q = 1$ and $q = Q$) formed at time $t-1$ obtained using the same multifactor model for both portfolios.

The graph shown in Figure 17-10, reproduced from Carhart's (1997) paper, illustrates the insight that can be brought with this procedure regarding the potential length of performance persistence.

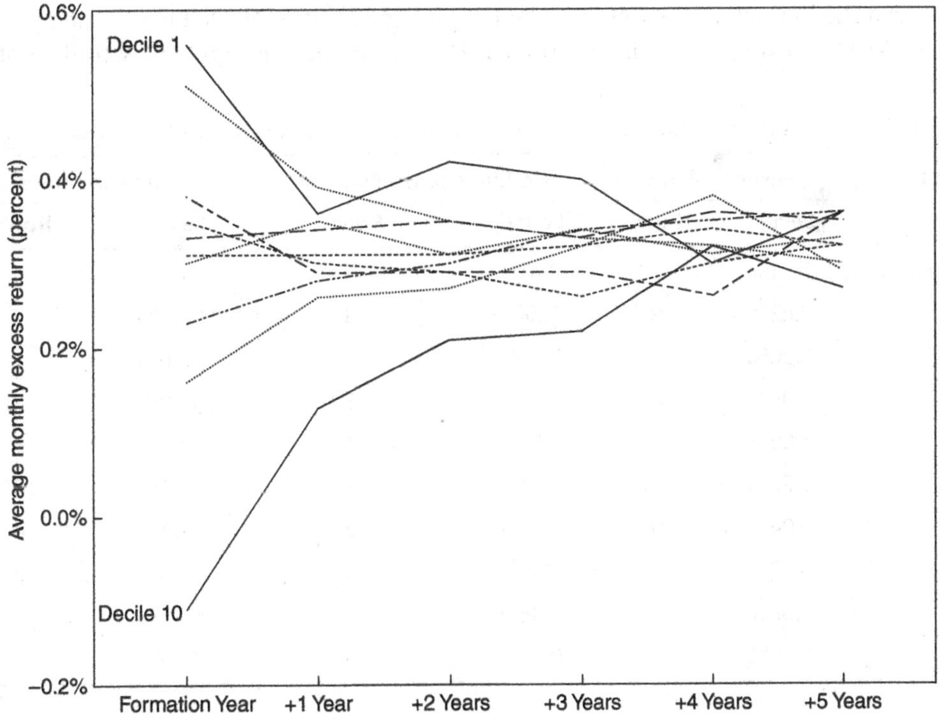

FIGURE 17-10 Illustration of average returns of calendar portfolios over different horizons. *Source*: Carhart (1997), Figure 2.

The ten decile portfolios are formed on the basis of total returns, from the best ($q = 1$) to the worst one ($q = 10$). This ranking criterion explains why the "Formation Year" returns are so different on the vertical axis, especially between the first and the tenth decile. Portfolio compositions are then kept constant and the returns are tracked for yearly horizons $\theta = 1$ to 5 years. The author shows that their cumulative returns eventually converge but mentions that $\overline{R}_{1,1} - \overline{R}_{10,1}$, i.e., the difference between the one-year returns of the first and the tenth decile portfolios, is significantly different. This finding feeds Carhart's (1997) conjecture that most of the persistence in returns is related to a momentum effect: winners remain winners, and losers remain losers.

PrediLab example (continued)

Following the same approach as in Table 17-4 for the first period, Predilab's analyst decides to switch from (i) Jensen's alpha to (ii) the modified Jensen's alpha and (iii) a composite measure based on the combination of the modified Jensen's alpha and the Active share, based on the results of Figure 17-8. Specifically, the composite measure is written as $m_{P,1} = -2.75\% + 0.75\ \widehat{m\alpha}_{P,1} + 0.094\ AS_{P,1}$.

The application of all three measures on the sample of returns over period 1 produces the following sets of values and associated rankings for the ten funds.

Given the limited number of funds in the peer group, it is decided to use the results of Table 17-10 to create two median portfolios ($H1$ with the top five and $H2$ with the bottom

TABLE 17-10 Predilab example – Performance measures and rankings for period 1.

Fund	Jensen's alpha		Modified Jensen's alpha		Composite measure	
	Level	Rank	Level	Rank	Level	Rank
Thematic	1.21%	2	3.47%	3	3.88%	5
B1	0.63%	8	1.54%	8	0.75%	7
B2	1.36%	1	3.49%	2	7.10%	1
B3	1.04%	6	3.81%	1	6.30%	2
B4	1.06%	5	1.68%	6	1.89%	6
B5	1.20%	3	1.64%	7	−0.31%	10
B6	−0.04%	9	−0.09%	9	5.56%	4
B7	0.73%	7	3.20%	5	0.48%	8
B8	1.08%	4	3.46%	4	6.13%	3
B9	−0.20%	10	−0.40%	10	0.25%	9

five funds) and to track their returns over the second period. The outcome is summarized in Table 17-11.

TABLE 17-11 Predilab example – Performance measures of ranked funds for period 2.

Rank (Period1)	Jensen's alpha				Modified Jensen's alpha				Composite measure			
	F	$R_{P,2}$	$\alpha_{P,2}$	$m\alpha_{P,2}$	F	$R_{P,2}$	$\alpha_{P,2}$	$m\alpha_{P,2}$	F	$R_{P,2}$	$\alpha_{P,2}$	$m\alpha_{P,2}$
1	B2	3.69%	0.77%	2.64%	B3	7.63%	4.23%	7.67%	B2	3.69%	0.77%	2.64%
2	Th	4.09%	0.99%	2.55%	B2	3.69%	0.77%	2.64%	B3	7.63%	4.23%	7.67%
3	B5	2.85%	−0.25%	−0.64%	Th	4.09%	0.99%	2.55%	B8	5.61%	2.75%	10.92%
4	B8	5.61%	2.75%	10.92%	B8	5.61%	2.75%	10.92%	B6	6.01%	2.71%	5.41%
5	B4	5.36%	1.40%	1.62%	B7	3.20%	0.16%	0.45%	Th	4.09%	0.99%	2.55%
6	B3	7.63%	4.23%	7.67%	B4	5.36%	1.40%	1.62%	B4	5.36%	1.40%	1.62%
7	B7	3.20%	0.16%	0.45%	B5	2.85%	−0.25%	−0.64%	B1	3.46%	0.24%	0.53%
8	B1	3.46%	0.24%	0.53%	B1	3.46%	0.24%	0.53%	B7	3.20%	0.16%	0.45%
8	B6	6.01%	2.71%	5.41%	B6	6.01%	2.71%	5.41%	B9	3.31%	0.29%	0.87%
10	B9	3.31%	0.29%	0.87%	B9	3.31%	0.29%	0.87%	B5	2.85%	−0.25%	−0.64%

The application of the recursive portfolio method of the two median portfolios whose allocation is made according to the three candidate performance measures involves averaging the returns of the five funds, entering their composition during the second period, and computing the performance measures on the resulting median portfolio returns. We miss information in order to perform statistical inference on the basis of the sample, but the application of this principle on the median portfolios based on the data of Table 17-11 already yields insightful and easily interpretable results from their visual inspection, as shown in Figure 17-11.

(continued)

(continued)

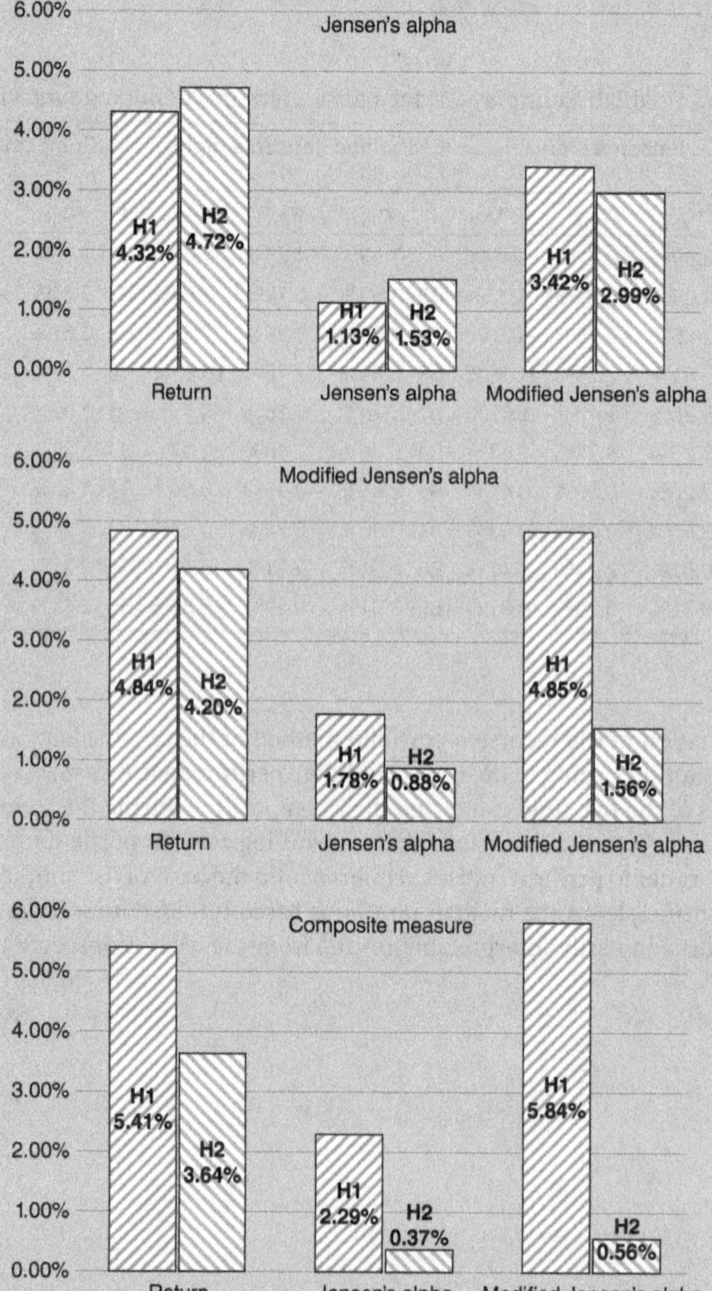

FIGURE 17-11 Predilab example – Performance measures of the median portfolios in period 2.

The comparison of the histograms on the left (total returns) does not leave a clear impression of superior persistence results of the first over the second median portfolios. The picture radically changes when the Jensen's alphas (middle bars) or the modified Jensen's alphas (right bars) are matched in period 2. The discriminating power of the modified Jensen's alpha (in the middle chart), and especially the composite measure (in the bottom chart), becomes visible. For both the Jensen's and modified Jensen's alphas, the first median portfolio produces economically significant positive values, whereas they are close to zero for the second median portfolio. The composite measure provides the strongest difference, which confirms the previous analysis made using the parametric cross-sectional persistence approach.

17.3.3 Alternative use of outputs

The quantile portfolios may exhibit persistence in performance because of the capacity of fund managers to consistently outperform the market over time. However, besides persistence, the performance measure chosen for the sorting of portfolios may also help forecast other outputs, such as fund flows, fees, or risk exposures, as already discussed in Section 17.1.2.1. The setup presented above can easily be adapted to test the predictability of these types of variables.

Another interesting type of forecast is the survival probability of a fund. Having a global sample of N funds and observing, at each point in time t, that there are N_t surviving funds and d_t funds that disappear, represents precious information, both in the portfolio formation and testing phases. In a context similar to the recursive portfolio method, Cogneau and Hübner (2015) propose using a linear combination of performance measures $m_{i,\rightarrow t-1} = c(m_{i,1,\rightarrow t-1}, \ldots, m_{i,K,\rightarrow t-1})$ in order to create the quantiles. Then, they use two approaches to test the capacity of past performance to predict the likelihood of a fund's survival.[16]

The first approach is to use the quantile portfolios illustrated in Figure 17-9 but, instead of performing the types of tests used for performance persistence, they assign a constant penalty rate of return to each quantile portfolio every time that one of its components disappears. Thus, the "graveyard-corrected" quantile portfolio return $R^{\dagger}_{q_{t-1},t}$ can be defined as

$$R^{\dagger}_{q_{t-1},t} = R_{q_{t-1},t} - \frac{1}{n_{q_{t-1}}} \sum_{i \in q_{t-1}} \pi \times 1_{\{i \in d_t\}} \tag{17-34}$$

[16]There exist some alternative approaches. The one proposed among others by Zalewska and Zhang (2020), consists of comparing the characteristics of the group of funds that disappear over a certain period compared to the ones of a control group of funds that do not disappear over the same period. Another approach is to use the Cox regression model to directly assess the fund's disappearance time, as in Cameron and Hall (2003).

where $R_{q_{t-1},t}$ is the raw quantile portfolio return as defined in Equation (17-28), π is the penalty return (in %) associated with the occurrence of a fund's disappearance (liquidation, merger, or inactivity) from the database, and $1_{\{i \in d_t\}}$ is an indicator function that takes a value of 1 if fund i belongs to the set d_t of disappearing funds, and 0 otherwise. Note that if $\pi = 0$, then $R^{\dagger}_{q_{t-1},t} = R_{q_{t-1},t}$.

The rationale underlying Equation (17-34) can be understood with a simple example. Consider five quintile portfolios ($Q = 5$). At time t, the first and last quintile portfolios, both featuring $n_{q_{t-1}} = 20$ funds, deliver the same rate of return: $R_{1,t} = R_{5,t} = +2\%$. Nevertheless, there have been no defunct funds in the first quintile, but four funds belonging to the fifth quintile have disappeared, hence posting no return for the corresponding funds in the database for that period. If we assign a penalty of $\pi = 5\%$ to each of these funds, the graveyard-corrected return of the portfolio becomes $R^{\dagger}_{5,t} = R_{5,t} - \frac{1}{20}\sum_{i \in q5} 10\% \times 1_{\{i \in d_t\}} = 2\% - \frac{1}{20} \times 5\% \times 4 = 1\%$. If a similar phenomenon (i.e., a substantially larger proportion of defunct funds in the highest quintile portfolio) regularly occurs, the impact of disappearing funds on the quantile portfolio returns could become very material.

The second approach uses the quantile-related information obtained in the portfolio formation period in the scope of a pure parametric survivorship analysis. Considering, as before, a horizon of θ periods for the prediction, this analysis consists of fitting a logistic function that connects a fund's characteristics with the event of disappearance in the following generic form:[17]

$$1_{\{t<\delta_i\leq t+\theta\}} = \frac{\exp\left(\beta_0 + \sum_{q=1}^{Q} \beta_q 1_{\{i \in q_{t-1}\}} + \sum_l \varphi_l \varphi_{i,l,t-1} + \nu_{i,\tau}\right)}{1 + \exp\left(\beta_0 + \sum_{q=1}^{Q} \beta_q 1_{\{i \in q_{t-1}\}} + \sum_l \varphi_l \varphi_{i,l,t-1} + \nu_{i,\tau}\right)} \tag{17-35}$$

where $1_{\{t<\delta_i\leq t+\theta\}}$ is an indicator function that takes a value of 1 if the disappearance time of fund i, denoted by δ_i, is earlier than or equal to the prediction horizon θ and 0 otherwise.

Coefficient β_q indicates the sensitivity of the probability of disappearance to the fund's belonging to quantile q. If the portfolio quantiles are relevant for the prediction of fund failure, there should be a significant difference in the levels of the β_q across quantiles. Consider for instance that $Q = 5$ (quintile portfolios), $\beta_1 = -2$, and $\beta_5 = +2$. This means that if a fund belongs to the first (best) quintile at time $t - 1$, this classification entails a contribution of $\beta_1 1_{\{i \in q1_{t-1}\}} = (-2) \times 1 = -2$ to the argument of the logistic function, whereas another fund belonging to the fifth (worst) quintile has a contribution of $\beta_5 1_{\{i \in q5_{t-1}\}} = (+2) \times 1 = +2$ to the argument of the logistic function. Thus, everything else remaining equal, one expects the fifth quintile fund to disappear faster than the first quintile fund.

Unlike the first method, for which the consequence of the funds' rankings directly impacts the returns of the quantile portfolios, it is necessary to establish a criterion for the quality of the logistic regression and to assess the relevance of the associated set of predictors. The traditional approach for such an assessment is to examine the receiver operating characteristic

[17] Other survivorship functions can be considered, like the probit function, or a Poisson counting process in the case of a portfolio.

(ROC) curve, which is well known in the context of credit risk for instance. In the current context, the ROC curve reflects the relationship between the false-positive rate (FPR) of disappearance prediction (i.e., the ratio of the number of funds that were predicted to disappear according to the criterion being among the worst $x\%$ rated funds, but did not, divided by the total number of disappearing funds) and the true-positive rate (TPR) (i.e., the ratio of the number of funds that were predicted to disappear according to the criterion being among the worst $x\%$ rated funds, and that actually did, divided by the total number of disappearing funds). The FPR is equivalent to one minus the specificity (i.e., propensity to generate the Type-I error) of the model, whereas the TPR is called the sensitivity (i.e., ability to avoid the Type-II error). A random prediction system would, on average, yield the same FPR and TPR for whichever threshold x, so that the ROC curve takes the form of a 45° straight line.

Applied to a sample of mutual funds, Cogneau and Hübner (2015) show how the use of the logistic model of Equation (17-35) graphically translates into an ROC curve, as shown in Figure 17-12.

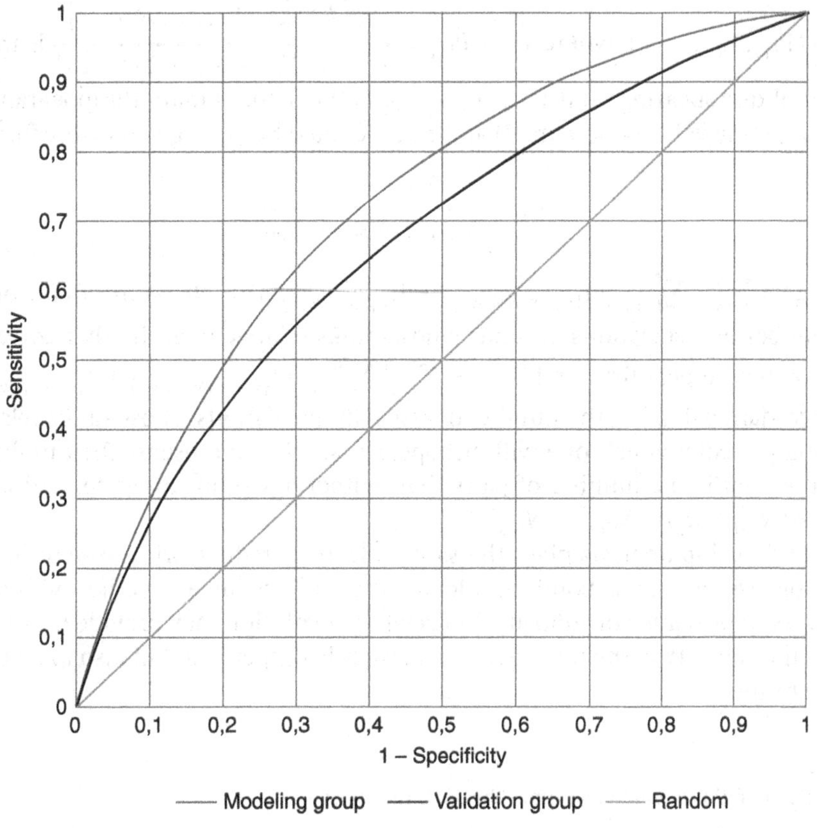

FIGURE 17-12 Illustration of the quality of a fund survivorship prediction model. *Source*: Cogneau and Hübner (2015), Figure 1.

Figure 17-12 shows the quality of the best calibration of the logistic function represented by Equation (17-35) for two sub-samples of funds: the "modeling group" (in-sample), on which the logistic function has been estimated and its parameters optimized, and the "validation group" (out-of-sample) on which the output of the model has been tested without parameter recalibration. The inputs are measured over a lagged three-year period ($h = 36$ months) and the prediction horizon is one year ($\theta = 12$ months).

The higher the ROC curve, the better the model predictive performance. Logically, the in-sample estimation (the observations are used in order to find the model parameters that provide the best fit) produces an ROC curve that lies above that of the validation sample. It is further necessary to evaluate the quality of the predictive model. Visually, it is related to the magnitude of the area under the curve (AUC). From a quantitative perspective, given the structure of the model (a continuous predictor function and a binary response variable), it is customary to use Somers' (1962) D statistic as an equivalent indicator of the quality of the model.[18]

In the survivorship analysis case, each fund $i = 1, \ldots, N_{t-1}$ is characterized by a pair $(x_{i,t}, y_{i,t}) \equiv (\widehat{\Pr}_{i,t}, 1_{\{t<\delta_i \le t+\theta\}})$, where $x_{i,t} \equiv \widehat{\Pr}_{i,t} = \frac{\exp\left(\beta_0 + \sum_{q=1}^{Q} \beta_q 1_{\{i \in q_{t-1}\}} + \sum_l \phi_l q_{i,l,t-1}\right)}{1+\exp\left(\beta_0 + \sum_{q=1}^{Q} \beta_q 1_{\{i \in q_{t-1}\}} + \sum_l \phi_l q_{i,l,t-1}\right)}$ is the predicted probability of disappearing, and $y_{i,t} \equiv 1_{\{t<\delta_i \le t+\theta\}}$ is the actual binary disappearance variable. The corresponding value of Somers' D at time t, denoted by D_t, is given by the formula

$$D_t = \frac{N_{\text{Con}_t} - N_{\text{Dis}_t}}{N_{\text{Con}_t} + N_{\text{Dis}_t} + N_{\text{Inc}_t}} \tag{17-36}$$

where $N_{\text{Con}_t} = \sum_{i=1}^{N_{t-1}} \sum_{j=1, j \neq i}^{N_{t-1}} (1_{\{x_{i,t}<x_{j,t} \& y_{i,t}<y_{j,t}\}} + 1_{\{x_{i,t}>x_{j,t} \& y_{i,t}>y_{j,t}\}})$ is the sum of concordant pairs, i.e., the number of associations of funds whose ranks relative to each other correctly predict which one will disappear first, and $N_{\text{Dis}_t} = \sum_{i=1}^{N_{t-1}} \sum_{j=1, j \neq i}^{N_{t-1}} (1_{\{x_{i,t}<x_{j,t} \& y_{i,t}>y_{j,t}\}} + 1_{\{x_{i,t}>x_{j,t} \& y_{i,t}<y_{j,t}\}})$ is the sum of discordant pairs, i.e., the number of associations of funds whose ranks relative to each other wrongly predict which one will disappear first. N_{Inc_t} represents the number of inconclusive pairs, that is the number of pairs that neither agree nor disagree, and is defined as $N_{\text{Inc}_t} = d_t \times (N_{t-1} - d_t) - N_{\text{Con}_t} - N_{\text{Dis}_t}$.

This survivorship analysis plays the same role as a credit scoring system in the context of defaultable assets such as bonds and loans. Past performance, together with other candidate variables, represents portfolio attributes whose evolution may provide useful insight not only about the capacity of the manager to consistently outperform but also to let the portfolio survive over time.

---

[18] Formally, Somers' D is equal to two times the AUC minus one.

PrediLab example (continued)

None of the ten funds disappeared over period 2. However, extending the prediction window further, the PrediLab analyst observes that three funds have disappeared from the database. These are funds B1, B5, and B7.

The basis for the survivorship analysis is the same as for the performance persistence. Funds are first scored on period 1 according to their Jensen's alpha, their modified Jensen's alpha and the composite measure based on the combination of the modified Jensen's alpha and the Active share. Then, the ROC curve is built on the basis of the inverse of the ranking (the worst performer is ranked #1, the second worst is ranked #2, and so on). As a way to make the graph intuitive, we illustrate in Figure 17-13 the relation between the fund ranking (horizontal axis) and the cumulative defunct proportion (vertical axis) for the three ranking systems.

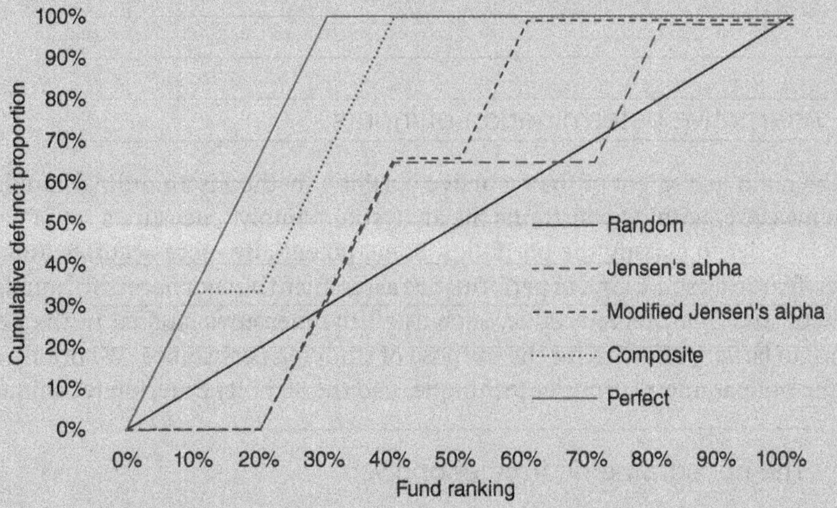

FIGURE 17-13 Predilab example – Survivorship predictive power of the three scoring systems.

The 45° line corresponding to the random prediction and the piecewise-linear continuous line corresponding to the perfect prediction (i.e., the bottom three funds are the defunct ones, so that each of these funds accounts for 33.3% of the total defunct funds) draw a triangle whose area corresponds to a perfect prediction. The ranking using Jensen's alpha ranks defunct funds as #3, #4, and #8. This is a poor predictive performance that represents graphically as quasi-erratic movements along the 45° line (spaced dashed line). The modified Jensen's alpha (medium dashed line), which ranks defunct funds #3, #4, and #6, does

(continued)

(continued)

slightly better. As for the persistence analysis, the best predictive performance is achieved by the composite score, which ranks defunct funds #1, #3, and #4 (i.e., almost perfectly).

These insights are confirmed by the Somers' *D* scores of the three ranking systems, whose computation is summarized in Table 17-12.

TABLE 17-12 Predilab example – Somers' *D* for the three ranking systems.

Pairs count	Jensen's alpha	Modified Jensen's alpha	Composite measure
Concordant	12	14	19
Discordant	9	7	2
Somers' D	***14.29%***	***33.33%***	***80.95%***

17.3.4 Alternative determination of inputs

Because the main ingredient of the recursive portfolio method is an ordinal ranking and not a cardinal measure, nothing constrains the analyst to "simply" measure a set of performance indicators in order to classify the portfolios. Some potentially more accurate and innovative techniques, featuring some kind of performance assessment but not necessarily under the form of a synthetic and interpretable value, such as all the measures studied in the first chapter, could prove to be very effective for the purpose of studying persistence. We briefly review two of them: the nonparametric frontier technique, and the stability criterion technique.

17.3.4.1 The nonparametric frontier analysis

After all, portfolio performance measurement can be seen as a way to assess the efficiency of the portfolio transformation process from an input (risk) into an output (return). The exact same logic is adopted in the context of nonparametric frontier analysis (NFA) but without the need to impose a strict structure that connects the outputs to the inputs. Its most popular version is probably the data envelopment analysis, introduced in the performance measurement literature by Gregoriou, Sedzro, and Zhu (2005), but there have been various improvements proposed in the context of the measurement of portfolio performance, such as the free disposable hull model.[19]

[19]A simpler application of this type of analysis is proposed with the efficiency measure examined in Equation (6-15) of Chapter 6 as an alternative to the Sharpe ratio.

In the context of performance persistence with the recursive portfolio method, the use of NFA has been proposed by Abdelsalam, Duygun, Matallín-Sáez, and Tortosa-Ausina (2014). The basis for the analysis is a set of J fund-related heterogeneous and non-negative inputs $\mathbf{x}_{i,t-1} = (x_{i,1,t-1}, \ldots, x_{i,J,t-1})$, whose interpretation should be related to a "cost" for the portfolio manager (e.g., beta, variance, kurtosis, VaR, CVaR, etc.), and a set of K fund-related heterogeneous and non-negative outputs $\mathbf{y}_{i,t-1} = (y_{i,1,t-1}, \ldots, y_{i,K,t-1})$, considered as a "reward," such as mean return, excess return, skewness. The first step is to define, from every possible combination of inputs and outputs, the "best practice production set" as the convex set of undominated input–output combinations:

$$\widehat{\boldsymbol{\Psi}}_{t-1} = \{(\mathbf{x}_{t-1}\mathbf{y}_{t-1})|\mathbf{x}_{t-1} \leq \mathbf{x}_{i,t-1}, \mathbf{y}_{t-1} \geq \mathbf{y}_{i,t-1}, i = 1, \ldots, N_{t-1}\} \tag{17-37}$$

under the constraint that the pair $(\mathbf{x}_{t-1}, \mathbf{y}_{t-1})$ is attainable.

In studies that focus on the performance of mutual or hedge funds, it is commonly accepted to stick to one single output per fund $y_{i,t-1}$. Then, the output-oriented efficiency indicator, which serves as a way to classify funds, is represented by the expression

$$\tilde{\varphi}_{i,t-1} \equiv \tilde{\varphi}(\mathbf{x}_{i,t-1}, y_{i,t-1}) = \sup\{\varphi|(\mathbf{x}_{i,t-1}, \varphi y_{i,t-1}) \in \widehat{\boldsymbol{\Psi}}_{t-1}\} \tag{17-38}$$

where $\tilde{\varphi}_{i,t-1} = 1$ if the fund is efficient, and $\tilde{\varphi}_{i,t-1} > 1$ if it is not. This coefficient can be seen as the necessary multiplier in output for fund i to reach the same level as that of the best (efficient) fund.

Since it is possible to obtain the indicator $\tilde{\varphi}_{i,t-1}$ for every fund at every point in time, we can simply define $m_{i,\to t-1} \equiv 1 - \tilde{\varphi}_{i,t-1} \leq 0$ for the purpose of classification in the context of Figure 17-9.

17.3.4.2 The stability criterion technique

In order to assess future persistence in performance, why not use past persistence as a potentially reliable indicator? Even though this idea might appear to be quite natural, its operational adaptation is challenging, mostly because of the necessity of having a sufficiently long time window to assess past persistence, together with strong enough evidence about the significance of this persistence.

An elegant solution to this challenge is provided by a dedicated application of the stability criterion developed in Section 4.4.1 of Chapter 4. Its principle consists of the identification of the frequency at which funds are ranked in the top k% according to some criterion (in our case the chosen performance measure $m_{i,\to t-1}$) over a repeated number of distinct classifications. A fund would then be contained in the "stable set" for percentile k if it belongs to this percentile with a minimum frequency of π%. This method has been adapted in the context of portfolio management by Grau-Carles, Doncel, and Sainz (2019).[20]

[20]The complete explanation of the stability criterion is performed in Chapter 4. We simply summarize it here.

How can this methodology be adapted in the context of the recursive portfolio method? As explained in Chapter 4, depending on the chosen threshold π, it is possible to rank funds according to the order with which they enter the stable set for decreasing values of k. It is thus necessary to (i) select a ranking criterion $m_{i,\to t-1}$, (ii) rank funds according to this criterion during n different (possibly overlapping) periods of time in the past (i.e., rank them according to measures $m_{i,\to t-n}, m_{i,\to t-n-1}, \ldots, m_{i,\to t-1}$), (iii) identify the fund that first enters the stable set according to the stability criterion and tag its last reported performance as $m^{\#1}_{\to t-1}$, and (iv) then identify the second-best fund and tag it as $m^{\#2}_{\to t-1}$, and so on until the last fund is identified. According to this nonparametric procedure that uses multiple past classifications, we obtain the list $\boldsymbol{S}_{(\to t-1)}$ that appears in Figure 17-9. The rest of the recursive portfolio methodology (i.e., the analysis of outputs) remains unchanged.[21]

Take for instance an example adapted from Chapter 4. Imagine that we have $N_{t-1} = 100$ funds that are ranked, from the best (#1) to the worst (#100), according to their Sharpe Ratio ($m_{i,\to t-1} \equiv \mathrm{SR}_{i,t-1}$) over a period of three years with weekly observations. We reproduce this ranking with a rolling window sliding back in the past, month per month, going back three years in time. We thus have 36 alternative (but relatively close) rankings of the same 100 funds. For the stability criterion, a rule of $\pi = 75\%$ is adopted. This means that a fund is considered as "stable" for percentile k if it appears in this percentile in at least 27 lists out of 36 ($\pi = 27/36$).

The determination of the final ranking is illustrated in Figure 17-14, which looks similar to Figure 4-8 of Chapter 4, but serves a different purpose.

The curve on the figure connects the ranking cutoff k with the associated cardinality $|\hat{\Lambda}^{\mathrm{SR}}_{k;75\%}|$ of the stable set, i.e., the number of funds that it contains for that cutoff using the Sharpe ratio and the threshold of $\pi = 75\%$.

In the example, we observe that the first fund that is considered as "stable" is the 47th one in the sample ($i = 47$). It is already included in the stable set for $k = 2$, which means that it belonged to the top two funds at least 27 times over the past 36 ranking periods. It is thus considered as the best fund according to the Sharpe ratio. In Figure 17-9, it would be on top of the list with associated performance $m^{\#1}_{\to t-1} = \mathrm{SR}_{47,t-1}$. The next fund that enters the stable set is $i = 88$. It is included in the top five list at least 27 times. This fund is ranked second, with $m^{\#2}_{\to t-1} = \mathrm{SR}_{88,t-1}$. The list continues to be incremented according to the increase in k: more and more funds enter the stable set, one by one, and they are ranked accordingly.

[21] Another application of the stability criterion in the context of performance persistence is to select, for a given percentile k, those funds that enter the stable set with a sufficient frequency so as to be considered as consistently superior over several time periods. If their subsequent (future) performance exceeds that of their peers, they are considered as persistent in their capacity to outperform. The set of performance measures whose out-of-sample test on the persistent funds is economically most significant is then selected as the "most powerful" $m_{i,\to t-1}$. The method does not only identify the most persistent funds but also the most anti-persistent ones by adapting the procedure to the reverse rankings (from the worst to the best one). The end-to-end innovative methodology and its associated industrial application framework have been patented by the Belgian fintech company Sopiad (`www.sopiad.com`).

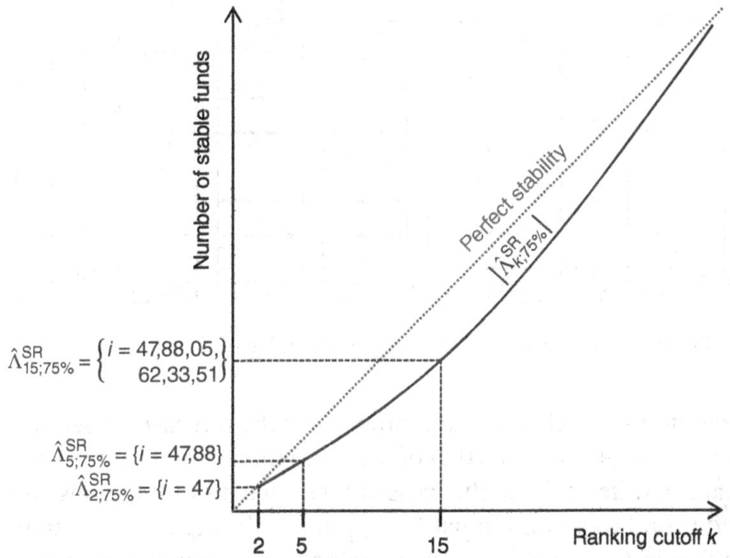

FIGURE 17-14 Illustration of the use of stability selection in the context of performance persistence.

For instance, when $k = 15$, there are a total of six funds in the list. In order to obtain the first decile of funds, it is thus necessary to loosen the selection criterion further. The quantile portfolios are thus constituted by moving k further and further to the right until we reach the end of the list ($k = 100$), in which case all funds are classified by definition.

17.4 RELATIVE PERSISTENCE WITH MATCHED RANKINGS

The recursive portfolio method can be viewed as a semi-parametric approach for predictability. The outcome of an estimation period appears as a ranking, which involves a simplification of the information gathered with the precise computation of a performance measure. However, looking at Figure 17-9, it turns out that the ranking information is used in a parametric manner within the forecasting period, as the returns of the quantile portfolios are studied over different prediction horizons.

The contingency table method is fully nonparametric, as it relies on ordinal measures both during the estimation and the prediction periods. In the first part, it uses the same type of input as the recursive portfolio method. The difference lies in the treatment of this information over the second part of the time frame, namely over the prediction horizon. Instead of creating quantile portfolios and updating them regularly, each fund is tracked over time and ranked according to its observed posterior performance (possibly using a different metric). Thus, the only material that happens to be exploited for the analysis is a pair of rankings. The procedure is illustrated in Figure 17-15, which adopts the same structure as Figure 17-9.

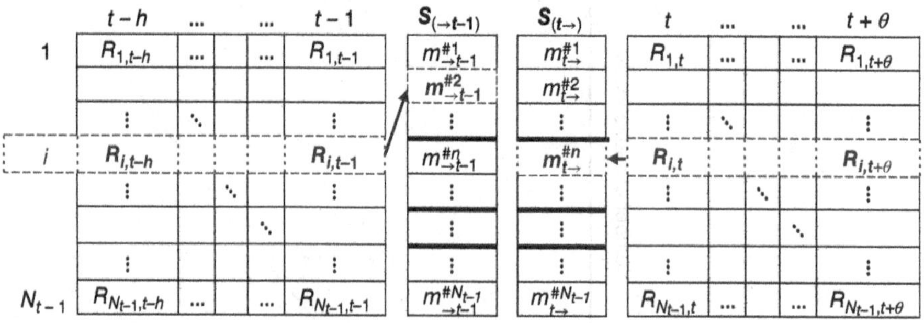

FIGURE 17-15 Illustration of the matched ranking methodology.

Zooming on fund i, the classification process for the forecasting period starting at time t and leading to horizon $t + \theta$ mirrors that of the estimation period from $t - h$ to $t - 1$. The fund will likely be ranked differently on the basis of these two disjoint periods, as illustrated in the graph (the fund is ranked second in list $S_{(\to t-1)}$ made during the formation period, but only at the nth position in the list $S_{(t\to)}$ corresponding to the testing period, therefore belonging to different quantiles). Eventually, the analyst is left with two rankings $S_{(\to t-1)}$ and $S_{(t\to)}$ for the analysis, and persistence will be evidenced if a significant connection can be discovered between them. At this point, several options are possible. These include a simple analysis of contingency tables, a wider examination of the complete rankings, or a dynamic approach based on Markov chains.

17.4.1 Contingency table analysis

Instead of trying to deal with the full information contained in rankings $S_{(\to t-1)}$ and $S_{(t\to)}$, a somewhat more modest standpoint is to split both lists into quantiles, as in the recursive portfolio method, and to check whether funds that belong to a given quantile in the first list have the tendency to still belong to the same quantile in the second list through a "contingency table." According to this approach, persistence is evidenced if the transition from one quantile to another is not due to luck but to a pattern that is at least partly deterministic. The use of contingency tables has the merits of being fully nonparametric and of allowing the identification of persistence with a very limited set of assumptions. The price to pay for this flexibility is the necessity of relying on large samples leading to a very unstructured type of persistence relationship.

The most commonly used contingency table method is to split both lists into two equal parts from the median. Funds are then categorized as "winners" or "losers" according to where they rank according to each list. The occurrences of each pair of possible outcomes are counted and serve as the basis for the statistical analysis.[22] This logic is represented in Table 17-13.

[22]If the amount of funds is a small and odd number, the median fund can be either considered in the first or second half, then the whole analysis is performed in both cases, and the average result is adopted.

TABLE 17-13 Structure of the 2 × 2 contingency table.

Prior ranking $S_{(\to t-1)}$	Posterior ranking $S_{(t\to)}$	
	$Rk(m_{i,t\to t}) < \frac{N_{t-1}}{2}$ "future winner"	$Rk(m_{i,t\to}) > \frac{N_{t-1}}{2}$ "future loser"
$Rk(m_{i,\to t-1}) < \frac{N_{t-1}}{2}$ "past winner"	$w_{t-1}w_t$	$w_{t-1}l_t$
$Rk(m_{i,\to t-1}) > \frac{N_{t-1}}{2}$ "past loser"	$l_{t-1}w_t$	$l_{t-1}l_t$

The main diagonal cells represent situations of agreements between the two rankings, i.e., repeat winners or losers. They stand respectively as $w_{t-1}w_t = \sum_{i=1}^{N_{t-1}} 1_{\{Rk(m_{i,\to t-1})<\frac{N_{t-1}}{2}\&Rk(m_{i,t\to})<\frac{N_{t-1}}{2}\}}$ for "winner–winner," which represents the sum of occurrences where the fund is ranked in the top half of both lists, and $l_{t-1}l_t = \sum_{i=1}^{N_{t-1}} 1_{\{Rk(m_{i,\to t-1})>\frac{N_{t-1}}{2}\&Rk(m_{i,t\to})>\frac{N_{t-1}}{2}\}}$ for "loser–loser," which represents the sum of occurrences where the fund is ranked in the bottom half of both lists. Similarly, the off-diagonal cells represent situations of disagreements between the rankings. These are respectively equal to $w_{t-1}l_t = \sum_{i=1}^{N_{t-1}} 1_{\{Rk(m_{i,\to t-1})<\frac{N_{t-1}}{2}\&Rk(m_{i,t\to})>\frac{N_{t-1}}{2}\}}$ ("winner–loser") and $l_{t-1}w_t = \sum_{i=1}^{N_{t-1}} 1_{\{Rk(m_{i,\to t-1})>\frac{N_{t-1}}{2}\&Rk(m_{i,t\to})<\frac{N_{t-1}}{2}\}}$ ("loser–winner").

From this basis material, the most straightforward treatments of information are the use of the cross-product ratio (CPR) and the repeat winner approaches. Both allow hypothesis testing on the basis of the standard normal distribution provided that the number of funds is sufficiently large.

The CPR approach, introduced by Brown and Goetzmann (1995) in the context of asset management, posits the randomness of the transition from the state of being a winner or loser to the next state as a winner or loser. If this is the case, then the product of the cell on the main diagonal of Table 17-13 should be equal to the product of the off-diagonal cells. The cross-product ratio at time t is just the ratio of these two products: $CPR_t = \frac{w_{t-1}w_t \times l_{t-1}l_t}{w_{t-1}l_t \times l_{t-1}w_t}$. The CPR Z-statistic follows a standard Gaussian distribution under the null hypothesis and is written as

$$\hat{z}_{CPR=1} = \frac{\log CPR_t}{\sigma(\log CPR_t)} \tag{17-39}$$

where $\sigma(\log CPR_t) = \sqrt{\frac{1}{w_{t-1}w_t} + \frac{1}{l_{t-1}l_t} + \frac{1}{w_{t-1}l_t} + \frac{1}{l_{t-1}w_t}}$.

The repeat winner approach of Malkiel (1995) also posits the randomness of transitions, but from the perspective of a binomial argument. The focus is put on the top row of

Table 17-13 – thus using less information than the CPR test – in which it is checked whether the proportion of repeat winners (upper left cell), denoted by $\mathrm{RW}_t = \frac{w_{t-1}w_t}{w_{t-1}w_t + w_{t-1}l_t}$, effectively accounts for half of the transitions, i.e.,

$$\hat{z}_{\mathrm{RW}_t=50\%} = \frac{w_{t-1}w_t - 0.5 \times (w_{t-1}w_t + w_{t-1}l_t)}{0.5\sqrt{(w_{t-1}w_t + w_{t-1}l_t)}} \tag{17-40}$$

A similar argument can be made for the repeat losers, in which only the bottom row is considered:

$$\hat{z}_{\mathrm{RL}_t=50\%} = \frac{l_{t-1}l_t - 0.5 \times (l_{t-1}l_t + l_{t-1}w_t)}{0.5\sqrt{(l_{t-1}l_t + l_{t-1}w_t)}} \tag{17-41}$$

The repeat winner/loser test is less comprehensive than the CPR test, because it uses less information. Nevertheless, it makes it possible to detect whether persistence is positive or negative, depending on whether the significance is different using Equation (17-40) or (17-41).

Finally, a more general approach of the contingency table method is the Chi-square approach introduced by Kahn and Rudd (1995). Again relying on large samples, this type of analysis compares the actual matrix of quantile transitions with the theoretical one, under the assumption of independent rankings. The underlying mechanism is illustrated in Table 17-14, which can be viewed as a generalization of Table 17-13.

The actual transitions from a given quantile in ranking $S_{(\rightarrow t-1)}$ to another quantile in ranking $S_{(t\rightarrow)}$ are represented in the table with the notation $j_{t-1}k_t = \sum_{i=1}^{N_{t-1}} 1_{\{i \in j_{t-1} \& i \in k_t\}}$. Under the null hypothesis of independent rankings, the N_{t-1} funds are spread equally across the $Q \times Q = Q^2$ cells of the table. Thus, one expects each cell to contain the same number $\frac{N_{t-1}}{Q^2}$ of observations.[23]

TABLE 17-14 Structure of the $Q \times Q$ actual and expected contingency tables.

$S_{(\rightarrow t-1)}$ Prior quantile	$S_{(t\rightarrow)}$ Posterior quantile						
	q = 1		q = 2		...	q = Q	
	Actual	Predicted	Actual	Predicted	...	Actual	Predicted
q = 1	$1_{t-1}1_t$	$\frac{N_{t-1}}{Q^2}$	$1_{t-1}2_t$	$\frac{N_{t-1}}{Q^2}$	...	$1_{t-1}Q_t$	$\frac{N_{t-1}}{Q^2}$
q = 2	$2_{t-1}1_t$	$\frac{N_{t-1}}{Q^2}$	$2_{t-1}2_t$	$\frac{N_{t-1}}{Q^2}$	...	$2_{t-1}Q_t$	$\frac{N_{t-1}}{Q^2}$
⋮	⋮	⋮	⋮	⋮	...	⋮	⋮
q = Q	$Q_{t-1}1_t$	$\frac{N_{t-1}}{Q^2}$	$Q_{t-1}2_t$	$\frac{N_{t-1}}{Q^2}$	...	$Q_{t-1}Q_t$	$\frac{N_{t-1}}{Q^2}$

[23] Naturally, the reasoning can be extended to a non-squared matrix, notably if some funds disappear between time $t-1$ and the expiration of the forecasting horizon $t+\theta$. In this case, the average number of defunct funds can be used as the expected number of disappearances, for instance. The expression corresponding to Equation (17-42) then becomes slightly more complex, but shares the same interpretation.

In this simple form, the Chi-square test performs a cell-by-cell comparison of the actual and predicted frequencies. It takes the squared deviation for each observation, sums them up, and takes their average. Starting from the structure of Table 17-14, it can be expressed as

$$\hat{\chi}^2_{(Q-1)^2} = \frac{1}{N_{t-1}} \sum_{j=1}^{Q} \sum_{k=1}^{Q} \left({}_{j_{t-1}}k_t - \frac{N_{t-1}}{Q^2} \right)^2 \tag{17-42}$$

where $\hat{\chi}^2_{(Q-1)^2}$ follows a Chi-squared distribution with $(Q-1)^2$ degrees of freedom under the null hypothesis of absence of persistence.

Because the test focuses on the deviations, it does not matter whether the departure from the expected transition frequencies are positive or negative – indeed they offset each other across the table. Thus, one important caveat with this method is that it allows us to test whether there is evidence of persistence, but not whether this persistence is positive or negative.

As a special case of Equation (17-42), it is possible to perform the test on the 2 × 2 contingency table of Table 17-13. In that case, the equation simplifies to:

$$\hat{\chi}^2_1 = \frac{1}{N_{t-1}} \left[\left(w_{t-1}w_t - \frac{N_{t-1}}{4} \right)^2 + \left(l_{t-1}l_t - \frac{N_{t-1}}{4} \right)^2 + \left(w_{t-1}l_t - \frac{N_{t-1}}{4} \right)^2 + \left(l_{t-1}w_t - \frac{N_{t-1}}{4} \right)^2 \right] \tag{17-43}$$

The test explicitly takes into account all information contained in the contingency table. In that sense, it can be viewed as the most specific test but also the one requiring the largest number of observations because the critical values of the Chi-squared distribution with one degree of freedom are very large for most confidence levels. It should be recommended for a large number of funds.

PrediLab example (continued)

It is decided to focus on (i) Jensen's alpha and (ii) the modified Jensen's alpha in order to construct the 2 × 2 contingency tables and perform the associated hypothesis tests. For that purpose, the rankings obtained in Table 17-10 are used for period 1, whereas the performance values of Table 17-11 provide the rankings for period 2. This leads to the contingency tables for both measures (Table 17-15).

(continued)

(continued)

TABLE 17-15 Predilab example – 2 × 2 contingency tables for Jensen's alpha and the modified Jensen's alpha.

	Jensen's alpha		Mod. Jensen's alpha	
	w_t	l_t	w_t	l_t
w_{t-1}	3	2	4	1
l_{t-1}	2	3	1	4

For both measures, the sum of the cells equals the number of funds in the list ($N_1 = 10$). There are four funds that switch from winner to loser (or vice versa) with Jensen's alpha, whereas this happens with only two funds with the modified Jensen's alpha. This tends to confirm the impression of a superior ability to predict future performance with the latter performance measure. Note that the fact that the tables are symmetric for both measures, as is the case here, is not automatic.

The three tests (cross-product ratio, repeat winner/repeat loser, and Chi-square) are performed on this very small list, bearing in mind that these tests are only valid for a much larger number of funds and that we are too far from the standard normal distribution to draw decisive conclusions about statistical significance from the observed values. The outcome of these tests is summarized in Table 17-16.

TABLE 17-16 Predilab example – Outcomes of the statistical tests on the 2 × 2 contingency tables.

	Jensen's alpha	Mod. Jensen's alpha
CPR_t	2.25	16
$\log CPR_t$	0.81	2.77
$\sigma(\log CPR_t)$	1.29	1.58
$\hat{z}_{CPR=1}$	0.63	1.75
$\hat{z}_{RW_t=50\%}$	0.45	1.34
$\hat{z}_{RL_t=50\%}$	0.45	1.34
$\hat{\chi}_1^2$	0.1	0.9

Not surprisingly given the content of Table 17-15, the tests all reveal more favorable results for the modified Jensen's alpha. Moreover, the test on the CPR provides a larger Z-statistic thanks to the use of the whole set of observations. However, even though the value of 1.75 could be thought as weakly significant in standard inference, this conclusion cannot reasonably be drawn here because of the too small number of observations.

17.4.2 Analysis of rankings associations

The problem underlying Figure 17-15 is a classical one in statistics. Evidencing predictability using performance indicators would imply finding a significant connection between the prior and posterior portfolio rankings. Even though this potential connection involves the existence of a causal relationship (the past influences the future and not vice versa), it suffices in this context to demonstrate the existence of an association between the rankings.

The main types of estimators of the association between two rankings have been discussed both in Section 4.4.2 of Chapter 4 and Section 11.4.1 of Chapter 11. These feature Spearman's rank correlation coefficient (Equation (11-6)), Cohen's kappa (Equation (11-7)), and Kendall's tau (Equation (11-8)).[24]

In the context of persistence analysis, the statistical use of these association coefficients for hypothesis testing can be considered as fairly classical. The null hypothesis is the absence of association between rankings $\boldsymbol{S}_{(\to t-1)}$ and $\boldsymbol{S}_{(t\to)}$. Since both ordered lists have been constituted according to two consecutive and non-overlapping time periods using information about returns of actively managed funds, the only source of potential association under the null hypothesis would be the presence of serial correlation between the returns, which is precisely the effect corresponding to the alternative hypothesis. Thus, the rankings can be considered as statistically "clean," and traditional inference techniques can be used.

Whichever association measure is adopted, and considering that the sample size (number of funds) is sufficiently large so as to apply statistical inference based on the Student distribution, the generic $\boldsymbol{t}$-statistic for the test of the absence of persistence is written as as

$$\hat{\boldsymbol{t}}_{\rho^x_{m_{\to t-1}, m_{t\to}}=0} = \frac{\hat{\rho}^x_{m_{\to t-1}, m_{t\to}}}{\sigma(\hat{\rho}^x_{m_{\to t-1}, m_{t\to}})} \tag{17-44}$$

[24]Note that Somers' D, which has been introduced in Section 17.3.1.2, is closely related to Kendall's tau.

TABLE 17-17 Estimates of the standard deviation of the rank association measures.

Association measure	Symbol x	Standard deviation $\sigma(\widehat{\rho}^x)$
Spearman's rank correlation	Σ	$\frac{\sqrt{1-(\widehat{\rho}^{\Sigma})^2}}{\sqrt{N_{t-1}-2}}$
Cohen's kappa	κ	$\frac{2\sqrt{(\widehat{\rho}^{\kappa})^2(ww+ll)+(1-\widehat{\rho}^{\kappa})^2(wl+lw)-\frac{N_{t-1}}{4}(1-\widehat{\rho}^{\kappa})^2}}{N}$
Kendall's tau	τ	$\frac{\sqrt{2(2N_{t-1}+5)}}{\sqrt{9N_{t-1}(N_{t-1}-1)}}$

where $\widehat{\rho}^x_{m_{\to t-1},m_{t\to}}$ is the estimated association coefficient between the list $S_{(\to t-1)}$ using the prior measure $m_{\to t-1}$ and the list $S_{(t\to)}$ using the posterior measure $m_{t\to}$, with $x=\Sigma$ for Spearman's rank correlation coefficient (Equation (11-6) of Chapter 11), $x=\kappa$ for Cohen's kappa (Equation (11-7) of Chapter 11) and $x=\tau$ for Kendall's tau (Equation (11-8) of Chapter 11).

The denominator $\sigma(\widehat{\rho}^x_{m_{\to t-1},m_{t\to}})$ of Equation (17-44) represents the standard deviation of the estimate in large samples, and is obtained for various measures through Table 17-17 (using the shortcut $\sigma(\widehat{\rho}^x)\equiv\sigma(\widehat{\rho}^x_{m_{\to t-1},m_{t\to}})$ for the clarity of notations) where, for Cohens' kappa, the expressions for ww, ll, wl and lw are similar to those of the 2×2 contingency table examined in the previous subsection.

PrediLab example (continued)

Using information from Table 17-11 on the modified Jensen's alpha, we can compare the rankings obtained by the ten funds during periods 1 and 2. The results are presented in a similar form to Table 17-5, which was initially constructed with Jensen's alpha.

Table 17-18 shows that the match of rankings is far from perfect. Nevertheless, it does not look erratic either. This calls for further statistical analysis of the various rank association coefficients.

TABLE 17-18 Predilab example – Match of consecutive rankings with the modified Jensen's alpha.

$m\alpha_{P,1}$	Fund	Fund	$m\alpha_{P,2}$
3.81%	B3	B8	10.92%
3.49%	B2	B3	7.67%
3.47%	**Thematic**	B6	5.41%
3.46%	B8	B2	2.64%
3.20%	B7	**Thematic**	**2.55%**
1.68%	B4	B4	1.62%
1.64%	B5	B9	0.87%
1.54%	B1	B1	0.53%
−0.09%	B6	B7	0.45%
−0.40%	B9	B5	−0.64%

Applying statistical inference to the three association measures (Spearman's rank correlation, Cohen's kappa, and Kendall's tau) to both sets of rankings provides the outcome presented in Table 17-19.

TABLE 17-19 Predilab example – Statistical inference on the three association measures.

	Jensen's alpha			Mod. Jensen's alpha		
	$\hat{\rho}^x$	$\sigma(\hat{\rho}^x)$	$\hat{t}_{\hat{\rho}^x=0}$	$\hat{\rho}^x$	$\sigma(\hat{\rho}^x)$	$\hat{t}_{\hat{\rho}^x=0}$
Spearman's rank correlation	1.8%	35.3%	0.05	46.67%	31.27%	1.49
Cohen's kappa	20.0%	21.9%	0.91	60%	33.47%	1.79
Kendall's tau	−6.7%	24.8%	−0.27	33.3%	24.8%	1.34

As expected from the visual impression left with Jensen's alpha, the three association measures confirm the noisy character of the link between both rankings. Regarding the modified Jensen's alpha, the association is much better, and even becomes (weakly) statistically significant when Cohen's kappa is used, even though this result should again be considered with caution given the low number of observations.

17.4.3 Dynamic analysis of ranking transitions

The classical use of contingency tables discussed above adopts a static perspective. All tests listed from Equation (17-39) to (17-43) involve a single pivotal point between the past and the future. If one wants to study persistence over several periods, the test has to be reproduced at each chosen date and considered in isolation.

Dealing with multiple points in time in a simultaneous fashion involves dealing with overlapping measurement periods for the estimation of portfolio performance. The design of the test must take this into account. Fortunately, there exists a similar challenge that is well studied in the context of credit risk with the issue of rating transitions. Starting from this analogy, and bearing in mind the differences in interpretation, Hereil, Mitaine, Moussavi, and Roncalli (2010) develop a persistence methodology based on the use of Markov chains.[25]

Consider the contingency table represented in Table 17-14. It has the same structure as a credit rating transition matrix. The prior quantile represents the initial state of a fund, and the posterior quantile represents its final state. Dividing the number of observations in each cell by the existing number of funds at inception, we define the transition probability at time $t-1$ as $p_{jk,t-1} = \frac{j_{t-1}k_t}{N_{t-1}}$. Collecting the data from time h (the number of periods necessary to estimate the performance measure used for the rankings) until time $T-1$, we have the necessary material to estimate the parameters of a time-homogeneous Markov chain. A powerful and popular approach is to use maximum likelihood estimation. Under standard distributional assumptions, the estimate for the steady transition probability is simply obtained as

$$\widehat{p}_{jk} = \frac{\sum_{t=h+1}^{T} j_{t-1}k_t}{\sum_{t=h+1}^{T} N_{t-1}} \tag{17-45}$$

The associated one-period transition matrix $\widehat{\Pi}$ is simply defined as the squared matrix containing all the $\widehat{p}_{jk}$ elements.

In order to study performance persistence, Hereil et al. (2010) suggest working in a continuous time setup. This involves two additional steps in order to compute the transition matrix that applies to any investment horizon. First, it is necessary to obtain the Markov generator associated with the estimated transition probabilities of Equation (17-45). This matrix, called $\widehat{\Lambda}$, is defined as

$$\widehat{\Lambda} = \begin{pmatrix} -\lambda_1 & \lambda_{12} & \cdots & \lambda_{1Q} \\ \lambda_{21} & -\lambda_2 & \ddots & \lambda_{2Q} \\ \vdots & \vdots & & \vdots \\ \lambda_{Q1} & \lambda_{Q2} & \cdots & -\lambda_Q \end{pmatrix} \tag{17-46}$$

[25]The authors use the Morningstar ratings as the basis for their empirical study, but their method can be adapted to any ranking criterion.

where $\lambda_{jk} = \log(1 + \hat{p}_{jk})$ for $j \neq k$ and $\lambda_j = \sum_{k=1,k\neq j}^{Q} \lambda_{jk}$, so that the sum of each row equals 0. Then, the transition matrix from time h to time $h + \theta$ (that is, with a prediction horizon of θ periods) is obtained by

$$\hat{\Pi}_{h,h+\theta} = \exp(\hat{\Lambda}\theta) = I_Q + \sum_{s=1}^{\infty} \frac{\hat{\Lambda}^s \theta^s}{s!} \tag{17-47}$$

where I_Q is an identity matrix of order Q.

In order to assess the persistence in performance, the perspective adopted in this context is to consider how much time a fund is likely to keep the same rating (i.e., to remain in the same quantile). The longer this stability period is, the more persistent the ranking system.

For this purpose, it is necessary to assess the "discrepancy rate," i.e., the probability that a fund remains within a given quantile during a certain horizon θ minus the probability that the fund ends up in a different quantile. This probability, denoted by $\delta_q(\theta)$, is given by the following expression:[26]

$$\delta_q(\theta) = \hat{p}_{qq}^{\theta} - (1 - \hat{p}_{qq}^{\theta}) = 2\hat{p}_{qq}^{\theta} - 1 \tag{17-48}$$

where $\hat{p}_{qq}^{\theta}$ is the qth diagonal element of matrix $\hat{\Pi}_{h,h+\theta}$.

The persistence time associated with each quantile q, denoted by τ_q is then defined as the shortest horizon for which the discrepancy rate becomes negative:

$$\tau_q = \inf_{\theta>0} \{\delta_q(\theta) \leq 0\} \tag{17-49}$$

Even though this method has, to date, only been applied to external fund ratings, it has the potential to address any quantile portfolio construction criterion based on performance measures. It is possible to test different ways to partition the rankings (median, tercile, quartile, quintile or decile portfolios, for instance) and check where persistence is the most pronounced.

The main limitation of the Markov chain analysis is, however, that the method is designed so as to identify the within-quantile persistence. If a fund is in the top 10% (first decile) and very likely to remain in the top 30%, for instance, the system will only uncover part of its potential persistence. Furthermore, there is no criterion for the assessment of the critical values of τ_q that define the presence or absence of persistence. The only objective assessment criterion is the comparison of the values of τ_q for different quantiles. The bigger the difference between two quantiles, the more persistence is found for one quantile compared with the other one.

[26] As an alternative to the approach of Hereil et al. (2010), Wessels and Flint (2017) claim that persistence is found if a fund remains within the same quantile during the *whole* period. The associated probability is naturally much lower.

Key Takeaways and Equations

- The links between performance and predictability are generically of four possible kinds:
  - Intrinsic pure performance prediction, which connects a specific portfolio's past and future performance;
  - Multiple pure performance prediction, which does it simultaneously for several portfolios;
  - Generalized performance prediction, which extends the set of predictors to other relevant variables;
  - Generic prediction using performance, which uses performance measures in order to forecast another type of portfolio-specific indicator.
- The set of potential predictors of future performance, beyond past performance itself, relates to six different dimensions: (i) the fund (size, age, expense ratio, and cash flows), (ii) the manager (education and stake), (iii) the market (cycles, liquidity, and volatility), (iv) the industry (nature, competitiveness, and interdependences), (v) the holdings and trades (concentration, turnover, and return gap), and (vi) the exposures (significance, style choice, and risk indicators).
- We can generically distinguish absolute persistence from relative persistence types of analysis. The former focuses on the individual portfolio and is most useful for the investor, whereas the latter looks at a group of comparable funds and mostly addresses the needs of managers.
- Under the rolling windows approach to absolute persistence, the key considerations are to detect the frequency of outperformance and the presence of a time trend. A simple approach is to use the frequency indicator

$$f_x(m_P^{(\tau)} > m^*(\tau)) = \frac{1}{T-L+1} \sum_{\tau=1}^{T-L+1} 1_{\{p(m_P^{(\tau)})<x\}} \tag{17-7}$$

and the linear trend regression

$$m_P^{(\tau)} - m^*(\tau) = a_P + b_P \tau + \varepsilon_{P,\tau} \tag{17-9}$$

- The assessment of a portfolio's length of performance persistence can be performed by an extension of the original K-ratio:

$$\text{eK-R}_P(H) = \frac{\hat{g}_{P,H}}{\sigma_{\hat{g}_{P,H}}} \tag{17-13}$$

With this measure, the persistence horizon can be written as

$$H^*_{m_p,x} = \sup_{H \leq T} \left(\text{eK-R}_P(H) \geq t_{(H-1);1-\frac{x}{2}} \right) \tag{17-14}$$

- In order to determine the capacity of a manager to sustain their performance over time, the Hurst exponent is computed by regressing the rescaled range of the portfolio excess returns on the horizon through the following equation:

$$\log \Lambda_P(\theta) = \log c + \mathcal{H}_P \log \theta + \varepsilon_{P,\theta} \tag{17-17}$$

The null hypothesis of the absence of absolute persistence is then tested with the statistic

$$\hat{Z}_{\mathcal{H}_P=0.5} = (\mathcal{H}_P - 0.5)\sqrt{T} \tag{17-18}$$

- As a way to simultaneously assess the absolute persistence for a group of portfolios, one generally adopts a two-stage Fama–MacBeth procedure in which current alphas are regressed on their lagged estimates:

$$\hat{\alpha}^{\text{MF}}_{i,\tau} = \lambda_{0,\tau} + \lambda_{1,\tau}\hat{\alpha}^{\text{MF}}_{i,\tau-1} + \nu_{i,\tau} \tag{17-22}$$

There are a number of possible variations that are meant to improve the estimation of this equation.

- The first classical approach used in relative persistence analysis is the recursive portfolio method. It uses quantile portfolio returns defined as

$$R_{q_{t-1},t} = \frac{1}{n_{q_{t-1}}} \sum_{i \in q_{t-1}} R_{i,t} \tag{17-28}$$

- Using this type of material, the assessment of persistence can take two major forms.
  - The global performance of the actual quantile portfolios through the test

$$\hat{t}_{\overline{R}_1-\overline{R}_Q=0} = \frac{\sqrt{\theta-1}(\overline{R}_1 - \overline{R}_Q)}{\sigma(R_1 - R_Q)} \tag{17-29}$$

  - The performance of the quantile portfolios with constant allocation through the test

$$\hat{t}_{\overline{R}_{1,\theta}-\overline{R}_{Q,\theta}=0} = \frac{\sqrt{T-\theta-h-2}(\overline{R}_{1,\theta} - \overline{R}_{Q,\theta})}{\sigma(R_{1,\theta} - R_{Q,\theta})} \tag{17-32}$$

(continued)

(continued)

- Alternatively, it is possible to study the impact of fund survivorship either by imposing a penalty for defunct funds:

$$R^{\dagger}_{q_{t-1},t} = R_{q_{t-1},t} - \frac{1}{n_{q_{t-1}}} \sum_{i \in q_{t-1}} \pi \times 1_{\{i \in d_t\}} \tag{17-34}$$

or by using a logistic regression of the type

$$1_{\{t<\delta_i \le t+\theta\}} = \frac{\exp\left(\beta_0 + \sum_{q=1}^{Q} \beta_q 1_{\{i \in q_{t-1}\}} + \sum_l \varphi_l q_{i,l,t-1} + \nu_{i,\tau}\right)}{1 + \exp\left(\beta_0 + \sum_{q=1}^{Q} \beta_q 1_{\{i \in q_{t-1}\}} + \sum_l \varphi_l q_{i,l,t-1} + \nu_{i,\tau}\right)} \tag{17-35}$$

- The inputs for the recursive portfolio approach can also be obtained through alternative techniques, such as the use of nonparametric frontier analysis:

$$\tilde{\varphi}_{i,t-1} \equiv \tilde{\varphi}(\mathbf{x}_{i,t-1}, y_{i,t-1}) = \sup\{\varphi | (\mathbf{x}_{i,t-1}, \varphi y_{i,t-1}) \in \widehat{\Psi}_{t-1}\} \tag{17-36}$$

or the stability criterion technique, in which funds are ranked according to the order with which they enter the stable set for various thresholds.
- The second classical approach used in relative persistence analysis is the matched ranking method. It is based on the comparison of the fund rankings in the formation and the test periods.
- The analysis of contingency tables represents the widest application of this approach. In its simplest (2 × 2) version, it serves as the basis for three tests:
  - The cross-product ratio test:

$$\hat{z}_{\mathrm{CPR}=1} = \frac{\log \mathrm{CPR}_t}{\sigma(\log \mathrm{CPR}_t)} \tag{17-39}$$

  - The repeat winner test (also applicable for repeat losers):

$$\hat{z}_{\mathrm{RW}_t=50\%} = \frac{w_{t-1}w_t - 0.5 \times (w_{t-1}w_t + w_{t-1}l_t)}{0.5\sqrt{(w_{t-1}w_t + w_{t-1}l_t)}} \tag{17-40}$$

- The Chi-squared test:

$$\widehat{\chi}_1^2 = \frac{1}{N_{t-1}}\left[\left(w_{t-1}w_t - \frac{N_{t-1}}{4}\right)^2 + \left(l_{t-1}l_t - \frac{N_{t-1}}{4}\right)^2 + \left(w_{t-1}l_t - \frac{N_{t-1}}{4}\right)^2 + \left(l_{t-1}w_t - \frac{N_{t-1}}{4}\right)^2\right] \quad (17\text{-}43)$$

- It is also possible to directly analyze the rankings associations with the test:

$$\widehat{\boldsymbol{t}}_{\rho^x_{m_{\rightarrow t-1}, m_{t\rightarrow}}=0} = \frac{\widehat{\rho}^x_{m_{\rightarrow t-1}, m_{t\rightarrow}}}{\sigma(\widehat{\rho}^x_{m_{\rightarrow t-1}, m_{t\rightarrow}})} \quad (17\text{-}44)$$

where $\widehat{\rho}^x_{m_{\rightarrow t-1}, m_{t\rightarrow}}$ can be set as Spearman's rank correlation coefficient, Cohen's kappa, or Kendall's tau, for instance.

- Finally, a dynamic approach consists of studying the matrix of transitions from one quantile to another. In this case, the discrepancy rate (the probability that a fund remains within a given quantile during a certain horizon θ minus the probability that the fund ends up in a difference quantile) is used in order to assess the persistence time for each quantile as

$$\tau_q = \inf_{\theta>0}\{\delta_q(\theta) \leq 0\} \quad (17\text{-}49)$$

REFERENCES

Abdelsalam, O., Duygun, M., Matallín-Sáez, J. C., and E. Tortosa-Ausina (2014), Do ethics imply persistence? The case of Islamic and socially responsible funds. *Journal of Banking & Finance*, Vol. 40, pp. 182–194.

Amihud, Y., and R. Goyenko (2013), Mutual fund's R^2 as a predictor of performance. *The Review of Financial Studies*, Vol. 26, pp. 667–694.

Baks, K. P., Metrick, A., and J. Wachter (2001), Should investors avoid all actively managed mutual funds? A study in Bayesian performance evaluation. *The Journal of Finance*, Vol. 56, pp. 45–85.

Barras, L., Scaillet, O., and R. Wermers (2010), False discoveries in mutual fund performance: Measuring luck in estimated alphas. *The Journal of Finance*, Vol. 65, pp. 179–216.

Berk, J. B., and R. C. Green (2004), Mutual fund flows and performance in rational markets. *Journal of Political Economy*, Vol. 112, pp. 1269–1295.

Bollen, N., and J. Busse (2001), On the timing ability of mutual fund managers. *The Journal of Finance*, Vol. 56, pp. 1075–1094.

Bollen, N., and J. Busse (2005), Short-term persistence in mutual fund performance. *The Review of Financial Studies*, Vol. 18, pp. 569–597.

Boyson, N. M. (2007), Hedge funds performance persistence: A new approach. *Financial Analysts Journal*, Vol. 64 (6), pp. 27–44.

Brown, S., and W. Goetzmann (1995), Attrition and mutual fund performance. *The Journal of Finance*, Vol. 50, pp. 679–698.

Brown, S., Goetzmann, W., Ibbotson, R., and S. Ross (1992), Survivorship bias in performance studies. *The Review of Financial Studies*, Vol. 5, pp. 553–580.

Bu, Q., and N. Lacey (2009), On understanding mutual fund terminations. *Journal of Economics and Finance*, Vol. 33, pp. 80–99.

Busse, J. A., and P. J. Irvine (2006), Bayesian alphas and mutual fund persistence. *The Journal of Finance*, Vol. 61, pp. 2251–2288.

Cameron, A. C., and A. D. Hall (2003), A survival analysis of Australian equity mutual funds. *Australian Journal of Management*, Vol. 28, pp. 209–226.

Carhart, M. M. (1997), On persistence in mutual fund performance. *The Journal of Finance*, Vol. 52, pp. 57–82.

Chevalier, J., and G. Ellison (1997), Risk taking by mutual funds as a response to incentives. *Journal of Political Economy*, Vol. 105, pp. 1167–1200.

Cogneau, P., and G. Hübner (2015), The prediction of fund failure through performance diagnostics. *Journal of Banking & Finance*, Vol. 50, pp. 224–241.

Cogneau, P., and G. Hübner (2020), International mutual funds performance and persistence across the universe of performance measures. *Finance*, Vol. 41, pp. 97–176.

Conrad, J., Wahal, S., and J. Xiang (2015), High-frequency quoting, trading, and the efficiency of prices. *Journal of Financial Economics*, Vol. 116, pp. 271–291.

Cremers, K. J. M., Driessen, J., Maenhout, P., and D. Weinbaum. (2009), Does skin in the game matter? Director incentives and governance in the mutual fund industry. *Journal of Financial and Quantitative Analysis*, Vol. 44, pp. 1345–1373.

Cremers, K. J. M., Fulkerson, J. A., and T. B. Riley (2019), Challenging the conventional wisdom on active management: A review of the past 20 years of academic literature on actively managed mutual funds. *Financial Analysts Journal*, Vol. 74 (4), pp. 8–35.

Cremers, K. J. M., and A. Petajisto (2009), How active is your fund manager? A new measure that predicts performance. *The Review of Financial Studies*, Vol. 22, pp. 3329–3365.

Cuthbertson, K., Nitzsche, D., and N. O'Sullivan (2022), Mutual fund performance persistence: Factor models and portfolio size. *International Review of Financial Analysis*, Vol. 81, 102133.

Darolles, S., Gagliardini, P., and C. Gouriéroux, (2014), Contagion and systematic risk: An application to the survival of hedge funds. Working Paper.

Droms, W. G. (2006), Hot hands, cold hands: Does past performance predict future returns? *Journal of Financial Planning*, Vol. 19 (5), pp. 60–69.

Elton, E. J., Gruber, M. J., and C. R. Blake (1996), Survivorship bias and mutual fund performance. *The Review of Financial Studies*, Vol. 9, pp. 1097–1120.

Europerformance (2006), *Méthodologie de l'Europerformance-Edhec style rating*. Technical document.

Fama, E. F., and K. R. French (2010), Luck versus skill in the cross-section of mutual fund returns. *The Journal of Finance*, Vol. 65, pp. 1915–1947.

Fama, E. F., and J. D. MacBeth (1973), Risk, return, and equilibrium: Empirical tests. *Journal of Political Economy*, Vol. 81, pp. 607–636.

Fays, B., Hübner, G., and M. Lambert (2022), Harvesting the seasons of the size anomaly. *Journal of Asset Management*, Vol. 23, pp. 337–349.

Goldman, E., Sun, Z., and X. Zhou (2016), The effect of management design on the portfolio concentration and performance of mutual funds. *Financial Analysts Journal*, Vol. 72 (4), pp. 49–61.

Grau-Carles, P., Doncel, L. M., and J. Sainz (2019), Stability in mutual fund performance rankings: A new proposal. *International Review of Economics and Finance*, Vol. 61, pp. 337–346.

Gregoriou, G. N., Sedzro, K., and J. Zhu (2005), Hedge fund performance appraisal using data envelopment analysis. *European Journal of Operational Research*, Vol. 164, pp. 555–571.

Grinblatt, M., and S. Titman (1992), The persistence of mutual fund performance. *The Journal of Finance*, Vol. 42, pp. 1977–1984.

Harvey, C. R., and Y. Liu (2014), Evaluating trading strategies. *The Journal of Portfolio Management*, Vol. 40 (5), pp. 108–118.

Harvey, C. R., Liu, Y., and H. Zhu (2016), ... and the cross-section of expected returns. *The Review of Financial Studies*, Vol. 29, pp. 5–68.

Hendricks, D., Patel, J., and R. Zeckhauser (1993), Hot hands in mutual funds: Short-run persistence of performance, 1974–88. *The Journal of Finance*, Vol. 48, pp. 93–130.

Hereil, P., Mitaine, P., Moussavi, N., and T. Roncalli (2010), Mutual fund ratings and performance persistence. Working Paper.

Hoberg, G., Kumar, N., and N. Prabhala (2018), Mutual fund competition, managerial skill, and alpha persistence. *The Review of Financial Studies*, Vol. 31, pp. 1896–1929.

Huij, J., and J. Derwall (2008), Hot hands in bond funds. *Journal of Banking & Finance*, Vol. 32, pp. 559–572.

Hurst, H. E. (1951), Long-term storage of reservoirs: An experimental study. *Transactions of the American Society of Civil Engineers*, Vol. 116, pp. 770–799.

Jensen, M. C. (1968), The performance of mutual funds in the period 1945–1964. *The Journal of Finance*, Vol. 23, pp. 389–416.

Kacperczyk, M., Sialm, C., and L. Zheng (2005), On the industry concentration of actively managed equity mutual funds. *The Journal of Finance*, Vol. 60, pp. 1983–2011.

Kacperczyk, M., Sialm, C., and L. Zheng (2008), Unobserved actions of mutual funds. *The Review of Financial Studies*, Vol. 21, pp. 2379–2416.

Kacperczyk, M., van Nieuwerburgh, S., and L. Veldkamp (2014), Time-varying fund manager skill. *The Journal of Finance*, Vol. 69, pp. 1455–1484.

Kahn, R. N., and A. Rudd (1995), Does historical performance predict future performance? *Financial Analysts Journal*, Vol. 51 (6), pp. 43–52.

Kaplan, S. N., and A. Schoar (2005), Private equity performance: Returns, persistence and capital flows. *The Journal of Finance*, Vol. 60, pp. 1791–1823.

Kestner, L. N. (1996), Getting a handle on true performance. *Futures*, Vol. 25 (1), pp. 44–47.

Kestner, L. N. (2013), (Re)Introducing the K-ratio. Working Paper.

Khorana, A., Servaes, H., and L. Wedge (2007), Portfolio management ownership and fund performance. *Journal of Financial Economics*, Vol. 85, pp. 179–204.

Kosowski, R., Naik, N. Y., and M. Teo (2007), Do hedge funds deliver alpha? A Bayesian and bootstrap analysis. *Journal of Financial Economics*, Vol. 84, pp. 229–264.

Kosowski, R., Timmermann, A., White, H., and R. Wermers (2006), Can mutual fund 'stars' really pick stocks? New evidence from a bootstrapping analysis. *The Journal of Finance*, Vol. 61, pp. 2551–2595.

Linnainmaa, J. (2013), Reverse survivorship bias. *The Journal of Finance*, Vol. 68, pp. 789–813.

Malkiel, B. G. (1995), Returns from investing in equity mutual funds 1971 to 1991. *The Journal of Finance*, Vol. 50, pp. 549–572.

Mamaysky, H., Spiegel, M., and H. Zhang (2007), Improved forecasting of mutual fund alphas and betas. *Review of Finance*, Vol. 11, pp. 359–400.

Mandelbrot, B. B. (2004), *The (Mis)Behavior of Markets. A Fractal View of Risk, Ruin and Reward.* Basic Books.

Massa, M., and V. Yadav (2015), Investor sentiment and mutual fund strategies. *Journal of Financial and Quantitative Analysis*, Vol. 50, pp. 699–727.

Pástor, L., Stambaugh, R., and L. Taylor (2017), Do funds make more when they trade more? *The Journal of Finance*, Vol. 72, pp. 1483–1528.

Riley, T., and Q. Yan (2022), Maximum drawdown as predictor of mutual fund performance and flows. *Financial Analysts Journal*, Vol. 78 (4), pp. 59–76.

Somers, R. H. (1962), A new asymmetric measure of association for ordinal variable. *American Sociological Review*, Vol. 27, pp. 799–811.

Weron, R. (2002), Estimating long-range dependence: Finite sample properties and confidence intervals. *Physica A*, Vol. 12, pp. 285–299.

Wessels, J., and E. Flint (2017), *Alternative and new methods for measuring persistence in fund performance.* Working Paper.

Zalewska, A., and Y. Zhang (2020), Mutual funds' exits, financial crisis and Darwin. *Journal of Corporate Finance*, Vol. 65, 101738.

CHAPTER 18

Agency Issues and Illusion of Performance

INTRODUCTION

Portfolio management is typically delegated to professional managers acting on behalf of investors. That delegation can be the source of distortions between investors' investment goals and portfolio managers' professional objectives. The financial economics literature has developed a framework, referred to as agency theory, for analyzing these distortions. Agency theory has been applied to various contexts, such as labor economics or corporate finance. More recently, it has focused on delegated portfolio management.

This chapter first reviews the *standard agency framework* and its application to the money management industry. After discussing some of the typical conflicts of interest between investors and portfolio managers (PMs), we examine how these conflicts can be mitigated through managerial compensation or governance mechanisms.

Next, the role of performance measurement is explicitly analyzed through the lens of agency. On the one hand, agency issues impact the quality of performance measurement. Supervisors monitoring the skills of portfolio managers need to understand the *financial and professional incentives* they are granting them. Some of these incentives can be counterproductive if they represent possibilities for managers to alter or manipulate performance scores in their favor. On the other hand, the design and implementation of performance measures is not neutral. We review some sources of agency conflict exacerbation that are driven by how performance is assessed.

In light of these potential agency issues, some research has been conducted to design performance measures that would be impervious to manipulation. We review the ideal properties that such measures should exhibit and revisit the *manipulation-proof performance measure* of Goetzmann, Ingersoll, Spiegel, and Welch (2007). Some techniques to detect fund manipulation (through misreporting or return smoothing for instance) are also examined.

Finally, beyond agency issues, we discuss the *role of luck* in performance measurement. Many scholars have claimed for decades that active management only yields an illusion of performance, invoking the strong efficiency of financial markets that cannot be beaten. The real contribution of active portfolio managers has been revisited on both the theoretical and empirical fronts. It is now argued that management skills should be measured through value creation and not returns. Under this perspective, skill appears to be prevalent in the mutual fund industry but rewarded mostly through management fees. The rent that portfolio managers seem to be extracting from investors is a new agency puzzle that future research will have to address.

The On Behalf Investment Example

On Behalf Investment (OBI) is an asset management firm offering the opportunity to invest in various funds. It has received a mandate from a client whose investment goal is to maximize the Sharpe ratio over the next period of evaluation.

The management of the investor's wealth is delegated to a portfolio manager employed by OBI. To reward and incentivize its PM, OBI grants a compensation. How should it design the fee structure for its managers to ensure that portfolio allocations are consistent with the investor's investment goal? To what extent does the measure of performance interfere with the compensation design? If the PM is indeed acting opportunistically (through misreporting or return smoothing), how can this manipulation be detected? These are some of the questions to be investigated throughout the chapter.

18.1 THE STANDARD AGENCY FRAMEWORK

18.1.1 Principal–agent relationship

18.1.1.1 Standard agency problem

In financial economics, a standard agency relationship involves a "principal" requesting the services from an "agent" to perform one or several tasks on the principal's behalf. The agent has supposedly superior abilities (skill, experience, availability, etc.) to complete the tasks, which results in potentially higher economic benefits for the principal. To this end, the two parties write a contract that usually describes the actions that the agent is supposed to take on and defines the compensation the agent will receive.

However, along with the benefits derived from letting the agent perform the tasks, inefficiencies associated with the agency relationship are also considered. These inefficiencies find their origin in the conflicts of interest between the two parties. When the agent pursues their own goals, their actions may deviate from the so-called "first-best" ones that maximize the principal's welfare. That misalignment in objectives represents the first source of *agency costs*. Of course, the principal is well aware of that problem and has at least two non-exclusive possibilities to try and mitigate its economic impact:[1]

- Control the agent *ex ante*. That solution consists in adding terms in the contract to reduce the agent's leeway to carry out their actions, forcing them to better comply with the principal's objectives. That solution only works if the additional terms can be enforced in practice, which is usually costly. Moreover, reducing the agent's flexibility could also harm their ability to perform the first-best actions. Finally, it may take time and transaction costs for the two parties to agree on these restrictive provisions in the contract.
- Control the agent *ex post*. That solution consists in regularly auditing the agent's actions. These monitoring efforts made by the principal typically come with their own costs.

These two attempts at controlling the agent's actions are therefore expensive. They represent the second source of agency costs. Figure 18-1 shows a schematic representation of the agency relationship.

The challenge for the two parties thus resides in implementing a contract and designing its terms to reduce the total agency costs while preserving the economic benefits from the agency relationship.

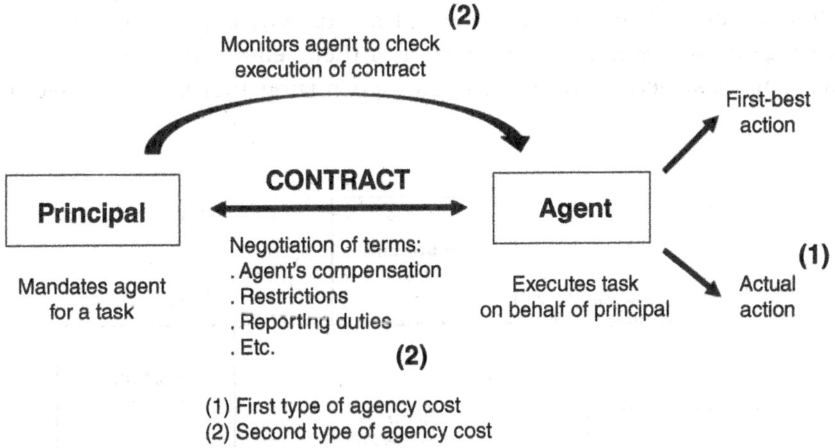

FIGURE 18-1 Schematic representation of the agency relationship.

[1]Another possibility is to search for another, more "obedient" agent. However, the extra costs induced by that search could be higher than the benefits generated by the improvement in the agency relationship.

18.1.1.2 Agency with delegation

In a slightly more complex agency relationship, the principal might want to delegate the monitoring of the agent to an intermediary. Such an agency structure might induce a loss of control from the principal, but it is worth considering when the intermediary can perform the monitoring task more efficiently than the principal (Strausz, 1997; François and Missonier-Piera, 2007). These benefits from delegation may arise for instance when there are multiple agents (i.e., supervision is costly) or when monitoring requires specific skills (i.e., supervision is highly technical).

Gryglewicz and Mayer (2023) make a distinction between *delegated monitoring*, where the principal is contracting with both the intermediary and the agent, and *delegated contracting*, where the principal enters into an agreement with the intermediary only, who, in turn, deals with the agent. Although delegated contracting implies higher contracting costs, such a structure can better cope with severe agency conflicts (and difficulties in monitoring) as it provides stronger incentives for both the intermediary and the agent. In other words, the intermediary has more "skin in the game" under delegated contracting and therefore plays their supervisiory role with enhanced diligence.

18.1.2 Application to the asset management industry

Based on the above discussion, the graph shown in Figure 18-2 shows the simplest agency structure encountered in the asset management industry.

The structure depicted in Figure 18-2 may represent, for instance, the structure of an open-end mutual fund where the investment firm is directly monitoring the performance of portfolio managers (henceforth PM) on behalf of their retail investors/clients. In this typical two-layer agency structure, investors aim at maximizing after-tax, net-of-fees returns, the

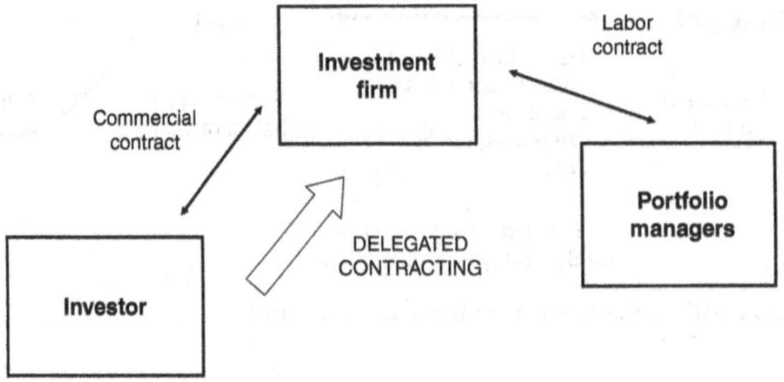

FIGURE 18-2 Basic agency structure in asset management.

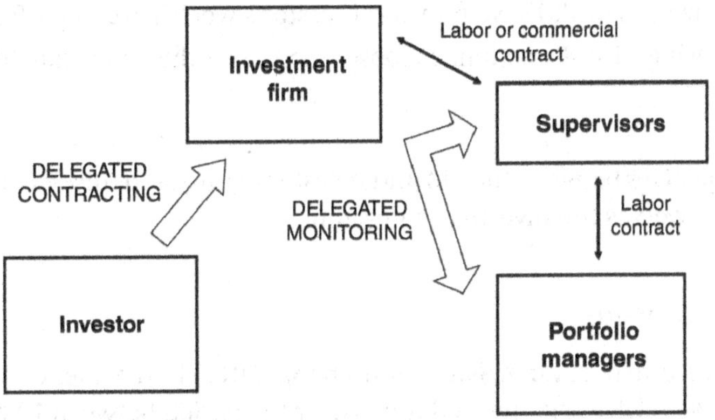

FIGURE 18-3 More advanced agency structure in asset management.

investment firm wants to maximize fees (which implies increasing the assets under management (AUM)), and PMs wish to maximize their compensation (salary, bonuses, etc.) while keeping an eye on longer-term goals (career concerns).

For the largest asset managers (such as BlackRock, Fidelity, or Vanguard), the agency structure becomes more complex with additional layers of intermediation. This complexity multiplies the agency relations and may therefore magnify the related agency costs. Figure 18-3 is one example of a more developed agency structure.

In the structure shown above, supervisors monitor the PMs on behalf of the investment firm. If the supervision is performed in-house (i.e., the supervisors, the PMs, and the investment firm belong to the same organization), the investment firm is engaged in a delegated monitoring relation with its PMs. Alternatively, supervisors and their PMs can form a distinct entity (i.e., supervision can be outsourced to a separate company), in which case the investment firm applies delegated contracting. This situation may arise, for example, when the investment firm is a commercial bank.

As pointed out by Lakonishok, Shleifer, and Vishny (1992), institutional investors (such as sponsors of pension funds, trustees of foundations, or treasurers of corporations) often delegate their investments to several layers of agents. The superior monitoring ability of institutional investors (relative to retail investors) may not compensate for the complex agency structure they have to deal with. As a result, the agency costs borne by institutional investors do not always compare favorably with those incurred by retail investors (see James and Karceski, 2006, for evidence).

18.1.3 Agency conflicts in delegated portfolio management

How do agency issues arise in the delegated portfolio management structures depicted above? The general answer is that agency conflicts occur whenever the following two conditions are met:

- The maximization of PM's welfare and investor's wealth are imperfectly aligned goals.
- The monitoring of PM's actions is loose enough so that they can adopt opportunistic behavior.

Diverging objectives between the PM and investor manifest themselves through the choice of risk exposure as well as the investment horizon.

18.1.3.1 Risk exposure

As far as risk is concerned, Huang, Sialm, and Zhang (2011) find evidence of risk shifting on a sample of almost 3000 US equity mutual funds over the period between 1980 and 2009. As the authors point out, risk shifting is not necessarily detrimental to investors. It may, for instance, be an indication of active management taking advantage of stock selection and timing skills. However, using a risk-shifting measure impacted by changes in portfolio composition but not affected by market conditions, the authors document the underperformance of funds that are more prone to increases in risk level. After eliminating alternative explanations, Huang et al. (2011) attribute this phenomenon mostly to an agency conflict.

The misalignment in risk preferences may be caused by the asymmetric relation between fund flows and performance documented by Starks (1987), Chevalier and Ellison (1997), or Huang, Wei, and Yan (2007), among many others. That is, investors tend to allocate more money to well-performing funds but do not withdraw money in the same proportions from bad performers.[2] Consequently, if PM compensation is related to the fund flows (for example, when fees are related to the assets under management), they have an incentive to raise their risk exposure primarily to increase their reward.

A recent study on US mutual funds by Mazur, Salganik-Shoshan, and Zagonov (2017) documents that the flow-performance sensitivity is convex in the high-performance region and concave in the low-performance region as shown in Figure 18-4. The convexity (concavity) is stronger for retail (institutional) funds.

The concavity region suggests that the agency conflict regarding risk exposure can also arise in the opposite direction, i.e., PMs may be tempted to actually decrease the risk profile of their portfolios when their past performance has not been good. Interestingly, career concerns produce a similar behavior among PMs (Chevalier and Ellison, 1999; Scotti, 2012). If contract termination is closely related to performance, PMs (especially the younger ones) may prefer to avoid unsystematic risk and to hold conventional portfolios (i.e., "herding"). As Scotti (2012) argues, such a "churning" behavior, adopted by the most uninformed PMs, does not worsen on average the agency conflict (i.e., the return expected from delegated portfolio management).

[2]This behavior suggests that investors rely on past returns to evaluate the funds, which may indicate low sophistication. In their international study, Ferreira, Keswani, Miguel, and Ramos (2012) find that the flow-performance relation exhibits less asymmetry when investor sophistication is higher.

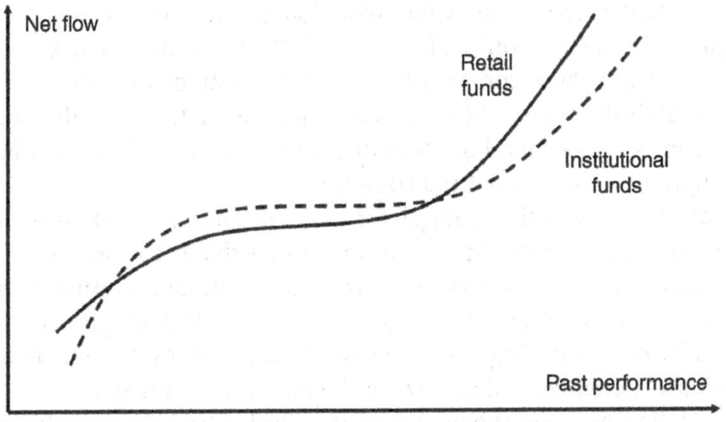

FIGURE 18-4 The flow-performance sensitivity as documented by Mazur et al. (2017).

It does, however, increase the performance gap between uninformed and informed PMs, which may represent an opportunity for the selective investor.

Taken together, these risk incentives lead to a U-shaped relation between risk level and prior performance, as modeled and empirically documented by Hu, Kale, Pagani, and Subramanian (2011). When past performance is satisfactory and the PM does not feel that their position is threatened, the incentive for taking on more risk prevails. As performance deteriorates, the PM becomes concerned about job termination and is tempted to adopt safer investment strategies. This holds up to a certain point where prior performance is so bad that the PM may drastically increase risk in a desperate attempt to recover profitability (such "gambling for resurrection" behavior has originally been documented in Brown, Harlow, and Starks, 1996).

18.1.3.2 Investment horizon

Another dimension of conflict between the investor and the PM is the investment horizon. As pointed out by Goldman and Slezak (2003), when the tenure of the manager is shorter than the horizon of the investor, then the PM is evaluated on the value improvement of a portfolio inherited from the preceding manager. As a consequence, the PM may not trade immediately on all information. More specifically, long-term information may be discarded if deemed to be revealed in asset prices after the PM's tenure. Such trading behavior (which the authors refer to as a "lock-in" effect) may, of course, be at the expense of the investor's best interests.

18.1.3.3 Monitoring

The magnitude of agency conflicts caused by risk or horizon distortions critically depends ultimately on the monitoring of the PM's actions. In their analysis of almost 10 000 US equity funds, Almazan, Brown, Carlson, and Chapman (2004) find that investment constraints contribute to mitigating the agency conflict between the PMs and investors. A similar conclusion is reached by Liu (2015). These constraints include restrictions on short selling, borrowing, and the holding of derivatives and illiquid assets. Direct restrictions are also coupled with governance mechanisms such as fund boards of directors, managerial career concerns, and peer monitoring through the existence of fund complexes.

Almazan et al. (2004) show that fund performance is neither economically nor statistically affected by the level of constraints. This seems to indicate that the level of monitoring adopted by the fund industry may not be too far away from the optimal investment contract, i.e., the one that trades off the costs with the benefits of monitoring. The adoption of restrictions (and therefore the quality of monitoring) increases with the proportion of inside directors within the board, the PMs' experience, and the size of the management team.

Finally, the relation between the quality of monitoring and the complexity of the agency structure is not unambiguous. It is impacted, as mentioned earlier, by the resort to delegated monitoring versus delegated contracting. Almazan et al. (2004) find that the number of investment restrictions is inversely related to the size of the organization. That is, under delegated monitoring, the layers of management delegation seem to play at the expense of the investor. By contrast, Gervais, Lynch, and Musto (2005) argue that fund families (working under delegated contracting) improve monitoring and help reveal information about PM quality to investors. That quality screening is more effective when the fund family monitors a large number of PMs.

18.2 HOW TO MITIGATE AGENCY CONFLICTS?

Since the presence of agency conflicts is almost inevitable in the context of the asset management industry, it is necessary to design mechanisms in order to mitigate as much as possible its potential negative consequences for the principal, namely the investor in this case. These mitigating actions take two main forms: managerial compensation, through performance payment or fund ownership mechanisms, and governance solutions. They are investigated in this section.

18.2.1 Linear performance pay

As emphasized by Stracca (2006) in his survey on delegated portfolio management, the PM compensation plays a key role in the mitigation of agency conflicts with investors. In a realistic setting, the investor hardly observes the effort made and the risk exposure taken by the PM. Therefore a "first-best" contract rewarding the PM that can credibly commit to acting in the best interest of the investor cannot be written. The alternative ("second-best") contract consists in offering the PM the compensation that will best align their interests with those of the investor.

A rich literature has examined the effects of various compensation packages on the agency of portfolio management. An important result (Stoughton, 1993; Admati and Pfleiderer, 1997) establishes that simple linear compensation contracts do not effectively incentivize PMs. Suppose the manager's compensation takes the following form:[3]

$$h_1 + h_2(R_P - R_B) \tag{18-1}$$

where R_P is the return on the portfolio, R_B is the return on a benchmark (predetermined or stochastic), h_2 is the incentivization parameter (selected by the principal), and h_1 is a constant to satisfy the agent's participation constraint. Suppose also that the return on the portfolio is a linear function of factors and some noise:

$$R_P = \alpha + \sum_{k=1}^{K} \beta_k F_k + \varepsilon \tag{18-2}$$

Once the PM receives signals $(\widehat{F}_k)$ about the values of the factors, they can adjust the portfolio allocation to try and match R_P. As a consequence, the PM's compensation rather looks like

$$h_1 + h_2\left(\alpha + \sum_{k=1}^{K} \beta_k \widehat{F}_k + \varepsilon - R_B\right) \tag{18-3}$$

which can be rewritten in the form

$$u_1 + \sum_{k=1}^{K} u_{2,k} \widehat{F}_k + u_3 \varepsilon \tag{18-4}$$

where $u_{2,k}$ and u_3 are coefficients adjusted by the PM (agent) and no longer controlled by the investor (principal).

The simple example above highlights one specific feature of the agency relation in delegated portfolio management, namely that the agent (the PM) can, at least partially, control in a linear way and at no cost the scale of their response action. That specific feature does not say whether the magnitude of the agency conflict is high or not. This merely implies that the linear compensation scheme cannot do much about it.

18.2.2 Nonlinear performance pay

The limitations of the linear compensation scheme explain the nonlinear, sometimes complex forms of PM remuneration observed in the industry. Recent evidence on PM compensation in the US mutual fund sector is provided by Ma, Tang, and Gomez (2019). Their sample consists of 4597 unique mutual funds from 479 fund families managed by 744 investment advisors, observed between 2006 and 2011. Table 18-1 is directly reproduced from their Table 1.

[3]We neglect here the time index for clarity of exposition.

TABLE 18-1 Compensation structure for a sample of US mutual fund portfolio managers.

Compensation	% of sample
Fixed salary	1.32
Nonfixed salary	98.68
Performance pay	79.04
Advisor-profit pay	50.89
AUM pay	19.61
Deferred compensation	29.41

Source: Ma et al. (2019).

As can be seen from Table 18-1, variable compensation that is linked to performance is the dominant form of remuneration for PMs. There are three such main mechanisms associated with the nonlinear performance compensation, namely standard option-based pay, high water-mark-based pay, and clawback-based pay.

18.2.2.1 Standard option-based pay

In their general study, Li and Tiwari (2009) consider a PM that can invest in the risk-free asset, a market index, and a stock. They examine four (non-exclusive) types of compensation: (i) fixed payments, (ii) proportional asset-based fees, (iii) benchmark-linked fulcrum (symmetric) fees, and (iv) benchmark-linked option-type "bonus" incentive fees. Formally, the PM's compensation takes the following form:

$$h_1 + h_2 R_P + h_3(R_P - R_{B1}) + h_4 \max(R_P - R_{B2}, 0) \tag{18-5}$$

Li and Tiwari's (2009) general conclusion is that, if the benchmark is chosen appropriately, the option-type "bonus" incentive fee effectively mitigates the agency conflict.[4] Conversely, the bonus actually harms the PM's incentive for effort if the benchmark is poorly chosen. The benchmark therefore appears as a double-edged sword while designing the PM compensation scheme. More specifically, Li and Tiwari (2009) show that the benchmark will yield the right incentives for the PM only when the benchmark weight on the passive asset and the manager's allocation to the passive asset are close enough. As mentioned by the authors, this result advocates for the use of style benchmarks.

[4]Starks (1987) argues that symmetric fees are preferable to bonuses because the latter encourage the PM to increase their risk exposure. That conclusion focuses on *risk* incentives, whereas Li and Tiwari (2009) determine the optimal contract according to *outcomes*.

In their empirical study, Ma et al. (2019) confirm that performance-based pay (in practice translated into "performance fees") and deferred compensation are more likely to prevail in PM compensation when agency conflicts are severe.[5] They also find that performance-based compensation is a substitute for other monitoring mechanisms that mitigate agency problems. These other mechanisms include investor sophistication, PM's ownership of the fund (examined in Section 18.2.3), or threat of dismissal.

The exact mitigation effect on agency conflicts of performance-based compensation remains open to debate. Ma et al. (2019) report that there is little difference in future performance among funds depending on their compensation structure. They attribute this finding to a possible contracting equilibrium found by the industry (in the same spirit that Almazan et al., 2004, concluded about monitoring restrictions). However, Foster and Young (2010) theoretically find that performance-based compensation hardly allows investors to screen out good PMs from bad ones. They further show that neither deferred compensation nor clawback provisions (discussed below) help separate the skilled from the unskilled PMs. The authors rather advocate for enhanced transparency through reporting and disclosure (examined in Section 18.3). Lee, Trzcinka, and Venkatesan (2019) find that the option-like feature of the bonus incentive encourages mutual fund managers to shift risk, especially when their performance is close to that of the benchmark (that is, when the vega of the option, defined as the sensitivity of the price to the volatility of the underlying, is the highest).

On Behalf Investment (continued)

A general compensation scheme similar to that in Equation (18-5) is considered. That is, total fees received by the PM are given by

$$F = h_1 + h_2 R_P + h_3(R_P - R_{B1}) + h_4 \max(R_P - R_{B2}, 0)$$

where R_{B1} and R_{B2} are two benchmarks.

Since these benchmarks are constant, the expression for fees can be rewritten as follows:

$$F = k_0 + k_1 R_P + k_2 \max(R_P - R_{B2}, 0)$$

with $k_0 = h_1 - h_3 R_{B1}$, $k_1 = h_2 + h_3$, and $k_2 = h_4$. Since we are interested in comparing fees between portfolios, we can set $k_0 = 0$ without any loss in generality. Thus, the final expression is

$$F = k_1 R_P + k_2 \max(R_P - R_{B2}, 0)$$

(continued)

[5]Given the characteristics of their sample data, the authors measure the intensity of agency conflicts at the level between the investment advisor and the PM.

(continued)

where k_1 accounts for the symmetric (fulcrum) fees and k_2 accounts for the option-type bonus fees.

The risk-neutral PM aims at maximizing the expectation of the expression above. Under the assumption that portfolio returns R_P are normally distributed with mean μ_P and standard deviation σ_P, the total expected fees are

$$E(F) = k_1\mu_P + k_2[(\mu_P - R_{B2})\Phi(z) + \varphi(-z)\sigma_P]$$

where $z = \frac{\mu_P - R_{B2}}{\sigma_P}$ and, as usual, $\varphi(.)$ and $\Phi(.)$ denote the standard normal density and cumulative distribution functions, respectively.

Table 18-2 indicates the PM's expected fees E(F) (in basis points) for six different funds (with $\sigma_P = 20\%$ or $\sigma_P = 30\%$ and Sharpe ratios equal to 0.25, 0.5 or 0.75). Three compensation schemes are considered: symmetric fees only ($k_1 = 1\%$, $k_2 = 0$), symmetric fees with a high-benchmark call option bonus ($k_1 = 0.5\%$, $k_2 = 0.5\%$, $R_{B2} = 20\%$), and symmetric fees with a low-benchmark call option bonus ($k_1 = 0.5\%$, $k_2 = 0.5\%$, $R_{B2} = 5\%$). The risk-free rate is 5%.

TABLE 18-2 OBI example – Expected fees for various funds and compensation schemes.

Fund	A	B	C	D	E	F
Expected return (μ_P)	0.1	0.15	0.2	0.125	0.2	0.275
Standard deviation (σ_P)	0.2	0.2	0.2	0.3	0.3	0.3
Sharpe ratio	0.25	0.5	0.75	0.25	0.5	0.75
Expected fees (bps)						
Symmetric only	10	15	20	12.5	20	27.5
Symmetric + high-benchmark call	14.87	16.13	17.98	19.20	21.97	25.68
Symmetric + low-benchmark call	12.96	16.05	19.69	18.18	22.82	28.29

The investor wishes to invest in funds C and F, but the compensation package introduces a slight distortion with the manager's preferences. Across all compensation schemes, the manager invests in fund F as a priority. However, the manager's second-best choice is fund E, not C. The fee structure is indeed sensitive to the fund's return volatility, much less to its Sharpe ratio. The introduction of a bonus-type fee reinforces the misalignment of interests between the investor and the PM, that is, the gap in expected fees between funds C and F widens. Note that this gap further increases as the benchmark gets easier to beat and the call becomes deeper in the money.

18.2.2.2 High water mark and clawback-based pay

As far as hedge funds are concerned, one common specific form of performance-based fee is the high water mark contract. According to this provision, the PM receives a periodic compensation only if the value of the assets under management exceeds a running maximum value (i.e., the high water mark). That compensation is usually a fraction of the value increase relative to the high water mark. Figure 18-5 provides an example of the high water mark mechanism.

Every quarter the running maximum value of assets under management is updated. At the end of the second quarter (Q2), the high water mark increases from HWM1 (the highest value of AUM during Q1) to HWM2. There is a last potential update at the end of Q3, but, because of a relatively poor performance during that quarter, the running maximum remains at HWM2. Finally, the terminal value of AUM at the end of the year is compared to the latest high water mark (HWM2 in that case), and the performance fee is calculated as a fraction of AUM(Q4) – HWM2.

As noted by Panageas and Westerfield (2009), the high water mark compensation scheme can be viewed as a collection of call options on the value of the fund. Every updated high water mark corresponds to a reset of the strike price, and each payment of the performance fee is the exercise of one call option while the PM holds another call option for the next evaluation period. Of course, such a compensation scheme provides the incentive to keep improving the fund performance. However, despite the option analogy, Panageas and Westerfield (2009) show that high water marks do not necessarily encourage risk shifting from the PM. Indeed, by raising fund volatility, the PM not only increases the chances of beating the latest high water mark (a short-term gain) but also increases the chances of updating the high water mark, which will be more difficult to beat in the next period (a longer-term loss). Therefore, the exact risk incentive will depend on how the PM trades off current with future gains. Drechsler (2014) argues

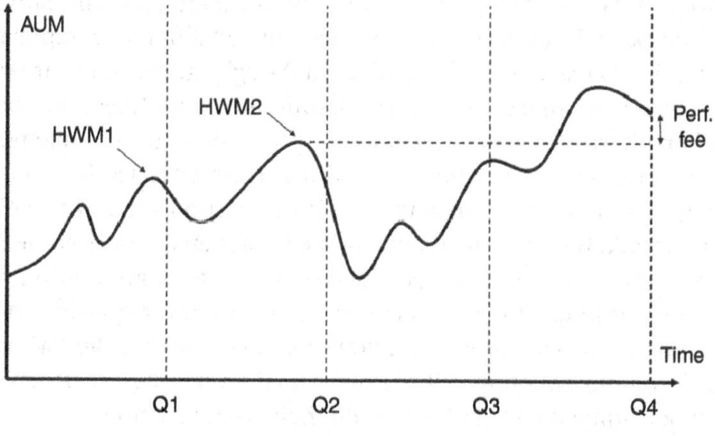

FIGURE 18-5 Example of annual performance fee with quarterly high water marks.

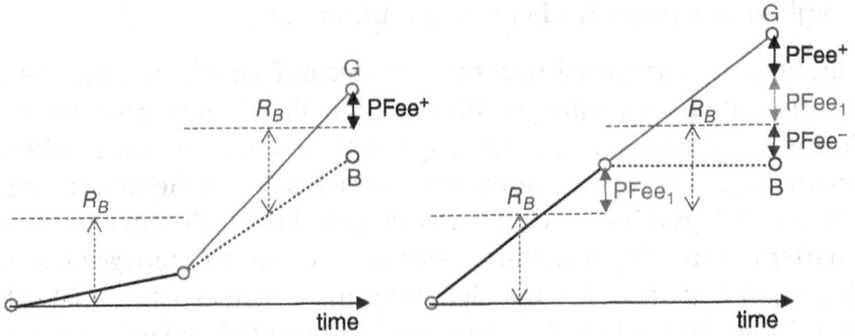

FIGURE 18-6 Illustration of the difference between the high water mark (left) and clawback (right) mechanisms.

that the high water mark compensation scheme combined with the investor's threat of fund termination further mitigates the incentive to shift risk.

Clawback provisions represent another way to potentially mitigate agency conflicts. This contractual feature entails that a fraction of the performance-based pay is deferred and will eventually only be freed out if the cumulative return of the portfolio exceeds the corresponding cumulative hurdle rate. Compared with the high water mark, whose effectiveness is related to the memory of previous poor returns that must be compensated for before the performance-related pay can be granted, the clawback provision works well when past performance has been good, but the subsequent one is poor. In that case, it is perfectly possible that the fees previously earned by the PM must be returned to the investors. The difference is illustrated in the graph shown in Figure 18-6.

Figure 18-6 shows different situations arising in a two-period setup. The left chart illustrates the high water mark mechanism. After the first period, the portfolio return does not match the hurdle (benchmark) rate R_B, and no performance fee is paid. In the second year, two cases can arise. If the portfolio reaches level G on the graph, its cumulative return exceeds that of the benchmark, and a performance fee is paid on the difference (represented by $PFee^+$). Otherwise, the fund only reaches level B, and, even though the second-year return exceeds the hurdle rate, the cumulative one is insufficient in order to obtain the option-based payment.

The right chart illustrates how the clawback provision can be implemented. In year 1, the portfolio return exceeds its hurdle rate, and a performance fee is earned. Nevertheless, it is not definitely acquired. In the second year, if the portfolio reaches level G, there is still no problem, and an additional performance-related compensation is earned, corresponding to $PFee^+$ on the graph. However, if the portfolio only gets to B, all the first year's gains have been lost, and the PM is forced to *reimburse* a fraction of their previously earned performance fee. This shows that a clawback provision allows us to ensure that the PM does not consider their past variable remuneration as definitely granted after it has been recorded, because a subsequent poor performance would then erode their compensation.

Because it involves a potential reimbursement, the clawback mechanism can only be implemented in situations that involve a multiperiod contract between the investor and the PM. This is the reason why it is mostly met in situations that involve a closed-end fund with a long horizon, like in the private equity industry. In that case, the PM's incentive payment is partly accumulated as a carried interest during the fund's lifetime, and the clawback amount is calculated at fund termination. The clawback provision can also be met in multi-year personal portfolio management contracts, for instant through the activities of a family office.

From a dynamic perspective, the implementation of a high water mark system can be combined with a clawback provision in an effective manner to ensure proper incentivization of the PM for a long period. The high water mark memorizes bad past events, whereas the clawback accounts for the good past ones. Over the course of the portfolio life, their combination guarantees that the multi-year variable compensation approaches as precisely as possible the one that would be obtained in a single period.

On Behalf Investment (continued)

The manager is considering investing in a newly established Fund G, an illiquid investment vehicle that offers different share classes A, B, and C. The first two are relatively simple in the calculation of fees:

- Class A shares entail a flat yearly management fee of 1.2% of the AUM;
- Class B shares entail a management fee of 1.0% and a performance fee of 20% of the outperformance over a constant hurdle rate $R_B = 4\%$ per year.

Based on the past three years' returns of a similar fund, the manager decides to simulate the outcome of this remuneration system with realized returns $R_{P1} = 0\%$, $R_{P2} = +10\%$, and $R_{P3} = -4\%$. The results are summarized in Table 18-3 (ignoring the compounding effect for simplicity).

TABLE 18-3 OBI example – Yearly fees for Class A and Class B shares.

	$R_{P1} = 0\%$	$R_{P2} = +10\%$	$R_{P3} = -4\%$
Class A	MFee = **1.2%**	MFee = **1.2%**	MFee = **1.2%**
Class B	MFee = 1.0%	MFee = 1.0%	MFee = 1.0%
	PFee = 0.0%	PFee = 20% × (10%–4%) = 1.2%	PFee = 0.0%
	Total 1.0%	**Total 2.2%**	**Total 1.0%**

(continued)

(continued)

It appears that, under the scenario considered, the Class B shares are relatively expensive because the performance fee for the second year neither accounts for the disappointing first year nor for the negative third year. Therefore, Fund G's portfolio manager is asked to create a new share Class C that would be similar to Class B but with three possible combinations of high water and clawback provisions:

- Class C1 = Class B with a high water mark (HWM);
- Class C2 = Class B with clawback (CB);
- Class C3 = Class B with a high water mark and clawback (HWM+CB).

The results according to the same scenario as in Table 18-3 are reported in Table 18-4 (only performance fees are considered).

TABLE 18-4 OBI example – Yearly fees for Class C shares.

	$R_{P1} = 0\%$	$R_{P2} = +10\%$	$R_{P3} = -4\%$
Class B	**0.0%**	20%x(10%–4%) = **1.2%**	**0.0%**
Class C1 (HWM)	**0.0%**	20%x(10%–8%) = **0.4%**	**0.0%**
Class C2 (CB)	**0.0%**	20%x(10%–4%) = **1.2%**	20%x(6%–8%) = **−0.4%**
Class C3 (HWM+CB)	**0.0%**	20%x(10%–8%) = **0.4%**	20%x(6%–8%) = **−0.4%**

Both types of provisions contribute to aligning the performance fees with the fund's history. The high water mark alone (C1) reduces the year-2 performance fee by accounting for the poor first-year return but does not induce a subsequent correction for the negative third year. The clawback alone (C2) allows the PM to reap a high performance fee in year 2, but a fraction of it is redeemed in year 3. Only the combination of these provisions (C3) simultaneously corrects for the year-1 and year-3 disappointing outcomes. Note that, in year 3, the deduction is limited to the amount previously paid, but the penalty is potentially larger.

To conclude, the manager should only subscribe to Class C3 shares as these are the only ones whose cumulative performance fee of 0% is in line with the poor cumulative fund performance of 0% + 10% − 4% = 6%, below the cumulative hurdle rate 3 × 4% = 12%.

18.2.3 Fund ownership

A standard way to mitigate the agency conflict between a company's shareholders and its management team is to reward the latter with stock options. Presumably, managers who are also shareholders will have a stronger incentive to maximize the value of the firm. The same logic applies to the fund industry. Granting PMs partial ownership of the fund might realign their interests toward those of the investors.[6]

Several empirical studies have documented how PM fund ownership contributes to mitigating agency problems. Khorana, Servaes, and Wedge (2007) and Evans (2008) find that managerial ownership relates positively to fund performance and negatively to turnover – two outcomes that are consistent with a reduction in agency conflict. Ma and Tang (2019) show that PM fund ownership is also associated with lower risk-taking. Among mutual funds with manager ownership, the authors observe a reduction in total risk (mitigating the incentives from the convex flow-performance relation) as well as in downside risk (alleviating career concerns). Aragon and Nanda (2012) find a similar negative relation for hedge funds.

However, fund ownership may have limitations in curbing agency issues. Ferris and Yan (2007) study the case of namesake funds. A namesake fund has the special characteristic that it shares its names with its manager. The PM of a namesake fund usually serves as fund director and chairs the board. They have significant ownership of the fund, but, as Ferris and Yan (2007) note, they also associate their reputation with the fund. The PM therefore has both direct and intangible ownership.

The authors highlight the ambiguous impact of ownership structure on agency conflicts. On the one hand, the strong level of PM ownership typically provides a stronger alignment with the interests of investors. On the other hand, with PMs of namesake funds being their own supervisors and enjoying their reputational capital, one could argue that they work under looser monitoring, have fewer career concerns, and benefit from a stronger bargaining power *vis-à-vis* the investors. In line with these conjectures, Ferris and Yan (2007) find that namesake funds assume greater levels of unsystematic risk and charge higher fees. Their performance, however, is not significantly different from that of non-namesake funds, which might indicate that the positive and negative effects of this particular ownership structure on agency conflicts partially offset one another.

18.2.4 Governance solutions

In addition to managerial compensation, the governance of the fund can help alleviate the agency conflicts between the investors and PMs working on their behalf. Gil-Bazo and

[6] PM fund ownership has become the rule, not the exception. In a sample of US mutual funds studied by Ma and Tang (2019), 70% of the funds have at least one manager coinvesting, with an average participation of $540 000.

Ruiz-Verdú (2009) provide evidence that better fund governance brings fees more in line with performance. Two communication channels contribute to improving the monitoring of PMs: (i) reporting, which refers to the set of internal procedures designed to convey trading information from managers to their supervisors and investors, and (ii) disclosure, which refers to the regulatory environment that investment firms must comply with in order to communicate with their clients and the general public. In addition, the composition of the board can also play an active role in PM monitoring.

18.2.4.1 Reporting

From a supervisory perspective, the quality of data is instrumental in assessing the PM's behavior. Depending on how information is managed within the fund, supervisors can evaluate the PMs on return data or on holdings data, and these data can be reported at various frequencies. While analyzing risk exposure for instance, holdings data (versus return data) help determine how risk may be shifted.

Higher frequency data not only enable supervisors to determine the timing of trades in a more accurate manner, but they also allow them to detect round-trip transactions. Elton, Gruber, Blake, Krasny, and Ozelge (2010) find less evidence of momentum trading or tournament behavior[7] with monthly (rather than quarterly) mutual fund holdings data. However, reporting fund holdings at lower frequency delays the incorporation of private information into prices and therefore prevents copycat funds from mimicking winning strategies (see Frank, Poterba, Shackelford, and Shoven, 2004, for evidence).

The concern for misreporting is even stronger for hedge funds, which are not allowed to advertise performance or to fully disclose portfolio positions. The practical question is therefore whether it is possible to detect misreporting (and possibly fraud) from the mere observation of reported returns. The literature obtains mixed results on this issue. For instance, Bollen and Pool (2008) argue that conditional serial correlation in returns is an indication of return smoothing (i.e., PMs fully reporting gains but delaying the reports on losses). However, Cassar and Gerakos (2011) show that suspected return smoothing can be explained in part by misreporting but for the most part by asset illiquidity.[8] Another example is the kink around zero[9] often observed in the return distribution of hedge funds that has been interpreted by some as evidence of return manipulation (Bollen and Pool, 2009). However, Beaver, McNichols, and Nelson (2007) attribute this pattern to a tax effect, while Jorion and Schwarz (2014) argue that it is a consequence of asymmetric incentive fees (through high water mark provisions, for example).

[7]Tournament behavior refers to PMs underperforming in the beginning of the year and shifting risk in the latter part of the year to potentially improve their ranking at the end of the monitoring period.
[8]See Sections 12.3 and 12.4 of Chapter 12 for a complete discussion of these issues.
[9]Such a kink is created by an abnormally low number of small losses and an abnormally large number of small gains.

In sum, the quality of fund management can benefit from a more comprehensive and transparent set of reporting practices (see Chapter 15 for a more detailed analysis of communication around performance). However, reporting alone does not appear as a definitive solution to eradicate agency distortions, nor does it represent a major channel to exacerbate them.

18.2.4.2 Disclosure

The investment firm's disclosure policy conveys information about fund management practices on a wider scale than reporting. As such, disclosure rules are expected to act as an even more effective monitoring device that mitigates the risk of opportunistic behavior from PMs.

Edelen, Evans, and Kadlec (2012) examine the specific impact of expenditure disclosure on fund performance. They document the lower returns of funds that used to bundle their operational costs with brokerage commissions (a practice that is now banned) in contrast to the funds that transparently expensed those costs. They conclude that bundling payments via commissions is a way to hide costs, and that clearer disclosure reduces agency costs in delegated portfolio management.

However, too much transparency may cause some unintended consequences. The 2004 regulatory change imposed by the SEC on the US mutual funds served as a natural experiment for several studies. After that date, the disclosure of portfolio composition became mandatory at the quarterly (instead of semi-annual) frequency. "Informed" funds (i.e., funds trading stocks subject to greater informational asymmetry) lost part of their informational advantage and experienced poorer performance after the new regulation (Agarwal, Mullally, Tang, and Yang, 2015). The 2004 regulatory change also increased herding among mutual funds according to Deng, Hung, and Qiao (2018) as it made mimicking strategies easier to implement. Dyakov, Harford, and Qiu (2022) further argue that the imposed enhanced transparency increased managerial skill-reassessment risk, which mostly penalized high volatility funds. These funds responded by increasing fees and lowering risk at the expense of investors.

Finally, the monitoring benefits from disclosure rules find a major limitation with the practice of "window dressing." This expression refers to temporary portfolio rebalancing made shortly before deadlines when portfolio compositions are disclosed. With window dressing, PMs aim at impressing sponsors and investors through their stock selection skills, and not just through aggregate portfolio performance. Evidence on window dressing has been reported for pension funds (Lakonishok, Shleifer, Thaler, and Vishny, 1991), equity mutual funds (Meier and Schaumburg, 2004), and bond mutual funds (Morey and O'Neal, 2006), but the extent of that practice is still open to debate.

18.2.4.3 Board composition

A stream of empirical research supports the idea that board independence contributes to the overall reduction in agency conflicts.[10] For instance, independent directors are more effective

[10] Part of this research was fostered after 2004 when the SEC set a rule to impose 75% of independent members in US mutual fund boards.

in terminating underperforming seasoned PMs (Fu and Wedge, 2011; Ding and Wermers, 2012). They are particularly effective in improving the performance of team-managed funds, as opposed to individually managed funds (Adams, Nishikawa, and Rao, 2018). As an incentive mechanism akin to the one applied to PMs, agency issues can be further mitigated if board directors have ownership of the fund (Cremers, Driessen, Maenhout, and Weinbaum, 2009; Fricke, 2015). However, Meschke (2019) finds that mutual funds with a higher proportion of independent directors charge lower fees but at the expense of lower performance.

Despite their much looser regulation, hedge funds do have a majority of outside board members. Clifford, Ellis, and Gerken (2018) examine a sample of more than 5000 hedge funds between 2009 and 2013 and find that the median board has three directors, two of them being outsiders. These outside directors serve on many boards at the same time, and because of these multiple positions, they can serve independently on behalf of investors, as argued by the authors.

18.3 PERFORMANCE MEASUREMENT AND AGENCY ISSUES

Delegating the management of a portfolio generates agency conflicts that neither contractual nor governance solutions can perfectly mitigate. It leaves room for potential manipulation of performance. We first review some classic, non-informed trading strategies that will mechanically embellish the measure of performance.

18.3.1 Performance manipulation strategies

If PMs know they are evaluated according to a given performance measure, then they might behave opportunistically by manipulating that measure while still pursuing their own objectives (e.g., fee maximization). Goetzmann et al. (2007) identify three general strategies for manipulating a performance measure:

- Altering the underlying distribution of returns to positively affect the measure (distributional manipulation).
- Playing with the time variation into the return distribution while the measure assumes stationarity (dynamic manipulation).
- Inducing a positive bias in the estimation of the measure by mixing distributional and dynamic manipulation.

The authors examine several performance measures (including the Sharpe ratio, Jensen's alpha, the Sortino ratio, and the Hendriksson–Merton and Treynor–Mazuy timing measures) and show that dynamic strategies that involve leveraging or trading in options can effectively improve the measure even with high transaction costs. Below we examine the potential manipulations of the Sharpe ratio.[11]

18.3.1.1 Distributional manipulation

Let us first examine altering the underlying distribution of returns. As discussed in Chapter 5, adding a short position on a call option to an initial long position in the stock (covered call strategy) introduces negative skewness in the return distribution. With a metric like the Sharpe ratio (or Jensen's alpha for instance), such asymmetric reduction in variance is not taken into account. The covered call strategy is therefore a simple way for the PM to overstate their performance. More generally, so will do trading strategies that yield a nonlinear payoff structure compared to the one of a reference index.[12]

The principle is rather simple and explained by Jagannathan and Korajczyk (1986): if the investors' dislike of high volatility and negative skewness translates into positive risk premiums for these two types of risks, then a PM can obtain the same average rate of return as that of a passive index by swapping a lower volatility (less risk) for a lower skewness (more risk). It is thus highly likely that, as a result, the Sharpe ratio (which only uses volatility as a risk input) will be inflated by the maneuver.

Consider the situation where the underlying stock returns follow a Gaussian distribution. It is currently worth \$100, and it grows at 15% per year with a return volatility of 20%. The investment horizon and the call option maturity are both set to 1 year. The risk-free rate is 3%. Sharpe ratios for covered call strategies using various call option strikes K are represented by the solid line in Figure 18-7. For comparison, the Sharpe ratio for the long position in the underlying stock is represented by the dashed line. The best Sharpe ratio-enhancing strategy consists in selling a slightly out-of-the-money call.

The following example illustrates the manipulation of return distribution with a simple real-life case. Consider the monthly total returns of the S&P500 index over a 10-year period (120 observations from July 2012 to June 2022). We contrast five mechanical trading strategies: (i) a long-only investment in the index; (ii) a strategy consisting of buying the index and writing, at the beginning of each month, one near-at-the-money (nATM) call with a strike price equal to the index price multiplied by a factor 1.025 (i.e., if the index price is 1000, then the strike is 1025) and a one-month maturity (the proceeds of this sale are invested in the index as well); (iii) a strategy similar to the previous one but with an out-of-the-money (OTM) call with strike multiplier 1.05; (iv) a similar strategy with a deep-out-of-the-money (dOTM) option with strike multiplier 1.075; and finally (v) a strategy similar to strategy (iii) but writing two calls instead of one. Strategies (ii) to (v) correspond to covered calls, i.e., strategies featuring the purchase of an asset and the sale of a call option on this same asset. We call these strategies (i) Linear,

[11]The reader is referred to the original article of Goetzmann et al. (2007) for the manipulation of other performance measures.

[12]We have already discussed it in the context of the CAPM in Figure 5-14 of Chapter 5.

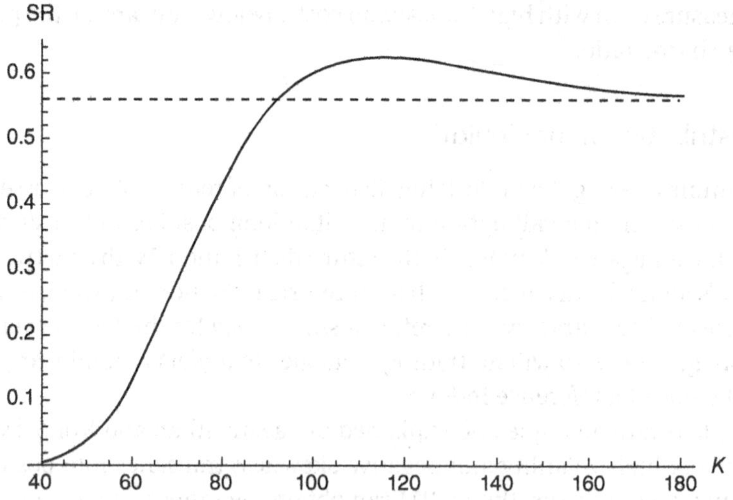

FIGURE 18-7 Sharpe ratios of the covered call strategy as a function of the call strike.

(ii) nATM CC, (iii) OTM CC, (iv) dOTM CC, and (v) 2OTM CC. Each option is priced according to the Black–Scholes formula and, in order to replicate the prevailing conditions at each point in time as faithfully as possible, we track the one-month T-Bill rate over time and use the six-month forward-looking market volatility as inputs.

These five strategies involve no discretionary trading decision. At the end of each month, the option payoff is recorded and is deduced from the portfolio value, resulting in a bonus (if the option is not struck, with a terminal payoff of zero) or a loss. This is illustrated in Figure 18-8, which reports the two most contrasting strategies, namely (i) Linear and (v) 2OTM CC.

The Linear strategy (crosses) delivers returns that are obviously equal to the S&P500 returns: The realizations are aligned on a straight line with a slope of one. The 2OTM CC strategy (circles) shows two distinct patterns. Whenever the market return is lower than 5%, the sale of the two options represents a cash inflow that generates an additional yield that enhances the index investment. The distance with the index return depends on how expensively the options were sold. If the market return exceeds 5%, the options are exercised. If only one option was sold, the trend would be horizontal, and the total return would be floored at 5%. However, because of the sale of two options, there is a potential loss, which is represented graphically as a downward trend.

The graph clearly suggests that (i) the covered call strategy displays a lower volatility than the Linear one (less vertical dispersion), but (ii) it displays a concave trend compared to the Linear one. This concavity typically translates into an asymmetric distribution between losses (potentially unlimited) and gains (much less pronounced). This leads to a more negative skewness of the return distribution. Table 18-5 translates these notions into concrete risk, return, and performance indicators, considering an average interest rate of 0.60% per annum.

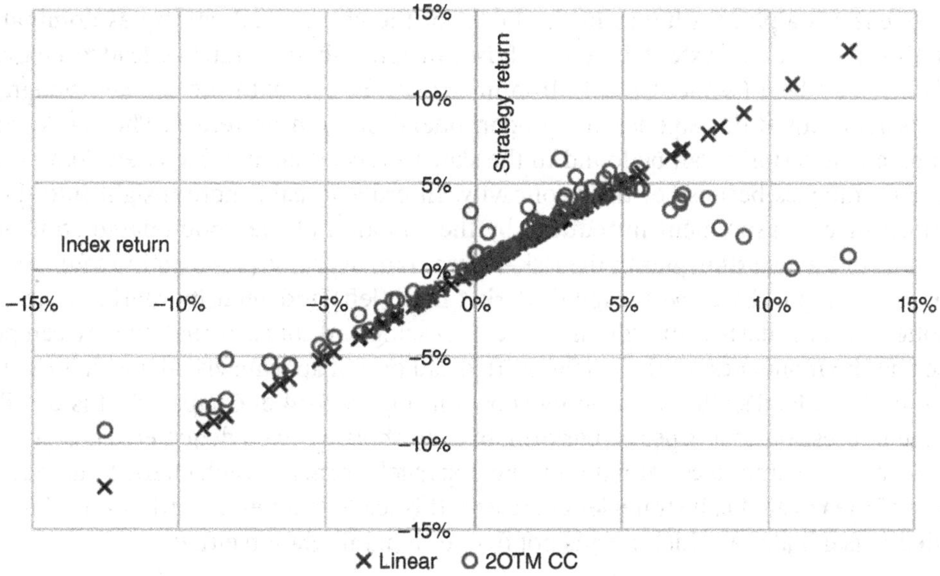

FIGURE 18-8 Returns of the Linear and 2OTM CC trading strategies.

TABLE 18-5 Risk, return, and performance indicator of five mechanical strategies on the S&P500.

	Strategy				
Indicator	**Linear**	**nATM CC**	**OTM CC**	**dOTM CC**	**OTM 2CC**
Mean return	12.01%	10.18%	12.01%	12.38%	12.01%
Volatility	13.87%	10.31%	12.08%	13.07%	11.11%
Sharpe ratio	***0.82***	***0.93***	***0.94***	***0.90***	***1.03***
Correlation	1.00	0.93	0.97	0.99	0.87
Beta	1.00	0.69	0.85	0.93	0.70
Jensen's alpha	***0.00%***	***1.69%***	***1.73%***	***1.11%***	***3.45%***
Skewness	−0.46	−1.41	−0.98	−0.69	−0.96
Excess kurtosis	1.42	1.83	0.93	0.86	0.77

As could be expected from the nature of the covered call strategies, both the Sharpe ratio and the Jensen's alpha (in italics in the table) of the covered call strategies dominate the long-only to a substantial extent. In terms of risk, all option-based strategies lead to a reduction in volatility and beta (without much drop in the correlation with the market though), but this does not occur at the expense of a proportional drop in mean return. The key reason for this apparent superiority can be found in the skewness coefficient, which deteriorates for all nonlinear strategies because of their concavity. In order to gain more insight into the bias in performance measurement introduced by the adoption of the option-based strategy, the positioning of the five strategies in the risk–return frameworks is provided in Figure 18-9.

On each graph, the *ex post* Capital Market Line (left) and Security Market Line (right) are plotted with the dashed straight line. The increasing and concave relation between performance and the moneyness of the single shorted call option appears visually well, in a similar fashion to the Leland's (1999) reasoning shown in Figure 5-14 of Chapter 5. It is possible to leave the impression of a superior performance, by shorting two adequately chosen options as shown by the diamond coordinates on the upper-left corner of each chart. Note that, since the beta of the covered call strategies decreases, this leads to an even further inflation of the modified Jensen's alpha, which is thus not free from manipulation either.

18.3.1.2 Dynamic manipulation

Another way to provide the illusion of outperformance, even though the manager has not used any particular information (and thus has displayed no particular skill), is *dynamic manipulation*. It is related to modifying leverage conditionally of past results, i.e., making the portfolio's risk contingent to its past performance. The principle of this performance manipulation can be summarized as follows. If a manager considers their performance "through the cycle," they can reasonably ascertain what could be the average rate of return they can obtain over a long period of time. Thus, after a certain period of time – say, in the middle of a reference period – they can assess whether the market conditions have been much more or much less favorable than their initial expectations. This very simple consideration could lead them to modify the risk level of the portfolio and thus its ability to capture the market risk premium. If the manager increases their exposure to the market after a worse-than-expected (low return) period or, conversely, reduces their exposure after better-than-expected times, the resulting performance measure has a high likelihood of being higher than that of a purely passive portfolio. Goetzmann et al. (2007) show that both the Sharpe ratio and the Jensen's alpha will be positively affected by this behavior, which does not use *per se* information about the market but simply makes the portfolio beta conditional on the past portfolio returns. This is illustrated in Figure 18-10 retrieved from their article.

The chart illustrates the "lucky" case of a manager who has obtained very good returns with their initial exposure to the market and then decides to cut their beta by a factor λ for the subsequent period. This looks like market timing, but it is not.

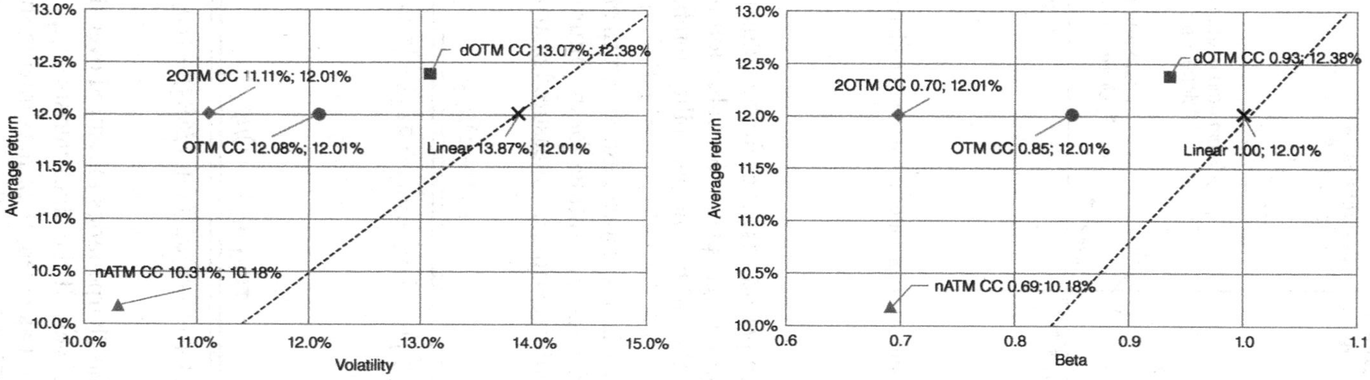

FIGURE 18-9 Risk–return coordinates of the five strategies with volatility (left) and beta (right).

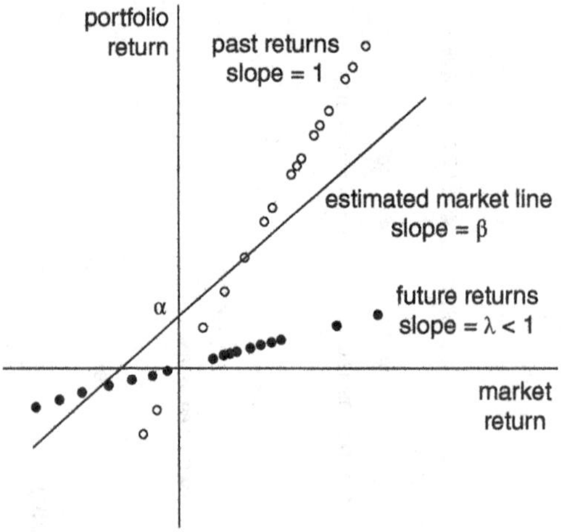

FIGURE 18-10 Illustration of the outcome of a conditional modification of beta.
Source: Goetzmann et al. (2007).

The example below is a two-period case that further illustrates dynamic manipulation. The Sharpe ratio calculated over a single period of evaluation is invariant to leverage. However, consider a situation where the PM has the possibility to rebalance their portfolio at some intermediate date τ $(0 < \tau < 1)$ during the period of evaluation (normalized to 1 for simplicity). At time τ, the PM has achieved a historical mean excess return of $\mu_{P,1}$ with standard deviation $\sigma_{P,1}$. Let $\mu_{P,2}$ and $\sigma_{P,2}$ denote those same quantities for the future portfolio (i.e., from time τ to time 1). At the end of the evaluation period, the measured Sharpe ratio will be:

$$\mathrm{SR}_P = \frac{\tau + (1-\tau)\mu_{P,2}}{\sqrt{\tau(\mu_{P,1}^2 + \sigma_{P,1}^2) + (1-\tau)(\mu_{P,2}^2 + \sigma_{P,2}^2) - [\tau\mu_{P,1} + (1-\tau)\mu_{P,2}]^2}} \tag{18-6}$$

or, equivalently,

$$\mathrm{SR}_P = \frac{\tau\mu_{P,1} + (1-\tau)\mu_{P,2}}{\sqrt{\tau\mu_{P,1}^2(1 + 1/\mathrm{SR}_1^2) + (1-\tau)\mu_{P,2}^2(1 + 1/\mathrm{SR}_2^2) - [\tau\mu_{P,1} + (1-\tau)\mu_{P,2}]^2}} \tag{18-7}$$

where SR_1 and SR_2 stand for the Sharpe ratios measured over the first period $[0, \tau]$ and over the second period $[\tau, 1]$, respectively. If the characteristics $(\mu_{P,2}, \sigma_{P,2})$ of the portfolio during the second period are considered as given, then maximizing the overall Sharpe ratio SR_P is equivalent to maximizing SR_2. That maximization problem remains invariant to leverage.

However, at time τ, the PM can revise their target for the mean excess return $\mu_{P,2}$ to reach a new maximum for SR. Treating SR_P as a function of $\mu_{P,2}$, the first-order condition yields

$$\mu^*_{P,2} = \begin{cases} \mu_{P,1}\dfrac{1 + 1/SR_1^2}{1 + 1/SR_2^2} & \text{if } \mu_{P,1} > 0 \\ \infty & \text{if } \mu_{P,1} \leq 0 \end{cases} \tag{18-8}$$

This means that the overall Sharpe ratio can be improved by leveraging at some intermediate point in time to revise the targeted mean excess return. That portfolio correction allows the PM to adjust their portfolio depending on the performance achieved during the first period.

Suppose, for instance, that the PM has been lucky in the first period by achieving a historical Sharpe ratio $SR_1 = 0.4$ (with $\mu_{P,1} = 10\%$), whereas the anticipated one is $SR_2 = 0.2$. Figure 18-11 shows the overall Sharpe ratio that can be obtained after one year if the portfolio can be rebalanced after one quarter ($\tau = 0.25$, gray line), two quarters ($\tau = 0.5$, dashed black line), or three quarters ($\tau = 0.75$, solid black line).

In all three cases, the optimal target for the mean excess return over the second period is $\mu^*_{P,2} \approx 2.79\%$, indicating that the PM has the incentive to reallocate their portfolio to a safer position to secure the good performance achieved in the first period. The resulting overall Sharpe ratio depends on how long the PM has been lucky: The higher τ is, the higher the SR. In all cases, it is clearly above SR_2. Thus, by manipulating the overall Sharpe ratio through leverage, the PM's management skills can be falsely evaluated.

18.3.1.3 Estimation bias

The first two types of manipulation examined thus far (distributional and dynamic) implicitly assumed the absence of estimation error. The fact that the evaluator of the PM's performance

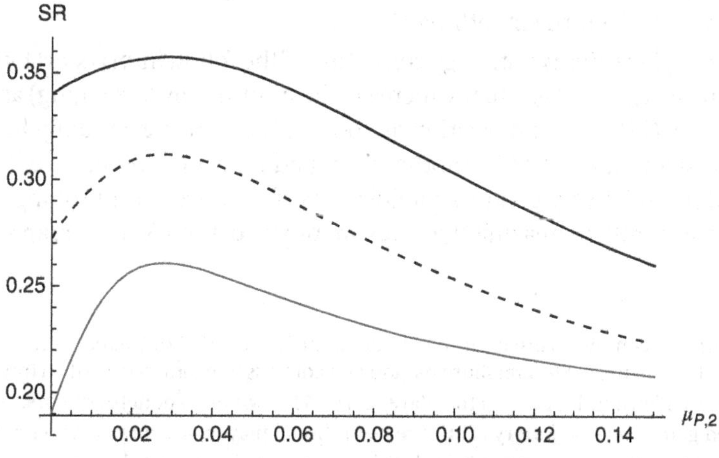

FIGURE 18-11 Overall Sharpe ratios as a function of the newly targeted mean excess return.

must estimate moments of the return distribution only increases the scope for manipulation. As discussed in Chapter 5, even though Sharpe ratios are at least as hard to estimate as mean returns, the difference in Sharpe ratios can be estimated more precisely. However, as Goetzmann et al. (2007) point out, such a property likely no longer holds for the return distributions of manipulated portfolios.

Investment strategies creating positive estimation bias are commonly referred to as "informationless." They merely consist of enhancing the measure of performance by systematically affecting the statistical estimation of means, variances, or measures of association. However, since they can be applied to any asset at any time, these strategies convey no information about the PM's selection or timing skills. Weisman (2002) gives some examples of such strategies. They typically tilt the risk–return ratio favorably while showing low correlation with systematic factors.

- *Short volatility investing* is a strategy consisting of selling an insurance policy against a low-probability event (such as writing an out-of-the-money option or a wide strangle with short maturity). The fund collects the premiums from the short positions, which seemingly increases the mean return while not affecting the volatility (since the strategy is in fact exposed to a long-maturity volatility event). As long as the PM is evaluated on a period that does not include a major volatility event, their performance will be positively assessed, no matter the market direction. The sanction associated with this estimation error is that the fund will strongly underperform when the volatility event materializes.
- *Return smoothing* is a strategy consisting of spreading gains and losses over time to reduce the estimated return volatility. Funds invested in illiquid assets are particularly prone to such manipulation because it is difficult to report an accurate net asset value (NAV) on a high-frequency basis. PMs may therefore opt to invest in illiquid securities when they are evaluated with a performance metric that is very sensitive to the historical return volatility, such as the Sharpe ratio. The example in the boxed text below provides an illustration of return smoothing.[13]
- *St-Petersburg investing* is a strategy consisting of the following: (i) start by investing a unit amount in an asset, (ii) gradually increase the position (by leveraging) as long as returns are negative, (iii) close the position as soon as the return eventually becomes positive, (iv) reinvest a unit amount in another asset and repeat the procedure.[14] Such a strategy can exhibit a relatively good risk-adjusted performance for a prolonged period. However, by constantly increasing the investment stake, the PM may reap some short-term

[13]Several unsmoothing techniques are examined in detail in Section 12.3 of Chapter 12.

[14]The name is in reference to the St-Petersburg paradox – a coin-tossing lottery described by eighteenth century mathematician Daniel Bernoulli in which the player earns \$$2^{n-1}$ where n denotes the first coin throw yielding tails. The expected gain from that lottery is infinite, yet rational players accept paying a limited sum of money to enter the game. The lottery is an example in decision theory to illustrate risk aversion.

benefits but exposes the fund to a higher risk of bankruptcy. Performance measures that miss higher order moments and/or that are applied on a too narrow time frame might not detect this type of manipulation.

On Behalf Investment (continued)

The manager decides to invest in Fund C. The performance is evaluated over a one-year horizon. Three reporting patterns are examined:

1. A daily mark to the market of the NAV.
2. A monthly update of the NAV (because of many illiquid assets in the fund).
3. A 21-trading day moving average of the NAV reported daily (return smoothing).

The daily evolution of the NAV is simulated as a discretized geometric Brownian motion with drift $\mu = 20\%$ and volatility $\sigma = 20\%$. Figure 18-12 shows one of the 1000 simulated paths.

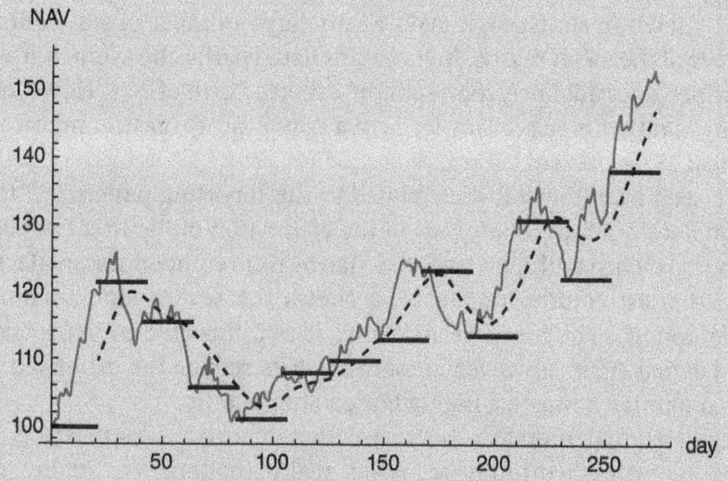

FIGURE 18-12 Simulation of the NAV with three different reporting patterns.

The initial value of the fund is set to 100. The daily NAV is plotted with the gray line (reporting pattern #1) over 13 months. The black solid line represents the NAV updated once every 21 trading days (reporting pattern #2). The dashed black line is the 21-trading moving average (reporting pattern #3), which starts only after one month.

(continued)

(continued)

The mean and standard deviation of the log-returns from the three time-series are calculated between day 21 and day 273, and so is the corresponding Sharpe ratio. Table 18-6 reports the average of these three metrics across the 1000 simulated scenarios.

TABLE 18-6 OBI example – Sharpe ratios with three different reporting patterns.

	Reporting pattern		
	#1	#2	#3
Mean	15.74%	15.64%	15.84%
Standard deviation	20.00%	19.85%	4.12%
Sharpe ratio	0.5369	0.5360	2.6294

As is well known in statistics, it takes a very large number of simulations to obtain a reliable estimate of the mean return. In these simulated paths, the average growth rate of the fund is 15%, which does not fairly represent the expected drift of 20%. However, the estimate of the volatility is rather precise. This leads to a downwardly biased empirical Sharpe ratio (relative to the 0.75 theoretical value).

As can be seen from the statistics related to the reporting pattern #2, the mere delay of information does not induce any bias in the estimation of the first two moments of the return distribution. The resulting estimated Sharpe ratio is therefore unaffected.

However, the last column of the table shows the severe manipulation that return smoothing can induce. The mean performance is not impacted by gains and losses being evenly spread across time. However, smoothing does reduce the estimated volatility by a considerable amount, leading to a highly biased Sharpe ratio.

The investor should therefore be aware that reporting frequency is not necessarily related to reporting truthfulness. What really matters for quality monitoring is that the investor can correctly associate the fund's cash flows to their corresponding trading date.

In conclusion, as long as a gap persists between the performance metric monitored by supervisors or investors and the PMs' personal goals, the latter keep their incentive to manipulate the performance measure to look better than what they actually do. The question addressed in the next subsection is whether the design of the performance measure can play a role in mitigating the agency conflict.

18.3.2 Performance measurement and manager's incentives

Up to now, our analysis of agency issues has been conducted for a given performance metric (say, e.g., the Sharpe ratio). In the examples described above, the performance metric is clearly not neutral in the agency conflict. For instance, the PM will manipulate skewness if they know the metric they are evaluated with ignores that higher moment. This leads us to wonder whether the design of a performance measure could have an impact on the PM's opportunistic behavior.

The literature has identified some cases where the implementation of commonly accepted performance metrics can improve (or worsen) the alignment of the investor's and the PM's goals. We review these cases below.

18.3.2.1 Linear benchmarking

As discussed previously, linear benchmarking hardly contributes to correctly incentivizing the PM. Admati and Pfleiderer (1997) formalize the intuition for this result in the CAPM framework. The investor's optimal allocation in this context is characterized by a two-fund portfolio (see Chapter 2). It can be obtained, for instance, with the conditional minimum variance portfolio (that the investor and the PM can both determine) and a second fund adjusting for the investor's preference toward risk. The agency conflict therefore applies on two levels: (i) the uninformed (i.e., unskilled) PM could invest in the unconditional minimum variance portfolio and (ii) the risk adjustment could be made according to the PM's risk preferences (and not the investor's).

Admati and Pfleiderer (1997) show that it takes a very specific design of the PM's compensation contract (parameters h_2 and h_3 in Equation (18-5)) to avoid issues (i) and (ii). Furthermore, benchmarking does not help because it rewards the PM for deviating from the optimal allocation. In fact, benchmarking reduces incentives to collect information and encourages passive strategies.

Dybvig, Farnsworth, and Carpenter (2010) extend this analysis and show that linear benchmarking is a second-best contract[15] when trading restrictions are applied. These restrictions may apply to the universe of assets, the positions held in those assets, the management of those assets (e.g., style of stocks, bond credit ratings, and use of derivatives), and to portfolio risk measures (e.g., duration, beta, and tracking error). Not only are trading restrictions essential to the optimal contract,[16] the authors argue, but additional incentives for risk must be provided if the PM can manipulate information. Otherwise, PMs could collect fees for active management while adopting passive strategies.

[15]Following the authors' terminology, second-best optimality is defined in a world where the investor can observe the PM's private information (through reporting and monitoring) but not their effort. In a third-best world (where neither private information nor effort is observable), the compensation contract must provide incentive to report signals truthfully. Dybvig et al. (2010) show that such a contract is more complex than mere benchmarking.

[16]Without them the PM can undo the incentives from the compensation contract (see Section 18.2.1).

Another issue inherent in benchmarking is time consistency. Mullally and Rossi (2022) document frequent changes in benchmarks in the US mutual funds (which is currently allowed by SEC regulation). Around 36% of funds in their sample made changes to their prospectus benchmarks at least once over the 2006–2018 period. On average, funds add indexes with low past returns and drop indexes with high past returns. Benchmark changes appear to be based on realized not expected returns. These findings are consistent with voluntary manipulation to bias the assessment of performance.

18.3.2.2 Factor-based performance metrics

If a PM's investment strategy is evaluated with a mean–variance measure (such as the Sharpe ratio or Jensen's alpha), they will have the incentive to load on negative co-skewness risk and reap the associated premium. Kostakis (2013) provides evidence from the UK equity fund industry that is consistent with that conjecture. The performance of the sample funds is substantially reduced when the Sharpe ratio is replaced with the downside Sharpe ratio (using negative semi-variance) or when Jensen's alpha is replaced with the Harvey–Siddique alpha.[17] Moreover, the funds that exhibit the highest Jensen's alpha are precisely the ones with the highest loadings on the negative co-skewness factor. Kostakis (2013) interprets this evidence as a bias in managers' incentives caused by too simplistic performance measures.

More generally, if the PM identifies a factor that is rewarded by the market, but that is not incorporated into the performance measure, they will be inclined to load their portfolio allocation on that unrecognized factor to generate returns that the investor will deem "abnormal" and therefore attribute it to the PM's skills.

18.3.2.3 Peer group comparisons

PMs are often evaluated in comparison to other managers within the investment firm or across other investment firms. These peer group comparisons are designed to foster competition among PMs, which should be for the benefit of investors.

However, this also creates a "tournament" effect whereby PMs ranked as strong contenders have the incentive to increase the volatility of their portfolio, and PMs ranked at the top tend to reduce that volatility to secure their leading position. The evidence on tournament effects is mixed for mutual funds (see, e.g., Brown et al., 1996; Qiu, 2003; Karoui and Meier, 2015) and weak for hedge funds (Brown, Goetzmann, and Park, 2001; Aragon and Nanda, 2012).

18.3.2.4 Horizon setting

The choice of a specific horizon for measuring portfolio performance may not be neutral. The horizon of investors is usually relatively long, but agency theory suggests that evaluating

[17]The Harvey-Siddique alpha is the intercept obtained from regressing realized returns on the market factor and a negative co-skewness factor.

the performance over shorter periods induces a tighter monitoring. However, the repeated maximization of a performance metric over short periods may not be equivalent to the maximization of the overall performance over the investor's horizon. In fact, the property of horizon invariance among performance measures is the exception rather than the rule.

Cvitanić, Lazrak, and Wang (2008) specifically study this problem for the Sharpe ratio. In a simplified investment environment where asset returns are independent and identically distributed, they show that the ratio between the five-year and the quarterly optimal Sharpe ratios varies from 126% to 168% depending on the level of the target return. In an investment environment where asset returns are mean-reverting, the impact of short termism on performance is aggravated, and the five-year Sharpe ratio can be 20 or 30 times its quarterly counterpart.

The authors find that a short-term Sharpe ratio maximizer implements a highly path-dependent trading strategy. Notably, they will increase (decrease) risk in the second half of the performance measurement period after a poor (good) performance in the first period. Thus, the risk manipulation typically observed around the mid-assessment period and attributed to tournament effects can also be explained by short-term performance goals imposed on PMs.

On Behalf Investment (continued)

In agreement with the investor, the manager of OBI forms a portfolio made of Fund C (with weight w) and the risk-free asset (with weight $(1 - w)$). To simplify the exposition, the dynamics of the Fund C value (denoted by F_t) is represented by a binomial tree compatible with normal returns with 20% drift and 20% volatility. Specifically, normalizing the initial value of Fund C to $F_0 = 100$ and using a quarterly time step, we obtain the tree as presented in Table 18-7.[18]

TABLE 18-7 OBI example – Binomial tree for the quarterly fund value.

t = 0	t = 0.25	t = 0.5	t = 0.75	t = 1
100	110.52	122.14	134.99	149.18
	90.48	100.00	110.52	122.14
		81.87	90.48	100.00
			74.08	81.87
				67.03

(continued)

[18] The tree is built along the Cox, Ross and Rubinstein specification where underlying fund value is multiplied or divided by a factor $u = \exp(\sigma\sqrt{\Delta t}) = \exp(0.2\sqrt{0.25}) \approx 1.10517$ over each period. The probability of fund value going up is $p = [\exp(\mu\Delta t) - \exp(-\sigma\sqrt{\Delta t})]/[\exp(\sigma\sqrt{\Delta t}) - \exp(-\sigma\sqrt{\Delta t})] \approx 0.73095$.

(continued)

The investor has mandated OBI to maximize the Sharpe ratio over the one-year horizon. More precisely, OBI is requested to solve for $\min(\text{Var}(R_{0,1}))$ subject to $E(R_{0,1}) \geq b$, where b is a minimum return requirement[19] and

$$R_{s,t} = w\frac{F_t}{F_s} + (1-w)1.05^{t-s}$$

denotes the gross return on the investor's portfolio between time s and time t.

To solve for the investor's program, the portfolio weight in Fund C (the risky asset) can be revised in each state and on every quarter. We denote these weights $w_{j,t}$ for state j and time t, where states are numbered from bottom to top (i.e., j counts the number of times when the value of Fund C has gone up). The expected gross return $E(R_{0,1})$ is calculated as the probability-weighted average of all terminal wealth obtained from an initial \$1 investment. There are $2^4 = 16$ different paths with probability $p^j(1-p)^{4-j}$. Similarly, the variance of gross return is calculated as $\text{Var}(R_{0,1}) = E(R_{0,1}^2) - (E(R_{0,1}))^2$. The solution to the optimization problem is reported in Table 18-8 (we set $b = 1.15$, but the corresponding maximal Sharpe ratio does not depend on b; see Goetzmann et al., 2007 or Cvitanić et al., 2008).

TABLE 18-8 OBI example – State- and time-dependent portfolio weights that maximize the one-year Sharpe ratio.

t = 0	t = 0.25	t = 0.5	t = 0.75
$w_{0,0} = 0.79$	$w_{1,1} = 0.45$	$w_{2,2} = 0.27$	$w_{3,3} = 0.16$
	$w_{0,1} = 1.25$	$w_{1,2} = 0.69$	$w_{2,3} = 0.40$
		$w_{0,2} = 2.07$	$w_{1,3} = 1.07$
			$w_{0,3} = 3.84$

The solution entails that $E(R_{0,1}) = 1.15$ (the constraint is binding), $\text{Var}(R_{0,1}) \approx 0.00977$, and the maximal Sharpe ratio is 1.01172. Notice how the weights in the risky asset decrease with state j, reflecting the incentive to lock in prior good performance and, conversely, the need to "catch up" after bad performance.

Let us now suppose that OBI reviews the performance of its PMs every six months on the basis of the Sharpe ratio they have achieved. The PM is therefore incentivized to solve for $\min(\text{Var}(R_{0,0.5}))$ subject to $E(R_{0,0.5}) \geq b$ and then for $\min(\text{Var}(R_{0.5,1}))$ subject to $E(R_{0.5,1}) \geq b$. Following the same binomial approach as $b = \sqrt{1.15}$, the solutions to these two optimization problems are shown in Table 18-9.

[19]The minimum return constraint is binding to obtain the solution.

TABLE 18-9 OBI example – State- and time-dependent portfolio weights that maximize the six-month Sharpe ratio.

$t = 0$	$t = 0.25$	$t = 0.5$	$t = 0.75$
$w_{0,0} = 0.66$	$w_{1,1} = 0.38$	$w_{0,2} = 0.66$	$w_{1,3} = 0.38$
	$w_{0,1} = 1.02$		$w_{0,3} = 1.02$

Notice that the weight at time $t = 0.5$ is reset to its initial value since the PM is solving for the same optimization problem as at time $t = 0$. Over the six-month period, the solution yields $\mathrm{E}(R_{0,0.5}) = \mathrm{E}(R_{0.5,1}) = \sqrt{1.15}$, $\mathrm{Var}(R_{0,0.5}) = \mathrm{Var}(R_{0.5,1}) \approx 0.00538$, and the maximal Sharpe ratio is 0.65001.

The misalignment in the investment horizon induces the PM to solve for a variance minimization program that is suboptimal from the investor's perspective. The agency conflict is material as the maximal Sharpe ratio drops from 1.01 to 0.65.

18.4 DESIGNING A NORMATIVE PERFORMANCE MEASURE

The potential presence of agency conflicts highlights the non-neutral aspect of performance assessment. The design and implementation of a performance measurement method may induce biases in the evaluation of PMs' skills. Agency issues can be mitigated or aggravated because of the performance metric. That conclusion has led the academic literature to study performance measurement from a normative angle. What properties *should* a performance measure display to correctly evaluate (and possibly rank) the managers' abilities?

18.4.1 Axioms for performance measurement

In this section, we review the contributions that aim at laying the theoretical foundations for a sound portfolio performance metric. As will be seen, this literature is still under development and no strong consensus has yet emerged. One major sticking point is the extent to which the performance measure should be specific to the investor. The trade-off is difficult to find between a generic score that can be largely applicable and a tailored measure that captures the investor's preferences (through a utility function, for instance).

Chen and Knez (1996) are arguably the first authors to present an axiomatic for performance measurement. In their approach, a portfolio manager has access to a given investment universe. There is a set of returns that they can attain by following strategies that rely on public information only. In addition, the PM can take advantage of a private signal about future returns. The goal of the performance measure is to assess the extent to which the PM effectively exploits the signal to improve the investment performance.

18.4.1.1 Admissible performance measure

A performance measure is said to be admissible if it satisfies the following four conditions:

1. The measure assigns a zero score to any portfolio return that an investor with public information can achieve.
2. The measure is linear. This entails that any recombination of portfolios does not alter the score.
3. The measure is continuous. This entails that managers producing indistinguishable returns will obtain the same score.
4. The measure is non-trivial, meaning that it assigns a non-zero score to any traded security. This avoids the situation where a fund whose excess return is proportional to some asset's gross return does not necessarily obtain a zero score.

The first two conditions have an interesting implication in terms of benchmarking. They indeed imply that the reference return does not impact the performance score provided it is achievable with public information. To see this, let $\Theta(R_P - R_B)$ denote the performance score assigned to portfolio return R_P in excess of benchmark return R_B. Consider R'_B as an alternative benchmark and assume that both R_B and R'_B can be achieved with public information. From the first condition, we can write that $\Theta(R'_B - R_B) = 0$. By linearity (second condition), this yields that $\Theta(R'_B) = \Theta(R_B)$. Linearity also entails that $\Theta(R_P - R_B) = \Theta(R_P) - \Theta(R_B)$, which is therefore equal to $\Theta(R_P) - \Theta(R'_B) = \Theta(R_P - R'_B)$.

Chen and Knez (1996) establish that the law of one price is a necessary and sufficient condition for the existence of an admissible performance measure. This, of course, does not entail that all commonly known performance measures are admissible. That existence theorem can be extended if one adds a fifth condition to characterize an admissible positive performance measure:

1. The measure is positive. That is, $\Theta(R_P - R_B) \geq 0$ whenever $R_P - R_B \geq 0$, and $\Theta(R_P - R_B) > 0$ whenever $R_P - R_B > 0$.

Then, Chen and Knez (1996) further establish that the absence of arbitrage is a necessary and sufficient condition for the existence of an admissible positive performance measure.

These admissible positive performance measures do not rely on any asset pricing model in particular. They are only related to the absence of arbitrage. As such, they can be represented with a positive stochastic discount factor (SDF) d (see, e.g., Cochrane, 1996) in the sense that there exists a scalar $\eta > 0$ such that, for every return R_P:

$$\Theta(R_P - R_B) = \eta \mathrm{E}(d(R_P - R_B)) \tag{18-9}$$

With this approach, the specification of the stochastic discount factor d corresponds to the choice of an asset pricing model.[20]

Alternatively, Chen and Knez (1996) show that the set $\mathcal{D}$ of SDFs of all investors admits an upper bound that can be expressed in terms of alpha:

$$\overline{\alpha}_P = \sup_{d \in \mathcal{D}} \mathrm{E}(d(R_P)) - 1 \tag{18-10}$$

where $\overline{\alpha}_P$ (the highest expected alpha) results from the best performance that can be expected from portfolio P. Assuming heterogeneity among investors, Chrétien and Kammoun (2017) examine a sample of US mutual funds, and empirically extract the range of possible alphas that are compatible with a restriction on the highest achievable Sharpe ratios.[21] The spread across alphas that the authors obtain reflects the disagreement among investors. For a given fund, the highest alpha obtained from Equation (18-10) corresponds to its best clientele (i.e., the set of investors that value this fund the most). Interestingly, focusing on best clienteles enhances the estimated performance of mutual funds. Chrétien and Kammoun (2017) argue that this evidence helps revisit the controversial performance of active portfolio management (see Section 18.5): The skills of PMs might not be fairly assessed when their funds are analyzed through the lens of a representative investor instead of their best clientele.

18.4.1.2 Properties of admissible performance measures

All admissible performance measures will assign a score of zero if the fund is achievable by an uninformed investor. However, if one fund is found to have a zero score with one admissible performance measure, it does not entail that this fund is not benefitting from an informed PM. It could well be that some other measures will capture the added value that is specific to that fund. An empirical implication of that property is that performance should be evaluated through the lens of many possible measures. In other words, the search for robustness pays off while identifying superior portfolio performance.[22]

Chen and Knez (1996) further point out that the score assigned by *positive* admissible performance measures is an increasing function of $R_P - R_B$ (see Equation (18-9)). This ensures that all positive admissible performance measures will provide a consistent ranking across funds. The ranking consistency property is not guaranteed, however, for admissible performance measures that do not satisfy the positivity condition.

[20] Farnsworth, Ferson, Jackson, and Todd (2002) show how to apply the stochastic discount factor methodology to the evaluation of mutual fund performance.

[21] This approach, pioneered by Cochrane and Saa-Requejo (2000), is referred to as the good-deal bounds. It imposes reasonable limits on the investment performance that can be achieved in incomplete markets.

[22] This is one of the reasons why this book has tried to present a view that is as exhaustive as possible on performance measurement.

18.4.1.3 Further axiomatic construction of performance measures

Additional developments related to the axiomatic characterization of a performance measure are provided by De Giorgi (2005) and Cherny and Madan (2009). These authors choose to design a score on terminal payoffs, not on returns.[23] Among the properties they put forward are:[24]

1. Linearity (as in Chen and Knez, 1996) or, alternatively, quasi-concavity is defined as follows. For two portfolios yielding the terminal payoffs X_1 and X_2, respectively, such that $\Theta(X_1) \geq x$ and $\Theta(X_2) \geq x$, then for any scalar $\lambda \in [0,1]$, $\Theta(\lambda X_1 + (1-\lambda)X_2) \geq x$.
   The quasi-concavity condition prevents the manipulation of the performance score by separating single positions.
2. Monotonicity. If the terminal payoff X_2 dominates X_1 in the sense that $X_2 \geq X_1$, then $\Theta(X_2) \geq \Theta(X_1)$.
3. Scale invariance. For any scalar $\lambda \in [0,1]$, $\Theta(\lambda X) = \Theta(X)$.
   Scale invariance is a desirable property as it prevents the manipulation of the performance score by leveraging the portfolio.
4. Law invariance. If X_1 and X_2 have the same distribution, then $\Theta(X_1) = \Theta(X_2)$.
   As discussed in Cherny and Madan (2009), law invariance is a debatable property. On the one hand, it allows for the practical implementation of the performance measure. On the other hand, it discards the investor's personal situation from the assessment procedure. For instance, if law invariance is an accepted property for performance measurement, then the correlation between the risky portfolio under study and the investor's marginal utility is simply ignored.
5. Second-order stochastic dominance. For any increasing concave function U, if $\mathrm{E}[U(X_2)] \geq \mathrm{E}[U(X_1)]$, that is, if X_2 stochastically dominates X_1,[25] then $\Theta(X_2) \geq \Theta(X_1)$.

That latter property illustrates the difficulty of fully incorporating investors' preferences into performance measurement. Even if the axioms abstract from any reference to a specific utility function, a certain relation to the standard preference theory must nevertheless prevail. Second-order stochastic dominance is the solution proposed by De Giorgi (2005) and Cherny and Madan (2009). It entails that investors make decisions that are compatible with expected utility. Note, however, that expected utility is not scale invariant. Therefore, the performance measures defined along these axioms aim at going beyond the expected utility framework.

---

[23] As noted by Zakamouline (2014), performance measures that are defined over returns automatically ignore the investor's wealth and only capture the risk preferences of a representative investor.
[24] Some of these properties were originally examined in the risk management literature to characterize coherent risk measures, already discussed in Chapter 6 (see Artzner, Delbaen, Eber, and Heath, 1999).
[25] See Chapter 16 for more details on stochastic dominance.

18.4.2 Manipulation-proof performance measure

The quest for a normative performance measure might be too ambitious for practical purposes. In response to potential agency issues, a more modest goal would be to design a performance measure that is not prone to manipulation.

18.4.2.1 A definition

Goetzmann et al. (2007) provide a general reflection on how to design a performance metric that is immune to manipulation. With such a manipulation-proof performance metric, the investor would not even have to worry about any agency conflict. Indeed, any misbehaving portfolio manager would be instantly penalized and identified through a bias-free performance score.

Assume that we observe a collection of (periodic) returns $R_{P,t}$ on the PM's portfolio. The returns on the risk-free asset are $R_{f,t}$. The evaluation period includes T observations. Let $\Theta(\{R_{P,t}\}_{t=1}^{T})$ denote the performance score assigned to the observed returns. To prevent dynamic manipulation, the authors first posit a time independence property, namely the fact that the relative ranking of future realized observations should not be impacted by the history of preceding observations. Formally, if:

$$\Theta(\{R_{P,t}^{0}\}_{t=1}^{\tau}, \{R'_{P,t}\}_{\tau+1}^{T}) > \Theta(\{R_{P,t}^{0}\}_{t=1}^{\tau}, \{R''_{P,t}\}_{\tau+1}^{T}) \tag{18-11}$$

then it must be that

$$\Theta(\{R_{P,t}\}_{t=1}^{\tau}, \{R'_{P,t}\}_{\tau+1}^{T}) > \Theta(\{R_{P,t}\}_{t=1}^{\tau}, \{R''_{P,t}\}_{\tau+1}^{T}) \tag{18-12}$$

for any history $\{R_{P,t}\}_{t=1}^{\tau}$.

Taking advantage of the fact that a ranking function displays this independence property if and only if it has an additive representation, Goetzmann et al. (2007) propose the following specification:

$$\Theta(\{R_{P,t}\}_{t=1}^{T}) = \Upsilon\left(\frac{1}{T}\sum_{t=1}^{T}\theta_t(R_{P,t})\right) \tag{18-13}$$

where the functions $\Upsilon(\cdot)$ and $\theta_t(\cdot)$ are all increasing.

In addition, to prevent static manipulation, the functions $\theta_t(\cdot)$ must be concave, so that the performance score is not improved by simply increasing unrewarded risk. Finally, the authors suggest that the functions $\theta_t(\cdot)$ be power functions to ensure that the compounding of observed returns $\theta_t(R_t)$ can represent a proxy for returns in different outcome states. They ultimately arrive at

$$\Theta(\{R_{P,t}\}_{t=1}^{T}) = -\frac{n}{\gamma}\log\left[\frac{1}{T}\sum_{t=1}^{T}(1+r_{P,t}^{g})^{-\gamma}\right] \tag{18-14}$$

which is equivalent to the manipulation-proof certainty equivalent (mpCE^j_P) already examined in Chapter 9 (see Equation (9-27)). In Equation (18-14), n is the number of observations per year, $r^g_{P,t}$ represents the geometric excess return, i.e., $r^g_{P,t} = \frac{1+R_{P,t}}{1+R_{f,t}} - 1$, and γ is a parameter to be determined.

The expression (18-14) allows us to interpret the performance score as the annualized continuously compounded excess return certainty equivalent of the portfolio. That is, a risk-free portfolio yielding a return $\exp(\log(1 + R_{f,t}) + \Theta/n)$ for each period would obtain a score of Θ.

Furthermore, the parameter γ can be adjusted to associate the performance score with a benchmark (with periodic return $R_{b,t}$). If $1 + R_{b,t}$ were log-normally distributed, then one should set

$$1 + \gamma = \frac{\log(\mathrm{E}(1 + R_{b,t})) - \log(1 + R_{f,t})}{\mathrm{Var}(\log(1 + R_{b,t}))} \tag{18-15}$$

and the quantity $1 + \gamma$ can then be interpreted as a risk-aversion coefficient.

The metric designed in Equation (18-14) is an interesting first step toward making performance evaluation robust to manipulation. However, it comes at the cost of having a rigid approach to assessing the PM's skills. In particular, one might worry that the designed performance measure does not entirely respond to the investor's investment objective. In light of the plethora of performance metrics analyzed in this book, the metric in Equation (18-14) is only one among many others whose exposure to manipulation risk remains to be clarified. Clearly, research in this area is only in its infancy. Eventually, one relevant question is whether the magnitude of the agency conflict justifies resorting to such a manipulation-proof performance measure possibly at the expense of the investor's, the investment firm's, and the PM's investment and business goals.

18.4.2.2 Practical implementation

Brown, Kang, In, and Lee (2010) empirically investigate whether the manipulation-proof certainty equivalent of Equation (18-14) can actually detect fund manipulation. They work on a sample of 1710 hedge funds with returns observed between January 2004 and July 2007. The sample period thus includes the subprime mortgage crisis, which arguably provided incentives for poorly performing PMs to manipulate their returns.

The first step of their analysis consists of replicating hedge funds to construct a time series of non-manipulated returns. To this end, the authors apply Hasanhodzic and Lo's (2007) linear five-factor model.[26] The estimation of the restricted model (i.e., no constant and the sum of coefficients set equal to 1) on a hedge fund's actual returns ($R_{P,t}$) yields the estimated returns

[26]The factors are an equity index return, a corporate bond index return, the US dollar currency return, a credit spread, and a commodity index return.

$R^*_{P,t}$. Then, the "clone" returns ($\widehat{R}_{P,t}$) are calculated as follows:

$$\widehat{R}_{P,t} = \frac{\sigma_{R_P}}{\sigma_{R^*_P}} R^*_{P,t} \tag{18-16}$$

That is, the clone returns are the volatility-adjusted estimated returns $R^*_{P,t}$. By construction, they are not subject to manipulation because they are obtained from market factors.

Next, the authors apply nine different performance measures on the series of original returns ($R_{P,t}$) and clone returns ($\widehat{R}_{P,t}$).[27] They compute the hedge fund ranking correlation among these nine measures and three manipulation-proof certainty equivalents (with levels of risk aversion of 2, 3, and 4) for both the original and the clone returns. In the absence of manipulation, all 12 performance measures (the nine standard plus the three manipulation-proof) should yield similar rankings among hedge funds, and their ranking correlation should therefore be very high. By contrast, if the three manipulation-proof certainty equivalents yield rankings that substantially differ from those given by the nine other measures, then manipulation can be suspected. Table 18-10 summarizes the findings of the authors.

We see from Table 18-10 that, in the universe of clone returns (Panel A), all Spearman correlations exceed 90%, and there is a strong consensus among all performance measures, be they manipulation-proof or not. The picture is very different in the universe of original returns (Panel B). The three manipulation-proof measures appear to be in disagreement with all other

TABLE 18-10 Rank correlations between performance measures in the Brown et al. (2010) study.

	Spearman correlation	
	Lowest	Highest
Panel A: Clone returns		
Among the nine standard measures	0.9963	0.9999
Between the three manipulation-proof measures and the nine standard measures	0.9251	0.9662
Panel B: Original returns		
Among the nine standard measures	0.8314	0.9969
Between the three manipulation-proof measures and the nine standard measures	0.5788	0.7588

[27]The selected performance measures are: The Sharpe, modified Sharpe, Omega, Sortino, Calmar, Sterling, and Burke ratios, the Kappa, and the excess return on Value-At-Risk.

nine standard measures as their rank correlation with them lies within 58% and 76% (whereas the nine standard measures seem to agree with each other as their rank correlation is higher than 83%).

All in all, these results support the ability of the manipulation-proof certainty equivalent to provide a performance score that is not contaminated by potential PMs' fraudulent actions. A further step consists of identifying those funds that seem to be prone to manipulation.

18.4.2.3 Detecting potential manipulation

To further document manipulation, Brown et al. (2010) implement several detection methods:[28]

- The return discontinuity around zero may indicate misreporting (Bollen and Pool, 2008).
- The conditional serial correlation may indicate return smoothing (Bollen and Pool, 2009).
- A good score for the market timing measure of Treynor and Mazuy (1966) can also indicate performance manipulation (Goetzmann et al., 2007).

As far as the discontinuity analysis is concerned, a much simpler, yet similar detection method is the Bias Ratio (BR_P) given by

$$BR_P = \frac{\sum_{t=1}^{T} 1_{\{R_{P,t} \in [0, \sigma_{R_P}]\}}}{1 + \sum_{t=1}^{T} 1_{\{R_{P,t} \in [-\sigma_{R_P}, 0[\}}} \tag{18-17}$$

where T is the number of observed returns. That is, the Bias Ratio is the count of positive returns over (one plus) the count of negative returns within one standard deviation of the return distribution. A manager manipulating the fund will tend to avoid reporting negative returns. The Bias Ratio might capture such behavior as it detects a strong asymmetry between positive and negative returns. It should not be interpreted in absolute values. Rather, comparing the Bias Ratios among a group of funds (e.g., hedge funds within the same style family) might help detect the potentially manipulated ones.

Brown et al. (2010) find that the discrepancy in ranking between the standard measures and the manipulation-proof measures becomes even stronger when calculated for funds that were previously detected as potentially manipulated. This leads them to design a detection tool built directly from the manipulation-proof certainty equivalent.

[28]The first two methods were briefly discussed in Section 18.2.4.1 in this chapter. Details about the timing measure can be found in Chapter 7.

The metric mpCE_P^j in Equation (18-14) is a decreasing function of risk aversion. However, Brown et al. (2010) point out that in the presence of manipulation (i.e., an unusually high number of positive excess returns), that metric will become similar across various levels of risk aversion. Therefore, they suggest defining the Doubt Ratio (DR_P) as follows:

$$\text{DR}_P = \frac{\text{mpCE}_P^j|_{\gamma=2}}{\text{mpCE}_P^j|_{\gamma=2} - \text{mpCE}_P^j|_{\gamma=3}} + 2 \tag{18-18}$$

That is, if there is manipulation, the manipulation-proof certainty equivalent calculated with a risk-aversion coefficient of $\gamma = 3$ will be very close to the one calculated with $\gamma = 2$, thereby inflating the DR.

Using a linear approximation, Brown et al. (2010) further show that

$$\text{DR}_P \approx \frac{2\overline{R}_{P-f}}{\hat{\sigma}^2_{P-f}} \times \frac{T}{T-1} + 1 \tag{18-19}$$

where $\overline{R}_{P-f}$ and $\hat{\sigma}^2_{P-f}$ denote the mean and the sample variance of *excess* returns, respectively. As can be seen from Equation (18-19), the DR is closely related to the Sharpe ratio with the notable difference that risk is measured as the variance of excess returns.

On Behalf Investment (continued)

A supervisor of OBI undertakes a closer analysis of the daily returns reported by the manager of Fund C. The fund has exhibited a historical performance of 20% average return with a 20% standard deviation. In the absence of manipulation, a histogram of daily returns (1000 observations over the last four years) could look like that shown in Figure 18-13.

We note a relatively symmetric, bell-shaped distribution of returns. Out of these 1000 observations, 173 lie within 0 and one daily standard deviation ($0.2/\sqrt{250}$), and 175 lie within minus one daily standard deviation and 0. This yields a Bias Ratio of $\text{BR}_C = \frac{173}{1+175} \approx 0.983$. The Bias Ratio is close to 1, indicating the fairly similar occurrence of positive and negative returns. The daily Sharpe ratio calculated from this sample is 0.0497.

Suppose now that the manager of Fund C is tempted to misreport those returns that are slightly negative. More precisely, all returns lying within -0.002 and 0 are reported equal to 0 (there are 59 of them). The distribution of returns would look like that shown in Figure 18-14.

(continued)

(continued)

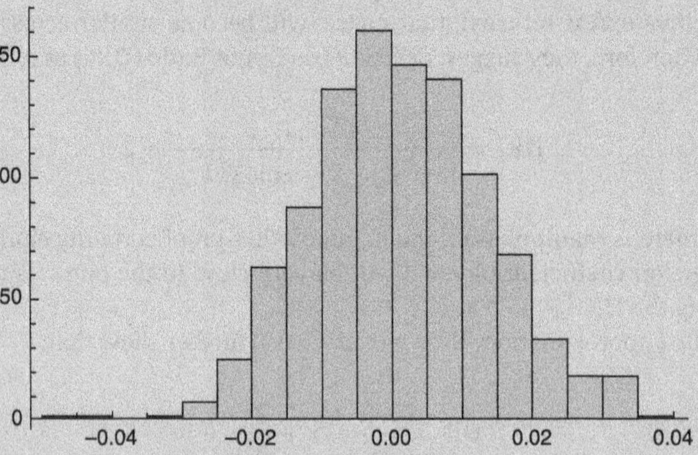

FIGURE 18-13 Histogram of Fund C daily returns – No manipulation.

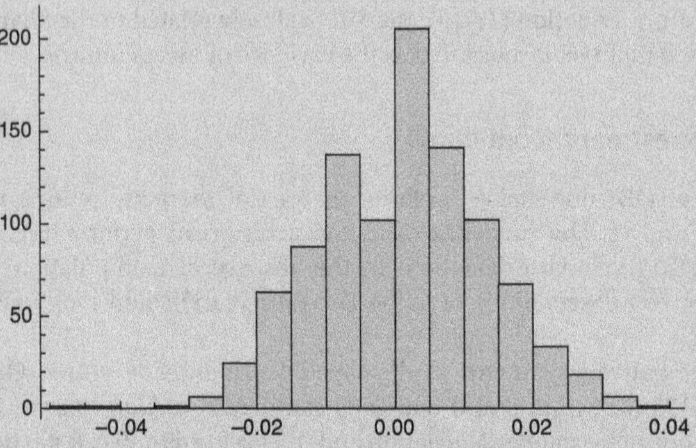

FIGURE 18-14 Histogram of Fund C daily returns – Manipulation.

The manager's manipulation translates into a slight distortion of the return distribution and a lack of regularity in its bell shape. There are now 405 observations lying within 0 and one daily standard deviation and 292 observations lying within minus one daily standard deviation and 0. The revised Bias Ratio is $BR_C = \frac{405}{1+292} \approx 1.382$. Its departure from one should alert the supervisor of a possible misreporting. Note that the daily Sharpe ratio calculated from this new sample is 0.0548.

18.4.2.4 Hunt which fund or fund a witch hunt?

Despite legitimate concerns for potential agency conflicts, investing in methods to identify misbehaving PMs can become counterproductive to a certain degree. As pointed out by Wermers (2011), the detection of manipulated funds is a filtering exercise typically associated with two sources of errors: attributing skills to an ill-intentioned manager (Type I error) and falsely accusing an honest (and possibly skillful) manager (Type II error).

Clearly, Type I errors can be very costly for the investor, the investment firm, its supervisors, and everyone having a stake invested in the PM's competence. Agency models typically emphasize the importance of incentives. If Type I errors are frequently committed, and managerial misbehaviors are not sanctioned enough, then PMs would have a strong incentive to take full advantage of the agency conflict.

However, Type II errors can also have huge repercussions. First, in terms of missed investment opportunities, i.e., investors refusing to invest in funds whose managers should have been trusted. Second, in terms of managing human resources. A manipulation detection method that overestimates the cases of fraud induces a sort of "witch hunt" among PMs, which might discourage the most skilled ones. The best supervision of PMs certainly stems from a sound balance between Type I and Type II errors.

18.5 THE ROLE OF LUCK IN PERFORMANCE MEASUREMENT

Beyond the question of PMs' intentions (are they taking advantage or not of an agency conflict with the investors?), a long-standing (and certainly more fundamental) issue has been debated about PMs' skills. Do these management skills really exist, or is the performance of PMs only the result of luck? In the latter case, is performance measurement reduced to nothing more than a search for an illusion of performance?

18.5.1 Disentangling skill from luck

Many empirical studies on mutual funds have documented the great difficulty for PMs to outperform passive benchmarks. For decades, the general conclusion from this evidence has been that financial markets are efficient, and PMs do not have enough skill to beat them. As a corollary, those PMs who exhibited positive alphas have been suspected to achieve that by luck. As noted by Berk (2005), that interpretation is not satisfactory as it leads to another puzzle: If investors view performing PMs as lucky, then why would they entrust these PMs with the management of their wealth? Why would the asset management industry even exist?

18.5.1.1 The statistical problem

In the same spirit of the filtering problem examined in Section 18.4.2.4, while disentangling skilled performance from manipulation, one may wonder whether good performance is correctly attributed to skill and not chance. The notions of Type I and Type II errors still apply in this context, as explained below.

Considering a sample of funds, it is possible to compute some performance metric (e.g., an alpha) and test whether that metric statistically indicates skill (e.g., the alpha is positive). Table 18-11 summarizes all the cases encountered during the tests, with π standing as proportions of the entire population of funds.[29]

If we work with a population of N PMs, we would be interested in knowing $\pi_0 = N_0/N$ or $\pi_+ = N_+/N$ that would yield the proportion of skilled managers. However, the presence of false discoveries (i.e., Type I errors) and false negatives (i.e., Type II errors) complicates the statistical inference.

Barras, Scaillet, and Wermers (2010) apply the false discovery rate (FDR) technique to a sample of US mutual funds whose alphas are calculated from a four-factor model estimated on after-fee returns. The false discovery rate is the fraction of Type I errors over all discoveries ($\frac{\pi_{t_+}|\pi_0}{\pi_{t_+}}$), and the FDR technique consists of controlling that fraction to an acceptable level. Their main results can be summarized in Figure 18-15.

Based on a long-term study with a multifactor model considered as robust, Barras et al. (2010) conclude that the average observed alpha of truly skilled and unskilled funds are equal to +3.8% and −3.2%, respectively. This corresponds to average t-statistics of 3.0 and −2.5. Given their respective variances, the distributions of the observed t-statistics for the unskilled, zero-alpha (no skill), and skilled funds are reported in the upper part (Panel A) of Figure 18-15. Setting a significance level of $x = 90\%$ corresponding to a critical value of the Student t-statistic of ±1.65, this entails that a proportion of zero-alpha funds would be wrongly classified as skilled (black area) and unskilled (gray area).

TABLE 18-11 Classification of multiple hypothesis tests.

	Null hypothesis is true: Manager has no skill or is unskilled	Alternative hypothesis is true: Manager is skilled	Total
Test is significant	Type I errors ($\pi_{t_+}|\pi_0$)	True positives ($\pi_{t_+}|\pi_+$)	π_{t_+}
Test is not significant	True negatives ($\pi_{t_0}|\pi_0$)	Type II errors ($\pi_{t_0}|\pi_0$)	π_{t_0}
Total	π_0	π_+	1

[29] We only focus on the skilled (positive alpha) and no-skill (zero alpha) PMs, leaving aside the unskilled (negative alpha) PMs in this example for the sake of readability.

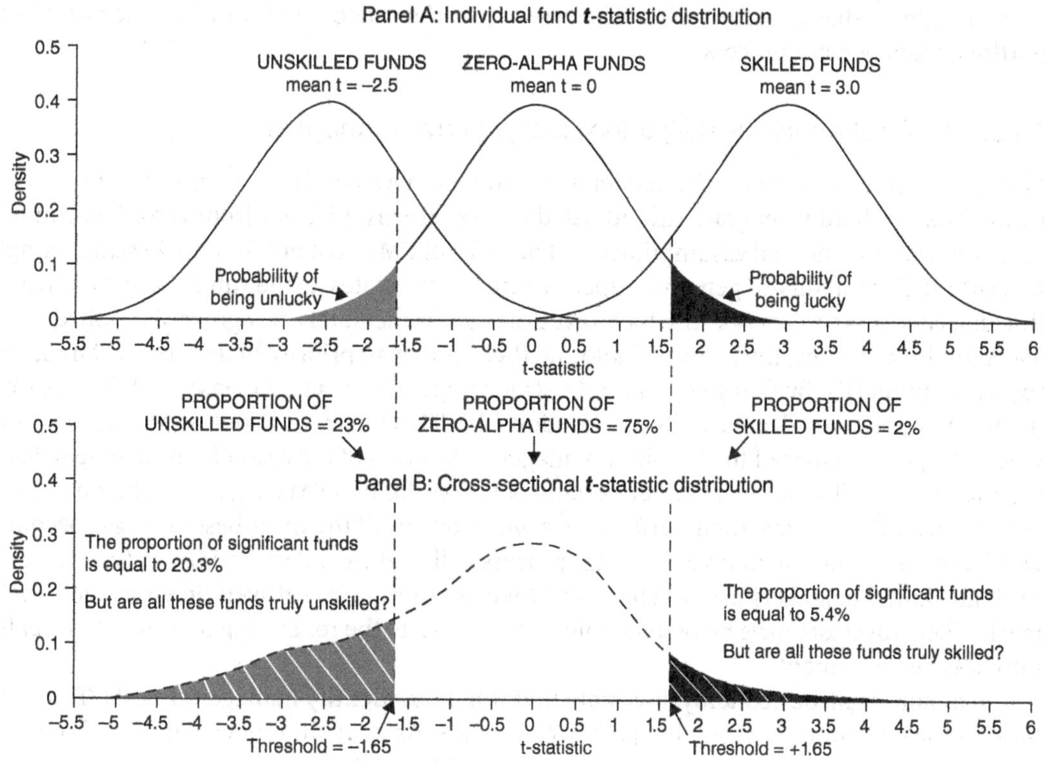

FIGURE 18-15 Individual and cross-sectional *t*-statistic distributions. *Source*: Barras et al. (2010), Figure 1.

The observer's problem is to distinguish those lucky (or unlucky) fund managers from the true ones on the basis of the aggregate cross-section distribution of *t*-statistics reported in Panel B. The question asked by the authors is thus: "*Out of the 5.4% of funds with significant alpha (at a* $\frac{1-x}{2} = 5\%$ *significance), what is the proportion of just lucky ones?.*" Fortunately, from a long-run perspective, we can assess that the estimated proportions of skilled, no-skill and unskilled funds equal $\pi_+^{LT} = 2\%$, $\pi_0^{LT} = 75\%$, and $\pi_-^{LT} = 23\%$. Hence, the answer to their question about the Type I error corresponds to the proportion of zero-alpha funds multiplied by the significance level, or $E(\pi_{t_+}|\pi_0) = \pi_0^{LT} \times \frac{1-x}{2} = 75\% \times 5\% = 3.75\%$. Furthermore, the misclassified truly skilled funds (Type II error) are obtained as $E(\pi_{t_0}|\pi_+) = \pi_+^{LT} \times \frac{1-x'}{2} = 2\% \times 9\% = 0.18\%$, where $x' = 82\%$ corresponds to the confidence level for a rejection of the hypothesis of a skilled PM (average *t*-statistic of 3.00) if the critical level is 1.65 as shown in Panel A. Consequently, the expected proportion of truly skilled funds corresponds to the observed proportion of significant *t*-statistics corrected with Type I and Type II errors and equals $E(\pi_+) = \pi_{t_+} - E(\pi_{t_+}|\pi_0) + E(\pi_{t_0}|\pi_+) = 5.4\% - 3.75\% + 0.18\% = 1.83\%$. Thus, in this sample, only about one-third of the statistically significant alphas are expected to be genuinely due to skilled PMs. The rest is just the outcome of a lucky outcome of the portfolio management process.

18.5.1.2 A rationale for skilled (not lucky) active managers

Berk and Green (2004) develop a model with rational investors that explains why, in equilibrium, PMs can hardly generate risk-adjusted excess returns different from zero. Their model relies on two fundamental assumptions: (i) The skills of PMs exist but they are in scarce supply and (ii) the PMs' ability to generate superior returns dissipates as the fund size grows. Let us first consider this framework in which investors can immediately recognize the skilled managers. In this economy, investors will allocate their money in priority to the first-best manager (by assumption (i)). By doing so, that PM's scale of operations will increase, and their performance will gradually decrease (by assumption (ii)). This effect will continue until the point where the performance of the first-best manager equals that of the second-best manager, leading investors to allocate their money equally between the two PMs. Again, as the operations of the two best PMs grow, their performance will erode until the third-best manager becomes worthy of consideration for investors. This process will continue, Berk and Green (2004) argue, until all skilled managers are solicited, and their performance is driven down to the benchmark. Then, investors have no better choice but to allocate the remaining non-invested wealth into passive investment.

In a more realistic economy, investors find it hard to identify managerial skills. They will have to learn about it by observing past performance. As a result, money will flow from past poor performers to past good performers. The fund flows thus appear as a manifestation of investors learning and rationally reallocating their money to those PMs that have exhibited skill. However, once this reallocation process is performed, the same performance erosion effect will apply, driving risk-adjusted excess returns down to zero.

The important conclusion from this reasoning is that superior performance from active management is hard to detect not because capital markets are efficient and managers are unskilled, but because capital markets are efficient and the asset management industry is competitive. Markets clear when the marginal return one can expect from active management equals the one obtained from the alternative investment opportunity, i.e., the benchmark. From that perspective, the finding of Barras et al. (2010) comes in support of Berk and Green's (2004) argument.

Another implication of Berk and Green (2004) is that the PMs' precise level of skill remains difficult to assess. Their equilibrium reasoning explains why it cannot be directly measured from performance. However, the existence of PM skillsets is consistent with the amount of fees that investors are willing to pay for fund management. In a calibration exercise, Berk and Green (2004) match some model outputs with observed quantities (after-fee return of active managers, fund survival rate, performance/flow relation), and infer a distribution of alpha. They find that around 80% of the distribution lies above the average level of management fees, leading to the (flattering?) conclusion that most PMs are skilled.

18.5.2 Assessing the level of portfolio managers' skill

18.5.2.1 Skill reflected through value, not return

In the direct continuity of Berk and Green's (2004) line of reasoning, Berk and van Binsbergen (2015) introduce a new way to measure PMs' skill. They suggest using the dollar value added by active portfolio management. Let $q_{P,t}$ denote the assets under management in fund P at time t. The value added between time $t-1$and t is

$$V_{P,t} = q_{P,t-1}(R^g_{P,t} - R_{B,t}) \tag{18-20}$$

where $R^g_{P,t}$ is the gross (before fees) return on fund P and $R_{B,t}$ is the benchmark return.

In Berk and Green's (2004) model of the rational and competitive asset management industry, risk-adjusted excess returns are driven to zero and thus tell nothing about PMs' skills. However, skilled managers, if correctly identified by investors, attract fund flows. Their skills should therefore manifest through the amount of extra money they can generate from assets under management. It should be noted that Equation (18-20) involves the fund's gross return. Thus, the added value $V_{P,t}$ is made of two components: the dollar value of all fees charged and a residual dollar value returned to investors (if any).

Berk and van Binsbergen (2015) compute the benchmark returns in two ways, either from a standard four-factor model or from a portfolio of tradable Vanguard index funds. Then they calculate their added value metric on a sample of roughly 6000 mutual funds from the CRSP and Morningstar databases over the 1977–2011 period. About 40% of funds generate positive added value. The distribution of $V_{P,t}$ is right-skewed leading to a positive average of $140 000 generated each month. This positive asymmetry in the distribution means that even if some funds destroy value, most of the capital is allocated to skilled managers whose talent more than offsets the losses of poor performers. All these results are robust to the choice of benchmark.

Another important finding of Berk and van Binsbergen (2015) is that the added value is persistent. Through a fund sorting exercise, they show that funds whose added value lies in the top (bottom) deciles are likely to stay in the same deciles in the next periods. Such persistence is detected over a horizon as long as 10 years. Assuming that PMs' skill is a permanent trait, this evidence indicates that investors do a relatively good job at identifying which PMs are the most skilled.

Barras, Gagliardini, and Scaillet (2022) extend the approach of Berk and van Binsbergen (2015) by incorporating scalability into the measure of PMs' value creation. This idea is directly related to Berk and Green's (2004) second assumption that PMs' ability to add value erodes with the scale of operations. Thus, some fund managers may distinguish themselves from others in their greater capacity to scale up good investment ideas. To formalize the authors' insight, Equation (18-20) can be rewritten as

$$V_{P,t} = \mathrm{E}[q_{P,t-1}\alpha^g_{P,t}] \tag{18-21}$$

where $\alpha^g_{P,t}$ is the gross alpha of fund P. If the following linear relation is assumed:

$$\alpha^g_{P,t} = a_P - b_P q_{P,t-1} \quad (18\text{-}22)$$

The (fund-specific) a_P coefficient can be interpreted as the PM's pure skill, i.e., their ability to add value from the first dollar invested (that is, in the absence of any scale constraint), and the (fund-specific as well) b_P coefficient represents the fund's sensitivity to diseconomies of scale.

In their study of US equity funds over the 1975-2019 period, Barras et al. (2022) obtain the following results. First, they confirm that skill is prevalent across PMs, even positive for more than 80% of them. Second, funds appear to be highly sensitive to diseconomies of scale, thereby validating Berk and Green's (2004) hypothesis. Third, the best performing funds achieve a certain balance between skill and scalability (their a_P and b_P coefficients are around the average across funds). Finally, small cap funds tend to create more value than large cap funds, as their relatively high skill level (high a_P) more than offsets their issues with scaling (high b_P).

18.5.2.2 Where is the reward to skill?

Mutual fund managers are typically rewarded with fees. The fact that fees are calculated from fund size (assets under management) and not from fund return is an indication that PMs might capture most of the benefits driven from their skills. In their theoretical analysis, Berk and Green (2004) already suspected that PMs extract the full rent from their skills and charge fees in such a way that, in equilibrium, investors are marginally indifferent between dealing with active managers or indexing passively. Berk and van Binsbergen (2015) empirically confirm that conjecture. They find that it is very difficult for investors to obtain a positive net alpha when dealing with the best managers. In other words, the added value defined in Equation (18-20) is mostly made of fees.

Of course, this is an equilibrium outcome. This means that investors, at least temporarily, from time to time, might obtain an extra redistributed gain (i.e., a piece of $V_{P,t}$). However, evidence indicates that, in the long run, PMs adjust their compensation to extract the full rent.[30] Ironically, such a conclusion brings us back to an agency problem. How do investors who are entrusting PMs to manage their wealth end up paying the full price for accessing PMs' skills? Is managerial talent so scarce that it puts investors in a very weak bargaining power to negotiate the terms of PM compensation? These are questions that require additional investigation.

[30] Hübner and Lambert (2019) provide hedge fund evidence pointing towards this same rent extraction interpretation. They show that high-volatility hedge funds charge higher fees and deliver lower net-of-fees Sharpe ratios than do their low-volatility peers. This can be an indication that these hedge funds fully exploit their competitive advantage on the high volatility segment that constrained institutional investors can hardly occupy.

Key Takeaways and Equations

- The business model of asset management relies on delegated portfolio management, which inevitably induces agency relations between industry participants. Depending on how complex the organizational structure is, there are at least two layers of agency: (i) the investor (principal) dealing with an investment firm (agent) to design and execute an investment strategy and (ii) the investment firm (principal) mandating portfolio managers (agents) to implement said strategy.
- One major source of conflict of interest between investors and PMs is risk exposure. The flow-performance sensitivity provides a strong incentive for PMs to shift risk. Successful past performance induces PMs to increase risk to attract more fund flows. Unsuccessful past performance, however, may have the opposite effect due to PMs' job termination concerns.
- Beyond monitoring, which is an *ex post* costly solution, the severity of agency conflicts between investors and PMs can be mitigated by *ex ante* mechanisms such as compensation and governance.
- Managerial compensation consists of *fees* and *fund ownership*.
  - As far as fee is concerned, a generic form of remuneration scheme is

$$h_1 + h_2 R_P + h_3(R_P - R_{B1}) + h_4 \max(R_P - R_{B2}, 0) \tag{18-5}$$

    where the last term represents the nonlinear performance-based pay that has become pervasive in the mutual fund industry. Whether compensation effectively aligns PMs' incentives with investors' interests is controversial. The choice of benchmarks plays a critical role, while the option-like component may encourage risk shifting.
  - Performance-based fees commonly take the form of high water marks in hedge fund contracts. Their ability to mitigate risk shifting is assessed positively. They can be complemented with clawback provisions, often observed in the private equity industry.
  - PMs' fund ownership better aligns incentives, but some studies have argued that it may reduce the quality of monitoring.
- Governance mechanisms include *reporting*, *disclosure*, and *board composition*. They all contribute to enhancing the quality of monitoring. However, their cost–benefit analysis has been challenged empirically.
- Agency issues directly impact performance measurement through (i) distributional manipulation, (ii) dynamic manipulation, and (iii) biased estimation.

(continued)

(continued)

- *Distributional manipulation* consists of altering the distribution of portfolio returns (e.g., through derivatives trading).
- *Dynamic manipulation* consists of rebalancing the portfolio (notably through a change in leverage) during the evaluation period.
- *Biased estimation* consists of altering the statistical estimation of means, variances, or measures of association by implementing "informationless" strategies, such as short volatility investing, return smoothing, or St-Petersburg investing.

- A radical response to the risk of manipulation is to resort to *manipulation-proof performance* metrics. Goetzmann et al. (2007) present the following score:

$$\Theta(\{R_t\}_{t=1}^T) = -\frac{n}{\gamma} \log \left[\frac{1}{T} \sum_{t=1}^{T} (1 + r_{P,t}^g)^{-\gamma} \right] \tag{18-14}$$

  where $1 + \gamma$ can be interpreted as a risk-aversion coefficient. Research in this area is still limited.

- Alternatively, one should be aware that the design and implementation of a performance measure may provide unwanted incentives for PMs. Among the sources of agency conflict exacerbation are:
  - Linear benchmarking and its impact on PMs' incentive for risk and for active management.
  - Factor-based performance metrics and PMs' incentive to overinvest in omitted factors.
  - Peer group comparisons and their associated tournament effects.
  - Horizon discrepancies between investors' investment goals and PM monitoring frequency.

- Scores that can help detect manipulation include the *Bias Ratio* (BR) and the *Doubt Ratio* (DR):

$$\text{BR}_P = \frac{\sum_{t=1}^{T} 1_{\{R_{P,t} \in [0, \sigma_{R_P}]\}}}{1 + \sum_{t=1}^{T} 1_{\{R_{P,t} \in [-\sigma_{R_P}, 0[\}}} \tag{18-15}$$

$$\text{DR}_P = \frac{\text{mpCE}_P^j|_{\gamma=2}}{\text{mpCE}_P^j|_{\gamma=2} - \text{mpCE}_P^j|_{\gamma=3}} + 2 \tag{18-16}$$

- In addition to being opportunistic and good-performing, PMs have also been suspected of being lucky. Recent theoretical and empirical work has, however, shown that the apparent difficulty in active management of beating the market results from a rational and highly competitive asset management industry. There is evidence of value creation (i.e., skill) from a majority of mutual funds.

- Funds differ in their ability to create value either through pure skill (good investment ideas) or through scalability.
- Current evidence suggests that the reward for PMs' skills manifests through management fees and is captured for the most part as a rent from investors.

REFERENCES

Adams, J. C., Nishikawa, T., and R. P. Rao (2018), Mutual fund performance, management teams, and boards. *Journal of Banking & Finance*, Vol. 92, pp. 358–368.

Admati, A. R., and P. Pfleiderer (1997), Does it all add up? Benchmarks and the compensation of active portfolio managers. *Journal of Business*, Vol. 70, pp. 323–350.

Agarwal, V., Mullally, K. A., Tang, Y., and B. Yang (2015), Mandatory portfolio disclosure, stock liquidity, and mutual fund performance. *The Journal of Finance*, Vol. 70, pp. 2733–2776.

Almazan, A., Brown, K. C., Carlson, M., and D. A. Chapman (2004), Why constrain your mutual fund manager? *Journal of Financial Economics*, Vol. 73, pp. 289–321.

Aragon, G. O., and V. Nanda (2012), Tournament behavior in hedge funds: High-water marks, fund liquidation, and managerial stake. *The Review of Financial Studies*, Vol. 25, pp. 937–974.

Artzner, P., Delbaen, F., Eber, J. M., and D. Heath (1999), Coherent measures of risk. *Mathematical Finance*, Vol. 9, pp. 203–228.

Barras, L., Gagliardini, P., and O. Scaillet (2022), Skill, scale, and value creation in the mutual fund industry. *The Journal of Finance*, Vol. 77, pp. 601–638.

Barras, L., Scaillet, O., and R. Wermers (2010), False discoveries in mutual fund performance: Measuring luck in estimated alphas. *The Journal of Finance*, Vol. 65, pp. 179–216.

Beaver, W. H., McNichols, M. F., and K. K. Nelson (2007), An alternative interpretation of the discontinuity in earnings distributions. *Review of Accounting Studies*, Vol. 12, pp. 525–556.

Berk, J. B. (2005), Five myths of active portfolio management. *The Journal of Portfolio Management*, Vol. 31 (3), pp. 27–31.

Berk, J. B., and R. C. Green (2004), Mutual fund flows and performance in rational markets. *Journal of Political Economy*, Vol. 112, pp. 1269–1295.

Berk, J. B., and J. H. van Binsbergen (2015), Measuring skill in the mutual fund industry. *Journal of Financial Economics*, Vol. 118, pp. 1–20.

Bollen, N. P., and V. K. Pool (2008), Conditional return smoothing in the hedge fund industry. *Journal of Financial and Quantitative Analysis*, Vol. 43, pp. 267–298.

Bollen, N. P., and V. K. Pool (2009), Do hedge fund managers misreport returns? Evidence from the pooled distribution. *The Journal of Finance*, Vol. 64, pp. 2257–2288.

Brown, S. J., Goetzmann, W., and J. Park (2001), Careers and survival: Competition and risk in the hedge fund and CTA industry. *The Journal of Finance*, Vol. 56, pp. 1869–1886.

Brown, K. C., Harlow, W. V., and L. T. Starks (1996), Of tournaments and temptations: An analysis of managerial incentives in the mutual fund industry. *The Journal of Finance*, Vol. 51, pp. 85–110.

Brown, S. J., Kang, M., In, F. H., and G. Lee (2010), Resisting the manipulation of performance metrics: An empirical analysis of the manipulation-proof performance measure. Working Paper, available at SSRN 1536323.

Cassar, G., and J. Gerakos (2011), Hedge funds: Pricing controls and the smoothing of self-reported returns. *The Review of Financial Studies*, Vol. 24, pp. 1698–1734.

Chen, Z., and P. J. Knez (1996), Portfolio performance measurement: Theory and applications. *The Review of Financial Studies*, Vol. 9, pp. 511–555.

Cherny, A., and D. Madan (2009), New measures for performance evaluation. *The Review of Financial Studies*, Vol. 22, pp. 2571–2606.

Chevalier, J., and G. Ellison (1997), Risk taking by mutual funds as a response to incentives. *Journal of Political Economy*, Vol. 105, pp. 1167–1200.

Chevalier, J., and G. Ellison (1999), Career concerns of mutual fund managers. *The Quarterly Journal of Economics*, Vol. 114, pp. 389–432.

Chrétien, S., and M. Kammoun (2017), Mutual fund performance evaluation and best clienteles. *Journal of Financial and Quantitative Analysis*, Vol. 52, pp. 1577–1604.

Clifford, C. P., Ellis, J. A., and W. C. Gerken (2018), Hedge fund boards and the market for independent directors. *Journal of Financial and Quantitative Analysis*, Vol. 53, pp. 2067–2101.

Cochrane, J. H. (1996), A cross-sectional test of an investment-based asset pricing model. *Journal of Political Economy*, Vol. 104, pp. 572–621.

Cochrane, J. H., and J. Saa-Requejo (2000), Beyond arbitrage: Good-deal asset price bounds in incomplete markets. *Journal of Political Economy*, Vol. 108, pp. 79–119.

Cremers, M., Driessen, J., Maenhout, P., and D. Weinbaum (2009), Does skin in the game matter? Director incentives and governance in the mutual fund industry. *Journal of Financial and Quantitative Analysis*, Vol. 44, pp. 1345–1373.

Cvitanić, J., Lazrak, A., and T. Wang (2008), Implications of the Sharpe ratio as a performance measure in multi-period settings. *Journal of Economic Dynamics and Control*, Vol. 32, pp. 1622–1649.

De Giorgi, E. (2005), Reward–risk portfolio selection and stochastic dominance. *Journal of Banking & Finance*, Vol. 29, pp. 895–926.

Deng, X., Hung, S., and Z. Qiao (2018), Mutual fund herding and stock price crashes. *Journal of Banking & Finance*, Vol. 94, pp. 166–184.

Ding, B., and R. Wermers (2012), Mutual fund performance and governance structure: The role of portfolio managers and boards of directors. Working Paper, available at SSRN 2207229.

Drechsler, I. (2014), Risk choice under high-water marks. *The Review of Financial Studies*, Vol. 27, pp. 2052–2096.

Dyakov, T., Harford, J., and B. Qiu (2022), Better kept in the dark? Portfolio disclosure and agency problems in mutual funds. *Journal of Financial and Quantitative Analysis*, Vol. 57, pp. 1529–1563.

Dybvig, P. H., Farnsworth, H. K., and J. N. Carpenter (2010), Portfolio performance and agency. *The Review of Financial Studies*, Vol. 23, pp. 1–23.

Edelen, R. M., Evans, R. B., and G. B. Kadlec (2012), Disclosure and agency conflict: Evidence from mutual fund commission bundling. *Journal of Financial Economics*, Vol. 103, pp. 308–326.

Elton, E. J., Gruber, M. J., Blake, C. R., Krasny, Y., and S. O. Ozelge (2010), The effect of holdings data frequency on conclusions about mutual fund behavior. *Journal of Banking & Finance*, Vol. 34, pp. 912–922.

Evans, A. L. (2008), Portfolio manager ownership and mutual fund performance. *Financial Management*, Vol. 37, pp. 513–534.

Farnsworth, H., Ferson, W., Jackson, D., and S. Todd (2002), Performance evaluation with stochastic discount factors. *Journal of Business*, Vol. 75, pp. 473–583.

Ferreira, M. A., Keswani, A., Miguel, A. F., and S. B. Ramos (2012), The flow-performance relationship around the world. *Journal of Banking & Finance*, Vol. 36, pp. 1759–1780.

Ferris, S. P., and X. Yan (2007), Agency conflicts in delegated portfolio management: Evidence from namesake mutual funds. *Journal of Financial Research*, Vol. 30, pp. 473–494.

Foster, D. P., and H. P. Young (2010), Gaming performance fees by portfolio managers. *The Quarterly Journal of Economics*, Vol. 125, pp. 1435–1458.

François, P., and F. Missonier-Piera (2007), The agency structure of loan syndicates. *Financial Review*, Vol. 42, pp. 227–245.

Frank, M. M., Poterba, J. M., Shackelford, D. A., and J. B. Shoven (2004), Copycat funds: Information disclosure regulation and the returns to active management in the mutual fund industry. *The Journal of Law and Economics*, Vol. 47, pp. 515–541.

Fricke, E. (2015), Board holdings, compensation and mutual fund manager turnover. *Journal of Financial Services Research*, Vol. 47, pp. 295–312.

Fu, R., and L. Wedge (2011), Board independence and mutual fund manager turnover. *Financial Review*, Vol. 46, pp. 621–641.

Gervais, S., Lynch, A. W., and D. K. Musto (2005), Fund families as delegated monitors of money managers. *The Review of Financial Studies*, Vol. 18, pp. 1139–1169.

Gil-Bazo, J., and P. Ruiz-Verdú (2009), The relation between price and performance in the mutual fund industry. *The Journal of Finance*, Vol. 64, pp. 2153–2183.

Goetzmann, W., Ingersoll, J., Spiegel, M., and I. Welch (2007), Portfolio performance manipulation and manipulation-proof performance measures. *The Review of Financial Studies*, Vol. 20, pp. 1503–1546.

Goldman, E., and S. L. Slezak (2003), Delegated portfolio management and rational prolonged mispricing. *The Journal of Finance*, Vol. 58, pp. 283–311.

Gryglewicz, S., and S. Mayer (2023), Dynamic contracting with intermediation: Operational, governance, and financial engineering. *The Journal of Finance*, Vol. 78, pp. 2779–2836.

Hasanhodzic, J., and A. W. Lo (2007), Can hedge-fund returns be replicated? The linear case. *Journal of Investment Management*, Vol. 5, pp. 5–45.

Hu, P., Kale, J. R., Pagani, M., and A. Subramanian (2011), Fund flows, performance, managerial career concerns, and risk taking. *Management Science*, Vol. 57, pp. 628–646.

Huang, J., Sialm, C., and H. Zhang (2011), Risk shifting and mutual fund performance. *The Review of Financial Studies*, Vol. 24, pp. 2575–2616.

Huang, J., Wei, K. D., and H. Yan (2007), Participation costs and the sensitivity of fund flows to past performance. *The Journal of Finance*, Vol. 62, pp. 1273–1311.

Hübner, G., and M. Lambert (2019), Performance sharing in risky portfolios: The case of hedge funds returns and fees. *The Journal of Portfolio Management*, Vol. 45 (4), pp. 105–118.

Jagannathan, R., and R. A. Korajczyk (1986), Assessing the market timing performance of managed portfolios. *Journal of Business*, Vol. 59, pp. 217–235.

James, C., and J. Karceski (2006), Investor monitoring and differences in mutual fund performance. *Journal of Banking & Finance*, Vol. 30, pp. 2787–2808.

Jorion, P., and C. Schwarz (2014), Are hedge fund managers systematically misreporting? Or not? *Journal of Financial Economics*, Vol. 111, pp. 311–327.

Karoui, A., and I. Meier (2015), Fund performance and subsequent risk: A study of mutual fund tournaments using holdings-based measures. *Financial Markets and Portfolio Management*, Vol. 29, pp. 1–20.

Khorana, A., Servaes, H., and L. Wedge (2007), Portfolio manager ownership and fund performance. *Journal of Financial Economics*, Vol. 85, pp. 179–204.

Kostakis, A. (2013), Performance measures and incentives: Loading negative coskewness to outperform the CAPM. In: *Asset Management and International Capital Markets. Routledge*, pp. 47–70.

Lakonishok, J., Shleifer, A., Thaler, R. H., and R. W. Vishny (1991), Window dressing by pension fund managers. *American Economic Review*, Vol. 81, pp. 227–231.

Lakonishok, J., Shleifer, A., and R. W. Vishny (1992), The structure and performance of the money management industry. *Brookings Papers on Economic Activity: Microeconomics*, pp. 339–390.

Lee, J. H., Trzcinka, C., and S. Venkatesan (2019), Do portfolio manager contracts contract portfolio management? *The Journal of Finance*, Vol. 74, pp. 2543–2577.

Leland, H. (1999), Beyond mean-variance: Performance measurement in a nonsymmetrical world. *Financial Analysts Journal*, Vol. 55 (1), pp. 25–36.

Li, C. W., and A. Tiwari (2009), Incentive contracts in delegated portfolio management. *The Review of Financial Studies*, Vol. 22, pp. 4681–4714.

Liu, W. L. (2015), Investment constraints and delegated portfolio management. Working Paper, available at SSRN 2231905.

Ma, L., and Y. Tang (2019), Portfolio manager ownership and mutual fund risk taking. *Management Science*, Vol. 65, pp. 5518–5534.

Ma, L., Tang, Y., and J. P. Gomez (2019), Portfolio manager compensation in the U.S. mutual fund industry. *The Journal of Finance*, Vol. 74, pp. 587–638.

Mazur, M., Salganik-Shoshan, G., and M. Zagonov (2017), Comparing performance sensitivity of retail and institutional mutual funds' investment flows. *Finance Research Letters*, Vol. 22, pp. 66–73.

Meier, I., and E. Schaumburg (2004), Do funds window dress? Evidence for U.S. domestic equity mutual funds. Unpublished Working Paper, HEC Montréal and Kellogg School of Management.

Meschke, F. (2019), An empirical examination of mutual fund boards. *Quarterly Journal of Finance*, Vol. 9, #1950015.

Morey, M. R., and E. S. O'Neal (2006), Window dressing in bond mutual funds. *Journal of Financial Research*, Vol. 29, pp. 325–347.

Mullally, K., and A. Rossi (2022), Moving the goalposts? Mutual fund benchmark changes and performance manipulation. Working Paper, available at SSRN 4145883.

Panageas, S., and M. M. Westerfield (2009), High-water marks: High risk appetites? Convex compensation, long horizons, and portfolio choice. *The Journal of Finance*, Vol. 64, pp. 1–36.

Qiu, J. (2003), Termination risk, multiple managers and mutual fund tournaments. *Review of Finance*, Vol. 7, pp. 161–190.

Scotti, M. (2012), Delegated portfolio management with career concerns. *Journal of Economic Behavior & Organization*, Vol. 84, pp. 829–839.

Starks, L. T. (1987), Performance incentive fees: An agency theoretic approach. *Journal of Financial and Quantitative Analysis*, Vol. 22, pp. 17–32.

Stoughton, N. M. (1993), Moral hazard and the portfolio management problem. *The Journal of Finance*, Vol. 48, pp. 2009–2028.

Stracca, L. (2006), Delegated portfolio management: A survey of the theoretical literature. *Journal of Economic Surveys*, Vol. 20, pp. 823–848.

Strausz, R. (1997), Delegation of monitoring in a principal–agent relationship. *The Review of Economic Studies*, Vol. 64, pp. 337–357.

Treynor, J., and K. Mazuy (1966), Can mutual funds outguess the market? *Harvard Business Review*, Vol. 44, pp. 131–136.

Weisman, A. B. (2002), Informationless investing and hedge fund performance measurement bias. *The Journal of Portfolio Management*, Vol. 28 (4), pp. 80–91.

Wermers, R. (2011), Performance measurement of mutual funds, hedge funds, and institutional accounts. *Annual Review of Financial Economics*, Vol. 3, pp. 537–574.

Zakamouline, V. (2014), Portfolio performance evaluation with loss aversion. *Quantitative Finance*, Vol. 14, pp. 699–710.

Index

T